COLLINS

CLASSICAL MUSIC
ENCYCLOPEDIA

EDITORIAL DIRECTION: Sonya Newland
DESIGN: Helen Courtney
PICTURE RESEARCH: Bridget Tily

DEVELOPMENT DIRECTOR: Ian Powling
CONCEPT/CREATIVE DIRECTOR: Nick Wells

Special thanks to:
Elisabeth Ingles and Ursula Payne (editorial)
Tully Potter (discography)

Thanks also to: Myles Archibald, Richard Abram, Frances Banfield, Ray Barnett, John Bimson, Lucy Bradbury, Robbie Capp, Claire Dashwood, Clare Double, Lucinda Hawksley, Stephen Jackson, James Jolly, Lesley Malkin, Geoff Newman, Heather Newell, Bob Nirkind, Brenda Ralph Lewis, Karen Villabona, Polly Willis and Nicholas Williams.

HarperCollinsPublishers
77-85 Fulham Palace Road
London
W6 8JB

Visit the HarperCollins Website – www.fireandwater.com

First published 2000

01 03 02 00

1 3 5 7 9 10 8 6 4 2

Produced by Flame Tree Publishing, a part of
The Foundry Creative Media Company Ltd
Crabtree Hall, Crabtree Lane,
Fulham, London, SW6 6TY

The CIP record for this book is available from the British Library.

ISBN 0 00 472390 2

COLLINS

CLASSICAL MUSIC
ENCYCLOPEDIA

GENERAL EDITOR: STANLEY SADIE

FOREWORD BY VLADIMIR ASHKENAZY

HarperCollins*Publishers*

CONTENTS

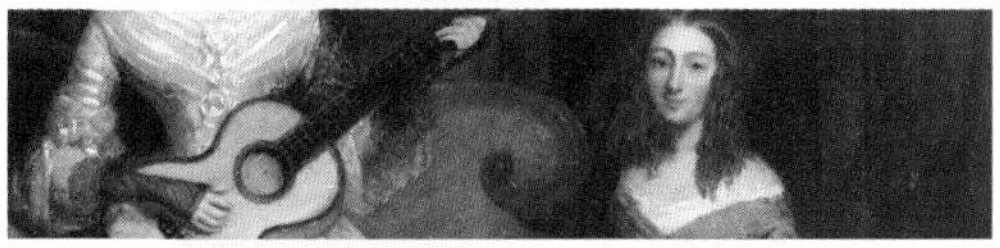

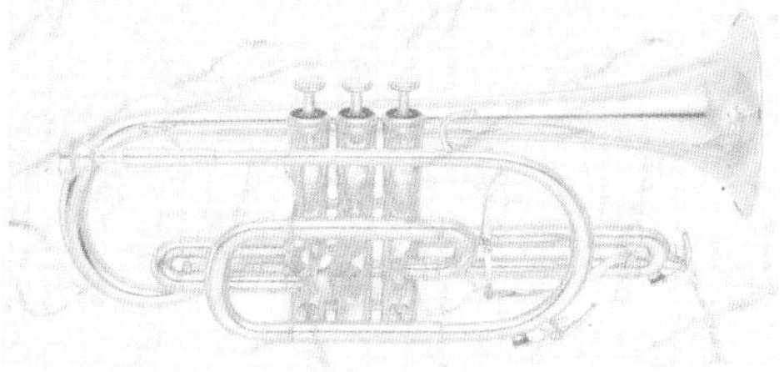

HOW TO USE THIS BOOK

ABOUT THE ENCYCLOPEDIA

The Encyclopedia comprises an introductory section on ancient musics from across the globe (The World of Music), followed by nine chronologically organized chapters, from The Medieval Era to The Late 20th Century.

Each chapter is divided into a series of sections. Common to each chapter are the following:

ERA INTRODUCTION

Gives vital information about the relevant period, including the major events of the time, clarifying the backdrop against which the music developed and setting it in its social and cultural context.

PERSONALITIES

Biographies of the key music figures of the day, their style and major works. In the two chapters on the twentieth century, this section is broken down for ease of use into a series of entries on the major composers of the era, followed by shorter entries on conductors, singers and instrumentalists.

STYLES AND FORMS

Details the creation of new musical styles and the development of those that already existed.

INSTRUMENTS

A guide to the popular instruments of the time, including, where relevant, their inventors, the craftsmen who made them, and information about how they were played, their construction and their role in the music of the period.

LISTENING GUIDE

Takes one of the most significant pieces of the era and discusses its history and influence, with a musical timeline for readers to follow with a recommended recording; four further pieces are also discussed. In the Late 20th Century, a time in which music had become more stylistically disparate than any other, four major pieces are detailed equally.

Some chapters have additional sections as appropriate. Most feature extended biographies of the best-known and most influential composers of each era in a Key Composers section and the rise of opera is charted in a section in The Late 20th Century.

THEMES

Six themes run throughout the book, the entries for which can be found in colour-coded boxes in a fixed position on each spread:

ARTS AND CULTURE

Embraces artistic, craft and cultural activities, and people that relate to, and help contextualize the music-makers.

INSIDE THE MUSIC

Covers the emergence and development of music theory, technology and musicology.

THE VOICE

Traces the history of significant singers, events, developments in, and contributions to, vocal music.

PERFORMANCE

Includes the significant performers and performance events, premières, debuts, audience reception and consequences.

WOMEN IN MUSIC

Covers the role women have played in the classical music tradition.

INFLUENCES

Allows the reader to follow connection in two directions, indicating the influence composers had on subsequent generations, and the people and music that influenced their own style.

FEATURE BOXES

In addition to these themes, other feature boxes emphasize information on key events, musical milestones, places, and highlight timelines and lists of works.

Popular Melody boxes can be found on the top of the right-hand page; these introduce pieces of music that may be familiar to the reader through their use in the popular media.

A thematic entry is indicated by an active icon at the top of the spread. The page references lead to the previous and following examples of the relevant theme.

page 139 ◀◁ WOMEN IN MUSIC ▷▶ page 203

ACTIVE

◀◁ WOMEN IN MUSIC ▷▶

INACTIVE

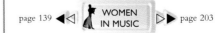

USING THE ENCYCLOPEDIA

The information in the Encyclopedia can be accessed in a number of different ways.

- The text can be read sequentially, through the chronologically organized chapters to gain a holistic view of the development of music since the earliest times.

- The themes listed on page 6 can be traced throught the book using the buttons at the top of each spread, which give page references to the previous and following boxes of the same theme.

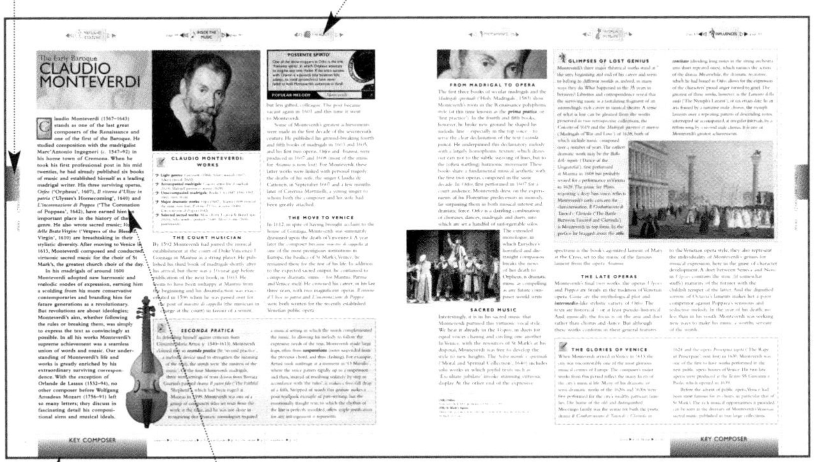

- The introductory paragraph in each section provides a summary of information, acting as a quick reference guide and allowing the reader to explore the subject without reading the entire section.

- Information on a particular element of classical music, such as the development of styles and forms or intruments, can be accessed using the tabs at the bottom of each page, which identify the different sections.

CROSS REFERENCING

A system of cross-referencing has been used in which terms or names that have an entry elsewhere in the encyclopedia are emboldened, with a page reference listed at the bottom of the spread.

- Terms: any terms that may require further explanation appear in bold in the text the first time they appear in a *section*; the cross-reference at the bottom of the left-hand page leads to the appropriate entry in the glossary on pages 356–363.
- Names: people who have an entry in one of the Personalities sections throughout the book appear in bold the first time they are mentioned in a section. The cross reference at the bottom of the right-hand page leads to the appropriate entry. Names are not cross-referenced within the Personalities sections if the person has his or her own entry in the same chapter.

Names and Dates

Full names and dates are given for all musicological figures the first time they appear in a chapter.

PHONETIC SPELLINGS

Phonetic spellings are given for all foreign names in the Personalities sections (excluding the shorter entries on conductors, singers and instrumentalists in The Modern Era and The Late 20th Century). These are intended only as a basic guide to pronunciation and have therefore been kept as simple as possible.

PRONUNCIATION GUIDE

Symbol	Example	Symbol	Example	Symbol	Example	Symbol	Example
a	at	ē	eat	ô	scorn	o͞o	moon
ā	ate	i	in	ö	schön	u	up
ä	awful	ī	mile		(German)	ü	une (French)
â	air	kh	sich (German)	oi	boy	z	zoo
à	art	o	hot	ou	how	zh	azure
e	egg	ō	old	oo	book		

PITCHES

A number of systems have been developed to indicate pitch in print. This encyclopedia uses a system based on upper and lower case letters used in conjunction with apostrophes. Middle C is represented by a lower case c with one apostrophe (c'), one octave above this is indicated by a lower case c with two apostrophes (c''), one octave below middle C is indicate by an upper case C, an octave below this C' etc.

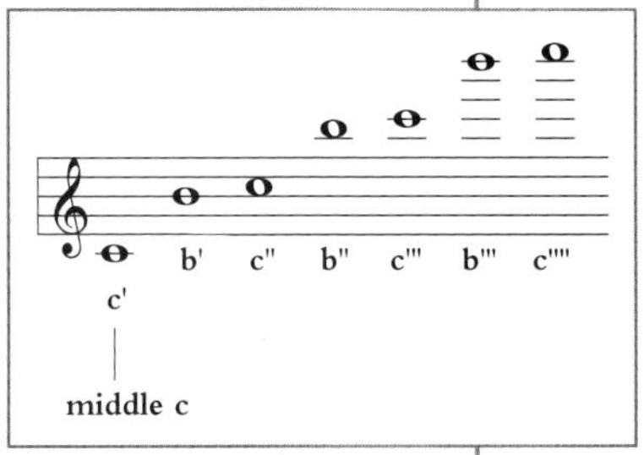

INSTRUMENTS

Each entry in the Instruments section is tagged with an icon indicating to which family of instruments it belongs:

STRINGED

WOODWIND

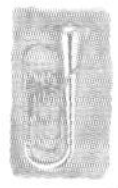
BRASS

KEYBOARD

ELECTRONIC

PERCUSSION

ODDBALL

CAPTIONS

Picture captions appear on the inside left- or right-hand page of each spread. For ease of use, pictures have been captioned clockwise from the inside left to the inside right of the spread. Thus *(BL)* means the bottom picture on the left-hand page, *(TR)* means the top picture on the right-hand page etc. Where two pictures appear on the same level, they are indicated Near *(N)* and Far *(F)*.

KEY

(T)	*Top*	*(M)*	*Middle*	*(R)*	*Right*	*(F)*	*Far*
(B)	*Bottom*	*(L)*	*Left*	*(N)*	*Near*		

FOREWORD

I often wonder how long some people will insist on calling classical music 'elitist'? True, many centuries ago music was a science, and later its main function was for a long time mostly religious; then when music gradually became more secular, it served for some time only a select few. But today the accessibility and availability of classical music is beyond question – the Proms, the American summer outdoor venues, the great number of easily affordable concerts, the classical radio stations, are all proof of this.

Like many of my colleagues, I believe that the benefits of being associated with classical music cannot be overestimated: the great music of Mozart and Beethoven, Sibelius and Tchaikovsky, engages our mind and soul, stimulates our spiritual entity to a degree seldom achieved by other manifestations of human expression, and one of the inner impulses in my musical activity has always been to do my best to bring awareness of it to as many people as possible, be it through debating on various aspects of music, introducing less well-known areas in music or generally sending a message that there is nothing elitist about the great music of the past and present. On the contrary, its mission simply reflects our existence: the effort required to participate in the musical process and receive its message is not enormous, but the rewards are incalculable.

This encyclopedia serves admirably the purpose of reaching out to a very broad spectrum of people – without being too unnecessarily scientific, it combines depth of insight with a high degree of accessibility which is achieved without being trivial or condescending. The scope of this innovative volume is all-embracing, and at the same time it allows the reader to find easily his or her area of interest. Here we have probably the best illustrated comprehensive and 'non-elitist' music encyclopedia available, and I have every reason to hope that many readers will benefit from it – I certainly will.

INTRODUCTION

This book offers a new approach to the presentation of information about music. It is designed for the intelligent music-lover, curious to find out more about the music he or she listens to and enjoys – and who wants to enrich his or her background knowledge in order to listen to it and enjoy it with a deeper understanding of how and why it came to take the form it does, and how it relates to the world around it.

Unlike other reference works, this book is broken down, by period, into chapters; the centre of each chapter is a dictionary-like section, arranged alphabetically, with entries on the main composers and personalities belonging to the era concerned. Near to the beginning of the chapter there are separate discussions about the very greatest among them – the Bachs, Mozarts, Beethovens and Wagners. These are the men whose music we listen to and love the most of all, the composers whose achievement and importance far transcends their own time.

Other features of the musical life and the broader social and political background of the period concerned are discussed alongside the chief composers. Accordingly, each chapter opens with a general outline of this background, the canvas on which the cultural events of the time are drawn and which gives them shape and meaning – for music has never been a hermetic art, insulated from the 'real' world, but an expression of that world, and without its context its meaning is diminished.

Each chapter also includes a discussion of the styles and the forms that music has taken in the period concerned; this enables the reader to see something of the musical context in which composers worked and explains why the music of one period, in its sound, its structure, its colours, is unlike that of any other. In addition, each chapter has a section describing the instruments used during the era. Finally, every era is rounded off by a section in which representative works of the period are cited and the music and its performance are discussed. In the chapters on the twentieth century, to help relate the book to the reader's musical experience, there are additional entries, not just on composers, but also on performers: conductors, singers, instrumentalists.

Music, it is sometimes said, is an international language. This is not entirely true: every culture has developed a musical language or style of its own. The style that originated in western Europe in the Middle Ages, and has continued to develop as western society has changed – and has been carried not only across the whole of Europe, but also to the New World (the Americas, north and south, Australia and New Zealand, much of Africa and Asia) – is only one, though a very highly developed one, among many. Other cultures have entirely different types of musical language, based on different instruments, different rhythmic schemes, different relationships between musical pitches: they demand different types of musical awareness from the listener. These musics, in a time when ethnic groups are so mobile, and travel and communication is relatively easy, have become increasingly available during the late years of the twentieth century. The western listener now has ready access to them – but, conditioned by western music, may find it difficult to come to terms with them. The first chapter of the book, therefore, serves to introduce the music of a variety of world cultures to the westerner, by describing their musical systems and helping the reader towards their understanding.

The remaining nine chapters cover, in more or less a traditional series of period divisions, from medieval times to the present day. But the book does not demand to be read continuously or even necessarily in sequence. It is planned and designed so that it might be read in a variety of ways, skipping from one chapter to another without losing continuity. It incorporates sections that interrelate across the period structure of the chapters. There are a number of particular themes that run through the book, for example, there are discussions of the great musical cities of Europe and the New World, of the human voice and its music and of the ways composers have absorbed influence and in turn passed it on. And the book does not confine itself to the music of only half the human race: the contribution of women composers and the nature of women's participation in the making of music is a distinctive theme of the book.

STANLEY SADIE

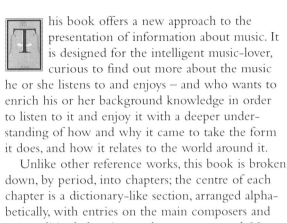

THE WORLD OF MUSIC

In order to put Western classical music into a global and historical context, one must survey the music of ancient civilizations as well as the traditions of the non-Western world. From what is known of this music it was – and is – performed in a vast range of cultural environments and with many functions other than for entertainment in a concert hall. Music is a vital element in ritual, worship, celebration, in coping with life's crises, work and warfare.

THE EARLIEST ROLES OF MUSIC

Archeological findings suggest that humans have made music from earliest times and that music, dance and ritual were inseparable in many prehistoric cultures. Excavations have unearthed many sound-producing artefacts and rock paintings depicting primitive instruments. The great civilizations of China, India, Mesopotamia and Egypt elaborated the role music played in prehistoric times. Although very little is known about how this ancient music actually sounded, archeologists have found clues as to the circumstances and meaning of this music-making. Depictions of an arched harp have been found in Sumeria and the Indus Valley, suggesting a historical link between two of the world's oldest civilizations. Images in ancient Egyptian tombs tell of supposed music in the afterlife. In other parts of the world, information comes from more recent records, such as those of the sixteenth-century Spanish conquerors of the New World, or James Cook's accounts of his explorations in the Pacific in the eighteenth century. The discovery and subsequent study of all these artefacts has significantly broadened our understanding of the meaning and role of music in the ancient world.

The World of Music

INTRODUCTION

Music was closely bound to the myth and beliefs of ancient cultures. The Indian *rāga*, for example was associated not only with specific moods, but also with particular times of the year and religious ceremonies. In many parts of the world this relationship between music and belief persists. The myths of China tell that their musical systems are rooted in the legendary cutting of bamboo pipes. In ancient times Egyptians, Native Americans, Indonesians and Hindus regarded their music as a gift from the gods. The appearance and sound of instruments had symbolic significance for Egyptians and Sumerians; then and now, around the world, some instruments are commonly classified as male and others as female. Many Oceanic people, Native Americans and others still see music as the expression of sacred beings.

FUNCTIONS OF MUSIC

Whereas classical music today is heard primarily as an entertainment art form, this is just one of the ways in which it functions throughout the world. From the earliest civilizations to the present day, in almost every culture, including those of the West, music has played an important role in religious practice. In ancient Mesopotamia, temple musicians were members of powerful élite classes; for modern Sufi sects, music and dance continue to be a route to ecstatic religious experiences. In Africa, music is considered to be thoroughly integrated in the fabric of life, being a part of work, life transition rites, war and celebration. Traditional Native Americans rarely perform music for itself. Rather, it is crucial for affirming cultural identity by accompanying a range of social activities.

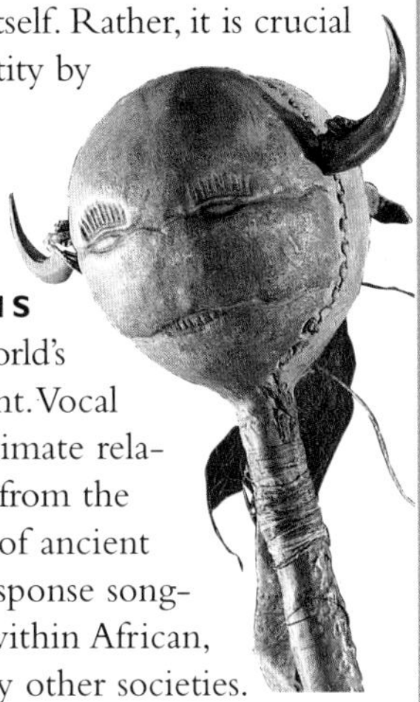

VOCAL AND MUSICAL FORMS

The human voice is the world's primary musical instrument. Vocal music has long had an intimate relationship to oral history – from the intoned Homeric poems of ancient Greece to the call-and-response song-forms that predominate within African, Native American and many other societies.

The relationship of music to time varies greatly. The duration of musical concepts can range from the few seconds of the shortest Southeast Asian gong-chime cycle to ceremonies in Oceania lasting over a year. The characteristic that perhaps most distinguishes classical music from other musical traditions is its development of harmony. Other cultures have followed different paths. In India, small ensembles produce intricate improvised melodies around a single drone note according to strict guidelines. In Southeast Asia, gong-chime ensembles play layered polyphonic music based on cycles.

GLOBAL INFLUENCES

Musical influences have flowed between peoples in all parts of the world, between continents and across centuries. **Claude Debussy** (1862–1918) and **Maurice Ravel** (1875–1937) were entranced when they encountered gamelan music from Java in the nineteenth century; **Olivier Messiaen** (1908–92) found inspiration in a thirteenth-century Indian treatise; and minimalist composer **Steve Reich** (b. 1936) was influenced by the traditional musics of Africa and Asia.

In the Americas, the Native Americans in the north have retained a musically discrete identity, whereas Amerindian music in the south has profoundly cross-fertilized with European forms. The Greeks left a legacy of scales, modes, theory and acoustics. Indeed, all the cultures discussed here have left a legacy whose influence on the West continues to the present day.

MUSICAL THEORIES

Most musical compositions and theories about music have been preserved over the generations in oral tradition. The great musical traditions of Africa, and those of indigenous peoples of the Americas and Australia, have been sustained through word of mouth alone. In other ancient civilizations – India, China, Persia, Arabia – complex written treatises have amplified and elucidated music that was relayed from teacher to student. Such is the case for Western classical music, which relies on both oral and written tradition: the subtle points of performing practice explained in music lessons and demonstrated by the great masters are discussed in dictionaries, scores and theoretical texts.

Treatises and Formal Systems

References to music in writings, such as the *Vedas* in India and the works attributed to Confucius in China, set out the role of music in life and religion, in the state and in entertainment. The *Natyasastra* ('Treatise on Drama', probably second century AD), an early Indian treatise, explains the theory, functions and meaning of music and the arts, and also serves as a production manual for plays and dances. In China and Greece, independent yet comparable systems were devised to divide the octave into 12 intervals. The Chinese used the cutting and blowing of pipes, whereas Pythagoras in Greece made his calculations by sub-dividing the lengths of a string. Musical notation has been most thoroughly developed in the West, although other cultures use tablature, cipher notation and other rudimentary systems. The instruments of Western classical music have kindred types in many another culture, where, as in the West, they are classified according to the material from in which they are made and the way in which they produce sound.

CHINA

The earliest recorded dynasty in China, the Shang (*c.* 1766–*c.* 1122 BC), developed the system of writing that today offers a record of Chinese musical activity and legend spanning 5,000 years. From these writings can be gained information on the destruction and reinvention of music theory through centuries of change: its mythological origins, theoretical basis, an inventory of court instruments, and the role of music in court life, sacred and secular.

THE TWELVE LÜ

According to legend, in 2697 BC, Emperor Huang-ti ('Yellow Emperor') sent one Ling Luen ('Music Master') to the western mountains to make musical pipes cut from lengths of bamboo (*lü*) tuned to the songs of the phoenix. Some key ideas underpinning ancient Chinese music – the harmony between humans and nature, and the relationship of accurate pitch to orderly government – were derived from the sound of these pipes. When, by tradition, subsequent sets of pipes were made, the first one gave the foundation note and was called the 'yellow bell' (*huang-chung*). Its length was a standard measure. It was used to cut and tune the full set of 12 pipes; the resulting set of 12 notes had the same proportional relationships as the mathematical ratios discovered by the Greek theorist Pythagoras in the sixth century BC.

THE 'EIGHT SOUNDS'

The traditional classification for instruments was called *pa-yin* ('eight sounds'). According to this system, each of the eight materials from which instruments were made had particular significance. For example, the skin of a drum was related to the north, the season of winter, and to water. The idea was to combine musical sounds so as to evoke the balance between different aspects of nature. The 'eight sounds' and associated instruments are shown in the table above.

chung	metal	bells
ch'ing	stone	chimes
yü	wood	boxes that were scraped or struck
hsuan	clay	globe-like ocarinas that were blown into
ko	skin	drums with stretched animal skins
ti and *chih*	bamboo	pipes and flutes
sheng	gourd	mouth organs
ssu	silk	stringed instruments

Among the earliest instruments found in China are bronze bells, stone-chimes and ocarinas from the second millennium BC. Stone reliefs from the Christian era show panpipes, drums, bells, stone chimes and zithers, all being played to accompany dances. The pre-eminent classical Chinese instrument is the *ch'in*, a long zither with seven silk strings. Other classical string instruments include the *sê*, a zither with 25 strings, and the *cheng*, a plucked zither used for personal and popular entertainment. The *p'i-p'a*, a four-stringed fretted lute, remains a popular solo instrument. The arrival of the Chinese *sheng* in Europe inspired the development of free-reed instruments in the early nineteenth century, such as the mouth organ.

MUSICAL THEATRE

China boasts over 300 forms of regional theatre; the most esteemed of these is Beijing (Peking) opera. This genre developed in the late eighteenth century in tea houses, with their atmosphere of casual conversation and social mingling. The typical characters include: male characters and generals (usually baritones); unbearded scholar-lovers (falsettos); the virtuous daughter or faithful wife (high falsetto); and the flirtatious woman. The stock repertory of some 30 tunes encompasses the required set of moods. The singers are accompanied by bowed and plucked strings, drums, clappers, gongs, cymbals, bamboo flutes and oboes. After the formation of the Chinese People's Republic (1949), Beijing opera was reformed according to the ideology of Mao Tse-Tung and during the Cultural Revolution, traditional opera virtually disappeared. A new repertory was composed to celebrate the triumphs of Marxist socialism, emphasizing patriotism and eliminating gestures of obeisance.

CULTURAL INFLUENCES

Politics, philosophy and music became entwined in China. Chinese thinkers, notably Confucius (551–479 BC) and his followers, expounded theories about music's effect on the mind, on emotions and on its role in education. As with Greek scholars Plato and Aristotle, they acknowledged the power of music over behaviour, and advocated state regulation of this powerful art form. Confucianism remained the state religion from the Han dynasty (206 BC–AD 220) until the fall in 1911 of China's last dynasty, the Ch'ing. During this 2,000-year period, with each new dynasty, an imperial bureau would re-define standards of musical pitch and oversee ceremonial court music. For example, the ministry of music in the Chou dynasty (1111–255 BC) determined the role of music in education, at court, in divination ceremonies and ancestor worship. The ideals of Confucius formed the basis for a twofold division of music into *ya-yüeh* ('elegant music') and *su-yüeh*, ('popular music'). Since the disappearance of the imperial courts in the twentieth century, however, *ya-yüeh* has been performed only in Confucian temples. The notion of state control over music was still current in the Chinese Cultural revolution (1966–68).

(BL) Native American Rattle
Rattles were used to accompany ceremonial songs and rituals in the ancient world.
(ML) Lute Player
Teracotta figure playing the lute, from the Chinese Sui dynasty, AD 581–618.
(TL) Harp Player
Egyptian wall painting showing a harp player and his audience.
(R) Banquet and Concert
Anonymous painting depicting ladies of the T'ang imperial court, enjoying a feast and music.

Debussy ▶ p. 282 Messiaen ▶ p. 293 Ravel ▶ p. 294 Reich ▶ p. 328

SOUTH ASIA

The South Asian region is centred on India and includes the neighbouring modern nations of Afghanistan, Pakistan, Bangladesh, Nepal, Bhutan and Sri Lanka. The region now called Pakistan saw the rise and fall of the Indus Valley civilization, one of the oldest in the world. Scarce archeological objects showing drums and an arched harp give a glimpse of a musical culture from around the third millennium BC. Between *c.* 2000 and *c.* 600 BC, Aryans from the Asian steppes invaded the Indus Valley and the Dravidian peoples in southern India. From the thirteenth century AD onwards, Muslims from Central Asia invaded, dominating northern India until the nineteenth century.

The two great classical music traditions of South Asia are the North Indian (including Pakistan and Bangladesh) and the Karnatic (southern India). In neither tradition did a highly developed system of musical notation occur. Also, the absence of harmony and simpler four-square rhythms meant that music was not played in large ensembles. Instead, Indian oral traditions followed a course of creativity entirely different from classical music in Europe, fostering a refined art of solo improvisation in expressive modal forms called *rāgas* ('melody types') and intricate rhythmic frameworks called *talas*.

THE *VEDAS* AND MUSICAL TREATISES

Indian music was intimately linked to the mythological and religious world view of the *Vedas* (lit. 'knowledge', *c.* 1400–*c.* 500 BC). The legacy of the Aryans, this was an enormous collection of sacred lore and ritual, originally oral and written down much later. The *Vedas* prescribed the correct forms of *nāda* (sound vibrations) for successful sacrifices and for a connection with the spiritual world. The earliest known Indian treatise to discuss music is the *Natyasastra*, attributed to the sage Bharata, which became the source for centuries of music theory. It describes a musical system with 22 intervals (*śruti*) per octave (smaller than the modern Western 12 intervals), details ranges of scales (*murchana*) and modes (*jāti*), and outlines a theory about emotions in music called *rasa*. Other notable treatises include the *Brihaddesi* ('The Great Treatise on Desi', *c.* ninth century AD), the *Manasottasa* ('Diversions of the Heart', 1131), the *Sangitaratnakara* ('The Jewel Mine of Music', thirteenth century). The last of these inspired the twentieth-century composer Messiaen to write the complex rhythms of his *Livre d'orgue* ('Organ Book', 1951). From the sixteenth century onwards, theoretical treatises continued to standardize and synthesize Indian music, moulding ancient concepts to suit the performing practice of the day.

HINDUSTANI AND KARNATIC STYLES

Hindustani musicians are predominantly Muslims, their forefathers having converted to Islam, the religion of the Mughal court. Yet their hereditary musical traditions reflect the hierarchical social order embedded in Hinduism: teacher is higher than student, soloist than drummer. Great twentieth-century performers such as Ravi Shankar (b. 1920) reverently touch the feet of their gurus and even bow to the stage out of humility to their art. The most sober Hindustani form, the *dhrupad*, is attributed to musicians in the great Moghul courts of Gwalior, notably Mayen Tansen (*c.* 1500–1589), to whose lineage many great twentieth-century musicians claimed allegiance. The more modern and lyrical vocal form, *khyal*, flourished in the eighteenth-century court of Muhammad Shah, displacing the stately *dhrupad* style.

In Karnatic music, three saint-musicians, Tiruvottiyur Tyagaraja (1764–1847), Muttusvami Diksitar (1775–1835), and Syama Sastri (1762–1827), are worshipped. Between them, they composed hundreds of *kriti*. These vocal compositions combine improvisation with composed sections based on some 10,000 (mainly devotional) texts. Slow introductory passages (*alapana*), variations and virtuosic sequences complete these beautiful pieces. In concert, a vocalist and instrumentalist (*vina*, flute) will perform *kriti* to evoke for audiences the well-known texts associated with the familiar tunes.

INSTRUMENTS

Indian musicians excel on stringed instruments, chiefly lute, and on the drums. North Indians use two plucked lutes: the *sitar*, with four melody strings, three drone strings and 13 sympathetic strings, and the *sarod*, with six melody, two drone, and additional sympathetic strings. South Indians play the *vīnā*, a long-necked lute with four melody and three drone strings. Also important are the *bin*, a zither, and the European violin. The classical drums are tuned to the main pitch of the *rāga*. The main Karnatic drum is the double-headed *mṛdangam*. The Hindustani *tabla* is a pair of small single-headed drums. The drone is constantly played on a *tambura*, a long-necked fretless lute.

(BL and TL) Indian Musicians
Statues of musicians at the Temple of the Sun complex at Konarak.
(TR) Indonesian Musicians
Relief showing musicians in scenes from the life of the Buddha.
(BR) Gamelan Gongs
The Javanese gamelan orchestra has influenced much Western music, most notably that of Debussy and Ravel.

INDIAN MUSICAL FORMS

Most Indian classical music has three main components: a solo melody line, a rhythmic accompaniment, and a drone. Vocal music is predominant, although modern Western audiences are more aware of instrumental genres. Improvisation, a key feature of Indian music, is based on the elaborate rules of the *rāgas* and *talas*, which are the principal formal concepts of classical Indian music. A *rāga* is a framework for playing melodies; a performer of a particular *rāga* improvises a melody while following the performance guidelines associated with it. These can include how fast to play, what mood (*rasa*) to convey and the appropriate time of day for performance. Of the thousands of ragas in theoretical writings, around 50 are played in the North Indian tradition and 50 in the Karnatic. The common structure of a *raga* would comprise a slow improvisatory section, followed by a fixed composition, leading to faster virtuosic interplay between soloist and drummer, culminating in an explosive finale. The word *tala* means 'beating together', suggesting the hand-clapping and small cymbal-striking used to keep time in Indian music. A *tala* is a framework for combining rhythms, and Indian drummers must memorize the characteristic patterns and phrases of the *talas* in their repertory.

cadence ▶ p. 356 *rāga* ▶ p. 362 *tala* ▶ p. 362

SOUTHEAST ASIA

The vast Southeast Asian region includes the island republics of Indonesia and the Philippines, and the mainland states of Burma, Thailand, Cambodia, Laos, Vietnam, Malaysia and Singapore. The mainland countries, particularly Vietnam, have been greatly influenced by Chinese culture and the Buddhist religion. Indonesia has been influenced by Hinduism and Islam, and the Philippines by Islam and Christianity. Each nation comprises many minority peoples and local languages. The geography of Southeast Asia, a region disturbed by earthquakes and volcanic eruptions, has influenced its musical development. Minorities, with their diverse indigenous folk music styles, tend to live in upland areas, whereas the dominant ethnic populations live in the lowlands. Within Southeast Asia's diversity of musical culture, two phenomena stand out: gong-chime and gamelan orchestras.

THE GAMELAN

Gamelan music had a great influence in the West, notably at the 1889 Grand Universal Exhibition in Paris, where the shimmering timbre of the orchestra made a profound impression on Debussy and Ravel. The gamelan was introduced to the United States at the Chicago World's Columbian Exposition in 1893. This musical style comes from the very diverse Indonesian culture that embraces peoples living in more than 3,000 islands speaking over 250 languages, variously subject to Mongol, Arab, Indian, Chinese and European influences. The music is made up of homogeneous percussive sounds, with a rich timbre and intricate patterns. A full gamelan has two sets of instruments, each using one of the two principal scales, the five-note *slendro* and the seven-note *pelog*. These can be performed in several modes (*pathet*) that specify the correct pitches, **cadences**, and time of day. The compositions employ polyphony and interlocking patterns, with each player adding notes to the total melody to produce fast, complex pieces without making excessive demands on any one musician.

The Javanese gamelan is the best known and most thoroughly studied style. With typically 25 instrumentalists in an ensemble, gamelan is played in concert and to accompany religious and state ceremonies, theatre, dance and puppet plays. The gamelan of Bali shares many features with that of Java, but is distinguished by the paired metallophones – one tuned slightly higher than the other – that give it a uniquely transparent, shimmering texture.

THE GONG-CHIME CULTURES

Southeast Asian countries are classified musically as gong-chime cultures. The region's huge variety of gong-chime ensembles play combinations of gongs, drums, flutes, string instruments, xylophones and metallophones. The composition and size of the ensembles vary from country to country, with Javanese *gamelan* having up to 75 instruments. Gong-chime ensembles reflect the stratified societies that foster them. The large gong is the most venerated and is thought to be the spiritual centre of the ensemble. It is blessed with ritual offerings. Smaller instruments and gong chimes are lower in status and are played for ornamentation and improvisation. Music is played in time cycles (Javanese, *gongan*), marked by the large gong. Repetitions of the cycle include minute variations and carefully controlled improvisations. A single cycle may last for a few seconds or several minutes. The accompanying instrumental parts weave together in an interlocking style. A solo melody played on lute, flute or oboe, or sung, may overarch several rhythmic cycles.

INSTRUMENTS

Southeast Asian gongs are made of bronze, brass, or iron, and hang in frames or are placed on racks or cases. Many ornately carved and painted instruments are prized for their beauty. They have magical powers attributed to them and receive ritual offerings. The forging of gongs is treated as a sacred activity and ritual protections are provided for the gong-maker, particular during the tempering or tuning of the instruments. Gongs often have a central knob called a 'boss', and are tuned to a pitch in the local scale (many with equidistantly-spaced intervals) – usually pentatonic (five-note) or heptatonic (seven-note). These rare equidistant scales are also found in East Africa, suggesting the possibility that sea traders introduced such tunings to Madagascar and the coastal region of modern Mozambique. The names of many instruments are onomatopoeic, mimicking their sounds – for example, large and small hanging bronze gongs (*gong ageng, kempul*), bronze kettle gongs (*kenong, ketuk*), gong-chimes (*bonang*), metallophones (*saron, gender*), xylophones (*gambang*). Together they may accompany one or more vocalists, flute (*suling*) or a bowed spike-fiddle (*rebab*) of Middle Eastern origin.

HISTORY OF MUSICAL PERFORMANCE

Java's temples offer information about the island's 2,000-year musical history. Bas-reliefs on Hindu temples show Indian influences from the fifth century AD. Reliefs on the Borobuduran Buddhist *stupa* (temples, *c.* AD 800) depict a wealth of instruments: trumpets, flutes, oboes, mouth organs, lutes, zithers, harps, drums, xylophones, bells and kettle gongs. Early Javanese *Kawi* literature tells of noisy percussion ensembles accompanying battles, masked dances and shadow puppetry. Wind and string instruments were also played for women's court dancing. The *Smaradhana* (*c.* twelfth century) mentions Islamic influences on local music, and the *Serat Centhini*, an encyclopedic poem (most popular version from 1800), lists compositions and describes music, dance and theatre.

Throughout Southeast Asia, music is intimately linked to the theatrical arts – plays, masked plays, puppet shows, shadow-dramas, dance-dramas and operas. Many of these genres have roots in ancient animistic rites for placating nature spirits. Later dramatic texts were based on foreign sources, especially the Hindu *Ramāyāṇa* and *Mahābhārata* epics, and the *Jataka* tales of the life of the Buddha. Between *c.* 1300 and *c.* 1750, Chinese theatrical forms were introduced to the northern mainland, and during the same period, extensive Arabic influences reached the southern mainland and the islands.

THE AMERICAS

The ancestors of the indigenous peoples of North and South America migrated from Asia across the frozen Bering Strait over 20,000 years ago. Even after millennia, some characteristics are shared between Oriental and Amerindian music: monophonic forms, large intervals, a tense vocal style, rattles and framedrums, and the importance of music in healing rituals. In the present day, as in centuries past, music is central to Amerindian culture, accompanying life rites, social and ritual gatherings, dances, hunting and story telling. Music is rarely performed for itself, as it is in Western concert settings.

The word 'Amerindian' is used to refer to the indigenous peoples of the Americas rather than the term 'Indian' (mistakenly coined by Columbus in 1492). More particularly, native groups from Canada choose to be called 'First Nations'; from the United States 'Native Americans'; and from Central and South America 'Amerindian'.

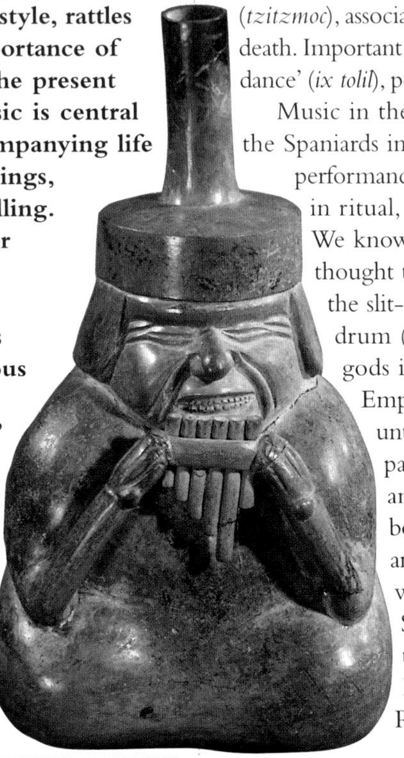

THE GHOST DANCE

The government-enforced isolation of Native Americans in the United States has fostered cultural independence, in contrast to the marked musical acculturation between the Hispanic-speaking and Amerindian societies in South America. But in modern times, North American groups have tended to set aside tribal differences and seek a pan-tribal cultural unity. The 'Ghost Dance', a religious cult led by Jack Wilson, was an early pan-tribal movement. Wilson proclaimed the 'Ghost Dance' would bring all dead Indians and dead buffalo back to life and drive the white man into the sea. The cult originated in the Great Basin (Utah, Nevada) during the 1880s, and soon caught hold in the Plains. The Ghost Dance style had a limited melodic range and simple form, generally with pairs of musical phrases (for instance AA, BB, CC). Although the cult was outlawed in the 1890s, its songs are still sung.

CENTRAL AND SOUTH AMERICAN CIVILIZATIONS

Sixteenth-century Spanish records provide a glimpse of the spectacular musical cultures of the Aztec, Maya and Inca empires. The Maya civilization of the Mexican Yucatán peninsula reached its pinnacle around AD 300–900. Mayan instruments included clay and wooden trumpets, clay flutes, vertical flutes with six fingerholes and panpipes. Manuscripts show the *kayum* drum was played barehanded. The only metal instrument was the pellet-bell rattle (*tzitzmoc*), associated with *Ah-Puch*, the god of death. Important dances included the 'ribbon dance' (*ix tolil*), performed as recently as 1941.

Music in the Aztec Empire (crushed by the Spaniards in 1521) embraced ensemble performance, song and dance; it was played in ritual, courtly and peasant settings. We know that certain instruments were thought to have supernatural powers and the slit-drum (*teponaztle*) and cylindrical drum (*huehuetl*) were believed to be gods in earthly exile. The Inca Empire dominated the Pacific coast until its demise in 1534. Early Inca panpipes (*c.* AD 500), trumpets, and flutes were made of clay and bone. 100-strong flute orchestras and smaller ensembles of panpipes were documented by the Spaniards. Trumpeters were said to enjoy high social status in the Inca Empire, as they did in Renaissance Europe.

NORTH AMERICA

Many Native Americans hold that music has been handed down since the beginning of time. New songs are thought to come in the dreams or visions, with few songs having named composers. Sung epics, origin myths and healing chants are passed on orally by shamans, medicine men and priests. The repertory of women is rich with lullabies, puberty songs, and social dance songs with their sometimes religious, sometimes teasing lyrics.

The best-known style is from the Great Plains, including Blackfoot, Comanche, Crow, Pawnee, Sioux and other peoples. Plains songs have descending melodies and pentatonic scales, sung with an unmistakable tense, hard vocal sound, in a high (even falsetto) range. Songs are often accompanied by the drum and rattle. The Pueblo peoples of the south-west share much with those in the Great Plains grouping.

However, the Yuma of the south-west and Californian groups use a relaxed vocal style, and musical forms with short repeated sections. The complex singing style of the Athabascan-speaking tribes of the south-west (Navajo, Apache) is light and nasal. The Iroquois and the Wabanaki confederations (of the north-east), the Cherokee, Creek, Seminole (south-east) and Chippewa (the Great Lakes) sing short call-and-response songs with simple rhythms and undulating melodies. In the present day, one important role of the music is to promote Native American identity through pan-tribal pow-wows or meetings.

AMERINDIAN INSTRUMENTS

The widest range of instruments is found in Central and South America, particularly in the Andean region. Flutes, whistles and rattles are widespread. An early example is the notched flute (*quena*) from the Chavin era (900–200 BC), sometimes made from human bone. Panpipes are popular in the Andes – they have one or two rows of pipes, are often tuned in thirds and can produce a complete scale. Clarinets are played in Argentina, Bolivia, Guyana and by remote groups along the Orinoco and Amazon rivers. Some of the most complex Amerindian music can be heard in the Andes, where European harps, guitars, violins and lutes are combined with indigenous flutes and panpipes.

Many South American instruments are believed to have magical or religious significance. For example, the Brazilian Coazárini tribe associate the clarinet with the serpent of evil, and the trumpets of the Tupí-Witoto of Brazil and the Piaroa of Venezuela are considered sacred. By contrast, Native Americans have few instruments. The flute is the main melodic instrument; rattles, clappers, and drums are used to accompany song and dance. The Apache fiddle (or 'Navajo violin') is a hybrid instrument, combining the Western violin with the archaic Native American bow.

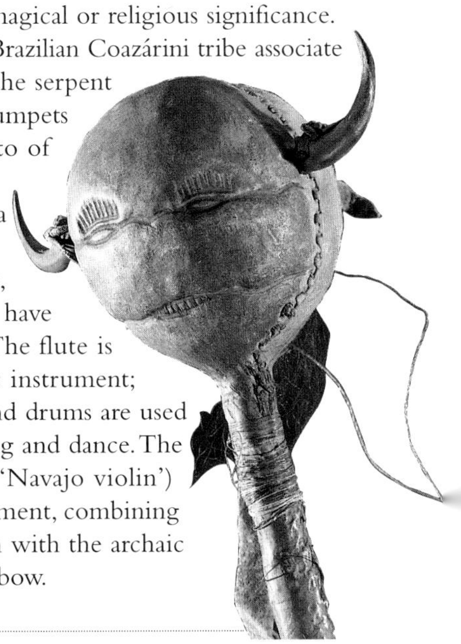

(BL) Native American Rattle
Plains Indians would accompany their songs with drums and rattles such as this.
(TL) Inca Statue
Early Inca flutes were made of clay and bone; many instruments were thought to have supernatural powers.
(R) Tahitian Nose Flute
Nose flutes were made of bamboo and were played by means of nasal breath.

diatonic ▶ p. 358

AFRICA

Since classical antiquity, the varied cultures of Africa have fascinated Europeans, but only in the twentieth century did musicologists overcome concepts of 'primitivism' to discover the richness of the continent's music. African performing arts are intimately bound to life – the music is woven into the fabric of society and culture. It is inseparable from other performing arts such as dance, drama and pantomime, and is such an integral part of life that many African languages do not have a separate word for 'music'.

MUSICAL STYLES

With few written treatises, African music is passed on by oral tradition. The typical form for African music is call-and-response, of which there are myriad variations. African melodies are often **diatonic** and so can sound less foreign to Western ears than do the pentatonic scales of East Asia or the modal forms of the Near East and India. Africans think of melodies as 'voices' and the typical call-and-response form as a 'conversation'. Inner parts in complex polyphonic structures may also 'converse'. Melodies follow the rhythm and stress of the local language. Because these have musical qualities, speech and song often overlap. More recent understanding of rhythm in African music suggests that Africans perceive the flow of simultaneous melodies not as 'polyrhythmic' but more as a maypole with many ribbons of flowing bright colours – uniting, crossing, twisting and reuniting.

CULTURAL FUNCTIONS OF MUSIC

African music is an essential part of religious rituals, for work and life transitions such as marriage. Many musical events involve all members of a community singing, playing, acting and dancing. Music for civic occasions is performed on a grand scale, as is the large repertory in many African societies of music for warfare. Political song is common throughout the continent and is a special preoccupation in West Africa, where the praise singers (*jali*) comment on the famous and infamous deeds of leaders, and recite the history and genealogy of their people. Most African societies boast vocal and instrumental virtuosos. Professional musicians were once sponsored by traditional ruler-patrons, whose modern equivalents are national cultural councils, broadcasters, and record companies.

INSTRUMENTS

African peoples play a host of instruments in addition to the many drums often written of in older reports. (The portrayal of Africa as a continent of drums persisted well into the twentieth century). Instruments serve four roles: they may be played solo, in ensembles, or to accompany the voice; they are thought to mediate between humans and gods: they are used to transmit messages (e.g. the famous *atumpan* 'talking drums' of Ghana); and instruments such as trumpets and drums reinforce prestige and authority. Blown instruments include flutes, wooden, metal and animal-horn trumpets, and single- and double-reed pipes. Idiophones range from simple rattles and bells to the complex giant xylophones of East Africa.

African chordophones include the full complement of harps, lutes, musical bows, zithers, lyres, and hybrid types such as the Gambian *kora* (harp-lute). Harps are played mainly north of the equator in a broad band across the continent from the western savannah to Uganda. Most African chordophones are used for self-accompaniment to sung poetry; the typical form has ostinato figures and interlocking polyphonic melodies. The lamellophone (*mbira, sansa*), is unique to Africa and the African diaspora; the *mbira* of southern Africa has a single or double keyboard of metal tongues (which are plucked) fastened to a board or box resonator and mounted in a dried calabash. Such melody instruments are often played with percussive techniques (plucked strings, struck keys), allowing the typical interlocking rhythms to be easily heard.

OCEANIA

The Oceania region includes three principal areas – Melanesia (from the Bismarcks to Fiji), Polynesia (Hawaii, Tonga, Tahiti and Samoa) and Micronesia (north of the equator and west of the International Date Line). The music of the Pacific islands (some 7,000 to 10,000) has been shaped by the alternating forces of isolation, migration and contact within their vast ocean setting. Our understanding of Pacific music dates from accounts of early explorers and missionaries, including Captain James Cook, whose ships' logs (1768–79) tell of a unified musical style throughout the islands – still largely true.

MUSICAL STYLES AND INFLUENCES

Music and dance throughout the Pacific are linked with poetry. Vocal music predominates and many of the smaller remote atolls have no local instruments. The most common style of singing is monophonic, a single line in unison or octaves, with call-and-response forms. Melodies are often limited to the range of a third. Music and dance accompany long ceremonial cycles, some even lasting more than a year. The influences of Western church music, whalers' shanties, and popular music were felt from the second half of the eighteenth century. In New Zealand and Hawaii, however, a concerted attempt has been mounted to preserve local music; and on more remote islands older forms still survive.

INSTRUMENTS

Most instruments of the Pacific islands serve many roles: for signalling (using the conch-shell trumpet), as lures, as toys to imitate the voices of supernatural beings and in rituals. Instruments are fairly uncomplicated, for example, bamboo mouth flutes and nose flutes (sounded by nasal breath). Single-headed hourglass drums are common and the open end is often carved to form the mouth of a bird or crocodile. 'Slit-drums' (hollowed-out tree trunks beaten with sticks) are also widespread. A few local instruments are unique to the Pacific. One such is the friction blocks of New Ireland – three or four wooden plaques rubbed with the hands. Instruments introduced from overseas include the Hawaiian ukulele, a native form of the Portuguese mandolin, brought to the islands in the 1870s. The Solomon Islands are distinguished by a complex polyphonic panpipe repertory. The composers of these panpipes pieces have documented their theoretical system for this music.

THE NEAR EAST

The Near East includes two of the world's earliest civilizations, in Mesopotamia and Egypt. From the few artefacts found in Mesopotamia something is known about Sumerian instruments and the circumstances in which music was played. The Egyptian musical culture shared characteristics with that of Mesopotamia; they played similar instruments and music was also closely associated with rituals and worship. Within the Bible lands lived the Hebrew peoples, whose musical culture was an important influence on music in the West because it formed the basis of early Christian liturgy. Much later, a distinctive relationship between music and religion was formed in the Islamic world.

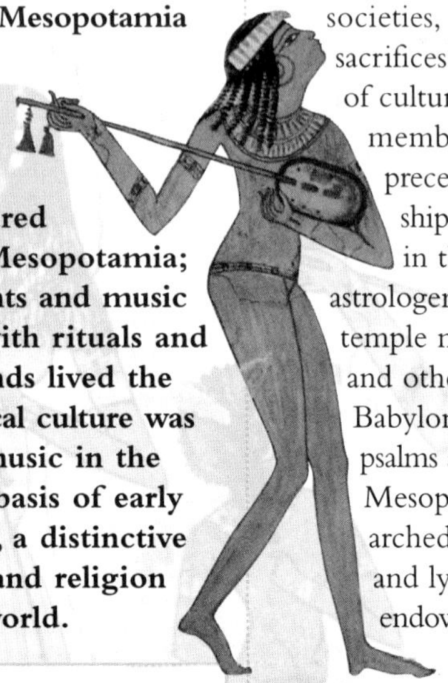

IMAGES OF MUSIC

The bas-reliefs, statues and hieroglyphs of ancient Egypt illustrate a musical culture that flourished from the third millennium BC until Roman times: the musicians, song texts and the social and religious contexts in which music was played. According to legend, Egyptian music and the arts were bequeathed to man by the god Osiris, 'Lord of the *sistrum*' (frame rattle). The god of music and dance was Bes (the 'dwarf god'), depicted with a harp or kithara in hand. Instruments had symbolic associations with their gods. Animals were depicted playing them and were featured on the decoration of instruments.

Scenes of Music-making

Reliefs in the royal tombs at Thebes show scenes of music-making intended to provide entertainment in the afterlife. There is currently no evidence that notation was developed in ancient Egypt, but there are depictions of cheironomy (hand signals that might have indicated pitches, rhythms, or fingerings for musicians and singers) from the third century BC,. Musicians are shown playing in groups – sometimes with singers, cheironomists and dancers – on a range of instruments (harps, lyres, flutes, double clarinets, frame drums, trumpets and rattles, including the *sistrum*). In Hellenistic times, instruments such as the *aulos* were also introduced from Greece.

MESOPOTAMIA

Cuneiform texts, bas-reliefs and archeological finds provide information about the music of the Tigris-Euphrates valley civilizations, from around 3,000 BC to Hellenistic times. These included the kingdoms of Sumeria, Akkadia, Chaldea, Babylonia and Assyria. In Mesopotamian societies, music was central to religious rites, sacrifices and festivals. Temples were centres of cultural life and temple musicians were members of social élites. Sumerian precentors, who led the singing in worship, had their own guilds and moved in the same circles as mathematicians, astrologers and priests. Babylonian castes of temple musicians included lament singers and other specialists. After around 1830 BC, Babylonian liturgical services comprised psalms and hymns with **antiphonal** styles. Mesopotamian instruments included arched harps, flutes, drums, frame drums and lyres. Certain instruments could be endowed with cult symbolism: for example, the soundbox of a lyre from the Royal Cemetary at Ur was shaped like a bull, symbolizing power and fertility.

THE BIBLE LANDS

...Praise Him with the sound of the trumpet
Praise Him with the psaltery and harp
Praise Him with the timbrel and dance
Praise Him with stringed instruments and organs...

Excerpt from Psalm 150

The Bible offers a vivid picture of music-making for worship and in the daily lives of the ancient Jews. The Hebrew lyrics (*c.* 1200–100 BC) of the Old Testament tell of victories celebrated with women's choirs, of music in religious festivals and of trumpet signals in war. In the great age of Hebrew music (1002–970 BC), the Levites, the hereditary priestly caste, performed instrumental and vocal music over generations. When Jesus worshipped in the Temple of Herod, he probably heard monophonic (single line) vocal music. The earliest instrument of worship, the *shofar* (ram's-horn trumpet), came from a former nomadic epoch. Instruments were played in King Solomon's temple (*c.* tenth century BC) but were later banned by the rabbis, forging an intensely spiritual style of sacred song. After the destruction of the Second Temple at Jerusalem in AD 70, worship shifted to the synagogue and a new system of cantillation ensued that persists to the present day.

MUSIC IN THE ISLAMIC WORLD

From the seventh century AD, Islamic music spread from Arabia and was nurtured in Persia, Syria, and Greece. To speak of 'Islamic music' is certainly a contradiction in terms, as music is banned from worship by orthodox Muslims; although the Qur'an does not speak against music, early Islamic scholars formulated prohibitions against it from the sayings of the prophet Muhammad. The chanting from the Qur'an by a soloist, usually with vocal ornamentation, is regarded as heightened speech, not song. Nevertheless, over the years and in many far-flung regions, song and dance (as commonly understood by non-Muslims) has been performed by Muslims in celebration of their faith. Sufi groups have expressed Islamic mysticism by drawing upon musical forms derived from indigenous music. The Mevlevî 'whirling dervishes' of Turkey perform a graceful ceremonial dance (condemned by orthodox Muslims) that leads devotees to religious ecstasy.

(BL and TL) Egyptian Musicians
Egyptian paintings showing double flute and lute.
(ML) Islamic Musicians
Illustration from an arabic book showing a musical entertainment.
(TR and MR) Greek Musicians
Statues of two Greek girls playing the lute and kithara.
(BR) Roman Musicians
Roman mosaic depicting an organ player and horn blower.

THE MAQAM

The fundamental characteristics of Arab classical music are described in splendid treatises including those by al-Kindi (*c.* AD 801–873) and al-Farabi (d. *c.* AD 950), in which we read of melodic and rhythmic modes, aesthetics and the physics of sound. The classical music of the Arab world is unified by a system of modes called ***maqam*** – analogous to the Indian system of *ragas*. Each *maqam* has its individual scales, extra-musical associations, tonal centres, final tones, and formulae for melodies and cadences. Thus Arab classical music sounds curiously exotic to Western ears, because the scales of the *maqam* modal system are seldom diatonic. Some 900 treatises in Arabic, Persian and Turkish were written between AD 900 and AD 1900 on the classical and religious musical traditions of the Islamic nations.

antiphonal music ▶ p. 356 *maqam* ▶ p. 359

GREECE AND ROME

M*ousiké*, the Greek word for music, came from the 'Muses' – nine sister goddesses who embodied the arts. Music was a part of public and private life: marriage and funeral rites, festivals, banquets, ceremonies and sporting events. Music was closely associated with poetry and dance, and was shaped first and foremost by poetic metre. The earliest composers of ancient Greece were poets – Homer, Archilochus, Sappho, Pindar and Sophocles – who intended their masterpieces to be intoned. It was the theory of Greek music, however, that was speculatively revived in later medieval treatises, and came to influence the musical thought of Western Europe.

WRITTEN MUSIC AND INSTRUMENTS

Some 40 fragments preserved on stone, papyrus, and in manuscripts are the only records of ancient Greek music. The earliest is probably a fragment of Euripides' *Iphigenia in Aulis* (*c.* 406 BC). Musical life is also shown on vases, frescoes and mosaics. Two systems of musical notation were developed, both using alphabetical or quasi alphabetical signs. One was for vocal, the other for instrumental music. Notable among Greek instruments were the lyre, associated with the god Apollo, the aulos, a reed-blown pipe with a shrill, licentious, oboe-like sound, and the kithara, a large lyre performed mainly by professionals. Tambourines (*tympana*), castanets (*krotala*) and cymbals (*kymbala*) featured in orgiastic cults such as that of Dionysus.

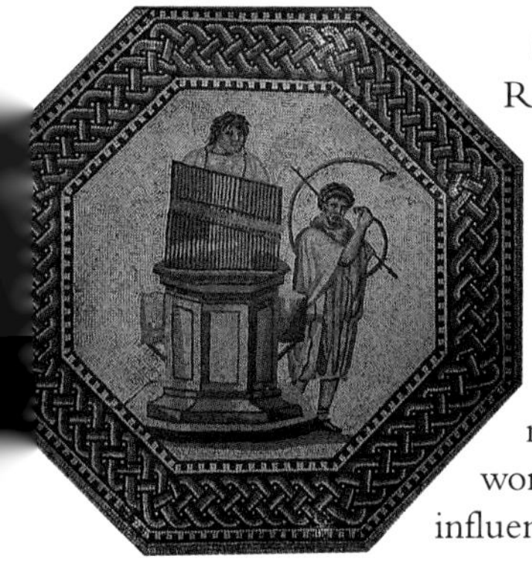

ROMAN MUSIC

Research in the twentieth century has dispelled the notion of ancient Romans as an unmusical people. Roman music was heard in diverse settings: religious, public, martial, theatrical and work. Rome absorbed musical influences from the Etruscans, the Greeks and the Orient. New genres were influenced by the music of conquered kingdoms: Macedonia, Syria and Egypt. In what can be considered the golden age of Roman music (27 BC–AD 192), slave musicians and dancers were recruited from throughout the Roman Empire, virtuosos (mainly Greek) played for a living, and Greek and Roman musicians had professional organizations. Musical theatre flourished, despite being denounced as 'demoralizing and effeminate' by Tacitus and others. Rome's most notorious musician was the emperor Nero (AD 37–68), whose artistic pretensions led him to give public performances on the kithara.

The diversity of instruments of ancient Rome reveals the international nature of this society. The kithara and lyre had been adopted, with their number of strings increased and the body size expanded. Asian harps and lutes were played in public and domestic settings. Frame drums, cymbals and other idiophones were used in mystery cults as well as the theatre. The invention of the hydraulis organ is credited to Ctesibius, an Alexandrian engineer (third century BC). Its loud sound was ideally suited for the great Roman amphitheatres. According to Pliny, the brilliant sound of trumpets (*tuba*) could banish evil spirits during sacrificial rites. In battle, they were indispensible, broadcasting vital signals – Attack! Onwards! Retreat!

INTO THE MIDDLE AGES

Roman culture preserved the musical ideas of Greek civilization; after the fall of the Roman Empire in AD 476, the music of antiquity was transmitted by European joculators (travelling players) to the thinkers of the Middle Ages. Early Christian music also grew from the practice of the Jewish Temple. The symbolic sacrifice of the Mass drew on the sacrifice of a lamb at the Temple; and the Mass borrowed hymns and rituals from Passover. As early Christianity spread from Jerusalem, it adopted music from West Asia, Africa and Europe. Hymns and psalm singing were borrowed from Syria and spread by way of Byzantium to Italy. Pliny the Younger (*c.* AD 112) described hymns of worship. During the sixth century, Pope Gregory codified the Western chants and by the eighth century, the Roman *Schola cantorum* further served music in the church.

Early church fathers (St Ambrose, St Augustine and others), wrote of the power music (and fear of the power of music), as did the Greeks before them. In *Confessions* (10:33), St Augustine pleads for self-control when hearing music: 'weep with me, and weep for me, you who can control your inward feelings.'

GREEK MUSICAL THEORIES

Pythagoras (*c.* 580–*c.* 500 BC) was the leading figure in Greek musical theory. He held that the motions of the planets produced a 'music of the spheres', a higher order of music of which earthly music was a mere reflection. His studies set out the mathematical relationships between string lengths and musical intervals: an octave resulted from a ratio of 1:2, a fifth from the ratio 2:3, a fourth from the ratio 3:4, and so on. The great philosophers Plato and Aristotle defined and rationalized the sacred, moral and therapeutic powers of music. Plato argued that the powerful forces of music required government control. Aristotle's student, Aristoxenus (fourth century BC) formalized the Greek scheme of modes that included Ionian, Dorian, Phrygian and Lydian. Each mode was thought to provoke a distinctive character – the Dorian could instil bravery, for example.

COURTESANS, NUNS AND OTHER MUSICIANS

Women have always made music, and women in the ancient world were no exception. The most famous female musician and poet of ancient Greece was Sappho (b. *c.* 612 BC) from the island of Lesbos. Her music has not survived, but she is known to have accompanied her poetry on a variety of harp-like instruments. Sappho's work includes love songs to other women and *epithalamia* (choral wedding songs).

Elsewhere in ancient Greece women worked as instrumentalists, singers and dancers. Many professional female musicians were slaves or courtesans, such as the *hetairai*, highly educated and cultured women who regularly provided the musical entertainment at parties. Although there were renowned female performers who were regarded as respectable women, the association of women musicians with prostitution doubtless led to their exclusion from singing in the church services of the early Christian era. Perhaps it was felt this was justified by Paul's famous warning: 'Let your women keep silent in the churches'.

Nevertheless, several women are known to have composed Byzantine chant. The best known is Kassia, born *c.* AD 810 into an aristocratic family. She was a potential bride for Emperor Theophilos, but displeased him with her quick wit and therefore retired to a convent. At least 23 of her liturgical works have survived with words and music, including the well-known composition 'The Fallen Woman'.

THE MEDIEVAL ERA

'Medieval' as a concept is very hard to define, and the period is just as difficult to delineate. It was a term invented by writers in the Renaissance who wished to make a distinction between their modernity and what had gone before. Although the onset of the Renaissance is often taken to be around the beginning of the fourteenth century, it was some time before the ideas associated with it took hold outside Italy and infiltrated all art forms.

DEFINING MEDIEVAL

Determining what in musical terms constitutes medieval and what Renaissance is a matter for constant debate. There is no question that from the fourteenth century composers considered here as medieval were working alongside such Renaissance luminaries as Petrarch, Boccaccio and, a little later, Brunelleschi. However, music did not belong to the core of humanistic studies and it was not, therefore, considered worthy

The Medieval Era
INTRODUCTION

The seven centuries covered here saw, essentially, the making of modern Europe. They saw the rise of the papacy and its numerous conflicts. They saw the shaping and reshaping of nations and empires. Yet beyond, and often because of, these conflicts and changes, they also saw the formation of great cultures. As nation met nation in war and on diplomatic missions, ideas were exchanged, influences transmitted. Where there was stability great courts thrived, harbouring circles of musicians and poets and enabling wonderful works of art to be created. Seats of learning such as Paris and Oxford produced philosophers and theologians renowned for their ideas about science, music and art. A powerful church erected many of Europe's greatest cathedrals: Romanesque buildings as at Durham; Gothic constructions of Notre Dame in both Paris and Chartres; and, in their wake, Cologne Cathedral and Westminster Abbey, to name but a few. Ecclesiastical institutions had *scriptoria* ('writing-rooms') and, later, urban centres also became important in manuscript production; beautifully decorated books were created for the church and for wealthy patrons.

The most enduring and romanticized aspect of medieval life is the idea of courtly love – the pure and chaste (yet romantic) love of a knight for his lady. It inspired great literature, such as the romances of Chrétien de Troyes (fl. *c.* 1160–90) and the *Roman de la Rose*, as well as smaller-scale poetic works, some of which were set to music.

One of the main problems in exploring medieval music is the uncertainty surrounding the identity and biographies of many composers. However, its wider context – the historical circumstances in which it was written and to which it sometimes refers – is accessible and makes a good starting-point when approaching an era so far removed from our own.

THE HOLY ROMAN EMPIRE

The earliest part of the medieval period was dominated by the empire of the Carolingian kings, Pippin III, 'the Short' (AD 751–68), and Charlemagne (AD 768–814). The Carolingians actively promoted missionary work carried out by monks of the Benedictine order and thus formed a mutually beneficial alliance with the papacy. As a result the pope crowned Pippin 'King of the Franks'. Charlemagne further expanded the kingdom of the Franks, and Pope Leo III rewarded him by anointing him 'Emperor of the Romans', so reconstituting, to some degree, the Roman Empire (which had collapsed over three centuries earlier). It was against this backdrop of the unification of the western church that the first music came to be written down, marking the beginning of the history of western music.

KEY EVENTS

800	Charlemagne is crowned 'Emperor of the Romans'
c.1030	Guido of Arezzo produces antiphoner (book of chant) with new staff notation
1066	Norman Conquest of England
1095	First Crusade is declared
c.1163	Work starts on the new cathedral of Notre Dame, Paris; *Magnus liber organi*
1204	Capture of Constantinople by crusaders
1248	Completion of Sainte-Chapelle, Paris
1307	Dante writes *Commedia*
1309	Papacy transfers to Avignon
c.1316	Completion of expanded version of the *Roman de Fauvel*
c.1322	Philippe de Vitry's *Ars nova* ('New art')
1337	Outbreak of Hundred Years' War
1353	Boccaccio writes *Decameron*
1378	Great Schism begins
1386	Chaucer writes the *Canterbury Tales*
1415	English defeat the French at Agincourt; Jan Hus burnt as a heretic at the Council of Constance
1416	Death of John, Duke of Berry, great patron of the arts; illumination of his most famous manuscript, the *Très Riches Heures*, left uncompleted
1417	Great Schism ends
1436	Dedication of S Maria del Fiore, Florence
1453	Fall of Constantinople; end of the Hundred Years' War
1454	Invention of printing by Gutenberg

Forma plenissime absolutionis et remissionis in vita
Misereatur tui
Forma plenarie remissionis in mortis articulo
Misereatur tui

The period from the ninth to the twelfth centuries was characterized on the political front by the fragmentation of the empire and invasion on all sides by 'barbarian' forces; the papacy's efforts to take the reins of power; and by the loss and reappropriation of territories by ruling authorities, especially between France and England. From the late eleventh century in particular there was also a renewed religious fervour as the pope ordered the Crusades, responding to Muslim invasions of the Byzantine Empire and appealing both to Christian piety and to the desire for new lands and wealth.

ESTABLISHMENT OF HIGH MEDIEVAL CULTURE IN FRANCE

At the beginning of the thirteenth century the French regained many of the lands that they had lost to the English Crown during the previous century, prompting the French monarchs to consolidate their power over the dukes and counts of their land. King Louis IX (later St Louis; 1226–70) dedicated himself to creating the ideal Christian monarchy, in the process winning the overwhelming support of his subjects, and under his rule medieval culture flourished. Many magnificent churches were built and the University of Paris grew to scholastic pre-eminence, attracting many of the great minds of the age.

THE INFLUENCE OF THE PAPACY

Without the church, music would probably have developed more slowly and in a very different way. The papacy was instrumental in the creation of the Holy Roman Empire, and the consequent standardization of the empire's liturgy (order of worship) along Roman lines led to the writing down of the plainchant repertory. After this early intervention, sacred music developed along its own lines largely unaffected by the popes (despite their periodic efforts to curb the use of polyphony in churches), and by the later fourteenth century the papal court had its own flourishing tradition of polyphony. At this time the papacy was based in Avignon in France. Clement V (r. 1305–14) had transferred his administration there in a bid to escape the factional atmosphere of Rome, as it became clear that the papal dream of ruling over a Christian empire would never be fulfilled. A series of French popes ruled in lavish style until 1376, when the papacy moved back to Rome under growing public pressure.

THE SCHISM

On the death of Gregory XI in 1378, an Italian was appointed Pope Urban VI, and he began a programme of reform, reducing the cardinals' incomes. Outraged, they immediately appointed a pope of their own and retreated to Avignon; thus began the Great Schism, one of the richest episodes for music of this period. Clement VII, the Antipope, restored the lifestyle of the Avignon papacy during his reign (1378–94), which had all the trappings of a secular court. A manuscript now held in nearby Apt records some of the sacred music heard there, including works by **Philippe de Vitry** (1291–1361), while some of the secular music in the Chantilly Manuscript can also be linked to the schismatic court.

The Schism was exacerbated by the outcome of the Council of Pisa (1409), which deposed both popes and elected a new one. As neither the Avignon nor the Roman pope recognized the authority of the Council, there was, for a time, a three-way schism. Finally, at the Council of Constance (1414–18) the church was reunited under one pope, Martin V.

Many composers were associated with the papal court in Rome, both during and after the Schism, including **Johannes Ciconia** (*c.* 1370–1412) and his contemporary Antonio Zacara, and **Guillaume Du Fay** (*c.* 1397–1474). The councils were also important forums for musicians, especially the Council of Constance, at which the courts of both popes were convened.

(BL) Canterbury Pilgrims
Illumination depicting an additional Canterbury Tale, by John of Lydgate (c. 1420).
(TL) Printing
Fragment of an historical work, produced on Gutenberg's first printing press.
(TR) Medieval Choir
Miniature from an antiphon, showing monks singing in a choir.
(BR) The Black Death
Flagellant atoning for the sins of the people; the plague was seen as a punishment from God.

MUSIC AND RELIGION

Religion had an overriding influence on the music of the whole medieval period: the first musical notation was for the church, and for well over two centuries sacred works were the only ones to be written down. Little or nothing is known about the origins of plainchant, but it is clear that from earliest times music was used as part of Christian worship. With the founding of the great monastic orders, music became an integral part of the liturgy, used around the clock in the chanting of the Hours and in the Mass.

Sacred music was not all associated with the liturgy and the Eucharist, however. Dramatic works are found in some of the earliest sources of monophony, and miracle plays were an important part of lay celebrations of religious feasts in the Middle Ages. Among these were English dramas such as the Chester miracle plays (*c.* 1375). Also in the vernacular were sacred songs such as the Spanish *Cantigas de Santa Maria* ('Songs of Saint Mary', *c.* 1250–80), *laude spirituali* ('spiritual songs') written in Italy from the fourteenth century, and English carols.

THE HUNDRED YEARS' WAR

The Hundred Years' War began in 1337 as an extension of the rivalry between England and France that had started with the Norman Conquest. The reasons for the outbreak of war were numerous, but the principal cause was a dispute between Edward III of England and Philip VI of France over the French monarchy. Although conflict could probably have been avoided, the pervading culture of heroism and chivalry prevailed and a long series of battles began; it did not end until 1453. Despite inflicting crushing defeats on the French in the earlier years of the war, the English eventually lost all their French lands except the port of Calais. The war took its toll on France far more than on England. More or less all the fighting took place in France, and its countryside suffered greatly at the hands of soldiers who pillaged even when not fighting. Meanwhile, the whole of Europe was suffering from the effects of the Black Death, which devastated the population in 1348–49, and again in 1361–62.

Fascinating details about life in France in these war- and plague-ravaged years are found in the works of the poet-composer **Guillaume de Machaut** (*c.* 1300–77). He was in the service of King John of Bohemia, who was killed at the Battle of Crécy (1346). Machaut also witnessed and survived both outbreaks of plague and the Siege of Reims (1359–60), and was probably at the signing of the Treaty of Brétigny in 1360 – events on which he cast a not-always dispassionate eye.

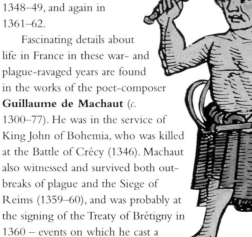

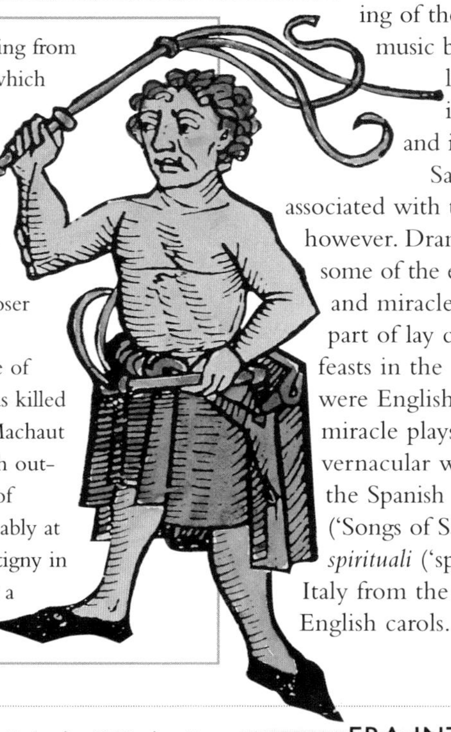

Ciconia ▶ p. 27 Du Fay ▶ p. 27 Machaut ▶ p. 29 Vitry ▶ p. 31

TOO WORLDLY FOR WORSHIP

The church sometimes commented on the part that music played in worship. Theologians such as Albertus Magnus and Thomas Aquinas wrote about the way it influences a worshipper's mind. Less benignly, from time to time the authorities issued edicts rebuking composers for writing music that was deemed too worldly for worship. One such Bull was that of Pope John XXII, the 'Docta sanctorum' (1325), in which he spoke out against the use of any kind of **mensural music** in the church. Thankfully for us, his edict was defied by many.

Many composers of the medieval period were at least partly dependent on the church for their income. Some, like Du Fay, were priests; others were lay singers in cathedrals; still others, such as Machaut, were awarded secular canonicates for services rendered to their royal patrons. Although the papacy often acted as an enemy of the developing musical art, the popes had vast courts which played host to many gifted musicians, resulting in some of the greatest music of the late fourteenth and fifteenth centuries.

MUSIC IN THE COURTS

It is not easy to trace the development of music for secular courts until the eleventh century, when it was first written down. There were

> **FROM REGIONALISM TO INTERNATIONALISM**
>
> Throughout the ages when the geographical dissemination of ideas was a slow process, artistic activity was cultivated most in places where there was a lively cultural atmosphere – in monasteries, courts and cities. Composers, poets and philosophers gravitated there for their education or in search of patronage. These places became the great centres of musical activity, though they were not necessarily great cities; in England, courts in relatively small towns – perhaps ducal seats – attracted the most talented composers of their age.
>
> The problem of communication ensured that different regions preserved their identities, which is why the music of Paris in the early fourteenth century is so different from that of Florence during the same period. But even as early as the fifteenth century, when composers began to travel a long way for their work, these strong regional traditions started to break down and a more international style was born.

minstrels who played and sang, providing courtly entertainment, but theirs was an art based on memorization and improvisation. In the late eleventh century troubadours began to flourish. They were poet-musicians from the area that is now southern France. Although some of them rose from low social origins to respected troubadour status, many were born into the nobility. The troubadours' most significant contribution to western literary culture was the idea of *fin' amours* ('pure love',

later called 'courtly love') the idealized feelings of a lover for a lady. The influence of the troubadours spread northwards into France, giving rise to the trouvères, and into Germany, where the tradition of Minnesang took root. *Fin' amours* dominated secular music throughout the medieval period.

PATRONIZING POET-MUSICIANS

The musico-poetic art that began with the troubadours was ideally suited to a courtly setting, and poet-musicians were actively patronized by the nobility. Besides the church, the courts were the only major source of patronage in the Middle Ages. Members of the nobility employed courtiers as entertainers and chroniclers; courts also had their own chapels – groups of clerics and singers who travelled with the court entourage. Many composers were employed for at least part of their adult lives in these chapels, which were a rich source of sacred music in the medieval period and beyond.

> **THE RISE OF GOTHIC**
>
> The two great architectural styles of the medieval age were the Romanesque and the Gothic. The Romanesque, with its round-arch forms borrowed from classical buildings, is a massive style, characterized by solid pillars supporting the great stone roof vaults that were a new feature of construction. It is often crowded with imaginative sculpture.
>
> During the twelfth century, architects began to incorporate novel elements into their church designs, which soon developed into a new style, the Gothic. The most striking early example is Abbot Suger's rebuilding of the Abbey of St Denis near Paris, dating from about 1140. By the end of the century pointed arches, ribbed vaults and flying buttresses enabled great weights to be supported in very high structures, allowing more delicate construction and larger windows. The greatest cathedrals brought the construction arts together with sculpture and music for the glorification of God.

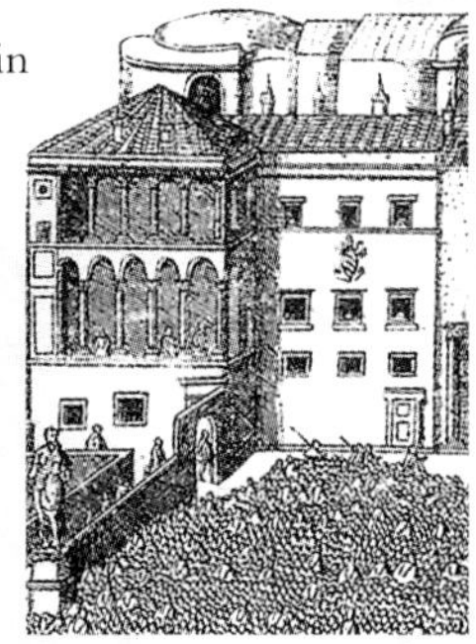

mensural music ▶ p. 360

One of the consequences of having musicians in the entourage of an itinerant court was that when nobles met, perhaps on diplomatic missions or for celebrations (for instance, weddings between members of great families), their musicians met as well. This was one of the ways ideas were exchanged and artists learnt from each other; cultures met and influence spread.

INSTRUMENTAL MUSIC

Very little instrumental music was written down in the medieval period, so it is really only possible to speculate about what instrumentalists played, which is why this chapter deals primarily with vocal music. There are some manuscripts of keyboard music (organists and other keyboard players were educated in universities and could therefore read music); they either contain arrangements of vocal pieces or demonstrate the art of improvisation.

THE MANUSCRIPT TRADITION

Manuscripts are fascinating documents of their time. Each was written by an individual scribe or a group of scribes for a specific purpose and is therefore a unique product. A music manuscript gives a snapshot of the repertory in a particular place at a particular time.

Categories of musical manuscripts from the medieval period include liturgical books (some with plainchant), collections of polyphony for use in churches, Books of Hours for private devotions and compilations made for wealthy patrons. Many of these were not intended for music-making but were richly illuminated for show. Manuscripts used in performance are generally less attractively decorated than these 'presentation manuscripts'. Among those used by performers or, perhaps, for study, were single-sheet documents with just one or two pieces – these must have been much more common than books, but because they were less valuable in both real and aesthetic terms, many have been lost, destroyed or re-used for binding other books.

Manuscripts are valuable not only for the music that they preserve, but also for the way they preserve it. They frequently represent regional tastes, both for repertory and for style. They may also present personal preferences – of the manuscript's first owner or scribe or even, in rare cases, of the actual composer.

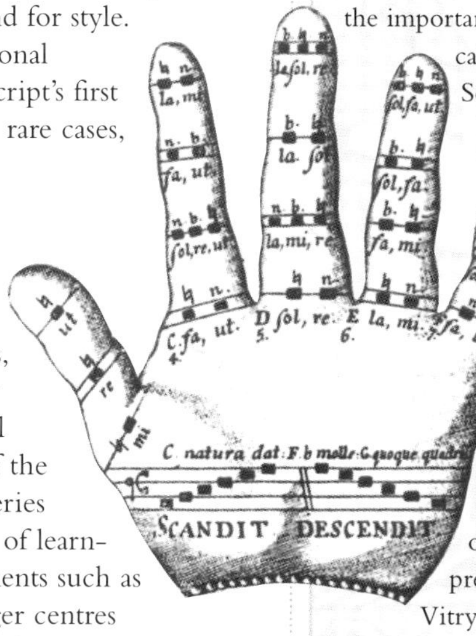

EDUCATION

For centuries, education lay in the domain of the church and the monasteries, whose schools kept literacy alive and enriched medieval culture. With the growth of the cities, however, the monasteries were superseded by centres of learning based around establishments such as cathedrals. Some of the larger centres became universities; among the most important were in Oxford, Paris and Bologna. The curriculum offered in the universities, the *studium generale*, included the seven 'liberal arts': grammar, rhetoric, arithmetic, logic, astronomy, geometry and music. Music theorists were part of the new urban educational culture. They were to influence the course of music history through their innovative thought and teaching.

THEORISTS

Music theorists were writers who recorded developments in music for the benefit of students of the art. Change in the music of the medieval period was rapid, and to a large extent our understanding of it is dictated by the surviving theoretical writings, as they frequently explain (in their own terms, of course) how it was written and how it was perceived.

There are many theorists about whom nothing is known – not even their names. The cataloguing of such anonymous writings has meant that some are now identified by collection (for example the 'Vatican organum treatise') or by number, as with the important theorist who has simply been called Anonymous IV (fl. *c.* 1275). Some names are known, such as Guido of Arezzo, Johannes de Garlandia (fl. *c.* 1240), as well as people such as Vitry – and something is known of their lives. Vitry and **Johannes Tinctoris** (1430–after 1511), for instance, were composers; the majority must also have been teachers. But all of them documented ideas about musical composition and notation, either writing about their own innovations or summarizing previous developments. For example, Vitry and Franco of Cologne (fl. 13th century) were influential because their new ideas affected the later course of music; Johannes de Garlandia summarized recent developments; Anonymous IV was and still is important for his history of music spanning at least a century, not only describing musical techniques, but also listing composers, teachers, singers and scribes, both in France and England.

FEMALE MINSTRELS

There are specific words for female minstrels in many medieval languages, such as *jougleresse* (Provençal), *ménestrelle* (Old French) and *gliewméden* (Middle English). The Provençal word *trobairitz* was used for female troubadours. Over 20 of these women are known by name, including Azalais de Porcairages (b. 1140) from Montpellier, Bieiris de Romans (fl. early 13th century); Dame Castelloza (b. *c.* 1200), a noblewoman from the Auvergne whose lyrics are full of misery; and Beatriz de Dia (fl. late 12th century). Beatriz de Dia is the only *trobairitz* whose music survives: her defiant song 'A Chantar m'er de so qu'eu no volria' ('I Must Sing of That Which I Would Rather Not') has been preserved alongside its text.

There were also female trouvères. Works survive with both music and text by Maroie de Dregnau of Lille (fl. 13th century) and Blanche of Castile (1188–1252), wife of Louis VIII of France. The popular trouvère Marie de France (fl. 1160–1215), originally from Normandy, was a member of the court of Eleanor of Aquitaine and Henry II of England. She wrote a famous collection of lais (short narrative poems) which she may have performed to her own harp accompaniment.

(ML) Guillaume Du Fay
Du Fay, like many others, was a priest and relied on the church for his income.
(TL) Minstrels
Music was disseminated across Europe by wandering minstrels, who played at royal courts.
(TR) Music Manuscript
Fourteenth-century French music manuscript, the Bible Historiale, *by Pierre le Manyeur.*
(MR) Guidonian Hand
Guido of Arezzo devised a system for showing the notes of the scale, the 'hand' was one way in which music could be taught.

Tinctoris ► p. 31

The Medieval Era
PERSONALITIES

Adam de la Halle

(A'-dàn de la'Al) c. *1250–1300*
FRENCH TROUVÈRE

Adam de la Halle was one of the last trouvères, and he composed works in almost every genre of the late thirteenth century, including monophonic and polyphonic songs and motets; his poetry is also important. He wrote three plays with musical interludes and an epic poem, now incomplete. His monophonic songs follow the tradition of the trouvères, but their melodies are considerably advanced in style for the age; his polyphonic songs (usually referred to as **rondeaux** but actually encompassing a variety of forms) are interesting in that they foreshadow the music of the fourteenth century.

Bernart de Ventadorn

(Ber-nàr' də Vàn'-ta-dôrn) c. *1135–95*
FRENCH TROUBADOUR

Bernart is regarded as perhaps the finest and most musically important of the troubadours. More of his melodies have survived than any other troubadour's; one, 'Quan vei la lauzeta mover' ('When I See the Lark Open His Wings'), was extremely popular and inspired poems to be sung to its melody in four different languages. Bernart travelled widely, and it is possible that he was responsible for bringing the art of the troubadour poet-composer to northern Europe, thus initiating the tradition of the trouvères.

Binchois, Gilles

(Bansh-wà', Zhēl) c. *1400–60*
FRANCO-FLEMISH COMPOSER

Binchois spent his formative years in Mons (now Belgium) and appears to have led a remarkably static life. In the late 1420s he joined the itinerant Burgundian court chapel, and served there with distinction until his retirement in the early 1450s, continuing to draw a pension until his death. Although he left a substantial amount of sacred music, he is best known for his songs. He was a supremely gifted melodist, at times surprising, often charming and always memorable. He possibly had a formative influence on Ockeghem, who may have come into contact with him in his youth. The younger composer wrote a lament on Binchois' passing, 'Mort tu as navré de ton dart' ('Death, You have Sorrow in your Arrows', 1460).

Busnoys, Antoine

(Bün-wà', Àn-twàn') c. *1435–92*
FRENCH COMPOSER

Busnoys was a younger contemporary of Ockeghem and worked alongside him in Tours in the early 1460s, when he may already have been serving the future Duke Charles the Bold of Burgundy in an unofficial capacity. His association with the Burgundian court probably continued after Charles's death in 1477, though evidence for this is sketchy. He is principally known as a composer of songs (of which there are several dozen), but his sacred music also had a profound impact on the composers of the next generation. His Mass *L'homme armé* ('The Armed Man') was one of the most influential works of the fifteenth century.

DU FAY AND HIS PATRONS

A large number of Du Fay's musical works can be linked directly to particular events or to his service with specific patrons. His ecclesiastical career, which proceeded apace despite his illegitimate birth, was probably given an early boost by a relative who was a canon of Cambrai Cathedral, where Du Fay seems to have been actively encouraged. By his early twenties he was working at the court of Carlo Malatesta in Rimini. His music provides the evidence for this in the form of a motet in honour of one of the Malatesta family before her wedding and a rondeau, 'Hé compaignons', which mentions several musicians of the Malatesta household. When Du Fay moved to Bologna in 1428 he continued to write music for the Malatesta family; his *Missa Sancti Jacobi* ('St James Mass') is linked with Bologna.

Rome

Du Fay's next move, also in 1428, was to the papal chapel in Rome, where he stayed for five years. During this time he successfully petitioned the pope for benefices to advance his ecclesiastical career. Several important works are datable to these years, most notably the motets 'Ecclesie militantis', Balsamus et munda cera' (1431) and 'Supremum est mortalibus' (1433), all written for papal occasions. In 1433 he was recruited by the Duke of Savoy, at whose court he is known to have met Binchois and Martin Le Franc. He returned to the papal chapel for two years (*Nuper rosarum flores*, written for the dedication of S Maria del Fiore in Florence, dates from this time) but was back in Savoy in 1437. The principal backdrop at this period was the Schism, and when a new schism was formed in 1439 by the appointment of the Duke of Savoy as Antipope Felix V, thus creating a conflict between his most important patrons, Du Fay retreated north to attend to his benefices in Cambrai and Bruges. He stayed in Cambrai for 10 years, continuing to compose for Italian patrons, including a Mass, probably written for the 1450 dedication of Donatello's altar in the basilica of S Antonio in Padua.

Cambrai

After the abdication of Felix V, Du Fay spent six years in Savoy, but then in 1458 returned to Cambrai, where he spent the rest of his life. In this last period he received many visitors, including Tinctoris, Ockeghem and Busnoys. Loyset Compère (*c.* 1445–1518) may also have been among them. His song 'En triumphant' ('In Triumph') may have been written during this time, on the death of Binchois in 1460. It may be that his own obituary Mass, *Ave Regina celorum* ('Hail, Queen of Heaven'), was first heard at the dedication of Cambrai Cathedral in 1472.

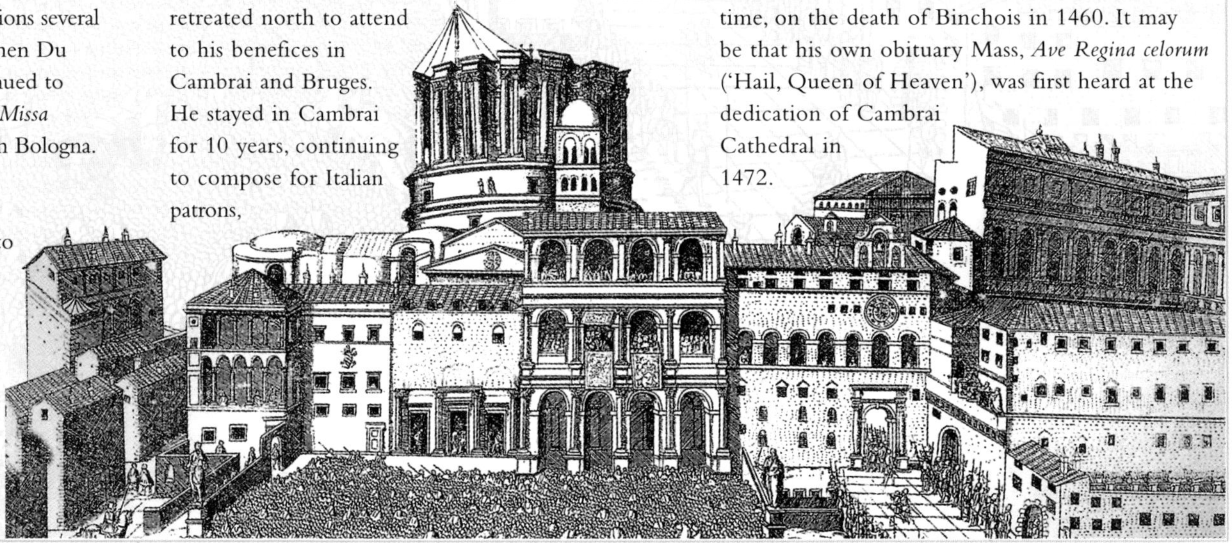

cantus firmus ▶ p. 356 *formes fixes* ▶ p. 358 *opéra comique* ▶ p. 361 rondeau ▶ p. 362

Ciconia, Johannes

(Sē-kōn'-yà, Yō-àn'-nez) c. *1370–1412*

FRANCO-FLEMISH COMPOSER AND THEORIST

Ciconia was active principally in Italy. For many years he was regarded as the main link between Machaut and Du Fay, and although other influential composers have now come to the fore, he is still seen as one of the most important figures of his generation. He wrote songs in French and Italian, music for the Mass and motets. His works cover a wide range of styles. Some of his songs are in a conventional fourteenth-century Italian style, and typically Italian features are also seen in some motets; a few works show the influence of the French Ars Subtilior. However, some of his songs are in a completely new compositional style, with the meaning of the words matched to the music. Strangely, for a composer who is regarded as the most innovative of his time, his theoretical writings are very old fashioned and do not deal with polyphonic music at all.

Du Fay, Guillaume

(Dūfā', Gē-yōm') c. *1397–1474*

FRENCH COMPOSER

Du Fay is regarded as the leading musical figure of his generation, and his reputation in his own time is underlined by his employment at many of the important musical centres in Europe. He grew up in Cambrai, where his skills were recognized early by the ecclesiastical authorities, and in his late teens he was taken into the retinue of a senior churchman. Thus began a life of service to the church, noble patronage and travel around Europe. Much of his biography can be written in minute detail, although some remains conjecture.

His music covers virtually all the polyphonic genres of his day: songs in the ***formes fixes***, Masses, motets (both isorhythmic and freely composed) and hymns. He employed a number of techniques, including ***cantus firmus*** settings, plainchant paraphrases (where one of the voices elaborates on the chant melody) and *fauxbourdon* (two notated voices, one an octave higher than plainchant, the other forming sixths and octaves below it), often combining these procedures. There is a gradual shift from a slightly disjunct late medieval style, in which small melodic motifs abound in a context of fast-moving upper voices and slower rhythm in the lower parts, to a smoother and more homogeneous rhythmic and melodic texture. His response to the music of his older contemporary Dunstaple is clear in a number of ways: for example, in his interest in *fauxbourdon*, which can be related to the English discant style, and in his later Mass cycles based on a *cantus firmus*.

MUSICAL PIONEER

In his isorhythmic motets Du Fay referred both to the works of Ciconia and to French music of the fourteenth century, producing densely textured works structured with isorhythm and related techniques in all voices. Some of these pieces, such as *Nuper rosarum flores* (1436) and 'Ecclesie militantis', are very impressive in structure and sound. His freely composed settings of texts for ceremonial or liturgical use, sometimes called cantilenas, are among his most interesting works. This was a relatively new way of composing music for such texts, and he ranged from simple settings of melodies resembling plainchant to complex textures similar to those in his isorhythmic motets.

Much attention has justifiably been given to Du Fay's Masses His earliest works are isolated movements or pairs. One of his first Mass cycles shares musical material with his song, 'Resveilliés vous' ('Awaken', 1423) and another cycle, the *Missa Sancti Jacobi*, is a so-called plenary Mass – one with settings of the Proper as well as the Ordinary. His later Masses show the influence of the 'Caput' Mass of *c.* 1440 (for many years he was thought to have been the composer of this work as well). The Mass *Ave Regina celorum*, written late in his life and based on his motet of the same name, seems to epitomize his approaches to music for the Mass throughout his career.

THE ULTIMATE TROUVÈRE

Adam de la Halle appears as something of a Janus figure at the end of the thirteenth century, at once looking back to his forebears and forwards into the fourteenth century and beyond. Born in Arras, the centre of much trouvère activity, he was probably educated in Paris and travelled widely in the service of noble patrons. His monophonic chansons were a culmination of the trouvère activities of the preceding century; his motets, based on plainchant tenors (lit. 'holding parts'), are rather unadventurous. While the musical style of the polyphonic chansons is also relatively conservative, the idea of setting secular texts polyphonically outside the motet tradition was new, and the poetic forms used foreshadow those seen in the next century. *Le Jeu de Robin et Marion* ('The Play of Robin and Marion') is the most famous of his three plays with music. While seemingly well ahead of their time (they are sometimes compared with the much later ***opéra comique***), they are more in the tradition of narrative *pastourelle* poems, which had musical interludes – a tradition that continued in the *dit* form of the fourteenth century.

(BL) Rome
Du Fay moved to the papal chapel in Rome in 1428; his five years here resulted in some of his most important works.
(TR)
Fifteenth-century illumination showing musicians, including a lute player; an anvil is being used as a percussion instrument.

Dunstaple, John [Dunstable]

c. *1390–1453*

ENGLISH COMPOSER

Dunstaple was the best known of an influential group of English composers which included Power. To judge by the number of his works in continental manuscripts, he was probably one of the most important composers of his day in Europe, although he may not have travelled particularly widely. He wrote early Mass cycles, including what is perhaps his most famous work, the Mass *Rex seculorum* ('King of Ages'), isorhythmic motets and some songs. He is reputed to have influenced the styles of Du Fay and Binchois, who, according to one writer, took on the *contenance angloise* in emulation of him. This may have had to do with the triadic nature of Dunstaple's musical style; he used what sound to the modern ear like major chords both in his melodies and especially in his harmonic writing. His use of thirds and sixths was part of the intrinsically English discant style, which then percolated through to continental Europe.

Hildegard of Bingen

(Hĭl-dĕ-gart of Bĭn'-gen) 1098–1179

GERMAN ABBESS AND COMPOSER

Hildegard of Bingen was abbess of a convent at Rupertsberg near Bingen in Germany. When she was in her forties, Hildegard started to produce remarkable works of theology, science, healing, drama, history and music. She advised religious and secular rulers as well as undertaking preaching tours. Hildegard presented her work as the word of God, told to her through intensely dramatic visions, which was probably the only way that, as a woman, she would have been allowed to communicate her ideas to a wider public.

Music, which Hildegard saw as a way of recapturing the beauty of paradise and reconnecting the human to the divine, played a vital part in the mystical atmosphere of her convent. Her main musical work is the *Symphonia harmoniae caelestium revelationum* ('Symphony of the Harmony of the Heavenly Revelations'). This is a collection of 77 liturgical songs for which she wrote both text and music. The vividly individual lyrics are matched by sensual and unusually elaborate melody, always a freely composed single line. Hildegard also wrote one of the earliest surviving morality plays with music, *Ordo Virtutum* ('Play of the Virtues'), which depicts the battle between the Devil and the 16 Virtues for the human soul.

Jehannot de Lescurel

(Zhä-nō' de Les-ko͞o-rel') fl. early 14th century

FRENCH POET AND COMPOSER

Very little is known about Jehannot de Lescurel; his works survive only in an appendix to the most important manuscript of the *Roman de Fauvel*. This constitutes a collection of some 32 monophonic songs, a polyphonic rondeau and two longer poems. The works are ordered alphabetically but the sequence, obviously incomplete, is cut off at the letter 'G'. The songs form the largest collection of their time and show one stage in the development of the poetic *formes fixes*. Also important is the way the melodies demonstrate how older elements of composition and performance became part of the emerging compositional style.

Landini, Francesco

(Làn-dē'-nē, Frän-chä'-skō)

c. *1325–97*

ITALIAN COMPOSER

Blind as the result of an attack of smallpox as a young child, Landini turned to music, learning to play the organ and several other instruments. He also sang and wrote poetry. Over 150 musical works by him survive, forming over one quarter of the known repertory of the fourteenth century. Most of his pieces are in the predominant Italian form of the period, the ballata, and he wrote a few madrigals, a **caccia** and a **virelai**. This last French form is a manifestation of his increasing interest in the forms and techniques of his French contemporaries. His works took on stylistic elements of the French Ars Nova, and he later seems to have merged the French and Italian styles successfully. He was well known and respected by other musicians, scholars and poets of his time. He may have written much of the poetry that he set to music.

Leonin

(Lā'-ō-nān) fl. c. *1150–1201*

FRENCH COMPOSER

Leonin is thought to have compiled the *Magnus liber organi* ('Great Book of Organum') – the collection of polyphony for Notre Dame Cathedral, Paris – and to have composed at least some of it. Although no music is directly ascribed to him, it is possible that some of the works in a new edition of the *Magnus liber* put together by Perotin (fl. *c.* 1200) were by Leonin. The theorist Anonymous IV, from whose writing both composers are known, said that Leonin was 'the best worker with **organum**', which may imply that he composed in other forms too. In any case, his achievement in compiling this extremely important collection cannot be overstated.

THE *CONTENANCE ANGLOISE*

The term *contenance angloise* ('English manner'), was first coined by the poet Martin Le Franc in his poem 'Le Champion des Dames' (*c.* 1440–42), in which he described new French music and implied that Du Fay and Binchois had 'taken on the *contenance angloise* and followed Dunstaple'. Although the poet did not define the term, the text immediately before this passage speaks of the 'elegant concord' in the new music. This seems to accord with one of the most striking characteristics of English music in the late fourteenth and early fifteenth centuries: the harmonic predominance of thirds and sixths. (English carols of the fifteenth century are dominated by this harmonic style; a well-known example is 'There is no Rose', with all three parts moving principally in parallel thirds and sixths.) In contrast, the third was still treated as a kind of **dissonance** in continental music. Fourths and fifths – which sound bare and austere to modern ears – were considered the consonant intervals. Another feature of the English style that was partly taken over by continental composers was the use of long duet sections in pieces for three or four voices.

caccia ▶ p. 356 dissonance ▶ p. 358 organum ▶ p. 361 solmization ▶ p. 362 virelai ▶ p. 363

Machaut, Guillaume de

(Ma-shō', Gē-yōm' da) c. *1300–77*

FRENCH COMPOSER AND POET

Machaut was the most important poet-composer of fourteenth-century France and had a wide and enduring influence. He was in constant demand by the greatest noble patrons of his day, and his music reflects this patronage. He was unusual, although probably not unique, among medieval writers in that he made an effort to collect his works – both poetic and musical – and six lavishly decorated manuscripts exist today (at least one and possibly more have been lost). Between them they preserve what is probably his complete output.

SONGWRITER

After Jehannot de Lescurel, Machaut is the first composer of the fourteenth century from whom a coherent body of songs survives. It is in his music that the song forms that were to dominate music for the next 150 years or more can be seen settling into their fixed patterns. Most of his music is secular: a total of 118 songs survive, the largest proportion of which are ballades (42), followed by virelais (33), rondeaux (22), lais (19) and one each of the old forms *complainte* and *chanson royal*. Little is known of other secular music immediately before and during Machaut's time – no songs by Vitry, perhaps his most likely model, appear to survive. So Machaut is always seen as an innovator.

EARLY POLYPHONY

The development of Machaut's style and compositional practice is clear. His earliest polyphonic songs are in two parts, with a fast-moving upper voice above a slow-moving tenor, much in the manner of a motet (one early song is even isorhythmic, although the rest were freely composed). In his first three-part songs the text-bearing voice is sandwiched between the tenor and an upper voice, the triplum, but he later settled on a combination with the voice carrying the words clearly audible on the top of the texture, above the tenor and contratenor. He also wrote some very complex songs in four parts. His virelais are mostly monophonic, in keeping with the tradition of this form as a dance-song, and the lais are also mostly for one voice, following the convention for this old trouvère form.

GUIDO OF AREZZO

Guido of Arezzo (b. *c.* AD 990/5) was perhaps the most influential music theorist of all time. He not only wrote one of the most widely read treatises of the Middle Ages, the *Micrologus*, but he also invented the system of lines for notating music that is still used today and, in addition, a method of teaching melodies using the syllables *ut, re, mi, fa, sol* and *la*.

During his early career Guido built a reputation as a gifted teacher, able to train singers to learn chants very quickly. It was probably during this period that he and a colleague began to write out an antiphoner (a book of chant) in a new system of notation. Later he wrote a prologue to the antiphoner, explaining the notation. He pointed out the advantages of a system where each pitch was represented on a line or in a space; and he showed that an indication of which lines represented C and F meant that singers knew immediately where the semitones fell, without having to know the mode of the melody.

In his new teaching method, a tune to the words of the hymn 'Ut queant laxis' was used as a mnemonic to aid the recognition of intervals and phrases. The syllables at the beginning of each line of the hymn form the sequence *ut–re–mi–fa–sol–la*, and although it is not clear whether Guido himself used these syllables for teaching melodies by interval (**solmization**) they were certainly adopted for this purpose later. The use of the hand to indicate where certain intervals should be sung was not his invention, but he may well have developed something like the well-known diagram of the hand showing the solmization syllables (the so-called 'Guidonian hand'); however, it did not appear in manuscript until the twelfth century.

MEDIEVAL CONVENTS

In the medieval period, as in later eras, the convent was one of the few places where women could gain a thorough musical education and find a valued forum for their music-making. Liturgical music, organized by the *cantrix* of the convent, was performed several times a day and formed a central element of the nuns' spiritual and artistic lives.

Hildegard of Bingen was not alone as a female composer of medieval sacred music. Herrad of Landsberg (fl. 1167–95), abbess of Hohenbourg near Strasbourg, was responsible for compiling the *Hortus delicariarum* ('The Garden of Delights'), a religious encyclopedia which included several of her own lyrics set to music. Several other manuscripts created for use in various European convents have survived, providing a clear indication of the music that nuns performed. Where the music is anonymous and not found in other named sources, it is reasonable to conclude that it was written by the nuns themselves. Manuscripts include the Kloster Wienhausen Hymnbook from a thirteenth-century German convent and a fifteenth-century hymnbook from Barking Abbey in England.

Until recently, scholars assumed that women did not perform works with more than a single line of music, but polyphonic manuscripts originating from convents show otherwise. The best known of these is the Las Huelgas Codex, compiled by Abbess Maria Gonzalez de Aguero for the Cistercian Monasterio de Santa Maria la Real de Las Huelgas in Spain. This large collection includes a vocal exercise used in teaching the nuns to sing polyphony.

(BL) Hildegard of Bingen
A view of Bingen (far left) and an illustration of the abbess and composer receiving inspiration.
(TR) Guillaume de Machaut
Contemporary portrait of the poet and composer.
(BR) Female Musicians
Musical education for women was largely confined to convents in medieval times.

SACRED MUSIC

Machaut's sacred music is much easier to see in context. Of his 23 motets at least one, 'Aucune gent/ Qui plus aimme/Fiat voluntas tua', his earliest four-part motet, was directly modelled on a motet by Vitry. In it he struggled with the complexities of isorhythmic and notational practices. By the time he wrote his last four-voice motets, having come to terms with the genre, he was making his own innovations, such as the inclusion of two-part textless 'introductions' which fall outside the isorhythmic structure.

Machaut's *Messe de Nostre Dame* is probably his most famous composition. Written in Reims in the early 1360s, it is perhaps the earliest setting of the entire Ordinary of the Mass. It represents a culmination of his work on isorhythmic construction and his development of harmonic writing, and this mastery was echoed in the songs and motets that were written around this time – arguably his best works in these genres. Here we see a composer at the peak of his powers.

POPULAR CULTURE

One of the most striking features of popular musical culture in the late twentieth century was a renewed fascination in music of the medieval period. In particular, there was an upsurge of interest in recordings of plainchant. It seems that its new-found popularity was due at least in part to the atmospheric serenity of modern recordings and its consequent marketing as 'mood music'. However, such interest also went beyond plainchant. The spectacularly successful recording *Officium* (1993) by jazz saxophonist Jan Garbarek (b.1947) was a collaboration with vocal group the Hilliard Ensemble, in which he improvised around their performances of medieval works. Medieval sources were used by the rock group Enigma as the basis for some of their music, and early music ensembles took part in their live performances. The Mediaeval Baebes sold large numbers of a Christmas-related album of medieval songs and dances. However, such interest did not extend to the more scholarly efforts of a large number of specialist performers, whose recordings and concerts are still, in the twenty-first century, very much a 'niche' market.

Ockeghem, Johannes

(Ō'-kă-gem, Yo-ăn'-nes) c. *1425–97*
FRANCO-FLEMISH COMPOSER

Born in St Ghislain near Mons (now in Belgium), Ockeghem is first recorded as a singer at the Church of Our Lady, Antwerp, in 1443. He joined the French royal chapel in 1451, becoming chapel-master by 1454. In 1459 King Charles VII appointed him treasurer of the abbey of St Martin of Tours. This prestigious royal post suggests a certain influence, and a document of 1471 refers to him as 'counsellor of the king'. He retained all his titles until his death on 6 February 1497.

Ockeghem's securely attributed output is small in relation to his reputation: scarcely more than a dozen Masses, barely 20 songs, only a handful of motets. Yet he was undisputedly the leading composer of his generation, and one of the most influential. His style is as memorable as it is difficult to describe. He frequently disguised the music's usual points of articulation, thus creating a seamless impression. His songs show him to be a sublime melodist; his Masses reveal a formal imagination of visionary power. He is best known for feats of technical skill, such as the *Missa prolationum* ('Prolation Mass'), but in fact his music is a classic case of art concealing art.

Oswald von Wolkenstein

(Ōz'-vält fun Vōl'-ken-shtīn) c. *1376–1445*
SOUTH TYROLEAN POET

A particularly interesting figure, Oswald von Wolkenstein has been called the most important poet writing in German between Walther von der Vogelweide and Johann Wolfgang von Goethe (1749–1832). He is known to have been a singer and was also very active in the political sphere. Well over 100 poems can be attributed to him, but it is not clear how many of their settings, both monophonic and polyphonic, were composed by him. It seems likely that much of the music to which he set poetry was composed by other musicians; this certainly applies to polyphonic settings (he most often used French chansons, but he also used Landini's ballata 'Questa fanciulla' ('This Girl') for a contrafactum, a work in which a new text has replaced the original one). However, he may have composed at least some of the monophonic melodies himself. His is a particularly interesting output, showing as it does the overlap between an increasingly sophisticated international repertory and older local traditions.

JACOB DE SENLECHES AND THE ARS SUBTILIOR

The so-called Ars Subtilior was an isolated phenomenon of the end of the fourteenth century. It seems that small cliques of composers wrote extremely difficult music for studying and performing among themselves, perhaps with the aim of outdoing each other in musical and notational complexity. Although some composers remain only names in the manuscripts, there are biographical details of others. One such is Jacob de Senleches (fl. 1378–95), a French composer who, as the text of one of his ballades, 'Fuions de ci' ('Escape from Here'), tells, was in the service of Eleanor of Castile when she died in 1382. He then entered the service of an Aragonese cardinal, Pedro de Luna (later Antipope Benedict XIII). Documents from this period state that Jacob was a harpist; perhaps his most interesting piece is called *La harpe de mélodie*, which in one manuscript is written in the shape of a harp. It is his most difficult composition, using canonic techniques described in its own poetic text.

mensural music ▶ p. 360

Perotin

(Pā-rō-tan') fl. c. *1200*

FRENCH COMPOSER

Perotin was named by the theorist Anonymous IV as the reviser of the *Magnus liber organi* originally compiled by Leonin for Notre Dame Cathedral, Paris. He stated that Perotin was a gifted composer of works in two, three and four parts, and some surviving pieces are directly attributable to him, for instance the well-known organa *Viderunt omnes* and *Sederunt principes*. These, as well as other large-scale and smaller works, are impressive for their sense of design and structure. His book, and therefore his works, remained in use all over Europe for a considerable time and had a profound influence on the music of later composers.

Power, Leonel

d. 1445

ENGLISH COMPOSER

Power was a contemporary of Dunstaple and, although rather less famous than the latter, was nonetheless an important figure in a period when English music was extremely influential. The majority of his works are movements from the Mass Ordinary. He (along with Dunstaple) broke new ground in the composition of Mass cycles, linking the movements of his Mass pairs and one definitely attributable complete Mass cycle by musical means. A large proportion of his works are preserved in the Old Hall manuscript; others are found in north Italian manuscripts of the first half of the fifteenth century. His style is not always easily distinguishable from that of Dunstaple.

Tinctoris, Johannes

(Tink'-tôr-is, Yō-än'-nes) 1430–after 1511

FRENCH THEORIST

Tinctoris attended university at Orléans and worked for most of his adult life at the Aragonese court in Naples. There he produced the most authoritative body of theoretical writing on music of his time. He was very familiar with current musical practices, and he dedicated one of his treatises to his contemporaries Ockeghem and Busnoys. His writings demonstrate the influence of humanism on his thinking: his Latin style is modelled on that of Cicero. His surviving compositions testify to a practical musician of real inspiration.

(TL) Medieval Dance
Fifteenth-century illustration of a basse dance, with cornetto players on the balcony.
(NR) Troubadour
Fourteenth-century manuscript illuniation showing a troubadour (above), leading musicians.

THE LAST TROUVÈRE?

Guillaume de Machaut is the quintessential medieval composer. Although his most famous work is probably his Mass, most of his music was secular, composed for courtly or popular purposes. He was known not only for his music but also for his poetry, and in writing both words and music he was more or less the last in the long tradition of the trouvères – a tradition reflected in his writing of large-scale forms such as the lai. His fame as a poet equalled and perhaps surpassed his renown as a musician; he almost certainly met Geoffrey Chaucer, who was heavily influenced by his poetry and translated some of it into English.

He is a fascinating figure, partly because so much is known about him. From details in his works and other documents a nearly complete

biography can be at least tentatively constructed. In addition, Machaut actually wrote about himself. He showed an extraordinary level of self-awareness, writing his own character into his long poems. In some poems the narrator is identified as 'Guillaume', and in an allegorical tale called *Remède de Fortune* ('Fortune's Remedy') the protagonist is a courtier capable, as all good courtiers should be, of writing love poetry; furthermore, seven musical works are woven into the story line (a feature once again reminiscent of the trouvères as well as of an older literary tradition going back to the ancient philosopher Boethius).

Vitry, Philippe de

(Vē-trē', Fē-lēp' de) 1291–1361

FRENCH THEORIST AND COMPOSER

As a result of his treatise *Ars nova* (*c.* 1322) Philippe de Vitry was the most musically influential figure of his day. It described new developments in **mensural notation**, allowing composers more rhythmic flexibility and therefore compositional variety. According to one writer, Vitry not only invented the *quatre prolacions* – a reference to his notational innovations – but was also responsible for new-style motets and songs. Unfortunately, no songs known to be by Vitry have survived, but a number of motets are ascribed to him in manuscripts, and still more can be attributed to him on stylistic grounds. His accomplished use of isorhythm sets him apart from other composers, as do aspects of melodic and harmonic use. Some of his motets are included in the most important manuscript of the *Roman de Fauvel.*

Walther von der Vogelweide

(Vol'-ter fun dâr Fō'-gel-vī-da) fl. c. *1200*

GERMAN MINNESINGER

Both in his time and in ours Walther von der Vogelweide has been considered the leading figure in medieval German poetry, and his music was specifically mentioned for its excellence by his contemporaries. His poetic works are found in a large number of manuscripts – an indication of his popularity – but little of his music has survived (although it is certain that the poetry was written to be sung). His poetry is most valued now for its transformation of the genres of German lyric from their rather restricted and formal tradition, into a freer and more expressive idiom.

TOUTE BELLE

Toute Belle is a character in Machaut's long collection of poetry with music, *Le Voir Dit* ('The True Poem', *c.* 1363). She is a young noblewoman, described as 'the best singer born in a hundred years', who initiated an intense correspondence with the ageing composer by sending him one of her own rondeaux. It has been suggested that Toute Belle actually existed; she may have been Agnès de Navarre-Champagne (b. *c.* 1320) or Peronelle d'Armentières (b. 1340). Whether she was fact or fantasy, Toute Belle's musical talent and intelligence tends to indicate that late-medieval women were excellent performers and understood the complex polyphonic music of their time.

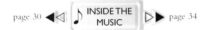

The Medieval Era

STYLES AND FORMS

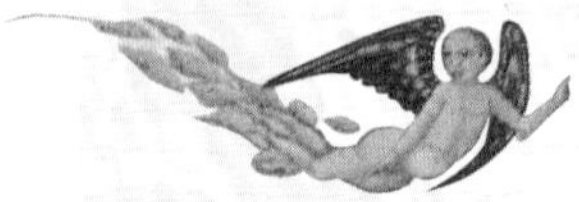

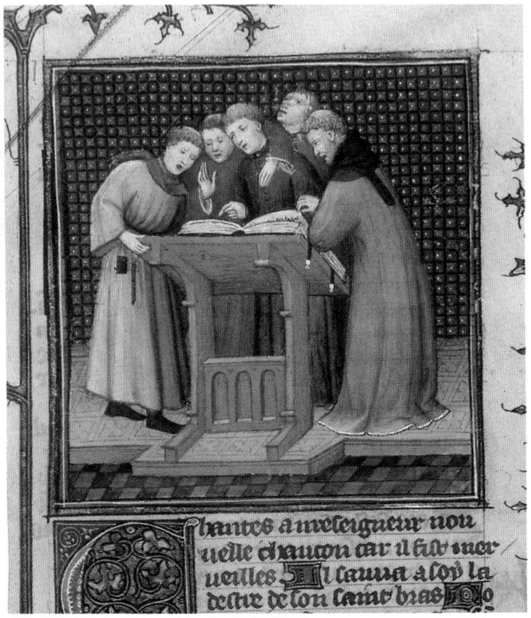

Before music was written down, musicians either memorized or improvised what they played or sang. Very little is known about the earliest European music because it was not recorded in notation. The music theorist Isidore of Seville (*c.* AD 559–636) even said that melodies could not be written down, and two centuries passed before a system of notation was established. This happened during the reigns of Pippin III and Charlemagne, when the need arose to organize the plainchant repertory. Early developments in notation are thus bound up with the history of music for the church; secular music continued to be based in traditions of memorization and improvisation until the eleventh century. The interaction between the tradition of improvisation and the need for notation is at the heart of the history of medieval music, and it led to the development of diverse techniques of musical composition, both sacred and secular.

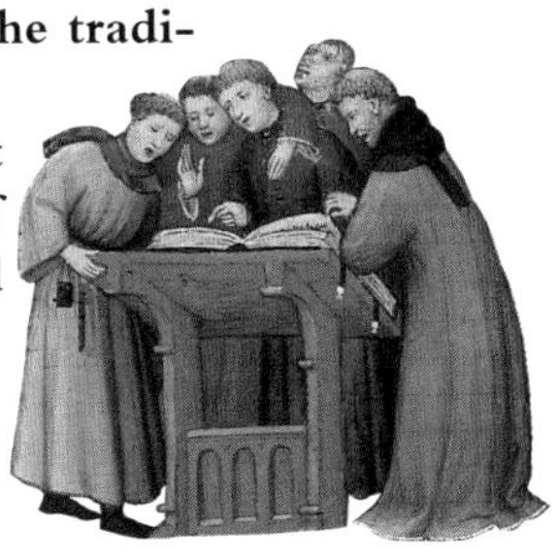

THE DEVELOPMENT OF NOTATION

Methods of encoding pitch using letters had been proposed from the sixth century, but the earliest notation – dating from the eighth – was made up of neumes, which were shapes indicating the contours of the melody. Because plainchant melodies were largely memorized, singers did not need precise pitches to be notated. In about 1030, Guido of Arezzo set out a new system of pitch notation based on a staff of lines representing notes a third apart. Alphabetical letters (C or F) at the start of a line indicated pitch, as did the use of differently coloured lines – yellow for C and red for F. The notes themselves were written on the staff as traditional neumes (although the shapes no longer strictly represented melodic contours). In theory it was possible at this stage for a person to sight-read a melody accurately. Later sources of polyphony, such as those from Aquitaine, use Guidonian notation with a four- or five-line staff, and are notated in a type of score.

Notating Rhythm

In the late twelfth century a method of notating rhythm was developed, possibly in response to singers who habitually slipped into trochaic (long–short) or iambic (short–long) rhythm. The system of rhythmic modes indicated rhythmic patterns by the way that notes were grouped together. It was superseded in about 1260–80 by a new system of rhythmic notation devised by the German theorist Franco of Cologne. Now, for the first time, the shape gave the singer fundamental information he needed about its likely duration. Franco set out rules for the relationship between three main note values (long, breve and semibreve): there could be either three or two of a smaller value within the next value up, depending on whether the music was in perfect (triple) or imperfect (duple) time. This method of measuring the relationships between note values is called **mensuration**. A further development is found in the works of the French theorist Petrus de Cruce (fl. *c.* 1290), who divided the breve into up to seven semibreves; the resulting smaller note values became known as minims.

In fourteenth-century France, the minim achieved independent status with **Vitry**'s *Ars nova*. There were again three principal levels of mensural relationship, with each note except the minim divisible into two or three. As the length of a note could only be exactly known from its context, and not by its shape, a number of rules governed the way that successive note values affected each other. Coloured notes (usually red) or sometimes void ones indicated temporary changes in mensuration, but the mensuration itself had to be worked out from the context; signs for indicating mensuration were not commonly used until some time later.

Notation in Italy

Italian notation in the fourteenth century was quite different from the Italian system, and it is clear that it was based on Petrus de Cruce's innovations. Marchettus of Padua set out rules whereby the breve (the fundamental unit) could be divided, in multiples of two or three, into up to 12 notes, with the shorter notes represented as minims. Intricate rhythms could be represented by different note shapes – unlike in French notation. These possiblities permitted a particularly elaborate melodic style, whereas the French tended towards complicated rhythms between voice-parts, as allowed by the several levels of mensural relationships in Ars Nova notation. Later in the fourteenth century, Italian musicians incorporated some French rhythmic conventions while preserving features of their own notation.

In the fifteenth century, scribes started to use white or void notes as normal practice. Composers in the latter part of the century began to use simpler notation based on the mensural system, also writing in arabic numerals to indicate relationships between note values. It was not until the sixteenth century that features from instrumental music for notating smaller note values were incorporated into the old system, forming the beginning of modern notation.

melisma ▶ p. 360 mensural music ▶ p. 360 mode ▶ p. 360 trope ▶ p. 363

Plainchant

Plainchant is the name given to the simple melodies used in church worship; it is frequently also called Gregorian chant. Legend has it that it originated when a dove dictated music to Pope Gregory the Great (r. AD 590–604) for the Roman Mass and Office, which he then wrote down. However, although 'Gregorian' is the name by which the western European plainchant repertory is now generally known, the melodies used for worship in the churches were actually much older than this, with roots in Jewish traditions and probably in pagan music too. The chants sung at each service were (and still are) prescribed by the liturgy, or order of worship, throughout the year. The Mass (or Eucharist) – the most important part of the Christian liturgy – is a re-enactment of the Last Supper; less important is the Office, a calendar of prayers said at set hours throughout each day.

NOTATING PLAINCHANT

Plainchant melodies were originally held in singers' memories and passed down orally. Repertories varied from place to place: for example, the Ambrosian chant tradition, named after the fourth-century Bishop Ambrose of Milan, is still used today in that city, while quite separate traditions evolved in Spain, Byzantium and other Eastern centres. Plainchant was first written down in the later eighth century, as part of the Carolingians' process of political (and therefore liturgical) unification, to ensure that the same melodies were sung throughout their empire. Many regional traditions were thus abolished. On the positive side, though, the new notation system helped church musicians in their work. The outline of the melody was shown by a system of symbols, or neumes, but precise pitches were not written down at this stage – the melody still had to be learnt by ear before the singers could 'read' it accurately from the page.

At approximately the same time as notation appeared, the Gregorian chant repertory took on a new system of classifying the melodies according to their characteristics: the note on which they ended (called the 'final'), the principal reciting note and the range of pitches used. This system divided the chants into eight broad melodic types, or **modes**, and must also have helped in the learning process.

The corpus of plainchant melodies became the most stable repertory in western European music. The melodies formed the underlying structure of the vast majority of sacred polyphonic works in the medieval period, and they are still used today – both on their own in Christian worship and as the basis for sacred (and occasionally secular) music.

THE NOTRE DAME SCHOOL

The large amount of music associated with Notre Dame in Paris was compiled to provide the newly built cathedral with a musical repertory. The main body of music – organa, clausulae and conductus – originated in an essentially improvisatory tradition, and was mostly written down between about 1165 and the early thirteenth century. The two principal composers that we know about are **Leonin** and **Perotin**. Leonin was credited with compiling the *Magnus liber organi*, a collection of two- and possibly three-part organa for liturgical use in the cathedral. Perotin, probably working slightly later, is thought to have revised the *Magnus liber*, adding his own pieces and reworking others. The music of the *Magnus liber* was frequently copied and remained in use throughout Europe possibly well into the fourteenth century.

The Earliest Polyphony

The practice of polyphony – more than one part played or sung at a time (from Gk *polyphōnos*, 'many-voiced') – is much older than the earliest notated examples. The first polyphony to be written down was simply embellished plainchant; it is found in two music treatises from the ninth century. One or more parts have been added to short extracts of plainchant, and they generally move mostly in austere, 'open'-sounding parallel intervals. The Winchester Troper is an important early eleventh-century manuscript from which polyphony, written in neumes, was sung. In a group of twelfth-century sources from Aquitaine the music is written in a more precise form of notation, the note-against-note style has been superseded by one in which several notes of a melody are sounded above one long note.

Organum and its Descendants

Organum is the name originally given to the practice of singing a part added above or below a plainchant melody. In the earliest organum the parts moved at the same speed; by the time the Aquitanian sources were compiled there was also a practice of singing florid music, or **melismas** above the long chant notes. These two types of organum, the syllabic and the melismatic, gradually became distinct from each other. The syllabic form came to be known as discant and the newer, more ornate sort began to dominate and thus took over the original term 'organum'.

The most important flowering of organum began in the later twelfth century at the cathedral of Notre Dame in Paris. A system of six rhythmic patterns was developed by about 1180, and it appears that an entire repertory of organa was selectively 'updated' to be performed rhythmically. Thus the two types of organum diverged further. The syllabic, note-against-note discant style became rhythmicized. Meanwhile melismatic organum split into two types: one style, still called 'organum', remained unrhythmicized; another adapted to the modal rhythms. A further split, not in style but in function, took place when the ornate upper part was given a different text from the chant melody. This was a form of **trope** and became known as motet. New sections of organum, called clausulae, were written to fit into older works. By the beginning of the thirteenth century, changes in what was harmonically permissible allowed for the writing of large-scale organa, for example Perotin's *Viderunt omnes*. In such music the plainchant was sung in long notes in the tenor (lit. 'holding' part), with two or three higher voices singing fast, rhythmicized polyphony above it.

CONDUCTUS

Another type of composition, the conductus, developed alongside organum in the south of France near the turn of the twelfth century. Its musical style was similar, but it was based on newly composed tenors and texts, sometimes secular. The defining feature of conductus is the fast speed at which the words are declaimed. In the late thirteenth century, it was subsumed into the broad category of works now known as motets.

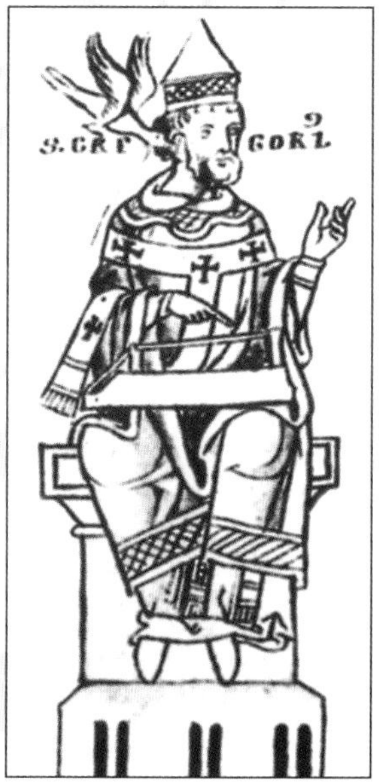

(BL) Music Manuscript
Developments in notation can be traced through the manuscripts that survive from this period.
(TL) Squarcialupi Codex
Page from the codex, showing one of Landini's comopsitions.
(BR) Pope Gregory
Illustration showing Pope Gregory recording the first plainchant, dictated to him by a dove.

Leonin ▶ p. 28 Perotin ▶ p. 31 Vitry ▶ p. 31

The Early Motet

The motet (from Fr. *mot*, 'word') evolved in the early thirteenth century, when poetic texts in French or Latin were added to the upper voices of clausulae over the slow-moving tenor. The practice of using already existing clausulae rather than composing new music continued for some time, mainly because it was impossible to notate fast-moving rhythms for syllabic text setting; the singers therefore fitted the new words to the rhythm of the melismas they knew. Most motets in the first half of the thirteenth century were for two voices. Later in the century, there were three- and sometimes four-voice works, and the advent of mensural notation meant that poetry could be set to new music. The repetition of tenor melodies and their rhythmic structures developed into a technique known as isorhythm.

MUSICAL CENTRES

Paris

In the second half of the twelfth century, the new cathedral of Notre Dame was the focus of an extraordinary effort by Leonin and others to create a whole new musical liturgy. Thanks to their efforts and to the presence of the increasingly independent University of Paris, whose curriculum was aimed towards ecclesiastical careers, the city became a leading musical centre. From Paris emanated the most important developments in musical notation in the twelfth, thirteenth and fourteenth centuries, the motet genre and, probably, the secular *formes fixes*.

Florence

Poetic works from fourteenth-century Florence sometimes mention the activities of its artistic community. Giovanni da Prato's *Paradiso degli Alberti* describes gatherings of poets and musicians at the home of the poet Antonio degli Alberti; Landini was among those who attended these meetings. Some musicians referred to in this and other poems are represented in the Squarcialupi Codex. Another great poem of the time, Boccaccio's *Decameron*, shows how music played a part in everyday life.

Burgundy

The dukes of Burgundy were important and generous musical patrons and the many composers whose work they fostered have collectively become known as the 'Burgundian school', even though most of their activity was focused in the courts of the Low Countries (e.g., Lille, Bruges and Brussels). The dukes had the finest chapel of their age, employing musicians such as **Binchois** and **Busnoys** and, later **Alexander Agricola** (*c.* 1446–1506); eventually the Burgundian tradition merged with that of the Spanish court to produce one of the most important institutions of the Renaissance.

Ars Nova and the Secular Song

The earliest known songs are those of the troubadours, trouvères and Minnesinger (e.g. canso, lai, bar form). The poetry they set to music was usually **strophic**, with a simple structure. By the end of the thirteenth century, a greater range of forms was beginning to emerge, probably with origins in unwritten traditions such as dance music. They are seen in the rondeaux of **Adam de la Halle** and, slightly later and more defined, in the songs of **Jehannot de Lescurel**.

The author of a fifteenth-century treatise wrote that Vitry 'found [i.e. founded] the manner of motets, ballades, lais and simple rondeaux', but none of his songs survives. However **Machaut**, his

SOURCES OF EARLY MUSIC

Winchester Troper: one of the earliest sources of polyphony, an English manuscript dating from the early eleventh century and originally used in Winchester; now in Christ's College, Cambridge.
Montpellier Codex: an important source of motets, compiled during the thirteenth century; now in the Bibliothèque interuniversitaire, Montpellier.
Roman de Fauvel: a satirical poem about the church written in the early fourteenth century. The most important manuscript has 167 musical items inserted in and appended to the poem, including works by Vitry. It is now in the Bibliothèque nationale, Paris.
Robertsbridge Codex: the earliest surviving manuscript of keyboard music (*c.* 1360), a fragment containing arrangements of two motets from the *Roman de Fauvel*, a hymn and three estampies (dances); now in the British Library, London.
Machaut manuscripts: six manuscripts (*c.* 1350 to *c.* 1390) representing his works from different periods of his career. Most are richly illuminated; some may have been made under his supervision. Five are now in the Bibliothèque Nationale, Paris, the other is in a private collection in New York.
Chantilly Manuscript: one of the two principal sources for the music of the Ars Subtilior. Its origin is unknown; now in the Musée Condé, Chantilly.
Old Hall Manuscript: an English manuscript of the early fifteenth century, probably compiled at the court of Thomas, Duke of Clarence, containing sacred music by such composers as Dunstaple.
Squarcialupi Codex: a major source of fourteenth-century Italian music, compiled in Florence *c.* 1410–15; now in the Biblioteca medicea Laurenziana, Florence.
Trent Codices: a group of seven manuscripts containing music from 1400–75. The music is by composers from all over Europe. Six are now in the Museo provincale d'artre, Trento, the other is the Biblioteca capitolare.

ARS ANTIQUA – ARS NOVA – ARS SUBTILIOR

The terms Ars Antiqua ('old art'), Ars Nova ('new art') and Ars Subtilior ('more subtle art') describe separate stages of musical development in the thirteenth and fourteenth centuries. In the fourteenth century, theorists coined the phrase Ars Antiqua to denote music that came before Vitry's treatise *Ars nova*. It covers a range of styles from early motets to the more complicated works of Petrus de Cruce. Vitry's treatise, with its flexible notational system, ushered in a new style: motets became longer and more elaborately structured and the *formes fixes* also took on his innovations. Ars Subtilior is a term invented by twentieth-century scholars to describe works of the late fourteenth century, in which the composers vied with each other to write ever-more complicated music, extremely difficult to decipher and perform.

ballade ▶ p. 356 canon ▶ p. 356 *cantus firmus* ▶ p. 356 rondeau ▶ p. 362 strophic ▶ p. 362 virelai ▶ p. 363

younger contemporary, wrote well over 100 songs in which the short strophic forms of **ballade**, **rondeau** and **virelai** (known as the *formes fixes*) are clearly defined. Machaut's mature polyphonic songs feature ornamented, agile melodic lines over slower-moving lower voices. His monophonic songs – mostly virelais and lais – generally have simple, tuneful melodies. In the fourteenth century the ballade was the dominant form, but by the mid-fifteenth century it was all but obsolete, having been superseded by the rondeau.

MASS CYCLES

Machaut's Mass was the first Mass cycle. Written in the early 1360s, it sets all the movements of the Ordinary, the dismissal, Ite missa est ('Go, the Mass is ended'), and its response, Deo gracias ('Thanks be to God'). Although not all the movements are based on chant (the 'Kyrie', 'Sanctus', 'Agnus Dei' and 'Ite missa est' are based on their respective plainchant melodies, in isorhythm, whereas the 'Gloria' and 'Credo' are set to freely composed syllabic polyphony), the Mass uses four-part scoring and similar vocal ranges thorughout.

Oddly, Machaut's Mass did not noticeably influence many later composers, although they must certainly have been aware of it. Around the beginning of the fifteenth century the focus shifted to England, where **Dunstaple** and his contemporaries were composing Masses (mostly in three voices) based on a *cantus firmus* in the tenor. The most influential of these compositions was the anonymous *Missa 'Caput'*. Based on a *cantus firmus*, but with the addition of a fourth, freely composed line below the tenor, it revolutionized Mass composition. It is structured by a masterful series of proportional relationships and it influenced later continental composers to do the same: it was used as a model by both **Ockeghem** and **Jacob Obrecht** (*c.* 1450–1505). For these features, and for its sonorous texture, it was justly famous in its day, and it is perhaps one of the most important pieces ever to have been composed.

Formes Fixes

While the *formes fixes* were emerging in France, the ballata, caccia and madrigal began to appear in Italy. The ballata, probably the oldest of the three, is related to the virelai and to similar forms from other countries. The text of the caccia (It., 'hunt') often took a hunting theme and the voices usually sang in **canon**. The strophic madrigal was relatively short-lived and was unrelated to the through-composed sixteenth-century madrigal genre.

Isorhythm

Isorhythm (from Gk *isos*, 'identical', and *rhythmos*, 'rhythm') is a compositional technique that had its heyday in the fourteenth and early fifteenth centuries. Composers took a melody – usually a section of plainchant – and allocated rhythm to it, normally in long note values. It was repeated several times. They then wrote music to fit over the tune, its melody and slow rhythm providing the ideal base for fast-moving upper voices. Isorhythmic works are structured around the repeated melody, often in quite subtle and complex ways. There might be two such themes sung at the same time, for example, or the rhythmic pattern might be different in length from the melodic one. Overlaps allowed the composer to work on several structural levels at once.

(FL) Courtly Love
A minnesinger being lifted up to his lady's window.
(NL) Manuscript Decoration
Decoration from an illuminated manuscript from the musical centre of Burgundy.
(BR) The Mass
Handwritten Mass dedicated to Margaret of Austria.

Music for the Mass

Most of the earliest polyphony consists of settings of the Proper of the Mass (the parts that change from day to day). There are very few early polyphonic settings of the movements of the Ordinary – Kyrie, Gloria, Credo, Sanctus and Agnus Dei – and complete Mass settings seem not to have appeared before the fourteenth century. Of the several surviving fourteenth-century Masses only one, Machaut's *Messe de Nostre Dame*, forms a unified work, and it is therefore the first Mass cycle.

From the late fourteenth century, composers concentrated their efforts on creating Mass settings in which the movements were musically related to each other. There are many instances in the late fourteenth and early fifteenth centuries of pairs of Mass movements ('Gloria'–'Credo'; 'Sanctus'–'Agnus Dei') related through their scoring, mensuration schemes or textural patterns. In addition, English composers began to base all the movements of a Mass on the same plainchant ***cantus firmus***. This technique was adopted by continental musicians and became one of the principal methods of cyclical Mass composition. In the fifteènth century secular melodies began to be used as *cantus firmi*; the most famous of these was the melody 'L'homme armé'. The final innovation, whose beginnings are evident in **Du Fay**'s Mass *Ave Regina celorum*, is the basing of Mass cycles on material from the whole of an existing work (not just a single melody); this – the parody – was to become very important for Renaissance composers.

Musical Style in the Fifteenth Century

By the end of the fourteenth century, music in France had become so complex that a change of direction was inevitable. The necessary impetus came from Italian composers who, at around the same time, began to merge their native style with that of the French. Although at the beginning of the fifteenth century some Italian composers continued in the Ars Subtilior style, there was also a marked movement towards less complicated and more melodic music, emphasizing the words. This trend spread quickly to northern composers. By the 1420s and 30s some chansons had quite consonant harmonies (far more 'modern'-sounding than their fourteenth-century counterparts) and a clean, clear texture without so much of the rhythmic complexity of earlier songs. This style also permeated sacred music such as Du Fay's vocal lines. Meanwhile, the even more consonant sound of English music was influencing composers in Burgundy, leading to a genuinely international style.

However, there were still vestiges of the old obsession with structure and form: the isorhythmic motet, relegated to use only for grand ceremonial occasions, remained a way for composers to demonstrate their musical ingenuity; this was also transferred to the Mass cycle, which came to supersede the motet as an 'intellectual' form.

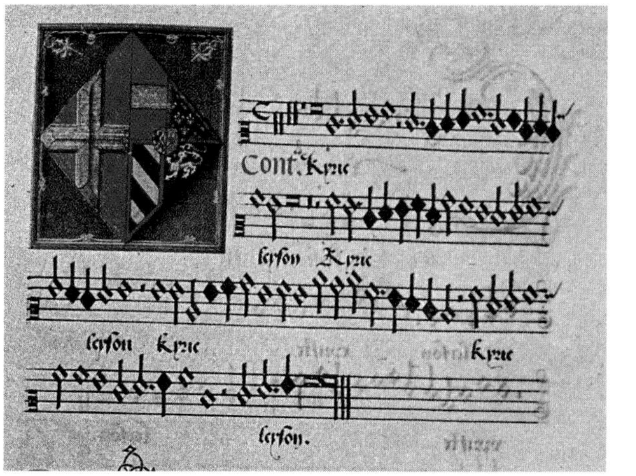

Adam de la Halle ▶ p. 26 Agricola ▶ p. 48 Busnoys ▶ p. 26 Du Fay ▶ p. 27 Dunstaple ▶ p. 28 Jehannot de Lescaurel ▶ p. 28 Machaut ▶ p. 29 Obrecht ▶ p. 55 Ockeghem ▶ p. 30

The Medieval Era

INSTRUMENTS

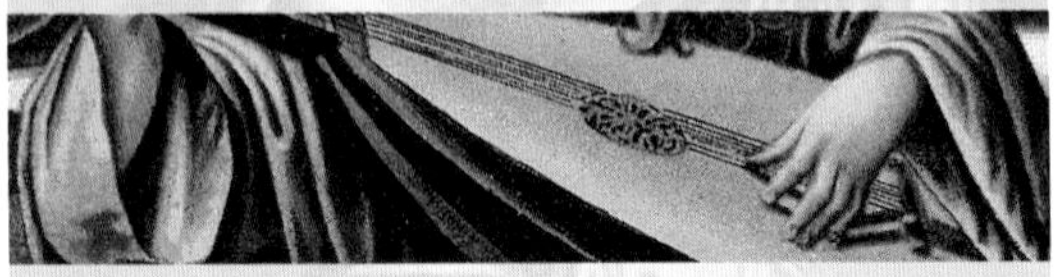

Lyre and Crwth

The medieval plucked lyre had six strings which passed over a bridge resting on the front of a hollow resonant body. They were secured at the base of the instrument and were fixed to a yoke which consisted of a crossbar between two arms projecting upwards from the sides of the body. The lyre rested in the lap and the right hand plucked the strings near the bridge.

The bowed lyre is now generally called by its Welsh name, 'crwth' (pronounced 'crooth'). Its arm and crossbar construction was altered: a fingerboard gave it a double arch, so the instrument as a whole looked like a face. It was held up against the chest to allow it to be bowed. The left hand grasped its 'nose' (the fingerboard) and the six strings were fixed to a row of pegs across the 'forehead'. The bridge – the mouth – was flat, so any melody was continuously accompanied by a drone on the other strings.

The Harp

The medieval harp was built on a roughly triangular frame, with the hollow soundbox held against the player's body and the strings running from it to the top part of the triangle, positioned like the crossbar of a bicycle frame. The strings were made variously of twisted sheep's intestines, horsehair and metals such as brass, silver and gold. They were fixed to the soundbox with L-shaped pins called 'brays'. The brays were designed to interfere with the vibration of the string just enough to create an extra buzzing sound as it was plucked. Harps at this time were readily portable laptop instruments. Because they did not interfere with the player's breathing, they were ideal for singers to use to accompany themselves.

Psaltery, Cittole and Gittern

The medieval psaltery was a flat box with strings running across its top; it was plucked either by the fingers or by a quill held in each hand. The harp-psaltery, or rote, took the form of a right-angled triangle

with the apex pointing into the mucisian's lap. Although played like a harp, in construction it was more similar to a psaltery as the soundbox lay behind the strings and filled the entire triangle.

The cittole and the gittern are two instruments of the thirteenth and fourteenth centuries much confused with each another. Both were held across the body and played like a guitar, plucked with the right hand and the strings were stopped by the left hand. The gittern had a pear-shaped body with a curved back, tapering into a neck ending in a peg box. The cittole was flat-backed and shaped in a figure-of-eight. To release the sound from the hollow body, the former had a series of holes puncturing the front like a lute rose and the latter a pair of C-shaped holes, not unlike a violin.

Pipe and Tabor

The medieval pipe was played by blowing directly into a mouthpiece, like a recorder or penny whistle. Although it usually had only three holes to finger, by varying the force of blowing, players could achieve a working range of about one-and-a-half octaves. It was played with the right hand; the left hand held a thick, stubby beater to play a type of drum called a tabor. Traditionally associated with clowns and jesters, the pipe and tabor were used in dance music. Three pipes were found on the ship *Mary Rose*, which sank off Portsmouth in 1545.

Bagpipe

The medieval bagpipe consisted of an animal-skin bag and a series of wooden pipes. The player held the bag under the arm and inflated it by blowing down one of the pipes. A second pipe, the 'chanter', contained a series of holes on which to play a melody, while the remainder, the 'drones', maintained a continuous, unvarying background chord. By keeping a steady pressure on the bag, the player was able to pause for breath without interrupting the continuity of sound. Once widespread, bagpipes survive best where industrialization has least disturbed traditional ways of life or where there has been a post-medieval folk revival, such as Scotland.

Trumpet

At the beginning of the Middle Ages, the trumpet was a straight piece of cylindrical metal tubing, running from a mouthpiece to the wide ending known as a 'bell'. A medieval instrument rescued from the mud of the River Thames in London in the 1980s was made of sections of metal sheet (brass or copper) which were rolled up and joined to form a tube. The joins were soldered together and a boss was wrapped around the join to strengthen it. Perhaps modelled on the Roman and Byzantine tuba, or perhaps on Islamic brass instruments seen during the crusades, this early trumpet was 1.2–1.5 m (4–5 ft) long.

After becoming a more manageable S-shape around 1400, the trumpet settled down as a loop. The later Middle Ages saw experiments with crooks and a slide. The former were extra lengths of metal tubing which could be fitted into the basic trumpet structure to alter the overall length

of the column of air inside and thus the emerging note. The latter was a kind of miniature telescope close to the mouthpiece; by opening or closing it, the player could make the trumpet longer or shorter.

Portative Organ

Although the early church had been hostile to instrumental music, the organ was gradually adopted by Christianity following its rediscovery in the eighth and ninth centuries. Since then it has been a largely ecclesiastical instrument, though chamber organs have also been used for secular music in aristocratic houses.

Most medieval organs were small, especially by modern standards. Indeed, the portative organ was small enough to be carried by a strap while the player was walking. It could be balanced on the left knee, played with the right hand and pumped with the left. No such instrument survives and carvings and paintings are the only source of information we have about them. They suggest that, until the fourteenth century, there were two rows of pipes, allowing a two-octave compass; from their size, it seems that middle C was the bottom note.

Positive Organ

The larger positive organ was not intended to be moved. The biggest difference between medieval and modern organs is that the positive organ's pipes were all of the same diameter; the pitch was defined by the length. This caused variation in tone quality across the range, making it 'flutier' as the pipes became shorter. Gradually organ-builders introduced 'reed' pipes, which concealed a vibrating reed and had an oboe-like sound. Some flue pipes were open tubes like a recorder; others were stopped – they had their ends plugged to drop their pitch by an octave, widening the compass of the instrument.

All organs require air to be pumped through pipes; the journey of the air and the choice of the pipe (and thus the note), is made by playing a keyboard. Graded by size, the pipes of the positive organ sat inside a series of matching openings in a windchest, where the pressure built up as air was fed in from manually operated bellows. The entrance to each pipe from the windchest was concealed by a pallet, a kind of hinged doorway or valve. It could be deliberately opened or closed by a mechanism of rods which were directed by the keyboard or 'manual'.

Hurdy-Gurdy, Organistrum, Sinfonye and Geigenwerk

Because the name 'hurdy-gurdy' was abducted by the nineteenth-century barrel organ, this instrument is rarely taken as seriously as it deserves. Known as the 'organistrum' from the tenth to twelfth centuries, it was a stringed instrument played by a cranked resined wheel, not a bow. It required two operators, one of whom would crank and one play, and it was associated at first with the clergy in choir schools. In the thirteenth century it developed into the 'sinfonye', a secular instrument, and could be worked by an individual. There are likely to have been strings besides the controlled ones which sounded throughout as a running accompaniment. The sinfonye has survived best in France.

A Renaissance version of the sinfonye is to be found in the Brussels Collection. This uses not the single 5- or 7.6-cm (2- or 3-in) wheel of the medieval period, but four wheels, each 17.8 cm (7 in) in diameter, their rims covered in parchment. The wheels are intended for different strings and turn at different speeds, the bass slower than the treble, allowing for greater refinement of performance. Made in Germany, it is called by its German name of 'Geigenwerk', or mechanical violin.

Bells

The bell may have been the instrument most widely and frequently heard in the European Middle Ages. Handbells had survived into the medieval period from antiquity; in addition, large bells were hung in church towers. Their loud sound was believed to keep away demons, so they may have offset the fear of churchyards. Bells were made of bronze; the small ones were sounded by being shaken, the large ones swung by means of ropes. Though they are not usually struck directly, bells are classified as tuned percussion instruments: a loose clapper or 'tongue' inside the hollow dome of the bell strikes at its sides.

BOWED INSTRUMENTS

The early medieval bow looked not unlike the weapon: a convex, dramatically curved wooden structure with horsehair where the archer's bow-string would have been. There was no attempt at standardization, and construction seems to have varied as different styles were tried out. Even by the late Middle Ages, the bow had only settled down in design terms to some degree. Length ranged between 50 and 80 cm (20 and 31 in). On some arched models there was a handle, held in the fist to allow for a vigorous application. Other bows were in the flat style with the hair and wood running in parallel; the player gripped both the wood and the bowhair, separating them in part with the fingers.

A number of new bowed instruments evolved, some assembled out of shaped pieces of wood, some carved from single blocks. Normally three strings were fixed over a flat bridge, to be played with the bow sloping one way or the other, or held level. By the fifteenth century, the development of a curved fingerboard and bridge made it easier to play individual strings, and more were added.

Medieval bowed instruments were held against the chest or shoulder, unlike the violin which is tucked under the chin. Although Arabs had already begun playing a kind of rebec placed upright on the lap, this position was not used in western music until the viols and the bass members of the violin family emerged at the beginning of the sixteenth century.

(BL) A Game of Chess
Medieval musicians on trumpets, tabor and bagpipes, entertaining chess players.
(TL) Early Instruments
Illuminated letter showing monks playing early instruments, including the psaltery.
(TR) Trumpets
Fifteenth-century French miniature depicting the Fall of Jericho at the trumpets of Joshua.
(BR) Bowed Instruments
Medieval bowed instruments were held against the chest or shoulder.

The Medieval Era

LISTENING GUIDE

Guillaume Du Fay
Nuper rosarum flores

WORK: Guillaume Du Fay, *Nuper rosarum flores*, composed 1436
SCORING: Unaccompanied chorus
EXCERPT: Track 6. Duration: 6 min 54 sec
TIMINGS BASED ON: *Missa L'homme armé* and motets, Hilliard Ensemble directed by Paul Hillier (see Recommended CDs)

On 25 March 1436, Florence Cathedral was consecrated in a splendid and solemn ceremony. Begun centuries earlier, the building had lain incomplete for years because no one could find a way of erecting the dome over the crossing: the area to be covered was simply too big. The man who solved this riddle of engineering was the architect Filippo Brunelleschi. The pope himself agreed to officiate, and to celebrate the event Guillaume Du Fay – the most celebrated composer of the age – composed music for the inauguration. The four-voice motet *Nuper rosarum flores* is a fitting musical counterpart to Brunelleschi's achievement.

THE COMMEMORATIVE MOTET

For the late medieval composer, a motet was the natural way to mark a great event or honour a famous person. The text was written specially, and the composer could show great ingenuity in devising a musical structure sophisticated enough to reflect the importance of the occasion. Like most sacred music of the medieval period, *Nuper rosarum flores* is built upon pre-existent material. Du Fay chose 14 notes of plainchant from the liturgy for the dedication of a church, setting the words 'Terribilis est locus iste' ('This place is awe-inspiring'). The choice of a liturgically appropriate plainchant was crucial to the omposer's purpose, even though very few notes were used.

COMPOSERS IN ARMS

Du Fay's Mass *L'homme armé* (tracks 1–5 of Recommended CD 1) was one of the first of several dozen Masses of that name composed between the years 1450 and 1700. 'L'homme armé' ('The Armed Man') was a popular, probably satirical, tune which may have been aimed at the less-valiant members of the French army during the last stages of the Hundred Years' War. Attracted by its tunefulness and its simple form, composers began writing Masses using it as a ***cantus firmus***. The first of these may have been **Ockeghem**, around 1450, but others soon followed suit. In fact, a sort of rivalry ensued as composers sought to outdo each other in presenting the tune in new and ingenious ways. Two sections of Du Fay's Mass illustrate this musical exhibitionism: in the Credo (track 3) at the words 'Genitum non factum' ('Begotten not made'; 3':24"), Du Fay makes the four voices sing at four different speeds simultaneously, resulting in a complex and exciting sound. In the third Agnus Dei (track 5, from 3':28") he begins by stating the tune (in the middle of the texture) at half speed and back-to-front, and from 5':28" it appears at normal speed the right way round. Younger composers such as **Busnoys** and **Josquin des Prez** (*c.* 1440–1521) responded to these tricks in various ways, and still others joined in, creating ever more contrived and sometimes witty devices. The list includes most of the Renaissance's most famous names, and some, like Josquin and **Giovanni Pierluigi da Palestrina** (1525/6–94), found the subject so fascinating that they wrote not one, but two, Masses based on it.

1. 0':00" The first section of the motet begins with a duo.
2. 0':34" The two voices imitate each other, singing the same music at a different pitch.
3. 1':08" The first tenor (*cantus firmus*) enters.
4. 1':10" The second tenor (*cantus firmus*) enters.
5. 1':52" The pope's name, Eugenius, is given special emphasis.
6. 2':20" The second section starts with a new duo.

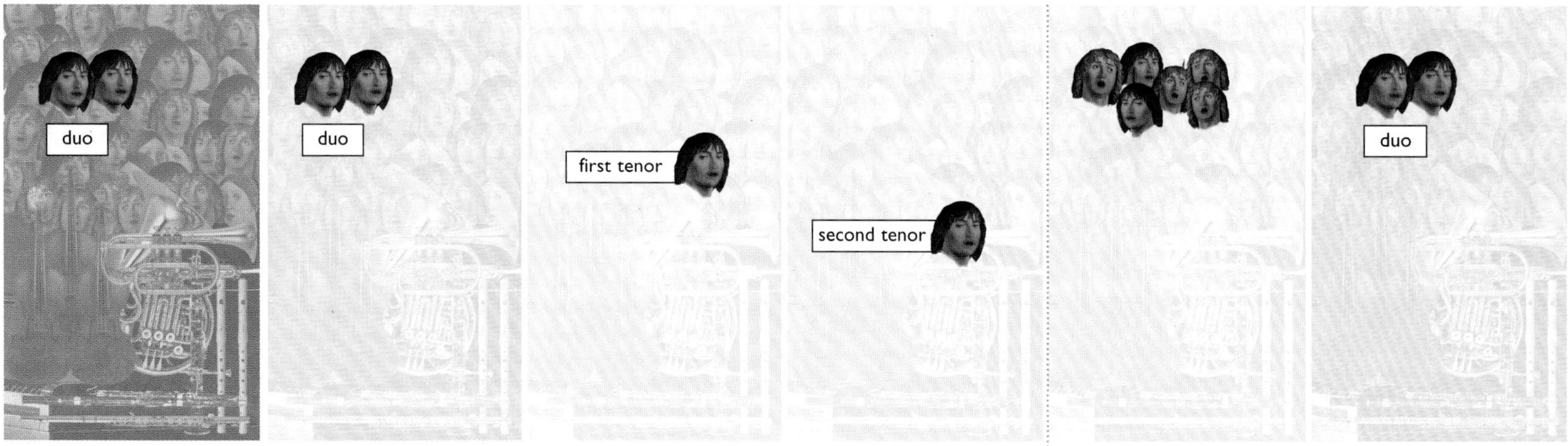

cantus firmus ▶ p. 356

This group of notes, called the *cantus firmus*, is heard in the two low voices, each starting on a different pitch (D is heard first, then G). They move very slowly to begin with, but over the course of the piece's four sections they are repeated four times at different speeds (using the technique of isorhythm). These speeds are in the proportion of 6:4:2:3, creating an overall effect of forward movement; the harmony becomes livelier and livelier as the piece evolves. Each section begins its own freely composed introductory duo, and the piece concludes with a magnificent acclamation, as for the first time the four voices say the same word together: 'Amen'.

MUSIC AS SOUNDING NUMBER

The structuring of a piece of music on a numerical plan may appear artificial to modern listeners, but to medieval musicians it was an audible representation of the structure of the universe. Simple ratios were thought to govern both the orbits of the planets around the earth, and correspond to the acoustic relationships between musical intervals. When used in music they were believed to reflect nothing less than the divine order. At the same time, people were keenly alive to music's beauty, its power to move and its ability to represent human things. They would have noted the way Du Fay underlines important words: the pope's name, Eugenius, is underscored by the addition of an extra voice. When he is described as the 'successor' of St Peter, the two upper voices sing that word one after the other (i.e. in succession). Du Fay included other clues that Brunelleschi and others would have appreciated. It has been observed that the proportions mentioned above are identical with those of the biblical temple of Solomon; and the way the two presentations of the *cantus firmus* overlap in the lower voices recalls the structure of Brunelleschi's dome, which includes interlocking inner and outer shells. The piece's perfect proportions are matched by the splendid effect of the four-part harmony. One chronicler reported that the beauty of the music and the magnificence of the occasion moved many of the congregation to tears.

(TR) Florence
Fifteenth-century view of Florence, showing the cathedral on the left-hand side.
(MR) Astrological Manuscript
The movement of the planets and the structure of the universe played a significant role in composition.

RECOMMENDED CDs

1. Guillaume Du Fay: *Missa L'homme armé* and motets. Hilliard Ensemble. Paul Hillier, director. EMI Reflexe CDC 5 55207-2

2. Guillaume Du Fay: Complete Secular Music. Medieval Ensemble of London. Peter and Timothy Davies, directors. Decca 452 557-2 (5 CDs)

   This contains all of Du Fay's songs, spanning the whole of his career, from youth through to the accomplished mastery of old age.

3. John Dunstaple: Motets. Hilliard Ensemble. directed by Paul Hillier, director. Virgin Classics VER5 613342-2

   Motets from Du Fay's elder English contemporary, whose style was a major influence on continental composers of Du Fay's time.

4. Johannes Ockeghem: Mass *De plus en plus* and songs. Orlando Consort. Archiv 453 419 2

   Music from Du Fay's great younger contemporary. The Mass represents a late stage of medieval music, in which songs of courtly love (rather than plainchant) could be used as borrowed material.

5. The Medieval Romantics. Gothic Voices. Christopher Page, director. Hyperion CDA 66463

   A perfect introduction to the diversity of musical styles and genres at the turn of the fifteenth century and beyond, including some of Du Fay's early songs, and music that influenced him.

7. 3':11" The second statements of the *cantus firmus* begin.

8. 4':06" The third and shortest section opens with another duo and more imitation.

9. 4':32" The third statements of the *cantus firmus* begin.

10. 5':00" The fourth section starts with the final duo.

11. 5':19" Du Fay introduces a third voice moving in tandem with the lower voice of the duo.

12. 5':41" The fourth statements of the *cantus firmus* begin.

13. 6':28" The four voices join together in a final acclamation.

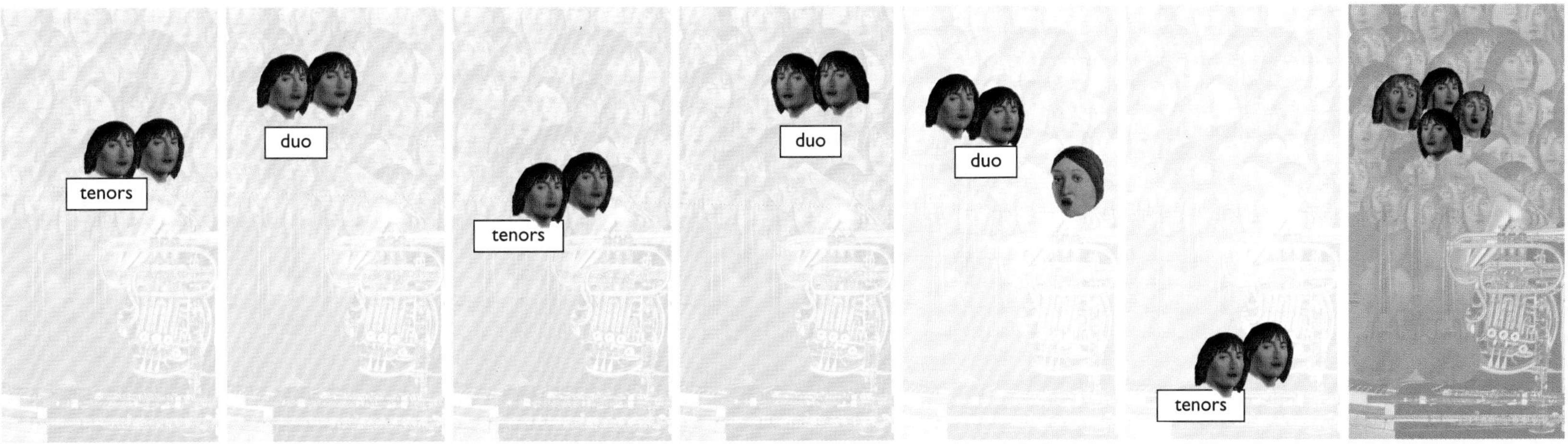

Busnoys ▶ p. 26 Du Fay ▶ p. 27 Dunstaple ▶ p. 28 Josquin des Prez ▶ p. 53 Ockeghem ▶ p. 30 Palestrina ▶ p. 56

CHANTS DE L'ÉGLISE DE ROME

Most recordings of medieval music are of polyphony. However, during the Middle Ages performances of polyphony were not the norm but the exception, reserved for special occasions. In church, the everyday musical fare was plainchant. Most regions had their own liturgical traditions, of which chant was an integral part. Equally, there must have been a corresponding diversity of local practices as regards performance, but they are difficult to reconstruct. Over the past 20 years, the French Ensemble Organum has specialized in the recovery of these local traditions and transformed the received aural image of plainchant.

Alongside regional variations, there was constant cultural exchange between communities. One instance of this occurred during the seventh and eighth centuries, when a number of Byzantine bishops were elected to the papacy. They brought to Rome the singers and repertories of their native region. To recreate this influence, Marcel Pérès collaborated on several of the ensemble's recordings with the Greek singer Lycourgos Angelopoulos, whose knowledge of Byzantine approaches to ornamentation in the Orthodox liturgy guided the singers of the Ensemble. Two particularly striking features of this style deserve mention: the use of **microtonal** ornaments, and the presence on many tracks of an *ison*, or pedal tone, sung by deep basses and underpinning the singing of the chant. Pérès has said of his reconstructions that they have only a 40 per cent chance of being 'right'. Some might say that is a very generous estimate, but despite the controversy they generate (especially in Anglo-Saxon countries), his recordings capture the ecstatic quality of plainchant in a highly dramatic way.

RECOMMENDED CD

Chants de l'église de Rome, sung by the Ensemble Organum. Marcel Pérès, director. Harmonia Mundi HMC 901218.

PEROTIN: *VIDERUNT OMNES*

Perotin was the best-known composer of **organum** at the turn of the thirteenth century and was the first composer of music for four voices whose name we know. Two four-voice organa of his survive: *Sederunt principes* for the feast of St Stephen (26 December) and *Viderunt omnes* for Christmas Day. Each employs a plainchant *cantus firmus* that runs through the length of the piece in very long notes. Around it the composer writes three additional voices moving at a much faster pace. These 'free' voices are arranged according to strictly defined patterns known as rhythmic modes. The clashes between them results in a subtle counterpoint of **dissonances** and resolutions which is at times surprisingly similar to the way in which dissonances produce tension in tonal music.

The Ensemble Gilles Binchois has made a speciality of interpreting the earliest notated polyphony. Its recording of *Viderunt omnes* takes the music at a slower tempo than most performances: it lasts over 17 minutes rather than the more usual 12. This allows both the singers and the listener to savour the interplay between the voices, and increases the music's spiralling effect. The CD also includes pieces for two and three voices by Perotin and others. Some are written in the conductus style, with the voices singing the text in a declamatory manner, often syllabically as in *Mundus vergens*.

RECOMMENDED CD

Ecole de Notre-Dame de Paris. Ensemble Gilles Binchois. Dominique Vellard, director. Harmonic H/CD 9349.

THE ORIGINAL *CARMINA BURANA*

Everyone has heard of Carl Orff's masterpiece, but few know that the texts he used were first written down by medieval Bavarian monks. Once a year, rules were relaxed, and the monks sang light-hearted parodies of their usual sacred chants.

POPULAR MELODY *Orff*

MACHAUT: *MESSE DE NOSTRE DAME*

Machaut's Mass is surely the best-known piece of the entire medieval period. Dating from the early 1360s, it is the first surviving setting of the Mass Ordinary (the five sections of the liturgy that are common to the vast majority of celebrations of the Mass) by a single composer. In addition, Machaut set the dismissal and its response. The Mass is composed in two sharply contrasted styles, both of which were common in the sacred music of Machaut's time. The four sections, 'Kyrie', 'Sanctus', 'Agnus Dei' and 'Ite missa est' (and the 'Amen' sections of the 'Gloria' and 'Credo'), have very short texts, and are set isorhythmically, like Du Fay's motet *Nuper rosarum*. In these movements one clearly hears the difference between the faster-moving upper voices. and the slower-moving lower pair. The 'Sanctus' uses the technique of hocket, in which single notes are exchanged between two voices in a 'hiccup' effect. In the Gloria and Credo the amount of text to be got through is much greater

RECOMMENDED CD

Messe de Nostre Dame. Taverner Consort and Choir. Andrew Parrott, director. Virgin ZM4 89982 2.

LE VOIR DIT

Machaut's poem *Le Voir Dit* is a sequence of letters between a young lady and a poet whose work she admires. The poem indicates that the two met and, if the narrative poetry linking the letters is to be believed, the relationship became more than educational and went even beyond the dictates of courtly love. Many scholars believe this to be an autobiographical poem, the events taking place in the early 1360s when Machaut was at least 60 years old. *Le Voir Dit* also mentions poems and music that Machaut sent to the lady, and it contains fascinating details about the way he composed.

It is tempting, given the nature of his work and his effort to collect his works in single manuscripts, to view Machaut as more modern than his contemporaries. However, most of what he did – even the complete-works manuscripts – has some precedent, and he should therefore be regarded as a man very much of, rather than ahead of, his time.

dissonance ▶ p. 358 microtone ▶ p. 360 minimalism ▶ p. 360 organum ▶ p. 361 triad ▶ p. 363

than in the other four movements, so it is set syllabically; all four voices declaim the text together. This harks back to the conductus style of the twelfth and thirteenth centuries.

In these longer movements there are short connecting passages for two voices without text. Until relatively recently it was assumed that the absence of text implied the use of instruments, and most recordings of the Mass were made with both voices and instruments. But Andrew Parrott's recording of 1983 used only voices, on the grounds that in Reims Cathedral, where Machaut served as a canon, all instruments were banned – even the organ. Since Parrott's recording, most others have tended to use only voices. Parrott's approach was radical in other respects, too: he used only a single voice on each part and a high tenor (as opposed to a countertenor) sang the top line; he employed the so-called 'Pythagorean' tuning-system that was universal in Machaut's time; and the Latin was pronounced in a way that the composer might have recognized. Finally, he presented the Mass as part of an imaginary reconstruction of a service in Reims Cathedral.

ANON: *MISSA 'CAPUT'*

Like most of the music before the advent of printing, this Mass survives without the name of a composer attached to it. This is true even of influential works – and few pieces were as influential in their time as this, probably one of the first four-voice settings of the five movements of the Mass Ordinary by a single composer since Machaut's *Messe de Nostre Dame*. It was written around 1440 by an English composer, and it introduced several ideas that had a profound impact on Mass composition in the fifteenth century and beyond.

Each movement begins with the same music (a motto or head-motive) for two voices. After a few bars, two other voices enter, one of which sings the *cantus firmus*, a fragment from the chant for Maundy Thursday. Like the motto, it is repeated in each movement. The use of a *cantus firmus* is of course not new, but below it the composer introduces a fourth voice, a bass. This is a departure from the music of the preceding period, and it allows the composer to control the flow of the harmony in a much freer, more flexible manner. This innovation took the musical world by storm, encouraging composers of the stature of Du Fay and **Binchois** to rethink their styles in response. The Gothic Voices capture this feeling of excitement in their performance, creating a constantly shifting kaleidoscope of sound, glorious and almost defiantly **triadic**. This must have been the *contenance angloise*, the 'English manner' described by a contemporary poet. It is also heard in the much simpler settings of carols included on the disc.

(FL) Medieval Choir
Plainchant was the traditional form of medieval music; polyphony was used on church occasions.
(TR) Psaltery
Tenth-century illustration showing a king playing the psaltery.
(BR) Guillaume de Machaut
Machaut's Messe de Nostre Dame *is one of the best-known pieces from the medieval era.*

RECOMMENDED CD

Missa 'Caput'. Gothic Voices. Christopher Page, director. Hyperion CDA66857.

THE MEDIEVAL INFLUENCE

Composers of the twentieth century and up to the present have often been drawn to the music of the medieval and Renaissance periods. A relatively early example is **Igor Stravinsky** (1882–1971), who became interested in the fourteenth-century technique of hocket and in the harmonic experiments of the Italian composer **Carlo Gesualdo** (*c.* 1561–1613). Hocket has since inspired many composers, both modernist (**Harrison Birtwistle**, b.1934, for instance, in his *Carmen Arcadiae Mechanicae Perpetuum*, 1984) and **minimalist** (Louis Andriessen, b. 1939: *Hocketus*). The canonic processes of Ockeghem find their way into the Requiem of 1963–65 by **György Ligeti** (b. 1923), and even the 'Caput' plainchant melody turns up in *Unsichtbare Farben* ('Invisible Colours') by **Brian Ferneyhough** (b. 1943). The possible list is extensive and includes neo-tonal composers like **Arvo Pärt** (b. 1935), who draws on the music of **Perotin**, **Steve Reich** (b. 1936) and **Alfred Schnittke** (1934–98). The diversity of styles is perhaps surprising, but composers are often drawn to the same music for entirely different reasons. Perhaps the common thread engaging their fascination is that so-called 'early music' suggests alternatives to the principle of thematic development (structuring music by the development of themes) that is typical of most tonal composition: for example, considerations of sonority, texture or notation.

Binchois ▶ p. 26 Birtwistle ▶ p. 324 Ferneyhough ▶ 325 Gesualdo ▶ p. 51 Ligeti ▶ p. 326 Machaut ▶ p. 29 Pärt ▶ p. 327 Perotin ▶ p. 31 Reich ▶ p. 328 Schnittke ▶ p. 328 Stravinsky ▶ p. 280

THE RENAISSANCE

Renaissance' is a French word meaning 'rebirth'. It has been used since the nineteenth century to describe the period between *c.* 1300 and 1600. Three hundred years is a long time for a single historical or cultural period, and the strain shows in any attempt to define the term 'Renaissance'.

THE RISE OF HUMANISM

The cultural phenomenon central to the Renaissance was a revival of interest in the literature, philosophy and architecture of classical antiquity. Early Christian leaders had been eager to put the polytheistic culture of imperial Rome behind them, and they did this with considerable success. But in the fourteenth century, with the power of the church on the wane and secular education on the rise, the wealthy educated classes started paying attention to the relics of Greek and, more particularly, Roman, civilization that lay unexamined around them. This *studia humanitas*, now known as Humanism, is first evident in the works of the Italian poet Francesco Petrarch. By the fifteenth century, scholars such as Poggio Bracciolini, artists like Donatello and architects like Filippo Brunelleschi were eagerly recovering, imitating and evaluating the artefacts of the classical world.

CLASSICAL IDEALS

Music was an important part of the humanist educational curriculum from the early fifteenth century, and by its last quarter more dramatic developments were being made; we have thus marked the beginning of the Renaissance at 1475, but it should be remembered that many of the ideals and practices of the Renaissance overlap with those of the late medieval period. The application of Renaissance ideals to musical composition at this time was difficult. Few works survived from classical times, and those that did were difficult to interpret. It was not possible in music, as it was in architecture and sculpture, to copy ancient models. There were, on the other hand, many references to music in classical texts, and humanists turned to these with enthusiasm.

The Renaissance

INTRODUCTION

Classical ideals began to show up in musical treatises in the late fifteenth century, especially in the writings of Johannes Tinctoris (1430–after 1511), who claimed that music had been reborn in the works of John Dunstaple (*c.* 1390–1453) and his followers around 1440. Also central to Renaissance thinking about music was the belief in the power of music to move the passions and the association of this power with specific modes (scales and melodic formulas). In his *Dodecachordon* (1547), the Swiss theorist Heinrich Glarean (1488–1563) expanded the medieval system of 8 modes to 12 and gave each a Greek name borrowed from modes found in Greek writings (Dorian, Phrygian and so forth). Later humanists realized that their modal system was, in fact, unrelated to the Greek one; but the names stuck and, along with them, the sense that this primary musical material was important in determining the effect of music on the hearer.

In practical terms, the most important influence came not from the study of musical treatises, but from those on oratory and drama. Quintilian's first-century *De institutione oratoria,* discovered by Bracciolini in 1416, became a central text for the important field of rhetoric. The belief that music could persuade, led composers to draw on the principles of rhetoric – at least unconsciously – in their composition.

Theorists like Joachim Burmeister (1564–1629) turned to rhetorical models to explain music. Oddly, the most important musical genre to arise from the study of ancient texts was one that belongs chronologically to the Baroque era. It became clear that classical drama had been sung throughout; attempts to revive this, in late sixteenth-century Florence, led to the creation of the first operas.

KEY EVENTS

1477	Geoffrey Chaucer's *Canterbury Tales* (written *c.* 1386) first printed by William Caxton
1478	Ferdinand and Isabella establish Spanish Inquisition, led by the infamous Torquemada
1485	Richard III defeated at Bosworth Field; Henry VII becomes first Tudor monarch in England
1492	Christopher Columbus embarks on his journey that ends with the discovery of the Americas
1494	Beginning of the Italian Wars between the major European powers
1495	Leonardo da Vinci paints *Last Supper* in monastic refectory in Milan
1504	Francesco Petrarch's *Rime* (written 14th century) published by Italian linguistic reformer Pietro Bembo
c.1510	Raphael's *School of Athens* painted
1517	Martin Luther nails '95 theses' to door of castle church in Wittenberg
1520	Henry VIII of England and François I of France meet at the 'Field of the Cloth of Gold'
1527	Sack of Rome by imperial forces
1528	Baldassare Castiglione's *Il libro del cortegiano* published in Italy
1531	Henry VIII establishes himself Supreme Head of Church of England
1535	Michelangelo begins *Last Judgement* in Sistine Chapel
1540	Jesuit order confirmed by Pope Paul III
1545	Beginning of Council of Trent
1555	Peace of Augsburg; Holy Roman Empire allows Protestant as well as Catholic states
1572	Massacres of St Bartholomew's Day in Paris and other French cities, start a rash of persecution of Protestants in France
1587	Mary, Queen of Scots executed on order of Elizabeth I
1589	Battista Guarini publishes influential pastoral tragicomedy, *Il pastor fido*
1599	On death of Alfonso II d'Este, the pope assumes control of Ferrara and Este court moves to Modena

HUMANISM

Defined simply as 'the study of classical texts and thought', humanism in practice was more far-reaching, embodying many of the ideals gleaned from these studies. Among the most important was the glorification of the individual, clearly articulated in *On the Dignity of Man*, an essay by the great fifteenth-century humanist Pico della Mirandola. Pico propounds a concept central to humanist thought: the importance of human achievement and self-will, as distinct from the power and will of God.

Humanists were fascinated by heroes of classical mythology and drama such as Ulysses and Jason. They were represented in art – in a highly idealized physical form – and praised in literature. In music the most important classical hero was Orpheus, whose story was accordingly treated many times in the fifteenth and sixteenth centuries.

(BL) Florence
View of fifteenth-century Florence, showing Filippo Bruneschelli's classically-inspired cathedral dome (far left).
(TL) The Last Supper by Leonardo da Vinci
Da Vinci has been described as the archetypal Renaissance man; his works embodied humanism in all its forms.
(R) Protestant Reformers
Martin Luther (far left), one of the leaders of the Protestant Reformation, with his protector John Frederick the Magnanimous, Elector of Saxony.

HUMANISM IN THE ARTS

Among the earliest humanist projects was the recovery and study of classical architecture. Many buildings from the Roman period still stood (some stand today); others were in ruins from which the originals could just be discerned. Study of these remains with reference to recently recovered classical architectural treatises led to a new school of architecture. Its leader was Filippo Brunelleschi. A native Florentine, he went to Rome early in the fifteenth century to study classical architecture. The result of his study is evident in his first major achievement, the dome of Florence Cathedral. Brunelleschi worked on a plan in which a single measurement dominated the entire architectural structure. This gave his buildings a sense of balance and perfection that still strikes visitors today. S Maria Maggiore in Rome, built 1442–65, is a gem of squares, rectangles and circles all in harmonious proportion to one other.

Late fifteenth- and sixteenth-century painters drew on classical architecture both literally – in the incorporation of architectural features into their paintings – and more generally in the use of proportion, perspective and other features learned from architectural theory. A brilliant example of both is Raphael's *School of Athens* (*c.* 1510), in which a classical subject allows for the representation of an architectural space, which in turn lends perspective to the group.

mode ▶ p. 360

It is no coincidence that the first major operas, a *Euridice* by each of **Jacopo Peri** (1561–1633) and **Giulio Caccini** (*c.* 1545–1618) and *Orfeo* by **Claudio Monteverdi** (1567–1643), take as their theme this half-man, half-god whose singing had the power to charm the gods and tame the beasts. His story encapsulates two central tenets of humanist thought: the unlimited resources of the individual and the liberating power of music.

PROTESTANT REFORMATION

The sixteenth century was marked by unprecedented upheaval in the Christian world. The Protestant revolution begun by Martin Luther had a deep and lasting effect. An Augustinian monk who had studied law, Luther publicly criticized the Catholic church when he visited Rome in 1510. In 1517 he took the fateful step of nailing his '95 theses' to the door of the castle church in Wittenberg. The theses outlined his opposition to corruption in the church institution, notably the selling of 'indulgences' (where people paid to reduce the amount of time they might spend in purgatory). Luther believed the Bible should be the source of all faith and that any religious practices or doctrines not founded on this were abuses. His teachings were condemned by the church authorities and in January 1521 he was excommunicated. Called to the Diet of Worms – a meeting of secular and ecclesiastical leaders – in April 1521, and asked to recant, he refused. By this time he already had a large following (and a noble patron) and the die was cast for widespread reinterpretation of Catholic doctrine. Luther's ideas spread rapidly and divergent views were soon expounded by different leaders. The Reformed Church had most success in German university towns and free imperial cities – places with no resident nobility and a strong middle class, and a tradition of intellectual debate.

Early important centres were Wittenberg, Leipzig and Nuremberg. Outside German territory Protestant fortunes varied. In the strong Catholic centres of Italy and the Iberian peninsula there was no significant presence. Luther's teachings came early to England, where Henry VIII took from them what was expedient to his political needs but condemned the rest as heretical and politically dangerous. France was perhaps the most complicated region. It was to be ravaged by religious wars for 100 years. Like Switzerland and Scotland, it was particularly influenced by the doctrines of Luther's follower Jean Calvin, a French theologian who was converted to Lutheranism between 1528 and 1533, and founded his own strict form of Puritanism, Calvinism.

INVENTION OF PRINTING

In the 1450s, after years of experimentation, Johannes Gutenberg of Mainz, Germany, produced a printed Bible. The technique caught on and spread quickly; by the mid 1470s, printers all over Europe were producing new books and, even more, 'old' ones, including the recently discovered classics.

The impact of the development of the printing press on European culture was profound and extensive. Books became both more readily available and much more affordable than before. When handwritten, their ownership had been the luxury of a chosen few, but by the sixteenth century most middle- and upper-class families owned several printed books. In turn, wider availability gradually led to increased literacy – people needed to learn to read as increased reliance on the printed word grew.

Music Printing

Music printing was a different – and more difficult – enterprise. The first whole book of printed music, Ottaviano Petrucci's *Harmonice musices odhecaton A*, was published in Italy in 1501. Petrucci used a triple-impression process: the paper went through the press three times, once each for staffs, notes and words. The result was a luxury item little more affordable than a manuscript and written music remained the province of a privileged few. This changed in the late 1520s when Pierre Attaingnant in France developed a single-impression method which was faster and so made the products more affordable. His technique was copied a decade later by other printers in France, Italy and the Low Countries. By the 1540s music printing was an efficient and economical process.

As with the printed word, this led to dissemination of music to a wider geographical area and a broader social span than previously. It was not unusual for a well-to-do merchant to own a few books of music, perhaps jointly with some friends. In the realm of sacred music, small parish churches could now afford the published works of major composers. As notation was made more widely available, music became easier to read and musical literacy spread.

Caccini ▶ p. 80 Dunstaple ▶ p. 28 Monteverdi ▶ p. 76 Peri ▶ p. 84 Tinctoris ▶ p. 31

PROTESTANT MUSIC

Luther loved music and believed in its ability to serve religion. He encouraged the use of polyphony in church services, but made one addition, which was to be enormously important both for worship and for music: he added congregational singing of hymns, or **chorales**. Some were familiar tunes, drawn from Latin chant or popular song. Others were newly composed, in song style. Broadsheets and collections of melodies were published from the early 1520s. In 1524 Luther called on the Wittenberg composer Johann Walter (1496–1570) to write some polyphonic hymns using these tunes as their ***cantus firmus***. The result was the first Lutheran hymnal, the *Geystliches gesangk Buchleyn* ('Book of Spiritual Songs').

The other important musical development came from Calvin, who believed the Bible should be the source of congregational song. Psalms were translated into French by various poets, beginning with the important humanist Clément Marot; they were set to music by **Claude Goudimel** (*c.* 1514–72), **Claude Le Jeune** (*c.* 1530–1600) and others.

COUNTER-REFORMATION

Many people now prefer the term Catholic Reformation to Counter-Reformation, because it reflects positively the spirit of self-examination and the desire for reform that originated within the Roman church. Nonetheless, the instigating crisis, if not the actual root, of the Counter-Reformation was the defection of the faithful to Luther and his followers. In 1536, Pope Paul III called for an ecumenical council, the nineteenth in the church's history. The Council of Trent, as it has come to be known, finally began its discussions nine years later. The issues addressed over the ensuing 18 years of the council's sitting were many and varied, ranging from profound theological questions such as the doctrine of Transubstantiation to details of administration like the awarding of offices in the church.

MUSIC AND THE COUNTER-REFORMATION

Of music the councillors actually had little to say. The topic was addressed in the twenty-second session, in 1562, and resulted in a set of guidelines concerning music in worship. It was to be 'uplifting', with clearly intelligible texts, and all traces of 'lascivious and impure' subject matter were to be avoided. In this third point the councillors seem to have been objecting to the practice of basing Masses on secular melodies or polyphonic songs, which were, admittedly, often incongruously irreverent. Masses of this kind continued to be written, but there was a clearly distinguishable preference on the part of some composers for sacred, or at least more serious, models. In the second half of the sixteenth century these same composers developed a polyphonic language that served the audibility of the text – the other great concern of the council. New devotional musical genres arose in the wake of Trent: spiritual madrigals and chansons. The ***lauda***, a form with a long history, also enjoyed renewed popularity in the late sixteenth century.

THE RENAISSANCE COURTS

Music thrived at court as it had in the later Middle Ages. The court of Burgundy, whose most glorious era was the early fifteenth century, remained a cultural centre into the sixteenth. More importantly, it became the model for other Renaissance courts, which sponsored increasingly lavish musical entertainments. They became the best places for musicians to make names for themselves.

The Spanish courts of Aragon and Castile – unified under Ferdinand and Isabella – which had strong ties through marriage to the Burgundians, were perhaps the most immediately influenced by that court. The Catholic monarchs had both survived war and internal conflict to gain their thrones and they were keen to reinforce power through state pageantry. They also valued the new humanist education for their children. Juan, the heir, owned a large collection of instruments and was known to sing polyphony with members of his chapel.

CULTURAL RIVALRY

The first half of the sixteenth century was dominated by what became known as the Italian Wars, in which the great European powers attempted to seize control of the small independent Italian states. Alongside this empirical rivalry was a cultural rivalry in which the various courts, notably France and England, vied in splendour and learning. This reached its peak in the early part of the reigns of Henry VIII and François I. Henry VIII was a musician of some talent; his court ceremony showed a debt to Burgundian pageantry. Renaissance humanism came early to the French court. Under the rule of François I, Paris was home to humanist philosophers, poets and artists. His musical patronage was no less impressive, and his chapel included **Claudin de Sermisy** (*c.* 1490–1562). The monarchs' rivalry came to head in 1520 at the 'Field of the Cloth of Gold', a site near Calais in France, where the two met to discuss an alliance. Both chapels (the musicians of the court) were present, and they sang constantly both together and separately, offering their members an enviable opportunity for the exchange of musical ideas. After the deaths of Henry and François, both courts were rocked by religious and political upheaval which cast a pall on court culture. In England, it was revived during the reign of Henry's daughter, Elizabeth I. The Elizabethan court was one of the richest, most culturally sophisticated centres of the Renaissance.

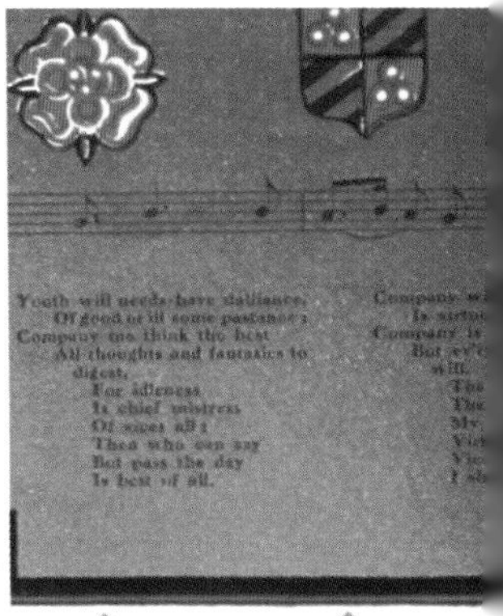

cantus firmus ▶ p. 356 chorale ▶ p. 357 frottola ▶ p. 358 *lauda* ▶ p. 359

MANTUA AND FERRARA

The small neighbouring courts of Ferrara and Mantua had a wonderful century in the realm of music patronage. Connected by marriage in 1490 when the 15-year-old Isabella d'Este of Ferrara married Francesco Gonzaga of Mantua, the two cities remained close allies and cultural rivals throughout the sixteenth century. Isabella had been given the finest humanist education and under her enlightened patronage the court at Mantua became the home of a new genre, the **frottola** – a light, secular form suited to performance by four voices or (probably more often) one voice and lute. Isabella was an accomplished lutenist, who no doubt played and sang frottolas herself.

Ferrara was also an important musical centre in the early years of the sixteenth century, visited by the likes of **Josquin des Prez** (*c.* 1440–1521) and **Cipriano de Rore** (*c.* 1515–65). But it was at the end of the century that this city shone most brightly. With the accession of Duke Alfonso II in 1579, a new era of courtly secular performance was inaugurated. During his reign a group of singing noblewomen at court, the *concerto delle dame*, was transformed from an amateur, recreational group into the most famous and imitated professional secular ensemble in Europe.

THE ITALIAN INFLUENCE

From the early fifteenth century the Medici family emerged from the role of leading burgher of Florence to become Grand Dukes. A series of family weddings in 1539, 1568, 1589 and 1600 plots the development of the relationship between music and drama that culminated in opera. Entertainment for these occasions was provided by the most famous musicians of the time: Francesco Corteccia (1502–71), Alessandro Striggio (*c.* 1540– 92) and Francesca Caccini (1587–*c.* 1638), to name a few.

A number of small Italian courts contributed to music patronage well beyond what might be expected, given their small role in international politics. Among these, the most outstanding were Mantua and Ferrara; other important centres were Urbino (where the dialogues in Castiglione's *Il libro del Cortegiano* are meant to have taken place), Milan and Naples.

(BL) Henry VIII
Henry VIII conducting his court musicians.
(ML) Italian Singers
Carving of boys singing, from the cathedral S Maria del Fiore in Florence.
(TR) Singer, Flautist and Lutenist
Castiglione's book, Il cortegiano, *emphasised the importance of musical accomplishment.*
(BR) Court Ball
Catherine de' Medici (left) attending the wedding of the Duchess Anne de Joyeuse.

CASTIGLIONE'S *CORTEGIANO*

Baldassare Castiglione's *Il libro del cortegiano* ('The Book of the Coutier') was published in 1528 and became the most influential book of manners of its time. It was reprinted into the eighteenth century and translated into many languages. The *Courtier* presents a series of evening conversations purported to have taken place at the court of Urbino, some 20 years before the book's publication, in 1506–07, during the reign of the musical duchess Elisabetta Gonzaga. The discussions, as represented by Castiglione, centre around the task of defining the ideal courtier. There are scattered references to musical performance as an important accomplishment for the well-rounded courtier. Improvisation to accompaniment lute is recommended, and the reading of music.

Equally interesting for musicians is Castiglione's term *sprezzatura*, an Italian word with no exact English equivalent implying a certain nonchalance. It was adopted by Caccini in 1602 to describe the ideal way to sing the solo song of his day – with expressiveness and rubato. But its implications for music are richer than this. The ideal of competence with no sign of effort, which Castiglione applies to all endeavours, gives an idea of contemporary performers' attitude towards their art.

THE NEW MIDDLE CLASS

The Renaissance saw the development of a consumer class outside the aristocracy and its hangers-on: the bourgeoisie. It consisted of merchants, traders and court officials who grew both numerically and in financial terms over the course of the fifteenth and sixteenth centuries. In the train of economic security came a desire for luxury and, especially, status.

Members of the middle class strove to give their children the same education and training as their models at court, or at least a scaled-down version of it. The recommendations of Castiglione and other writers on manners were followed as avidly by the middle class as by the aristocracy, to whom much of what Castiglione said was not new. Musical education was in his programme and included training on instruments – in particular the lute and small keyboards – as well as singing. With the advent of music printing, singers had increasingly to learn to read notation from partbooks.

A published literature of practical music theory for the amateur arose to fill a new market. *The Plaine and Easie Introduction to Practicall Music* (1597) by **Thomas Morley** (*c.* 1557–1602), which includes both rudimentary theory and an introduction to music appreciation, was the outstanding example. Similar books were published in other languages, however.

The most significant effect of consumerism was on the music itself. The demand for new pieces to sing gave rise to unprecedented numbers of works. Most stunning are the statistics for the Italian madrigal: thousands were published between the late 1530s and 1600. Similarly affected were the secular chanson in France and, later, the English madrigal.

Goudimel ▶ p. 51 Josquin des Prez ▶ p. 53 Le Jeune ▶ p. 54 Morley ▶ p. 55 Rore ▶ p. 56 Sermisy ▶ p. 56

The Renaissance

PERSONALITIES

Agricola, Alexander

(A-grē-kō-lä, Al-eks-än'-der) c. *1446–1506*

FRANCO-FLEMISH COMPOSER

Probably born in what is now Belgium, Agricola was employed by, or associated with, some of the most brilliant courts in Europe, including those of Galeazzo Maria Sforza in Milan, Lorenzo de' Medici in Florence, Burgundy and the French royal court. He composed Masses, motets, chansons and instrumental arrangements of chansons by other composers. Among the last category are no less than five arrangements of one of the greatest hits of the fifteenth century, *De tous biens plaine* by Hayne van Ghizeghem (*c.* 1440–72). Agricola died of the plague.

Animuccia, Giovanni

(An'-nē-mōō-chya, Jō-van'-e) c. *1500–71*

ITALIAN COMPOSER

Animuccia, who lived and worked in Rome in the 1550s and 1560s, was one of the earliest composers of music for the Catholic Counter-Reformation. For Filippo Neri and his Oratorians he composed two books of *laudi spirituali*, simple devotional songs with Latin or Italian texts. His first book of Masses (1567) was, by his own account, written in accordance with

the musical deliberations of the Council of Trent. This book is one of the few surviving examples of music clearly intended to rise to the challenges issued by the Council.

Arcadelt, Jacques

(Är'-kä-delt, Zhäk) c. *1505–68*

FRENCH COMPOSER

Although probably of French birth, Arcadelt spent much of his adulthood in the great Italian cities of Florence, Rome and Venice. He is best known for madrigals (although he composed Masses, motets and chansons as well), including some of the genre's most precious gems. They are almost all easy to sing, but their simplicity is deceptive. The justly famous 'Il bianco e

'A MIGHTY FORTRESS IS OUR GOD'

This hymn, which appears in most modern Protestant hymnals, was composed by Martin Luther himself as 'Ein feste Burg ist unser Gott'. Its easily learnt 'AAB' form is typical of popular German songs of Luther's day.

POPULAR MELODY *Luther*

dolce cigno' ('The White and Gentle Swan'), with its play on the term 'death', uses word-painting and other devices to amuse and delight its singers. For example, the poem's final line, 'If this is death, I would like to die 1,000 deaths a day' (*mille morte il dì*) is set to a musical joke: each singer repeats the phrase many times in a figurative 1,000 deaths.

Banchieri, Adriano

(Bän-kyā'-rē, Ä-drē-ä'-nō) *1568–1634*

ITALIAN COMPOSER

Banchieri is known for his books of music theory and for his contribution to a small, but fascinating repertory: the madrigal comedy. *L'organo suonarino* ('The Sound of the Organ', 1605), a handbook for church organists, is one of the earliest sources of practical advice for realizing a ***basso continuo***. His madrigal comedies – collections of madrigals and canzonettas organized around a narrative thread – owe much to the ***commedia dell'arte***. The most interesting is *La barca veneta* ('The Venetian Boat'), with its cast of stereotypes articulating the prejudices of provincial northern Italy at the turn of the seventeenth century.

(L) Concert by Ercole Roberti
Contemporaneous painting of a lutenist and singers.
(TR) William Byrd
Byrd's collaboration with Thomas Tallis was one of the earliest successful musical partnerships.
(BR) The Adoration of the Magi by Benozzo Gozzoli
Lorenzo de' Medici (pictured on the white horse) extended his patronage to Alexander Agricola.

RELIGIOUS UPHEAVAL

Once hailed by the Pope as 'Defender of the Faith' against Martin Luther, Henry VIII made an about-face when he declared himself primate of the Church of England in order to grant himself a divorce from his first wife, Catherine of Aragon. The political, religious and social results of Henry's action are well-known; the impact on music was also far-reaching. In the century leading up to 1536, England had established a musical ascendancy unprecedented in its history, exporting its style to France. The state of English sacred music at the beginning of the sixteenth century can be ascertained from the Eton Choirbook, a beautiful manuscipt of polyphony from the last generation of great Catholic composers in England. It contains works by the major English musicians of the reigns of Henry VII and Henry VIII, including five pieces by Cornysh.

A Bad Climate for Composers

Although Henry VIII's restructuring of the church was more political than spiritual, the ensuing upheaval – and in particular the danger faced by any public figure showing reluctance to affirm the king's claims – had a discouraging effect on composition for the rest of his reign. After his death in 1547, the tumultuous reigns of the Protestant Edward VI and the Catholic Mary I, with their profound changes not only in orthodoxy but in liturgical detail, provided an even less welcoming climate for composers. Matters improved with the accession of the music-loving Elizabeth I in 1558, although religious tensions were still present. A few brave and flexible musicians did leave their mark. Among these Tallis stands out for his ability to survive and flourish under four Tudor monarchs, writing whatever music was the order of the day and, apparently, keeping his own counsel about his beliefs.

It was in this spiritual minefield that Byrd lived his life. Unlike Tallis, he was a single-mindedly devoted Catholic. That he managed not only to survive fines and imprisonment, but also to have a successful and productive career, is a tribute not only to his talent but also to Elizabeth's relative tolerance – and perhaps to her love of music as well.

basso continuo ▶ p. 356 *cantus firmus* ▶ p. 356 *commedia dell'arte* ▶ p. 357 eye music ▶ p. 358

Bull, John

c. 1562–1628

ENGLISH COMPOSER AND KEYBOARD PLAYER

Bull was by all evidence an extraordinary musician. His name headed the list of members of the Chapel Royal who attended the funeral of Elizabeth I in 1603. He was also an organ-builder and a scholar. A Catholic with a difficult personality, he often found himself in trouble in England. In 1613, following charges of adultery, he left the country permanently to settle in Brussels. Bull's surviving keyboard works represent a cross-section of keyboard genres at the turn of the sixteenth century: dances such as almans, galliards, corantos; free forms like the fantasia; and works on sacred ***cantus firmi***.

Byrd, William

1543–1623

ENGLISH COMPOSER

Byrd's early life is shrouded in mystery. He may have been born in Lincoln, but his formative years must have been spent at least partly in London; at some point in his youth he studied with Tallis. In 1563 he was made organist and master of the choristers at Lincoln Cathedral. He married in 1569 and in 1570 moved to London, where he was appointed a Gentleman of the Chapel Royal. During his first successful years in London he was associated with a number of powerful patrons, as well as with his teacher Tallis. In 1575 he and Tallis were granted a monopoly on music printing. The inaugural publication from the press, Byrd's first book of *cantiones sacrae* (1589–91), was dedicated to Queen Elizabeth I. Soon after this his fortunes took a downward turn.

In 1577 his wife, Juliana, was cited for recusancy (refusal to attend Church of England services) and the family endured harassment from that point on. Byrd seems to have remained unintimidated; in 1583 he attended a high-profile gathering in honour of two notorious Jesuits – at that time perhaps the most hated representatives of Roman Catholicism. Byrd himself was cited for recusancy in 1585 and in 1587 was briefly taken into custody. Yet in spite of increasing personal difficulties, Byrd's professional life seems to have been undamaged by his unwavering and undisguised Catholicism. In the mid 1580s he composed celebratory pieces for the queen, including the famous 'Rejoice Unto the Lord', written for Accession Day in 1586.

GOING SOLO

In 1587 he revived his career as a publisher, now without his partner Tallis, who had died two years previously. During the 1570s and 80s Byrd composed religious music in both Latin and English. His three books of *cantiones sacrae* (1575, 1589 and 1591) are Latin motets in the style of Palestrina. Latin was not banned in the Elizabethan church, and the queen herself seems to have preferred it; textually the motets were thus suited to both Anglican and Catholic worship. The large scale and technical difficulty of the music suggests that much of it was intended for the Chapel Royal.

In 1591 Byrd moved with his second wife, Ellen (Juliana had died in 1586), to Essex, where they probably joined a Catholic community under the patronage of the Catholic Petre family. He remained officially on the rolls of the Chapel Royal, but seems to have had little to do with London during this time. His publications after 1590 appear to be a courageous effort to provide a body of music for Catholic worship in England. They include three Masses – one each for four, five and six voices, published in the years 1593–95 – and two books of *gradualia* (1605 and 1607). The Masses and *gradualia* are smaller in scale than the earlier *cantiones sacrae*, in keeping with their intended use by underground Catholic communities lacking large resources. Byrd also left an important repertory of keyboard music, much of it preserved in the manuscript *My Ladye Nevells Book*, which bears the date 1591. The genres represented include fantasias, variations and a large number of dances.

AN EVENING OF MADRIGAL SINGING

In his *Dialogo della musica* ('Musical Dialogue'), published in 1544, Antonfrancesco Doni describes two performances, one in an all-male academy, the other at a more informal gathering including a woman. The singing of madrigals by contemporary composers is interspersed with conversation. Is this a realistic picture of a social gathering in mid-sixteenth century Italy? Diverse clues suggest that it is.

Madrigals were published in partbooks: each singer held a book containing only his or her line of music. Many surviving collections bear the hand-written inscription 'property of so-and-so and his friends', suggesting that groups of friends purchased collections together. Further evidence of Doni's realism comes from the music itself which, until the later 1540s, was rarely of great technical difficulty, suggesting that it was composed for amateurs. Finally, although many works are beautiful to listen to, much of their appeal is most evident to the singers. Notational features like **eye music**, in which the musical notation is itself a pun on the text (for example, the sudden appearance of black notes for the word 'night'), can only be seen. Even text-expressive devices that are audible are much more noticeable to the singer than the listener. So perhaps, following Doni, we can imagine men and women gathering for a social evening and, when the conversation lags, they take out their partbooks to sing.

Cabezón, Antonio de

(Kà-bà-thōn', An-tōn'-yō da) 1510–66

SPANISH KEYBOARD COMPOSER AND PLAYER

Blind from birth, Cabezón learnt the organ from an early age and became one of the great keyboard players of his day. He began his career as organist to Queen Isabella. After her death he worked for her children, later attaching himself solely to the future king, Philip II. Cabezón's works are all for keyboard and include intabulations of vocal works by other people's freely composed forms. Among the latter his tientos (a Spanish form of fantasia) are among the finest of the genre.

Campion, Thomas

1567–1620

ENGLISH POET AND COMPOSER

Campion first distinguished himself as a poet and poetic theorist. His treatise, *Observations in the Art of English Poesie* (1602), included controversial opinions regarding metre and rhyme, revealing the musical basis of his poetry. He published four books of lute-songs. Some are humanist experiments in setting classically accentuated poetry, but the best are light love lyrics set to simple, memorable tunes. Campion also contributed, as both poet and composer, to court masques for James I.

Carver, Robert

c. *1490*–c. *1546*

SCOTTISH COMPOSER

Carver's first composition may have been for the coronation of James V (1513); the *Dum sacrum mysterium* Mass is composed in 10 parts. Four of his other Masses remain extant and demonstrate the influence of Franco-Flemish style of composition characteristic of Josquin and others of the age.

Casulana, Maddalena

(Cà-sü-la'-na, Mad'-dà-là-na) c. *1540–90*

ITALIAN SINGER AND COMPOSER

Casulana worked as a professional singer and composer in Venice and Milan. The first of several volumes of her madrigals appeared in 1568 – the earliest-known printed collection by a woman. In Casulana's words, it aimed 'to show the world ... the vain error of men that they alone possess intellectual gifts, and who appear to believe that the same gifts are not possible for women'.

Clemens non Papa

(Kle'-menz nōn Pà'-pà) c. *1510–55*

FRANCO-FLEMISH COMPOSER

His given name was Jacob Clemens, and it is not known how he came to be called Clemens non Papa (one translation of 'non papa' is 'not the pope' – a rather unlikely mistake, it would seem). He composed some works in his native Dutch, the best-known of which are the *souterliedekens*. These three-voice, mostly homophonic settings of the psalms in Dutch translation, illustrate the spreading use of the vernacular in worship during the first half of the sixteenth century. In contrast, his Masses and motets have Latin texts and are densely polyphonic, with long, melismatic lines.

Cornysh, William

c. *1465–1523*

ENGLISH COMPOSER

Cornysh served at the courts of both Henry VII and Henry VIII as a poet, actor and musician. His greatest moment was being chosen to head the Chapel Royal at the famous 'Field of the Cloth of Gold' in June 1520. Five polyphonic works by him are preserved in the Eton Choirbook; he also composed early examples of English-language secular song, such as the **canon**, 'Ah Robyn, gentil Robyn'.

Dowland, John

1563–1626

ENGLISH COMPOSER AND LUTENIST

Dowland was the greatest lute-song composer of the early seventeenth century. His conversion to Catholicism in the early 1580s may have contributed to his lack of professional success. Twice disappointed in applications for a post at court, he travelled and then worked on the continent. By November 1598 he was employed at the court of Christian IV of Denmark where he stayed until 1606. Dowland's best songs, such as the bittersweet 'Now oh now I needs must part', have an air of melancholy. Though intended for voice and lute, they can be sung by four unaccompanied voices. This melancholy is epitomized in his set of variations *Lachrimae* (1604).

Escobar, Pedro de

(Es-kō-bär', Pà'-drō dà) c. *1465*–c. *1535*

PORTUGUESE COMPOSER

Although Portuguese by birth, Escobar spent his career in Spain, including 10 years in the chapel of Isabella of Aragon and a stint as *maestro de capilla* at Seville Cathedral. The date of his death is unknown; he was last heard of around 1535. His motet 'Clamabat autem mulier' shows him to have been a composer of great skill and expressive power. The high esteem in which his music was held is evidenced by its wide distribution – some works have been found in sixteenth-century Mexican and Guatemalan manuscripts.

Ferrabosco

(Fer-ra-bos'-ko)

ITALIAN MUSICAL FAMILY

This family produced four generations of musicians. Domenico (1513–74), of Bologna, was a composer of early madrigals in the style of Arcadelt. His son Alfonso (1543–88) moved to England as a young man and spent most of his life at the court of Elizabeth I. Morley praised him for his 'deep skill' and placed him alongside such worthies as Marenzio. Much more prolific than his father, he wrote many madrigals, motets and chansons. His son (also Alfonso, *c.* 1575–1628) and grandson, John (1626–82), completed the dynasty.

Gabrieli, Andrea

(Gàb-rē-ā'-lē, Àn-dra'-à) c. *1510–86*

ITALIAN COMPOSER

After spending some time in Munich as a colleague of Lassus, in 1566 Gabrieli became *maestro di cappella* at St Mark's, Venice. There, with the resources of its great choir at his disposal, he composed an impressive repertory of music for various combinations of voices and instruments. His style – in sacred and secular genres – is characterized by clear textures and lively incisive rhythms. He made a contribution to the pre-history of opera by composing choruses for an Italian-language production of Sophocles' *Oedipus tyrannus*, performed at Vicenza, in 1585.

***(BL)* Group of Singers in a Landscape**
Mid sixteenth century painting capturing the importance of music during the Renaissance.
***(TR)* Columbus in the New World**
Natives greeting Columbus as he lands in the Americas; music proved an important method of converting the inhabitants of the New World to Christianity.
***(BR)* Belshazzar's Feast**
Nobles enjoying musical entertainment at a feast, by an unknown artist of the Flemish School, c. 1600.

cadence ▶ p. 356 canon ▶ p. 356 canzona ▶ p. 356 dissonance ▶ p. 358

Gabrieli, Giovanni

(Gàb-rē-ā'-lē, Jō-vàn'-nē) c. *1553–1612*

ITALIAN COMPOSER

Gabrieli was taught by his uncle Andrea Gabrieli and, like him, was first employed in Munich with Lassus. After Andrea's death Giovanni became principal composer for St Mark's, Venice, and like Andrea, he wrote much of his music with its choir (and building) in mind. His musical debt to his uncle is evident in the *Concerti* (1587), a collection of motets and madrigals for various combinations of voices and instruments by both men. Giovanni's lively instrumental **canzonas** and sonatas, which often use contrasting 'choirs' of instruments', have remained popular and are available on numerous recordings. His *Sonata pian e forte*, published in 1597, is an early example of the use of specified dynamics.

Galilei, Vincenzo

(Gà-lē-lā'-ē, Vin-chānt'-zō) c. *1520–91*

ITALIAN THEORIST AND MUSICIAN

The father of Galileo Galilei, Vincenzo, also had a scientific mind. His experience as a lutenist and composer formed the practical basis for a significant body of music theory. His later works, especially, are heavily influenced by contemporary humanist enquiry into the nature of ancient music and, in particular, the work of the classical scholar Girolamo Mei. In the *Dialogo della musica* (1581), Galilei condemned polyphony on the basis that ancient music had been entirely monophonic. His argument that ancient drama had been sung throughout formed one of the theoretical bases of early experiments in opera.

Gastoldi, Giovanni

(Gàs-tōl'-dē, Jō-vàn'-nē) c. *1550s–1622*

ITALIAN COMPOSER

Gastoldi spent much of his career in Mantua, where in the early 1590s, he composed music for a production of Battista Guarini's famous play, *Il pastor fido* ('The Faithful Shepherd'); although the production was scrapped, Gastoldi published some of his music in 1602. He is best known, however, for his ballettos. (The form is a light-hearted, homophonic relative of the madrigal.) Extremely popular in England, they were the primary source of the style of the light 'fa la la' madrigals of Morley and others.

THE NEW WORLD

When Christopher Columbus accidentally stumbled on Central America in 1492, he unwittingly introduced to his fervently Catholic patrons, Ferdinand and Isabella, two continents of potential converts. The Spanish monarchs wasted no time: Catholic missionaries, first mostly Franciscans, and later Jesuits – arrived in the area within a few years. By 1528 Mexico City had a cathedral and a bishop. Music, an important tool of conversion, took root and flourished. Manuscripts from sixteenth-century Mexico include music by Spanish composers such as Escobar and Morales. Among music history's eeriest artefacts of cultural exchange are two hymns in honour of the Virgin, very Spanish in sound, with texts in Nahuatl, the language of the Aztec Empire.

Gesualdo, Carlo

(Jā-zōō-āl'-dō, Kär'-lō) c. *1561–1613*

ITALIAN COMPOSER

Gesualdo may be more famous than he deserves to be. Everyone loves a good story and Gesualdo, who brutally murdered his wife and her lover, provides one of the most colourful and scandalous in all music history. A nobleman of minor rank, he found, strangely, that his marital history did not make him a bad match: his second wife was Leonora d'Este, sister of the duke of Ferrara. Gesualdo's music, which makes extreme use of **dissonance**, is interesting for its own sake, but had little far-reaching influence.

Gibbons, Orlando

1583–1625

ENGLISH COMPOSER

Although he made his living as a keyboard player, it is for his vocal music that Gibbons is best remembered. His anthems, for combinations of soloist, choir and instruments, are still heard both in church and in the concert hall. In the simple but deeply moving *This is the Record of John*, a five-part chorus echoes and expands upon an alto solo. Gibbons' only book of madrigals includes the famous, elegiac 'The Silver Swanne'. With Byrd, Farnaby and Bull, he was one of the founders of the English keyboard school in the early seventeenth century.

Gombert, Nicolas

(Gôm-bâr, Nē-kō-làs') c. *1495–1560*

FLEMISH COMPOSER

Joining the Burgundian court around 1525, Gombert travelled widely with the emperor, Charles V, and composed music for state occasions. The composer Hermann Finck (1527–58) said of Gombert's style that 'he avoids pauses', and this somewhat blunt observation is a key to the seamless melodic tapestry of his music. At a time when many composers were moving towards a style based on clear enunciation of the text and balanced phrases, Gombert wrote complex polyphony with long-breathed melodic lines, unbroken by clear **cadences**.

Goudimel, Claude

(Gōō-dē-mel', Klōd) c. *1514–72*

FRENCH COMPOSER

Goudimel worked with the French music publisher Nicolas du Chemin, first as proofreader and later as partner. He corresponded with French humanists and writers such as Pierre Ronsard, some of whose verse he set. However, he is most important for his psalms, based on French translations begun by Clement Marot and published with melodies in Calvinist psalters from the 1530s. He set them in a variety of styles ranging from strict homophony, where the tune appears in the top line, to motet-like counterpoint with the melody providing material for all voices. After spending some years in Metz, a Huguenot stronghold, Goudimel moved to Lyons. He was murdered, along with hundreds of other Protestants, in the St Bartholomew's Day massacres of 1572.

Hassler, Hans Leo

(Häs-ler, Hänts Lā'-ō) *1562–1612*
GERMAN COMPOSER

Hassler was the most important member of a family of musicians. Trained by his father, he travelled in 1584 to Venice, where he studied with Andrea Gabrieli. Hassler's large surviving repertory reflects the religious diversity of German-speaking lands during his lifetime. He spent much of his early career in the service of members of the Catholic Fugger family in Augsburg, and his Latin-texted music was probably composed for them. But Hassler himself was a Protestant; among his many chorale settings is Martin Luther's 'Ein feste Burg ist unser Gott' ('A Great Castle is Our God').

Henry VIII

1491–1547
KING OF ENGLAND AND COMPOSER

From his coronation in 1509 until his death in 1547 Henry VIII led his country in a permanent split from the Catholic church, and he depleted the savings accumulated by his parsimonious father in a series of wars he lost against France. On the brighter side, he was a generous patron of music. An avid amateur performer, he seems to have been something of a composer as well. A manuscript known as 'Henry VIII's Book' contains some 37 songs and instrumental works ascribed to the king, the best and most famous is the jolly song 'Pastyme with Good Company'.

Isaac, Heinrich

(Ē'-zäk, Hīn'-rikh) c. *1450–1517*
FLEMISH COMPOSER

Isaac worked in Florence from the mid 1480s until 1494, when the changing fortunes of the Medici family cost him his job. In 1497 he was hired by the Habsburg emperor Maximilian I, to the appointment of *Hofkomponist* ('court composer'). Although he remained in Maximilian's pay for the rest of his life, he travelled and lived in various places in Austria, Switzerland and Italy. Ten years in Italy left a lasting impression on his musical style. In their simple homophony his many German songs resemble the Italian **frottola**. His most famous work, 'Insbrugk, ich muss dich lassen' ('Innsbruck, I Must Leave Thee', 1583) is a tender farewell to a city he knew well. In 1508–09, Isaac began work on the *Choralis constantinus*, a set of polyphonic Mass music for the entire liturgical year. This enormous project remained unfinished at his death; edited posthumously by his student Senfl, it was finally published in 1550–55. The twentieth-century composer **Anton Webern** (1883–1945) received his doctorate for his study of Isaac.

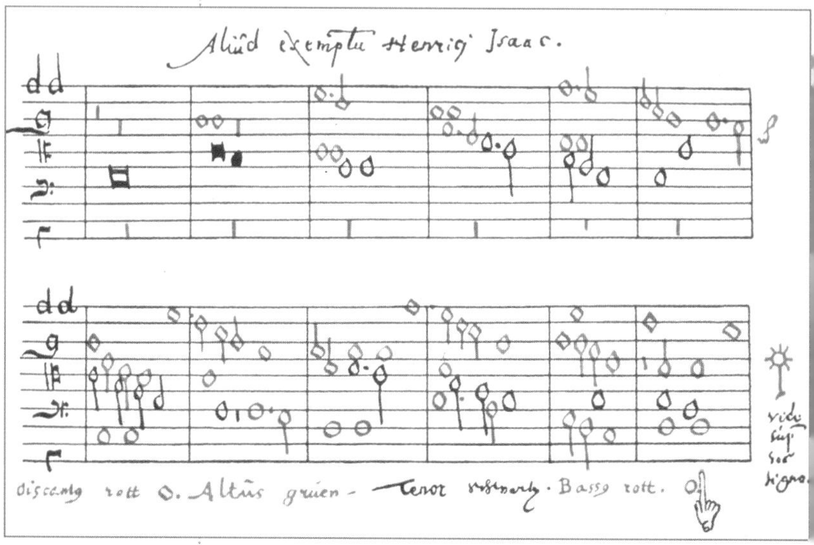

Janequin, Clément

(Zhän-kan', Klā-män') c. *1485–1558*
FRENCH COMPOSER

Janequin's failure to procure a stable and lucrative job may have been due to the fact that he spent most of his career outside Paris, the centre of French culture. Nevertheless, he became the principal exponent of the narrative chanson, a form popular in the mid sixteenth century. These songs are often relatively long and have texts bursting with active imagery that lends itself to musical mimesis. A famous example is 'Le chant des oiseaux' ('The Song of the Birds'), which consists largely of an ornithological survey, with the music imitating various types of birdsong.

DISCOVERING JOSQUIN

In the late fifteenth and early sixteenth centuries, there were at least five musicians by the name of Josquin belonging to musical establishments around Europe. Most were singers, with perhaps a small-time composer among them. One, however, was the greatest composer of his generation – among the greatest of the Renaissance. Untangling the strands of references to the various Josquins, in order to trace the biography of the composer, has proven a daunting and absorbing task. It is not helped by the state of the sources containing his music. At the end of Josquin's life the new technology of music printing was just taking hold, and printers were eager to publish works by well-known composers. Thus, in the 30 years after his death, a substantial body of music appeared in print attributed to Josquin. Unfortunately, of this impressive repertory little can actually be proved to be by him, and much of it can be shown to be by someone else. Figuring out exactly what Josquin wrote is a worthy pursuit, for among the works attributed to this mysterious character are some of the most heart-rendingly beautiful pieces ever written.

'IN DULCI JUBILO'

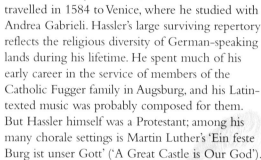

The melody of this popular Christmas carol, also known by the English title 'Good Christian Men Rejoice', was already being sung in the Middle Ages. Among today's harmonizations is one by the Renaissance composer and music theorist Michael Praetorius.

POPULAR MELODY *Praetorius*

(TR) De Musica Poetica
Handwritten composition by Heinrich Isaac, in four parts, using different colours.
(TR) Missa de Venerabili Sacramento
Three examples from the score of Josquin's hymn book, showing mensural notation.
(BR) Elizabeth I
Elizabeth was one of the greatest female patrons of the arts and her court was a centre of cultural and artistic excellence.

APPROACHES TO HOMAGE

Cantus firmus technique, in which a pre-existent melody forms the basis of a new composition, lends itself well to musical homage, and it is likely that the selection of *cantus firmi* was often influenced by the dedicatee or patron. This might mean the choice of a favourite song, or a section of plainchant whose text held some personal meaning for the dedicatee. In the case of Josquin's *Missa Hercules Dux Ferrariae*, the homage is absolutely clear, if somewhat technical. The Mass was dedicated to Ercole d'Este, duke of Ferrara, and its *cantus firmus* is made up of **solmizations** based on the syllables in the words of the title (re–ut–re–ut–re–fa–mi–re). Around this unpromising tune Josquin wove a beautiful Mass.

One of Josquin's most poignant works is the motet-chanson *Nymphes des bois* ('Wood Nymphs', composed in memory of his friend **Johannes Ockeghem** (*c.* 1425–97). In this four-voice piece, the top three parts sing a French text lamenting Ockeghem's death while the bottom line serves as a *cantus firmus*, borrowing text and music from his Requiem Mass: 'Requiescat in pacem' ('Rest in Peace').

chorale ▶ p. 357 frottola ▶ p. 358 solmization ▶ p. 362

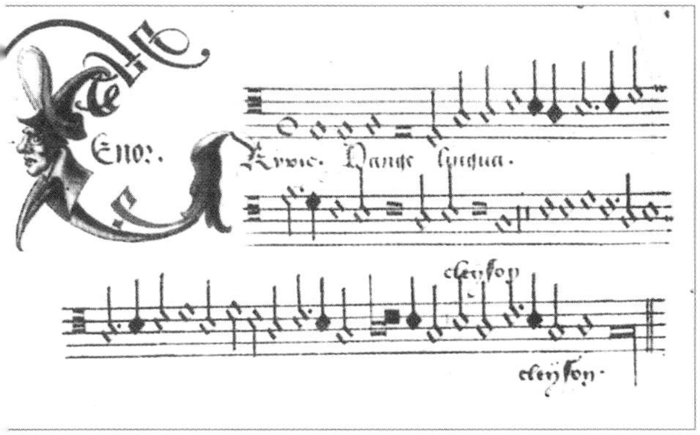

Josquin des Prez

(Zhōs-kan' dā Prā) c. *1440–1521*

FRANCO-FLEMISH COMPOSER

Much ambiguity surrounds the composer Josquin; other musicians of the period shared his name and it is doubtful that all the works attributed to him were his own; any biographical details are thus bound to be tentative. Current opinion is that he was probably born in Tournai in the 1440s, although he seems to have moved early to Condé. The first documentation that definitely refers to him dates from 1477–78 when he was at the court of René of Anjou in Aix-en-Provence. He seems to have remained in France until 1483, when he moved to Milan, beginning an Italian period that was to last until 1504. In that year he returned to Condé, where he spent the rest of his life.

A number of works can be firmly attributed to Josquin, and several can be dated with some precision. Among his compositions are approximately 18 Masses, 112 motets and around 70 chansons. Pieces from the 1470s bear the marks of a young composer learning his trade by imitating contemporary masters **Guillaume Du Fay** (*c.* 1397–1474) and Ockeghem. Among these is the lovely song 'Adieu mes amours' ('Goodbye My Loves'). Even at this early stage in his career, Josquin was developing the imitative four-voice style for which he is famous. The motet 'Ave Maria Virgo Serena' ('Hail Mary, Happy Virgin', now known to have been composed in the 1470s), was long thought to be the prime example of his mature style.

In 1502 Ottaviano Petrucci published a book of five Masses by Josquin – the first volume of music devoted to a single composer. Mostly composed in the 1490s, they have an astounding technical mastery. The book includes both of the composer's Masses using the famous 'L'homme armé' ('The Armed Man') melody as a *cantus firmus*. In the *Missa L'homme armé super voces musicales*, the tune is set a step higher in each succeeding movement, bursting into the top voice in the Agnus Dei. The *Missa Fortuna* is an imitation Mass, using all three voices of the anonymous song on which it is based.

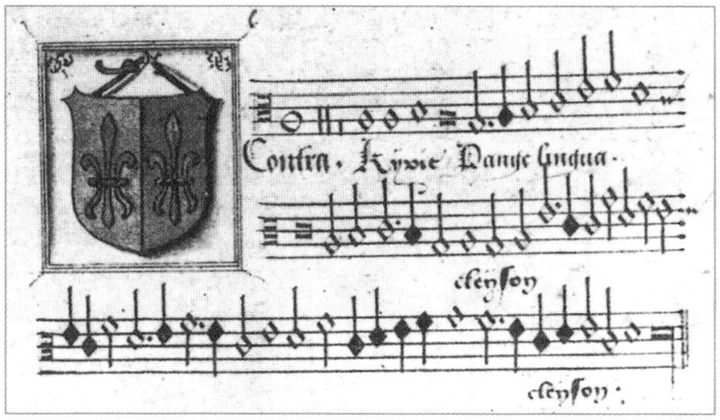

La Rue, Pierre de

(Là Rü, Pē-âr' de) c. *1460–1518*

FLEMISH COMPOSER

Like Isaac, La Rue joined the Habsburg court after spending some years working in Italy. He served under four rulers: Maximilian, Philip le Beau; La Rue may have composed his Requiem for him), Margaret and Charles (the future Emperor Charles V). His works do not show the influence of Italian music, unlike those of Isaac. Instead, he preserved and developed the Franco-Flemish style long cultivated by Burgundian composers such as **Antoine Busnoys** (*c.* 1435–92) and **Gilles Binchois** (*c.* 1400–60). Travelling extensively with the court, he passed this style on to other musicians, especially Spaniards like Juan de Peñalosa (*c.* 1515–79) and Escobar.

A FEMININE ART?

During the Renaissance, European noblewomen were taught to sing and play particular instruments deemed suitable for them, such as the harp, lute and keyboard. Improvising songs with accompaniment was an important aspect of such music-making but, as in other improvising traditions, few women of this class ever wrote down the music they created, so it has not survived. There are many reports of musically talented noblewomen of the early sixteenth century, such as Polissena Pecorina (fl. 1534–70) from Venice, who sang and accompanied herself on the lute, and the ill-fated English queen Anne Boleyn (*c.* 1507–36), who was reputed to compose as well as perform. Courtesans were also frequently praised for their musical talents. One notable example was Tullia d'Arogana (1510–56), who ran a salon, published poetry, sang and played the lute.

It was difficult for women to work as professional musicians since, unless they entered a convent, they were excluded from participation in church music. The church provided male musicians with both their education and their subsequent career. Nevertheless, professional female musicians did find training and work; usually they performed rather than composed. In late fifteenth-century Naples, for example, special housing was provided for the women musicians employed at the court, one of whom was referred to as 'Anna Inglese' (fl. late fifteenth century). Female musicians at other Italian courts included Laura Ruggeri, who worked for Pope Paul II in the 1530s and 1540s; Virginia Vagnoli, a singer who accompanied herself on the lute and was employed by the court at Urbino *c.* 1566–70; Maddalena Casulana, who composed and sang professionally in Venice and Milan; and the *concerto della dame* at Ferrara.

Women as Patrons

Many noble and royal women of the Renaissance were renowned as musical patrons. Isabella d'Este did much to promote the composition of specifically Italian forms, such as the frottola, at her court in Mantua. Margaret of Austria (1480–1530), governor of the Netherlands in the early sixteenth century, was herself a performer and composer, as well as being responsible for two important chanson manuscripts with works by local composers such as Josquin, Isaac and Obrecht . Elizabeth I of England was another enthusiastic musician who ensured that music flourished during her reign.

Binchois ▶ p. 26 Busnoys ▶ p. 26 Du Fay ▶ p. 27 Ockeghem ▶ p. 30 Webern ▶ p. 299

LASSUS'S OP. I

Lassus's first publication, in 1555 when he was in his early twenties, was one of the most audacious débuts in the history of composition. The book was clearly designed as a sample of his talents. Its title page boasts the variety of its contents (motets, madrigals, villanescas and chansons), and the range and self-assurance of the compositions is astonishing for a composer just beginning his career. The five motets reveal that Lassus had been studying the works of Rore. Secular music is represented by three genres in two languages. Among the villanescas is now the ribald 'Matona mia cara', one of his most famous works. With its uncomplicated music, the genre was decidedly low-brow (though still extremely popular). However, in the secular realm, the genre in which a young composer needed to prove himself was the madrigal. And the madrigals in op. 1 show a composer of great musical gifts. The poetry is of a deliberately chosen weightiness, including works by Petrarch, Sannazaro and Ariosto. The poems vary in length, from a setting of a single sonnet quatrain (Petrarch's 'Occhi piangete' – 'Crying Eyes') to an extensively worked six-part madrigal cycle on the sestina 'Del freddo Rheno'.

Lassus, Orlande de

(Làs'sōōs, Ōr-lànd' de) 1532–94

FRANCO-FLEMISH COMPOSER

Lassus went to Italy at the age of 12 as a singer in the choir of Ferrante Gonzaga, a minor member of the important family of music patrons who ruled the duchy of Mantua. He spent the next 10 years in Italy, travelling to Naples and then Rome, where for a time he was *maestro di cappella* at S Giovanni Laterano, one of the city's great basilicas and the employer of many important musicians over the course of the sixteenth century. He assumed this prestigious position in 1553 and two years later began his career as a published composer with the appearance of his op. 1. In 1556 he joined the court of duke Albrecht V of Bavaria in Munich, where he remained for the rest of his life. His marriage in 1558 produced two sons, Ferdinand (*c.* 1560–1609) and Rudolph (*c.* 1563–1625), who both became musicians. Lassus journeyed widely and received offers of employment from some of the leading courts of Europe, but he seems never to have seriously considered leaving Munich. Indeed, evidence shows that he was happy there and had exceptionally good relationships with Albrecht V and his son Wilhelm V, who succeeded his father in 1579.

VOCAL MUSIC

Lassus was a prolific composer of all genres of vocal music. In the sacred realm he composed Masses, motets, music for the Office – including over 100 Magnificats – and settings of all four Passions. His contributions to secular music include madrigals, villanellas (also called villanescas), chansons and Lieder.

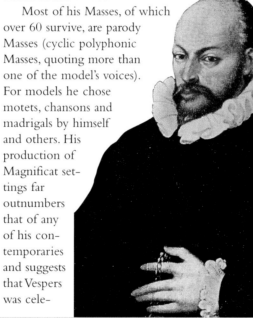

Most of his Masses, of which over 60 survive, are parody Masses (cyclic polyphonic Masses, quoting more than one of the model's voices). For models he chose motets, chansons and madrigals by himself and others. His production of Magnificat settings far outnumbers that of any of his contemporaries and suggests that Vespers was celebrated with some ceremony at Munich. In 1604 Lassus's two sons paid tribute to their father – and did future music lovers a great service – by compiling and publishing the *Magnum opus musicum*, a complete edition of Orlande's motets. The compositional achievement collected here is, quite simply, breathtaking. The breadth of text types is astonishing, including occasional, devotional, liturgical, didactic and even humorous works. The music shows an equally broad stylistic and expressive range. His five-voice motet, *In me transierunt*, (1562) was chosen by the music theorist Burmeister in 1606 as a model of musical rhetoric.

Lassus composed secular music to Italian, French and German texts with equal ease. His genius is notably evident in the Italian works. From the sublime madrigal 'Solo e pensoso' (1555) to the ridiculous (not to say obscene) villanella 'Matona mia cara' (1581), Lassus demonstrated himself a genius of the musical handling of text. The spiritual cycle *Lagrime di S Pietro* ('The Tears of St Peter'), composed at the end of his life and published after his death, is a remarkable swan-song: an accumulation of 40 years of compositional experience in a searingly beautiful religious statement.

LASSUS'S LETTERS

An extraordinary correspondence between Lassus and his young patron, the future Wilhelm V, gives a glimpse of the composer's personality that is very rare in this period. The letters were written in the 1570s, a decade during which Lassus travelled extensively in France and Italy. As a record of the composer's wit and linguistic virtuosity this correspondence is matched in music history, only by the letters of **Monteverdi** and **Mozart**. Like those of Mozart, Lassus's letters are full of humour, both sophisticated and childish. The wordplay is brilliant and many letters are written in a mixture of languages: French, Italian, German and Latin. Not surprisingly, the subject of music arises frequently. A letter referring to an enclosed compostition, which Lassus says he hopes to perform for Wilhelm, is a rare example of the day-to-day workings of musical patronage in the sixteenth century. Other letters are sprinkled with musical puns; even the composer's signature could be a play on words. In its Italian form – Lasso – his name is formed of two solmization syllables (la–sol). He often signed with musical notation indicating them.

(L) Orlande de Lassus
Portrait of Lassus (BL) and a picture of the composer playing the spinet at the Bavarian court chapel (TL).
(FR)* Saint Cecilia *by Giuseppe Martinelli
Saint Cecilia is honoured as the patron saint of music and musicians.
***(NR)* First Booke of Canzonets**
Title page from Morley's First Booke of Canzonets to Two Voyces, *published in 1595.*

chromaticism ▶ p. 357

Le Jeune, Claude

(Le Zhön, Klōd) c. *1530–1600*

FRENCH COMPOSER

Le Jeune mixed in French humanist circles, participating in the Académie de Poésie et de Musique, a circle of poets and musicians dedicated to reviving the ideals of classical sung verse. He was the principal composer to experiment with *musique mesurée*, the attempt to set text according to the principles of ancient declamation. Like his contemporary Goudimel, he was a Huguenot and made an important contribution to the polyphonic psalm repertory.

Marenzio, Luca

(Mà-rents'yō, Lōō'-kà) c. *1553–99*

ITALIAN COMPOSER

Marenzio spent most of his adult life in Rome, in the service of various cardinals and other patrons. Although he composed Masses and motets, his fame rests on his madrigals. In the 1580s he developed the canzonetta style of madrigal, borrowing the clear textures and lively rhythms of the canzonetta but applying them to a larger and more sophisticated canvas. In the last decade of his life he explored a variety of new, serious, expressive styles. His final book, published in 1599, is mostly devoted to the poetry of Petrarch. In the opening measures of his famous setting of Petrarch's 'Solo e pensoso', the poet's 'slow and heavy tread' is portrayed in the soprano line, which moves slowly up and then back down a **chromatic scale**.

Monte, Philippe de

(Mōn'-tà, Fē-lēp' dā) 1521–1603

FLEMISH COMPOSER

In his early years Monte travelled in Italy and, although his maturity was spent at the Habsburg court, he became one of the most prolific composers of Italian madrigals, publishing more than 1,100 of them. His career lasted for over 50 years, making him a good measure of changing tastes in madrigal composition. In particular, he responded to the rise of pastoralism in the 1570s and the related move towards themed madrigal volumes: his last book of madrigals is devoted entirely to texts from Guarini's *Il pastor fido*.

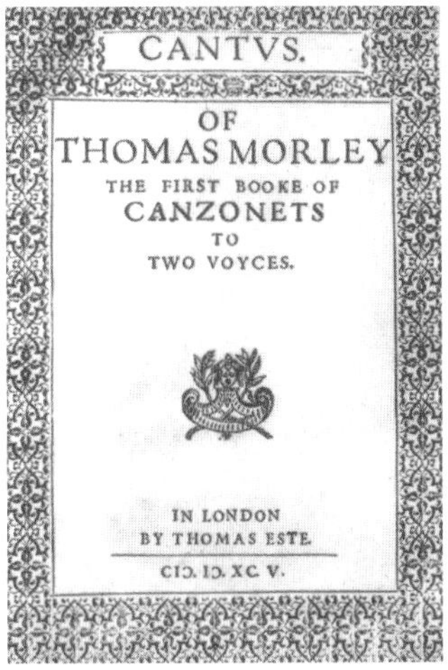

Morales, Cristóbal de

(Mō-rà'-lās, Krē-stō'-bàl dā) c. *1500–53*

SPANISH COMPOSER

Morales spent much of his career at the papal court, serving under Leo X and Paul III. He wrote little secular music and his fame rests on his sacred works, which include Masses, motets, lamentations and a book of Magnificat settings. Widely disseminated in sixteenth- and seventeenth-century Latin America, Morales's compositions had an important influence on the development of sacred music in the New World. His motet 'Parce mihi, Domine' ('Spare Me, Oh Lord') was sung in Mexico City in 1556 on the occasion of the death of Holy Roman Emperor Charles V.

Morley, Thomas

c. *1557–1602*

ENGLISH COMPOSER AND THEORIST

Morley was the most important composer involved in developing the English Elizabethan madrigal from its Italian counterpart. In the 1580s and 1590s he published some English translations of Italian madrigals with newly composed English works of his own, which imitated the Italian style. His most famous works are the 'fa la la' madrigals: pieces with a nonsense refrain, such as the wonderful 'Now is the Month of Maying'. Morley is also known for his treatise *A Plaine and Easie Introduction to Practicall Musicke* (1597). In addition to advice for the amateur, the book includes assessments of contemporary music and musicians that reveal opinions of the time and have remained influential to this day.

Mouton, Jean

(Mōō-tôn', Zhàn) c. *1459–1522*

FRENCH COMPOSER

Having held various church jobs in France, Mouton joined the French royal court in 1502 and remained there for the rest of his life. Many of his motets are occasional works – written for a personage or event at court. He was probably among the musicians present at the famous 'Field of the Cloth of Gold' in 1520. One of the favourite composers of the music-loving Pope Leo X, he composed a motet for his election on the appropriate text, *Christus vincit* (1513).

Obrecht, Jacob

(Ōb'-rekht, Yà'-kōb) c. *1450–1505*

FRANCO-FLEMISH COMPOSER

Obrecht, who has long lived in the shadow of his more famous contemporary Josquin, may begin to receive the attention he deserves now that changes in Josquin's biography show that many of the musical developments once attributed to him first appeared in Obrecht's music. Innovator or not, Obrecht was a composer of considerable talent. He worked throughout his life in the Low Countries, though he travelled in southern Europe, notably to Ferrara in 1487. He was most prolific in Mass composition and around 25 of these are extant; he later wrote in the parody Mass form and chansons.

FERRARA'S FEMALE MUSICIANS

In 1580, Duke Alfonso II d'Este of Ferrara founded his famous *concerto delle dame*, a group of upper-middle class women officially employed as 'ladies-in-waiting' to the duchess, but in fact chosen specifically for their musical talents (and paid more than the duke's *maestro di cappella*). The three original women – Laura Peverara, Anna Guarini and Livia d'Arco – were joined in 1583 by Tarquinia Molza. The group sang madrigals and accompanied themselves on lute, viol or harp in solo songs. Their musical expertise soon made them famous and imitated throughout Italy, opening up new opportunities for professional female musicians.

At the same time there were renowned female musicians in the convents of Ferrara: San Silvestro, San Antonio and especially San Vito. The woman in charge of the music at San Vito was Rafaella Aleotti, known as Vittoria before she became a nun. Aleotti published two volumes of madrigals (1591 and 1593) and a collection of sacred motets (1593). Furthermore, she was famous as an organist and as the conductor of the vocal and instrumental ensemble of the San Vito convent. It unusually included cornet and trombone players and received high praise from all who heard it.

Monteverdi ▶ p. 76 Mozart ▶ p. 144

Palestrina, Giovanni Pierluigi da

(Pä-lēs-tre'-nä, Jō-vän'-e Per-lōō-e'-jē da) 1525/6–94

ITALIAN COMPOSER

Palestrina is named after a small town near Rome, where he is thought to have been born. He was educated in Rome; in 1537 he was a choirboy at the basilica of S Maria Maggiore, one of the city's principal churches and an important musical establishment. By 1544 he was back in Palestrina, in his first post, as organist at the cathedral. He spent the next seven years there, marrying Lucrezia Gori in 1547. In 1551 he returned to Rome, where he remained for the rest of his life.

Palestrina's first position was the prestigious one of *maestro di cappella* at the Cappella Giulia, the choir of St Peter's. Subsequently he served in most of the major institutions in Rome: the Cappella Sistina (the pope's personal choir) briefly in 1555; S Giovanni Laterano (1555–60); S Maria Maggiore (1561–66); and back to the Cappella Giulia from 1571 until his death. From 1567 to 1571 he was in the private service of the powerful cardinal Ippolito d'Este, a member of the ruling family of Ferrara. Palestrina's reputation spread across Europe during his lifetime and he turned down job offers from other parts of Italy and abroad.

QUANTITY AND QUALITY

Palestrina's life spanned the first 50 years of the Counter-Reformation, which had an impact on his career and was in turn defined, musically, by his contribution. He was personally affected by the reforms when in 1555, after only a few months in the Cappella Sistina, he was dismissed along with all other married men in the chapel, by the strict reformist pope, Paul IV. However, in general, the atmosphere of the Counter-Reformation was beneficial to Palestrina. Music, which had always been an important part of Catholic worship, came under new scrutiny by church leaders eager to stem the tide of defectors to the Protestant cause. When the reformers wanted a revision of the church's plainchant, they turned to Palestrina and another Roman, Annibale Zoilo (*c.* 1537–92). Although the project was not finished in Palestrina's lifetime, much of the resulting publication – the *Editio Medicea* of 1614 – was undoubtedly his work. His predominance in the realm of sacred music is a matter of quantity as much as quality. One hundred and four Masses and nearly 500 other sacred works, including motets and various liturgical genres, have survived. His fourth book of motets, published in 1584 and devoted entirely to texts drawn from the Bible's beautiful and erotic Song of Songs, is a *tour de force* of musical imagery within the context of contrapuntal refinement.

Palestrina's contribution to secular music is often downplayed, and indeed he was undecided about this side of his compositional personality. Nevertheless, he published four books of madrigals, and many more appeared in anthologies. About a third of them are religious; the rest are on the same decidedly secular themes as those of his contemporaries. His most famous madrigal is the five-voice 'Vestiva i colli' (1566), which was widely reprinted and used a basis for parody works by a number of composers.

PALESTRINA AND THE COUNTER-REFORMATION

Among the concerns of Counter-Reformation churchmen interested in music was the intelligibility of text. By the 1540s, the predominant melodic and contrapuntal styles made it very difficult to understand. With the extensive use of **melisma**, individual words were often stretched out over many notes, and natural speech rhythms were obliterated. Further, the vocal lines were combined in close, dense, counterpoint. The result was often a web of sound without audible words or phrases.

On 28 April 1565, the singers of the Cappella Sistina gathered in the home of the reforming cardinal Vitellozi to 'sing some Masses and test whether the words could be understood'. An early biographer of Palestrina claimed that the composer's *Missa Papae Marcelli* ('Pope Marcellus Mass') was sung here and that it convinced the cardinals that the texts of polyphonic music could be intelligible. Unfortunately, the story – the basis of **Hans Pfitzner**'s (1869–1949) opera of 1917 – seems to have no foundation in fact. But there is no question that many of Palestrina's Masses are models of textual clarity. Melisma is moved to the end of a vocal phrase, and the beginning often has an incisive rhythm that clearly articulates the text. The carefully balanced imitative style, with a cadence structure linked to the sense of the text, also helps to convey the meaning of the words with no sacrifice of richness.

Praetorius, Michael

(Prī-tō'-rē-ōōs, Mēkh'-ä-el) c. 1571–1621

GERMAN COMPOSER AND THEORIST

Born into a strict Lutheran household, Praetorius became one of the greatest and most prolific early composers in the Protestant tradition. He composed over 1,000 sacred works – mostly hymns based on Lutheran chorales, but also German psalm settings and some Latin-texted works. Today, however, Praetorius is best known from his *Syntagma musicum* ('Musical Survey', 1614–20), a three-volume theoretical/pedagogical work. The most important section is the second book, 'De organographia', a detailed discussion of the instruments of his day, illustrated with beautiful and intricately detailed woodcuts, providing evidence about the construction and nomenclature of early instruments.

Rore, Cipriano de

(Rō'-rä, Chē-prē-ä'-nō dä) c. 1515–65

FRANCO-FLEMISH COMPOSER

Rore spent much of his relatively short life in Italy, first in Ferrara and then in the brilliant musical circle around Willaert in Venice. Rore was cited by Monteverdi as a pioneer of the ***seconda pratica***, and modern critics tend to emphasize the serious, intellectually rigorous side to his musical personality. But madrigals like the dawn song 'Dalle belle contrade oriente'

melisma ▶ p. 360 *prima pratica* ▶ p. 361 *seconda pratica* ▶ p. 362

('The Beautiful Country of the East') show that he was also quite comfortable in the less self-consciously highbrow language of the madrigal.

Senfl, Ludwig

(Zen'-fal, Lōōd'-vikh) c. *1486–1542/3*

SWISS COMPOSER

Senfl joined the choir of Holy Roman Emperor Maximilian I as a choirboy in 1498 and became Isaac's star pupil. On Isaac's death in 1517, Senfl succeeded him in the position of *Hofkomponist*. From 1523 until his death he was in Munich, at the court chapel of Duke Wilhelm IV of Bavaria. Although he spent his career working for Catholic patrons and composed in the traditional Catholic genres of Mass and motet, Senfl corresponded with Martin Luther and also made a contribution to the repertory of Protestant music, which was then still in its infancy.

Sermisy, Claudin de

(Sâr-mē-se', Klō-dan' da) c. *1490–1562*

FRENCH COMPOSER

Sermisy spent most of his adult life in Paris and was the leading exponent of the genre known as the 'Parisian chanson'. Mostly for four voices, his songs are similar in style to the early madrigal, which was developing at the same time. They are relatively easy to sing, with lively rhythms, straightforward melodies and an essentially homophonic texture. The texts are light and often playful. He was also an important composer of motets in the French style of Josquin.

Tallis, Thomas

1505–85

ENGLISH COMPOSER

Athough undoubtedly a fine composer, Tallis is also worth mentioning for his amazing ability to sustain a successful career spanning the religious upheavals of the reigns of Henry VIII and his three children. Beginning as a good Catholic, he composed Latin Masses and motets. When change came, he changed too and turned out to be one of the greatest Anglican composers of all time. Particularly memorable are his English anthems, some of them, like 'If Ye Love Me', of an ineffably sweet simplicity.

(NL) Syntagma Musicum
Page from Praetorius's best-known work, a valuable source of information about early instruments.
(FL) Palestrina
Portrait of the composer (TL) and title page of one of his many Masses, showing the composer giving his work to Pope Julius III (ML).
(R) Printing Patent
Page from the Cantiones Sacrae *showing the royal patent granting Tallis and Byrd the right to print and sell music.*

Taverner, John

c. *1490–1545*

ENGLISH COMPOSER

Taverner's career fell entirely within the reign of Henry VIII. Apparently on good terms with the king's most powerful ministers (first with Wolsey and then with Cromwell), he must have been an astute politician. Most of his music, which is thought to have been composed mostly in the 1520s and 30s, is firmly in the medieval Catholic tradition; this is the subject of **Peter Maxwell Davies**'s (b. 1934) opera of 1975. Taverner was the unwitting founder of the *In nomine*, a type of contrapuntal fantasy built around a theme in the Benedictus movement from his *Missa Gloria tibi trinitatis*.

Verdelot, Philippe

(Vâr-da-lō', Fē-lēp') c. *1480s–1530s*

FRENCH COMPOSER

Although French by birth and the composer of chansons and motets, Verdelot went to Italy early in his life, and is best known as one of the founders of the madrigal. He seems to have composed most, if not all, of his madrigals in the 1520s, the genre's first decade. Many of them are indistinguishable from frottolas with their simple, homophonic, four-voice texture. Some were composed for specific occasions; three refer to the Sack of Rome in 1527.

Victoria, Tomás Luis de

(Vik-tôr'-yà, Tō-màs' Lōō-ēs' dā) 1548–1611

SPANISH COMPOSER

After training as a choirboy at Avila Cathedral, Victoria spent his early adult life in Rome, principally at the Jesuit Collegio Germanico, as both pupil and teacher. He returned to Spain permanently in the 1580s, where he became the chaplain to Philip II's sister, Maria; he remained there as organist after her death in 1603. The Counter-Reformation intensity of Victoria's music encourages comparison with the paintings of his contemporary El Greco. Not as prolific as Palestrina or Lassus, Victoria published 20 Masses and a variety of smaller liturgical works. His Christmas motet *O magnum mysterium* (1572), on which he based a parody Mass, opens with a poignant setting of the solemn text 'Oh Great Mystery' and closes with a jubilant Alleluia.

Weelkes, Thomas

1576–1623

ENGLISH COMPOSER

Weelkes was one of the leading composers of the English madrigal. The unusual text of 'Thule the Period of Cosmographie' (1660) is a list of marvels, each of which he matches with appropriately descriptive music. Also famous is 'As Vesta Was, from Latmos hill descending' (1601), his contribution to *The Triumphs of Oriana*, a book of madrigals collected by Morley and dedicated to Elizabeth I. Weelkes's Anglican church music includes a number of brilliant anthems.

Wilbye, John

1574–1638

ENGLISH COMPOSER

Although not as prolific as some of his contemporaries, Wilbye made a substantial contribution to the English madrigal. Like Weelkes, he was influenced by Morley's light-hearted canzonets and ballets; later he turned to a more serious style, producing some of the repertory's most poignant works. Madrigals like 'Weepe O Mine Eies' (1598) and 'Draw on, Sweet Night' (1609) remain among the most loved examples of the genre.

Willaert, Adrian

(Vil-lârt, À'-drē-àn) c. *1490–1562*

FLEMISH COMPOSER

Willaert was one of an important group of composers who settled in Italy and there adapted the Franco-Flemish style. He spent most of his career as *maestro di cappella* at St Mark's, Venice. He gathered around him an influential group of musicians, including Rore and the great theorist Zarlino. His most influential publication was *Musica nova*, a collection of madrigals and motets probably composed some time before the book came out in 1559.

Zarlino, Gioseffo

(Tsâr-lē'-nō, Jō-zef'-fō) 1517–90

ITALIAN THEORIST AND COMPOSER

Zarlino's early musical experience was in the circle around Willaert in Venice in the 1540s. He was *maestro di cappella* at St Mark's, Venice, from 1565 until his death. In 1558 Zarlino published his *Institutioni harmoniche*, the first of a number of books that remain central to the canon of music theory. In its third part, he set out an exposition of the rules of classical counterpoint that would form the core of the ***prima pratica*** for future generations.

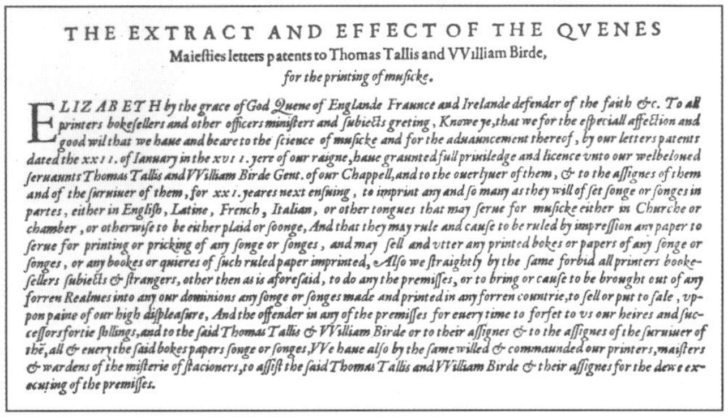
THE EXTRACT AND EFFECT OF THE QVENES
Maieſties letters patents to Thomas Tallis and VVilliam Birde,
for the printing of muſicke.

ELIZABETH by the grace of God Quene of Englande Fraunce and Irelande defender of the faith &c. To all printers bokeſellers and other officers miniſters and ſubiects greting, Knowe ye, that we for the eſpeciall affection and good wil that we haue and beare to the ſcience of muſicke and for the aduauncement thereof, by our letters patents dated the xxII. of Ianuary in the xvII. yere of our raigne, haue graunted full priuiledge and licence vnto our welbeloued ſeruaunts Thomas Tallis and VVilliam Birde Gent. of our Chappell, and to the ouerlyuer of them, & to the aſſignes of them and of the ſuruiuer of them, for xxI. yeares next enſuing, to imprint any and ſo many as they will of ſet ſonge or ſonges in partes, either in Engliſh, Latine, French, Italian, or other tongues that may ſerue for muſicke either in Churche or chamber, or otherwiſe to be either plaid or ſoonge, And that they may rule and cauſe to be ruled by impreſſion any paper to ſerue for printing or pricking of any ſonge or ſonges, and may ſell and vtter any printed bokes or papers of any ſonge or ſonges, or any bookes or quieres of ſuch ruled paper imprinted, Alſo we ſtraightly by the ſame forbid all printers bookeſellers ſubiects & ſtrangers, other then as is aforeſaid, to do any the premiſſes, or to bring or cauſe to be brought out of any forren Realmes into any our dominions any ſonge or ſonges made and printed in any forren countrie, to ſell or put to ſale, vppon paine of our high diſpleaſure, And the offender in any of the premiſſes for euery time to forfet to vs our heires and ſucceſſors fortie ſhillings, and to the ſaid Thomas Tallis & VVilliam Birde or to their aſſignes & to the aſſignes of the ſuruiuer of thē, all & euery the ſaid bokes papers ſonge or ſonges, VVe haue alſo by the ſame willed & commaunded our printers, maiſters & wardens of the miſterie of ſtacioners, to aſſiſt the ſaid Thomas Tallis and VVilliam Birde & their aſſignes for the dewe executing of the premiſſes.

Pfitzner ▶ p. 293 Davies ▶ p. 325

The Renaissance

STYLES AND FORMS

The main opportunities for professional music-making in the Renaissance continued to be provided by the church and by royal and ducal courts, particularly those in Italy. They sponsored musical entertainment both on a large scale, such as the lavish Florentine *intermedi*, and on a more intimate level, in the form of the madrigal. The influence of humanism balanced the attempts of militant Catholic authorities in Italy and Spain to clamp down on what they saw as the seductive and profane excesses of music. Composers and theorists returned to ancient classical texts to justify their search for new means of expression, their concern to reflect the mood and meaning of the text, and their belief in the power of music to convey and evoke human emotions.

On a more practical level, the economic prosperity of many European cities in the late fifteenth century and the development of music printing and publishing created a new market. The emerging middle classes were eager to buy books of music that they could perform for their own entertainment.

The Mass

A setting of the Latin Mass was among the most important works a Renaissance composer could write, and its words inspired some of the finest music of the age. The movements of the Mass consisted of the Kyrie, Gloria, Credo, Sanctus and Agnus Dei. Many composers structured and unified their Mass settings by basing all five of these movements on the same tune. This tune – sometimes plainchant, but often taken from a secular song – is called a ***cantus firmus*** ('fixed melody'). One of the most famous examples is 'L'homme armé': **Du Fay**, **Ockeghem**, **Busnoys**, **Josquin** and **Obrecht** were among the earliest composers to write a *Missa L'homme armé*, a competitive tradition that continued in the sixteenth century.

Some of the most prolific composers of Mass settings in the sixteenth century were the Spaniards **Morales** and **Victoria**, and, above all, the Italian **Palestrina**, whose 104 Masses combine technical mastery with expressive power and are considered the epitome of the Renaissance Mass style. England's strong tradition developed rather separately from that on the continent; among the most beautiful English Masses are those of **Taverner** and **Byrd**.

RENAISSANCE POLYPHONY

Renaissance polyphony (Gk., 'many sounds', 'many voices') is a style of music characterized by the equal participation of voices in exchange and imitation of motifs and phrases. According to sixteenth-century theorists the art of polyphony lay in the clarity and beauty of the texture, themes and text-setting, and in the careful control of structure and **dissonance**. Achieving such clarity and consonance while each voice is singing a different line of music requires considerable skill, yet in the hands of the best composers the result appears effortless. The words and phrases of each voice come through the texture clearly, their combination creating a richly expressive whole. Among the finest examples are the Masses and motets of the Franco-Flemish composers Ockeghem, Obrecht and Josquin in the fifteenth century, and of Lassus, Byrd, Victoria, and, above all, Palestrina in the sixteenth; the Franco-Flemish style was also influential in the development of the polyphonic Italian madrigal.

The Spanish 'Golden Age'

Artistic and cultural life flourished in Spain during the reigns of Charles I, later Holy Roman Emperor Charles V, and Philip II, which spanned most of the sixteenth century, though as a result of the Inquisition many composers felt obliged to focus on sacred music. Three composers stand out in this 'golden age' of Spanish music: Morales, Francisco Guerrero (1528–99) and especially Victoria. All three were masters of the techniques of Renaissance polyphony – Palestrina's music was a great influence on Victoria, who, like Morales, spent much of his career in Rome – and their Mass settings and motets are works of great expressiveness and emotional power.

The Development of Compositional Process

The 'classical' polyphony of the Renaissance, where each voice is equal in function, stands at the mid-point of the progression from the strict compositional practices of the Middle Ages, in which a piece was constructed line by line around a tenor voice, to the chord-based language of the Baroque, in which textures were conceived vertically and polarized around a bass line and a melody line. Although singers still performed mainly from partbooks that contained only their own line, music scores (with all voices aligned vertically) began to be used for study purposes in the mid sixteenth century. In Renaissance vocal music, much of the impetus for change came from the search for new ways of responding to the words set: musical language expanded and previously inviolable rules were broken in the name of expression and musical rhetoric. While improvisation was nothing new in the Renaissance, composers now tried to capture its essence in notated music.

Prima Pratica, Seconda Pratica

Monteverdi coined the terms *prima pratica* (It. 'first practice') and *seconda pratica* (It. 'second practice') to describe traditional and modern styles of composition in the sixteenth century. In response to criticism from the conservative theorist Giovanni Maria Artusi (*c.* 1540–1613), who had attacked some of Monteverdi's madrigals for breaking the rules of

(BL) Palestrina
Pierluigi da Palestrina was one of the most prolific composers of Masses of the Renaissance era; 104 of his settings survive.

(R) Meistersinger
German tenor Herman Winkelmann as Walther von Stolzing in Wagner's opera, Die Meistersinger.

cantus firmus ▶ p. 356 dissonance ▶ p. 358

MEISTERSINGER

Meistersinger (the singular and plural forms are identical) were German men predominantly from the lower and middle classes who were members of town guilds formed to encourage the composition and performance of songs known as *Meisterlieder*. The genre had its origins in the fourteenth century and flourished for three centuries. It was essentially an oral tradition: not all *Meistersinger* could read music, so they relied on learning their songs by heart.

Meistersinger guilds – celebrated in **Richard Wagner**'s (1813–83) famous opera – were subject to the control of the municipal authorities and were organized according to strict regulations. Each guild had elected officials, including directors and treasurers, and new members began by being apprenticed to an existing singer. *Meisterlieder* were educational and edifying in purpose, in keeping with the spirit of the Lutheran Reformation. Many of their texts are based on Luther's German translations of the Bible, though some took historical themes, including the history of *Meistersinger* tradition itself.

Meisterlieder

Just as the structure of the guilds was strictly controlled, so the creation of *Meisterlieder* was carefully controlled by tradition: there was always an odd number of verses (a minimum of three) and both text and music had to share the same structure – bar form, using a broad AAB format for each verse. Often the specific form used was taken from a work by an earlier *Meistersinger*. Each line of verse was supposed to be of a length that could easily be sung in one breath. Meisterlieder were performed, without accompaniment, by a solo singer or by a chorus in unison. In the surviving manuscripts only the pitch of the melodies is indicated, not the rhythm, and the assumption is that they were declaimed following the rhythms and stresses of the words.

counterpoint, the composer explained that these so-called errors arose from the desire to create a new style that was expressive of the text. *Prima pratica* prized above all the correct use of counterpoint, and *seconda pratica*, which Monteverdi used, aimed 'to make the words the mistress of the harmony and not the servant'.

The Motet

The Renaissance motet was a relatively small-scale sacred form, performed during Mass and outside church as private devotional entertainment. Early fifteenth-century motets could be either strict *cantus firmus* compositions or freer works. The motets of Josquin bridge the change from the fifteenth century to the sixteenth. Expression of the text was his main concern, and his settings are full of contrasts – of imitative and chordal writing, of passages for all voices and passages for just two or three, and of sections in duple and triple time.

Sixteenth-century composers in Venice developed these contrasts of texture into the technique of *cori spezzati* (It. 'divided choirs'). The motets of Victoria and Palestrina represent the culmination of the conservative Renaissance style, while those of **Lassus** are at the other end of the stylistic spectrum: the emphasis is on the depiction of the individual words of the text, using rhetorical techniques familiar from the madrigal.

Melismas

The Counter-Reformation zeal of Pope Paul III had a great impact on music through the decrees issued by the Council of Trent. These stated that all church music was to be purged of the 'lascivious and impure', and that in all sacred vocal music the words were to be as clear as possible. In order to comply, composers had to avoid using 'seductive' melismas and complex contrapuntal writing. The new style, setting the text in a predominantly chordal and declamatory manner so that it could be clearly understood, is seen in some (though by no means all) Mass settings by Roman composers in the late sixteenth century.

Antiphonal Singing

In antiphonal or polychoral music, a choir is divided into two or more groups that sing in alternation; echo effects and contrasts of volume or range may be exploited, and the groups may be placed some distance apart. The technique known as *cori spezzati*, associated particularly with St Mark's in Venice, was very popular in the sixteenth century. Motets and psalm settings for many *cori spezzati* were often used for ceremonial occasions and exploited the spatial contrasts possible in the basilica. The music tends to be built up of chordal phrases with clear harmonic progressions that are passed to and fro among the various groups of voices to resounding effect.

POLYPHONY IN FLANDERS

From the Middle Ages music had played a prominent role in various areas of life in the Low Countries (the term 'Netherlands' in the Renaissance included the modern Netherlands, Belgium, Luxembourg and part of north-eastern France). Professional musicians were employed in churches, cathedrals and monasteries, as well as at court and in municipal bands. Moreover, theorists from the region also produced many important music treatises.

The Netherlandish Golden Age

This flourishing musical life was partly the result of the keen patronage of the powerful European Habsburg family, especially Maximilian I and Charles V, Duke of Burgundy and King of Spain. It is often referred to as the 'golden age' of Netherlandish music, when Franco-Flemish composers frequently travelled to southern Europe, assimilating cosmopolitan musical influences and helping to disseminate their style.

Du Fay wrote in most of the major forms of his day (notably the Mass, motet and chanson), while **Binchois** is known chiefly for his chansons. They were followed by Ockeghem, whose Mass settings developed the richly woven contrapuntal textures that characterize Netherlandish polyphony, and Josquin, whose highly expressive music achieved something close to legendary status even in his own day. With the main composers of the next generation, **Gombert** and **Clemens non Papa** (both of whom remained based in the Netherlands), equal-voiced polyphony gradually evolved into a more declamatory and chordal style.

In the mid sixteenth century, the final decades of the Netherlandish 'golden age' were populated by composers who made their mark mainly in Italy, including **Rore** and **Monte**. By combining the legacy of their native contrapuntal traditions with new expressive styles of writing, these composers made an invaluable contribution to the development of the Italian madrigal.

Binchois ▶ p. 26 Busnoys ▶ p. 26 Byrd ▶ p. 49 Clemens non Papa ▶ p. 50 Du Fay ▶ p. 27 Gombert ▶ p. 51 Josquin des Prez ▶ p. 53 Lassus ▶ p. 54
Monte ▶ p. 55 Morales ▶ p. 55 Obrecht ▶ p. 55 Ockeghem ▶ p. 30 Palestrina ▶ p. 56 Rore ▶ p. 56 Taverner ▶ p. 57 Victoria ▶ p. 57 Wagner ▶ p. 226

Protestant Hymn and Psalm Settings

The introduction of congregational singing was perhaps the most important musical development of the Reformation: rather than listening to a professional church choir perform in Latin, worshippers could take a more active role, singing in their own language. The first Protestant hymn book was published by the Bohemian Brethren in 1505, and the first collection of Lutheran hymns was published in 1524. Original English hymns first appeared in 1562. Composers such as Byrd and Tallis wrote harmonizations, probably intended for domestic use or choirs rather than for congregational singing. The Calvinists used psalm texts rather than composing new verses; the Calvinist Psalter of 1551 included the tune (by Loys Bourgeois, *c.* 1510–61 or later) now known as the 'Old Hundredth' – one of the most familiar English hymns.

Chanson

Chanson is simply the French word for 'song', but in the late Middle Ages and the Renaissance it refers to a specific body of French songs for several voices. Many early examples survive in beautifully decorated manuscript collections known as 'chansonniers', and some use intricate rhythms and notation.

At the start of the sixteenth century, chansons began to appear in print rather than in manuscripts. Composers based in Paris in the 1530s and 40s developed a new style, simple and lyrical,

often using light-hearted texts. Of this group **Janequin** is perhaps best known for his witty, descriptive chansons, such as 'La guerre' and 'Le chant des oiseaux', in which the voices depict the sounds of war and birdsong respectively.

Frottola

The frottola, a setting for three or four voices generally of light-hearted love poetry, flourished in Italy during the Renaissance. The composer provided music for the first verse and it was repeated for the subsequent verses. As a result, although there may be a close connection between the structure and rhythms of the verse and the music, the music is less likely to reflect the meaning of the text. Settings are usually chordal, with simple rhythms, clear phrases and the melody in the top voice; sometimes the tunes of popular songs were incorporated. Bartolomo Tromboncino (*c.* 1470–1535 or later) and Marchetto Cara (*c.* 1470–*c.* 1525) are the best-known frottola composers.

Madrigal

The madrigal – a setting for several voices (usually four to six) of a secular poetic text – was one of the most popular forms of the Renaissance. It originated in Italy and its influence spread to other countries with cosmopolitan courts and flourishing publishing cultures. Petrarch's bittersweet love poems enjoyed a revival in the early sixteenth century and were emulated by new poets. Composers responded with music that captured this richly expressive poetic style. The first madrigals appeared in manuscript form during the 1520s and in print a decade later. The greatest contributions of that time were by three Franco-Flemish musicians who worked in Italy – **Verdelot**, **Willaert** and **Arcadelt**. In the mid-century madrigals of Rore, a more vividly expressive style developed: he used smaller note values to create a rapid *parlando* (It. 'speaking') effect, contrasted with long, slow chords and poignant dissonances.

The lighter style seen in the madrigals of **Andrea Gabrieli** and several younger composers was very popular in England, and many fine settings of English texts were created. The polyphonic madrigal culminated in the late sixteenth century in the works of composers who drew on both the lighter and the serious styles, notably **Morley**, **Marenzio** and, above all, **Monteverdi**.

Intermedio

The *intermedio* was an interlude presented between the acts of a play or other entertainment. At its simplest, it consisted of instrumental music alone, but the more elaborate courtly *intermedi* were series of performances which involved singers, dancers and actors and were intended both to reflect the themes of the main play and to impress the aristocracy in the audience. The most spectacular Renaissance *intermedi* were those staged with lavish costumes, scenery and special effects in Florence, and music survives for two, performed at Medici wedding celebrations in 1539 and 1589. The music for the 1589 *intermedi*, by Marenzio and Cristofano Malvezzi (1547–99), ranged from virtuoso solo songs to danced choruses involving large numbers of singers and instruments.

MUSIC MANUSCRIPTS

One of the best-known Renaissance music manuscripts, the *Fitzwilliam Virginal Book*, was compiled by the musician Francis Tregian (1574–1619) during his imprisonment in London for recusancy from 1609 until his death. The manuscript contains an unusually wide-ranging collection of nearly 300 keyboard pieces by English composers (many of them also known for their Catholic sympathies), including Tallis, Byrd and Bull. Continental musicians such as **Jan Pieterszoon Sweelinck** (1562–1621) are also represented and there are arrangements of madrigals by Italian composers.

Other Important Manuscripts

Earlier manuscripts of keyboard music include the *Buxheimer Orgelbuch*, an important source of over 250 German organ works compiled in about 1470; the *Lublin Tablature*, compiled by the Polish organist Jan z Lublina (fl. *c.* 1540) between 1537 and 1548 and containing dances, preludes, works on plainchant and arrangements of vocal pieces by composers from all over Europe; and the *Mulliner Book*, a collection of pieces mainly for organ compiled in the mid sixteenth century by the English composer Thomas Mulliner (fl. 1563).

An important source of Italian lute music from the early sixteenth century is the *Capirola Lutebook*. This beautifully illuminated manuscript, which includes a preface on the technique of lute playing, contains ricercares, dances and arrangements of chansons, motets and other vocal works by Vincenzo Capirola (1474–after 1548), a nobleman and lutenist. It was prepared by one of Capirola's pupils in about 1517.

(BL) Organ Player
Compilations of organ music began to appear across Europe in the early 1400s.
(TL) Renaissance Singers
During the Renaissance, the French chanson started to appear in printed, rather than manuscript, form.
(TR) Court Ball
The European aristocracy staged lavish entertainments, including intermedi, *at court weddings and balls.*
(BR) Venice
The Italian courts used music to demonstrate the wealth and taste of the ruling families.

canzona ▶ p. 356 consort ▶ p. 357 ricercare ▶ p. 362 tablature ▶ p. 362 toccata ▶ p. 362

Keyboard Music

Until the late Baroque period, music for keyboard was usually intended for whatever instrument was available – generally an organ for church music and a harpsichord, spinet or virginal for dance music. Manuscript collections containing keyboard music survive from the fifteenth century, but these tend to consist of arrangements of vocal works. Keyboard music really emerged as a genre in its own right in the sixteenth century. Composers began to develop idiomatic styles, embellishing melodic lines with runs to help maintain the flow of sound (unlike the piano, neither the organ nor the harpsichord can sustain a note once the key has been released). Dances and arrangements of sacred and secular vocal pieces were still common, but new forms, such as the prelude, **toccata**, **ricercare** and **canzona**, also developed. English keyboard music of the sixteenth century – much of which survives in manuscript rather than print – was quite progressive in establishing what became typical keyboard idioms, notably the use of ornaments, lively bass lines and varied repeats.

Lute-Song

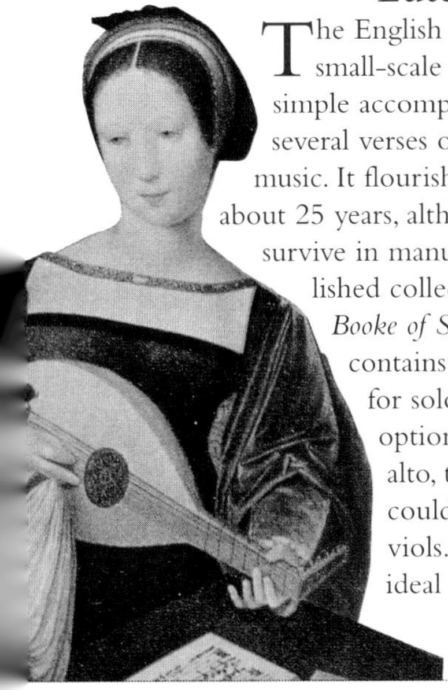

The English lute-song, or ayre, is a small-scale form of song with simple accompaniment, often setting several verses of text to repeated music. It flourished in print for only about 25 years, although later examples survive in manuscript. The first published collection, **Dowland**'s *First Booke of Songes or Ayres* (1597), contains 21 songs with parts for solo voice and lute, with optional additional parts for alto, tenor and bass, which could be sung or played on viols. Lute-songs were thus ideal for domestic music-making, since they could be performed by any combination of voices and instruments that was available. Some of Dowland's best songs, such as 'His Golden Locks' (1597) are also his most poignant, and those of John Danyel (1564–*c.* 1626), notably 'Can Dolefull Notes' (1606), are similarly expressive. The ayres of the poet and composer **Campion**, such as 'When to her Lute Corinna Sings', are in a much lighter and simpler style.

LUTE MUSIC

Several important developments took place in lute music during the Renaissance. Lutenists began using the fingers of the right hand rather than a plectrum, which allowed them to play more than one string at once, and they shifted from generally improvising to performing pre-composed music. Linked to both of these changes was a vital development in the notation of lute music: the use of **tablature**. Unlike conventional musical notation, this uses a system of letters or numbers, which represent the frets, on horizontal lines, which represent the strings. Rhythms are indicated by stems without note-heads above the staff.

Many of the composers writing for the lute in the early fifteenth century were also accomplished lutenists. Much lute music was aimed at professional virtuosos, but there was also a growing demand for pieces suitable for amateurs to play at home. This domestic market was particularly strong in England. It was fed by publications of instruction books which covered various aspects of lute playing (e.g. fingering and ornamentation) and included pieces of varying degrees of difficulty by composers such as Dowland and the **Ferrabosco** family.

English Viol Music

The popularity of music for virginal and for lute in sixteenth-century England was matched by that of music for viols. The first viol players in the country were probably the Italians employed by **Henry VIII**. They were soon replaced by English professional players, and by the end of the century viol-playing was a well-established pastime among amateurs too; many wealthy Elizabethan families owned a **consort** of viols. Composers such as Tallis, Byrd and Gibbons wrote fantasias, dances and *In nomines* for consorts as well as music for solo viol which was more virtuoso in style – full of ornaments and divisions (rapid embellishments on a melodic line). Viols were also used to accompany voices, and treble and bass viols were played in mixed consorts with lute, cittern, bandora and flute.

Instrumental Forms

The fantasia, often known as the 'fancy' in England, was a form in which composers were free to exercise their imagination, often including virtuoso runs and brilliant contrapuntal passages. Among the best examples are pieces by Francesco Canova da Milano (1497–1543), Bakfark Balint (1507–76) and Dowland for lute, and by Sweelinck, Byrd and Gibbons for keyboard. The lute or keyboard ricercare was a similar composition, often characterized by imitative or fugal writing. Sometimes it functioned as a sort of prelude, perhaps based on a vocal piece. Dance forms were popular in music for keyboard, lute or ensemble, often in linked pairs – for example the pavan (a sedate dance in duple time) and galliard (faster and in triple time in a simple homophic style). In the hands of composers like Byrd and Dowland such pieces are elevated from simple dance music to skilful, weighty and even moving works.

THE ITALIAN COURTS

Music was an important part of courtly life in sixteenth-century Italy, serving not only to accompany worship and as entertainment, but also to reflect the wealth and good taste of the ruling family. The Florentine court is well known for its cultivation of lavish staged entertainment, the *intermedi* and later the development of the first operas, but the Este dukes at Ferrara and the Gonzaga dukes at Mantua were also important patrons of music. Towards the end of the fifteenth century, Duke Ercole I d'Este built up an impressive musical chapel, employing some of the best musicians of the day from Italy and abroad. Under Duke Alfonso II, the court composer Luzzasco Luzzaschi (?1545–1607) wrote many ornate madrigals for performance by the renowned *concerto della dame*, a group of virtuoso female singers who gave private concerts for the duke and his guests. The poets Guarini and Torquato Tasso, whose pastoral plays were important in the development of music drama, were also in the service of the Este court. Tasso addressed some of his love poems to Peverara, a member of the *concerto*; she was also honoured by many of the finest composers of the day in a series of three madrigal anthologies.

Arcadelt ▶ p. 48 Campion ▶ p. 50 Ferrabosco ▶ p. 50 A. Gabrieli ▶ p. 50 Henry VIII ▶ p. 52 Janequin ▶ p. 52 Marenzio ▶ p. 54
Monteverdi ▶ p. 76 Morley ▶ p. 55 Sweelinck ▶ p. 86 Verdelot ▶ p. 57 ▶ Willaert p. 57

The Renaissance
INSTRUMENTS

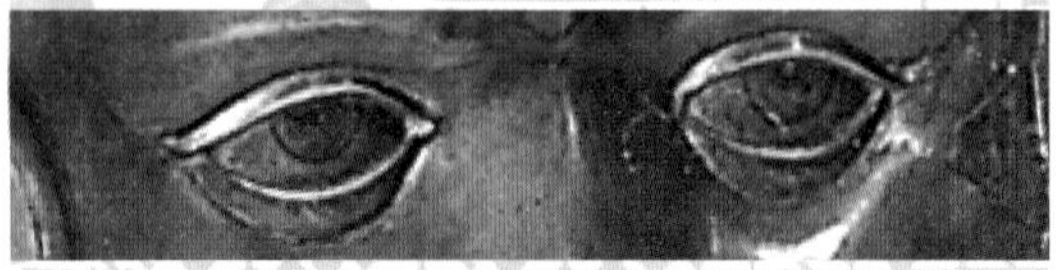

Viol and Violin

It is still possible to find old books which explain cheerily that the viol was an early version of the violin, now superseded. It is worth saying straight away that this is not true. These two related but different families of instruments both evolved from the early sixteenth century in northern Italy, but made different sounds and were played in different repertories. The violin was from the outset associated with dance music and was part of the entertainment end of music, a bit like the saxophone or the electric guitar in the twentieth century. The viol was in a higher social class altogether and the music written for it was intended to be played for (or even by) the nobility. It is usually judged to be a bowed version of the vihuela. Originally played in Spain, this instrument became popular in Italy at the time of the Spanish Borgia popes. Notable Renaissance composers for the viol included **Byrd** and **Gibbons**.

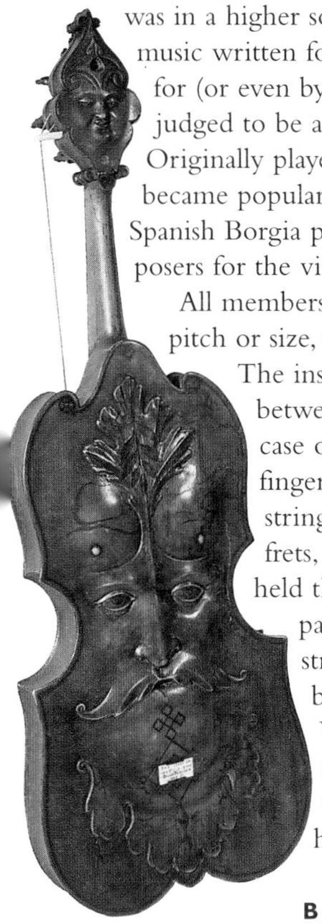

All members of the viol family, of whatever pitch or size, were played in the same way. The instrument was held upright between the player's knees (or in the case of the smallest, on the lap). The fingers of the left hand stopped the strings, pulling them down on to gut frets, to alter the pitch; the right hand held the bow in an underhand grip, palm upwards, and crossed the string at right angles midway between bridge and fingerboard. While something similar is true of the cello, the violin and viola were from the beginning held higher and more horizontally.

BEGINNINGS OF THE VIOLIN

At the end of the Middle Ages, there were a number of bowed instruments that were held in the left hand and wedged against the shoulder or chest. Often with three strings, they were made in a variety of shapes and carried various names, such as the rebec and the medieval fiddle. The *lira da bracchio*, a surviving example of which can be seen in the Ashmolean Museum in Oxford, had five strings running along the fingerboard and over the bow, plus another two to one side, which could be bowed but not fingered. The term 'viole' replaced that of 'lira' early in the sixteenth century, developing into 'violino'.

In the early sixteenth century a bowed shoulder-instrument developed, with the number of strings fixed at four and the tuning settled more or less at e'', a', d' and g, marking the beginning of the history of the violin itself. The tunings of the other family members also settled down: at a', d', g', c for the viola, and the same an octave lower for the cello.

The strings of both viol and violin families were tuned by pegs slotted into a peg box at the end of the instrument's neck. They were wound aound the pegs and the pegs turned to increase or relax the tension, thus causing the string to go up or down in pitch. The peg box of the violin family was invariably carved to the shape of a scroll and that of the viol to a figure, such as a woman or an animal.

Lute

The Renaissance lute had a flat front and a rounded back made out of a series of curved strips of wood (usually yew or sycamore) fitted together. At the centre of the front was the soundhole, called the 'rose', which was round and intricately decorated. The instrument's neck was glued and nailed to the top block of the body, a thick lump of wood. The strings ran from where they were fixed to a bridge across the front, up the fingerboard (which was fitted with gut frets), to a peg box set back at an angle of about 80 degrees. The lute was cradled against the chest, with the fingers of the left hand stopping the strings to vary the pitch and produce chords, those of the right plucking near the rose.

As the strings – particularly the upper ones – were often paired (two neighbouring strings were

(NL) Lutenist and Singers
The Renaissance lute was held against the chest, the fingers of the left hand stopping the strings and the right-hand plucking.
(FL) Lira da Braccio
One of the earliest violins, a lira da braccio, *with ornate carving.*
(NR) Cittern
The cittern was played with a quill plectrum rather than being plucked with the fingers.

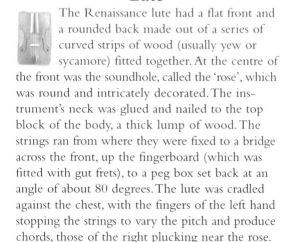

tuned to the same note and played at the same time), lutenists tend to talk about the number of courses on an instrument. This term disregards whether the strings are single or double, counting only the number of different pitches to which they are tuned. Most early lute music was intabulated from chansons. The six-course lute was popular in the sixteenth century and was most frequently used in ricercares and fantasias. Elizabethan and Jacobean music was written largely for seven- and eight-course instruments, while in the Baroque period, **Johann Sebastian Bach** (1685–1750) would have known a 13-course lute.

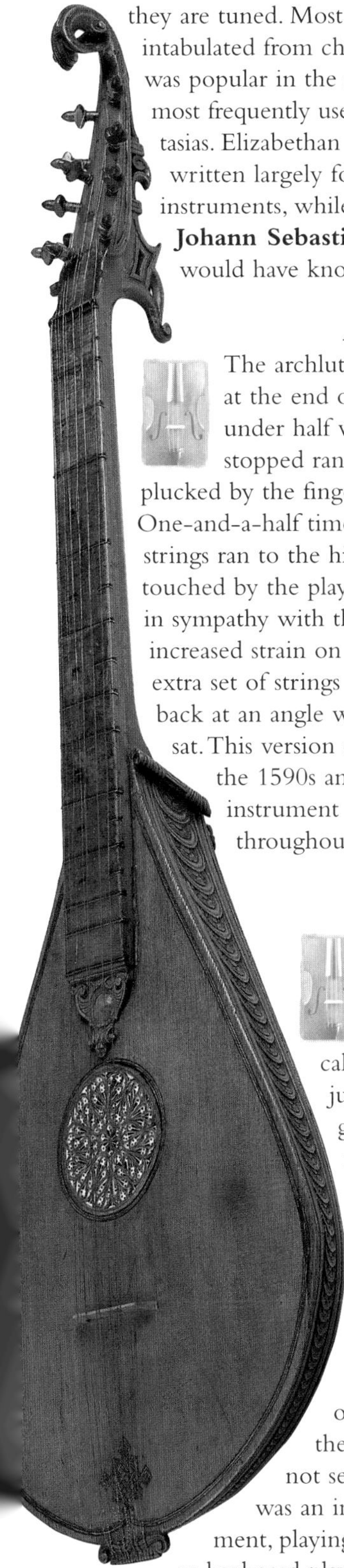

Archlute

The archlute had two peg boxes, one at the end of the neck and one just under half way up. The strings to be stopped ran to the lower one and were plucked by the fingernails of the right hand. One-and-a-half times as long, the unstopped strings ran to the higher one and were not touched by the player – they simply resonated in sympathy with the plucked notes. The increased strain on the neck of tensioning an extra set of strings was offset by setting it back at an angle where the lower peg box sat. This version of the lute developed in the 1590s and was used both as a solo instrument and in a continuo role throughout the seventeenth century.

Theorbo

An alternative to the archlute was the theorbo. It had a set of unstopped bass strings called 'diapasons' which lay just to one side of the fingerboard and ran directly from where they were attached to the bridge to a peg box at the end of a long neck. The stopped strings ran to a second peg box placed, as in the archlute, a little under half way up the neck. The theorbo's neck was straight and the peg box at the end was not set at an angle. The theorbo was an important continuo instrument, playing with the bass viol, cello or keyboard player's left hand.

ORIGINS OF THE LUTE

Although types of lute can be found in many societies, both ancient and modern, the structure and indeed name of the Renaissance lute derived from an Arabic instrument, *al-ud* ('the ud'). Like the western Renaissance lute, the ud consisted of a large curved soundbox, a short neck ending in a peg box and a series of strings to be plucked. As the Spanish-Portuguese peninsula consisted of a patchwork of Christian and Muslim kingdoms until the end of the Middle Ages, with a high level of trade and a changing pattern of diplomatic and military alliances, Spain is generally thought to be the place where the Arabic instrument was adopted and westernized.

Cittern

The cittern was a plucked stringed instrument of the sixteenth and seventeenth centuries. It was strung with wire and played not with the right fingers but using a quill plectrum, rather like the cittole and gittern of the medieval era. The body was flat both back and front, with a pear-shaped face. The fingerboard lay on the front of a short neck ending in a peg box, usually carved. Known in classical Rome and in the Dark Ages, the instrument originally had an elongated, tapering body and no fingerboard. The fingerboard that it acquired had on its surface a series of wooden graduations descending to the peg box, rather than the gut frets used on lutes and viols.

Vihuela and Guitar

The vihuela had a waisted body but it cannot be said to have been figure-of-eight shaped, for the inward curve was slight. It was flat both front and back and could have several roses. Like the lute, it carried gut strings in pairs – usually six or seven courses. The fingerboard was crossed by gut frets. More popular in Spain than the lute, the vihuela was among the accomplishments of both Ferdinand of Aragon and Isabella of Castile; it seems to have been an instrument of the elite.

The name of the guitar has encouraged some to trace its origins to the ancient Greek *kithara*. The biggest question, however, is whether it was adopted from Arabic musicians or already native to western Europe by the Middle Ages. Like the cittern, the Renaissance guitar had a flat back and front body, with a gentle waist. Held across the body of the player at a rising angle, with the fingering left hand higher than the plucking right, it was smaller and quieter than the modern instrument. Sixteenth-century guitars had four or five courses; the four-course was preferred for polyphonic music and the five-course as an accompanying instrument.

Harp

Between medieval and Renaissance times, the harp underwent some simple developments: it grew a little larger and the number of strings increased to 24. Other than that, it was made and played in the same way as it had been in the Middle Ages. An open triangle supported a sounding box on the side against the player's body and the player could reach the strings from both sides. There were some regional variations: in his *Syntagma musicum*, **Praetorius** contrasts what he calls a 'simple common harp' with an Irish harp. The former had a straighter, slimmer forepillar and a narrower soundbox (which we know from surviving instruments was carved out of a single block of wood), while the Irish instrument was heavier and more curved.

Double Harp

During the sixteenth century the harp was in danger of falling into disuse as chromatic keyboards raised composers' expectations of what plucked strings could achieve. But in the third quarter of the century, instrument-builders began to experiment with the double harp, constructed with a second row of strings running next to the first. Arrangements of strings varied as makers attempted to discover how to distribute them between the two rows in a way that would best suit fluent playing (an interesting parallel could be drawn with the modern QWERTY keyboard). The double harp (and its further extension the triple harp), were superseded by later developments in harp-making. It survived longest in Wales, where it was a folk and gypsy instrument until revived in the nineteenth century under the influence of Lady Llanover, who encouraged makers and players to settle on her estate; it continues to be played there.

J. S. Bach ▶ p. 106 Byrd ▶ p. 49 Gibbons ▶ p. 51 Praetorius ▶ p. 56

Recorder

The recorder was played by blowing directly into a beak-shaped mouthpiece and the pitch varied by changing the fingering on the holes – a set of seven on the front of the instrument and a single thumb-hole at the back. In the Renaissance it was generally made of a single piece of wood, but now it usually has three jointed sections: a head containing the mouthpiece; a middle section with six of the finger-holes; and a foot joint which has the seventh hole. The bore of the Renaissance recorder was almost cylindrical. In the Baroque recorder it narrowed and became more conical in shape, making the instrument sound less reedy, sweeter and fuller.

The Renaissance recorder had a working range of about an octave and a sixth, achieved by varying the blowing as well as changing the fingering. (Baroque players seem to have expected to cover about two octaves.) Sylvestro di dal Fonrego Ganassi (1492–mid sixteenth century), in his treatise *Fontegara* (1535), suggested that the compass of the recorder could be extended to two octaves and a sixth by means of special fingering. In fact, most of the Renaissance repertory of dance music played by recorders only required the less ambitious range.

A CONSORT INSTRUMENT

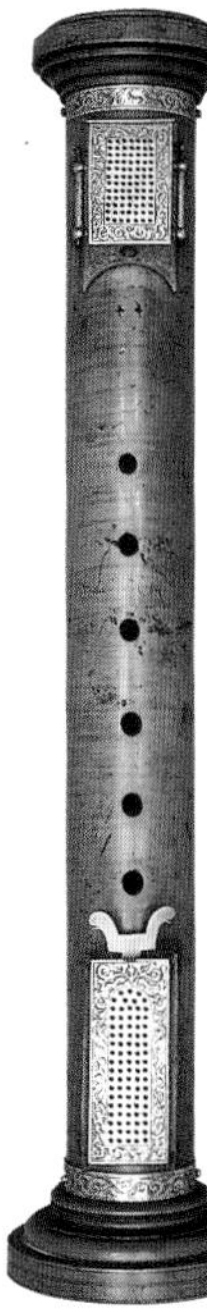

Recorders came in different sizes, giving them different ranges and sound qualities. Today, they are normally referred to (from high to low) as descant or soprano, treble or alto, tenor and bass recorders. There are also more rarely great bass and double bass instruments and at the top end, sopraninos.

The Renaissance recorder was a consort instrument, to be played in groups, with each member playing a different part. Praetorius's *Syntagma musicum* depicts a consort of recorders, from the massive 2.5 m (8 ft 3 in) great bass to the tiny garklein, which played an octave above the descant. **Henry VIII** is on record as having owned 76 recorders, though none is known to have survived.

The recorder failed to maintain its position in the developing orchestra and by the end of the eighteenth century had been usurped by the flute. After almost total invisibility in the nineteenth century, it made a surprise comeback in the hands of Arnold Dolmetsch (1858–1940), who both made and played it. He promoted Renaissance repertory and led the way for a full-scale resurgence as the most widely used **chromatic** teaching instrument and as a tool in the hands of avant-garde composers.

Shawm

In use from the late Middle Ages to the seventeenth century, the shawm was a wooden instrument, often made out of boxwood, with a conical bore opening out from top to bottom. At the top, a cut and scraped reed was fitted over a small brass tube called a 'staple'. The hollow reed was housed in a mouthpiece or 'pirouette', which was placed against the performer's lips and produced a sound not unlike blowing on a blade of grass. As the reed was entire and hollow (rather than a single piece of cane vibrating against a solid mouthpiece) the shawm is classed within the woodwind category as double reed.

Shawms came in families of different-sized instruments, of which the larger were called 'bombards' (the name *Pommer* was used in Germany for alto, tenor and bass shawms). *Hautbois* ('loud wooden instrument') was the French term, for shawms were famously loud. Adopted into English, this was corrupted to 'oboe' and applied to the shawm's indirect Baroque offspring. In the medieval and Renaissance periods, the shawm was particularly popular in outdoor dance bands and was also used for military purposes.

Racket, Dulcian, Curtal

The racket was a short double-reed instrument that looked like a kaleidoscope. It had nine parallel bores, all connected at alternate ends to form a continuous tube, with eight of them arranged around a central ninth. In this last a reed was inserted on a staple, much as in a shawm. The finger-holes were at the front and sides of the racket; it was fingered by both hands in parallel, not left above right as in almost all other wind instruments. Some rackets were made of hard wood, others of ivory.

Further double-reed instruments from the Renaissance include the dulcian and the curtal. An early version of the bassoon, the dulcian was made in one piece rather than in the separable three of the later bassoon. 'Curtal' was the name normally used in England for both dulcian and bassoon until the modern term was adopted in the eighteenth century.

Crumhorn

Instantly recognizable, the crumhorn (also known as the krummhorn or cromorne) was made out of wood – usually boxwood – that had been bent rather than carved. The bell turned dramatically upwards like a hook, and the narrow cylindrical body flared only slightly, making the instrument lower in pitch than one with a conical bore of the same length. Like the recorder, there was a thumb-hole

broken consort ▶ p. 356 chromaticism ▶ p. 357 consort ▶ p. 357

at the back of the instrument and a set of seven finger-holes running down the front. Concealed inside a wind cap was a reed on a staple, as in a shawm. The wind cap was put to the lips rather than the reed itself. It produced a soft buzzing tone.

In the early sixteenth century, Sebastian Virdung illustrated four sizes of crumhorn, but his description mention just three: descant; a middle size covering the alto and tenor range; and bass. A century later, Praetorius referred to five standard sizes, with the lowest instruments extended by means of sliders.

Sackbut

Originating in the fifteenth century, the sackbut, ancestor of the modern trombone, seems to have evolved from the medieval slide trumpet. Credit is usually given to the workshop of Hans Neuschel the Elder of Nuremberg (d. 1503/4) for significantly improving the emerging instrument. The bore was smaller than that of the modern trombone, producing a quieter, sweeter-sounding tone, and the mouthpiece was flatter than its rounded modern descendant. Heard in cathedrals and particularly grand churches, the sackbut was used to accompany choirs.

(NL) Harpsichord
Double-manual harpsichord by Jacob Kirckman, of the famous London family of instrument-makers.
(FL) Recorders
Recorders come in different sizes, offering a variety of ranges: descant, alto, tenor and bass.
(R) Spinet
The spinet was essentially a small version of the harpsichord and was normally used in the home rather than for public performance.

CONSORTS

Most instrumental music of the Renaissance was written for small ensembles. At the time, the major distinction was between the **consort** and the **broken consort**. The former consisted of a set of instruments from the same family. The fact that recorders, shawms, viols, violins and many others existed not as single instruments but as a whole range – from large and deep to small and shrill – meant that each range could exist self-sufficiently if its players chose.

The broken consort brought together instruments of different families. The lute often joined a group of viol players, for example. Most published music stated that the composer expected it to be played by various instruments, or by various combinations of voices and instruments. A broken consort might consist of two plucked, two bowed and two woodwind instruments – maybe lutes, viols and flutes. Four-part vocal music could indeed have been performed by four voices, but also by, for example, two singers and two instrumentalists.

Harpsichord

Most famous of all the early keyboard instruments, the harpsichord was first mentioned in 1397, and the earliest representation to have survived dates from 1425. The harpsichord rose to prominence in the sixteenth century and flourished for a while before its harmonic limitations caused its gradual displacement by the piano in the eighteenth century.

The harpsichord consisted of a wooden frame on which a series of metal strings were mounted, starting with the lowest on the left. The frame was essentially a right-angled triangle whose longest side swept inwards. Across the shortest side lay the keyboard. On depressing any of the keys, the player set in motion a lever device which made a jack jump up and fall immediately back into place. The quill plectrum protruding from the jack thus rose and plucked the strings a single time. Each note sounded much the same every time it was played; there was little of the dynamic variance (except by stopping) so important on a modern piano.

NATIONAL STYLES

Italian harpsichords were light constructions with two complete sets of strings operated by a single keyboard, while Flemish and English makers – among them the famous Ruckers family of Anwerp and the Kirckmans of London – made instruments that had two keyboards, one placed above and behind the other, like two steps of a staircase. Decoration of the case also set instruments from different countries apart: while the English and Germans stuck to the techniques of cabinet-making using some modest marquetry, the Flemish, French and Italians, particularly, went in for extravagant use of gold leaf and painted scenes – sometimes under the lid, which was lifted for performance in the manner of a modern concert grand piano, sometimes over the entire body of the instrument.

Spinet and Virginal

Almost invariably with just one keyboard and a single set of strings and jacks, the spinet was essentially a smaller version of the harpsichord. Its name meant 'little thorn' (referring to the quill) and the mechanism for plucking the string and the resulting sound were both like those of the harpsichord. However, while the harpsichord's strings were attached immediately behind the keyboard and ran away from the player in straight lines, those of the spinet were mounted obliquely to run diagonally from left to right. The spinet, essentially an early harpsichord, was generally used in domestic settings.

The virginal (or virginals) was another form of small harpsichord, usually with one set of strings and jacks and invariably with only one keyboard. The term was used in England to denote all quilled keyboard instruments throughout the Renaissance, which has led to some confusion. It is now taken to refer to instruments with transverse strings – running at right angles to the keys. The longest (therefore deepest-sounding) strings were placed at the front, enabling makers to build virginals in a wide variety of shapes – rectangular, pentagonal and polygonal. These were desk-top instruments, and tended not to be made with a set of built-in legs as harpsichords were. The Fitzwilliam Virginal Book is made up of nearly 300 pieces by the leading composers for this instrument, including Bull and Byrd.

Clavichord

The playing mechanism of the clavichord was quite different from that of the harpsichord family. It was a simpler lever system, working like a seesaw. As the player's fingers landed on the key, its other end rose and struck the string from below. In sound production, the clavichord was thus similar to the dulcimer and the piano. But, unlike on the piano, performers could keep the hammer in touch with the string, changing the pressure on the key to produce an effect like vibrato on a violin. Playing more forcibly produced a louder sound, but the clavichord's construction only really allowed a range of very quiet to slightly less quiet. Because of this, it was largely an instrument for the home, suitable for practice, composition and private performance. The repertory written for it in the twentieth century is surprisingly large.

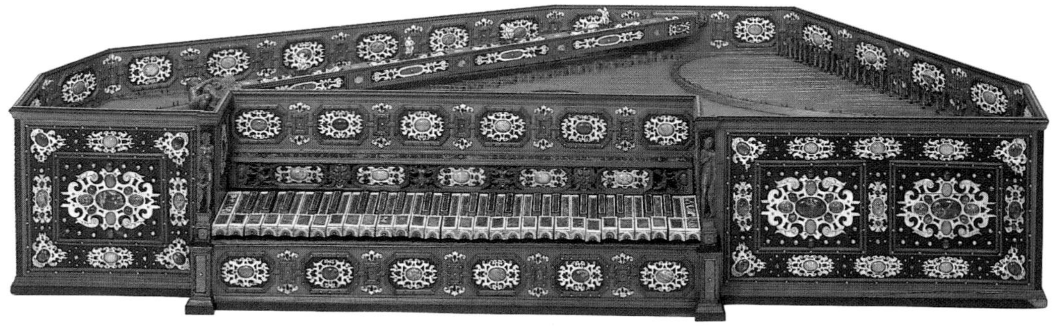

Henry VIII ▶ p. 52

The Renaissance

LISTENING GUIDE

Josquin des Prez

Pater Noster/Ave Maria

WORK: Josquin des Prez Pater noster/Ave Maria, composed before 1521
SCORING: Unaccompanied chorus
EXCERPT: Track 7. Duration: 8 min 35 sec
TIMINGS BASED ON: Music of the Sistine Chapel. Taverner Consort directed by Andrew Parrott (see Recommended CDs)

RECOMMENDED CDs

1. Music of the Sistine Chapel. Taverner Consort. Andrew Parrott, director. Virgin Classics VER5 61309-2

   The Taverner Consort has aimed to recreate a late sixteenth-century performance in the Sistine Chapel. During Josquin's time there, castratos would not have been allowed and the top line – sung here by female sopranos – would have been performed by countertenors.

2. Josquin des Prez: Mass *Pange lingua*. Ensembles Organum and Clément Janequin. Marcel Pérès and Dominique Visse, directors. Harmonia Mundi HMC 901239

   This is probably Josquin's last Mass, and certainly his most famous. It is sung here as part of the feast of Corpus Christi, complete with the appropriate plainchant.

3. Cipriano de Rore: Mass *Praeter rerum seriem* and motets. Tallis Scholars. Peter Phillips, director. Gimmell CD GIM 029

   A Mass by one of Josquin's successors at the court of Ferrara, based on another of his six-voice motets. Rore's setting is sumptuous, for seven voices, and refers to Josquin's piece in several ways.

4. Alexander Agricola: Mass, motets and songs. Huelgas Ensemble. Paul van Nevel, director. Sony Classical SK 60760

   One of the early Renaissance's most distinctive voices, this older contemporary of Josquin was singled out in his time for a certain 'strangeness of manner'. The CD offers a wide-ranging introduction to his work.

5. Orlande de Lassus: *Lagrime di San Pietro*. Ensemble Vocal Européen. Philippe Herreweghe, director. Harmonia Mundi HMC 901483

   Lassus's last masterpiece, completed days before his death, is a cycle of sacred madrigals describing the grief of St Peter at his betrayal of Christ.

In May 1504, Josquin was appointed Provost of the collegiate church of Notre Dame of Condé-sur-Escaut in northern France. In this, he was following the established practice of many Franco-Flemish composers, who usually retired to their homeland after a lifetime of travelling and singing at courts and churches throughout Europe. During his retirement he continued to compose: his best-known Mass, *Pange lingua*, is thought to date from this period. In his last years he also concentrated on a series of songs and motets for six voices which were to have a profound influence on the next generation of composers. Perhaps the best-known of these is the double motet *Pater noster/Ave Maria*. The setting of the Lord's Prayer and the Hail Mary is the musical equivalent of the rosary, and Josquin intended this as an artistic last will and testament. Here too, he was following a tradition established by his elders: both Ockeghem and Du Fay wrote motets with a similar valedictory purpose (Du Fay even stipulated in his will that his work be sung at his death-bed).

MUSIC AS AN ADJUNCT TO PRAYER

Given its probable importance for its composer, it is not surprising that *Pater noster/Ave Maria* sums up both Josquin's style and his technical preoccupations: the syllables are most often sung by several voices simultaneously, so that the words are projected as clearly as possible. It is sometimes claimed that Josquin was the first composer to be truly concerned with the projection and illustration of text. Like many such claims, this is a vast oversimplification; but there is no denying that the clarity of text declamation is one of *Pater noster/*

1. 0':00" The motet begins with the Lord's Prayer.
2. 0':07" The tenor (first canonic voice) enters.
3. 0':13" The altos (second canonic voice) enters a fifth above the tenor.
4. 0':36" A new point of imitation is introduced at 'hallowed be Thy name'.
5. 1':57" 'On earth as it is in heaven': antiphonal exchanges.

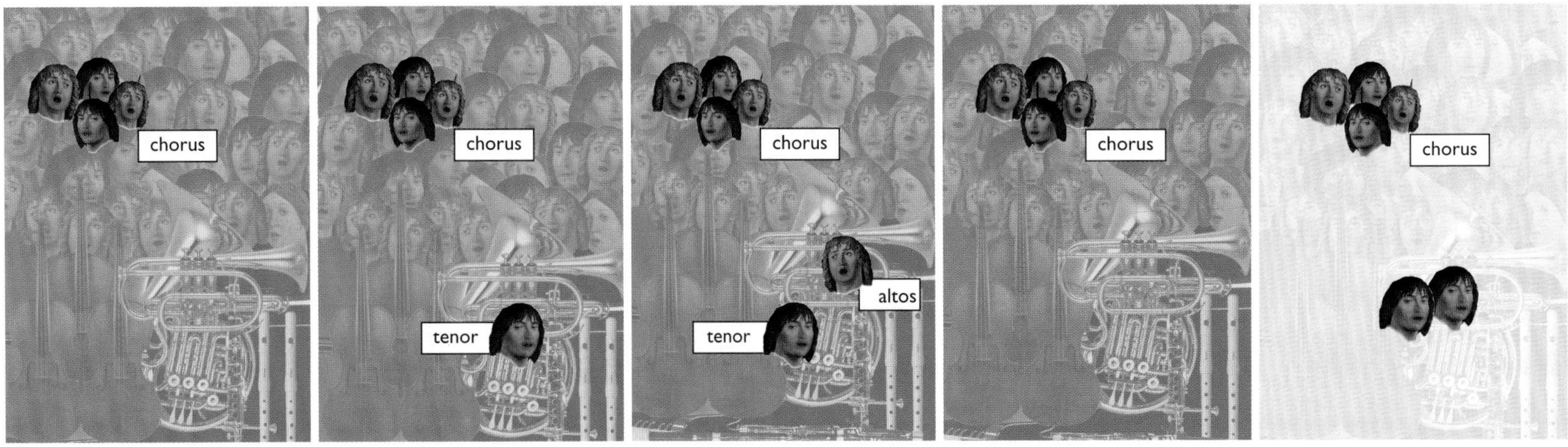

antiphonal music ▶ p. 356 canon ▶ p. 356 castrato ▶ p. 357

Ave Maria's most striking features – one that typifies the music of the High Renaissance. In its directness, simplicity and economy of expression it looks forward to the music of that quintessential Renaissance church composer, **Palestrina**.

HIDDEN SUBTLETY: ART DISGUISING ART

However, a few tricks of the composer's trade lie concealed under the apparent simplicity. One of Josquin's favourite devices is **canon**, a principle whereby two or more different voices sing the same music, but not at the same time: one voice begins, then several bars are allowed to elapse before the next enters. A further twist is that the voices need not start on the same note, but they may be higher or lower relative to each other. In the notation of the time, the singers of these canonic voices read from the same part, so that only five parts are actually written even though six voices are heard. In the *Pater noster*, the two canonic voices are separated by the interval of a fifth, and by a time-distance of three bars. In the *Ave Maria* they are again separated by three bars, but they begin at the same pitch.

The canonic line quotes the plainchant melodies of both texts, in a mildly ornamented form. Around them, Josquin arranges the freely composed voices so that the musical flow is smooth and uninterrupted. The combination of voices used at any given time is constantly changing, creating the kaleidoscopic effect that is so typical of vocal music of the medieval and Renaissance periods. Another choral effect that Josquin introduces, to underline important phrases, is **antiphony**, whereby different groups of singers exchange the same music in a 'statement and response' fashion. This can be heard clearly in the Recommended CD: 'Sancta Maria/regina celi/dulcis et pia/O mater Dei' ('Holy Mary/queen of heaven/sweet and pious/O mother of God'). The CD also includes several motets by Palestrina and other composers who worked in Rome later in the sixteenth century.

SINGER-VIRTUOSOS

Just as virtuoso composer-violinists dominated the instrumental scene in the seventeenth century, and composer-pianists in the eighteenth and nineteenth, so were singers in constant demand throughout the medieval and Renaissance periods. In northern France and modern Belgium and the Netherlands, a rich tradition of cathedral choirs produced a thriving community of singers who travelled throughout Europe, spreading their style of performance far and wide. In their native lands the most successful ones became choirmasters at cathedral and collegiate institutions, or sang in the court chapels of kings or dukes. Some travelled further afield, to Italy for instance, attracted by the long purses of noble music-lovers. The dukes of Milan and Ferrara went to extraordinary lengths – including poaching each other's singers – to maintain private chapels of the highest standard.

Usually, composers were singers who also wrote music. Some would have been paid far less than colleagues who happened to be better singers. Not until the early sixteenth century did musicians begin to draw regular salaries specifically for composing. Over time, composition was increasingly valued (and remunerated) in its own right, but even the most successful composers were employed as performers. **Ockeghem** was renowned as one of the finest basses of his time, and Lassus is said to have been kidnapped several times in boyhood on account of his voice. Rather like the experience of **Joseph Haydn** (1732–1809) in service at the court of Eszterháza centuries later, the everyday life of even these famous musicians was punctuated by the daily obligations of attendance at Mass and holy Offices.

During both the medieval and Renaissance periods, choral ensembles employed either boys or countertenors (also called falsettists) on the top lines, since women were banned from participating in liturgical singing alongside men. During the sixteenth century, countertenors were gradually replaced in some institutions by **castratos** – adult males who had undergone surgery in boyhood to retain their high voices permanently. Women were not banned from all singing, however: in the late Renaissance, virtuoso female sopranos were increasingly sought-after at courtly entertainments.

(TL) Flemish Danse Basse
Miniature from a manuscript showing a Flemish Danse Basse from Josquin's time.
(TR) Josquin Des Prez
Engraving of the Franco-Flemish composer.

6. 4':12"
For the first time all six voices are heard together.

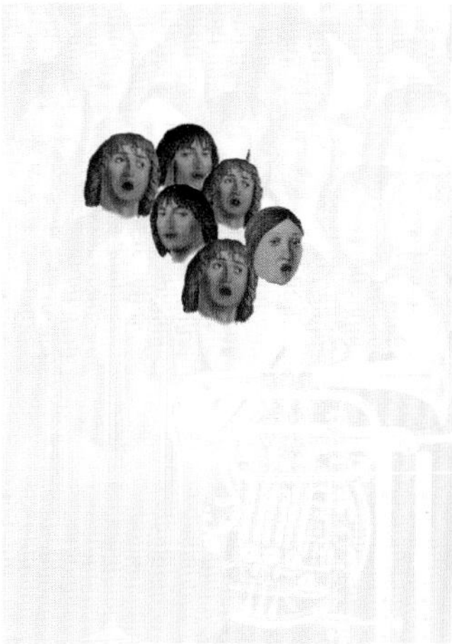

7. 5':06"
'Hail Mary': the second part begins, the tenor enters.

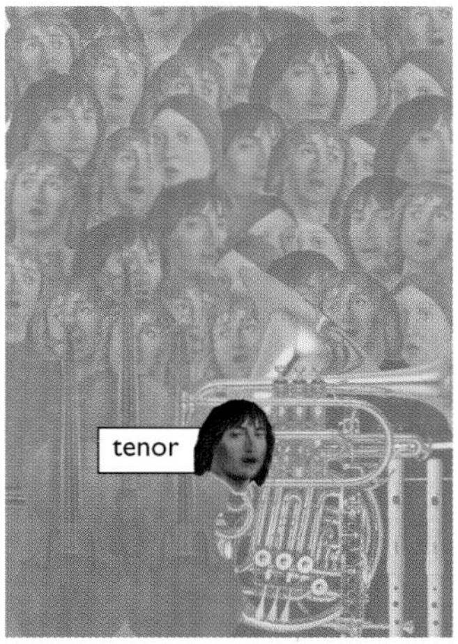

8. 5':14"
The altus enters at the unison (i.e. on the same pitch as the tenor)

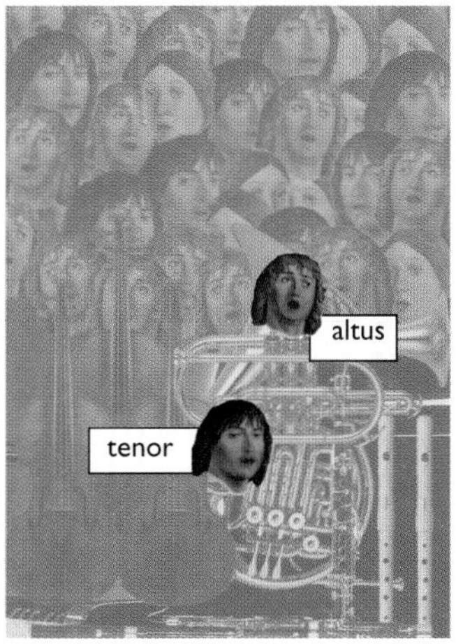

9. 6':58"
There is an antiphonal exchange between two groups of three voices, at 'Holy Mary, queen of heaven'.

10. 8':13"
The voices all sing together for the second and last time.

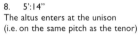

Du Fay ▶ p. 27 Haydn ▶ p. 140 Josquin des Prez ▶ p. 53 Ockeghem ▶ p. 30 Palestrina ▶ p. 56

THE ART OF THE NETHERLANDS

Twenty-five years from its publication, this collection remains the best-rounded anthology of the late fifteenth and early sixteenth centuries, and still the best introduction to the music of the early Renaissance. The director David Munrow was both a pioneer of the early music movement and a free spirit – qualities that are reflected in his choice of pieces and in the manner of their presentation. The collection is equally divided between secular (vocal and instrumental) and sacred genres (motets and Masses). Munrow's approach to the latter is typically resourceful: rather than perform a single Mass, he takes a single movement from five highly contrasted and original works. He includes a Kyrie by **Tinctoris** in which the basses regularly descend to low C and an astonishing 12-voice Gloria by Josquin's contemporary Antoine Brumel (*c.* 1460–*c.* 1515). There are gems among the motets too: Ockeghem's incomparable five-voice 'Intemerata Dei mater' ('Undefiled Mother of God'), which again has some very low bass writing.

The section devoted to songs today sounds the most dated of the set, but Munrow's colourful approach to instrumental participation in the vocal pieces produces some lovely surprises. (As with sacred music of this period, the involvement of instruments in texted music is a matter of contention, but it is now believed that in the early Renaissance, voices and instruments were kept apart more than was thought likely when Munrow made these recordings. Undoubtedly, custom and practice differed from place to place.) The purely instrumental genres are generously represented, allowing Munrow's virtuosity to come to the fore. The anthology includes more works by Josquin than by any other composer but, ironically, several of them have since been shown to be incorrectly attributed to him.

> **RECOMMENDED CD**
>
> The Art of the Netherlands. Early Music Consort of London. David Munrow, director. Virgin Classics 5 61334 2 (2 CDs).

GOMBERT

Gombert served as singer and chapel-master to the emperor Charles V. His style, in common with that of his contemporaries, extends the principle of imitation so that it pervades the music to an unprecedented degree. It is structured, in effect, like a series of musical paragraphs: each section of text has its own motif (called a point of imitation) which, presented in one voice, works its way through all the others in turn (often more than once) before being replaced by the next. Because a new point of imitation is usually introduced before the previous one has been fully exhausted, the texture has a seamless quality that is found in all of Gombert's music, whether sacred or secular. His style changes little between genres. Compare a song like 'Je prens congie' ('I Take Leave') with the motet 'Media vita' ('In the Midst of Life'); the same procedure governs both. This method of pervasive imitation influenced composers of the following generations and was central to the style of the most famous Renaissance composers, **Tallis**, **Byrd** and **Victoria** among them.

> **'GREENSLEEVES'**
>
> 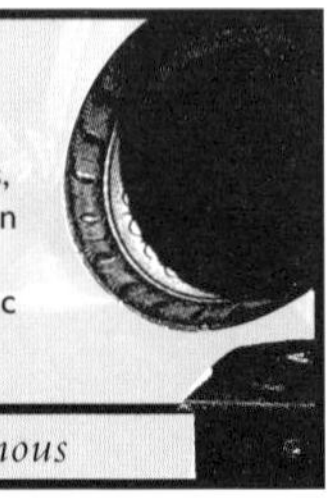
>
> 'Greensleeves' is perhaps the best-known Renaissance tune in English-speaking countries, and it is often incorrectly thought to have been composed by Henry VIII. Like many myths, it has its basis in truth: Henry was an enthusiastic musician who wrote several pieces.
>
> **POPULAR MELODY** *Anonymous*

Gombert's sound-world is typically dense and dark because he tends to use all the available voices most of the time. This gives his work a brooding quality that is very involving, and reminiscent at times of Ockeghem in the previous century. Another striking feature of Gombert's music is his use of telling and pungent **dissonances**, which he sometimes uses to illustrate the text, as in 'Media vita' at the words 'pro peccatis nostris' ('for our sins').

> **RECOMMENDED CD**
>
> Nicolas Gombert: 'Regina caeli', 'Media vita', 'Je prens congie', *Missa Paschale*, etc. Huelgas Ensemble. Paul van Nevel, director. Sony Classical SK 48249.

LASSUS: CHANSONS

Lassus was music's archetypal 'Renaissance man', expert in all the genres available to him, whether sacred or secular. He was equally adept at setting German songs (he lived for most of his life in Munich), Italian madrigals and lighter texts (his formative musical experiences took place in Italy) or Latin motets. However, his mother-tongue was French and, perhaps for this reason, his most personal contribution was in the domain of the chanson, where he followed in the footsteps of

> **'AUTHENTICITY'**
>
> Since the 1950s, a growing interest in early music has sparked much research into the performance practices of the Middle Ages and the Renaissance. The aim has been to recreate as closely as possible the sound and the performance style of the music, drawing from as many sources of information as possible. Where original instruments are unavailable, for example, copies are made from contemporary illustrations in theoretical treatises or even paintings; the same paintings can also give clues as to how the instrument was played. Eye-witness accounts and payment records provide information about the precise forces used in a given performance. And in the case of ensemble music of later periods, orchestral parts indicate even the smallest details of tempo, ornamentation and phrasing. All this information must be interpreted and evaluated, and performer and musicologist often work closely together. For dramatic works the principle has sometimes been extended to include staging, costumes, dance and gestures. Necessarily, there are limits to this quest for so-called 'authenticity'. No matter how precisely we could re-create a given performance (and certain aspects can only be guessed at), we can never put ourselves in the place of a listener from the past. Experience can only be contemporary.
>
> 

diminutions ▶ p. 358 dissonance ▶ p. 358

THE VOICE IN EARLY MUSIC

Although researchers continue to make discoveries about the way music was performed in the Middle Ages and the Renaissance, little is known about one of its most crucial aspects: how did singers actually sound? Many medieval theorists and writers mention performers with voices 'like those of angels', and words such as 'sweetness' occur again and again; equally, the same authors criticize others for 'braying like asses'. But although such remarks tell us how people felt about 'good' or 'bad' singing, it does not help modern performers to recreate the sort of sounds singers made. It is difficult to know how far modern vocal techniques can be applied to early music. Peter Phillips, the director of the Tallis Scholars, has observed that if we were to hear a choir from the fourteenth century, we might be horrified! In recent years, a number of groups, like the French Ensemble Organum, have deliberately adopted a style of singing that challenges received notions of 'beauty'.

Janequin and **Sermisy**. Lassus's extraordinary sensitivity to text is everywhere in evidence, whether painting a musical picture of a nocturnal landscape ('La nuit froide et sombre'), serenading a lady ('Las! Me faut-il') or describing a scurrilous anecdote ('En un chasteau, Un jeune moine'). His wit and lightness of touch are obvious, but to these qualities Lassus adds a psychological acuity that is truly modern and sets him apart from many chanson composers. The songs give an idea of Lassus's tastes: 'Vignon, vignon' is a delightfully whimsical drinking-song, addressing wine in almost personal terms.

RECOMMENDED CD

Orlande de Lassus: Chansons et Moresche. Ensemble Clément Janequin, Dominique Visse, director. Harmonia Mundi HMA 901391.

His complex character had a darker side, however, that led to the deep depression of his final years; 'O foible esprit' is in this more troubled vein. In modern times Lassus might have been diagnosed as manic-depressive. There is a hint of this in 'Lucessit jam o socii', whose text is split between Latin phrases (biblical references) and the interjections in French of a group of drinking companions. The Ensemble Clément Janequin cleverly underscores it by dividing the instrumental accompaniment between the organ (sacred) and the lute (courtly). This French group has long specialized in the chanson repertory, and they respond to every shade of Lassus's inspiration, delivering the bawdier pieces with an energy that certainly challenges the popular view of Renaissance polyphony as 'monk-music'. Besides, Lassus's monks are usually up to no good.

BYRD: COMPLETE KEYBOARD MUSIC

Given the excellence and diversity of his vocal music, it could come as a surprise that Byrd is also often considered the first great keyboard composer. He wrote everything from short preludes to extended contrapuntal fantasias on various subjects, similar in idiom to vocal music. There are sets of variations on popular tunes and stylized dance movements of the sort that eventually led to the suites of **J. S. Bach**. Such dances were often presented in pairs, with a slow one in duple time followed by a fast one in triple time. Very common in England at the end of the sixteenth century, was the pavan and galliard pairing; Byrd wrote many of these. The structure of the two movements is the same: three sections (each usually of eight or 16 bars, but sometimes as many as 32) are presented one after the other. Each is immediately repeated. These repeats involve **diminutions** – that is, ornaments and embellishments designed to show off the performer's skill.

This seven-CD set includes all of Byrd's keyboard music, recorded by the harpsichordist and organist Davitt Moroney over a period of several years.

RECOMMENDED CD

William Byrd: The Complete Keyboard Music. Davitt Moroney (harpsichords, muselar [Flemish virginal], organ, chamber organ, virginal and clavichord). Hyperion CDA 66551/7 (7 CDs).

(BL) King David Playing the Psaltery *by Girolamo da Santa Croce*
Copies of early instruments such as the psaltery are made when recreating contemporary sounds.
(TL) Lutenist
French manuscript showing a lutenist wooing his lover.
(TR) William Byrd
Byrd wrote prolifically for the keyboard, incorporating popular melodies into his pieces.
(BR) Henry VIII
Henry VIII is known to have been an enthusiastic musician and composer.

J. S. Bach ▶ p. 106 Byrd ▶ p. 49 Gombert ▶ p. 51 Janequin ▶ p. 52 Lassus ▶ p. 54 Sermisy ▶ p. 56 Tallis ▶ p. 57 Tinctoris ▶ p. 31 Victoria ▶ p. 57

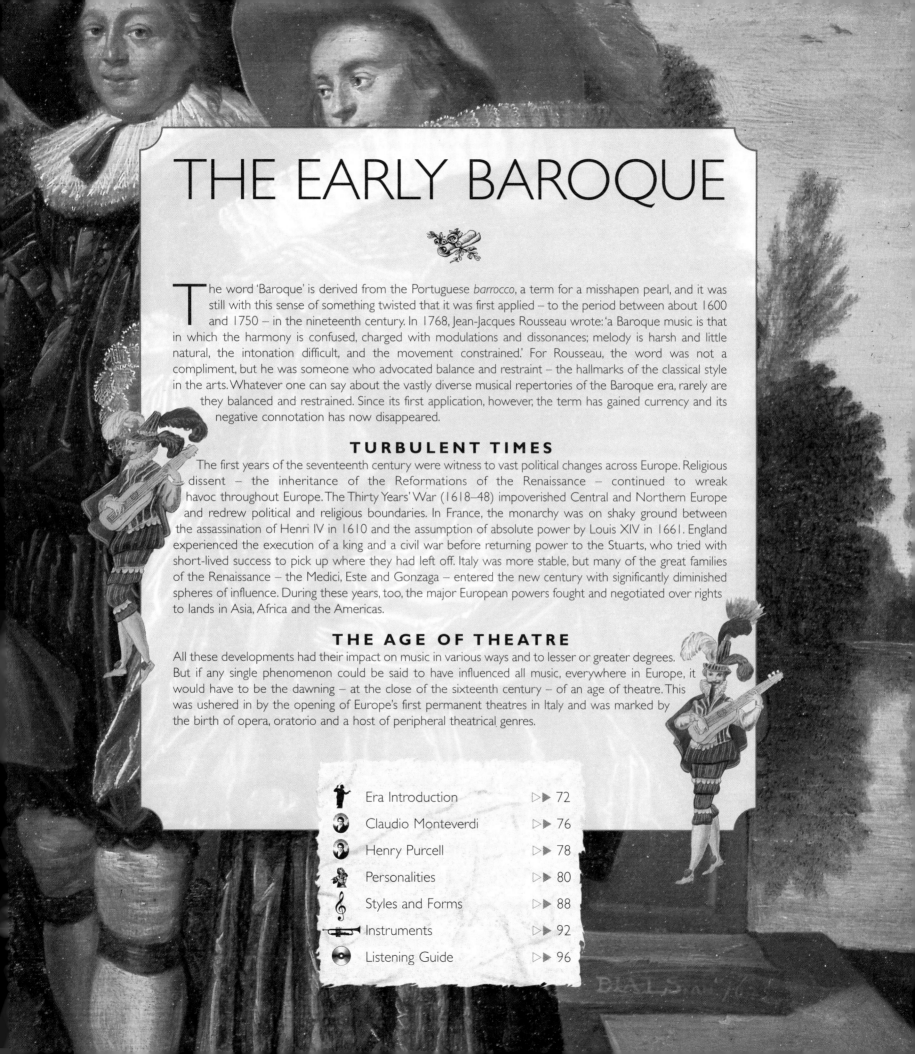

THE EARLY BAROQUE

The word 'Baroque' is derived from the Portuguese *barrocco*, a term for a misshapen pearl, and it was still with this sense of something twisted that it was first applied – to the period between about 1600 and 1750 – in the nineteenth century. In 1768, Jean-Jacques Rousseau wrote: 'a Baroque music is that in which the harmony is confused, charged with modulations and dissonances; melody is harsh and little natural, the intonation difficult, and the movement constrained.' For Rousseau, the word was not a compliment, but he was someone who advocated balance and restraint – the hallmarks of the classical style in the arts. Whatever one can say about the vastly diverse musical repertories of the Baroque era, rarely are they balanced and restrained. Since its first application, however, the term has gained currency and its negative connotation has now disappeared.

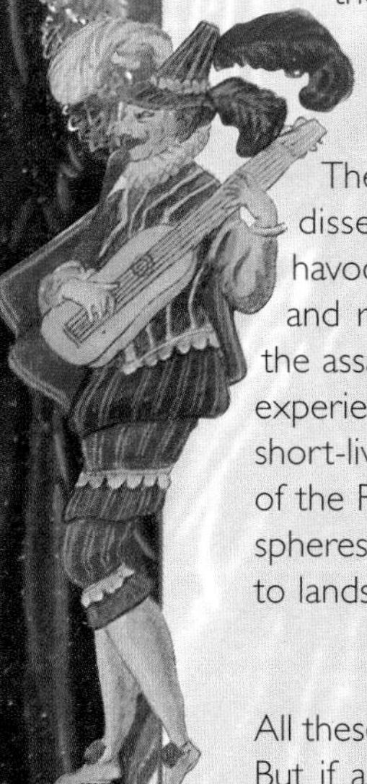

TURBULENT TIMES

The first years of the seventeenth century were witness to vast political changes across Europe. Religious dissent – the inheritance of the Reformations of the Renaissance – continued to wreak havoc throughout Europe. The Thirty Years' War (1618–48) impoverished Central and Northern Europe and redrew political and religious boundaries. In France, the monarchy was on shaky ground between the assassination of Henri IV in 1610 and the assumption of absolute power by Louis XIV in 1661. England experienced the execution of a king and a civil war before returning power to the Stuarts, who tried with short-lived success to pick up where they had left off. Italy was more stable, but many of the great families of the Renaissance – the Medici, Este and Gonzaga – entered the new century with significantly diminished spheres of influence. During these years, too, the major European powers fought and negotiated over rights to lands in Asia, Africa and the Americas.

THE AGE OF THEATRE

All these developments had their impact on music in various ways and to lesser or greater degrees. But if any single phenomenon could be said to have influenced all music, everywhere in Europe, it would have to be the dawning – at the close of the sixteenth century – of an age of theatre. This was ushered in by the opening of Europe's first permanent theatres in Italy and was marked by the birth of opera, oratorio and a host of peripheral theatrical genres.

The Early Baroque

INTRODUCTION

The revival and imitation of ancient theatrical genres in sixteenth-century Italy bore fruit in seventeenth-century England and France in the works of the great dramatists of those countries: William Shakespeare and Christopher Marlowe, Pierre Corneille and Jean Racine. In Italy, however, the sixteenth-century innovations in spoken drama were followed in the next century not by a great national spoken theatre, but by the creation of opera. If Shakespeare and Corneille were the heirs of Renaissance theatre in England and France, their counterpart in Italy was Claudio Monteverdi (1567–1643).

Opera was not the only musical genre to grow from the roots of theatre. In between the acts of spoken drama the Italians placed *intermedi*, musical interludes that could be as simple as a madrigal or as grand as the famous *intermedi* of 1589. *Intermedi* continued to be composed in Italy well into the seventeenth century; in fact they were sometimes performed in the intermissions of operas. They also served as inspiration for courtly entertainment outside Italy, giving rise to the masque in England and the *ballet de cour* in France.

SACRED MUSIC

Opera, masque and *ballet de cour* are theatre music, but it is also possible for music to be theatrical without being intended for the theatre. It is the development of theatrical modes of expression, in all music, that shows the extent of the influence theatre had on Baroque music. In sacred music this is most evident in the oratorio, which is essentially an unstaged religious opera, but a more general sense of theatre infused other sacred genres as well. Texts, even of conservative genres like the motet, increasingly focused on the speaker's emotional response to biblical events, especially to the Passion, the gospel account of the Crucifixion. The dramatic possibilities of the Passion held a strong attraction for Protestants, who produced increasingly elaborate settings which were to culminate in the famous Passions of **Johann Sebastian Bach** (1685–1750).

KEY EVENTS

1598 Huguenots granted freedom of worship and equal rights in the Edict of Nantes
1599 Globe Theatre, home of Shakespeare's plays, built in London
1602 Persecution of Protestants in Bohemia and Hungary
1603 Death of Elizabeth I; James VI of Scotland becomes first Stuart king of England as James I
1606 Shakespeare writes *King Lear* and *Macbeth*
1610 Assassination of Henri IV of France, who is succeeded by nine-year-old Louis XIII; Galileo uses telescope to observe Jupiter's satellites
1611 Authorized 'King James' Bible issued
1618 Beginning of Thirty Years' War
1619 Hamburg and Venice banks founded; Pilgrims leave Plymouth, England, for North America
1628 Harvey publishes discovery of blood circulation
1630 Tirso de Molina writes *El burlador de Sevilla*, first dramatization of Don Juan legend
1632 Rembrandt paints *Anatomy Lesson*
1637 Descartes inaugurates modern study of mathematics; Corneille writes *Le Cid*
1642 English Civil War breaks out between Charles I and Parliament
1645 Gianlorenzo Bernini starts *Ecstasy of St Teresa*
1661 Louis XIV begins personal absolute rule in France
1666 Great Fire of London destroys many buildings in the city but wipes out the plague
1675 Christopher Wren rebuilds St Paul's Cathedral, London

This theatrical aesthetic can even be traced in purely instrumental genres. Of central importance to Baroque instrumental music is the fundamentally dramatic principal of contrast: between forces, between dynamics, between textures and – most important for the development of musical technique – between harmonies. The need to place harmonic areas in opposition to one another was the primary impetus for the development of functional tonality and, in this sense, even this most important technical development was a theatrical one.

EMPIRICISM: HARVEY, GALILEO, DESCARTES

Broadly speaking, empiricism, from the Greek *empeiria* ('experience'), is a philosophical tradition that accepts as fact only what can be verified by observation, or experience, through the use of the five senses. Galileo Galilei's support of Copernican theory was a result of his observation of the planet Venus through a telescope. His insistence that what he saw was more authoritative than the traditional teachings of the church brought down on him the persecution of the Catholic Inquisition. In contrast, when William Harvey published the results of his observations on the circulation of blood in 1628, he avoided persecution. Instead of attacking the church's dogma directly, he concentrated on overturning Galenic theory (based on the second-century writings of Claudius Galen and at the core of medieval and Renaissance medical thought). More controversial than Harvey, and less easily identified as heretical than Galileo, was René Descartes, whose famous soundbite *Cogito ergo sum* ('I think, therefore I am') claimed that the only proof of human existence is our own awareness of ourselves.

THE SPREAD OF OPERA

The greatest and most enduring result of the dramatic impulse of the Baroque era was opera, a genre that draws together art, architecture, music and literature. The operas of the seventeenth century are an index of the latest developments in all these arts. The scenery, in imitation of the scenery used in Renaissance theatre, drew on new experiments in perspective and illusion. The theatres themselves, often designed by the leading architects of the day (Buontalenti in Florence, Palladio in Parma) drew on classical and modern principles of performance space. The plots of operas were mostly drawn, in the seventeenth century, from either mythology or history. But the telling of the tales reflected the most up-to-date literary ideals. The librettos of Monteverdi's last two operas, for example, were written by the experimental poet Giovanni Francesco Busenello. And, of course, the music itself was on the cutting edge, from the early experiments in recitative at the turn of the sixteenth century, to the development of new aria forms throughout the middle and late seventeenth.

From the beginning, opera was an elite art. The first operas were created and performed for small invited audiences at wealthy courts: Florence,

ballet de cour ▶ p. 356 *intermedio* ▶ p. 359

Mantua, Parma and Rome. The 'invitation only' nature of the genre changed forever when the first public opera theatre opened in Venice in 1637. It would be a mistake to overestimate the impact that event had on the class of opera goer, however. The Venetian opera houses were funded by Venice's patrician families and were paid for mostly by the sale of subscription boxes to wealthy families. From the start, opera was expensive to produce, and access to the results were limited to those with money to spare.

COLONIZING THE 'NEW WORLD'

If the sixteenth century was the age of discovery, then the seventeenth was the age of colonization. Asia, Africa and the Americas all became the target of European settlers, fuelled by various motives. The English East India and West African companies and the Dutch West India Company were among the purely capitalist ventures. Religious groups such as the Puritans, who settled in what is now Massachusetts in the 1620s, sought places to found communities based on their religious ideals. Other religious emigrants went in search of potential converts: Catholic missionary activity – led by the Jesuits and Franciscans, who focused on Central and South America – was at fever pitch. In all cases the settlers found people who were already settled, with customs, economies and religions of their own, and the result was rarely a positive one for the native people. In the face of hardship and local hostility, the emigrants turned to music for solace and, in the case of the Catholic missionaries, as a tool of conversion. From Nova Scotia to Peru, European musical genres took root and thrived.

(TL) Court Musician
Example of a ballet costume worn at the court of the French king, Louis XIV.
(TR) The Pilgrim Fathers
Many groups left England to found religious communities in the New World.
(BR) Anatomy Lesson by Rembrandt
Dissection allowed greater knowledge of the physiological make-up of the human body.

THE THIRTY YEARS' WAR

Of the religious conflicts that rocked Europe during this period, the most devastating was the Thirty Years' War. Focused in Central Europe, its repercussions were felt across the continent. Although the war 'officially' began in 1618, it was part of a series of conflicts reaching back to Martin Luther's lifetime (1483–1546). By the time peace was declared in 1648, the power structures of the area had been radically reshaped. Among the losers were the Habsburgs, who emerged with significantly reduced power; among the winners, France and Sweden expanded their territorial holdings. Music had winners and losers too. Dresden, the once-dazzling capital of Saxony was now poverty stricken and unable to pay its most glorious musician, **Heinrich Schütz** (1585–1672); Hamburg, however, emerged from the war a new musical power.

NEW LUTHERAN MUSIC

The development of chorale-based genres was localized at first and reflected the fortunes of individual musical centres; of these, the most fortunate was Hamburg. Situated in a prime position on the North Sea and far enough from the centres of conflict to maintain neutrality, Hamburg hummed along while its southern neighbours languished. The city's culture was enriched by influxes of people from all over Europe fleeing religious per-secution, in particular Protestants from the Spanish Netherlands and Jews from Portugal. During the first half of the seventeenth century, Hamburg attained a cultural ascendancy that it was to maintain into the eighteenth century. As home to a series of great organists, including **Dietrich Buxtehude** (*c.* 1637–1707), it became the centre of the burgeoning repertory of Protestant organ music.

SCIENTIFIC REVOLUTIONS

In science, the turn of the century was witness to the rise of the empirical method as opposed to the established mode of reliance on, and refinement of, a canon of written authority. The artisitic potential of a scientific method based on observation and demonstration was not lost on Rembrandt. In his *Anatomy Lesson* (1632), the anatomist gestures elegantly as the well-dressed students crane their necks for a better view of the displayed corpse. Dissection allowed scientists to develop observation-based theories of human physiology and biology. The science of astronomy was similarly affected by new instruments which made it possible to observe the planets and stars. The ongoing argument of the place of the earth in the universe was now subjected to observed phenomena, giving support to Copernican theory (that the earth rotated round the sun, not the other way round) and undermining the authority of the Catholic church's claim that the earth was at the centre of the universe.

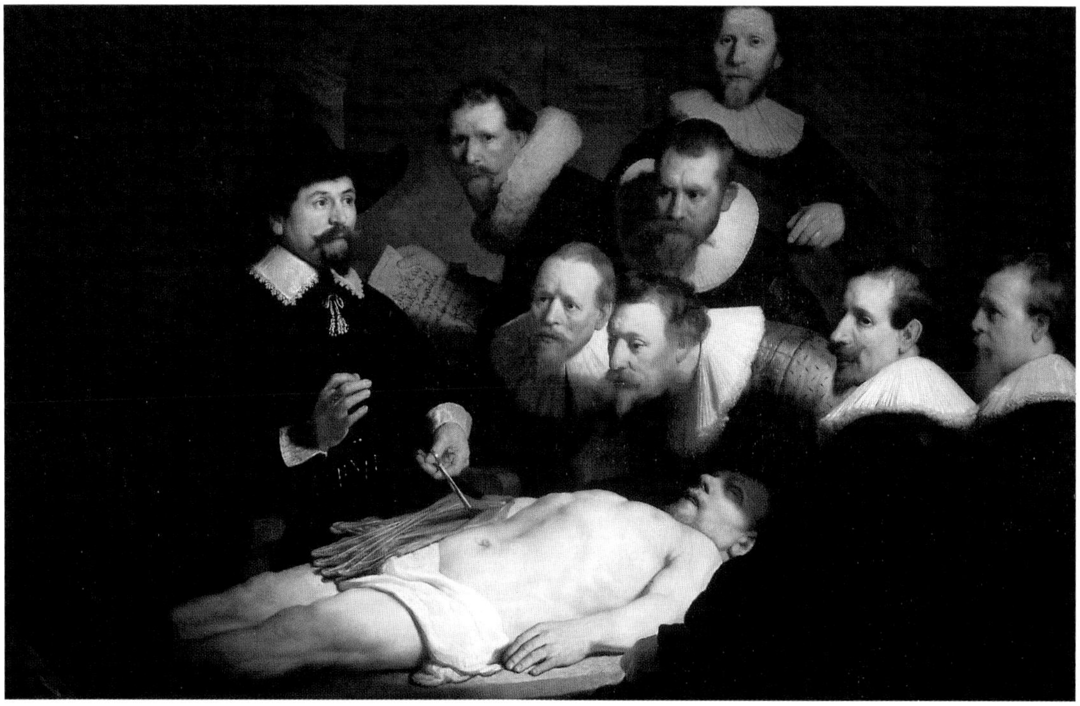

J. S. Bach ▶ p. 106 Buxtehude ▶ p. 80 Monteverdi ▶ p. 76 Schütz ▶ p. 86

MASQUE AND *BALLET DE COUR*

In the first part of the seventeenth century, two traditions of absolute power were struggling to maintain their hold. In England, after the death of Elizabeth I in 1603, the Stuart dynasty fought for survival for 40 years. Then the dream crumbled in the face of civil war and the execution of the king, Charles I, in 1649. Eleven years later Charles II was restored to the throne and proceeded with absolute rule in England and Scotland; James II followed the same route until he was driven out in 1688. In France the chronology was reversed: 50 years of turmoil following the assassination of Henri IV in 1610 were ended in 1661 when Louis XIV seized absolute power.

Both the Stuarts and Louis XIV took a cue from sixteenth-century Italian rulers in making musical theatre a tool of power. The English masque and the French *ballet de cour* brought together the finest writers, composers, performers and artists the countries had to offer. But whatever the genres' artistic merits, their *raison d'etre* was the glorification of the ruling class, in particular the king. The masque's loosely constructed plots were designed to allow frequent oblique reference to contemporary politics: *Britannia triumphans* ('Britain Triumphant', 1638), for example, included remarks supporting recent policy decisions and ridiculing the Puritans. Similarly, Louis' insatiable need for pageantry was met by plot structures that allowed mythological stories to be fitted loosely around the central theme of the king's majesty. An engraving survives that shows him performing in the *Ballet du Roy des Festes de Bacchus* ('The King's Ballet on the Feast of Bacchus', 1651) as the god Apollo, a role that inspired Louis' epithet of 'Sun King'.

Audience Participation

Both genres also included audience participation. In England the bulk of the work was performed by courtiers, offering them the chance to dress up and be noticed. In the *Masque of Blackness* (1605), the queen and some of her ladies masqueraded as the daughters of Niger. Audience participation could itself be an instrument of power: in the *ballet de cour* it was reserved for the final *grand ballet*, and Louis used this opportunity not only to show off his own excellent dancing skills, but also to impose what must have been a nearly paralysing authority over many of his closest courtiers who were lucky enough to be invited to participate.

Underlying all empirical research was a philosophical attitude that set human experience above faith and imagination. Apart from its impact on science, therefore, empiricism was to have a lasting influence on the discipline of philosophy.

REPERCUSSIONS OF THE PROTESTANT REFORMATION

A century after Martin Luther wrote his '95 theses' (1517), condemning the corruption of the Catholic church, and nailed them to the door of the castle church in Wittenberg, Germany, all of Northern Europe was mired in religious conflict. The Thirty Years' War was the most significant consequence of the sixteenth-century reformations, but was far from the only one. As is often the case, however, in the midst of human tragedy, music flourished. The early seventeenth century saw the invention and development of a repertory of Protestant music to stand alongside the Catholic musical heritage. At its core was the **chorale**, or monophonic congregational hymn. Congregational singing, which had been introduced by Luther, was central to Protestant worship. The chorale served as a structural framework for a variety of new polyphonic genres, as chant had done centuries earlier for Catholic music.

REPERCUSSIONS OF THE COUNTER-REFORMATION

The Council of Trent was finally called by Pope Paul III as a reaction against the Protestant crisis and was intended to reaffirm and redefine Catholicism. Implicit in the decrees of the Council of Trent was the goal of stimulating the faithful to piety by stirring them emotionally. This call to reach out to the community of believers and actively work to evoke religious fervour by appealing to the emotions, was one of the most fundamental changes to come out of Trent.

Of primary importance in the Catholic church's outreach programmes were two relatively new religious groups: the Oratorians, founded by Filippo Neri, and the Jesuits of Ignatius Loyola. Both used theatre to draw the populace to religious worship. It was in the Chiesa Nuova in Rome, home to the Oratorians, that the *Rappresentatione di Anima, et di Corpo* ('Representation of the Soul and Body', 1600) by **Emilio de' Cavalieri** (*c.* 1550–1602) was first performed. This work played an important part in the rise of the oratorio – the dramatico-religious form takes its name from the halls where the Oratorians met.

The Jesuits' primary purpose was education, and Rome was the home of a number of Jesuit colleges, including the Seminario Romano, the Collegio Germanico and the Collegio Inglese. In all these, sacred drama served both as an educational tool and an instrument of worship. Dramas with music were produced as early as the first years of the sixteenth century. A landmark event was the production at the Collegio Germanico, in the Carnival of 1606, of the first sacred opera, *Eumelio*, with music by Agostino Agazzari (1578–1640).

BARBARINI ROME

In spite of the work of the Oratorians and Jesuits, Rome in the first years of the seventeenth century was shrouded in Counter-Reformation severity. Pope Clement VIII grew increasingly hostile to secular music in the later years of his reign, and the climate of austerity continued under Paul V. A new age was ushered in with the crowning of Maffeo Barbarini as Urban VIII in 1623. Like all popes, Barbarini set himself immediately to the task of placing his own family in strategic positions throughout Rome. Two nephews were elevated to the cardinalate (in 1623 and 1627) and a third married into the Colonna family, one of Rome's oldest and most prestigious dynasties. Other powerful positions were distributed among the pope's friends and associates.

An amateur poet, Barbarini was a lover of all the arts. His favourite artist was Gianlorenzo Bernini, whose sculptures still grace many of Rome's piazzas and churches. Among Bernini's projects was the rebuilding of the Palazzo alle Quattro Fontane, which held the Teatro Barbarini. The Teatro opened in 1632 with a religious opera, *Il Sant'Alessio* ('Saint Alexis'), influenced by the oratorio and sacred Jesuit drama. The text was by one of Urban VIII's close associates, Cardinal Giulio Rospigliosi, later Pope Clement IX. The music

chorale ▶ p. 357 *comédie-ballet* ▶ p. 357 semi-opera ▶ p. 362 *tragédie lyrique* ▶ p. 363

RESTORATION LONDON

After the restoration of Charles II to the throne in 1660, the monarchy never resumed the absolute authority of pre-civil-war England. Artistically, the victim of the Civil War was the royal masque. It was replaced – in its role of praising the monarchy – by the anthem and, especially, the ode. The major events of the reigns of Charles II, James II and William and Mary can be traced in the odes and welcome songs of **Henry Purcell** (1659–95) and his contemporaries.

The Civil War and Commonwealth left their mark on music in two important ways. First, domestic music-making, which had long held an important place in English life, was revitalized as the dispersal of the court left musicians to seek posts in private homes, and the upper classes had to fall back on their own resources for entertainment. The masque moved from the court to the home, where it was performed with more modest means than before. Second, royalists who fled to the continent were exposed to the latest music in France and Italy; when they returned they brought their newly formed musical tastes with them. These two changes came together in the music theatre of the Restoration. Stripped of its pageantry and focus on royal glorification, the masque gained both formal unity and dramatic intensity, and under influence from continental Europe it was transformed into a new genre: the **semi-opera**, to which **John Blow** (1649–1708) contributed *Venus and Adonis* (1685) and Purcell *Dido and Aeneas* (1689).

was by **Stefano Landi** (*c.* 1586–1639). Other operas, both sacred and secular, followed and for a brief but significant period in the 1630s, Rome became the centre of opera production in Italy.

MEDICI FLORENCE

The pageantry of the Medici court had an oddly symbiotic relationship with the city's intellectual life. Since the fifteenth century, Florence had been one of Europe's intellectual centres, with learning concentrated not in one of the great universities but in small groups or academies of varying formality. Among these was a group of scholars, poets and musicians who began meeting in the 1570s in the home of the nobleman Giovanni de' Bardi. It is referred to in various contemporary accounts as the 'Camerata' (lit. 'society'), and under that name it has come to hold an almost mythical place in the history of opera. The Camerata's actual history is complex, but its contribution to opera is unequivocal. In 1598 the 'first opera', *Dafne*, with a libretto by member Ottavio Rinuccini and music by **Jacopo Peri** (1561–1633) was performed at the home of the group's then-patron, Jacopo Corsi (d. 1604). Although only a couple of choruses survive from this experiment, it set the stage for the future of opera.

The wedding of Grand Duke Ferdinando I and Christine of Lorraine in 1589 marked the beginning of the Medici family's last great reign. The family continued to rule Florence – and play the role of patron – into the eighteenth century; but never after Ferdinando's death in 1609 would they equal their former splendour. A breathtaking succession of important musical events was inaugurated by the wedding festivities of 1589, which included elaborate *intermedi* sung by the next generation's leading composers and singers of monody: **Giulio Caccini** (*c.* 1545–1618), Peri and Vittoria Archilei (*c.* 1545–1618).

LOUIS XIV'S PARIS

Louis XIV, who had become king of France at the age of four, assumed full power in 1661, following years of political uncertainty and the dictatorial ministries of cardinals Richelieu and Mazarin. Learning the lessons of his childhood, Louis took all possible steps to make his leadership absolute. He relied heavily on patronage of the arts to reflect and even invent his majesty. During his reign academies were established for painting and sculpture, science, music and other artistic and intellectual disciplines.

At the king's side throughout was an Italian-born musician and dancer, **Jean-Baptiste Lully** (1632–87). Lully joined Louis' court shortly after the king assumed power and remained its central musical – indeed artistic – figure until his death. In the early years of Lully's leadership, the principal courtly musical genre was the *ballet de cour*. In the 1660s, *ballets de cour* gave way to ***comédie-ballet***, on which Lully collaborated with the actor-playwright Molière, notably *Le bourgeois gentilhomme* ('The Middle-Class Gentleman') in 1670. *Comédies-ballets* began to decline in the 1670s under the influence of Italian opera. The French response, to all intents and purposes invented by Lully with Philippe Quinault, was the ***tragédie lyrique***. Although still under the umbrella of royal patronage, the *tragédie lyrique*, which incorporated ballet, was performed in public theatres before a wider audience than its predecessor, and solely by 'professionals'. Lully's *Armide* (1686) continued to be performed up until the Revolution.

(L) Commedia dell' Arte
Scene from an Italian comedy; the court in Florence, in particular, hosted many lavish theatrical entertainments.
(TR) Armide
Costume design for Lully's popular opera Armide.
(MR) The Restoration
The English king, Charles II, lands at Dover to reclaim the throne after 11 years of the Republic.
(BR) Versailles
The Palace of Versailles, home to the court of Louis XIV, the 'Sun King'.

Blow ▶ p. 80 Caccini ▶ p. 80 Cavalieri ▶ p. 81 Landi ▶ p. 83 Lully ▶ p. 84 Peri ▶ p. 84 Purcell ▶ p. 78

The Early Baroque

CLAUDIO MONTEVERDI

Claudio Monteverdi (1567–1643) stands as one of the last great composers of the Renaissance and one of the first of the Baroque. He studied composition with the madrigalist Marc'Antonio Ingegneri (*c.* 1547–92) in his home town of Cremona. When he took his first professional post in his mid twenties, he had already published six books of music and established himself as a leading madrigal writer. His three surviving operas, *Orfeo* ('Orpheus', 1607), *Il ritorno d'Ulisse in patria* ('Ulysses's Homecoming', 1640) and *L'incoronazione di Poppea* ('The Coronation of Poppaea', 1642), have earned him an important place in the history of that genre. He also wrote sacred music; *Vespro della Beata Vergine* ('Vespers of the Blessed Virgin', 1610) are breathtaking in their stylistic diversity. After moving to Venice in 1613, Monteverdi composed and conducted virtuosic sacred music for the choir of St Mark's, the greatest church choir of the day.

In his madrigals of around 1600 Monteverdi adopted new harmonic and melodic modes of expression, earning him a scolding from his more conservative contemporaries and branding him for future generations as a revolutionary. But revolutions are about ideologies; Monteverdi's aim, whether following the rules or breaking them, was simply to express the text as convincingly as possible. In all his works Monteverdi's supreme achievement was a seamless union of words and music. Our understanding of Monteverdi's life and works is greatly enriched by his extraordinary surviving correspondence. With the exception of Orlande de Lassus (1532–94), no other composer before Wolfgang Amadeus Mozart (1756–91) left so many letters; they discuss in fascinating detail his compositional aims and musical ideals.

CLAUDIO MONTEVERDI: WORKS

- **Light genres:** *Canzonette* (1584), *Scherzi musicali* (1607), *Scherzi musicali* (1632)
- **Accompanied madrigals:** *Concerto: settimo libro de madrigali* (1619), *Madrigali guerrieri et amorosi* (1638)
- **Unaccompanied madrigals:** Books 1–6 (1587, 1590, 1592, 1603, 1605, 1614)
- **Major dramatic works:** *Orfeo* (1607), *Arianna* (1608; most of the music now lost), *Il ritorno d'Ulisse in patria* (1640), *L'incoronazione di Poppea* (1642)
- **Selected sacred works:** Mass (1610), *Vespro della Beata Vergine* (1610), *Selva morale e spirituale* (1640), *Messa et salmi* (1650; posthumous)

THE COURT MUSICIAN

By 1592 Monteverdi had joined the musical establishment at the court of Duke Vincenzo I Gonzaga in Mantua as a string player. He published his third book of madrigals shortly after his arrival, but there was a 10-year gap before publication of the next book, in 1603. He seems to have been unhappy at Mantua from the beginning and his dissatisfaction was exacerbated in 1596 when he was passed over for the post of *maestro di cappella* (the musician in charge at the court) in favour of a senior, but less gifted, colleague. The post became vacant again in 1601 and this time it went to Monteverdi.

Some of Monteverdi's greatest achievements were made in the first decade of the seventeenth century. He published his ground-breaking fourth and fifth books of madrigals in 1603 and 1605, and his first two operas, *Orfeo* and *Arianna*, were produced in 1607 and 1608 (most of the music for *Arianna* is now lost). For Monteverdi, these latter works were linked with personal tragedy: the deaths of his wife, the singer Claudia de Catteneis, in September 1607 and a few months later of Caterina Martinelli, a young singer to whom both the composer and his wife had been greatly attached.

'POSSENTE SPIRTO'

One of the show-stoppers in *Orfeo* is the aria 'Possente spirto', in which Orpheus attempts to sing his way into Hades. If the aria's success with Charon is equivocal (the boatman falls asleep), its vocal pyrotechnics have never failed to hold Monteverdi's audiences in thrall.

POPULAR MELODY *Monteverdi*

THE MOVE TO VENICE

In 1612, in spite of having brought acclaim to the house of Gonzaga, Monteverdi was summarily dismissed upon the death of Vincenzo I. A year later the composer became *maestro di cappella* at one of the most prestigious institutions in Europe, the basilica of St Mark's, Venice; he remained there for the rest of his life. In addition to the expected sacred output, he continued to compose dramatic music – for Mantua, Parma and Venice itself. He crowned his career, in his last three years, with two magnificent operas. *Il ritorno d'Ulisse in patria* and *L'incoronazione di Poppea* were both written for the recently established Venetian public opera.

SECONDA PRATICA

In defending himself against criticism from Giovanni Maria Artusi (*c.* 1540–1613), Monteverdi claimed that in ***seconda pratica*** (lit. 'second practice', a melodic device used to strengthen the meaning of the text), the words were 'the mistress of the music'. Of the four Monteverdi madrigals, three were settings of texts drawn from Battista Guarini's pastoral drama *Il pastor fido* ('The Faithful Shepherd'), which had been staged at Mantua in 1598. Monteverdi was one of a group of composers who set texts from the work at the time, and he was not alone in recognizing that dramatic monologues required a musical setting in which the words complemented the music. In allowing his melody to follow the expressive needs of the text, Monteverdi made large leaps, often from **suspensions** (notes suspended from the previous chord, and thus clashing). For example, Artusi took umbrage at a moment in 'O Mirtillo', where the voice patters rapidly up to a suspension and then, instead of resolving sedately by step in accordance with 'the rules', it makes a free-fall drop of a fifth. Stripped of words this gesture makes a poor textbook example of part-writing, but the emotionally fraught text, to which the rhythm of the line is perfectly moulded, offers ample justification for any infringement it represents.

intermedio ▶ p. 359 *prima pratica* ▶ p. 361 *seconda pratica* ▶ p. 362 *stile concitato* ▶ p. 362 suspension ▶ p. 362

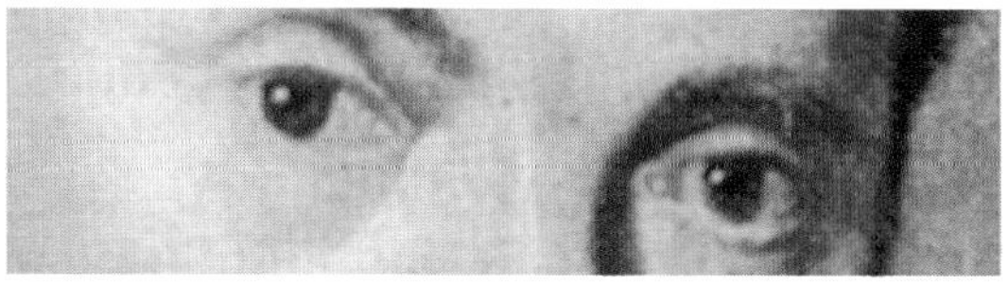

FROM MADRIGAL TO OPERA

The first three books of secular madrigals and the *Madrigali spirituali* ('Holy Madrigals', 1583) show Monteverdi's roots in the Renaissance polyphonic style (at this time known as the ***prima pratica***, or 'first practice'). In the fourth and fifth books, however, he broke new ground: he shaped his melodic line – especially in the top voice – to serve the clear declamation of the text (*seconda pratica*). He underpinned this declamatory melody with a largely homophonic texture, which draws our ears not to the subtle weaving of lines, but to the (often startling) harmonic movement. These books share a fundamental musical aesthetic with the first two operas, composed in the same decade. In *Orfeo*, first performed in 1607 for a court audience, Monteverdi drew on the experiments of his Florentine predecessors in monody, far surpassing them in both musical interest and dramatic force. *Orfeo* is a dazzling combination of choruses, dances, madrigals and duets, into which are set a handful of unforgettable solos.

The extended monologue, in which Eurydice's horrified and distraught companion breaks the news of her death to Orpheus, is dramatic music as compelling as any future composer would write.

SACRED MUSIC

Interestingly, it is in his sacred music that Monteverdi pursued this virtuosic vocal style. We hear it already in the *Vespers*, in duets for equal voices chasing and circling one another. In Venice, with the resources of St Mark's at his disposal, Monteverdi was free to develop the style to new heights. The *Selva morale e spirituale* ('Moral and Spritual Collection', 1640) includes solo works in which joyful texts such as 'Excultate jubilate' invoke stunning virtuosic display. At the other end of the expressive spectrum is the book's agonized lament of Mary at the Cross, set to the music of the famous lament from the opera *Arianna*.

GLIMPSES OF LOST GENIUS

Monteverdi's three major theatrical works stand at the very beginning and end of his career and seem to belong to different worlds as, indeed, in many ways they do. What happened in the 35 years in between? Librettos and correspondence reveal that the surviving music is a tantalizing fragment of an astoundingly rich career in musical theatre. A sense of what is lost can be gleaned from the works preserved in two retrospective collections, the *Concerto* of 1619 and the *Madrigali guerrieri et amorosi* ('Madrigals of War and Love') of 1638, both of which include music composed over a number of years. The earliest dramatic work may be the *Ballo delle ingrate* ('Dance of the Ungrateful'), first performed at Mantua in 1608 but probably revised for a performance in Vienna in 1628. The music for Pluto, requiring a deep bass voice, reflects Monteverdi's early concern for characterization. *Il Combattimento di Tancred e Clorinda* ('The Battle Between Tancred and Clorinda') is Monteverdi in top form. In the preface he bragged about the ***stile concitato*** (dividing long notes in the string orchestra into short repeated ones), which mimics the action of the drama. Meanwhile, the dramatic recitative, which he had honed in *Orfeo*, allows for the expression of the characters' proud anger turned to grief. The greatest of these works, however, is the *Lamento della ninfa* ('The Nymph's Lament'), of uncertain date. In an aria framed by a narrative male chorus, the nymph laments over a repeating pattern of descending notes, interrupted or accompanied, at irregular intervals, by a refrain sung by a second male chorus. It is one of Monteverdi's greatest achievements.

THE LATE OPERAS

Monteverdi's final two works, the operas *Ulysses* and *Poppea* are firmly in the tradition of Venetian opera. Gone are the mythological plot and ***intermedio***-like stylistic variety of *Orfeo*. The texts are historical – or at least pseudo-historical. And, musically, the focus is on the aria and duet rather than chorus and dance. But although these works conform in their general features to the Venetian opera style, they also represent the individuality of Monteverdi's genius for musical expression, here in the guise of character development. A duet between Seneca and Nero in *Ulysses* contrasts the stoic (if somewhat stuffy) maturity of the former with the childish temper of the latter. And the dignified sorrow of Octavia's laments makes her a poor competitor against Poppaea's sensuous and seductive melody. In the year of his death, no less than in his youth, Monteverdi was seeking new ways to make his music a worthy servant of the words.

THE GLORIES OF VENICE

When Monteverdi arrived in Venice in 1613, the city was uncontestably one of the most glorious musical centres of Europe. The composer's major works from this period reflect the many facets of the city's musical life. Many of his dramatic or semi-dramatic works of the 1620s and 1630s were first performed for the city's wealthy patrician families. The home of the old and distinguished Mocenigo family was the venue for both the poetic drama *Il Combattimento di Tancredi e Clorinda* in 1624 and the opera *Proserpina rapita* ('The Rape of Proserpine'; now lost) in 1630. Monteverdi was one of the first to have works performed in the new public opera houses of Venice. His two late operas were produced at the Teatro SS Giovanni e Paolo, which opened in 1639.

Before the advent of public opera, Venice had been most famous for its choirs, in particular that of St Mark's. The rich musical opportunities it provided can be seen in the diversity of Monteverdi's Venetian sacred music, published in two large collections.

(NR) Orfeo
Scene from the ENO's production of Orfeo in 1996.
(FR) St Mark's Square
Monteverdi spent most of his adult life working in the magnificent basilica of St Mark's in Venice.

The Early Baroque
HENRY PURCELL

Purcell

Henry Purcell (1659–95) was, without doubt, the most distinguished English composer of the seventeenth century. Equally at home writing for the church, the theatre or the court, he also set a number of bawdy catches for which it is likely he also wrote the words.

Unfortunately, little is known about Purcell's private life. His date of birth is generally believed to have been in 1659, since the inscription on his memorial tablet in Westminster Abbey states that he died on 21 November 1695 in his 37th year. We know that his father and uncle were Gentlemen of the Chapel Royal; he was a Child of the Chapel Royal and served under four monarchs. Purcell married at the age of about 20 and his wife, Frances, bore him seven children; all but two of these died in infancy. He remained in the employment of the royal court until his untimely death at the age of 36.

EARLY YEARS

The Westminster in which Purcell was born was then quite a small place in the parish of St Margaret's, concentrated around the Abbey Church of St Peter, now known as Westminster Abbey. When Purcell's father, Henry, died in 1664, his uncle Thomas took responsibility for his nephew's musical and general education, and young Henry became a Child of the Chapel Royal when he was six years old. He enrolled under the confirmed royalist Captain Henry Cooke, and in addition to learning singing and sight-reading he was given lessons on the lute, theorbo, violin and harpsichord. The first musical composition attributed to Purcell, aged 11, is *An Address of the Children of the Chapel Royal to the King, and their Master, Captain Cooke, on His Majesty's Birthday, AD 1670.*

HENRY PURCELL: WORKS

- **Operas and semi-operas:** *Dido and Aeneas* (1689), *The Prophetess, or The History of Dioclesian* (1690), *King Arthur, or The British Worthy* (1691), *The Fairy-Queen* (1692), *The Indian Queen* (1695), *The Tempest, or The Enchanted Island* (*c.* 1695)
- **Selected anthems, services and other sacred works:** 'Rejoice in the Lord Alway' (*c.* 1682–85), 'I was Glad' (1685), 'My Heart is Inditing' (1685), 'The Blessed Virgin's Expostulation' (1693), 'Thou Know'st, Lord, the Secrets of our Hearts' (1695)
- **Selected odes and songs:** 'Welcome, Viceregent' (1680), 'From Silent Shades' or 'Bess of Bedlam' (1683), 'Sound the Trumpet' (1687), 'Welcome, Welcome, Glorious Morn' (1691), 'Hail Bright Cecilia' (1692), 'Music for a While', from *Oedipus* (*c.* 1692), 'Nymphs and Shepherds, Come Away', from *The Libertine* (*c.* 1692), 'Celebrate this Festival' (1693), 'Come, Ye Sons of Art, Away' (1694), 'From Rosie Bowers', from *Don Quixote* (1694–95), 'The Knotting Song' (1695)
- **Selected catches:** 'A Health to the Nut-brown Lass' (1685), 'Full Bags, a Brisk Bottle' (1686), 'Bring the Bowl and Cool Nantz' (*c.* 1693–4)
- Incidental music and songs for plays, duets, string and wind music, harpsichord and organ works

'SOUND THE TRUMPET'

Purcell had written the music for the ode 'Sound the Trumpet' for King James II's birthday in 1687. It was so rousing and popular that he resuscitated it in 1689, changing the words to welcome the new king, William of Orange, from his home in Flanders, when he came to take the English throne. He used it again to great effect in 1691 for the chaconne in *King Arthur*.

POPULAR MELODY *Purcell*

COURT EMPLOYMENT

At the age of 14, Purcell was appointed 'keeper, mender, maker, repairer and tuner of the regals, organs, virginals, flutes and recorders and all other kinds of wind instruments whatsoever, in ordinary, without fee, to his Majesty and assistant to John Hingeston'. Hingeston (d. 1688) was an organist and viol player who had been a member of Charles I's band and Keeper of the Organs under Oliver Cromwell during the Republic. In 1677, Purcell was appointed 'Composer in Ordinary with fee for the Violin to His Majesty' in place of **Matthew Locke** (*c.* 1622–77). Purcell and Locke had been friends and neighbours, and on the latter's death Purcell wrote a personal tribute: 'What Hope for us Remains now he is Gone?' (it was published in *Choice Ayres Book II* in 1679).

In 1678, Purcell became a Bishop's Boy at St Peter's College, Westminster. Bishop's Boys received scholarships through a trust fund set up by the

(BL) London Coffee House
By the end of the early Baroque era, coffee houses had replaced many alehouses and taverns as social meeting places in London.
(TR) King Arthur
Title page from Purcell's opera, with text by John Dryden.

THE CITY OF LONDON

In the latter half of the seventeenth century, renewed vitality had come back into people's lives after 11 years of Puritanism during the Commonwealth (1649–60). With the restoration of Charles II in 1660, majesty was reinstated by a king who rode in a gilded coach and wore colourful clothes.

London at this time was an agricultural centre surrounded by green fields, and the City itself was still walled. The taverns, alehouses and eating houses, of which there were over 100 in the square mile that constituted London proper, were an integral part of daily life. In the eighteenth century, many of these were replaced by coffee houses.

The principal artery of London was the River Thames, the only main highway. It was quicker to travel by water than on land and boats could be hired at the quay near Palace Yard, Westminster. In the streets the noise was intolerable, with the constant rumble of wooden and iron wheels on cobbled streets, together with the ear-splitting cries of hawkers. Moreover, sanitation was unknown: the gutters were running with effluent and the stench was horrific; chamber pots and slop pails were emptied in the streets without any thought for the passers-by.

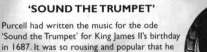

entr'acte ▶ p. 358

PURCELL'S USE OF LANGUAGE

Purcell's special gift as a composer lay in his settings of the English language. *Dido and Aeneas* is a fine example. On Aeneas's first entry, he sings: 'Let Dido smile, and I'le defie, The feeble Stroke of Destiny.' There is the gesture of a drawn sword in his rising phrase, strengthened by the wide-mouthed, bright insistence of the repeated vowel 'I'. Here Purcell turns the weakness of the poetry to musical advantage. After the climax of 'defie', the word 'feeble' sinks with no strength; the 'k' of 'Stroke' then cuts like a knife and the voice drops to a low level to express scorn. This talent is again apparent in his odes to celebrate the Feast of St Cecilia. In 'Welcome to All the Pleasures', Purcell uses an alto ground for 'Here the deities approve', and in the final chorus 'In a consort of voices' a sustained tonic chord supports the four voices as they gradually fade in succession, finishing with the basses. Such word-painting is evident in a number of his other Cecilian odes, including 'Raise, Raise the Voice' and 'Hail, Bright Cecilia'.

Bishop of Lincoln. Presumably he had to discontinue his education in 1679, as he was appointed organist of Westminster Abbey, succeeding his master **Blow**.

CHANGES IN THE MONARCHY

In 1682, Purcell was appointed one of three organists in the Chapel Royal. They shared duties on the days of solemn feasts and when not playing they sang in the choir. This posed no problem for Purcell as, when his voice broke, he developed into a bass who could also sing countertenor.

Three years later, the Catholic James II ascended the throne. Although Purcell contributed two of the anthems sung at the Coronation, 'I was Glad' and 'My Heart is Inditing', he and other Protestant court musicians fared rather badly under the new king, who had no interest in music. Purcell lost his two most important appointments to Catholic rivals. He was merely required to play the harpsichord, although some months later he was sworn in to the king's 'Private Music in Ordinary'. Thus Purcell seriously turned to writing for

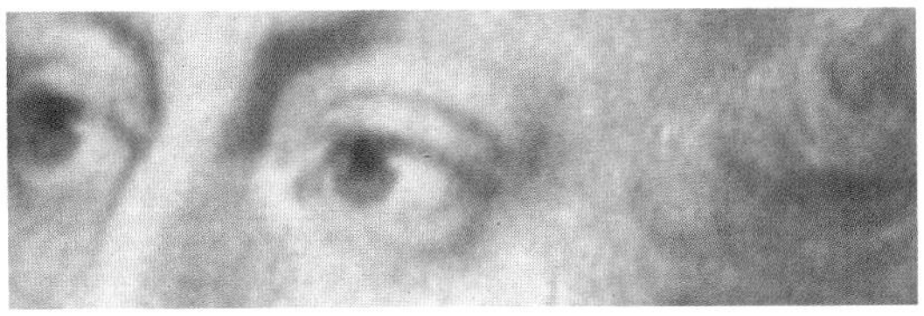

the theatre. (The incidental music he wrote for the play *Abeldazar* found renewed fame at the hands of **Benjamin Britten** (1913–76), in his *Young Person's Guide to the Orchestra, Variations and Fugue on a Theme of Purcell*).

In 1688, James II's principal opponents secretly invited the Dutch William of Orange to invade England and take the throne; James and his family fled to France. William was first and foremost a military man who had little interest in music, but his joint sovereign, Queen Mary, was genuinely fond of it. Purcell wrote six odes to celebrate her birthday – two of the best-known are 'Welcome, Welcome, Glorious Morn' (1691) and 'Celebrate this Festival' (1693).

PURCELL AND DRYDEN

From this time onwards, Purcell was busy composing odes for the royal birthdays, anthems for the church and songs and **entr'acte** music for the theatre. In 1690, Thomas Betterton, the distinguished actor-dramatist with whom Purcell

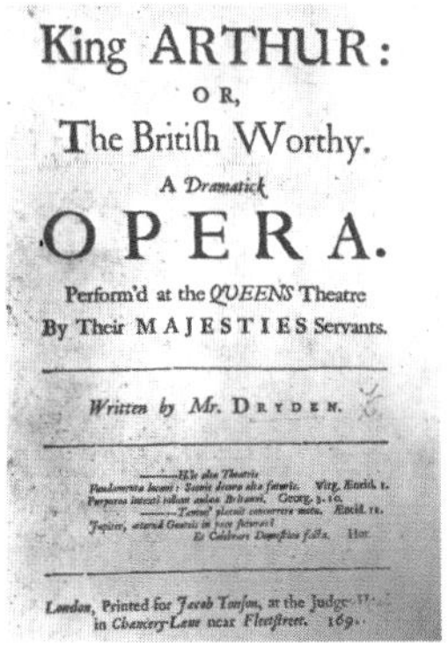

King ARTHUR:
OR,
The Britifh Worthy.
A Dramatick
OPERA.
Perform'd at the QUEENS Theatre
By Their MAJESTIES Servants.
Written by Mr. DRYDEN.
London, Printed for Jacob Tonson, at the Judge's ... in Chancery-Lane near Fleetstreet. 169.

had collaborated in numerous stage productions, decided to adapt the libretto of *The Prophetess, or The History of Dioclesian* by John Fletcher and Philip Massinger and asked Purcell to provide all the music. It was a great success and brought about a meeting between the composer and the poet John Dryden. This was a turning point in Purcell's life, leading to several productions, including *Amphitryon* (1690) and *King Arthur* (1691). Two outstanding examples of his dramatic writing are the 'Frost' scene in *King Arthur*, where every voice and instrument shivers, and the scene of the drunken poet in *The Fairy-Queen* (1692), where voices and accompaniment appropriately sway and swerve to create a musical effect that had not previously been heard on the London stage.

SOLEMN MUSIC

In December 1694, at the age of 32, Queen Mary died of smallpox, and Purcell was asked to write music for her funeral. He composed a march played on trumpets and trombones accompanied by muffled drumbeats, and the anthem 'Thou Know'st, Lord, the Secrets of our Hearts' (1695).

In November 1695 Purcell himself became ill, probably from tuberculosis, a common disease at the time (then known as consumption). On what was to be his deathbed he wrote one last song for a production of *Don Quixote* (1694–95). 'From Rosie Bowers' offers another example of Purcell's gift for creating atmosphere: it is a cry of real despair and the setting of the word 'death' is bone-chilling. He died on 21 November. Five days later most of the music he had written for Queen Mary's funeral was played at his own.

PACKING THE THEATRES

The year 1680 was an eventful one for Purcell: he completed his fantasies for viols (except for one unfinished movement); he wrote his first welcome ode for Charles II, 'Welcome, Viceregent', marking the king's return from Windsor to Whitehall; and, as far as we know, he made his first contribution to music for the theatre. He wrote the incidental music and several songs for Nathaniel Lee's tragedy *Theodosius, or The Force of Love*.

The London stage, as Purcell would have known it, was attempting to rehabilitate itself after its deprivation during the Commonwealth. The theatres that had survived were built in the old Elizabethan pattern, with an open courtyard and two or three roofed-in galleries round the sides where the nobility sat. The common people, often as many as 400, crowded into the courtyard, paying twopence to stand.

THE FIRST ENGLISH OPERA

Although many attempts had been made to introduce Italian opera to England, no one had truly succeeded. The spoken drama was far too deeply rooted in the hearts of the English people for a musical equivalent to take its place. Ironically, it was when the Puritans suppressed the drama that masques assumed a more dramatic form and English opera could emerge. After the Restoration, performances gradually assumed a more operatic style, but it is *Dido and Aeneas* – libretto by Nahum Tate and music by Purcell – that is now regarded as the first English opera. Its premise can be seen with hindsight as one of the most important events in Purcell's involvement with the theatre, even though it took place privately in a girls' school in Chelsea. We have no details of how it was performed or who took the male roles. The date is generally believed to be 1689, but recent research provides an argument for placing it earlier. Of the opera itself, the most memorable part is Dido's famous lament 'When I am Laid in Earth', which is considered to be one of the most moving and perfect pieces of writing in the history of English music.

Blow ▶ p. 80 Britten ▶ p. 287 Locke ▶ p. 83

The Early Baroque

PERSONALITIES

Biber, Heinrich Ignaz Franz von

(Bē'-ber, Hīn'-rikh Ēg'-nàts Frants fun) 1644–1704

GERMAN COMPOSER

Biber was a violin virtuoso and one of the most imaginative composers of his time. He was employed at the Moravian court of Kromeriz (near Brno in today's Czechoslovakia) during the 1660s, but from the early 1670s worked at the Salzburg court of the Prince-Archbishop, where he subsequently became *Kapellmeister* ('chapel master'), in 1684. Biber's compositions include operas, sacred vocal music with instruments and pieces for solo violin and for instrumental ensemble. Among these are the rhythmically colourful *Battalia* ('Battle', 1673) and *Fechtschule* ('Fencing School'), and 16 *Mystery (Rosary) Sonatas* (*c.* 1676) for violin and continuo, in which he demonstrates his skill in the art of ***scordatura*** (retuning of the violin strings) and in evoking – sometimes poignantly, sometimes exuberantly – events from the life of Christ.

Blow, John

1649–1708

ENGLISH COMPOSER

Blow held various court appointments and served as the first Composer of the Chapel Royal (1700). His greatest gifts lay in the composition of vocal music, notably anthems and services for the church. Among the finest of his verse anthems is 'God spake sometime in visions', for the coronation of James II (1685). In this piece, his individual approach to harmony and **modulation** is a distinctive feature. As well as organ voluntaries and miscellaneous keyboard compositions, Blow wrote a single stage work, *Venus and Adonis*. Incorporating features of French musical drama and of the Italian chamber cantata, it was a significant precursor to **Purcell**'s *Dido and Aeneas*. He also composed an ode on the death of Purcell, whom he succeeded as organist of Westminster Abbey (1695).

Böhm, Georg

(Böm, Gā-ôrg') 1661–1733

GERMAN COMPOSER

Böhm was a Lutheran organist-composer who studied with members of the Bach family before becoming organist at Lüneburg. At an early age he travelled to Hamburg, where he encountered **Johann Adam Reincken** (1623–1722), one of the most influential North German organists. Böhm contributed to the principal forms popular with the organists of this region, notably the **toccata** and the organ **chorale**, which he imbued with a high level of virtuosity. He was especially resourceful in his harpsichord *partite*, or variations, usually on a chorale melody. He also composed harpsichord suites, following models established by Froberger, sacred cantatas, Passions and songs.

Buxtehude, Dietrich

(Bōōks-te-hōō'-de, Dēt'-rikh) c. *1637–1707*

GERMAN COMPOSER

Buxtehude was born in Scandinavia, but from 1668 until his death, held the post of organist at St Mary's, Lübeck. The position did not require him to provide much in the way of vocal music; he also wrote cantatas and arias for the *Abendmusiken* (public concerts) in which he was deeply involved. His cantatas, of which *Alles, was ihr tut* ('All That You Do') is an attractive example, incorporate elements of instrumental sonata, *concertato*, aria and chorale. They served as effective models for the next generation of composers. As well as composing music for solo organ and harpsichord, some of it requiring technical virtuosity, Buxtehude wrote a number of trio sonatas.

Caccini, Giulio

(Kà-chē'-nē, Jōōl'-yō) c. *1545–1618*

ITALIAN COMPOSER

Caccini was a singer and instrumentalist at the Medici court. His most important publication was *Le nuove musiche* ('The New Music', 1602), which contained madrigals and **strophic** songs with ***basso continuo***. Its preface, in which ornamentation and **figured bass** are discussed, outlines the *stile rappresentativo*. In this new monodic style he sought to follow the rhythm and **cadences** of ordinary speech (*sprezzatura*) in order to affect the senses and engage the passions. These were among the foremost aspirations of the Florentine Camerata hosted by Giovanni de' Bardi, of which Caccini was a member. The preface is now recognized as an important source of early Baroque performance practice. Caccini's daughter, Francesca (1587–*c.* 1638), also composed and published monody; with *La Liberazione di Ruggerio dall'isola d'Alcina* ('Ruggerio's Escape from the Island of Alcina'), performed in 1625, she became the first woman to compose an opera.

Carissimi, Giacomo

(Kà-rēs'-sē-me, Jà'-kō-mō) 1605–74

ITALIAN COMPOSER

Carissimi was the most important composer of oratorios of his time. He was born in Rome where, in about 1630, he became *maestro di cappella* at Sant'Apollinare, the church of the Jesuit Collegio Germanico,

CASTRATOS

From the late sixteenth century, castratos were engaged as singers by the Sistine Chapel in Rome. Although castration had been forbidden by Pope Gregory XIII, some children who had suffered mutilation were trained as castrato singers. Their voices were found to be much stronger, and their vocal ranges wider, than those of falsettists, whom they gradually replaced in the papal chapel. Initially castratos were engaged solely as church musicians, but with the growth of opera their careers diversified and there was a great demand for them both in Italy and in many foreign countries. In 1639 Johann Georg II, the Elector apparent at Dresden, engaged Giovanni Andrea Bontempi (*c.* 1624–1705) as the court's first Italian castrato.

As Italian opera grew in popularity, the demand for castrati intensified. By the end of the seventeenth century singers such as Giovanni Francesco Grossi, 'Siface' (1653–97) and Pier Francesco Tosi (*c.* 1653–1732), now remembered chiefly for an influential singing treatise *Opinioni de' cantori antichi e moderni* ('Theories on Ancient and Modern Songs', 1723) were among the highest-paid musicians of their day. In the eighteenth century castratos were often international celebrities, creating most of the great roles as heroes and lovers (Handel's Julius Caesar, Gluck's Orpheus), and commanding almost any fee they liked.

basso continuo ▶ p. 356 cadence ▶ p. 356 chorale ▶ p. 357 *concertato* ▶ p. 357 *entrée* ▶ p. 358 figured bass ▶ p. 358 *intermedi* ▶ p. 359 modulation ▶ p. 360 *scordatura* ▶ p. 362 strophic ▶ p. 362 *style brisé* ▶ p. 362 toccata ▶ p. 362 tombeau ▶ p. 362

renowned for its musical tradition. Carissimi composed masses and motets, but is chiefly admired for his cantatas and his harmonically affecting oratorios, in which a narrator (*historicus*) recounts the events while solo voices, both in contrast and in combination, further enliven the story. Choruses provide an additional dramatic dimension to a fundamentally ***concertato*** style. Carissimi was a celebrated teacher who may have numbered Charpentier among his pupils.

Cavalieri, Emilio de'

(Kä-väl-yä'-rē, Ā-mēl'-yō dā) c. *1550–1602*

ITALIAN COMPOSER

Cavalieri was born in Rome and was a teacher, dancer and diplomat at the Medici court. In 1589 he organized the celebrated Florentine ***intermedi*** for the wedding of Grand Duke Ferdinando I and Christine of Lorraine. He was associated with the Florentine Camerata of Giovanni de' Bardi, whose members experimented with musically continuous dramas. His *Rappresentatione di Anima, et di Corpo*, considered the first work of its kind, was performed in Rome in 1600. It contains passages of extended monodic recitative, solo airs and pieces in madrigal style. It is the earliest known score to be printed with figured-bass instrumental parts.

(BL) Farinelli
Farinelli (real name Carlo Broschi) was one of the most famous castratos of the Baroque era.
***(TR and BR)* Il pomo d'oro**
Two illustrations recording performances of Cesti's opera in 1666.

Cavalli, Francesco

(Kä-väl'-lē, Frän-ches'-kō) 1602–76

ITALIAN COMPOSER

Cavalli was born Caletti but took the name of his first patron. His life was centred on the basilica of St Mark's, where his teacher, **Monteverdi**, was *maestro di cappella*. He became second organist there in 1639, principal organist in 1665, and *maestro di cappella* in 1668. He was the most gifted and celebrated of Monteverdi's successors in Venetian opera. Almost 30 by him are known. His first opera, *Le nozze di Teti e Peleo* ('The Marriage of Teti and Peleo'), was staged at the Teatro San Cassiano in 1639. Among later successes were *Egisto* (1643), *Ormindo* (1644) and *Giasone* (1648–49), the last of which was played more than any other of his operas during his lifetime. Between 1660 and 1662 Cavalli worked in Paris, at the invitation of Cardinal Mazarin. *Xerse* (1654), performed for the wedding of Louis XIV and the Infanta Maria Theresa of Spain, was followed by *Ercole amante* ('Hercules in Love', 1662), which failed disastrously. Both contained splendid danced ***entrées*** by Lully.

Cesti, Antonio

(Chās'-tē, Än-tōn'-yō) c. *1623–69*

ITALIAN COMPOSER

Cesti was a Franciscan monk who studied music in Rome. Employed as a singer at the Florentine and Sienese courts, he then travelled to Venice, where his first opera

Orontea (1649) was successfully performed at the Teatro di SS Apostoli. Following an affair with a singer, Cesti moved to Innsbruck, Austria, where further operas were performed. In 1658 Cesti revisited Rome and joined the papal choir. Released from his Franciscan vows in 1661, he returned to Innsbruck as a secular priest. In 1666 he was appointed to a post at the Vienna court. There his greatest works, *Le disgrazie d'Amore* ('Love's Misfortunes', 1667) and *Il pomo d'oro* ('The Golden Apple', 1668), which celebrates the marriage of Leopold I and the Infanta Margherita of Spain, were performed.

Chambonnières, Jacques Champion, Sieur de

(Shan-bun-yâr, Zhak Shamp-yôn' Syör da)

c. *1601–72*

FRENCH COMPOSER

Chambonnières is generally considered the founder of the French harpsichord school. He developed a style in harpsichord writing adapted from the lute idiom of ***style brisé***, characterized by broken, arpeggiated chordal textures. In 1641, he began a twice-weekly series of concerts, later inheriting his father's position as *gentilhomme ordinaire* of the king's chamber. During the 1650s he danced in several court entertainments. His two collections of harpsichord pieces were both published in 1670. He was sought after as a teacher and numbered among his pupils Nicolas-Antoine Lebègue (*c.* 1631–1702), Guillaume Gabriel Nivers (*c.* 1632–1714) and Jean-Henri d'Anglebert (1635–91), who composed a ***tombeau*** for solo harpsichord in his memory.

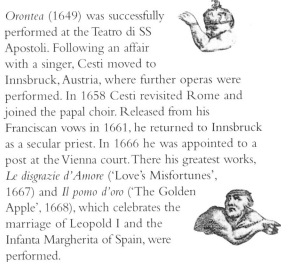

Monteverdi ▶ p. 76 Purcell ▶ p. 78 Reincken ▶ p. 120

Charpentier, Marc-Antoine

(Shär-pont-yā', Märk An-twän') 1643–1704

FRENCH COMPOSER

Charpentier studied in Italy during the 1660s. There he familiarized himself with the instrumental and vocal forms of Carissimi and above all, that of the oratorio. When he returned to Paris he joined the musicians of the Duchess of Guise and in 1673 became associated with Molière's Comédie Française. In 1687, Charpentier composed his popular *La Descente d'Orphée aux enfers* ('Orpheus's Descent into Hell'), based on Ovid's *Metamorphoses*. Though he never held a court appointment, he received commissions from many sacred institutions and in 1698 became *maître de musique* (master of music) of the Jesuit Sainte-Chapelle. He was equally accomplished in sacred and secular forms. Compositions of particular merit include a single lyric tragedy, *Médée* ('Medea', 1693), a dramatic motet, 'Le reniement de St Pierre' ('The Denial of St Peter'), a religious drama, *David et Jonathas* ('David and Goliath', 1688), a Mass, *Assumpta est Maria* ('Mary is Risen', 1698–1702), and many tenebrae (matins and lauds for Holy Week) and psalm settings. He described keys in terms of their expressive characters in his *Règles de Composition* ('Rules of Composition', *c.* 1692)

Corelli, Arcangelo

(Kō-rel'-lē, Ärk-än'-jel-ō) 1653–1713

ITALIAN COMPOSER AND VIOLINIST

Corelli studied in Bologna, but by the mid 1670s was living in Rome, where he acquired a reputation as one of the city's foremost violinists. His first patron in Rome was the exiled Queen Christina of Sweden, to whom he dedicated his earliest printed collection, 12 trio sonatas op. 1 (1681). Next he worked as director of music for Cardinal Pamphili. From 1690, Corelli's most important patron was Cardinal Ottoboni, with whom he remained until his death. Ottoboni offered Corelli a secure and artistically stimulating environment in which he was able to perfect styles of composition and performance that were taken as models by younger musicians at home and further afield. It was here that he produced his popular op. 5 (1700), consisting of 12 sonatas. In 1706, Corelli was admitted to the Accademia degli Arcadi, perhaps the most exclusive of many such existing institutions.

Although his only collection of ***concerti grossi***, op. 6, was issued posthumously in 1714, it is evident that Corelli had been preparing them for publication for some time. The concertos fall into two distinct types, ***concerti da chiesa*** (church concertos), whose movements are of a predominantly serious nature, and ***concerti da camera*** (chamber concertos), which are more closely allied to the dance suite. In all of them, a ***concertino***, typically two violins and a cello, is contrasted with the full complement of instruments, the ***ripieno***.

In his concertos, as in his sets of solo and trio sonatas, Corelli codified and refined the classic Baroque language of the seventeenth century.

Fischer, Johann Caspar Ferdinand

(Fish'-er, Yō'-han Käs'-pâr Far'-dē-nänt) 1656–1746

GERMAN COMPOSER

Fischer, who was *Hofkapellmeister* at the court of Baden, contributed to the dissemination of Lully's French orchestral style with his eight suites published as *Le journal du printemps* ('Spring Diary', 1685). These follow the seventeenth-century French practice of five-part string writing, with the addition of two trumpets. Fischer was an imaginative keyboard composer, whose range of ideas is contained in his 1696 *Musicalisches Blumen-Büschlein* ('Musical Bouquet'), consisting of eight dance suites for harpsichord, *Ariadne musica* (1702), whose preludes and fugues for organ may have provided **J. S. Bach** with a model for his *Well-Tempered Clavier* (1720), and *Musicalischer Parnassus* ('Musical Parnassus', 1738).

'CHRISTMAS PASTORALE'

The most famous piece from Corelli's *concerti grossi* is the 'Pastorale ad libitum' at the end of Concerto no. 8, with its Christmas associations. Its origins lie in Italian folk tradition – it is shepherds' music in the 12/8 rhythm of a Siciliano. The drone bass evokes the *piva* or folk bagpipe.

POPULAR MELODY *Corelli*

Frescobaldi, Girolamo

(Fres-kō-bäl'-dē, Ji-rō'-lä'mo) 1583–1643

ITALIAN COMPOSER

Frescobaldi was appointed organist at St Peter's Basilica, Rome, in 1608 and, apart from occasional leaves of absence – of which the longest was between 1628 and 1634, when he served at the ducal court in Florence – he remained in the post for the rest of his life. Frescobaldi wrote madrigals, Masses and other miscellaneous vocal pieces, but he acquired fame on the strength of his compositions for organ and harpsichord and as a keyboard virtuoso. In both his *Toccate e partite* ('Toccata and Partita', 1615) and *Fiori musicali* ('Musical Flowers', 1635) Frescobaldi addresses the performer, emphasizing the importance of responding to the emotions by playing with imagination and expressive freedom. Frescobaldi's keyboard music often has a pronounced individuality which can be found, above all, in his toccatas, dances and variations on popular melodies.

Froberger, Johann Jacob

(Frō'-bâr-ger, Yō'-hän Yä'-kōp) 1616–67

GERMAN COMPOSER

Froberger was the most important German harpsichord composer of the first half of the seventeenth century. In about 1637, he became imperial court organist at Vienna, where he benefitted from a sympathetic patron in Emperor Ferdinand III, himself a gifted musician. Soon after his appointment, Froberger took leave to study in Rome with Frescobaldi. Further periods of travel followed before Froberger eventually settled in Vienna in 1653. His deeply felt *Lamentation* on the death of Ferdinand in 1657 suggests a warm rapport between musician and employer. Froberger was receptive to both Italian and French musical styles: his **canzonas**, **toccatas** and **ricercares** betray Italian influences, while the dance suites owe more to France.

(TL) Marc-Antoine Charpentier
Caricature of the French composer.

***(NR)* Sonata a Tre**
Title page from Arcangelo Corelli's Sonata a Tre; *this would have been published earlier than the handwritten date of 1748.*

canzona ▶ p. 356 *concertino* ▶ p. 357 *concerto da camera* ▶ p. 357 *concerto da chiesa* ▶ p. 357 *concerto grosso* ▶ p. 357 consort ▶ p. 357 ricercares ▶ p. 362 ripieno ▶ p. 362 toccata ▶ p. 362 *tragédie lyrique* ▶ p. 363

Humfrey, Pelham

1647–74

ENGLISH COMPOSER

Humfrey's precocious gifts became apparent when, as a chorister, he started to compose anthems for the Chapel Royal. In 1664 he set out for France and Italy to familiarize himself with continental styles in music. He returned to England in 1667 and was appointed a Gentleman of the Chapel Royal. Much of Humfrey's sacred vocal writing has an Italian bias, while his deployment of instruments reveals a debt to Lully. These skills, notwithstanding the contrary opinion of his contemporary, Samuel Pepys, enhanced Humfrey's distinctively expressive handling of the English language with its vivid word-painting.

CHARPENTIER'S *MÉDÉE*

The restrictions that Lully imposed upon the larger-scale dramatic endeavours of other French composers meant that while he was alive he had no rivals in the sphere of French serious opera, or ***tragédie lyrique***. The most gifted musician to suffer under Lully's monopolistic practices was Charpentier. When Lully died in 1687, composers were suddenly free to write operas and many did, most famously **Elisabeth Jacquet de la Guerre** (1665–1729) and **Marin Marais** (1656–1728); others included Pascal Collasse (1649–1709) André Campra (1660–1744) and André Cardinal Destouches (1672–1749). Charpentier was quick off the mark with his religious drama *David et Jonathas*. It was followed by *Médée*, a *tragédie lyrique* with a libretto by Thomas Corneille, and the composer's dramatic masterpiece. While adhering to the formal structure of Lullian opera, with its prologue and five acts, Charpentier greatly enriched and diversified the static harmonies of his predecessor with a wealth of ideas inspired by his Italian training. Although Charpentier proved himself brilliantly imaginative in his musical characterisation, *Médée* was not well received by a public whose senses were, perhaps, anaesthetized by the comfortable, undemanding nature of Lully's music. Maybe the composer and cleric, Sébastian de Brossard, an admirer of Charpentier's *Médée*, was near the truth when he blamed its failure on 'the intrigues of the envious and the ignorant'.

Landi, Stefano

c. *1586–1639*

ITALIAN COMPOSER

Although Landi was active as a church musician, he is chiefly recognized nowadays as one of the most gifted and successful opera composers of the period between Monteverdi's Florentine dramas and those that he wrote for Venice. During the 1630s, the focus on *dramma per musica* ('drama through music') shifted from Florence to Rome where, in 1632, Landi's most impressive opera, *Il Sant'Alessio*, inaugurated the Teatro Quattro Fontane. This drama, recounting the story of the modest, self-effacing St Alexis, was among the first to be based on history rather than legend. The machinery it required for extravagant scenic effects conforms with the Roman taste of the time.

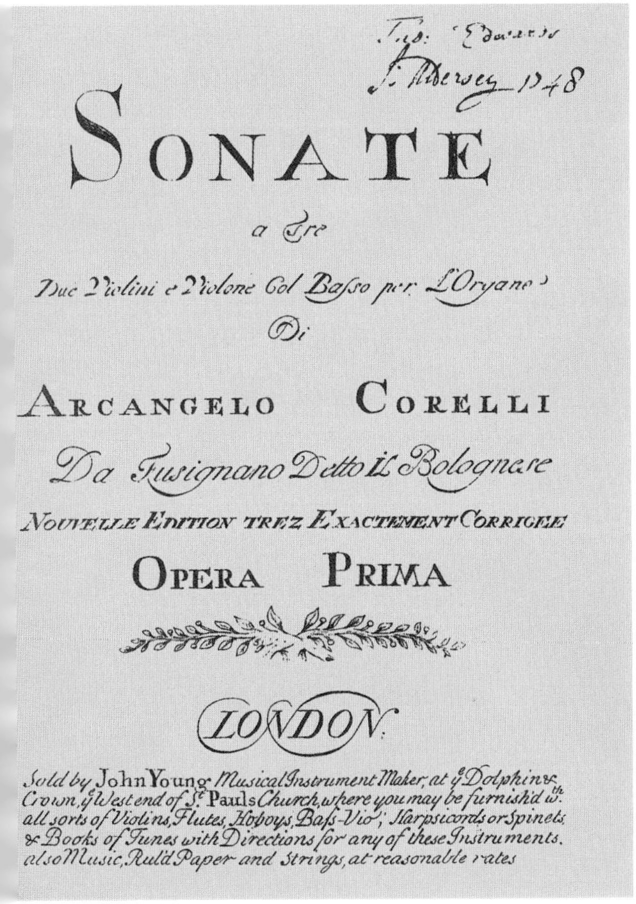
SONATE

a tre

Due Violini e Violone Col Basso per L'Organo

Di

ARCANGELO CORELLI

Da Fusignano Detto il Bolognese

NOUVELLE EDITION TREZ EXACTEMENT CORRIGEE

OPERA PRIMA

LONDON

Sold by John Young Musical Instrument Maker, at ye Dolphin & Crown, ye West end of St Pauls Church, where you may be furnish'd wth all sorts of Violins, Flutes, Hoboys, Bass-Viol's, Harpsicords or Spinets, & Books of Tunes with Directions for any of these Instruments. also Music, Ruld Paper and Strings, at reasonable rates

Lawes, Henry

1596–1662

ENGLISH COMPOSER

Henry Lawes served in the Chapel Royal of Charles I and, in the early part of his career, composed theatre music known as masques. By the early 1630s, Lawes had cultivated a friendship with the poet John Milton, with whom he collaborated in two masques, *Arcades* (1630), whose music has not survived, and *Comus* (1634). The latter is the piece for which Lawes is perhaps best remembered, and it was performed to celebrate the establishment of John Egerton as President of Wales. The composer himself played the part of the Attendant Spirit in the first performance. Many of Lawes' songs are settings of texts by the Cavalier poets, among them Thomas Carew and Robert Herrick. In these Lawes aimed, in his own words, to shape 'Notes to the Words and Sense'. Lawes provided a setting of the anthem 'Zadok the Priest' for the coronation of Charles II in 1660.

Lawes, William

1602–45

ENGLISH COMPOSER

William Lawes, like his brother Henry, was a musician at the court of Charles I. Although he too composed songs and theatre music, his greater strength lay in **consort** music for viols or members of the violin family. Lawes' consort music in four, five and six parts probably dates from the 1620s. In these pieces the composer reveals a manner that is individual and often intensely expressive. His two sets of fantasia suites for one and two violins, bass viol and organ, share common ground with the Italian trio sonata. Lawes fought for the royalist cause and his death at the Siege of Chester prompted many tributes.

Locke, Matthew

c. *1622–77*

ENGLISH COMPOSER

While a chorister at Exeter Cathedral, where he learnt to play the organ, Locke met Christopher Gibbons (1615–76), with whom he later collaborated on the music for the masque *Cupid and Death* (1653). Locke's revision of the piece in 1659 has survived in autograph and is the only known complete score of a seventeenth-century English masque. In 1656, Locke was one of five composers who provided music for Sir William Davenant's *The Siege of Rhodes*, but none of this has survived. He contributed music to the coronation of Charles II and after the Restoration held various court appointments. His last publications were *Melothesia* (1673), containing keyboard pieces, and *Tripla Concordia* (1677), an anthology of music for two violins and bass violin. In these, as elsewhere, his distinctive melodic ideas and often dissonant harmonies strike an individual and experimental note. He numbered Purcell among his pupils.

J. S. Bach ▶ p. 106 Jacquet de la Guerre ▶ p. 118 Marais ▶ p. 119

Lully, Jean-Baptiste

(Lü-lē', Zhàn Bä-tēst') 1632–87

FRENCH COMPOSER

Lully was an Italian by birth, but as a youth accompanied the Chevalier de Guise to Paris, where he remained for the rest of his life. In 1653, Lully danced with the young King Louis XIV in the *Ballet de la nuit*, from which point began his meteoric rise at court. At first he composed court ballets and *intermèdes* for imported Italian operas by Cavalli, performed in celebration of the king's marriage. In 1661, the king appointed him to the specially created post of *Surintendant de la musique et compositeur de la musique de la chambre* ('overseer and composer of court music') – the highest position in court music. He became a naturalized Frenchman in the same year.

The next decade saw crucial developments in Lully's style and *modus operandi*. He wisely collaborated with France's leading comic playwright, Molière, in highly successful ***comédies-ballets***, then gradually altered the balance of drama and music to favour the latter. Following Pierre Perrin's failure to establish opera academies, Lully, with the backing of the king and his finance minister Colbert, created a uniquely French form of opera or *tragédie lyrique* with *Cadmus et Hermione* (1673), which served political as well as artistic ends. Through a series of restrictive measures guaranteed by the king, Lully gained almost exclusive rights to mount large-scale music productions for the French stage. His sacred compositions include a 'Te Deum' and 'Miserere' that were much admired.

Muffat, Georg

(Moo'-fät, Gā-ôrg') 1653–1704

GERMAN COMPOSER

During the 1660s, Muffat worked with Lully in Paris, later visiting Vienna, Prague, Salzburg and Rome. The deep impression that his Italian and French studies made is reflected in four important collections. *Armonico tributo* (1682) consists of five sonatas modelled on Corelli's concertos. These were revised and included along with six new concertos in his last publication, *Ausserlesene Instrumental-Musik* (1701). Between these two Italian-dominated collections came the Francophile *Florilegium primum* (1695) and *Florilegium secundum* (1698), consisting of five-part orchestral suites, together with instructions for performing them.

Pachelbel, Johann

(Päkh'-el-bel, Yō'-hän) 1653–1706

GERMAN COMPOSER

Pachelbel was court organist at Eisenach (he taught J. S. Bach's eldest brother Johann Christoph) before taking up the post at Erfurt, where he published his first organ music, *Musicalischen Sterbens-Gedancken* ('Musical Meditation on Death', 1683). In 1690 he moved to Stuttgart and then Gotha before becoming organist at the Sebaldkirche in Nuremberg, where he served for the last decade of his life. His chorale-based works, for organ and for voices, illustrate his skill both in imitative part-writing and in ornamental variation. His suites for two violins and continuo – *Musicalische Ergötzung* – were published in the 1690s and his *Hexachordum Apollinis* for organ or harpsichord, dedicated to Buxtehude, in 1699. Today he is best known for his three-part canon in D major.

Pasquini, Bernardo

(Päs-kwē'-nē, Bâr-när'-dō) 1637–1710

ITALIAN COMPOSER

Pasquini was a keyboard virtuoso and teacher working in Rome, who numbered Muffat, Francesco Gasparini (1668–1727) and Domenico Zipoli (1688–1726) among his pupils. He benefited from several of the leading Roman patrons of the time, including the cardinals Pamphili and Ottoboni, as well as from the exiled Queen Christina of Sweden. He served as organist of S Maria in Aracoeli from 1664, but involved himself in a varied musical life which brought him success and membership of the Accademia dell'Arcadi (1706). He wrote operas, oratorios, cantatas and a wide variety of inventive and virtuosic keyboard pieces, including toccatas, variations, sonatas and suites, whose dance sequence he did much to establish.

LE BOURGEOIS GENTILHOMME

Unlike the music of other court composers, Lully's was sung and whistled by Paris's man in the street. One of his most celebrated dances is a minuet from the *comédie-ballet Le bourgeois gentilhomme*. It occurs in a scene from the second act when Monsieur Jourdain, the hero of the play attempts, with the assistance of his music master, to dance in his nightgown.

POPULAR MELODY *Lully*

Peri, Jacopo

(Pā'-rē, Yä-kō-pō) 1561–1633

ITALIAN COMPOSER

Peri was a Florentine who held a post as musician at the Medici court. He was probably a member of Bardi's Camerata in Florence, but by 1592 was enjoying the patronage of the amateur composer, Corsi. One of the poets of Corsi's household was

L'EVRIDICE
COMPOSTA IN
MVSICA
In Stile Rappresentatiuo da
GIVLIO CACCINI
detto Romano.

comédie-ballet ► p. 357 obbligato ► p. 360

Rinuccini, whose pastoral poem *Dafne* was partly set to music by Corsi then completed by Peri. It was first played at Corsi's palace in 1598 and repeated at court in 1599 and 1600. *Dafne* was the first full-length opera ever written. It was followed by *Euridice* (1600), another Peri–Rinuccini collaboration, with additional music by Caccini. In each of these works Peri sought a compromise between singing and speech which came to be called *stile recitativo* ('dramatic style'), reflecting the previous experiments of the Camerata members.

Rossi, Luigi

(Rôs'-sē, Lōō-ē'-jē) 1598–1653

ITALIAN COMPOSER

Rossi was one of the early Roman composers of opera and cantata. After studying in Naples he entered the service of the Borghese family in Rome in 1621. In 1633 he was appointed organist of S Luigi dei Francesi and in 1641 moved to the Barberini's. His first opera, *Il palazzo incantato* ('The Enchanted Palace'), was lavishly produced for the Barberini theatre in 1642. In 1645 the Barberinis moved to France, and in 1647 Rossi's second opera *Orfeo* was successfully presented in Paris at the Palais Royal. After a brief return to Rome he travelled once more to Paris, but with the advent of xenophobic Fronde he found himself unwelcome there.

Rossi, Salamone

(Rôs'-sē, Sà-lā-mō'-nā) c. *1570*–c. *1630*

ITALIAN COMPOSER

Rossi was a Mantuan composer, teacher and instrumentalist associated with the court music of Duke Guglielmo Gonzaga. He lived in the Jewish quarter of Mantua, where he may have died after the city was sacked in 1630. His five books of madrigals are progressive in their requirement of an instrumental bass with and without figures, as are his four collections of assorted pieces, variously for solo keyboard and instrumental ensemble. *Hashirim asher lish'lomo* ('The Songs of Solomon', 1622–23) contains settings of Hebrew songs for synagogue use, and he also contributed music for staged entertainment at the Gonzaga court.

THE POWER OF LULLY

Because of his astute political judgment, and his secure position at court, Lully was able to wield musical influence within France seldom if ever realized anywhere by any composer. His restrictive monopolies removed the threat of all serious competition, both by other French composers and from visiting musicians. If such control inevitably exercised a stranglehold on French musical diversity, Lully's achievements were nevertheless varied and far-reaching.

Among his greatest contributions were his disciplined handling of instrumental ensembles, in which he laid the foundation of the modern orchestra; the creation of *tragédie lyrique*, whose outline and character endured – with modifications – for almost a century; the definition that he gave to instrumental dances; and the establishment of the French overture, as one of the major forms of the late Baroque era. With a sharply dotted rhythm in its introductory bars followed by a faster fugal section, the style was widely imitated throughout Europe.

Johann Sigismund Kusser (1660–1727) and Muffat, both pupils of Lully, disseminated his overture and dance style in Germany, providing models for composers of the next generation such as J. S. Bach, **George Frideric Handel** (1685–1759) and **Georg Philipp Telemann** (1681–1767). The Italians were less receptive, but the French overture principle appears in the music of **Antonio Vivaldi** (1678–1741) on at least one occasion. Although he made many enemies, Lully saw his achievements recognized during his lifetime and they were acknowledged after his death too. Among the composers who wrote music in his memory are **François Couperin** (1668–1733), Marais, **Jean-Féry Rebel** (1666–1747) and d'Anglebert, who arranged several of the overtures, dances and airs from his operas for solo harpsichord.

Scheidt, Samuel

(Shīdt, Zä'-mōō-el) 1587–1654

GERMAN COMPOSER

Scheidt – a pupil of Sweelinck, organist, composer and himself a teacher – served as *Kapellmeister* to the Halle court from 1619. He published seven collections of sacred music: the earliest, *Cantiones sacrae* ('Holy Songs', 1620), contains eight-voice polychoral motets. One calls for instrumental doubling of parts; the musical style blends Italian and Netherlandish influences with that of the German chorale. Scheidt's remaining sacred publications are *Pars prima concertuum sacrorum* (1622), which includes obbligato instrumental parts, four volumes of *Geistliche Concerten* for a small vocal ensemble with continuo (1631–40) and *Liebliche Krafft-Blümlein* (1635), concertos for two voices and continuo. He also published a voluminous dance anthology, *Paduana, galliarda, courante, alemande, intrada, canzonetto...* (1621) – and chorale variations for solo organ, the *Tabulatur-Buch* (1650), which confirm his reputation as an imaginative keyboard composer.

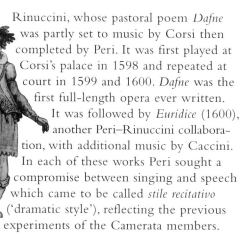

Schein, Johann Hermann

(Shīn, Yō-hän Hâr'-män) 1586–1630

GERMAN COMPOSER

Schein trained at Dresden, Naumburg and Leipzig. Following a short appointment at Weimar, he took charge of the music at St Thomas's, Leipzig, in 1616. His first vocal music collection, *Cymbalum Sionium* (1615), brings together settings of Latin and German texts in a variety of styles. A more modern outlook, embracing the Italian idiom and demonstrating greater personal expression, is reflected in his three- to five-voice chorale settings with *basso continuo, Opella nova* ('New Service', 1618). The second volume (1626), for three to six voices with **obbligato** instruments reveals his skill in word-painting. More than half the pieces are settings of biblical texts; the remainder are chorale-based. Two further publications reflect progressive and traditional influences respectively: *Fontana d'Israel* ('Israel's Fountain', 1623) sets Old Testament texts in Italian madrigal style while the *Cantional* ('Song Book', 1627) is a vast anthology of Lutheran hymns designed for use in the Leipzig churches. A colourful collection of instrumental dances, *Banchetto musicale* ('Musical Banquet'), was published in 1617.

(BL) Euridice
Woodcut for the score of Caccini's opera; Peri also used the popular story for his own opera.

(TL) Armide
Detail of a tapestry showing Louis XIV at a performance of Lully's opera Armide.

(TR) Jacopo Peri
The composer dressed up to model one of his costumes.

(BR) Samuel Scheidt
Scheidt published both sacred and secular music while serving as Kapellmeister *at Halle.*

Couperin ▶ p. 117 Handel ▶ p. 112 Rebel ▶ p. 120 Telemann ▶ p. 122 Vivaldi ▶ p. 122

Schütz, Heinrich

(Shüts, Hīn'-rikh) 1585–1672

GERMAN COMPOSER

Schütz received his early training at the Collegium Mauritianum at Hessen-Kassel. From there he went to Marburg University to study law. In 1609, Landgrave Moritz of Hessen-Kassel, of whom Schütz was a protegé, sent the young composer to Venice where he studied with **Giovanni Gabrieli** (*c.* 1553–1612). He returned to Kassel in about 1613, but after visiting Dresden became a permanent member of the household of Elector Johann Georg I of Saxony. He held the post of *Kapellmeister* at the Dresden court for almost half a century. Schütz's fame grew rapidly both in Germany and abroad, but he was prevented from publishing many of his large-scale pieces by the difficult economic conditions caused by the Thirty Years' War. He suffered much personal sadness, including the deaths of his young wife in 1625, his close friend Schein in 1630 and his two brothers (1638 and 1655).

VENICE AND DRESDEN

Schütz paid a second visit to Venice in 1628, following the production of his opera *Dafne* (now lost) for the wedding celebrations of the Elector's daughter and Landgrave Georg II of Hessen-Darmstadt. He met Monteverdi and published the *Symphoniae sacrae* ('Holy Symphony') in Venice the following year. Back in Dresden in 1630 he composed the motet 'Das ist je gewieslich wahr' at the dying request, and in memory, of Schein.

Schütz's principal responsibilities at the Dresden court were the provision of theatre and occasional music for special functions, and the supervision of vocal and instrumental resources. He rebuilt and reorganized court music after the Thirty Years' War, recruiting many musicians from Italy. Such were the privations inflicted on German cultural and economic life by this, that during the 1630s and early 1640s, Schütz divided his time between the Dresden court and that of King Christian of Copenhagen. The king appointed Schütz his *Kapellmeister* in 1633, and in 1639 the composer took up an additional *Kapellmeister's* post at Hildesheim. Schütz returned to Dresden in 1645 and struck an agreement with the Elector to work for him just six months a year over the following decade. In 1656, Johann Georg I died and his successor appointed Schütz *Ober-Kapellmeister*, at the same time releasing him from the responsibilities of supervising the court music and musicians. He continued to travel and compose almost until his death.

PASSION

Schütz's music spans over half a century and embraces old and newly emerging compositional styles. By introducing Italian developments to Germany he laid the foundations of eighteenth-century German sacred music. Among his finest collections are *Psalmen Davids* ('The Psalms of David', 1619), and *Cantiones sacrae* (1625), both of which reveal a masterly *rapprochement* between Italian expression and Lutheran tradition, the strikingly organized *Musicalische Exequien* (1636), *Geistliche Chor-Music* ('Spiritual Choir Music', 1648) and the stylistically forward-looking and emotionally affecting *Die sieben Wortte Jesu Christi am Kreuz* ('The Seven Words of Jesus Christ on the Cross', 1885). The *Weinachtshistorie* ('Christmas Story', 1660) also demonstrates his talent for magnificent orchestration.

Stradella, Alessandro

(Stră-del'-lă, Ā-lel'-săn'-drō) 1644–82

ITALIAN COMPOSER

Stradella was born in Rome. By the age of 20 he was composing for the exiled Queen Christina of Sweden who appointed him *servitore di camera* (servant of the chamber). He enjoyed the patronage of several leading families, but was forced to leave Rome briefly in 1669 after attempting to embezzle money from the church. An ill-judged affair with one of his pupils led to his murder in Genoa.

Stradella made important contributions to several musical forms, anticipating *concerto grosso* principles later established by Corelli in a *sonata di viole* and in the orchestral disposition of his most dramatic oratorio *San Giovanni Battista* ('Saint John the Baptist'), performed in Rome in 1675.

Strozzi, Barbara

(Strŏt-sē, Bâr'-bră) 1619–64

ITALIAN COMPOSER AND SINGER

In the 1630s, Strozzi was a central figure of the Venetian Accademia degli Unisoni, established by her adopted (or perhaps natural) father, the poet Giulio Strozzi, to provide a forum for her renowned vocal performances. A pupil of Cavalli, she published eight volumes of over 100 madrigals, motets, arias and cantatas; she probably wrote most of them to sing herself. Her music is characterized by lyricism, frequent **melismas** (prolonging one syllable over many notes) and careful word-painting.

Sweelinck, Jan Pieterszoon

(Svā'-lingk, Yän Pe'-ter-sun) 1562–1621

NETHERLANDISH COMPOSER

Sweelinck was a composer, organist and teacher, numbering Scheidt among his pupils. He was enormously influential in the development of north and mid-German organ music, later prompting the most important writer on music of the German Baroque, **Johann Mattheson** (1681–1764), to describe him as the 'creator of Hamburg organists'. He worked all his life in Amsterdam, where he was organist at the Oude Kerk. He mastered the traditional form of the motet and created a synthesis of European styles, above all in his keyboard works, of which none was printed in his lifetime. His published vocal music includes *Cantiones sacrae* (1619) and secular songs.

(TR) Johann Sebastian Bach
The Bach dynasty reached its peak with Johann Sebastian, shown here at the keyboard.
(BR) Adriana Basile
The Italian Basile was renowned for her performances in Monteverdi's operas.

melisma ▶ p. 360

THE BACH DYNASTY

During the early seventeenth century a remarkable dynasty of musicians emerged, culminating in the genius of J. S. Bach. His musical forebears are too numerous to consider individually, but a handful of them were sufficiently accomplished and imaginative as composers to deserve a mention. Their music is increasingly finding a place in present-day concert programming.

Their multifarious gifts and musical versatility embraced singing, playing, teaching, composing and instrument-building. Their skills became legendary in their native Thuringia (central Germany) and their surname synonymous with the science and performance of music. An entry in the Eisenach town records relates that in 1672 Ambrosius Bach – father of J. S. Bach – 'the new director of town music played at Easter upon the organ, the violin, the trumpet and the kettledrums, and also sang, something which has never been known in the history of Eisenach'.

The Roots of Genius

The motet 'Unser Leben ist ein Schatten' ('Our Life is a Shadow') by Johann Bach (1604–73) paints an affecting picture of the frailty of human life and may have been inspired by the terrible hardship of the Thirty Years' War. Johann Bach's brother Heinrich (1615–92) was also an able composer. His sons Johann Christoph Bach (1642–1703) and Johann Michael Bach (1648–94) were the most original of J. S. Bach's ancestors. Both were fluent in the art of the chorale motet, but it is the vocal concertos of Johann Christoph that perhaps provide the most striking evidence of his talent. He was highly regarded by other members of the family, including J. S. Bach, who described him as a 'profound composer' and later **Carl Philipp Emanuel Bach** (1714–88) added to his father's opinion, 'this is the great and expressive composer'.

Torelli, Giuseppe

(Tō-rel'-lē, Jōō-sep'-pē) 1658–1709

ITALIAN COMPOSER

Torelli was born in Verona, but moved to Bologna in the early 1680s where, like Corelli, he became a member of the Accademia dei Filarmonici. He was a violin virtuoso and teacher who studied with Giacomo Antonio Perti (1661–1756) in Bologna. There he joined the orchestra of S Petronio. He travelled to Germany and Austria during the 1690s; the Dresden violinist and composer, Johann Georg Pisendel (1687–1755) became one of his pupils. He wrote prolifically for trumpet and strings and played an important role in the development of the concerto. His 12 most stylistically advanced pieces were published shortly after his death as *Concerti grossi con una pastorale per il Ss Natale.*

ON THE STAGE AND IN THE CONVENT

The rise of opera in the early Baroque period provided increased musical opportunities for women, especially as singers, but also as composers. One of the earliest female opera singers was Vittoria, who worked for the Medici court in Florence. Her career was overshadowed by that of another Medici employee, composer and singer – Francesca Caccini – who by the 1620s was the highest-paid musician at the Medici court. Caccini wrote the music for many court entertainments. Unfortunately only one has survived: her opera *La liberazione di Ruggiero dall'isola d'Alcina* (1625), the first Italian opera to be performed outside its native country.

Operatic productions in France did not use castratos and thus provided more opportunities for female singers, who also performed in the choruses that were so popular on the French operatic stage. The dramatic soprano Marthe le Rochois (*c.* 1658–1728) appeared as *première actrice* in the original productions of Lully's *tragédies lyriques*. The English soprano Katharine Tofts (*c.* 1685–1756), working in London, was one of the earliest female singers to attract the intense media attention that was to become associated with the operatic *prima donna*. An unusual example of a noblewoman working as an opera singer is Faustina Bordoni (1700–81) from Venice, whose international career included singing for Handel in London in the 1720s and thereafter for her husband, the German composer **Johann Adolf Hasse** (1699–1783), in Dresden and Venice.

Musical Nuns

While working on the stage was not regarded as a reputable female occupation, retiring to a convent remained an option that allowed women to devote themselves to music while retaining their respectability. The sixteenth-century decrees of the Council of Trent, banning nuns from performing polyphonic music, were often ignored and many Italian convents continued to be renowned for their music. Several nuns, such as Caterina Assandra (fl. 1609–18) and Chiara Margarita Cozzolani (1602–*c.* 1676), both from convents in or near Milan, wrote a wide range of liturgical and sacred vocal music which became known outside Italy. Isabella Leonarda (1620–1704), a nun at the Collegio di Santa Orsola in Novara, published a remarkable series of 20 volumes of music, containing over 200 liturgical and sacred works. These include the earliest surviving set of instrumental pieces to be published by a woman, her op. 16 sonatas, which appeared in 1693.

C. P. E. Bach ▶ p. 156 G. Gabrieli ▶ p. 51 Hasse ▶ p. 160 Mattheson ▶ p. 119

The Early Baroque

STYLES AND FORMS

Perhaps the most important developments in music around the year 1600 were the emergence of the *basso continuo* and the fashion for virtuosity. The presence of an independent bass line moved composition away from the flowing polyphony of the Renaissance, in which all voices played an equal role in the texture, leaving the upper voices free to indulge in expressive and impressive displays. It also helped to sustain larger-scale structures and provide continuity between contrasting sections. Whereas before music had two functions and styles – church and chamber – now a third was added: theatre. The boundaries between different functions and styles became less rigid so that, for example, dramatic elements (recitative and aria) began to appear in sacred genres and dance elements were incorporated into serious instrumental works, such as the suite and sonata. These changes gave rise to some of the most important musical forms: solo songs (monody), opera, oratorio, cantata, sonata and concerto.

The Development of Opera

The wealth and stability of Florence under the rule of the Medici Grand Dukes created the perfect environment for the development of opera at the end of the sixteenth century. Among the city's various formal and informal academies and salons was the Florentine Camerata, a group of friends who met at the house of the nobleman and composer Giovanni de' Bardi in the 1570s and 1580s, to discuss subjects such as the power of ancient classical music and how it could be recreated to reform and 'purify' modern music. (Bardi disapproved strongly of singers who ruined madrigals by adding badly improvised ornamentation merely in order to show off their voices.) Among the members of Bardi's Camerata were **Vincenzo Galilei** (*c.* 1520–91) and **Caccini**, the most important singer at the Florentine court.

Another court singer, **Peri**, was a member of a similar (though less academic) group which met at Corsi's home during the 1590s. Caccini and Peri, who were involved with many of the ***intermedi*** staged at the Florentine court, enjoyed a healthy rivalry in trying to develop a new style of singing in which, unlike much music of the time, clarity of the words was paramount.

Masque

England had a long tradition of staged allegorical plays and pageants that involved music and dancing but, unlike Italy and France, it had nothing that could be described as opera. What it did have in the seventeenth century was the masque, a lavish form of court entertainment which included speech, songs, choruses, instrumental music and dances. Visual impact – spectacular scenery, costumes, stage machinery and gesture – was very important, and in many Stuart masques these elements were designed by the famous architect Inigo Jones. The first masque for which a complete score survives is *Cupid and Death* (1659) with music by **Locke** and **Orlando Gibbons** (1583–1625).

Musical Drama

The first English musical drama to be sung throughout was William Davenant's *The Siege of Rhodes* (1656). The music, now lost, was by **Henry Lawes** and others. Davenant was among the first to incorporate speech into his music dramas (often based on heroic plays, especially Shakespeare's), to create a new genre known as **semi-opera**, which was also influenced by the French ***comédie-ballet*** of **Lully**. **Purcell** wrote five semi-operas, including *The Fairy-Queen*, based on *A Midsummer Night's Dream* – in which his music is limited to the masques at the end of each of the five acts – and one opera, *Dido and*

(BL) Venice
The courts at Venice and Florence played an important role in the development of seventeenth-century opera.

(TL)* The Party in the Country *by David Vinckeboons
The early Baroque period saw the first musical dramas in England; these were often based on heroic plays such as those of Shakespeare.

chorale ▶ p. 357 *comédie-ballet* ▶ p. 357 *da capo* ▶ p. 358 ground bass ▶ p. 358 *intermedio* ▶ p. 359 ostinato ▶ p. 361 *ritornello* ▶ p. 362 semi-opera ▶ p. 362

OPERA: *EURIDICE, ORFEO, POPPEA*

What distinguishes Peri's *Euridice* from other musical dramas staged at the time, and allows it to claim the status of the first opera, is the composer's use of a new style of singing, intended to imitate speech in song. It was partly the outcome of attempts to recreate the direct and expressive declamation of ancient Greek and Roman dramas, and partly the natural progress of composers seeking to express themselves in new ways; it led to the development of operatic recitative.

Peri's music for *Euridice* includes choruses that comment on the events and solos that either express the character's emotions in song or narrate the story in the new declamatory style of singing, *stile recitativo*. The declamation closely follows the rhythm of the words. Expressive details, such as dynamics and ornamentation (trills, runs and so on), are carefully notated to discourage singers from improvising, and the continuo accompaniment is carefully paced to match the 'passions' of the singer's words.

Monteverdi's *Orfeo*

The story of Orpheus and Eurydice is also the subject of **Monteverdi**'s opera *Orfeo*, first performed in Mantua in 1607. While the early Florentine operas can sound rather sparse, Monteverdi's music creates a richer sound-world that is derived from the *intermedi* tradition. What interested him was how to portray as vividly as possible the emotions and actions of the characters.

The accompaniment is provided by a large and varied orchestra. It includes lighter combinations of recorders, violins, chitarroni and harpsichord for pastoral scenes; darker trombones, bass viols and organs for the infernal scenes; and the whole range for the opening fanfare and many of the choruses, which often use lively dance rhythms. The emotional and musical heart of the opera is Orpheus's 'Possente spirto', in which he tries to charm the boatman Charon with his renowned singing powers so that he may cross the River Styx. Each of Orpheus's verses is punctuated by an instrumental *ritornello*, and the style and instrumentation change with each verse.

Poppea

Monteverdi's last opera, *L'incoronazione di Poppea* (some of the music is by other composers), was written many years later, in 1642. Although it uses a much simpler orchestra than *Orfeo*, Monteverdi's carefully structured music brings to life characters who are not mythological, as in the early Italian operas, but human – subject to human emotions and ambitions. The *stile recitativo* is now a much more intense representation of speech – notably in Octavia's recitative lament 'Disprezzata regina' ('The Scornful Queen'') – with characters often interrupting one another in recitative dialogues. The arias and duets are substantial, lyrical and richly expressive, particularly in Nero and Poppaea's final duet, 'Pur ti miro' ('I Look for You').

Aeneas, which includes Dido's famous haunting lament with its melancholy **ground bass**. Masques continued to flourish into the eighteenth century.

Ternary Aria

In seventeenth-century opera, the term 'aria' denotes a song, often (though not always) for a solo singer and usually in several verses (or 'strophes'). It is generally accompanied by continuo (perhaps using a repeating **ostinato** or ground bass) and instrumental ***ritornellos*** may be played between the strophes. Most seventeenth-century arias are in ternary form – that is, the first line (or lines) is repeated at the end of the strophe, giving the structure ABA; if the last line(s) is repeated instead, the structure is ABB. The music of the repeated lines may be exactly the same as at the first hearing or may be varied. ABA form gave rise to the ***da capo*** aria, the main type in the eighteenth century: after the aria has been sung once, the performer is instructed to repeat the first section *da capo* ('from the beginning'), adding additional ornamentation *ad libitum*.

The Rise of Oratorio

In February 1600, a new style of sacred drama set to music, **Cavalieri**'s *Rappresentatione di Anima, et di Corpo*, was performed at the Chiesa Nuova in Rome. Cavalieri had worked in Florence, and his *Rappresentatione* included choruses with dance rhythms, florid madrigal-like songs and solos in the new recitative style. Some of the finest examples of this style from the mid-seventeenth century are the Latin oratorios of **Carissimi** (such as *Jephte*). Here the individual characters are portrayed by soloists singing either in simple recitative or in a more lyrical aria style; instrumental *ritornellos* punctuate the vocal pieces.

By the late seventeenth century, the oratorio was continuing to flourish in Rome but was also spreading to northern Italy and even beyond, notably to Vienna. It developed from a devotional work to a form of entertainment, known as a *sepolcro*, often performed as an alternative to opera when the theatres were closed during Lent.

In Protestant Germany the vernacular oratorio was foreshadowed in the biblical settings, or *Historias*, of **Schütz** and developed by composers such as **Telemann**. Greater use was made of choruses than in Italian oratorios and **chorales** were incorporated. The German oratorio was to reach its peak with **J. S. Bach**.

Roman Church Music and the *Stile Antico*

Many composers in Italy in the early seventeenth century, such as Cavalieri, were developing new approaches in sacred vocal music, with more soloistic vocal writing and instrumental accompaniment. But the older style, epitomized by **Giovanni Pierluigi da Palestrina** (1525/6–94), persisted among some composers in Rome. This self-consciously archaic style was known as the *stile antico* and is found particularly in the works of his pupils, such as Gregorio Allegri (1582–1652), famous for his setting of the 'Miserere'. Many later composers, particularly in Germany, continued to hold up Palestrina's church music and the *stile antico* as worthy of emulation.

French *Grand Motet*

The *grand motet*, which flourished at the royal chapel of Louis XIV, developed in the mid-seventeenth century. As in other forms of Baroque music, the main element was contrast, here of solo voices (*petit choeur*) and chorus (*grand choeur*), the soloists accompanied by continuo instruments (bass viol, theorbo and harpsichord) and with the chorus often doubled by instruments. Lully's *grands motets* are typical: they begin with an orchestral introduction and the orchestra returns throughout the work to mark structural divisions. The text is set in sections for soloists, small groups and chorus. In the hands of **Michel-Richard de Lalande** (1657–1726) the *grand motet* came of age: the orchestra no longer merely doubled the voices, and expressive melodies and rich harmonies in the *récits*, *airs* and choruses underlined the text's meaning.

Villancico

In the sixteenth century the villancico – a song for several voices, setting a text made up of verses (*coplas*) and refrain (*estribillo*) – was one of the main forms of secular vocal music in Spain. By the early seventeenth century, however, sacred texts became common in the villancico and, in Latin America as in Spain, it was used in church services instead of the Latin motet. At the hands of composers such as Juan Blas de Castro (*c.* 1560–1631) and Juan Ridalgo (1614–85,) its form expanded to something more like the cantata: more *coplas* were included, set for solo voices with organ accompaniment. These were contrasted with movements for

J. S. Bach ▶ p. 106 Caccini ▶ p. 80 Carissimi ▶ p. 80 Cavalieri ▶ p. 81 Galilei ▶ p. 51 Gibbons ▶ p. 51 Lalande ▶ p. 118 H. Lawes ▶ p. 83 Locke ▶ p. 83
Lully ▶ p. 84 Monteverdi ▶ p. 76 Palestrina ▶ p. 56 Peri ▶ p. 84 Purcell ▶ p. 78 Schütz ▶ p. 86 Telemann ▶ p. 122

chorus accompanied by a small instrumental ensemble. In the eighteenth century the form developed further: *coplas* were replaced by recitatives and aria, instrumental sections became more prominent and dance rhythms were even introduced.

Protestant Motet in Germany

Schütz's *Psalmen Davids*, with their use of speech-like *stile recitativo* in both solo and choral writing, their **antiphonal** exchange between choirs and their instrumental accompaniments, are typical of the *grand motet* style in Lutheran Germany. His choral motets (such as the *Geistliche Chor-Music*, 1648) are notable for using the musical contrasts and responsiveness to the text characteristic of madrigal composition. Schütz and **Schein** were also influenced by the antiphonal style of Venetians such as **Giovanni Gabrieli**. Yet these large-scale works were beyond the performing capabilities of many groups; much more suitable were the *geistliche Konzerte*, or concerted motets, for reduced forces – even just solo voices and continuo, or perhaps with an accompanying instrumental ensemble.

ORGANS AND BUILDERS

Many of the famous German Baroque organs are what is known as *Werkprinzip* ('department principle') organs, built up of several separate 'departments' (i.e. a manual or pedal keyboard and its chest), all linked into the single console at which the organist plays. This method of construction means that organs can be tailored to specific requirements and added to over the years. Often it is obvious from the instrument's appearance that its final form is the result of several stages of building.

Organ-Building Families

German Baroque organ builders such as the Fritzsche and Compenius families and Andreas Silbermann (1678–1734) and his brother Gottfried (1683–1753) increased the size and quality of the instrument and the variety of stops. Others, such as Eugen Casparini (1623–1706), also introduced novel stops such as bells and drums and visual effects such as angels playing trumpets. Gottfried Fritzsche (1578–1638), who worked as an apprentice on the organs of St Thomas's and St Nicholas's, Leipzig, was a friend of **Michael Praetorius** (*c.* 1571–1621), Schütz and **Scheidt**; and J. S. Bach obviously took a great interest in the splendid new organs being built at this time: he knew Gottfried Silbermann, and is thought to have travelled when a young man to Hamburg to hear Reincken play and to Lübeck to hear Buxtehude play.

Anglican Anthem

In England, Latin had ceased to be the official language of the church in 1549, and by the end of the sixteenth century the anthem, not the motet, was one of the main features of the Anglican choral service. The most common form was the verse anthem, in which verses for solo voices with organ (or other instrumental) accompaniment alternated with verses sung by the full choir. But many composers, following the example of **William Byrd** (1543–1623), wrote both verse and full choral anthems. After the Restoration in 1660, composers such as Locke helped to lead the anthem away from the vestiges of Renaissance vocal writing towards a new style, also expanding the instrumental accompaniment to include a string group which played between verses. Purcell, like **Blow**, wrote full anthems, verse anthems and the new orchestral anthems.

Lutheran Chorale

One important aspect of Martin Luther's church reforms was an emphasis on the involvement of the congregation in the service. This was achieved in particular by singing hymns, called chorales, that were in German rather than Latin. They had short, rhyming verses and were set to easily remembered and easily sung tunes. By the end of the sixteenth century fewer new chorale tunes were being written, but composers were arranging chorales in simple four-part harmony, with the melody in the top voice for the congregation to sing. Books of chorales, culminating in the works of J. S. Bach, were published containing just the melody and a **figured bass**, which could be played on the organ in church or, for domestic use, on a smaller keyboard instrument.

Fugue

Fugue is a particularly strict technique of counterpoint, involving the imitation by each voice (a vocal or instrumental line) in turn of a theme stated by the opening voice (the term is derived from the Latin *fuga*, meaning 'flight', 'fleeing'). Imitation on a small scale can been found in music dating from at least medieval times, but it was only after 1600 that the large-scale fugue became an important technique of composition.

A fugue begins with the main theme, the 'subject', stated by a single voice. As the subject is completed a second voice enters with the 'answer', a repeat of the subject at a different pitch – usually at an interval of a fourth or fifth from that of the subject, in the **dominant** key. (If it is an exact repeat of the subject, it is known as a 'real' answer, if an inexact repeat, a 'tonal' answer.) The first voice, meanwhile, accompanies the answer with a 'counter-subject'. A third voice then enters with the subject, usually returning to the **tonic** and often an octave above or below the pitch of the first voice's entry; the second voice takes over the counter-subject, while the first voice moves to a second counter-subject. This opening section, in which each voice sets out the subject or answer, is called the **exposition**. After the exposition the subject is developed and varied, for example being heard in **augmentation** (longer note

(NR) Baroque Musicians
Lute player following a musical score held by an old man.
(FR) Louis XIV
Engraving showing Louis XIV dancing a minuet.

COUNTERPOINT

The term 'counterpoint' is derived from the Latin *contra punctum* ('[note] against note'). It is generally understood to refer to a technique of composition in which continuous lines move (horizontally) against each other, as opposed to chordal writing, in which the sound can be thought of in vertical blocks. Strictly speaking, these two types of writing are called polyphony ('many sounds') and homophony ('same sound'); chordal considerations are not absent from polyphony, nor melodic ones from homophony.

The sacred vocal works of Palestrina, in which each voice plays an equal role in the musical structure, are often described as one peak of the contrapuntal art, while, at the end of the Baroque era, the music of J. S. Bach represents another. Bach's fugues are the most obvious examples of his contrapuntal skill, but equally skilful is the counterpoint between voice and accompaniment in the arias of his vocal works, or the illusion of contrapuntal lines created in his works for solo instruments, particularly in the suites for unaccompanied cello.

antiphonal music ▶ p. 356 augmentation ▶ p. 356 cadence ▶ p. 356 diminution ▶ p. 358 dominant ▶ p. 358 exposition ▶ p. 358 figured bass ▶ p. 358 partita ▶ p. 361 suspension ▶ p. 362 tonic ▶ p. 363

values), **diminution** (shorter note values) or inversion (upside-down), or with 'stretto' entries (the voices entering more quickly after one another than in the exposition). Between the entries of the subject there may be a short connecting passage; in the exposition this is called a 'codetta', and after the exposition an 'episode'.

Figured Bass

Around 1600, musical textures moved away from the polyphony of the Renaissance, in which all voices were equal in function and could share the same material, towards a new texture in which the bass line had the specific function of providing harmonic support for the free melodic lines of the upper voices. This bass line is known by the Italian term *basso continuo* ('continuous bass'; the English term 'thoroughbass' is also found). In both vocal and instrumental music, the bass line was generally played by a keyboard instrument. Its part was not usually written out for two hands, but consisted of the bass line alone, with numbers (or 'figures') below the notes, indicating to the performer which chords to improvise above it; this is known as a 'figured bass'. The term *basso continuo* strictly refers to an independent bass line, while a keyboard part that simply doubles the lowest sounding voice at any time is called a *basso seguente* ('following bass'). The earliest figured basses are found in the dramatic works of Caccini, Peri, Cavalieri and Monteverdi, around 1600.

Trio Sonata

The trio sonata was one of the most important instrumental forms and textures of the Baroque period. It was written for two melody instruments and continuo, and the most common instrumentation was two violins with cello (bass viol or bassoon) and/or harpsichord, although at least one of the violin parts could be replaced by an instrument such as the treble viol, flute, recorder or oboe and the harpsichord by a chamber organ. The sonatas of Italian composers such as Giovanni Legrenzi (1626–90), Giovanni Battista Vitali (1632–92) are often described as being *da chiesa* (for church, often with four movements: slow–fast– slow–fast) or *da camera* (chamber, with three or four movements based on dances). In **Corelli**'s pieces, the two upper voices are often paired in thirds, drawing out sweet **suspensions**, or exchange imitative or fugal phrases. The trio-sonata texture was an important move away from the equal-voiced polyphony of the Renaissance.

Suite

The Baroque suite is a set of instrumental pieces in the same key, some or all of which are based on dances, typically the allemande (German), courante (French), sarabande (Spanish) and (after 1650) gigue (English). Other dances or variations (often called 'doubles') of these four could be added, as could a prelude or other introductory piece. Many suites of dances were published in Germany, England, France, Italy and elsewhere in the early seventeenth century.

In the second half of the seventeenth century suites were written by composers such as **Froberger** and **Buxtehude** (for keyboard) in Germany; Denis Gaultier (1603–72) (for lute), **Chambonnières** and **Couperin** (for keyboard) in France; and **William Lawes** (strings), Purcell (keyboard) and Locke (strings, keyboard) in England. Other composers wrote freer sets of pieces which do not necessarily use the standard dances, such as Lully's suites drawn from his stage works, **Marais**' five books of *pièces de viole* (1686– 1725) and Telemann's many orchestral suites.

NEW DANCE SOURCES

By this time, the dances of the suite had become very stylized, and the additional movements added to the four core dances were many and varied. The most notable composers of suites in the late Baroque were **Jean-Philippe Rameau** (1683–1764) for harpsichord, and **Handel** (mainly keyboard, but also the well-known orchestral *Water Music*, 1717, and *Music for the Royal Fireworks*, 1749). J. S. Bach's cello and violin suites, in particular, are technically challenging and much weightier compositions than the early suites of music. He also wrote keyboard suites (the so-called French and English suites and six harpsichord **partitas**) and four orchestral suites, the latter, in contrast, designed more for entertainment.

French Overture

The form of the French overture was established in the introductory music of Lully's ballet *Alcidiane* (1658). There are two contrasting sections, the first slow and stately, with dotted rhythms and ascending flourishes on upbeats, and the second faster and with busy imitative or fugal writing; both sections are repeated. As the form developed, further sections were sometimes added, such as an additional slow movement after the second section, or a dance movement after either section. This format was widely used for opera and ballet overtures in the second half of the seventeenth century and the early eighteenth, not just by Lully and other French composers, but also by composers in Italy, England and Germany.

Concerto Grosso

The first publication to use the word 'concerto', the *Concerti di Andrea et di Gio. Gabrieli* (1587), did not contain what we understand today as concertos, but was a collection of sacred and secular pieces that could be performed by various combinations of instruments and voices, sometimes involving exchange between contrasting groups. The term continued to be applied to works for voices with instrumental accompaniment for much of the seventeenth century in Italy.

The first instrumental concertos that pit a soloist or soloists against an accompanying group, were written in the second half of the seventeenth century by composers such as **Stradella**. In these pieces, the orchestra is divided into two groups, the *concerto grosso* ('large ensemble', also known as the *ripieno*, 'rest', or *tutti*, 'all') and the *concertino* ('small ensemble', or *soli*, 'soloists'). A work written for these forces is called a *concerto grosso*. At its simplest, it consists of music for the three voices of the trio sonata; sections in which the soloists play alone contrast with tuttis, where they are doubled by the rest of the orchestra. More characteristically, solo passages are punctuated by orchestral **cadences**, and phrases stated by the orchestra are echoed and elaborated by the soloists.

Blow ▶ p. 80 Buxtehude ▶ p. 80 Byrd ▶ p. 49 Chambonnières ▶ p. 81 Corelli ▶ p. 82 Couperin ▶ p. 117 Froberger ▶ p. 82 G. Gabrieli ▶ p. 51 Handel ▶ p. 112 W. Lawes ▶ p. 83 Marais ▶ p. 119 Praetorius ▶ p. 56 Rameau ▶ p. 120 Scheidt ▶ p. 85 Schein ▶ p. 85 Stradella ▶ p. 86

The Early Baroque INSTRUMENTS

Violin

The basic construction of the violin, with its waisted or figure-of-eight body (with a hard-wood back, usually maple, and a softer front, usually spruce), was established early in the sixteenth century. The strings (tuned, from the top downwards, as E, A, D and G) run from a peg box, where tension can be adjusted by turning the pegs, and along a fingerboard. Here the player's left hand alters the length of the vibrating string and thus its pitch by 'stopping' it (firmly placing a finger on the string) at different positions to produce different notes. The strings pass over a bridge to the tail piece, which is attached to the end of the violin by a loop of gut. The surface of the fingerboard is made of a hard wood, to survive the constant wear on it. The soundpost sits underneath the foot of the bridge and runs towards the back; it supports string and bridge pressure while carrying and balancing string vibrations.

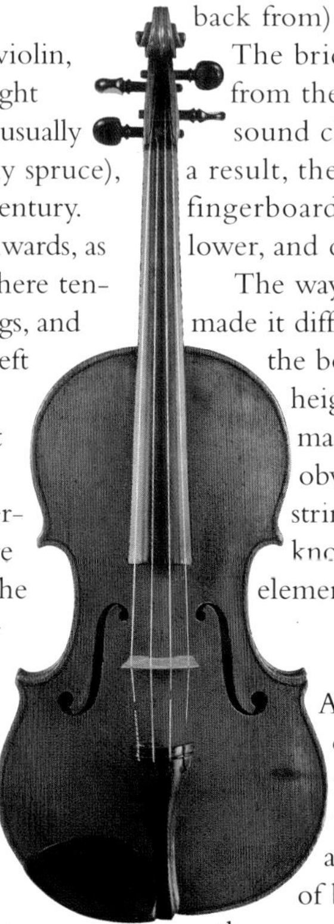

When their social status rose, violins began to be decorated with a marquetry inlay around the edge of the front (known as the 'belly') called 'purfling'. To allow the sound to escape from within the instrument, the belly was pierced on either side of the bridge by two sound holes shaped like an old-fashioned 'f'.

THE BAROQUE VIOLIN

The Baroque violin was different from the modern instrument in having its neck set perpendicular to (or only very slightly tilted back from) the line of the instrument's body. The bridge, which lifts the strings away from the body of the violin so that they can sound clearly, was lower than it is today. As a result, the strings lay slightly closer to the fingerboard, the tension on the strings was lower, and consequently the volume was less.

The way that the Baroque violin was set up made it difficult to change the string on which the bow was playing; the difference in height between the strings was less marked than it is today. This same set-up obviously made playing on two or more strings at once far easier. The technique, known as **double stopping**, is a notable element of Baroque music.

AN EVOLVING DESIGN

As the demands made by composers on the instrument increased, so its makers changed their designs. Necks were set back at a slightly greater angle and were made longer. Instead of being attached by glue and one nail, they were jointed in the top block (a chunk of wood at the top of the body, at the point where the neck joins it). Bridges became slightly higher. The soundpost, which sits inside the belly of the violin, underneath the bridge, to stop the pressure of the strings from driving it through the violin's front, was strengthened to take the increased tension.

Strings were initially made of pure gut before a technique was developed for wrapping them up by winding a silver thread around them in a spiral. Particularly on the deeper instruments in the violin family, a covered-gut string is easier to play.

PLAYING POSITION

The related viol was fretted and was held vertically either between the knees or on the lap by a seated performer. In general, it seems that fiddles were fretted for beginners and the frets were cut away once the player had learned the geography of the finger board. The fretless violin was always held against the upper body of the player – not under the chin as today. This clearly relates to its usage, for the violin was commonly played standing up, to accompany dancing. **Praetorius**'s *Theatrum instrumentorum* ('Theatre of Instruments') of 1620 includes a picture of the violin family, showing examples of the diminutive violins that we call 'kits', which were used by dancing masters. Various examples survive; they are also known as *pochettes* ('pockets'), since they were small enough to be tucked away in the pocket when the master wanted to free their hands in order to demonstrate a few steps.

(R) Antonio Stradivari
One of the 650 extant instruments made by Stradivari in the seventeenth century, the 'Emile Sauret Strad' (TR). Portrait of Stradivari, who remains the best-known maker of stringed instruments to this day (BR).

BOWS AND BOWMAKERS

In the early Baroque bow, the horsehair (which strokes the string and produces the sound) was fastened at the hand end, known as the 'heel', by an immovable 'nut' or 'frog', a kind of clip. During the seventeenth century, makers developed a frog in which the mechanism for attaching the horse hair could be released and then clipped back into a different notched position. This kind of ratchet system was abandoned in about 1700 and the earliest known bow to use the modern system, varying tension by means of turning a screw to draw the nut backwards in a groove, dates from 1694.

Styles of bowing changed as the bows themselves changed. The early Baroque cello, for example, seems to have been played either with the bow held palm-upwards, in the manner of a viol, or palm-down but with the hand as much as a quarter of the way along from the heel. During the eighteenth century, the balance of the bow changed, with the centre of gravity moving towards the heel. As a result, while the palm-down position won, the grip had to shift back to the heel. As the bow and bow-hold both developed, so greater control of the instrument became possible.

The most famous name in the history of bow-making is that of François Tourte (1747–1835). During his lifetime the bow became concave, and the modern forms of the point and the frog were designed. The length was finally fixed at about 75 cm (30 in) for the violin, with the viola a little shorter and the cello a little shorter again. Tourte's bows were made not of snakewood, which had been used earlier, but of pernambuco, a South American hardwood.

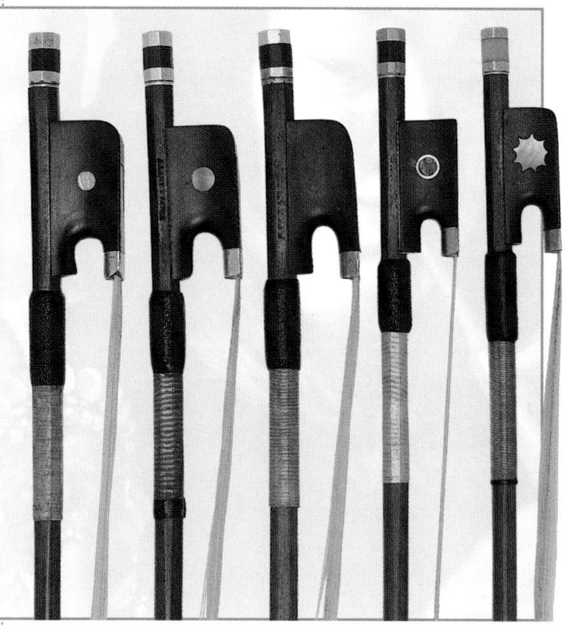

double stopping ▶ p. 358

Viola

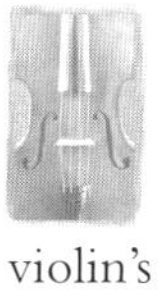

Developed to accompany the violin, the viola is tuned a fifth below it (losing the violin's top E string, it acquires instead a bottom C string) and plays alto to the violin's soprano. The viola was made as a slightly bigger violin, to be played in the same way.

It has been argued that if the makers had worked out the same size-to-pitch relationship for the viola as the violin, they would have come up with an instrument nearly half as big again, which would therefore have been played vertically, between the knees, like a small cello. Changes in design of the viola match those of the violin; they took place at the same time and were driven by the same musical forces.

THE BAROQUE VIOLA

The viola was harder to play than the violin. It took more time to get the thicker strings to 'speak' or sound musical. As a result, it was important to allow the viola player to have less to do and accordingly the viola line in Baroque music tends to be simple. There is little virtuoso music for the viola dating from the Baroque, though **Telemann** wrote three concertos for it.

During the Baroque era, a viola with seven bowed strings and seven concealed strings became popular. Called the viola d'amore, it is the size of a viola, but with a flat back like a viol. The sound holes are not 'f's but wavering lines, nicknamed the 'flaming sword'. The seven concealed strings run underneath the fingerboard and through, not over, the bridge. These vibrate in sympathy with the bowed strings. **Vivaldi** wrote several concertos for the viola d'amore (he actually wrote none for the viola).

BASS VIOL, VIOLONE AND BASS VIOLIN

The developing violin family did not immediately settle down into its modern designs, nor its modern grouping. Although the cello certainly existed during the early Baroque era, composers initially often wrote in preference for the bass violin. Slightly larger and heavier than the cello, with a gruffer sound and a lower tuning, it can be heard today in some historically informed (early music) performances of the music of **Purcell** and **Couperin**.

Few words in the musical lexicon are more confusing than 'violone'. Meaning simply a double-bass viol, the direct ancestor of the modern double bass, the term can be found in different documents referring to a surprisingly wide variety of different bass bowed string instruments, depending on where and when the document was written. It carried five or six strings and the tuning was variable. The bass viol or viola da gamba ('leg viol') has six or seven strings.

Although viols as a whole went into decline during the Baroque era, eclipsed by the upstart violin family like nobility by provincial gentry, the bass viol, joined by the double bass viol, enjoyed an extended life. The demand for instruments to accompany church choirs meant that bass viols were still being made at the time of the American Civil War (1861–65) and, indeed, the larger instruments were normally referred to as 'church basses'. In the mid nineteenth century, however, the much-delayed end came as more American churches bought reed or pipe organs.

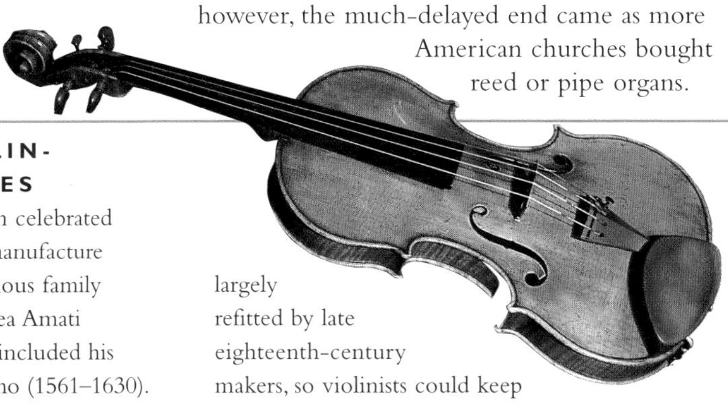

CREMONA'S VIOLIN-MAKING FAMILIES

The Italian city of Cremona has been celebrated since the sixteenth century for the manufacture of stringed instruments. The first famous family of makers there was the Amati. Andrea Amati (*c.* 1505–80) founded a dynasty that included his sons Antonio (*c.* 1538–95) and Girolamo (1561–1630). But it is the latter's son Nicolo (1596–1684) who is usually regarded as the most outstanding of the Amatis. His instruments tend to be rather larger than those of the preceding generation and as a result have a more powerful tone.

Andreas Guarneri (*c.* 1625–98) trained under Nicolo Amati, living in his house as an apprentice. His older son Pietro (1655–1720) moved to Mantua, but the younger, Giuseppe (1666–*c.* 1740), remained in Cremona and inherited Andreas's workshop. It is Giuseppe's son Giuseppe Antonio (1698–1744), known as 'Del Gesù' from his habit of labelling his instruments 'IHS' (*Iesus hominum salavtor*, 'Jesus, the Saviour of Mankind'), who is recognized as the most outstanding scion of this house.

Antonio Stradivari

No other maker has ever achieved the status of Antonio Stradivari (1644–1737). Known by the Latinized version of his name, 'Stradivarius', he may have studied with the Amati family, since his early instruments are held to reflect that maker's influence. Some 650 of his instruments survive – mostly violins, but also violas and cellos. Although any instrument by this man is bound to have a special aura, the golden period of his creativity is generally seen as the first two decades of the eighteenth century. Stradivariuses typically display an orange-brown varnish, flamed-maple backs and, most importantly, a rich, powerful sound.

While woodwind instruments wear out with use and get overtaken by technology, stringed instruments age well. They hold their value and they can be adapted to meet a new owner's demands. The older-style Baroque violins were largely refitted by late eighteenth-century makers, so violinists could keep up with the revolutions going on in music. In consequence, none of the Stradivariuses now in the hands of modern-day violinists look or sound the way they did when they left Stradivari's workshop.

Couperin ▶ p. 117 Praetorius ▶ p. 56 Purcell ▶ p. 78 Telemann ▶ p. 122 Vivaldi ▶ p. 122

Flute

Already a successful instrument in the Renaissance, the Middle Ages and indeed earlier, the flute has a long continuous history. The Renaissance flute was made of wood in one or sometimes two pieces, with a cylindrical bore and six finger holes. Its distinguishing feature was that it was not blown into directly like the recorder: the player held it sideways to the mouth (the 'traverse' position) and blew across a hole (a technique called 'cross blowing').

While the basic concept of cross blowing and traverse position remained constant, the flute's bore was changed to be conical in the third quarter of the seventeenth century. Instruments acquired a separate key for **chromatic** notes to be played by the little finger of the right hand, and they began being made in three pieces called 'joints'. It is traditionally the French Hotteterre family of players and makers that is credited with developing the Baroque flute. Pitched at A=392 (that is to say an entire tone below modern concert pitch), the instrument was written for particularly by **J. S. Bach** as well as Vivaldi and Couperin. At the end of the Baroque period, a four-piece flute established itself, still with one key.

J. J. QUANTZ

A significant name in the history of the Baroque flute is **Johann Joachim Quantz** (1697–1773), who wrote a treatise on playing the flute and was himself a maker, player and the composer of late Baroque/early classical flute music at the Berlin court of Frederick the Great. Quantz's instruments included something for which the modern instrument has no equivalent (because there is no need): *corps de rechange*. These were extra joints that could be fitted into the instrument and enabled it to be played at different pitches – pitch varied from region to region.

Bassoon

The bassoon, constructed in three parts, started being made in the mid-seventeenth century, perhaps in France in imitation of the flute and oboe. Built with three keys by the Denners of Nuremberg, the new instrument allowed greater virtuosity in the player than the one-piece curtal and dulcian, which began to decline in favour of the bassoon at the end of the seventeenth century. The playing position of the hands settled as left up, right down. A four-key instrument was developed in the early eighteenth century. It was to remain standard until the late classical period.

Made of pear or maple wood, the bassoon has a conical bore and is a tight U-shape, so the 'bell' or exit of the instrument is adjacent to the **crook**. This is the equivalent of the staple in an oboe: the reed that goes into the player's mouth is mounted on it. The sound of the Baroque bassoon was not unlike that of the oboe – similarly buzzing, but deeper. The bassoon was usually relegated to the bass line, supporting other instruments, but a number of more challenging solo pieces appeared for the bassoon at the hands of both Telemann and J. S. Bach; Vivaldi distinguished himself by composing no fewer than 37 concertos for it.

Cornett

Not to be confused with the modern valved brass-band cornet, which is a kind of small trumpet, the cornett (with that extra final 't') was made of two carved,

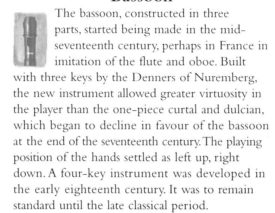

lightly curved pieces of European hardwood (such as pear) bound together and wrapped in leather. The instrument is further unusual in that it has an octagonal finish. To the body was added a mouthpiece, made variously of ivory, bone or silver. The result, a kind of wooden horn (for the mouthpiece does not contain a reed, like a

ORGAN TECHNOLOGY

The core of the organ's ability to make music is its ranks, or rows, of pipes, ranging from very large, for low pitches, to very small, for high pitches. Different pipe shapes and designs produce different tone qualities. Air is either pumped manually or, from the nineteenth century, produced by various mechanical means. It is held under pressure in a reservoir and admitted to the pipes by means of valves or 'pallets' operated from a keyboard.

Organs are notable for the variety of sounds they can produce. From the Middle Ages, organs had possessed levers or knobs known as 'stops' which, when moved, brought into play a different or additional row of pipes. The player could build up a 'chorus of principals' (the fundamental sound of the organ) or choose flute-like or reed-like effects.

Baroque organ builders sought to imitate a wider range of instruments. For example, the organ was capable of a brass effect. The Epistle organ in the Cathedral of Segovia in Spain was built in 1702 and 70 years later was joined by an identical twin organ opposite it. It is remarkable for its *trompeteria*, a feature of the late-Baroque Spanish organ. Horizontally mounted and pointing straight out at the base of the organ pipes like the ranked cannon on a man-o'-war of the time, these spectacular 'trumpets' were activated by an organ stop. Horizontal trumpets, which were very rare outside Spain in the Baroque period, can also be seen at St Maximin, Provence.

chromaticism ▶ p. 357 crook ▶ p. 358 *concerto grosso* ▶ p. 357

shawm), belongs mostly to the fifteenth to eighteenth centuries. It was played by fingering sixholes at the front and one thumb hole at the back. The compass was g" until the seventeenth century, when the music shows it reached d'".

VARIANTS OF THE CORNETT

There were also two variant cornetts: the straight cornett, usually made of boxwood, and the mute cornett, also of boxwood and straight, but with no detachable mouthpiece.

The cornett frequently appeared in the company of the sackbut. The instrument is associated with virtuosic display music, particular from Venice, where composers wrote demanding and exciting music for cornetts and sackbuts.

Oboe

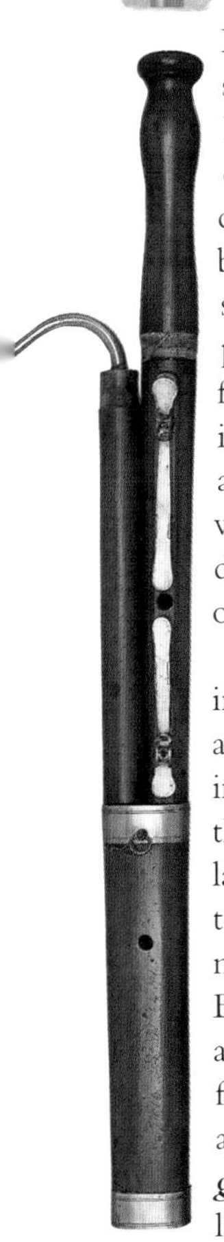

The oboe was developed in the mid seventeenth century and the credit is usually given to Jean Hotteterre (*c.* 1605–90/2), a shawm player at the court of Louis XIV. Its immediate predecessor was the shawm and the oboe took over the French name for smaller shawms, *hautbois* or 'loud woodwind instrument'. The distribution of the finger holes and the bore was changed, the instrument was shortened and it was made in three jointed pieces, not one. This last alteration allowed for a subtler tapering and greater precision in construction. The reed was mounted on a staple clear of the body of the instrument, without the shawm's pirouette, to be held directly in the mouth. Like the flute, the oboe acquired an extra chromatic key.

The modifications created a new instrument – one capable of a more refined and controllable sound and able to participate in mixed ensembles. In addition, it possessed the full chromatic compass that the shawm lacked. As a result, where the shawm had tended to be played out of doors, the oboe moved indoors and into the developing Baroque orchestra. It was quickly accepted as a standard instrument, being written for by Vivaldi, Handel and Telemann, and acting as soloist in some Baroque ***concerti grossi***. Purcell wrote the oboe into all his larger works after 1690.

(BL) Three Musicians *by Jacob Jordaens*
Baroque musicians playing wind instruments, including flutes and pipes.
(TL) Bassoon Player
Seventeenth-century German print showing a bassoon player.
(FR) Baroque Organ
Baroque organs such as this (c. 1627) took on grand and ornate appearances.

THE BAROQUE OBOE

The Baroque oboe was first built with two hinged levers called 'keys'. These stopped the holes at the lower end of the instrument (the D-sharp and the low C) mechanically, rather than directly by the fourth and fifth fingers. Interestingly, the low C key was made in the shape of a fish tail, in such a way that the instrumentalist could play with the hands in either position, suggesting that the modern practice of left above right had yet not become fixed. To ensure it could be played by either left- or right-handed people, it carried alternative extra keys, one on each side of the instrument. The alto variant of the oboe, known as the oboe d'amore, was also popular in the Baroque era. J. S. Bach used it in more than 60 of his works.

Organ

Unlike all other instruments, the organ can actually form part of the building in which it performs and its effect on church architecture has been matched only by that of the choir. While the internal workings of the organ have changed little over the centuries, one thing that has changed is the organ case. Every instrument needs to be put away in a case or bag and the organ is no exception. However, as the organ is fixed, so the case too needs to be a permanent fixture. Organ cases help blend and direct the sound, as well as being a major decorative feature.

EARLY ORGANS

The case of the medieval and Renaissance organ looked a bit like an altarpiece. The organ on the west wall of the Cathedral of Notre Dame at Valère sur Sion in Switzerland dates from the mid fifteenth century and is generally referred to as the oldest playable organ in the world. The doors over its face look like the wings on a medieval altarpiece. As Baroque principles took over in art and architecture, so the grand appearance of the Baroque organ developed.

The organ in the Sint Bavo Kerk, Haarlem, the Netherlands, was built between 1735 and 1738 and was played by the young **Mozart**. Here, the complex assemblage of pipes is gathered into a series of bundles, making it look like a regal gathering of stooks in a jewelled cornfield, and the whole is topped off by a host of statuary.

Although some organ pipes were made of wood, the most common material was a tin-lead alloy. This was hard and could be polished to a high sheen. Sometimes zinc or copper were used if the tin-lead alloy was judged too expensive. The metal was cast as a sheet, the shape cut out and then beaten round a 'mandrel' rather as shoe leather is shaped round a last, and the resulting joint soldered.

RELIGION AND POLITICS

Because they were so closely associated with the church, organs found themselves mixed up in the religious and political upheavals of the Renaissance and Baroque periods. Organs were smashed in the Netherlands in 1566 and in some parts of Protestant Europe they were removed from churches. Liturgical development, relative local affluence and patterns of trade and contact created different schools of organ building. In brief, while Protestant churches sought power from their instruments, Roman Catholic ones were looking for a wide palette of sounds. Thus organs in the Netherlands and Lutheran North Germany grew bigger, but Italian, French and South German organs built up a wider range of 'colours' – pipes imitating string instruments, percussion stops, echo departments and other effects. In fact, the organ was growing all round. Instruments from the late Baroque period sometimes have five manuals or 60 stops.

In addition to these built-in, site-specific organs, there were also far smaller chamber organs in use. Designed for private or domestic use, the later Baroque saw them played in concert rooms and pleasure gardens, as continuo instruments.

J. S. Bach ▶ p. 106 Mozart ▶ p. 144 Quantz ▶ p. 120

The Early Baroque

LISTENING GUIDE

Claudio Monteverdi
Vespers *of 1610*

WORK: Claudio Monteverdi, *Vespro della Beata Vergine* ('Vespers of the Blesses Virgin'), composed 1610.
SCORING: Soloists and chorus; *fifari*, recorders, cornettos, trombones, strings and continuo. In this recording, the *fifari* parts are played by high recorders, and the cornetto parts by trumpets.
EXCERPT: *Magnificat*, Tracks 2–13 of CDII. Duration: 19 min 58 secs
TIMINGS BASED ON: Vespers, Monteverdi Choir and Orchestra conducted by John Eliot Gardiner (see Recommended CDs).

RECOMMENDED CDs

1. *Vespers*. Monteverdi Choir and Orchestra, Salisbury Cathedral Boys' Choir, Philip Jones Brass Ensemble, David Munrow Recorder Ensemble. Soloists: Jill Gomez, Felicity Palmer, James Bowman, Robert Tear, Philip Langridge, John Shirley-Quirk, Michael Rippon. John Eliot Gardiner, conductor. Decca 443 482-2 (2 CDs)

   A fine recording on modern instruments, coupled on a mid-price Double Decca set with motets by Monteverdi, Gabrieli and Giovanni Bassano.

2. *Vespers*. Les Arts Florissants, les Sacqueboutiers de Toulouse. Soloists: Sophie Marin-Degor, Maryseult Wieczorek, Artur Stefanowicz, Fabián Schofrin, Paul Agnew, Joseph Cornwell, François Piolino, Thierry Félix, Clive Bayley. William Christie, conductor. Erato 3984-23139-2 (2 CDs)

   Monteverdi's music is supplemented by plainchant and instrumental works by Giovanni Paolo Cima. 'Lauda, Jerus alem' and the 'Magnificat' are sung at the lower pitch that some scholars believe to be correct.

3. *Vespers*. Taverner Consort, Choir and Players. Andrew Parrott, conductor. Virgin Veritas 5 61347 2 (2 CDs)

   A performance that sets the Vespers in the liturgical context of the Feast of the Assumption (15 August). Different plainchant but the same pieces by Cima as on the Christie recording, and the same adjustment to the pitch.

4. *Vespers*. Monteverdi Choir, London Oratory Junior Choir, English Baroque Soloists, His Majesty's Sagbutts and Cornetts. Soloists: Ann Monoyios, Marinella Pennicchi, Michael Chance, Mark Tucker, Nigel Robson, Sandro Naglia, Bryn Terfel, Alastair Miles. John Eliot Gardiner, conductor. DG Archiv 429 565-2AH2 (2 CDs)

   Gardiner's second recording, this time on early instruments. Also available on video, it was made in the spectacular setting of St Mark's, Venice, which may have played host to a performance during Monteverdi's lifetime.

In his long life, Monteverdi spanned the transition from the polyphonic or contrapuntal style of the Renaissance, where each strand in the musical texture is of equal importance, to the monodic or homophonic style of the Baroque, where the emphasis is on an expressive melodic line supported by a slow-moving bass. In 1610 he published a volume of church music, dedicated to the pope and printed in Venice, which was almost certainly a bid for employment. It failed in the short run, but in 1613 Monteverdi was appointed *maestro di capella* at St Mark's, Venice. He had to perform some of his own music as part of the selection process for the job and it is very likely that he chose the main work from the 1610 volume, which was a setting of the *Vespers* interspersed with motets for solo voices.

MIXTURE OF STYLES

The *Vespers* get off to a brilliant start, with Monteverdi clearly showing that he is looking both forwards and backwards. The two choirs chant the words on one chord, a technique that would have been familiar to members of the congregation. What they would have found novel is the use of his instrumental **toccata** which Monteverdi adapted from his first opera, *Orfeo*, composed three years earlier.

This mixture of styles is continued in the five Vesper psalms. Each one is based on a plainchant melody. In 'Dixit Dominus' the opening tag is heard in one voice after another, at different levels of the contrapuntal texture. Monteverdi continues in the old style with more chanting, this time in free rhythm; but at 'Iuravit Dominus' the plainchant in the bass is overlaid with a solo tenor duet in a more declamatory style. The contrast is

1. 0'58" (*Magnificat*)
The chorus opens with a bold statement of 'Magnificat', answered (0'34") gently by a solo soprano.

2. 1'31" (*Et exultavit*)
The solo tenors express joy in imitative counterpoint, while the chorus altos continue the plainchant melody in long notes (0'07").

3. 1'56" (*Quia respexit*)
A solo tenor intones the melody, accompanied in turn by sopranino recorders, trombones and treble recorders. The chorus tenors join in at 'omnes generationes' (1'42").

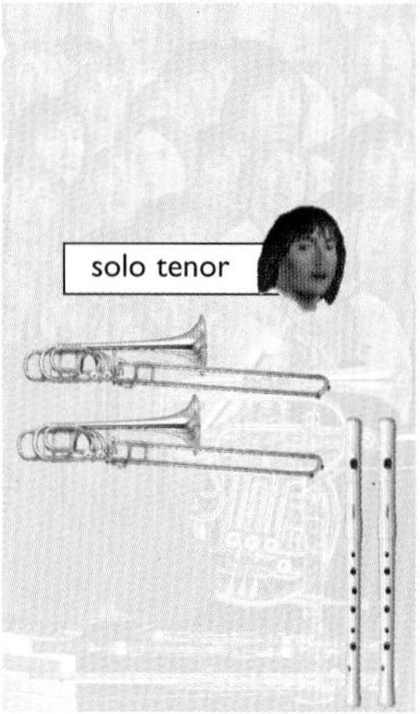

4. 1'05" (*Quia fecit mihi magna*)
A robust section for two solo basses, whose jerky, 'dotted' rhythm is matched in the violins. The plainchant is again sung by the altos.

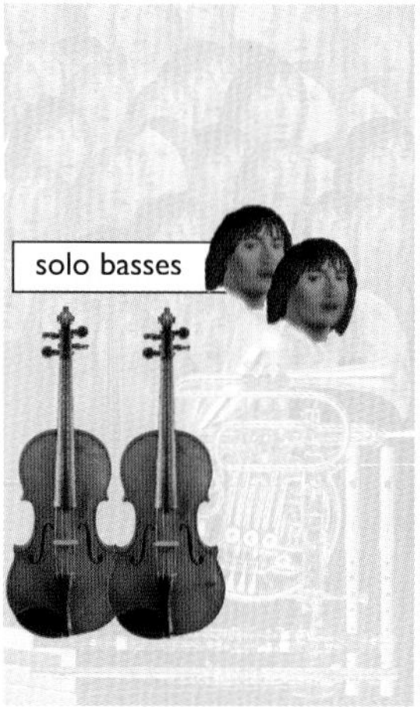

5. 2'35" (*Et misericordia*)
The chorus is divided into upper and lower groups, each in three parts, which alternate before combining at the end (2'00").

6. 1'00" (*Fecit potentiam*)
A solo countertenor has the tune while the violins dance round him.

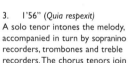

obbligato ▶ p. 360 toccata ▶ p. 362

THE MONTEVERDI REVIVAL

Monteverdi's operas lay forgotten for nearly three centuries. The extent to which his scores depended on the performing conventions of his time made it difficult for modern performers to revive it in anything like 'authentic' form. The first modern revival of *Orfeo* was in 1911, in an edition by **Vincent d'Indy** (1851–1931); other composers – **Carl Orff** (1895–1982), **Ottorino Respighi** (1879–1936) – preparted versions in the 1920s, but the first revivals that sought to recreate the work as Monteverdi wrote it followed the scholarly edition of Monteverdi's works prepared by **Gian Francesco Malipiero** (1882–1973) or that of Jack Westrup, given in Oxford in 1925. D'Indy was also involved in early revivals of *Il ritorno d'Ulisse in patria* and *L'incoronazione di Poppea*. It was not until the 1960s and 70s that these works began to enter the opera-house repertories; the revivals in the colourful realizations prepared by Raymond Leppard for Glyndebourne, along with works by **Cavalli**, did much to arouse public interest. More recent revivals, such as those under Nikolaus Harnoncourt, Alan Curtis or Roger Norrington, have tried to recreate the kind of sound and musical texture that the composer might have imagined.

even more explicit in 'Laudate, pueri, Dominum': starting at 'Sit nomen Domini' the soloists sing florid runs and scales which come across as secular or even operatic. As if to stress his modern credentials, Monteverdi gives the final 'Amen' not to the full choir but to the solo tenors. In 'Nisi Dominus', where the melody is concealed in the middle of the texture, the music goes back and forth between the two choirs, a technique that was especially suitable for the musicians' galleries in St Mark's.

In the hymn 'Ave maris stella' the plainchant first appears, slow and stately, in the full choir. It is then transformed into a flowing, triple-time melody, heard five times with instrumental interludes before the return of the solemn opening. The 'Sonata sopra "Sancta Maria"' is an instrumental piece with soprano **obbligato**. After a dance-like opening, the instruments play in short, jerky phrases while the soprano repeats a fragment of plainchant. At the end, the vocal and instrumental melodies are heard simultaneously.

VARIETY OF VOCAL LINES

In the psalms, Monteverdi shows his ability to combine old and new styles. In the four motets, or concertos, he concentrates on monody. Here the rhythm is free, almost improvisatory. 'Nigra sum', for solo tenor, is a setting of words from the Song of Solomon in the Bible: 'I am black but comely'. A simple rising scale illustrates the words 'Rise up, my love, my fair one, and come away.' In 'Duo Seraphim' the two vocal lines leapfrog sensuously before competing with each other in rapidly repeated notes. A third singer joins in at 'There are three who bear witness in heaven', and the three graphically become one at 'And these three are one'. In 'Audi coelum' the ornate solo line is shadowed by an echo which responds to the text. Only at the crucial name 'Maria' does the echo answer exactly.

In the concluding 'Magnificat' (see the featured movement), Monteverdi reverts to combining old and new. A plainchant melody is heard throughout, surrounded here and there by counterpoint of the old school. But he also provides virtuoso parts for the instruments, recalling the great aria in *Orfeo*, 'Possente spirito'. The most exciting music comes towards the end. Accompanied only by the continuo, the trebles sing the plainchant while the two solo tenors – one of them an echo – proclaim the Gloria with all the melodic devices of the new Baroque style.

7. 2'33" (*Deposuit potentes*) Two cornettos (trumpets here) duet high above the solo tenor, succeeded by two solo violins (1'11").

8. 1'28" (*Esurientes implevit bonis*) A swinging tune in the brass alternates with the unaccompanied boys' choir, joining forces in the closing bars (1'14").

9. 1'27" (*Suscepit Israel*) The two solo sopranos sing gently in canon while the plainchant melody is intoned in the tenors.

10. 0'53" (*Sicut locutus est*) With the plainchant back in the altos, the violins and trumpets take it in turns to weave a lively accompaniment.

11. 2'44" (*Gloria Patri*) A solo tenor, with the second tenor providing a distant echo, sings a florid line, full of scales and trills, as the trebles quietly repeat the plainchant.

12. 1'39" (*Sictut erat in principio*) Choir and instruments are all heard together for the first time since the opening 'Magnificat'. The solid textures of 'Sicut erat' are followed by a joyous, almost jaunty 'Amen' (1'06").

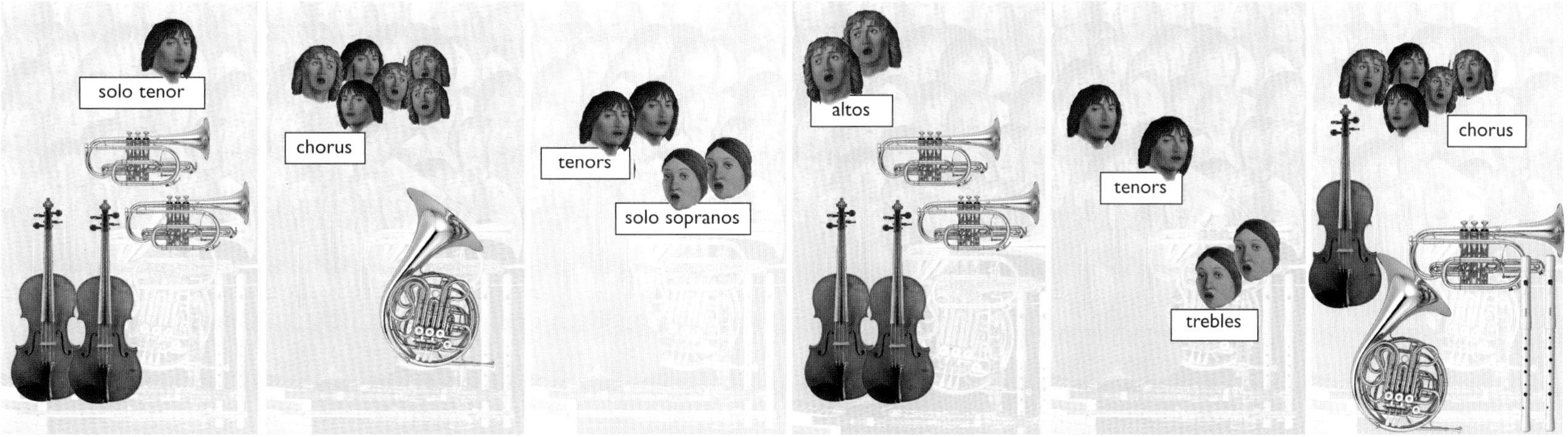

Cavalli ▶ p. 81 d'Indy ▶ p. 244 Malipiero ▶ p. 292 Monteverdi ▶ p. 76 Orff ▶ p. 293 Respighi ▶ p. 295

HEINRICH SCHÜTZ: *WEIHNACHTSHISTORIE*

The *Weinachtshistorie* ('Christmas Story') dates from the end of **Schütz**'s life. It was published in Dresden in 1664, but probably first performed there in 1660. When Schütz was a young man he spent several years in Venice as a pupil of **Giovanni Gabrieli**, whose influence can still be heard in the rich orchestration of the piece.

The opening chorus proclaims simply 'The birth of our Lord Jesus Christ, as it has been recorded by the holy Evangelists'. The biblical story then begins in recitative, which Schütz directed should be sung by a 'good, light tenor' at conversational speed. The Evangelist's narration is interspersed with eight ***intermedi***, passages in direct speech with instrumental accompaniment.

In the first *intermedium*, the angel announces Christ's birth to the shepherds in the field, with two tenor viols chasing each other over a rocking, bass. The heavenly host takes over – a six-part choir praising God, accompanied by two violins.

Then it is the shepherds' turn: three altos with bassoon and, appropriately, the rustic sound of two recorders. Schütz assigned violins and bassoon to the three wise men, and for the chief priests and scribes he employed the dignified sound of trombones. In all these movements the music is predominantly contrapuntal, with blocks of homophony at key moments such as **cadences**.

The bright tone of trumpets is heard for the only time when Herod commands the wise men to travel to Bethlehem. In a variant of his music in the first *intermedio*, the angel warns Joseph to take his family to Egypt, with a notable **melisma** on the word *fleuch* ('flee'). In the following recitative, the prophecy of Rachel lamenting her children is graphically portrayed by the normally dispassionate Evangelist. The angel returns to advise Joseph, the Evangelist concludes the story and the work ends with a chorus of rejoicing.

RECOMMENDED CD

Heinrich Schütz: *Weihnachtshistorie* ('Christmas story'). Taverner Consort, Choir and Players. Soloists: Nigel Rogers (Evangelist), Emma Kirkby (Angel), David Thomas (Herod). Andrew Parrott, conductor. Virgin Veritas 5 61353 2.

Nigel Rogers, an expert performer in early Baroque music, with a known sense of style, delivers the Evangelist's music in a well-defined, rather reedy tone.

MARC-ANTOINE CHARPENTIER: *LA DESCENTE D'ORPHÉE AUX ENFERS*

Unlike his better-known contemporary **Lully**, **Charpentier** held no official position at the court of Louis XIV. He benefited instead from the patronage of Marie de Lorraine, the Duchesse of Guise, and it was for her that he composed *La descente d'Orphée aux Enfers* ('Orpheus's Descent into Hell') – a short opera – in about 1687. Charpentier, who was employed as singer as well as composer, took a small part at what was probably its only contemporary performance. It is on a modest scale, quite different from Lully's operas and from Charpentier's own setting of *Médée*.

The story is taken by the unknown librettist from Ovid's *Metamorphoses*. Orpheus, encouraged by his father Apollo, descends to Hades to reclaim his bride Eurydice, who was fatally bitten by a snake on their wedding day. Pluto, beguiled by

'TE DEUM' IN D

Millions of people know a piece by Charpentier, though they might not realize it. In the early 1950s, the Prelude to his 'Te Deum' was chosen to be the signature tune for Eurovision. In the US, it introduced Masterpiece Theatre. The martial opening on the trumpets sums up all the splendour of the Baroque. But the rest of the *Te Deum* is just as good.

POPULAR MELODY *Charpentier*

THE GROUND BASS

Three arias and the 'Triumphing Dance' in **Purcell**'s *Dido and Aeneas* are composed on a **ground bass**. This was a short phrase repeated several times, usually but not always in the bass. Such self-imposed restriction stimulated the composer to be inventive in melody and other parts of the texture. In particular, the apparent monotony of a bass line repeated over and over again was countered, in the best examples, by fluidity in the top part. The listener's ear is intrigued and diverted by phrases that do not coincide with those in the bass. The effect of this overlapping is to propel the music forward.

In Dido's first air, 'Ah! Belinda', the ground is heard 21 times, with a brief change of key at 'I languish'. In the 'Triumphing Dance' the first violin is in the limelight for a moment before the ground re-enters in the bass. 'Oft she visits this lone mountain' – the air for the Second Woman – is sung over a smoothly running bass with almost no alteration.

Of all Purcell's wonderful ground basses, the most famous is 'When I am laid in earth'. The ground, a five-bar descending phrase first heard quite unadorned, spurs Purcell into writing a similarly asymmetrical opening line for Dido. A four-bar phrase is followed by one of five bars, which allows for a poignant repetition of 'no trouble'. And at the end, after varying the position above the bass of 'Remember me!' in a simple but masterly way, Purcell gives a mournful phrase to the first violin which echoes and extends the **chromatic** line of the bass.

OPERA IN FRANCE IN THE REIGN OF THE SUN KING

Under Louis XIV, who took full power in 1661 and reigned until 1715, France experienced a renaissance of artistic and literary activity. The great palace of Versailles was begun in 1662, its gardens laid out by Le Nôtre. The tragedies of Corneille and Racine dominated the dramatic scene, as did the comedies of Molière, and Charles Lebrun was active as a painter, director of the Gobelins tapestry factory, and a theorist.

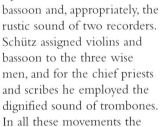

In music, the most important composer by far was Lully, who was employed by Louis from the age of 20, initially to compose music for the court ballets. Unscrupulous in his dealings, he was able to secure a monopoly to write and produce operas, which he did virtually every year from 1672 until his death in 1687.

Most of Lully's operas were tragedies, but they did not set the plays of Corneille or Racine, whose verse did not lend itself to musical setting. Instead, he used the librettist Philippe Quinault. Drawing on the same source of Greek or Roman legends, he provided Lully with plenty of opportunities for spectacle, in the form of ***divertissements***. These might depict scenes of battle, celebration or magic, and invariably included dancing.

The whole point of the operas was to praise the king, whom the hero of the story was generally understood to represent. More specifically, the king would be praised in the prologue, though not by name. However, in Charpentier's masterpiece *Médée*, which was dedicated to the king, the opening words are 'Louis est triomphant, tout cède à sa puissance' ('Louis is triumphant, everything yields to his power'). Although modern audiences find such sycophancy absurd and undramatic, it was exactly what the absolutist court of Louis XIV expected and required.

arioso ▶ p. 356 cadence ▶ p. 356 chromaticism ▶ p. 357 *concerto grosso* ▶ p. 357 *divertissement* ▶ p. 358 double stopping ▶ p. 358 fugue ▶ p. 358 ground bass ▶ p. 358 home key ▶ p. 359 *intermedio* ▶ p. 359 melisma ▶ p. 360 semi-opera ▶ p. 362 *sonata da camera* ▶ p. 362 *sonata da chiesa* ▶ p. 362

RECOMMENDED CD

Marc-Antoine Charpentier: *La descente d'Orphée aux Enfers*. Les Arts Florissants. William Christie, conductor. Erato 0630-11913-2.

This is the only recording of the piece, made after a series of performances. It is dominated by the wonderfully expressive Orpheus of Paul Agnew and the beautiful viol playing of Philippe Pierlot and Anne-Marie Lasla.

Orpheus's musical eloquence, permits him to take Eurydice, provided he does not look round on their journey back to the surface. Charpentier's opera ends here; the story is complete in itself, but there may be a missing third act where, as in other operatic versions (including that by **Christoph Willibald von Gluck**, 1714–87), Orpheus loses Eurydice for a second time.

Charpentier studied for several years in Rome, perhaps with **Carissimi**, and there is an Italianate flavour to such pieces as the nymphs' duet near the beginning. Similarly, Orpheus's plea to Pluto is, in its tunefulness and regular metre, more like an aria than the flexible recitative typical of French opera.

HENRY PURCELL: *DIDO AND AENEAS*

Purcell earned his living primarily as a church musician, but he was equally at home when writing for the stage. He provided incidental music for countless plays and wrote full-length settings of *King Arthur* by John Dryden and *The Fairy-Queen*, an adaptation of Shakespeare's *A Midsummer Night's Dream*. The latter are known as **semi-operas**. *Dido and Aeneas*, however, is a true opera and the earliest English opera that is still seen on stage today. It was modelled on *Venus and Adonis* by Purcell's master and friend **Blow**, and may have been written for a private entertainment at court. Its only known performance in Purcell's lifetime was at a girls' school in Chelsea in the late 1680s.

The libretto, by Nahum Tate, is based on Virgil's *Aeneid*. Aeneas has escaped from Troy after its conquest by the Greeks. He arrives at Carthage, on the North African coast, where he and the widowed queen Dido fall in love; but a sorceress, in the guise of the god Mercury, commands him to found a new Troy in Italy. Nothing is left for the broken-hearted Dido but death.

Purcell's writing is a mixture of flexible ***arioso*** and aria. The style is simple and direct, with the vocal line flowering on words such as 'storms' and 'pursued'. There are also choruses and dances in the French manner. Dido's first aria has a ground bass, the repetitions of the short phrase conveying the obsessiveness of her as yet unrevealed love.

Aeneas, who is not given any arias, remains a shadowy figure by comparison, although he does respond in impassioned *arioso* to the false Mercury. The climax of the opera is Dido's lament, 'When I am laid in earth'. Over a descending chromatic ground bass, Dido expresses her grief in broken phrases, the accompanying strings taking over as she falls silent. It is one of the great moments in opera.

(BL) Louis XIV
The French king as the sun in the Ballet de la Nuit.
(ML and TL) Heinrich Schütz
Portrait of the composer (TL) and Moritzburg Castle, where he was Kapellmeister *from 1665 (ML).*
(R) Dido and Aeneas ***by Gerard de Lauresse***
Portrait of the legend from which Purcell drew inspiration for his opera of the same name.

ARCANGELO CORELLI: SONATA FOR VIOLIN AND *BASSO CONTINUO*, OP. 5 NO. 5

Corelli was a virtuoso violinist who composed almost exclusively sonatas and concertos. The 12 sonatas that make up his op. 5 were published in Rome in 1700. They were extremely popular, appearing in many editions in Italy and abroad, and they were adapted as ***concerti grossi*** by his pupil **Francesco Geminiani** (1687–1762), who published them in the 1720s. In theory, the set consists of six church sonatas (***sonata da chiesa***) and six chamber sonatas (***sonata da camera***). In fact there is much overlapping: for instance, two of the church sonatas end with a jig and there are movements in the chamber sonatas that are not dances.

RECOMMENDED CD

Henry Purcell: *Dido and Aeneas*. St Anthony Singers, English Chamber Orchestra. Soloists: Janet Baker (Dido), Raimund Herincx (Aeneas), Patricia Clark (Belinda), Monica Sinclair (Sorceress), John Mitchinson (Sailor). Anthony Lewis, conductor. Decca 466 387-2.

This recording from 1962 has attained classic status, thanks to Janet Baker's powerful and moving account of Dido.

The fifth in the set is one of the *sonate da chiesa* with a final jig. Typically, all the movements are in the **home key** of G minor. The opening slow movement is in two sections, each of which is repeated. In the second Corelli uses the characteristic Baroque device of the sequence, which extends the melody by passing the same phrase briefly through different keys.

The next movement begins, as one would expect in a *sonata da chiesa*, in the style of a **fugue**. Here the violin's **double stopping** temporarily adds an extra line to the texture, a technique further developed by **J. S. Bach** in his sonatas for solo violin and solo cello. After this fast movement another slow one follows. Here the violin part, which is very plain on the printed page, would have been treated by the player simply as a blueprint, giving the opportunity for ear-tickling embellishments.

RECOMMENDED CD

Arcangelo Corelli: 12 Violin Sonatas, op. 5. The Locatelli trio: Elizabeth Wallfisch (violin), Richard Tunnicliffe (cello), Paul Nicholson (harpsichord and organ). Hyperion CDA66381/2

In No. 5, as elsewhere, Elizabeth Wallfisch decorates the Adagios with what may be Corelli's own embellishments. The recorded sound is so natural that you almost think the players are actually in the room.

The penultimate, fast movement introduces a dialogue between violin and continuo, who pass a six-note figure back and forth. After a while the violin lays claim to all the interest, but the continuo has the last word, with the violin relegated to a chordal accompanying role. The violin reasserts its supremacy in the jig, which is in two repeated sections with the suggestion of a reprise. Some people make the mistake of equating a major key with joy and a minor key with sorrow; this is a good example of a jaunty tune in the minor.

J. S. Bach ▶ p. 106 Blow ▶ p. 80 Carissimi ▶ p. 81 Charpentier ▶ p. 82 G. Gabrieli ▶ p. 51 Geminiani ▶ p. 117 Gluck ▶ p. 158
Lully ▶ p. 84 Purcell ▶ p. 78 Schütz ▶ p. 86

THE LATE BAROQUE

The late Baroque era (1700–50) was a time of major political change throughout Europe, involving a shift in the balance of power between sovereign states. Across the continent it was a period of almost continuous warfare, the effects of which were later felt in other parts of the world as a result of conflicting ambitions among the various trading empires consolidated in the previous century. Certain European nations witnessed, in the process, a decline in their international influence and status; others rose to new prominence, seriously affecting the peace and security of their neighbours. Spain, for example, though still in possession of an immense South American empire, never regained the great-power role it had enjoyed in the sixteenth and seventeenth centuries. Sweden, meanwhile, lost its hold on extensive areas of northern Europe which had turned it into a major international player during the late seventeenth century. In Italy, the Republic of Venice finally gave up its long and costly struggle against the Turks in the Mediterranean and entered a slow but perceptible period of decline.

THE POWER OF RUSSIA AND PRUSSIA

The two states whose meteoric success made them forces to be reckoned with on Europe's new political map were Russia (in the past often called the Empire of Muscovy) and Prussia (formerly the principality of Brandenburg, it became a kingdom in 1712). Under the dynamic Tsar Peter I ('the Great'), Russia seized Swedish territory around the Baltic, together with much of what is now Ukraine. This Great Northern War (1701–21) established it as a major European power. By challenging the Austrian Habsburg dynasty, Prussia to the west laid the foundations of what would eventually become a united Germany.

THE INFLUENCE OF FRANCE

France continued to hold on to the power, influence and wealth that it had enjoyed during the earlier decades of the reign of Louis XIV. Following Louis' death the extravagant court of Versailles flourished under the regency of the Duke of Orléans, and the Parisian aristocracy lavishly patronized the various arts. However, French supremacy in Europe, both military and economic, was now being contested by the British. Great Britain was benefiting from the union of the English and Scottish kingdoms as a single nation in 1707 and swiftly gaining economic strength as a trading and industrial power. London expanded steadily in the early eighteenth century; its reputation for growth made the city a magnet to musicians from all parts of Europe.

The Late Baroque
INTRODUCTION

More sophisticated diplomatic relations between states in the late Baroque era resulted in a time of relative peace – for a short period at least – during which the arts flourished. As in the Renaissance and early Baroque eras, writers, artists and musicians turned to the classical antiquity of Greece and Rome for their standards and their inspiration. At the same time a new interest in realism in the arts spread across Europe. The rise of printing meant that new ideas were disseminated rapidly to increasingly literate populations, and many standard musical forms, most notably opera, underwent a rush of development. Then came the War of the Austrian Succession, bringing such development to a temporary halt as the music of the period became propagandist in nature, or was forced to take a back seat while money and attention were focussed on more pressing matters.

CLASSICAL INFLUENCES

During the early eighteenth century, several art forms achieved greater purity and rigour in an attempt at closer emulation of classical styles. Architecture, especially in Britain, was inspired by the so-called 'Palladian' idiom based on the reinterpretation of Roman buildings originally made by the sixteenth-century Venetian architect Andrea Palladio. Many poets cultivated the satirical vein of Latin writers such as Horace and Juvenal, while among those writing for opera, **Pietro Metastasio** (1698–1782) gained international celebrity status as a librettist who set new standards of seriousness and idealism for musical drama.

KEY EVENTS

1702 Outbreak of War of the Spanish Succession
1706 Thomas Newcomen invents the first practical working steam engine
1709 Battle of Poltava: Peter the Great, Tsar of Russia, consolidates power by defeating Swedish army of Charles XII
1710 Bishop George Berkeley publishes *A Treatise Concerning the Principles of Human Knowledge*
1713 Treaty of Utrecht ends War of the Spanish Succession; Habsburg Emperor Charles VI names his daughter Maria Theresa as his heir
1718 Gabriel Fahrenheit invents the mercury thermometer
1719 Daniel Defoe publishes *Robinson Crusoe*
1720 The South Sea Bubble, the first international stock market crisis, causes financial panic in London and Paris
1726 Jonathan Swift publishes *Gulliver's Travels*
1728 John Gay's *Beggar's Opera* opens in London
1733 John Kay invents the flying-shuttle loom
1739 John Wesley founds the Methodist movement; David Hume publishes *A Treatise on Human Nature*
1740 War of the Austrian Succession begins; Samuel Richardson publishes *Pamela*
1742 Handel's *Messiah* is first performed in Dublin
1745 Second Jacobite Rebellion led by Prince Charles Edward Stuart
1748 Peace of Aix-la-Chapelle concludes War of the Austrian Succession
1749 Henry Fielding publishes *Tom Jones*

PRINCELY COURTS

During the eighteenth century, European rulers made a deliberate attempt to emulate the image-building and self-aggrandizement that had characterized the court of Louis XIV. Using Versailles (created by Louis le Vau, Charles Le Brun and André le Nôtre) as a model, kings and princes created handsome new residences containing suites of grand staterooms and surrounded by formal gardens. The paintings on the walls and ceilings of the various apartments, often by distinguished Italian artists such as Giovanni Battista Tiepolo and Sebastiano Ricci, celebrated rulers' achievements, ancestors or the virtues they purported to uphold. Such palaces were intended to act as showcases for their occupants, displaying them as sovereigns endowed with good taste as well as power and money.

Status and Subservience

Music provided an important indicator of taste, wealth and social status – whether professional court opera performances in the prince's private chapel or in semi-amateur performances, where members of the royal or noble family took part, assisted by professional musicians. Almost every composer of any note found himself attached to a court establishment of some sort. **Johann Sebastian Bach** (1685–1750) spent several years as *Kapellmeister* (music director) to Prince Leopold of Anhalt-Cöthen, and **George Frideric Handel** (1685–1759) wrote various important works for the Duke of Chandos. **Domenico Scarlatti** (1685–1757) spent most of his career in the service of Princess Maria Barbara of Portugal, later queen of Spain, and many of the major works of **Antonio Caldara** (1670–1736) were written for the Imperial chapel and court theatre in Vienna. However highly regarded their skill, though, composers were frequently treated as little better than talented servants, subject to the whims and high-handedness of their employers and expected to wear a uniform. This subservient position remained a standard feature of a musician's life at court (with the exception of Handel) until the end of the eighteenth century, when the French Revolution undermined aristocratic assumptions of power, and Romanticism's subsequent glorification of the artist helped to elevate the status of composers and performers.

REPRESENTATIONS OF LIFE

At the same time, artists in France, Italy and England were being drawn towards the representation of ordinary life in all its complexity. In London, William Hogarth used satirical painting and engraving as means of offering serious criticism of contemporary manners and morals. The French painter Jean-Baptiste Chardin turned to domestic scenes and still lifes to create an alternative world to the fantasy and glitter of the court at Versailles.

In literature, this aim for greater realism was manifested in the transformation of the novel from prose romance to an important weapon of social criticism and more debate. An ever-widening readership embraced stories of daily life, featuring figures such as thieves, prostitutes and servants as their principal characters. Novels, including Samuel Richardson's *Pamela* and Henry Fielding's *Tom Jones*, had significant international impact. Each was soon turned into an opera libretto as part of a developing enthusiasm for comic operas based on contemporary themes.

POPULAR MEDIA

This was the first great age of print journalism: the newspaper and the magazine established themselves as indispensable features of civilized living. Wider access to knowledge and informed opinion, together with the growth of literacy – especially in northern Europe – brought about greater interest in science, exploration and the natural world. This was followed in turn by a more critical, questioning approach to accepted forms of religion and government. The late Baroque era saw the beginnings of European Enlightenment, a period when writers on politics, art and philosophy such as Voltaire, Montesquieu and Hume became important opinion-formers. They challenged popular prejudice, religious dogma and assumptions of superiority among governing elites.

Musical culture, meanwhile, witnessed the evolution of a whole range of standard forms, such as the sonata, the concerto and the cantata, which had made their earliest appearances during the previous century. Among instrumental genres, the trio sonata, epitomized by the opp. 1–4 of **Arcangelo Corelli** (1653–1713), emerged as one of the favourites, disappearing almost as rapidly in the decades after 1750. The most notable newcomer during the first 50 years of the eighteenth century was the symphony, deriving from the three-movement Italian opera overture but receiving its first important impetus from composers working in Germany. The form was, however, in its early stages during the Baroque era and it was not until the next century that it came to fruition.

(ML) Gulliver in Brobdingnag
Illustration from Jonathan's Swift's political satire Gulliver's Travels.
***(TL)* The Beggar's Opera**
Performance of John Gay's immensely popular ballad opera.
(TNR) David Hume
Hume was one of the leading philosophers of the late Baroque era.
***(TFR)* Music for the Royal Fireworks**
Handel's famous piece was composed for the official celebration of the end of the War of the Austrian Succession.
(BR)* March of the Guards to Finchley *by William Hogarth
Hogarth was well known for his satirical paintings, through which he made social comments about contemporary life.

THE WAR OF THE AUSTRIAN SUCCESSION

The War of the Austrian Succession (1740–48) involved practically every major European nation, either directly or peripherally, in a long, costly and ultimately inconclusive contest over claims to the crown of Austria and the Holy Roman Empire. The disputed succession to the throne of the emperor, Charles VI, claimed by his daughter Maria Theresa and the Elector of Bavaria, masked several far more significant rivalries. France, supporting the Elector, was keen to wear down or altogether destroy Austria as a European power. Britain, meanwhile, backing Maria Theresa, feared French colonial ambitions in India and America. In his first important campaigns, the young king of Prussia, Frederick II, 'the Great', sought to profit from Austria's weakness by seizing its province of Silesia and attacking the neighbouring state of Saxony. By the end of the war, which also witnessed fighting in Italy and Scotland, Prussia had emerged as a major military force. Britain and France stood ready to renew their colonial power struggles more fiercely in the Seven Years' War, which began barely a decade later.

The Effects of War

The effects of the war on civilian life, and hence on the arts, varied inevitably according to its intensity in the different spheres of military activity. In Britain, for example, music was directly harnessed to propaganda purposes in the aftermath of the 1745 rebellion, in which Prince Charles Edward Stuart, seeking to drive George II from his throne, was defeated at Culloden Moor. At least two of Handel's oratorios, *Judas Maccabaeus* (1746) and the *Occasional Oratorio* (1746), seem to have been intended to boost pro-government support by emphasizing the preservation of popular liberties. It was Handel whose *Music for the Royal Fireworks* (1749) accompanied the official London celebration of the Peace of Aix-la-Chapelle, marking an end to hostilities.

In continental Europe, the war's deepest impact on musical life was felt in Saxony. Its capital, Dresden, had boasted a superb musical establishment, attracting performers and composers from neighbouring states and featuring talents such as those of **Johann Adolf Hasse** (1699–1783) and **Jan Dismas Zelenka** (1679–1745). However, mounting financial problems resulting from Saxony's involvement in the war affected the range and quality of Dresden's musical life during this period. Many court musicians were forced to seek alternative employment, several of them entering the service of the victorious Frederick the Great at the court of Potsdam.

J. S. Bach ▶ p. 106 Caldara ▶ p. 116 Corelli ▶ p. 82 Handel ▶ p. 112 Hasse ▶ p. 160 Metastasio ▶ p. 161 D. Scarlatti ▶ p. 121 Zelenka ▶ p. 123

THE IMPORTANCE OF OPERA

Opera was the most widely cultivated musical form during this period, surrounded by its own social and economic subculture and engaging many of the finest composers. By the beginning of the eighteenth century, most of the principal European cities had imported opera from Italy. In many centres the patronage of kings and princes, together with singers and composers, had helped to establish performances on a regular basis. The Italian operatic style could be modified to suit the taste of local audiences, as in the case of northern Germany, where it became intermingled with the French style established in Paris by **Jean-Baptiste Lully** (1632–87) for his ***tragédies lyriques***. France tended largely to ignore the Italian operatic form in favour of the *tragédie lyrique*, with its significant use of ballet. This extended narrative dance form developed into an independent entertainment, ***opéra-ballet***, with its own stars.

ITALIAN STAR SYSTEM

The star system dominated opera first in Italy. Throughout the eighteenth century, the Italian **castrato** (a male singer whose testes had been removed during boyhood, enabling him to continue singing at soprano, mezzo-soprano or alto pitch thereafter) reigned supreme in many European opera houses from Vienna to Prague and London to Lisbon. Most heroic roles were assigned to this voice and, for composers such as Handel, it was taken for granted that the success of a new opera was based to a considerable extent on the technique and personal attractiveness of the castrato or *musico*, as he was also called.

(L) Armide
A court performance of Lully's opera Armide.
(TR) Pianoforte
The pianoforte made its first appearance during the late Baroque era.
(BR) Castrato Farinelli
Most European opera in the eighteenth century was geared towards the voice of the castrato.

SOCIAL ENTERTAINMENT

Musicians have always enjoyed a significicant role as providers of social entertainment. In the early eighteenth century, this aspect of music-making gained greater importance, as the middle-classes in European towns and cities cultivated the art of courtly dancing in such forms as the minuet, the bourée and the gavotte. Most of the era's major composers, including J. S. Bach, Handel and Telemann, featured the rhythms and styles of popular dance music in their works. Dancing also took place at some of the London pleasure gardens, whose bands provided concerts with varied programmes made up of popular operatic and orchestral items. The growing popularity of public concerts enouraged traditions of musical amateurism in several countries. Non-professional performers assembled as orchestras or small chamber groups, and some the era's most distinguished figures in areas other than music were noted for their prowess as instrumental performers. Prussia's Frederick the Great, for example, was a gifted flautist, employing composers such as **Johann Joachim Quantz** (1697–1773), as well as writing his own music for the instrument.

STANDARD FORMS

A crucial centre for the emergence of the symphony was the electoral court at Mannheim, where the orchestra achieved an international reputation under its director **Johann Wenzel Anton Stamitz** (1717–57). Elsewhere in Europe, orchestral music figured significantly in the mixed programmes of the public concerts that formed a feature of musical life in many cities from the early 1700s. There was a greater focus than ever before on instrumental virtuosity, and the age saw the earliest appearance of the extended solo concerto, developed by composers like **Antonio Vivaldi** (1678–1741) into a medium that combined sensitive exploration of the individual sonorities of an instrument with opportunities for technical display.

The use of certain instruments began to decline as others became more attractive to performers, composers and audiences. The popularity of the transverse flute, for example, owed much to the enthusiasm of its most distinguished amateur player, Frederick the Great. The viola da gamba, on the other hand, even if it did not fade into obscurity until the century's close, was increasingly relegated to an accompanying role. The cello was favoured with eloquent suites and sonatas by J. S. Bach and sonatas by Vivaldi. Among newer sounds, clarinets were heard for the first time around 1710 and horns found their way somewhat later into the opera-house. The pianoforte (or fortepiano) made its earliest appearance in Florence in 1698, when Bartolomeo Cristofori (1655–1731) experimented with a percussion keyboard; later, in Germany, grand pianos made by Gottfried Silbermann (1683–1753) attracted the interest of J. S. Bach.

castrato ▶ p. 357 *opéra-ballet* ▶ p. 360 *opera buffa* ▶ p. 360 *opera seria* ▶ p. 361 *tragédie lyrique* ▶ p. 363

Many castratos profited materially from their singing careers and the most successful of all – Carlo Broschi (known as Farinelli, 1705–82) – achieved considerable backstage influence at the court of Spain through the therapeutic effect of his singing on the melancholy Philip V.

Farinelli was a friend of Metastasio, the poet whose attempt at raising the artistic standards of opera both poetically and dramatically had the strongest effect on the form during this period. As ***opera seria*** ('serious opera') tended towards a greater purity of outline and expression, the comic elements freely incorporated in the musical dramas of the seventeenth century became separated. The late Baroque saw the development of an entirely independent form which later became known as ***opera buffa*** ('comic opera'). The earliest examples were composed in Naples, with its rich traditions of popular comedy and street entertainment, by masters such as **Giovanni Battista Pergolesi** (1710–36) and his teacher Leonardo Vinci (*c.* 1690–1730), both famous for their serious operas.

THE AUDIENCE

Audiences for late Baroque opera have often been represented as mere affluent consumers of a costly and elite art form, to whose finest points they paid little serious attention. Although performances were not received, as today, in total silence, and although composers were already complaining of the excessive focus on stars at the expense of the music itself, there is plenty of evidence that opera at the time was taken seriously, as a means for underlining contemporary ideals and moral values. Perhaps the strongest proof of audience attentiveness lies in the simple fact that copies of the libretto were always available. The condition of many of those surviving suggests that they were actively consulted during performances. Many people subscribed for the whole season and attended multiple performances of the same work.

TRAVELLING MUSICIANS

Many musicians had grown accustomed to travelling far from their native cities or countries in search of employment, or in response to invitations from rulers of different states. By 1700 this existence had become a standard feature of musical life in Europe, involving singers, instrumentalists and composers in sometimes permanent separation from home and family.

Musical styles could thus be carried long distances from the cultures in which they had evolved. The presense of an Italian master such as Agostino Steffani at the courts of Hanover and Dusseldorf in the late 1600s had an important influence on contemporary north German musicians, including Handel. While in Germany, however, Steffani fused his Venetian operatic idiom with the French mannerisms of Lully's Versailles. Some composers working within alien traditions felt tempted to absorb the local styles of regional folk music: Domenico Scarlatti, for example, made use of dance rhythms and melodies encountered during nearly 40 years in Portugal and Spain.

Another musical exodus occurred in Italy. Although plenty of opportunities existed there for regular work in theatres and churches, lucrative employment offers drew them north across the Alps. In London and Stockholm, Lisbon and Vienna, the presence of expatriate Italian composers, singers and poets was accepted as part of the musical infrastructure.

German composers frequently followed a similar nomadic pattern, though they often stayed within German-speaking domains. **Georg Philipp Telemann** (1681–1767) was born in Magdeburg and worked in Leipzig, Silesia, Eisenach, Frankfurt and Hamburg. J. S. Bach studied in Lüneburg, became organist to the Duke of Saxe-Weimar, spent five years at the court of Cöthen and, even when finally settled in Leipzig, may have hoped to find work in the Saxon Elector's service at Dresden.

Lully ▶ p. 84 Pergolesi ▶ p. 119 Quantz ▶ p. 120 Stamitz ▶ p. 162 Telemann ▶ p. 122 Vivaldi ▶ p. 122

The Late Baroque

JOHANN SEBASTIAN BACH

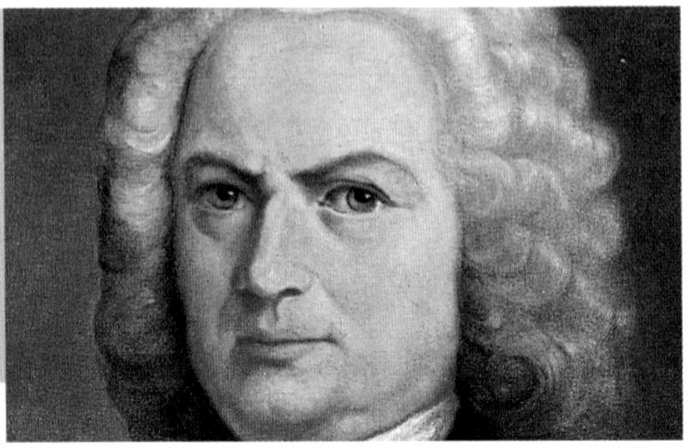

Johann Sebastian Bach (1685–1750) was born into a closely knit musical family of which he was rightly proud. His father Johann Ambrosius Bach (1645–95) had an identical twin brother, Johann Christoph (1645–93), who was like a second father to the young Sebastian. Johann was such a common name that almost all boys called Johann were known by their second name.

In 1671, when Christoph moved to Arnstadt, Ambrosius and Maria Elisabetha set up home in Eisenach, where Ambrosius took up a post as town musician. The couple were to have eight children, and it was in Eisenach that their youngest son, Johann Sebastian, was born on 21 March 1685. Young Sebastian's musical talents were evident from his boyhood. He was able to sponsor the last stages of his schooling through his vocal abilities, and later to get his first paid job as a violinist. But it was his ability as an organist and keyboard player that was to earn him the greatest respect throughout his career. His employment in both Arnstadt and Mülhausen centred on his organ playing. He moved to Weimar as a chamber musician and court organist and only later added to this the position of *Konzertmeister*, which carried with it the obligation to compose church cantatas. After some years devoted to chamber music in Cöthen, Bach took the position of *Kantor* in Leipzig, where he was to remain for the rest of his life.

LIFE TIMELINE

1685	Born on 21 March and baptized on 23 March in St George's, Eisenach
1695	Orphaned; moves to Ohrdruf to live with brother Johann Christoph Bach
1700	Leaves Ohrdruf for Lüneburg where he becomes chorister and completes his education
1703	Occasional job as court musician in Weimar; permanent post as organist in Arnstadt
1705	Study trip to Lübeck to hear great organist Dietrich Buxtehude
1707	Takes post as organist in Mühlhausen; marries Maria Barbara
1708	Moves to court position in Weimar; birth of first child
1714	Offer of Halle organist post; birth of Carl Philipp Emanuel Bach
1717	Refusal of duke to release Bach from service; imprisonment and move to Cöthen
1720	Death and burial of Maria Barbara in Bach's absence
1721	Dedication of 'Brandenburg' Concertos; marriage to Anna Magdalena
1722	Publishes first book of the *Well-Tempered Clavier*
1723	First of Anna Magdalena's 13 children born; move to St Thomas's School, Leipzig
c. 1727	First performance of *St Matthew Passion* at St Thomas's Church
1729	Directorship of *collegium musicum*
1733	Official state mourning of Elector Friedrich Augustus I of Saxony
1747	Accepts membership into Mizler's Society of Musical Sciences
1750	Two eye operations in March and April, followed by a stroke and death on 28 July

LIBRETTISTS AND POETS

Bach's vocal works all required a written text. Composers had a wide selection of authors from which to choose, as large quantities of devotional literature were published in this period. However, Bach was very particular about words and frequently altered the printed version.

Throughout his career he collaborated with poets rather than using published books. Mühlhausen pastor Georg Christian Eilmar wrote some of the texts for the early cantatas. In Weimar Bach worked with the court librarian Salomon Franck and in Leipzig he continued to set his texts. Bach used five sources by the academic cleric Erdmann Neumeister, three in Weimar and two in Leipzig. Neumeister's pupil, the infamous Arnstadt-born plagiarist Menantes (Christian Friedrich Hunold) wrote the librettos for a number of Bach's secular cantatas in Cöthen.

In Leipzig Bach enjoyed working with his neighbour Christiane Mariane von Ziegler and the colourful tax collector Picander (Christian Friedrich Henrici). However, many of the texts of the Leipzig cantatas are anonymous and it has been suggested that Bach wrote them from the scriptural material stipulated for the week; he certainly had a library of theological reference works large to have helped him understand the significance of the biblical readings.

'AIR ON THE G STRING'

The melody now known as 'Air on the G String' comes from Bach's third orchestral suite and was arranged in 1871 by August Wilhelmj, who stipulated that the opening melody be played on the lowest violin string. This produces the dreamy sound for which the piece has become well known.

POPULAR MELODY *J. S. Bach*

SEBASTIAN'S SCHOOLING

The musical Bach family had lived for generations in Thuringia, the cradle of Lutheranism. What better educational beginning could Johann Ambrosius and Maria Elisabetha have wished for their sons than the Latin school at Eisenach, where Martin Luther had been a pupil 200 years earlier?

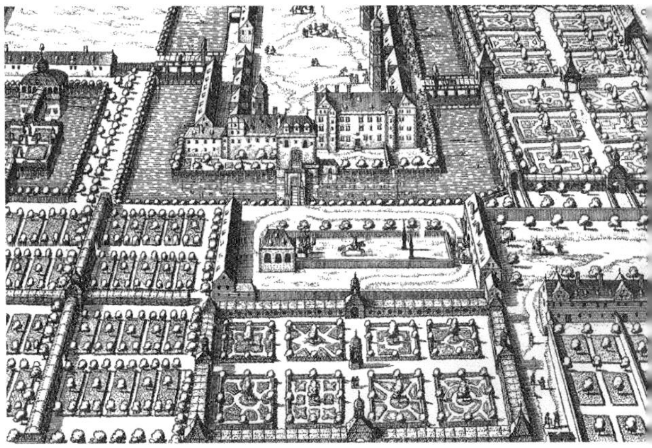

Children began school when they were seven years old. They sat in large classes and were moved up according to achievement rather than age, normally spending two years at each level. Bach began at the Latin school in 1692 and was in the first class ('Quinta') for two years. He was 47th of 81 at the end of his first year and 14th of 74 in his second, whereupon he was promoted to the next class ('Quarta'). Sickness and bereavement disrupted his education, causing him to be absent in his first year for 96 half-days, in his second for 59 and in his third for 103.

ORPHANED

In 1693 Bach's 'second father' – his uncle Johann Christoph Bach – died, followed in May 1694 by his own mother. Six months later Johann Ambrosius remarried, which facilitated the day-to-day care of his two youngest children, Johann Jakob (1682–1722) and Johann Sebastian. However, within three months Johann Ambrosius

(BL) Cöthen
The country seat of Prince Leopold, Bach's patron at Cöthen.
(TR) Bach's House
A room at the Bach's family home in Eisenach.
(BR) Church Concert
The 18-year-old Bach was appointed organist at Arnstadt in 1703.

arioso ▶ p. 356 recitative ▶ p. 362

also died. Unable to finance the upbringing of the two boys, Bach's stepmother Barbara Margaretha was obliged to send them to live with their closest relative, their eldest brother Johann Christoph.

OHRDRUF

Johann Christoph Bach had been organist at St Michael's Church in Ohrdruf since 1690 and had married in October 1694. Thirteen-year-old Johann Jakob and ten-year-old Johann Sebastian went to live with their older brother and his wife in March 1695, just a few weeks after their father's death. The boys' schooling continued at the Ohrdruf Lyceum, where Johann Sebastian in particular was to excel. By the age of 14 he had been promoted to the fifth class ('Prima'), whereas at the same age Johann Jakob had reached only the third. The brothers were separated when Johann Jakob was apprenticed to his late father's successor, Johann Heinrich Halle, in Eisenach. Johann Sebastian remained with Johann Christoph and his growing family until he was 15. At this time, a classmate from Ohrdruf, Georg Erdmann, left school with the intention of moving to Lüneburg to be employed as a chorister in return for a monthly fee, free tuition, board and lodging at St Michael's Gymnasium (the equivalent of a sixth-form college). This seemed the ideal next stage for Johann Sebastian too, and so in March 1700 the two teenagers moved to Lüneburg.

MUSICAL TRAINING

Bach's musical talents were encouraged in the early days by his father and uncle, and by Andreas Christian Dedekind, the *Kantor* at the Latin school in Eisenach. Bach had an unusually fine treble voice and probably sang in the choir of St George's, Eisenach, where Dedekind was *Kapellmeister*. The five years in Ohrdruf allowed him to establish his keyboard technique under the strict eye of brother/surrogate father Johann Christoph.

The move to Lüneburg exposed Bach to many new cultural experiences. He travelled several times to Hamburg to hear the famous organist of St Catharine's, **Johann Adam Reincken** (1623–1722), and he encountered French taste, which at the time was considered by many to be the height of refinement. The Ritterakademie, a school for sons of noblemen, was next door to St Michael's and through his musical contacts Bach made the acquaintance of several fencing, dancing, French-speaking young gentlemen there. He also visited the court in the nearby town of Celle, where the duke had formed an orchestra to play fashionable contemporary French music.

MONUMENTAL MASTERPIECES

The story of Christ's suffering and crucifixion – the Passion story, recorded in the Bible by the evangelists Matthew, Mark, Luke and John – is the text on which all Passion music is based. From at least the fifteenth century these texts for Holy Week, leading up to Easter Day, had special musical settings. By Bach's time there was a tradition of Protestant Passion music on which he could build.

Passion Poet Picander

Inspired by a published Passion text by the poet, librettist and tax collector Picander, Bach persuaded him to collaborate on a similar work based on the gospel of Matthew. Ideas came not only from the Bible, but from a series of Passion sermons by Heinrich Müller. Bach owned a copy of them, and it may have been his, rather than Picander's, idea to incorporate Müller's sentiments. The libretto is made up of many short sections, interspersing the biblical narrative (sung by the Evangelist) with comments (in the form of ***arioso*-like recitative**) and reflection (presented in arias).

The *St Matthew Passion* received its première in St Thomas's Church on either 11 April 1727 or 15 April 1729. During the first performances, Bach made several changes and so before it was heard again on 30 March 1736 he wrote the music out afresh. The 1736 version is arranged in two complete 'choirs' of vocal quartet and orchestra.

Bach's *St Matthew Passion* has been hailed as 'the most monumental dramatic masterpiece before Wagner's *Ring*'. Its 1829 performance, directed by **Felix Mendelssohn** (1809–47), ushered in a revival of interest in Bach's works.

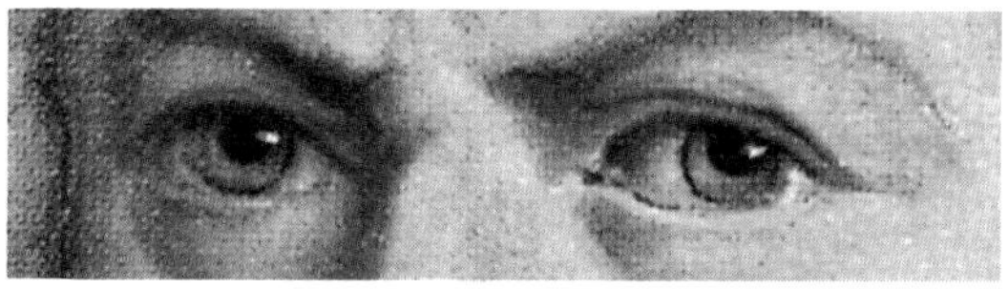

At some point during his time in Lüneburg Bach's voice broke, bringing to an end the secure benefits of St Michael's, but by this time he was an accomplished violinist and keyboard player, able to earn his keep by performing. He returned to his home region, where there were many relatives able to give him good recommendations for work. In 1703 he found an occasional job as a violinist in the court orchestra of Weimar, just 45 km (28 miles) from Ohrdruf. But it was keyboard skills that were to win him his first permanent post.

ARNSTADT AND MÜHLHAUSEN

In July 1703 the new organ for Arnstadt's rebuilt church was complete. Bach, a little-known 18-year-old, was called in to test it. A week later he gave a recital that aroused so much interest, there was pressure from the congregation to appoint him immediately as organist. On 14 August 1703 he was promised a handsome salary in return for playing for public worship and maintaining the organ. But trouble soon began. One night he drew his sword on an arrogant youth. Six months later he extended four weeks' study leave to four months, enraptured by the organist **Dietrich Buxtehude** (*c.* 1637–1717). To compound his wrongdoings, he was accused in 1706 of unlawfully admitting a young lady into the organ loft. He needed to move on.

Buxtehude ▶ p. 80 Mendelssohn ▶ p. 197 Reincken ▶ p. 120

FRUSTRATION AND LACK OF FREEDOM

In June 1707, Bach was invited to audition for the post of organist at St Blasius's Church in nearby Mühlhausen. He requested the same inflated salary he was paid in Arnstadt, a far larger sum than the previous organist had received, and left Arnstadt on 29 June.

The attractions of Mühlhausen were to be short-lived, and here the theologians proved to be a great source of frustration to him. The young organist was possibly ignorant of the divisions caused by Pietism and Orthodoxy within the Lutheran church at this time. The recently deceased theologian Philipp Jacob Spener had emphasized a subjective and devotional expression of the faith. Unfortunately this piety (hence 'Pietism') caused his many followers to limit the use of music in worship. Johann Adolf Frohne, Bach's pastor at St Blasius, was a firm advocate of Spener's teaching, and gave little opportunity to his young organist to elaborate **chorale** melodies or write worship music such as cantatas. Bach sought advice from the Orthodox pastor at St Mary's Church, Georg Christian Eilmar, and found not only wise counsel, but also friendship.

Bach's letter of resignation from Mühlhausen makes clear his lack of freedom to develop the church music: 'I should always have liked to work toward the goal, namely, a well-regulated church music, to the glory of God ... yet it has not been possible to accomplish all this without hindrance, and there are at present hardly any signs that in the future a change may take place.'

MARRIAGE AND DEPARTURE

Within two months of moving from Arnstadt, Bach's maternal uncle, Tobias, had died, leaving him 50 gulden (more than six months' salary). This extra cash enabled him, on 17 October 1707, to marry the young woman from the Arnstadt organ loft, his second cousin Maria Barbara Bach. On the understanding that Bach returned to oversee the rebuilding of the St Blasius organ, the young couple was released from Mühlhausen on 26 June 1708, wiser in the ways of the world and the church.

WEIMAR

Bach was familiar with the Weimar court because of his earlier job as violinist for Duke Johann Ernst. In 1708 he arrived in Weimar as court organist and chamber musician for Duke Wilhelm Ernst, older brother of Johann Ernst. His new employer enforced strict rules upon the courtiers, imposing a curfew with candles snuffed at 8 p.m. in winter and 9 p.m. in summer, forbidding traditional feast-day dances and encouraging his subjects to attend the sermons preached in the court chapel.

The first years in Weimar seem to have been stable for the growing Bach family until he was offered an organist's post in Halle in 1714. A contract was drawn up, but at the last moment Bach backed out. Meanwhile his Weimar master had increased his salary in line with the Halle offer and promoted him to the rank of *Konzertmeister*. Bach roundly denied using the Halle appointment to procure a rise in salary.

CANTATAS AND ORGAN WORKS

In Weimar the promotion to *Konzertmeister* in 1714 carried with it the obligation to compose and perform a cantata each month in the court chapel. Bach began this task with great zeal, frequently enlisting the help of Salomo Franck to provide texts; cantata production ceased, though, as the relationship with the duke cooled.

The majority of Bach's organ music was written in or before 1717, when he was employed as an organist. In Weimar he had two organs at his disposal: the dizzyingly high Himmelsburg organ in the court chapel and that of the town church St Peter and St Paul's, where his second cousin Johann Gottfried Walther (1684–1748) was organist. Walther was also music teacher to the young Prince Johann Ernst – nephew of Bach's employer Duke Wilhelm – until his early death.

JEALOUSY AND IMPRISONMENT

By 1716 the relationship between Bach and his duke had deteriorated. Jealous of the popularity of his co-regent, Duke Ernst August, and disdainful of Ernst August's taste in Italian music, Duke Wilhelm Ernst imposed a fine of 10 thaler (roughly two weeks' salary) on any employee who participated in activities at Ernst August's Red Castle. Bach blatantly flouted the rule, joining festivities celebrating the young duke's marriage and performing a birthday cantata (BWV 208) in his honour, clearly precluding any further promotions in Weimar. Recognizing

(L) J. S. Bach
Nineteenth-century engraving showing Bach at the organ.
(FR) Georg Philipp Telemann
Bach asked Telemann to be godfather to his son Carl Philipp Emanuel.
(NR) Memorial to Bach
Statue commemorating the composer in Eisenach, Germany.

MUSIC FOR THE GLORY OF GOD

Pushed to the limits by the circumstances of his employment, Bach sometimes vented his frustration on paper. We can be thankful that, on two occasions, the frustration led him to spell out his philosophy as a Christian musician. On 25 June 1707, in his letter of resignation to the Mühlhausen town council, he wrote that he had been offered a post that promised him the possibility of achieving his goal of composing 'a well-regulated church music to the glory of God without further vexation'.

The standard of musicians and choristers at Bach's disposal in Leipzig was on a steep decline. His memorandum to the Leipzig town council of 23 August 1730 is entitled 'Short but most necessary draft for a well-appointed church music'. Besides the inadequate quality of instrumentalists he classified his 54 singers as '17 usable, 20 not yet usable and 17 wholly unsuitable'.

Lowering Standards

Appalling standards of musical performance in worship would have been anathema to the Lutheran. Bach saw his creative activities as services to God. Many of his scores are headed J. J. (*Jesu Juva* – 'with Jesus's help') and end with the letters S. D. G. (*Soli Deo Gloria* – 'to God alone be the glory'). One can only begin to imagine the torment occasioned by the lack of funding to hire good performers.

After 1730 he wrote few church cantatas and, not surprisingly, turned to less painful forms of music-making. Perfecting the art of composition in works that did not stipulate an instrumentalist was one solution.

chorale ▶ p. 357 chromaticism ▶ p. 357 fugue ▶ p. 358

Bach's talents, Prince Leopold of Anhalt-Cöthen (Ernst August's brother-in-law), made the irresistible offer of a large salary and an immediate cash gift if the young composer would become *Kapellmeister* in Cöthen. Duke Wilhelm Ernst was furious, and refused to release him from his obligations. He had Bach put in prison in 1717 for safe-keeping, but after four weeks reluctantly granted his release.

FAMILY CIRCUMSTANCES

Bach and his first wife Maria Barbara kept in contact with the Mulhausen pastor and poet, Eilmar, choosing him to be godfather to their first child Catharina Dorothea, born on 29 December 1708. Two years later Eilmar's daughter, Anna Dorothea Eilmar, was godmother to Wilhelm Friedemann. All six children born to Maria Barbara were baptized in Weimar. Sadly the twins, Maria Sophia and Johann Christoph, died in March 1713 within three weeks of birth. Fourteen months later a very healthy son; **Carl Philipp Emanuel Bach** (1714–88), was born and, perhaps prophetically, the most illustrious composer of that period, **Telemann**, was asked to be godfather. Bach took great trouble to train his sons as musicians. Later he did the same for several more distant relatives.

VOCAL ABILITY

Bach's first experience of making great music was with his voice. He had an uncommonly good treble voice and was able to use it as a chorister to sponsor the last few years of his education. He had always been attracted by good vocal skills. It seems that his first wife sang illegally in the organ loft at Arnstadt, and his second wife, Anna Magdalena was a court, singer at Cöthen. His brief in Leipzig was primarily to develop a strong choir with the students at St Thomas's School, but their poor voices and 'bad ears' made this difficult.

Bach wrote some of the world's most powerful vocal music. The large Passion settings exploit the colours and range of the human voice masterfully. Bach tended to use the bass for Christ's words and the tenor as the storyteller or Evangelist. The soprano is frequently the voice of the soul, making a spiritual comment on the action, and the alto represents the Holy Spirit.

THE WELL-TEMPERED CLAVIER

The Well-Tempered Clavier was published by Bach in two volumes of 24 (1722, 1742). The preludes and **fugues** in each volume are paired by tonality, with one for each major and minor key of the **chromatic** scale. Book One was put together from various sources, including the *Clavier-Büchlein* for his first son **Wilhelm Friedemann Bach** (1710–84), and a beautiful copy was made in 1722. Bach used it as teaching material for students with advanced keyboard skills. His title page reads: 'For the use and profit of the musical youth desirous of learning and for the pastime of those already skilled in this study'. He intended the pieces to be played on any keyboard instrument (*clavier*) – harpsichord, clavichord or organ. Book Two was compiled with the help of Anna Magdalena between 1739 and 1742, and in 1744 Bach's pupil and son-in-law-to-be, Johann Christoph Altnickol (1719–59), made a fair copy.

Posthumous Success

There had been much discussion in the early 1700s about systems of tuning keyboard instruments to enable works in every key to sound tolerably in tune. The theorist Andreas Werckmeister (1645–1706) coined the phrase 'well-tempered' to describe acceptable tuning systems. It is not known for certain what type of tuning Bach used, but having such a good ear and great technical knowledge of keyboard instruments he must have taken a delight in the challenge of temperament.

The two books of *The Well-Tempered Clavier* were not published during Bach's lifetime. However, although his sons continued to use them as teaching material and some preludes and fugues were circulated in manuscript after his death – which is how **Wolfgang Amadeus Mozart** (1756–91) became acquainted with them in 1782 – it was not until 1801 that the first complete edition was published.

C. P. E. Bach ▶ p. 156 W. F. Bach ▶ p. 157 Mozart ▶ p. 144 Telemann ▶ p. 122

THE CÖTHEN YEARS

Prince Leopold of Anhalt-Cöthen was a gifted musician and longed to establish a *collegium musicum* like those he had seen in various European courts. When the king of Prussia disbanded his orchestra in Berlin, Leopold brought seven of the experienced musicians to Cöthen. By the time he was 21 and old enough to rule, there were 18 musicians in his *collegium musicum*. A year later, flush with the optimism of youthful power, and sizing up the sorry state of affairs in Weimar, Leopold offered the leadership of the musicians to Bach. He arrived in 1717.

The Cöthen post gave Bach creative space and financial security in which to produce some magnificent compositions. With a fine instrumental ensemble at his disposal, his compositional productivity focused on chamber music, concertos and orchestral arrangements of keyboard works. In 1721 he dedicated the 'Brandenburg' Concertos to Margrave Christian Ludwig of Brandenburg. The violin concertos and the Concerto for Two Violins in D minor were written in Cöthen, probably for the leader of the ensemble, Joseph Spiess, and Martin Friedrich Marcus, both from the disbanded Berlin orchestra. The suites for unaccompanied cello and solo violin were likewise written for members of the *collegium musicum*. Much of the keyboard music from this period, on the other hand, stemmed from a need for teaching material – either for family members, as in the case of the two *Clavier-Büchlein* for Wilhelm Friedemann and Anna Magdalena, or for pupils.

FAMILY TRAGEDY

In May 1720, Bach left with a light heart to accompany the prince on a two-month trip to Carlsbad. He returned to find that during his absence Maria Barbara had died and been buried. He was now a widower with responsibility for four children, just as his father had been 25 years earlier. In February 1721 death struck again, taking Bach's older brother Johann Christoph. It must have been a cheerless 12 months.

JOHANN SEBASTIAN BACH: WORKS

For a comprehensive overview of Bach's works consult *Bach-Werke Verzeichnis* – Kleine Ausgabe (Breitkopf, 1998), ed. Dürr and Kobayashi. The BWV catalogue was originally compiled by Wolfgang Schmieder in 1950 as an index to the complete Bach edition, with a BWV number assigned to each work as it appeared in the bound volumes. The numbers do not reflect the chronology of composition. A number of works originally listed have now been shown to be spurious.

- **Sacred and secular cantatas:** BWV 1–222 (1706–42); the music of at least 20 cantatas has been lost.
- **Large choral works:** BWV 225–30 motets; BWV 232 B Minor Mass (assembled 1747–49; the different sections were written between 1714 ['Crucifixus'] and 1735 ['Agnus Dei II']); BWV 233–42 Masses; BWV 243 *Magnificat* in E flat (1723) and D (*c.* 1728–31); BWV 244 *St Matthew Passion* (1727, 1729, 1736, 1740 in revised versions); BWV 245 *St John Passion* (1724, 1725, *c.* 1730, 1740s in revised versions); BWV 246 *Luke Passion* is spurious; BWV 247 *St Mark Passion* (1731 and now lost); BWV 248 *Christmas Oratorio* (performed in 6 parts 25 December 1734 to 6 January 1735); BWV 249 *Easter Oratorio* (1725 revised 1732–5)
- **Chorales and sacred songs.** BWV 250–524
- **Organ works:** BWV 525–748; BWV 599–644 is the *Orgel-Büchlein* (1714–16)
- **Other keyboard works:** BWV 772–994, including BWV 846–93 *The Well-Tempered Clavier*, the '48' preludes and fugues, book 1 (1722) and book 2 (1738–42); BWV 971 *Italian Concerto* (1735); BWV 988 *Goldberg Variations* (1741–42)
- **Lute music:** BWV 995–1000
- **Chamber music:** BWV 01–1040, including BWV 1001–6 Sonatas and partitas for solo violin (1720); BWV 1007–12 6 Suites for solo cello (c. 1720)
- **Orchestral music:** BWV 1041–71, including BWV 1046–51 'Brandenburg' Concertos (1721)
- **Canons and fugues:** BWV 1072–126, including BWV 1079 *Musical Offering* (1747); BWV 1080 *The Art of Fugue* (1742–49)

But fortune smiled and in September 1721 the aged widow of his mother's Uncle Tobias bequeathed him 500 thalers (well over a year's salary). Before the end of the year Bach married again. His bride, Anna Magdalena Wilcke (1701–60), was 16 years his junior, an instrumentalist, and a court singer from a musical family. Eight days later Prince Leopold also married. Unfortunately for Bach and his family, the new princess had little time for music. Leopold's enthusiasm for the art dwindled and Bach grew restless. His sons needed a broader education and exposure of their musical talents to a wider audience. He was approached about the position of *Kantor* at St Thomas's School. This was the most prestigious musical appointment in Leipzig, with responsibility for the city's four principal churches.

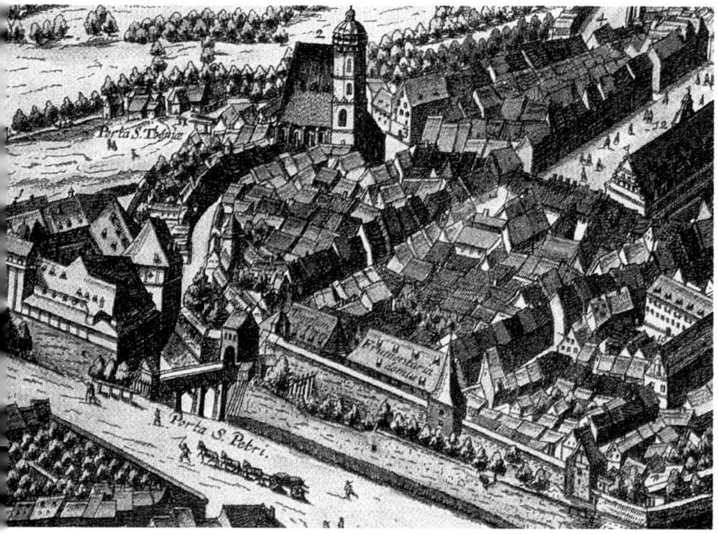

LEIPZIG

Bach was not the first choice of candidate for the Leipzig post. Telemann, who had been associated with Leipzig for many years, was offered the position in August 1722, but declined as he could not obtain release from his situation in Hamburg. Three other candidates were considered before Bach and Johann Christoph Graupner (1683– 1760) joined the contest. Graupner was appointed in January 1723, but as he had the same problem with contractual obligations as Telemann, the post was finally offered to Bach, and on 28 May 1723 the household moved into the newly renovated school apartment.

It was political rather than musical issues that had weakened his application initially. The selection board was made up of members whose loyalty was primarily either to Elector Friedrich August II, who desired total power, or to the Estates party, which wanted to curb the absolute power of the Elector and place it in the hands of local government. The Estates party members favoured a traditional *Kantor*, able to teach subjects other than music, hence they supported Georg Friedrich Kaufmann (1679–1735), Bach and Georg Balthasar Schott (1686–1736). The Absolutists favoured high-profile composers who would bring glamour to Leipzig through their compositions, particularly operas, hence their support of Telemann, Graupner and Johann Friedrich Fasch (1688–1758). Although an Absolutist, the mayor, Gottfried Lange, saw Bach's potential and voted in his favour.

(BL) Leipzig
Scene showing Leipzig in Bach's day, with St Thomas's Church (top centre).
(TL) Kantor at Leipzig
Engraving showing a kantor at work with his pupils in Leipzig.
(TR) The Bach Festival
Leaflet for the 1999, 9th London Bach Festival, a prelude to the 250th anniversary of his death in 2000.
(BR) Felix Mendelssohn
Mendelssohn was responsible for the centenary revival of Bach's St Matthew Passion.

ST THOMAS'S SCHOOL

As *Kantor* of St Thomas's School, Bach was third in rank beneath the Rector (headmaster) and Con-Rector (deputy headmaster). The *Kantor* had to teach grammar and Latin – a task Bach quickly delegated to a junior teacher – as well as share mundane duties, such as waking the boys in time for 5.15 a.m. prayers. St Thomas's School provided the choristers for the Leipzig churches, and Bach tried with limited resources to furnish them with wonderful choirs.

The politics of his position within St Thomas's School frequently made his job difficult. He was allowed to delegate teaching duties, but had many problems with the school authorities. On several occasions he appealed to the Elector himself for a just judgement on school issues. Circumstances in the school reached an all-time low for Bach under the headship of Johann August Ernesti (installed in 1734), who had such a low opinion of music in the curriculum that he would admonish any child that was found practising.

BACH'S CHILDREN

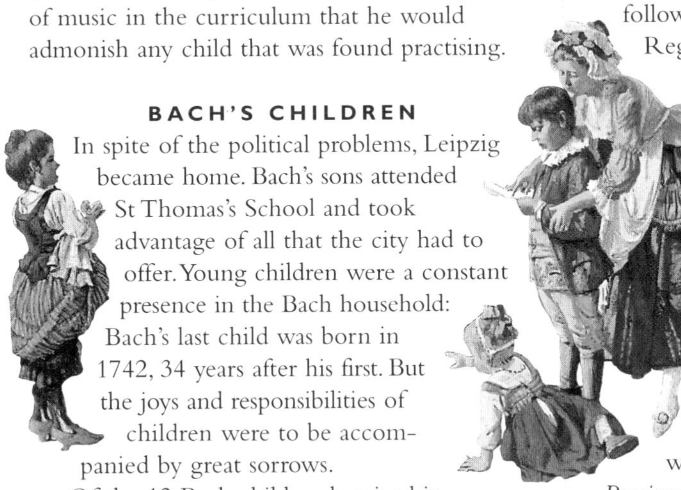

In spite of the political problems, Leipzig became home. Bach's sons attended St Thomas's School and took advantage of all that the city had to offer. Young children were a constant presence in the Bach household: Bach's last child was born in 1742, 34 years after his first. But the joys and responsibilities of children were to be accompanied by great sorrows.

Of the 12 Bach children baptized in St Thomas's Church, only six were to outlive their father. Three newborn babies died within a week of birth, in 1727, 1730 and 1733, but still more devastating must have been the death of strong, healthy toddlers. In June 1726 Anna Magdalena's first child Christiana Sophia Henrietta, who had been baptized in Cöthen, died at the age of three. Two years later Christian Gottlieb died aged three-and-a-half. In 1732 18-month-old Christiana Dorothea died, followed in 1733 by four-and-a-half-year-old Regina Johanna. An indispensable 'second mother' in the household, Friedelina Margaretha Bach, died in 1729, having lived with the family since 1709.

FINAL YEARS

Bach was to remain in Leipzig for the rest of his life, and his first years there proved extremely prolific. Amongst the church music he composed at this time were the *St John* and *St Matthew Passions* and five annual cantata cycles. Later he turned to secular music, composing the *Christmas Oratorio* in 1734, then in the last decade of his the life, *Musical Offering* and his unfinished *Art of Fugue*.

Bach himself was physically robust, and it was complications following eye surgery that foreshortened his life. In April 1750 he underwent two operations for cataracts, suffered a stroke and died on 28 July. His passing was marked with public honour. The household was disbanded, his young children taken in by members of the family, but sadly, Anna Magdalena was left with no financial independence and in 1760 died in poverty.

B-A-C-H THEME

As the letter h is used for b natural in Germany and Austria (b denotes b flat in German musical orthography), the name Bach can be 'read' in the music pitches b flat, a, c, b natural. Bach was aware of this, and his lexicographer cousin, Walther mentions it in the short entry on him. In the final unfinished movement of his *Art of Fugue* (1742–49) Bach quotes the four notes. Many composers since, including **Robert Schumann** (1810–56), **Franz Liszt** (1811–86) and **Ferrucio Busoni** (1866–1924) have consciously used the figure as inspiration.

Bach's works are the apotheosis of contrapuntal and harmonic style. Teachers, composers and musicians of every taste have used his compositions as a reference point and they continue to do so today.

'Essentially 'Ways to Bach' – a prelude to the 250th anniversary'
31 October - 12 November 1999

MENDELSSOHN'S REVIVAL OF THE *ST MATTHEW PASSION*

After Bach's death in 1750, his compositions were naturally performed less frequently than in his lifetime. Soon they became virtually unknown. The Berlin-born composer and conductor Carl Friedrich Zelter (1758–1832) admired the works of C. P. E. Bach and was delighted to meet W. F. Bach, who introduced him to his late father's compositions. Zelter became an avid collector of Bach's works and as director of the Berlin Singakademie introduced them to pupils and friends. Mendelssohn and Edvard Devrient (1801–77) both heard the *St Matthew Passion* in Zelter's class. Mendelssohn desperately wished to own a copy, and his wish was granted in 1823 when his grandmother arranged for him to have a copy as a Christmas present.

In 1827 Mendelssohn began to assemble a small choir for weekly practices of rarely heard works. With encouragement from Devrient, the idea of performing the *St Matthew Passion* with the Singakademie choir was hatched. Having obtained approval of the plan from Zelter, the choir and the orchestra, Mendelssohn conducted the famous revival 100 years to the day (according to their knowledge) of the première, on 11 March 1829, in the large hall of the Singakademie in Berlin. The performance was such a success that *St Matthew Passion* has never again left the repertory.

The Late Baroque

GEORGE FRIDERIC HANDEL

George Frideric Handel (1685–1759) is one of the best known of all Baroque composers. His gift for melody, his instinctive sense of drama and vivid scene-painting, and the extraordinary range of human emotions explored in his vocal compositions, make his music instantly accessible. Works such as *Messiah* (1741), *Water Music* (1717) and *Music for the Royal Fireworks* (1749) have guaranteed him enduring popularity. Born in Germany, Handel formed a personal style based mainly on the French and Italian music of the period, but he spent most of his working life in England. Unlike most of his musical contemporaries, he was not (except very briefly) attached to a royal court or a religious institution, and financial independence helped him to maintain his individual profile as a composer. Handel's early career was dominated by opera, but he became increasingly interested in the possibilities of the oratorio form, which he established as a leading feature of English musical life. He showed equal mastery as a writer of cantatas, anthems and concertos and was greatly admired for his virtuosity as an organist and harpsichordist. His mature style had a major influence on the native English composers of his time.

LIFE TIMELINE

1685	Born on 23 February at Halle
1702	Appointed organist of Halle Cathedral
1703	Leaves for Hamburg, where he joins orchestra at Gänsemarkt theatre
1705	First opera, *Almira*, performed in Hamburg
1706	Embarks on a journey to Italy, visiting Florence and Rome
1707	Composes his *Dixit Dominus*
1708	Oratorio *La Resurrezione* performed in Rome
1710	Opera *Agrippina* runs for a triumphant 27 nights in Venice; arrives in Hanover and is appointed *Kapellmeister* to the Elector; almost immediately makes plans to visit England
1713	*Te Deum* and *Jubilate* performed at St Paul's Cathedral, London, to celebrate Peace of Utrecht
1717	*Water Music* performed on the River Thames
1719	Royal Academy of Music established
1728	Collapse of Royal Academy
1729	Begins a new opera company, the so-called 'Second Academy'
1734	First season at Covent Garden
1737	Handel's opera project collapses
1740	Publishes op. 6 *concerti grossi*
1742	*Messiah* premièred in Dublin; returns to London to begin yearly seasons of oratorio
1749	*Music for the Royal Fireworks* performed to celebrate the Peace of Aix-la-Chapelle
1750	During the completion of *Jephtha*, eyesight deteriorates
1753	Becomes totally blind
1759	Dies in Brook Street, London, on 14 April and is buried in Westminster Abbey on 20 April

THE 'HALLELUJAH' CHORUS

Messiah has retained its immense popularity since the very first performance in 1742. With its universal message of hope and victory over suffering, expressed at its strongest in the stirringly affirmative 'Hallelujah' Chorus, it has become one of the most frequently performed of all the great choral works.

POPULAR MELODY *Handel*

EARLY LIFE

Handel was born on 23 February 1685, as Georg Friederich Händel (he later anglicized his name), in the German city of Halle. His father was a well-respected barber-surgeon, whose much younger wife was the daughter of a Lutheran minister. This middle-class background, combined with a good education at local schools, whose curricula were among the most advanced in Europe, might have destined the boy to a professional career, and Dr Händel evidently intended his son to become a lawyer. A single year spent at Halle's university in 1702 may have been devoted to legal studies, but by this time Handel's father was dead, and he had developed into a composer and instrumental performer of real promise.

It was one of Dr Händel's aristocratic patrons, the Duke of Saxe-Weissenfels, who had urged him to allow his son to study music. The young Handel's teacher was Friedrich Wilhelm Zachow (1663–1712), an outstanding organist and well known as a composer of Lutheran cantatas. Little of Handel's student work survives, but the evidence suggests that Zachow's teaching was extremely thorough. His pupil was encouraged to examine a wide range of music by other masters – German and Italian – and this laid the basis of the eclectic style Handel developed in his artistic maturity.

***(BL)* Music for the Royal Fireworks**
First performance of Handel's Music for the Royal Fireworks, *held in Green Park, 1749.*
(R)* Handel's Choir *by William Hogarth
Sketch by Hogarth showing Handel's choir singing Willem de Fesch's oratorio Judith.

THE HANOVERIAN ROYAL FAMILY

The Hanoverian royal family is traditionally represented as boorish and dysfunctional, but the truth was more complex. However much they hated and quarrelled with one another, they all expressed enthusiasm for Handel's music. Both George I and his son George II, who succeeded him in 1727, were loyal supporters of the composer in the opera-house, and his anthems were sung at two royal weddings. Handel gave music lessons to George II's daughters. His anthem 'The ways of Zion do mourn' was written expressly for the funeral of their mother Queen Caroline in 1737. Its allusions to works by **Heinrich Schütz** (1585–1672) and Johann Philipp Krieger (1649–1725) recall the German origins the Hanover queen shared with Handel. Even the son she despised, Frederick, Prince of Wales (who never became king), having patronized the Opera of the Nobility as a deliberate gesture of political opposition to his parents, became reconciled to Handel during the late 1730s. Frederick's son, as George III, showed an almost obsessive devotion to the composer's music. To him we owe the acquisition of almost all of Handel's autograph scores, which eventually passed from the royal collection to the British Library, where they remain today.

serenata ▶ p. 362

THE HAMBURG YEARS

After a one-year contract as organist at Halle Cathedral in 1702, Handel moved to Hamburg to join the orchestra at the Gänsemarkt opera-house. This northern city was one of Germany's largest and most cosmopolitan, a wealthy international trading centre, which had imported the fashionable new entertainment form of opera during the late seventeenth century. Influences at the Gänsemarkt theatre were chiefly French and Italian: ballet and spectacular stage effects recalled Louis XIV's Versailles, while the style of the librettos was marked by a mixture of serious and comic elements derived from Venetian opera.

Handel gained valuable experience in Hamburg as an orchestral violinist, while making his earliest attempts at composing for the theatre. The leading operatic master at the Gänsemarkt was **Reinhard Keiser** (1674–1739), from whose work Handel borrowed ideas throughout his career. He became great friends with a younger composer-singer, **Johann Mattheson** (1681–1764), but in December 1704 the pair quarrelled and fought a duel outside the theatre. The sword-fight, Mattheson tells us, 'might have ended unfortunately had not God graciously ordained that my blade, in thrusting against my opponent's metal coat-button, should be shattered'. The pair were reconciled and Mattheson took a leading role in Handel's first opera *Almira*, which successfully premièred in 1705.

THE ITALIAN JOURNEY

In autumn 1706 Handel set out for Italy, perhaps at the invitation of a member of the ruling Medici family of Florence. Italian music – vocal and instrumental – had had a major influence on the rest of Europe during the previous century. A passion for opera had taken hold in centres such as Venice and Naples, with inevitable consequences for church and chamber music, and Italy remained a magnet for European composers until the end of the Baroque era.

The Italian journey was to prove influential in a number of ways. While visiting Venice he met **Domenico Scarlatti**, who accompanied him back to Rome, where he eventually settled, gaining entry to the musical household of Cardinal Pietro Ottoboni and found an enthusiastic admirer in another equally wealthy cardinal, Benedetto Pamphili. It was Pamphili who wrote the libretto for Handel's earliest oratorio, *Il trionfo del Tempo e del Disinganno* ('The Triumph of Time and Disenchantment', 1707) and who provided verses for some of the many chamber cantatas he composed for Marchese Francesco Maria Ruspoli. Handel lived for a time in Ruspoli's palace and accompanied him to his country villa north of Rome. These Roman grandees seem to have treated the composer as a distinguished foreign virtuoso, rather than giving him the sort of servant status most musicians would have been accorded at the time.

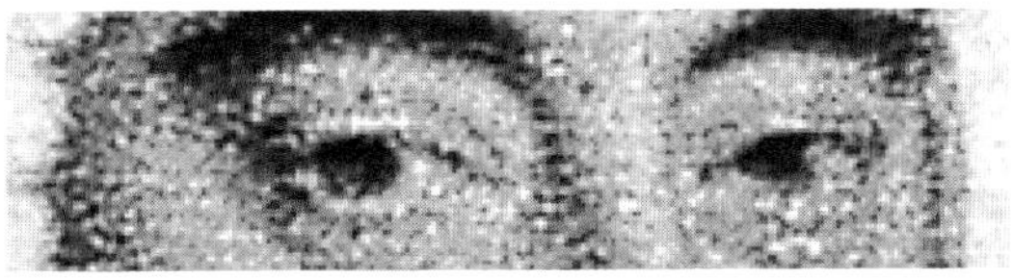

THE MUSE OF ROME

Although Handel clearly profited financially from his Italian trip in 1706, the fact that he could afford to undertake it in the first place points to a social and economic independence that remained an important element throughout his life and was later to influence several of his most crucial career decisions.

Handel's most important Roman commission was a series of psalm settings, including the great *Dixit Dominus* (1707). Some of them were probably composed for a solemn vesper service at the Carmelite church of S Maria del Monte Santo. There was no opera in Rome, because of a papal ban, but in 1707 Handel wrote *Rodrigo* for performance in Florence, where he was lavishly rewarded by Prince Ferdinando de' Medici. Returning to Rome, he produced the oratorio *La Resurrezione* ('The Resurrection', 1708), sumptuously presented in Ruspoli's palace, before journeying south to Naples. There the Austrian Imperial viceroy was a Venetian cardinal, Vincenzo Grimani, who provided Handel with a witty satirical libretto for the opera *Agrippina*. In January 1710, this was produced at Grimani's family theatre in Venice, San Giovanni Crisostomo, and ran for 27 nights – a triumphant conclusion to Handel's Italian journey.

HANOVER AND LONDON

On his return to Germany in 1710, Handel spent some time at Hanover as *Kapellmeister* to Elector Georg August, who in 1714 was to become king of Great Britain as George I. In 1711, during his first visit to London, Handel scored an immediate success with the opera *Rinaldo*, composed for the recently built Queen's Theatre in the Haymarket. Three further operas were written for the theatre with excellent, mainly Italian casts and elaborate staging, before mounting expenses temporarily halted performance. Handel, meanwhile, had made useful contacts in London society and seems to have been employed as an unofficial conduit of information by Hanoverian diplomats during the last years of Queen Anne.

ANGLICAN INFLUENCES

When George I succeeded Queen Anne, he did not immediately appoint Handel to an official court position, although two of the composer's sacred works were performed in the Chapel Royal to celebrate the king's arrival in London. The story that *Water Music* was written to regain the king's favour has no sure basis in fact. During the years 1717–19 he engaged on a series of 11 anthems for the private chapel of the immensely rich Duke of Chandos at Cannons, north of London. The experience of writing these, together with the *Te Deum* and *Jubilate* composed to celebrate the Peace of Utrecht in 1713, brought Handel into contact with the Anglican choral tradition of **Purcell** and **John Blow** (1649–1708). Significant use of the chorus was also made in two dramatic works written with the help of poets in Chandos's circle, including Alexander Pope and John Gay: the **serenata** *Acis and Galatea* and the oratorio *Esther* (both 1718).

Blow ▶ p. 80 Keiser ▶ p. 118 Mattheson ▶ p. 119 Purcell ▶ p. 78 D. Scarlatti ▶ p. 121 Schütz ▶ p. 86

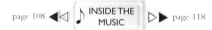

THE ROYAL ACADEMY OF MUSIC

In 1719, a scheme was initiated by a group of prominent noblemen, politicians and army officers for creating a suitably staged annual season of performances in Haymarket's King's Theatre (as it had now become). It was to feature Italian operas starring the best available singers and would be financed as a joint-stock company under royal charter. Known as 'The Royal Academy of Music', the enterprise involved Handel as principal composer, along with other prominent composers such as **Giovanni Bononcini** (1670–1747). Although the project did not always run smoothly, the Academy initially was a success and several of Handel's finest stage works, including *Giulio Cesare* (1724), *Tamerlano* (1724) and *Rodelinda* (1725), were written for these Academy seasons.

Handel, meanwhile, had acquired English nationality and his acceptance by London society was reflected in his adoption of an anglicized form of his name. He settled in a fine new house in Brook Street in the city's most elegant quarter, and led the life of a gentleman amid a circle of cultured friends, several of whom were aristocrats. He never married and, although there are a few hints as to relationships with female singers, almost nothing is known of his private life.

THE SECOND ACADEMY

The Royal Academy entered a troubled phase in 1726 when its patrons decided to challenge the reigning *prima donna* Francesca Cuzzoni (*c.* 1698–1770) with a rival, the Venetian soprano Faustina Bordoni (1700–81). Partisanship surrounding the pair (who eventually came to blows on stage) attracted ridicule, and the reluctance of subscribers to defray mounting production costs, together with the immense success that greeted John Gay's *The Beggar's Opera*, which began a new trend for 'ballad opera', brought the Academy to a halt in 1728. The following year Handel went to Italy to engage singers for a new season, and the subscription system was revived for a further series of operas, among them *Orlando* (1732), in which the composer returned to the world of magic with which he had entranced London at *Rinaldo*'s première 21 years earlier.

Although this 'Second Academy' featured several outstanding stars, its finances were always insecure. Handel's promotion of his own music at the expense of recent Italian operatic successes was increasingly criticized. Early in 1733 a group of aristocrats, building on resentment against 'the Dominion of Mr Handel', gathered to form what became known as the 'Opera of the Nobility'. The scheme, patronized by Frederick, Prince of Wales, involved poaching most of the best singers from the King's Theatre. It was the most significant challenge encountered by Handel in his career so far.

GEORGE FRIDERIC HANDEL: WORKS

- **Operas:** *Almira* (1705), *Agrippina* (1709), *Rinaldo* (1711), *Radamisto* (1720), *Giulio Cesare* (1724), *Tamerlano* (1724), *Rodelinda* (1725), *Orlando* (1732), *Ariodante* (1735), *Alcina* (1735)
- **Selected oratorios and dramatic works to English texts:** *Il trionfo del Tempo e del Disinganno* (1707), *La Resurrezione* (1708), *Acis and Galatea* (1718), *Esther* (1718), *Deborah* (1733), *Athalia* (1733), *Alexander's Feast* (1736), *Saul* (1738), *Israel in Egypt* (1738), *Ode for St Cecilia's Day* (1739), *L'Allegro, il Penseroso ed il Moderato* (1740), *Messiah* (1741), *Samson* (1741), *Semele* (1743), *Belshazzar* (1744), *Occasional Oratorio* (1746), *Judas Maccabaeus* (1746), *Joshua* (1748), *Solomon* (1748), *Theodora* (1749), *Jephtha* (1751)
- **Selected sacred works:** *Dixit Dominus* (1707), *Utrecht*, *Te Deum* and *Jubilate* (1713), *Brockes Passion* (1716), Coronation anthems, including 'Zadok the Priest' (1727), 11 Chandos anthems
- **Selected instrumental works:** *Water Music* (1717), Chamber Music solos op. 1 (1732), trio sonatas op 2 (1732), *Concerti Grossi* op. 3 (1734), Organ Concertos op. 4 (1738), op. 7 (1740s), Trio Sonatas op. 5 (1739), *Concerti Grossi* op. 6 (1739), *Music for the Royal Fireworks* (1749)

A RETURN TO ORATORIO

In 1733, however, Handel returned to oratorio. The two dramatic works written for the Duke of Chandos, *Esther* and *Acis and Galatea*, had been performed by friends of Handel the previous year, followed by pirate performances by rival groups and Handel planned to put *Esther* on at the King's Theatre. The possibility of staging it was thwarted by a veto from the Bishop of London, but even unstaged it attracted sufficient interest for Handel to produce another oratorio – *Deborah* – the following season. This work's grandiose performance requirements were unprecedented in London. During the summer of 1733 Handel visited Oxford, where the premiere of *Athalia*, the earliest of his oratorios to show real mastery of the sacred dramatic form, was performed at the annual degree ceremony.

THE FATE OF HARMONY

Continuing to attract audiences, the Opera of the Nobility moved into the King's Theatre. Handel, meanwhile, enjoyed the facilities of the newly built Covent Garden, where his operas *Ariodante* and *Alcina* (both 1735) were enhanced by ballets featuring the brilliant French dancer Marie Sallé. In the later 1730s, a need to sustain his London public seems to have brought Handel close to nervous exhaustion and he had a series of strokes. This created real alarm among his circle of friends, who were concerned that 'ye Fate of Harmony depends upon a single life'. None of his operas composed at this time drew sufficient audiences, but although non-dramatic vocal works, such as *Alexander's Feast* (1736) and *L'Allegro, il Penseroso ed il Moderato* ('The Merry, the Thoughtful and the Modest', 1740), provided an outlet for his refinement and originality, he was not yet prepared to forsake the stage completely.

DUBLIN AND *MESSIAH*

The collapse of Handel's final opera season at Lincoln's Inn Fields Theatre in 1741 coincided

(BL and TR) Rodelinda and Orlando
Twentieth-century productions of Handel's operas Rodelinda *and* Orlando.
(TL) Giulio Cesare
Contemporaneous performance of Handel's Giulio Cesare.
(BR) Messiah
Frontispiece to Handel's best-known work, Messiah, *first performed in Dublin in 1742.*

INSTRUMENTAL WORKS OF THE 1730s

Instrumental works were always something of a sideline for Handel, but in the 1720s and 30s a number of his instrumental works were published. He was a virtuoso harpsichordist, so it isn't surprising that books of his harpsichord suites were first to appear. In the early 1730s, 12 sonatas for a melody instrument (violin, flute, recorder or oboe) and continuo were issued as his op. 1, followed by six trio sonatas as his op. 2. A set of concertos, chiefly for strings and oboes, appeared as his op. 3 (1734); most had been written years before, but his publishers knew that there would be a public demand for them from many music societies that ran subscription concert series. They also printed collections of his opera overtures. In the mid 1730s, Handel started playing organ concertos as interval music in his oratorios, and a set of six was gathered for publication as op. 4. 1739 saw the issue of more trio sonatas as well as the creation of his finest instrumental works, the 12 'Grand Concertos', op. 6: these highly original works are the last great essay by a Baroque composer in the style made famous by **Corelli**.

with an invitation to visit Ireland by the Lord Lieutenant, the 3rd Duke of Devonshire. Its capital, Dublin, was a rapidly expanding city, where Handel found a ready welcome. Spending almost a year there, he presented a successful concert season, crowned by the first performance of his oratorio *Messiah*. The text was arranged from the Old and New Testaments by Charles Jennens, a wealthy amateur. Jennens deeply admired Handel, though he was often critical of him. The success of their collaboration can be measured as much from *Saul* (1738) – a work of epic grandeur and arguably Handel's finest achievement in the field of dramatic oratorio – as from *Messiah* itself. Jennens' imaginative design shapes a narrative outline from the biblical story, contributing greatly to the work's impact and originality.

THE ORATORIOS OF THE 1740s

Returning from Ireland in 1742, Handel devoted himself to composing oratorio. It may be that the public for these works derived to some extent from the London bourgeoisie rather than the aristocracy and gentry who had dominated his opera audience. English texts made these works more accessible and their appeal was due partly to a new seriousness in matters of religion. Works such as *Samson* (1741), *Joshua* (1748) and *Solomon* (1748) also made an impact because of Handel's vivid use of the chorus as a key element in the drama, whether as commentator on the action or to highlight a particular mood.

The oratorios gained a popular following through allusions to contemporary political events, such as the Jacobite rebellion of 1745. *Messiah*, meanwhile, began to establish itself as a favourite with the public, after performances at the newly built Foundling Hospital for the reception of abandoned babies and orphans. Handel was made a governor of the hospital in May 1750 and his interest in the project led to regular *Messiah* performances there from this time onwards.

HANDEL'S LAST YEARS

As he grew older, Handel's friends often remarked upon his robust constitution. Summer visits to the country and trips to spas and watering places helped him to relax and prepare new scores. During the composition of *Jephtha*, however, he noted the gradual weakening of his left eye and by 1753 he had become completely blind. His musical activities continued, though, since he could still prepare and direct performances and play the organ. His amanuensis since 1719 was John Christopher Smith (1683–1763). Smith was a composer and assisted Handel in making the necessary revisions to his works to accommodate new singers for the annual oratorio seasons.

Handel's health began to fail during the early months of 1759. After a *Messiah* performance on 6 April he took to his bed, dying early on the morning of the 14th, aged 74. He left the considerable sum of £20,000, almost a third of which involved charitable legacies.

HANDEL'S LEGACY

A solemn funeral in Westminster Abbey demonstrated the veneration in which Handel was held by his adopted country. His music soon began to find admirers outside England, and its influence can be heard in several works by **Joseph Haydn** (1732–1809), as well as Mozart, composed towards the end of the eighteenth century. **Ludwig van Beethoven** (1770–1827) was generous in his praise of Handel, declaring, 'I would uncover my head and kneel down at his tomb'. Yet with the exception of *Messiah*, a few dramatic oratorios and favourite pieces such as the coronation anthem 'Zadok the Priest' (1727), the bulk of Handel's output fell rapidly into neglect. He began to be compared unfavourably with his contemporary **J. S. Bach** and his music became associated with a particular strain of English Protestant religious solemnity encouraged by such occasions as the annual Handel festivals at London's Crystal Palace.

It was not until the twentieth century that the scope of Handel's achievement was adequately revealed. Most of his operas were revived and several of them now form part of the general operatic repertory. New performing styles, closer to those of Handel's own time, were found for the English oratorios. Handel is now regarded as one of the most powerful of eighteenth-century musical personalities: cosmopolitan, versatile, unorthodox and endlessly resourceful.

MESSIAH

Handel composed *Messiah* during August and September 1741, and the work was given its first performance the following April at the music room in Fishamble Street, Dublin. Its immediate popularity owed much to the skill with which Jennens had arranged the libretto from biblical sources, dwelling on Christ's nativity, his Passion and his triumph over death at the resurrection. Handel used a simple orchestra, consisting of strings (oboes and bassoons were added in his later versions), with trumpets and drums added in certain of the choruses. The individual arias were tailored to the abilities and limitations of specific singers, among them Susanna Maria Cibber (1714–66), whose private life had given her a dubious reputation. Hearing her sing 'He was despised' however, a Dublin clergyman, quoting Jesus's own words, exclaimed 'Woman, for this be all thy sins forgiven thee'. As with his other oratorios, Handel made a great many alterations to *Messiah* during later years, and after his death it was reorchestrated by **Mozart**, amongst others.

J. S. Bach ▶ p. 106 Beethoven ▶ p. 150 Bononcini ▶ p. 116 Corelli ▶ p. 82 Haydn ▶ p. 140 Mozart ▶ p. 144

The Late Baroque

PERSONALITIES

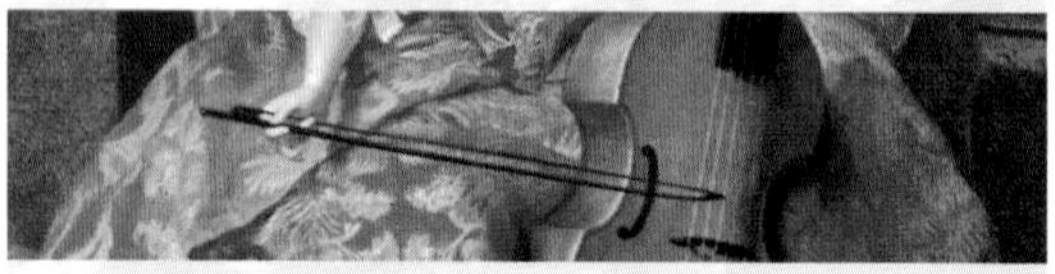

Albinoni, Tomaso

(Ál-bē-nō'-nē, Tō-mä'-zō) 1671–1751

ITALIAN COMPOSER

Albinoni considered himself a *dilettante*, depending for a living neither on the success of his compositions nor on his ability as a performer. Although he was a prolific composer of operas, several of which were performed outside Italy, Albinoni is recognized chiefly for his concertos the first of which (op. 2, 1700) were the earliest published Venetian concertos. A distinctive feature of his op. 7 and op. 9 collections (1715, 1722) is the inclusion of concertos for one and two oboes. Their slow movements often reveal Albinoni's considerable melodic gifts. Some of his music was known to **J. S. Bach**, who may have been attracted by his leaning towards counterpoint.

Avison, Charles

1709–70

ENGLISH COMPOSER

Avison was a teacher, writer, concert promoter and organist of St Nicholas's Church, Newcastle-upon-Tyne, from 1735. He was a pupil of Geminiani. As well as composing several sets of his own concertos, published over a period of some 30 years, he arranged 12 of Domenico Scarlatti's harpsichord sonatas as ***concerti grossi*** (1744), orchestrating them skilfully. Along with almost every English composer of note, Avison subscribed to Thomas Roseingrave's publication of a selection of Scarlatti's sonatas (1739). He organized successful subscription concerts in Newcastle and Durham where both his own music and that of other composers, including Rameau, was performed. In 1752 he published *An Essay on Musical Expression*, which deals with both performance practice and emotional responses to music.

Bononcini, Giovanni

(Bō-non-chē'nē, Jō-vän'-ē) 1670–1747

ITALIAN COMPOSER

Bononcini came from a musical family in Modena; his father Giovanni Maria was the *maestro di cappella* of Modena Cathedral and his younger brother, Antonio Maria, was a talented cellist and composer. He was also a cellist and studied music in Bologna. He worked in Milan, then Rome – where he wrote several operas – and Vienna, where he produced further operas as well as writing oratorios and cantatas. In 1719 he was invited to London to compose for the Royal Academy of Music which had recently been set up under **Handel**'s direction. His *Astarto* was successfully played during the 1720 season and for a time his operas offered serious rivalry to those of Handel. In 1727 he was exposed for passing off an opera by Antonio Lotti (*c.* 1667–1740) as his own. He left London shortly after this, visiting Paris and Lisbon before going to Vienna, where he died in 1747.

CONCERTO IN D MINOR

Albinoni's concertos for one and two oboes with string orchestra are among his most appealing instrumental compositions. The central movement of the Concerto in D minor (op. 9, no. 2) is a lyrical *adagio* whose wistful melody with its accompaniment of gently undulating arpeggios makes it one of the composer's outstanding achievements and one of the most familiar pieces from the Baroque era.

POPULAR MELODY *Albinoni*

Caldara, Antonio

(Kál-dá'-rá, Án-tōn'-yō) 1670–1736

ITALIAN COMPOSER

Caldara was a Venetian composer whose career was divided almost equally between Italy and Austria. He sang under Giovanni Legrenzi (1626–90) at St Mark's and in 1699 was appointed *maestro di cappella* at the Mantuan court. In 1708 he left Mantua for Rome, where his oratorio *Il martirio di San Caterina* ('The Martyrdom of St Catherine') was performed. After visiting Spain he returned to Rome, becoming *maestro di cappella* to Marchese Ruspoli, for whom he composed cantatas, operas and oratorios. When Fux succeeded Marc'Antonio Ziani (*c.* 1653–1715) as *Kapellmeister* at the Viennese court in 1715, the post of *Vice-Kapellmeister* was filled by Caldara, who retained it for the remainder of his life. He wrote oratorios and operas for Vienna, setting texts by the court poet Apostolo Zeno and by his successor **Metastasio**.

(BL) Travelling Musician
Music was disseminated by means of travelling musicians, who played and sold their music across Europe.
(MFR) French Dancer
Eighteenth-century French music was more dance-orientated than in other European countries.
(BR) François Couperin
Couperin was known as 'le grand' and came from a long line of musicians and composers.

THE SPREAD OF ITALIAN MUSIC

Individual patrons, the church and the various Italian political states were generous supporters of the arts throughout the sixteenth, seventeenth and eighteenth centuries. Among the chief centres of musical activity were Rome, Venice, Florence and Naples, though many other cities became known for particular aspects of musical entertainment or instrumental craftsmanship. With such a favourable artistic climate, and with generous funding, it is not surprising that new ideas, styles and forms developed by Italian musicians spread further afield. Opera, oratorio, cantata, sonata and instrumental concerto were the major forms that emerged from seventeenth-century Italy; all were to some extent assimilated into the established conventions of countries throughout Europe. Elements of opera, above all, penetrated almost every other musical form, sacred and secular, instrumental and vocal.

Travelling, Publishing and Theorizing

The means by which Italian music was disseminated abroad were varied. Itinerant musicians travelling from one centre to another, court and city alike, not only played their music but often carried manuscripts of it, which could be copied or perhaps even bought. Music publishing, notably in Amsterdam, Hamburg and London, enabled connoisseurs and professional and amateur performers to encounter the latest sonatas and concertos of Corelli and Vivaldi. Meanwhile the growing taste for public concerts in Hamburg, Frankfurt, Paris, London and many other cities attracted Italian singers and instrumentalists. Manifestos and treatises, which were avidly sought by music-lovers and intellectuals, also played their part in the spread of Italian ideas. By the beginning of the eighteenth century, Italian theories, vocal and instrumental techniques, concepts, forms and means of expression had influenced virtually every aspect of music throughout Europe. One particular aim was to express the emotions of a text faithfully and in such a way as to stir the emotions of an audience. This aspiration to move audiences by a variety of oratorical gestures was as much present in instrumental as in vocal music.

concerto grosso ▶ p. 357 *ordre* ▶ p. 361 *petit motet* ▶ p. 361

Clarke, Jeremiah

c. 1674–1707

ENGLISH COMPOSER

Clarke was a chorister of the Chapel Royal when he sang at the Coronation of James II in 1685. He became organist of St Paul's Cathedral, then Gentleman Extraordinary and one of the organists of the Chapel Royal. In 1704 he succeeded **Blow** as Master of the Choristers at St Paul's. He composed anthems, odes, keyboard pieces and theatre music. Though one of the leading English church composers of his time – one of his anthems was sung at Queen Anne's coronation in 1702 – Clarke is nowadays chiefly remembered for his Trumpet Voluntary (1697), which was long attributed to **Purcell**.

Couperin, François

(Kōō-per-àn', Fràn-swä') 1668–1733

FRENCH COMPOSER

Couperin, known as *le grand*, was the most gifted member of an illustrious French musical family. He lived and worked in Paris where, at the age of 18, he inherited the post of organist at St Gervais, which had previously been held by his father and uncle. In 1693 he was appointed one of king's organists at Versailles and in 1717 he replaced Jean-Henri d'Anglebert (1635–91) as *Ordinaire de la musique de la Chambre du Roi pour le clavecin* ('member of the king's chamber for keyboard'). He held both posts until 1730.

Couperin's earliest known music is for solo organ. His *pièces d'orgue* were issued in manuscript with engraved title pages in 1690. An interest in uniting the characteristics of Italian and French styles became apparent soon after this when he wrote trios and quartets in the manner of **Corelli** and small-scale sacred vocal pieces (***petits motets***) modelled on those of **Marc-Antoine Charpentier** (1643–1704) who had studied in Rome. Two extended trios, *L'Apothéose de Corelli* (1724), and *L'Apothéose de Lully* (1725), bear witness to Couperin's fascination with national styles and their unification.

Couperin is recognized, above all, for his solo harpsichord music, issued in four collections of *pièces de clavecin* between 1713 and 1730. The works are assembled into 27 ***ordres***, a term that Couperin used to denote groups of pieces in related keys, falling somewhere between a suite and an anthology. Their meticulous craftsmanship and delicately expressive inflexions, which depend upon adherence to the composer's precisely notated ornamentation, represent his most sustained achievement.

Fux, Johann Joseph

(Fōōks, Yō'-hàn Yō'-sef) 1660–1741

GERMAN COMPOSER, ORGANIST AND THEORIST

There are large gaps in the biographical knowledge of Fux. It is known that he was born into a peasant family, but where he learnt his musical skills remains a mystery. In 1698 Emperor Leopold I appointed Fux *Hofcomponist* ('head composer') at the Vienna court, and in 1700 Fux travelled to Rome where he studied with **Bernardo Pasquini** (1637–1710). In 1705 he became *Vice-Kapellmeister*, later *Kapellmeister*, of St Stephen's Cathedral, Vienna. A year later Leopold appointed him court *Vice-Kapellmeister* and in 1715 *Kapellmeister*. Fux composed Italian oratorios, around 80 masses, motets and other church music, and Italian operas; *Costanza e Fortezza* ('Patience and Fortitude', 1723) was performed in Prague at the coronation of Emperor Charles VI as king of Bohemia. *Concentus musico-instrumentalis* ('Instrumental Collection', 1701) contains some of his most ambitious orchestral suites (*partite*). His Latin treatise on counterpoint, *Gradus ad Parnassum* ('Steps to Parnassus', 1725), was studied by **Haydn**, **Mozart** and **Beethoven**, remaining influential until the turn of the twentieth century.

Geminiani, Francesco

(Jă-mēn-yà'-nē, Fràn-chäs'-kō) 1687–1762

ITALIAN COMPOSER AND VIOLINIST

Geminiani was born in Lucca and studied in Rome with Corelli. In 1714 he went to England, where he remained for the rest of his life. Geminiani established a fine reputation as a teacher, composer and violin virtuoso. His earliest concertos – arrangements of Corelli's celebrated sonatas for violin and continuo (op. 5) – were printed in 1726. In 1732 he published six *concerti grossi* of his own (op. 2) and in the following year his finest collection (op. 3), which in the opinion of music historian **Charles Burney** (1726–1814) 'placed him at the head of all masters then living, in this species of composition'. A further set was issued in 1746 (op. 7). A staged pantomime called *The Enchanted Forest*, scored for strings, wind and timpani, and performed in Paris in 1754, was among his last compositions. Geminiani's many treatises on performance practice include *The Art of Playing the Violin* (1751) which laid the foundations of modern string technique.

FRENCH AND ITALIAN STYLES OF COMPOSITION

The aims of codifying and cultivating the concept of national style can be found in the music of some European countries well before the beginning of the Baroque era. But awareness of national traits in composing and playing music intensified during the seventeenth and eighteenth centuries. At the same time, authors of treatises and manifestos became increasingly interested in the ideas and performing styles of other countries. As in most matters concerning style and form, Italian musicians and thinkers provided the models. In vocal music the emphasis lay on an 'affective' treatment of words, in which virtuosity played an ever-increasing part. While this provided other European countries with a model it was one that needed to be tailored to the particular requirements of different languages and traditions.

Resisting Influences

The country that throughout the seventeenth century was most resistant to the style of Italian music was France. In its instrumental music, France was more dance-orientated. Particularly in music for lute and keyboard, French music showed a predilection for precise and profuse ornamentation. Their propensity manifested itself often in structural ways rather than merely decorative ones. Italian forms such as the sonata and concerto only began to interest French composers towards the very end of the seventeenth century, and even then ornamentation and a close relationship to dance remained characteristic and distinguishing features of French music.

J. S. Bach ▶ p. 106 Beethoven ▶ p. 150 Blow ▶ p. 80 Burney ▶ p. 157 Charpentier ▶ p. 82 Corelli ▶ p. 82 Handel p. 112 Haydn ▶ p. 140 Metastasio ▶ p. 161 Mozart ▶ p. 144 Pasquini ▶ p. 84 Purcell ▶ p. 78

Jacquet de La Guerre, Elisabeth-Claude

(Zhă-kā' de lă Găr, E-lēs-ă-bĕt' Klōd) 1665–1729

FRENCH COMPOSER AND HARPSICHORDIST

Jacquet de la Guerre was a child prodigy. The daughter of an organ builder, she was described by the *Mercure Galant* in 1678 as *la merveille de notre siècle* ('the marvel of our century'). After performing for Louis XIV, she was taken to live at Versailles, where her education was supervised by his mistress Madame de Montespan. She married the organist Marin de la Guerre and continued to perform and compose throughout her life. Jacquet de la Guerre's earliest published work was a collection of sparkling harpsichord pieces (1687). Two years earlier she had written the ballet *Les Jeux à l'honneur de la victoire* ('Games of Honour and Victory'), dedicated to the king. Her other large-scale dramatic work, the five-act opera *Céphale et Procris*, received its première in 1694. A second set of harpsichord pieces was published in 1707 and her other music includes songs, violin sonatas, trio sonatas and three volumes of cantatas.

Keiser, Reinhard

(Kī'-zer, Rīn'-härt) 1674–1739

GERMAN COMPOSER

Keiser studied at St Thomas's School, Leipzig. His first operas were performed at the Brunswick court during the early 1690s. In 1695 he moved to Hamburg, where he became director of the Gänsemarkt theatre in 1702. He wrote over 60 operas, mainly for Hamburg, but periods of absence did not further his cause. In 1721 Telemann, who had been appointed new music director of Hamburg's five churches, additionally assumed directorship of the opera-house. Keiser was skilled in writing comic scenes and imaginative in his lively handling of recitative. He also wrote oratorios and Passions, of which one, at least – *St Mark* (*c.* 1717–18) – was well known to J. S. Bach. Mattheson called Keiser 'the greatest opera composer of the world' and he greatly influenced Handel.

Kuhnau, Johann

(Kōō'-nou, Yō'-hăn) 1660–1722

GERMAN COMPOSER

After studying at Dresden and Zittau, Kuhnau went to Leipzig, where he became organist in 1684 and in 1701 *Kantor* at St Thomas's Church. He was a learned and energetic man. He wrote many cantatas and other sacred works which were technically and musically resourceful – with their lyrical lines and powerful **fugues** – and often dramatic; he also composed much harpsichord music, including suites and a well-known set of *Biblische Historien* ('Biblical Stories'), sonatas which portray, ingeniously if sometimes naïvely, the emotional states aroused by events described in the Bible. His successor at the Thomaskirche was J. S. Bach.

Lalande, Michel-Richard de

(Lă län de, Me-shel' Rē'-shăre de) 1657–1726

FRENCH COMPOSER

During the mid 1660s Lalande, along with Marais, was a member of the choir at St Germain-l'Auxerrois in Paris and later, as an organist, he was the mentor of Couperin. In 1683 he was appointed one of four *sous-maîtres* of the Chapelle Royale, gradually acquiring all the other major musical positions at Versailles following **Lully**'s death in 1687. He composed music for the stage and for the church. An attractive by-product of his theatre music is the collection of instrumental dances put together in the mid-twentieth century under the title *Symphonies pour les soupers du Roi* ('Symphonies for the King's Supper').

Lalande's greatest talent lay in the sphere of the ***grand motet***, of which 64 have survived. This was the favoured musical style of Louis XIV during the services at the Chapelle Royale and one to which Lalande introduced a rewarding stylistic diversity, ranging from supple, often contrapuntal choruses to the tender intimacy of recitatives and airs with **obbligato** instruments.

CONCERTO IN E MINOR

In his two sets of six violin concertos (op. 7, 1737, and op. 10, *c.* 1744), Leclair produced the finest Baroque concertos by a Frenchman. His blend of Italian virtuosity with the simpler, often dance-orientated character of his native airs resulted in music of *galant* charm and distinction. The Concerto in E minor (op. 10, no. 5) provides a sustained example of his expressive gift.

POPULAR MELODY *Leclair*

Leclair, Jean-Marie

(Le-klâr, Zhăn Măr-rē) 1697–1764

FRENCH COMPOSER AND VIOLINIST

Born in Lyons, Leclair came from a family of musicians. He studied the violin in Italy under Giovanni Battista Somis (1686–1763). By the

(TL) Michel-Richard de Lalande
Lalande was a master of the grand motet*; 64 of his pieces survive altogether.*
(BR) Madame Henriette
Louis XV's daughter playing the viola da gamba at the king's court, where Leclair served from 1733.

VIRTUOSITY

Novelty, exuberance and contrast were among the many disparate features of Baroque art that helped to enrich its expressive content. The oft-declared aim of the Baroque composer to stir the emotions was entrusted to the performer, whose affective vocabulary was increasingly enlarged by developments taking place in singing techniques, with their emphasis on challenging ornaments and dazzling passagework, and in the craft of instrument-building. Modena, Bologna, Cremona and Venice were active centres of instrument-making, while Naples played host to singing techniques that were quickly disseminated abroad – though not always without resistance. Already by the late 1620s composers such as Biagio Marini (*c.* 1587–1663) and Carlo Farina (*c.* 1600–*c.* 1640) were experimenting with new techniques in their aim to introduce an element of extravagant display into their violin writing. Later, composer-performers like **Girolamo Frescobaldi** (1583–1643) on the harpsichord, Reincken and J. S. Bach on the organ, and Corelli, Geminiani, Vivaldi, Locatelli and Leclair on the violin, developed the virtuoso content of their music to unparalleled heights of sophistication.

The chief vehicle for display in vocal music of the late Baroque was the aria, whose three-part ***da capo*** structure afforded the singer an opportunity for brilliant vocal display ***coloratura***). Such technically advanced singing was not confined to opera or other secular entertainment, but was often a feature of oratorios, sacred cantatas and the varied musical components of the liturgy. Increasingly, virtuoso solo singing, usually in the soprano and alto voice ranges, together with elaborate, colourful costumes and scenery, became the chief attraction for visitors to the opera.

coloratura ▶ p. 357 *da capo* ▶ p. 358 fugue ▶ p. 358 *grand motet* ▶ p. 358 intermezzo ▶ p. 359 obbligato ▶ p. 360 tombeau ▶ p. 362

1720s he was establishing a reputation as a violinist in Paris. In 1728 he made his début at the *Concert Spirituel*, playing his own sonatas and concertos. In 1733 Louis XV appointed him *Ordinaire de la musique de la chambre du Roi* ('member of the king's musicians'). His sonatas and concertos, most of which are for violin, contain a pleasing juxtaposition of French and Italian styles and are, both technically and formally, among the most advanced by a French composer of the time.

Locatelli, Pietro Antonio

(Lō-kă-tel'-lē, Pē-ā'-trō Ăn-tōn'-yō) 1695–1764

ITALIAN COMPOSER AND VIOLINIST

Locatelli studied at Bergamo and Rome, where he played for Cardinal Ottoboni. After a short appointment as *virtuoso da camera* ('court virtuoso) at the Mantuan court (1725–27), Locatelli travelled throughout Austria and Germany appearing as a virtuoso – on one occasion with Leclair. He settled in Amsterdam in 1729 where he taught, composed and published his music. Five sets of concertos were issued between 1721 and 1762; the earliest is stylistically indebted to Corelli. Notably in his *L'arte del violino* (op. 3, 1733), Locatelli explored wider virtuosic possibilities in violin technique.

Marais, Marin

(Mă-rā', Mă-ran') 1656–1728

FRENCH COMPOSER AND VIOL PLAYER

Marais was a pupil of Sainte-Colombe (1691–1701). He was associated with the Académie Royale de Musique and the French court for most of his life. Marais' idiomatic and expressive viol playing won him European renown. Between 1686 and 1725 he published five collections of *pièces de violes*; the first was dedicated to Lully, his mentor. They contain over 500 works of which three ***tombeaux***, character pieces and others with a programmatic element, are striking for their expressive variety. The most celebrated and successful of his operas was *Alcyone* (1706), whose atmospheric Tempest scene was greatly admired and widely imitated.

Marcello, Benedetto

(Mär-chel'-lō, Bā-na-dāt'-tō) 1686–1739

ITALIAN COMPOSER AND SATIRIST

Marcello was a Venetian nobleman and younger brother of the composer Alessandro Marcello (1669–1750). Benedetto trained as a lawyer and held various public positions in Venice, including those of chamberlain and governor. He was not dependent upon music for a living and consequently styled himself *dilettante*. His compositions included concertos, sonatas, sinfonias and sacred vocal music. Fifty psalm paraphrases in the vernacular, published under the title *Estro poetico-armonico* ('Theories on Poetic Harmony', 1724–26), were admired by Telemann, Mattheson and others. His celebrated satire on Italian opera, *Il teatro alla moda* ('The Theatre in Fashion', 1720), ridiculed the operatic practices of Vivaldi on its title page and those of Venetian opera in general throughout.

Mattheson, Johann

(Măt'-te-zōn, Yō'-hän) 1681–1764

GERMAN COMPOSER AND THEORIST

Mattheson was the most important writer on music during the Baroque era. His *Die Vernünfftler*, which translated the *Tatler* and *Spectator* of Addison and Steele, was the first German weekly (1713). He befriended Handel when he arrived in Hamburg in 1703 and sang the leading tenor role in Handel's first opera, *Almira* (1705). He was one of the few composers whose operas were performed regularly at the Gänsemarkt theatre, where they attracted an enthusiastic public. Among his other compositions were an oratorio, cantatas and solo keyboard music. Mattheson was an excellent organist and became music director of Hamburg cathedral in 1715. He turned increasingly to writing as his hearing, declined founding a critical journal on music and writing the famous *Grundlage einer Ehren-Pforte* ('Foundation for a Triumphal Arch', 1740), a dictionary of composers. His lifelong friend Telemann conducted the music that Mattheson had composed for his own burial service after his death in 1764.

Pergolesi, Giovanni Battista

(Pâr-gō-lā'-zē, Jō-văn'-nē Băt-tēs'-tă) 1710–36

ITALIAN COMPOSER

Pergolesi studied in Naples with Francesco Durante (1684–1755). He received his first commission in 1731 and the following year was appointed *maestro di cappella* to the equerry of the Viceroy of Naples. Pergolesi composed comic and serious opera, sacred music and a small quantity of instrumental music. He is chiefly remembered for two works of a disparate character. *La serva padrona* ('The Maid as Boss', 1733) is a comic **intermezzo** which was performed in Naples as a companion piece to his serious opera *Il prigionier superbo* ('The Haughty Prisoner', 1733). Lively plot, credibly drawn characters and engaging music made it a popular dramatic entertainments. The *Stabat Mater* for soprano, mezzo-soprano and strings was among Pergolesi's last compositions; its style approaches the idiom of contemporary Italian opera.

Frescobaldi ▶ p. 82 Lully ▶ p. 84

Quantz, Johann Joachim

(Kvänts, Yō'-hän Yō-ä'-khem) 1697–1773

GERMAN COMPOSER AND FLAUTIST

After training in Merseburg, Quantz went to Dresden and Vienna, where he studied with Fux and Zelenka (1716). Further travels took him to Prague, Rome, Paris and London, where he met Handel. In 1727 he became a member of the Dresden court. In the following year he gave flute lessons to Prussian crown prince Frederick ('the Great') during a visit to Berlin. This encounter determined the remaining course of Quantz's life, and in 1741 he became Frederick's court composer, flautist and director of chamber music. Quantz was a prolific composer of sonatas and concertos for the flute and the author of a treatise *Versuch einer Anweisung die Flöte traversière zu spielen* ('On Playing the Flute', 1752), whose content sheds important light on late-Baroque performance practice.

Rameau, Jean-Philippe

(Rä-mō', Zhän Fi-lēp') 1683–1764

FRENCH COMPOSER AND THEORIST

Rameau was born in Dijon, where he was first taught music by his father. During his early years he held organist's posts at Avignon and Clermont-Ferrand, Paris (where he published his first harpsichord pieces in 1706), Dijon (1709), Lyons (*c.* 1713), and once more at Clermont-Ferrand (1715). He finally settled in Paris in 1722. In the same year he published his first theoretical work, *Traité de l'harmonie* ('Treatise on Harmony'). Other treatises followed, and he produced further collections of harpsichord pieces in 1724 and *c.* 1729. During this period he also wrote chamber cantatas and music for the Parisian fair theatres (comic stage shows).

His first, controversial ***tragédie lyrique***, *Hippolyte et Aricie* (1733), was followed by *Castor et Pollux* (1737) and *Dardanus* (1739). Rameau also produced two ***opéra-ballets*** during this decade, *Les Indes galantes* ('The Gallant Indians', 1735) and *Les fetes d'Hébé* ('The Festival of Summer', 1739). This type of entertainment, developed by André Campra (1660–1744), placed great emphasis on spectacle and dance, allowing Rameau scope to demonstrate his outstanding talent as an orchestrator. Among the many original and musically satisfying products of later years are a bitter-sweet ***comédie-lyrique***, *Platée* (1745), an ***acte de ballet***, *Pigmalion* (1748), and a *tragédie lyrique*, *Zoroastre* (1749).

Rebel, Jean-Féry

(Re-bel', Zhän Fā-rē') 1666–1747

FRENCH COMPOSER

Rebel belonged to a family of court musicians. At the age of eight, his violin playing attracted the attention of Lully. From then onwards he occupied posts both at the Académie Royale de Musique and at court. Rebel's *Sonates à II et III parties*, written towards the end of the seventeenth century, but not published until *c.* 1712, reveal his skill in blending elements of Italian and French styles. His solo violin sonatas were among the first of their kind in France. Although his one opera, *Ulysse* (1703), failed he was successful in choreographed *symphonies de danses*.

THEORETICALLY SPEAKING...

From the earliest years of the Baroque era musicians, scientists and assorted intellectuals, mainly from Italy, wrote treatises and manifestos discussing the theories, aesthetics and musical practice of a new style of music. By the early eighteenth century almost every country in Europe was producing writers who aimed to define musical styles and concepts. They attempted to rationalize and, to an extent, codify emotional responses to music. Although the results were often imprecise and inconsistent, the declared aim of music to move the passions was universally accepted.

The most profound and influential writer on musical science was Rameau, whose theories form the basis of modern tonal harmony. Among the early eighteenth-century theorists who attempted a definition and categorization of musical style were the composers Sébastien de Brossard (1655–1730; *Dictionnaire de musique*, 1703) and Johann Walter (*Musicalisches Lexicon*, 1732). Their ideas and others were later discussed and developed by a profusion of composers, theorists and lexicographers among whom Mattheson, Quantz and Avison made important contributions to the debate. Mattheson, in addition to his many theoretical writings, produced the first lexicon to include biographical information on German musicians (*Grundlage einer Ehren-Pforte*, 1740), while *Memoirs of the Life of the Late George Frederic Handel* (1760) by John Mainwaring (*c.* 1724–1807) was the first monograph of a composer.

CASTOR ET POLLUX

Rameau was very skilled at composing emotionally charged vocal airs. One of the most celebrated, 'Tristes apprêts, pâles flambeaux', occurs in Act I of his *tragédie lyrique Castor et Pollux*. It is delicately scored for soprano, strings and a bassoon.

POPULAR MELODY — *Rameau*

Reincken, Johann Adam

(Rīn'-ken, Yō-hän Ä'-däm) 1623–1722

NETHERLANDISH/GERMAN COMPOSER

Reincken studied the organ with Heinrich Scheidemann (*c.* 1595–1663) at St Catharine's, Hamburg, becoming his assistant then successor. Reincken was both teacher and virtuoso organist. Many musicians travelled to hear him play, including **Georg Böhm** (1661–1733), **Buxtehude** and J. S. Bach. In 1720 Bach himself played on the organ of St Catharine's before an audience that included the 97-year-old Reincken. Little of his organ music has survived, but an indication of his virtuosity can be found in the extended chorale variations, *An den Wasserflüssen Babylon* ('By the Waters of Babylon, 1720) – on which Bach improvised during his recital. Reincken also wrote chamber music, of which only *Hortus musicus* ('Park Music', 1687) has survived.

Scarlatti, Alessandro

(Skär-lät'-tē, Äl-es-sän'-drō) 1660–1725

ITALIAN COMPOSER

Scarlatti was born in Sicily but spent most of his working life in Rome, where he studied, and Naples. He made important and prolific contributions to opera, oratorio, serenata and cantata forms, composing a much smaller quantity of instrumental and keyboard music. His musical talent attracted the attention of many leading patrons in Rome including the Ottoboni and Pamphili families and the exiled Queen Christina of Sweden. In spite of early successes, Scarlatti left in 1684 for Naples, where he was appointed *maestro di cappella* to the Viceroy. He remained there for 18 years, composing extensively in all the major vocal forms of the time. In 1702 he travelled to Florence, where he enjoyed the patronage of Prince Ferdinando de' Medici. Scarlatti returned to Rome in 1703, again entering

(L) Ballet Costume
Costume for a Greek in one of Jean-Philippe Rameau's opéra-ballets.
(TR) Platee
Twentieth-century production of Rameau's opera Platee.
(BR) Italian Chamber Music
Domenico Scarlatti (at the keyboard), with other Italian composer-musicians, including Tartini and Locatelli.

acte de ballet ▶ p. 356 *comédie lyrique* ▶ p. 357 *opéra-ballet* ▶ p. 360 *pastorale héroïque* ▶ p. 361 serenata ▶ p. 362 *tragédie lyrique* ▶ p. 363

RAMEAU – AN INNOVATIVE COMPOSER OF OPERA

Although Rameau considered his theoretical writings to be his most important contribution to music, he is now recognized first and foremost as an innovative and brilliant composer for the stage. His first three operas, *Hippolyte et Aricie*, *Castor et Pollux* and *Dardanus*, preserve Lully's pattern of a prologue and five acts; essentially, the Lullian formula of the *tragédie lyrique* had not changed over the preceding half-century. But in the remaining two, *Zoroastre* and *Les Boréades* ('The Sons of Boreas', 1760), Rameau broke with tradition by omitting the prologue – which customarily had nothing to do with the plot. He was musically more imaginative than his predecessors, with a technique that enabled him to express emotions and evoke atmosphere by means of rich and varied harmonics. Such originality, however, did not endear his operas to Lully's followers.

Light Entertainment

As well as writing serious opera, Rameau proved himself highly skilled in composing lighter entertainment of a kind that was enjoying ever-increasing popularity, both in court circles and in Parisian society. This was *opéra-ballet*, which typically consisted of a prologue and three to five acts or *entrées*, but without a continuous plot. In Rameau's hands, the form was given an unparalleled luxuriousness of orchestral colour and spectacle. His masterpieces were *Les Indes galantes* and *Les fetes d'Hébé*. In these works – which might almost be regarded as antecedents of the twentieth-century revue – and in various related forms, such as *acte de ballet* (*Pigmalion*), and **pastorale héroïque** (*Zaïs*, 1748; *Naïs*, 1749), Rameau's imaginative concept of orchestral colour and intuitive feeling for dance reached full fruition. He also wrote two *comédies lyriques*; *Platée* was considered by some of his contemporaries to be his greatest achievement.

the service of Cardinal Ottoboni. In 1706 he was admitted to the select Accademia dell'Arcadia. For the remainder of his life he divided his time between Rome and Naples, where he died. His cantatas, mostly for solo voice and continuo, number at least 600. They are sophisticated pieces which, like the larger-scale **serenatas**, were written mainly for the cultivated audiences of his wealthy and influential patrons.

Scarlatti, Domenico

(Skär-lät'-tē, Dō-män'-ē-kō) 1685–1757

ITALIAN COMPOSER AND HARPSICHORDIST

Domenico Scarlatti was the son of Alessandro Scarlatti. He was born in Naples and lived there until 1704, when he joined his father in Rome. The following year he travelled to Florence and Venice, where he met Handel. He returned to Rome in 1708 and entered the service of the exiled Polish queen, Maria Casimira the following year. He provided her with an oratorio and several operas including *Tetide in Sciro* ('Thetis on Skyros', *c.* 1712) of which only 10 arias have survived. In 1714 Scarlatti was appointed *maestro di cappella Giulia* and also to the Portuguese ambassador. He resigned from both positions in 1719 and left Rome for Palermo. His opera *Narciso* was staged in London the following year. By 1724, he had accepted the post of *maestro di cappella* at the Portuguese court in Lisbon, where he taught the king's daughter, Maria Barbara. In 1729 she married Crown Prince Ferdinando of Spain, making Scarlatti her *maestro di musica*. He continued to serve her for the rest of his life. Scarlatti wrote more than 500 inventive and highly original harpsichord sonatas, almost all of which are single-movement lessons (*essercizi*). Although 30 were published under the title *Essercizi per gravicembalo* ('Lessons on the Harpsichord') in London in 1738, the bulk of the sonatas, copied out in Spain between 1742 and 1757, remained in manuscript books, unpublished during his lifetime.

Tartini, Giuseppe

(Tär-tē'-nē, Jōō-sep'-pā) 1692–1770

ITALIAN COMPOSER AND THEORIST

Tartini was born in Pirano and studied law at Padua, where he was appointed *primo violino e capo di concerto* ('first violin and concertmaster') at the Basilica in 1721. In 1728 he founded a school of violinists there which became known as the *Scuola della Nazioni* ('School of Nations'), as it attracted students from all over Europe. Tartini's musical reputation for fiery gestures and virtuoso passagework has been romanticized because of the fame of his violin sonata, *The Devil's Trill* (1713). Yet his sonatas and concertos are often more noteworthy for their 'singing' style, which anticipates the classical period. Many of his pieces carry poetic mottoes, sometimes in code and mainly drawn from Metastasio's opera libretti, establishing their intended character. His most important theories are contained in the published *Trattato di musica secondo la vera scienza dell'armonia* ('Second Treatise on the True Science of Harmony', 1754) and *Traité des agréments de la musique* ('Treatise on the Charms of Music', 1771).

Böhm ▶ p. 80 Buxtehude ▶ p. 80

Telemann, Georg Philipp

(Te'-le-män, Gä-ôrg' Fē-lēp') 1681–1767

GERMAN COMPOSER

Telemann was born in Magdeburg and showed early promise as a musician. While a law student at Leipzig Univeristy he founded a *collegium musicum*, directed the Leipzig Opera and was commissioned to write cantatas for St Thomas's Church. In 1705 he became *Kapellmeister* to Count Erdmann of Promnitz, whose residence in Sorau (Zary) brought him into contact with Polish folk music. Together with influences from France and Italy, this contributed a distinctive ingredient to the formation of his style. By 1708 he was court *Konzertmeister* at Eisenach, where he met J. S. Bach. In 1712 he moved to Frankfurt-am-Main as director of the city's music, *Kapellmeister* at the Barfüsserkirche and director of the Frauenstein Society. Telemann made his final move, to Hamburg, to be *Kantor* of the Johanneum and director of the five main churches, in 1721.

Among his most important compositions are an orchestral/instrumental anthology, *Musique de Table* (1733), 72 sacred cantatas, *Der harmonische Gottesdienst* (1725–40), six *Nouveaux Quatuors* (1738) and *Essercizii Musici* (*c.* 1740). Some of his most original and forward-looking compositions belong to the last years of his life and include the cantata *Der Tageszeiten* (1757), the oratorio *Der Tag des Gerichts* (1762) and the dramatic cantata *Ino* (1765).

Vivaldi, Antonio

(Ve-väl'-dē, Än-tōn'-yō) 1678–1741

ITALIAN COMPOSER AND VIOLINIST

Vivaldi was born in Venice. After learning the violin with his father, and possibly other teachers too, he joined the orchestra of St Mark's. He was ordained in 1703, later acquiring the nickname *Il prete rosso* ('the Red Priest'), because of his red hair. Partly because of fragile health and partly perhaps as a result of his musical talent and ambition, Vivaldi abandoned the priesthood shortly afterwards. In the same year as his ordination he was engaged as *maestro di violino* by the Pio Ospedale della Pietà, one of four Venetian charitable institutions for orphaned or abandoned children. Boys were usually apprenticed to various trades at an early age so the adolescent/adult population of the *ospedali* was entirely female.

TELEMANN – EDUCATIONALIST AND PUBLISHER

One of Telemann's great achievements, notably in Hamburg, was to widen the accessibility of music. He did this by engraving and printing many of his own compositions, by establishing student or amateur *collegia musica* and by instituting public concerts. Thus he fostered an ideal that music was to be played and heard by many and not just by those from a privileged background. In 1728 Telemann launched the first instalment of a weekly music journal, *Der getreue Music-Meister* ('The Constant Music Master'). He engraved the pewter plates himself and issued each instalment by subscription, under his own imprint. They mostly contained his music, though contributions by other composers – among them J. S. Bach, and Zelenka – were sometimes included. Promoting and circulating his music in this way enhanced his reputation and widened his popularity both in Germany and further afield.

Public concert life flourished in Leipzig, Frankfurt and Hamburg under Telemann's seemingly tireless and vital direction, and Handel's music was brought to a wider audience under Telemann's promotion at this time. Among his many achievements was the release of sacred music from a purely ritual function to provide entertainment in the concert hall. Many of his later Passion-oratorios were first heard either privately or in Hamburg's Drillhaus. Telemann also directed concerts in his home but, mainly owing to the thriving concert life of the city, for which Telemann deserves most of the credit, a new purpose-built concert hall was erected in 1761 – the first of its kind in Germany.

FOUR SEASONS

Vivaldi's four seasons are, to some extent, evocations of Arcadia – the classical landscape that provides the backdrop to so many Baroque cantatas. They contain minutely descriptive music in which orchestral *ritornellos* conjure up familiar sounds from a pastoral world, such as the birdsong in the second concerto, 'Summer'.

POPULAR MELODY *Vivaldi*

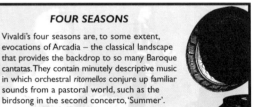

NEW OPPORTUNITY IN THE PIETÀ

Vivaldi's responsibilities lay foremost in teaching stringed instruments and probably wind instruments as well. Unofficially, he may also have been expected to direct concerts and to provide music for his talented pupils. In 1713, Francesco Gasparini (1668–1727), who had been in charge of music at the Pietà since 1701, took leave of absence, creating an important opportunity for Vivaldi. As acting *maestro di coro* (1713–19) he was responsible for providing new music for services at the Pietà chapel. Among the works that he almost certainly composed for the Pietà are two settings of the 'Gloria', the psalm 'Dixit Dominus', a 'Stabat Mater' (RV 621) and several solo motets and **antiphons**. It was also for the Pietà that Vivaldi wrote his only surviving oratorio, *Juditha triumphans* (1716). The work contains allegorical references to the Ottoman war in which Venice had been recently victorious; it is scored for female voices and an exceptionally varied assembly of instruments. Its recitatives and arias and, to some extent, its characterization, measure up to the finest of his operas. The earliest, *Ottone in villa*, had already been performed in Vicenza (1713).

(TFL) Georg Philipp Telemann
Telemann's works showed the mixed influences of French, Italian and Polish music.
***(TNL)* The Four Seasons**
Cover for the Orpheus Chamber Orchestra's recording of Vivaldi's famous Four Seasons.
(R) The Ospedali
View of the room in which Vivaldi taught at the Ospedali in Venice.

antiphon ▶ p. 356 *capriccio* ▶ p. 356 *ripieno* ▶ p. 362 *ritornello* ▶ p. 362

THE INFLUENCE OF PUBLISHING ON VIVALDI

Vivaldi's music was widely disseminated in Europe and his reputation was greatly enhanced by his publishers. The most important of these were Estienne Roger and, after 1722, his successor, Michel-Charles Le Cène. They were based in Amsterdam, one of the most important centres for music printing during the eighteenth century.

Twelve collections of instrumental pieces – sonatas and concertos – were published during Vivaldi's lifetime. Most of them were for his own instrument, the violin. The first was issued by the Venetian publisher Giuseppe Sala in 1705, as the composer's op. 1. It contained trios for two violins and bass in the manner of Corelli. Vivaldi seems to have paid tribute to him in the Twelfth Sonata, a set of variations on the Spanish *folia* dance; the older composer had written variations on the same theme (op. 5, no. 12). His second set, issued by a different Venetian printer, Antonio Bortoli, consisted of 12 sonatas for violin and bass. These pieces demonstrate a greater degree of individuality than the earlier trios, though a distinctively Vivaldian style is as yet only faintly impressed upon the music.

A Publishing Triumph

Vivaldi's remaining printed sets were published in Amsterdam. In 1711 his first concertos (op. 3) appeared under the title *L'estro armonico* ('Harmonic Caprice'). Here he created 12 pieces of striking individuality, whose orderly discipline provided models that were to be applauded and imitated. *L'estro armonico* was immensely successful in Vivaldi's lifetime: it ran to at least 14 editions and put the composer decisively on the international map. Among its admirers was the young J. S. Bach, who arranged five of the concertos for solo keyboard and a later sixth for four harpsichords and strings.

COMPOSER OF OPERA

Although Vivaldi's association with the Pietà lasted intermittently for most of his career, his activities and influence extended far beyond its confines. Between 1713 and 1739 he was frequently occupied in opera production – as composer, arranger and impresario. Of the 94 operas that he himself once claimed to have penned, 16 have survived complete. They were written for many centres: Venice; other Italian cities such as Mantua (*Tito Manlio*, 1719), where Vivaldi worked between 1718 and 1720; and outside Italy for Prague, which he visited in 1730–31; and Vienna. If they lack the strong characterization and skilful pacing of Handelian opera, they are generously provided with beguiling melodies and opportunities for vocal display.

In addition to opera, Vivaldi composed chamber cantatas, mainly for female voices, solo motets and three serenatas. The most extended of these is *La Senna festeggiante* ('The Seine *en fête*'), which he composed in honour of the French royal house of Bourbon during the 1720s.

INNOVATIVE INSTRUMENTAL COMPOSER

Gifted and successful though he was in writing for the voice, it was as an instrumental composer that Vivaldi made his most innovative and far-reaching contributions to the development of music. Many of his sonatas and concertos were written for his pupils at the Pietà. They played a wide variety of instruments for which Vivaldi catered generously in his solo writing, as well as demonstrating a distinctive flair for colourful groupings. Their versatility and virtuosity were remarked upon by visitors to Venice and the orchestra of the Pietà enjoyed an international reputation of the highest quality. Vivaldi himself was, of course, a virtuoso violinist.

TOWARDS THE SOLO CONCERTO

In op. 4, *La stravaganza* ('The Extravaganza', *c.* 1714), Vivaldi comes a step closer to the solo concerto. In this set he consolidates the concerto-movement form, typically consisting of five ***ritornellos*** and four alternating solo sections. The solos are often more extended than previously and are of greater expressive variety. The 12 works are fertile in invention and their slow movements – more varied than those of his predecessors – are rich in expressive nuances. In 1725, Vivaldi issued 12 concertos under the title *Il cimento dell'armonia e dell'inventione* ('The Contest Between Harmony and Invention', op. 8). It included the music for which he has become best known, *Le quattro stagione* ('The Four Seasons'). These pieces were soon to enjoy wide currency throughout Europe, especially in France, where they were variously arranged as well as performed at the Concert Spirituel in Paris. With descriptive captions in the score, they have a specifically programmatic element.

Two years later, Vivaldi published his op. 9, *La cetra* ('The Lyre'). It contains fine examples of the composer's mature style and provides many instances of his lyrical gifts, his highly developed sense of fantasy and his assured deployment of solo and ***ripieno*** forces.

Zelenka, Jan Dismas

(Ze-leng'-kä, Yän Dēz'-mäs) 1679–1745

BOHEMIAN COMPOSER

Zelenka was born near Prague but worked for most of his life in Dresden, where he was double bass player in the court orchestra. He studied with Fux in Vienna and Antonio Lotti (1667–1740) in Venice. Although he wrote three oratorios and at least 20 Masses, and was eventually appointed *vice-Kapellmeister* of church music, Zelenka is better known for a small number of instrumental works. These include six trio sonatas for two oboes and bassoon, and five orchestral ***capriccios***. Much of this music requires an instrumental virtuosity seldom encountered elsewhere at the time, other than in the works of J. S. Bach.

The Late Baroque
STYLES AND FORMS

In the late Baroque era music both consolidated earlier developments and looked forward to the new styles of the classical era. The output of the two greatest composers of the time, J. S. Bach and Handel, reflects the general trends in music. The main forms – notably the sonata, concerto and opera – became longer and more complex, placing increasing emphasis on technical virtuosity. Traditional, strict compositional techniques such as fugue were combined with new styles such as expressive, aria-like melodies with a subordinate accompaniment. The desire to express shifting emotions in music was a primary force, not just in text-inspired vocal pieces but in instrumental works too. Towards the mid-eighteenth century, the old distinctions between church, chamber and theatre styles began to break down. Thus operatic recitatives and arias are found in sacred cantatas, and chamber suites and sonatas include dance movements. National styles also became more fluid – the works of J. S. Bach and Handel show the influence of German, Italian, English and French music. Finally, while domestic music-making continued to flourish, public concerts were increasingly common, with audiences paying to hear their favourite performers.

Concerto Grosso

The *concerto grosso* is a work in which music for the orchestra (*concerto grosso* means 'large ensemble'; it is also called the *ripieno*, 'rest', or *tutti*, 'all') alternates with sections for the *concertino* ('small ensemble', or *soli*, 'soloists'). The form reached maturity in the late Baroque era in the works of **Vivaldi** and J. S. Bach. Vivaldi's *concertos*, notably those in his first published collection, *L'estro armonico*, were popular and influential in Italy and elsewhere. The well-known *concerto grosso* for two violins from this set (op. 3 no. 8, in A minor) is typical of his creative and innovative style. It is in three movements, the outer two fast, bold and energetic, the middle one slow, stately and lyrical. In the first movement, the opening statement by the full ensemble is made up of not one theme but several. These themes return separately and in various combinations throughout the movement, punctuating the soloists' more virtuoso passages and even being taken up by the soloists. J. S. Bach was greatly influenced by Vivaldi's *concerti grossi* (he transcribed six from op. 3). His development of Vivaldi's model into much more complex, dense and virtuoso works is summed up in the three *concerti grossi* (nos 2, 4 and 5) in his famous 'Brandenburg' Concertos, each for a different combination of instruments. A similar variety of styles is found in Handel's op. 6.

Solo Concerto

Following the development of the solo concerto by **Giuseppe Torelli** (1658–1709), Vivaldi and J. S. Bach contributed works to the genre that are still in the standard repertory today. Vivaldi is believed to have written about 350 solo concertos, many for violin, but some for instruments such as the flute, oboe and even mandolin. Their structure is broadly similar to that of his *concerti grossi*. Vivaldi, himself a virtuoso violinist, was ahead of his time in specifying technical details of bowing and fingering for the performer; he also used effects such as ***pizzicato*** ('plucking') and muted playing. His best-known violin concertos are the programmatic 'Four Seasons', their gently lyrical slow movements showing the influence of the operatic aria. The Italians **Locatelli** and **Tartini** also wrote virtuoso violin concertos, while J. S. Bach wrote solo concertos for violin and for harpsichord; his famous 'double' Concerto in D minor for two violins includes a fugal first movement. Organ concertos were an invention of Handel's. He performed them himself between the acts of his oratorios, probably on a small organ (only one has a pedal part), and allowed plenty of opportunity to display his virtuosity and improvisatory skill at the keyboard.

Handel's Contribution to Musical Development

Handel grew up in Germany, spent some time in Italy and worked for much of his career in England. His cosmopolitan life is reflected in his music, in which the styles of these countries

(BL) Orlando
Modern interpretation of Handel's opera Orlando.
(TL) Concert at Rome
A performance of the Italian cantata La Contessa de Numi, with a libretto by Metastasio.
***(TR)* The Beggar's Opera**
John Gay's popular opera started a trend for sairical pieces in the genre.
(BR) George Frideric Handel
Handel composed in most of the popular forms of the day, as well as developing the English oratorio and the organ concerto.

ariette ▶ p. 356 *arioso* ▶ p. 356 *da capo* ▶ p. 358 dissonance ▶ p. 358 *opera seria* ▶ p. 361 *pizzicato* ▶ p. 361 *ritornello* ▶ p. 362 suspension ▶ p. 362 *tragédie lyrique* ▶ p. 363

THE DEVELOPMENT OF OPERA

By the late seventeenth century, Italian opera had moved away from the noble ideals of its originators in Florence. The emphasis was increasingly on satisfying public demand for entertainment and providing showpieces for the virtuoso singers (particularly sopranos and castratos). Arias, now often with orchestral rather than simple continuo accompaniment, were becoming longer and more elaborate, and were clearly differentiated from the brisk, speech-like recitatives. The ***da capo*** aria allowed an opportunity for vocal display as the singer embellished the repeat of the aria's opening section, and the whole structure expanded as vocal phrases were interspersed with recurring instrumental phrases known as ***ritornellos***. This style is seen in operas such as **Alessandro Scarlatti**'s *Mitridate Eupatore* (1707), which also uses an orchestral sinfonia in place of a French overture (such sinfonias, influenced by the Italian concerto's fast–slow–fast structure and its contrasts between full ensemble and soloists, were forerunners of the early symphony).

These conventions were consolidated in serious Italian operas (***opera seria***) during the early eighteenth century. Heroic and historical tales were common. The dialogue and action took place in recitative while the characters pondered on their situation or feelings in arias. Handel wrote nearly 40 operas in the Italian style during his years in London. These are made up mainly of recitatives and arias, the latter written to display the skills of the 'star' singers who took the leading roles. Handel's arias are by no means empty virtuoso vehicles for lyrical singers, however, but express a great range of emotions.

These sophisticated and serious Italian works were not the only operas available to English audiences in the early eighteenth century: in stark contrast, down-to-earth, satirical operas, sung in English to simple ballads, were also popular. *The Beggar's Opera* by John Gay is the best-known example.

French Opera

The situation was rather different in France, where opera remained more closely linked with courtly entertainment and with the strong traditions of ballet and spoken drama. **Lully**'s operas (called ***tragédies lyriques***), written in the 1670s and 1680s, combine French and Italian elements. Recitative receives greater emphasis than in Italian opera, while the airs are shorter and simpler in style than Italian arias. The chorus and orchestra play prominent roles, as do dancers. Lully's orchestral overtures are also important, and in *Persée* (1682), he used the full orchestra to accompany dramatically important recitatives.

French opera flourished again towards the mid-eighteenth century with the *tragédies lyriques* of **Rameau**. He developed the Lullian model into a work of greater dramatic power, writing ***ariettes*** that were longer and more virtuoso than the *air* – more like Italian arias. He also used the orchestra more boldly to evoke and heighten moods, notably in recitatives, where the sentiments voiced by the singer are underlined by rich **dissonances** and **suspensions** in the accompaniment.

and of France (which he is not known to have ever visited) are blended. He combined the rich contrapuntal writing of the high Baroque with the new developments in Italian opera. Renowned in his day as a virtuoso organist and harpsichordist and a highly skilled improviser, he is known to many today mainly for his oratorio *Messiah* and orchestral pieces such as the *Water Music* and *Music for the Royal Fireworks*. Handel wrote outstanding works in most of the main forms available, both instrumental and vocal, for church, chamber and theatre, even developing two new forms: the English oratorio and the organ concerto.

Handel was an eminently flexible composer; he excelled at finding the most suitable idiom for a particular occasion. The *Water Music* and *Music for the Royal Fireworks* were designed for outdoor performance, for example, and so use clear, solid phrases and harmonies, since any more subtle effects would be lost. He was also a superb dramatic composer, responding to the text with great sensitivity and creating music to portray a huge spectrum of situations and moods. His operas are the best examples of this skill, but it is also seen in his oratorios, whose movements range from large-scale choruses to intimate solo arias, matched by a variety of styles. Even in smaller-scale works this dramatic impulse is evident – the growing sense of anticipation at the opening of the anthem 'Zadok the Priest' is a fine example.

The Cantata in Italy

The cantata (the term is derived from the Italian *cantare*, 'to sing') emerged in Italy early in the Baroque era. During the seventeenth century it expanded from a fairly short work for one or two voices and continuo to a more substantial series of recitatives and arias with orchestral accompaniment – an opportunity for operatic writing on a smaller scale. Secular Italian cantatas often take as their subject tales of love, especially in a pastoral setting, but historical and mythological subjects are also found.

Alessandro Scarlatti's 600 or so cantatas (mainly for solo voice, usually soprano) built on those of his predecessors such as **Giacomo Carissimi** (1605–74), **Alessandro Stradella** (1644–82) and **Barbara Strozzi** (*c.* 1619–64). Scarlatti bridged the change between recitatives and arias with ***arioso*** passages (a style of singing halfway between recitative and aria). In his arias – often moving representations of the passions of the unrequited lover – he developed the *da capo* form that was to become standard.

Handel's Italian cantatas match his operas in dramatic and expressive effect. Most are for solo voice, though some are for two or three voices, and the accompaniment ranges from a simple continuo to a small orchestra (generally a string ensemble, sometimes with additional wind instruments). The chamber cantata flourished most notably in Venice in the first half of the eighteenth century, with contributions by Vivaldi and **Marcello**. Vivaldi also wrote sacred cantatas, which were essentially Latin motets given a more operatic treatment.

J. S. Bach ▶ p. 106 Carissimi ▶ p. 81 Handel ▶ p. 112 Locatelli ▶ p. 119 Lully ▶ p. 84 Marcello ▶ p. 119 Rameau ▶ p. 120 A. Scarlatti ▶ p. 120 Stradella ▶ p. 86 Strozzi ▶ p. 86 Tartini ▶ p. 121 Torelli ▶ p. 87 Vivaldi ▶ p. 122

The Cantata in Germany

Whereas in Italy the cantata was basically a secular work, in Protestant Germany the church cantata dominated. The finest examples are those by J. S. Bach. While Bach was *Kantor* in Leipzig he had to provide a cantata every Sunday, for performance between the gospel reading and the Creed. In his church cantatas Bach synthesized the Italian solo cantata style with the German motet and **chorale** tradition. Bach's church cantatas are made up of a series of choruses, recitatives and arias, often arranged in a symmetrical pattern, beginning with a strong, contrapuntal chorus or perhaps an orchestral movement, and ending with a simple chorale harmonization. They set a mixture of biblical passages, chorale texts and free devotional poetry, all in German. The arias, always beautifully expressive, are usually in *da capo* form and are sometimes for more than one voice. They may use an **obbligato** accompaniment – an independent instrumental line weaving around the voice and matching it in virtuosity and expressiveness, perhaps played by a solo violin, flute or oboe. In some cantatas (such as *Christ lag in Todes Banden*, 'Christ Lay in Swaddling Clothes', 1707/08) the chorale melody appears in every movement; it may be sung as a ***cantus firmus*** under an obbligato line, as in *Wachet auf, ruft uns die Stimme* (1731).

J. S. Bach's Contribution to Musical Development

J. S. Bach made important contributions in most of the main musical forms of the late Baroque, with the notable exception of opera. His output partly reflects his career: as a church and court musician he had plenty of opportunities to write organ music, chamber and orchestral music and sacred vocal works, but none to write for the theatre. Yet in works such as the *St Matthew Passion*, it is clear from the vivid and intensely expressive portrayal of both the individual characters and the chorus that he had a feeling for dramatic characterization. The essence of Bach's music lies in the sublime beauty that comes from absolute mastery of the strict compositional techniques of his day, the cerebral rigour of counterpoint and fugue combined with the more sensual appeal of expressive melodies and the simplicity of the Lutheran chorale. The Easter and Christmas oratorios are good examples of this.

Bach was himself a highly accomplished organist and harpsichordist, and he had no hesitation in making considerable technical demands on the performer in his compositions. He was perhaps freer to do this than, for example, was Handel, since as *Kapellmeister* and *Kantor* he was writing for performers under his own direction rather than for a broader public. In his instrumental works – notably the suites for solo violin and solo cello and much of the harpsichord music (some of which was designed as teaching material) – this combination of technical virtuosity and contrapuntal, especially fugal, intricacy is made to appear effortless.

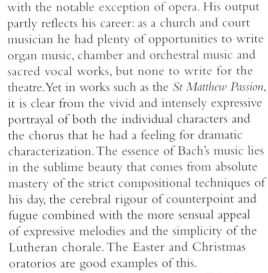

Suites for Keyboard, Cello and Violin

By the late Baroque, the dances of the suite had become very stylized, and the additional movements added to the four core dances (allemande, courante, sarabande and gigue) were many and varied. The most notable contributors to the suite's final flowering were Rameau, Handel and J. S. Bach.

Rameau's harpsichord suites include virtuoso movements with descriptive titles as well as dances with ornamented repeats ('doubles'). Handel's suites are mainly for keyboard, but also include the well-known orchestral *Water Music* and *Music for the Royal Fireworks*. The movements of his keyboard suites are often linked thematically. Bach's cello and violin suites in particular are technically challenging and much weightier compositions than the suites of music to accompany dancing in which the form had its origins. He also wrote

(L) *J. S. Bach*
Bach was perhaps the most influential composer of the Baroque era.
(R) *Harpsichord*
Domenico Scarlatti wrote prolifically for the keyboard, including over 500 sonatas for the harpsichord.

adagio ▶ p. 356 arpeggio ▶ p. 356 binary form ▶ p. 356 *cantus firmus* ▶ p. 356 chaconne ▶ p. 357 chorale ▶ p. 357 ground bass ▶ p. 358 obbligato ▶ p. 360 partita ▶ p. 361 *style brisé* ▶ p. 362 toccata ▶ p. 362

THE EVOLUTION OF EARLIER FORMS

Forms such as the **toccata** and prelude, which began in the Renaissance as improvised 'warm-up' pieces, became more substantial virtuoso keyboard compositions in the late Baroque era, though they retained their introductory function. Alessandro Scarlatti's harpsichord toccatas expanded the form to embrace a series of contrasting sections, some of them in strict styles – perhaps fugal or variations on a **ground bass**. J. S. Bach's harpsichord toccatas continued this practice, moving between free rhapsodic sections, free sections in regular rhythms, sombre ***adagios*** and lively fugues. His organ toccatas may be genuine introductory pieces followed by a separate fugue, or, like those of **Buxtehude**, they may combine free and fugal writing. The famous Toccata and Fugue in D minor is typical of his style: after a short free introduction, the toccata itself is not rhapsodic but rhythmically insistent, with a dense texture of rapid notes ranging up and down the keyboards.

J. S. Bach's organ preludes similarly precede fugues. Those for harpsichord may be paired with fugues (as in *The Well-Tempered Clavier*) or begin a suite of dances (as in the English suites). The influence of Italian and French styles is evident: the contrasts of texture and pace characteristic of the Italian concerto are found in some of the preludes for organ and harpsichord, while those of the English suites reflect French harpsichord style in their use of ornaments and ***style brisé*** (spreading out the notes of a chord in order to sustain the sound).

keyboard suites (the so-called French and English suites and six harpsichord **partitas**), and four orchestral suites, the latter, in contrast, designed more for entertainment. The cello suites and English suites follow the traditional pattern of dances most closely, adding an opening prelude and often a pair of dances (such as minuets, bourrées or gavottes) before the final gigue. In contrast, the harpsichord and violin partitas include a greater variety of extra movements, including, in the second violin partita in D minor, a **chaconne** that is a technical *tour de force* and seems to overshadow the preceding dances.

Development of the Sonata

After 1700 the trio sonata, epitomized by the works of **Corelli**, began to be replaced by sonatas for solo instrument and continuo. These were usually in four movements (slow-fast-slow-fast, or some variation of this pattern), and the third and fourth movements were often based on dances such as the sarabande and gigue. The violin was the most popular instrument, perhaps because many of the composers of such sonatas were themselves accomplished violinists. However, sonatas were also written for instruments such as the oboe, flute and cello. Italian composers flourished at home (notably Vivaldi and Tartini) and abroad (Locatelli in Amsterdam, **Geminiani** in London). Sonatas for keyboard alone were written by **Domenico Scarlatti** and Marcello among others. The Italian sonata was influential in France too, where Rameau wrote sonatas accompanied by a violin or flute. In Germany and Austria sonatas such as those by **Telemann** (who wrote more than 200) and J. S. Bach were most often unaccompanied. Handel wrote solo sonatas for keyboard and other instruments as well as more old-fashioned trio sonatas, which remained popular in London.

Stylistically, the late Baroque sonata was a cosmopolitan combination of the traits previously associated with particular countries, and the influence of opera is seen in the use of lyrical, aria-like slow movements. Whereas earlier sonatas could be played on whatever instruments were available, composers now explored the idioms and capabilities of a specific instrument.

SUBSCRIPTION CONCERTS

During the Renaissance, the performance of serious music outside sacred or ceremonial occasions took place in mainly private and domestic contexts – at courts, academies or individuals' homes – in front of small groups of friends. By the end of the Baroque era, in contrast, public performances – larger-scale entertainments before a paying audience – were well established. This had long been the case in Venice; not having the luxury of funding from a ducal court, the city sought patronage from the public and opened the first public opera house in 1637. This had a significant effect on the music, as composers focused increasingly on providing virtuoso display arias to satisfy the audiences, who paid to hear their favourite star singers.

Public concerts of instrumental music followed a little later. England seems to have led the way, perhaps because the lack of royal patronage in the mid-seventeenth century encouraged alternative means of funding performances. The first public subscription concerts were given in London in 1672 by the violinist John Banister (*c.* 1625–79). Public concerts of solo, chamber and orchestral music became popular all over England in the eighteenth century. Handel performed at many and his music, like that of Corelli and Geminiani, remained popular in England for decades. One important promoter of such concerts was Johann Peter Salomon (1745–1815), himself a concert violinist. He began staging subscription concerts in England in 1783 and managed to engage famous performers from all over Europe, notably **Haydn**, who wrote his 'London' symphonies (also known as the 'Salomon' symphonies) for his visits in 1790–91 and 1794–95.

DOMENICO SCARLATTI'S HARPSICHORD SONATAS

Domenico Scarlatti wrote over 500 sonatas for harpsichord (though a few were probably intended for the fortepiano and a few for organ). All of them are in one movement, made up of two sections (this is called **binary form**). Written in honour of Maria Barbara, the daughter of the Portuguese king John V, they are works of great originality and virtuosity. They are generally not based on the development of a melody so much as on a series of contrasting motifs and phrases, and they explore techniques such as hand-crossing, rapid runs and **arpeggios** that cover the whole keyboard and quick repetition of one note or chord. Repetition was perhaps inspired by the guitar music he heard during his years working in Portugal and Spain. Scarlatti used bold harmonies, unexpected chord progressions and clashes that resolve at the last minute, or even not at all. His music still sounds modern and unpredictable today.

Buxtehude ▶ p. 80 Corelli ▶ p. 82 Geminiani ▶ p. 117 Haydn ▶ p. 140 D. Scarlatti ▶ p. 121 Telemann ▶ p. 122

The Late Baroque INSTRUMENTS

Cello

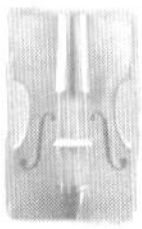

Originally (and still occasionally) known as the 'violoncello', or 'little violone', the cello is tuned in fifths like the violin and viola, running bottom to top, C, G, d, a, the same tuning as a viola, but an octave lower. There were early experiments with a smaller five-stringed instrument (with an additional E string to give it an extended upper range) called a *violoncello piccolo*. **J. S. Bach** composed the last of his six solo cello suites for this instrument.

The larger size of the instrument meant that a fingering technique different from that of the violin and viola was necessary. In the early eighteenth century, players started to rest the left thumb (kept tucked behind the neck by violinists) across the strings when playing in higher positions, taking the left hand along the fingerboard to produce higher notes.

From its essentially routine role in the early Baroque, the cello rose to a position of importance in the late Baroque as a continuo instrument and frequently accompanied the vocal line in opera and cantatas. **Vivaldi**, **C. P. E. Bach** and **Tartini** were among those who wrote concertos for the cello.

CONTINUO

Continuo, or *basso continuo* ('continuous bass'), is the name both for a kind of bass-line music and the group of performers who played it. Given the florid, exciting melodic line, it is not surprising that Baroque composers usually felt the need to provide solid harmonic underpinning. The music was not usually composed in full; instead, the bass notes were written on the staff, with numbers indicating which chords to improvise above them. This **figured bass** was a code governed by rules about the choice of common chords. Where the composer wanted something out of the ordinary, the figures gave the basic information; players were expected to improvise, adding notes and shaping the music, according to their own judgement.

Double Bass

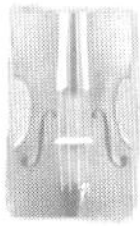

The double bass is the only survivor from the viol family to have found a regular place in the orchestra. Like other members of the viol family, it initially carried frets – tiny knotted pieces of gut that measured out the fingerboard. As it was adopted into the violin family, it settled down as a four-stringed instrument, shed its frets and standardized its tuning in fourths from bottom to top: E', A', D, G (the same string names as the violin's, but in the reverse order). The size of the instrument makes it difficult to get around quickly. Doubling the cello's line but an octave lower, the bass has a story not unlike that of the viola.

Essentially an accompanying instrument with a role in continuo groups, it achieved prominence when classical composers like **Carl Ditters von Dittersdorf** (1739–99) began to write lively lines for it and even treated it as the soloist in his concertos, some of which have recently been revived.

VIOLIN TUTORS AND THE GROWTH OF AMATEUR PLAYING

As the violin family acquired the musical respectability previously enjoyed by the viols, so the upper-middle classes began to take an interest in becoming amateur players. Accordingly, a market grew up for tutors, or instruction books.

The earliest known volume devoted to the violin was *The Gentleman's Diversion* (1693) by John Lenton (d. 1718) and this served as a model for most early eighteenth-century English violin methods. Intended for beginners, they sometimes offered advice of dubious merit. One early authority advised that when tuning a violin, the musician should wind up the 'first or Treble string as high as it will bear' and follow by tuning the other strings 'from the note thus produced', a procedure that must have broken a lot of E strings.

Publications

The initial tutors explained basic fingering and ornamentation to the amateur player, offering guidance on posture and how to hold both instrument and bow. The two publications most frequently consulted by modern players as offering invaluable insight into the thinking of some performers of the time are *The Art of Playing on the Violin* (1751) by **Geminiani** and *Versuch einer gründlichen Violinschule* ('An Attempt at Learning the Violin', 1756) by Leopold Mozart (1719–87). The question is, do these publications reflect what Baroque string players were actually doing, or what their authors hoped to persuade them to do?

Clarinet

The clarinet is a wooden instrument with a cylindrical bore and a single beating reed. Instead of being a kind of flattened drinking straw wedged on to a thin metal tube, as in the case of the oboe and bassoon, it is more like a thin spatula tied on to an open-topped recorder mouthpiece. A single-reed woodwind instrument called the chalumeau had evolved in the seventeenth century, possibly as a development of the recorder. The clarinet was invented at the beginning of the eighteenth century, probably by Johann Christoph Denner of Nuremberg (1655–1707), and was conceived as a kind of chalumeau with the added ability to produce higher notes, known as the 'clarino' register. Both instruments were played with the reed against the upper lip (the opposite of the modern clarinet). At the back of the clarinet was a 'speaker key', operated by the left thumb to open a small hole some way down the instrument. This opening allowed 'overblowing' at the 12th rather than at the octave. Despite this, the clarinet continued to be weak in these lower notes and the chalumeau therefore went on being used alongside it throughout the eighteenth century.

The first known concertos for solo clarinet were written by the Karlsruhe court composer Johann Melchior Molter around 1745, but it was not really until the late eighteenth century and the Quintet in A and the Clarinet Concerto by **Mozart**, that the instrument was taken seriously.

broken consort ▶ p. 356 *concertino* ▶ p. 357 *concerto grosso* ▶ p. 357 figured bass ▶ p. 358 fugue ▶ p. 358 *pizzicato* ▶ p. 361 *ripieno* ▶ p. 362

Trumpet and Horn

The context in which the trumpet was played – solo and in trumpet ensembles – did not greatly alter in the Renaissance. Meanwhile, its compass expanded upwards. Then in the Baroque period, the bell throat become progressively narrower and, like the horn, it was provided by makers with purpose-built extra lengths of tubing. These could be fitted to extend the length of the instrument pipework and thus allow it to play notes appropriate to the key of the music.

During the seventeenth century, the trumpet began to be included in mixed ensembles. Previously part of a musically illiterate tradition, trumpeters now learnt to read music and match their sound to the indoor company of string and woodwind players. Whereas before they had placed a premium on loudness, now they found themselves praised for playing quietly. Many of the orchestral trumpeters of this period 'doubled' on French horn. Horns (which may have been developed in seventeenth-century France, although this is not certain) can be heard in **Handel**'s *Water Music* (1717) and it is likely that J. S. Bach's cantatas include a horn part, though the exact nature of the specified 'corno da tirarsi' remains unclear.

(TL) **The Concert** *by Gabbiani*
Musicians of the Modena court, showing violins, cello and harpsichord.
(NR) Trumpet Player
Contemporary illustration showing a travelling trumpet player.
(FR) Jean-Baptiste Lully
The orchestra that Lully established in the second half of the seventeenth century provided a model for other court orchestras in the later Baroque period.

Harpsichord

The basic harpsichord mechanism of a sprung lever with a quill plectrum plucking the string a single time, remained largely unchanged since its origins. However, a small series of stops was developed, allowing the sound quality of the instrument to be varied between a brighter sound and a muted ***pizzicato***. Because these changes were effected mechanically, by pulling out or pushing in the stops, they could not be gradual; they were stepped, not sloped.

Such was the instrument for which J. S. Bach wrote his solo Italian Concerto (BWV 971, 1735), which contains passages marked *piano* ('soft') and *forte* ('loud').

As harpsichord sound decays rapidly and dynamic variation is limited, Baroque composers were faced with a double challenge. They responded by developing ornamentation and trills, by building up and then dissipating the density of the texture (as in a **fugue**) and by moving from slow to fast and back to slow.

Bagpipes

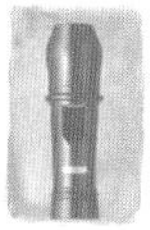

The bagpipe consists of drones, or reedpipes, which are connected to a windbag. The windbag is held under the arm and is squeezed by the elbow to pass air into the pipes. The windbag is inflated by means of a blowpipe or bellows, and the melody is played by means of a chanter, a pipe with fingerholes.

Although the bagpipe was essentially a folk instrument, it was played at court in several periods. Certainly **Henry VIII** (1491–1547) of England's courtiers heard it and in Baroque France the *musette* (which is fed by a small hand-pumped bellows) and the *cornemuse* (which has a conical chanter) joined the court's instrumental ensembles. These French instruments had embroidered bags and ivory pipes; they are to be heard to wonderful effect in music such as the shepherd's dance in **Rameau**'s *Les fêtes d'Hébé*. The bagpipe's association with pastoral life combined quite naturally with a literary fashion for such subjects inherited from classical Greek verse.

THE BAROQUE ORCHESTRA

Modern writers refer to the mixed instrumental chamber ensembles of the Renaissance as **broken consorts**. Different kinds of instruments were brought together with choirs for special occasions such as royal weddings and funerals. But there was no large ensemble encompassing different families of instruments, with settled instrumentation, and performing its own recognizable genres of music, until the Baroque period. Indeed, rivalries, discrepancies in tuning and different attitudes to reading notation all conspired to keep string, brass and woodwind ensembles apart.

The introduction by **Claudio Monteverdi** (1567–1643) of string players into the 16-strong brass ensemble of St Mark's, Venice, at the beginning of the sixteenth century, is usually seen as a significant indicator of the way things were going. The development of opera as a new musical genre at this time contributed to the emergence of the orchestra. For *Orfeo* (1607) Monteverdi required harpsichords, organs, chitarroni, violins, violas, cellos, cornetts, sackbuts, sopranino recorders and others, making a total of 30 different instruments. They included bowed and plucked strings, woodwind, brass and keyboards.

Changes in the Orchestra

Away from the opera pit, the early Baroque orchestra that developed became string-heavy. **Lully**'s Paris orchestra, playing in five parts rather than the three or four favoured in Italy, consisted of a substantial number of violins, a smaller number of alto and tenor instruments of different sizes, tuned like the viola but assigned to three different parts in the music, and a group of bass violins (tuned like the cello though a tone lower), with a supporting role for wind instruments, usually a combination of oboes and bassoon.

This orchestra provided a model that other court orchestras followed. But in the later Baroque, the revolution in wind instruments that French makers had pioneered in the mid and late seventeenth century, meant that the flute, recorder, oboe, bassoon and horn (and more rarely the sackbut) all began to secure regular employment as orchestral instruments. Trumpet and timpani were included more occasionally, the former often doubling on horn. There was invariably a continuo group within the orchestra providing support to the bass line. In ***concerti grossi*** there would be a division between a smaller group of instruments, the ***concertino***, and a larger one, the ***ripenio***.

C. P. E. Bach ▶ p. 156 J. S. Bach ▶ p. 106 Dittersdorf ▶ p. 158 Geminiani ▶ p. 117 Handel ▶ p. 112 Henry VIII ▶ p. 52 Lully ▶ p. 84
Monteverdi ▶ p. 76 Mozart ▶ p. 144 Rameau ▶ p. 120 Tartini ▶ p. 121 Vivaldi ▶ p. 122

The Late Baroque

LISTENING GUIDE

George Frideric Handel
Messiah

WORK: George Frideric Handel, *Messiah*, composed in 1741
SCORING: Soloists and chorus; trumpets, timpani, strings and continuo (Handel later added oboes, bassoons and horns)
EXCERPT: Part One, first half ('Sinfony'–'For unto us'). Duration: 39 min 00 sec
TIMINGS BASED ON: *Messiah*, English Concert and Choir conducted by Trevor Pinnock (see Recommended CDs)

RECOMMENDED CDs

1. *Messiah*. English Concert and Choir. Soloists: Arleen Auger, Anne Sofie von Otter, Michael Chance, Howard Crook, John Tomlinson. Trevor Pinnock, conductor. DG Archiv 423 630-2.

   In this recording, the alto arias are divided between a contralto and a countertenor. John Tomlinson rages splendidly in 'Why do the nations?' and Pinnock secures lively and robust singing and playing from choir and orchestra.

2. *Messiah*. Les Arts Florissants. Soloists: Barbara Schlick, Sandrine Piau, Andreas Scholl, Mark Padmore, Nathan Berg. William Christie, conductor. Harmonia Mundi HMX 2901498.99.

   For the various revivals of *Messiah* in his lifetime, Handel adapted and recomposed according to the forces available. Here it is the soprano arias that are shared between two singers.

3. *Messiah*. Gabrieli Consort and Players. Soloists: Dorothea Röschmann, Susan Gritton, Bernarda Fink, Charles Daniels, Neal Davies. Paul McCreesh, conductor. DG Archiv 453 464-2.

   As with the first two recordings, the orchestra includes the oboes, bassoons and horns that Handel is known to have added for his London performances. Some listeners might find the speeds too fast, but the overall effect is exhilarating.

4. *Messiah*. Royal Philharmonic Orchestra and Chorus. Soloists: Jennifer Vyvyan, Monica Sinclair, Jon Vickers, Giorgio Tozzi. Sir Thomas Beecham, conductor. RCA 09026-61266-2.

   This recording, made in 1959, is an indirect descendant of the Handel commemorations in Westminster Abbey, with Sir Eugene Goossens' reorchestration for modern symphony orchestra as a counterpart to the gargantuan forces of the 1780s. Sceptics should try 'Thou shalt break them', with its roll on the cymbal introducing Jon Vickers' passionate singing.

Handel and his great contemporary J. S. Bach had much in common: both were born into the Protestant tradition of northern Germany, both were composers of church music and music for all combinations of instruments and both were brilliant keyboard players. In at least two respects, however, they were quite different. Handel travelled to Italy and England, whereas Bach never left his native land; and Bach did not write any operas.

Messiah **is probably Handel's best-known work in the English-speaking world, but although he wrote a certain amount of festive religious music after settling in London, it was as a composer of Italian operas that he made his reputation. Between 1712 and 1741 he wrote nearly 40 operas for the London stage, only abandoning them when he hit financial difficulties. He also applied his dramatic skills to the writing of oratorios, for performance not in church but in the theatre.**

AN ATYPICAL WORK

Most of Handel's oratorios are dramas; some could even be staged. Their principal difference from the operas lies in his substantial use of the chorus. *Messiah* is atypical: although the layout is that of a three-act opera, there are no characters. Rather than dramatic conflict and resolution, it features description and commentary. Part One deals with the foretelling of the coming of Christ,

1. 3'22"
('Sinfony')
Handel begins with a solemn French overture: after the slow opening section, played twice, the fugal fast section is introduced by the first violins (1'21").

2. 3'26"
('Comfort ye my people')
The solo tenor sings a gentle *arioso* before becoming more forthright at 'The voice of him' (3'04").

3. 3'32"
('Every valley')
The tenor continues with a vigorous air, graphically illustrating the text with rising figures on 'exalted' (0'34") and jagged phrases at 'the crooked straight'.

4. 2'51"
('And the glory of the Lord')
The prophecies of Isaiah continue with a joyful chorus. The swinging, triple-time rhythm is dislocated at important moments (0'41", 1'56" and 2'27").

5. 1'36"
('Thus saith the Lord')
This is the counterpart, for solo bass, to 'Comfort ye'. Vivid representations of 'I'll shake' give way to the rhetoric of 'The Lord whom ye seek' (1'05").

6. 4'45"
('But who may abide')
The solo alto sings a deceptively lilting tune before fireworks erupt with string *tremolandos* at 'For he is like a refiner's fire'. The opening section returns briefly.

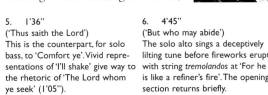

da capo ▶ p. 358 obbligato ▶ p. 360

THE HANDEL COMMEMORATION OF 1784

In 1784, the directors of the 'Concert of Ancient Music' mounted a festival to mark both the centenary of Handel's birth (incorrectly thought to have been 1684) and the 25th anniversary of his death. Five concerts were arranged – all but one in Westminster Abbey – including two performances of *Messiah*.

Burney, who was closely involved with the festival, published a detailed account the following year. His book includes illustrations showing the tiered seating for the performers at the west end of the nave and the throne and boxes for the royal family and other dignitaries. An organ was installed high up by the west window, connected by 'keys of communication' with the keyboard of the conductor, Joah Bates.

An Event to Remember

The forces were enormous: a choir of over 250 and an orchestra nearly as big, including 95 violins, 26 bassoons and six trombones (a rare instrument in England at the time). There was great public excitement: the doors opened at 9 a.m. and the Abbey was soon full, with a long wait until the performances started at 12 noon.

Despite the possibility of disaster, with only one rehearsal and Bates having to keep everything going from his position seated at the keyboard, all went well. In his description of the first of the *Messiah* performances, Burney refers to 'this wonderful band' and the 'superlative excellence' of the chorus, and praises most of the soloists.

and his nativity; Part Two ranges from Christ's Passion to Whitsun; Part Three is a meditation on the general theme of resurrection.

Messiah is unique among Handel's oratorios in having a text drawn entirely from the Bible. It was put together by Charles Jennens, who had collaborated with Handel on two earlier oratorios and now hoped to interest him in a third. Handel's response was almost immediate, and he composed the work between 22 August and 14 September 1741. Three weeks to complete *Messiah* may seem an amazing achievement, but such speed was nothing unusual for Handel. By the end of September he had started on *Samson*, which he finished a month later.

Messiah was first performed in Dublin on 13 April 1742, in a charity concert during what we would now call a Handel festival. It was a great success and was repeated a few weeks later. It failed at Covent Garden in London the next year, largely because of a hostile press campaign against the supposed blasphemy of performing a religious work in the theatre, but eventually gained acceptance through a series of annual performances in aid of the Foundling Hospital in Coram Fields, London.

THREE PARTS

Part One is divided into two sections. Most of the first is taken from the book of Isaiah in the Old Testament and prophesies the birth of Christ. The music is shared between the choir and the four soloists. All four choruses are buoyant and cheerful, including the one in a minor key ('And he shall purify'). Contrast is provided by the soloists, whose music ranges from the reassuring ('Comfort ye') to the mysterious ('For behold, darkness shall cover the earth'). The second part moves from a vivid depiction of the shepherds abiding in the field to prophecy and commentary. In 'Glory to God', the trumpets lightly accompanying the heavenly host fall silent as the music seems to disappear with the angels into thin air.

In Part Two, the action is swift. Only the air for contralto, 'He was despised', moves at a leisurely pace. This is a ***da capo*** aria, a form directly transplanted from opera but used much less frequently in Handel's oratorios. The chorus ranges from monolithic blocks of sound, in 'Lift up your heads' and 'The Lord gave the word', to the fugal 'And with his stripes' and 'He trusted in God'.

Although Part Three is the shortest, it is the most spaciously laid out, with two new features. Handel introduces an **obbligato** trumpet, which lends a martial air to 'The trumpet shall sound'. And the duet 'O death, where is thy sting' has a particularly strong impact, standing out as the only ensemble in the piece. After the first section of the extended fugal 'Amen', Handel keeps the trumpets and timpani silent. Their splendid reappearance in the closing bars makes a thrilling end to the work.

(NL) The Royal Philharmonic Orchestra
The RPO have made one of the finest and most popular recordings of Handel's Messiah.
(TR) Handel Commemoration
Engraving depicting the festival to commemorate Handel, held at Westminster Abbey.

7. 2'25"
('And he shall purify')
The chorus returns with imitative entries, and striking melismas on 'purify'. At 'that they may offer' (0'48') the music of the melismas is taken over by the strings while the chorus reverts to block harmonies.

8. 0'30"
('Behold, a virgin shall conceive')
The first of one of the very few secco (lit. 'dry', i.e. without orchestral accompaniment) recitatives, which simply introduces the next air.

9. 5'30'
('O thou that tellest')
The contralto engages in a dialogue with the first violins, the opening of the tune following the contours of 'But who may abide'. The chorus takes up and reinforces her message (3'46").

10. 3'03"
('For behold, darkness shall cover')
Mysterious phrases in the violins at the bottom of their register lead to a bass arioso.

11. 3'56"
('The people that walked in darkness')
The brooding figure of the previous number is developed to illustrate the people's wanderings.

12. 4'04"
('For unto us a Child is born')
The chorus expresses its joy with long melismas on 'born'. A new, dotted rhythm is introduced by the tenors and repeated by the whole chorus.

J. S. Bach ▶ p. 106 Burney ▶ p. 157 Handel ▶ p. 112

ANTONIO VIVALDI: *LE QUATTRO STAGIONI*

As teacher of the violin at the Pio Ospedale della Pietà, **Vivaldi** wrote concerto after concerto for the school orchestra. However, *Le quattro stagioni* ('The Four Seasons') was probably composed for the orchestra of the Bohemian count Wenzel von Morzin, to whom the published score is dedicated. The collection in which it appears, *Il cimento dell'armonia e dell'inventione*, came out in 1725, but it dates from some years earlier.

The concertos are in the standard Vivaldi three-movement form, fast–slow–fast. What is unusual is that each one is prefaced by a sonnet, and the music illustrates the lines of the poem at various specified points.

'Spring'

The opening movement of the first concerto, 'Spring', covers the first two stanzas of the sonnet. The orchestral ***ritornello*** announces the arrival of spring; the soloist, with two other solo violins, imitates birdsong before the whole ensemble depicts flowing brooks and gentle breezes. Thunder and lightning break out, but the birds soon return. Here, as in the other fast movements in the set, the contrast between the solo instrument and the orchestra is clearly defined, but such features as the extra violins in the birdsong mean that it is never predictable.

The slow movement covers the third stanza. The violins, in thirds, portray the rustling meadow, while the solo violin's long-drawn-out melody represents a dozing goatherd. With the cellos and double basses silent, the bass line is taken by the violas, whose two-note repetitions convey the barking of the herdsman's dog.

The last movement, a pastoral dance, is devoted to the fourth stanza. A **drone** bass imitates the sound of bagpipes as nymphs and shepherds dance, with just a hint of cloud in the central minor-key section.

RECOMMENDED CD

Antonio Vivaldi: *Le quattro stagioni*, with Oboe Concertos in A minor, RV461, and D minor, RV454. The Amsterdam Baroque Orchestra. Soloists: Andrew Manze (violin), Marcel Ponseele (oboe). Ton Koopman, conductor. Erato 4509-94811-2.

These most hackneyed of works come up fresh in this recording which is played on period instruments.

J. S. BACH: CONCERTO FOR TWO VIOLINS IN D MINOR

The Concerto for Two Violins (*c.* 1720) is in the three-movement form popularized by Vivaldi. Unlike the 'Brandenburg' Concertos, which make use of a variety of instruments, it is scored simply for two solo violins, strings and continuo.

The first movement begins with the usual orchestral *ritornello*, a virile theme with rising phrases balanced by falling ones. What is unusual is that it is a fugal **exposition**, with the second violins leading, the first violins answering in the **dominant**, and the cellos and double basses restating the subject in the **tonic**.

After 20 bars the solo first violin, who has been playing along with the *tutti*, emerges with a wide-ranging theme, full of leaps and scales. The second violin soon echoes this, almost in a spirit of competition. Their roles are reversed a few bars later, after the orchestra has joined them with fragments of the fugal material. The dialogue continues to the end, punctuated and rounded off by restatements of the *ritornello*.

Building Momentum

In the slow movement the orchestra has a simple accompanying role. The soloists, starting this time with the second violin, engage in a lilting duet. The mood is one of sensuous delight, especially in the two passages where one instrument creates a momentary discord by sustaining a note for a fraction too long.

The *ritornello* of the finale is given to the solo instruments in a rhythmically teasing chase. The opening three-note figure, lightly touched in by the orchestra, pervades the whole movement. Slightly extended, it accompanies memorable passages where both solo violins play repeated double-stopped chords. The sense of momentum is enhanced by a triplet figure which pushes the work to its unyielding conclusion.

TOCCATA AND FUGUE IN D MINOR FOR ORGAN

Any compilation of 'Bach's Greatest Hits' would include the Toccata and Fugue in D minor. It was probably not written originally for the organ, and might not even be by Bach, but the opening twiddle ('diddle-dee') makes it instantly recognizable. It was featured in the film of Jules Verne's *20,000 Leagues Under the Sea*.

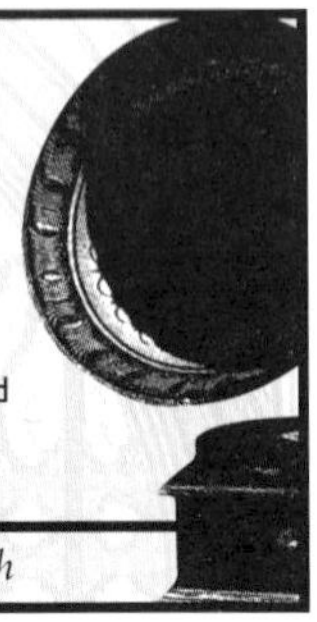

POPULAR MELODY *J. S. Bach*

RECOMMENDED CD

Concerto in D minor for Two Violins, Violin Concertos in A minor and E, Concerto in D minor for Oboe and Violin. Les Solistes Romandes, New Philharmonia Orchestra. Soloists: Arthur Grumiaux, Herman Krebbers (violins), Heinz Holliger (oboe). Arpad Gereçz, Edo de Waart, conductors. Philips 420 700-2.

Grumiaux and Krebbers might be a little heavy for those who prefer period instruments, but the speeds are just right and the phrasing is exquisite.

J. S. BACH: CANTATA NO. 140, *WACHET AUF*

Wachet auf ('Sleepers, wake') was composed in November 1731. It is based on a **chorale** by Philipp Nicolai (1556–1608) which deals with the coming of Christ as looked forward to by the wise virgins (the foolish ones of Jesus's parable are

binary form ▶ p. 356 chorale ▶ p. 357 dominant ▶ p. 358 drone ▶ p. 358 exposition ▶ p. 358 *ordre* ▶ p. 361 *ritornello* ▶ p. 362 tonic ▶ p. 363

RECOMMENDED CD

J. S. Bach: Cantatas 140 (*Wachet auf*) and 147 (*Herz und Mund und Tat und Leben*). Monteverdi Choir, English Baroque Soloists. Ruth Holton (soprano), Anthony Rolfe Johnson (tenor), Stephen Varcoe (baritone). Sir John Eliot Gardiner, conductor. DG Archiv 463 587-2 (1990).

Gardiner's lightness of touch is particularly evident in the first movement, which dances along in a most engaging way. Although the Monteverdi is not the all-male choir that Bach wrote for, Ruth Holton does sound uncannily like a boy treble.

not mentioned). Nicolai's three stanzas are interspersed with Bible-based recitatives and duets by an unknown poet, where Christ the Bridegroom achieves union with the Soul as Bride.

The opening movement presents the chorale melody in long notes in the sopranos while the orchestra and the rest of the chorus weave an elaborate and wide-ranging accompaniment. Strings and wind engage in a dialogue independent of the voice parts and the soprano line is doubled by a horn.

A short *secco* recitative for tenor, 'He comes, he comes, the Bridegroom comes!', introduces the first duet for Jesus (bass) and the Soul (soprano). The orchestra is silent, save for the continuo and a *violino piccolo* ('small violin', usually tuned a fourth higher than the violin) which, over a slow-moving bass, plays an impassioned serenade as Christ and the Soul duet in decorous fashion.

Glorious Melody

The following movement, 'Zion hears the watchmen singing', reverts to Nicolai. The solo tenor, or the chorus tenors, have the chorale melody: as in the first movement, its entry is delayed by the orchestra. Here Bach gives violins and violas in unison a glorious, long-breathed tune which is probably as well known as the chorale.

In the second recitative Christ, accompanied by the strings, welcomes and reassures the Soul. The second duet, 'My friend is mine!' is a rapturous *da capo* dialogue, the soprano and bass sometimes alternating, sometimes uniting. A solo oboe takes the role of the *violino piccolo* in the earlier duet, introducing the vocal outpourings and complementing them. The last movement consists of the chorale unadorned, with the solo horn reappearing for the only time.

THE OSPEDALI IN VENICE

Vivaldi was appointed *maestro di violino* at the Pio Ospedale della Pietà in 1709. He was later promoted to *maestro de' concerti*. His association with the place continued on and off for years: he was *maestro di cappella* from 1735 to 1738 and was still providing concertos the year before his death in 1741.

The four Venetian *ospedali* were the Pietà, the Mendicanti, the Incurabili and the Ospedaletto. Of these the Pietà, which took in foundlings, was both the largest and the most musical. Its most talented girls were trained to sing and play for chapel services and 'occasional' entertainments. The choice of instruments on offer to an aspiring performer was unusually varied and in Vivaldi's time included the mandolin, chalumeau, the newly developing clarinet and the viola d'amore. During the first half of the eighteenth century the Pietà was able to field one of the best-disciplined orchestras in Europe and its virtues were recognized by connoisseurs and travellers throughout the continent.

(BL) 20,000 Leagues Under the Sea
Still from the Jules Verne film that brought Bach's Toccata and Fugue in D Minor for organ to a new audience.
(TL) Antonio Vivaldi
In the 'Spring' movement of his Four Seasons, *Vivaldi evokes sounds such as birdsong, flowing water and spring breezes.*

J. S. BACH AND THE CANTATA

Bach was appointed *Kantor* of St Thomas's School, Leipzig, in 1723. He had many non-musical duties, but he soon shed them to concentrate on his musical responsibilities, which included the provision of music for the city in general and for its four principal churches in particular.

The school provided the choir for no less than three churches. Each Sunday its 'first choir' sang a cantata at either St Nicholas's or St Thomas's; at the main festivals of the church year the cantata performed at one in the early morning would be repeated at the other in the afternoon. Bach had the task of composing these cantatas, sometimes at the rate of one a week; he also had to copy out parts and rehearse the performers, including an orchestra drawn from town and gown.

Bach had occasion to complain about the quality of his schoolboys, who sang all the vocal lines. However, the virtuosity of some of his solo vocal and instrumental writing shows that he had at least some first-rate performers at his disposal. The cantatas were each based on a chorale, and the stanzas were separated by recitative and aria. In the elaborate opening movements, the boys on the top line were often supported by a cornett as a safety measure. Bach, ever the practical musician, sometimes alleviated his burden by adapting previously written secular material to sacred words.

FRANÇOIS COUPERIN: *QUATRIÈME LIVRE DE PIÈCES DE CLAVECIN* ('FOURTH BOOK OF HARPSICHORD PIECES'), ORDRE NO. 20

Couperin, organist and harpsichordist at the French court, published four major books of harpsichord pieces, each containing between five and eight ***ordres***. The first collection, published in 1713, includes miscellaneous pieces which had been in circulation for some years; the *ordres* in the later books, on the other hand, are carefully designed as entities in themselves.

All of the *ordres* in Books 3 and 4 are made up of pieces with descriptive titles. Book 4 was published in 1730. The writing throughout the *ordre* is generally in two parts, one for each hand; the effect is spare but never dull. Most of the pieces are in **binary form**, with two unequal parts, each played twice, but the first in the 20th *ordre* is in three sections. Named after Marie Leszczynska, who married Louis XV and was one of Couperin's pupils, it reflects her gentle nature and acknowledges her origins with an 'Air in the Polish style'. 'La Bouffone' is a gigue, with no evident buffoonery about it. The reference in the next title is equally obscure: 'Les Chérubins ou L'aimable Lazure', which starts in the minor and moves in its second section to the major, perhaps portrays two youngsters.

'La Croûilli ou la Couperinéte' is also in two sections. Croûilly was Couperin's childhood home in the country, and the rustic setting is suggested by the harpsichord simulating the drone of a *musette*, or bagpipe. An optional *contrepartie* for viol adds to the charm. 'La Fine Madelon' and 'La Douce Janneton' may be complementary portraits of an actress at the Comédie-Française, Paris. Nicolas Sezille held a financial post at court; 'La Sezile' uses the lower register of the harpsichord and, as in the previous piece, the player has to cross hands. 'Les Tambourins' consists of two short dances. They may be alternated *ad infinitum*, but 'one must always end with the first one'.

RECOMMENDED CD

François Couperin: *Quatrième livre de clavecin*. Kenneth Gilbert (harpsichord). Harmonia Mundi HMA 190359.60 (2 CDs).

Kenneth Gilbert, an authority on Couperin, recorded and edited all four of his books in the 1970s. The 20th *ordre*, right at the beginning of this set, serves as an excellent preparation for the more elaborate movements in the later ones.

Couperin ▶ p. 117 Vivaldi ▶ p. 123

THE CLASSICAL ERA

The very name, 'Classical Era', speaks for itself: it proclaims a period that is regarded as 'Standard, first-class, of allowed excellence', with manifestations that are 'simple, harmonious, proportioned, finished', to quote a dictionary definition. The period from 1750 to roughly 1820 is widely recognized as one of exceptional achievement in music – it is the time of all the main works of Haydn, Mozart and Gluck, and most of those of Beethoven, as well as the earlier music of Schubert and much of the output of Rossini. The word, of course, reflects attitudes to the classicism of ancient civilizations, Greece and Rome; and it was the middle and late eighteenth century that, through its archeology, truly began to discover classical antiquity. This period was not, however, a time of stability, but one of enormous social change, provoked by Enlightenment thinking and scientific progress; this all had its effect on many aspects of musical life across Europe.

CLASSICAL MASTERS

In music, this was a time – at least until the first decade of the new century – when composers were happy to pursue the same basic ideas as to how music should be constructed and presented. The idea of balance between different keys and between different sections helped to orient the listener and make clear to him or her the design of a piece and what was to be expected of it. It has been said that there was no classical period in music, only a classical style. But the rules or conventions within which Haydn, Mozart and Beethoven created their masterpieces were not laid down by them alone, nor were they exclusive to those three men: they had evolved over many decades and were common property. These three composers were simply their supreme masters.

The Classical Era

INTRODUCTION

The Enlightenment was a great wave of thought in the eighteenth century that combated mysticism, superstition and the supernatural – and to some extent the dominance of the church. Its origins lie in French rationalism and scepticism and English empiricism, as well as in the new spirit of scientific enquiry. It also affected political theory in the writings of such men as François-Marie Voltaire and Jean-Jacques Rousseau in France, and Thomas Paine in the US. Enlightenment thinking had its effect on music: naturalness and simplicity were watchwords for the new generation of composers. Baroque counterpoint was giving way by the middle of the eighteenth century to agreeable, elegant and affecting melody. The writer J. A. Scheibe said: 'Who can listen to a symphony by Hasse or Graun without pleasure and benefit?' – as opposed, he meant, to the learned complexities of Bachian counterpoint.

ENLIGHTENMENT OPERAS

Increasingly, the vernacular forms of opera (Singspiel, *opéra comique*, ballad opera, even *opera buffa*, often with its local, Neapolitan and Venetian dialects), based on direct, everyday human drama about ordinary people, gained ground over serious, heroic Italian opera. One vernacular opera is *Le devin du village* ('The Village Soothsayer', 1752), by Jean-Jacques Rousseau himself, which although a slender piece, was widely translated and played beyond France. The ultimate Enlightenment operas, however, are those of **Christoph Willibald von Gluck** (1714–87), with their rational reforms, their rejection of unmotivated elaboration and their basis in simplicity and direct emotional appeal, and *Die Zauberflöte* ('The Magic Flute') by **Wolfgang Amadeus Mozart** (1756–91), with its triumph of Wisdom, Reason and Nature, through the brotherhood of man, over the forces of darkness. **Joseph Haydn** (1732–1809), in *The Creation* and *The Seasons*, and **Ludwig van Beethoven** (1770–1827), in his Choral Symphony, carried the same serene confidence in man and God into the world of choral music, with its symbolic embrace of 'alle Menschen' ('all mankind').

KEY EVENTS

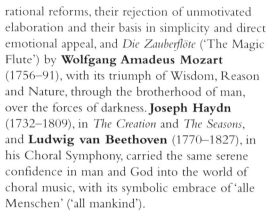

1750	Johann Stamitz appointed leader of Europe's finest orchestra, the Mannheim
c. 1762	Robert Adam's Syon House echoes classical Roman architectural styles
1770s	Haydn's early mature works; classical era in music reckoned to start
1775	American Revolution against the British begins
1776	Declaration of Independence in United States; the multi-volume *Encyclopédie* is published, edited by Diderot in collaboration with Voltaire and Rousseau;
1785	*The Oath of the Horatii* by Jacques-Louis David, a landmark neo-classical painting
1789	French Revolution begins; the Bastille is stormed
1791	Mozart dies, leaving his *Requiem* unfinished
1804	Napoleon Bonaparte crowns himself Emperor, to the disapproval of Beethoven
1812	Napoleon's French army retreats from Moscow; 600,000 lives lost
1814	The Congress of Vienna restores a balance of power between the European great powers: France, Britain, Russia, Austria and Prussia
1827	Ludwig van Beethoven dies

LITERATURE: RATIONAL AND REVOLUTIONARY

This was an era in which seminal reference works were produced. Samuel Johnson completed his *Dictionary of the English Language* in 1755. The first *Encyclopedia Britannica* was issued in 1771 by a Society of Gentlemen in Scotland. One of the greatest collective achievements of the age was the multi-volume *Encyclopédie* (1751–76), edited by Denis Diderot. Its rational humanism undermined the legitimacy of the French aristocracy (*ancien régime*). Diderot's collaborators included two great French writers – Voltaire, the free-thinking satirist who wrote the philosophical tale *Candide* (1759), and Rousseau, whose *Emile* (1762) would influence the Romantic movement. French writers were heralding the twilight of late Baroque certainty and the dawn of modern anxiety. These *philosophes* ('philosophers') laid the groundwork for the French Revolution.

(TL) Voltaire
The Enlightenment brought with it a wave of scientific and political enquiry in the works of men such as the French author-philosopher Voltaire.
***(TR) Scene from Goethe's* Faust**
The emphasis on emotion encapsulated in the literary movement Sturm und Drang *was adopted by composers, artists and other exponents of the arts.*
(FR)* The Oath of the Horatii *by Jacques-Louis David
The revived interest in classical antiquity was reflected in art, literature and music.
(NR) The Declaration of Independence
The classical era was characterized by political unrest, building up to events such as the French Revolution and the independence of the American colonies.

ROCOCO

The dominant style in art at the start of the classical era was the Rococo (from *rocaille*, 'shellwork'). Created in early eighteenth-century France, its leading figures in the graphic arts were Antoine Watteau and François Boucher. The closest musical analogue is not Mozart (as once was traditionally argued) but **François Couperin** (1668–1733) – the late Baroque generation, in fact, for the Rococo is essentially a breaking-down of the Baroque. Rococo ideas and mannerisms were exported, especially to southern Germany and Austria, and manifested themselves in, for example, the Munich court opera house, by François Cuvilliès, and in the elaborate shellwork and scrollwork to be seen in the otherwise Italianate churches of the region. The decorative, mannered style had its musical counterpart, initially in Couperin's ornamentation, but later too:its influence can be felt in the figuration used in much *galant* music, for example the graceful cadence figures of **Johann Christian Bach** (1735–82), in the lines and flourishes of **Carl Philipp Emanuel Bach**'s (1714–88) keyboard music (the 'Empfindsamer Stil', 'sensitive style') and, even as late as the 1780s and 90s in the florid detail of **Luigi Boccherini**'s (1743–1805) chamber music. And in Mozart too: one Rococo-decorated church is St Peter's Abbey in Salzburg, where Mozart's C minor Mass had its first (partial) hearing, and if the florid but expressively intense **coloratura** music of the 'Et incarnatus' was sung on that occasion in 1783, the consonance of idiom, the delight in luxuriant lines, between music and architecture must have been obvious. This is musical Rococo carried to its highest level.

coloratura ▶ p. 357

STORM AND STRESS

The literary movement known as *Sturm und Drang* ('Storm and Stress') takes its name from a play of 1776 by Maximilian Klinger, about the American Revolution. Confined to the German-speaking lands, although it had parallels elsewhere, it contradicted (or reacted to) much current 'enlightened' thinking, by emphasizing the emotional, the passionate, the irrational, the terrifying. It belonged initially in the theatre, where it was taken up by Friedrich von Schiller, especially in *Die Raüber*, ('The Robber', 1780–81), and Johann Wolfgang von Goethe, and passed to the graphic arts – the paintings of John Henry Fuseli, and the fashion for storms and shipwrecks and gothic dungeons; other manifestations of the same spirit are found in the pseudo-primitive Ossian ballads. In music, the melodramas popular in northern Germany, by **Georg Benda** (1722–95) in particular, show the agitation and terror typical of the movement. A strong case can be argued for Haydn's being influenced by *Sturm und Drang* in his symphonies of this time, those with numbers in the 40s, several of them in minor keys and passionate in tone; minor-key symphonies by others (Johann Baptist Vanhal, 1739–1813, J. C. Bach, Mozart) should be included, too, among the products of this curious outburst, which subsided after some five years, as suddenly as it had arrived.

In Britain, Henry Fielding's 'comic epic' *The History of Tom Jones* (1749) and the sentimental *Clarissa* (1748) by Samuel Richardson gave impetus to the British novel. The enigmatic William Blake expressed his personal worldview in paintings, engravings and poems such as *Jerusalem* (1804). Literature also revealed the Enlightenment's darker side – the sexual cynicism of *Dangerous Liaisons* (1782) by Choderlos de Laclos, and the cruel ethics of the Marquis de Sade, as in his *Justine* (1791). *The Castle of Otranto* (1764) was published anonymously by Horace Wimpole; it was the first of a genre of Gothic novels.

CLASSICISM

To the man and woman of the late eighteenth century, Classicism meant ancient Greece and Rome. In the 1740s, archeologists had unearthed the remains of Pompeii: artists drew them, engravers copied them for wider circulation, theorists calculated the principles behind their design. Historians and aestheticians, J. J. Winckelmann prominent among them, studied and praised the works of classical antiquity; Edward Gibbon charted the decline and fall of the Roman Empire (1788). Joshua Reynolds held that the highest achievement in painting depended on the choice of Greek or Roman subjects and their representation of heroic or suffering humanity, a principle shared with Jacques-Louis David, the official artist to the French Revolution and painter of the famous *The Oath of the Horatii* (1785), the three brothers who resolve to die for their country. The same spirit suffused many of the sculptures of Antonio Canova. Above all, interest in the classical era was seen in the architecture of the time. This is the age of the British Museum in London, the White House in Washington D.C. and the Winter Palace in St Petersburg. Classicism also permeated country house and domestic architecture, for example Thomas Jefferson's house at Monticello (1775) or the work of Robert Adam, who designed Syon House (1762–69). The more detached, intellectual approach of the classically minded artist did not preclude strong emotion; rather, it gave emotion a powerful context. In opera, classical topics came increasingly to be preferred to the historical and fanciful ones favoured by the previous generation: all but one of Gluck's 'reform' operas have a basis in classical antiquity. Haydn's last opera was based on the story of Orpheus, Mozart's on that of the emperor Titus.

AN AGE OF REVOLUTION

Although a classical age, it was also a turbulent one politically. When it began, Frederick the Great's Prussia was invading Saxony and humiliating Austria, and England and France were at loggerheads over their colonial ambitions – resolved in England's favour in Canada and India in 1759. England had less success in 1776, however, when her American colonies declared themselves independent. In 1789, Europe was shaken by the French Revolution, followed by the Terror of the next four years (including the execution of Louis XVI and Marie Antoinette, as well as several leading figures of the Revolution).

The central figure after the Revolution was Napoleon Bonaparte. He took over the French government in 1799; in 1804 he declared himself Emperor, to the dismay of Beethoven, who promptly removed Napoleon's name from the dedication of his *Eroïca* symphony. By this time, Napoleon had conquered most of Europe. The reversal in fortune of his French army's disastrous retreat from Moscow in 1812, culminated in his defeat by the English at the Battle of Waterloo in 1815.

C. P. E. Bach ▶ p. 156 J. C. Bach ▶ p. 156 Beethoven ▶ p. 150 Benda ▶ p. 157 Boccherini ▶ p. 157 Couperin ▶ p. 117 Gluck ▶ p. 158 Haydn ▶ p. 140 Mozart ▶ p. 144

CLASSICISM IN MUSIC

The classical era in music is usually reckoned to begin in earnest with Haydn's early maturity – the mid-1770s, or perhaps his op. 33 string quartets of 1781 – to the death of Beethoven in 1827, although by that date it would be hard to deny that the Romantic period had also begun. More than any other individual, Haydn was responsible for its establishment, with his development of what has been called 'obbligato homophony', a style harmonic rather than polyphonic, but where each voice (instrumental or vocal) plays an essential role in the texture of the music. This differentiates it from the late Baroque style, where there is a continuo part, playing an accompanying role. It is an idiom in which modulation is used to establish large-scale structure, with harmonic rhythms articulating the smaller structural elements; it is also deeply indebted to Italian opera and the Italian language for its rhythmic character. Not content with the routine homophony and sluggish harmonic rhythms of lesser composers, Haydn and Mozart, in their mature works, often enriched the texture with contrapuntal elements, particularly in the developments of their sonata-form movements. Haydn, with his close thematic argument and his capacity to construct entire movements from a single thematic idea (Mozart occasionally did the same, but his melodic fecundity made it unnecessary), laid the foundations for more extended movements, and Beethoven went further in the string quartets, sonatas and symphonies of his maturity.

VIENNA

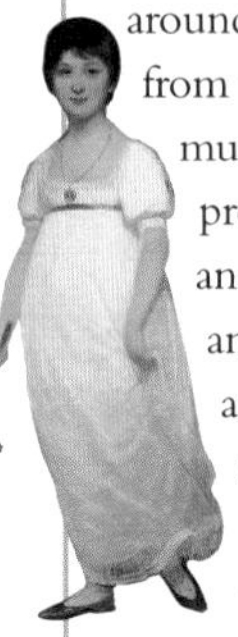

The capital of the Austrian Empire and the Holy Roman Empire, Vienna, was a particular magnet to musicians. It had its own court, of course, at which the musicians (to the irritation of Mozart and others) were chiefly Italian, through a long tradition; but around it there were numerous noble families from various parts of the empire, which included much of northern Italy as well as most of present-day Austria and Hungary, the Czech and Slovak republics, much of Romania, Croatia and Slovenia and parts of the Low Countries, and there were links with Spain. Naturally, many musicians came to try their fortune in Vienna, because of the patronage available there from the rich and cultured families, many of which had their own musical establishments. Musical styles converged there, too: the native Austrian-German traditions, Italian opera, even (during the reign of Maria Theresa) opera and ballet from the empire's traditional foe, France, and the instrumental skills of Austria's Bohemian neighbours. It was this wealth and cosmopolitanism, helped by the social and other reforms initiated by Joseph II when he became emperor in 1765, that made Vienna the melting-pot of musical styles from which the idiom of Classicism was forged by the three great composers whose lives centred on the city, Haydn (born nearby), Mozart and Beethoven (both drawn to it by the opportunities they thought it offered), while the next great Viennese, **Franz Schubert** (1797–1828), was born there before the century was out.

MUSICAL DEVELOPMENTS

This was the period when the familiar genres of music crystallized. The sonata, the concerto, the symphony and opera all became newly defined in forms that proved to be durable, through the work of Haydn and Mozart. The two men did not themselves create them (had they never lived, there would still have been sonatas, concertos and so on); but the sheer excellence of their work gave these genres their life and importance and laid down models for later generations. All these genres have their basis in the so-called 'sonata form' or 'sonata style'. This type of structure – which applies to single movements, not entire sonatas, and also to the symphony (and a few other types of work) as well as the sonata – became basic to the musical language of the classical era; its treatment of tonality and theme pervades music of the era, not only instrumental music, but also opera arias, church music and everything else. The centre of these developments was Vienna, but other cities also had significant roles. In Italy, Venice and Naples retained their importance in the development of opera, to be joined by Milan (the centre of Italian rule and a home of intellectual ferment in this period) as well as Bologna, the centre of learning; Paris and London, the two great commercial capital cities, had more wealth and a wider public than anywhere else; while in Germany Mannheim (until 1778) was the centre of orchestral music, Dresden remained a major operatic centre, Berlin was growing in cultural importance and Leipzig was becoming a centre of publishing, both for music criticism and music itself.

INSTRUMENTS

It is always difficult to determine – in the sense of the chicken-and-the-egg issue – whether instruments develop to meet needs, or styles develop to accommodate the opportunities opened up by technical changes to instruments. This is nowhere more pertinent that in the mid-eighteenth century. Musical style now demanded a much more flexible approach to dynamics, and as it did so the piano became popular. Its early models are usually called 'fortepiano', as they often were at the time, because it could move gradually between *forte* and

(BL) Society Ball
Concerts and balls became a part of middle-class life for the first time in the second half of the eighteenth century.
(TR) Jane Austen
Austen's novels demonstrate the improved status of musical accomplishment for women in domestic circles.

piano (loud and soft) and could shade the music as the instrument it displaced, the harpsichord, could not. In 1750, the harpsichord was still the standard domestic instrument; by the end of the century it had been overtaken by the piano. The early piano was quite modest in the volume it could produce (the harpsichord was long preferred for accompanying in the opera house, where the fortepiano's sound was readily lost), but was favoured as the domestic instrument for its capacity for the light and shade needed for the expressive performance of the music of this period. About the same time, the control of volume, sustaining power and articulation on the violin and other stringed instruments was improved by the development of the bow, especially by the Parisian François Tourte in the 1780s. The only significant addition to the orchestra in this period was the clarinet, which gradually achieved a regular place in the orchestra towards the end of the eighteenth century.

SOCIAL CHANGES

Changes in society and technical developments had their effects on many aspects of musical life. As industrialization proceeded and the world of commerce developed, the old systems of patronage began to break down. Haydn had taken it for granted that he would work for a noble family. Mozart, too, at first worked for the church and sought employment at court, but ended up as a freelance. Beethoven was always a freelance, though he expected (and for a time received) support from aristocratic patrons. He expected it as of right: for him, the artist was no servant, to supply entertainment as a duty, to wear livery (as Haydn had) along with the cooks and the valets, but the equal of any man – indeed the superior to most as the creator of great music: 'there are many princes but only one Beethoven'.

The age of the artist as hero had begun. The development of a new middle class, eager to emulate the taste of the upper classes of the past and interested in buying sheet music and in going to concerts, created a new public for composers – as Haydn happily discovered for himself in his late years, when his music sold in quantity and he was sought out to compose for the audiences in the great capital cities. Large quantities of music poured from the presses, aided early in the new century by the new process of lithography, to meet the needs of the growing numbers of amateur musicians – young ladies especially played the harpsichord or the piano, men favoured the violin or the flute (there even arose a new genre, the 'accompanied sonata', with the main interest in the piano part and a simple violin part, which flourished for a while to accommodate the social need that this situation brought about; it developed into the classical violin and piano sonata). This new public, literate but not confident of its taste, gave rise to another new phenomenon, the music critic, who reported in daily newspapers – not often well informed, but sufficient to guide the tastes of those who read his words.

THE MANNHEIM ORCHESTRA

One of the catalysts of eighteenth-century music was the Palatine court at Mannheim under Elector Carl Theodor, who reigned from 1742 until he became Elector of Bavaria in 1778 and the court dissolved. Carl Theodor appointed **Johann Stamitz** (1717–57) leader of the orchestra in the 1740s and director in 1750. Stamitz assembled an orchestra of unprecedented skill, many of them composers; **Charles Burney** (1726–1814) called them 'an army of generals, equally fit to plan a battle as to fight it'. They developed a new style of orchestration – arising directly out of their virtuoso abilities – that played an important role in defining the way an orchestra would function, how different roles in different kinds of passages would be distributed among the instruments. Similar developments were taking place elsewhere, for example in Italy, Vienna and Berlin, but the Mannheim School presented theirs more powerfully and had a direct influence on Mozart (who visited the city four times) and possibly, indirectly, on Beethoven. The Mannheim court orchestra also helped create the multiple concerto, or sinfonia concertante, a form much favoured there for the opportunities it offered to the skilled assembly of players.

WOMEN AT THE KEYBOARD

As keyboard instruments, from the harpsichord to the new-fangled pianoforte, became more easily available in a variety of European households, they were widely played by well-to-do young ladies, eager to develop what was seen as an important accomplishment. Jane Austen's novels present illuminating portrayals of women amateurs, from those to whom playing was simply a way of attracting a husband to those for whom music was an important part of their life. The increasing numbers of talented amateur female keyboard players provided a healthy market for certain new domestic genres, such as the accompanied sonata, typically performed by a woman playing the dominant keyboard part and a man playing the accompanying flute or violin (neither of which were considered suitable for women to play).

There were also growing numbers of women pianists who performed in public. Mozart wrote several of his keyboard works for female performers, such as Josepha Barbara von Auernhammer (1756–1820), who performed with him in the early 1780s and supervised the printed editions of his keyboard sonatas, or Barbara Ployer (fl. 1770–90), for whom he wrote two of his piano concertos. The blind Viennese pianist and composer Maria Theresia von Paradis (1759–1824) toured throughout Europe and had keyboard works written for her by Haydn, Mozart and **Antonio Salieri** (1750–1825). In England there were several well-known professional pianists who also wrote piano music, such as Maria Hester Park (1760–1813), who worked in Oxford and London and published a piano concerto (*c.* 1795). There was also the child prodigy Jane Guest (*c.* 1765–after 1824), who wrote numerous sonatas, concertos and smaller pieces.

Burney ▶ p. 157 Salieri ▶ p. 162 Schubert ▶ p. 182 Stamitz ▶ p. 162

The Classical Era

JOSEPH HAYDN

Joseph Haydn (1732–1809) was the most celebrated musician of the late eighteenth century and the first of the great triumvirate (Haydn, Mozart, Beethoven) of Viennese classical composers. A tireless explorer and innovator, he did more than anyone to develop the dramatic potential of the sonata style. When he composed his cheerful F major *Missa brevis* in 1749, the Baroque was being eclipsed by the newly fashionable *galant* manner. By the time of his last great work, the *Harmoniemesse* ('Wind-Band Mass') of 1802, European music stood on the threshold of Romanticism.

Haydn's characteristic juxtaposition of serious and comic, learned and popular, was often misunderstood in the nineteenth and early twentieth centuries, when he was patronizingly dubbed 'Papa Haydn'. Today he is revered for his mastery of wit and irony, his inspired play with the listener's expectations, and the sheer speed and subtlety of his musical thought. Less appreciated, though, are the depth and moral seriousness of much of his music: the elevated slow introductions to the London symphonies, for instance, or the profound spirituality of movements in the late Masses and string quartets.

LIFE TIMELINE

1732 Born in Rohrau, 31 March
1738 Receives his first formal musical instruction
1739 Enters the choir school of St Stephen's Cathedral in Vienna
1749 Dismissed from the choir school; ekes out a living teaching and playing
1757 First salaried post, as music director to Count Morzin; composes first symphonies
1760 Marries Maria Anna Keller
1761 Becomes vice-*Kapellmeister* to the Esterházy family
1766 Promoted to *Kapellmeister* on the death of Gregor Werner
1768 Eszterháza opera house inaugurated with Haydn's *Lo speziale*
1772 Composes the 'Farewell' Symphony and the op. 20 string quartets
1783 Composes his final opera for Eszterháza, *Armida*
1785 Receives commission from Paris to compose six symphonies
1786 Composes *The Seven Last Words* to a commission from Cádiz
1790 Composes the op. 64 string quartets; Prince Nikolaus Esterházy dies
1791 Arrives in England on New Year's Day
1792 Returns to Vienna
1794 Second visit to London
1795 Composes last two symphonies, nos. 103 and 104; returns to Vienna
1797 Composes *The Creation* and the op. 76 quartets
1798 Composes the 'Nelson' Mass; first private performance of *The Creation*
1799 Composes last complete string quartets, op. 77; first public performance of *The Creation*
1801 Completes *The Seasons*
1802 Composes his last major work, the *Harmoniemesse*
1808 Makes last public appearance, at a performance of *The Creation*
1809 Dies in Vienna on 31 May

THE EARLY YEARS

Franz Joseph Haydn was born in the Austrian village of Rohrau, south-east of Vienna, on 31 March 1732. His parents, Mathias and Anna, were both musical, and Anna would often sing in the evenings accompanied by her husband on the harp. In time the pair would be joined by Joseph, who by the age of five was showing unusual talent as a singer. His younger brothers Johann Michael (1737–1806) and Johann Evangelist (1743–1805) were also musically gifted, and would likewise become professional musicians.

By 1738 young 'Sepperl', as he was always called, was receiving music lessons, and a year or two later he won a place at the elite choir school of St Stephen's Cathedral in Vienna, where he was taught singing, the harpsichord and the violin, learnt basic musical theory and cut his teeth as a composer. Various anecdotes suggest that Haydn had a mischievous sense of humour and it was one of his typical pranks – cutting off the pigtail of the boy in front of him in the choir stalls – that caused his dismissal from St Stephen's in 1749. So on a damp November evening, the 17-year-old Haydn found himself on the streets of Vienna, 'with three mean shirts and a worn coat'.

THE EMPEROR'S HYMN

Haydn's most famous melody, 'Gott erhalte Franz den Kaiser' (1797), was composed as the Austrian national anthem. Known in English as the hymn 'Glorious Things of Thee are Spoken', Haydn used the sublime theme in his 'Emperor' Quartet, op. 76 no. 3. It was later appropriated by the Nazis before being adopted as the present German national anthem.

POPULAR MELODY *Haydn*

FREELANCE IN VIENNA

By Haydn's own admission, his first years as a freelance musician in the imperial capital were hard. He was forced 'to eke out a wretched existence' by teaching, composed 'diligently, but not quite correctly' and supplemented his paltry income by playing in serenade parties. As luck had it, though, he found himself living in the attic of the same house as the famous poet **Pietro Metastasio** (1698–1782), who introduced him to the old Italian opera composer Nicola Porpora (1686–1768). Through Porpora, Haydn claimed to have learnt 'the true fundamentals of composition'; and certainly the works he wrote after about 1754 show a new italianate fluency and sophistication. Gradually the young composer's reputation grew; and around 1755 he was invited to play in musical parties at the country estate of a music-loving aristocrat, Baron von Fürnberg. It was for these occasions that Haydn composed his first string quartets. Although these works, known as op. 1 and op. 2, are a far cry from Haydn's later quartet masterpieces, their melodic freshness and impeccable sense of proportion already mark their composer as someone special.

IMPROVED FORTUNES

In 1757 Baron von Fürnberg recommended Haydn for his first salaried post: music director to Count Morzin, who lived in Vienna but spent his summers at his castle in Bohemia. For Morzin's small orchestra Haydn wrote his earliest symphonies, most of them in three movements and imbued with the composer's own brand of driving energy and quirky humour.

(BL) The Esterházy Theatre
Haydn was responsible for everything to do with music at the Esterházy court, and was forbidden to compose for anyone else.
(TR) The Heavenly Quartet
Nineteenth-century representation of (l-r) Beethoven, Schubert, Mozart and Haydn.
(BR) Opus 31
Autographed manuscript sketches for an unfinished string quartet by Haydn.

adagio ▶ p. 356 fugue ▶ p. 358

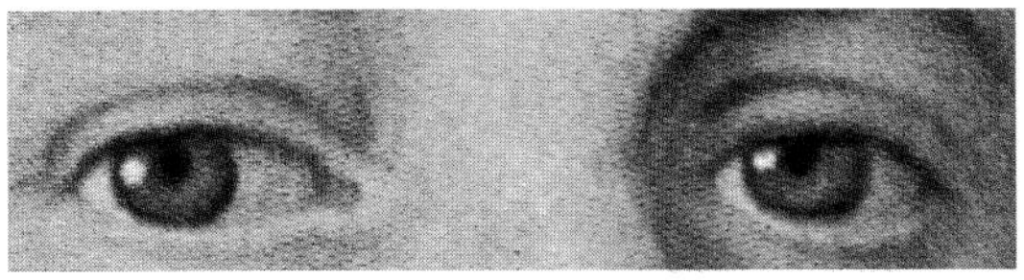

By 1760, Haydn felt secure enough financially to marry, and as with Mozart, his bride was the sister of his first love, in Haydn's case because that first love, a wigmaker's daughter called Therese Keller, had already wed. The marriage to Maria Anna Keller, however, turned out to be loveless: a story of petty quarrels, infidelities and growing bitterness.

By early 1761 Morzin found himself close to bankruptcy, and he was forced to dismiss his musicians. But the composer at once landed the job of vice-*Kapellmeister* to the Esterházys, an enormously rich and influential family of Hungarian aristocrats. Haydn took up his post at the Esterházy palace in Eisenstadt in the spring of 1761.

AT THE ESTERHÁZY COURT

Haydn's duties as vice-*Kapellmeister* to Prince Paul Anton Esterházy involved taking charge of the orchestra and managing the court's musical affairs. His contract placed him under 'permanent obligation to compose such pieces of music as his Serene Highness may command', and forbade him from composing music for anyone else. He was, in addition, responsible for the musical instruments, and for instructing the court singers. He was also required to perform with the orchestra as leader and soloist. Paul Anton died the following year and was succeeded by his younger brother, Prince Nikolaus, a passionate music lover and a talented performer on the baryton.

HAYDN AND MOZART

It was probably in the winter of 1783–84 that Haydn first met Mozart, 24 years his junior, in Vienna and over the next few years they formed one of the closest of all musical friendships. There are contemporary accounts of the two men playing quartets together, with Haydn on first violin, Mozart on viola and the composers **Carl Ditters von Dittersdorf** (1739–99) and Jan Krtitl Vanhal (1739–1813) on second violin and cello. We know, too, that Haydn attended rehearsals of *Così fan tutte* ('Thus are All Women') in the winter of 1789–90.

Mozart revered Haydn above all other living composers. His six string quartets now known as the 'Haydn' quartets (1785) were dedicated to the older composer; several movements show the patent influence of Haydn, especially his so-called 'Russian' quartets, op. 33 (1781). On hearing the last three of the set (K458, K464 and K465), Haydn famously told Mozart's father, Leopold: 'Your son is the greatest composer known to me either in person or by name. He has taste and, what is more, the most profound knowledge of composition.' Haydn may even have been a little overawed at Mozart's genius. In London, in the presence of the English music historian **Burney**, he remarked: 'I have often been flattered by my friends that I have some genius; but he was much my superior.' Haydn was grief-stricken at Mozart's premature death, and may well have composed the gravely beautiful *adagio cantabile* of Symphony No. 98 (1792) as a tribute to his young friend.

In his early years with the Esterházys, Haydn composed in all the main genres except church music, which remained the province of the *Kapellmeister*, Gregor Werner. For his crack orchestra he wrote a stream of brilliant symphonies, beginning with the *Times of Day* trilogy, Nos. 6–8 (1761), whose star turns for almost every instrument were guaranteed to endear him to his players. There is even more flamboyant solo writing in the *Hornsignal*, No. 31, which celebrates the prince's passion for hunting with virtuoso parts for four horns. At the other end of the spectrum is Symphony No. 22 (1764), whose solemn, incantatory opening ***adagio*** spawned the piece's nickname 'The Philosopher'.

KAPELLMEISTER

In 1766 Werner died and Haydn was promoted to *Kapellmeister*, which meant an increase in privileges and the opportunity to flex his muscles as a composer of church music. Over the next few years he composed two large-scale Masses: the imposing, if stylistically eclectic, C major *Missa Cellensis* (1766); and the more intimate 'Great Organ Solo Mass', coloured by the plangent sound of English horns. Even finer is the 1767 setting of the 'Stabat mater', with its dramatic power and piercing harmonic expressiveness.

The minor-keyed intensity of the 'Stabat mater' also left its mark on Haydn's instrumental music. He now embarked on a series of symphonies in minor keys, including the 'Mourning' Symphony, No. 44 (1771), so-called because Haydn allegedly wanted the beautiful, consolatory *adagio* to be played at his funeral, and the 'Farewell', No. 45 (1772). These turbulent minor-keyed works have attracted the label *Sturm und Drang*, though the German literary movement of that name lay several years in the future.

THE STRING QUARTETS

Haydn has commonly, if erroneously, been dubbed 'the father of the symphony'. He could, with far more justification, be called the father of the string quartet, a form he almost single-handedly raised from humble origins in the outdoor serenade, to a supreme vehicle for sophisticated musical discourse. Haydn's three sets of works composed between 1769 and 1772, op. 9, op. 17 and op. 20, mark the string quartet's coming of age. With their weighty four-movement structures and mastery of rhetoric and thematic development they are a world away from the divertimento-like quartets of the 1750s.

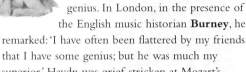

Op. 20

Fine as op. 9 and op. 17 are, the six quartets of op. 20 (1772) are the first indisputably great works in the medium. What immediately astonishes about them is their enormous expressive variety, from the rapt, inward-looking *Affetuoso e sostenuto* ('Affection and Support') of No. 1 in E flat, through the hilarity and gypsy pungency of No. 4's finale, to the two contrasting quartets in minor keys: the acerbic, highly strung No. 3 in G minor and No. 5 in F minor.

The thematic development has a power and resource unmatched by any of Haydn's contemporaries. The composer now realizes the dynamic potential inherent in the smallest motifs, and the recapitulations of sonata-form movements begin to re-interpret rather than merely restate the material. Textures in op. 20 are more imaginative and democratic than in any previous quartets: No. 2 in C, for instance, opens with a long cello solo, while three of the works close with **fugues**, the most democratic texture of all: a Baroque technique which Haydn had perfected in his church music.

Beethoven ▶ p. 150 Burney ▶ p. 157 Dittersdorf ▶ p. 158 Metastasio ▶ p. 161 Mozart ▶ p. 144

THE OPERA IMPRESARIO

From the late 1760s, the court spent more and more time at Prince Nikolaus's sumptuous new pleasure palace, Eszterháza, in the remote Hungarian marshes. During the following decade, the prince's musical establishment grew more and more lavish, to include not only his own orchestra but a full-blown Italian opera company. Haydn was responsible for everything to do with opera at Eszterháza, from engaging the singers to rehearsing and directing the performances, writing operas of his own and adapting those of other composers.

Though Haydn was proud of his operas, they have always been overshadowed by Mozart's masterpieces of a decade later. Often hampered in the theatre by slow-moving, far-fetched plots, they lack Mozart's innate sense of dramatic pacing and depth of human insight. But they are full of vivid and richly worked music, sometimes of a sensuous beauty not readily associated with Haydn; and if the characters, both serious and comic, tend to be the stock-in-trade of Italian opera, there are some sharp and witty individual portraits, such as the fast-talking Pasquale in *Orlando Paladino* (1782), with his two irresistible patter songs.

INTERNATIONAL CELEBRITY

In 1779, Haydn had renegotiated his contract with Prince Nikolaus on more favourable terms; and, crucially, he had the clause removed forbidding him to compose music for anyone else. Like Beethoven after him, Haydn was not above selling so-called 'exclusive' rights to two or three publishers simultaneously.

Much of Haydn's music in the 1780s was initially written for consumption beyond the confines of the Esterházy court. His string quartets from op. 33 (1781) to op. 64 (1790) and symphonies are both more popular in tone and even more sophisticated in craftsmanship than the great works of the 1770s. The most prestigious and lucrative commission of the decade came in 1785 from the famed Concert de la Loge Olympique in Paris, for whom Haydn composed the six 'Paris' symphonies, Nos. 82–87. More unexpected was a request in 1786 from distant Cádiz, southern Spain, for a sequence of orchestral meditations on the Seven Last Words of Christ: the result was perhaps the loftiest and most fervently Catholic music that Haydn ever composed.

JOSEPH HAYDN: WORKS

- **Symphonies**: 104 plus two unnumbered symphonies, including Nos. 6–8 ('Le matin', D, 'Le midi', C, 'Le soir', G, all 1761); No. 22 in E flat, 'The Philosopher' (1764); No. 44 in e, 'Mourning' (1771); No. 45 in f sharp, 'Farewell' (1772); No. 48 in C, 'Maria Theresa' (1769); No. 49 in f, 'La passione' (1768); No. 53 in D, 'L'Imperiale' (1778–79); No. 60 in C, 'Il distratto' (1774); No. 73 in D, 'La chasse' (1781); No. 82 in C, 'The Bear' (1786); No. 83 in g, 'The Hen' (1785); No. 85 in B flat, 'La Reine' (1785); No. 88 in G (1787); No. 92 in G, 'Oxford' (1789); Nos. 93–104, the 'London' symphonies (1791–95)
- **String quartets**: 68 including op. 20 (1772); op. 33 (1781); op. 50 (1787); op. 54 and op. 55 (1788–90); op. 64 (1790); op. 71 and op. 74 (1793); op. 76 (1797); op. 77 (1799)
- **Piano sonatas**: 62 including No. 33 in C (1771); No. 59 in E flat (1789); No. 60 in C (1794); No. 62 in E flat (1794)
- **Concertos**: two Cello Concertos (in C, *c.* 1762; in D, 1783); Concertos and Divertimentos for keyboard and orchestra, including Concerto in D (*c.* 1780); Trumpet Concerto in E flat (1796)
- Sinfonia Concertante in B flat (1792)
  Die Sieben letzten Worte unseres Erlösers am Kreuze (1786; later arranged by Haydn for string quartet, and as an oratorio, 1796)
- **Masses**: 14 including *Missa Cellensis* (1766); *Missa in tempore belli* (1796); 'Nelson' Mass (1798); *Harmoniemesse* (1802)
- **Oratorios**: *Il ritorno di Tobia* (1775); *The Creation* (1798); *The Seasons* (1801)
- **Operas**: *c.* 25 including *Lo speziale* (1768); *Le pescatrici* (1770); *L'infedelta delusa* (1773); *L'incontro improvviso* (1775); *Il mondo della luna* (1777); *La vera costanza* (*c.* 1778); *L'isola disabitata* (1779); *La fedeltà premiata* (1780); *Orlando paladino* (1782); *Armida* (1783); *L'anima del filosofo* (1791)
- Dances, divertimentos, cassations, baryton trios, other choral works, songs and partsongs, including the 'Emperor's Hymn' (1797)

THE FIRST LONDON VISIT

Haydn must have found it providential when, in the autumn of 1790, the ageing Prince Nikolaus Esterházy died and his successor, Prince Anton, disbanded the opera company and most of the orchestra. Haydn was still on the Esterházy payroll, but was now virtually freed from his official duties. Within a few weeks he had concluded a deal with the violinist and impresario Johann Peter Salomon to visit London, an event that heralded the happiest years of his entire career.

Life at Eszterháza had hardly prepared Haydn for the feverish musical and social activity of the English capital. Shortly after his arrival in January 1791 he wrote: 'Everyone wants to know me. I had to dine out six times up to now, and if I wanted to I could have an invitation every day; but first I must consider my health, and second my work.' The main part of Haydn's deal with Salomon was the provision of six new symphonies over two seasons – the works known as Nos. 93–98. These include his most sensational success of all, the 'Surprise', no. 94 (1791), in which Haydn mischievously inserted a sudden loud chord in the *andante* to startle any listeners whose attention had begun to waver.

THE SECOND LONDON VISIT

Haydn certainly found his high-pressure existence in London exhilarating. But the constant noise and bustle and the endless social engagements took their toll on a man of 60; and in the summer of 1792 he left for Vienna, with an agreement to return to England the following season. He remained in Vienna for the next 18 months,

(BL) Crossing to London
Haydn in a storm during his journey to London; the stormy crossing may have influenced the writing of his oratorio, The Creation.
(TR) Haydn in Vienna
Haydn spent his time in Vienna teaching a young Beethoven and fulfilling his official duties for Prince Anton.
(BR) Paradise Lost
Haydn based The Creation *on the Genesis chapter of the Bible and John Milton's epic poem* Paradise Lost.

fulfilling occasional official duties for Prince Anton and giving lessons to a bright and original young pupil named Beethoven. For his planned return visit to England he wrote six magnificent string quartets (opp. 71 and 74, 1793), full of bold effects suitable for the public concert hall.

Haydn eventually set off for London early in 1794, and immediately plunged again into the hectic musical and social round. He composed six new symphonies for Salomon's concerts, including the 'Military', No. 100, the 'Clock', No. 101, the 'Drum Roll', No. 103, and the 'London', No. 104. These great works are not only Haydn's most glittering and worldly symphonies but also his most searching and intellectually rigorous. His melodies are now more spacious and more popular, his forms still freer and his treatment of the orchestra more imaginative. In London Haydn also composed his final triptych of piano sonatas (1794), and a wonderful series of piano trios whose harmonic expansiveness and relaxed, intimate lyricism often foreshadow Schubert.

THE LATE HARVEST

Although Haydn was tempted to remain in England, he opted, at 63, to return to the security of the Esterházy family. The latest prince, Nikolaus II, made limited demands on Haydn's time, leaving him free to play his role in Viennese musical life. Until he was 70 Haydn composed with an unquenched vigour and sense of exploration matched only by **Leoš Janáček** (1854–1928) at a comparable age. The eight string quartets of opp. 76 and 77 (1797–99) are the absolute summit of the genre.

Haydn's final phase was dominated above all by choral music. The six Masses he composed for Princess Esterházy between 1796 and 1802, with their masterly fusion of Handelian counterpoint and symphonic drama, are the supreme expressions of the composer's reverent, essentially optimistic religious faith. This faith permeates the two masterpieces that crown Haydn's career: *Die Schöpfung* ('The Creation', 1798) and *Die Jahreszeiten* ('The Seasons', 1801). *The Seasons* has always suffered by comparison with its predecessor. If its subject is less exalted, however, it is a poetic and exuberant celebration of an idealized rural world; more than any of Haydn's works, it looks forward, via Beethoven's Pastoral Symphony, to the Romantic nature music of **Schubert** and **Carl Maria von Weber** (1786–1826).

THE FINAL YEARS

After completing *The Seasons* in 1801, Haydn wrote two more Masses for Princess Esterházy and composed two movements of a string quartet, known as op. 103. But this was destined to remain a fragment. What Haydn called 'nervous weakness' forced him to give up composing entirely at the end of 1804. He lived on for another few years, well cared for by the Esterházy family. His last public appearance was

at a performance of *The Creation* in March 1808, just over a year before he died, on 31 May 1809.

In 1802 Haydn replied to a letter he had received expressing admiration for *The Creation*: 'Often, when I was struggling with all kinds of obstacles ... a secret voice whispered to me: "There are in this world so few happy and contented people ... perhaps your labour will become a source from which the careworn ... will for a while draw peace..."' Haydn's hopes were fulfilled in his own lifetime. His humane, life-affirming vision, expressed with consummate mastery of the sonata style he did so much to perfect, can refresh and uplift the spirit more, perhaps, than any other composer.

CONSUMMATION: *THE CREATION*

The Creation was Haydn's most popular work in his lifetime and remains so today. Its literary origins were the Book of Genesis and, more obliquely, John Milton's *Paradise Lost*, its initial musical inspiration the oratorios of **George Frideric Handel** (1685–1759). Conscious that he was writing the masterpiece that would ensure his lasting reputation, Haydn worked on the score between autumn 1796 and the end of 1797; and it was first heard, in private, on 30 April 1798. The audience was overwhelmed, one of the guests reporting that 'in the moment when Light broke forth for the first time, one would have said that light-rays darted from the composer's blazing eyes. The enchantment of the electrified Viennese was so profound that the performers could not continue for several minutes'.

'Long Live Father Haydn'

The first public performance of *The Creation*, involving a huge complement of nearly 200 singers and players, took place in Vienna's Imperial Burgtheater on 19 March 1799. It was the greatest triumph of Haydn's career. An eyewitness wrote that 'the whole went off wonderfully. Between the sections of the work, tumultuous applause; during each section, however, it was as still as the grave. When it was over, there were calls, "Haydn to the front!", which crowned the celebration. Finally, the old man came forward and was greeted with tumultuous applause and with cries, "Long live Father Haydn! Long live music!" Their imperial majesties were all present and joined in the "bravo" calls.'

Within a few years, Haydn's joyous, idyllic celebration of an ordered, enlightened universe, an ideal vision that contrasted poignantly with the turbulence of the Napoleonic wars, was being performed throughout Europe. Rarely before or since has a work been so perfectly attuned to the spirit of the age and appealed to listeners on every level.

Handel ▶ p. 112 Janáček ▶ p. 291 Schubert ▶ p. 182 Weber ▶ p. 205

The Classical Era

WOLFGANG AMADEUS MOZART

The 'miracle which God let be born in Salzburg' – to quote his father, Leopold – came into the world on 27 January 1756 and was baptized the next day as Joannes Chrysostomus Wolfgangus Theophilus; he normally used only the last two names, in the forms Wolfgang Amadeus or Wolfgang Amadè. His father, a violinist, came from an artistic family, from the Augsburg area; his mother, Maria Anna *née* Pertl, was from near Salzburg. Wolfgang was the second of their surviving children; his sister, Maria Anna, usually called Nannerl, born in 1751, was an accomplished musician and keyboard player. His musical gifts were obvious when he was three or four. There are many anecdotes about his extraordinary precocity: about his insisting on joining in on the violin during family music-making, and doing so perfectly; about his noticing that a friend's violin was tuned a quarter-tone different from the pitch he was used to at home; about his writing down music he had composed, full of ink blots – and when his father said it was too difficult to play, claiming it was a concerto, so it had to be difficult. When he was five he was writing short pieces, and at that age he first played the harpsichord in a public concert.

LIFE TIMELINE

1756	Born in Salzburg, 27 January
1762	Performances at the Vienna court
1763	Tour of western Europe, including Paris and London begins
1770	Makes the first of three visits to Italy (until 1773)
1777	Sets off on visits to Mannheim and Paris
1781	*Idomeneo* given in Munich; Mozart settles in Vienna
1782	Marriage to Constanze Weber; première of *The Abduction from the Harem*
1784	The height of his concert career: the great piano concertos and string quartets
1786	Première of *The Marriage of Figaro*
1787	First visit to Prague: return for première of *Don Giovanni*
1788	Composition of the last three symphonies, E flat, G minor, 'Jupiter'
1789	Journey to Dresden, Leipzig and Berlin
1790	Première of *Così fan tutte*, Vienna
1791	Premières of *La clemenza di Tito* in Prague and *The Magic Flute* in Vienna; composition of part of *Requiem*; death in Vienna (5 December)

EINE KLEINE NACHTMUSIK

No piece of Mozart's is better known than *Eine kleine Nachtmusik* ('A Little Night Music' or 'Nocturne'). This piece, for strings (solo or orchestral), was written in the early part of 1787 and has become one of the most familiar pieces in Mozart's repertory.

POPULAR MELODY *Mozart*

EARLY TRAVELS

Leopold Mozart saw it as his duty to display publicly the miracle of his son's musical precocity; it could also help the family finances. When Wolfgang was six he was taken to Vienna, where he and Nannerl played at the imperial court and at lesser courts on the way. He played at sight, improvised in various styles, played with a cloth covering the keys and accompanied other musicians. In 1763 the family embarked on an extended European tour, with the archbishop's permission and probably with financial backing from Salzburg friends and business people. They went to the main courts of southern and western Germany, including those at Munich, Stuttgart and Mannheim, then up the Rhine to Brussels and on to Paris. There they charmed Louis XVI and Marie Antoinette, and Mozart's earliest publications, sonatas for harpsichord and violin, were issued. They went on to London, where they spent 15 months, and played to the royal family and in public; there Mozart wrote his first symphonies and met **J. C. Bach**, who became a friend and was a lifelong influence. They returned via Amsterdam and, again, Paris, then home through Switzerland and southern Germany. They arrived back in Salzburg at the end of 1766, laden with gifts – gold rings, watches and snuffboxes – but less actual money than Leopold (and presumably his backers) had hoped. Mozart met many musicians during these travels and was quick to learn from everything he heard; his cosmopolitan upbringing had far-reaching effects on his development as man and musician.

CHILDHOOD WORKS

The Paris sonatas were soon followed by another group printed in London and a third in The Hague. Also from these years are some lively symphonies, written in London and the Low Countries, in a style much affected by his father's but showing his awareness of J. C. Bach and others whose music he

(BL) Court Wedding
A young Mozart (centre), attending the marriage of Joseph II to Isabella of Parma.
(TL) Mozart as a Child
Portrait of Mozart dressed in court gala costume, c. 1762.
***(TR) Twentieth-Century Performance of* The Marriage of Figaro**
Operas were written to suit the voices of the first performers. Two arias in The Marriage of Figaro *were rewritten for the opera's second run.*
(BR) Mozart with his Father and Sister, Paris, 1763
Leopold Mozart, an excellent musician himself, had a profound influence on his son.

castrato ▶ p. 357 serenata ▶ p. 362

MOZART AND HIS SINGERS

Writing operas for major opera-houses brought Mozart into contact with some of the finest singers in Europe. He had met well-known singers during his travels, particularly in Vienna and London, and had taken some lessons from a leading Italian **castrato**. When composing an opera, it was normal to design the music specifically for the singers taking part in the first performances: composers wrote their music for the occasion, not for posterity – most operas had only one run of performances, and if given again they would be revised. So he did not compose *Mitridate* or *Lucio Silla* until he reached Milan and could hear the actual voices; he prepared the recitatives in advance but not the arias. Then he would submit each one to the singer, and try it over, as it were, for size (he once wrote that an aria should fit the singer's voice like a well-made suit of clothes). In the case of *Mitridate*, most of the singers asked for revisions, and one complained so much that Mozart made five attempts at an aria before he accepted it. Even later in his life, Mozart, like many other composers, worked in this way: when *The Marriage of Figaro* was revived, three years after its composition, he rewrote two arias for a new singer in quite a different style to suit her voice.

had heard. Back in Salzburg, he wrote music for a school opera and part of an oratorio. The family went to Vienna in 1767–68 for 15 months, where he wrote an Italian comic opera in the manner of those he had heard there (it remained unperformed) and a little German comedy, *Bastien und Bastienne*; he also composed a Mass for the dedication, before the Emperor, of a new orphanage church.

THE ITALIAN JOURNEYS

To most Germans and Austrians, Italy was the land where much of the best new music came from, opera especially. Leopold was eager to take his son there, partly to complete his musical education, partly to capitalize on his gifts while he was still young enough to be a source of wonderment. They left in December 1769 for Milan, the centre of Austrian government, pausing on the way to play to potential patrons. It was arranged in Milan that Mozart would compose the opera to open the next winter season; then they moved on – to Bologna, where Mozart visited the theorist and teacher Padre Martini, and to Rome, where he wrote out from memory, after a single hearing, the Sistine choir's exclusive showpiece, Gregorio Allegri's (1582–1652)

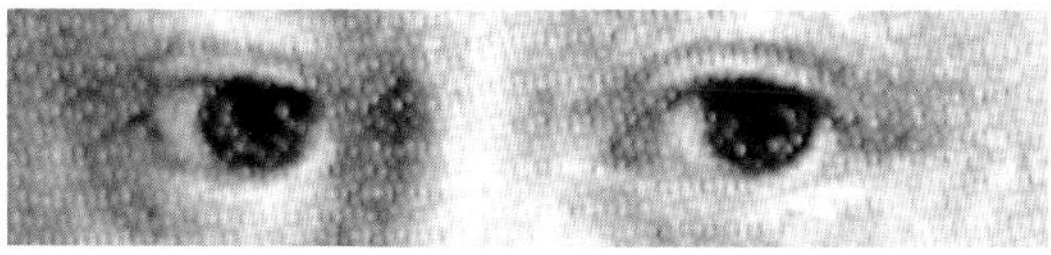

Miserere. They went to Naples, seeing Pompeii and Vesuvius, then back to Rome, where Mozart received a papal knighthood; Bologna again, where he was admitted to the esteemed Accademia Filarmonica; and back to Milan, where he composed the opera *Mitridate*, given on 26 December 1770: Mozart himself directed the first performances. Father and son returned home in March after a trip to Venice. They had picked up further Italian commissions and went back to Milan in October 1771 for the performance of a serenata, *Ascanio in Alba*, in honour of a royal marriage. More large-scale works followed: an oratorio commissioned for Padua, a **serenata** to celebrate Archbishop Schrattenbach's anniversary but, when he died, was adapted and used instead to celebrate the enthronement of his successor, and then another opera for Milan, *Lucio Silla*, for which Mozart and his father returned at the end of 1772. Leopold also made enquiries about a post for his son in Italy, but evidently drew a blank.

SALZBURG

Salzburg, in what is now Austria, close to the Bavarian border, was a handsome city in an Alpine setting containing many churches and squares. Politically, it was independent from the Austrian Empire; it was in 'church lands', ruled by its own Prince-Archbishop, who was usually appointed from a leading aristocratic family. The archbishop employed a substantial orchestra of some 40 musicians, in which Leopold Mozart was a violinist and vice-*Kapellmeister*. The emphasis lay on church music, but the archbishop, Sigismund von Schrattenbach, encouraged his musicians to study in Italy and to write new works, instrumental as well as vocal, for the court and the spacious Baroque cathedral that adjoined his Residence, and also to compose for the local Benedictine university. His successor, Hieronymus Colloredo, a Viennese, was a reformer and modernizer who simplified the church services, reducing the amount of music performed; instrumental music was largely eliminated and this led to the court composers writing chiefly for patrons from among the local nobility.

LEOPOLD MOZART

While Mozart was greatly affected by the various composers and musical styles he encountered, the most dominant influence on him, personally and musically, was his father. Leopold Mozart was an excellent musician; he wrote an important treatise on violin playing and composed a great deal, especially church music and symphonies, although he gave up composing in the early 1760s when he came to realize the extraordinary nature of his son's gifts and saw that fostering them had to be his chief responsibility. He has often been accused of exploiting Wolfgang in a selfish way, and later of trying to dominate him. But it is absurd to condemn Leopold according to the criteria of modern child psychology. There is little doubt that he educated Wolfgang (not only in music) diligently and lovingly and that he felt he had a duty – a duty to God – to show this wonder to the world; he also tried to help his son (as any father might) to behave responsibly and develop a satisfactory career. Possibly he passed on to his son a certain suspicion of his fellow musicians and of the motives behind their behaviour. The later disagreements between father and son are of the kind that might arise between any cautious parent and a young man coming into adulthood. Leopold never quite attained the recognition he deserved; a friend in Salzburg said, on his death, that although he was a man of wit and wisdom he 'had the misfortune always to be persecuted here and was far less loved than in other great places in Europe'. His best testimony is the superb musical technique that he passed on to his son.

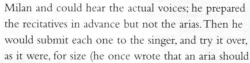

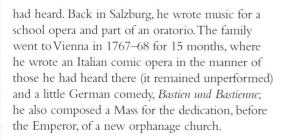

J. C. Bach ► p. 156

THE YOUNG *KONZERTMEISTER*

One of Archbishop Colloredo's first actions had been to appoint Mozart, then 16, as a salaried *Konzertmeister*; until then he had been unpaid for his services – playing the violin in the orchestra and composing for court and cathedral. However, the Mozarts were discontented: Salzburg employment limited their opportunities. They had a spell in Vienna in 1773, investigating the situation there, but evidently returned disappointed. Mozart's contact with new Viennese music was fruitful, however, as his compositions of the period show: among them are six string quartets, his first piano concerto and some violin concertos, several serenades for Salzburg university ceremonials and a series of symphonies – a fiery one in G minor and a spirited, lyrical one in A are the earliest to have firm places in today's repertory. These years also saw the composition of a quantity of church music, notably a group of Mass settings. Larger works from this time are a serenata, *Il re pastore* ('The Shepherd King'), written for an archduke's visit to Salzburg, and a comic opera, *La finta giardiniera* ('The Pretend Gardener Girl'), for performance in Munich.

SEEKING A BETTER JOB

In 1777 they lost patience: Mozart, with his mother to watch over him, went off to seek his fortune elsewhere. Offered nothing in Munich, he moved on to Mannheim, where he evidently made a great impression – but was politely turned down. Perhaps employers were not keen to have restless geniuses at their courts. There he fell in love with a fine singer, the soprano Aloysia Weber. His father, infuriated by his dawdling, directed him on to Paris, where he composed a symphony for the famous orchestra and finished groups of sonatas begun at Mannheim. But tragedy struck: his mother was taken ill and died. He broke the news gently to his father in a letter saying that she was ill, writing of her death to the family priest and asking him to tell his father. It was also becoming clear that there was no job to be had in Paris. Eventually his father arranged for him to return home to take up an improved post as *Konzertmeister*-organist. Mozart did so, reluctantly and slowly – and an encounter with Aloysia on the way, at which she rejected him, deepened his misery.

FAMILY CORRESPONDENCE

Much of our information about Mozart's life comes from the family correspondence. On the early tours, Leopold wrote numerous letters to his landlord, a good friend and probably one of those who underwrote the journey; much of the information was commercial, for circulation among a group in Salzburg. When father and son went to Italy, they reported home regularly to Mozart's mother and sister. When Mozart and his mother travelled, they in turn reported to Leopold and Nannerl, and Leopold often sent detailed instructions, as well as reports on events back home, to the travellers. In later years, Mozart kept a correspondence going with his father. Here and there, especially during the Mannheim–Paris journey, irritation creeps in, where Leopold feels that his son is behaving

(L) Mozart Manuscript
Autographed manuscript of part of a soprano aria, dating from the early 1780s and showing scoring for strings and horn.
(TR) Mozart at the Piano
In 1781, Mozart decided to become a private tutor in Vienna and took on a number of wealthy pupils.
(BR) Mozart Statue
Mozart's music was to influence musicians of his own generation as well as those for many years to come.

MOZART'S TRAVELS

Mannheim

Mannheim was one of the liveliest courts in Germany. Presided over by the Elector Carl Theodor, it had a fine orchestra, created by **Stamitz**, which developed a new style of orchestral playing. Mozart was eager to be part of this distinguished group and quickly made friends there. He even composed a piano sonata picturing the character of the *Kapellmeister* Cannabich's daughter – 'anyone can see it was composed in Mannheim', wrote Leopold when he saw it, so distinctive is the Mannheim flavour. The style left its mark: several of Mozart's works of the next years show its influence.

Paris

Paris was one of the largest musical centres in Europe. Mozart went in 1778 to seek a position there, or make a living by composing, playing and publishing his works – and perhaps by composing a work for the Opéra. He had good connections and soon had music performed at the Concert Spirituel, which gave concerts during Holy Week and on other religious holidays. Its orchestra was famous for its showy performances and Mozart exploited its virtuosity in his Paris Symphony (No. 31). But he did not like the French, and apparently made that clear: with half the talent and double the shrewdness, a friend told Leopold, he would have flourished in Paris.

Vienna

When Mozart came to settle in Vienna in 1781 he was embarking on a career in the principal musical metropolis of central Europe. Vienna, royal capital of the Austrian Empire and imperial capital of the Holy Roman Empire, was a musical melting-pot: full of Bohemians, Italians and Hungarians as well as Austrians and Germans. There were court appointments for musicians, mostly held traditionally by Italians, and many church appointments; and the assemblage of nobility from distant parts of the Empire for the main season, some of them with domestic musical establishments, provided opportunities for musicians, who gave concerts in their salons. There was a court opera at the Burgtheater, run as a German opera house or Nationaltheater from 1778 to 1782 as part of Joseph II's reforms, but then reverting to Italian opera – primarily comic, mainly because Joseph was unwilling to pay the much higher fees demanded by singers of serious opera. There was also some concert activity, mainly in the Easter season and at Advent, occasionally in the summer, but public concerts were given only occasionally and generally on a speculative basis by individual performers.

tremolando ▶ p. 363

unwisely; and occasionally Mozart himself tells half-truths. But the letters, especially Mozart's own, are written in lively fashion, with much information on Mozart's own music and performances, on musicians and musical events more generally, day-to-day happenings, events in Salzburg and much else besides.

IDOMENEO

Mozart again dawdled on his way home, pausing at Mannheim and Munich – to which, after the War of the Bavarian Succession, the Mannheim court had moved. There followed nearly two years (1779–80) in Salzburg, during which he wrote several sacred works (including the popular Coronation Mass), a richly scored and deeply felt Sinfonia Concertante for violin and viola, three symphonies and part of an opera (*Zaïde*, which he never completed). Then in summer 1780 he was invited to write a serious opera in Italian, *Idomeneo*, for production in Munich. He went there in the autumn to hear the singers and to compose it. Mozart's correspondence with his father, acting as intermediary with G. B. Varesco, who prepared the text from its French original, tells us much about Mozart's attitudes to musical drama and his composition process. *Idomeneo* is a work of great richness and expressive force, much enhanced by the orchestral writing for the former Mannheim players.

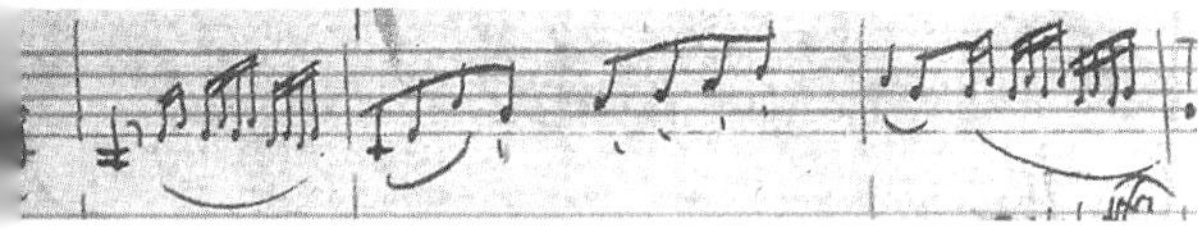

Mozart was still in Munich when a message arrived: he was to go at once to Vienna, to attend Archbishop Colloredo during the celebrations of the accession of Joseph II as emperor.

FREELANCE COMPOSER

In May 1781, Mozart reached crisis point in his relationship with Archbishop Colloredo, who required him to refuse an invitation to play before the emperor. He angrily resigned, and was literally kicked out by the archbishop's steward. Leopold was dismayed and fearful for his own job in Salzburg. Mozart, however, relished the prospect of a freelance life in Vienna, where he would combine teaching (a well-paid activity, since lessons were normally given daily) with playing and composing. He took on several noble or bourgeois young ladies as pupils, and published some new sonatas, a traditional way of raising one's profile as a composer. He made occasional appearances at court, notably in a piano contest with the visiting Italian virtuoso **Muzio Clementi** (1752–1832). And he obtained a commission to compose for the opera: it was to be a German piece, *Die Entführung aus dem Serail* ('The Abduction from the Harem'). It was given in July 1782; Joseph II is alleged to have reacted: 'Too many notes, my dear Mozart', to which Mozart responded, 'Just as many as are needed, Your Majesty'. The story is unlikely, but plausible in that the opera is far more elaborately composed, and much longer, than those of other composers given at the same theatre.

MARRIAGE

When he left the archbishop's employment, Mozart moved into lodgings. The Weber family (related to the composer), whose second daughter, Aloysia, he had fallen in love with in Mannheim, now lived in Vienna; they took him in. He became attached to the third daughter, Constanze, and her mother and her guardian (the father had died) began pressing him to marry her. He was 26, she was 20; she was a capable but not professional singer. Leopold was against it: he felt that Mozart's career was not yet established. But Mozart was eager, and the couple were married on 4 August 1782: Leopold's grudging assent arrived the next day.

MOZART AND HIS CONTEMPORARIES

It was partly because he was impressionable, and partly because he was intensely competitive, that Mozart was so affected by the different musical styles he encountered in his childhood, youth and early manhood. In London he imitated J. C. Bach; in Italy he wrote in the light, crisp orchestral style cultivated by such men as **Giovanni Paisiello** (1740–1816) and Pasquale Anfossi (1727–97); after his visits to Vienna of 1768 and 1773, he was using the richer, more developed Viennese orchestral manner; after his months in Mannheim he was drawing on the orchestral effects (crescendos, ***tremolandos***, 'rockets') cultivated by the composers there; and after his stay in Paris he was ready to write an opera that had echoes of **Gluck** and **Niccolò Piccinni** (1728–1800), whose supporters had been at loggerheads during his visit. Once, passing through Munich, he commented approvingly on the piano and violin sonatas of a minor composer, Joseph Schuster: those he wrote a few weeks later use the same processes – but incomparably better and more interestingly.

Mozart was not a borrower. What he did was to note the methods and the processes, then draw what he valued from them and adapt it to his own needs. He was competitive: he saw what others were doing and proved to himself and the world that he could do it better. In his mature years external influences diminished, although he was clearly affected by his contact with **Haydn** from the early and middle 1780s onwards. This synthesizing procedure lies at the heart of Mozart's genius, his ability to absorb, to develop his own unique style by blending others together; this accounts for the universality of his music.

Clementi ▶ p. 158 Gluck ▶ p. 158 Haydn ▶ p. 140 Paisiello ▶ p. 161 Piccinni ▶ p. 162 Stamitz ▶ p. 162

CHAMBER MUSIC

A project particularly dear to Mozart in these years was the composition of six string quartets (this was the standard number for a set to be published). He began in 1782 and did not complete the task until 1785: these works, in a genre regarded as his most intimate, serious and personal, are written with a keen awareness of Haydn's masterpieces, but are also highly individual in the way the medium is handled, especially in the dialogue between instruments. Mozart dedicated the set not to a patron (who would have provided a handsome gift in return), but to Haydn. Mozart wrote four further string quartets, as well as piano trios and quartets; perhaps his crowning achievement in chamber music is the pair of string quintets, K515 and 516, of 1787, works of a new richness, warmth and depth of feeling.

WOLFGANG AMADEUS MOZART: WORKS

K denotes number in Köchel catalogues, First to Third editions; number following / is from the sixth edition (1965), with improved chronology; incl = including; inc. = incomplete

- **Sacred works:** 16 Masses, incl. Coronation Mass, C, K317 (1779); Mass, c, K427/417a (inc., 1782–83); Requiem. d. K626 (inc., 1791); 4 Litanies; 2 Vesper settings; many motets etc., incl. 'Exsultate jubilate' K165/158a, 'Ave verum corpus' K618; 17 church sonatas
- Oratorios, cantatas, incl. La Betulia liberata K118/74c (1771); masonic cantats
- **Operas etc.:** *Mitridate re di Ponto* K87/74a (1770); *Lucio Silla* K135 (1772); *La finta giardiniera* (1775); *Il re pastore* K208 (1775); *Idomeneo* K366 (1781); *Die Entführung aus dem Serail* K384 (1782); *Le nozze di Figaro* K492 (1786); *Don Giovanni* K527 (1787); *Così fan tutte* K588 (1790); *Die Zauberflöte* K620 (1791); *La clemenza di Tito* K621 (1791)
- About 60 arias, mostly for soprano and orchestra; about 30 songs, voice and piano; canons
- **Symphonies:** about 60, incl. No. 21, A, K134 (1772); no. 26, E flat K184/161a (1773); no. 25, g, 183/173dB (1773); no. 29, A, K202/186a (1774); no. 28, C, K200/189k (1774); no. 31, D, K297/300a (1778), 'Paris'; no. 32, G, K318 (1779); no. 33, B flat, K319 (1779); no. 34, C, K338 (1779); no. 35, D, K385 (1782), 'Haffner'; no. 36, C, K425 (1783), 'Linz'; no. 38, D, K504 (1786), 'Prague'; no. 39, E flat, K543 (1788); no. 40, g, K550 (1788); no. 41, C, K551 (1788), 'Jupiter'
- **Miscellaneous orch.:** *c.* 10 orch. serenades incl. D, K250/248b (1776), 'Haffner'; D, K320 (1779), 'Posthorn'. 3 wind serenades: B flat, K361/370a (1781–84); E flat, K375 (1781); c, K388 (1782–83). Divertimentos, 6 for strings, 14 for wind. *Eine kleine Nachtmusik* K525 (1787), many dances (minuets, contredanses, German danses) and marches
- **Concertos:** 23 for piano, incl. E flat, K271 (1777); A, K414/385p (1782); E flat, K449 (1784); B flat, K450 (1784); D, K451 (1784); G, K453 (1784); B flat, K456 (1784); F, K459 (1784); d, K466 (1785); C, K467 (1785); E flat, K482 (1785); A, K488 (1786); c, K491 (1786); C, K503 (1786); D, K537 (1788), 'Coronation'; B flat, K595 (1791)
- **Concertos for other insts:** bassoon, B flat, K191/186e (1774); 5 for violin, incl. G, K216, D, K218, A, K219 (all 1775); 2 for flute, G, K313/285c (1778), D K314/285d (1778, also for oboe, in C); flute and harp, C, K299/297c (1778); violin, viola, Sinfonia concertante, E flat, K364/320c (1779); 4 for horn, E flat, K417 (1783); E flat, K447 (1784–87), E flat, K495 (1786), D, K412/386b and 514 (1791, inc.); clarinet, A, K622 (1791)
- **Chamber music for strings:** 6 quintets, incl. C, K515 (1788); g, K516 (1788); D, K593 (1790); E flat, K614 (1791). 26 quartets, incl. 6, F, A, C, E flat, B flat, d, K168–73 (1773); G, K387 (1782); d, K421/417b (1783), E flat, K428/421b (1783); B flat, 458 (1785), 'Hunt'; A, 464 (1785); C, K465 (1785), 'Dissonance'; D, K499 (1786); D, K575 (1789); B flat, K589 (1790); F, K590 (1790). 2 trios, incl. E flat, K563 (1788). 2 duos, G, B flat, K423–4 (1783)
- Chamber music, wind and strings, incl. 2 quintets, horn, strings, K407 (1782), clarinet, strings, K581 (1789); 5 quartets, 4 for flute, strings (1777–78, 1786), 1 for oboe, strings, F, K370 (1781)
- **Chamber music with piano:** quintet, with oboe, clarinet, bassoon, horn, E flat, K452 (1784); 2 quartets, with strings, g, K478 (1785), E flat, K493 (1786); 7 trios, incl. B flat, K502 (1786), E, K542 (1788); 33 sonatas with violin, incl. 7 (1778), 8 (1781) and B flat, K454 (1784), E flat, K481 (1785), A, K526 (1787), F, K547 (1788)
- **Piano:** 18 sonatas: C, F, B flat, E flat, G, K279–83/189d-h (1775); C, K309/284b (1777); D, K311/284c (1777); a, K310/300d (1778); C, A, F, K330–32/300h, i, k (1783–84); B flat, K333/315c (1783); c, K457 (1784); F, K533 (1788); C, K545 (1788); B flat, K570 (1789), D, K576 (1789); 17 sets of variations, many single pieces (minuets, rondos etc.); for piano duet: 4 sonatas, incl. F, K497 (1786), C, K521 (1787); for 2 pianos, sonata, D, K448/375a (1781)
- **Miscellaneous:** for mechanical organ, Adagio and Allegro in f, K594 (1790), Fantasia, f, K608 (1790); pieces with glass armonica

THE DA PONTE OPERAS

But Mozart's chief ambition, expressed many times in his letters, lay in opera. In 1783 he had met **Lorenzo da Ponte** (1749–1838), who had become court poet in Vienna. Two years later Da Ponte supplied him with an operatic version of the Beaumarchais play *Le mariage de Figaro*, its subversive political content somewhat watered down: the opera, *Le nozze di Figaro*, was finally given on 1 May 1786. This brilliant comedy of social and sexual tensions greatly extends the range of ***opera buffa***, with its powerful depictions of the grief of the neglected countess and the jealous fury of Figaro; but its chief achievement lies in the way Mozart used ensembles, especially the long act finales, to portray the action, using symphonic structures and changes in metre, key, tempo and orchestral colour to convey the situations and emotions of the characters. *Figaro* was a success, particularly in Prague, which he visited at the beginning of 1787; he returned home with a commission to write an opera for the Bohemian capital on the Don Juan story. Da Ponte prepared a libretto (based on an existing one) and the new opera was given on 29 October 1787 (and revived in Vienna the next year).

Like *Figaro*, *Don Giovanni* is concerned with class and especially sexual tensions, and although Mozart still treats it as a topic for ***opera buffa***, it has darker, demonic aspects – as he makes clear with his powerful, stormy D minor music for the appearance of the 'stone guest' (the statue of the murdered father of Donna Anna, whom Giovanni had sought to violate), who consigns the sinner to the flames.

(BL)* A Young Man at the Piano *by Joseph Siffred Dupplessis
Mozart began composing short pieces at the age of five, already showing signs of the brilliance that was to characterize his later works.
(TL) Mozart and Haydn
Mozart dedicated his six string quartets, begun in 1782, to Joseph Haydn.
(TR) Mozart in Prague
Mozart visited what was then the Bohemian capital five times during his lifetime and it was here that he composed some of his best-known works, including Don Giovanni.
(BR) Requiem
Mozart conducting his requiem from his deathbed.

MOZART'S COMPOSING METHODS

Tradition has it that Mozart wrote entire movements in his head before putting a note on paper. Certainly he had extraordinary gifts for planning a piece and visualizing its broad shape. However, the sketches and manuscripts he left make it clear that the music did not spring fully developed from his brow. He tended, when composing, to write out first the main line – often the first violin part, or the vocal line in an aria – with some of the bass line, and indications of detail in the accompaniment or in passages where the main line was discontinuous. Then he would go back and fill in the harmonies, the accompaniments, the orchestration: remarks in his letters, too, suggest that he regarded composing as a two-fold process, the initial act of creation, the secondary act of completion (once he even talked of composing a second movement while orchestrating the first). It was not easy, though, as writers have suggested and as the polished results might seem to imply. It was hard work, demanding long hours and intense concentration, and in some kinds of music – the six string quartets composed in 1782–85, for example – the original manuscript makes it clear how much effort he put into bringing the music to its final form.

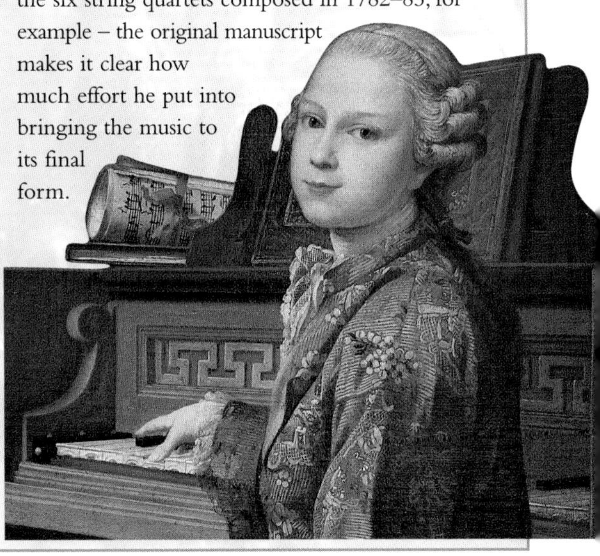

opera buffa ▶ p. 360

MOZART'S FINANCES

Life as a freelance musician was not easy. Mozart hoped for a court position, and obtained one at the end of 1787, as Chamber Composer at 800 gulden per annum. This was a good salary and the duties were modest. However, Mozart had got into financial difficulties. Times were hard in Vienna, as Austria was at war: concert life was at a low ebb, the flow of pupils had dried up and interest in him seems to have waned among the notoriously fickle Viennese public. He earned some money by publishing, and wrote a few works for the purpose. Operas brought in a fee, but not a large one. Mozart in fact earned much more than most musicians, but seems to have spent heavily, partly because of the obligations imposed by the circles in which he moved and partly because of Constanze's health (she had had several pregnancies). He repeatedly had to borrow from a fellow Freemason (he had joined them in 1784), and was still in debt, although prospects were probably improving, at the time of his death.

THE LAST SYMPHONIES

Mozart, Constanze and their one surviving son moved away from their central apartment by the cathedral at the end of 1787; they moved again in spring 1788 to the suburbs. There, in the early summer, he wrote three symphonies – probably he was contemplating a concert series, and interest in piano concertos had diminished. These three works, in E flat, G minor and C, called nos. 39, 40 and 41 (the numbering bears little relation to reality: he had written more than 50), represent his final symphonic testimony. No. 39 is distinguished for its warm lyricism. No. 40 is usually regarded as a tragic work; its tone of passion is to most listeners unmistakable. No. 41, 'Jupiter', is a noble piece in the tradition of C major works, with the military rhythms and the trumpets and drums of its first movement; but its *andante* is lyrical and deeply felt, and the finale, using fugal processes within sonata form, has a richness and grandeur of its own.

THE MOZART PIANO CONCERTOS

The series of piano concertos Mozart wrote in the years 1784–86 represent one of the peaks of his creative achievement. He had composed a handful of piano concertos before (including one remarkable work just before he left for Mannheim in 1777). Now, however, mainly for the concert series he was giving in Vienna, he wrote several more: a dozen, over three years, each one a distinctive masterpiece. In them he forged a new kind of relationship between soloist and orchestra, related to that of the earlier concerto and especially the aria (with the piano, as it were, taking the place of the voice), in which the allocation and interchange of material is handled with great subtlety and imagination; the rich writing for the orchestral wind instruments helps give each concerto its particular character. Some are highly virtuoso works (K450, 451), others are more lyrical (such as K453, 456 and 488), while those of 1785 and 1786 – including the two in minor keys, D minor K466 and C minor K491, and the two C major works K467 and 503 – have an increasingly symphonic quality.

PRAGUE

The capital of Bohemia in Mozart's time was to some extent a musical outpost of Vienna. Mozart's visit at the beginning of 1787 when he performed the symphony now known as the 'Prague', No. 38 – was the first of five: the second was for *Don Giovanni*. He had friends in the city and passed through twice in 1789; then in 1791 he was invited to write the opera to be given in celebration of the coronation as king of Bohemia of Leopold II, Joseph's successor as emperor and to conduct his Coronation Mass. The opera, *La clemenza di Tito* ('The Clemency of Titus'), was not particularly successful with the king or queen, but Mozart was admired in Prague and seems to have been happy there.

LATE TRAVELS

In 1789 Prince Karl Lichnowsky, who had been a patron of Mozart's, asked the composer to accompany him on a journey north. They went to Prague, Dresden (where he played at court) and Leipzig – here he visited the Thomaskirche and played on the organ that had been **Johann Sebastian Bach**'s (1685–1750). In Berlin and Potsdam they visited the court of Friedrich Wilhelm II, and he went back to Leipzig to give a concert. He may have been commissioned to write some music for the king. But the journey as a whole was unprofitable and there is reason to think that his relationship with Lichnowsky deteriorated. The next year he went to Frankfurt for the coronation of Leopold II as Holy Roman Emperor: he was not in the court retinue, to his distress, but went anyway as he felt he might profit from the gathering of people. He gave a concert, with two piano concertos: it was 'a success as regards honour and glory, but a failure as far as money was concerned'.

THE LATE WORKS

At the beginning of 1790, the third of Mozart's operas written with Da Ponte, *Così fan tutte*, had its première: his graceful and heartfelt music adds depth to this ostensibly lightweight tale about two officers who test their fiancées' fidelity and find it wanting. (The title is difficult to translate: it means literally 'Thus Do All Women', and might be rendered 'All Women are Like That'.) In spring 1791 the prospect of financial security came closer when it was agreed that Mozart would be appointed *Kapellmeister* at St Stephen's Cathedral on the death of the elderly incumbent. Two operas followed in the summer. Working with Emanuel Schikaneder, singer, actor, manager and librettist, he wrote *Die Zauberflöte* ('The Magic Flute') for a popular theatre in a Viennese suburb: given on 30 September, it was an immediate success, with its mixture of comic pantomime and solemn, masonic-influenced ritual, paralleled in music that embraces catchy songs, entrancing arias and duets, spectacular display pieces and noble choruses. A few days later Mozart completed his Clarinet Concerto.

On 6 September the coronation opera *La clemenza di Tito* had been given in Prague; commissioned late, it had been written in some haste (allegedly in 18 days). Another important commission had come during the summer, for a Requiem, to be composed secretly for a nobleman, recently widowed, who wanted to pass it off as his own tribute to his late wife. The fee was generous and Mozart accepted, but work had to await the completion of the other commissions. In fact the Requiem was never finished. Mozart is said to have had premonitions of his end while writing it, although his letters of the time show him in good spirits. In November he was taken ill, and on 5 December he died. The cause is uncertain; probably it was rheumatic fever or infective endocarditis. He was buried simply, according to the custom of the time, in an unmarked grave. On 10 December, parts of the Requiem (completed by his pupil Franz Xaver Süssmayr, 1766–1803) were sung at St Michael's Church, Vienna, in his memory.

J. S. Bach ▶ p. 106 Da Ponte ▶ p. 158

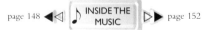

The Classical Era

LUDWIG VAN BEETHOVEN

Ludwig van Beethoven (1770–1827) is one of the greatest composers in history – perhaps the greatest. Standing at the crossroads between the classical and Romantic eras, he created music that belongs not just to its period but to all time. He excelled in virtually every genre of his day, and had enormous influence on the composers who succeeded him. His music possesses tremendous emotional and intellectual depth. Its impact on the listener is often so immediate and direct that no prior knowledge of music is needed to appreciate its power. On the other hand, some of the procedures he uses are so sophisticated and complex that even the most learned experts are continually finding new things to admire in it. Its range is vast: from the despair of the 'Appassionata' Sonata to the ecstasy of the 'Ode to Joy' in the Ninth Symphony; from the wit and frivolity of one of his many scherzos to the profound mysticism of the *Missa solemnis*; and from the tiniest bagatelles and canons to the awesome size of the *Grosse Fuge* and the 'Diabelli' Variations. Beethoven's originality is equally astounding. Each major work explores some new concept or device, and he was forever stretching the boundaries of what was possible, without straying beyond them into lawlessness and unmusicality.

BEETHOVEN'S CHILDHOOD

Beethoven's father Johann (*c.* 1740–92) was a professional singer at the court of the Elector of Cologne, whose seat was in Bonn. There was a long tradition of music-making at this court, although the size of the establishment fluctuated, depending on what funds were available. Johann's own father, Ludwig, or Louis, van Beethoven (1712–73), had been appointed as *Kapellmeister* at the court in 1761, and Beethoven always revered his grandfather, even though the latter died when Beethoven was only three years old.

Beethoven began showing musical interest at about the age of four, and his father was soon teaching him the piano. Under Johann's strict régime, Beethoven made such rapid progress that eventually a new teacher had to be found. Luckily there arrived in Bonn in 1779 a very able musician called Christian Neefe (1748–98), who taught Beethoven the rudiments of composition.

LIFE TIMELINE

1770	Born in Bonn, 16 December, the second of seven siblings (only two brothers survived infancy)
1783	First sonatas published; magazine article on Bonn musicians praises him
1792	Leaves Bonn to study with Haydn in Vienna
1795	First public performance in Vienna, and publication of his opp. 1 and 2
1796	Visits Prague, Dresden and Berlin
1800	Gives benefit concert in Vienna, including première of First Symphony
1802	In despair over increasing deafness, writes Heiligenstadt Testament
1803	Second benefit concert, including première of Second Symphony and Third Piano Concerto
1805	Première of opera *Leonore*, shortly after French invasion of Vienna
1806	Extremely productive year, including two concertos, three string quartets, Fourth Symphony and revision of *Leonore*
1808	Third benefit concert, including première of Fifth and Sixth Symphonies
1809	Granted annuity, providing regular income for life, by three aristocratic patrons
1812	Meets the great writer Goethe during a visit to Teplitz, Bohemia
1815	Brother Carl dies, and Beethoven claims guardianship of nephew Karl
1818	Increasing deafness forces him to use conversation books for communication
1819	Begins *Missa solemnis*, intended for enthronement of Archduke Rudolph as Archbishop
1820	After several legal battles, is finally confirmed as guardian of nephew
1823	Copy of *Missa solemnis* finally presented to Archduke Rudolph, three years late
1824	Final benefit concert, including première of Ninth Symphony
1827	After prolonged illness, dies on 26 March, during a thunderstorm

THE NINTH SYMPHONY

The theme of the finale of Beethoven's Ninth Symphony has been adopted as the official theme of the EU. It is intended to portray the joy that can bind all mankind together as brothers, and its simple stepwise tune seems so obvious one wonders why nobody else thought of it first.

POPULAR MELODY *Beethoven*

BEETHOVEN'S SKETCHES

Beethoven's approach to composition was strikingly different from that of his predecessors, in that he made a vast amount of rough drafting and sketching for each work. Although many of these sketches were discarded or lost, a large number survive – probably about 10,000 pages altogether, with nearly all his works represented.

These sketches provide fascinating insights into exactly how he composed individual masterpieces – what problems he had, how else he might have written them, and in what order the bits were put together. They reveal, for example, that he normally composed successive movements of a work in the order in which they finally appeared, but that during work on one movement he was repeatedly jotting down possible ideas for later ones.

Despite their fascination, many of these sketches have still not been studied in detail; this is partly because there are so many, but also because they are generally very difficult to decipher. In addition, sketches for several works are often jumbled up on one page, while those for a single work may now be scattered around several libraries in different parts of the world.

Some of the sketches were written in ink in actual manuscript books known as sketchbooks, but until 1798 they were all simply jotted on loose sheets of paper. During his late period, many were written in pencil in pocket-sized sketchbooks which he used on long walks, while others were still being written on loose sheets or in full-sized sketchbooks.

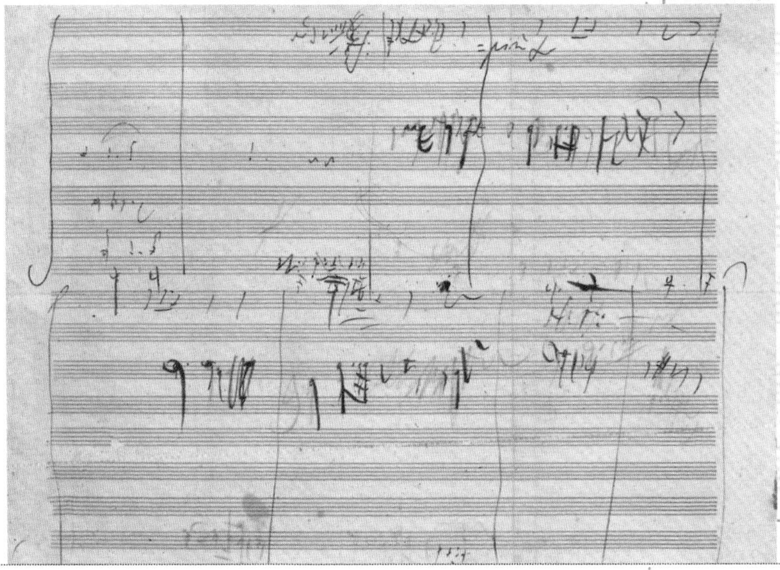

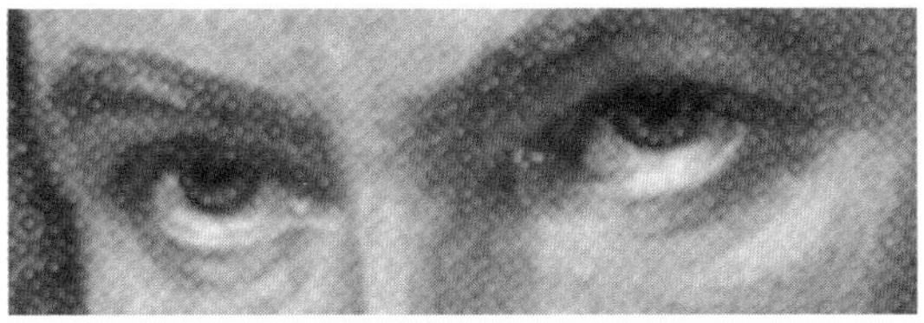

Again Beethoven made rapid progress, and Neefe arranged for publication of some of his earliest compositions, including a set of variations in 1782 and a set of three piano sonatas in 1783. All of these show considerable originality.

THE YOUNG COURTIER

Beethoven had been deputizing as a musician at court for some years by the time he was officially appointed as court organist alongside Neefe. By 1787 it had been decided to send him to **Mozart** in Vienna to improve his skills still further, since there was little in music that he could still learn from anyone in Bonn. His visit to Vienna proved short-lived, however, for almost immediately after arriving he heard that his mother was terminally ill. He hurried back to Bonn, and she died shortly after his return. He resumed his duties at court, taking part in many operatic productions (probably often as a viola player). His father, meanwhile, was rapidly descending into alcoholism and had to be pensioned off. Beethoven thus assumed responsibility as head of his household, which included his two brothers Carl (1774–1815) and Johann (1776–1848); four other siblings had died in infancy.

Hardly any compositions by Beethoven survive from the late 1780s, but in 1790 he wrote two large-scale cantatas – on the death of Emperor Joseph II and on the accession of Emperor Leopold II. These evidently proved so difficult for the performers, however, that neither of them progressed beyond the rehearsal stage.

THE MOVE TO VIENNA

During Christmas 1790, **Haydn** arrived in Bonn en route from Vienna to London, and met some of the musicians who lived there. He visited them again on his way back in July 1792, and was almost certainly shown some of Beethoven's compositions, including one of the cantatas and probably other recent works such as concertos, arias, piano music and chamber music. It must have been at the second meeting that he agreed to give Beethoven tuition in Vienna. Mozart had died suddenly the previous year and Haydn possibly hoped that Beethoven might be able to fill the void felt in Vienna. During the summer Beethoven made final preparations for his departure, and in October his friends began writing farewell messages in a little album. The message from Count Waldstein, one of Beethoven's leading supporters in Bonn, was the most prophetic, predicting that Beethoven would receive 'Mozart's spirit from Haydn's hands': Beethoven's early works in Vienna do show much of Mozart's influence, although this never completely eclipses his own personal style. Beethoven finally set out in early November, arriving in Vienna about a week later.

VIENNA: THE EARLY PERIOD

Contrary to some accounts, Beethoven seems to have struck up a warm and friendly relationship with Haydn, and instruction continued for over a year. Haydn then left Vienna for his second trip to England, and Beethoven transferred to Johann Georg Albrechtsberger (1736–1809). Albrechtsberger was the leading composer in the old, learned style of fugal counterpoint, and his instruction of Beethoven appears to have been much more rigorous than Haydn's easygoing manner. Beethoven systematically followed through Albrechtsberger's course for 18 months, and the teacher's markings on Beethoven's exercises – most of which still survive – reveal much about Albrechtsberger's diligence and skill.

During his year with Haydn, Beethoven composed several works, including a wind octet and a now lost oboe concerto. The following year he produced less (he was probably too busy completing Albrechtsberger's numerous exercises), but in 1795 he was ready to burst into the limelight. At his public debut that March he performed a new piano concerto (probably No. 1 in C), and a few months later published what he now designated as his op. 1, a set of piano trios. These were shortly followed by op. 2, a set of sonatas which he dedicated to Haydn.

BEETHOVEN'S INSPIRATION

One of the most significant early influences on Beethoven's music was his teacher Christian Neefe, who gave him instruction in theory and composition. Neefe was probably responsible for some of the loftiness of aim that permeates Beethoven's music. So, too, was **J. S. Bach**, whose *Well-Tempered Clavier* (1722) Beethoven learned under Neefe's instruction. The Bachian ideal re-emerged more profoundly during Beethoven's late period, when he even contemplated writing an overture on the notes B-A-C-H (H is the German for b natural; B denotes b flat).

The two main composers in whose footsteps Beethoven followed, however, were Mozart and Haydn. Much of Beethoven's vocal and wind writing is indebted to Mozart, while his ingenious manipulation and development of small motifs is based on Haydn's example. In general Mozart's influence is clearer in opera and concerto, Haydn's in symphony and string quartet. Beethoven also became a great admirer of **Handel** – especially his ability to create great movements out of the simplest materials, a skill that is evident in many of Beethoven's works.

Beethoven in turn became an enormous influence on many succeeding composers. Poetic works such as his Pastoral Symphony (No. 6, 1808) were to inspire **Hector Berlioz** (1803–69) and

Franz Liszt (1811–86) among others, while the grandeur of the 'Choral' Symphony (No. 9, 1823) paved the way for **Gustav Mahler** (1860–1911). His song cycle *An die ferne Geliebte* ('To the Distant Beloved', 1816) was the first of many in this genre.

Meanwhile his 'pure' music, such as his string quartets and most of his symphonies, provided models for such composers as **Robert Schumann** (1810–56) and **Johannes Brahms** (1833–97) and for twentieth-century composers such as **Arnold Schoenberg** (1874–1951), **Michael Tippett** (1905–98) and **Brian Ferneyhough** (b. 1943). Without Beethoven, the history of music in the last two centuries would have been very different.

(BL) Beethoven Sketch
'Sketch for Dle Welhe des Hauses, op. 24 (1822).
(TR) Franz Liszt
The Hungarian composer Franz Liszt was influenced by Beethoven's 'Pastoral' Symphony; he later became a musical legend in his own right.
(MR) Haydn and Beethoven
Artist's impression of Beethoven with Haydn, with whom he studied for a brief period.

J. S. Bach ▶ p. 106 Berlioz ▶ p. 186 Brahms ▶ p. 240 Ferneyhough ▶ p. 325 Handel ▶ p. 112 Haydn ▶ p. 140 Liszt ▶ p. 194 Mahler ▶ p. 250
Mozart ▶ p. 144 Schoenberg ▶ p. 295 Schumann ▶ p. 201 Tippett ▶ p. 330

'FRIENDS AND RENOWN'

By the end of 1795 Beethoven had won both 'friends and renown', as he put it, and had settled in Vienna, where he had been joined by his two brothers. The following year he set off on a tour to Prague, Dresden and Berlin. He performed at the piano in each of these cities, and composed several works for the musicians of Prague and Berlin. These included his Cello Sonatas op. 5 (1796) for the Berlin court cellist Jean-Louis Duport (1749–1818). Beethoven visited Prague again in 1798, by which time he had composed many more works, including several piano sonatas, and had also begun work on a symphony and a set of string quartets. The symphony that eventually emerged in 1800 was No. 1 in C, which was performed on 2 April that year, along with his Septet, at a benefit concert that he gave in Vienna. The concert also included works by Haydn and Mozart, and an extemporization on the piano – a skill at which Beethoven greatly excelled. Also completed that year, after several revisions, was his set of six string quartets op. 18, which he dedicated to Prince Franz Lobkowitz one of several aristocratic patrons who supported him at this time.

THE DEAFNESS CRISIS

Soon after completing his First Symphony, Beethoven began work on his Second, and in 1801 he wrote a highly successful ballet, *Die Geschöpfe des Prometheus* ('The Creatures of Prometheus'). He was by now greatly admired as a composer and was generally prospering, but unfortunately his hearing was becoming seriously impaired. First signs of deafness had appeared in about 1797 and the condition gradually became worse over many years, although it fluctuated somewhat. At first Beethoven tried to keep it secret, but he consulted various doctors in an attempt to find a cure, and confided his problems in letters to close friends in 1801. In 1802, as a final attempt at a cure, he moved to the quiet village of Heiligenstadt, just north of Vienna, for six months. This plan, too, proved unsuccessful, and in October Beethoven wrote a moving account of his despairing mental state in a document which became known as the 'Heiligenstadt Testament'. Addressed primarily to his brothers, but also to the world at large, it begins: 'O you men who think or say I am hostile, peevish, or misanthropic, how greatly you wrong me. You do not know the secret cause that makes me seem so to you.'

ARCHDUKE RUDOLPH

Of all Beethoven's aristocratic patrons, Archduke Rudolph (1788-1831) seems to have been the most devoted and enduring. Rudolph's poor health made him unsuitable for military training and instead he entered the church. He developed a great love of music in general, and of Beethoven's music in particular, and from about 1808 was a close friend of the composer, despite their difference in status.

Archduke Rudolph was one of the three patrons who, in 1809, granted Beethoven a lifetime annuity, and in that year began taking composition lessons from him. Beethoven had previously refused to teach anyone composition, but it says much for Rudolph's gentle nature and skilled arts of persuasion that Beethoven made this single exception.

Beethoven dedicated more works to Rudolph than to anyone else. Particularly noteworthy are the sonata op. 81a, 'Les adieux' ('The Farewell', 1809), written to mark his patron's departure from and return to Vienna; the 'Archduke' Trio; the 'Hammerklavier' Sonata (1818), written specially for him; and the *Missa solemnis*, which was intended for his enthronement as Archbishop of Olmütz in 1820, but was not completed in time.

CONTINUITY AND ENDING

Beethoven was the first composer to realize the full implications of the fact that a piece of music, like a good story, should have a good ending and a sense of narrative continuity. First, his music tends to have a great sense of rhythmic drive and momentum. Secondly, although movements in Beethoven's day customarily were divided into sections, he was constantly seeking ways of smoothing over the joins. This striving for continuity increasingly resulted in links between whole movements: many of his slow movements lack a full termination but run straight on into the finale, and in his later works he sometimes linked other movements.

Even where movements were kept separate, Beethoven often created subtle motivic relationships between them. Perhaps the most obvious example is the Fifth Symphony, where the opening four-note motif not only generates most of the thematic material for the first movement, but is echoed in various ways in each of the subsequent movements. The Fifth Symphony is also a prime example of an overall trajectory that spans the entire work, progressing from minor to major, from darkness to light, from the anguish of the opening movement to the triumph of the finale.

The Finale Problem

Beethoven was the first to be fully aware of, and to solve, the 'finale problem' that plagued so many of his successors, where the last movement needs to create a sense of satisfactory completion and achievement. He also treated endings of individual movements as particularly important, often writing a lengthy **coda** to provide a kind of summing up, in which unstable elements heard earlier were somehow rounded off: a rhythmic pattern would perhaps be reversed, or an incomplete melodic shape finally extended to its natural conclusion. Whatever the means, the last bar always possesses an unmistakable air of finality.

coda ▶ p. 357

THE SYMPHONIES

Since they were first composed, Beethoven's symphonies have formed one of the cornerstones of orchestral repertory. Building on Haydn's example, Beethoven turned the symphony as a genre into what it has remained for almost all subsequent composers: a grand, unified structure to be regarded with awe by composer and audience alike. Whereas Haydn's symphonies often came in batches of three or six, Beethoven's were produced singly or, at most, in a pair. Moreover, each of his symphonies is highly individual and original, while retaining many traditional elements and typically Beethovenian features.

Beethoven's originality is evident right from the first chord of No. 1 – an out-of-key discord with unusual scoring. His Third Symphony, the 'Eroica' (1803), embodies the concept of heroism and dwarfs all previous symphonies. Its massive first movement builds up to a ferocious climax during the development section, and its second movement is a slow, lengthy funeral march. The finale borrows its main theme from his heroic ballet *Prometheus*.

The Fifth to the Tenth

The Fifth (1807) is perhaps the most celebrated, with its compressed intensity built out of the famous opening motto. The Sixth (1808), the *Pastoral*, could not be more different. It combines symphonic breadth with the pastoral idiom, in which each of its five movements evokes some particular aspect of the countryside which Beethoven loved so much. The Seventh (1812) is different again, with its emphasis on strong repeated rhythmic cells giving it a dance-like character.

Beethoven's last completed symphony, the Ninth (1823), surpasses all previous ones in power and scale. Like the Fifth, it progresses from minor to major; but whereas the Fifth added trombones and piccolo for the finale, the Ninth adds solo and choral voices – never previously used in a standard symphony. As for the Tenth, it was apparently to have been a much more intimate work; but how it would have turned out, we shall never know.

THE SHADOW OF NAPOLEON

Beethoven's life and work are customarily divided into three periods – early, middle and late; although such divisions are obviously an over-simplification, they do to some extent reflect the nature of his personal development. In 1802 he overcame his deafness crisis by plunging himself into composition with renewed vigour, and began a series of works of great power and originality. The first of these was his oratorio *Christus am Oelberge* ('Christ on the Mount of Olives', 1803–04), a profound depiction of Christ's suffering, evidently written in response to Beethoven's own. More famous was his next major work, the enormous 'Eroica' Symphony No. 3. This was originally intended for Napoleon, whom Beethoven greatly admired as a champion of liberty; but when Napoleon proclaimed himself Emperor in 1804, Beethoven tore up the dedication.

Beethoven was a vociferous opponent of all forms of tyranny and in 1804–05 he wrote an opera on the subject. Known at first as *Leonore* but later as *Fidelio*, it deals with a man's wrongful imprisonment and rescue by his wife. It was first performed in November 1805, but Napoleon had just invaded Vienna, and the theatre was almost empty.

***(BL) Ludwig van Beethoven** by Willibrod Joseph Mähler*
Beethoven, like many other composers, faced the challenge of giving his works a suitably memorable finale.
(TL) Napoleon Bonaparte
Beethoven originally dedicated his 'Eroica' Symphony to Napoleon, but destroyed the dedication when Napoleon declared himself emperor.
(TR) Beethoven Composing a Symphony
Later artist's impression of what Beethoven saw while composing his symphonies.

CORNERSTONES OF THE REPERTORY

Despite the disastrous première of *Leonore* in 1805, Beethoven revised it a few months later, and during the next three years he wrote many works that have become cornerstones of the orchestral, chamber or solo repertory, including three symphonies (Nos. 4–6), three string quartets for Count Razumovsky, two concertos, his Mass in C, the *Coriolan* Overture, the Cello Sonata in A, two piano trios (op. 70) and the Choral Fantasia. Many of these, like the 'Eroica', were on an unusually large scale. His style was continually advancing, and although some musicians felt his music to be too learned, complex, elevated or simply bizarre, he always had plenty of supporters who recognized his genius and appreciated the outstanding originality and ingenuity of his works.

By now he was performing on the piano less frequently, partly because of his deafness. In December 1808, however, he was permitted a benefit concert at which he directed several of his latest works, including his Fifth and Sixth Symphonies and his Fourth Piano Concerto (in which he played the solo part). It was a huge programme that lasted four hours with the audience enduring freezing temperatures, but the music itself was greatly admired.

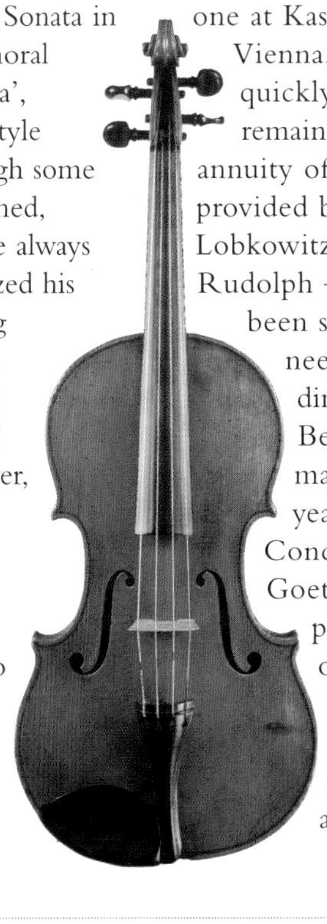

A REGULAR INCOME

Since the lapsing of his salary from Bonn in 1794, Beethoven had supported himself mainly by selling compositions to publishers. He also received intermittent support from various patrons, and Prince Karl Lichnowsky granted him a small but regular payment for a few years from 1800. Beethoven would have preferred a regular position, however, and he was offered one at Kassel in 1808. His supporters in Vienna, realizing they might lose him, quickly arranged a deal whereby he would remain in the capital, supported by a regular annuity of 4,000 florins for life. Funds were provided by three aristocrats – Prince Lobkowitz, Prince Kinsky and Archduke Rudolph – and the annuity should have been sufficient to provide for all his basic needs, although its value was soon diminished somewhat by inflation.

Beethoven continued with further major works during the next few years, including the 'Emperor' Concerto (No. 5), incidental music for Goethe's *Egmont* and two more symphonies. He also embarked on a series of settings of British and continental folksong melodies, at the request of George Thomson of Edinburgh, making 179 settings altogether over a 10-year period.

THE IMMORTAL BELOVED

Beethoven never married, but he was often in love in his younger days. He may have proposed to Countess Josephine Deym in 1805, and to Therese Malfatti in 1810, but if so he was refused in both cases. In 1812 he fell in love again, with a woman whose identity has never been confirmed. While on holiday in Teplitz, Bohemia, he wrote a passionate letter to her in which he does not mention her name but simply refers to her by such phrases as 'my angel' and 'immortal beloved'. She was probably Antonie Brentano, a married woman with several children, who is known to have been in close contact with him that year.

In 1813 Beethoven's productivity declined markedly, but towards the end of the year he composed *Wellingtons Sieg* ('Wellington's Victory', often known as the 'Battle Symphony'), which celebrated the defeat of the French army by the Duke of Wellington at the Battle of Vitoria. The work was originally suggested by Johann Maelzel (1772–1838), the inventor of the metronome. Beethoven later fell out with Maelzel, but was the first major composer to use metronome marks, and even provided some retrospectively for symphonies composed several years earlier.

FAMILY OBLIGATIONS

Beethoven reached the heights of popular acclaim in 1814 with a series of politically inspired works that are little known nowadays. The following year, however, his personal life was thrown into turmoil with the death of his brother Carl. Beethoven at once attempted to become guardian of his nine-year-old nephew Karl, claiming that the boy's mother Johanna was unsuitable. His claims had some justification, since she was known to be dishonest, badly educated and of poor reputation, whereas Beethoven himself always had high moral values. The result was a series of legal battles that lasted until 1820 and absorbed much of his energy, but he was eventually successful in excluding Johanna from the guardianship.

Meanwhile, however, his thinking was becoming increasingly profound. He displayed growing interest in religious matters, including the writings of Indian mystics. He also turned to the music of Bach for inspiration, and adopted a more complex contrapuntal style in which every instrumental line developed thematic material. His last two cello sonatas are the first works in which this late style is clearly apparent, and the final movement of No. 2 consists of a **fugue**, as do several other movements in his late period.

LUDWIG VAN BEETHOVEN: WORKS

- **Symphonies:** Symphony No. 1 in C (1800); Symphony No. 2 in D (1802); Symphony No. 3 'Eroica' in E flat (1803); Symphony No. 4 in B flat (1806); Symphony No. 5 in c (1807); Symphony No. 6 'Pastoral' in F (1808); Symphony No. 7 in A (1812); Symphony No. 8 in F (1812); Symphony No. 9 'Choral' in d (1823)
- **Concertos:** Piano Concerto in E flat (1784); Violin Concerto in C (fragment) (*c.* 1791); Oboe Concerto in F (fragment) (1793); Piano Concerto No 1 in C (1795, rev. 1800); Piano Concerto No. 2 in B flat (*c.* 1788, rev. 1798); Piano Concerto No. 3 in c (1803); Triple Concerto in C (1804); Piano Concerto No. 4 in G (1806); Violin Concerto in D (1806; also arranged as Piano Concerto); Piano Concerto No. 5 'Emperor' in E flat (1809)
- **String quartets:** Six quartets op. 18 (1798–1800); three 'Razumovsky' quartets op. 59 (1806); 'Harp' Quartet in E flat, op. 74 (1809); Quartet in f, 'Serioso', op. 95 (1810); Quartet in E flat, op. 127 (1824); Quartet in a, op. 132 (1825); Quartet in B flat, op. 130 (1825–26); *Grosse Fuge*, op. 133 (1825, original finale to op. 130); Quartet in c sharp, op. 131 (1826); Quartet in F, op. 135 (1826)
- **Piano trios:** Three trios op. 1 (1795); Two trios op. 70 (1808); 'Archduke' Trio in B flat, op. 97 (1811); and shorter works
- **Violin sonatas:** Three sonatas op. 12 (1798); Sonata in a, op. 23 (1800); 'Spring' Sonata in F, op. 24 (1801); Three Sonatas op. 30 (1802); 'Kreutzer' Sonata in A, op. 47 (1802–03); Sonata in G, op. 96 (1812)
- **Cello sonatas:** Two sonatas op. 5 (1796); Sonata in A, op. 69 (1807); Two sonatas op. 102 (1815)
- **Piano sonatas:** Three 'Electoral' sonatas (1783); Three sonatas op. 2 (1795); Two sonatas op. 49 (1796–97); Sonata in E flat, op. 7 (1797); Three sonatas op. 10 (1798); 'Pathétique' Sonata in c, op. 13 (1798); Two sonatas op. 14 (1798); Sonata in B flat, op. 22 (1800); Sonata in A flat, op. 26 (1801); Two sonatas *quasi una fantasia* (No. 2 in c sharp: 'Moonlight', 1801); 'Pastoral' Sonata in D, op. 28 (1801); Three sonatas op. 31 (No. 2 in d: 'Tempest', 1802); 'Waldstein' Sonata in C, op. 53 (1803–04); Sonata in F, op. 54 (1804); 'Appassionata' Sonata in f, op. 57 (1805); Sonata in F sharp, op. 78 (1809); Sonata in G, op. 79 (1809); Sonata in E flat, Das Lebewohl ('Les Adieux'), op. 81a (1809); Sonata in e, op. 90 (1814); Sonata in A, op. 101 (1816); 'Hammerklavier' Sonata in B flat, op. 106 (1818); Sonata in E, op. 109 (1820); Sonata in A flat, op. 110 (1821); Sonata in c, op. 111 (1822)
- **Major choral works**: *Christus am Ölberge* (1803–04); Mass in C (1807); Choral Fantasia in C (1808); Mass in D, *Missa solemnis* (1819–22)
- **Operas and ballets:** *Ritterballett* (1791); *Die Geschöpfe des Prometheus* (1801; ballet); *Leonore* (1805, rev. 1806; opera), rev. as *Fidelio* (1814); two one-act Singspiels (1811): *Die Ruinen von Athen* and *König Stephan*
- Music for stage, dance music, marches, orchestral music, chamber music, piano music, choral music, arias with orchestra, songs, folksong settings, canons, counterpoint exercises (fugues etc.), music for mechanical clock

DECLINING POWERS?

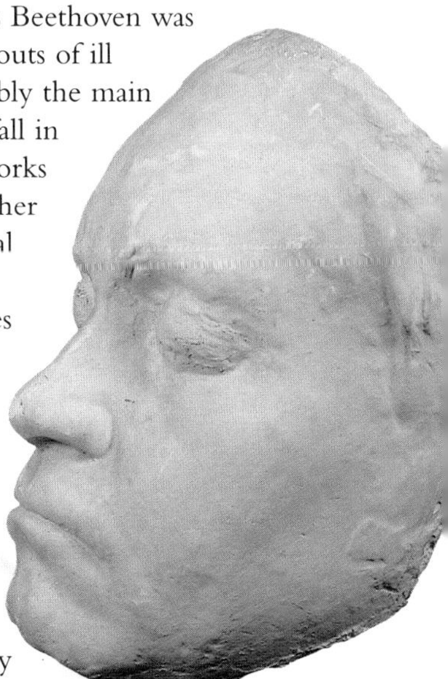

For the next few years Beethoven was plagued by frequent bouts of ill health. This was probably the main cause of a substantial fall in the number of new works produced, although other factors, such as his legal disputes, his changing domestic circumstances and his efforts to provide for his nephew, also contributed. During 1817 he composed virtually nothing, and there was to be a similar creative silence for much of 1821. He may also have been searching for a way forward in the development of his music, for he jotted down many ideas that were not brought to fruition – most notably a piano concerto in D (1815) and a piano trio in F minor (1816).

The key to progress was found in expansion. Just as his 'Eroica' and several works written shortly afterwards had exhibited unprecedented length, so now he embarked on a series of works in which the size and scale were expanded still further. These included the 'Hammerklavier' Sonata of 1818; the Ninth Symphony, begun in earnest about the same time; and the 'Diabelli' Variations and the *Missa solemnis*, both begun in 1819.

(FL) Portrait of Beethoven
Beethoven, shown in a classical setting, with the Temple of Apollo in the background.
(NL and TR) Mask and Memorial Statue
Mask of the composer's face and statue of the composer in the Beethovenplatz, Vienna.
***(BR)* Beethoven Frieze**
Klimt's piece for the Secession building in Vienna was inspired by Wagner's description of Beethoven's Ninth Symphony.

fugue ▶ p. 358

VOCAL MUSIC

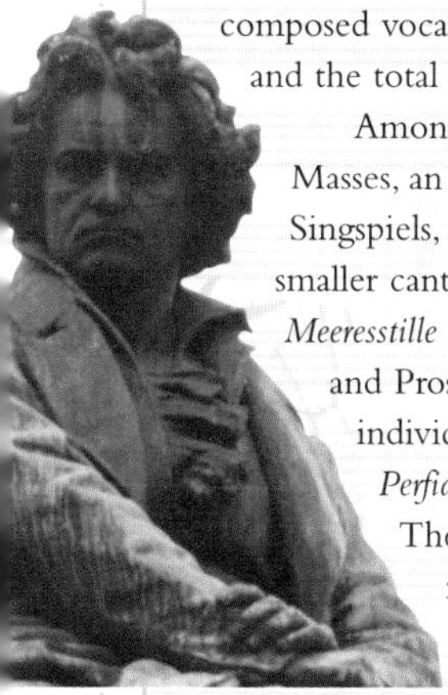

There is a widespread misconception that Beethoven did not write much for the voice, that what he did produce is not very good, and that much of it is virtually unsingable. In view of the enormous amount of attention that has been given to his instrumental music, such notions are understandable, but they are far from the truth. Beethoven composed vocal music at every stage of his life, and the total amount is considerable.

Among his larger works are two Masses, an oratorio, an opera, two Singspiels, three large-scale cantatas, several smaller cantatas such as the beautiful *Meeresstille und glückliche Fahrt* ('Calm Sea and Prosperous Voyage', 1815), and some individual concert arias such as *Ah! Perfido* ('Ah! Treacherous One', 1796). There are also about 90 songs, including the first proper song cycle for voice and piano, *An die ferne Geliebte* ('To the Distant Beloved', 1816), and nearly all were written before any of **Schubert**'s. To these can be added numerous folksong settings, and about 40 short canons for two or more voices.

Many of these works are extremely fine. The *Missa solemnis* was described by Beethoven himself, with some justification, as his greatest work, and its combination of profundity and directness is unsurpassed. Even his folksong settings, which were neglected or disparaged for many years, have proved on closer inspection to be outstandingly innovative and well crafted.

Beethoven always made great efforts to capture both the rhythm and the meaning of the words. This sometimes prompted him to extreme solutions – hence the allegations of difficulty; but his instrumental music is equally challenging for performers. In both instrumental and vocal music, the difficulties are not there for their own sake, but because he wanted to stretch his ideas to the limits of human capability.

RESURGENCE

The symphony, the variations and the Mass were all set aside for a time, but were taken up again in 1822–23. Beethoven's output, which had for some years been rather meagre, showed a sudden resurgence, as he completed his last three piano sonatas, various minor pieces, and then the three gigantic works begun earlier. For the *Missa solemnis*, Beethoven made a careful study of the text and then set it in a way that embodied its grandeur and depth of meaning, drawing out its implications in every possible way. The 'Diabelli' Variations were based on a trivial waltz tune by Anton Diabelli, who had invited all Vienna's composers to write a single variation. While 50 other composers duly wrote their variation, Beethoven responded with 33, each developing some aspect of the theme in an unexpected way. The Ninth Symphony, besides its unprecedented length, introduces solo and choral voices in its finale, in a setting of Friedrich Schiller's ode *An die Freude* ('To Joy'). Beethoven, by now almost completely deaf, directed its première as best he could on 7 May 1824, at a concert that also included movements from his *Missa solemnis*.

THE LATE QUARTETS

By May 1824 Beethoven was under pressure to return to the medium of the string quartet, and he spent his next two and a half years almost entirely occupied by this genre, producing works of extraordinary originality. Three were sent to the Russian Prince Galitzin (1794–1866) – op. 127 in E flat, op. 132 in A minor, and op. 130 in B flat – and two more followed (op. 131 in C sharp minor and op. 135 in F). Here Beethoven employed what he called 'a new kind of part-writing', in which all the instruments have melodic interest and the motivic material is shared out in novel and unexpected ways.

Beethoven also explored structural and formal innovations: the finale of op. 130, for example, was a massive fugue that rather dwarfed the rest of the quartet, and he eventually replaced it by a new finale of more normal size, publishing the original one separately as *Grosse Fuge* ('Great Fugue'). He then embarked on a string quintet, but by now his health was failing. A strained relationship with his nephew had led to the latter attempting suicide in August 1826, and he left to join the army the following January. Beethoven remained in bed, suffering from dropsy and liver failure, and finally died on 26 March 1827.

Schubert ▶ p. 182

The Classical Era

PERSONALITIES

Abel, Carl Friedrich

(Á'-bel, Kärl Frē'-drikh) 1723–87

GERMAN COMPOSER

Abel was born at Cöthen, where his father played in **J. S. Bach**'s group. In 1759 he settled in London, becoming a chamber musician to Queen Charlotte and, with J. C. Bach, establishing in 1764 a concert series that brought new continental music to English audiences. He wrote sonatas, quartets and other chamber works, as well as concertos and symphonies (one was long thought a youthful work of **Mozart**'s), in a graceful, genial, *galant* style. Abel was the last great viola da gamba player; there is a fine Gainsborough portrait of him with his instrument.

Arne, Thomas Augustine

1710–78

ENGLISH COMPOSER

Arne was the son of an upholsterer in Covent Garden. As a Roman Catholic, he had no access to the usual opportunities for advancement as a musician through a church appointment. In the 1730s, he became involved with putting on English-language opera performances in London, earning a reputation as a skilful theatre composer, and was also active in the music for the pleasure gardens.

His numerous theatre works include masques (notably *Comus*, 1738, and *Alfred*, 1740), operas (including *Thomas and Sally*, 1760) and incidental music, and among his songs are many delightful and popular Shakespeare settings (for example 'Where the bee sucks'). In 1762 he wrote the fine *Artaxerxes*, an English opera in the Italian style, for which he translated the libretto from the Metastasio original. Reportedly not the most agreeable of men, Arne had a fine gift for the setting of English words and a fresh melodic style very much his own.

Bach, Carl Philipp Emanuel

(Bākh, Kärl Fē'-lip E-mä'-nōō-el) 1714–88

GERMAN COMPOSER

In the eighteenth century, 'Bach' usually meant C. P. E. Bach, not his father Johann Sebastian. Born in Weimar, he studied under his father, then read law at the university in Frankfurt an der Oder. He took up a post in Berlin at the court of Prince Frederick, later Frederick the Great, serving there, accompanying the flute-playing king and his orchestra for nearly 30 years, composing keyboard sonatas, chamber music and concertos in a forward-looking, often intensely expressive style (the 'empfindsamer Stil'). But opportunities there were circumscribed and in 1768 he moved to Hamburg as city music director, responsible for teaching and for the music in five churches. He composed church music and also wrote symphonies of a markedly individual, dramatic and fiery character. He was the leading north German composer of his time and an important musical thinker; his enormously influential *Essay on the True Art of Keyboard Playing* (1753, 1762) is widely used to establish performance style in mid eighteenth-century music.

BOCCHERINI MINUET

The 'Boccherini minuet' – an extract from one of his string quintets – is a very familiar tune. It was used in *The Lavender Hill Mob*, where the crooks deceive their landlady into thinking they are innocently and delicately playing chamber music by putting on a record of the minuet.

POPULAR MELODY *Boccherini*

Bach, Johann Christian

(Bākh, Yō'-hän Krēst'-yän) 1735–82

GERMAN COMPOSER

J. S. Bach's youngest son was known as the London Bach. Earlier he was the Milan Bach: after studying with his father and his half-brother Carl Philipp Emanuel in Berlin, he had gone to Italy, studying in Bologna, embracing Roman Catholicism and becoming organist at Milan Cathedral, and composing operas for theatres in Turin and Naples. In 1762 he went to write operas in London, where he settled as music master to Queen Charlotte and became a fashionable teacher. His instrumental music won favour at the concerts he gave with Abel and more widely. Later he wrote operas for Mannheim and Paris. But his reputation faded and he died young, in straitened circumstances. His music – piano sonatas (he was an early exponent of the forte-piano), quintets and other chamber works, concertos (for piano and for groups of instruments) and many symphonies – is characterized by its warmth, its elegance and its clarity of design. The fusion of German and Italian elements, and his desire to write pleasingly for London audiences, produced music of a unique grace and polish that much influenced the young Mozart.

(BL) Johann Christian Bach by Thomas Gainsborough
Gainsborough's painting immortalizes Johann Sebastian's youngest son, known as the 'London Bach'.
(ML) Elizabeth Billington
The famous opera singer in Thomas Arne's Artaxerxes.
(TR) The 'Boccherini Minuet'
Boccherini's minuet is an extract from one of his string quintets; it has become familiar through its use in the film The Lavender Hill Mob.

WRITERS ABOUT MUSIC

It was in the late eighteenth century, as Enlightenment thinking developed, that the business of writing about music for an informed public began to flourish. There were historians, such as Padre Martini, in Italy, La Borde in France, Friedrich Wilhelm Marpurg in Germany and Charles Burney in England; there were lexicographers; and there were theorists, eager to codify compositional practices.

There were also pedagogical writers, explaining performance techniques for the benefit of students and amateurs. This tradition goes back to the late Baroque, but there are three important mid-century writers who between them summarize many aspects of performance: C. P. E. Bach on the keyboard, Leopold Mozart on the violin and **Johann Joachim Quantz** (1697–1773) on the flute. A little later comes D. G. Türk's book on the keyboard. The growing world of amateur music-making was well served.

In France, musical lexicography flourished from the beginning of the century, and the rationalist spirit found its greatest outlet in the *Encyclopédie* of Diderot and D'Alembert, which gave extensive coverage to music. Several French aestheticians wrote on music as an imitation of nature. Rameau's writings take rationalist music theory to its ultimate. The polemical pamphlet also flourished, especially in the numerous operatic disputes.

Bach, Wilhelm Friedemann

(Bákh, Vil'-helm Frē'-da-mán) 1710–84

GERMAN COMPOSER

The eldest son of J. S. Bach, Wilhelm Friedemann studied with his father and at Leipzig University. He was organist at the Dresden Sophienkirche and, from 1746, at the Liebfrauenkirche in Halle, but in the 1760s he embarked on a precarious freelance career, ending up in Berlin. He composed church cantatas, keyboard, chamber and orchestral music, more conservative in style than that of his brothers but showing striking originality in his melodic lines, his harmony and his counterpoint: his keyboard polonaises in particular contain music of remarkable intensity. However, the disturbed circumstances of his life meant that his gifts were never quite fully realized.

Benda, Georg

(Ben'-dá, Gā-ôrg) 1722–95

BOHEMIAN COMPOSER

Born at Staré Benátky in Bohemia into a family of musicians (his brother Franz was a violinist and composer at Frederick the Great's court in Berlin), Benda went to Germany as a young man and spent most of his working career as *Kapellmeister* at Gotha; he retired in 1778. He is remembered chiefly for his German operas and especially his melodramas, in which a spoken text is illustrated by a highly expressive background of instrumental music. His *Ariadne auf Naxos* (1774), *Medea* and *Romeo und Julie* (1776) greatly impressed Mozart, who imitated their style in works of his own.

Boccherini, Luigi

(Bŏk-ker-ē'-nē, Loō-ē'-gē) 1743–1805

ITALIAN COMPOSER

The son of a musician in Lucca, Boccherini was trained by his father and in Rome as a composer and cellist. He made his début at 13 and undertook several journeys to play in Vienna. In 1766 he went on a concert tour which took him to Paris and Madrid, where he was offered a post in the service of the Infante. He spent the rest of his life in Spain, working for various patrons, also composing for Friedrich Wilhelm II of Prussia, to whom he posted many chamber works. Boccherini wrote symphonies, cello concertos (which he originally played himself) and much chamber music, including over a hundred string quintets (mostly with two cellos) and almost as many quartets and trios. He favoured a gentle, rather melancholy manner, laying much stress on highly decorative lines, colourful, dynamic textures and a suave, graceful melodic style; he sometimes experimented with cyclic forms, ingeniously interleaving sections of movements.

THE BACH DYNASTY

Musical abilities often pass down through generations. In no family have they displayed themselves for as long or as extensively as in the Bach's.

The earliest known musician was Veit Bach, a baker, probably from what is now Bratislava in Slovakia, who settled in the Thuringian village of Wechmar in the mid-sixteenth century (his bakery still stands): he was also a 'Spielmann' (fiddler or minstrel). After four generations there were 11 Bachs pursuing musical careers in the area; there were 19 in the next (including J. S.) and 25 in the one after. The last, W. F. E. Bach, J. S. Bach's grandson, died in 1845.

Many were humble town musicians, paid by the municipality to play in bands on ceremonial and religious occasions, or to play hymns from church towers. Others were *Kantors* (teachers and music directors), church organists, *Kapellmeisters* (directors of musical establishments) or court musicians. Bachs are found across Thuringia, especially in the cluster of small towns around Eisenach, Ohrdruf, Erfurt and Amstadt, but also further afield. The family sustained this position until the traditions of local Lutheranism and, in particular, the social systems that gave rise to the prevalence of family traditions through trade guilds dissolved.

Boyce, William

1711–79

ENGLISH COMPOSER

A Londoner, Boyce was a chorister at St Paul's and a pupil of Maurice Greene (1696–1755) and J. C. Pepusch (1667–1752). He held posts as organist, notably at the Chapel Royal, and became Master of the King's Musick in 1755. In that capacity he composed many court odes; he also wrote sacred music and stage works (his operas include *The Chaplet*, 1749, and *The Shepherd's Lottery*, 1751; there is also a serenata, almost voluptuous in tone, on the Song of Solomon). His instrumental music includes fine trio sonatas and overtures. His sure technique and sturdy, tuneful tone are distinctive. Boyce was a keen musical antiquarian and produced an important edition of *English Cathedral Music* (1760–73).

Burney, Charles

1726–1814

ENGLISH MUSIC THEORIST AND WRITER

Burney, the most important English writer on music of his time, was born in Shrewsbury and brought up in Chester. There he met Arne, to whom he was apprenticed. Later he took posts as organist and worked in the London theatres. In the 1770s he made two long journeys through France, Italy, Germany and the Low Countries, meeting numerous musicians and reporting in two books on the state of music. These were a preparation for his four-volume *General History of Music* (1776–89), which although lacking in historical sympathy is remarkably rich and elegantly written. Burney composed (rather feebly), knew **Handel** and **Haydn** and wrote about both, produced numerous letters, diaries and memoirs and was always full of ideas and ambitions. He was a member of the Thrale circle of intellectuals and a friend of Dr Johnson, who said of him: 'I much question if there is in the world such another man for mind, intelligence, and manners.'

Cimarosa, Domenico

(Chē-má-rô'-zá, Dō-mā'-nē-kō) 1749–1801

ITALIAN COMPOSER

Trained in Naples, Cimarosa quickly launched himself on an operatic career with successes in Naples, Rome and Venice. In 1787 he was invited to St Petersburg. On the way home he paused at Vienna, where his *Il matrimonio segreto* ('The Secret Marriage') had a huge success in 1792 – uniquely, the entire opera was encored. Back in Naples, he got into trouble because of his Republican sympathies, so he went to Venice, where he died (possibly poisoned). He was thought in his day the equal of Mozart and Haydn for his 70-odd operas, serious as well as comic; it is the latter that survive, for their sparkle, vivacity and melodic warmth.

J. S. Bach ► p. 106 Handel ► p. 112 Haydn ► p. 140 Mozart ► p. 144 Quantz ► p. 119

Clementi, Muzio

(Klā-mān'-tē, Mōōdz'-yō) 1752–1832

ITALIAN PIANIST AND COMPOSER

Born in Rome, at about 15 Clementi went to England and spent seven years in Dorset becoming an accomplished keyboard player. Most of his career was in London, where he was involved in piano manufacture and publishing, playing and composing. He undertook extended concert tours on the continent, competed with Mozart and published works by **Beethoven**. He wrote some symphonies but is chiefly admired for his many piano sonatas, fluently written, sometimes technically very demanding and often highly expressive. He was the leader of a group of London composers eager to establish a new style of piano writing.

Da Ponte, Lorenzo

(Da Pōn'-tē, Lō-rĕn'-tsō) 1749–1838

ITALIAN LIBRETTIST

Da Ponte was born in Ceneda (now Vittoria Veneto) as Emanuele Conegliano, and took the name Da Ponte when his family converted from Judaism. He trained for the priesthood, but his political and sexual liberalism and his literary gifts led him elsewhere. As court poet in Vienna (1783–91) he wrote librettos, notably for Mozart (*Le nozze di Figaro*, *Don Giovanni* and *Così fan tutte*). He worked at theatres in London during 1794–1805, then went to the US, where he taught, traded and translated. He wrote or arranged some 50 librettos, showing an extraordinary skill and fluency as a writer and a sharp, perceptive wit.

Dibdin, Charles

1745–1814

ENGLISH COMPOSER

Dibdin began as a chorus singer at Covent Garden Theatre, London. He composed many English operas and other dramatic pieces, spending most of his life around the London theatres and pleasure gardens (with journeys to France to elude his creditors and other enemies). His chief success came with his one-man 'Table Entertainments', songs and readings, often in comic accents; he also wrote novels, librettos, memoirs and travel books. Above all, Dibdin was a gifted composer of songs, but his awkward personality obstructed the realization of his gifts.

Dittersdorf, Carl Ditters von

(Dit'-ters-dôrf, Kärl Dit'-ters fun) 1739–99

AUSTRIAN COMPOSER

One of the most important Viennese composers in the age of Haydn and Mozart, Dittersdorf held posts as violinist, composer and *Kapellmeister* in Vienna, Grosswardein (now Oradea, Romania) and other courts in the Austrian Empire. He was a prolific composer, particularly of symphonies (among them 12 based on texts from Ovid's *Metamorphoses*), chamber music including some admired string quartets, and operas, of which those to German texts (Singspiels, for example *Doktor und Apotheker*, 'Doctor and Apothecary', 1786) are particularly successful for their spirited, popular melodies and their effective use of ensembles. He was an ingenious composer, working in a style similar to Haydn's, with a vein of wit very much his own.

Galuppi, Baldassare

(Gá-lōōp'-pē, Bál-dás-sá'-rā) 1706–85

ITALIAN COMPOSER

Galuppi had great influence on the development of ***opera buffa***. Most of his career was spent in his native Venice, apart from spells in London in the 1740s and St Petersburg in the 1760s. He was *maestro di cappella* at St Mark's and worked at the girls' orphanage-conservatories. His music is notable for its fluent, elegant melody and its fresh, lucid style. Most of his comic operas are to librettos by the Venetian dramatist Carlo Goldoni; with him he created the 'chain finale', where successive sections in different rhythm, tempo and texture, responding to the dramatic situation, convey the flux of emotions portrayed.

ORFEO

Gluck's *Orfeo* has one number known beyond its original context: the 'Dance of the Blessed Spirits', a hauntingly beautiful dance, heard when Orpheus enters the Elysian Fields. The floating melody, with its softly moving accompaniment, perfectly captures the unearthly joy of the moment.

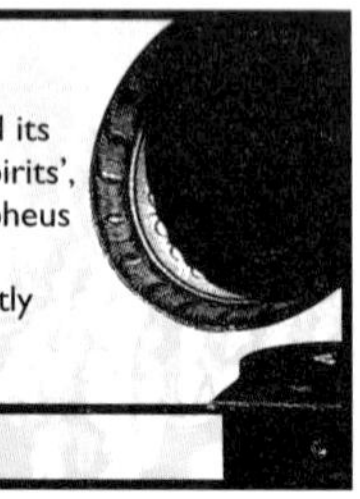

POPULAR MELODY *Gluck*

Gluck, Christoph Willibald von

(Glōōk, Khrēs'-tōf Vil'-lē-bált fun) 1714–87

BOHEMIAN COMPOSER

Gluck was born in Erasbach, by the Czech-German border; his native language may well have been Czech. His father, a forester, was opposed to a musical career, but the boy left home at 13 to study in Prague, where he took musical posts and went briefly to the university. At about 20 he went to Vienna, obtaining work as a musician in an aristocratic household; after two years he took a similar post in Milan. Opera was, and remained, his central interest, and in 1741 his first opera, *Artaserse*, opened the season at Milan's main opera-house. More followed, there and in other Italian centres. In 1745 he went to England, where he gave two new operas in London. More travel followed, with opera performances in several centres (Copenhagen, Dresden, Naples, Prague), but in 1752 Gluck settled in Vienna as director of a princely musical establishment. There he became involved with the court theatres, organizing performances including several of French ***opéras comiques*** and composing works in Italian for court entertainments. By 1759 he held a salaried post at the court theatre.

GLUCK'S REFORM OF OPERA

Gluck was not the only reformer of opera. A number of Italians, notably Jommelli and Traetta, had worked along similar lines, but Gluck, although his purely musical gifts were circumscribed, was the greatest and the most influential. He described the reforms in the famous preface to the published score of *Alceste* (1767): 'When I undertook to write the music for *Alceste*, I resolved to divest it entirely of those abuses, introduced by the misguided vanity of singers or the excessive complaisance of composers, that have so long disfigured Italian opera and made it ... so ridiculous and boring'. This involved making the music serve the drama through its expression of the situations and their attendant emotions without interruption by orchestral ***ritornellos*** or florid and ornamental singing; making the overture relevant to the drama and the orchestration apt to the emotions expressed; avoiding the gratuitous repetition of words, and breaking down the 'artificial' divisions between recitative and aria so as to produce a more continuous texture – 'in short, to abolish,' he wrote, 'all those abuses against which good sense and reason have long cried out in vain'.

He also abandoned the complex historical and dynastic plots used by Metastasio and his followers, full of disguises and intrigues and subplots, in favour of simple, direct, classical ones, in which poetry, dance, scenery and music were at one. He sought 'a beautiful simplicity'; and in his finest works, *Orfeo* (1762), *Alceste* and *Iphigénie en Tauride* (1774), his capacity for the expression of profound emotion – ranging through serenity, grief, terror, fury and passionate love – in a manner entirely his own gives his operas a unique force and visionary power.

opera buffa ▶ p. 360 *opéra comique* ▶ p. 361 *ritornello* ▶ p. 361

OPERA IN THE VERNACULAR

Opera was essentially an Italian genre: it had been born in Florence, come to its first maturity in Venice and developed next in Naples and Rome. However, Italian art of all sorts was admired across Europe, and opera soon took root in France, Austria, Germany, England and Spain, even in distant Sweden and Russia.

At first this was Italian opera, particularly in the courtly establishments where this luxury entertainment could be afforded and where Italian could be understood. Centres for Italian opera in the early to mid-eighteenth century included Vienna, Munich, Stuttgart, Dresden, London, Prague and St Petersburg. But with the development of public opera-houses and the advent of a merchant class eager to savour the pleasures that had generally been the preserve of the aristocracy, a need arose for opera in a language these audiences could understand.

German Opera

In Germany, opera in the vernacular began early: in 1678 an opera-house opened in Hamburg – a trading city with no court, but with a large middle class. Leipzig, another city with no court, soon followed. But these and similar enterprises ran foul of church authorities and floundered. A firm German-language operatic tradition had to wait until the mid-eighteenth century, when works of the genre now called Singspiel (originally meaning simply a play with music) were given, chiefly translations of works from England. In Vienna, Emperor Joseph II established a Nationaltheater to give German opera in 1776, but it had limited success and was scrapped in 1783. Nevertheless, a new genre had been created: German opera, with songs and spoken dialogue.

Anglo-French Influences

In France there was a different situation. There, an Italian-born composer, **Jean-Baptiste Lully** (1632–87), had established a new type of opera, drawing on Italian style and French traditions of theatrical declamation. The rise of a middle-class opera came about through the popular Paris fair theatres, where troupes put on lively, often scandalous musical entertainments. This eventually led to the rise of *opéra comique*, French-language opera with spoken dialogue. In England, *The Beggar's Opera*, a political and social parody with songs culled from a variety of sources, had in 1728 created a scandal. This was a 'ballad opera' – an opera based on popular ballads – as were many in the succeeding years, but more were freshly composed, with songs and English-language dialogue.

In these countries, and others, vernacular opera avoided the elaborate plots used in serious opera in favour of simpler tales, often in a rural setting, predominantly about young lovers whose happiness is threatened by parents or elderly lechers. Composers of this genre used a much more direct musical style than those who wrote serious Italian operas, with less florid vocal writing, which suited the Italian language far better than any other anyway.

CHANGE OF DIRECTION

Up to this time, most of Gluck's works had been fairly traditional in manner, within the usual style of Italian serious opera. But now, in collaboration with two other artists strongly influenced by Enlightenment ideals, the poet Raniero Calzabigi and the choreographer Gasparo Angiolini, he experimented with new styles. First, they produced together a ballet based on the Don Juan story, given in 1761 – a *ballet d'action* in which the dance is designed to be dramatic and expressive of the action rather than purely decorative (as it had generally been until then). This was found powerful and rather alarming by the audiences. Their next work, the following year, was the opera *Orfeo ed Euridice* (given in celebration of the emperor's nameday, it had to have a happy ending, with Eurydice restored to life).

Orfeo is the first of what are known as Gluck's 'reform' operas, in which he took radical steps to create a new kind of work in which all elements were allied to serve the drama and to appeal directly and powerfully to the audience's emotions. It was followed up, in 1767, with *Alceste*, in which his and Calzabigi's new dramatic principles were carried a stage further; both operas were immensely successful in Vienna, although a third, *Paride ed Elena* (1770), was not.

REVISING FRENCH OPERA

Gluck, however, was not content with success in Italian opera in Vienna: he wanted to apply his principles to French opera (in which to some extent they had originated). In 1774 he gave two operas in Paris, *Iphigénie en Aulide* and a much-revised French version of *Orfeo*. He challenged tradition even more squarely in 1776, when he wrote *Armide*, of which Lully had made a setting that was regarded as a classic. He went on to a French revision of *Alceste* (1777) and the noble *Iphigénie en Tauride* (1779); this, his greatest success in Paris, was quickly followed by his greatest failure, *Echo et Narcisse* (1779).

Gluck finally returned to Vienna in 1779; he wrote some songs and made some revisions to his operas. But with uncertain health, and no pressing need to work (he had married well, and received a pension appropriate to his high standing), he abandoned plans for a journey to London and Paris and was ready for retirement. He heard and admired operas by Mozart, but regarded Salieri as his heir in the world of opera. He died in 1787.

(L) Christoph Willibald von Gluck
Gluck travelled extensively in Europe and incorporated the styles he found there into his works.
***(BR)* Parnaso Confuso**
Contemporaneous performance of Gluck's opera.

Beethoven ▶ p. 150 Lully ▶ p. 84

Gossec, François-Joseph
(Gu-sek', Frän-swä Zhō-zef') 1734–1829
BELGIAN (FRENCH) COMPOSER
Born in what is now the French-speaking part of Belgium, Gossec spent most of his career in Paris as a theatre composer, violinist and director of musical organizations, including the Concert Spirituel, the Ecole Royale de Chant and (after the Revolution) the band of the Garde Nationale. He wrote operas and ballets for the Opéra and the Comédie-Italienne and also revolutionary hymns and sacred and instrumental works; later he taught at the new Conservatoire. A prolific composer, he was important chiefly as the leading writer of symphonies in France in his time and for his post-Revolution role as civic composer and 'democratizer of art'.

Graun, Carl Heinrich
(Groun, Kârl Hīn'-rikh) 1703/4–59
GERMAN COMPOSER
Graun worked in the opera at Dresden and then at Brunswick (where he wrote six operas), before becoming *Kapellmeister* in 1735 to Frederick, the Prussian prince, promoted to royal *Kapellmeister* when Frederick (the Great) acceded in 1740. He was in charge of the new Berlin court opera, for which he wrote 26 works (some, including the admired *Montezuma*, 1755, have librettos by Frederick). Graun was particularly admired for his intense, richly inventive Passion, *Der Tod Jesu* ('The Death of Jesus', 1755). His brother Johann Gottlieb (1702/3–1771), *Konzertmeister* at the Berlin opera, was a prolific and gifted instrumental composer.

Grétry, André-Ernest-Modeste
(Grā'-trē, Än-drā Âr-nest' Mō-dest') 1741–1813
BELGIAN (FRENCH) COMPOSER
Born in Liège, Grétry studied in Rome and in 1767 settled in Paris. With the success the next year of *Le Huron* he quickly became the leading composer of *opéra comique*, having particular successes with *Zémire et Azor* (1771), *La caravane du Caire* ('The Caravan of Cairo', 1783) and *Richard Coeur-de-Lion* ('Richard the Lionheart', 1784); he also wrote, less successfully, for the Opéra, although he helped fuse the comic and the serious in parallel to developments in Italian opera. He was a gifted melodist, drawing on Italian traditions as well as those of French declamation, and he characterized effectively through his fresh, expressive music.

Hasse, Johann Adolf
(Häs'-se, Yō'-hän Ä'-dolf) 1699–1783
GERMAN COMPOSER AND TENOR
Born just outside Hamburg, Hasse became the leading Italian opera composer of his time. He began his career as a tenor, went to Italy for training (under **Alessandro Scarlatti**, 1660–1725, and others), and had operas given in Naples; he married Faustina Bordoni (1700–81), a famous soprano who had sung for Handel in London. He held a post as *Kapellmeister* at the Italianate Dresden court, but was in constant demand elsewhere, especially in Naples, Venice and above all Vienna. Metastasio favoured him above all others who set his librettos; a graceful and polished melodist, he was called by Burney 'the most natural, elegant, and judicious composer of vocal music, as well as the most voluminous'. In his late years he chiefly wrote sacred music.

Hiller, Johann Adam
1728–1804
GERMAN COMPOSER
Hiller worked for most of his life in Leipzig, where he directed concerts, had charge of the music for various churches, founded choirs, a music school and a musical society, wrote criticism for an influential music periodical, published musical treatises and eventually became *Kantor* of St Thomas's Church (the post once held by J. S. Bach). His most important contribution, however, lay in his theatre works: he provided incidental music, lively and expressive, to middle-class comedies, so playing a central role in the creation of the north German Singspiel as well as fuelling the development of a German song tradition.

Hook, James
1746–1827
ENGLISH COMPOSER AND ORGANIST
Born in Norwich, Hook was musically precocious, performing in public when he was six and composing an opera at eight. At 17 he settled in London as an organist, and soon obtained posts as organist and composer at Marylebone Pleasure Gardens and then (in 1774) at Vauxhall, retiring in 1820. A fluent composer, he wrote numerous light and tuneful sonatas and songs, concertos (he played one every night in the season at Vauxhall) and comic operas, as well as didactic works for his teaching (*Guida di Musica*). Influenced by J. C. Bach and later by Haydn, he was the leading native British composer in the *galant* style.

Jommelli, Nicolò
(Zhō-me'-lē, Nik'-kō-lō) 1714–74
ITALIAN COMPOSER

Among the many opera composers of this period hailing from Naples, Jommelli was the greatest. His first comic opera was given in the city in 1737. It was in Rome that his first serious opera was performed, in 1740, and he then moved first to Bologna and after that to Venice, occupied as much with sacred music as with the opera-house. His most important works were written for the Württemberg court at Stuttgart, where he was resident 1754–69; after that he composed mainly in Italy and, by correspondence, for Lisbon. He wrote about 100 stage works, 60 of them serious operas, mainly to librettos by Metastasio. He was much concerned with creating effective musical drama and reducing the primacy accorded to singers: he added accompanied recitatives, ensembles, choruses and dances, used more flexible forms, removed superfluous elements, and handled the orchestra vividly to enhance the drama. He also wrote many oratorios and cantatas as well as liturgical works.

Krebs, Johann Ludwig
(Kreps, Yō'-hän Lōōd'-vikh) 1713–80
GERMAN COMPOSER
Like his father, Johann Tobias (1690–1762), Krebs was a pupil of J. S. Bach; he attended St Thomas's School in Leipzig for nine years and won a warm testimonial from the great man. He was organist at Zwickau from 1737, then from 1744 at Zeitz and finally at Gotha (he applied unsuccessfully for the succession to Bach at Leipzig in 1750). Admired for his 'full and masterly manner of playing the organ', he was primarily a composer for the keyboard, influenced by Bach in his adherence to contrapuntal writing at a time when it was becoming unfashionable, but also affected by the new *galant* style. He wrote prolifically for the organ and published many suites and other works for the harpsichord; he also produced sacred and instrumental music.

Martín y Soler, Vicente
(Mär'-tī-nī So-le, Fi'-thēn-ti) 1754–1806
SPANISH COMPOSER
Martín y Soler had moved to Naples by 1777, when his *Ifigenia in Aulide* was staged there. By the early 1780s, his operas were being given in north Italy and he moved to Venice; from this time on he wrote only comic operas. Three years later he was in Vienna, where he had important successes in operas

minuet ▶ p. 360 *opera seria* ▶ p. 361

to texts by Da Ponte, among them *Una cosa rara* ('A Rare Thing', 1786 – remembered through Mozart's quotation of it in the *Don Giovanni* supper scene). Later he went to St Petersburg, where his works included an opera to a text by Catherine the Great, to London, where he collaborated again with Da Ponte, and back to Russia where he died. He was admired for his lyrical, pastoral style, full of melodic grace and charm; in his day, his operas won at least as much popularity as Mozart's.

Martini, Giovanni Battista

(Mär-tē'-nē, Jō-vän'-nē Bät-tēs'-tä) 1706–84

ITALIAN THEORIST AND COMPOSER

Padre Martini, as he was always known, was the most influential theorist and musical thinker of his time. He was born in Bologna, traditionally a centre of learning, where he studied with his father and leading musicians before entering a monastery. He returned to Bologna as organist and then as *maestro di cappella* at San Francesco, and was ordained in 1729. He composed much music, conservative in style, had many students, wrote an extended history of music and several theoretical works, and conducted a lively correspondence on musical matters with composers and others (some 6,000 letters survive); J. C. Bach, Grétry, Jommelli and Mozart are among those who had lessons with him. He was revered as the ultimate arbiter on matters musical. Burney wrote that, 'upon so short an acquaintance, I never liked any man more; and I felt as little reserve with him after a few hours' conversation, as with an old friend or beloved brother'. Martini assembled a large library and a fine collection of musicians' portraits, which are preserved today in the Civico Museo Bibliografico Musicale in Bologna.

Metastasio, Pietro

(Met-tä-shtä-syō, Pi-ēt'-trō) 1698–1782

ITALIAN LIBRETTIST AND POET

Metastasio was the leading Italian librettist of his era, and creator of the tradition of a particular kind of serious opera. He was born in Rome, worked initially there and in Venice, and settled in Vienna in 1730 as poet to the imperial Habsburg court. He wrote numerous texts for music, elegant and mellifluous in style, of which the most famous were his 27 for three-act heroic operas, usually with elaborate plots on classical, historic or dynastic themes and with a strong moral content, featuring noble behaviour and inner conflict (usually duty v. passion) and showing the triumph of virtue and reason as well as divine (or royal) benevolence. Metastasio's librettos, of which the most popular were *Alessandro nell'Indie* ('Alexander in India') and *Artaserse* ('Artaxerxes'), provided the back-bone for Italian ***opera seria*** throughout Europe; many were set repeatedly and modified as tastes changed. He took a deep interest in their settings and corre-sponded voluminously with the various composers.

Monn, Matthias Georg

(Mon, Mät-tē'-äs Gā'-ōrg) 1717–50

AUSTRIAN COMPOSER

Although he died at the middle of the century, Monn was an important figure in the development of the symphony. A Viennese (he was organist at the Karlkirche), he wrote some 21 symphonies, which make early use of the procedures of classical sonata form; all are in three movements except one, from 1740, which is probably the first four-movement symphony, with a **minuet** as third movement. His concertos, including seven for harpsichord and one for cello (of which **Schoenberg** made an edition), also foreshadow later classical forms. Monn's brother J. C. Monn (1726–82) was also a composer.

Paisiello, Giovanni

(Pī-sē-el'-lō, Jō-vän'-nē) 1740–1816

ITALIAN COMPOSER

Paisiello was trained in Naples and had early successes as an opera composer there and in north Italy. He served as court composer to Catherine the Great in St Petersburg, 1776–84; there, in 1782, he wrote *Il barbiere di Siviglia*, his most admired comic opera. He returned to Italy and spent most of his time in Naples, except for a spell in Paris, directing the music for Napoleon's chapel. Most of his operas are comic, written in a lively, spirited style, but some are sentimental comedy (*Nina*, 1789), warmer and more colourful in manner. Later in his life he wrote mainly serious works.

LONDON PLEASURE GARDENS

The London Pleasure Gardens, open from the late spring until the early autumn each year, were an important site for music-making. The earliest, among them Marylebone, were founded about 1660. All social classes met and mixed in the gardens; there were promenades, stalls, sideshows and restaurants (it was said that for a shilling you could buy a slice of beef or ham, carved so thin that you could read a newspaper through it). Their heyday was in the middle and late eighteenth century, when three in particular – Marylebone, Ranelagh and above all Vauxhall – provided music regularly, and of a high order, as the central evening's entertainment.

These and several others had specially designed features for music-making. In Ranelagh there was a large Rotunda for concerts and balls; Vauxhall had a concert room, 'the Umbrella', and a raised, open-air bandstand shaped as a Moorish-Gothic temple, as well as a statue of Handel by Roubiliac erected in 1738 (which the *Daily Post* thought fitting, since Handel's harmony had 'so often charm'd even the greatest crouds into the profoundest calm and the most decent Behaviour'). Many eminent London composers, including Arne, Samuel Arnold (the Westminster Abbey organist) and Hook, held appointments as musical directors at the pleasure gardens; Handel himself and J. C. Bach appeared there. And at this time of the year – out of the concert and opera seasons – the London orchestra musicians could find work there. The concerts included symphonies and concertos, songs, glees, choruses and sometimes short operas; many com-posers, notably Arne, J. C. Bach and Hook, wrote music specially. Changing social circumstances led to the gradual closing down of the gardens, mostly in the early nineteenth century.

(BL) Montezuma
Costume for the Classical German opera Montezuma, *by Carl Heinrich Graun*
(TL) Nicolò Jommelli
Jommelli originally wrote comic opera, but moved to serious opera in 1740.
(R) Vauxhall Gardens
Pleasure Gardens such as Vauxhall increased in popularity throughout the Classical era.

A. Scarlatti ▶ p. 120 Schoenberg ▶ p. 295

Philidor, François-André-Danican

(Fē-lē-dôr', Frān-swä Ān-drā' Dä-nē-kān) 1726–95

FRENCH COMPOSER

Coming from a large family of musicians associated with the French court, Philidor was a pupil of André Campra (1660–1744). He achieved international fame as a chess player and played much in England as well as in France. His main musical contribution came in his *opéras comiques*; he wrote more than 20, of which the best known is *Tom Jones* (1765); they show Italian influence in their expressive melody and their well-managed ensembles. Philidor also wrote serious operas, notably *Ernelinde* (1767), the first French opera with Italian-style arias rather than the traditional airs.

Piccinni, Niccolò

(Pit-chin'-nē, Nik'-kō-lō) 1728–1800

ITALIAN COMPOSER

Piccinni trained in Naples and had operas, serious as well as comic, staged there from 1754; he held posts at the cathedral and at court. In 1760 he enjoyed a spectacular success in Rome with *La buona figliuola* ('The Good Son'), to a Goldoni libretto after Samuel Richardson's *Pamela*; this was only one of nearly 100 operas, serious and comic, from the years up to 1776. That year he went to Paris to write French *tragédies* for the Opéra and (briefly) to direct an Italian *opera buffa* company. He was praised for the vigour and animation of his Italian operas; his originality and his rich orchestral writing; and his achievement in Paris of synthesizing French and Italian elements helped establish an international style.

Salieri, Antonio

(Säl-yâr'-ē, Än-tōn'-yō) 1750–1825

ITALIAN COMPOSER

Born in north Italy, Salieri went to Vienna when he was 15. He had several early successes and at 24 became court composer and conductor of the opera, and *Kapellmeister* 14 years later. He visited Italy where, in 1778, he wrote the opera for the opening of La Scala, Milan, and in the 1780s Paris, where he was regarded as Gluck's true successor (that was also Gluck's view) and enjoyed successes with *Les Danaïdes* ('The Danaids', 1784) and *Tarare* (1787), works of an exalted, original and rather austere post-Gluckian style. His later music is more conventional. Salieri served the Viennese court for 50 years; he was an admired teacher and a generous man and did much for music and musicians in the city.

Schobert, Johann

(Shō'-bârt, Yō'-hän) c. 1735–66

GERMAN COMPOSER

Schobert went to Paris about 1760 and became established as a harpsichordist and composer in the employment of the Prince of Conti. He wrote 43 sonatas (or sinfonias) for harpsichord – most of them with accompaniments for strings – and five harpsichord concertos; they are warm and fresh in expression and often technically demanding. Mozart drew on them for his early concerto arrangements. Schobert died, along with his family, from eating poisonous mushrooms.

Stamitz, Johann Wenzel Anton

(Shtä'-mit, Yō'-hän Vent'-zel Än'-tōn) 1717–57

BOHEMIAN COMPOSER

Born in Bohemia, by 1741 Stamitz was at the Mannheim court, where he became leading violinist in 1743, *Konzertmeister* soon after, and director in 1750. He made the Mannheim orchestra the most famous in Europe for its discipline and its capacity to achieve new effects. Although he composed concertos and chamber music, it is principally for his symphonies that he is important. He was the first to write four-movement works consistently, and he introduced a new style of orchestration, in which the roles assigned to the wind instruments – often used for sustaining and giving harmonic support – are distinct from those of the strings. Influenced by Italian composers, especially Jommelli, and by the virtuosity of his orchestra, he developed a new, dynamic style of orchestral composition. Stamitz's sons, Carl (1745–1801) and Anton (1750–*c.* 1800), were also composers.

FRENCH OPERATIC DISPUTES

When, at the beginning of the eighteenth century, French critics came into contact with Italian opera, many felt that the musical freedom of the Italians offered something that French opera, so closely tied to theatrical declamatory traditions, made impossible. The Abbé Raguenet, enamoured of Italian singing and the supporting instrumental skills, mocked French opera, which was staunchly defended as more 'rational' by Le Cerf de la Viéville.

The operatic début of **Jean-Philippe Rameau** (1683–1764) was also greeted by criticism. Most writers sided with the Ramistes, acknowledging the splendour of his *Hippolyte et Aricie* (1733), but a few conservative Lullistes accused him of betraying the Lully tradition and admitting Italian features.

The most heated of the disputes was the Querelle des Bouffons of the early 1750s, when an Italian troupe gave brief, farcical operas in the exalted surroundings of the Opéra. This was closely linked to constitutional, political and religious disputes of the time, which led to the *coin du roi* ('king's corner') asserting the noble traditions of the tragédie lyrique and criticizing the Italians' emphasis on the aria and the feebleness of recitative, while the *coin de la reine* ('queen's corner'), along with the 'rationalist' Encyclopédists, praised the relative clarity of Italian line and harmony. The controversy flared up in 1753 and petered out the next year, as quickly as it had risen.

Gluck's Influence

Gluck's arrival provoked a fresh controversy: Gluckistes v. Piccinnistes. Piccinni was imported in 1776 as Gluck's rival, a role he neither wanted nor felt himself able to fulfil and indeed specifically disclaimed. Matters grew worse when the two composers were set to work on the same topics – to fuel the dispute, both were to compose a *Roland*, and later an *Iphigénie en Tauride*. Gluck abandoned *Roland*. Piccinni agreed to set *Iphigénie* only if his would precede Gluck's, but it was delayed two years and was only moderately successful, partly because the leading soprano was drunk at the second performance (it was dubbed *Iphigénie en Champagne*). While the Gluckistes aimed to create a new, reformed French opera, the Piccinnistes wanted to show the superiority of Italian music; the rivalry was essentially one of styles. Gluck, ultimately, was the victor; Piccinni was an able dramatist but his gifts were not on the scale of Gluck's and the marriage of Italian music and French forms was always ill-conceived.

Storace, Stephen

1762–96

ENGLISH COMPOSER

Born in London of Italian and English parentage, Storace studied in Naples and first worked in Florence. He was back in London in the 1780s and spent time in Vienna, where his sister Nancy was a singer (she was the first Susanna in Mozart's *Marriage of Figaro*); he was a friend of Mozart's. Back in London in 1787, he became involved in theatrical life, in particular as a composer of operas, in which his songs vary from simple folk-like melodies to elaborate, italianate bravura arias. Notable successes were *No Song, No Supper* (1790) and *The Pirates* (1792).

Traetta, Tommaso

(Trā-ât'-tē, Tō-mà'-zō) 1727–79

ITALIAN COMPOSER

Trained in Naples, Traetta began his career as an opera composer there and in Rome. He was appointed to the Parma court in 1758, where his first few operas included two based on translations of texts used by Rameau, so bringing French structure into Italian opera (*Ippolito ed Aricia*, 1759; *I tintaridi*, 'The Heavenly Twins, 1760, after *Castor et Pollux*). Further operas to French-based texts followed, at Vienna as well as Parma. Traetta moved to Venice as director of the Ospedaletto conservatory in 1765, and to St Petersburg in 1768, where he composed *Antigone* (1772) and other works for Catherine the Great's court; he returned to Venice in 1777. His music shows exceptional richness of colour and dramatic force.

Wagenseil, Georg Christoph

(Vä'-gen-zīl, Gā'-ôrg Krēs'-tof) 1715–77

AUSTRIAN COMPOSER

A Viennese, and a pupil of **Johann Joseph Fux** (1660–1741), he obtained a post as court composer in 1739 and held it all his life. His early compositions are largely sacred music, including richly scored, elaborately written Masses, and in 1745–50 he wrote several operas. He is principally important for his instrumental music, consisting of 15 keyboard sonatas, keyboard concertos (mostly on a chamber-music scale) and a large number of symphonies, central to the form's development in Vienna.

(L) La Grotta di Trofonio

Illustration from the title page of a programme for Salieri's comic opera.

(NR) Samuel Sebastian Wesley

S. S. Wesley was the grandson of the famous founder of the Methodist movement in Britain; the family consisted of many talented musicians and made an enormous contribution to English church music.

(FR) Anna Amalia

Frederick the Great's sister, Duchess Anna Amalia, was a great music patron in Berlin, and built up an impressive library of works.

Wesley

ENGLISH MUSICAL FAMILY

The Wesley family, remembered primarily through the religious leader John Wesley (1703–91), made a deep and long-lasting contribution to English music. John's brother Charles (1707–88), the hymn writer, had two musician sons, Charles (1757–1834) and Samuel (1766– 1837). The young Charles, though a prodigy, never developed as a composer, but was a professional organist.

Samuel was a prolific composer for the church (Catholic as well as Anglican), of organ and other keyboard music and of orchestral works, including some symphonies of striking originality; he played a central part in the Bach revival. His illegitimate son, Samuel Sebastian Wesley (1810–76), was the leading English church composer of his time.

WOMEN PATRONS AND PERFORMERS

During the classical era women, usually from the nobility or royalty, continued to play an important role in promoting music. In Berlin, Frederick the Great's sister, Anna Amalia (1723–87), encouraged the performance of earlier music by building an impressive library of works by such composers as **Giovanni Pierluigi da Palestrina** (1525/6–94), J. S. Bach and **Georg Philipp Telemann** (1681–1767). Another Anna Amalia, the Duchess of Saxe-Weimar (1739–1807), established a highly artistic court at Weimar, where theatre and opera were particularly encouraged. Women also established important and influential salons, including that run by the Viennese musician Marianne von Martinez (1744–1812), which was attended by Mozart and Haydn. She was a talented composer herself, and her works included four Masses for soloists, choir and orchestra. She also established a singing school.

Women in the Trade

It would have been unthinkable for women of the upper classes to establish professional careers as musicians. But, like their male contemporaries, women from other classes were able to embrace most aspects of the music profession, working as singers, instrumentalists, composers, teachers and instrument makers. These women usually came from musical families and were taught the family trade – playing, singing and composing – by their parents. Corona Schröter (1751–1802) worked as a singer and actor at the Weimar court of Anna Amalia, where she also wrote incidental music for plays, including Goethe's *Die Fischerin* ('The Fisher Girl', 1782). Schröter published Lieder, as did her younger contemporary Louise Reichardt (1779–1826), who supported herself by working as a singing teacher in Hamburg. In France the singer, actress, playwright and composer Julie Candeille (1767–1834) made her debut at the Paris Opéra at the age of 14. Her comic opera *Ida, ou L'orpheline de Berlin* ('Ida, or the Orphan of Berlin', 1807) was based on the life of a female harpist.

The English singer Harriet Abrams (1760–1822) was unusual in not coming from a musical back-ground – her parents are thought to have been servants. Abrams sang in opera, oratorio and at private parties, while organizing concerts and publishing her own vocal music. Another English musicians career was that of Sophia Dussek (1775– *c.* 1830). Born in Edinburgh into a musical family of Italian origin, she worked as both singer and pianist, marrying a musician from the well-known Dussek family. After he abandoned her she turned to the more lucrative activities of teaching and publishing. She published numerous compositions and arrange-ments for the profitable amateur market under the gender-ambiguous name S. Dussek.

Fux ▶ p. 117 Palestrina ▶ p. 56 Rameau ▶ p. 120 Telemann ▶ p. 122

The Classical Era

STYLES AND FORMS

Developments in philosophy during the early decades of the eighteenth century saw rationalist and humanist ideals displacing mysticism in a new age of 'Enlightenment'. By the middle of the century, principles of natural order and balance were being explored in the arts. Composers attempted to give a clear sense of where their music was going in terms of themes and tonality, and graceful melodies with a light accompaniment replaced the heavy counterpoint of the Baroque period. The most important developments took place in Austria, where elements of Italian opera, French dance and Germanic instrumental music came together in the classical style of Haydn and Mozart.

The social dimension of music was also changing: culture began extending to the middle classes, as seen, for example, in the rise of light operas dealing with ordinary people, in contrast to the classical and mythological subjects of serious Italian opera. Developments in technology and publishing meant that the middle classes could own a keyboard instrument, such as a fortepiano, and buy sheet music to play at home. Indeed, keyboard skills became an important social skill for young women. Composers thus produced music that could be played by amateurs, yet which had taste and elegance. Concert life also began to take off as people played in groups both for their own pleasure and for the public who came to listen.

The Mass

The Mass flourished in Italy and in southern Germany and Austria during the classical period. Among composers writing in the Italian style, Hasse combined traditional Neapolitan principles with a *galant* approach. Therefore, although the structure of the Mass remained sectional, and the choral writing was generally in the 'antique' style, his solo parts were strongly lyrical.

Meanwhile, Viennese composers were beginning to introduce a more integrated structure to the genre, joining, for example, the sections of the 'Gloria' and 'Credo' more convincingly. Haydn composed six Masses between 1796 and 1802 which employ striking symphonic techniques alongside more traditional practices. The 'Kyrie' is often in a variant of sonata form, and the 'Kyrie' and 'Sanctus' sometimes have a slow introduction leading into an *allegro* movement. Mozart also combined traditional textures with a more modern approach. His Coronation Mass (1779) contains symphonic devices, such as the recapitulation of material in the 'Gloria', and an almost operatic intensity and complexity in the solo voices. His later Masses, in contrast, show his cultivation of the 'antique' style, following his interest in the fugues of **J. S. Bach** and **Handel**.

The Oratorio

Sacred and secular cantatas declined in importance after the mid-eighteenth century; in contrast the oratorio became more popular. In Italy the *oratorio volgare* (in Italian rather than Latin), which retained the Baroque two-part structure, was favoured. The texts of **Metastasio** were frequently set, and there was emphasis on solo singing, especially in ***da capo*** form. Occasionally these oratorios were staged; they were differentiated from opera only by their sacred subject matter and their two-part structure. Pietro Alessandro Guglielmi (1728–1804) was one of the practitioners of the genre; his *Debora e Sisara* (1789) was a particularly fine work.

There were two types of German oratorio: the dramatic, biblical type, similar to the Italian oratorio, of which Johann Rolle (1716–85) was the most prolific composer, and the contemplative type, which emphasized lyrical and sentimental expression, inspired by religious events and by nature. The Messiah and the Passion were popular subjects. This type of oratorio was performed liturgically, as a substitute for the cantata, and in public concerts. The most significant oratorios of the late classical period are those of Haydn. His *Die Schöpfung* embraces his mature symphonic style but also includes poetic and pictorial descriptions of nature.

THE *GALANT* STYLE

Although the French term *galant* came into use to describe music in about 1700 and gained currency as a style in the 1720s, it was only towards the middle of the century that it became prevalent throughout Europe. It implied sensuous pleasure with a certain elegance, embodied in flowing melodies with a light, often static, accompaniment. Characteristics included supporting (rather than driving) bass-lines, 'singing' melodies, dance rhythms and short two- or four-bar phrases; the voice and flute were particularly ideal for conveying this new style, and the clavichord enabled more delicate dynamic nuances than the harpsichord.

The chamber music of **J. C. Bach** exemplifies the *galant* style; his two-movement keyboard sonatas and trios for two violins and viola or continuo (comprising a slow movement and a **minuet**) are characteristically lyrical. His six quintets for flute, oboe, violin, viola and continuo op. 11 (1774) combine melodic charm with formal elegance, and present dialogue between different groups of instruments. The keyboard sonatas of **Galuppi** are also good examples of the *galant* style; his use of short, well-balanced, melodic phrases and his simple harmony reflect his experiences as an opera composer.

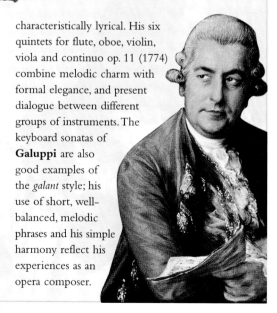

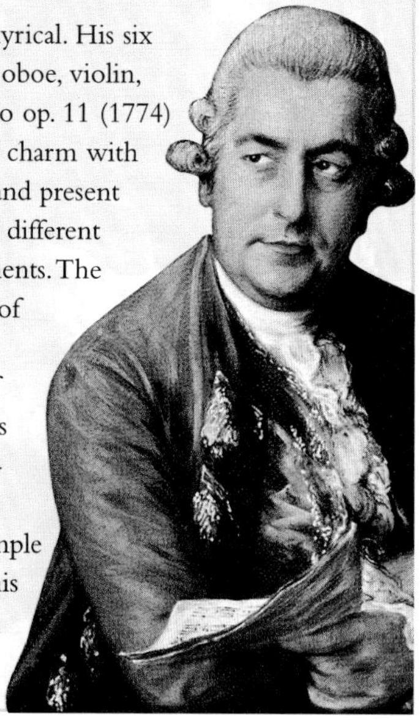

da capo ▶ p. 358 minuet ▶ p. 360 *opera buffa* ▶ p. 360 *opéra comique* ▶ p. 361 *opera seria* ▶ p. 361

CLASSICAL OPERA

Opera in the mid-eighteenth century was dominated in Italy, Germany, Austria and England (as well as in Scandinavia and Russia) by serious Italian opera, or ***opera seria***. It was even occasionally performed in Paris, despite nationalist resistance. Composers such as **Hasse**, **Jommelli** and **Traetta** generally set librettos by Metastasio, and brought to opera the new and graceful melodic style of the *galant*. Their operas consisted almost entirely of highly decorated arias (in which a character expressed his or her feelings) linked by recitatives (in which the action took place).

Around 1750, however, the structure of *opera seria* began to be challenged by lighter forms, such as ***opera buffa*** (Italy), ***opéra comique*** or *comédie mêlée d'ariettes*, a kind of comic miscellany (France), ballad or comic opera (England) and Singspiel (Germany). Except in Italy, they consisted of a more realistic and flexible structure of spoken dialogue interspersed with songs. Such works were in the language of the country, and dealt with ordinary people; the music was in a simpler style.

Opera Seria and *Opera Buffa*

Gluck was the most important figure in the reform of *opera seria*. He effectively created a new kind of opera which melded aspects of the comic and serious types, and combined different national styles. *Orfeo ed Euridice* (1762) is a tale of love explored in a continuous sequence of linked numbers, including ensembles and choruses, all with orchestral support. Gluck depicted the emotions of humans in classical mythology using simple yet powerful means, and achieved a convincing fusion of dance, drama, chorus and song.

Mozart achieved a similar effect in *opera buffa*. The characters in his operas are not the caricatures usually found in comic theatre at this time, but recognizable, complex human beings. Moreover, melodic lines, suggestive harmony and rich orchestration all help to convey character and emotion. The songs for Count Almaviva and his wife in *Le nozze de Figaro*, for example, are distinct in tone from those for their servants; the music communicates their social backgrounds and the sexual tensions that lie at the heart of the opera. The action is even reflected in the structure of the work: long, elaborate finales divided into sections as the changes in the action propel the plot forward and sustain the tension.

MUSICAL CENTRES

The political situation in Europe in the second half of the eighteenth century helped to shape musical developments in different countries. The political stability and economic health of England and France enabled London and Paris to develop as significant urban centres, each with a strong and varied musical culture. The decentralization of Germany and Italy conversely created a number of cities, towns and courts, each with their own small and self-sufficient musical establishment. Austria was a combination of the two models: although numerous provincial towns and estates had their own musical cultures, nobility from all over Europe came to Vienna for part of the year, bringing a concentration of resources comparable to those of London and Paris. This cosmopolitanism was perhaps one of the reasons for the synthesis in Vienna of national styles drawn from the rest of Europe; it attracted ambitious young composers and performers including Gluck, Mozart and **Beethoven**.

London was an important centre for Italian opera in Europe and attracted foreign singers and composers. It was also well known for its numerous subscription concerts, including those organized by Johann Peter Salomon (1745–1815), at which Haydn appeared in the 1790s. In contrast to the mainly upper- and middle-class audiences attracted by these two types of event, the pleasure gardens such as Vauxhall were visited by a cross-section of the public. Here, evening concerts included a range of vocal and orchestral works, both sacred and secular, serious and popular in tone.

French Revolutionary Hymns

In France, following the fall of the Bastille in 1789, musical performance was expected to conform to the social and political ideas of the new régime. Sung texts were chosen to help consolidate national identity and unity, and were performed at festivals – often in the open air – in the 1790s. A 'Te Deum' by **Gossec** was written for the first great festival in 1790, and represents the beginning of the Revolutionary hymn. **Luigi Cherubini** (1760–1842), **Etienne-Nicolas Méhul** (1763–1817) and others also contributed to the genre. Such works were generally characterized by four-square phrases and harmony, militaristic rhythms and woodwind and brass accompaniment; later hymns made the simple vocal parts more flexible, even contrapuntal, and introduced alternating chorus and solo parts. Many songs were sung in the street, and some found their way into stage works and operas. Indeed, much of this music became known outside France by way of Napoleon's soldiers on their campaigns. The *Chant de guerre pour l'armée du Rhin* ('Song of War for the Army of the Rhine', 1792), later known as the *Marseillaise*, by Claude-Joseph Rouget de Lisle (1760–1836), was adopted as an official national song in 1795.

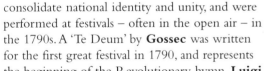

(BL) Johann Christian Bach
J. C. Bach's chamber music provides fine examples of the galant *style – characterized by flowing lyricism.*

(ML) Ladies at the Harpsichord
Developments in technology meant that more of the middle classes could own keyboard instruments.

(TL and BR) Pleasure Gardens
Pleasure gardens were open to a cross-section of society, which meant that a variety of music was available to the public for the first time and was no longer the domain of the upper classes.

(TR) Christoph Willibald von Gluck
Gluck's reforms of opera seria *saw a melding of serious and comic elements and a mixture of national styles.*

J. C. Bach ▶ p. 156 J. S. Bach ▶ p. 106 Beethoven ▶ p. 150 Cherubini ▶ p. 189 Galuppi ▶ p. 158 Gluck ▶ p. 158 Gossec ▶ p. 160 Handel ▶ p. 112 Hasse ▶ p. 160
Haydn ▶ p. 140 Jommelli ▶ p. 160 Méhul ▶ p. 197 Metastasio ▶ p. 161 Mozart ▶ p. 144 Traetta ▶ p. 163

The Early Sonata

During the classical period the sonata was generally in three movements (fast-slow-fast), although there were variations on this structure, including slow introductions, additional movements, thematic links between movements and even the playing of movements without a break. The first two movements were usually in sonata form, with the final and any additional movements in variation or rondo form, or in minuet, scherzo or other dance forms.

Following the flowering of the solo keyboard sonata in the Baroque period, **C. P. E. Bach**, **Boccherini** and Haydn developed a style characterized by two-bar melodic units, simple harmonic and key relationships and repetitive accompanying figures such as the Alberti bass. Gradually, more dissonant decorative figures and richer and more varied textures and rhythms were introduced. Haydn's Sonata in C minor No. 36 (1771) marks his decisive move away from the light, dance-music style; its emotional contrasts and combination of drama and reflective melody mark the inauguration of the Viennese classical style.

The Classical Sonata

More extended and complex themes were progressively introduced into the classical sonata, together with richer textures, more varied accompaniments and a broader harmonic vocabulary. Mozart preferred clarity rather than technical

display, and his later piano sonatas, although they show harmonic ingenuity and melodic richness, are spare, elegant and lyrical. In contrast, **Clementi** introduced a more abrasive melodic style and laid the foundations of the piano style of the next generation. He exploited the new pianoforte, with its capacity for brilliant, dramatic effects and rhetorical gestures, and despite the predominantly light nature of his works foreshadowed the textural richness of Beethoven and **Frédéric Chopin** (1810–49). Beethoven's 'Pathétique' Sonata (op. 13, 1798) has an orchestral quality and shows the composer's growing dissatisfaction with the limits of classical form.

Just as numerous, although of less artistic and historical importance, were the accompanied sonatas for keyboard, usually with violin (sometimes optional), and the piano trio (usually for piano, violin and cello). Only towards the end of the period, in the mature violin sonatas and piano trios of Mozart and Beethoven, however, were string and keyboard instruments treated equally. A fine example is Mozart's Violin Sonata in A major (1787), which includes virtuoso exchanges between the violin and right-hand piano part.

SONATA FORM

Sonata form was the most important principle of musical structure during the classical period, and has remained so up to the present day. It applies most often to a single movement, part of a sonata, symphony or quartet, but an independent movement, such as an overture, may also be in sonata form. Its principles affect the structural features of other works, including the Mass. Sonata form is most clearly seen as the expansion of the **binary form** of Baroque dances, but other genres, including the aria and the concerto, also influenced its development. Essentially, sonata form presents and develops contrasting musical ideas at length, while providing a convincing unity to the whole. Examples of the form can be found in the works of Haydn, Mozart and Beethoven.

The Sonata Structure

A typical sonata-form movement consists of three main sections, based on a two-part key structure:

1. Exposition. This opening section sets out the main themes of the movement. It is divided into a first-subject group in the **tonic** and, after transitional material, a second-subject group in another key, usually the **dominant** in major movements (the relative major in minor movements). A short codetta, reinforcing the new key, often rounds off the section.
2. Development. In this section, music from the exposition is treated in a variety of ways. The themes may be fragmented or treated contrapuntally, or be the basis of new ideas; they usually move through a number of keys and create rhythmic and melodic tensions.
3. Recapitulation. In this final section both main themes are repeated, usually both in the home key, thus resolving the tension created by the dominant (or relative major) in the exposition. There may also be temporary visits to other keys, but the return of the original material in the home key marks the culmination of the movement. To the three-section structure of sonata form a slow introduction and a **coda** may also be added.

Another form used frequently in the classical era was the sonata-rondo. As its name suggests, it combined the idea of the sonata (in which the tension created by presenting thematic material in two keys is resolved by restating the themes in the home key) with that of the rondo (in which a main section recurs between subsidiary sections). The tonal plan of sonata form is thus combined with the thematic structure of the rondo.

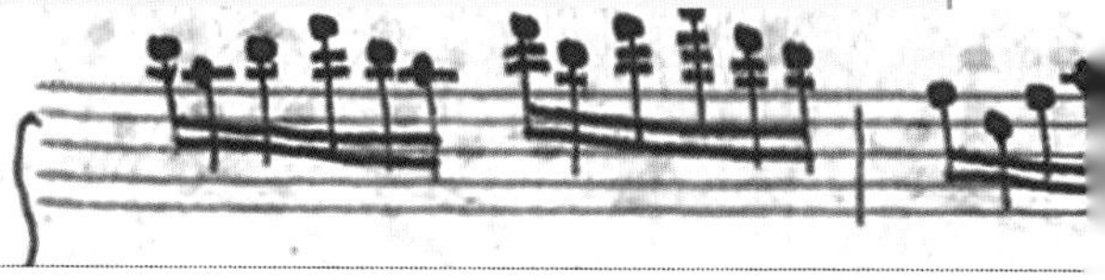

binary form ▶ p. 356 coda ▶ p. 357 dominant ▶ p. 358 tonic ▶ p. 363

Early Development of the String Quartet

The string quartet, usually scored for two violins, viola and cello, was not firmly established until the time of Haydn. With his op. 9 quartets (1769–70) a four-movement scheme was established (fast-slow-minuet-fast), with a generally well-distributed four-part texture. The first, second and final movements are usually in sonata form, although variations were also frequently introduced in all except the first movement. In his op. 33 quartets (1781), which introduce the scherzo into the genre, Haydn achieved a new clarity of structure and balance of texture, though brilliant writing for the first violin always remained part of his style.

Italian composers, including Giuseppe Cambini (1746–1825) and Boccherini, developed a more lyrical style, often with virtuoso first violin writing. This style was taken up in France by **Giovanni Battista Viotti** (1755–1824) and others; here the *quatuor brillant* ('brilliant quartet') became a popular genre in which the first violinist, usually a travelling virtuoso, was given solistic prominence while the other players formed an accompanying ensemble. The *quatuor concertant* ('concert quartet'), in which all the instruments have equal weight, was also popular in late eighteenth-century Paris. Its most characteristic texture was that of dialogue, in which players exchanged roles, and each had a solo moment.

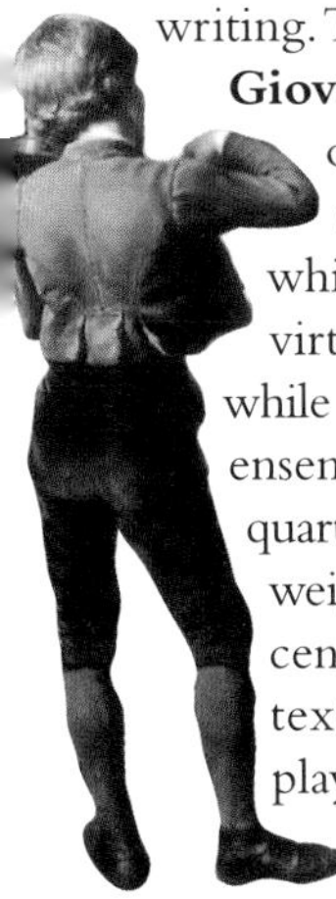

The Mature String Quartets of Haydn and Mozart

By the end of the eighteenth century, string quartets, formerly a genre exclusive to the private salon, were performed in concerts. This shift in practice is reflected in Haydn's quartets. Many of his earlier works begin softly with the statement of a theme, but his opp. 71 and 74 quartets (1793) start with a loud arresting gesture – necessary to quieten a waiting audience. His op. 76 quartets (1797) exhibit ingenious variations, complex fugal writing, folk-influenced melodies, perfect ensemble writing and a range of expression.

Mozart's early quartets were influenced by the Milanese style of Giovanni Battista Sammartini (1700/01–75), with their 'singing allegros' dominated by the first violin, and it was not until he wrote the set, dedicated to Haydn (1782–85), that he attained a fully integrated quartet style. The first of the group opens in rich four-part harmony, then moves into dialogue with the same phrase passed between the instruments. He also used chromatic effects and counterpoint to intensify the impact of the music. His 'Hunt' Quartet (1784), named after its galloping opening and hunting-horn motif, is a serious attempt at a four-part texture; the *adagio* in particular has a rich, almost Romantic, quality.

(BL) The Quartet
The string quartet was fully established in the mid eighteenth century.
(TR) Eighteenth-Century Dancing
Engraving of contemporary English dance.

The Quintet

The early history of the quintet for two violins, two violas and cello is similar to that of the string quartet, though the repertory is smaller. Boccherini was one of the most prolific composers in the genre, although usually using two cellos and only one viola. As a cellist, he often called upon that instrument to play rapidly and brilliantly. He aimed for rich and varied textures and cultivated a gentle, graceful melodic style, often ornate and fine in detail. Some of his quintets involve the imitation of non-musical sounds, for example birdsong and street cries. In op. 20 (1776) his ideas are more fully worked, the moods more strongly defined and sustained, and each piece has a marked character. He also adapted some quintets to include the guitar.

Although the string quintet was a relatively uncommon genre in Mozart's day, he seems to have been particularly drawn to it. The C major and G minor quintets (1787) represent a peak in his chamber music; he drew richly on the opportunities that the extra instrument (a second viola) provided for different kinds of symmetry and richness of texture. His Clarinet Quintet (1789), written for his friend the clarinettist Anton Stadler (1753–1812), contains a wide variety of colours and beautiful melodies, and imaginatively explores the clarinet's range.

Divertimento

The divertimento was a prominent musical form in the classical period. The title was commonly applied to a light piece for keyboard, or, more often, for an ensemble of soloists. There are usually up to nine movements. Neither polyphonic nor extensively developed like the sonata, its function was to please and entertain rather than express deep emotion. The genre overlaps with other forms of outdoor music or table music (including the serenade, *notturno*, partita, *Tafelmusik*), but by 1780 'divertimento' was the most commonly used term.

Early divertimentos were written for three main types of instrumentation: keyboard, with or without accompanying instruments; wind ensemble; and strings, sometimes augmented by a pair of wind instruments or horns. The genre sometimes blurred with the string trio, quartet, even symphony and concerto. Haydn's keyboard divertimentos, and those for three instruments or orchestra, are usually in three movements; those for four or five instruments are in five movements. Mozart's *Eine kleine Nachtmusik*, for string quartet and double bass (although often played by a small string orchestra today), is the most famous example of the genre.

C. P. E. Bach ▶ p. 156 Boccherini ▶ p. 157 Chopin ▶ p. 190 Clementi ▶ p. 158 Viotti ▶ p. 204

The Early Classical Concerto

The three-movement solo concerto developed by **Antonio Vivaldi** (1678–1741) and J. S. Bach, with the quick movements in ***ritornello*** form, survived into the classical period. The first movements of C. P. E. Bach's harpsichord concertos from the 1770s elaborate on this *ritornello* model, alternating solo episodes with orchestral passages. His concertos are often expressive three- or four-movement works in the minor key, with engaging ideas and **modulations**. In some of his later concertos, as in his symphonies, the movements follow each other without a break, and material recurs between movements. His style was influential on Haydn's early concertos. In contrast, J. C. Bach had a more fluent, Italianate melodic style and clearly defined themes. He favoured the *galant* two-movement form, and introduced distinct secondary themes in the dominant for the soloist. Mozart's five violin concertos (1773–75) show this Italianate influence, with expressive *cantilenas*, or lyrical themes, in the slow movements and clearly differentiated subject groups. His wind and horn concertos show his sensitivity to the limitations and character of each instrument, and an attention to melodic beauty rather than to technical display.

Musikalisches Vielerley.
Herausgegeben
von
Herrn Carl Philipp Emanuel Bach,
Musik-Director zu Hamburg.
Hamburg,
gedruckt und verlegt von Michael Christian Bock.
1770.

MOZART'S PIANO CONCERTOS

In the eighteenth century, early pianos were not really powerful enough to compete with the orchestra, and the Baroque concerto form, in which solo episodes alternated with orchestral *ritornellos*, continued. However, Mozart developed a more intrinsic relationship between piano and orchestra, and expanded the concept of the genre, combining *ritornello* and sonata forms more completely. The orchestra states some of the themes and provides accompaniment, while the piano develops such themes and provides new ones. Importantly, the piano has an opportunity for technical display, and brings the movement to a climax in a **cadenza** – a virtuoso solo passage. Initially Mozart achieved this formal flexibility by allowing themes to proliferate; they are linked by brilliant passage-work or orchestral *tuttis* rather than developments. In later works, however, he tended to use shorter, more motivic ideas, which helped to unify the work, as, for example, in Piano Concerto in C K467 (1785). K450 in B flat (1784) also shows the influence on Mozart of the Mannheim composers: the orchestral sonority is expanded, and a distinct wind section engages in dialogue with the strings in the outer movements.

The Early Classical Symphony

Features of the classical symphony can be traced to the Italian overture of the late seventeenth century in three movements (fast-slow-fast). Composers such as Boccherini continued the developments made by the previous generation of Italian opera composers, and composers active in London, Paris and elsewhere also contributed to the genre's progress. However, it was in Austria and Germany that a richer, more developed style evolved, and that a dance movement in triple time (usually a minuet) was added before the finale. C. P. E. Bach's symphonic works are full of unexpected effects and contrast with the *galant* style of his contemporaries. For example, he would employ rapid scales and **arpeggios**, and run movements together in dramatic ways as he disliked breaking the flow of the music. His six 'Hamburg' Symphonies (1773), written for Baron van Swieten, later to become a patron of Mozart, are particularly original examples of the genre. J. C. Bach favoured the three-movement Italian symphony form in which he presented florid melodies and well-defined contrasts of theme and colour, bringing together aspects of German technique and Italian grace in a popular, vital style.

EMPFINDSAMKEIT

The term *Empfindsamkeit* ('sensitivity') is associated with a particular aesthetic outlook prevalent in north Germany in the mid-eighteenth century. It refers to an intimate, melancholic expression, the ideals of which are found in the music and writings of C. P. E. Bach. His style is often rhetorical, with sudden pauses and changes of key, and expressive leaning appoggiaturas and chromatic notes. One of his fantasias is said to represent Hamlet's famous soliloquy. His keyboard sonatas are best played not on the harpsichord with its even dynamics (the strings are plucked), but on the clavichord or piano, which allows finer gradations of tone (the strings are struck).

ORCHESTRATION

During the Baroque era, the orchestra gradually began to assume a standard form. In Italy, string groups were used in the opera houses; in France, the court had its famous '24 violons du roi', which also played in the opera house with wind instruments, and this was imitated at the English and the major German and Austrian courts. A typical opera orchestra of the early eighteenth century might have 15 violins, 10 lower strings, possibly four oboes and two bassoons. By the classical era, the manner of writing for the orchestra was more standardized: strings formed the backbone, wind supported the loud, *tutti* passages and sometimes had solos of their own. To play this repertory, a court would need a string group of 10 to 20, two oboes and two horns; often the oboists could also play the flute if needed, and there would generally be one or two bassoons. Clarinets were beginning to come into regular use by the 1770s, and trumpets and timpani would be called in for more festive pieces. Sometimes a court or opera orchestra would hire these extra instruments from the local military band; and in some cities trombones were used in church music, supporting the choir and adding a note of solemnity. The classical orchestra was directed from the harpsichord, in collaboration with the leading violinist.

arpeggio ▶ p. 356 cadenza ▶ p. 356 modulation ▶ p. 360 *ritornello* ▶ p. 361 ternary form ▶ p. 362

(NL) Joseph Haydn
Haydn's early works were strongly influenced by the concertos of C. P. E. Bach.
(FL) C. P. E. Bach's **Musical Periodical**
The works of C. P. E. Bach encompass the ideals of the musical aesthetic Empfindsamkeit *('sensitivity').*
(TR) Leader of the Orchestra
The classical orchestra was led by the harpsichordist.

The Mature Classical Symphony

In the later classical symphony the first movement (the longest and most important) was usually in sonata form, often with a slow introductory section. The second movement too was usually in sonata form, although Haydn often preferred variations. The minuet was in **ternary form** (A-B-A), and was sometimes replaced by the livelier scherzo. The finale was in sonata form, and in later works it became more substantial, to balance the weight of the first movement.

Haydn is often referred to as the 'father of the symphony', and his 104 symphonies include many fine examples, in which he often built whole expositions on a single thematic idea, or minimized the contrast between the first and second subjects to preserve a structural unity in more extended works. His last 12 symphonies (nos. 93–104), written for London in 1791–95, include popular works which have since earned themselves nicknames – the 'Surprise' with its loud chord to wake any sleepers in the audience, the 'Clock' with its ticking figure in the slow movement. Mozart wrote 41 symphonies, which combine Italian influences (derived partly from his friendship with J. C. Bach) with harmonic depth, subtlety of phrasing and orchestral virtuosity. In the finale of his 'Jupiter' Symphony (No. 41, 1788) he combines six separate themes in an astonishingly inventive coda.

Symphonie Concertante

The *symphonie concertante* or *sinfonia concertante* was a concert genre of the late eighteenth and early nineteenth centuries for solo instruments (usually two, three or four) and orchestra. Closer to a concerto than a symphony, it also resembles the classical divertimento in its light-hearted character. It is usually in a major key and in two or three movements. From *c.* 1770 to 1790 the genre was particularly popular in Paris, where it satisfied a taste for virtuoso display, colourful sonorities and a pleasing melodic line. Notable contributors to the genre include Gossec, Cambini and Ignace Pleyel (1757–1831). Mannheim composers, particularly Cannabich and Karl Stamitz (1745–1801), also contributed to the early flowering of the *symphonie concertante*.

In London, J. C. Bach's feeling for orchestral colour attracted him to the *symphonie concertante* in the 1770s. The number of solo parts in his pieces, often written for leading London virtuosos, varies from two to nine; most were in three movements, some in the *galant* two-movement form. Bach's attitude to the solo group was never rigid, and he sometimes added an instrument or two from the *tutti* if required. Outstanding examples of the genre are Mozart's for violin and viola (1779) and Haydn's for oboe, bassoon, violin and cello (1792).

PARIS AND NAPLES

The reputation that Paris enjoyed for elegance and culture also attracted many foreign visitors to the city. While Italian opera was occasionally performed, French-language serious and comic opera predominated. The city's most famous concert series was the Concert Spirituel, founded by Anne-Danican Philidor (1681–1728) in 1725. By the middle of the century, the mainly sacred repertory had expanded to include instrumental and secular works. Although the music and musicians were predominantly French, Italian opera virtuosos and German orchestral players performed as well, effectively disseminating foreign music and styles.

Naples was the largest city in Italy in the eighteenth century and one of its leading musical centres. Its conservatories attracted musicians from all over Italy and Europe. There were no public concerts, although there were private celebrations and religious festivals and, from 1777, the Accademia de' Cavalieri, which put on concerts for its members and their guests. The connections between *opera seria* and the court were particularly close, and Neapolitan tastes were recognized as being old-fashioned for much of the second half of the century.

ROCKETS AND SIGHS

A group of composers at the electoral court of Mannheim between about 1740 and 1778 developed a style which was to be important both to the development of the orchestra and to the history of the symphony. They were best known for their dynamic effects, influenced by Italian opera, which included a kind of crescendo passage, known as a 'roller', that was apparently so thrilling that audiences would rise in their seats with it, and perhaps more famously the 'Mannheim rocket', a leaping triad, and the 'Mannheim sigh', an expressive falling phrase. The high performance standards of the orchestra members perhaps encouraged this flamboyant compositional style; they knew how to exploit their talents to create new and bold effects. The orchestra's first musical director, **Stamitz**, was also influential in the early development of the symphony; he was strongly influenced by the Italian overture, and was the first composer to write symphonies consistently in four movements (with a minuet). He favoured a large orchestra with a full wind section, and developed new and imaginative instrumental styles, giving more emphasis to the wind section. His sons and his pupils, most notably Christian Cannabich (1731–98), continued his developments in the second half of the century.

Stamitz ▶ p. 162 Vivaldi ▶ p. 122

The Classical Era

INSTRUMENTS

Fortepiano

When the player's fingers press down its keys, the lever mechanism of the fortepiano (meaning 'loud-soft') causes the string to be struck once by a covered hammer, rather than plucked as in a harpsichord. The mechanism allowed it to play variously loudly or softly, and in an age producing music of increasing emotional diversity the dynamic range of the fortepiano quickly became essential.

In their experiments with the new instrument, many eighteenth-century fortepiano makers used knee levers and other devices to alter the sound. In addition to the 'damper' effect, which modern pianos preserve (nick named the 'soft pedal'), there were pedals or stops to operate drums, triangles, bells and cymbals, and there were even bassoon, harpsichord and buzzer stops. Later makers abandoned these and concentrated instead on producing fortepianos that possessed two qualities: a wider compass and greater dynamic breadth.

The fortepiano was found to be more versatile than the harpsichord, which at that time composers used. While **Haydn**'s early keyboard pieces can be performed on a harpsichord, the later sonatas cannot. They include markings such as sforzando ('accented, forced') and crescendo ('gradually getting louder'), effects which were impossible on a harpsichord. Certainly, Haydn was pleased with the developing fortepiano.

Glass Armonica

Perhaps with medieval Persian origins, the glass armonica entered into the Western musical mainstream only in the eighteenth century. A series of glass vessels could be tuned by having the appropriate quantity of water poured into them; they were then struck like bells to produce a ringing sound, or the rims were dampened and then rubbed. **Gluck** played a concerto on such an instrument in the 1740s, but it was the American Benjamin Franklin (1706–90) who in 1761 took on the task of producing a serious instrument. Carefully grading the size of the vessels and mounting them to ensure they were secure and that the rims were close together, he achieved an instrument on which chords and runs were possible.

Although in 1791 **Mozart** composed a quintet for glass armonica, flute, oboe, viola and cello for the famous blind performer Marianne Kirchgessner (1769–1808), the instrument was out of fashion by the mid-nineteenth century.

Clarinet

The clarinet is a wooden instrument of cylindrical bore, with a single vibrating reed in a mouthpiece. Clarinets began to appear in music by **J. C. Bach** and **Arne** in the 1760s; the Mannheim orchestra championed it. Mozart wrote parts for it in his Divertimento K113. His operas make extensive, if straightforward use of clarinets, probably the five-keyed boxwood instruments in C, B flat and A, which began to be available from about 1770.

At the same time, as the lower notes of the instrument – now known as the 'chalumeau register' – became more playable, so the ancient chalumeau was dropped. This continued to be a time of experiment and several different competing and complementary instruments were on the market. Mozart wrote for a deeper clarinet called the basset horn in his *Requiem*. His friend, the virtuoso Anton Stadler (1753–1812), developed a variant known to us as the 'basset clarinet' in around 1789. Again a little deeper than the modern clarinet, it was the instrument for which Mozart wrote both his Clarinet Concerto (1791) and his Clarinet Quintet (1789). The early nineteenth century saw the development of 13-keyed instruments.

French Horn

Beginning as the simple pastoral and hunting instrument that its name suggests, the seventeenth-century horn was a brass tube with three coils, with a conical 'bore', or inner measurement, opening outwards from the funnel-shaped mouthpiece to the concluding 'bell'. Pitch was controlled through breath pressure. This instrument, included by **Handel** in his *Water Music* (1717) and by **J. S. Bach** in his *Brandenburg* Concerto No. 1 (1721), had no means of changing key; players sometimes sat on stage with more than one, changing instrument as the key changed.

The Viennese instrument maker Michael Leichnamschneider (1676–after 1746) realized that by jointing in different extra metal hoops, the overall length of metal tubing could be varied, and these hoops, known as 'crooks', transformed the life of the horn. Some players found they could alter pitch by putting their hand more deeply or shallowly into the bell, and makers like Raoux and Courtois in Paris concentrated on reducing dimensions so that hand movements could become smaller, although the hand-stopped notes were of a different quality or 'colour' from the natural open tones. Mozart's three horn concertos in E flat and one in D all date from the period 1783–91 and were written for this natural horn.

Wind Bands

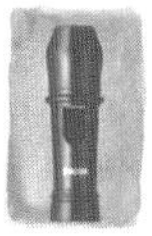

The Classical period saw the rise of the 'Harmonie', a small wind band of up to a dozen instruments. Usually this consisted of a mixture of brass and reeds, such as horns, clarinets, oboes and bassoons: **Beethoven**'s octet op. 103 (1792) is written for two of each of these (the 1796 op. 71 sextet leaves out the oboes). Mozart wrote two octet serenades, but his K361/ 370a requires 12 winds plus a double bass. However, there were no fixed rules; when, at the end of the classical age, **Felix Mendelssohn** (1809–47) wrote an overture for Harmonie, op. 24 (1824), it was for no fewer than 23 winds plus percussion.

Because of their carrying power, wind ensembles are able to play successfully out of doors or in a noisy environment, something which has helped the development of military bands (there are no traditions of military string quartets). The Harmonie thus specialized in easy listening, such as pleasant background music during dinner: an example of this practice comes during the supper scene in Mozart's *Don Giovanni*. Mozart opera provides another nice example of the wind band at work, in his *Così fan tutte*, where a serenade is performed in the garden scene as a seduction is being prepared.

(TR) The Classical Orchestra
Plan showing the position of players in the classical orchestra, as arranged for Handel's Commemoration in Westminster Abbey in 1784.
(BR) Orchestration
Nineteenth-century orchestra, showing the importance of the harpsichord.

Baryton

A baryton is a bass string instrument, similar in appearance to a viol. It is held between the performer's knees and played with a bow; it usually carries six strings which the bow sounds directly. It has a number of strings (up to 40) which are concealed and which can be plucked by the thumb or allowed to vibrate in sympathy. These run underneath the fingerboard over which the six active strings are stretched, across the belly and over a low bridge, to be attached near the base of the tailpiece. They were often (though not always) tuned D, G, c, e, a', d' like a bass viol; the decoration of the few surviving examples suggests they may largely have been owned by aristocratic amateurs. Haydn's patron Prince Nikolaus I Esterházy was such a one, and as a result Haydn wrote chamber music for the instrument.

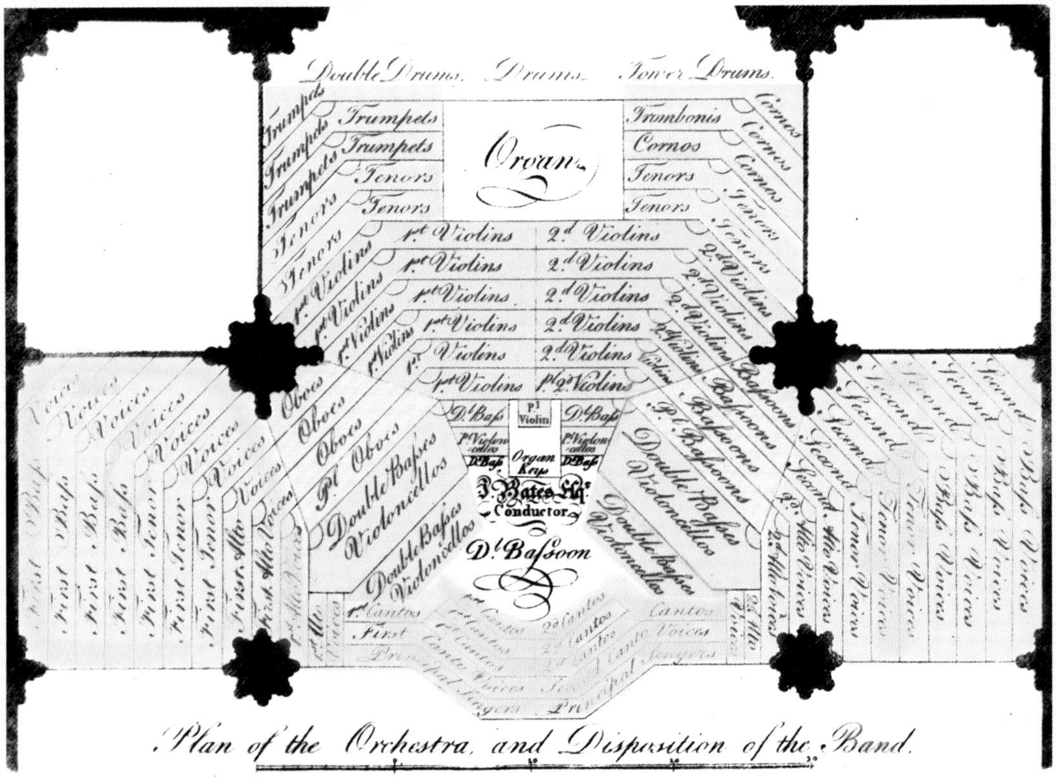

TURKISH SOUNDS

In the seventeenth century, a Turkish army was driven back from the walls of Vienna. As diplomatic relations replaced hostilities, Turkish embassies in Vienna used 'janissary' or military bands as part of their parade and a Turkish band was presented to the Polish king by the Sultan. In the eighteenth century a fashion for Turkish sounds such as shawms, bass drums, jingles, cymbals and bells developed as admiration for the troops grew in military circles.

As the orchestral bass drum is descended from the Turkish military *daval*, it is not surprising that when Mozart wanted to create the right exotic effect in his *Die Entführung aus dem Serail* he wrote a part for it. Other effects which composers called on included the triangle, in attempting imitation of the jingles used by the janissary armies. Special effects in fortepianos allowed jingles to be played in *alla Turca* piano music, such as the finale of Mozart's piano sonata in A K331. A Turkish march can even be found in Beethoven's Ninth Symphony (1823).

ESTABLISHMENT OF THE CLASSICAL ORCHESTRA

Just as the individual instruments were changing, so the way in which they were grouped together was also changing. As virtuosity became possible on a wider range of instruments, so the domination of violins in the ensemble was reduced and the more balanced four-part string section (first violins, second violins, violas and cellos) emerged. The recorder was dropped in favour of the developing flute.

Direction of the classical orchestra, continuing to follow the Baroque model, was shared between a violin-playing concert master, leading from the first violins, and a director playing the harpsichord, located in the continuo group. As the fortepiano proved capable of undertaking more of what the classical composer required, the harpsichord was dropped. By the first few years of the nineteenth century the entire continuo section found itself disbanded, and the piano was to return to the orchestra as a regular member only in the modern age.

In the early classical period, the orchestra was still not standardized. Haydn wrote a part for the *oboe da caccia* ('oboe of the hunt', an ancestor of the modern English horn) in his Symphony No. 22, first played by the orchestra at Eisenstadt in 1764, but he had to rewrite it for performances elsewhere, since the instrument was not otherwise available.

Nevertheless, improved communications meant that news travelled and comparisons were made between different orchestras. The Mannheim ensemble was particularly influential in orchestral development, but commentators at the time also noted the Elector of Saxony's orchestra and the opera orchestra in Turin. The classical orchestra settled down as a four-part string section plus two each (sometimes three or four) of flutes, oboes, clarinets, bassoons, horns and trumpets, plus timpani.

Arne ▶ p. 156 J. C. Bach ▶ p. 156 J. S. Bach ▶ p. 106 Beethoven ▶ p. 150 Gluck ▶ p. 159 Handel ▶ p. 112 Haydn ▶ p. 140 Mendelssohn ▶ p. 197 Mozart ▶ p. 144

The Classical Era

LISTENING GUIDE

Wolfgang Amadeus Mozart

Piano Concerto No. 20

WORK: Wolfgang Amadeus Mozart, Piano Concerto No. 20 in D minor, K466, composed 1785.

SCORING: Flute, pairs of oboes, bassoons, horns, trumpets and timpani, strings

EXCERPT: Third movement (Track 3)

TIMINGS BASED ON: Piano Concerto No. 20 in D minor, Murray Perahia and the English Chamber Orchestra (see Recommended CDs)

RECOMMENDED CDs

1. Piano Concerto No. 20 in D minor, K466; Piano Concerto No. 27 in B flat, K595. English Chamber Orchestra. Murray Perahia, piano and conductor. Sony Classical SK 42 241. Recorded 1977 (K466), 1979 (K595).

   Murray Perahia combines smoky tone with virile yet sensitive phrasing to give a near-ideal performance of the D minor concerto. Excellent support from the ECO.

2. Piano Concerto No. 20 in D minor, K466; Piano Concerto No. 21 in C, K467. English Chamber Orchestra. Mitsuko Uchida, piano. Jeffrey Tate, conductor. Philips 416 381-2. Recorded 1985.

   The ECO is not on quite such good form, but Mitsuko Uchida's performance is as muscular as Perahia's, and as limpid. She plays Beethoven's cadenzas.

3. Piano Concerto No. 20 in D minor, K466; Piano Concerto No. 18 in B flat, K456. Orpheus Chamber Orchestra. Richard Goode, piano. Nonesuch 7559-79439-2. Recorded 1996.

   The American pianist Richard Goode shows himself to be a stylish Mozartian. Unlike Murray Perahia, he plays Beethoven's cadenza in the first movement, and one of his own composition in the last. He plays the Romance straight, with no decoration.

4. Piano Concerto No. 20 in D minor, K466; Piano Concerto No. 21 in C, K467. English Baroque Soloists. Malcolm Bilson, fortepiano. John Eliot Gardiner, conductor. DG Archiv 419 609-2. Recorded 1986.

   This performance on period instruments is particularly interesting, as Malcolm Bilson plays on a copy of Mozart's own fortepiano. He improvises his own cadenzas in the outer movements.

When Mozart arrived in Vienna in March 1781, he was still in the employ of the Archbishop of Salzburg. Fresh from Munich, where he had just had a great success with his opera *Idomeneo*, he resented his lowly status as a menial. He secured his release from the Archbishop's service in June with much mutual ill-feeling, and launched himself as a freelance pianist, composer and teacher. The following 18 months saw the première of *Die Entführung aus dem Serail*, his marriage to Constanze, sister of his earlier love Aloysia Weber, and the composition of the first three in the sequence of piano concertos that occupied him on and off for the rest of his life.

FIRST MOVEMENT

Although some were written for his pupils, most of the concertos were played by Mozart himself at concerts put on for his own benefit. Six appeared in 1784, all, like their predecessors, in a major key. Even if he had written no others, they would have been enough to establish Mozart's reputation as master of the form, with their brilliance, spaciousness and symphonic working-out of the thematic material.

However, the Piano Concerto in D minor, composed early in 1785, plumbs greater depths. If the earlier concertos were formal, even courtly, K466 is mysterious, passionate and violent. It begins quietly, syncopated chords in the upper strings accompanying dark rumblings in the bass. The syncopations continue as the woodwind and horns are added to the texture, until the arrival of a fierce *tutti*. The mood softens briefly with an abrupt change to the major, but the striding theme of the *tutti* soon returns, heralding the entry of the soloist.

1. 0'00"
The piano begins with a virile theme based on a rising arpeggio.

2. 0'11"
The orchestra enters with the same material, leading to…

3. 0'28"
… rising and (0'37") falling chromatic phrases.

4. 0'59"
The piano enters with a new theme in the tonic.

5. 1'27"
A secondary theme is heard in the remote key of F minor.

6. 2'11"
Flute, oboe and bassoon introduce the jaunty second subject, in F major.

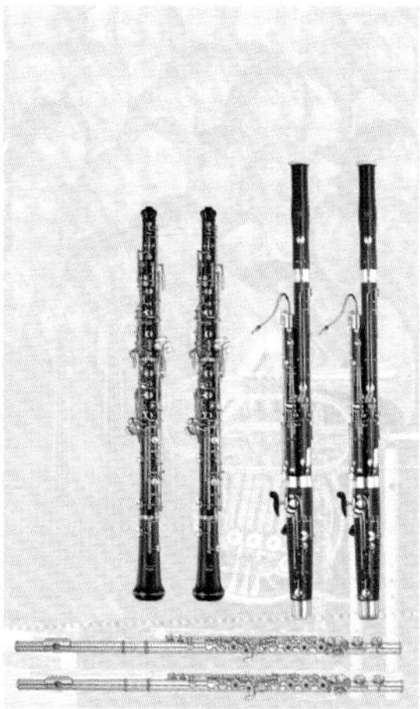

cadenza ▶ p. 356

STURM UND DRANG

Sturm und Drang ('Storm and Stress'), a name taken from a play of the time, began as a literary movement that flourished in Germany and Austria in the second half of the eighteenth century. Easier to recognize than to define, its manifestations included the 'horrid' world of the Gothic novel and, in the visual arts, the paintings of Fuseli and the drawings of Giambattista Piranesi. In the violence it expressed and the terror it was intended to evoke, *Sturm und Drang* was very different from the delicate 'sensibility' of the period, though a work such as Goethe's *Die Leiden des jungen Werthers* ('The Sorrows of Young Werther', 1774), with its lengthy passages taken from James MacPherson's spurious *Ballads of Ossian*, partook of both worlds. The fashion did not last long, and was soon overtaken by the 'Classical' style associated with the Enlightenment.

The term can also be cautiously applied to music, especially opera, referring to the heightened forms of expression and swift changes of mood in the orchestrally accompanied recitatives of the time. And the choruses and dances of the Furies in Act II of **Gluck**'s *Orfeo ed Euridice* (1762) are certainly 'stormy'; even more so is the end of his ballet of the previous year, *Don Juan* (1761), a work that Mozart must have had in mind when despatching his own *Don Giovanni* (1787) in the same key of D minor.

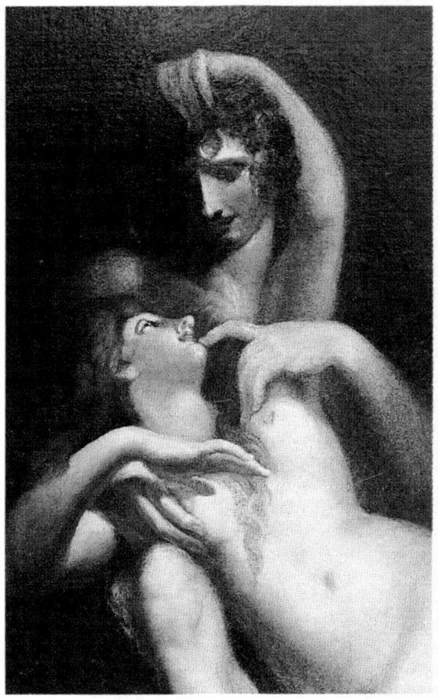

Away from the stage, many of the works that Haydn was writing in the 1760s are notable for a similar violence and passion, especially the minor-key Symphonies Nos. 26, 39, 44, 49 and 52. They are milestones on the journey between the general abstractions of the Baroque and the expressions of personal crisis that characterize the late classical and the Romantic periods, of which the D minor Piano Concerto of Mozart is a particularly fine example.

The piano begins with what seems like a new theme but which is in fact related to one already heard on the flute. When the syncopated opening is restated, semi-quavers in the piano increase the tension by stressing the beginning of each beat. The gentler second theme, or subject, is heard first on the piano and echoed by the woodwind. From the next *tutti*, piano and orchestra engage in a continuing dialogue, the rumbling figure never absent for long. Even the second theme loses its tenderness when it reappears in the minor. The movement ends with dark mutterings from the whole orchestra.

(TR) Adam and Eve *by Henry Fuseli*
Paintings such as this formed part of the artistic movement, encompassing literature, music and the visual arts, that became known as Sturm und Drang.

ROMANCE AND THIRD MOVEMENT

The Romance brings a change of mood: it begins with a simple, lyrical melody in two parts, each part played first by the piano and then by the orchestra. The piano continues with a solo, to a chugging accompaniment on the strings; the mood is still tranquil, but the return of the opening melody is interrupted by an outburst on the piano, which rages away, accompanied mainly by the wind, until calm descends.

Passion and vigour return in the rocketing opening to the last movement, where the orchestra takes up the piano's theme and develops it with angry rising and falling chromatic scales. When the soloist re-enters, his theme follows the contours of his opening statement in the first movement. A jaunty tune in the woodwind brings respite, but not for long, and its next appearance is back in the minor before a final outburst from the orchestra before the **cadenza**.

Mozart then springs two surprises. The first is that the orchestra does not enter after the cadential trill: instead, the piano restates the rocketing tune, ending with a rhetorical gesture followed by a pause. The key moves to the major and the jaunty tune reappears on the oboe, with an almost facetious accompaniment on the bassoon. Then, on its third appearance, it is followed by a humorous six-note tag that pervades the rest of the movement as if turning its back on all the previous storms and tempests. Neither opera had yet been written; but they are foreshadowed as here the demonic passion of *Don Giovanni* gives way to the joyous laughter of *Le nozze di Figaro*.

7. 2'38"
Restatement of the opening.

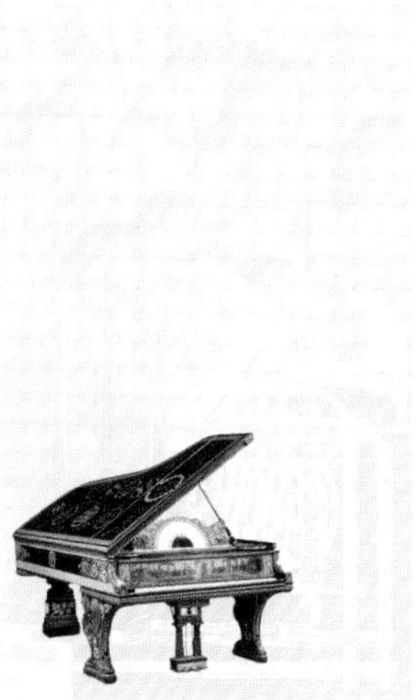

8. 3'20"
Flute and bassoon develop the rising arpeggio.

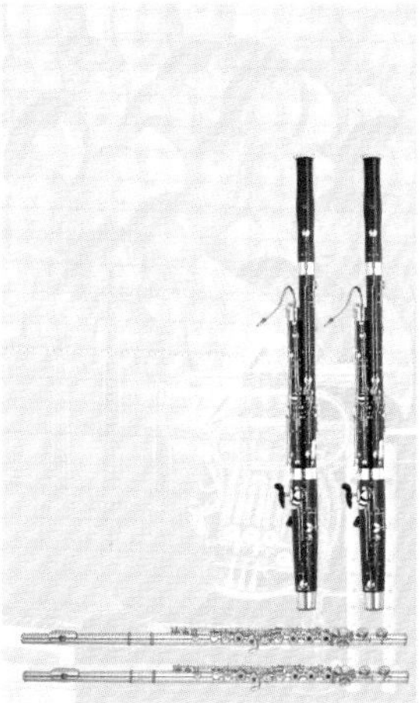

9. 4'15"
The F minor theme returns in the tonic.

10. 4'44"
The second subject returns in the minor.

11. 5'26"
Beginning of the cadenza.

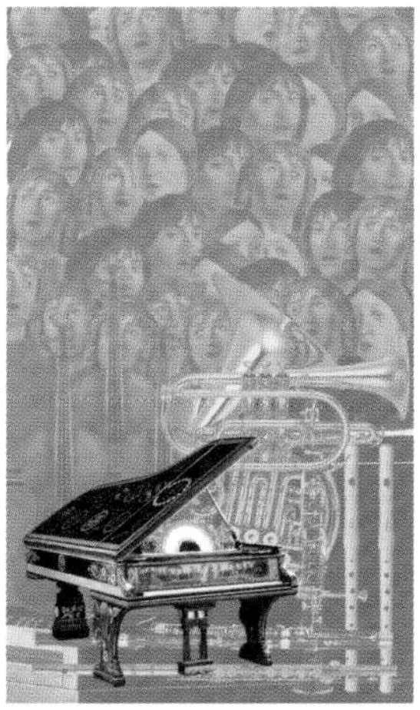

12. 5'56"
Key changes to D major with the second subject on the oboe.

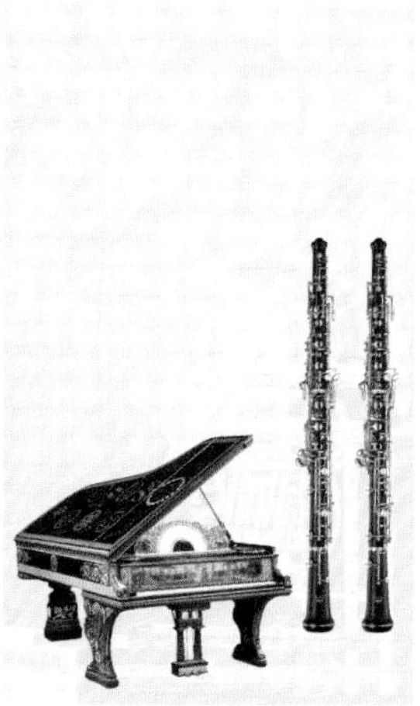

Gluck ▶ p. 158 Mozart ▶ p. 144

GLUCK: *ORFEO ED EURIDICE*

The première in Vienna on 5 October 1762 of *Orfeo ed Euridice* is one of the most significant occasions in the history of opera. Composed to celebrate the name day of Emperor Franz I, husband of Maria Theresa, it was an immediate success.

It is ironic that it was billed as an *azione teatrale* ('theatrical action'): the term was invented by **Metastasio**, the court poet, whose influence Gluck was struggling to counter. Together with his librettist, Raniero Calzabigi, Gluck wrote three works, now known as his 'reform' operas: *Orfeo ed Euridice*, *Alceste* and *Paride ed Elena*. Their intention was to rid the stage of 'abuses' ranging from sub-plots to empty displays of virtuosity.

The Story

Orpheus has lost his wife, Eurydice, who has been fatally bitten by a snake. He is allowed by Jupiter (via Cupid, the third character in the opera) to rescue her from the underworld, provided he does not look at her on their journey back to the world of mortals. In Act II, standing at the entrance to the underworld, he is challenged by the Furies, who threaten him, singing in stark octaves; Orpheus, accompanying himself on the lyre, charms them into allowing him passage.

The darkness – literal and musical – gives way to the pure light of the Elysian Fields. Orpheus enters: his wonder at the beauty of his surroundings is illustrated by a melody on the appropriately pastoral oboe, round which a flute and a solo cello weave a filigree pattern. He is welcomed by a chorus of heroes and heroines in soft accents far removed from the hostility and despair of the Furies. Eurydice enters, and the pair silently leave. In the third act, Eurydice dies a second time when Orpheus is finally unable to resist looking at her, but Cupid reappears to restore her to life and arrange a happy ending.

RECOMMENDED CD

Christoph Willibald von Gluck: *Orfeo ed Euridice*. Nancy Argenta, Michael Chance, Stefan Beckerbauer. Stuttgart Chamber Choir. Tafelmusik. Frieder Bemius, conductor. Sony SX2K 48 040 (2 CDs).

The pure, rather unearthly tones of Michael Chance's countertenor make a refreshing change from the usual mezzo-soprano or contralto Orpheus. This recording of the original 1762 version also benefits from the clarity of the period-instrument orchestra.

MOZART: STRING QUARTET IN C, K465, 'DISSONANCE'

Mozart composed this quartet in January 1785, a month before the D minor Piano Concerto. It is the last of six that he dedicated to his 'dearest friend', Haydn. The feeling of four individuals conversing on equal terms shows that Mozart had studied Haydn's six quartets op. 33 (1781).

The first movement is unusual on two counts: it is the only one of Mozart's quartets to have a slow introduction, and that introduction is highly **chromatic**. The *allegro* is launched with a two-bar phrase in the first violin, accompanied by repeated quavers in the second violin and viola. This phrase virtually dominates the whole movement: it is soon treated in imitation, from the cello up to the first violin, and although new material is introduced in the dominant, it returns to round off the **exposition**, or first section. The development section is entirely devoted to this phrase and its even shorter derivative, as is the **coda** that follows the recapitulation.

The Final Movements

The slow movement begins with a heartfelt melody for the first violin, followed by a tender dialogue with the cello. When the melody returns, it is embellished in the manner of an operatic aria. In between, and subsequently, comes a series of overlapping phrases for the three upper instruments, to poignant effect.

There are more surprises in the third movement, with a chromatic slant to the **minuet**, and a trio in the minor featuring wide leaps in the first violin. And the finale, so carefree on the surface, is full of descending chromatic phrases, as well as unusual **modulations**, unexpected pauses and restarts, too: a joke that Haydn was fond of perpetrating, and one that he would have enjoyed here.

PIANO CONCERTO IN C

The slow movement of Mozart's Piano Concerto in No. 21 in C, K467 has become one of his best-known pieces because of its use in the film *Elvira Madigan* (1967). Its floating melodic line, and its almost painfully poignant harmony, lend it a unique poetic quality.

POPULAR MELODY *Mozart*

RECOMMENDED CD

Mozart: String Quartet in C, K465, 'Dissonance'; String Quartet in B flat, K458, 'Hunt'. Alban Berg Quartet. Teldec 2292-43037-2. Recorded 1978.

The Alban Berg Quartet are fully at home in this music, playing at speeds that allow it to breathe.

DISSONANCE IN THE 'DISSONANCE' QUARTET

Mozart's 'Dissonance' Quartet takes its title from the 22-bar *adagio* introduction to the first movement. It begins with softly repeated quavers on the cello. The note is C, the tonic, which is only to be expected. But expectation is soon confounded: the violin enters on A flat, followed by the second violin on E flat. The viola moves down to G, but if we are expecting a chord of C minor, we are in for a shock, because the first violin enters on a high A natural, almost clashing with the A flat before it follows the viola down to G.

With the completion of the first violin's rising phrase after another harmonic near-miss, the process is repeated a tone lower. The throbbing cello quavers continue in a slow **diatonic** descent from A flat to E flat as the viola embarks on a rising chromatic phrase. This is heard three more times, on the first violin, cello, and viola again, and once upside-down on the second violin. The dissonance caused by these phrases rising and falling continues to tease the ear. By the sixteenth bar the part-writing is less sinuous and the music seems to be approaching a **cadence** in C minor. In bar 21, however, the goal is clearly C major, despite unsettling chromaticisms involving C sharp and A sharp; and C major is confirmed at last with the arrival of the *allegro*.

There are chromatic inflections in the third and fourth movements. These also produce **dissonances**, such as the chain of seventh chords towards the end of the exposition of the finale, though none are as stark as those in the introduction to the first movement.

cadence ▶ p. 356 canon ▶ p. 356 chromaticism ▶ p. 357 coda ▶ p. 357 diatonic ▶ p. 358 dissonance ▶ p. 358 exposition ▶ p. 358 minuet ▶ p. 360 modulation ▶ p. 360 obbligato p. 360

CASTRATO, CONTRALTO AND COUNTERTENOR

From the mid-seventeenth to the mid-eighteenth century, heroic roles were generally composed for castratos: male sopranos or altos who had been castrated before puberty to preserve their high voice. Castratos disappeared from the stage in the early nineteenth century, though they were kept on in the choir of the Sistine Chapel in Rome; the last survivor lived long enough to make gramophone recordings. The question then arose: how to perform the music written for them? One solution, favoured in Germany, was to transpose it down an octave for tenor or baritone. This was unsatisfactory, because it introduced an alien timbre and caused problems in ensembles.

The most common solution is to assign the roles to a woman, soprano or alto. **Berlioz** did this in his conflation of the two versions of Gluck's *Orfeo ed Euridice*, and it was in the role of Orpheus that the contralto **Kathleen Ferrier** (1912–53) made her name. But however skilful the costume and make-up, one is always conscious of watching a woman dressed as a man.

With the advent on stage in the twentieth century of the countertenor, the integrity of both pitch and appearance is preserved: singers such as James Bowman or **Andreas Scholl** (b. 1967) can be wonderfully convincing, although the actual sound is quite different from the castrato's. Soprano castrato parts, however, which remain outside the countertenor's range, continue perforce to be sung by women.

HAYDN: *MISSA IN ANGUSTIIS* ('NELSON' MASS)

The 'Nelson' Mass is the third in the series of six Masses that Haydn wrote for the name day of Princess Maria Hermenegild, the wife of his employer. It was first performed at Eisenstadt, the Esterházy family's castle, in September 1798. Haydn called it *Missa in angustiis* ('Mass in Straitened Times'), but it soon became associated with Nelson, who – though Haydn did not know this at the time – defeated the French at the Battle of the Nile while the Mass was being composed.

The unusual scoring – no woodwind or horns, only trumpets, timpani and organ **obbligato** in addition to the usual strings – reflects the fear and unease of the times. The magnificent *Kyrie* opens with menacing fanfares alternating with the solemn tread of the violins, producing an effect of grandeur intensified when the chorus enters. The solo soprano provides a more gentle contrast at 'Christe eleison', but the solemn mood soon returns. The tension is increased at the reprise of the opening material, the soprano soaring above the chorus.

The *Gloria*

The *Gloria* is a joyful outpouring in the major key, with a contrasting solo at 'Qui tollis' and a brief restatement before the fugue at 'in gloria Dei Patris'. Haydn shows off his contrapuntal skills in the first section of the *Credo*, which is a strict canon at the fifth up to the closing bars.

The menacing fanfares recur at the reference to Pontius Pilate and, even more remarkably, in the *Benedictus*. The cheerfulness and vigour of 'Dona nobis pacem' suggests that the suppliants are expecting, rather than pleading for, peace to be granted.

RECOMMENDED CD

Haydn: *Missa in angustiis* ('Nelson' Mass); Handel: *Zadok the Priest*; Vivaldi: *Gloria*. Choir of King's College, Cambridge. London Symphony Orchestra. Academy of St-Martin-in-the-Fields. Sylvia Stahlman, Helen Watts, Wilfred Brown, Tom Krause, Elizabeth Vaughan, Janet Baker. David Willcocks, conductor. Decca 458 623-2.

This recording made a great stir when it came out in 1962, and it still packs a punch. With its authentically all-male choir, excellent soloists and the LSO in top form, it is a winner.

BEETHOVEN: SYMPHONY NO. 5 IN C MINOR, OP. 67

Though shorter than the Third Symphony (the 'Eroica'), the Fifth (1807) is on a similarly epic scale. The beginning is one of the most famous openings in all music: three short notes and a long one, the rhythm used ('V' for Victory, in Morse code) for broadcasts to occupied Europe in World War II. This rhythmic, fateful figure builds up into an extensive paragraph and not only introduces but underpins the gentle second theme. In the development section, it is reduced first to pairs of chords played by the wind and brass alternating with the strings; then it is refined still further to single chords, the music getting quieter and quieter until, eventually, a *fortissimo* outburst leads to the recapitulation.

The Slow, Third and Fourth Movements

The slow movement is a series of variations, one of them in the minor key, on a singing melody for violas and cellos. Contrast is provided by a martial theme on the trumpets and horns. On the singing melody's last appearance it, too, is played *fortissimo*, with the wind attempting to follow the

strings in **canon**. The tempo increases for the coda, led off by a wistful bassoon, but the original speed soon returns.

The third movement contrasts another four-note figure in the minor with gruff phrases from the cellos and double basses in the major. There is a touch of Gothic horror about the sinister drum-taps that lead from the mysterious coda to the joyful C major of the fourth movement, which follows without a break.

Here, for the first time in a symphony, the orchestra is joined by three trombones, as well as a piccolo. The clouds are dispelled, but Beethoven brings back the goblins, as E. M. Forster famously called them in *Howard's End*, for one last frisson before the triumphant mood returns with a reprise followed by a *presto* coda.

RECOMMENDED CD

Beethoven: Symphony No. 5 in C minor, op. 65; Symphony No. 7 in A, op. 92. Vienna Philharmonic Orchestra. Carlos Kleiber, conductor. DG 447 400-2. Recorded in 1974.

This recording stands the test of time brilliantly. Carlos Kleiber, a conductor of rare distinction, makes you hear the symphony as though for the first time.

(FL) Opera Costumes
Designs for costumes from four of Gluck's operas, including a Fury from Orfeo *(BL).*
(TL) The Heavenly Quartet
Nineteenth-century depiction of (l-r) Beethoven, Schubert, Mozart and Haydn.
(TR) King's College Choir
The choir at King's College, Cambridge, who made a recording of Haydn's 'Nelson' Mass.
(BR) Esterházy Theatre
The stage and orchestra – for which Haydn was responsible – at the Esterházy court.

Beethoven ▶ p. 150 Berlioz ▶ p. 186 Ferrier ▶ p. 303

THE EARLY ROMANTIC

The first half of the nineteenth century was essentially a period of insurgence in Europe, from the French Revolution in 1789 to the series of uprisings that rocked the continent around 1848. Meanwhile, the Industrial Revolution was also underway, beginning in Britain, then spreading south through the rest of Europe. With these two strands of revolution came transformations in society, including the growing awareness of national identity, social development, the growth of cities and important advances in technology, all of which were reflected by and embodied in the arts.

THE SENTIMENTS OF THE AGE

Culturally, the first two decades of the nineteenth century marked the rejection of the scientific certainty that had characterized the Enlightenment: classical balance, symmetry and simplicity were gradually replaced by Romantic expressivity, individualism and grand gestures. Distinctive traits (many of which derived from the writings of the French philosopher Jean-Jacques Rousseau) included an interest in Nature, the supernatural, the relatively recent past (particularly the Middle Ages) and national and individual identity. Closer links were forged between the arts and social and political reality. In literature, Goethe's *Faust* and the chivalric novels of Walter Scott were seen as embodying the sentiments of the age. Of all the arts, however, it was music, particularly absolute music, that came to be seen as the ideal means of expression, partly because of its ambiguous, indefinable quality.

MUSICAL DEVELOPMENTS

Although classical structures were retained in music, they were expanded, and new ways to shock or move were sought. Thus opera increasingly used realistic settings and historical events for its subjects; orchestral music was often inspired by literary or historical themes; and virtuoso concertos and intimate mood pieces focused on the expression of the individual. The most influential developments in opera took place in France and Italy, while instrumental music flourished in the German-speaking lands.

The Early Romantic
INTRODUCTION

Following the social and political upheaval of the French Revolution and the Napoleonic Wars, Europe enjoyed a short period of relative stability with Napoleon's exile, the restoration of the Bourbon monarchy in France and the establishment of the Vienna Peace Settlement in 1815. However, in the early 1820s a number of minor revolts broke out in Naples and the Iberian peninsula, and in 1822 Europe was drawn into the Greek War of Independence.

A second, more serious, wave of revolts occurred around 1830. The Bourbons were overthrown in France, then the Belgians' gained independence from the Dutch; these events were followed by risings in Poland, Italy and Germany, by civil war in Spain and Portugal, and by the overthrow of Wellington and the Tories in Britain. This wave of revolts effectively confirmed liberalism as an important political and social force in Western Europe, while the problem of nationalism took precedence over everything else east of the Rhine. Meanwhile, the colonies of South and Central America were gaining independence, and Europe turned its empire-building efforts east.

The following decades built to the crisis of 1848, when revolution broke out almost simultaneously in cities across Europe, triggered by a crisis in agriculture and economics. Although these uprisings were largely unsuccessful, the urge towards national unity was crystallized, and the principles of universal suffrage were established.

KEY EVENTS

1808	Part I of Goethe's *Faust* published
1812	French invasion of Russia
1815	French defeated at Waterloo; Napoleon is exiled, the Bourbon monarchy is restored in France, and the Vienna Peace Settlement is signed; Johann Nepomuk Maelzel patents his metronome
1820	Revolts crushed in Naples, Spain and Portugal
1822	Start of Greek War of Independence, following uprising against the Turks the previous year
1824	Death of Byron at Missolonghi, fighting for the Greeks
1829	Stephenson's *Rocket* locomotive built
1830	July Revolution in France: Louis-Philippe comes to the throne; Belgian revolt, reputedly sparked by a performance of Auber's *La muette de Portici*; foundation of the Societé des Concerts du Conservatoire
1831	Michael Faraday discovers electromagnetic induction; circumnavigation by Charles Darwin
1832	Reform Bill in Britain; Metternich issues repressive decrees in Germany; Giuseppe Mazzini founds 'La Giovane Italia' with the aim of national independence for Italy; completion of first continental railway, from Budweis to Linz
1837	Death of William IV, succession of Victoria in Britain; Louis Daguerre invents the daguerreotype, the first practicable process of photography
1840	Death of Friedrich Wilhelm III of Prussia, succession of Friedrich Wilhelm IV
1842	Verdi's *Nabucco* performed; the chorus 'Va pensiero' later becomes a provisional national anthem in Italy; *Gazzetta musicale di Milano* first published in Italy
1845	Wagner's *Tannhäuser* performed in Dresden
1846	Irish potato famine
1848	Uprisings throughout Europe; abdication of Ferdinand I of Austria, succession of Franz Joseph; abdication of Louis Philippe; French Republic proclaimed, with Louis-Napoleon as president

MUSIC AND JOURNALISM

With the advances in print technology, a new wave of music journal publishing began in Europe which aimed at comprehensive coverage. The *Allgemeine Musikalische Zeitung* ('General Musical Journal'), founded in Leipzig in 1798 by the publishers Breitkopf & Härtel, set new standards, reporting on a range of topics rather than promoting the specific interests of the company. Its contributors included **E. T. A. Hoffmann** (1776–1822). In 1834, **Robert Schumann** (1810–56) founded the *Neue Zeitschrift für Musik* ('New Music Journal'); although it covered a similar breadth of topics, Schumann saw it as a forum for the creative artist, promoting Romanticism.

France, Britain and Italy were rather slower to produce quality music journals. However, *La revue musicale* ('The Musical Review'), established by François-Joseph Fétis in 1827, was read all over Europe. In 1835 it was absorbed by the *Gazette musicale de Paris* ('Paris Musical Journal'); **Hector Berlioz** (1803–69) and Fétis himself were among its contributors. In Britain, the first comprehensive music journal to appear was *The Musical World*, founded in 1836 by Alfred Novello. It was largely modelled on its German and French predecessors. Eight years later Novello established *The Musical Times*, which remains the oldest of all musical journals with a continuous record of publication. The first significant music journal to appear in Italy was the *Gazzetta musicale di Milano* ('Milan Musical Gazette'), which first came out only in 1842; in contrast to the international flavour of other journals, it focused primarily on Italian music.

THE GREEK WAR OF INDEPENDENCE

Only one of the uprisings in southern Europe during the early 1820s had any lasting success. This was the Greek revolt in 1821, which led ultimately to Greece's independence from the Ottoman Turks. Despite the risk of widespread unrest in the Balkan states, the four major European powers – Britain, France, Austria and Russia – were initially unwilling to come to the aid of the Greeks. However, public opinion was fully in favour of the rebels; philhellenic committees were set up in Western Europe, and money and volunteer fighters were sent to Greece. The war was viewed primarily as a people's insurrection, and became the inspiration of international liberalism, effectively rallying the radicals in Europe. The most celebrated philhellene was Byron, who formed the 'Byron Brigade', gave money and inspiration to the insurgent Greeks, and died of fever while training rebel troops at Missolonghi in 1824.

Many artists, writers and composers were inspired by the revolt. Notable works include paintings by Eugène Delacroix, such as *The Massacres of Chios* (1824) and *Greece Expiring on the Ruins of Missolonghi* (1826), and *La révolution Grecque* ('The Greek Revolution', 1825–26), a *scène grecque* by Berlioz). *Maometto II*, an opera by **Gioacchino Rossini** (1792–1868), adapted for the Paris Opéra as *Le siège de Corinthe* ('The Siege of Corinth', 1826), was also in part a response to the Greek War.

LITHOGRAPHIC PRINTING OF MUSIC

The Industrial Revolution brought many transformations as it spread from England to the rest of Europe. Rapid technological progress in instrument manufacture and stage machinery led to developments in the composition and performance of music and opera. And wide-reaching innovations in printing, as methods became quicker and cheaper, meant that music was disseminated much more widely.

At the beginning of the nineteenth century, the main method of printing music was by engraving, a technique that had been developed in the seventeenth century in which a steel plate was scored or punched, and the music was then printed directly from the plate. Paris, London and Amsterdam were the main centres of music publishing at this time. However, in 1796 a new process of music printing was developed. Lithography, invented by Alois Senefelder, involved preparing a stone surface so that some parts of it would accept a greasy ink and others would repel it. The image of the music was inscribed on such a surface, and it was used to print further copies. This led to a diversification of music publishing, particularly in Vienna. By the middle of the century, following the developments of Louis Daguerre and W. H. Fox Talbot, the process was speeded up as photographic transfers were made on to stone and zinc.

(FL) Gazetta Musicale di Milano
The Gazetta was the first quality music journal in Italy.
(NL) Printing
Advances in printing and lithography allowed a more rapid dissemination of music.
(R) Franz Liszt
Liszt was one of the many young composers drawn to the new centre of music in Europe: Paris.

1830: THE TRIUMPH OF ROMANTICISM IN FRANCE

In France, not only did 1830 mark the year of an important political revolution – the ousting of the Bourbons and the crowning of the 'Citizen King', Louis-Philippe; it also marked the moment at which Romanticism was officially recognized in the theatre. Throughout the 1820s there had been heated discussions between classicists, protectors of tradition, and Romantics, who sought modernity and realism in the arts. In 1830 the drama *Hernani*, by the leader of the French Romantics, Victor Hugo, was seen as throwing off the shackles of classical restraint, bringing to the Théâtre Français something of the realism, emotion and shock that had characterized popular drama for the past decades. Culturally it was a culminating moment. The same year, Delacroix's *Liberty Leading the People* was exhibited at the Academy's Salon; he similarly rejected the classical subject matter and smooth style of painting of Jean-Auguste-Dominique Ingres and others, presenting a picture that was at once more immediate, more rough, more dramatic.

The *Grand Opéra*

Musically, too, these were important years in Paris. In 1827 the first significant French music journal, *La revue musicale*, was founded, and the following year saw the première of the first *grand opéra*, *La muette de Portici* ('The Mute Girl of Portici') by **Daniel-François-Esprit Auber** (1782–1871), performances of Beethoven's symphonies conducted by François-Antoine Habeneck (1781–1849) and the founding of the Société des Concerts du Conservatoire. In 1830, with the mood of the 'bourgeois revolution', censorship was temporarily dropped, and the following year the Opéra, for so long viewed as part of the establishment, became a commercial venture run by a series of investor-directors. Throughout the decade, foreign virtuosos and composers, including **Franz Liszt** (1811–86), **Frédéric Chopin** (1810–49), **Gaetano Donizetti** (1797–1848) and a young **Richard Wagner** (1813– 83), came to Paris the new musical capital of Europe.

Auber ▶ p. 186 Berlioz ▶ p. 186 Chopin ▶ p. 190 Donizetti ▶ p. 192 Hoffman ▶ p. 193 Liszt ▶ p. 194 Rossini ▶ p. 200
R. Schumann ▶ p. 201 Wagner ▶ p. 226

ROMANTICISM

Romanticism has always been difficult to define, despite a certain number of recurring characteristics in the various arts. Some writers sought to suggest the uniqueness of the individual; carried to an extreme, this led to a sense of isolation or alienation, as exemplified in *Die Leiden des jungen Werthers* ('The Sorrows of Young Werther', 1774) by Johann Wolfgang von Goethe, and the works of the second generation of English Romantic poets. Similarly, the paintings of Caspar David Friedrich frequently depict an individual contemplating a powerful landscape, suggesting man's insignificance, but also his longing for the infinite. At around the same time Joseph Mallord William Turner developed new techniques with which to create a total, impressionistic impact in his dramatic landscapes.

Some writers returned to the past; François-René de Chateaubriand, Novalis and Walter Scott romanticized the medieval period, depicting an age when society provided the individual with security and a sense of belonging. Their works were frequently adapted for the stage. In art, Delacroix introduced a theatricality and sense of movement into his often melodramatic paintings of episodes from literature and history.

Composers addressed similar issues. Broadly, they infused classical forms with new meaning, evoking a range of impressions and emotions through more varied orchestral colours, extra-musical inspirations and programmes, and emphasis on the individual.

EXPANSION

Rather than a break with classical rules, Romanticism in music was essentially an expansion of existing forms and structures. **Ludwig van Beethoven** (1770–1827), who straddles the classical and early Romantic periods, embodies this growth in his orchestral works; his Ninth Symphony (1824), for example, is twice the length of his earliest symphonies, and calls for voices in addition to the orchestra. Similarly, French *grand opéra* was longer in duration than earlier French opera, and employed more choruses, soloists and instrumentalists, as well as more artists, technicians and stage-hands.

All aspects of music were effectively expanded and loosened without destructive effect. Thus harmonic language was extended; more remote key relationships and fluent modulations were explored; added and altered notes and unprepared

and unresolved dissonances were introduced. Melody also acquired new importance; dazzling display was often replaced by a more complex, expressive style whether in opera, song, or in instrumental genres. Rhythm was expanded through folk music, particularly dances, in which irregular phrase and bar lengths were common, although the classical eight-bar period was retained. The orchestra was also greatly enlarged, and a new emphasis was placed on the specific qualities of individual instruments in unusual combinations, notably by **Carl Maria von Weber** (1786–1826) and Berlioz. Moreover, technical advances allowed greater flexibility and power. In sum, more importance was given to emotional and expressive demands than to formal developments.

ROMANTICISM AND THE CULT OF THE INDIVIDUAL

An important aspect of Romanticism was its focus on individual feeling and expression, in contrast to the universal strictures of classical form and style. This led inevitably to a concept of the artist as a misunderstood genius, battling against the world. The second generation of English Romantic poets, including Percy Bysshe Shelley and Lord Byron, contributed significantly to this idea. Their extravagant lifestyles, their travels abroad and their early deaths meant that their biographies and letters became as important for Romanticism as their poetry. Furthermore, the critical writings and lectures of William Hazlitt and others described poetry and drama with new psychological appreciation and emphasis on the creativity of the individual.

A similar focus on the personal can be seen in music. Donizetti favoured inner psychological conflict as a central feature in many of his serious operas, such as *Maria Stuarda* ('Mary Stuart', 1835). In instrumental music, Shakespearean soliloquies, notably that of Hamlet, proved inspirational; Berlioz's *Symphonie fantastique* similarly paints a personal, albeit phantasmagorical, journey. In the concert hall, virtuoso soloists such as Liszt and **Nicolò Paganini** (1782–1840) came to be seen as creative geniuses, musical heroes of the age.

EXTRAMUSICAL INSPIRATION

Although at the beginning of the nineteenth century instrumental works relied on strict musical codes to convey 'meaning' and to establish a coherent structure, with the expansion and loosening of classical forms, extramusical associations became increasingly significant, both in providing inspiration and structure and in eroding them. This new interest in the extramusical was manifested in various ways. The inspiration of specific landscapes lay behind the broadly programmatic 'Italian' and 'Scottish' Symphonies (1833, 1842) by **Felix Mendelssohn** (1809–47) and the 'Spring' Symphony (1841) by Robert Schumann, each of which can be seen as a response to Beethoven's Sixth Symphony, the 'Pastoral' (1808). In contrast, a more personal, psychological programme inspired Berlioz's *Symphonie fantastique* ('Fantastic Symphony', 1830). Meanwhile, newly expressive genres were often inspired by plays or by historical events. Examples include the symphonic poems by Liszt based on characters such as Hamlet, Tasso and Prometheus, and many of Berlioz's orchestral works, which defy categorization altogether. In *Harold en Italie* (1834) and *Roméo et Juliette* (1839) expression is more important than traditional form; the former is described as a 'symphony with obbligato viola', a merging of symphony and concerto; the latter as a 'dramatic symphony' – a symphony with voices.

HISTORY AND FRENCH OPERA

The Romantic era saw a growing fascination with the past. In France, a need was felt to forget the turbulence of recent times and re-establish a continuity with more distant national history. Thus nostalgic plays about the first Bourbon king became popular, as did dramas about national heroes such as Joan of Arc. Yet there was also a need to understand the horrors of the 1790s, and in the late 1820s, plays and operas based on revolts that had (for reasons of censorship) taken place in a distant place or time became popular. Auber's *La muette de Portici*, for example, harked back to a peasant rebellion in seventeenth-century Italy. Parallels with 1789 were recognized, and from 1830 the opera's relevance to French politics was openly acknowledged; its protagonist, Masaniello, was seen as a national hero for much of the nineteenth century.

In the 1830s, grand operas by **Giacomo Meyerbeer** (1791–1864) and others depicted more familiar historical conflicts, recalling events such as the St Bartholomew's Day Massacre of 1572 (*Les Huguenots*, 1836). These works were openly ambiguous in their political implications, a result of the relaxation in censorship under the new régime. The subjects were inherently dramatic and spectacular, and lent themselves to depiction on the stage of the Opéra, where an astonishing accuracy of historical detail was achieved in the costumes and scenery, and sometimes even in the music.

THE EMERGENCE OF NATIONALISM IN OPERA

During this era of political instability, there was an emerging awareness of the importance of national identity. Whether in countries moving towards unification, or states breaking away from oppression, opera was an obvious means of expressing nationhood. The genre resented the opportunity to use the vernacular language, to depict familiar landscapes, events and rituals, and to employ native folk tales and music.

Italian opera continued to dominate Europe, but alongside it increasingly popular German Singspiel operas evoked the supernatural, and the dark, mysterious forests of German Romanticism. Meanwhile, in independent nations such as Russia and Poland, where vernacular opera was considered an expression of patriotism, *A Life for the Tsar* or *Ivan Susanin* (1836) by **Mikhail Ivanovich Glinka** (1804–57) was recognized as the first 'national' opera. The member states of the Habsburg Empire tended to graft vernacular opera on to existing traditions, perhaps because of their links with Vienna. They were to produce their greatest national operas in the second half of the century.

In the Italian peninsula, it was not until the violent clashes of the *Risorgimento* in the 1840s that opera was linked explicitly with national identity. The operas of **Giuseppe Verdi** (1813–1901) were seized on for their apparent political messages, most famously the chorus of the Hebrew exiles from *Nabucco* (1842).

LONDON CONCERT LIFE

During the first half of the nineteenth century, London became the financial and commercial capital of the world, its population expanding to two and a half million. Concert life had stagnated at the turn of the century, but by 1810 development was quickening, reflecting the growth of the city. In 1813, the Philharmonic Society grew out of a need for an organization to provide regular concerts of orchestral music. It was dependent on aristocratic patronage, but managed by professional musicians, many of whom formed the core of the orchestra. Programmes usually consisted of music that was new to London, including, for example, Beethoven's overtures and Fifth Symphony. The players were effectively Europe's first fully professional symphony orchestra.

By the late 1830s, however, despite continuing prosperity in the city, musical life was becoming uncertain, and dependent on fashion. Audiences at the Philharmonic Society were declining, and it was criticized for its conservative programmes, poor performance standards and the low wages paid to its musicians – in effect a complete reversal of its initial ideals. Meanwhile, however, other types of concert flourished, notably chamber music performances and 'cheap' concerts, such as the Promenade Concerts (from 1838) and the amazingly popular Concerts d'Hiver (1841) started by Louis Jullien, in which fine performance was combined with showy display.

(BL) Lord Byron
The poet Byron contributed to the cult of the individual as a theme of Romanticism.
(TL)* The Wayfarer Above Sea of Fog *by Caspar David Friedrich
Caspar David Friedrich's paintings encapsulated the new Romanticism, represented by the individual in isolation.
(FR) Concert Life
Promenade concerts, such as this in London's Covent Garden Opera House, flourished from 1838.
***(NR) Character from* Les Huguenots**
Meyerbeer's operas concentrated on recent historical events, such as the expulsion of the Huguenots or the St Bartholomew's Day Massacre.

Beethoven ▶ p. 150 Glinka ▶ p. 192 Mendelssohn ▶ p. 197 Meyerbeer ▶ p. 198 Paganini ▶ p. 198 Verdi ▶ p. 230 Weber ▶ p. 205

The Early Romantic
FRANZ SCHUBERT

Described by Liszt as 'the most poetic of all composers', Franz Schubert (1797–1828) was both the heir to the great Viennese classical tradition of Joseph Haydn (1732–1809), Wolfgang Amadeus Mozart (1756–91) and Beethoven, and the first true Romantic composer. In his short life, spent almost entirely in Vienna, he was known almost exclusively as a composer of songs and piano pieces. Yet he composed prolifically in virtually all the major genres; and the full range of his achievement was only gradually realized after his death.

Schubert's early death spawned a welter of sentimental myths and half-truths. For well over a century the image lingered of the complaisant, happy-go-lucky composer, blithely scribbling melodies on the back of the nearest available menu. Onlyin recent decades have scholars identified a darker, depressive, even neurotic strain in his make-up, which manifested itself above all in the bleak *Winterreise* ('Winter's Journey') song cycle and the great chamber works of his last years.

Schubert's sexual orientation, too, has come under scrutiny and while this may remain the subject of speculation, the charges of fecklessness once levelled against Schubert have been well and truly discredited. Far from being the unselfcritical 'clairvoyant' composer of popular legend, he was unswerving in his sense of purpose, and would often make extensive sketches before a piece satisfied his stringent demands. And while he is rightly loved as the creator of some of the world's supreme melodies, he is now equally revered for his mastery of large-scale structures and his innovative, even visionary, approach to harmony.

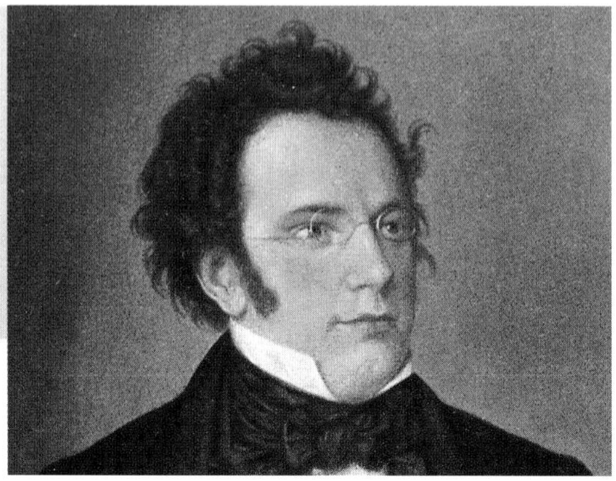

KEY EVENTS

1797	Born 31 January in the poor Himmelpfortgrund district of Vienna, the son of a schoolmaster
1806	Studies organ and harmony with Michael Holzer, organist at the parish church of Lichtental
1808	Becomes choral scholar in the Imperial Court Chapel choir
1811	Writes first surviving song, 'Hagars Klage'
1812	Mother dies; begins lessons with Salieri
1813	Composes First Symphony; enters imperial teacher training college
1814	Composes his first Goethe songs, including 'Gretchen am Spinnrade'
1815	Now a teacher at his father's school, composes 145 songs, including 'Heidenröslein' and 'Erlkönig'
1816	Composes Fourth and Fifth symphonies and over 100 songs; first Schubertiads held
1817	Meets the baritone Johann Michael Vogl, who begins to champion his songs
1818	Spends summer as music master to Count Johann Esterházy in Hungary
1819	Summer holiday with Vogl in Upper Austria; composes Piano Sonata in A major, D664, and the 'Trout' Quintet
1820	Briefly arrested, with several friends, for suspected political subversion; composes *Quartettsatz* in C minor and music for *Die Zauberharfe*
1822	Composes the two movements of the 'Unfinished' Symphony; contracts syphilis, probably at the end of the year
1823	Admitted to hospital for several weeks. Composes *Die schöne Müllerin* and the opera *Fierrabras*
1824	Second spell as music master to Count Esterházy; composes Octet and string quartets in A minor and D minor
1825	Tours in Upper Austria with Vogl; begins work on 'Great' C major Symphony
1826	Composes G major Piano Sonata and G major String Quartet
1827	Health begins to fail; composes *Winterreise* and B flat Piano Trio; is a torchbearer in Beethoven's funeral procession on 29 March
1828	Completes 'Great' C major Symphony; composes E flat Mass, the 14 songs published as *Schwanengesang*, the last three piano sonatas and the String Quintet; dies in Vienna, 19 November, buried in the Währing cemetery, close to Beethoven

SCHUBERT'S CHILDHOOD

Franz Peter Schubert was born on 31 January 1797 in a cramped apartment in the Himmelpfortgrund suburb of Vienna. Both his father Franz Theodor, the local elementary school teacher, and his mother Elisabeth originally hailed from northern Moravia, on the fringes of the sprawling Austrian Empire. Franz was their twelfth child; three sons survived to adulthood, as did a subsequent daughter.

'THE TROUT'

'The Trout' (1817) shows Schubert's genius at its most lovable. The folksong-like melody is enhanced by the accompaniment depicting the darting fish. Schubert later reused the song in the 'Trout' Quintet, where it appears in various guises before finally emerging with its original leaping piano accompaniment.

POPULAR MELODY *Schubert*

From early on, Franz's musical talents were nurtured by his affectionate family. He received piano lessons from his brother Ignaz and violin lessons from his father. Ignaz later wrote that 'within a very short time he progressed so far that I had to recognize in him a master who far out-stripped me'; and before his tenth birthday Franz had bluntly announced that he had no further use for his piano lessons and would continue on his own. By this time he was receiving instruction in organ and music theory from Michael Holzer, choirmaster of the local Lichtental parish church. It was probably Holzer who introduced Franz to the venerable **Antonio Salieri** (1750–1825), famous as Mozart's rival. On Salieri's recommendation the boy competed for a position as chorister in the Imperial Court Chapel and a place at the Stadtkonvikt, a boarding school run by Piarist monks. He sailed through his audition and exam; and at the end of 1808 he left his family home for the spartan régime of the Stadtkonvikt.

EARLY INFLUENCES

Franz no doubt suffered from the Stadtkonvikt's inadequate food and iron discipline. But in compensation he was exposed to an exciting new world of music-making. He soon became the star treble in the chapel choir, and came to know symphonies by Haydn, Mozart and Beethoven as a violinist in the school orchestra under a young university student Josef von Spaun, who was to become a lifelong friend. Two of the young Schubert's particular favourites were Mozart's Fortieth Symphony and Beethoven's Second, both of which were to leave their mark on works of his own. His first surviving composition, for piano duet, dates from 1810, and his earliest complete song, 'Hagars Klage' ('Hagar's Lament'), from the following year.

When his voice broke in 1812 he left the chapel choir and found himself with more free time to compose. He had already begun composition lessons with Salieri, who introduced the boy to the grave splendours of **Christoph Willibald von Gluck** (1714–87) and classical ***opera seria***. In October 1813 he composed his first symphony, in D, obviously indebted to

opera seria ▶ p. 361

Mozart and Beethoven, but exuding extraordinary youthful confidence and élan. Probably in the same month, the 16-year-old Schubert left the Stadtkonvikt and, under pressure from his father, who had recently remarried after Elisabeth's death the previous year, entered the imperial teachers' training college in the Annagasse, close to St Stephen's Cathedral.

THE GALLEY YEARS

By the autumn of 1814, Schubert was a reluctant teacher at his father's school, continuing his studies with Salieri and singing, now in a light, falsettoish tenor, in the Lichtental church choir. For all the day-to-day schoolroom drudgery, the years 1814 to 1816 were crucial in Schubert's development as a composer. In the spring of 1814 he received his first commission, to compose a festive Mass for the Lichtental church; and the upshot was the Mass in F, an imposing, large-scale work in the Haydn tradition. The soprano in the first performance of the Mass, on 16 October, was a schoolmaster's daughter, Therese Grob, with whom Schubert was in love and whom for a time he hoped to marry. Whether or not fired by his longing for Therese, he set a clutch of love poems by Goethe at this time, including his earliest masterpiece, 'Gretchen am Spinnrade' ('Gretchen at the Spinning Wheel').

ANNUS MIRABILIS

Schubert's absorption in the poetry of Goethe continued during 1815, an *annus mirabilis* that saw the creation of four stage works, two symphonies (Nos. 2 and 3), church and chamber music and no fewer than 145 songs, among them such popular favourites as the folklike 'Heidenröslein' ('Wild Rose') and the sinister ballad 'Erlkönig' ('The Erl-King'). In the autumn of 1815 he made the acquaintance of Franz von Schober, a wealthy *dilettante* who tried to persuade Schubert to give up his teaching and devote himself to composing. But it was to be another year before Schubert

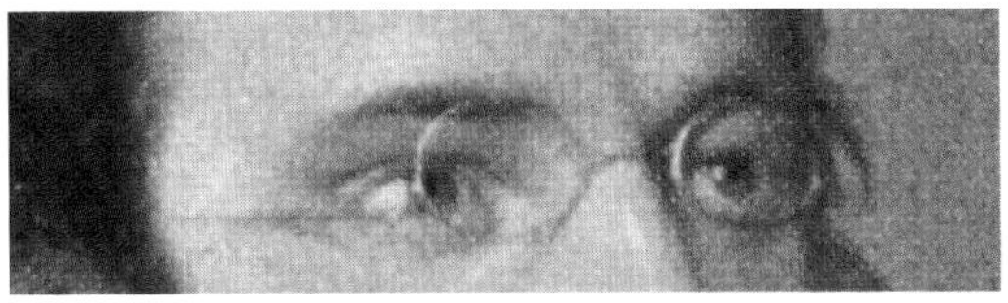

finally made the break and took lodgings in the home of Schober's mother.

Schubert's phenomenal productivity continued throughout 1816, the year of the Fourth and Fifth Symphonies, several string quartets and over 100 songs, including 'Der Wanderer' ('The Wanderer'), a song of Romantic alienation whose popularity during the composer's lifetime was second only to that of 'Erlkönig'. This was the year, too, of the first so-called Schubertiads, convivial evenings devoted to music, poetry-reading and punch-drinking held in Spaun's lodgings. Besides Spaun himself and Schober, regulars at these gatherings included the saturnine, mis-anthropic poet Johann Mayrhofer, and Anselm Hüttenbrenner, a cheerful, extrovert character and a moderately gifted amateur composer.

'GRETCHEN AM SPINNRADE'

Schubert composed his first song at the age of 14. By the time of his premature death in 1828 his tally of songs numbered over 600, many of them among the most sublime creations of Western art. In instrumental music he was deeply conscious of the Viennese tradition of Haydn, Mozart and Beethoven; but in song he was less aware of his predecessors. He did, though, have the suggestive power of the recently evolved piano, whose expressive possibilities had been richly explored by Beethoven, and the stimulus of the new German lyric poetry, with its immediate sensuous appeal.

Supreme among Schubert's poets was Goethe, whose spontaneity of feeling and ecstatic eagerness to seize and glorify the moment inspired most of the finest songs from Schubert's teens, including 'Gretchen am Spinnrade'. Composed on 19 October 1814, 'Gretchen' is an impassioned *scena*, rising from numb pathos to near-hysteria, and miraculously unified by an accompanying figure that at once evokes the rotation of the spinning wheel and mirrors every phase of the girl's agitation – a synthesis of pictorial illustration and emotional insight characteristic of many of Schubert's greatest songs.

GROWING INDEPENDENCE

By December 1816 Schubert had left his family home and moved to the luxurious apartment of Schober's mother, although he was still forced to earn his meagre living teaching at his father's school. At the Schober's, he had a fine six-octave piano at his disposal, which may well have stimulated the composition of a series of piano sonatas in the spring and summer of 1817. This was the year, too, of such famous songs as 'Die Forelle' ('The Trout') and 'Ganymed', and of Schubert's first meeting, at Schober's behest, with the operatic baritone Johann Michael Vogl. The distinguished singer was initially condescending: 'There is something in you,' he remarked, 'but you are too little of a comedian, too little of a charlatan.' But a few weeks later they performed several Schubert songs before a group of friends, initiating a partnership which was to spread the composer's name through Vienna's middle-class salons.

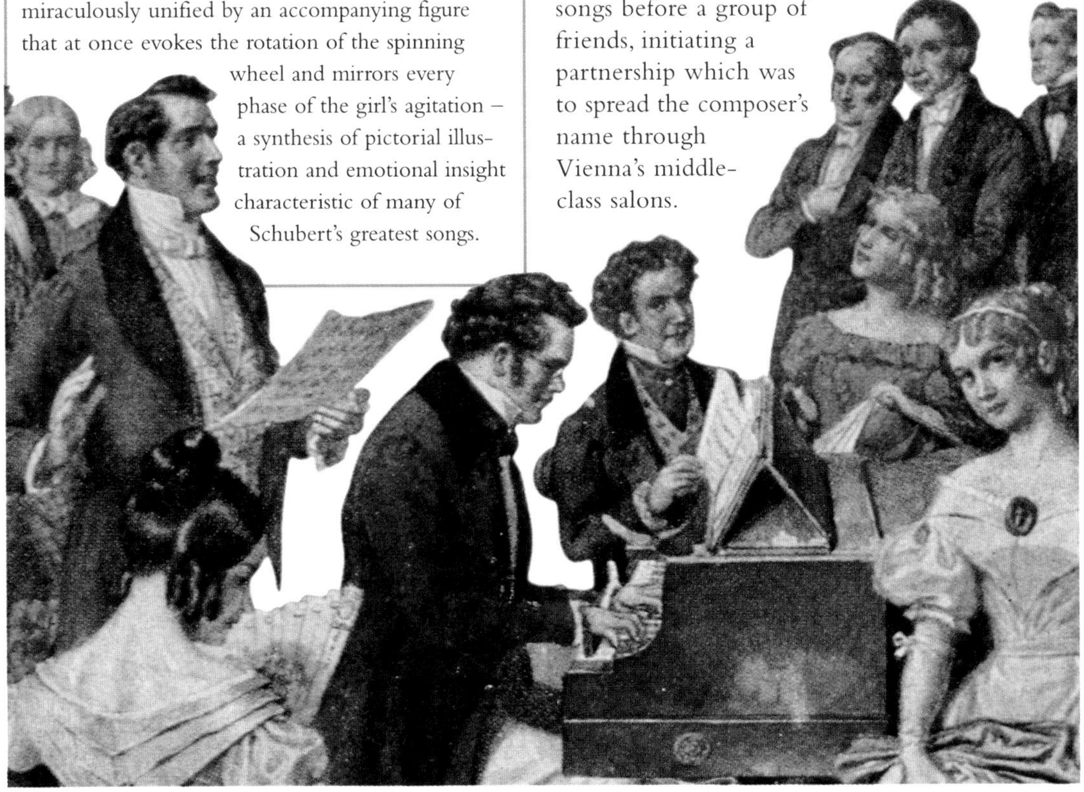

(BL) Schubert Playing the Organ
Schubert initially gained his skills at the keyboard with the help of his brother Ignaz.
(NR) The Quartet
Schubert playing in a quartet with his father and friends.
(FR) Schubert and von Spaun
Schubert entertains at an evening hosted by Josef von Spaun.

Beethoven ▶ p. 150 Gluck ▶ p. 158 Haydn ▶ p. 140 Mozart ▶ p. 144 Salieri ▶ p. 162

SCHUBERT AND VOGL

Encouraged by Vogl's championship and increasing public performances of his songs and piano pieces, Schubert finally broke with his father's school in July 1818 and, like Mozart before him, chanced his arm as a freelance composer. He immediately took up a summer job as music master to the children of Count Johann Esterházy at their summer residence at Zseliz in Hungary. On his return to Vienna he moved in with Mayrhofer, whose poetry, often based on classical myth, inspired many of the finest songs of 1817–19, among them 'Memnon' and 'Der Schiffer' ('The Boatman'). Meanwhile, Vogl had secured Schubert's first major paid commission, for the operetta *Die Zwillingsbrüder* ('The Twin Brothers'), which was finally given in the summer of 1820.

In the summer of 1819, Schubert and Vogl undertook the first of several walking tours to Upper Austria. They spent some time in Vogl's birthplace, Steyr, delighting audiences with recitals of Schubert's songs. And it was probably in these idyllic surroundings that the composer embarked on one of his sunniest, most relaxed works: the much-loved 'Trout' Quintet for piano and strings.

OPERATIC AMBITIONS

First staged on 14 June 1820, with Vogl doubling the roles of the twin brothers, *Die Zwillingsbrüder* was only moderately successful. But it did lead to another major commission, to compose incidental music for the melodrama *Die Zauberharfe* ('The Magic Harp'): the upshot – much glorious, prophetic music attached to a preposterous drama – set the pattern for most of the stage works that dominated his output over the next few years. In fact, Schubert's lack of opportunism and theatrical flair proved fatal in a Vienna intoxicated by **Rossini**; and his two most ambitious operas, *Alfonso und Estrella* (1821–22) and *Fierrabras* (1823), were rejected for performance by the Court Theatre. By the end of 1823 his operatic hopes had collapsed.

MISBEHAVIOUR

There was, however, compensation in the ever-growing popularity of his songs and piano pieces, both in public performances and through publication. By the end of 1821 Schubert had left Mayrhofer's lodgings and moved back to the Schobers' family apartment. According to others in the Schubert circle, the composer was in thrall to the charismatic Schober, who now encouraged him in a hedonistic lifestyle. Besides hints of sexual profligacy, there are reports of Schubert's uncouth behaviour in public at this time, and of his gratuitous rudeness to friends, including Vogl.

FRANZ SCHUBERT: WORKS

- **Over 600 songs, including:** 'Gretchen am Spinnrade' (1814); 'Erlkönig' (1815); 'Heidenröslein' (1815); 'Wanderers Nachtlied I' (1815); 'Der Wanderer' (1816); 'Ganymed' (1817); 'Der Tod und das Mädchen' (1817); 'An die Musik' (1817); 'Wanderers Nachtlied II' (?1822); 'Du bist die Ruh' (1823); *Die schöne Müllerin* (song-cycle, 1823); 'Die junge Nonne' (1824); 'Fischerweise' (1826); 'Nur wer die Sehnsucht kennt' (1826); *Winterreise* (song-cycle, 1827); *Schwanengesang* (song cycle, 1828); 'Der Hirt auf dem Felsen' (1828)
- Many choruses and partsongs
- **Piano works including:** Sonata in A, D664 (1819); 'Wanderer' Fantasy, D760 (1822); Sonata in A minor, D784 (1823); Sonata in A minor, D845 (1825); Sonata in D, D850 (1825); Sonata in G, D894 (1826); Sonatas in C minor, D958, A, D959, and B flat, D960 (1828). Many dances and other shorter pieces, including two sets of Impromptus (1827) and six *Moments Musicaux* (1823–28)
- Many works for piano duet, including *Grand Duo* in C (1824) and *Fantaisie* in F minor (1828)
- **String quartets and quintets:** *Quartettsatz* in C minor (1820), Quartets in A minor and D minor (1824) and Quartet in G (1826); String Quintet in C (1828); Octet in F (1824); 'Trout' Quintet (1819); Piano Trio in B flat (1827); Piano Trio in E flat (?1828)
- **Symphonies, nine plus several fragments including:** No. 4 in C minor, 'Tragic' (1816); No. 5 in B flat (1816); No. 8 in B minor, 'Unfinished' (1822); No. 9 in C major, 'Great' (1825–28)
- **Stage works including:** *Die Zwillingsbrüder* (1819); *Die Zauberharfe* (1820); *Alfonso und Estrella* (1821–22); *Die Verschworenen* (1823); *Fierrabras* (1823); *Rosamunde* (incidental music, 1823)
- Church music, including 6 Masses; oratorio *Lazarus* (unfinished, 1828)

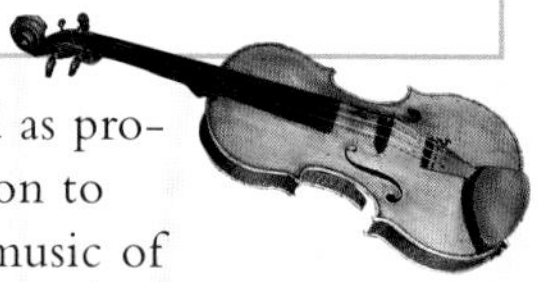

Yet he still composed as prolifically as ever. In addition to *Alfonso und Estrella*, the music of 1820–22 includes the Mass in A flat, which marries liturgical grandeur with Schubert's own personal, often disturbing vision, and two powerful instrumental masterpieces which, like many of the works composed between 1818 and 1822, he left as torsos: the so-called *Quartettsatz* (quartet movement) in C minor (1820), and the 'Unfinished' Symphony in B minor (1822), with its tragic, almost confessional tone and its extreme contrasts of violence and lyrical pathos.

ILLNESS AND FATALISM

At the end of 1822, within weeks of composing the two movements of the B minor Symphony, Schubert was seriously ill with the first symptoms of syphilis, contracted, no doubt, in Viennese brothels. With periods of respite, the affliction was to undermine his health for the remaining years of his life. The only known treatment in those days was mercury, itself a toxin; and he spent part of the spring and summer of 1823 in hospital, where he probably composed some of the songs that make up the song-cycle *Die schöne Müllerin* ('The Fair Maid of the Mill'). While it would be a romantic exaggeration to say that Schubert lived out the rest of his life in the shadow of death, a new note of fatalism is discernible in his letters. His friends often found him distracted and withdrawn; and in his music the sense of yearning, of the evanescence of beauty, deepens and darkens. The Viennese *Gemütlichkeit* of the 'Trout' Quintet and the exquisite A major Piano Sonata (D664) is never entirely lost. It reappears, for instance, in the Octet of 1824, which raises the alfresco eighteenth-century divertimento to a supreme level. But the other major instrumental works of 1823–24 seem to peer into the abyss: the bleak, concentrated A minor Piano Sonata, D784; the A minor Quartet, perhaps Schubert's most poignant expression of nostalgia for a lost innocence; and the grim, uncompromisingly argued 'Death and the Maiden' Quartet in D minor, so-called because its andante variations are based on the song of that name.

REPRIEVE

By the spring of 1824 the symptoms of primary syphilis were in abeyance. And on 25 May Schubert left Vienna to spend the summer once more in Zseliz, where he seems to have fallen in love with one of the Esterházy daughters, Caroline, then nearly 20. Though often lonely and depressed at Zseliz, he did produce some of his finest music for piano duet to play with his pupils, including the almost symphonic *Grand Duo*, D812. Back in Vienna, his health seemingly restored, he moved in February 1825 to a suburban house near the home of his artist friend Moritz von Schwind.

adagio ▶ p. 356

SCHUBERT'S SONG CYCLES

With the modest exception of Beethoven's *An die ferne Geliebte* ('To the Distant Beloved,' 1816), there were no precedents for Schubert's great song cycles to poems by Wilhelm Müller: *Die schöne Müllerin* (1823) and *Winterreise* (1827). Each is in effect a musical drama unfolded in an extended sequence of songs. But while the narrative of the later cycle is largely interior, *Die schöne Müllerin* charts a chronological sequence of events: the young man's arrival at the mill, his love for the miller's daughter, his rejection in favour of the glamorous huntsman, his despair and suicide, and, in the haunting final lullaby, the benediction of the millstream, the protagonist's companion and confidant throughout the cycle.

In a sense, *Winterreise* begins where *Die schöne Müllerin* leaves off. The jilted miller has now become the archetypal romantic wanderer, condemned, like Goethe's Harper and the solitary, pitiable figures in the landscapes of Caspar David Friedrich, to remain on the margins of existence. The springing rhythms and water music of the earlier cycle give way to the wanderer's increasingly weary footsteps and musical emblems of bareness and frozen stillness as Schubert explores a mind hovering between delusion, ironic self-awareness and bleak nihilism.

As in 1819, he spent the summer of 1825 with Vogl in Upper Austria, walking, giving impromptu concerts and visiting old friends. At Gastein he composed the expansive, open-hearted Piano Sonata in D, D850, and at Gmunden 'worked at a symphony' which grew into the 'Great' C major, though this probably only reached its final form in March 1828. The work recalls the Dionysian rhythmic power of Beethoven's Seventh Symphony, though its leisurely time-scale and intense, romantic lyricism are uniquely Schubertian.

WINTERREISE

Meanwhile, Schubert's reputation in Vienna continued to grow. His concerts with Vogl were renowned events and he was negotiating with several publishers. 1826 saw the creation of his last great Goethe songs (settings of poems from the novel *Wilhelm Meister*), the mysteriously serene G major Piano Sonata and the G major String Quartet, the most violent and tonally unstable of all his major works – a world away from the companionable, lyrical Schubert, but an expression of an equally crucial aspect of his musical personality.

In February 1827, Schubert composed a group of what he called 'terrifying songs' from Wilhelm Müller's sequence of poems *Winterreise*, and sang them through at Schober's 'in a voice wrought with emotion'. The following autumn, suffering from headaches and frequent suffusions of blood to the head, he added a further 12 songs, completing the greatest and most harrowing of all song cycles.

Though Schubert was depressed and ailing at the end of 1827, it would be dangerous to regard *Winterreise* as an autobiographical statement, all the more so as the same period also saw the creation of one of his happiest and most spontaneously tuneful works, the Piano Trio in B flat. In the first months of 1828 both his spirits and his health seemed to revive. He was negotiating with several publishers in Vienna and abroad there were frequent public performances of his songs and piano music and in March he gave a full-scale benefit concert devoted entirely to his own music, including the recently composed Piano Trio in E flat.

THE FINAL YEAR

Even by Schubert's standards, 1828 was a year of phenomenal productivity, comparable to 1791 for Mozart. It was as if both composers somehow had a premonition that time was running out. In the summer he composed the great E flat Mass and the songs published posthumously under the sentimental title of *Schwanengesang* ('Swansong'), among them 'Ständchen' ('Serenade'), the most sensuous and beguiling of his many serenades, and the searing, apocalyptic 'Der Doppelgänger' ('The Double'). Then, in the autumn, Schubert wrote his final trilogy of piano sonatas and the sublime String Quintet in C. The first two of the sonatas, in C minor and A, though wholly characteristic of Schubert, are more specifically indebted to Beethoven than any of his other instrumental works. But the third sonata, in B flat, is utterly un-Beethovenian. The contemplative ecstasy of its first two movements is a quintessentially Schubertian experience of the kind first glimpsed in his 1815 setting of Goethe's 'Wanderers Nachtlied' and found again in the ethereal, disembodied ***adagio*** of the String Quintet.

(FL) Schubert and Vogl
Schubert's association with the bartitone Vogl was to help widen his reputation across Vienna.
(NL) Quartet in B Flat Minor
Manuscript of one of Schubert's Quartets, as a work in progress.
(TR) Schubert Statue
Statue situated in Schubert's home town of Vienna.
(BR) Winterreise
This painting of Schubert was probably inspired by his song-cycle Winterreise.

'A RICH POSSESSION'

In October, the month he completed the Quintet, Schubert became troubled by recurrent headaches; and in early November he developed a continuous high fever and was increasingly confined to his bed. The exact cause of his death, on 19 November, has been much debated. But it is now generally agreed that he contracted typhoid fever in the last weeks of his life when he was already suffering from the active tertiary stage of syphilis.

The poet Franz Grillparzer's famous epitaph on Schubert's tomb – 'The art of music here has buried a rich possession, but still fairer hopes' – reminds us that works like the 'Unfinished' and 'Great' C major symphonies and the String Quintet, and with them the full scope of his genius, remained unknown for many years after the composer's death. Today we contemplate that genius with mingled awe and delight. Yet, with Schubert's visionary late works in our minds, it is hard – far harder than with Mozart – to escape a tragic sense of what might have been.

Rossini ▶ p. 200

The Early Romantic

PERSONALITIES

Auber, Daniel-François-Esprit

(Ō-bâr', Dân-yel' Frân-swà Es-prē') 1782–1871

FRENCH COMPOSER

Auber is renowned for his operas and was the leading composer of ***opéras comiques*** in nineteenth-century France. He studied with Cherubini in Paris, writing concertos and vocal music before turning his attention to operas. His most important work is *La muette de Portici* (1828), one of many collaborations with the librettist Eugène Scribe, which deals with the Neapolitan insurrection under Masaniello in 1647. Auber became director of the Paris Conservatoire in 1842 and remained there until its closure in 1870.

Balfe, Michael

1808–70

IRISH COMPOSER

Balfe was the most successful composer of English operas of the nineteenth century. He made his name as a singer with a fine baritone voice, and sang in Rossini's *The Barber of Seville* in Paris, as well as leading roles in Italy until 1833. His fame as a composer began in London with *The Siege of Rochelle* (1835). Balfe went on to compose operas for the Italian Opera (*Falstaff*, 1838) and the Opéra-Comique in Paris (*Le puits d'amour*, 1843), but all these successes were eclipsed by the huge popularity of *The Bohemian Girl* (1843). Although other contemporary English composers were more convincing dramatists, Balfe's skill was as a melodist, particularly as a writer of affectingly simple ballads.

FAUST IN PARIS

In the mid-1820s, three translations into French of *Faust* by Goethe were published in Paris; there were also two melodramas based on the story for the popular stage, and a series of paintings of scenes from the legend by Delacroix was exhibited at the 1827–28 salon.

It was Gérard de Nerval's translation of 1827 that particularly inspired Berlioz: 'the marvellous book fascinated me.' He planned to write the music for a *Faust* ballet for the Opéra, which sadly was never commissioned, and in 1828 he published, at his own expense, *Huit scènes de Faust* ('Eight Scenes from *Faust*') as his op. 1. This strikingly original collection of pieces, each scored for a different combination of forces and headed by a quotation from Shakespeare, reveals Berlioz's wit, sensitivity to text, and flexible treatment of traditional generic forms. Goethe was apparently unimpressed by the settings, and Berlioz himself changed his mind about them, destroying as many copies as he could find. However, much of the music found its way, almost unchanged, into *La damnation de Faust* ('The Damnation of Faust', 1846) nearly 20 years later.

Berlioz's *Faust*

The 'dramatic legend' *La damnation de Faust* is effectively an oratorio for concert performance, although it is often performed as an opera. Berlioz manages to retain the philosophical as well as supernatural aspects of Goethe's story in a breathlessly original range of pictorial music, from the poignant, lyrical solos for Marguérite, to the energetic number for the carousing students, to the wonderful mocking choral fugue on the death of a rat. A highlight is the apocalyptic 'Cours à l'abîme' ('Journey to the Abyss'), in which the galloping ride to Hell, mocking skeletons and jeering demons are all graphically depicted.

'MARCH TO THE SCAFFOLD'

Berlioz's 'March to the Scaffold' is the most famous movement in his *Symphony fantastique*. It provides a marvellously grim marching theme, with blaring brass and drums, as the artist dreams he has murdered his beloved and is being dragged to the scaffold.

POPULAR MELODY *Berlioz*

Bellini, Vincenzo

(Bel-lē'-nē, Vēn-chânt'-zō) 1801–35

ITALIAN COMPOSER

One of the most important opera composers of the nineteenth century, Bellini cultivated a ***bel canto*** (literally 'fine singing') melodic style that influenced not only other opera composers but also Chopin and Robert Schumann. He studied first with his grandfather, composing youthful sacred works, ***ariettas*** and instrumental pieces, and in 1819 moved to Naples and studied with Zingarelli at the conservatory. He had his first operatic success on completing his studies (*Adelson e Salvini*, 1825), and was soon invited to write an opera for La Scala, Milan. The resulting work, *Il pirata* ('The Pirate', 1827), laid the foundation of his operatic career. Bellini remained mostly in Milan until 1833, reaching his maturity as an opera composer, before visiting London and Paris. His finest works include *La sonnambula* ('The Sleepwalker', 1831), *Norma* (1831) and *I puritani* ('The Puritans', 1835). Bellini's style exudes emotional potency, with the expressive tension often being intensified throughout individual arias, and encompasses a broad range, from rich elegiac lyricism to more forceful and imposing drama.

Berlioz, Louis-Hector

(Ber-lyōz', Lōō-ē' Ek-tôr') 1803–69

FRENCH COMPOSER, CRITIC AND CONDUCTOR

Berlioz was the leading French musician of his age. His greatest achievements were with large-scale orchestral and vocal works, although he also wrote in other genres. He was rooted in classical traditions – his earliest influences included **Gluck** and the music of the French Revolution – but his interest in new and varied modes of expression and his passionate sense of colour and drama embodied the Romantic ideal.

Although admired today, Berlioz's talents as a composer were not generally recognized by his contemporaries in France. His idiosyncratic style, embracing irregular rhythms and phrases, contrapuntal textures and imaginative orchestration, was not appreciated. In his day he was

ariette ▶ p. 356 bel canto ▶ p. 356 idée fixe ▶ p. 359 opéra comique ▶ p. 361

more successful as a critic, and indeed this was largely how he earned his living. He wrote with wit, trenchantly defending composers he admired, notably Beethoven, while pouring scorn on what he saw as the frivolous musical style of Rossini and other Italian opera composers. His entertaining *Mémoires* are an important (if often misleading) source of our understanding of his life.

FORMATIVE YEARS

As a boy Berlioz learnt to play the flute and guitar, though conspicuously not the piano. Yet despite his early interest in performing and composing, on his father's insistence he spent two unhappy years studying medicine in Paris. From 1822, however, he attended composition classes with Jean-François Le Sueur (1760–1837), and in 1826 he enrolled at the Conservatoire. Compositions from these years include a number of romances and a *Messe solennelle* (1824), material from which he was to incorporate into later works.

In 1827 an important event took place that was to affect his personal and professional life fundamentally. He saw *Hamlet* performed by a visiting English troupe and, despite his difficulty in understanding the language, was profoundly moved. This marked the beginning of a life-long love of the works of William Shakespeare (to be reflected in many of his works), and the start of a mercurially intense relationship with the Irish actress Harriet Smithson, who played the part of Ophelia (they married in 1833, but separated nine years later). His *Symphonie fantastique* ('Fantastic Symphony', 1830), a huge, Beethovenian, narrative drama for orchestra, reflects his emotional turmoil at this time: it describes the progression of a violent, opium-induced love affair through five movements, and is unified by the recurrence of a theme, or ***idée fixe***, representing the artist's obsession.

(NL) I Puritani
Italian baritone Antonio Tamburini plays Riccardo in Bellini's I Puritani.
(FL) La Zingara
Score cover for La Zingara *('The Bohemian Girl'), Balfe's most successful composition.*
(BR) Ludwig van Beethoven
Beethoven's influence on succeeding generations of composers was immeasurable.

SUCCESS AND DISILLUSION

In 1831, having won first prize in the Prix de Rome, Berlioz went to Italy for 15 months to study. Although temporarily relieved of financial worries, he did not have a particularly happy time there, wanting to build on his growing reputation in Paris. However, the warmth and vitality of some of his later works reflect his response to the Italian landscape, notably *Harold en Italie* (1834), and *Benvenuto Cellini* (1838), a grand opera based on the life of the Renaissance sculptor which failed at the Opéra, although the brilliant overture 'Le carnaval romain' ('Roman Carnival', 1844), extracted from it, was to prove immensely popular.

Back in Paris, Berlioz was commissioned to write his *Grande messe des morts* ('Great Mass for the Dead', 1837), in the tradition of the massive Revolutionary works written for open-air performances. The dramatic symphony *Roméo et Juliette* (1839) and a number of more intimate works such as the song *Sara la baigneuse* ('Sara the Bather', 1834) also date from this period. However, there were few in Paris (Chopin and Liszt were notable exceptions) who appreciated Berlioz's talents as a composer.

THE RECEPTION OF BEETHOVEN'S MUSIC

The years 1826–28 saw the deaths of the three greatest composers of their respective generations, Weber, **Beethoven** and **Schubert**. Only in the years that followed could early Romanticism really forge its own identity. The 1830s saw the flowering of a new generation of great composers, including Chopin, Schumann, Berlioz, Liszt and Mendelssohn, and for each of these musicians the influence of their forebears, especially Beethoven, was enormous. When Beethoven died many of his works, especially from his last period, were little-known, barely understood and very difficult to play. Disseminating his works throughout Europe required performers of an enlightened and adventurous outlook; live performance was, of course, the only way of getting to know new music. So when François-Antoine Habeneck performed Beethoven's symphonies in Paris, including the first performances there of the Fifth and Ninth Symphonies (1828 and 1831 respectively), the sense of musical shock was tangible. Berlioz was inspired to compose his *Symphonie Fantastique*, while Liszt sketched the beginnings of a 'Revolutionary' Symphony (1830) and went on to become the leading exponent during the nineteenth century of Beethoven's piano sonatas. Other works of Beethoven remained mysterious for far longer, and the late string quartets in particular were rarely on board by early nineteenth-century composers (excepting perhaps Mendelssohn), and not until the quartets of **Béla Bartók** (1881–1945) was their influence thoroughly absorbed.

GREAT OPERA SINGERS

The early nineteenth century saw the rise of the operatic personality, or prima donna. Composers built working relationships with individual singers and tailored their roles to the vocal characteristics of their favoured performers. Meyerbeer, for example, carefully considered his performers' vocal nuances and technical capabilities, and if the singer he had in mind could not perform, he would find a replacement and re-write the part. The most celebrated of all Meyerbeer's interpreters was the great Swedish soprano Jenny Lind (1820–87), whom he discovered. Nicknamed 'the Swedish nightingale', Lind was principally a recitalist and oratorio singer, but her short operatic career made a huge impact, especially in Germany and England.

Another singer whose performances helped the success of Meyerbeer's work, specifically *Le prophète*, was the French mezzo-soprano Pauline Viardot. Similarly, Bellini wrote leading roles for another great operatic soprano of the era, Guiditta Pasta (1797–1865), including Amina in *La sonnambula* and the title role in *Norma*. During the 1830s Pasta was recognized as the greatest soprano in Europe, appearing in many Rossini operas, and contributing much to the success of works by Donizetti, including *Anna Bolena*. Her special combination of lyrical flair and dramatic potency was a great influence for Bellini. This illustrates the reciprocal relationship that existed between composers and performers, a co-operative spirit that was more important in the nineteenth century than ever before.

Bartók ▶ p. 285 Beethoven ▶ p. 150 Gluck ▶ p. 158 Schubert ▶ p. 182

ON TOUR

By the early 1840s, Berlioz's music was rarely performed in Paris, and he was composing little. Instead, he devoted his energies to literary activity, notably a treatise on orchestration (1843) and especially journalism, a profession he despised but which he was forced to pursue in order to earn a living and fund his composing.

However, his reputation abroad was growing, and he embarked on the first of several concert tours. He travelled to Germany, Belgium, Russia and London, where he found that his music and conducting skills were warmly appreciated in a way that they had never been in Paris. In 1852 Liszt revived *Benvenuto Cellini* and it enjoyed great success in Germany.

When in Paris, Berlioz continued to devote his time to writing, and conducted at several large-scale concerts, notably at the Universal Exhibition in 1855, where his *Te Deum* (1849) was first performed. His sporadic compositions during these years include the song cycle for voice and piano *Les nuits d'été* ('Summer Nights', 1841), *La damnation de Faust* and the oratorio *L'enfance du Christ* ('The Childhood of Christ', 1854), a legendary narrative.

THE LAST YEARS

In 1856, he turned his attention to an idea that he had been thinking about for some time: an epic opera based on Virgil's *Aeneid*. *Les Troyens* ('The Trojans') combined the classical grandeur and tragedy of Gluck's operas with the spectacle and national conflicts that characterized the Romantic grand operas of Meyerbeer still dominating the Parisian stage. Unable to secure its production at the Opéra, Berlioz split the five-hour work in two and had the second portion, *Les Troyens à Carthage*, performed with success at the Théâtre-Lyrique in 1863. The first part, *La prise de Troie* ('The Prize of Troy'), was not staged in his lifetime, and it was only in 1957 that the entire opera was first performed complete, in London.

Meanwhile, Berlioz revised Gluck's *Orphée* (1859), completed a comic Shakespearean opera *Béatrice et Bénédict* (1862), based on *Much Ado about Nothing*, and undertook further tours to Vienna and Russia. However, his last years were filled with illness, despair (particularly following the death of his son Louis in 1867) and bitterness at his lack of recognition as a composer in France. He died in 1869.

HECTOR BERLIOZ: WORKS

- **Operas:** *Benvenuto Cellini* (1838), *Les Troyens* (1858), *Béatrice et Bénédict* (1862)
- **Sacred works:** *Messe solennelle* (1824), *Grande messe des morts* (1837), *Te Deum* (1849), *L'enfance du Christ* (1854)
- **Orchestral works:** *Symphonie fantastique* (1830), *Harold en Italie*, with viola obbligato (1834), *Roméo et Juliette*, with voices (1839)
- **Overtures:** *Waverley* (1828), *Le roi Lear* ('1831), *Le carnaval romain* (1844)
- **Other vocal works:** *Lélio, ou La retour à la vie* (1832, rev. 1854), *La damnation de Faust* (1846), Les nuits d'été (1841, orchd 1856); Song Arrangements

THE PARIS CONSERVATOIRE

The Paris Conservatoire revolutionized music education in France. For most of the eighteenth century such education in Paris was rooted around church choir schools, but as these gradually closed the Ecole Royal de Chant was founded (1783), largely thanks to Gossec. This institution became the Institut National de Musique in 1793. By 1794 there were 80 pupils. On 3 August 1795 the Paris Conservatoire was founded out of this institution; the following year there were 351 pupils and 115 professors. At this time the five inspectors were Cherubini, Gossec, Grétry, Le Sueur and Méhul. The Paris Conservatoire was the first truly modern institution of its type, organized on a national basis and supported entirely from public funds.

The Foundation of Music Education

The Conservatoire trained a prestigious generation of instrumentalists. One of its functions was to provide music for public ceremonies, and as a result the teaching staff went from being mainly singers and those connected with the opera, to being instrumentalists, principally wind players: there were 19 'professors' of the clarinet and 12 of the bassoon. The Conservatoire's record at producing world-class singers was therefore less successful. A formal curriculum and examination statutes were put in place, although when Cherubini took over from François-Louis Perne as director in 1822, he introduced a more structured hierarchy of study, from counterpoint, harmony and fugue to composition, and laid the foundation of music education for years to come.

Berwald, Franz

(Bâr'-vàld, Fránts) 1796–1868

SWEDISH COMPOSER

Berwald played the violin in the court orchestra in Stockholm from 1812 until 1828. In 1829 he went to Berlin, where he worked on various operatic projects. His efforts were largely fruitless, and it was not until the 1840s that he met with success; all the works on which his reputation now rests date from this decade, including the four symphonies. He returned to Sweden in 1849, and continued his business activities outside music, as well as composing. He was appointed professor at the Swedish Royal Academy of Music in 1867. Appreciation of Berwald's work, including many first performances, had to wait until the twentieth century. His style was rooted in the harmonic language of Beethoven, Hummel and Spohr, although his best works (such as the *Sinfonie singulière*, 'Singular Symphony', 1845) show melodic freshness and originality of form. He is one of the most important and individual of all Swedish composers.

BERLIOZ AS CRITIC

Berlioz was better known and admired as a critic than as a composer by his compatriots, and wrote for the major musical journals of the day. He also published three collections of essays, including most famously *Les soirées de l'orchestre* ('Evenings in the Orchestra', 1852). His writings tended to be witty, provocative and deeply felt.

In broad terms, he valued expression, dramatic coherence and novelty in music, and admired such qualities in his idols, notably Gluck and Beethoven. In his famously savage dismissals of Rossini and other 'second-rate' composers – which, perhaps inevitably, make for a more interesting read – he attacked empty frivolity, formulaic harmony and melody, and unimaginative orchestration. Moreover, he abhorred the extremely popular arrangements and translations of foreign operas for the French stage which he believed violated the concept of the original work (although he was to engage in such 'mutilations' himself).

It is generally believed that Berlioz's battles as a critic were closely tied to his attempts to gain acceptance as a composer. If, for example, his readers could understand the beauties of Gluck, they might then be able to appreciate the same characteristics in his own music. However, if this was indeed a conscious strategy, it failed conspicuously.

strophic ▶ p. 362

THE SONGS OF BERLIOZ

Berlioz's songs owe much to the tradition of the *romance*, the simple and sentimental **strophic** poems of the eighteenth century that became so popular in *opéra comique*. Notable examples in the genre include the Romantic *Elégie en prose* ('Elegy in Prose', 1829), to a text by Thomas Moore, and the exquisite *Sara la baigneuse* (1834), a setting of a verse by Victor Hugo. Rather unusually, many of his songs are written for varied forces: *La mort d'Ophélie* ('The Death of Ophelia'), for example, can be performed either by a solo voice with piano accompaniment, or by a women's chorus with piano or orchestra.

His best-known songs are *Les nuits d'été*, a cycle of six pieces to verses by Théophile Gautier, for voice and piano. He later orchestrated them, transposing some for different voices. They include a wide range of styles and moods centring on the theme of love, from the sparkling 'Villanelle', through four varied slow songs, to the ebullient yet ironic *barcarolle* 'L'île inconnue' ('Unknown Island'). In many ways the French equivalent of the German Lied, they open the way for later generations of French song writers such as **Gabriel Fauré** (1845–1924) and **Henri Duparc** (1848–1933).

Boieldieu, François-Adrien

(Bwalď-yö, Frän'-swȧ Ȧ-drē-an') 1775–1834

FRENCH COMPOSER

Boieldieu was one of the leading opera composers of the early nineteenth century, concentrating on the *opéra comique* tradition. He studied with Charles Broche in his home town of Rouen, and was influenced by late eighteenth-century *opéra comique*, especially the works of **André-Ernest-Modeste Grétry** (1741–1813) and Méhul. His earliest operas were encouragingly received and in 1796 he moved to Paris, where he quickly became established as a prominent figure in musical life. After a brief, ill-fated marriage he went to St Petersburg in 1803 and was made director of the French Opéra. He returned to Paris in 1811 and the following year won great acclaim with *Jean de Paris*, an opera full of warmth and vigour. His next major triumph was with *La Dame blanche* ('The White Lady', 1825), his most enduring work. *Les deux nuits* ('The Two Nights', 1829) signalled a more adventurous approach, but it did not achieve the same lasting success. Harmonically, Boieldieu was more restricted than Méhul or Cherubini, but the freshness and elegance of his melodic invention greatly impressed his contemporaries.

(TNR) Harriet Smithson
Berlioz's wife, in the role that won his admiration – Ophelia in Hamlet.
(TFR) Ole Bull
Memorial statue to the Norwegian violinist and composer in Bergen.
(BR) Jean de Paris
1908 Berlin Opera House production of Boieldieu's opera, which opened to great acclaim in 1811.

Bull, Ole

(Bool, Ō'-le) 1810–80

NORWEGIAN VIOLINIST AND COMPOSER

Bull was one of the greatest violinists of the nineteenth century and a key figure in the development of Norwegian music. He went to Christiania (now Oslo) in 1828, where he soon became conductor of the Musical Lyceum, also devoting himself to theory and composition. In Paris in 1831, he was introduced to Paganini's style of violin playing. He toured Italy (1833–35) before returning to Paris to give a concert at the Opéra (apart from Paganini, he is the only violinist ever to do so). In 1840 he played Beethoven's 'Kreutzer' Sonata in London with Liszt. He continued to tour extensively, and in later years divided his time between Norway and the US. His compositions were largely designed to demonstrate his specific technical abilities, fostered by his use of a violin with some characteristics of a Norwegian peasant fiddle and a specially shaped bow. His best-known work is *Et saeterbesog* ('A Visit to the Mountain Pasture') for violin and orchestra.

Cherubini, Luigi

(Kā-rōō-bē'-nē, Lōō-ē'-jē) 1760–1842

ITALIAN COMPOSER AND TEACHER

Cherubini was a dominant figure in French musical life, particularly as a composer of operas, but also as director of the Paris Conservatoire. He studied with Giuseppe Sarti in Bologna and Milan (1778–81) before returning to his native Florence. After a brief period in London, where he composed *La finta principessa* ('The False Princess', 1785) for the Theatre Royal, he settled in Paris in 1786. When the Paris Conservatoire was founded in 1795 he was appointed one of its inspectors, becoming director in 1822. His most successful operas were *Médée* ('Medea', 1797) and *Les deux journées* ('The Two Days', 1800), which expanded the dramatic possibilities of *opéra comique*. However, his works soon became outmoded, replaced by the grand Romantic operas of Spontini and Meyerbeer; Cherubini's reputation faded and in the late nineteenth century he was remembered primarily for his treatise on counterpoint, although more recent revivals have led to a re-evaluation of his work.

Duparc ▶ p. 245 Fauré ▶ p. 248 Grétry ▶ p. 160

Chopin, Fryderyk Francisek (Frédéric François)

(Shō-pàn, Fri-drikh Frăn'-zhĕk [Fră-dă-rĕk' Fràn-swà']) 1810–49

POLISH COMPOSER

Chopin was unique among composers of the highest achievement and influence in that he wrote all his works, with the merest handful of exceptions, for the solo piano. Leaving Warsaw, which at the time offered only restricted musical possibilities, and living most of his adult life in Paris, he acquired a reputation as a pianist of exceptional poetic expression, despite a career that, unlike those of such contemporaries as Sigismund Thalberg (1820–71) and Liszt, largely avoided public appearances. Although he was not the founder of any compositional school, his daring and innovative harmony, complete understanding of the piano and its sonorities, development of Polish genre, such as the mazurka and polonaise, as well as 'narrative' forms such as the **ballade**, all had a profound influence on many composers. The contrast between his personal sensitivity and apparent fragility and the expressive drive and ardour of many of his compositions has contributed to a popular image of the composer as a pallid and otherworldly Romantic, an impression intensified by his early death from tuberculosis. Yet, during his 39 years, he wrote a body of music for the piano that defined the technique of the instrument, expanded its expressive world, and has never disappeared from recital programmes.

FRÉDÉRIC CHOPIN: WORKS

(all for solo piano unless otherwise marked)
Three Sonatas: c, b flat, b; Four Ballades: g, F/a, A flat, f; Four Scherzos: b, b flat, c sharp, E; 24 Études, opp. 10 and 25; 24 Preludes, op. 28; Three Impromptus, and Fantasy-Impromptu; Polonaises, including in A, op. 40, f sharp, op. 44, A flat, op. 53, and Polonaise-Fantasy, op. 61; F minor Fantasy, op. 49; c. 50 Mazurkas; 19 Nocturnes; 19 Waltzes; other works, including Berceuse, op. 57, Barcarolle, op. 60, 3 Nouvelles Études (1839), Rondos, Variations; Piano Trio, g, op. 8; Sonata for cello and piano, g, op. 65; 17 Polish songs, op. 74, voice and piano

EARLY LIFE IN POLAND

Chopin was born on 1 March 1810 in Zelazowa Wola, near Warsaw. His father was of French origin, his mother Polish. From an early age, his extraordinary ability on the piano was obvious, and although he had some lessons, he developed his very individual approach to the instrument largely by himself, away from any rigid school or method. At this early stage he also became familiar with Polish folk music, which was to have a profound impact on his mature compositions. Chopin did study composition for a number of years with Józef Elsner during his time at the Warsaw Conservatory. For Elsner, Chopin wrote his first piano sonata (1828), although it became clear that his talent was mainly to express itself in smaller, freer musical forms. The brilliant rondos and variations were written at this time, and would have provided Chopin with impressive concert pieces. The only pieces Chopin wrote for the very public medium of piano and orchestra also date from these years, including his two piano concertos, which he played with great success in Warsaw in 1830. The concertos

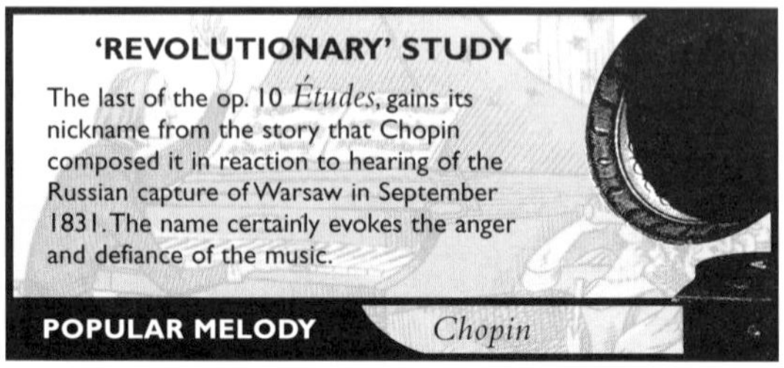

'REVOLUTIONARY' STUDY

The last of the op. 10 *Études*, gains its nickname from the story that Chopin composed it in reaction to hearing of the Russian capture of Warsaw in September 1831. The name certainly evokes the anger and defiance of the music.

POPULAR MELODY   *Chopin*

THE 24 *ÉTUDES*, OPP. 10 AND 25

With the two sets of studies that make up the 24 *Études* Chopin encapsulated the virtuoso technique of the Romantic piano, each piece already a demonstration of musical and technical mastery rather than a lesson in how to achieve it. There had already been sets of studies prompted by the rise of the piano as a virtuoso solo instrument, notably the *Gradus ad Parnassum* ('Steps to Parnassus') of **Muzio Clementi** (1752–1832), the studies of Johann Baptist Cramer (1771–1858) and the exercises of Czerny, but Chopin's were a new departure in their combination of musical and poetic interest with technical demands: they stand as complete concert pieces, and might easily have carried titles descriptive of their differing moods and atmospheres. Yet in each study a technical element – widespread **arpeggios**, double notes (thirds, sixths or octaves), rapid left-hand figures – forms the underlying texture out of which each piece develops.

Between Bach and Wagner

Musically, the studies both look back to the Baroque preludes of **J. S. Bach** in the first of op. 10, albeit in radically expanded keyboard textures, and also anticipate the chromaticism of **Wagner**, notably in the E flat minor study of op. 10. In mood they cover a wide range: serene beauty and lyricism (the studies in E major, op. 10, and A flat major, op. 25), mercurial lightness (G flat major, op. 10, F minor, op. 25), and turbulent heroism (C minor, op. 12, A minor, op. 25). With these two sets of studies, the first begun when he was only 19, Chopin defined piano playing and set challenges that pianists must confront even today.

(TNR) Chopin with George Sand
Chopin's affair with George Sand lasted nearly 10 years – his most productive period.
(FR) Chopin Monument
Memorial statue showing Chopin at the piano, in the Parc Monceau, Paris.
(NR) Manuscript
Manuscript of Chopin's 'Grande Valse Brillante' op. 18 in E flat major.

arpeggio ▶ p. 356 ballade ▶ p. 356

have sometimes been criticized for the imbalance between the solo part and that of the orchestra, which is certainly subsidiary, but they contain marvellously inventive and expressive piano writing, beautiful melodies and, in the finales, lively Polish folk tunes. After a tour of Europe taking in Dresden, Prague and Vienna, in September 1831 Chopin arrived in Paris, then the capital of the piano-playing world.

PARIS

Chopin gave his first Paris concert early in 1832, and it was not long before he became an important figure in the musical scene. Among the musicians he met were Liszt, Berlioz and Mendelssohn, and he also moved in literary circles that included Heinrich Heine and Honoré de Balzac. Many significant works date from the early 1830s: the *Études* op. 10 (completed in 1831) and op. 25 (1831–36), and the G minor Ballade, which Schumann described as the 'most spirited and daring' of Chopin's early works.

In 1836 Chopin met the novelist George Sand (her real name was Aurore Dudevant), who became the object of his most enduring love affair. Their relationship lasted for almost a decade from 1838, and it coincided with Chopin's most musically productive years. The 24 Preludes op. 28 were completed during a holiday Chopin spent with Sand in Majorca during the winter of 1838–39; their form testifies to Chopin's reverence for J. S. Bach – in number they relate to Bach's 48 Preludes and Fugues, and like Bach's set they follow a strict (though different) key scheme. By the end of the 1830s Chopin had written three of his four scherzos, two of the Ballades and the Second Sonata, as well as several sets of waltzes, nocturnes, mazurkas and polonaises.

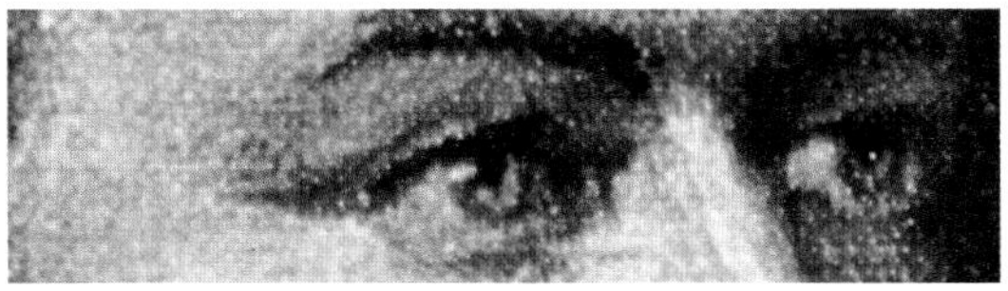

THE LAST DECADE

Chopin continued his relationship with Sand, by now apparently platonic, up till 1847, spending the summers at Sand's residence in Nohant and the winters in Paris. He now played only for private gatherings (often at aristocratic salons), but despite the advances of illness continued to compose and teach. The fourth Ballade (F minor, 1842) encapsulates the mature style of these last years: a theme developed with increasing complexity each time it returns, a growing use of counterpoint, almost operatic spans of melody, and great harmonic daring. Other works from the 1840s include the idyllic *Berceuse* (1843), the very original Polonaise-Fantasy, op. 61 (1846), and the Cello Sonata, op. 65 (1846), one of the very few works not for solo piano. Chopin's break with Sand coincided with a decline in his health, and in the last two years of his life he composed little. A visit to England and Scotland in the summer of 1848, when he again appeared in public as a pianist, only worsened his health, and in November of that year he returned to Paris. He died on 17 October 1849 in Paris, at 12 place Vendôme.

CHOPIN'S INFLUENCES

There are a number of musical influences that acted on Chopin. His early sets of variations, written as public display pieces, are close to the virtuoso styles of composer-pianists such as Ignaz Moscheles (1794–1870). Another composer-pianist of importance was Field, whose piano nocturnes formed a prototype for Chopin's own, with their flowing left-hand accompaniment and extended 'vocal' melodic style; Chopin's long, developing melodies in these pieces also recreate on the piano the *bel canto* style of Bellini's operas. Other influences that can be traced include J.S. Bach, whose preludes and fugues Chopin knew by heart, and **Mozart**. Polish folk styles (particularly in the mazurkas, which use the rhythms of folk dances as well as folk scales), were also influential. Yet the originality of Chopin's harmony, form and piano textures goes beyond any amalgam of outside influences.

Chopin's music in turn was to influence many later composers: his very chromatic harmonies anticipate Liszt and Wagner, while his piano style had a distinct effect on the textures of **Claude Debussy**'s (1862–1918) earlier piano pieces, and on the conception of some of his later works (Debussy's own set of 12 *Études* is dedicated 'à la mémoire de Frédéric Chopin'). Similarly, the early preludes and *études* of **Alexander Scriabin** (1872–1915) are close in style to Chopin. Among Polish composers, **Karol Szymanowski** (1882–1937) began by writing Chopinesque preludes and studies, before developing a more personal style.

CHOPIN AS A PERFORMER

The attempt to describe and recreate Chopin's style of playing has been a controversial subject, often relying on anecdote and subjective impressions. Many of his contemporaries tried to define the effect his playing could have – Schumann's description is one of the most poetic: 'At the end of the study [in A flat, op. 25] it seemed as if a blessed apparition had vanished – like one seen in a dream, which, now half awake, one tries to recapture.' Commentators agreed that Chopin achieved his impact at the piano more through subtle gradation of sound and rhythmic freedom ('rubato') rather than by force or brilliance; indeed, he allowed his pupil Adolph Gutman the first performance of his vigorous third Scherzo. Above all, Chopin valued beauty of tone (he encouraged his pupils to hear good singers, and then 'sing' through the piano).

In the few written notes he left towards a piano method he also stressed suppleness and a natural approach to the keyboard, recognizing the strengths and weaknesses of the hands, a far cry from the rigid technique previously taught. Heine summed up Chopin's art by writing that 'With Chopin I forget altogether his mastery of the piano, and sink into the sweet abyss of his music ...'.

J. S. Bach ▶ p.106 Clementi ▶ p. 158 Debussy ▶ p. 282 Mozart ▶ p. 144 Scriabin ▶ p. 296 Szymanowski ▶ p. 298 Wagner ▶ p. 226

Czerny, Carl

(Châr'-nē, Kärl) 1791–1857

AUSTRIAN PIANO TEACHER AND COMPOSER

As the pupil of Beethoven and the teacher of Liszt, Czerny occupies an important historical position as a pianist and pedagogue, and forms a vital link between these two masters. He was immensely prolific, writing over 1,000 works, including the many volumes of technical studies for which he is best known. His ability to present systematically different aspects of piano technique, at a time when the capabilities of the instrument were evolving rapidly, singles him out as a pedagogue of rare authority and enduring relevance. As well as hundreds of exercises Czerny composed many serious works, including 11 piano sonatas, six symphonies and numerous chamber works.

Danzi, Franz

(Dänt'-sē, Fränts) 1763–1826

GERMAN COMPOSER

At the age of 15 Danzi was a cellist in the famous Mannheim orchestra. He was appointed deputy *Kapellmeister* in Munich in 1798, and in 1807 became *Kapellmeister* in Stuttgart, where he befriended Weber, before holding a similar position in Karlsruhe. Danzi's positions as theatre *Kapellmeister* encouraged him to compose extensively for the stage, and his works include Singspiels and melodramas, where the music is interspersed with spoken dialogue. He was extremely prolific, composing choral works, songs, symphonies and concertos, and, most notably, much chamber music, which is still performed today.

Donizetti, Gaetano

(Dōn-it-set'-tē, Gä-ā-tä'-nō) 1797–1848

ITALIAN COMPOSER

Between the death of Bellini (1835) and the emergence of **Verdi**, Donizetti was the dominant figure in Italian opera. He studied with Mayr and Padre Mattei. After composing numerous apprentice operas and various sacred, orchestral and instrumental works, he had his first real success with *Zoraida di Granata* ('Zoraida of Granada', 1822), which gave him the opportunity to work in Naples. But the turning point of his career – and the opera that gave his work a truly international profile – was *Anna Bolena* ('Anne Boleyn', 1830). His subsequent operas, written with great speed, were not all successful, but *Lucia di Lammermoor* (1835), a cornerstone of Italian Romanticism, was a major hit in Naples. In 1838 Donizetti moved to Paris, hoping that the greater rewards on offer would enable him to retire. However, the operas he wrote there were not wholly successful, and in 1842 he took up a post as *Kapellmeister* to the Austrian court in Vienna, a position that allowed him time to pursue his career elsewhere. Donizetti's style is typical of its time and place, inevitably influenced by Rossini. His thematic vitality and sense of dramatic pacing keep his best works, including the comic operas *Don Pasquale* (1843) and *L'elisir d'amore* ('The Elixir of Love', 1832), firmly in the repertory.

THE NOCTURNE

John Field was the inventor of the nocturne; he was not only the first to use this title, but he originated the style of piano writing that became associated with the genre. With his nocturnes Field introduced the 'character piece', a short work that evokes a particular mood or atmosphere, without the contrasts of opposing thematic subjects associated with sonata form. The mood of the nocturne has been described as 'sadness consoled', and Field's nocturnes were, in essence, the first 'songs without words'. The principal characteristics of the nocturne style are a left-hand accompaniment often based on rocking arpeggios and sustained by the pedal, and an expressive melodic line played by the right hand, often ornamented with gentle arabesques. The genre reached its poetic flowering with the nocturnes of Chopin, which are more highly developed than Field's in expression and embellishment.

Dussek, Jan Ladislav

(Dōō'-sek, Yän Lä'-dē-slaf) 1760–1812

BOHEMIAN PIANIST AND COMPOSER

Dussek's fame as a pianist was widespread, and he made the acquaintance of Queen Marie Antoinette and Emperor Napoleon. Because of his connections with the aristocracy he was at risk at the time of the French Revolution, and escaped to London, where he set up a music publishing business with his father-in-law, Domenico Corri, and published many of his own works. The venture ran into debt and Dussek left his family and fled to Germany. He became *Kapellmeister* to Prince Louis Ferdinand of Prussia, and when the prince died in battle, Dussek wrote his best-known piano sonata, *Elégie harmonique sur la mort du Prince Louis Ferdinand de Prusse*, op. 61. Dussek died obese and alcoholic. His compositions are mainly for the piano and his style is brilliant and virtuosic.

Field, John

1782–1837

IRISH COMPOSER AND PIANIST

Field was the principal creator of the style of Romantic piano writing that reached its culmination in the works of Chopin, and invented the piano 'nocturne'. Born in Dublin to a Protestant Irish family, he moved to London in 1793, where he studied with Clementi. His reputation as a pianist spread and he was soon in great demand. In 1802 he went on a prolonged European tour with Clementi, ending up in St Petersburg. When Clementi left the following year, Field stayed on and was soon a celebrity among fashionable society, living in Russia for most of his remaining life. As well as nocturnes and other piano works, Field also composed seven piano concertos.

Flotow, Friedrich

(Flō'-tō, Frē'-drikh) 1812–83

GERMAN COMPOSER

Flotow was a prolific composer of operas. He studied at the Paris Conservatoire (1828–30) and was influenced by the major opera composers of the day, including Rossini, Meyerbeer and Donizetti, and later by his friendships with **Charles Gounod** (1818–93) and **Jacques Offenbach** (1819–80). His early operas are in the French lyric style, but his most successful works, *Alessandro Stradella* (1844) and *Martha* (1847), combine a German text with Italianate melodic traits. The first production of *Martha*, in Vienna, was a triumph, and the next production was conducted by Liszt in Weimar. Flotow never reached the same heights again. His style is characterized by melodic grace and textural clarity, but his harmonic language lacks variety and subtlety.

Glinka, Mikhail Ivanovich

(Glin'-kä, Mēkh'-ä-il Ē-vä-nō'-vich) 1804–57

RUSSIAN COMPOSER

Known as the 'father of Russian music', Glinka was the initial force behind nineteenth-century Russian nationalism. He grew up in a cosseted environment, and his early exposure to music was confined largely to the folksongs sung by his

1820 — 1850 EARLY ROMANTIC

nurse, the traits of which were later absorbed into his melodic style. After a couple of years in Italy, Glinka went to Berlin in 1833 to study with the distinguished teacher Siegfried Dehn, but the news of his father's death in March 1834 sent him back to Russia. He then embarked on his two most celebrated works, the operas *A Life for the Tsar* (1834–36) and *Ruslan and Lyudmila* (1837–42). These works demonstrate a fusion of Russian and Western styles, with the melodic and rhythmic shapes of Russian folksong permeating the music, which is nevertheless built on the Western tradition. In creating works that had a distinctive Russian flavour, he was a profound influence on **Mily Balakirev** (1837–1910) and other members of 'The Five', as well as **Pyotr Ilyich Tchaikovsky** (1840–93), all of whom openly acknowledged their debt to Glinka.

***(TL)* Martha**
Title page of the aria 'Martha, Martha, O Return my Love' from Friedrich Flotow's opera.
(FR) Fanny Mendelssohn
A talented pianist, Fanny lived somewhat in the shadow of her brother Felix.
(NR) Mikhail Glinka
The Russian composer working on Ruslan and Lyudmila.

Halévy, Jacques-François-Fromental

(Á-lā-vē', Zhák Frán-swá' Frō-mon-tál) 1799–1862

FRENCH COMPOSER

Halévy entered the Paris Conservatoire at the age of nine, and from 1811 studied with Cherubini, who was a great influence on him. Halévy won the Prix de Rome in 1819 and taught at the Paris Conservatoire from 1827 (where his pupils included Bizet and Gounod). He composed 40 operas. His first serious grand opera, *La Juive* ('The Jewish Girl', 1835), was his greatest success and is the work on which his fame rests. Halévy's style embodies a typical fusion of French and Italian operatic characteristics, and his best work was esteemed by both Berlioz and Wagner. He also composed vocal works and a small number of instrumental pieces.

Heinrich, Anthony Philip

1781–1861

AMERICAN COMPOSER

Heinrich was one of the most important figures in American musical life in the nineteenth century. Born in Bohemia to a German family, he tried unsuccessfully to set up business in America, and in 1817 he settled there to embark on a musical career, becoming the country's first professional composer, and being dubbed by some critics the 'Beethoven of America'. His reputation extended beyond his adopted country, and he spent several periods in Europe. He was essentially self-taught, and his compositions are mostly descriptive works, often either autobiographical or based on American themes. Although occasionally rough around the edges, his works are often strikingly original and deeply expressive.

Hensel, Fanny (Mendelssohn)

(Hĕn'-zĕl, Fá'-nē [Men'-del-sōn]) 1805–47

GERMAN COMPOSER

Fanny was the sister of Mendelssohn. They received identical musical education, but their conservative father expected Fanny to display her undoubted musical talents only within the semi-public world of the family's renowned Sunday concerts, which she organized and performed in as pianist and conductor. Encouraged by her husband, Hensel started to publish her work shortly before her sudden death at the age of 41. Her music consists largely of Lieder and piano pieces, including the cycle *Das Jahr* – a musical diary of an idyllic year spent in Italy – as well as chamber music and a few choral works.

Hoffmann, E. T. A. (Ernst Theodor Amadeus)

(Hof'-mán, Arnst Tā'-ō-dôr Á-má-dā'-ōōs) 1776–1822

GERMAN WRITER AND COMPOSER

Hoffmann's wide-ranging talents were the source of great inspiration throughout the nineteenth century, and composers who drew on his stories include Schumann (*Kreisleriana*) and Offenbach (*Les Contes d'Hoffmann*). He was also an astute and perceptive critic, and his review in 1810 of Beethoven's Fifth Symphony is justly famous. As a composer he has been neglected, although there was a revival of interest in both his writings and his music around the turn of the twentieth century. Hoffmann followed a family tradition and studied law at Königsberg, becoming a civil servant while trying to pursue his musical ambitions. His compositions are mostly for the stage, although there are also vocal and instrumental works, and much of this body of work has languished in obscurity since his death. Hoffmann's style draws on the dramatic characteristics of Gluck and Mozart, and his strengths lie in sustaining and developing his material rather than in the inherent beauty of the initial inspiration.

Balakirev ▶ p. 238 Gounod ▶ p. 249 Offenbach ▶ p. 253 Tchaikovsky ▶ p. 234 Verdi ▶ p. 230

Hummel, Johann Nepomuk

(Hoom'-mel, Yō'-hān Ne'-pō-mook) 1778–1837

AUSTRIAN COMPOSER AND PIANIST

A child prodigy, Hummel studied with Mozart soon after moving to Vienna at the age of eight, and later studied with Albrechtsberger and Salieri. From 1804 to 1811 he was *Konzertmeister* to Prince Esterházy, composing for the chapel (most of his sacred works date from this period), and was later *Kapellmeister* at Stuttgart. In 1818 he moved to Weimar, where he conducted at the court theatre; he became friends with Goethe and other leading intellectual figures, and his piano playing was something of a tourist attraction. He had a long-standing rivalry with Beethoven, which was reconciled only during Beethoven's final illness (Hummel was a pall-bearer at his funeral). As a composer Hummel is generally known for his virtuoso piano works, although he explored most genres (he never wrote a symphony). His style is essentially late classical, bridging the gap between Mozart and Chopin, characterized by clarity of texture, embroidered melodic lines, and harmonic and formal solidity. His reputation now rests, perhaps unfairly, on only a fraction of his large output. Basically a conservative, Hummel nevertheless paved the way for the revolutionary composers of early Romanticism.

Kuhlau, Friedrich

(Kōō'-lau, Frē'-drikh) 1786–1832

DANISH COMPOSER AND PIANIST

Along with C. E. F. Kuhlau Weyse (1774–1842) was the foremost Danish composer of the early Romantic period. He grew up in Germany, but when Napoleon invaded Hamburg in 1810 he fled to Copenhagen. He earned a living as a pianist and through various appointments (among them chamber court musician and chorus master), and to supplement his income he fulfilled the considerable demand for flute music, although not himself a flautist. His best-known works, however, are for the piano, including several sonatas, rondos, character pieces and sets of variations.

Liszt, Franz

(List, Frants) 1811–86

HUNGARIAN COMPOSER AND PIANIST

Liszt was one of the leading and most adventurous composers of the nineteenth century. His vast output is unusually complicated: many works exist in more than one version, and he was constantly revising and redrafting. His body of work may be somewhat uneven, but it should hardly be surprising if a composer at the leading edge of artistic exploration occasionally produces works in which experiment outweighs achievement. The greatest piano virtuoso of his time, he wrote piano music that includes some of the most taxing pieces ever written, and he did much to spread knowledge of other composers' works through his transcriptions. Absorbed by a spiritual longing, he was nevertheless also a man of broad social horizons. Few composers have aroused such contradictory opinions in their lifetime and since, and few have been so misunderstood; once seen as an eccentric and peripheral composer, he is increasingly viewed as one of the central figures of musical Romanticism.

LIEBESTRAUM

Liszt's *Liebestraum* No. 3 ('Dream of Love') contains one of his best-known melodies. Liszt originally wrote it as a song – although it is most famous as a piano piece – and the work's melting poetry makes it a great favourite for pianists, both in concert and on record.

POPULAR MELODY *Liszt*

YEARS OF PILGRIMAGE

Born in Raiding (then in Hungary, now in Austria), Liszt studied the piano with his father, an amateur musician, before moving to Vienna in 1822 to have lessons with Czerny. Thanks to Czerny's rigorous methods, his immense natural gift for the piano was given a sound technical

'THE WAR OF THE ROMANTICS'

During the mid-nineteenth century, and in particular Liszt's time in Weimar in the 1850s, there were many personal and idealistic tensions in the musical world. The cohesive spirit of early Romanticism during the years following Beethoven's death (1827) had become fragmented. Liszt had surrounded himself in Weimar with pupils who shared his musical ideals; they became known as the New German School, and Wagner and, at a distance, Berlioz were also associated with them. However, Liszt's passionate belief in musical progression – and his works that espoused this belief, specifically the symphonic poems, a form he invented – met with a deeply critical reaction. The chief argument was over the future of sonata form. Liszt's view was that the form should be developed and modified to suit his new expressive means, while **Johannes Brahms** (1833–97), Clara Schumann, Joachim and others believed that the classical tradition should be upheld. Liszt composed not symphonies but symphonic poems, in which the structure unfolds in a single movement and the music is associated with a literary or extra-musical programme; Brahms, on the other hand, wrote traditional four-movement symphonies. The arguments – programme music versus absolute music, form versus content, revolution versus reaction – were ultimately unresolvable. In the 1860s Brahms turned to the 'classical' medium of chamber music, while Liszt became increasingly isolated and withdrawn, leaving Wagner to occupy the revolutionary stage.

'METAMORPHOSIS OF THEMES'

Liszt's technique of 'metamorphosis of themes' represents his most lasting contribution to the history of musical form. It is essentially an advanced form of thematic development based on the technique of variation. A thematic idea or kernel is metamorphosed into a number of different forms – with a range of diverse characteristics conveying distinct emotional states – bound together by an underlying thematic unity. Liszt was building on a technique used before by many composers (Beethoven in his Ninth Symphony; Schubert in his 'Wanderer' Fantasy; Berlioz in his *Symphonie fantastique*), but he was the first to create entire musical structures from this technique. Although Liszt's technique was akin to Berlioz's *idée fixe* and Wagner's **leitmotif**, his application of it is different in that he did not seek explicitly to describe extramusical scenes or objects, but rather to translate into music the character and varying emotions of his subjects. He was concerned less with depicting external events than with contemplating more general poetic ideas. Liszt firmly believed that musical forms should be flexible, that content should dictate structure; 'new wine demands new bottles', he declared. Examples of works that are built upon the technique include the 'Faust' Symphony, the Second Piano Concerto, the B minor Piano Sonata and, above all, the 12 symphonic poems Liszt composed during his time at Weimar in the 1850s.

leitmotif ▶ p. 359

foundation. In 1823 he met Beethoven, his spiritual mentor, whose music he promoted throughout his life. When Liszt's father died in 1827, he settled in Paris with his mother and became deeply religious. He met Comtesse Marie d'Agoult, who was unhappily married with two children, and when in 1835 she became pregnant with Liszt's child the couple eloped to Switzerland. This period of Liszt's life is known as the 'Years of Pilgrimage', and his travels through Switzerland and later Italy are represented musically in the first two books of his *Années de pèlerinage*. Liszt continued to give concerts, and enjoyed the social trimmings associated with his success and fame, but this created tension in his relationship with Marie, who wanted him to concentrate on composing. In 1839 Liszt travelled to Vienna to give charity concerts in aid of the Beethoven monument, while Marie travelled with two of their children to Paris; it was the turning point of their relationship and the beginning of the most glamorous period of Liszt's career.

(TR) Lisztomania
Franz Liszt receiving an ecstatic response from adoring female fans.
(BR) Franz Liszt
Statue of the Hungarian composer and pianist on the Budapest Opera House.

LISZTOMANIA

The period from 1839 to 1847, when Liszt toured Europe from Lisbon to Moscow and from Dublin to Constantinople, playing to audiences that went wild with adulation, represents the most remarkable concert tour in the history of performance. The poet Heinrich Heine coined the term 'Lisztomania' to encapsulate the hysterical response of many (mostly female) admirers. In some quarters Liszt was viewed with suspicion: there was a belief that he was compromising his art and prostituting his talent. Liszt certainly knew how to maximize his theatrical effect, and some compositions (*Grand galop chromatique*; some of the opera fantasies) were designed unashamedly for show purposes, but he did much to raise the social status of performing musicians. His concerts were also highly innovative: he invented the term 'recital' and was the first performer to appear regularly without supporting artists; he was the first to turn the piano sideways, rather than sit facing the audience; and he was the first to play the full range of repertory (as it then existed) in the largest halls throughout Europe. It was also during this period that Liszt's unprecedented development of piano technique enabled him to introduce a range of new technical and expressive possibilities. Modern piano playing, in both its technique and presentation, owes much to Liszt's pioneering spirit during these years.

FOLLOWER AND LEADER

In terms of currents and counter-currents of influence, Liszt is one of the focal points of nineteenth-century music. He was influenced by, and was the influence for, a broad range of composers, from his absorption of styles as an impressionistic youth to the prophetic works of his old age, which were not really understood before the mid-twentieth century. The most striking influence on Liszt was that of the great violinist Paganini. In 1832, Paganini's performances in Paris inspired Liszt to recreate his incredible virtuosity on the piano. Liszt set about a systematic study of every facet of piano technique, and many of his most difficult works stem from this impulse, including the fearsomely difficult first versions of the *Transcendental Studies* and the *Paganini Studies*.

The Importance of Beethoven

However, a more lasting and profound inspiration was drawn from Beethoven. Beethoven was a more universally influential figure through the nineteenth century than Paganini, and to Liszt his importance was paramount. Liszt's approach to form, to a declamatory melodic style and use of dramatic instrumental recitative, and to pushing back the limits of his inherited expressive vocabulary, all stem from Beethoven. Liszt also made piano transcriptions of works by a long list of composers (often, generously, to promote their works), including all Beethoven's symphonies, Berlioz's *Symphonie fantastique* and *Harold en Italie*, and J.S. Bach's organ works. He learnt a lot from this detailed knowledge of great music. He was interested in composers from earlier centuries, and as well as J. S. Bach he transcribed works by **Orlande de Lassus** (1532–94) and **Giovanni Pierluigi da Palestrina** (1526–94), and drew on medieval plainchant in his oratorio *Christus*. His influence on others was equally widespread, and his innovations, both imaginative and technical, were far-reaching. The striking economy of means and tonal language of his late works anticipate ideas and procedures from the twentieth century. Bartók concluded that: 'For the future development of music Liszt's *oeuvre* seems to me of far greater importance than that of Strauss or even Wagner'.

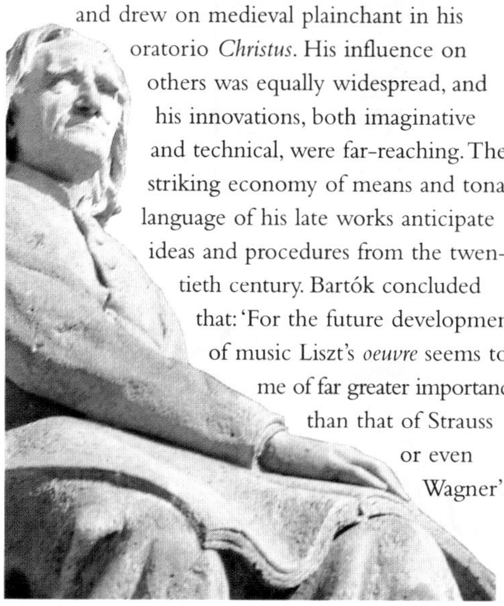

Brahms ▶ p. 240 Lassus ▶ p. 54 Palestrina ▶ p. 56

THE WEIMAR YEARS

In 1847, Liszt officially retired from the concert platform. Although he still occasionally played in public, he never again accepted a fee. After an arduous eight years of touring he wanted to concentrate on composition, and in 1848 he settled in Weimar as '*Kapellmeister* extraordinary' with the second great love of his life, Princess Carolyne Sayn-Wittgenstein. The resources of an orchestra and an opera-house helped Liszt to realize his ambitions as a composer, and much of his most important music was written at Weimar, including one of the greatest piano works of the Romantic era, the B minor Sonata. He also refined and published the final versions of many pieces originally written during his years as a performing virtuoso, including the *Transcendental Studies* and the *Années de pèlerinage*. His promotion of new music and his own orchestral compositions – particularly the symphonic poems – was the cause of much acrimony. As attacks on his work became more venomous and his patron, the Grand Duke Carl Alexander, gradually lost interest in his ideas, Liszt realized that his aim to make Weimar a great cultural and musical centre was increasingly futile. He eventually left in 1861, tired and disillusioned.

THE FASHION FOR SHAKESPEARE

During the early Romantic age there was enormous interest in Shakespeare, whose plays came to be known widely outside the English-speaking world for the first time in translation. As a dramatist he was admired by Romantic writers for his freedom from the classical strictures of form and taste, for his historical settings, and for his interest in the supernatural. This appeal was also recognized by Romantic composers. Mendelssohn's overture to *A Midsummer Night's Dream* (1826) was one of the earliest pieces of descriptive music specifically intended for the concert hall rather than the theatre. In the overture, and in the incidental music he wrote in 1843, the magical atmosphere of Shakespeare's world is evoked, and events and characters are described in music; rapid, high violin patterns suggest the fairies, for example. Berlioz also developed a passion for Shakespeare, and among other works he composed an overture to *King Lear* (1831) and a dramatic symphony on the theme of *Romeo and Juliet* (1839). Some composers wrote songs on Shakespeare's texts, while others created operas from them, such as Verdi (*Macbeth*, 1847). Shakespeare's popularity continued throughout the nineteenth century and into the twentieth.

FRANZ LISZT: WORKS

(Dates in brackets are of composition – Liszt was continually reshaping compositions and revising earlier works, so to give precise dates of composition is occasionally somewhat arbitrary)

- **Piano works:** Ballade No. 1 in D flat (1845–48); Hungarian Rhapsodies Nos. 1–19 (from 1846); *Consolations* (1848); *Années de pèlerinage*, 3 books (1848–55, 1839–49, 1867–77); *Etudes d'exécution transcendante* (1851); *Grandes études de Paganini* (1851); Sonata in b (1852–53); Ballade No. 2 in b (1853); Many other works; Numerous fantasies on operatic themes; Transcriptions
- **Orchestral works:** Les préludes, symphonic poem (1848, rev. before 1854); Piano Concerto No. 1 (1849); Piano Concerto No. 2 (1849); Totentanz, for piano and orchestra (1849); Orpheus, symphonic poem (1853–54); Faust-Symphonie (1854); 'Dante' Symphony (1856–57); Hamlet, symphonic poem (1858); 10 other symphonic poems; other works
- **Choral works:** *The Legend of St Elisabeth*, oratorio (1857–62); *Christus*, oratorio (by 1867); Hungarian Coronation Mass (1866–67)

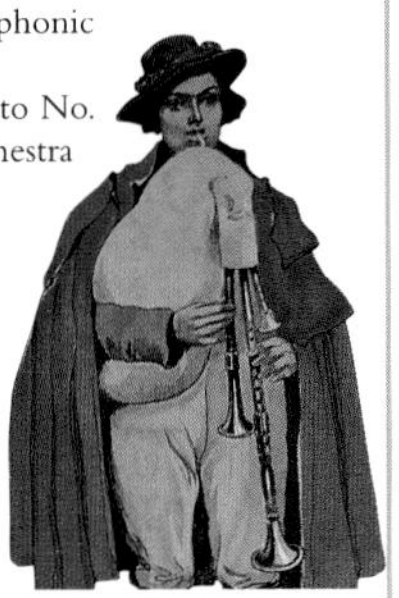

THE WEDDING MARCH

The famous Wedding March (1842) comes from Mendelssohn's incidental music to *A Midsummer Night's Dream*. Puck matches up the wrong people as he administers a love potion. All eventually turns out well, and the play concludes with the marriage of Theseus and Hippolyta that is celebrated in the March.

POPULAR MELODY *Mendelssohn*

THE FINAL YEARS

In October 1861, to coincide with his fiftieth birthday, Liszt had intended to marry Carolyne in Rome, but his attempts were thwarted by the Catholic church (because of problems to do with the annulment of her previous marriage). He settled in Rome and took minor orders in 1865, becoming known as Abbé Liszt; but the deaths of two of his children in 1859 and 1862, and his estrangement from his remaining daughter, Cosima, who had left her husband, his friend **Hans von Bülow** (1830–94), for Wagner, clouded his life. During these years he wrote two huge oratorios, *St Elisabeth* and *Christus*. From 1869, Liszt divided his time between Rome, Weimar and Budapest and gave regular masterclasses to some of the finest pianists of the day. He and Wagner were eventually reconciled, and he died on 31 July 1886, six days after attending the first Bayreuth performance of *Tristan und Isolde* (and three years after Wagner's own death). The music from Liszt's last years is radically different from his virtuoso works, and the sparseness of texture, harmonic ambiguity and dark expressive remoteness look forward daringly to the twentieth century.

Loewe, Carl

(Lö'-ve, Kärl) 1796–1869

GERMAN COMPOSER AND SINGER

Loewe studied first with his father and later with Daniel Türk at Halle. He was a gifted singer and performer and was appointed professor and *Kantor* at the Gymnasium and seminary in Stettin, where he spent the rest of his life. He was a devout Catholic, and his religion was an inspiration for his composition throughout his life. Loewe regularly went on tour as a singer, but his work as a composer was not seriously disrupted. He is best known for his songs, especially the narrative ballads, and his setting of Goethe's *Erlkönig* is a worthy alternative to Schubert's famous song. A stroke in 1864 seriously affected his work, and he died from another stroke five years later.

***(TL)* Undine**
Set for Lortzing's opera Undine *at the Berlin Opera House, 1897.*
***(R)* Der Vampyr**
Engraving showing a scene from Marschner's dramatic opera.

Marschner, Heinrich

(Marsh'-ner, Hīn'-rikh) 1795–1861

GERMAN COMPOSER

Marschner was the most important composer of German operas during the period between Weber and Wagner. Marschner grew up in Zittau and in 1815 met Beethoven in Vienna. In 1821 he moved to Dresden before settling in Hanover in 1830 as the conductor of the Hoftheater, where many of his operas were first performed. Marschner believed in a national German opera that was free of foreign influences, although his works draw on folk elements only when appropriate to the narrative. He was concerned primarily with the dramatic interaction of characters, exemplified in the opera *Der Vampyr* (1828), and his psychological approach reaches its height with his best-known opera, *Hans Heiling* (1831–32).

Mason, Lowell

1792–1872

AMERICAN COMPOSER AND EDUCATOR

Mason was a great pioneer of music education in America, especially in the schools of Boston. He was particularly involved in teaching vocal music to children and compiled a number of school music collections. Mason was also involved in a reform movement in American church music, and his ideals were based on European models: he composed much in the genre – his hymn tunes occupy a central place in American hymnals – and issued many collections of church music.

Mayr, Johannes Simon

(Mī'-er, Yō-hān'-es Sē'-mōn) 1763–1845

GERMAN COMPOSER

Mayr grew up in Bavaria and taught himself to play most string and wind instruments, before moving to Venice, where he studied composition with Ferdinando Bertoni. Mayr composed numerous operas, many for La Scala, Milan. Although his works exhibit diverse stylistic elements, his melodic and harmonic expression was rooted in the late Neapolitan operatic style. His melodies have sometimes been considered rather foursquare, but his use of the orchestra is highly imaginative, and his enduring legacy is his construction of broad dramatic sequences for his main characters. This is demonstrated in his finest operas, *Medea* and *La rosa*. He also composed over 600 sacred works, mostly unpublished.

Méhul, Etienne-Nicolas

(Mā-ül', Ā-tyen' Nē-kō-làs') 1763–1817

FRENCH COMPOSER

Méhul is known primarily for his many *opéras comiques* and for his symphonies. Between 1778 and 1779 he moved to Paris, where he studied with the composer Jean-Frédéric Edelmann. When the Paris Conservatoire was founded in 1795, Méhul was made one of its inspectors. Although heavily influenced by Gluck, he was one of the most original French composers of his time, renowned for his striking innovations in orchestration. *Joseph* (1807), his most famous *opéra comique*, was his last important stage work; Méhul became disillusioned with operatic composition and turned to symphonic writing, becoming the most important French composer of symphonies between **François-Joseph Gossec** (1734–1829) and Berlioz.

Mendelssohn, Fanny (see Hensel, Fanny)

FELIX MENDELSSOHN: WORKS

- **Symphonies:** Symphony No. 1 in c (1824); Symphony No. 2, 'Hymn of Praise' in B flat (1840); Symphony No. 3, 'Scottish', in a (1842); Symphony No. 4, 'Italian', in A (1833); Symphony No. 5, 'Reformation', in D (1830)
- **Other orchestral works:** *A Midsummer Night's Dream*, overture (1826); *The Hebrides*, overture (1830); Piano Concerto No. 1 in g (1831); Piano Concerto No. 2 in d (1837); Violin Concerto in e (1844)
- **Chamber works:** Octet, strings, op. 10 (1825); *Lieder ohne Worte*, piano (1829–35); 3 String Quartets, op. 44 (1838); String Quintet No. 2 in B flat (1845)
- **Oratorios:** *St Paul* (1836), *Elijah* (1846)
- Incidental music, overtures, piano concertos, string quartets, piano music, psalms, cantatas, motets and songs

Mendelssohn, Felix

(Men'-del-sōn, Fā'-lēks) 1809–47

GERMAN COMPOSER

Mendelssohn was born into a cultured banking family, who in 1816 converted from Judaism to Christianity, adding 'Bartholdy' to their name. Felix studied the piano, theory and composition, and showed early talent, writing his first piece at the age of 11. There were also important non-musical inspirations for his composing at this time, including visitors to his parents' salon and the writings of Goethe and Shakespeare. Indeed, literary, artistic and historical ideas continued to influence his dramatic and orchestral works throughout his life. His overture to *A Midsummer Night's Dream* (1826), for example, to which he later added incidental music, is a poetic evocation of Shakespeare's play. He also showed early talent as a conductor; his direction of the *St Matthew Passion* in 1829 in Berlin pioneered the revival of J. S. Bach's music.

FORMATIVE YEARS

In the early 1820s, Mendelssohn wrote a number of chamber works, which showed the influences of Bach, Haydn and Mozart. These included three piano quartets and a violin sonata, which were his first published opuses. A more personal style emerged decisively in his well-known Octet op. 20 for strings (1825), acknowledged as his first masterpiece. It encompasses a range of textures and styles, from the lyrical opening theme of the first movement, to the breathless rhythms of the scherzo, with its highly contrapuntal finale (a movement inspired by the 'Walpurgisnacht' in Goethe's *Faust*.

The string quartets composed between 1827 and 1847 show a similar range of stylistic influences and growing individualism. In Quartet op. 12 (1829), Mendelssohn confronts the musical language of Beethoven's late quartets, modelling the opening on Beethoven's op. 74, and reintroducing the Allegro theme at the end of the finale. The Three Quartets op. 44 (1837–38), are particularly fine works, and show a more classical orientation. The second quartet had a scherzo whose rhythmic patterns, like those of the scherzo of the Octet and the canzonetta of the Quartet op. 12, suggest the sparkle of *A Midsummer Night's Dream*.

TRAVELS IN EUROPE

Mendelssohn travelled through Europe in the early 1830s, giving recitals in England, Scotland, Italy and France; these experiences both enhanced his popularity and provided inspiration for a number of compositions. His atmospheric overture *The Hebrides* (1830), for example, contains descriptive passages in which the waves crashing on the shore are depicted and, more poetically, the mystery of Fingal's Cave is hinted at by echoing instrumental fanfares. Similarly, the 'Italian' Symphony, No. 4 (1832), captures a poetic vitality and warmth through imaginative scoring and its energetic finale is written in the style of a Neapolitan dance, the *saltarello*.

In 1833–35 Mendelssohn conducted in Düsseldorf, taking particular interest in the oratorios of **George Frideric Handel** (1685–1759), and in 1835 he became conductor of the Gewandhaus Orchestra in Leipzig, a post he was to retain for the rest of his life. He revived music by Baroque and classical composers including Bach and Mozart and promoted the works of his contemporaries, including Weber, Berlioz and Schubert, whose 'Great' C major Symphony he conducted at its première. In 1843 he founded the Leipzig Conservatory.

Bülow ▶ p. 243 Gossec ▶ p. 160 Handel ▶ p. 112

LATER YEARS
His compositions written during the 1840s include his beautiful String Quartet No. 6 (1847) and the 'Scottish' Symphony (1842). The Violin Concerto (1844) is widely recognized as the first great Romantic violin concerto, and in it Mendelssohn explores both the lyrical and the virtuoso potential of the violin within a slightly modified concerto form. The slow movement recalls the sentimentality of his *Lieder ohne Worte* ('Songs without Words', 1829–45) for piano, while the finale displays brilliant virtuosity.

Mendelssohn was at the peak of his career at this time, artistically fulfilled and in an important professional post. However, the vitality of his earlier works seemed to fade, despite his continued technical mastery. After a visit to England, during which he conducted his oratorio *Elijah* in Birmingham and London to great acclaim, he arrived home in spring 1847 to hear that his dear sister Fanny had died. He became ill himself and died some months later.

Mercadante, Saverio
(Mâr-kä-dàn'-tā, Sà-vä'-rē-ō) 1795–1870
ITALIAN COMPOSER
Mercadante was one of the greatest opera composers contemporary with Donizetti, Bellini and Verdi, although his works are now rarely performed. He studied composition with Zingarelli and wrote his first opera in 1819. His first major success was with *Elisa e Claudio* (1821), which established his European reputation. *Il giuramento* ('The Oath', 1837), one of his finest works, provides a link between the *bel canto* style of Bellini and Donizetti and the more melodramatic intensity of Verdi. In 1840 he succeeded Zingarelli as director of the Naples Conservatory, a post he held until his death. By 1862 Mercadante was blind, and composed by dictating. He was enormously prolific, composing 60 operas as well as ballets, cantatas, sacred works, orchestral sinfonias and chamber music.

Meyerbeer, Giacomo
(Mī'-er-bâr, Jà'-kō-mō) 1791–1864
GERMAN COMPOSER
Meyerbeer (like Mendelssohn) came from a wealthy German-Jewish family. He studied composition with Carl Friedrich Zelter and later with the renowned music theorist Georg Joseph Vogler. In 1831 he had a phenomenal success at the Paris Opéra with *Robert le diable* ('Robert the Devil'), which within three years was performed in 77 theatres in 10 countries, and he felt pressured for many years afterwards by the need to sustain and build on this achievement. His next major success was the historical opera *Les Huguenots* (1836), another of many collaborations with the librettist Eugène Scribe. Meyerbeer helped Wagner's early career, although his generosity (financial and professional) was reciprocated only by Wagner's adverse critical response to his work. Meyerbeer's fascination with singers – he was often attracted to premières by the performers rather than the music, and did much to promote the great Swedish soprano Jenny Lind – manifests itself through his lean orchestral accompaniment to extended solo vocal passages. He also explored highly innovative instrumental textures. His later operas include *Le prophète* (1849) and *L'africaine* (1865), and he wrote many songs and sacred works.

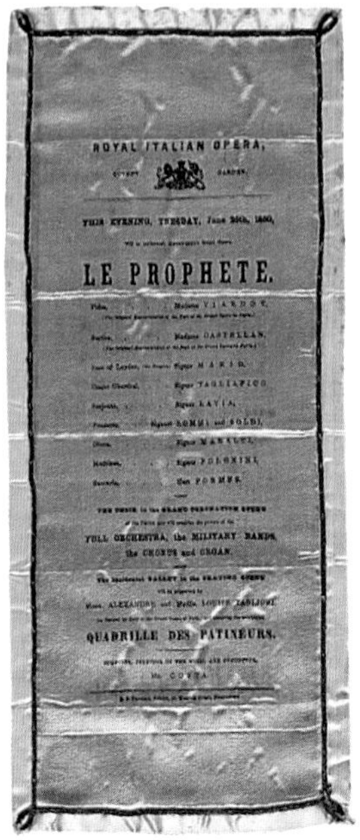

Moniuszko, Stanisław
(Mon-yōōsh'-kō, Stà'-nē-slwàf) 1819–72
POLISH COMPOSER
Moniuszko was the foremost composer of operas in nineteenth-century Poland, and his national importance is equivalent to that of **Bedřich Smetana** (1824–84) in the Czech lands and Glinka in Russia. He studied in Minsk (1830–37) and Berlin (1837–40) and began to write stage works in the mid-1840s. His opera *Halka* was staged in Warsaw in 1858 to great acclaim, and the work secured a reputation outside Poland. Moniuszko's style incorporates traits of Italian opera and French *opéra comique*, with widespread use of Polish national dances (polonaise, mazurka, krakowiak, kujawiak). He was also the most important Polish song composer of his time, writing around 360 songs.

Nicolai, Otto
(Nē'-kō-lī, O'-tō) 1810–49
GERMAN COMPOSER
Nicolai studied in Berlin with Zelter, and in 1833 became organist at the embassy chapel in Rome, but he resigned in 1836 to pursue a career as an opera composer. He quickly found fame with *Enrico II* ('Henry II', 1839) and *Il templario* (The Templar', 1840), and also made an impression as a conductor in Vienna, performing Beethoven's symphonies and *Fidelio*. Since he was one of many German contemporaries to study in Italy, Nicolai's style was grounded in Italian opera; his works epitomizedRomanticism's friction between intellect and emotion. His finest opera, the Shakespearean *Die lustigen Weiber von Windsor* ('The Merry Wives of Windsor', 1849), was at first rejected, but its popular national style, melodic inventiveness and comic situation soon established this work as a peak of early Romantic German opera.

Paer, Ferdinando
(Pà'-er, Fâr-dē-nàn'-dō) 1771–1839
ITALIAN COMPOSER
Paer was among the last of the group of Italian composers in demand as *maestri di cappella*, and together with Mayr dominated Italian opera in the first decade of the nineteenth century. He studied in Parma, but moved to Paris in 1807, when Napoleon, a great admirer of his work, appointed him *maître de chapelle*, and later director of the Opéra-Comique and the Théâtre-Italien. His operatic style owes much to Mozart, although his works often lack expressive concentration. He generally relied on vocal virtuosity rather than on harmonic devices for his dramatic effects; among his finest works are *Camilla, ossia Il sotterraneo* ('Camilla of the Underworld', 1799) and *Achille* ('Achillis', 1801), an ***opera seria*** based on the *Iliad*. In the 1820s his composition pupils included the young Liszt.

Paganini, Nicolò
(Pà-gà-nē'-nē, Nik'-kō-lō) 1782–1840
ITALIAN VIOLINIST AND COMPOSER
The foremost virtuoso in the history of the violin, Paganini contributed significantly to the development of the instrument's technique and drew Romantic

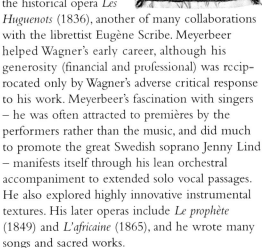

(BNL and R) Paganini
Caricatures showing the virtuoso violinist Paganini, who made a significant contribution to the development of violin technique.
***(BFL)* Les Huguenots**
Character from Meyerbeer's historical opera.
(TFL)* Elijah *Manuscript
Manuscript of the full score of Mendelssohn's oratorio Elijah.
***(TNL)* Le Prophète**
Early example of a silk programme for Le Prophète *at the Royal Italian Opera, 1850.*

opera seria ▶ p. 361 *pizzicato* ▶ p. 361

BEGINNING OF NATIONAL STYLES IN OPERA

Through a long history of tradition, the language of opera is Italian. The early history of the art-form is rooted in the language – Mozart's greatest operas are set to Italian librettos – and the wealth of Italian opera composers in the early nineteenth century (Rossini, Donizetti, Bellini, Cherubini, Spontini, Mercadante) is testimony to the richness of the tradition. But gradually composers of other nationalities, most notably German, began to forge their own national operatic voice. Mozart had written an opera to a German libretto (*Die Zauberflöte*, much imitated in the 1790s), but had not really created a German operatic style. Spohr, Weber, Nicolai and Marschner cultivated a dramatic vein that drew more heavily on German themes, on folklore and rustic scenes; their operas have a Germanic quality quite distinct from Italian opera, culminating with the music dramas of Wagner. The setting of different languages also influenced musical styles, as melodies were fitted to certain speech patterns (this is especially true of Slavonic languages), and as the wave of nationalism spread through eastern Europe later in the nineteenth century, so musical styles were diversified and enrichened.

composers, especially Liszt, to the potential of instrumental virtuosity in expanding expressive range and impact. Paganini first studied with his father, who made him practise long hours, and then with Antonio Cervetto and Giacomo Costa. An early influence was the Polish virtuoso Duranowski.

In 1801 he moved to Lucca, where he was involved with the court orchestra; around 1805 he composed his famous 24 Caprices, which contain some of the most difficult violin music ever written. He left Lucca in 1809 and built a growing reputation throughout Italy, mesmerizing audiences and continuing to compose violin works. In 1828 he ventured abroad, astonishing audiences in Vienna and Germany; the culmination of this extended tour was his series of concerts in Paris in 1831. Paganini's international career ended in 1834, when he returned to Italy; his six years of touring had provided him with wealth and fame, but had taken a terrible toll on his health, which continued to deteriorate until his death.

Paganini's best works show a great compositional facility and are still performed frequently, but it is his development of violin technique – left-hand ***pizzicatos***, single- and double-stop harmonics, 'ricochet' bowing and imaginative fingerings – that remains his most enduring legacy.

Reicha, Antonin

(Rī-khă, Ăn'-tō-nyēn) 1770–1836

CZECH/FRENCH COMPOSER

Born in Prague, Reicha studied the violin and piano with his uncle, Joseph Reicha. He then lived in Bonn, where he became a friend of Beethoven. After striving largely in vain for operatic success, he settled in 1801 in Vienna, where he formed a close friendship with Haydn. In 1808 he went to Paris, where he spent the rest of his life, teaching at the Conservatoire from 1818; his pupils included Liszt, Berlioz and César Franck (1822–90). He composed 17 operas, choral and solo vocal works, symphonies, concertos, chamber music and piano pieces. Many works combined theoretical and didactic aims with purely musical worth, and his theoretical writings had a wide currency during the nineteenth century.

THE RISE OF THE VIRTUOSO

One of the most startling developments in instrumental music during the first half of the nineteenth century was the rise of the virtuoso performer, particularly the composer-performer who wrote very difficult works to demonstrate his own flamboyant skills. Virtuoso performers were nothing new, of course – Mozart and Clementi were both dazzling pianists who wrote works for their own use, and J. S. Bach's powers as a performer are evident from his organ works – but during the 1820s and 30s a whole group of players emerged who pushed the boundaries of instrumental technique and development at an unprecedented pace.

A Thing of Beauty

Beethoven (e.g. 'Hammerklavier' Sonata) and Schubert (e.g. 'Wanderer' Fantasy) had each stretched the limits of instrumental capability in works of enduring power and depth, where the technical considerations are subordinated to the musical argument. But these 'modernist' works took many years to reap their full musical consequences. The virtuosos that subsequently flourished retreated to a more facile, brilliant showmanship, where the musical argument is often subordinated to the requirements of technical display. Pianists such as Thalberg, Kalkbrenner, Herz and Pixis were hardly great composers, yet they wrote works of impressive pianistic effect. However, the full importance of this new virtuosity was in works of genuine musical substance. Liszt's fusion of musical and technical exploration was ground-breaking, and his contribution to piano technique was unique. The works of the Russian Romantics **Modest Musorgsky** (1839–82), **Anton Rubinstein** (1829–94), the French Impressionists Debussy, **Maurice Ravel** (1975–1937) and the great pianist-composers **Ferruccio Busoni** (1866–1924), **Sergey Rachmaninov** (1873–1943) are all unthinkable without the realization by both Liszt and Paganini that virtuosity can be elevated to the status of great art. As **Camille Saint-Saëns** (1835–1921) later remarked: 'A difficulty overcome is a thing of beauty.'

Busoni ▶ p. 288 Musorgsky ▶ p. 253 Rachmaninov ▶ p. 256 Ravel ▶ p. 294 Rubinstein ▶ p. 256 Saint-Saëns ▶ p. 256 Smetana ▶ p. 258

THE 'WILLIAM TELL' OVERTURE

The last section of the overture to *Guillaume Tell* is well known as the theme to *The Lone Ranger*, accompanying the outlaws as they gallop across the plains chasing villains. Tell is a similar popular hero, a skilled marksman who frees Swiss peasants from Austrian oppression.

POPULAR MELODY *Rossini*

THE MANIA FOR WALTER SCOTT

Sir Walter Scott was perhaps the most popular literary figure in Europe in the 1820s. His adventurous tales set in chivalrous times captured an atmosphere of romance and mysticism, and exploited the vogue for Scottish subjects which was enveloping Europe. Rossini's *La donna del lago* ('The Lady of the Lake', 1819), was the first successful opera derived from Scott's works. The score included Scottish dance rhythms, hunting horns and a Chorus of Bards which was to become one of his most famous numbers and something of a patriotic anthem. Inevitably it was necessary to cut and simplify Scott's often long and involved plots in order to create a coherent opera. Indeed, Scott himself remarked that *Ivanhoé* (1826), a pastiche concocted from Rossini's music for the Théâtre de l'Odéon in Paris, was 'superbly got up … but it was an opera, and, of course, the story sadly mangled'. Composers of Italian opera continued to adapt his novels into the 1830s and 40s, and Donizetti's setting of *The Bride of Lammermoor* as *Lucia di Lammermoor* (1835) is perhaps the best-known Scott opera. *The Heart of Midlothian* inspired Scottish composer Hamish MacCunn's (1868–1916) *Jeanie Deans* (1894). Other works, including *Kenilworth* and *Waverley*, inspired further operas, songs, overtures and incidental music.

GIOACCHINO ROSSINI: WORKS

- **Operas:** *Tancredi* (1813), *L'italiana in Algeri* (1813), *Otello* (1816), *Il barbiere di Siviglia* (1816), *La Cenerentola* (1817), *Mosè in Egitto* (1818), *La donna del lago* (1819), *Semiramide* (1823), *Il viaggio a Reims* (1825), *Le comte Ory* (1828), *Guillaume Tell* (1829), 28 others
- **Other vocal music:** *Les soirées musicales* (1835), *Stabat mater* (1841), *Péchés de vieillesse* (1857–68), *Petite messe solennelle* (1863)
- Masses, cantatas, choruses, sinfonias, string sonatas, piano pieces

Rossini, Gioacchino

(Rōs-sē'-nē, Jō-äk-kē'-nō) 1792–1868

ITALIAN COMPOSER

Rossini dominated Italian opera during the first half of the nineteenth century, writing nearly 40 operas in less than 20 years. He established new conventions in the genre, and was the first Italian composer to abandon unaccompanied recitative in an attempt to create a more continuous flow in the music. He also developed rhythm and repetition as structural principles in their own right, and showed wit and humour in translating emotion and action into music. The immediacy and energy of his scores, together with his facility for melodies and love of noisy effects, were criticized by some, but his supporters were equally passionate, and during the 1820s and 30s he enjoyed success throughout Europe.

It was only in the 1840s that his popularity began to fade, as audiences turned to the less formulaic, more Romantic operas of Donizetti, Bellini and Verdi. The lack of singers able to perform his virtuosic music contributed to this decline. But during the twentieth century the comic operas gained a new popularity, and, particularly in the last 20 years, the *opera seria* are being performed again; this is due in large part to a new generation of **coloratura** singers who have developed the techniques so crucial to Rossini's style.

THE EARLY YEARS

Rossini was born into a musical family, and as a boy learnt to sing and play the horn. He studied in Bologna, and at the age of 18 wrote a one-act comic opera for Venice. Further commissions followed from other northern Italian opera-houses. His first works to win international success were the *opera seria, Tancredi* (1813), whose aria 'Di tanti palpiti' was reputedly sung by Venetian gondoliers, and the ***opera buffa*** *L'italiana in Algeri* ('The Italian Girl in Algiers', 1813), which displays Rossini's taste and talent for manic pacing and farcical scenes. But *L'italiana* also had a serious aspect, including a patriotic number, 'Pensa alla patria' ('Think of the Homeland'); this combination of moods was to characterize his later comic operas.

In 1815 Rossini moved to Naples as the director of the Teatro S Carlo, where he concentrated on writing serious opera. *Otello* (1816), a highly reductive and free adaptation of Shakespeare's play, despite a mediocre libretto, was much admired by other composers, including Meyerbeer and Verdi. It combined suggestions of Venetian local colour with forceful and dramatic vocal

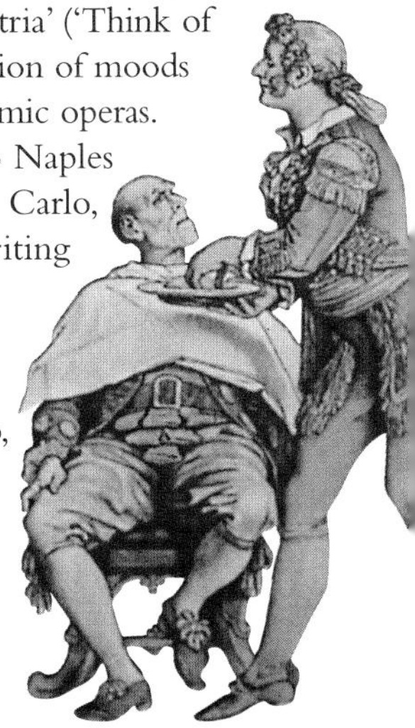

***(BNL)* The Barber of Seville**
Vienna Court Opera performance of Rossini's most enduringly popular opera.
***(BFL)* Rossini's Operas**
Giuseppe Ronzi de Begnis in Rossini's Mosè in Egitto *(ML) and Henrietta Sontag in* La donna del Lago *(FL).*
***(TL)* Le Siège de Corinthe**
The spectacular set for Rossini's opera at the Berlin Staatsoper, 1830.
***(TR)* Clara Schumann**
Clara was a pianist and composer, although she also promoted her husband's music.

coloratura ▶ p. 357 *opera buffa* ▶ p. 360

HIGH C

On Rossini's advice, the already established tenor Adolphe Nourrit (1802–39) took singing lessons in order to acquire an Italianate flexibility of tone. His subsequent performance in the première of Rossini's *Le siège de Corinthe* at the Paris Opéra in 1826 was a triumph, and in the same year he was made principal tenor of the Opéra. He appeared in each new work, including *Le comte Ory* (1828) and *Guillaume Tell* (1829), to great acclaim. However, the appointment of Gilbert Duprez as joint first tenor was to prove fatal. When in 1836 Duprez sang the role of Arnold in *Guillaume Tell*, instead of the usual weak high C, he sang the first ever high C from the chest (the sound that is produced by tenors today). Although Rossini, who was in the audience, declared it 'the squawk of a capon whose throat is being cut', Donizetti and Nourrit, who were also in the audience, recognized its power. Nourrit resigned from the Opéra and moved to Italy, where he committed suicide soon afterwards.

writing, notably in Desdemona's 'Willow Song' which precedes her murder in the final act. The number includes chromatic folk harmonies, ethereal orchestration and intense vocal expression, and its third act was one of the works by which Rossini wished to be remembered.

GROWING REPUTATION

While in Naples, Rossini continued to compose for other theatres, and his most popular comedy was written in Rome during this period: *Il barbiere di Siviglia* ('The Barber of Seville', 1816). Based on Beaumarchais' play, it featured the same characters as Mozart's *Le nozze di Figaro* ('The Marriage of Figaro', 1786). Rossini reportedly wrote the entire score in just two weeks; the energetic pacing of the music, crammed with memorable tunes, perhaps reflects this urgency. The best-known number is Figaro's 'patter song' 'Largo al factotum', which illustrates Rossini's famed mastery of crescendo and repetition as devices for building tension.

Rossini's critics mocked the ease and speed with which he turned out such operas. Berlioz, for example, criticized his 'eternal puerile crescendo', 'brutal bass drum' and 'melodic cynicism'. However, his supporters were equally vociferous. Indeed, the almost visceral effect of Rossini's music was admired by the French writer Stendhal, who reported in his biography of the composer that a specific key change in a later opera, *Mosè in Egitto* ('Moses in Egypt', 1818), led to 'more than 40 cases of brain-fever and nervous convulsions among young ladies with an over-ardent passion for music'.

TRAVELS

Rossini's success enabled him to travel further afield. In 1822, after marrying Isabella Colbran, the leading soprano in Naples and mistress of the impresario Barbaia, who had effectively launched Rossini's career at the S Carlo, he moved to Bologna. The following year the couple went to London, via Paris, where Rossini accepted the directorship of the Théâtre Italien, which he was to take up in 1824. His final opera written for Italy, *Semiramide*, had its première in Venice in 1823. The epic power of Voltaire's tragedy is suggested musically through dramatic ensemble numbers and through the dazzling, expressive coloratura of Semiramide herself.

In Paris Rossini adapted two of his Neapolitan operas for a French audience and wrote two new works for the Opéra. *Le comte Ory* ('Count Ory', 1828) was a masterly combination of farce (in one scene Ory's men, disguised as nuns, become drunk in the local convent), and seamless, energetic music; Berlioz described it as Rossini's 'absolute masterpiece', and it can even be seen as the source of French operetta of the later nineteenth century. In contrast, *Guillaume Tell* ('William Tell', 1829) is viewed as an early *grand opéra*, a precursor of Meyerbeer's grand heroic dramas. It depicts revolution, and includes great patriotic choruses, dramatic ballets and spectacular scenery.

FINAL YEARS

Tell turned out to be Rossini's last opera, although he participated in the running of the Théâtre Italien in the 1830s, promoting works by the emerging generation of Italian composers such as Donizetti and Bellini. In 1837 he returned to Italy, where he suffered from a long illness. Following the death of Isabella in 1845 he married Olympe Pelissier, with whom he had been living for the past 15 years. He composed little during this period, but in 1855 was drawn back to Paris. Almost every famous European composer came to his salon there, including Wagner in 1860; there he wrote the witty collections of short pieces for piano and voices, *Péchés de vieillesse* ('Sins of Old Age', 1857–68), and his *Petite messe solennelle* (1863). He died in Paris in 1868.

Schumann, Clara

(Shoo'-man, Kla'-ra) 1819–96

GERMAN PIANIST

Clara made her début at the age of 11 and soon became famous as a virtuoso soloist. She also composed music – usually for herself to perform. Early works include a piano concerto (1833–35) and several piano pieces. After a fierce battle with her father, she married Robert Schumann in 1840 and continued to perform, becoming the main exponent of her husband's music. As a composer she produced several collections of Lieder and a piano trio (1846). After her husband's death in 1856, she gave up composing to concentrate on an internationally concert and teaching career. She also developed a close friendship with Brahms.

Schumann, Robert

(Shoo'-man, Ro'-bârt) 1810–56

GERMAN COMPOSER

Robert Schumann, in his life and music, embodied many of the central themes of the German Romantic movement: steeped in German literary Romanticism, he composed Lieder combining the melodic simplicity of German folk tradition with expressive harmonic setting, wrote poetically titled miniatures, and composed music rich in literary inspiration and allusion. His life, too, epitomized that of the Romantic artist: rebelling against a training in law that had been expected of him, he threw himself into the study of music; he struggled against the wishes of his beloved's father to marry Clara Wieck; and he ultimately suffered from a mental disturbance and deterioration of health that led to his tragically early death.

EARLY YEARS

Robert Schumann was born on 8 June 1810 in the town of Zwickau in Saxony. He did not show the same prodigious musical facility at a young age that is associated with many great composers – indeed, although he played the piano as a child he was also greatly interested in literature, both as reader and writer, and only when he was about 20 years old did he devote himself fully to music. At the end of his teens (1828–29) he had even begun to study law, first at Leipzig University and then at Heidelberg, but with little enthusiasm. At around this time he began a course of piano lessons with Friedrich Wieck, a celebrated teacher, and would probably have had a career as a virtuoso pianist had it not been for a severe weakness in his right hand that has traditionally been attributed to use of a mechanical finger-strengthening device, but that may have resulted from the effect of mercury, used at that time as a treatment for syphilis.

PIANO WORKS

The energy that Schumann might have given to playing the piano was now channelled into writing music for it, and his first 23 opuses are for piano solo: the 'Abegg' Variations op. 1 show something of the virtuoso piano style of Moscheles and Herz, but also give an early example of a characteristic Schumann trait – the encoding into musical notation of names, phrases or ideas (here the theme A–B flat–E–G–G is suggested by the surname of a girl he knew). Soon there followed works of a more individual style: the colourful *Davidsbündlertänze*, a kaleidoscopic portrayal of various characters from Schumann's life and imagination, the *Carnaval* op. 9, the virtuoso *Symphonic Studies* op. 13, and the Fantasy op. 17, the grandest of the piano works. This imagination stretched to creating two alter egos, under whose names he also wrote: 'Eusebius', reflecting his calm and contemplative side, and 'Florestan', his tempestuous side.

ROBERT SCHUMANN: WORKS

- **Orchestral works:** 4 symphonies, No. 1 in B flat, 'Spring' (1841), No. 2 in C (1846), No. 3 in E flat, 'Rhenish' (1850), No. 4 in d (1841, rev. 1851); Piano Concerto, a (1841/45); Cello Concerto, a (1850); Violin Concerto, d (1853); Konzertstück for four horns (1849); overtures and fantasias
- **Choral works:** *Das Paradies und die Peri* (1843), *Requiem für Mignon* (1849), *Szenen aus Goethes Faust* (1853)
- **Piano solo:** *Davidsbündlertänze*, op. 6; *Carnaval*, op. 9; Sonata No. 1, f sharp, op. 11; *Symphonische Etüden*, op. 13; *Kinderszenen*, op. 15; *Kreisleriana*, op. 16; Phantasie, op. 17; Sonata No. 2, g, op. 22 (all 1834–38); *Album für die Jugend*, op. 68 (1848); *Waldszenen*, op. 82 (1849); many other pieces
- **Chamber works:** Quintet (op. 44, 1842) and Quartet (op. 47, 1842) for piano and strings; 3 string quartets, 3 piano trios, violin sonatas, etc.
- **Songs:** collections from 1840 include: *Liederkreis*, op. 24; *Myrthen*, op. 25; 12; Songs, op. 35; 'Liebesfrühling' songs, op. 37 (incl. 3 by Clara); *Liederkreis*, op. 39; *Frauenliebe und -leben*, op. 42; *Dichterliebe*, op. 48; about 250 songs in all
- *Genoveva*, opera (1847–49); other choruses and partsongs

CLARA AND THE SONGS OF 1840

Schumann's courtship of Wieck's daughter Clara – not only one of the leading pianists of the age but also a composer – was beset by difficulties, in particular the opposition of her father. Schumann and Clara successfully took legal action to force Wieck to agree to their marriage, though even this did not stop him circulating accusations against Schumann. They eventually married in September 1840. That year saw a complete switch in Schumann's creativity, from piano music to songs, and the song cycles of this year alone would place him as one of the greatest composers of the genre in Germany. Schumann's literary sensitivity led him to choose poems by leading Romantic poets, and the *Liederkreis* op. 24 to poems of Heine was followed by song cycles to texts by Eichendorff, Rückert and Goethe, among others. Schumann's talent for 'miniature' forms or mood-pieces, first shown in the piano music, is again manifest in the songs ('Mondnacht' from op. 39 is a beautiful example of how he can create a whole world of feeling and colour in two short pages). Being a pianist, he did not write merely functional accompaniments for the piano, but would allow it to create atmosphere and sometimes continue its commentary after the voice had ended.

PIANO CONCERTO IN A MINOR

This concerto avoids the empty display that Schumann so criticized. There is no shortage of drama: the piano's opening cascade, followed by the quietly melancholic woodwind theme, make this a favourite of pianists and audience alike.

POPULAR MELODY *R. Schumann*

1841 ONWARDS

Happily married, Schumann turned again to new genres – orchestral and chamber music, which were the main work of this period. It is probably the Piano Concerto op. 54 (begun in 1841 and completed four years later) that is now his most frequently heard orchestral work, rather than any of the four symphonies. The concerto was given its first performance in Leipzig in 1846 by Clara, who championed all of Schumann's piano works. There were now occasional signs of the mental disturbance that was to plague his last years: he had been severely depressed during a tour of Russia with Clara, and their move to Dresden in 1844 was initially fraught.

Other works of this decade include the marvellous *Konzertstück* for four horns and orchestra and the Quintet for

THE COMPOSER AS WRITER AND CRITIC

Schumann was one of the first generation of composers to express themselves in public not only through music, but also through the printed word – what we know of earlier composers' views has generally come through private correspondence. Schumann's classical education and early immersion in literature (mostly through his father's bookshop) gave him the ability and confidence not only to write poems and short stories, but also to begin a significant career in music journalism: he was founder of the highly influential *Neue Zeitschrift für Musik* in 1834, and was for 10 years its editor. He used the journal to promote the work of composers who accorded with his own aesthetic, or whom he generally admired: Berlioz's *Symphonie fantastique*, which must have seemed bizarre to most audiences of the time, was greeted with enthusiasm, and Schumann's response to the young Chopin – 'Hats off, gentlemen, a genius!' – is now legendary; Brahms, too, benefited from Schumann's patronage. Schumann's collected writings on music were published in 1854.

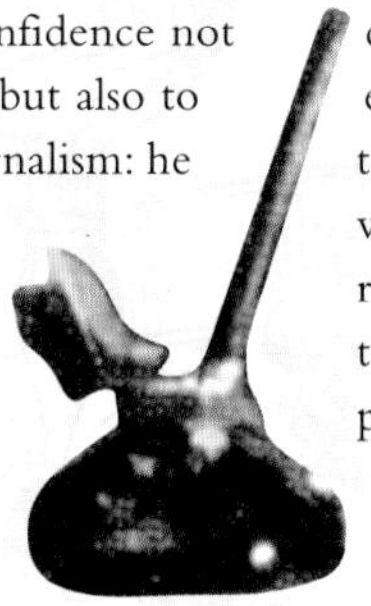

Perhaps the first really significant composer-critic of the nineteenth century, Schumann was equalled in this by Berlioz himself, who contributed regularly to the press and also wrote a volume of *Mémoires*, and Wagner, who published relentlessly on a wide range of subjects. In the early twentieth century Debussy, writing under the pseudonym 'Monsieur Croche', wrote music criticism more as an ironic commentator than as one of the fervent crusaders of the Romantic era.

DICHTERLIEBE

Like Schubert's song cycle *Winterreise*, the Heine poems that Schumann selected for *Dichterliebe* ('A Poet's Love') tell of suffering caused by lost love. The settings chart an emotional journey: the first song, 'Im wunderschönen Monat Mai' (In the Beautiful Month of May'), expresses the hope and yearning of the poet, who in the following songs seems briefly to have achieved happiness with his lover. But soon he is rejected, and the emotional pain of the songs draws from Schumann music of great variety and poignancy: 'Im Rhein, im heiligen Strome' matches in its music the Baroque grandeur of the cathedral it describes; 'Ich grolle nicht' suggests heroic defiance, a stance belied by the despair of some of the later songs such as 'Ich hab' im Traum geweinet'. In the final song, 'Die alten bösen Lieder', the poet tries to bury all memory of his love; but as the voice finishes the song is still unresolved, and it is left to the piano, in its serene postlude, to turn the mood from despair to one of calm – unlike the journey in Schubert's *Winterreise*, this one does not lead to madness but to acceptance and resignation.

Piano and Strings, one of his greatest and most characteristic works. Schumann also contemplated writing an opera on Goethe's *Faust* (fragments of this project became the *Szenen aus Goethes Faust* for chorus and orchestra); his one completed opera, *Genoveva*, was successfully performed in Leipzig in 1850.

MENTAL INSTABILITY

In 1850 Schumann took up the post of director of music at Düsseldorf, but his uneasy relationship with the orchestral committee and worsening mental state made this difficult. In late 1852 he began to suffer from aural hallucinations – sometimes in the form of music – and on 27 February 1854, having previously asked to be taken to an asylum, he attempted suicide by jumping off a bridge into the Rhine. Rescued by a passer-by, he was taken to an asylum at Endenich, where he spent the last two years of his life. He died on 29 July 1856.

WOMEN AS PROFESSIONAL PIANISTS

Given the long tradition of regarding the keyboard as a suitable and attractive instrument for a woman, it is not surprising that it was mostly as pianists that women made their names as professional virtuoso soloists in the early nineteenth century. The leading female pianist was undoubtedly Clara Schumann, who was acclaimed as one of Europe's leading players throughout an extremely long career. Schumann was largely responsible for introducing the piano recital, focusing on the composer rather than more showily on the performer. Her female contemporaries included two renowned pianists who both studied with Kalkbrenner and Moscheles: Leopoldine Blahetka (1811–87) and Marie (or Camilla) Pleyel (1811–75). Blahetka was very popular in Vienna in the 1820s. When she retired in the 1830s, she turned to teaching – as did the more successful Pleyel, seen by critics as embodying both masculine and feminine qualities in her playing, on her retirement in 1848. Lucy Anderson (1797–1878) became the first woman to play at the prestigious Philharmonic Society's concerts when she performed Hummel's B minor Piano Concerto in 1822. She taught the piano to Queen Victoria and her children. Later female virtuosos included the fiery Liszt pupil Sophie Menter (1846–1918); the Venezuelan pianist Teresa Carreño (1853–1917) and Anderson's pupil Arabella Goddard (1836–1922). Several of Clara Schumann's female pupils, including Fanny Davies (1861–1934), carried on the tradition of their teacher's style of playing in the course of highly successful solo careers.

(BL) Robert and Clara Schumann
Clara Wieck's father so opposed her relationship with Schumann that the couple had to take legal action to force him to agree to their marriage.
(TR) Robert Schumann
The composer working on his tale of love lost, Dichterliebe.
(BR) Sofie Menter
Piano virtuoso Sofie Menter was a pupil of Franz Liszt.

Spohr, Louis

(Shpôr, Lōō'-ēs) 1784–1859

GERMAN COMPOSER, VIOLINIST AND CONDUCTOR

Spohr was a prolific composer of instrumental music and also wrote operas that foreshadow Wagner's leitmotif technique. He first studied in his native Brunswick, and Mozart soon became his idol. He was a virtuoso violinist and between 1807 and 1821 went on many tours to the major European cities with his wife, the harpist Dorette Scheidler, and wrote works for them. He was briefly director at the Theater an der Wien (1813–15) and opera director at Frankfurt (1817–19). In 1822 he was appointed *Kapellmeister* at Kassel (a post suggested by Weber, who declined it himself), where he remained for the rest of his life. Spohr's musical style combines an adherence to classical form with a Romantic freedom of expression. His nine symphonies and 36 string quartets form an important proportion of his output, and his most influential operas were *Faust* (1813), *Zemire und Azor* (1818–19) and the successful *Jessonda* (1823). Although his works hold an important position historically, most are now forgotten, although he is remembered for being the first to conduct with a wooden baton.

THE IMPRESARIO BARBAIA

As a young man Domenico Barbaia (1778–1841) made millions running Italy's largest gambling empire. At the age of just 30 he obtained (by dishonest means) the licences of the Neapolitan royal opera-houses and eventually of La Scala, Milan, and the Viennese Kärntnertortheater and Theater an der Wien. Despite his blunt manner and self-confessed lack of education he became the era's most influential opera promoter, with enormous energy and a genius for recognizing talent. When a fire destroyed the S Carlo opera-house in 1816, King Ferdinand jokingly remarked how nice it would be to attend the ballet there on his next birthday, 11 months away. Barbaia rose to the challenge and had a new opera-house built, which still stands today. During his time at the S Carlo he inaugurated the new *opera seria* tradition in Naples, and hleped launch the careers of Rossini, Bellini and Donizetti among others. Rossini complained at the amount of work demanded of him, suggesting 'Barbaia would have put me in charge of the kitchen as well' (he was a renowned gourmet), but in these years he composed some of his most important operas including *Otello* and *La donna del lago*.

Spontini, Gaspare

(Spôn-tē'-nē, Gäs'-pä-rā) 1774–1851

ITALIAN COMPOSER

Spontini was the central figure in French serious opera between 1800 and 1820. Many of Spontini's early Italian comic operas are now lost, and he achieved only modest success before settling in Paris in 1803. He was composer for Empress Joséphine from 1805, and in 1810 was appointed director of the Théâtre-Italien. His reputation was secured before he moved to Berlin as general music director in 1820, but his tenure was soured by personal and national rivalry (Weber was generally viewed as the authentic German opera composer), and only the support of the king, a passionate admirer of his work, kept Spontini there until 1842. His final years were spent in Paris. Spontini was another in a long line of Italian émigrés whose music embodies a synthesis of Italian and French styles, infusing *opera seria* with Italianate lyricism. His success comes from his sense of dramatic evolution and pacing, and proper appreciation of his work often eludes the listener who knows only individual numbers. His finest operas include *La vestale* (1807) and *Fernand Cortez* (1809).

Viotti, Giovanni Battista

(Vē-ot'-tē, Jō-vän'-nē Bät-tēs'-tä) 1755–1824

ITALIAN VIOLINIST AND COMPOSER

The most influential violinist between **Giuseppe Tartini** (1692–1770) and Paganini, Viotti is con-sidered the founder of modern violin playing. He studied with Gaetano Pugnani and played in the royal chapel orchestra at Turin for five years (in the back desk of the first violins), before going on tour with his teacher. Viotti moved on to Paris and was an instant success, being recognized as one of the foremost players of his time. He continued to perform regularly before entering royal service in 1784; the French Revolution forced him to flee to London, ending the most successful period of his career. By 1801 he had retired from music, until his brief appointment in 1818 as director of the Paris Opéra. Viotti's most important compositions are his 29 violin concertos, which, while more restrained in virtuosity than was soon the norm, were highly influential.

canon ▶ p. 356

Wallace, Vincent

1812–65

IRISH COMPOSER

Between 1835, when he emigrated to Tasmania, and 1845, when he appeared in concert in London, he travelled across the globe establishing a considerable reputation as a virtuoso performer on the piano and violin, and initiating a number of fanciful tales of his expeditions that seemed to precede him wherever he went. Once back in London he composed a number of works for the stage. The most successful was *Maritana* (1845), which shows Wallace's absorption of a range of national styles presumably picked up on his travels. He also wrote a number of other stage works and numerous piano pieces.

Weber, Carl Maria von

(Vā'-ber, Kârl Mä-rē'-ä fun) 1786–1826

GERMAN COMPOSER

Weber was a central figure in the growth of the Romantic movement in Germany, and one of its most important composers. He resuscitated and spread an enthusiasm for German opera, to which his own three-act opera *Der Freischütz* ('The Freeshot', 1812) contributed. A gifted *Kapellmeister* and astute critic, he raised standards of performance and introduced fresh ideas, influencing many composers, most significantly Wagner.

He studied with Michael Haydn in Salzburg and Abbé Vogler in Vienna. Between 1804 and 1813 he held posts in Breslau, Karlsruhe and Stuttgart – each for a short period – and his performances throughout Germany won admiration and respect. Although he composed only intermittently during this period, he gained a thorough knowledge of Singspiels and French opera, and by the time he moved to Prague in 1813 he had composed six operas. In Prague he took up an appointment at the opera, and during his three-year tenure there he performed 62 operas by over 30 composers. Such detailed knowledge of the major operas of the day clearly inspired Weber in his own stage works.

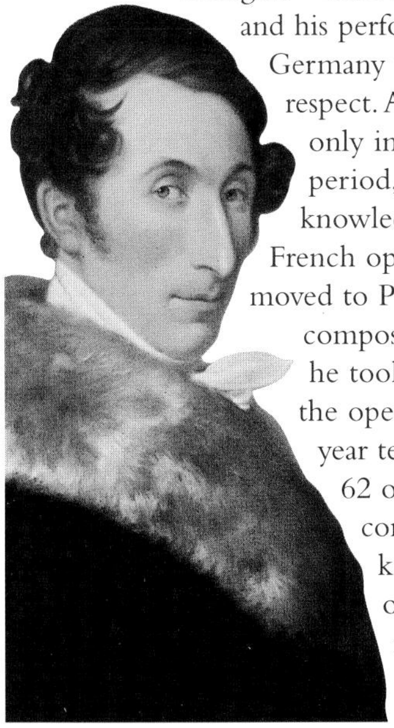

GERMAN NATIONAL OPERA

At the end of 1816 he was appointed Royal Saxon *Kapellmeister* and music director at Dresden, where his brief was to develop a German national opera. The operatic traditions of Dresden were based on Italian *opera seria*, and Weber was forced to work alongside an Italian, Francesco Morlacchi, who opposed most of his reforms and Germanic ideals. Nevertheless, Weber's most important works were composed in Dresden. In 1821 the première of *Der Freischütz* ('Free Shot') in Berlin was a triumph: based on German folklore and country life, this opera appealed to the search for a distinctive musical voice. It has remained popular throughout Europe. Weber continued to promote opera as a unification of art forms – a concept he considered a specifically Germanic aspect of opera – and this view was deeply inspirational to Wagner. In 1826, although desperately ill, to provide for his family's future Weber accepted a lucrative offer to go to London, but his health did not hold out and he died there. In 1844 Wagner arranged for the coffin to be brought back to Dresden.

Weber's best works rely on dramatic impulse, whether on the stage or in his instrumental works or songs. His tailoring of musical structure to elucidate narrative or pictorial ideas profoundly influenced later Romantic composers. In addition to *Der Freischütz*, his most important operas are *Euryanthe* (1822–23) and *Oberon* (1825–26). His other works include cantatas, two piano concertos and the excellent *Konzertstück*, two symphonies, a clarinet quintet, four piano sonatas and many songs.

A SHAPE OF GERMANY

Unlike the 'New German School' of Liszt and Wagner, Schumann did not pursue a path of radical experimentation in form and harmony; his style more aptly encapsulates German literary Romanticism in music, interpreting the rhythms and melodic shapes of German poetry and folk music through his own ardent and whimsical nature, and incorporating themes and ideas from Goethe, Tisch, Schlagel and Heine amongst others. Among earlier composers who were significant for him was J. S. Bach – occasional Baroque-style passages occur in many works, and he was also interested in counter-point, even writing a set of **canons** for pedal-piano (an instrument fitted with an organ-style pedal board). Schumann also revered Schubert – his *Papillons* op. 2 are very close to Schubert's own waltzes, and he is reported to have wept all night at hearing of Schubert's death. Perhaps a more significant influence than any one composer was that of German Romantic writers including Jean Paul Richter and E. T. A. Hoffmann, whose creations inspired such pieces as *Kreisleriana* op.16.

Schumann's A minor Concerto later served as a model both in form and gesture for Grieg's famous concerto in the same key; on a smaller scale, his *Album für die Jugend* ('Album for the Young') op. 68 and *Kinderszenen* ('Scenes from Childhood') op. 15 are the direct ancestor of much adventurous piano music written for children (or about childhood) by composers such as Debussy, **Dmitri Kabalevsky** (1904–87) and Bartók.

MUSICAL EDUCATION

During the nineteenth century, women amateurs of the middle and upper classes continued to be taught music privately, often receiving an extremely thorough musical education from the leading musicians of the day. Professional women musicians, like their eighteenth-century predecessors, often came from musical families and were traditionally taught by their parents. They also attended small private music schools, of which there were many in Europe, often run by women. From the early nineteenth century there was also the option to study at the conservatories that were being founded throughout Europe. Female students were admitted to most of these establishments from the start, although lessons were usually segregated and certain options (such as the study of counterpoint or the violin) were not available to women – especially in continental Europe – until later in the century.

The Royal Academy of Music

When the Royal Academy of Music in London opened in 1823 it had 40 female and 40 male students. The girls were taught harmony and counterpoint, piano, singing, harp, Italian, dancing and 'writing music'. The boys were taught the same subjects with the exclusion of dancing and the addition of the violin, cello and oboe. Female students soon outnumbered male and continued to do so throughout the century. In contrast, at the Leipzig Conservatory (founded in 1843) male students continually outnumbered female.

(BL) Agnes von Hohenstaufen
1829 staging of Spontini's serious opera, by the Berlin Staatsoper.
(TL) Louis Spohr
Photograph of the music room in Spohr's house.

Kabalevsky ▶ p. 292 Tartini ▶ p. 121

The Early Romantic

STYLES AND FORMS

The early Romantic era was a period that saw a move in all the arts towards greater expression and a loosening of structures and forms. In music this meant an expanding and freeing up of existing classical forms such as the symphony, and the development of newly expressive genres such as the symphonic poem. Opera took on bigger, more confrontational issues, often drawn from history, and instrumental as well as vocal works were frequently inspired by extra-musical ideas. Technological advances in instrument manufacture enabled composers to make more extreme demands of

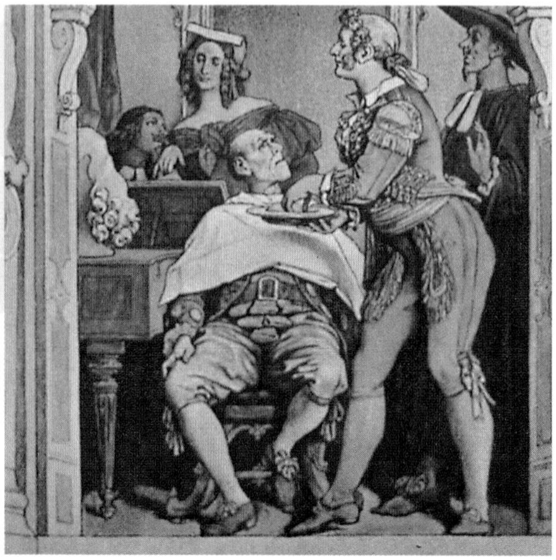

performers, and there was also a new interest in virtuoso composer-performers.

Distinctive ideas which characterized the period, in terms of inspirations and texts, included a preoccupation with Nature and the supernatural, a fascination with the recent (rather than ancient) past and an interest in establishing national identity following the upheaval of the French Revolution. Music was used variously to draw pictures, describe events and convey specific emotions. Moreover, in response to the growing interest in performing musics of the past, Romantic composers, with an eye towards posterity, became more interested in creating a distinct personal language.

EUGÈNE SCRIBE

Eugène Scribe (1791–1861) began his career as a dramatist for the Parisian popular stage, writing vaudevilles and comedies. This experience was crucial to his development of the French opera libretto, as he injected a new realism, pace and drama into serious and comic opera, and brought the two genres closer together. During his lifetime he wrote librettos for almost every major European opera composer. His early ***opéra comique*** collaborations with **Auber** paved the way for *La muette de Portici*, a grand opera whose libretto included fishermen, peasants and aristocratic characters and incorporated popular verse forms as well as traditional arias and recitative. Scribe went on to refine his grand opera librettos with **Meyerbeer**, drawing in all the characteristics of the Romantic novel, in terms of tragic conflicts, passionate love and spectacular effects. *Robert le diable* (1831), for example, is a variation on the Faust story that also contains two love stories and features devils and debauched nuns cavorting in a moonlit cloister. More fundamentally, *Les Huguenots* contains a personal dilemma played out against and within a public drama, a technique which became central to grand opera. Scribe also provided librettos for **Offenbach**, and for Italian composers drawn to the Paris Opéra, including **Rossini**, **Donizetti**, **Bellini** and **Verdi**.

IDÉE FIXE

The term *idée fixe* was first used by **Berlioz** to describe a melody, representing a character or feeling, which recurs in different movements of a work. In his *Symphonie fantastique* the main theme, symbolizing his obsession with his beloved – inspired by Harriet Smithson, with whom he famously fell in love – returns in each of the five movements, transformed on each occasion to chart the disintegration of the hero's opium-induced imaginary love affair. The theme enabled Berlioz to distinguish between the hero and his thoughts, and the circumstances in which he found himself. In *Harold en Italie* he took the concept a stage further, developing the 'Harold' motif, played by a solo viola. **Liszt** continued the process in his *Faust-Symphonie* (1857), a work dedicated to Berlioz. In each titled movement – 'Faust', 'Gretchen', 'Mephistopheles' – themes are subtly transformed to suggest character development; in the third movement those of the first are parodied grotesquely. The idea of a recurrent theme was used by many later composers, and anticipated the **leitmotif** technique of the second half of the century.

Italian Opera

By the beginning of the nineteenth century comic and serious genres had come closer together in Italian opera, often combining in a hybrid *opera semiseria*; the leading composers at this time were **Mayr** and **Paer**. But the early years of the century were essentially a period of transition, and it was not until 1813 that Italian opera found a new identity in the works of Rossini. He effectively codified practice for both serious and comic opera: a complex and ornate, ***bel canto***, melodic line was underpinned by a simple but strong harmonic structure, musical numbers were combined to make composite scenes, and the freedom of singers to ornament at will was curbed – instead their particular talents were written into the score. In his best-known comedy, *Il barbiere di Siviglia*, Rossini combined the brilliant virtuosity of 'patter songs' (in which humour is created by uttering a great number of words in a short space of time) with the gentle sentiment of arias and the confusion and momentum of ensemble scenes. His personal battery included a brilliant orchestral style, ornate flourishes in the vocal line and the ubiquitous *crescendo*.

(BNL) Harriet Smithson
Berlioz's wife Harriet inspired his famous Symphonie fantastique.
(BFL) Eugène Scribe
Scribe was a prolific librettists, working with many major composers of the time.
***(TL)* The Barber of Seville**
Rossini's best-loved opera demonstrates his brilliant orchestral style.
***(TR)* Bel Canto**
Rossini's style was further explored and developed by his successors.
***(BR)* Guillaume Tell**
Rossini's opera turned to history, its dramatic revolutions and heroes for inspiration.

bel canto ▶ p. 356 leitmotif ▶ p. 359 *opera comique* ▶ p. 361 Auber ▶ p. 186 Beethoven ▶ p. 150 Bellini ▶ p. 186 Berlioz ▶ p. 186 Boeildieu ▶ p. 189

SACRED MUSIC

At the end of the eighteenth century few major composers were writing sacred music. In France the churches were closed following the Revolution and it was only with Napoleon's elevation as consul for life in 1802 that they were reopened; sacred music was now written largely to celebrate state occasions. Similarly, although the Masses of the great classical composers still served a liturgical function, most Masses in early nineteenth-century Germany and Austria were written for concert performance or special occasions. In a departure from the decorative rococo of the previous century, sacred music acquired a new solemnity and grandeur.

The Requiem Mass

Mozart was the first to set the Requiem Mass on a large scale with instruments from the concert repertory (1791); Berlioz and later composers followed suit, employing huge forces. Perhaps the best-known early nineteenth-century Mass, the *Missa Solemnis* (1823) by **Beethoven**, combines serenity with militaristic declamation and contains strong dynamic contrasts and demanding passages for the soloists. Berlioz's *Grande messe des morts* similarly employs dynamic extremes, and is famed for its use of four brass bands in the 'Tuba Mirum'. the piece is unusual in being a Requiem created by a man of no religious belief.

In non-Catholic Germany and England, the oratorio took on new importance, often as the centrepiece of an outdoor festival. The oratorios of **Mendelssohn** and **Spohr** were performed alongside those of earlier composers; Mendelssohn's *Elijah* was particularly popular in England. Around the middle of the century the genre took off as a vehicle for individual (often secular) masterpieces, such as Berlioz's *L'enfance du Christ*, which is presented as an epic legendary narrative rather than as a spiritual experience.

Italian Opera after Rossini

Rossini's successors in the 1830s and 40s, Bellini and Donizetti among them, remained somewhat in his shadow, developing the *bel canto* style that he had established. But they also focused more keenly on characterizations and evolved personal styles. Bellini was known for his long, elegant and exquisite melodies, as typified by 'Casta diva' in *Norma* (1831); his emphasis on emotional power and his attention to the nuances of sentiments paved the way for Verdi and **Puccini**. Donizetti was known for his effortlessly appealing tunes, but he also brought a more complex and confrontational sense of drama into his operas, and developed pathos into a structural element of both the drama and the music. The heroine's mad scene in *Lucia di Lammermoor*, for example, uses musical and verbal reminiscence both to suggest madness and to unify the opera hematically. A now less well-known contemporary, **Mercadante**, developed a dramatic fluency in *Il Giuramento* (1837), which clearly foreshadowed Verdi. Each composer moved away from Rossini's by now rather predictable repetitions of melodic and harmonic patterns in an attempt to chart the drama more faithfully.

French Comic Opera

Opéras comiques in the decades following the Revolution tended to be tuneful, witty comedies, as typified by the works of **Boieldieu**. Following the enormous popularity of the operas of Rossini in Paris, however, French composers imitated his style; most *opéras comiques* of the 1820s and 1830s are clearly influenced by his formulaic use of harmony and rhythm, his lyricism and his frantic pacing. Although they still consisted of spoken dialogue interspersed with musical numbers, emphasis was increasingly placed on the chorus and ensembles rather than on solo arias, in an attempt to create a more realistic and dramatic whole. The most popular *opéra comique* of the period was Boieldieu's *La dame blanche* which embraced the fashion for Scotland and for the supernatural with its libretto based on three Walter Scott novels. Greeted at the time by some critics as France's alternative to Rossini, Boieldieu indeed shared Rossini's easy lyricism, wit and predilection for rhythmic repetitions, although he had a subtler use of instrumentation. The other major *opéra comique* composer of the period was Auber, whose *Fra Diavolo* (1830) exemplifies the charm, wit and melodic fluency that were so popular with audiences of the time.

French Grand Opera

In the 1830s and 40s public and critical interest in Paris focused on an emerging new genre. Following the lead of **Spontini** and **Méhul** in the first decades of the century, composers of serious opera were turning to historical subjects that had a resonance in the present. Past revolutions, religious conflicts and heroic national figures were all depicted on the Parisian stage. Such works were characterized by the fusion of the different elements of opera into a grandiose whole: usually in five acts, they featured large casts of soloists and several choruses, spectacular scenery and effects, and varied musical forms, including ballet and pantomime. The librettist Eugène Scribe was central to the consolidation of this new genre, collaborating with Auber on the first grand opera, *La muette de Portici*, which presented revolution on stage and in which the title-role was played by a dancer. Further examples of the genre followed, including Rossini's popular *Guillaume Tell* and *Les Huguenots* by Meyerbeer. Berlioz's epic *Les Troyens* was essentially a culmination of the genre, although others took on the mantle of grand opera in the second half of the century.

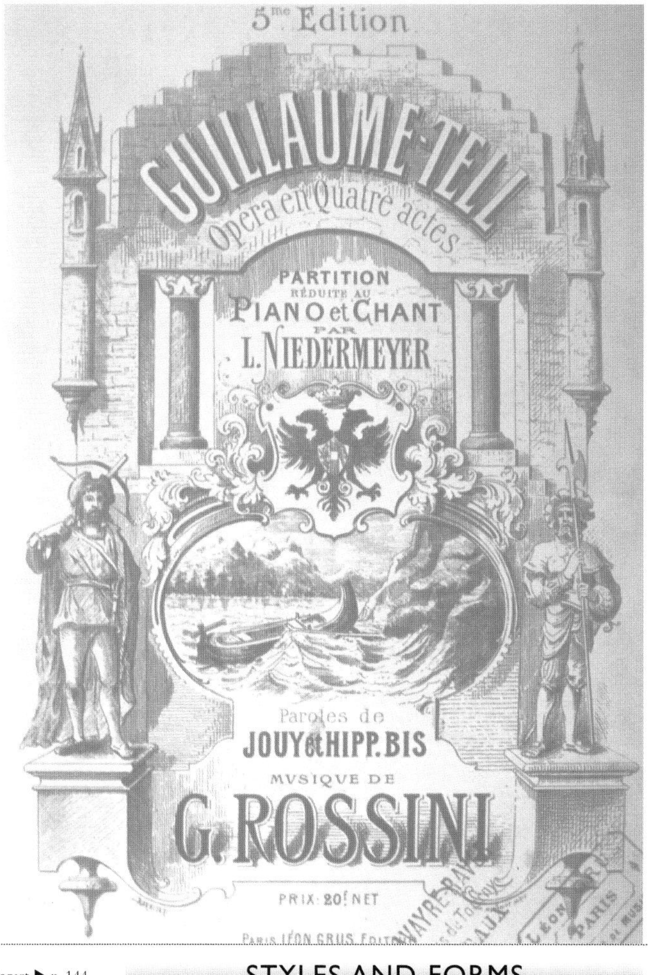

Donizetti ▶ p. 192 Liszt ▶ p. 194 Mayr ▶ p. 197 Méhul ▶ p. 197 Mendelssohn ▶ p. 197 Mercadente ▶ p. 198 Meyerbeer ▶ p. 198 Mozart ▶ p. 144
Offenbach ▶ p. 253 Paer ▶ p. 198 Puccini ▶ p. 254 Rossini ▶ p. 200 Spohr ▶ p. 204 Spontini ▶ p. 204 Verdi ▶ p. 230

German Opera

By the beginning of the nineteenth century, the distinction between Singspiel and serious opera in Germany and Austria was also becoming blurred. Subject matter was often drawn from folk tales and dominated by evocations of Nature and the supernatural. In Spohr's *Faust* and particularly in **Weber**'s *Der Freischütz*, the orchestra was used imaginatively to establish a type of 'local colour'. Diminished seventh chords, recurring motifs and precise instrumentation (usually involving brass instruments and low strings and woodwinds) were used to signify the presence of spirits, while folk-like melodies and horn calls represented peasant life. The use of recurring motifs was further developed by Spohr and **Marschner**, who in his *Der Vampyr* also explored chromatic harmony, varied orchestration and a type of heightened vocal style approximating speech. The operas of this period effectively ended the monopoly in German theatres of Italian opera, and were recognized as the beginnings of a national genre (a similar change was beginning in eastern Europe and in Russia). In the 1840s, **Nicolai** combined the distinctive German orchestral palette with Italian lyricism in a comic masterpiece, *Die lustigen Weiber von Windsor*.

Beethoven and his Symphonic Legacy

The gradual move in opera towards grander, through-composed works that drew on contemporary literary subjects was to a certain extent paralleled in (and, in Germany, derived from) orchestral music. The classical symphonic structure of three or four self-contained movements was expanded to four or five, which were sometimes linked together, and works were often inspired by extramusical themes. In his Symphony No. 3, 'Eroica' (1803), originally dedicated to Napoleon (although the dedication was later erased), Beethoven significantly expanded the scale of gestures and structures, and embraced the revolutionary ideal of the heroic human spirit. Beethoven continued this development in his later symphonies by using evolving and recurring themes and by evoking non-musical ideas. The Ninth Symphony (1824) is his most grandiose work, culminating triumphantly in a setting of Schiller's 'Ode to Joy', scored for soloists and chorus. It prefigures the epic pieces of Berlioz and **Wagner** which fuse poetry and orchestral music, communicating a new emotional intensity and spiritual depth.

Although the early nineteenth-century symphony is now typified by Beethoven, the French composer Méhul was also moving towards the idea of unifying. In his recently discovered Fourth Symphony (begun in 1810) he employed a complex network of rhythmic and thematic motifs linking movements.

The Development of the Romantic Symphony

More conservative Romantics such as Mendelssohn and **Robert Schumann** remained broadly faithful to the classical concept of the symphony, responding to aspects of Beethoven's developments rather than to his whole symphonic ideal. For example, they sometimes incorporated a limited programmatic tendency into their symphonies, as in Mendelssohn's No. 3, 'Scottish', the first bars of which were sketched on a visit to Holyrood Palace, and Schumann's No. 1, 'Spring', whose four movements were each given a descriptive title. More strikingly, great thematic unity is achieved in Schumann's Fourth Symphony (1841, rev. 1852): it is through- composed, with almost every significant theme deriving from motifs in the slow introduction. Some composers responded to the grandeur suggested by Beethoven. In Berlioz's *Symphonie fantastique*, for example, instrumental music is used to present a specific narrative drama, in a sort of opera without words. Although the symphonies of **Schubert** are essentially classical in concept, the last two display an approach to orchestral colouring that looks forward to the second half of the century. The 'Great' C major, for example, rather than blending instruments, presents an array of striking timbral colours, using imaginative combinations of woodwind and brass that were quite unknown in the classical symphony.

SYMPHONIC POEM

Liszt used the term 'symphonic poem' to describe an extended orchestral piece in one movement presented as the interpretation of a single non-musical idea. He wrote 13 such pieces, inspired by subjects taken from classical mythology, Romantic literature, recent history and his own imagination. The genre's programmatic origins lie with Beethoven's impressionistic overtures (such as *Coriolan*, 1807; *Egmont*, 1810), which show an independence from their theatrical inspirations; indeed Beethoven declared he wished to be known as a 'tone poet' rather than a composer. Liszt saw the genre as the expression of general ideas in music, and preferred to elaborate musically on poetic themes, such as the suffering of creative genius in *Prometheus*, rather than to engage in narrative or literal description. In *Hamlet*, for example, originally conceived as an overture to Shakespeare's play, he gives a striking psychological portrait of the prince waiting for revenge. The work consists of a slow introduction, a violent *allegro* (in which two short passages allude to Ophelia), and a slow final section which concludes with a funeral march. It is perhaps unsurprising to learn that many of Liszt's symphonic poems were originally written as overtures to plays.

cadenza ▶ p. 356

Programme Music

Liszt coined the term 'programme music' to describe works in which objects and events are depicted, and which have a preface to guide the listener. Such music has a narrative or descriptive element essential to its mood. The concept predates Liszt, of course: a feature of some eighteenth-century music, it can also be seen in Beethoven's Sixth Symphony and more literally in Berlioz's *Symphonie fantastique* as well as some music from the Renaissance and early Baroque. Liszt found programme music particularly effective when describing characters rather than events. In his second symphonic poem, *Tasso: Lamento e Trionfo* ('Tasso: Lament and Triumph', 1849–54), the reworking and revision of an overture written for Goethe's play *Torquato Tasso*, the sequence of the events of Tasso's life dictates the development of the music. A violent *allegro*, for example, symbolizes Tasso's sufferings, and an elegant, minuet-style section represents his time at the court of Ferrara. Liszt also favoured the depiction of general ideas rather than detailed descriptions. His *Héroïde funèbre* ('Funerary Heroic Piece', 1849–57) is a dignified funeral march originally conceived as a movement in a symphony responding to the revolutionary uprisings in Europe around 1848; its central section has a theme similar to the *Marseillaise*.

(BL) Hamlet
Kenneth Branagh's modern film production of Shakespeare's Hamlet.
(TL) Der Vampyr
Engraving of a scene from the first act of Marschner's dramatic opera.
(TR) Felix Mendelssohn
Although composers such as Mendelssohn remained largely faithful to the classical style of symphony, new elements were introduced that would evolve into a new Romantic style.

INSTRUMENTATION

The increasingly dramatic and descriptive nature of orchestral music for the concert hall embraced instrumental techniques used in the theatres. For example, particular theatrical effects were recreated by using specific registers and combinations of instruments. In his last two symphonies, Schubert's imaginative use of orchestral colour in building thematic and harmonic structure, and his strengthening of the brass section by adding three trombones, owe much to Weber's instrumentation, exemplified in his opera *Der Freischütz*.

Berlioz was a famously imaginative orchestrator, and he criticized his colleagues for using the same old effects; he was particularly vociferous about Rossini's laziness in resorting to loud brass and bass drums at moments of high drama. In his Symphonie fantastique Berlioz introduced such novelties as the E flat clarinet and English horn, and added extra percussion and important parts for harps. His develoment of the idée fixe also came to embrace instrmental qualities, such as in his use of the viola as a character in *Harold en Italie*.

BEETHOVEN'S PASTORAL SYMPHONY

Beethoven's Sixth Symphony, the 'Pastoral', comprises five movements, each with a programmatic title: i. Awakening of happy feelings on arriving in the country; ii. By the brook; iii. Peasants' merry-making; iv. Thunderstorm; v. Shepherds' song of thanksgiving after the storm. He wrote it in 1808 while staying outside Vienna in Heiligenstadt and Baden, and it can be taken to represent his love of the countryside. Indeed, he famously described it as 'more the expression of feeling than painting', and it was to lead the way for later Romantic evocations of atmosphere. The third movement, for example, is constructed over a drone suggesting bagpipes, and in the second bird-song is suggested by flutes, oboes and clarinets. The music, however, is able to stand independently from the pictorial idea, a concept that foreshadowed the symphonic poems of Liszt and other composers. The thunderstorm of the fourth movement, for example, with its dramatic trombones and piccolos, runs into the final movement without a break and can be understood as an extended transitional passage linking the third and fifth movements. This idea of a one-movement plan laid on to four movements was taken up by later nineteenth-century composers.

Orchestration

During the nineteenth century, orchestration became a crucial element of compositional technique. Technological advances enabled improvements to be made in instrumental mechanics, particularly for woodwind and brass instruments. Boehm, for example, made important modifications to the flute, giving it greater versatility; Sax invented the saxophone, and developed other similar instruments. Such changes enabled instruments previously used only for special effects to become permanent residents in the orchestra. As the power and flexibility of instruments increased, and the size of the orchestra grew, so internal balance became more important, as did the role of the conductor. Many theoretical works on orchestration were published, notably by the French theorist Jean-Georges Kastner (1810–67) and by Berlioz, as composers rarely had the opportunity that their eighteenth-century predecessors had to work regularly with an orchestra.

Violin and Clarinet Concertos

While the symphony was expanding and embracing Romantic ideas, so too was the other major orchestral genre of the period, the concerto. In his 12 violin concertos (1802–27), rather than simply providing an orchestral framework for the soloist, Spohr attempted to balance substance and virtuosity, giving the orchestra a more symphonic role. This recognition of the orchestra is also apparent in Beethoven's Violin Concerto (1806), which features sparring exchanges between soloist and orchestra. Mendelssohn in his Violin Concerto in E minor (1844) went still further, weaving the written-out violin **cadenza** into the structure of the work; it concludes with a virtuoso display that demands as much from the orchestra as it does from the soloist.

Meanwhile, the virtuoso concerto, influenced by Italian opera, remained extremely popular. Here the orchestra's primary purpose was to support the soloist's technical display. The soloist in the finale of Violin Concerto No. 1 (1817–18) by Paganini, for example, plays high chords, brilliant runs and 'ricochet' effects in which several bouncing notes are played on one stroke of the bow. Similarly, although Weber's clarinet concertos and the Concertino (1811) have beautifully slow and sonorous central movements, the finales display an almost operatic brilliance.

Marschner ▶ p. 197 Nicolai ▶ p. 198 Schubert ▶ p. 182 R. Schumann ▶ p. 201 Wagner ▶ p. 226 Weber ▶ p. 205

Piano Concertos

Beethoven was one of the first composers to recognize the potential of the piano concerto for dramatic conflict. Rather than delicate exchanges between the soloist and orchestra, with the piano merely repeating themes played by the orchestra, he gave both elements material to be played independently. In the 'Emperor' Concerto, No. 5 (1809), we see the piano almost dominating the texture. In contrast, for Chopin the genre was primarily a vehicle for the piano, and in his two concertos (1830) the orchestra plays a subordinate role, accompanying and introducing the virtuoso display of the soloist. Liszt, in his Second Piano Concerto (1857), was influenced by **Paganini**'s extreme concept of virtuosity. He treated the form more freely, and introduced an expressive display of rivalry between the soloist and the orchestra.

Mendelssohn took an important step in his First Piano Concerto (1831), dissolving the opposition between pianist and orchestra by replacing the virtuoso display of the soloist with more recitative-like drama; in his Second Concerto (1837) he wove the solo and orchestral parts together. Similarly, in Schumann's Piano Concerto (1841), the material is organized into a sustained dialogue between soloist and orchestra in which eloquence rather than virtuosity is displayed.

The String Quartet

Chamber music was also expanding its structures and to a certain degree changing the relationship between soloist and accompaniment. The string quartet made its most important advances in the early nineteenth century in Vienna. Beethoven's 'Rasumovsky' Quartets op. 59 (1806), for example, are characterized by an expansion of scale, elaborate contrapuntal textures and rich sonorities; the six late quartets (1823–26) push the genre to its emotional and formal limits and beyond. The *Grosse Fuge*, the final movement of op. 130, made such strenuous demands of the four performers that Beethoven reluctantly wrote an alternative finale, subsequently treating the *Grosse Fuge* as a separate work with its own opus number (133).

Other composers, however, were less radical in their explorations of the genre. In his later quartets Schubert gave predominant interest to the first violin and cello, and explored lyrical expression, partly the result of incorporating material from his songs, as in the Quartet in D minor (1824), whose second movement is a set of variations on *Der Tod und das Mädchen* ('Death and the Maiden'). Mendelssohn and Schumann in contrast often used more pianistic forms and idioms. Some composers, notably Spohr, Reicha and Cherubini, turned to the less formal, more virtuoso potential of variations on popular themes, potpourris and *quatuors brillants* in which the first violin dominated the texture.

Beethoven's Sonatas and their Legacy

During the first half of the nineteenth century sonatas were generally written for piano or for piano and one other instrument (usually violin or cello); the piano became as important to the sonata idea as the structural concept itself. Beethoven was the first to write violin sonatas that made the piano an equal partner. The 'Kreutzer' Sonata (1803), for example, contains dramatically passionate exchanges and demands virtuosity from both players. His piano sonatas explore the possibilities made available by technological advances to the instrument. The final movement of the *Appassionata* (1804–05) is introduced by dramatic crashing chords that would previously have been unthinkable, while the last four sonatas (opp. 106, 109–111) are of such extraordinary emotional and technical power as to defy description, going far beyond anything ever written before.

After Beethoven, composers tended to expand the classical three- or four-movement form without breaking with it, often emphasizing lyrical and symmetrical themes that contrasted with the tension of the high Classical sonata. Schubert's compositions in the genre display lyrical rather than virtuoso writing, but his late sonatas in particular (1828) nevertheless explore emotional extremes. Chopin's Third Sonata (1844), although criticized for its weak structure and thematic development, is a lyrical work with a huge sweep of shifting moods and sustained energy.

(NL) Frédéric Chopin
Chopin, perhaps the best-known piano virtuoso, explored and improved the potential of the instrument.
(FL) Ludwig van Beethoven
Beethoven's music was enormously influential on early Romantic composers.
(BR) The Lied
Schubert was a master at enhancing the meaning of words using voice and piano.

PIANO TECHNOLOGY

During the first years of the nineteenth century piano technology progressed at an astonishing rate. The range of notes was extended by two and a half octaves, the sustaining pedal and sound-board were developed, and in England the idea of using metal bracing to bear the tension of the strings was explored, enabling thicker strings and a fuller tone.

The repertory naturally reflected these developments in technology. The piano's new responsiveness was suited to powerful, showy concert works as well as to expressive, intimate salon pieces. Virtuoso performers such as Liszt and **Chopin** exploited the piano's potential in different ways. Liszt's bold and powerful approach created quasi-orchestral textures, while Chopin had a more profound understanding of the instrument and was famed for his long, sustained, almost vocal right-hand melodies. Simultaneously the role of the instrument in piano concertos, quartets and quintets, as well as in song, grew from being a mere accompaniment to being an equal partner in a musical dialogue. In Schubert's 'Trout' Piano Quintet, for example, the piano part is integrated with the textures of the strings, and has a high, light part that balances the weight of the double bass.

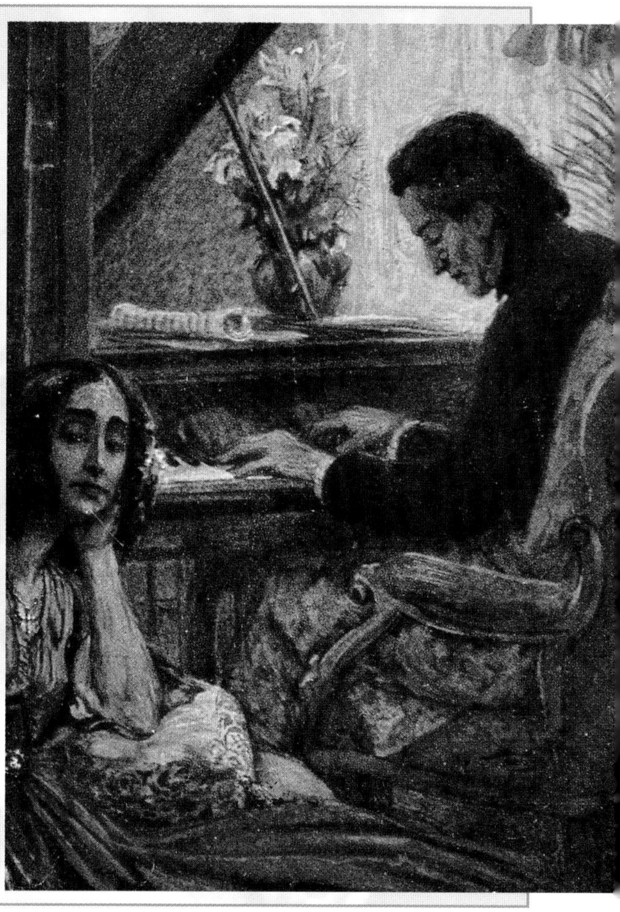

LIED AND BALLAD

In the nineteenth century, German vernacular song developed into an art form, the Lied, in which the meaning of the words was enhanced by their setting for voice and piano. The best-known practitioner of this genre was Schubert. His 'Gretchen am Spinnrade', for example, conjures up the image of a spinning wheel by providing recurrent circling semiquavers in the piano accompaniment; this pattern also reflects Gretchen's changing emotions, coming to a halt as she breaks down and starting up again as she recovers. *Erlkönig* similarly suggests the sound of galloping as a terrified young boy is carried through the forest by his father on horseback. As well as onomatopoeic sounds, Schubert suggested subtler, less pictorial ideas, associated with love, grief and sleep, in his accompaniments. His song cycles *Die schöne Müllerin* and *Winterreise* provide numerous examples of such techniques; poet, character, scene and singer, as well as lyric, dramatic and visual ideas, all become closely integrated.

Following in Schubert's Footsteps

Schubert's contemporaries and successors rarely matched his cohesion of text and music. The singer-composer **Loewe** was known in Vienna as 'the north German Schubert', but music was usually subordinate to the words in his Lieder. He did, however, use the music to achieve unity in the diverse scenes and dialogues of his narrative poems, and he had a particular talent for humorous narratives. His setting of *Erlkönig* (1818) bears comparison with that of Schubert. For Mendelssohn the reverse was true: the music was almost always independent, and the piano usually provided a simple accompaniment to the voice. But his genius for expressive melody was nevertheless influential on later composers in the genre.

It was Schumann who followed in Schubert's steps most closely. His cycle *Dichterliebe*, for example, tells the tragic story of the flowering of love, its failure, and the poet's longing for death. The piano does not simply become an equal partner in the piece, but has long solo preludes and postludes, and often communicates emotion more tellingly than the voice. Berlioz's cycle of six songs *Les nuits d'été* was his single-handed introduction of the song cycle into French music. They are gorgeous songs, attuned to the melancholic languor of the text, and he later orchestrated them all. However, they remain isolated examples of what was essentially a German genre.

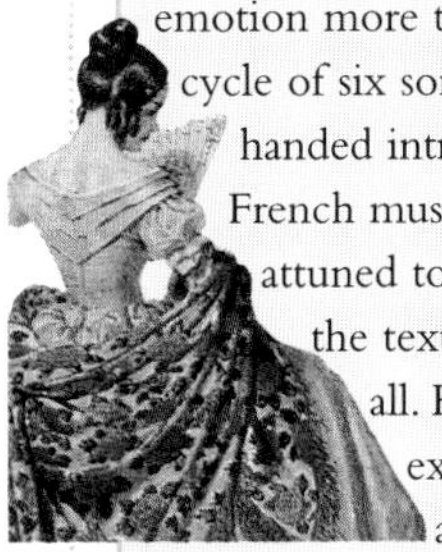

The Romantic Sonata

The classical form of the sonata provided a challenge for some composers, who searched for new means of unifying it. Schumann, for example, felt that the genre had become outmoded, and his sonatas are effectively fantasias although not as episodic in structure as this would suggest. Sonata No. 1 (1835), for example, is a rather disparate collection of movements with sudden key changes, thematic transformations and dramatic juxtapositions of contrasting expressions of emotion. Liszt and Charles-Valentin Alkan (1813–88) turned to programmes to provide structural unity, as with Liszt's *Après une lecture de Dante* ('After a Reading from Dante', 1837–49), a 'fantasia quasi sonata', and Alkan's *Grand sonate: les quatres ages* (1848), which describes the four stages in a man's life, each movement getting progressively slower after the initial scherzo. The recognized masterpiece in the genre, however, is Liszt's Piano Sonata in B minor (1853), dedicated to Schumann. A monumental work, it is cast as three movements to be played without a break, and carries the principle of thematic transformation to its limits: its unity derives from a series of thematic cells which grow and fuse, underpinning the structure of the entire piece.

GENRE PIECES

At a time when expression was more important than maintaining classical forms, freer structures that enabled the communication of a single mood or idea became particularly popular with pianists as an alternative to sonatas. Schubert, for example, is best revealed in his short lyric pieces in which his melodic expansiveness is not constrained. His *Moments Musicaux* (1828), a series of six intimate pieces, illustrate beautifully his ability to evoke intense emotion. Mendelssohn's *Lieder ohne Worte* ('Songs without Words', 1829–45), 48 miniatures published as six cycles, partly virtuoso, partly lyrical, are similarly exquisite mood pieces. Schumann also wrote on a more intimate scale; his *Davidsbündlertänze* ('Dances of the League of David', i.e. banded against the Philistines, 1837), is a series of 18 character pieces composed around a motto written by his wife Clara, and *Kinderszenen* (1838) consists of trance-like evocations of the past. Chopin found his own voice in a range of genre pieces. He particularly favoured dance forms from his native country, including the polonaise and the mazurka. He used these small works both to experiment with the modal and rhythmic ambiguities of Polish music, and to conjure up images of his homeland; they range from the melancholic and despairing to the fiery.

Transcriptions

In the early nineteenth century opera airs and orchestral pieces were frequently arranged for piano, for both domestic and concert performance. Transcriptions of opera arias were particularly popular with French composers. The 'caprices' and 'reminiscences' of Louis Jadin (1768–1853) and Daniel Steibelt (1765–1823), for example, were showy operatic fantasies which were not too technically demanding. However, Parisian audiences were even more delighted in the 1830s by the virtuoso transcriptions of composer-performers such as Thalberg and Liszt. Thalberg in particular delighted audiences in his operatic fantasies with his 'three hands' trick, in which he played the melody in the middle of the keyboard with his thumbs, while the other fingers swirled above and below. Liszt, however, was careful when drawing themes from an opera to encompass the work's dramatic and atmospheric range, and he communicated the poetic as well as the more obviously spectacular. In addition to the elaborate paraphrases based on the operas of Mozart, Wagner, Verdi and others, he made more straightforward arrangements. For example, he transcribed Schubert's songs and all Beethoven's symphonies for the piano in order to bring them to a wider audience.

Chopin ▶ p. 190 Loewe ▶ p. 196 Paganini ▶ p. 198

The Early Romantic
INSTRUMENTS

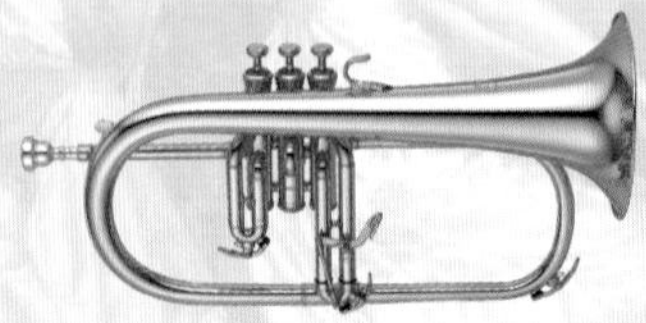

Pianoforte

Although the terms 'fortepiano' and 'pianoforte' were used indiscriminately by musicians of the time, for the sake of clarity the former term is now specifically used to indicate keyboard instruments of the late eighteenth and early nineteenth centuries, and the latter to mean the modern instrument.

The piano displaced the harpsichord musically and socially, taking over the latter's role in domestic music-making. A piano was an acquisition which brought with it an implicit confirmation of social standing. Although the modern world is used to plain wooden casework, the nineteenth century saw some highly decorated instruments being made. The part played by the piano in social relationships can be gauged from its appearance in the arts. Domestic music-making provided a meeting-ground for young men and

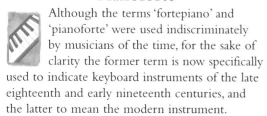

women in a society increasingly inhibited about such contacts. The piano skills of Jane Fairfax in Jane Austen's *Emma* (1815) indicated that the piano could play a significant role in courtship at the beginning of the nineteenth century. By contrast, later in the century, the upright piano in the background of the painting *The Awakening Conscience* (1853) by the Pre-Raphaelite William Holman Hunt suggests that it was seen as playing a part in seduction as well.

COMPETITION FOR THE AMATEUR

Towards the end of the Romantic age, the (usually upright) piano faced several competitors in the amateur market. One of these was the player piano, now usually known by the trade name of 'pianola'.

PIANOFORTE MAKERS

Johann Andreas Stein of Augsburg (1728–92) was the maker of instruments which both **Mozart** and **Beethoven** knew. Stein worked to improve both the escapement mechanism and the damping of the sound. The latter, which on a modern piano is achieved by means of a pedal, was in Stein's instrument controlled by a knee lever.

It was only after Stein's daughter Nanette and her husband J. A. Streicher set up a fortepiano business in Vienna that the German piano-making school can strictly be regarded as making the 'Viennese' action. Also working in Austria at this time were the firms of Bösendorfer (still a famous firm today) and Graf. Indeed, between 1791 and 1815 it is said there were more than 135 keyboard instrument-makers at work in Vienna alone.

The 'English' action was developed during the reign of George III. Instead of a wing-shaped instrument that looked like a harpsichord (or indeed a modern grand piano), Johannes Zumpe (fl. 1735–83) adopted the rectangular shape of the mid-eighteenth-century clavichord. With no built-in legs, these pianos were supported on trestles. They were without escapement, often tuned to uneven temperament, with a small soundboard to the right of the instrument, a reduced dynamic range and with lighter hammers.

The Broadwood Piano

This style of piano was developed by the Scottish cabinet-maker John Broadwood (1732–1812), who married the daughter of the Swiss-born instrument-maker Burkat Schudi. Within the shape, descended from the clavichord, of what had become known as a 'square piano', Broadwood developed a new foot-pedal mechanism and a divided bridge that was a departure from the harpsichord type of a single, long bridge. Both Beethoven, in his latter years, and **Chopin** famously played on Broadwood pianos. **Mendelssohn**, not surprisingly given his connections with Britain, was a Broadwood customer, as was **Hummel**. In 1853 three major piano manufacturers were founded: Bechstein (Berlin), Blüthner (Leipzig) and Steinway (New York). Alongside Bösendorfer, founded in Austria in 1828, and Yamaha, founded in Japan at the turn of the century, they were to dominate the piano market for a century and more.

PIANOFORTE TECHNOLOGY

The pianoforte was a direct development of the fortepiano: a keyboard sets in motion a mechanism which strikes the string with a hammer. The defining change which separates the two was the move towards an iron frame. Broadwood started using metal tension bars in 1808 and in the 1820s iron bracing became more and more necessary to ensure the instrument's ability to cope with the increasing tension of the strings. The earlier wooden frames would have collapsed under the strain. In addition, the old-style fortepiano could not withstand the new way of performing, with its greater emphasis on 'attack' and drama. Now that the frame was stronger, makers were able to try using heavier hammers and strings. Hammers had long been covered in a thin leather jacket. With the new mechanism, there was a risk of an ugly clanging sound as the hammers hit the strings. To avoid this, makers moved away from using leather and tried out thicker materials that would work in the more demanding mechanism: felt became the norm.

Double-Escapement

The escapement action had been an essential element in the fortepiano. It had meant that if players hit the key once, they got one note only: with a hammer action there is always the risk of a rebound, which would produce a faint echo of the original note, ruining the clarity. As the instrument became more powerful in the early nineteenth century, it grew heavier and slower. Rapidly repeating a note was no longer possible, as the key was so slow to return to its original position. The firm of Erard developed a complex system of levers called a double-escapement' action. This kept the hammer itself at a certain height even while the key was returning to its starting position, which meant that players could hit the key a second time and get a repeated note without waiting for the key to come back up.

Steinway

The Viennese and English actions were in competition throughout the nineteenth century. Eventually it was the American firm of Steinway which, working from the English model, produced a piano with a split-level design. Here the bass strings were built to run diagonally across the treble strings, rather like playing cards when you hold them in a 'fan'.

In 1859 the firm produced a piano which combined double-escapement, an iron frame and overstringing: this was the modern piano, and although some firms disliked it and were slow to adopt it, this was to be the design that all modern concert grand pianos would eventually follow.

crook ▶ p. 357

A second was the gramophone. The piano had been used throughout the nineteenth century to play not simply the recognized piano repertory, but also arrangements of popular tunes from opera and operetta, and reductions of orchestral works. As such, it had acted as the standard private window on to the world of art music, matched in the public arena by choirs and brass bands. The gramophone and the piano roll made this repertory, widely available, even to those possessing no instrumental music skills.

THE ECONOMICS OF PIANO-MAKING

Throughout the Romantic period, the economics of the piano continued to encourage experiment. Unlike violins, but like woodwind instruments, pianos wear out. Where a violin, sympathetically used, matures, a piano slowly deteriorates. There is therefore a continual need for a supply of new instruments. In addition, a piano is a sizeable investment. Customers want to be assured of the highest quality and the latest research, just as they now are when buying a computer or a car. Finally, the development of the repertory was a continual stimulus to solving problems and meeting the demands made by ever-more ambitious composers.

By the end of the eighteenth century, there was a number of competing companies producing fortepianos according to different methods of construction. These are often referred to as the English and the Viennese 'actions', since the significant difference was in the way the mechanism for producing the notes 'acted'.

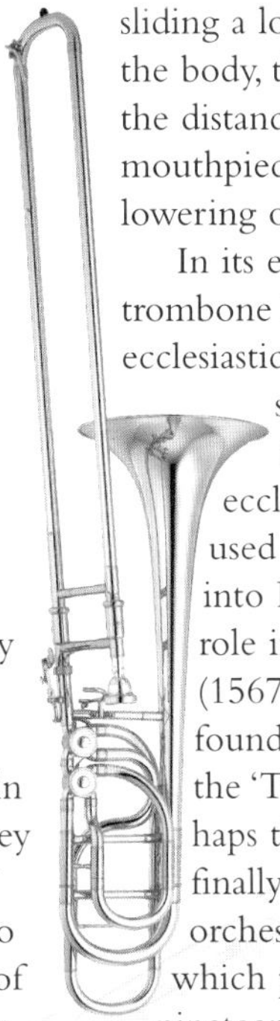

THE RISE OF THE SOLO PIANOFORTE

Just as the violin was the prince of the Baroque, so the piano was the ruler of Romanticism. Certainly the piano had already been important in the music and careers of classical composers such as Mozart and Beethoven (whose father had struggled in vain to turn him into a violinist): up to a point they can be regarded as role models for the life of a pianist-composer. But the piano is central to **Robert Schumann**'s work, and in the case of Chopin and **Liszt**, so central that without the piano their lives and music would have been utterly different. Both had careers as pianists that were closely tied to their composing. In Schumann's case, his ambition to be a virtuoso performer was abruptly halted by (perhaps self-inflicted) damage to his fingers in his early twenties. A century later **Rachmaninov** was not only a very late Romantic composer, he also matched the stereotype by being a highly regarded pianist.

During the Romantic period, the pianist acquired heroic status. The Polish pianist Ignacy Paderewski (1860–1941) became a cultural hero, the embodiment of his divided, conquered country's continuing cultural identity at a time when it was unable to have a political one. Indeed, such was his standing that, on the re-establishment of an independent Poland in the new Europe drawn up in the 1919 Treaty of Versailles, he was elected its president.

Trombone

The trombone developed the idea of the Renaissance slide trumpet. While the trumpet abandoned the slide in favour first of **crooks** and later of valves, the trombone pursued the slide method and perfected it. The trombone is shaped like a giant paper-clip. While the left hand holds the instrument close to the mouth, the right hand grasps a crossbar; by sliding a loop of tubing away from or closer to the body, the player can increase or decrease the distance that the wind travels between the mouthpiece and the terminating 'bell', thus lowering or raising the note.

In its early incarnation as the sackbut, the trombone led an honoured and busy life in ecclesiastical and royal music. It did not really settle into the orchestra until late in the eighteenth century. Retaining its ecclesiastical associations, the trombone was used to symbolize the afterlife, the descent into Purgatory or Hell. That had been its role in *Orfeo* by **Claudio Monteverdi** (1567–1643), and in similar vein it can be found in Mozart's sacred works, notably in the 'Tuba Mirum' of his *Requiem*. But perhaps the decisive reason why the trombone finally secured its place in the Romantic orchestra was that it was used in two works which probably had as much influence over nineteenth-century music as any other. Three trombones are to be found in the enlarged orchestra which Beethoven employed for his Fifth Symphony; and the instrument features in the concluding 'supper' scene of Mozart's opera *Don Giovanni*.

(TL) The Flirt *by Vittorio Reggianini*
Musical prowess was considered an important accomplishment for young ladies of the Romantic era.
(TR) *Steinway Piano*
Highly decorated pianos were extremely popular with the nineteenth-century aristocracy.
(BR) Trombone
Nineteenth-century trombone showing mouthpiece, sliding tube loop and 'bell'.

Beethoven ▶ p. 150 Chopin ▶ p. 190 Hummel ▶ p. 194 Liszt ▶ p. 194 Mendelssohn ▶ p. 197 Monteverdi ▶ p. 76 Mozart ▶ p. 144 Rachmaninov ▶ p. 256 R. Schumann ▶ p. 201

Valves in Brass

Baroque brass music was written for natural horns and trumpets. The classical period saw experiments with introducing keys into trumpets: the concertos for trumpet by **Haydn** and Hummel were both written with a keyed trumpet in mind. Trumpeters and horn players also experimented with using one hand in the bell to affect pitch. However, in the early Romantic period valves were introduced into the brass section.

Valves are really a mechanized version of the old Baroque crook. The difference is that instead of the crooks having to be slotted in or whipped out mid-performance, they are all permanently built into the instrument. The valve acts like a traffic policeman with a set of cones. When the valves are untouched, the player's breath passes straight down the 'high street' of the instrument. Each time a valve comes into play, the policeman cones off the main route, and the player's breath is forced down a diversion of varying length. These diversions are the crooks.

The invention of valves is attributed to Stölzel and Blühmel of Berlin in the late 1820s, and although older instruments were not abandoned overnight, it was certainly the valve trumpet that **Rossini** had in mind when he wrote *Guillaume Tell*. The French horn too became a valve instrument at this time. Schumann wrote for the valve horn in his *Konzertstück* op. 70 for four horns and orchestra.

The Early Romantic Orchestra

Berlioz's characteristic 'instrument' was the orchestra. While makers had sought to improve different woodwind instruments, Berlioz set himself the task of advancing the orchestra as his favourite instrument. He was always keen to know about the latest developments in instrument-making and performance technique, and made last-minute changes to his *Traite général d'instrumen-tation* ('General Treatise on Instrumentation') in response to the latest news. He adopted modern developments such as valved brass, pedal harps and Adolph Sax's inventions. He also brought into the symphony orchestra instruments previously considered as belonging to the military band or the opera-house: English

ADOLPHE SAX

The son of the Brussels wind-instrument maker Charles-Joseph Sax, Adolphe Sax (1814–94) studied the clarinet at the Conservatoire in Brussels. Accordingly, his first experiments with instruments were designs for improving the clarinet and then plans for a bass clarinet.

Sax patented the saxhorn in 1845. He took the existing valved brass instruments and came up with the idea of a group of such instruments, with a shared playing technique and a shared quality of sound. Initially copying the trumpet, he sub-sequently modelled the instruments on the tuba. His most famous invention, the saxophone itself, was patented in 1846. Crossing the single-reed woodwind family with the keyed-brass instruments of the early nineteenth century, he created a new instrument family.

His least-known instrument design is probably that for his timpani. Patented in 1855, this replaced the metal shell with an open frame, stretching the drum-head vellum over a long, conically shaped resonator. A pedal operated a series of shutters which allowed the pitch of the instrument to change, not by altering the tension in the vellum, but by changing the size of the resonator.

Sax's successes led to his winning a virtual monopoly in the supply of instruments to France's military bands. This, combined with his own self-esteem and quarrelsome temperament, led to a series of lawsuits involving other instrument-makers who claimed that he had patented already existing designs. As a result of this he was declared bankrupt in 1852, 1873 and 1877.

ADVANCES IN INSTRUMENT TECHNOLOGY

Flutes at the beginning of the nineteenth century were made of a wide range of materials. Boxwood instruments were still being made, as they had been in the Baroque era. Increased contact with Africa meant that ebony was also used. Ivory continued to be favoured, but also cocus wood. Brass, silver and pewter were all used for keywork.

The Renaissance flute had been played using fingerholes only. French innovations meant that the Baroque flute began the eighteenth century with a single key and ended it with eight. There the story largely rested until the intervention of Theobald Boehm (1794–1881).

Trained as a jeweller and watchmaker, Boehm had juggled the careers of goldsmith, flutemaker and flautist. On a visit to London in 1831, he took an interest in the instrument being played by a flautist called Charles Nicholson, which was remarkable both for its large fingerholes and for its fine tone. Boehm concluded that the flute had been hampered by attempting to place the holes within easy range of the flautist's fingers. He opted for large playing holes, evenly spaced. Initially he left the bore conical in shape, but he later moved the instrument over to a cylindrical bore, while the playing holes were now so large that any attempt to play them directly was abandoned and each was fitted with a padded cover and keywork to operate it.

String Instrument Modifications

Around 1820 the composer **Spohr** invented the chin rest, and as a result the violin was played tucked in at the side of the chin, with the head held slightly forwards and to one side in the modern manner. In the late eighteenth and early nineteenth centuries the violin's fingerboard was extended, and the neck made slimmer and bent back at a slightly more pronounced angle. In addition, the bridge became a little higher and more arched. Inside, the bass bar, which provided longitudinal support to the belly, was strengthened to prevent it from collapsing under the strain of the higher tension which the stronger style of strings could now sustain, and the soundpost, which stands directly under the bridge, grew thicker.

In addition to modifications like those of the violin, the cello's major change was to move away from being held resting on the player's calves to being supported by a spike or tail-pin. This grips the floor to stop the instrument slipping; it can be adjusted in length to suit the performer and even tucked away inside the instrument. Whether extended or withdrawn, the spike is held in position by a screw.

obbligato ▶ p. 360

horn or cor anglais, E flat clarinet, bells and novel percussion. In addition, he was given to providing very specific technical instructions in his scores, detailing how he wanted the instruments played; he also experimented with methods of playing: clarinets appeared in silk sacks in *La mort d'Orphée*.

SHIFTING EMPHASIS

The early Romantic period was a time in which the number and variety of instruments had only partly settled down. The flute, oboe, trumpet and French horn had all found their places in the ensemble; trombones gained a position in the orchestra at last. The coming of the bass tuba in the 1830s eased out the serpents, which had been introduced to provide some bass reinforcements for the trombonists. Meanwhile, the English horn made a comeback, and the E flat clarinet, which had been leading a military life as a band instrument, came into the orchestra in Berlioz's *Symphonie fantastique*, where its shriek forms part of the witches' sabbath rites in the final movement. The *Symphonie fantastique* also contains the first appearance in a symphony of a harp: its role in orchestral music had previously been minor.

SOUND WORLD OF THE FUTURE

In his search for the sound world of the future, Berlioz experimented with beaters with sponge heads for the timpani, to create a menacing sound. In his *Grande messe des morts* ('High Mass for the Dead', 1837) he wrote for two tenor drums, while his *Te Deum* (1849) requires six of them. He needed 16 drums in his *Requiem* (1837). His *Symphonie funèbre et triomphale* ('Funereal and Triumphal Symphony') requires four Turkish crescents, a jingling instrument consisting of bells arranged on a stick which is held upright and pounded on the floor. There are castanets in *Zaïde* and a distant bass drum in the 'Rákóczy March'. In *Les Troyens*, he scored for a drum called a 'tarbuka', a sistrum (a kind of ancient hand-held jingle) and a set of tuned bars, together with strokes of the tam-tam.

(TL) Valves
Valves enabled players of brass instruments to rapidly alter their sounding length.
(NR) Trumpet
By the early Romantic period, the trumpet had established its place in the ensemble.
(FR) Serpent
A curious-looking instrument, the serpent was eventually usurped by the tuba.

In the 1840s and 50s he began to use the bass tuba, sometimes to replace the ophicleide, sometimes as an alternative. The *Te Deum* is notable for being the first time an organ is given a prominent rather than a continuo or **obbligato** role in the orchestra. Its interventions in the piece, far from providing an underpinning, are dramatic and challenging. He used a double quartet of saxhorns in *Les Troyens* and a saxhorn *suraigu* (high-pitched) for the 'Marche troyenne' and the entry of the Trojan horse.

BEATING BEETHOVEN

Brahms wrote for the modest orchestra of Beethoven's age (the symphonic forces for which Beethoven had written at the end of the classical period were about 55), ignoring the technical developments that had transformed horns and trumpets into valved instruments with a full chromatic compass. Berlioz, like Brahms a passionate admirer of Beethoven, set himself the task of going beyond his hero. Beethoven had expanded the scale and ambition of the symphony. In 1824, his Ninth Symphony needed no fewer than 61 players (24 violins, 10 violas, 6 cellos, 6 double basses, 2 each of flutes, oboes, clarinets, bassoons, horns, trumpets and trombones, and 1 timpanist), not to mention a full chorus. Berlioz took it further down this road. Beethoven had demanded much of his instrumentalists: Berlioz would demand more.

Serpent

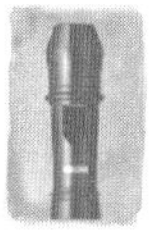

The serpent is the bass member of the cornett family and, like the cornett, is made of two carved pieces of wood which are fastened together and then bound in canvas and leather. Sinuously shaped like two Ss, one leading straight into the other, it has a cup mouthpiece on the end of a brass crook, a conical bore and a series of finger holes. At the beginning of the nineteenth century three or sometimes more keys were added to it. The serpent was eventually displaced when the tuba was invented.

Although often thought of as a Baroque oddity, the serpent had a long life as an instrument in church choirs of the kind Thomas Hardy writes about in *Under the Greenwood Tree*. Mendelssohn's *St Paul* (1836) has a part for serpentist which later generations have found it difficult to staff.

Arpeggione

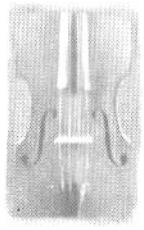

A bowed string instrument, the arpeggione was invented in Vienna by J. G. Stauffer in 1823–24. A kind of bass viol, with soundholes like a viol, it is waisted, but shaped more like a large guitar than a viol or double bass. Six-stringed and with metal frets, it was tuned E, A, d, g, b, e'. The arpeggione was played by Vincenz Schuster, who wrote a tutor for the instrument, and Heinrich August Birnback (1782–1848), who wrote a concerto for it. The main reason for the arpeggione's continuing fame, however, is a sonata written for Schuster by Schubert in November 1824. This piece is now normally played on either the cello or the viola.

Berlioz ▶ p. 186 Brahms ▶ p. 240 Haydn ▶ p. 140 Rossini ▶ p. 200 Schubert ▶ p. 182 Spohr ▶ p. 204

The Early Romantic

LISTENING GUIDE

Hector Berlioz
Symphonie fantastique

WORK: Hector Berlioz, *Symphonie fantastique*, op. 14, composed in 1830
SCORING: Two flutes (2nd doubles on piccolo), two oboes (2nd doubles on English horn), two clarinets, four bassoons, four horns, two cornets, two trumpets, three trombones, two ophicleides, timpani, percussion, two harps, strings
EXCERPT: Track 5, 5th movement ('Sabbath Night's Dream')
TIMINGS BASED ON: Royal Concertgebouw Orchestra, conducted by Sir Colin Davis (see Recommended CDs)

'In an artist's life,' Berlioz wrote in his memoirs, 'one thunderclap sometimes follows swiftly on another.' On 11 September 1827 he was bowled over by a double thunderclap, when an English company performed *Hamlet* in Paris, with an Irish actress called Harriet Smithson as Ophelia; and on 9 March 1828 Beethoven's Third Symphony, the 'Eroica', was played at the Paris Conservatoire, followed on 13 April by the Fifth Symphony. Both Shakespeare and Beethoven were largely unknown to the French. The general influence of Shakespeare on Berlioz was comparable to that of his adored Virgil, while the specific combination of Harriet Smithson and Beethoven led directly to the composition of his *Symphonie fantastique*.

Berlioz was obsessed with Harriet, as a present-day teenager might be with a pop star. In his case, worship from afar led to marriage, but it was a long and hard road. In 1830, with Harriet still unattainable, he poured out his feelings in this symphony, which is subtitled 'Episode in the Life of an Artist'. In a programme note, which he revised several times, Berlioz set out the story. A young musician, despairing of a hopeless love, experiences strange visions which are transformed into musical ideas. One in particular recurs, the *idée fixe* associated with the beloved.

RECOMMENDED CDs

1. *Symphonie fantastique*; **Romeo and Juliet* (Love scene and Queen Mab scherzo). Royal Concertgebouw Orchestra, *London Symphony Orchestra. Sir Colin Davis, conductor. Philips 446 202-2. Recorded 1974, *1968.

   Sir Colin Davis loves this music so much that he is sometimes prone to exaggeration. But everyone should have this recording by the supreme Berlioz interpreter of our time.

2. *Symphonie fantastique*. Dutilleux: *Métaboles*. Orchestre de l'Opéra Bastille. Myung-Whun Chung, conductor. DG 445 878-2. Recorded 1993.

   A vivid performance, beautifully recorded: just listen to the thwacks of the *pizzicato* strings in the first movement, and the bony skeletons at the *col legno* passage in the Finale.

3. *Symphonie fantastique*. Orchestre Révolutionnaire et Romantique. Sir John Eliot Gardiner, conductor. Philips 434 402-2. Recorded 1991.

   Gardiner conducts a brilliant performance on period instruments, with close attention to Berlioz's dynamic and *portamento* markings.

4. *Symphonie fantastique*. The London Classical Players. Sir Roger Norrington, conductor. EMI 7 49541 2. Recorded 1988.

   Norrington the pioneer led the way with this first recording on period instruments. Like Gardiner, he follows Berlioz's instructions for 'at least' two harps per part, and uses ophicleides rather than modern tubas to splendid effect.

VOLCANIC LOVE AND SUFFERING

The introduction to the first movement recalls the artist's melancholy and longing. The *idée fixe*, hinted at early on in the violins, is heard in full when the slow tempo gives way to the *allegro*. It is a long, asymmetrical melody that dominates the rest of the movement, which is given over to his 'volcanic' love and his suffering. The music has a Beethovenian energy, and the exposition is repeated as in a classical symphony, but it is far beyond anything that Beethoven would have recognized. In the development section, for example, shrieks in the woodwind are superimposed on rising and falling **chromatic** scales

1. 0'00"
Sinister rumblings in the bass alternate with shivers in the upper strings and mournful woodwind calls.

2. 1'28"
The shrill clarinet in C announces the arrival of the beloved in a speeded-up version of her motto.

3. 1'47"
A fuller statement of the *idée fixe*, distorted on the even shriller E-flat clarinet.

4. 3'00"
Deep bells sound, followed by an anticipation of the round dance.

5. 3'27"
Bassoons and tubas intone the *Dies irae*.

chromaticism ▶ p. 357 fugue ▶ p. 358 idée fixe ▶ p. 359

PREPARATIONS FOR THE PREMIÈRE

Berlioz made several attempts at the Prix de Rome, an annual prize for composers awarded by the Académie des Beaux-Arts of the Institut de France. The prize was a five-year scholarship: two years in Rome, one in Germany and two in Paris. Berlioz did not want to leave Paris, but he was short of money, and he needed to impress the mother of Camille Moke, a young pianist whom – having given up on Harriet Smithson – he was intending to marry.

As part of his preparations, Berlioz planned to put on a concert in May 1830, to include the first performance of his *Symphonie fantastique*. It never took place, partly because the stage and pit of the theatre were too small to accommodate the orchestra, and partly because other concerts arranged for the same day would have deprived him of many of his players and much of his audience. However, the rehearsals reinforced his faith in the work.

Ecstatic Reception

The postponement evidently did his prospects no harm; in August, a few weeks after Paris had been briefly convulsed by revolution, Berlioz heard that his entry, the cantata *Sardanapale*, had won the Prix de Rome. The first performance of the *Symphonie fantastique* eventually took place on 5 December 1830 at the Conservatoire. It was conducted by Habeneck and was a great success. The audience demanded – but did not get – an encore of the 'March to the Scaffold' and erupted at the end.

Berlioz was in ecstasies, not least because of the positive effect the symphony had on Camille Moke and her mother. Nonetheless, he was able to see where the work was flawed, and over the next few years he made alterations to the first two movements and completely rewrote the 'Scene in the Meadows'. He left for Rome at the end of December. His relationship with Camille did not survive; but Harriet Smithson, the negative inspiration of the work, became his wife three years later.

in the strings. After a dramatic pause, the *idée fixe* returns as though nothing had happened. The movement ends *religiosamente*, with a few quiet chords.

THE SHEPHERD'S CALL

In the second movement, the artist is at a ball. Hitherto, the harp had been associated with the opera, as in *Orfeo ed Euridice* by **Gluck**, a composer whom Berlioz worshipped. Here, Berlioz employs two harps to introduce a graceful waltz. Its progress is interrupted by the *idée fixe*. Later on the young man sees his beloved again for an instant, before he is swept up in the revelry.

In the 'Scene in the Meadows', the longest movement in the symphony, an English horn in the orchestra and an offstage oboe represent two shepherds calling to each other on their pipes. If Berlioz reminds the listener of Beethoven's 'Pastoral' Symphony, he also conjures up the landscape of the great French painter of the seventeenth century, Claude Lorrain. The *idée fixe* fills the artist with fears about his beloved's constancy. At the end, the first shepherd's call is answered only by distant rumbles of thunder, magically evoked by Berlioz with chords on four timpani.

It is the timpani that introduce the 'March to the Scaffold'. The artist has taken opium and dreams that he has been condemned to death for murdering his beloved. The march is alternately sinister and brash. Just before the end, the *idée fixe* is heard softly on the clarinet, before the guillotine falls with a crash and his head rolls into the basket.

(R)* Coastal Landscape *by Claude Lorrain
The 'Scene in the Meadows' from the Symphonie fantastique *conjures up the pastoral landscapes of Lorrain's work.*

A BLAZE OF SOUND

In the last movement, he dreams that witches and monsters have gathered for his funeral. The beloved arrives to join the witches, her motto perverted into a grotesque dance. Distant bells lead to the intoning on the lower wind and brass of the plainchant 'Dies irae' from the Mass for the dead. Berlioz then embarks on a **fugue** to depict the witches' round dance. Finally the dance and the 'Dies irae' are combined, and the symphony ends in a blaze of sound.

Berlioz's exploitation of the orchestra is without precedent. The wailing woodwind, the use of a cornet to add garishness to the ball, the timpani in the slow movement, the sinister writing for divided strings at the beginning of the finale, are the work of a master orchestrator. And his use of extreme dynamics, such as writing *pianissimo* and *fortissimo* in the same bar, demonstrate the fertility and the vividness of his unique imagination.

6. 5'21"
The witches' round dance begins, punctuated by a syncopated figure on the brass

7. 8'07"
The round dance and the 'Dies irae' are combined.

8. 8'36"
Violins and violas play *col legno* (with the wood of the bow), suggesting the rattling of skeletons.

9. 9'08"
A demented screech on the woodwind.

10. 9'14"
The last appearance of the *Dies irae* before the climax.

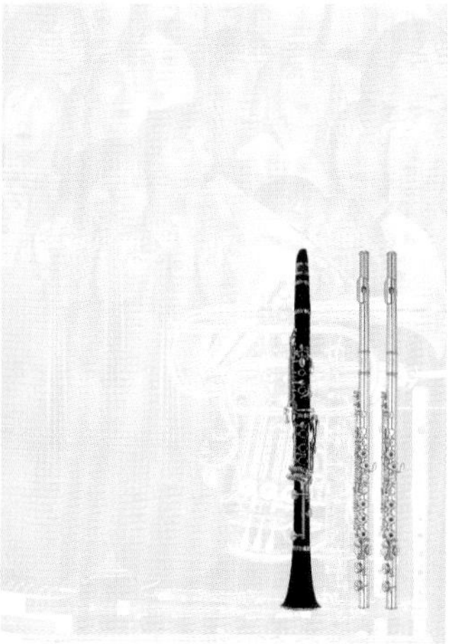

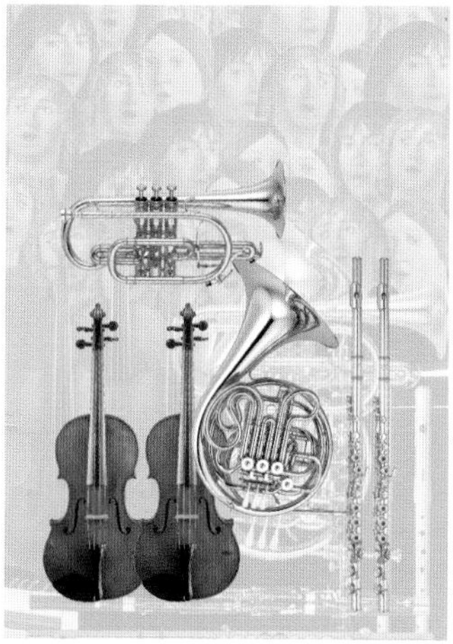

Beethoven ▶ p. 150 Berlioz ▶ p. 186 Gluck ▶ p. 158

FRANZ SCHUBERT: *DIE SCHÖNE MÜLLERIN*

One of the ironies of the world of music lies in a letter that the poet Wilhelm Müller wrote shortly before his death, expressing the hope that one day a 'kindred spirit' would be found whose ear would 'catch the melodies from my words'. Müller never knew that Schubert had already set *Die schöne Müllerin* from a volume of his verse published in 1821, and was even then working on a second sequence of his poems, *Winterreise*.

Die schöne Müllerin dates from 1823, a year when Schubert was in a state of depression, but no hint of his unhappiness is to be found in the music. The poems – sentimental and romantic – recount the story of a young miller who loves and loses the daughter of the house where he finds work. The narrative is advanced by connecting images and phrases; ever present is the brook, to which the boy confides his feelings.

RECOMMENDED CD

Franz Schubert: *Die schöne Müllerin* Dietrich Fischer-Dieskau, baritone. Gerald Moore, piano. EMI CDM 5669072

Fischer-Dieskau made several recordings of *Die schöne Müllerin*; this dates from 1961, when he was in his prime. He catches the bittersweet mood of the songs to perfection, and Moore is a true partner, never merely an accompanist.

The Journey

Of the 20 songs in the cycle, nine are **strophic**, where the same music is used for each verse. Examples of this include the first song, 'Das Wandern' ('Roving'), where the boy sets out on his journey, and the thirteenth, 'Mit dem grünen Lautenband' ('With the Lute's Green Ribbon'), where he muses on the girl's favourite colour. Others are continuous, with brief passages of recitative at heightened moments. They are also examples of the skill with which Schubert modulates into distant keys, returning to base with a harmonic sleight-of-hand. In 'Tränenregen' ('Shower of Tears'), the boy's tears and the impending shower of rain are suggested by an uneasy seesaw from minor to major and back again.

Perhaps the best-known song is 'Mein!', half-way through the cycle, where the lover calls on all nature to defer to his joy. The pounding accompaniment, representing the brook and the turning millwheels, provides an irresistibly energetic background to his delusion of happiness. At the very end, it is in the brook that he finds peace.

THE *BIEDERMEIER*

Biedermeier was originally a derogatory term, coined early in the twentieth century to describe the life and art of the middle classes in German-speaking countries from about 1815 to 1848. During this period, the Chancellor of Austria was Prince Metternich, whose aim in the aftermath of the French Revolution and the Napoleonic Wars was to re-establish the principle of absolute monarchy. Political activity was banned and any expression of dangerous revolutionary ideas was suppressed by strict censorship.

As a result, a cosy domesticity prevailed, the middle classes amusing themselves with musical evenings at home and family walks in the country. From art and music to interior decoration and fashion, the fine and applied arts all reflected a way of life that was seemingly idyllic, but which was considered grossly philistine by its detractors.

If public entertainment included dancing to the waltzes of Joseph Lanner (1801–43) and the elder Johann Strauss (1804–49), musical entertainment in the home was centred on the piano, especially in the shape of piano duets and Lieder. Schubert and the baritone Michael Vogl were much in demand in the salons of Vienna, and many of the composer's pieces were first heard at the 'Schubertiade', convivial gatherings of Schubert and his friends.

DEATH AND THE MAIDEN

The first movement of Schubert's String Quartet in D minor was used to tense effect in Roman Polanski's dark political thriller *Death and the Maiden*; the piece was also used in the ballet of the same name that premiered in London in 1937.

POPULAR MELODY *Schubert*

FRÉDÉRIC CHOPIN: BALLADE NO. 1 IN G MINOR

Many of Chopin's pieces were written for his pupils, but the four Ballades are among the larger-scale works that he wrote primarily for himself. The term suggests a derivation from an epic poem, but there does not appear to be any specific connection essential to understanding.

The First Ballade was composed in 1834 or 1835. Chopin was much admired for his extemporizations at the keyboard: this ballade (like many of his other pieces) has an improvisatory feel to it, without ever rambling aimlessly.

SCHUBERT AND GOETHE

Lied is simply the German word for song, but it is used (plural *Lieder*) specifically to mean a song in German. Schubert was not the first composer of Lieder, but he was the first composer for whom they were as important as symphonies or string quartets. Moreover, he used the themes of his songs as the basis of variation movements in two of his best-known compositions, the 'Death and the Maiden' quartet and the 'Trout' quintet.

Schubert set the verses of many poets, famous and obscure. Some of his finest songs are to words by Germany's greatest poet, Goethe, who seems to have been initially unimpressed with the composer, despite Schubert's sending him a handful of songs. 'Gretchen am Spinnrade', written when he was only 17, acutely conveys the girl's misery, the spinning-wheel figure in the accompaniment coming to a dramatic halt as Gretchen recalls her lover's kiss. 'Heidenröslein', with its echo of Mozart's *Magic Flute*, has the simplicity of a folksong. In *Erlkönig* ('The Erl King'), relentless triplets in the piano brilliantly depict the father's desperate ride through the night. Of Schubert's 60 or more Goethe settings, one of the best loved is 'Der Musensohn' ('Son of the Muses'). In its infectious good humour, when performed as an encore it never fails to send the audience home smiling.

coda ▶ p. 357 strophic ▶ p. 362 subdominant ▶ p. 362

Directed Improvisation

It starts with a solemn passage in octaves, a curtain-raiser to the drama that follows. The ballade is based on two contrasting tunes. The first is a rather hesitant waltz in the minor, the melody highlighted by a simple, syncopated accompaniment. Chopin toys dreamily with this theme before the mood changes to one of agitation.

A gentle figure in the left hand, like a horn call, leads to the second tune, in the major. On its first appearance it is lyrical, almost wistful; again, all the emphasis is on the tune, the accompaniment lightly etched in. A brief allusion to the first theme leads to a complete transformation of the second. Crashing chords and a wide-ranging accompaniment mark the first *fortissimo* outburst. If the ballade has a hero, this surely marks his arrival. Dazzling fireworks, rising rapidly through nearly four octaves, are followed by a repeat of the virile theme, still *fortissimo* but now at the lower pitch of its first appearance. The tentative first theme recurs for the last time, picking up strength as it leads into the **coda**.

Here, *Presto con fuoco* (very fast and fiery), the material is unrelated to what has been heard so far. But the octaves of the opening reappear just before the barnstorming conclusion.

RECOMMENDED CD

Frédéric Chopin: Ballade No. 1 in g (plus Ballades 2–4, Grande Valse brillante in E flat, op. 18; Grande Valse in A flat, op. 42; Nocturne in F, op. 15 No. 1; Mazurka in f, op. 7 No. 3; Mazurka in A minor, op. 17 No. 4; Mazurka in D, op. 33 No. 2; Etude in E, op. 10 No. 3; Etude in c sharp, op. 10 No. 4). Murray Perahia, piano. Sony SK 64399.

This excellent selection, recorded in 1994, makes an ideal introduction. Perahia has all the technique at his command, but he is never merely flashy.

ROBERT SCHUMANN: PIANO QUINTET IN E FLAT, OP. 44

In 1842, with two symphonies and other works behind him, Schumann's mind was on chamber music. He began the piece on 23 September and completed it in less than three weeks.

Schumann who pioneered the combination of piano and string quartet and his lead was followed by other composers. The first movement opens with a rising seventh which, extended to a rising octave, dominates the first group of melodies. The second subject is a softer, yielding tune on the cello, answered immediately in mirror fashion on the viola. The development section features the piano, busying away in virtually non-stop quavers, with the strings in a subordinate role. Equality is restored with the recapitulation.

Finale

The slow movement is in sonata rondo form, the measured tread of a march in C minor alternating with a flowing passage in the major and with a stormy section in the **subdominant** F minor. The scherzo boasts two sections, tranquil and impassioned respectively, both of which reflect the cello tune in the first movement. But it is in the Finale that Schumann really goes to town. He starts not in the home key of E flat, but in G minor; then he passes through remote keys, culminating in a long passage in E major. Finally, after solemn chords have prepared the listener for a peroration, he brings back the opening theme of the first movement in long notes, to which he adds the first theme of the Finale as a fugal counter-subject. Syncopations in the piano part propel the movement to a triumphant conclusion.

RECOMMENDED CD

Robert Schumann: Piano Quintet in E flat, op. 44 (coupled with Johannes Brahms: Piano Quintet in f). Kodály Quartet, Jenö Jandó, piano. Naxos 8.550406

A bargain issue that couples two of the best-known piano quintets in ideal performances. Made in 1990, this recording should be in everybody's collection.

FELIX MENDELSSOHN: VIOLIN CONCERTO IN E MINOR, OP. 64

Mendelssohn completed his Violin Concerto while on holiday in September 1844; it was first performed the following March by his friend Ferdinand David, the leader of the Leipzig Gewandhaus Orchestra.

There is no introduction. Over a murmuring accompaniment in the strings, the soloist enters with a singing tune, rich in potential for melodic and rhythmic development. Mendelssohn's audience would have expected an orchestral statement of this material right at the beginning: it comes eventually, but the soloist seizes a new phrase from the violins and oboes and launches into a frenzy of double stopping. The second subject, in the major, is first heard in the woodwind, the violin providing the bass by sustaining a low note.

Keeping Listeners on Their Toes

Mendelssohn has two surprises in store. The cadenza comes after the development section, rather than at the end of the movement. It is written out in full, not left for the soloist to

improvise. The second surprise occurs when another sustained note, on the bassoon, leads seamlessly into the slow movement. Here, accompanied by the strings and the lightest touch of woodwind, the soloist embarks on a lyrical tune. The contrasting second section in the minor hints at passion, but calm returns with the first tune, now with a more elaborate accompaniment.

The last movement begins with a short linking passage, insistent rather than urgent, before the movement proper is introduced by brass fanfares. The scurrying first subject, for the violin and two flutes, evokes the fairy world atmosphere of the overture to *A Midsummer Night's Dream*. This is never far away, even in the development of the martial second subject. Mendelssohn springs his last surprise by introducing an expansive melody that he combines with the fairy music, and the concerto ends with the soloist ascending like a rocket.

RECOMMENDED CD

Felix Mendelssohn: Violin Concerto in E minor (coupled with Concerto for Violin and String Orchestra in d [1822]). Kyoko Takezawa, violin. Bamberg Symphony Orchestra. Claus Peter Flor, conductor. RCA Victor 09026 62512 2. Recorded 1994.

Kyoko Takezawa starts as she means to go on: gloriously impassioned playing in the first movement and the transition to the last, and sweet-toned in the slow movement. Flor provides excellent support, with crisp *sforzandi* in the Finale.

(ML) Salons of Vienna
Schubert and Vogl were in demand in the salons of Vienna as well as amongst their friends.
(TL) Working Manuscript
Manuscript score by Franz Schubert of the Quartet in B flat major, Vienna, 1814.
(R) Robert Schumann
Schumann completed his Piano Quintet in E Flat, op. 44 in just three weeks in 1842.

Chopin ▶ p. 190 Mendelssohn ▶ p. 197 Schubert ▶ p. 182 R. Schumann ▶ p. 201

THE LATE ROMANTIC

The political structure of Europe changed greatly during the second half of the nineteenth century. Germany and Italy became united countries under supreme rulers. The Habsburgs' Austrian Empire, ruled from Vienna, became fragmented into Austria-Hungary. The borders of this new confederation contained the cauldron of difficulties that eventually developed into the confrontations which culminated in World War I in 1914.

INTELLECTUAL CONSEQUENCES OF POLITICAL CHANGES

The sense of a changing world gradually led to greater polarity between those bent on reforms and those wanting to resist and suppress change. The growing sense of political frustration in some cases led to more radical attempts to alter the status quo, which invited more stringent measures to suppress them. In other cases it led to an intellectual and artistic removal from world affairs, a personal withdrawal from reality to private dreams, self-absorption or despair. The presence of powerful, often repressive, centres of government led to increasing demands for self-determination by subjugated parts of Europe, often inspired by musical and other nationalist works of art. In the earlier part of the nineteenth century, Germany was challenging for the intellectual leadership of Europe, in instrumental music as well as in other fields. Germany used its own intellectual development to help define and secure its identity, and eventual unification, by an exploration of, and admiration for, its national folk-tales, ancient sagas and peasant ballads.

A SENSE OF THE PAST

German intellectual and artistic dominance led many other national groups to distance themselves and follow other paths. These included Russia, Bohemia, Hungary, Great Britain and, in particular, France and Italy. Ironically, many of these movements grew from an investigation of their national pasts, an interest which had stemmed from German ideas of the Enlightenment in the late eighteenth and early nineteenth centuries. Many of the most radical moves that appeared in this period, and which had so profound an effect on the twentieth century, sought to avoid tradition and break with the past by emphasizing their modernity.

The Late Romantic

INTRODUCTION

The 1860s saw a number of major reorganizations in European politics. Italy became a united country under the king of (former) Piedmont-Sardinia, Victor Emmanuel II, in 1861 and its new national government tried to retain the kingdom's liberal ideals, such as removing instances of operatic and intellectual censorship. However, Italy's liberalism was not aspired to by other European countries undergoing radical organizational changes. The Austrian Empire, for example, never truly coped with middle-class and intellectual desires for political representation and reform. The celebrated Viennese street plan, the Ringstrasse, was in part intended as a boulevard sufficiently broad to prevent insurrectionary barricades and to allow cavalry ease of access to suppress street violence.

One of the most symbolic measures of illiberalism throughout Europe was the growth of anti-semitism. The increasing number of prominent Jewish intellectuals, writers and musicians led to ever more hostile resentment, in many cases spawned by the rising tide of nationalism. In Russia, the promotion of the Slavonic identity led to an intolerance of all racial minorities and manifested itself in anti-Jewish pogroms.

The reign of Alexander II (1855–81) came closest to liberal tolerance, but the Tsar adamantly refused any national representational government. Consequently, his empire became the focus of increasingly radical revolutionary ideas and actions. Drastic anti-reform measures followed his assassination in 1881. The revolutions of 1905 and 1917 were the consequence of this repression of political reforms and the intellectual freedoms sought in this period.

KEY EVENTS

1861	Friedrich Wilhelm I becomes Prussian kaiser
1862	Bismarck made prime minister of Prussia
1865	American Civil War ends with surrender of Confederate Army
1869	Leo Tolstoy finishes *War and Peace*, begun in 1864
1871	France loses Franco-Prussian war; riots and Commune follow in Paris
1874	First Impressionist exhibition is held in Paris; includes Claude Monet's *Impression: Sunrise*
1876	Bayreuth Festspielhaus opens with the first complete performance of Wagner's *Ring*
1879	The Norwegian dramatist Henrik Ibsen's realist play *The Doll's House* first performed
1881	Tsar Alexander II assassinated; Dostoevsky completes *The Brothers Karamazov*
1885	The German philosopher Karl Marx finishes *Das Kapital*
1887	First performance of Verdi's *Otello*, libretto by Arrigo Boito, after Shakespeare
1894	Alfred Dreyfus, a Jewish-French army officer, accused and tried for treason, and imprisoned on Devil's Island
1898	In Paris, Pierre and Marie Curie discover radium and polonium
1900	In Vienna, Sigmund Freud publishes *The Interpretation of Dreams* about the unconscious

GREAT BRITAIN AND NORTH AMERICA

Liberal reforms were most evident in Great Britain where, more than in other countries, the government controlled the power of the monarchy and the aristocracy. Though the enormous growth in material prosperity led to urban poverty, the conditions of those in work were improved by the admission of workers' organizations and the founding of the Trades Union Congress (TUC) in 1868. Much of Great Britain's wealth depended on its worldwide empire, which was much envied by Germany, France and Italy. The growing power of Germany struck fear into the hearts of British governments, which as a result increasingly sought alliances with other countries.

The founding and amalgamation of states in North America, especially after the end of the Civil War (1861–65), led to considerable economic growth, but artistically the new country was still strongly dependent on its mostly

immigrant population's desire to emulate European models. Only later in this period were moves made to establish a distinctly American culture.

INTELLECTUAL BACKGROUND

In the early part of the nineteenth century, the German philosopher Georg Friedrich Hegel promulgated a profoundly influential, all-embracing theory of the inevitable progress of civilization and its synthesis with human self-fulfilment. For Hegel this historical 'progress' was demonstrated by the forward journey of a metaphysical 'spirit' (*Geist*) traceable in all human activities, not least

chromaticism ▶ p. 357

WAGNER AND WAGNERISM

Between 1860 and 1918 **Richard Wagner** (1813–83) became the most influential intellectual figure in Europe. For his *Gesamtkunstwerk* ('Complete Art-Work') he drew on a wide range of inspirations, including Greek tragedy, the symphonies of **Ludwig van Beethoven** (1770–1827) and his own historicist ideas of realizing the latent tendencies of all arts. This ensured that his music-dramas reached into almost every area of European artistic, philosophical and even political life.

The performance of the revised *Tannhäuser* (in Paris in 1861, though poorly received by many traditional opera-goers, profoundly affected the poet and critic Charles Baudelaire. Baudelaire's own portrayal of longing and the corruption of love in *Les Fleurs du Mal* ('The Flowers of Evil') found many echoes in Wagner's newly written opening scene in the Venusberg. Baudelaire's use of poetic 'correspondences' (suggestive parallels between feelings, expressed in poetry by transferring metaphors between the arts) also found common ground with Wagner's ideas of artistic synthesis. Several magazines and societies were founded in Paris to promote Wagner's ideas; in the 1870s and 80s almost no composer escaped his influence.

Intellectual Influence

The performance of Wagner's *Tristan und Isolde* in Munich in 1865 also proved highly influential. Its novel use of **chromaticism**, orchestral colour and flexible rhythm had profound effects in many intellectual spheres. The struggle to escape the musical influence of *Tristan* became one of the distinguishing features of the early modern period in music.

The opening of the specially built Festspielhaus in Bayreuth in 1876 attracted musicians, monarchs, writers and philosophers from all over the world. The effect of the four-opera cycle *Der Ring des Nibelungen* ('The Nibelung's Ring') was profound. The sunken orchestra pit and the darkened auditorium were much admired, though not copied, innovations. The presentation of many ideas in an opera house also changed the status of opera and the power and meaning of music. Music now had a new role as the articulator of unconscious feelings or ideas. Wagner's dramaturgy, especially its use of monologues and its deliberately powerful engagement of the audience, also had a lasting effect.

the arts – primarily music – and philosophy. **Felix Mendelssohn**'s (1809–47) innovatory sense of music's history, and his concept of what constituted musical excellence, were shaped by Hegel's ideas.

(BL) The Struggle for Italian Unity
Allegorical picture showing the signs of autocracy in 1860s' Italy being swept aside.
(TL) Charles Darwin
Darwin's theory of evolution revolutionized thinking about the origins of the human race.
***(TR)* Tristan und Isolde**
Poster for Wagner's influential opera.
(BR) Otto von Bismarck
Bismarck led the struggle for unification amongst all the German-speaking states.

Hegel's concept of 'historical progress' strongly influenced Karl Marx, and found parallels in Charles Darwin's *Origin of the Species by Means of Natural Selection* (1859), which attributed the evolution of man to 'the survival of the fittest'. These historically 'progressive' theories helped shape the nineteenth century's views of musical evolution, particularly German music. But after the defeat of the liberal revolutions of 1848, views that history showed the steady improvement of civilization started being challenged.

PROGRESSION AND REGRESSION

The material manifestations of progress, such as economic growth and expanding industrialization, came to be viewed as anything but progressive. Disillusion became widespread, and there appeared a growing sense that either the best times would never come, or that they had already been. The arts were increasingly seen as opposed to, or as an escape from, outward 'progress'. Science and art were perceived as antithetical.

Powerful proponents of these ideas were the philosophers Arthur Schopenhauer and Friedrich Nietzsche. Schopenhauer's *Die Welt als Wille und Vorstellung* ('The World as Will and Idea'), ignored when it first appeared in 1819, became widely read after 1848. Schopenhauer proposed a pessimistic, anti-Hegelian philosophy, in which unconscious selfishness was the prime motivator of mankind. This could be suspended only by pity, or by the arts, especially music, in which self-interest could be submerged. His ideas influenced many including Nietzsche, Sigmund Freud and Wagner. Wagner, exiled in Switzerland, was disillusioned with politics and progressivism. The effect of these ideas was profound, on the plots of his subsequent music-dramas as well as on his view of the primacy of music in them.

THE FRANCO-PRUSSIAN WAR

The Franco-Prussian War (1870–71) was arguably the most significant European political event of the late Romantic era. Following the final defeat of Napoleon at Waterloo (1815) the loose confederation of independent German-speaking states realized that only in unity could there be strength to resist outside domination, especially by France. In time, the aim of German unification was driven less by fear of domination and more by the assertion of independence and power. It took its lead from its most persistent advocate, Otto von Bismarck, who as prime and foreign minister of Prussia did everything in his power to unite all German-speaking states under Prussian military and political command. A series of short wars in the 1860s led to the North German Confederation, headed by Prussia, which significantly – as Bismarck wished – excluded one major German-speaking nation: Austria. Other south German states, such as the kingdom of Bavaria, remained reluctant to abandon sovereignty to Prussia, so Bismarck used a disagreement with the French over the succession to the Spanish throne to provoke a war with France, simultaneously bringing into line the recalcitrant states and defeating Germany's strongest Western political threat.

Political Unity

Prussia's defeat of France at the Battle of Sedan in 1871 led to the unification of Germany, the annexation of the French territories of Alsace and Lorraine, and the establishment of Berlin as the capital of the new Germany. The new German political unity and increased military prowess seemed to many Germans to provide a material manifestation of their intellectual and artistic (especially musical) hegemony. Between 1871 and 1918, the Romantic age could be said to have concluded just as the Modern Era was emerging from its smouldering embers.

Beethoven ▶ p. 150 Mendelssohn ▶ p. 197 Wagner ▶ p. 226

THE GOLDEN AGE

One example of the change in attitude to the past was the growth of collected editions of dead composers' works. The assembling of first-hand evidence of the history of music was sparked off originally by Leopold von Ranke in Berlin. The systematic collection of such material as the starting-point for dispassionate historical analysis was at first akin to Hegelian 'progress'. By the end of the nineteenth century in music, however, this material came to be viewed differently. Earlier composers such as the great triumverate of the classical era, came to seem, not stages to a better present, but custodians of a golden age and of an unsurpassable greatness. Musical modernity represented a decline of musical civilization.

PESSIMISM AND REALISM

The pessimistic view of history lay behind the rise of Realism in the nineteenth century. Opposed to the optimism of the last stages of Romanticism, novelists such as Gustave Flaubert, Emile Zola and Charles Dickens, and painters such as Gustave Courbet, avoided romanticized images and tried to portray ordinary life in a matter-of-fact way, in the process exposing some of its evils. In music, the influence of Realism was particularly apparent in the works of Russian composers such as **Modest Petrovich Musorgsky** (1839–81) who, in the first version of his *Boris Godunov* (1868–69), tried to reproduce everyday speech patterns in music. Even in the opera's heavily revised later versions his pessimistic historicism, in which the Russian people learn nothing from Tsar Boris's oppression, exemplified a typically 'realist' view of history. After the assassination of Tsar Alexander II in 1881 Russian censorship became more repressive and the arts moved away from realism towards nationalism and folk culture.

ROMANTICISM AND THE SELF

Realism concerned the outside world, but music was more affected by the changes in attitude to the individual's personal psychological world. Romanticism had already looked closely at the Self, but post-1848 disillusion increasingly changed what was perceived. The ideas of Schopenhauer became more influential, most significantly on Nietzsche. In his *Birth of Tragedy*, he described civilization as a struggle between 'untamed' Dionysian forces – expressed in the arts – and rational, conscious Apollonian forces. He argued that the latter had won and as a result created an imbalance in the individual's and in civilization's collective psychology. The dichotomy between rational and unconscious forces was close to Wagner's dramaturgical views, especially his post-Schopenhauerian ideas about the role of music in his dramas. Nietzsche's writings on individual liberation from the constraints of common morality gave confidence to many composers' anti-traditionalism.

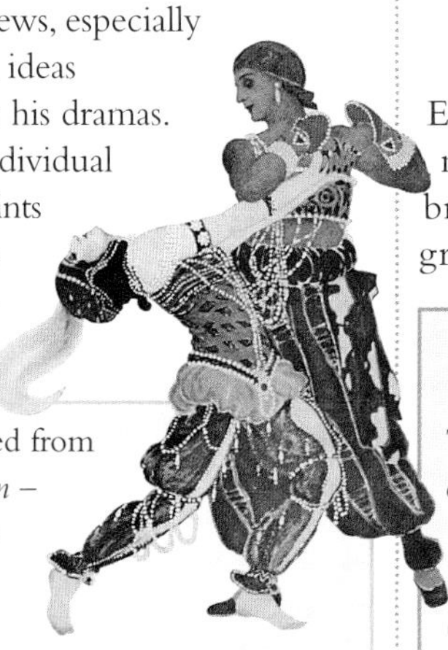

PARIS: AN ARTISTIC CENTRE

Provoked by its humiliating defeat in the Franco-Prussian War in 1871, France, despite an upsurge of political conservatism, began a period of artistic and intellectual re-examination, radicalism and creative activity.

Paris emerged as the centre for new ideas in the visual arts. In the 1850s and 60s, Realism had begun to replace the idealized images of Romanticism. Out of Realism emerged another artistic movement similarly wedded to painting the contemporary world, but turning away from Realism's social concerns. The movement's artists, rejected by the official French Academy, mounted an exhibition of their own in 1874. Their collective name, 'Impressionists', was derived from Monet's painting *Impression – Sunrise*. The Impressionists introduced new uses of colour, brushwork and draughtsmanship to capture fleeting moments, particularly effects of light. Though essentially a visual movement, Impressionism's radical transformation of colour-use and traditional forms led commentators to apply the term 'Impressionist' to other arts, notably (and controversially) music.

This emerging cultural centre was foremost in the search for alternatives to traditional art and German music. The city also saw influential performances of Russian music. Concerts of works by the 'Five', a group of Russian composers, sparked interest in the 1880s and 90s, but the most significant events were Sergey Diaghilev's series of 'Saisons russes' from 1907. Diaghilev's Ballets Russes, and ballets by Stravinsky such as *The Firebird* (1910) and *The Rite of Spring* (1913), helped confirm Paris as the artistic capital of pre-World War I Europe.

BREAKING AWAY FROM WAGNER

The enormous influence German music, and in particular Wagner, had on composers posed the dilemma of acquiescence or escape. In Paris, simultaneously with the growing Wagner cult, there emerged the Société Nationale de Musique in 1871 with its motto 'Ars Gallica' and its declared aim of promoting French chamber music. In effect, it began a process of establishing a distinct French musical culture, with composers such as **Gabriel Fauré** (1845–1924), **Camille Saint-Saëns** (1835–1921) and César Franck (1822–90) putting ever greater distance between themselves and German models.

Claude Debussy (1862–1918), at first a passionate Wagnerite, grew increasingly distrustful of Wagnerian style and aesthetics. His use of oriental features, plainsong modes, early polyphonic techniques and French classical dances all helped establish his separation from Wagner and the Germanic tradition. Other important influences on his artistic outlook were French poetry and art.

RADICALS

Even more radical, **Erik Satie** (1866–1925) managed further separation. His unemotional, brief works, often with comic or satiric programmes, established a very different aesthetic.

LINKS TO THE PAST

The sense of cultural and societal degeneration and decline affected both the subject-matter of music and, more intangibly, its forms and structures. Much of the music of **Johannes Brahms** (1833–97), for instance, deliberately invoked earlier models as a way of linking himself with his idea of a great but past tradition. He saturated his music with counterpoint and old-fashioned devices almost as a way of ensuring its permanent worth. His invocation of past models, such as Beethoven's Ninth Symphony in his Symphony No. 1 (1855–76), changed the working-out of material in a way that seems less triumphant than resigned.

Brahms was dubbed conservative, which outwardly was true of his forms, but not of his development of harmonic or other structural devices. He was, however, opposed to many modern, radical developments, notably the rise of programmaticism and the music-dramas of Wagner. Yet despite their differing techniques, a similar concern with things final, even a sense of despair, pervades their music.

In 1916, the writer Jean Cocteau took Satie as the model for the anti-Wagnerian in his *Coq et l'harlequin*. Cocteau had provided the scenario for Satie's ballet *Parade* (1916), in which ragtime, music-hall and popular rhythms and songs had all been part of the anti-Wagnerian vocabulary.

One means of escaping German models was to draw for inspiration on the pre-classical forms and styles of individual countries. French dances as much as English madrigals and most Baroque genres all provided ways of escaping the pervasive German features of sonata form, thematic development and harmonic structure. Modality as well as linear polyphonic styles were taken up and often harmony, which had previously provided the driving force of music for many composers, was relegated to a colour rather than a structural feature.

NATIONALISM

One of the most powerful driving forces helping to throw off Germanic philosophical influences was nationalism. The desire for political self-determination grew rapidly in the late nineteenth century, and often this was closely linked to the appearance of operas, books and plays on national subjects. Not only in content, but also through their very existence, these emphasized the importance and the distinctness of national languages and cultures. In the Austrian Empire the rise of distinct Czech, Bohemian and Moravian cultures was epitomized by composers such as **Bedřich Smetana** (1824–84), **Antonín Dvořák** (1841–1904) and **Leoš Janáček** (1854–1928).

(BL) Impression, Sunrise *by Claude Monet*
The painting that gave rise to the artistic movement known as Impressionism.

(TL) Sheherazade
Costume design by León Bakst for Rimsky-Korsakov's Sheherazade.

(BFR) Beethoven Frieze
Klimt's piece for the Secession building was inspired by Wagner's description of Beethoven's Ninth Symphony.

(BNR) Leoš ***Janáček***
The Czech composer Janáček studying the sound of the surf on the North Sea Coast in Holland.

AN EPITOME OF ENDING

If any city could be cited as epitomizing the sense of decline and despair in the late nineteenth century it would be Vienna. Heartland of the oldest existing European empire, its shift from the liberalism of the 1840s towards the political conservatism of the 1890s onwards was typical, as was the inability of its emperor and ruling aristocracy to deal with the growing desire for popular change. The public appeal to past values was exemplified in the series of buildings designed in historical style on the Ringstrasse, such as the classical parliament recalling Greek democracy and the Gothic town-hall representing medieval guilds. The lack of real political power led many Viennese to the arts as an expression of their anger or despair.

The most radical anti-establishment, anti-historicist movement was the *Sezession* ('Secession'). Begun in 1897, it attracted leading artists such as Gustav Klimt, Kolo Moser and Otto Wagner, and produced radical art and architecture. Examples of this were the sexually suggestive friezes by Klimt for various university faculties and the Beethoven Frieze for the Secession building, itself inspired by Wagner's description of Beethoven's Ninth Symphony.

Arguably the most distinctive nationalism in the early part of this period was found in Russia, where the exploration and inclusion of non-Western scales had permeated the music of **Mikhail Glinka** (1804–57) as early as the 1840s. Its particular church style also provided a unique voice for crowd scenes. Russia's growing Slavonic consciousness further stimulated its national arts to reflect this, inspiring works as different as Musorgsky's *Boris Godunov* (first version, 1868) and Dostoevsky's *Brothers Karamazov* (1879–80). After the assassination of the Tsar in 1881, Russian nationalism moved from the overtly historical to folk, mythical and rural subjects. These were greatly enriched by Diaghilev, whose *World of Art* magazine influenced not only such artists as Léon Bakst and Alexandre Benois, but was also the impulse behind the plots and designs of the Ballets Russes.

NATIONAL ROMANTICISM

The rise of National Romanticism, notably in Scandinavia and the Baltic states, produced distinctive ethnic features which influenced the architecture of the town hall in Stockholm and the Art Nouveau buildings in Riga. It also lay behind the art of such painters as the Finn Akseli Gallen-Kallela and the Swede Carl Larsson; their works can be strongly linked to composers such as **Jean Sibelius** (1865–1957) and **Carl Nielsen** (1865–1931).

The use of folk idioms and the search for national identity also transformed the music of such diverse composers as **Ralph Vaughan Williams** (1872–1958) and **Gustav Holst** (1874–1934) in Great Britain, and **Zoltán Kodály** (1882–1967) and **Béla Bartók** (1881–1945) in Hungary, each of whom had a deep influence on the musical development of the generation that followed them.

Bartók ▶ p. 285 Brahms ▶ p. 240 Debussy ▶ p. 282 Dvořák ▶ p. 245 Fauré ▶ p. 248 Glinka ▶ p. 192 Holst ▶ p. 290 Janáček ▶ p. 291 Kodály ▶ p. 293 Musorgsky ▶ p. 253 Nielsen ▶ p. 293 Saint-Saëns ▶ p. 256 Satie ▶ p. 295 Sibelius ▶ p. 256 Smetana ▶ p. 258 Vaughan Williams ▶ p. 298

The Late Romantic
RICHARD WAGNER

Richard Wagner (1813–83) is one of the most influential and controversial composers in the history of classical music. He was born in Leipzig and educated there and in Dresden. His later years were spent in Bayreuth, the home of the festival theatre and the yearly summer festival he founded, which still flourish today. The idea of Bayreuth, a small German town (now a city) in the north-east of Bavaria, is at the heart of the Wagnerian enterprise. The place was chosen as a peaceful retreat away from the hubbub of modern city life, where audiences could experience musical drama at its most profound level in a theatre specially constructed for the purpose. Wagner realized his vision only after years of struggle, public scandal and moments of near-poverty – a turbulent life that was notorious even before his death. He wrote the texts and the music of 13 operas, at least seven of which are still regarded as towering masterpieces. No one has ever doubted that Wagner's bold adventures in harmony and orchestration left an indelible mark on later music, instrumental as well as vocal.

LIFE TIMELINE

1828 Finishes *Leubald* and begins composition lessons
1834 Composes *Die Feen*, his first completed opera, and first essay on opera and début as an opera conductor
1837 Appointed musical director in Königsberg and Riga
1839 Meets Meyerbeer while travelling from Riga to Paris
1842 Successful Dresden première of his third opera *Rienzi*
1843 Accepts *Kapellmeister* post after première of *Der fliegende Holländer*
1845 Dresden première of *Tannhäuser*
1848 News of uprising in Paris and the start of the *Ring*
1849 Flees to Switzerland and writes *Art and Revolution*
1850 Première of *Lohengrin* in Weimar under Liszt
1851 Finishes essay *Opera and Drama* and expands the *Ring* cycle
1853 Publishes the *Ring* text and starts composing the first part, *Das Rheingold*
1854 Plans *Tristan und Isolde* after reading Schopenhauer's philosophy
1855 Conducts London concerts and meets Queen Victoria
1857 Breaks off work on third *Ring* opera, *Siegfried* (Act 2), to start *Tristan*
1859 Finishes *Tristan* in Lucerne and settles in Paris
1861 Revised *Tannhäuser* scandalizes the Paris Opéra
1865 Première of *Tristan* in Munich under Bülow
1867 Triumphant première of *Die Meistersinger von Nürnberg* in Munich
1869 Work on the *Ring* resumed
1872 Foundation stone of Bayreuth festival theatre laid
1874 Score of the *Ring* finally completed
1876 First Bayreuth festival and première of the entire *Ring* cycle
1878 Composition of *Parsifal* begun
1882 Second Bayreuth festival and première of *Parsifal*
1883 Ideas for symphonies left unrealized at Wagner's death

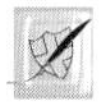

EARLY YEARS

Wagner was the youngest of seven children born to a police actuary, Carl Friedrich Wagner, and his wife Johanna, a baker's daughter. His father died six months after his birth. Nine months later his mother married a portrait painter, actor and poet, Ludwig Geyer, who for the next eight years became the only 'father' Wagner ever knew. There has been a great deal of speculation about whether Geyer was Wagner's natural father, as Johanna was acquainted with Geyer long before she married him.

'THE RIDE OF THE VALKYRIES'

Perhaps the most instantly recognizable piece of music by Wagner, this was extracted and arranged by Wagner from his opera *Die Walküre* (the second in the *Ring* cycle). Popular in his own day, the piece is familiar now as it is featured in Francis Ford Coppola's film *Apocalypse Now* (1979).

POPULAR MELODY *Wagner*

According to all available evidence, however, Wagner's natural father was Carl Friedrich, though the boy carried the name Geyer until he was almost 15 years old. Coincidentally, Richard's surname reverted to Wagner in 1828, the year in which he completed his first extant work. It was a sprawling five-act play called *Leubald*, which blended Shakespeare's *Hamlet* with *King Lear* and with works by German playwrights such as Kleist and Goethe. Wagner later joked that it was so vast and bloody that he ran out of characters before the end and had to bring most of them back as ghosts. The most important thing about it, however, was that it inspired him to compose. He began taking lessons with two local musicians and soon had a series of concert overtures, piano sonatas and even a string quartet and a symphony under his belt. Many of them are still extant. These pieces are technically competent, but haunted by the musical idols of his youth – **Wolfgang Amadeus Mozart** (1756–91), **Beethoven** and **Carl Maria von Weber** (1786–1826) – to such an extent that all traces of originality seem to have been frightened away.

TOWARDS PARIS

As Nietzsche later remarked in a positive appraisal of Wagner's achievements, there has seldom been a great composer who began so late and with so little promise. His first attempts at opera, for which he wrote both libretto and music, as he was to do throughout his life, were not much better than his early instrumental works. *Die Hochzeit* ('The Wedding') was aborted at an early stage, while *Die Feen* ('The Fairies'), based on Carlo Gozzi's play *La donna serpente*, was completed but never performed. His involvement in Leipzig with the so-called Young German movement – a group of intellectuals whose views were directed against Germany's fragmented feudal

(BL) Bayreuth
The festival house at Bayreuth, the heart of the musical empire that grew up around Wagner.
(ML) Wotan
Painting of the Norse God Wotan, from Wagner's Die Walküre.
(TR) Apocalypse Now
Frances Ford Coppola used The Ride of the Valkyries, *from Wagner's* Die Walküre, *in in his 1979 war film.*
(BR) The Flying Dutchman
1998 performance of Wagner's first masterpiece, premièred in 1843.

past – eventually brought about a change. In 1834, he published his first polemical article, 'German Opera', and turned Shakespeare's *Measure for Measure* into a grand comic opera, *Das Liebesverbot* ('The Ban on Love'). Both the article and the opera glorified Italian sensuality at the expense of German small-mindedness. The former was later banished from his collected writings by the mature Wagner and he dismissed the latter as a 'sin of his youth'. But these pieces set the tone for a lifetime of rebellion against the artistic and social norms of provincial Germany.

THE FIRST MASTERPIECE

It was at Paris that Wagner composed his first masterpiece: *Der fliegende Holländer* ('The Flying Dutchman'). It was based on a short story by Heinrich Heine about a Dutchman compelled by the Devil to roam the seas for eternity, but allowed back on to land every seven years to seek the woman who could redeem him. Having undertaken the hazardous journey to Paris and endured near-starvation with his first wife Minna faithfully at his side, Wagner saw the stark intensity of the story in part as a reflection of his own life. Shortly before the première of the opera

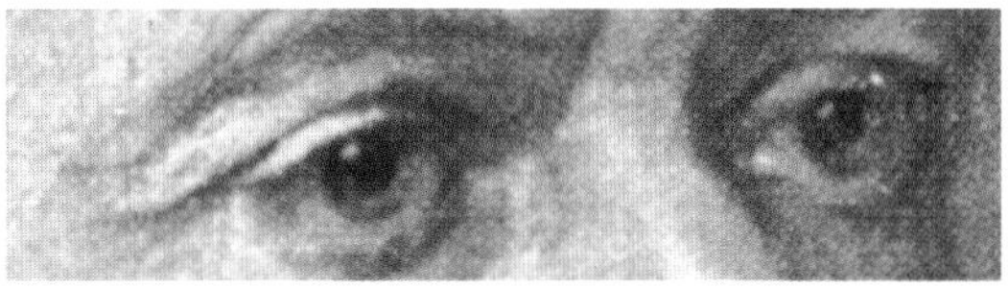

in Dresden on 2 January 1843, he changed the location of its story from Scotland to Norway, to match a short autobiography which was being published at the time. After his return to Germany from Paris, which he had grown to hate, life and art for Wagner had become inextricably intertwined.

DRESDEN AND REVOLUTION

After his first successes in Dresden, Wagner was appointed to the post of royal *Kapellmeister* at the Court Opera in 1843. The position brought with it financial security but burdensome duties. Wagner dedicated himself to a gradual, but radical, reform of the Opera, which earned him the gratitude of some of his colleagues, but few friends in high places. He also composed two remarkable operas based on medieval German sources, *Tannhäuser* and *Lohengrin*, which are essentially both parables about the artist in conflict with a society that fails to understand him. *Tannhäuser* was first performed at the Court Opera on 19 October 1845 and had a lukewarm reception. But its popularity steadily increased while its composer's relations with the royal court worsened. All eyes were turned towards *Lohengrin*; but plans for its production had to be abandoned. Along with other dissatisfied intellectuals, Wagner had been agitating openly for the abolition of the court and by the early months of 1849, the political situation had worsened so rapidly that a breach of the constitution by the king of Saxony led to a violent revolution in which Wagner took an active part. A warrant for his arrest was issued on 16 May 1849.

IN EXILE

With the help of **Franz Liszt** (1811–86), Wagner escaped to Switzerland and for the next 11 years was banned from Germany. However, his role in the Dresden revolution had made him much better known. *Lohengrin*, which in Wagner's absence had its belated première on 28 August 1850 in Weimar under Liszt's direction, and *Tannhäuser* became favourites in opera-houses all over Germany. News was also spreading that Wagner was working on a mammoth project called *Der Ring des Nibelungen*, a great parable of human existence spread over four evenings involving a vast orchestra, spectacular scenic effects with swirling rivers, a dragon and a live horse, and extremely taxing vocal parts. He had begun it as a single heroic drama and an allegory of revolution even before the Dresden uprising. Now it was a much broader project about the nature of power and the relation between nature and society. The many theoretical works that Wagner had published soon after his exile from Germany were in a sense also intended as an intellectual blueprint for it. Not only was he introducing a new way of writing librettos called *Stabreim* (irregular alliterative verse), he was also inventing a new kind of music that could reflect the complexities of drama in ways opera had never done before.

RIENZI

In 1837 Wagner began his third opera, based on Edward Bulwer Lytton's novel *Rienzi, the Last of the Roman Tribunes*. Planned in five acts, with spectacular scenic effects, it emulated French *grand opéra*, though it is hardly a slavish imitation, as some critics have claimed. In fact Wagner's *Rienzi* is the first of his works to show startling originality. At its centre, too, is the first of those famous Wagnerian heroic leaders who, in the face of calamity, attempt to save their respective worlds from despair and disarray.

Rienzi is ultimately too dependent on French models and too uneven musically to be called a masterpiece. But its enormous success in Dresden on 20 October 1842 marked decisively the beginning of Wagner's public career. It was the brilliant outcome of an odyssey of misfortune that had dogged Wagner since his days in Riga, where he had begun composing the opera in 1838. Pursued by creditors, he had fled Riga and had nearly been shipwrecked off the coast of Norway. After a short stay in London he spent three difficult years in Paris, at times on the verge of starvation, where his goal had been to get a hearing for one of his operas in the city that was then the dazzling centre of the operatic world. Keeping body and soul together with back-breaking work as a journalist and arranger, he signally failed to make a mark there.

Beethoven ▶ p. 150 Liszt ▶ p. 194 Mozart ▶ p. 144 Weber ▶ p. 205

PERSONAL AFFAIRS

Now settled in Zürich and dependent on private patronage, Wagner began composing the music of the *Ring* in 1853. Only a year later he was introduced to the philosophy of Schopenhauer and fell deeply in love with Mathilde Wesendonck, the wife of one of his patrons. Both experiences led to the conception of *Tristan und Isolde* and eventually, in 1857, to the interruption of work on the *Ring*. In the following months, Wagner set five of Mathilde's poems to music, two of which he described as 'studies for *Tristan*'. His marriage never recovered. His wife Minna intercepted one of his many letters to Mathilde, and this precipitated a crisis that led to his departure for Venice where, alone in the Palazzo Giustinian, he continued to compose *Tristan*.

THE ETERNAL WANDERER

His marriage in ruins, Wagner embarked on the most fragmented, yet creatively most productive, phase of his life. Still the eternal wanderer and now a political fugitive as well, he was hounded out of Venice by the police. He moved briefly to Lucerne in Switzerland to finish *Tristan*, and then to Paris where, after a series of complicated diplomatic manoeuvres, Napoleon III gave the order for the production of *Tannhäuser* at the Opéra. Wagner immediately set about revising parts of the work in the style of *Tristan*, a process that stimulated some of his most voluptuous and difficult music. The production in 1861 is one of the most famous musical scandals. The noisy protests of the audience, some of whom were using the occasion as a demonstration against the pro-Austrian policies of Napoleon, were frequently so loud that they drowned the singers and the orchestra. Wagner withdrew the score after only three performances.

CAUSE CÉLÈBRE

In the long run, the failure of *Tannhäuser* was actually a success. Wagner became an international *cause célèbre*, rallying not only influential artists and intellectuals to his cause (including the poet Charles Baudelaire), but also powerful diplomats who secured from Saxony a partial amnesty on his behalf. Under certain restrictions, Wagner was allowed to return to Germany and Austria where he unsuccessfully canvassed support for a performance of *Tristan* (the work was widely regarded as unperformable) and began serious work on his next project, *Die Meistersinger von Nürnberg* ('The Mastersingers of Nuremberg'). But in Vienna his weakness for extravagance and his mounting debts brought with them a serious threat of imprisonment. In 1864 he left the city in a hurry, intending to retire to the Swabian mountains to finish *Die Meistersinger*.

RICHARD WAGNER: WORKS

Operas: *Die Hochzeit* (1832, incomplete); *Die Feen* (1833–34); *Das Liebesverbot* (1835–36); *Rienzi, der Letzte der Tribunen* (1837–40); *Der fliegende Holländer* (1840–41); *Tannhäuser und der Sängerkrieg auf Wartburg* (1843–45; revised 1847, 1860); *Lohengrin* (1845–48); *Der Ring des Nibelungen* – Preliminary Evening: *Das Rheingold* (1851–54), First Day: *Die Walküre* (1851–56); Second Day: *Siegfried* (1851–57; 1864–71), Third Day: *Götterdämmerung* (1848–52; 1869–74); *Tristan und Isolde* (1854–59); *Die Meistersinger von Nürnberg* (1845; 1862–67); *Parsifal* (1865; 1878–81)
Orchestral works: A Faust Overture (1839–40; revised 1855), *Siegfried Idyll* (1870)
Songs: *Wesendonck Lieder* (1857–58)
Concert overtures, symphonies, chamber music, marches, songs, piano music, incidental music, arrangements

TOWARDS BAYREUTH

At the moment Wagner reached the nadir of his fortunes, Ludwig II, a great admirer of his art, succeeded to the throne of Bavaria at the age of only 18. The coincidence was like a fairy-tale: the young king agreed to settle the composer's debts and granted him a generous allowance. Wagner moved to Munich where again he made enemies, this time on account of his lifestyle and his adulterous liaison with Liszt's daughter Cosima, the wife of his friend and protégé **Hans von Bülow** (1830–94). Most importantly, Ludwig agreed to give Wagner a contract to finish the *Ring* and provided him with the means at last to produce *Tristan*. The opera was first performed on 10 June 1865 in the Munich Court Theatre, with Bülow conducting. Three weeks after the fourth performance, the tenor Ludwig Schnorr von Carolsfeld, who had sung Tristan, died unexpectedly. It was widely supposed that he was the victim of the role's huge physical demands, providing yet more ammunition for those critics who believed that Wagner's music was dangerous. Once more, life seemed to be imitating art, but this time not to Wagner's advantage.

DIE MEISTERSINGER VON NÜRNBERG

Die Meistersinger, best described as a comedy with tinges of profound melancholy, was based on sources describing the German Renaissance poet Hans Sachs and the singers' guilds of mid sixteenth-century Nuremberg. The subject allowed Wagner to embrace some more immediately attractive, if essentially pessimistic, themes about the nature of art and the community that supports it. Similarly, in the scenario of *Parsifal*, drafted only two months after the première of *Tristan*, he explored the more readily acceptable, though still highly fraught, subject of a divine moral code as the conqueror of social decay.

The première of *Die Meistersinger* on 21 June 1868 in Munich, again conducted by Bülow, was the most resounding public success of Wagner's career. From being an ambitious young artist emerging hungry in Paris, he was now a prince among artists looking towards the establishment of his own theatre at the heart of Germany. Scandal had forced him to leave Munich in 1865 and with Ludwig's permission he had settled in Tribschen, on Lake Lucerne where, in 1869 he resumed work on the *Ring*. The premières of the *Ring*'s first two operas, *Das Rheingold* and *Die Walküre*, took place in Munich on 22 September 1869 and 26 June 1870 respectively. He also began developing plans for a festival theatre which would be set apart from the intrusiveness of city life. On his 59th birthday, 22 May 1872, grim-faced and in terrible weather, he laid the foundation stone of his festival theatre in Bayreuth, a small town in the north-east of Bavaria, midway between Berlin and Munich. He marked the event by conducting Beethoven's Ninth Symphony, thus establishing a spiritual lineage at the heart of his life's work. The sheer boldness of the idea created sustained, and not always friendly, advance publicity. By the time the *Ring* cycle eventually received its first performance as a tetralogy in the newly completed theatre in August 1876, the Bayreuth Festival was already an established event, almost before any performances had actually taken place.

WAGNER'S INFLUENCES

Wagner always claimed that he was virtually self-taught, needing only the shortest time with his teachers to learn the basics of musical composition before setting off in the world to make his mark as a genius. The truth is more prosaic, and also more interesting. His greatest musical heroes were Beethoven and Weber. He emulated them in many of his early instrumental works, now mostly forgotten, and in parts of his operas up to *Lohengrin*. But the colourful symphonic style he developed by the time he began work on the music of the *Ring* also owed just as much to his study of early Romantic Lieder and in particular to **Franz Schubert**'s (1797–1828) uncanny sense of musical imagery. The effectiveness of his music in the theatre was also helped by a close study of French and Italian opera, especially that of **Giacomo Meyerbeer** (1791–1864) and **Vincenzo Bellini** (1801–35), and the colourful brilliance of **Hector Berlioz**'s (1803–69) music. He never publicly acknowledged their influence, though orchestrally he never looked back once he had heard Berlioz's music in Paris in 1839.

His Legacy

Wagner's own influence was far-reaching. Enthusiasm for *Tristan* practically verged on frenzy in Europe in the 1890s when the spirit of the *fin-de-siècle*, with its odd mixture of decadence and modernist ambition, seemed to match the hot-house aestheticism and stubborn individuality of Wagner's art. No one from **Richard Strauss** (1864–1949) and **Gustav Mahler** (1860–1911), or **Arnold Schoenberg** (1874–1951) and **Hans Pfitzner** (1869–1949) in Germany, to **Vincent D'Indy** (1851–1931) and Debussy in France or **Arrigo Boito** (1842–1918) and **Giacomo Puccini** (1858–1924) in Italy, would have seriously denied the influence of Wagner at this time. It was often not only Wagner's art, but also his philosophy that left a deep mark. Many became fervent Wagnerites, which usually meant that they were disciples not only of Wagner, but also of Schopenhauer and Nietzsche. For the Wagnerites, philosophy and politics were never far from music. Wagner's philosophy, however, never freed itself of controversy; his anti-semitism in particular has given rise to much discussion. The most lasting effects of his influence, however, have been musical: the fusion of harmony and instrumentation, the expansion of tonality to breaking point, and the experiments in large-scale structure that have characterized much of modern music since the late nineteenth century, would have been unthinkable without Wagner.

FINAL YEARS

In actual fact, the event turned out to be a financial disaster and the theatre had to close for the next six years. 'I can only blame Bayreuth,' Wagner wrote, 'to the extent that I chose it myself. Yet I did so with a great idea: with the support of the nation I wanted to create something thoroughly independent that would make the town important – a sort of Washington of Art.'

In the long run, Wagner was right: despite severe adversities, the festival theatre has withstood the test of time as one of the great cultural achievements of the nineteenth century, and is still a focal point of modern operatic life. But Wagner had to pay a high personal price for it. His final years were dogged by financial worries that took a severe toll on his health. The huge debts incurred by the 1876 festival were eventually settled by Ludwig, leaving Wagner with the time and energy to complete *Parsifal*, his final and perhaps greatest work, a masterly culmination of a lifetime rich in musical experience and reformist zeal. It was performed at the second Bayreuth Festival in 1882 to great acclaim and made an unexpected profit, which encouraged Wagner to announce further performances the following year. It was too late. Full of plans to write symphonies and to complete his autobiography, he died in Venice of a heart attack on 13 February 1883, a few months before his seventieth birthday. 'It is self-evident,' his doctor wrote, 'that the innumerable psychical agitations to which Wagner was daily disposed by his peculiar mental constitution and disposition, his sharply defined attitude towards a number of burning questions of art, science and politics, and his remarkable social position did much to hasten his unfortunate end'.

(BL) **Die Meistersinger**
German tenor Herman Winkelmann as Walther von Stolzing in Wagner's opera.
(TL) **The Concert Builders** ***by Adolf Oberländer***
Contemporary caricature depicting Wagner destroying classical music forms.
(TR) **Das Rheingold**
Scene from Das Rheingold, *part of Wagner's immense and influential* Ring *cycle.*
(BR) **Tristan und Isolde**
Wagner's opera, based on the famous legend, was famed for the explicit eroticism of its music.

TRISTAN UND ISOLDE

Wagner decided to write *Tristan und Isolde* after reading the philosophical writings of Arthur Schopenhauer. Overlaid with a provocative interpretation of Schopenhauer's metaphysics of sexual love, the opera became a *cause célèbre* after its première in 1865, largely because of the explicit eroticism of its music. Wagner's main literary source was Gottfried von Strassburg's medieval epic *Tristan* (*c.* 1215) – a work admired in the nineteenth century for its style and pilloried for its suspect morality in about equal measure. There were in fact several reasons for Wagner's sudden decision to adapt it, including its unusual subject of fated and enchanted, as opposed to courtly, love that leads to physical destruction and 'eternal death'. The idea was in tune not only with Wagner's newly awakened interest in Schopenhauer, who believed that the preconscious Will was an expression of the sexual drive and the road to salvation its negation, but also with his increasing love for Mathilde Wesendonck, the beautiful wife of his long-suffering patron Otto Wesendonck. Wagner's need to present unquenchable yearning and sexual passion in a convincing way led him to widen the scope of his musical resources so drastically that *Tristan* almost inevitably became one of the most important musical works of the nineteenth century. The unprecedented expansion of harmonic possibilities audible in the very first chord of the work (the so-called Tristan chord) and the sheer freedom and invention in the handling of individual chromatic lines mean that it is quite justifiable to speak of the music of *Tristan* as a harbinger of the new music of the twentieth century.

The Late Romantic

GIUSEPPE VERDI

Giuseppe Verdi (1813–1901) composed 28 operas over a period of 54 years. In his native Italy he became immensely popular early in his career, and by the time he died he was idolized as the greatest Italian composer of the nineteenth century. In other musical centres of Europe it took a little longer for Verdi's genius to be recognized. Audiences loved his operas, but critics were less impressed. The tremendous rhythmic vitality of his style, the memorability of his splendid tunes, just the things that captivated the ordinary opera-lover, did not appear as virtues to the London musical establishment. Gradually the critical climate changed, and after the production of his two final operas, *Otello* and *Falstaff*, universally acclaimed as masterpieces, even the critics were willing to admit that Verdi was a genius. After the composer's death, his reputation continued to grow, although it was not until 1951, the fiftieth anniversary of his death, that many of his early operas were disinterred and found to be, if not masterpieces, then extremely enjoyable in performance. In his long life Verdi cast a very long shadow over his Italian contemporaries. The early deaths of Bellini and Donizetti removed two possible rivals, and it was not until 1893, the year of Verdi's last opera, *Falstaff*, that the production of Puccini's *Manon Lescaut* heralded the arrival of his successor.

BEGINNINGS

Verdi was born on 10 October 1813 at Le Roncole, a village near Busseto in the Duchy of Parma. His parents were poor, but his musical ability was early recognized, and he was given lessons by the village organist. Sent to school in Busseto, he came to the notice of Antonio Barezzi, president of the local Philharmonic Society, who virtually adopted him. Donations from a charitable organization and support from Barezzi enabled the 18-year-old Verdi to go to Milan, but the Conservatory rejected him as too old, so he studied for two years with Vincenzo Lavigna, a conductor at La Scala opera-house. In 1836 Verdi married his benefactor Barezzi's daughter, Margharita. They had two children, both of whom died under the age of two. Verdi's first opera, *Oberto*, was finished by 1838 and rehearsed, but it had to be postponed owing to the tenor's illness. It was finally performed at La Scala on 17 November 1839, scoring a fair success. The publisher Giovanni Ricordi bought it for publication, and the Scala impresario Bartolomeo Merelli put Verdi under contract. While he was writing his next opera, *Un giorno di regno* ('King for a Day'), a comedy, his wife Margharita died of encephalitis. Verdi tried to break his contract, but Merelli refused to release him and *Un giorno* was given at La Scala on 5 September 1840. A total failure, it received only one performance. Verdi swore never to write another opera, but relented when Merelli gave him the libretto of *Nabucco*, concerned with the captivity of the Hebrews in Babylon. Produced at La Scala in 1842, *Nabucco* was a huge popular success.

LIFE TIMELINE

1813	Giuseppe Verdi born in same year as Richard Wagner
1836	Verdi marries Margharita Barezzi
1839	First opera *Oberto* produced at La Scala, Milan
1840	His wife Margharita dies
1842	*Nabucco*, first great success, produced at La Scala
1847	Verdi and the soprano Giuseppina Strepponi become lovers; Queen Victoria and Prince Albert attend performance of *I masnadieri*
1851	*Rigoletto* produced in Venice
1853	Verdi and Strepponi move to Sant'Agata, near Busseto; *La traviata* is greeted badly on its performance in Venice
1859	Verdi marries Giuseppina Strepponi
1861	Unification of Italy; Count Camillo di Cavour persuades Verdi to stand for Parliament
1862	Verdi goes to St Petersburg
1867	*Don Carlos* produced at Paris Opéra
1871	*Aida* produced in Cairo
1874	Manzoni *Requiem* performed in Milan
1879	Verdi meets Arrigo Boito in Milan
1881	*Simon Boccanegra* revised by Boito and Verdi
1887	*Otello* produced at La Scala, Verdi receives a standing ovation.
1893	*Falstaff* produced at La Scala
1897	Giuseppina Verdi dies
1901	Giuseppe Verdi dies

A NIGHT AT THE OPERA

In the film *A Night at the Opera*, the Marx Brothers invade an opera house during a performance of Verdi's *Il trovatore*, with disastrous results. Scenery rises and falls, Harpo Marx sails by on a rope, while the Monks chant a *Miserere* and the lovers bid each other farewell amid the chaos.

POPULAR MELODY *Verdi*

THE GALLEY YEARS

In the nine years between *Nabucco* (1842) and *Rigoletto* (1851), Verdi wrote 12 operas. He called this period his years in the galley, and it is undeniable that some of the operas are, to put it bluntly, pot-boilers. In 1843, he returned to La Scala with *I Lombardi alla prima Crociata* ('The Lombards at the First Crusade'). Asked to write an opera for the Teatro La Fenice, Venice, he

LIBRETTISTS

Verdi bullied his librettists unmercifully. Sometimes he wrote the text himself and merely let the librettist put it into verse; what he wanted in the early operas was a series of dramatic situations and confrontations. Temistocle Solera and Salvatore Cammarano provided exactly that. Solera, after revising the text of *Oberto*, wrote *Nabucco*, *I Lombardi*, *Giovanna d'Arco* and *Attila*. Cammarano contributed *Alzira*, *La battaglia di Legnano*, *Luisa Miller* and *Il trovatore*. Francesco Maria Piave, a personal friend of Verdi, whom he worshipped, always obeyed instructions to the best of his ability. He wrote *Ernani*, *I due Foscari*, *Macbeth*, *Il corsaro*, *Stiffelio*, *Rigoletto*, *La traviata*, *Simon Boccanegra* and *La forza del destino*. Eugène Scribe did not respond to bullying, and Verdi complained bitterly, but to no avail, about the text of *Les vêpres siciliennes*. Scribe also wrote *Gustave III, ou le bal masqué*, the original libretto on which *Un ballo in maschera* is based. A more congenial French librettist, Camille Du Locle, wrote *Don Carlos* in collaboration with Joseph Méry. Du Locle also provided the original libretto of *Aida*, which was translated into Italian by Antonio Ghislanzoni, a former baritone who had sung in *Ernani* in Paris.

obliged with *Ernani* (1844), based on a play by Victor Hugo that had caused a scandal in Paris. This, one of the better products of the Galley Years, was very popular.

Next he went to Rome, to put on *I due Foscari* (1844), based on Lord Byron's play *The Two Foscari*, at the Teatro Argentina. Only three months later he was back at La Scala for *Giovanna d'Arco* ('Joan of Arc', 1845), adapted from Friedrich Schiller's drama *The Maid of Orleans*. Verdi quarrelled

(BL) *Amelita Galli-Curci*
Italian opera singer Galli-Curci in the role of Violetta in La Traviata.
(TR) *Giuseppina Strepponi*
The Italian soprano Strepponi was Verdi's second wife; they married in 1859.
(BR) *Venice*
Engraving of St Mark's basilica, Venice.

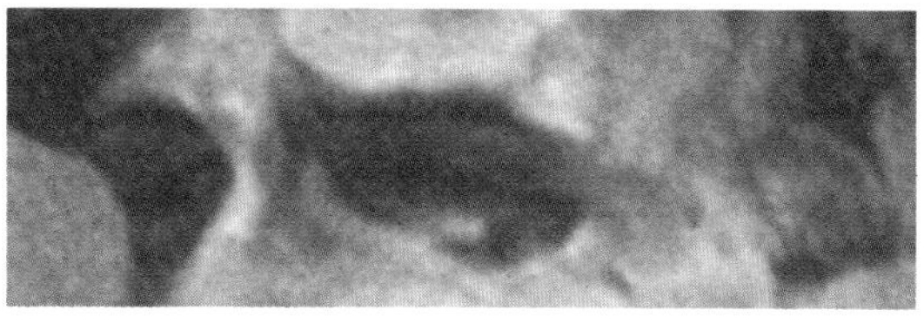

with Merelli and boycotted La Scala, so far as premières of his operas went, for 25 years. For the Teatro San Carlo, Naples, he wrote *Alzira* (1845), based on a drama by Voltaire about the Incas of Peru. This is possibly Verdi's weakest opera. *Attila* (1846) was much better, and the audience at La Fenice loved it. *Macbeth* (1847) at the Teatro della Pergola, Florence, was better still, and is of particular interest as Verdi's first attempt at setting a work by William Shakespeare, whom he revered. It was an enormous success and Verdi took 38 curtain calls.

JOURNEY TO LONDON AND PARIS

Verdi intended to go to London immediately after *Attila*, but he became ill with nervous exhaustion and the psychosomatic headaches and stomach cramps from which he frequently suffered during those years. In the event, he set out for London in early summer 1847. He was contracted to write an opera for Her Majesty's Theatre, and *I masnadieri* ('The Robbers'), an adaptation of a play by Schiller, was performed on 22 July, with Queen Victoria and Prince Albert attending the première. Verdi then left for Paris, to adapt *I Lombardi* for the Paris Opéra. He also had a private date to keep. Giuseppina Strepponi, the soprano who sang in *Nabucco*, was now living in Paris, having retired from the stage. Earlier, she had been involved in an affair with the tenor Napoleone Moriani. That affair was now over, and Giuseppina and Verdi, their mutual respect turning to passion, became lovers. Staying in Paris after the production of *Jérusalem* (as *I Lombardi* was renamed), Verdi wrote *Il corsaro* (1848), based on Byron's *The Corsair*, for the Teatro Grande, Trieste, but did not attend the première. He did go to Rome for *La battaglia di Legnano* ('The Battle of Legnano', 1849), which was taken to symbolize the efforts of the Italian states to drive out the Austrians.

DOMESTIC DRAMAS

Verdi went back to Paris, and then returned to Italy with Giuseppina. The couple took up residence at Sant'Agata, a few miles outside Busseto. Verdi's next two operas had domestic themes, and were important as transitional works in his development. *Luisa Miller* (1849), based on Schiller's tragedy *Intrigue and Love*, was given at the San Carlo, Naples, while *Stiffelio* (1850) received its première in Trieste. Neither work was very successful; indeed *Stiffelio*, about a Protestant minister whose wife commits adultery, shocked the Catholic audience. Some years later Verdi adapted the text to create *Aroldo*, about an English crusader from 'near Kenth' (sic) who went to 'Lago di Loomond'; that was not very successful either. Verdi frequently had trouble with the censor, as the difficulties with his next opera demonstrate. He chose a play by Victor Hugo, *Le roi s'amuse* ('The King is Amused') which had been banned after its Paris première. An opera about a licentious French king (François I) was not acceptable to the Austrian censor either, who called it 'revoltingly immoral, obscene and trivial'. Later, *La Maledizione* ('The Curse'), as it began life, was variously dubbed *Viscardello*, *Clara di Perth* and *Lionello*. We know it as *Rigoletto* (1851).

THE UNIFICATION OF ITALY

When Verdi was born in 1813, the Duchy of Parma was occupied by the French. After the Treaty of Vienna (1815), the Italian states were given back to their rulers, Lombardy was occupied by the Austrians, Rome belonged to the Papal States and the Bourbons regained Naples. The struggle for the unification of Italy continued underground, led politically by Count Camillo di Cavour. Verdi's great choruses, whether sung by the Hebrews in exile in Babylon or the Scottish refugees in England, were taken by Italian patriots as coded exhortations to rise against their oppressors, but the only direct propaganda in Verdi's operas is in *Il battaglia di Legnano*. The message it conveys is to follow the example of the Lombard League, who defeated the German Emperor Barbarossa by combining their forces. In 1848 there were revolutions in Venice and Milan, severely quashed by the Austrians; the short-lived Roman Republic was declared in 1849, but unification was not finally achieved until after the invasion of Sicily by Giuseppe Garibaldi. In 1861 Victor Emmanuel, the king of Sardinia, was proclaimed king of Italy.

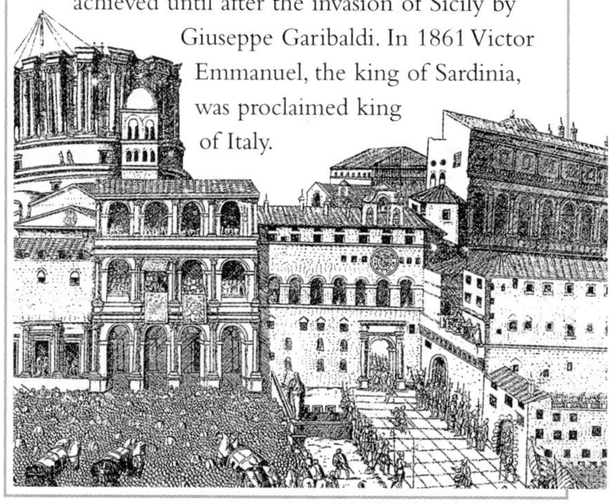

TWO TRIUMPHS AND A FAILURE

The première of *Rigoletto* at La Fenice in Venice, was a tremendous success. With the profligate French king now transformed into a fictional Duke of Mantua, the opera conquered all of Italy, then Paris, London and the rest of Europe. Verdi's next opera, *Il trovatore* ('The Troubadour'), based on a play by the Spanish dramatist Antonio García Gutiérrez, was equally successful, scoring a triumph at its première in Rome in January 1853. Although lacking in the subtle characterizations of *Rigoletto*, and with an all but impenetrable plot, it quickly became just as frequently played. Less than two months later Verdi was in Venice for the first performance of a work he had completed some time before, *La traviata* ('The Fallen Woman'), derived from the novel *La dame aux camélias* by Alexandre Dumas *fils*. This time La Fenice exploded in cat-calls and hisses, not applause. One reason for this was the generous size of the soprano, supposed to be dying of consumption, who evoked much laughter; the performance was also badly rehearsed, and the period of the action put back from 'the present day' (1850s) to the early eighteenth century. Restaged in 1854 at another Venetian theatre, better cast and properly rehearsed, *La traviata* was a huge success.

GIUSEPPE VERDI: WORKS

- **Operas:** *Oberto* (1838); *Un giorno di regno* (1840); *Nabucco* (1842); *I Lombardi alla prima Crociata* (1843); *Ernani* (1844), *I due Foscari* (1844); *Giovanna d'Arco* (1845), *Alzira* (1845); *Attila* (1846); *Macbeth* (1847); *I masnadieri* (1847); *Jérusalem* (1847); *Il corsaro* (1848); *La battaglia di Legnano* (1849); *Luisa Miller* (1849); *Stiffelio* (1850); *Rigoletto* (1851); *Il trovatore* (1853); *La traviata* (1853); *Les vêpres siciliennes* (1855); *Aroldo* (1857); *Simon Boccanegra* (1857); *Un ballo in maschera* (1859); *La forza del destino* (1862); *Don Carlos* (1867); *Aida* (1871); *Otello* (1884–86); *Falstaff* (1893)
- **Choral works:** *Inno delli nazioni* (1862); *Messa di Requiem* (1874); *Quattro pezzi sacri* (1888–97)
- String Quartet in E (1877)
- Songs

MORE TROUBLES WITH THE CENSOR

Les vêpres siciliennes ('The Sicilian Vespers', 1855), Verdi's first opera written especially for the Paris Opéra, caused him a great deal of trouble. Grand operas had to be in five acts, with spectacular effects, huge choruses and, most importantly, a ballet. Rehearsals dragged on for five months, but the première was surprisingly successful.

Translated into Italian as *I vespri siciliani*, the story of the massacre of the French by the Sicilians in 1282 ran foul of the censor. The opera became *Giovanna di Braganza*, *Giovanna di Guzman* and *Batilde di Turenna* before regaining its rightful name. *Simon Boccanegra* (1857) did not receive great acclaim in Venice, where it is set, but *Un ballo in maschera* ('A Masked Ball, 1859) caused a riot, though only after much trouble with the censor. Based on *Gustave III, ou Le bal masqué*, the opera dealt with the murder of King Gustavus of Sweden at a masked ball. It was originally intended for Naples, but the censor there refused to license it, even if the characters were changed. The Roman censor required many changes, and the setting was altered to pre-Independence America; the king became Riccardo, Governor of Boston. The reception was ecstatic and for the first time 'Viva Verdi' was shouted as a slogan, short for 'Viva Vittorio Emanuele, Re D'Italia' ('Long live Victor Emmanuel, king of Italy').

RUSSIA, AND PARIS AGAIN

In 1859 Verdi at last married Giuseppina Strepponi. He was elected to an Assembly in Parma, where he met his hero, Count Camillo di Cavour. On the unification of Italy in 1861, Cavour urged Verdi to stand as member for Busseto in Parliament, which he did. Later that year Verdi and his wife travelled to St Petersburg, where the Imperial Opera had commissioned him to write an opera. This was postponed, owing to the soprano's illness. In 1862 they returned to Russia where *La forza del destino* ('The Force of Destiny') was given a warm welcome. The work is tragic and has much noble, stirring music; but it also finds spare for a comic character, the jovial monk Fra Melitone. For a production at La Scala a few years later, Verdi revised the opera quite considerably. In 1865 he revised *Macbeth* for the Théâtre Lyrique, Paris, adding the obligatory ballet. He returned to Paris in 1867 for another commission at the Opéra, *Don Carlos*. There were the usual troubles that beset Verdi in Paris, and the long opera had to be cut severely at the last moment, to enable the first-night audience to catch the last trains back to the suburbs. The opera scored only a moderate success. Verdi returned to Sant'Agata and his life as a farmer. During the winter he and Giuseppina rented an apartment in Genoa.

OTELLO

Verdi was a fervent admirer of Shakespeare. He read and re-read the plays (in Italian translation) and made operas out of three, *Macbeth*, *Othello* and *The Merry Wives of Windsor* (*Falstaff*). *Macbeth* was one of his early successes. He wrote the text himself, in prose, for the librettist to turn into verse. He also had plans for *King Lear*, and once commissioned a libretto, but something always occurred to stop the actual composition. There was no suitable bass singer for Lear in the company, or the soprano he wanted to sing Cordelia was not available. Perhaps, in his heart, Verdi was frightened of tackling *King Lear*.

A True Music-Drama

Nearly 40 years after *Macbeth*, when Verdi came to consider the idea of turning *Othello* into an opera, the situation was very different. He had announced that he would compose no more operas after *Aida*. When **Boito** handed him a synopsis of a libretto based on the play, he was sorely tempted, but refused to commit himself. Boito's adaptation is a masterpiece in itself. He omits Shakespeare's first act, set in Venice, confining the action to Cyprus, and using some of the cut material for a love duet between Otello and Desdemona at the end of the opera's first act. In this way he preserves the unity of place and time. *Otello* is a true music-drama. The action is carried on through the music, which is continuous, as graphically as by the words. There are still a few arias embedded in the score, such as Iago's 'Credo' or Desdemona's 'Willow Song', but they derive from the context of the drama.

***(BL)* Rose Caron**
Caron played Desdemona at the first Paris performance of Verdi's Otello.
***(TL)* Rigoletto**
Titta Ruffo in the title role of Verdi's Rigoletto.
(TR) Arrigo Boito
Boito and Verdi worked together most famously on Otello.
(BR) Tito Gobbi
Italian Baritone Gobbi in his most popular role as Verdi's Falstaff.

FATHER AND DAUGHTER DUETS

Verdi wrote rewarding music for all vocal categories, but it is hard not to suspect that he favoured baritones. Not only did he give them splendid arias, he wrote a unique series of duets for baritone father and soprano daughter. These scenes occur throughout his operas and are often of great poignancy. In *Giovanna d'Arco*, the shepherd Giacomo betrays his daughter Joan to the English because he believes she is a witch. He then frees her so that she can die in battle. Luisa Miller and her father have a fine duet in which the old soldier warns her about the danger of loving a nobleman. Rigoletto and his daughter Gilda have two magnificent duets, one before and one after her seduction by the Duke. Simon Boccanegra recognizes in Amelia Grimaldi his long-lost daughter Maria. Amonasro, king of Ethiopia, accuses his daughter Aida of becoming a slave to the Egyptians. There are also surrogate father and daughter duets: in *Nabucco*, Abigaille discovers that she is not Nabucco's daughter but a slave; in *La traviata*, the elder Germont asks Violetta to give up her lover, his son Alfredo. In *La forza del destino*, Leonora, responsible for the death of her father, asks the Father Superior for shelter in his monastery.

CAIRO

Early in 1870, Verdi agreed to write an opera for Cairo Opera House, which had opened the previous year with *Rigoletto*, just before the opening of the Suez Canal. The work was based on a story by Auguste Mariette, a French Egyptologist, set in Ancient Egypt. Composition took only four months, but owing to the Franco-Prussian War the scenery for the opera was trapped in Paris, and *Aida* was not performed in Cairo until 24 December 1871. Verdi did not attend the première, but supervised the first Italian performance at La Scala on 8 February 1872 – a triumphant success.

In May 1873 the poet and novelist Alessandro Manzoni died at the age of 89. Verdi, who greatly admired him, offered to compose a Requiem; he would pay for printing the score, if the city of Milan would pay for the first performance. Using a duet cut from *Don Carlos* and the 'Libera me' from an unfinished Requiem in honour of **Gioachino Rossini** (1792–1868), Verdi finished the Manzoni *Requiem* in time to give the first performance at the church of S Marco, Milan, on the first anniversary of the poet's death. After three more performances at La Scala, the *Requiem* was toured to Paris, Vienna and London, where it filled the Albert Hall to overflowing. It still does.

THE 'CHOCOLATE IDEA'

After *Aida* and the *Requiem*, Verdi did not intend to compose another opera. But in 1879 at Milan he was introduced to the composer and writer Boito, who suggested Shakespeare's *Othello* as the subject for an opera, giving Verdi a synopsis he had prepared. Verdi was tempted, but could not make up his mind. Meanwhile, together with Boito, he revised *Simon Boccanegra* for La Scala, where it was received with acclaim in 1881. During this time Verdi and Boito were secretly working on what they called the 'chocolate idea'. Completed by the end of 1886, *Otello* was given at La Scala on 5 February 1887. The first performance was a major occasion. Musicians and critics from all over the world attended. Excitement mounted to fever pitch, both inside and outside the opera-house. At the final curtain Verdi and Boito received a standing ovation.

By contrast with the long gestation period of *Otello*, the birth of the comic opera *Falstaff* (1893) was relatively quick. Boito sent Verdi a synopsis of *The Merry Wives of Windsor*, with additions from *Henry IV*, parts 1 and 2. Verdi responded, 'Excellent! Excellent!', and three years later the opera was ready. At the première at La Scala familiar scenes of triumph took place. This was Verdi's last opera. His wife died in 1897, Verdi on 27 January 1901. They were buried in Milan, in the courtyard of the Casa Verdi, a home for elderly musicians founded and funded by the composer.

THE INFLUENCE OF VERDI'S SINGERS

Verdi, like most opera composers of his time, wrote his operas for a particular opera-house and specific singers, and therefore to a certain extent he was influenced by those singers. Giuseppina Strepponi, the soprano who became his second wife, helped his career significantly by recommending *Oberto* to the management of La Scala. Giorgio Ronconi, the baritone who first sang Nabucco, later became the first London Rigoletto. Felice Varesi, the first Rigoletto, also created Macbeth and Germont in *La traviata*. The tenor Gaetano Fraschini sang in six Verdi premières, including *Stiffelio* and *Un ballo in maschera*. Enrico Tamberlik, the tenor who created Don Alvaro in *La forza del destino*, was London's first Manrico in *Il trovatore*. The soprano Teresa Stolz, the first Italian Elisabeth in *Don Carlos*, Leonora in the revised *La forza del destino* and Aida, sang in the first performance of the Manzoni *Requiem*. In the revised version of *Simon Boccanegra* at La Scala in 1881, the tenor Francesco Tamagno sang Gabriele Adorno, while the French baritone Victor Maurel sang Boccanegra. Eight years later, Tamagno created Otello and Maurel created Iago. Both singers took part in the British première of *Otello*, while Maurel became the first Falstaff.

Boito ▶ p. 240 Rossini ▶ p. 200

The Late Romantic

PYOTR ILYICH TCHAIKOVSKY

Few composers from the second half of the nineteenth century have achieved as great a popularity as Pyotr Ilyich Tchaikovsky (1840–93). For many listeners, the secret lies in his special gift for broad, arching melodies and his tendency towards agonized self-expression, rooted in a series of crises in his personal life, which fall easy prey to lurid dramatization. In Russia he is acknowledged for so much more, above all for his innovations in the spheres of the symphony, opera and ballet music, which he raised to a whole new level. The subjective, Romantic vein in his music is frequently undercut by a return to classical models, above all his beloved Mozart. Far from being merely a 'Westernized' composer at loggerheads with nationalist Russian musicians, as he is often portrayed, Tchaikovsky, through his association with many of those figures, above all their leader Mily Alexeyevich Balakirev (1837–1910), produced many works robustly Russian in spirit, especially in his early years. He then composed a series of autobiographical masterpieces leading up to the time of his disastrous marriage in 1877. Although his sense of fate in hot pursuit never left him, the range of his music broadened with his many travels abroad. His sudden death in 1893 remains an enigmatic tragedy, the abrupt end of a composer at the height of his creative powers.

LIFE TIMELINE

1844	First composition, the song 'Our Mama in St Petersburg'
1859	Studies musical theory with Nikolai Zaremba at the Russian Musical Society while working as a clerk in the St Petersburg Ministry of Justice
1862	Becomes one of the first students at the newly opened St Petersburg Conservatory
1865	First public performance of his work: the *Characteristic Dances*, conducted by Johann Strauss II, at Pavlovsk outside St Petersburg; graduates from the St Petersburg Conservatory and leaves to take up a teaching post at the Moscow Conservatory
1869	Works under Balakirev's guidance on his first masterpiece, the fantasy overture *Romeo and Juliet*
1874	Refuses to alter the First Piano Concerto under severe criticism from Nikolai Rubinstein
1876	Tolstoy weeps on hearing the *Andante cantabile* from the String Quartet No. 1
1877	Disastrous première of *Swan Lake*; long-term patronage of Nadezhda von Meck begins; Tchaikovsky marries and swiftly separates from Antonina Milyukova; starts work on the Fourth Symphony and *Eugene Onegin*; start of long periods spent abroad, chiefly in Italy
1881	Death of his father-figure Rubinstein prompts the tribute of the Piano Trio
1884	*Ygevny Onegin* lavishly staged at the Bolshoi and Maryinsky Theatres six years after its modest student première
1886	Takes up the baton for the third time in his life with new-found confidence
1890	Two spectacular premières at the Imperial Theatres: *The Sleeping Beauty* in January, *The Queen of Spades* in December; patronage of Nadezhda von Meck inexplicably withdrawn
1891	Conducting tour of the US
1892	*The Nutcracker* opens in a lavish double-bill with the one-act opera *Iolanta*
1893	Sudden death in St Petersburg in November, nine days after the première of the Sixth Symphony, leaves several question marks

THE MUSICAL CIVIL SERVANT

Tchaikovsky was born in Votkinsk, some 600 miles east of Moscow, where his kindly and modestly cultured father was manager of the local ironworks. Four years into his studies at the St Petersburg School of Jurisprudence, when he was 14, his mother, whom he admitted worshipping 'with a sort of morbidly passionate love', died from cholera, the same disease that was supposedly to carry the composer himself away nearly 40 years later. Although Tchaikovsky dutifully followed his father's wishes and went on to become a lowly clerk in the Ministry of Justice in 1859, his heart already belonged to music and he was lucky to have the encouragement of leading figures in the recently founded Russian Musical Society. In 1862 he was among the first students admitted to the brand-new St Petersburg Conservatory, and after his graduation three and a half years later, he became a teacher of musical theory at its sister establishment in Moscow. At the age of 22, he had achieved what he promised his sister Sasha, to give up his clerical drudgery only when he was 'finally sure that I am an artist and not a civil servant'.

THE 'FANTASY' OVERTURE

The emotional core of Tchaikovsky's fantasy overture *Romeo and Juliet*, the love theme, contrasting with the solemn music of Friar Laurence and the dramatic skirmishes of Montagues and Capulets, has become the archetypal musical symbol (and occasionally the parody) of tragic love.

POPULAR MELODY *Tchaikovsky*

SUCCESSES AND SETBACKS

The conservatory years resulted in several accomplished scores, but it was not until he had spent some months in Moscow that Tchaikovsky began the first of his works that revealed stretches of poetic genius: the First Symphony (1866, rev. 1874), which he subtitled 'Winter Daydreams'. Working through the night when the symphony 'just would not come' brought him to the first of several suicidal breaking-points, but he was to look back on the end result with fondness. His early operas on Russian themes, *The Voyevoda* ('Dream on the Volga', 1867–68) and *The*

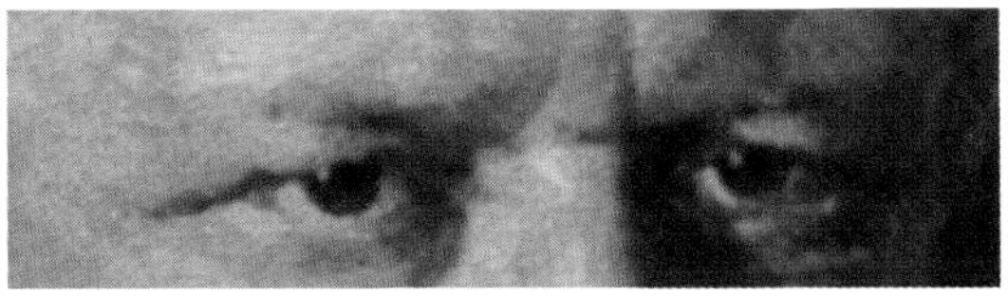

Oprichnik ('The Life Guardsman', 1870–72), were unsuccessful; his first true masterpiece, on the other hand, was a result of his meeting with the most influential of the nationalists, Balakirev, who provided both the programme and some crucial alterations to the fantasy overture *Romeo and Juliet* (1869, rev. 1870 and 1880). Balakirev was in no doubt over the quality of the now famous love-theme, telling Tchaikovsky, 'I play it often and I very much want to kiss you for it. Here are tenderness and the sweetness of love'.

A DUBIOUS RECEPTION

Balakirev's circle also went into raptures over the exuberant folksong finale of Tchaikovsky's Second Symphony (1872, rev. 1879–80), completed during happy times on the Ukrainian estate of his sister's family. His benefactor at the Moscow Conservatory, Nikolai Rubinstein, was less impressed by the First Piano Concerto (1874), rudely refusing to take on the difficult solo role as it stood when Tchaikovsky played it through to him on Christmas Eve 1874. Another masterpiece which got off to a doubtful start was Tchaikovsky's surprising attempt to write a full-length ballet score; the Bolshoi première of *Swan Lake* in 1877 was marked by inept choreography, sets and costumes cobbled together from bits and pieces and poor orchestral playing.

SWAN LAKE

The music of *Swan Lake*, however, lived on to grace a definitive production two years after the composer's death. Its balance of narrative drama with sheer melodic charm took to greater heights the achievements of the ballets by the French composer **Léo Delibes** (1836–91), *Coppélia* (1870) and *Sylvia* (1876). Tchaikovsky had not heard them when he composed *Swan Lake*, but he soon fell under their spell. For him, they came to represent the epitome of Gallic grace and charm, along with *Carmen* (1873–74) by **Georges Bizet** (1838–75) , which he saw in its unpopular early days, when he predicted that in 10 years it would become 'the most popular opera in the world'. Its influence on his music cannot be overestimated.

AESTHETIC INFLUENCES

'The aesthetic influences that one experiences in one's early years are of enormous significance,' wrote Tchaikovsky. At several points in his life he was happy to trace back his development to three early sources. The first was the figure whom no Russian composer from the mid nineteenth century onwards could ignore, the so-called 'father of Russian music' **Glinka**. Tchaikovsky saw his first great patriotic opera, *A Life for the Tsar* (1836), as a 10-year-old and his piquant scoring in later years was especially indebted to the fantastical colourings of Glinka's second stage masterpiece, *Ruslan and Lyudmila* (1842). Tchaikovsky also described himself as 'steeped from my earliest childhood in the indescribable beauty of Russian folk music with all its special characteristics'.

The influence of many Western composers popular in Russia, above all **Robert Schumann** (1810–56) and **Berlioz**, came later; but it was Mozart who inspired Tchaikovsky to a life dedicated to music. 'Perhaps it is precisely because as a man of my times I am broken and morally sick that I so love to seek peace and consolation in Mozart's music,' he declared shortly after the great crisis of his life in 1877. By then he had already composed the charming *Variations on a Rococo Theme* (1876) for cello and orchestra. He was to go on to pay direct homage to his idol in the arrangements of the Suite No. 4, 'Mozartiana' (1887), and the pastoral *divertissement* in the ball scene of the opera *The Queen of Spades* (1890).

In the meantime, he travelled to Bayreuth for the first ever four-day presentation of **Wagner**'s *Ring* cycle in 1876, and although he reacted to the event with bewilderment and animosity, the *Ring* made an impact on his most turbulent score to date, *Francesca da Rimini*, another fantasy overture, this time evoking the hellfire to which the Italian poet Dante had committed the adulterous lovers Francesca and Paolo in his *Inferno*.

A TIME OF CRISIS

The mournful themes Tchaikovsky had so memorably found for Shakespeare's and Dante's lovers spring from the composer's conviction, as he later put it, that he could experience 'the torments and at the same time the bliss of love' without ever having known 'complete happiness' in it. After his return from Bayreuth, the homosexuality to which he had many times given free rein became a torment to him, and he told his similarly orientated brother Modest that 'we must fight our natures to the best of our ability'. His solution was to seek a wife. The unfortunate candidate was a former conservatory student, Antonina Milyukova. She had written him a love-letter which he initially rejected, but as he began work on an opera based on Aleksandr Pushkin's verse novel *Eugene Onegin*, he became so involved in the lovable heroine Tatyana's candid confession of love and the hero Onegin's fateful rejection of it, that he determined to behave otherwise. He married Antonina in July 1877, fled from her shortly after the honeymoon and tried to commit suicide by submerging himself in the freezing waters of the Moskva River, which only served to improve his health. The already unbalanced Antonina, who was to spend the rest of her life in mental institutions, accepted a separation, and Tchaikovsky left immediately for southern Europe.

(BL) Romeo and Juliet ***by Ford Madox Brown***
Tchaikovsky based his fantasy overture on Shakespeare's tale of tragic love.

(R) Swan Lake
Tchaikovsky's ballet Swan Lake *proved to be his most popular and enduring work, despite its inauspicious start.*

Balakirev ▶ p. 238 Berlioz ▶ p. 186 Bizet ▶ p. 239 Delibes ▶ p. 245 Glinka ▶ p. 192 Mozart ▶ p. 144 R. Schumann ▶ p. 201 Wagner ▶ p. 226

PATRONESS AND FRIEND

The altered pattern of his life, which now entailed spending a substantial portion of the year abroad, had been made possible by a very different and far more acceptable kind of 'marriage'. The woman who stepped in to help him out of severe financial difficulties was a wealthy Moscow widow and music-lover, Nadezhda von Meck, whose only condition attached to the generous annual sum she provided was that they should conduct their relationship entirely through correspondence; on the few occasions they did meet, no word passed between them. Among the first of the 1,200 letters that have come down to us are those detailing Tchaikovsky's work on the symphony in which he gave vent to so many of the pressures of 1877 – the Fourth; and though the tragic programme he provided to Madame von Meck must inevitably have been adapted to her tastes, it gives a vivid sense of the autobiographical impetus behind his music of this period.

PYOTR ILYICH TCHAIKOVSKY: WORKS

- **Operas:** *Vakula the Smith*, op. 14 (1874, revised in 1885 as *The Slippers*); *Eugene Onegin*, op. 24 (1877–78); *The Maid of Orleans* (1878–79); *Mazeppa* (1881–83); *The Enchantress* (1887); *The Queen of Spades*, op. 68 (1890); *Iolanta*, op. 69 (1891)
- **Ballets:** *Swan Lake*, op. 20 (1875–76); *The Sleeping Beauty*, op. 66 (1888–89); *Nutcracker*, op. 71 (1891–92)
- **Symphonies:** Symphony No. 1 in G, op. 13 'Winter Daydreams' (1866, rev. 1874); Symphony No. 2 in C, op. 17 'Little Russian' (1872, rev. 1879–80); Symphony No. 3 in D, op. 29 'Polish' (1875); Symphony No. 4 in F (1877–78); Symphony No. 5 in E, op. 64 (1888); Symphony No. 6 in B, op. 74 'Pathétique' (1893)
- **Concertos:** Piano Concerto No. 1 in B flat, op. 23 (1874–75); Piano Concerto No. 2 in G, op. 44 (1879–80); Concert Fantasia, op. 56, for piano and orchestra (1884); Violin Concerto in D, op. 35 (1878); *Variations on a Rococo Theme*, op. 33, for cello and orchestra (1876)
- **Programme music and other orchestral works:** Fantasy Overture, *Romeo and Juliet* (1869, revised 1870 and 1880); Fantasy Overture, *Francesca da Rimini*, op. 32 (1876); *Marche Slave*, op. 31 (1876); *Capriccio Italien*, op. 45 (1880); *Serenade for Strings*, op. 48 (1880); *1812* Overture, op. 49 (1880); Suite No. 3 in G, op. 55 (1884); *Manfred Symphony*, op. 58 (1885); *Nutcracker* Suite, op. 71a (1892)
- **Chamber music:** String Quartet No. 1 in D, op. 11 (with *Andante cantabile* often performed separately, 1871); Piano Trio in A, op. 50 (1881–82); *Souvenir de Florence*, String Sextet, op. 70 (1887–92)
- Numerous piano pieces, including *The Seasons* (set of 12, 1875–76); two major choral works, including *Liturgy of St John Chrysostom*, op. 41 (1878); numerous songs, including 'None but the Lonely Heart'.

WANDERING AND RECOGNITION

Once in Italy, Tchaikovsky took something of a holiday from dark and tragic music. Over the next few years, his fame at last began to spread and by 1885 he had become a national hero. The operas he wrote during the 1880s departed from the utterly original and personal tone of *Eugene Onegin* to fit in with the public taste, a taste that was nurtured by a new era of splendour in the Imperial Theatres, initiated by the well-connected impresario Ivan Vsevolozhsky. In orchestral terms, Tchaikovsky spread his net wider, from the effective public-occasion piece of the *1812* Overture, to the subtleties of the work which immediately followed it in 1881, the *Serenade for Strings*, and the daring experiments in orchestration of his first three orchestral suites.

These helped to pave the way for the crowning glory of 'imperial style', *The Sleeping Beauty* (1888–89). Its lavish première in 1890 was a far cry indeed from the première of *Swan Lake* 12 years earlier; but the iridescent score, too, marks a considerable advance on the dashing if sometimes crude outlines of his first ballet. Its orchestral sophistication, though not its sheer dramatic scope, was to be capped by the score for *Nutcracker*, which opened in a double-bill with the one-act opera *Iolanta* in 1892. The opera that followed *The Sleeping Beauty* in 1890, *The Queen of Spades*, is its darker counterpart. Although the concision of Pushkin's precise supernatural story has been sacrificed to a certain amount of court spectacle, indulging along the way Tchaikovsky's love of Mozart, the chilling core of *The Queen of Spades* is perfectly realized in several scenes of pure music-theatre.

RUSSIAN MUSICAL LIFE

The musical climate of the Russia in which Tchaikovsky grew up hardly nurtured new talent; only a determined genius could forge ahead alone. There were no music colleges or conservatories when the first great Russian composer, Glinka, came to maturity. Although he did briefly undertake a systematic course of study in Germany, and despite the perfect scoring which graces nearly every page of his opera *Ruslan and Lyudmila*, Glinka was constantly to face the charge of dilettantism. The relatively late establishment of a conservatory in St Petersburg in 1862, shortly followed by a second in Moscow, had a curious impact on Russian musical life.

'The Five'

The fact that one of the two brothers who brought these institutions to fruition, **Anton Rubinstein** (1829–94), favoured German models in his conscientious, often frankly dull music, led to suspicions surrounding the solid academic training on offer. This was only heightened by the passionate nationalism of the leading musical figure who opposed the Rubinsteins, Balakirev. For a brief period in the 1860s, he devoted himself to the unofficial musical training of four other brilliant young men who had only been able to devote themselves part-time to music: the other members of The Five were the naval cadet **Nicolai Rimsky-Korsakov** (1844–1908), the former imperial guard **Musorgsky**, the engineering officer Cesar Cui (1835–81) and a respected chemistry professor, **Alexander Borodin** (1833–87). As one of the St Petersburg Conservatory's first students, Tchaikovsky was to suffer for being supposedly on the side of the academics, though he was soon to associate with Balakirev's 'mighty little handful' (*moguchaya kuchka*), with outstanding results.

EUGENE ONEGIN

Now that Tchaikovsky's *Eugene Onegin* (1877–78) is one of the best-loved operas in the world, it is hard to realize just how novel it was when it first appeared. The subtitle Tchaikovsky gave it, 'Lyric Scenes after Pushkin', hints at its special character. He wanted to get as far away as possible from what he saw as the cardboard cut-outs of a work like **Verdi**'s *Aida* and to portray instead 'ordinary, simple universal sensations far removed from high tragedy and theatricality'. To realize his dream, he needed young singers close to the tender ages of his three main characters – Tatyana, Onegin and the 18-year-old poet Lensky. This is by no means easy, given the mature vocal stamina required above all for the role of Tatyana; but Tchaikovsky's dream was realized when in March 1878 the première was given by students from the Moscow Conservatory. Ironically, it was a grand imperial treatment of the work in the 1880s that helped to turn Tchaikovsky into a national figure, and only in recent years has the Russian tradition of casting an ageing diva as Tatyana and, in one conductor's words, 'a pot-bellied baritone of 50' as Onegin begun to change.

PRIME OF LIFE

With many of his old ghosts laid at least temporarily to rest, Tchaikovsky was now a man at the peak of his career. He had mastered his terror of conducting so as to be able to promote his own music abroad, which he did with great success in a series of tours throughout Europe and the US starting in 1888. He had put a stop to his nomadic wanderings abroad by seeking his own home in the Russian countryside, finding his last haven in a handsome dacha north of Moscow in Klin, which is now one of the most beautifully preserved and presented house-museums anywhere in the world.

The help he had received throughout the years of struggle he now gave back to young composers and charitable causes. The conductor Alexander Mackenzie (1853–1929), who met him when he travelled to Cambridge to receive an honorary doctorate in June 1893, wrote how 'his unaffected modesty, kindly manner and real gratitude for any trifling service rendered contributed to the favourable impression made by a lovable man'.

THE 'PATHÉTIQUE'

Tchaikovsky's Sixth Symphony earned its belated subtitle, 'Pathétique' in the Russian or French sense of the word implying 'suffering', at the suggestion of his brother Modest. It has been so heavily linked with the circumstances of the composer's life and death that its enormous achievement simply as a piece of music can easily be overlooked. In the first movement, Tchaikovsky reveals his grasp of large-scale symphonic structure as he had only previously done in the equivalent movement in the Fourth Symphony, and his second movement is a gracious piece in the rare time-signature of 5/4 – unusual in the history of the symphony, but well-known in Russian folk music. But the real novelty is the reversal of the usual symphonic roles of the last two movements. The scherzo, which begins as a lightly scored fantasy, evolves into a march of such hectic brilliance that audiences invariably applaud its thunderous closing bars, unless the conductor has sufficient authority to keep them quiet. But Tchaikovsky then plunges us into the despairing gloom of an *Adagio lamentoso*. It is the first time in a symphony of stature that the slow movement comes last, and its final bars of total darkness, with the cellos and basses playing as quietly as possible – Tchaikovsky marks their parts with four *pianos*, *pppp* – provide a new, if unremittingly bleak, solution to the well-known 'finale problem' a composer faces in ending a symphony.

MYSTERIOUS DEATH

Tchaikovsky was able to exorcise the demons that had pursued him in the Fifth Symphony (1888), where dogged fate gives way to providence in the shape of a motto theme which turns from grimness to triumph, and in the Sixth Symphony, composed in what turned out to be the last year of his life, 1893. Although it ends in deepest tragedy, work on the Sixth during that spring turned out to be a positive and life-affirming experience. His attitude seems to have given no premonition of his death – 'sudden and simple … natural and unnatural' as Leo Tolstoy called it – a few months later.

There are conflicting accounts of its circumstances, and none has so far been established as the unquestionable truth. It could simply be that, against all precautions, Tchaikovsky had the misfortune to drink a glass of unboiled water in a time of cholera; though the details of his illness, and the dubious act of allowing the corpse's face to be kissed as it lay in state, have been questioned both by many contemporary witnesses and by medical experts. The theory of suicide at the decree of a court of old boys from his school, trying to hush up a homosexual scandal, has been advanced, but most students of Russian society of this period regard it as implausible. The manner of Tchaikovsky's death will always be cause for speculation and mythmaking; but the fact that the 'Pathétique' Symphony happens to reflect it, is pure coincidence.

***(BNL)* The Queen of Spades**
The gambling scene from Tchaikovsky's dark opera, based on Pushkin's supernatural story.
***(BFL)* Mily Balakirev**
Leading Russian nationalist musician Balakirev had a profound influence on Tchaikovsky.
***(TL)* Nadezhda von Meck**
Von Meck was a generous patron to Tchaichovsky; much of their correspondence survives.
***(TR)* Eugene Onegin**
The duel scene from the opera.
***(BR)* The House at Klin**
Tchaikovsky at last settled here at Klin, just north of Moscow.

Borodin ▶ p. 240 Musorgsky ▶ p. 253 Rimsky-Korsakov ▶ p. 256 Rubinstein ▶ p. 256 Verdi ▶ p. 230

The Late Romantic

PERSONALITIES

Albéniz, Isaac

(Àl-bā'-nēth, Ē'-zăk) 1860–1909

SPANISH PIANIST AND COMPOSER

Albeniz led the revival of a Spanish national musical style at the turn of the twentieth century. He studied composition with Felipe Pedrell (1841–1922), famous for his pioneering collections of Spanish folk and classical music that also inspired Albéniz's contemporary Enrique Granados and, a little later, **Manuel de Falla** (1876–1946). Aged 20, he abandoned his virtuoso career in favour of composition, producing, during nearly 30 years, over 250 piano works of Spanish character. Among the most popular are the suites *España*, *Tango*, *Navarra* and *Iberia* (1906–09), composed in Paris, where Albéniz studied from 1903 with **Paul Dukas** (1865–1935) and D'Indy. In his masterpiece *Iberia*, the pyrotechnics of **Liszt** and the exotic impressionism of **Debussy** are combined with Spanish dance rhythms, ingenious pianistic imitations of guitar sounds and flamenco or gypsy ornamentation.

Alkan, Charles Henri Valentin

(Àl-kăn', Shärl On-rē' Và-lon-tan') 1813–88

FRENCH PIANIST AND COMPOSER

One of the only virtuosos before whom Liszt, a contemporary, was believed to be anxious about playing, Alkan extended the technical challenges of piano repertory to astonishing new peaks. A child prodigy and young virtuoso, he performed alongside **Frédéric François Chopin** (1810–49), but thereafter became an eccentric recluse, seldom appearing in public. His death was as idiosyncratic as his life – he was crushed under a falling bookcase while clutching his beloved Talmud. His prolific output includes the Symphony and Concerto for piano, and many colourful character pieces and studies for piano and organ which still daunt all but the greatest interpreters.

Arensky, Anton Stepanovich

(À-ren'-shkē, Àn'-tōn Styā-pà-nō'-vēch) 1861–1906

RUSSIAN COMPOSER AND PIANIST

Arensky studied with Rimsky-Korsakov at the St Petersburg Conservatory but was also influenced by **Tchaikovsky** whom he met, along with Taneyev, while professor at the Moscow Conservatory. Among his pupils there were Rachmaninov, Glière and **Alexander Scriabin**. During a virtuoso career he was Director of the Russian Choral Society (1888–95), council member of the School of Church Music (1889–93) and successor to Balakirev as Director of the Imperial Chapel in St Petersburg (1894–1901). Best known are his Piano Trio in D minor, with its Tchaikovskian slow movement, and the Chopinesque Piano Concerto No. 1, with a 'Russian' finale. He also wrote three operas, symphonies, piano pieces and songs, and Variations on Tchaikovsky's 'Legend'.

Balakirev, Mily Alexeyevich

(Bà-lă'-kē-ref, Mē'-lē Àl-yek-sā'-ye-vich) 1837–1910

RUSSIAN COMPOSER

Balakirev's early piano fantasy on **Glinka**'s *A Life for the Tsar* won Glinka's approval in 1855 and in appreciation Glinka gave Balakirev two Spanish melodies, later reworked in the *Spanish Serenade*. Balakirev performed Beethoven's 'Emperor' Concerto before the Tsar, a highlight of a virtuoso career that culminated with his Chopin Anniversary recital in Warsaw in 1894. From the 1850s, Balakirev guided and inspired the nationalist group known as 'The Five'. He succeeded his conservative rival Rubinstein as conductor of the Russian Musical Society and promoted educational reforms as Director of the Free School of Music and later of the Imperial Court Chapel in St Petersburg. His best-known work is the Oriental Fantasy for piano *Islamey* (1869), which combines Listzian virtuosity with exotic **modes** and **chromaticism**. That synthesis also colours his many songs and orchestral works such as the *Overture on Three Russian Themes*, the tone-poem *Tamara* (1882), and two symphonies of his final years. It was left to Balakirev's last pupil, Sergey Lyapunov (1859–1924), to complete his Piano Concerto No. 2, begun 50 years earlier in 1862.

'BEAT OUT DAT RHYTHM'

In the film of *Carmen Jones*, although the stars had their singing voices dubbed by opera singers, Pearl Bailey sang herself. She was even given one of Carmen's songs, 'Les tringles des sistres tintaient', which as 'Beat Out Dat Rhythm on a Drum' became a tremendously popular hit number.

POPULAR MELODY *Bizet*

Beach, Amy

1867–1944

AMERICAN COMPOSER

Beach (née Cheney) made her début as a pianist in 1883, the year in which her first composition was published. In 1885 she married, and retired from a professional performing career. She did, however, continue to compose, writing large-scale works such as the 'Gaelic' Symphony in E minor op. 32 (1896) and the virtuoso Piano Concerto in C sharp minor op. 45 (1900), which were given prestigious, well-received performances. After her husband's death in 1910 Beach started playing professionally again, undertaking a very successful tour of Europe in the years before World War I. Her later, smaller-scale music shows a move away from the late Romantic language and Celtic idioms of her earlier works.

Without a long tradition of male-dominated music as in Europe, it appears to have been easier for women composers to be accepted in the US. Beach had several successful female contemporaries (or near-contemporaries) including Mabel Daniels (1879–1971), the first woman to take the score-reading class at the Munich Conservatory; her sister Bostonian Margaret Ruthven Lang (1867–1972);

chromaticism ▶ p. 357 mode ▶ p. 360

the West-Coast opera composer Mary Carr Moore (1873–1957) and the African-American composer Florence Price (1888–1953).

Bennett, (Sir) William Sterndale

1816–75

ENGLISH COMPOSER

Bennett was a leading figure of the 'London Piano School', a significant group of pianist-composers that included **Muzio Clementi** (1752–1832), Ignaz Moscheles (1794–1870) and Johann Baptist Cramer (1771–1858). A boy chorister at King's College, Cambridge, he began studies aged 10 at the Royal Academy of Music (RAM), where his teachers included Cipriani Potter. Close friends included **Mendelssohn**, under whom he often performed in Leipzig, and **Robert Schumann**, who wrote enthusiastically about him in the *Neue Zeitschrift für Musik* ('New Musical Journal'). Their influence can be found in his music, which includes four symphonies, an oratorio, *The Woman of Samaria*, cantatas and much compelling piano music, including the *Maid of Orleans* sonata. He founded the Bach Society (1849), conducted the Philharmonic Society (1856–66), and was Principal of the RAM (1866–75) where his students included Sullivan (1842–1900) and Parry.

Bizet, Georges

(Bē-zā', Zhôrzh) 1838–75

FRENCH COMPOSER

When Bizet died at the age of 37, he was considered a failure by the French musical establishment. He had had several operas produced in Paris, but none of them had been wholly successful; now his latest work, *Carmen*, had caused a scandal. Bizet's reputation was at its lowest ebb, but already the tide was turning. In less than 10 years Carmen swept across Europe and North America to become one of the world's best-loved operas.

GEORGES BIZET: WORKS

- **Operas:** *Le Docteur Miracle* (1857); *Don Procopio* (1859, performed 1906); *Ivan IV* (1862–65, performed 1948); *Les pêcheurs de perles* (1863); *La jolie fille de Perth* (1867); *Djamileh* (1872); *Carmen* (1873–74)
- **Orchestral works:** Symphony in C (1855, performed 1938); Symphony 'Roma' (1860–68); Suite from incidental music for *L'Arlésienne* by Alphonse Daudet (1872)
- Piano music, cantatas, songs

(FL) Arensky's Tomb

Detail from Arensky's tombstone at the Tikhvin Cemetery, St Petersburg.

(R) Georges Bizet

Bizet died thinking his opera Carmen *was a failure, today it is one of his most popular pieces.*

EARLY YEARS

Bizet was born in Paris on 25 October 1838. His father was a singing teacher, and Georges could read notes as soon as he could read words. At the age of 10 he was accepted into the Paris Conservatoire of Music. There he was influenced by Gounod, the future composer of *Faust*. At the age of 19, Bizet wrote a one-act operetta, *Le Docteur Miracle*, which won joint first prize in a competition organized by Offenbach, who produced it at his own theatre, the Bouffes-Parisiens. At the end of his studies at the Conservatory, Bizet won the Prix de Rome, a scholarship that paid him a stipend for five years, three of which were spent in Rome. During that period he wrote a two-act Italian comic opera, *Don Procopio*, which was not performed until 1906.

THE MARCH OF *CARMEN*

Carmen's worldwide popularity began in October 1875, when the opera was performed in Vienna with sung recitatives written by Bizet's friend Ernest Guiraud (1837–92). The opera scored a great success, and though Guiraud's recitatives are now considered stylistically wrong and have been abandoned, there is no doubt that they helped in the acceptance of the opera as a masterpiece.

London and New York heard *Carmen* in 1878, and soon every major opera house in the world had presented it. Orchestral suites and ballets were made of the music, whose catchy tunes and Spanish rhythms were irresistible; early gramophone records featured Carmen's 'Habanera' and 'Seguidilla', while Don José's 'Flower Song' was particularly popular with tenors. The cinema embraced *Carmen* with special warmth; there was a silent movie made in France in 1910, which lasted 16 minutes, while Cecil B. de Mille mounted a grand Hollywood spectacle in 1915, with the famous and beautiful American singer Geraldine Farrar as Carmen. *Carmen Jones*, a musical using Bizet's score with a new text by Oscar Hammerstein II, was produced on Broadway in 1943 with an all-black cast. The action was relocated from Seville to Chicago, while Escamillo, the toreador, became a champion prize-fighter. This ran for over 500 performances, and a hugely successful film version followed in 1954, with the voice of **Marilyn Horne** (b. 1934) in the title-role.

FIRST MATURE OPERAS

When his scholarship money ran out, Bizet had to earn his living. He gave piano lessons, he played for rehearsals at various theatres and made vocal scores and piano arrangements for music publishers. He continued to compose and wrote two operas for the Théâtre-Lyrique, an independent theatre whose director, Léon Carvalho, was one of his greatest admirers. *Les pêcheurs de perles* ('The Pearl Fishers') was produced in 1863, and *La jolie fille de Perth* ('The Fair Maid of Perth', loosely adapted from Walter Scott) in 1867. Both works received 18 performances, and were then forgotten until after Bizet's death. The outbreak of the Franco-Prussian War in 1870 caused the closure of all the Paris theatres. Bizet, though in poor health and exempt from military service as a winner of the Prix de Rome, joined the National Guard.

THE OPÉRA-COMIQUE

The ambition of all French composers was to write for one of the national theatres, the Paris Opéra or the Opéra-Comique. Between 1862 and 1865 Bizet worked on a grand opera, *Ivan IV*, but did not finish it. In 1872, he achieved part of that ambition when *Djamileh* was produced at the Opéra-Comique. This theatre did not only present comic operas, but works in which the musical numbers were separated by spoken dialogue rather than sung recitative as in the Italian style. It was a theatre where families went to celebrate engagements or weddings, and audiences expected a mildly amusing, sentimental opera with a happy ending. *Djamileh* fulfilled these specifications; *Carmen*, Bizet's next and final opera, performed there in March 1875, most certainly did not. Adapted from a story by Prosper Mérimée (1803–70), *Carmen*'s libretto was by Henri Meilhac and Ludovic Halévy, authors of several Offenbach operettas. They watered down the original story's plot, but nothing could disguise the tragic ending, when the gypsy Carmen is killed on stage by her former lover Don José. The audience at the Opéra-Comique was deeply shocked, as were many of the critics, who were unanimous in their condemnation of the opera. Bizet, who was not well, fled Paris to Bougival, just outside the city, where he died less than three months later. He never knew that Carmen would soon be among the most loved of all operas.

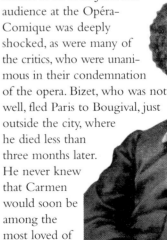

Chopin ▶ p. 190 Clementi ▶ p. 158 Debussy ▶ p. 282 Dukas ▶ p. 289 Falla ▶ p. 289 Glinka ▶ p. 192 Horne ▶ p. 334 Liszt ▶ p. 194 Mendelssohn ▶ p. 197 R. Schumann ▶ p. 201 Scriabin ▶ p. 296 Tchaikovsky ▶ p. 234

Boito, Arrigo

(Bō-ē'-tō, Ār-ī'-gō) 1842–1918

ITALIAN COMPOSER AND LIBRETTIST

Boito furnished the librettos for two of **Verdi**'s greatest Shakespearean masterpieces, *Otello* (1884–86) and *Falstaff* (1893). The première of his own operatic masterpiece *Mefistofele*, based on Goethe's *Faust*, at La Scala, Milan (1868), was greeted with whistles due to the work's extreme length (over five hours) and Germanic influences. As a result Boito for a while signed his work 'Tobia Gorrio', as in his libretto to Ponchielli's *La Gioconda* (1876). *Mefistofele* finally established itself in the repertory in a revised version in 1875. The music's great beauty and lyricism are matched by an eloquent libretto which, more than **Berlioz**'s or Gounod's versions, highlights the moral-philosophical debate, as explored in Boito's second opera *Nerone*, completed and first performed posthumously in 1924.

Borodin, Alexander

(Bô-rō-dēn', Ā-lex-ān'-der) 1833–87

RUSSIAN COMPOSER

Borodin joined Balakirev's circle known as 'The Five' while an army doctor in 1861. He later became a professor of chemistry and founded a school of medicine for women in St Petersburg, yet in his spare time composed a highly polished, if small, output. His melodic style draws on folk music reworked into compelling symphonic forms. He composed two important symphonies, the symphonic poem *In the Steppes of Central Asia* (1880), songs and chamber music, including three still-popular string quartets. His monumental opera *Prince Igor* (1869–70, completed 1874–87) is unified through the use of a few folk-like themes and abounds in spectacular tableaux and dances, including the famous 'Polovtsian Dances', spiced with percussion and chorus. Borodin's sudden death left his opera to be completed by Rimsky-Korsakov and Glazunov.

Brahms, Johannes

(Brāmz, Yō-hān'-nes) 1833–97

GERMAN COMPOSER

Brahms is a Janus-like figure in music history: he simultaneously faced the past and the future. Reviving and enlarging the classical principles of **Haydn**, **Mozart** and **Beethoven**, his music has often been seen as a conservative reaction against the 'new music' of Liszt and, in particular, **Wagner**. Yet Brahms's highly personal blend of Beethovenian dynamism, Schubertian lyricism and German folksong with the strict contrapuntal disciplines of the Baroque era, created a powerful new musical synthesis. His example was just as vital as Wagner's in the creation of the new music of the twentieth century. Though he appeared frequently as a pianist and conductor, after his thirties Brahms was financially successful enough to support himself as a freelance composer. Like Beethoven, he was a north German who based himself in Vienna, and remained a bachelor even though he was the centre of a large circle of influential musical friends.

WIEGENLIED ('BRAHMS'S LULLABY')

In 1868 Brahms celebrated the birth of a son to his Viennese friend Bertha Faber with one of the world's best-known lullabies. He blended a Viennese dialect love-song with a German folk-poem into an exquisite slow waltz, its tenderness directed equally towards mother and child.

POPULAR MELODY *Brahms*

HAMBURG, DÜSSELDORF, DETMOLD

Brahms, born on 7 May 1833 in a slum district of Hamburg, was the second of three children of Johann Jakob Brahms, a town musician, and Christiane Nissen, a seamstress. His musical talent was evident in early childhood; he grew up studying **J. S. Bach** with local piano teachers and playing in dockside taverns (bars and brothels) to augment the family's income. His first foray away

'THE FIVE'

Glinka, the 'father of Russian music', was the first composer to forge a distinctively Russian style. Previously, during the reigns of Peter the Great and Catherine the Great in the eighteenth and early nineteenth centuries, music at the Imperial court had been directed by leading Italian opera composers such as **Baldassare Galuppi** (1706–85), **Giovanni Paisiello** (1740–1816) and **Domenico Cimarosa** (1749–1801). Significantly, Glinka's musical training was European: after studies in Moscow with **John Field** (1782–1837), he toured Europe and absorbed the Italian operatic styles of **Bellini** and **Gaetano Donizetti** (1797–1848), and German Romanticism in Berlin. Glinka combined these sophisticated idioms with overtly Russian elements, peasant dances and choruses in his operas *A Life for the Tsar* (1836) and *Ruslan and Lyudmila* (1842), a synthesis seen also in the colourful *Kamarinskaya* (1848).

Glinka's Nationalism

Glinka's new awareness of his Russian musical heritage was to have a profound influence on another gifted Russian, Balakirev, who in the 1850s and 60s gathered around him a small coterie of like-minded artists eager to promote a truly Russian style. Musorgsky and Cui, and later Rimsky-Korsakov and Borodin, all of whom pursued music alongside full-time careers, developed their ideas guided by their mentor Balakirev, who influenced their compositions, suggesting literary subjects and folk themes. Vladimir Stasov, a powerful music critic sympathetic to their cause, first coined the term 'The Mighty Handful' in a review of one of their concerts at the Free School of Music. Cui became their spokesman, critical of the more pro-European conservative faction led by the Rubinsteins. Their nationalist style was coloured by folk themes, modal harmony, exotic orchestration, orientalism and a lyrical vocal style often, as in Musorgsky's case, influenced by speech patterns.

One of their final collective projects was the ballet-opera *Mlada* (1871), one act composed by each except for Balakirev. The group also supported each other by orchestrating or completing each other's works. Particularly through the modernist tendencies of Musorgsky's *Boris Godunov* and Rimsky-Korsakov's pupil **Igor Stravinsky** (1882–1971), 'The Five' exerted a powerful and decisive influence on Russian music in the twentieth century.

canon ▶ p. 356

LOOKING TO THE PAST

Brahms blended many influences into a potent and highly individual idiom. He felt that the programmatic music advocated by the 'New German School' was damaging the essentials of the art, and in 1860 he published an unsuccessful manifesto directed against Liszt and his followers – his only foray into public polemics. On the other hand, he admired Wagner, whereas Wagner resented Brahms's growing reputation and sought to belittle him as a mere academic. Brahms indeed was in the forefront of the nineteenth-century movement to arrive at a fuller and more accurate understanding of earlier masters, and studied their music more systematically than any composer before him.

Baroque and Classical Influences

The profound influence of Beethoven is obvious in the monumental First Piano Concerto and First Symphony, but Brahms was equally inspired by Mozart, Haydn and particularly **Schubert**, whose major works were only being rediscovered in the 1860s. Far more than most contemporaries, he was aware of **George Frideric Handel** (1685–1759) and J. S. Bach, whose music was gradually being published throughout the late nineteenth century. Moreover he collected, studied and performed music from the Renaissance and early Baroque periods, which taught him the value of strictly imitative contrapuntal forms such as **canon** and fugue. He also collected and arranged many German folksongs, which helped to develop his richly lyrical style of melody. This broad synthesis of influences, allied to his uniquely flexible sense of rhythm, created many new possibilities for the composers who came after him, notably Reger and **Schoenberg**.

from Hamburg in 1853–54 brought unexpected celebrity and the brief patronage of Robert Schumann. After Schumann's suicide attempt in February 1854, Brahms remained in Düsseldorf, helping Schumann's wife and family, until the older composer's death. During 1857–60 he divided his time mainly between Hamburg, where he conducted a women's choir, and an annual appointment at the small ducal court of Detmold. In 1858–59 Brahms spent time in Göttingen, where he became engaged to Agathe von Siebold, then almost immediately broke off the relationship. Although his music was becoming more widely known, he continued to base himself in Hamburg, evidently hoping to succeed the ageing conductor of the town orchestra, but while he was visiting Vienna for the first time in late 1862, the post was awarded to another.

FIRST YEAR AWAY FROM HAMBURG

Brahms left Hamburg in April 1853 as accompanist to the Hungarian violinist Eduard Rémenyi (1830–98), who introduced him to his fellow-countryman Joachim, already recognized as the greatest violinist of the age. When Rémenyi decided to go his own way, Joachim gave Brahms introductions to Liszt and Schumann. A walking tour of the Rhineland brought Brahms to Düsseldorf at the end of September. Here Schumann was astounded by his compositions and forthwith arranged for some of them to be published in Leipzig by the end of the year. In an article for the influential journal *Neue Zeitschrift für Musik* he hailed Brahms as 'the chosen one … destined to give the highest expression to the times'. In February 1854, Schumann's madness, suicide attempt and subsequent incarceration in an asylum left Brahms without a patron, yet he chivalrously assumed the role of protector of **Clara Schumann** (1819–96) and her numerous children.

JOHANNES BRAHMS: WORKS

- **Symphonies:** No. 1 in C (1862–76); No. 2 in D (1877); No. 3 in F (1883); No. 4 in E (1884–85)
- **Concertos:** Piano Concerto No. 1 in D (1854–59); No. 2 in B flat (1882); Violin Concerto in D (1878); Double Concerto (violin and cello) in A (1887)
- **Serenades:** No. 1 in D (1857–58); No. 2 in A (1858–59)
- **Overtures and variations:** *Academic Festival* (1879); *Tragic* (1880); *Variations on a Theme of Haydn* ('St Anthony Variations', 1873)
- **Choral works:** *A German Requiem* (1857–68); *Rinaldo* (1863–68); *Alto Rhapsody* (1869); *Song of Destiny* (1868–71); *Song of Triumph* (1870–71); *Nanie* (1880–81); *Song of the Fates* (1882)
- **Chamber works:** 2 string sextets; Clarinet Quintet; Piano Quintet; 2 string quintets; 3 piano quartets; 3 string quartets; Clarinet Trio; Horn Trio; 3 piano trios; 3 violin sonatas; 2 clarinet sonatas; 2 cello sonatas
- Motets, organ music, partsongs, piano music (including *Hungarian Dances*, 3 sonatas, variations) and songs

FRIENDSHIPS WITH CLARA SCHUMANN AND JOSEPH JOACHIM

Brahms was a solitary, difficult man, with a powerful need for friendship. Among his most significant relationships were those with Clara Schumann, widow of Robert Schumann, and the violinist-composer Joachim. Fourteen years his senior, Clara represented a romantic ideal of womanhood and was also one of the most gifted pianists of the century. Soon after their first meeting, Brahms realized he loved her. She returned his affection, though they are generally thought not to have been lovers. They remained very close for the rest of their lives, and Clara's advocacy as a performer helped to make Brahms's piano music widely known while identifying him in the public eye as Schumann's successor. Relations with the touchy and jealous Joachim were more chequered, but he helped the young Brahms gain confidence in composition and did much, both as violinist and conductor, to promote Brahms's cause. Brahms wrote several important works for him, notably the Violin Concerto and Double Concerto.

(NL) Johannes Brahms
Brahms's music, strongly influenced by the classical style, has often been seen as a reaction to the 'new music' by other composers of the Romantic era.
(FL) Borodin's Tombstone
The tomb of the Russian composer, with a score from his monumental opera Prince Igor.
(R) Brahms and Joachim
Joachim, a talented violinist and a composer himself, helped give the young Brahms confidence, although their relationship was often stormy.

J. S. Bach ▶ p. 106 Beethoven ▶ p. 150 Bellini ▶ p. 186 Berlioz ▶ p. 186 Cimarosa ▶ p. 157 Donizetti ▶ p. 192 Field ▶ p. 192 Galuppi ▶ p. 158 Handel ▶ p. 112
Haydn ▶ p. 140 Mozart ▶ p. 144 Paisiello ▶ p. 161 Schoenberg ▶ p. 295 Schubert ▶ p. 182 C. Schumann ▶ p. 201 Stravinsky ▶ p. 280 Verdi ▶ p. 230 Wagner ▶ p. 226

VIENNA, LIFE AND CONTACTS

The lack of recognition Brahms had found in his home town contrasted with the warm welcome he encountered in Austria from such new friends as the influential critic Eduard Hanslick. He spent increasingly long periods in Vienna, and essentially settled there from 1863, when he accepted the conductorship of an important choral society, the Singakademie, for a year. For three seasons (1872–75) he directed the concert series of the *Gesellschaft der Musikfreunde* ('Society of the Friends of Music'), but a permanent post did not suit him and he lived otherwise as a freelance composer, making occasional concert tours with friends and teaching selected piano pupils.

INTERNATIONAL REPUTATION

Brahms began to reach a mass audience with his waltzes and *Hungarian Dances* for piano duet, and with vocal quartets and songs. He was deeply affected by his mother's death in 1865, and his major choral work, *Ein deutsches Requiem* ('A German Requiem'), was written partly in her memory. First given in Bremen in 1868, and soon performed throughout Europe, it laid the foundation of Brahms's international reputation. This work and the subsequent *Triumphlied* ('Song of Triumph') were much performed as patriotic music during the Franco-Prussian War, further enhancing his profile in Germany. Meanwhile, his profound chamber and instrumental works attracted professionals such as the conductors Hermann Levi (1839–1900) and Bülow and amateurs like Brahms's erstwhile piano pupil Elisabeth von Herzogenberg. Thus he mastered each genre in turn, approaching the summit of his ambitions: the symphony.

THE 'THIRD B': EMINENCE IN LATER LIFE

From the time of the First Symphony (1876) Brahms's place in European musical life was assured, and he received many public honours. In 1889 he was awarded the freedom of his native city, Hamburg; in 1895 he was hailed as the 'third B' in a festival at Meiningen devoted to 'the three great B's – Bach, Beethoven and Brahms'. During his last 20 years, Brahms created his greatest masterpieces and established a fruitful relationship with the ducal orchestra in Meiningen. He aided many musicians out of his own purse and helped to further several notable careers, such as that of Dvořák. Brahms continued to travel widely, but this latter stage of his life was darkened by the deaths of many of his friends, and his music took on an increasingly elegiac character, for example in the autumnal Clarinet Quintet, and the *Vier ernste Gesänge* ('Four Serious Songs') to biblical texts, written after Clara Schumann's death in 1896. He died of cancer of the liver on 3 April 1897.

BRAHMS: SYMPHONY NO. 1

Although Schumann had prophesied in 1853 that Brahms would be pre-eminent in symphonic forms, he was diffident about coming before the public with a symphony. Many felt that Beethoven had already said all that there remained to say in this, the grandest of orchestral genres. So the eventual appearance of Brahms's First Symphony in 1876 was a major event. In many respects an 'answer to Beethoven', it is an intensely dramatic work in C minor, the key of Beethoven's Fifth Symphony. The great singing tune of the finale, and the trombones' suggestion of a **chorale**, clearly refer to the vocal music in the finale of Beethoven's Ninth (the 'Choral Symphony'), but Brahms here recreates vocal music in purely orchestral guise and blends it with Romantic imagery taken from nature (the finale's horn call imitates an Alpine shepherd's horn). The symphony therefore reinterprets Beethovenian ideas from a later perspective, and it was hailed by some critics as 'the Tenth Symphony', following on from Beethoven's Ninth. In fact, this direct confrontation with Beethoven enabled Brahms to concentrate on a more personal kind of symphonism in his three later symphonies, more lyrical and elegiac and (in the case of No. 4) reviving structural principles derived from J. S. Bach.

Bruch, Max

(Brōōkh, Māks) 1838–1920

GERMAN COMPOSER

Bruch studied first with his mother, a soprano, and then with Ferdinand Hiller (1811–85) in Cologne. He held conducting posts across Germany, as well as with the Liverpool Philharmonic Society (1880–83), and a professorship at the Berlin Academy from 1891. Late in his career he received honorary doctorates from the universities of Cambridge and Berlin and was honoured by the French Academy. His best-known masterpiece is the Violin Concerto in G minor, op. 26 (1868). It is one of several stirring works for solo strings and orchestra, including the *Scottish Fantasia* for violin and the more exotic *Kol Nidrei* for cello based on a traditional Hebrew melody. His style combines the formalism of Brahms with a love of **fugue** and counterpoint, rich Romantic orchestration and the pre-Wagnerian technique of motivic reminiscence, evident in the second of three operas, *Die Loreley* (1862). He excelled particularly in choral works and oratorios, of which *Moses* (1895) is an impressive example.

Bruckner, Anton

(Brōōk'-ner, Ān'-tōn) 1824–96

AUSTRIAN COMPOSER

Bruckner's Masses and symphonies, alongside those of Mahler, brought the Romantic symphonic tradition to its zenith. In contrast to Mahler's angst and irony, Bruckner's symphonies express triumphant faith, their almost cathedral-like proportions infused with exciting orchestral power and poetry.

Born in the small town of Ansfelden near Linz, where his father was schoolmaster, Bruckner grew up in an environment of rustic humility and devout Catholicism. After his father died, the talented 13-year-old began studies as a chorister at the nearby monastery of St Florian in 1837, where in 1845 he was appointed organist and schoolmaster for 10 years. He then obtained the prestigious appointment of organist at Linz Cathedral (1856–68), studying in Vienna with the famous

(NL) Bruckner Caricature
Caricature of the controversial composer, whose symphonies were condemned for their wildness.
(FL) Brahms in Vienna
Brahms settled in Vienna in 1863 and began work at the Singakademie.
(BR) Giuditta Pasta and Jenny Lind
The late Romantic era was the age of the diva, despite the belief that the theatre was no place for respectable women.

chorale ▶ p. 357 fugue ▶ p. 358 ostinato ▶ p. 361 *tremolando* ▶ p. 363

teacher Simon Sechter; he received a glowing recommendation from him in 1861. When he graduated from the Vienna Conservatory one of his examiners is said to have remarked, 'If I knew one tenth of what he knows, I'd be happy'.

FORMING A STYLE

The next few years were decisive for Bruckner's style: during his studies with Otto Kitzler, who conducted the Linz première of *Tannhäuser*, he first encountered – and was overwhelmed by – Wagner's music. He later attended the première of *Tristan* in Munich in 1865 and of *Lohengrin* and *The Flying Dutchman*, and received Wagner's approval to conduct the première of the finale to *Die Meistersinger* in 1868, prior to the opera's first production. These years also saw the composition of the three great masses and the first three symphonies (in F minor and No. 1 and one in D minor he numbered 0). In 1867 he was appointed successor to Sechter as court organist in Vienna and the following year he became professor of organ and theory at the Vienna Conservatory. He won international fame for his organ improvisations at competitions in Paris and London (1869–71), at Notre Dame and the Royal Albert Hall. His Mass in F minor, first given in 1872, was highly praised by Liszt.

OVERCOMING OBSTACLES

However, both his Symphony No. 1 and his first mature symphony, No. 2, were rejected by the Vienna Philharmonic for their 'wildness', while the Third Symphony received a catastrophic première under the composer's baton in 1875. Most of the audience left, and the orchestra too; the young Mahler was one of the few who stayed to congratulate the despairing Bruckner. Wagner observed that Bruckner was the 'only symphonist to approach Beethoven', but his alignment with the Wagnerians resulted in much criticism and subsequent revisions. The Fourth Symphony had to wait seven years for its 1881 première under **Hans Richter** (1843–1916). Again due to hostility, the Fifth and Sixth Symphonies were not played in Bruckner's lifetime. The turning point came with the successful première of the Seventh Symphony under **Arthur Nikisch** (1855–1922), and similar acclaim for the Eighth under Richter. At long last Bruckner's fame was assured. In his last years he was accorded the honours and accolades he so richly deserved, including a doctorate from the Vienna Conservatory (1891), and international commemorations for his 70th birthday, an appreciation of greatness which posterity has upheld.

BRUCKNER'S MASSES AND SYMPHONIES

Of Bruckner's seven Masses his three masterpieces are those in D minor (1864, rev. 1876, 1881), E minor (1866) and F minor (1868). The Mass in E minor, composed for the new Linz Cathedral, is unusually scored for choir and woodwind ensemble. It is modal and extremely contrapuntal in the style of Renaissance polyphony. Both the Masses in D minor and F minor are symphonic in scope with Wagnerian brass, cyclic structures, incisive fugues in the 'Glorias' and resonant choruses. Bruckner's *Te Deum* (1884) and *Psalm 150* (1892) crown his liturgical output, triumphant hymns of praise, each with climactic double fugues.

Bruckner's symphonies, though not 'programmatic' in the sense of Berlioz or Liszt, express a transcendent vision that is similar to the religious works, several of which are quoted. The influence of Beethoven's Ninth Symphony is strongly evident, particularly at the outset, often a string ***tremolando*** or **ostinato** with a bold theme etched above. Further stylistic hallmarks include vast block-like structures within which strident fanfares or soaring melodies build to huge climaxes, dramatic pauses, brass chorales and rich chromatic harmony. Bruckner's self-doubt, a reaction to criticism, resulted in extensive revisions to his symphonies. Impelled more by external pressure than inner conviction, these, in some cases rewritten by other hands, sometimes fall short of improving the original.

Bülow, Hans von

(Bü'-lō, Häns fun) 1830–94

GERMAN CONDUCTOR

One of the first great Wagner conductors, Bülow was a pupil of Liszt at Weimar and married Liszt's daughter Cosima in 1857. He was Head of Piano at the Berlin Conservatory (1855–64) and later, as director of the Munich Court Opera, conducted the premières of Wagner's *Tristan* (1865) and *Die Meistersinger* (1868). Although devastated when Cosima left him in 1869 to marry Wagner, Bülow nevertheless remained loyal to Wagner's cause. He was a legendary conductor and under his direction the Meiningen Court Orchestra became the most famous in Germany (1880–85). Though Bülow's tone poems and piano works are neglected, his seminal editions of the classics are still highly respected.

THE DIVA

The nineteenth century was the age of the great diva, the female opera-singer who performed roles in which she usually ended up mad, abandoned or dead, but who mesmerized audiences with the power of her voice. The theatre was not seen as a respectable workplace and for most of the century female opera-singers were not regarded as reputable women. They were often thought demanding and unreasonable, as can be seen in the changing meaning of the term 'prima donna'. Their talents were usually ascribed to natural gifts rather than the outcome of hard work and training, and their private lives were subject to intense media scrutiny. Early divas included Giuditta Pasta (1798–1865), who created the demanding title-role in Bellini's *Norma*, and the uninhibited Maria Malibran (1808–36). Malibran's younger sister Pauline Viardot-Garcia (1821–1910) impressed many of the leading figures of the day, including Berlioz, Dickens, Gounod, George Sand and Turgenev, with her intensely tragic performances.

An increasing respectability in the diva's reputation was largely the result of the image carefully cultivated by the 'Swedish Nightingale' Jenny Lind (1820–87), who always wore white, undertook charitable work and emphasized her devout Protestant Christianity. Nevertheless, before the middle-class American singer Clara Louise Kellogg (1842–1916) made her début in 1861, she told her friends she would understand if they never spoke to her again. The undoubted 'queen of song' during the nineteenth century was the coloratura soprano Adelina Patti (1843–1919), around whom sprang up numerous stories of irresponsible, capricious behaviour. Her voice was captured in early recordings in 1905.

Nikisch ▶ p. 300 Richter ▶ p. 300

Chabrier, Emmanuel

(Shăb-rē-ā', E-mă-el') 1841–94

FRENCH COMPOSER

After hearing Wagner's *Tristan* in Munich in 1879 with D'Indy and Duparc, Chabrier resigned his government post to become a full-time composer. The spectacular success of *España* (1883), a scintillating symphonic poem, proved him a master orchestrator. He composed two successful ***opéras comiques***, *L'étoile* ('The Star', 1877) and *Le roi malgré lui* ('King in Spite of Himself', 1887), and an opera, *Gwendoline* (1885), which utilizes Wagnerian **leitmotif**. His other orchestral works, songs and piano works show great melodic charm and zest, and include the famous *Bourrée fantasque* (1892), popularized in the orchestral version by his friend, the Wagner conductor Felix Mottl.

Chaminade, Cécile

(Shă-mē-năd', Să-sēl') 1857–1944

FRENCH COMPOSER

At the turn of the century, Chaminade's tuneful songs and piano pieces were extremely popular, partly due to her tireless promotion of her own music in performances throughout Europe and the US. The best known of these works is the wistful and dramatic piano piece 'Automne' from her *Etudes de Concert* op. 35 (1886). She was also the highly regarded composer of large-scale works such as the comic opera *La Sévillane* (1882), the choral symphony *Les Amazones* (1888) and a Concertino for flute and orchestra (1902). In 1913 she became the first female composer to be awarded the Légion d'Honneur.

Chausson, Ernest

(Shō-sôn', Âr-nest') 1855–99

FRENCH COMPOSER

After qualifying in law, Chausson studied with Massenet and Franck at the Paris Conservatoire and absorbed Wagnerian style, attending the Bayreuth première of *Parsifal* on his honeymoon. All three influences pervade his highly polished oeuvre in all genres. Best known are his masterly Symphony in B flat (1889), his sparkling concerto for piano, violin and string quartet and the sumptuous *Poème* (1882–90, rev. 1893) for violin and orchestra. He also wrote orchestral songs and *Le roi Arthus* (1886–95), an opera which uses leitmotif technique. Chausson was Secretary of the National Society of French Music from 1886 and his famous salons were attended by leading artists; his flourishing career was cut short by a cycling accident.

Cornelius, Peter

(Kôr-năl'-yoos, Pā'-ter) 1824–74

GERMAN COMPOSER

Although gifted as an actor, Cornelius studied music in Berlin and joined Liszt's circle in Weimar (1852), alongside Bülow, Joachim and others. He was a vociferous literary champion of the 'New German School' of Liszt and Wagner, yet his own works are surprisingly un-Wagnerian. They include many attractive Lieder, to his own poetry, and his opera *The Barber of Baghdad*, still considered one of the finest German Romantic comic operas. Its Weimar première (1858) aroused fierce opposition, leading to Liszt's resignation, but in 1884 it enjoyed posthumous success in Felix Mottl's revision. Cornelius composed two more operas, *Der Cid* (1865) and the unfinished *Gunlod* (completed 1891).

D'Albert, Eugene

(Dăl'-bēr, Oi'-gān) 1864–1932

GERMAN PIANIST AND COMPOSER

Born in Glasgow to a ballet composer, at 17 D'Albert moved to Vienna, befriending the great Wagner conductors Richter and Bülow, as well as Brahms and Liszt, with whom he studied. Widely admired as a piano virtuoso (several of his six wives were noted musicians), D'Albert was increasingly drawn to operatic composition. His 22 operas range from comic (*Der Rubin*) to occult (*Der Golem*) and introduced into German opera the gutsy realism of the Italian ***verismo*** style of Mascagni and Leoncavallo. His best-known opera, *Tiefland* ('Lowland'), combines Wagnerian intensity and Puccinian melody in its tale of jealousy, passion and violence.

D'Indy, Vincent

(Dān-dē', Vān-sōn') 1851–1931

FRENCH COMPOSER

An influential member of Franck's circle, D'Indy was a vociferous promoter of Franck's ideas, and his biographer. He was a prolific composer in every genre. He excelled in programme music, inspired by French and Swiss landscapes and nature.

'NEW WORLD' SYMPHONY

The slow movement of the 'New World' Symphony has become familiar through repeated use in film and television. The warm, mellow theme creates a sense of well-being in the listener that has ensured its continuing success.

POPULAR MELODY *Dvořák*

Best known are the colourful tone-poems for piano and orchestra, *Jour d'été à la montagne* ('Summer Day in the Mountains', 1905) and *Symphonie sur un chant montagnard français* ('Symphony on a French Mountain Song', 1886). He was influenced by both Franck and Wagner, particularly their use of cyclic techniques and leitmotif. These are employed in his three dramatic symphonies, piano sonata, symphonic poems and opera *Fervaal* (1889–95). He was co-founder and principal of the important Schola Cantorum in Paris, devoted to the study of plainchant, and as a conductor championed French music.

opéra comique ▶ p. 361 leitmotif ▶ p. 359 *verismo* ▶ p. 363

RUSALKA

Although Dvořák is viewed today mainly as a composer of orchestral and chamber music, he wrote 11 operas and, particularly towards the end of his life, considered himself to be foremost an operatic composer, which he believed to be 'the most suitable for the nation'. His music for stage included grand operas such as *Dimitrij* and comedies such as the hilarious *The Devil and Kate*. His greatest opera, however, was the 'lyric fairytale' *Rusalka*. Set in the Bohemian forest, it is essentially the story of Hans Andersen's 'Little Mermaid' transferred to the world of Czech folklore. Musically, it is a magical balance of symphonic development and exquisite lyricism. By far its best-known aria is Rusalka's 'Song to the Moon'. An early recording (1915) was made by the famous Czech soprano Emmy Destinn and in 1952 Dame Joan Hammond recorded her very popular version; since then it has been recorded by a range of the finest sopranos.

Dargomïzhsky, Alexander

(Där-gō-mēzh'-kē, Äl-yek-sän-der) 1813–69

RUSSIAN COMPOSER

From a landowning background, Dargomïzhsky was renowned in the salons of St Petersburg as a performer and composer, while pursuing a civil service career. Emulating the example of his contemporary Glinka, Dargomïzhsky followed his first opera *Esmeralda* (1839) by two works of overtly Russian character based on Pushkin, *Rusalka* (1856) and *The Stone Guest* (completed in 1870 by Cui and Rimsky-Korsakov). The exploration of speech inflection and realism in this last work had a profound influence on 'The Five', notably on Musorgsky's *The Marriage* (1868), based on Gogol, only one act of which was completed due to criticism of its radical style.

Delibes, Léo

(De-lēbz', Lā-ō') 1836–91

FRENCH COMPOSER

Known as 'the father of modern ballet', Delibes studied with Adolphe Adam and after his first ballet, *La Source* (1866), composed two enduring masterpieces: *Coppélia* (1870), which combines brilliantly orchestrated mazurkas, czardas, waltzes and boleros with dramatic symphonic music; and *Sylvia* (1876), best known as a concert suite, its delightful 'Pizzicato' popularized in film and television. Tchaikovsky greatly admired and was influenced by these works. After the *opéra-comique Le roi l'a dit* ('The King has Said It', 1873) came Delibes' operatic masterpiece, *Lakmé* (1883), influenced by both Bizet and Wagner, with its exotic 'bell song'. Delibes was awarded the Légion d'Honneur and was elected to the French Institut. *Kassya*, his last opera, was completed by Massenet, and staged in 1893.

ANTONÍN DVOŘÁK: WORKS

- **Symphonies:** Symphony No. 1 in C (1865); Symphony No. 2 in B flat (1865); Symphony No. 3 in E flat (1873); Symphony No. 4 in D (1874); Symphony No. 5 in F (1875); Symphony No. 6 in D (1880); Symphony No. 7 in D (1885); Symphony No. 8 in G (1889); Symphony No. 9 in E, 'From the New World' (1893)
- **Symphonic poems:** *The Water Goblin* (1896); *The Noonday Witch* (1896); *The Golden Spinning Wheel* (1896); *The Wood Dove* (1896); *The Hero's Song* (1897)
- **Concertos:** Piano in G (1876); Violin in A (1880); Cello in B (1895)
- **Orchestral works:** *Serenade* in E (1875); *Slavonic Dances* I (1878); *Serenade* in D (1878); *Slavonic Dances* II (1887)
- **String quartets, quintets and sextet:** String Quartet No. 5 in F (1873); String Quartet No. 6 in A (1873); String Quintet No. 2 in G (1875); String Quartet No. 8 in E (1876); String Quartet No. 9 in D (1877); String Sextet in A (1878); String Quartet No. 10 in E flat (1879); String Quartet No. 11 in C (1881); String Quartet No. 12 in F, 'American' (1893); String Quintet No. 3 in E flat (1893); String Quartet No. 13 in G (1895); String Quartet No. 14 in A flat (1895)
- **Piano trios, quartets and quintets:** Piano Quintet No. 1 in A (1872); Piano Trio No. 1 in B flat (1875); Piano Quartet No. 1 in D (1875); Piano Trio No. 2 in G (1876); Piano Trio No. 3 in F (1883); Piano Quintet No. 2 in A (1887); Piano Quartet No. 2 in E flat (1889); Piano Trio No. 4 in E, Dumky (1891)
- **Choral music:** *The Heirs of the White Mountain* (1872); *Stabat Mater* (1876); *The Spectre's Bride* (1884); *St Ludmila* (1886); Mass (1887); *Requiem* (1890); *Te Deum* (1892)
- **Songs and duets:** *Cypresses* (1865); *Moravian Duets* (1875–79); *Biblical Songs* (1894)
- **Piano music:** *Theme and Variations* (1876); *Poetic Tone Pictures* (1889)
- **Operas:** *Alfred* (1870); *The King and the Charcoal Burner* I and II (1871 and 1874); *The Stubborn Lovers* (1874); *Vanda* (1875); *The Cunning Peasant* (1877); *Dimitrij* (1882); *The Jacobin* (1888); *The Devil and Kate* (1899); *Rusalka* (1900), *Armida* (1903)
- Symphonies, symphonic poems, orchestral music, chamber music, choral music, songs and duets, piano music, operas

Duparc, Henri

(Düpärk', On-rē') 1848–1933

FRENCH COMPOSER

Duparc's small but exquisite output influenced the development of French 'mélodie' through Fauré and Debussy. Duparc studied with Franck, whose circle he joined alongside Chausson, Chabrier and D'Indy, absorbing the Wagnerian style through visits to Bayreuth and Munich. From 1868 to 1884 Duparc produced the 13 songs upon which his reputation is founded: each is a miniature gem, intimate and intense, with ravishing interaction between lyrical voice and expressive piano. His other works include *Feuilles volantes* ('Falling Leaves', 1867–69) for piano, and two symphonic poems, but he ceased composing in 1885 because of a nervous ailment, and spent his remaining years in increasing religious contemplation, finally moving to Switzerland.

Dvořák, Antonín

(Dvôr'zhäk, Än'-tō-nyēn) 1841–1904

CZECH COMPOSER

Dvořák was the pre-eminent composer of the Czech national revival. Arguably his achievement was less fundamental than Smetana's, but he developed a strong international profile and for millions his style epitomizes 'Czechness' in music. The Czech influence in his work is hard to demonstrate and he almost never quoted folk-song, but the appeal of his melodies, rhythmic drive, rich emotion and strong grasp of form, demonstrated in a huge number of works, have always proved seductive. The uncomplicated, direct melody and greater simplicity of form in works composed during his two stays in the US (1892–94 and 1894–95) have guaranteed that compositions such as 'From the New World' Symphony (No. 9) and the 'American' Quartet are among the most popular concert works ever composed.

ROOTS AND EARLY STRUGGLES

Dvořák was born to near-poverty in the village of Nelahozeves on the river Vltava, north of Prague. There was music in the family, but they made their living as innkeepers and butchers. Dvořák's musical talent soon became clear; eluding the family trade, he studied music and enrolled at the Prague Organ School in 1857. Two years later he graduated second in his class and took up a career as viola player in the Prague Provisional Theatre orchestra from its opening in 1862 until 1871. He lived in great poverty in these years, but acquired a range of musical experiences, including the music of Wagner, Smetana, Liszt and Verdi, and soon began to find his own voice. A decisive moment for his reputation in Prague came with the successful première of his cantata, *The Heirs of the White Mountain* on 9 March 1873.

(BL) Vincent d'Indy
D'Indy (second right at the back) collecting folk music; the composer was inspired by the landscapes and nature he saw on his travels.
(R) Antonin Dvořák
Dvořák conducting at the Chicago World Fair.

SUCCESS AND MATURITY

Later in 1873 Dvořák married Anna Čermáková. Tragedy and success marked the couple's lives in the mid 1870s. Three children were born and died between 1875 and 1877; at the same time Dvořák was awarded an Austrian state stipend for poor artists, which greatly increased his productivity. Judging candidates for the stipend brought Brahms into contact with Dvořák's music and he helped arrange the publication of the *Moravian Duets* in Germany. Their popularity was eclipsed by that of the *Slavonic Dances* (1878) which, in two years, transformed his reputation from a local to an international one. An invitation to London in 1883 resulted in a triumphant performance of his *Stabat Mater* and led to six more visits to England, for which he composed his Seventh Symphony, *The Spectre's Bride* and the *Requiem*. Dvořák was also extremely active at home writing, among much else, the operas *Dimitrij* and *The Jacobin*. During these years he developed links with important conductors, among them Richter, and became a firm friend of Brahms, Joachim and Tchaikovsky.

THE NEW WORLD AND AFTER

One result of Dvořák's burgeoning international reputation was the invitation by Mrs Jeanette Thurber to come to New York in 1892 as director of the National Conservatory of Music. Although there were many aspects of his stay that Dvořák found uncongenial, not least a pervasive homesickness, he made significant contributions to the Conservatory, encouraging black students and acting as inspiration to young American composers, while writing some of his best-known works. Symphony No. 9, 'From the New World', in part inspired by spirituals, and the Cello Concerto were composed in New York. Dvořák returned to Bohemia for good on 27 April 1895, devoting the rest of his life to the composition of symphonic poems and operas, largely based on Czech folklore. In his last four years he became increasingly retiring and died of a stroke on 1 May 1904, shortly after the disappointing *succès d'estime* of his last opera, *Armida*.

DVOŘÁK'S MUSICAL INFLUENCES

Dvořák composed in virtually every genre available to him, but those of opera, symphony and string quartet were ever present throughout his career. His early tendency towards symphonic gigantism in the mid 1860s turned to a period of acute experiment by the early 1870s, inspired to a considerable extent by Wagner and Liszt. The moderation of his style in the mid-1870s has often been attributed to Brahms's influence, but it was well under way before he encountered that master's music. Works like the Fifth Symphony and E major *Serenade* show the characteristics of his 'romantic-classic' style: balanced, attractive melody, a fine ear for instrumental **timbre**, and a remarkable, instinctive grasp of large-scale form. Exciting rhythm and a sense of identity with national tradition, even without direct quotation of folksong, added the exotic elements in his work that so commended him to international audiences.

DR. DVORAK'S GREAT SYMPHONY.

"From the New World" Heard for the First Time at the Philharmonic Rehearsal.

ABOUT THE SALIENT BEAUTIES.

First Movement the Most Tragic, Second the Most Beautiful, Third the Most Sprightly.

INSPIRED BY INDIAN MUSIC

The Director of the National Conservatory Adds a Masterpiece to Musical Literature

MR. SEIDL LEADING THE NEW DVORAK SYMPHONY.

'LAND OF HOPE AND GLORY'

It may have been Edward VII himself who first suggested putting words to the superb trio tune in *Pomp and Circumstance* March No. 1. The hint was taken up in the *Coronation Ode*. The words have since become Britain's alternative national anthem, 'Land of Hope and Glory'.

POPULAR MELODY *Elgar*

THE CAPACITY FOR SURPRISE

Alongside the symphonic and chamber music of the 1870s and 80s, Dvořák produced works such as the *Stabat Mater* which display a command of large-scale composition unparalleled in the Czech Romantic repertory. In this work, and in his operas, he showed an admiration for Italian music alongside the influences of Brahms and Wagner. But far from being an eclectic dominated by foreign impulses, Dvořák forged an inimitable style which emerges as strongly in such favourites as the A major Piano Quintet and the Seventh Symphony as in the *Requiem* and his operas. His 'American' works, composed deliberately for a less sophisticated audience, have a vitality and directness that have ensured success since their premières. The last part of his career shows a continued capacity for surprise in the astonishing neo-primitivism of his late symphonic poems (1896–97) and the ravishingly lyrical and finely characterized opera *Rusalka* (1900).

DVOŘÁK'S PRAGUE

Dvořák was born at a time of rapid advance in the Czech lands. For some 200 years Prague had been German-speaking, but owing to the industrial revolution and the gravitation of Czech-speaking country folk to the city, there was a gradual rise in interest in the native language and culture. Prague had always been a beautiful city, but towards the end of the nineteenth century it acquired buildings that celebrated its growing confidence as capital of the Czech nation with a Czech-speaking population rather than a major but provincial city of the Austrian Empire. The National Theatre was among the most striking, but even more spectacular were the later, Art Nouveau-influenced buildings such as the main station, designed by Josef Fanta, and the 'municipal house' designed by Antonín Balšánek and Osvald Polívka.

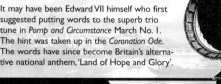

timbre ▶ p. 362

Elgar, (Sir) Edward

1857–1934

ENGLISH COMPOSER

Elgar was born at Broadheath, near Worcester. His father ran a music shop in Worcester, where Elgar embarked on a course of self-instruction that made him total master of music's craft and one of the world's greatest orchestrators. Brought up a Roman Catholic in a Protestant community and a tradesman's son, Elgar never felt socially at ease. His early fame was in Worcester, spreading only gradually to the other Three Choirs cities (Hereford and Gloucester), to more distant regional festivals, to London, and to the international scene, by which time he was 42. Milestones along the way are clear. His first Three Choirs commission produced the overture *Froissart*, a work entirely characteristic in its chivalrous panache. There followed choral works such as *King Olaf* (1896) for the North Staffordshire Festival and *Caractacus* (1898) for the Leeds Festival. It was an orchestral masterpiece, however, the 'Enigma' Variations, dedicated to 'my Friends pictured within', that launched the international career of the most significant British composer since **Henry Purcell** (1659–95).

(BL) *Prague*
Prague experienced a new nationalism, celebrating the Czech language and culture.

***(TL) Review of* From the New World**
A rave review after the first performance of Dvořák's From the New World.

(TR) Early Recording Studio
Elgar (far right) making an early recording.

(BR) Elgar and Menuhin
The elderly composer with the young violinist Yehudi Menuhin, who made the seminal recording of Elgar's Violin Concerto.

EDWARD ELGAR: WORKS

- **Choral works:** *The Black Knight* (1893); *The Light of Life* (1896); *Scenes from the Saga of King Olaf* (1896); *Caractacus* (1898); *The Dream of Gerontius* (1900); *Coronation Ode* (1902); *The Apostles* (1903); *The Kingdom* (1906); *The Music Makers* (1912); *The Spirit of England* (1917)
- **Orchestral works:** *Froissart* Overture (1890); *Imperial March* (1897); *Bavarian Dances* (1897); 'Enigma' Variations (1899); *Cockaigne* Overture (1901); *Pomp and Circumstance* Marches (1901–30); *In the South* Overture (1904); Symphony No. 1 in A flat (1908); Violin Concerto in B (1910); Symphony No. 2 in E flat (1911); *Falstaff* (1913); Cello Concerto in E (1919)
- Church music, partsongs, songs, works for small orchestra including *Chanson de matin*, chamber music, music for violin, piano, organ

EDWARDIAN LAUREATE

His fame as a great choral composer was consolidated by *The Dream of Gerontius* (1900) to text by Cardinal Newman, and by two oratorios of a projected trilogy on biblical texts compiled by himself, *The Apostles* (1903) and *The Kingdom* (1906). All three works demonstrated an orchestral virtuosity that equalled Wagner's and was perhaps superior to that of Richard Strauss or Mahler. Such concert pieces as the *Cockaigne* Overture (1901) and *In the South* (1904), the series of *Pomp and Circumstance* Marches (begun 1901) and the beautifully turned *Wand of Youth* suites consolidated his reputation. He was knighted in 1904.

At the end of 1907, he set aside plans for his third oratorio and began concentrated work on Symphony No. 1, which achieved remarkable success at its première (December 1908) and reached a total of 100 performances in hardly more than a year. An accomplished violinist himself, Elgar had long contemplated a violin concerto. This was completed in 1910 after consultation about the solo part with W. H. Reed and Fritz Kreisler, and had a triumphant reception from the outset.

DISILLUSION, WAR AND REVIVAL

The death of King Edward VII in May 1910 saw the end of an era, and Elgar's works written in the reign of George V were not greeted with the popular acclaim he had come to expect. Symphony No. 2 (1913) is a simpler construction than No. 1 and ends quietly. *Falstaff* (1913), a symphonic study of supreme mastery that emphasized the knightly qualities of the mostly disreputable Sir John, bewildered its early audiences. Success continued with works of minor importance, such as the *Crown of India* masque (1912), which celebrated in a somewhat bombastic manner the 1911 Delhi Durbar and transfer of the Indian capital from Calcutta, and *The Fringes of the Fleet* (1917), a wartime stage setting of poems by Rudyard Kipling (1865–1936) concerned with the exploits of British seamen.

Elgar made his first recording in 1914, and for the next 20 years he was closely associated with the gramophone, conducting many major works on disc and showing himself an incomparable interpreter of his own music. The post-war period produced little important Elgar apart from the nostalgic Cello Concerto (1919), the comparitive reticence of which seemed baffling at first; but the last *Pomp and Circumstance* March (1930) and the sketches for Symphony No. 3, completed by Anthony Payne in 1998, show that the old fires were still burning.

HANS RICHTER

The 'Enigma' Variations arose almost by accident when Elgar was improvising at the piano after a day's violin teaching in Malvern (October 1898). When he had completed them, Elgar was confident enough of their worth to submit them for consideration by Hans Richter, first conductor of Wagner's *Ring* and by now living mainly in England. Richter decided to give the première (19 June 1899). Thus began a close association, resulting in the dedication of Elgar's first symphony to Richter and Elgar's agreeing to succeed him as conductor of the London Symphony Orchestra in 1911. After the 'Enigma' triumph, Elgar could call on singers as renowned as Clara Butt and there was even tentative discussion of a *King Lear* opera with Chaliapin, the great Russian bass. Fritz Kreisler gave the first performance of the Violin Concerto. It was hoped he would record it, too, but eventually it was the combination in 1932 of the 75-year-old Elgar with the teenage **Yehudi Menuhin** (1916–99) that produced a version that is still unsurpassed.

Erkel, Ferenc

(Er'-kel, Fer'-enk) 1810–93

HUNGARIAN COMPOSER AND CONDUCTOR

A pioneer of Hungarian national opera, Erkel was conductor at the National Theatre in Pest from 1838 and later of the Budapest Philharmonic concerts. His early works in the *style hongroise* predate even Liszt's Hungarian works, and he forged a national operatic style in such works as *Hunyádi László* (1844), with its Hungarian melodies and dances, and *Bánk bán* (1861), composed with his son Gyula, the first work to incorporate a cimbalom. The later, more Wagnerian operas, such as *King István* (1885), show Gyula's notable contribution. Erkel was conductor of the National Choral Association and Director of the Music Academy in Budapest. One of his most famous works is the stirring Hungarian National Anthem (1845).

Menuhin ▶ p. 333 Purcell ▶ p. 78

Fauré, Gabriel

(Fō-rā', Gā-brē-el') 1845–1924

FRENCH COMPOSER

Fauré, a pre-eminent master of French song, studied with Saint-Saëns in 1866, whom he succeeded after 1896 as chief organist at the Madeleine. He was appointed Director at the Paris Conservatoire (1905–20) and also served as critic for *Le Figaro*. He was thus a powerful influence on twentieth-century French music, especially through his students who included **Maurice Ravel** (1875–1937) and **George Enescu** (1881–1955). Fauré's music is quintessentially French: lyrical, elegant, richly sonorous and harmonically beguiling, with a sensuous use of modes. Of nearly 100 songs, the most famous include *Clair de lune* ('Moonlight', 1887) and two Verlaine sets, *Cinq mélodies* (1890) and *La bonne chanson* (1892). His lyrical inspiration also pervades his *Requiem* (1887) and opera *Pénélope* (1913). His piano works owe much to Chopin, shown by their descriptions, impromptus, barcarolles and nocturnes, yet with distinctively French sonorities that also permeate the impassioned Second Violin Sonata (1917) and his piano quartets.

Fibich, Zdeněk

(Fē'-bikh, Zden'-yek) 1850–1900

CZECH COMPOSER

Fibich was conductor of the National Theatre, Prague and later of the Russian Orthodox Choir. Trained in Prague and Leipzig, he deployed Wagnerian techniques in his seven Czech operas, including *The Bride of Messina* (1884). The librettist of his opera *Šárka* (1897) was Anezka Schulzová, a pupil with whom he had a love affair, charted in an epic 'diary' for piano, *Moods, Impressions, Reminiscences* (1892–99), consisting of over 200 pieces including his popular *Poème*. Fibich was the earliest composer of Czech tone-poems, based on folk ballads; he also composed three 'cyclic' symphonies, many songs and chamber works and excelled in the genre of melodrama.

Gade, Niels

(Gā'-de, Nēls) 1817–90

DANISH COMPOSER

In Copenhagen, Gade, a pioneer of the modern Scandinavian school, was violinist in the Royal Orchestra where many of his earliest works were performed, including the prize-winning tone-poem *Ossian* (1841). His masterly Symphony in C minor (1843) was first given in Leipzig by Mendelssohn. The following year, Gade assisted Mendelssohn as conductor of the Gewandhaus Orchestra, succeeding him when he died in 1847. In 1848, at the start of the German-Danish war, Gade returned to Copenhagen and was influential as a conductor and co-founder of the Conservatory.

Glazunov, Alexander Konstantinovich

(Glā'-zōō-nof, Āl-yek'-sān'-der Kon-stān-tē-nō'-vich) 1865–1936

RUSSIAN COMPOSER

Glazunov was heir to the nationalism of 'The Five' and the cosmopolitanism of Tchaikovsky. He studied with Rimsky-Korsakov and completed many of Borodin's works after he died, notating the overture to *Prince Igor* from memory. In the 1880s and 90s he enjoyed international fame for works such as the tone-poem *Stenka Razin* (1885), the ballet *Raymonda* (1896–97) and early symphonies. While Director of the St Petersburg Conservatory (1905–22) he composed his finest works, the Seventh and Eighth Symphonies (1902, 1906) and concertos for violin and piano; after the 1917 Revolution he was honoured as People's Artist of the Republic. In 1928 Glazunov settled in Paris, but composed little apart from a masterly Saxophone Concerto (1931).

Glière, Reinhold Moritsovich

(Glē-âr, Rīn'-hōld Mō-rēt-zō'-vēch) 1875–1956

RUSSIAN COMPOSER

Glière studied with Taneyev and Arensky at the Moscow Conservatory where he was Professor, 1920–41. He was chairman of the Organizing Committee of USSR Composers (1938–48) and received many state awards. His style, in the tradition of Russian Romanticism, features expressive melody, brilliant orchestration and reflects the folk music of the Eastern provinces; for instance, Azerbaijan melodies appear in the opera *Shah Senem* (1934). Glière was a pioneer of Soviet ballet, and his best-known works in this sphere include *The Red Poppy* (1926–27) and *The Bronze Horseman* (1948–49). Soviet themes appear in three symphonies, *March of the Red Army* (1924) and *Victory Overture*, as well as many chamber works, songs and piano pieces.

'MORNING' FROM *PEER GYNT*

'Morning' from the *Peer Gynt* Suite No. 1 is one of the warmly lyrical movements that highlights Grieg's melodic and colouristic gift. The piece surpasses the original play in popularity, its appealing melody and atmospheric effects familiar from concert, ballet and film.

POPULAR MELODY *Grieg*

Gomes, Carlos

(Gō'-mās, Kār-lōōs) 1836–96

BRAZILIAN COMPOSER

Gomes was the son of a bandmaster, and after studies at the Imperial Conservatory of Music in Rio de Janeiro, settled in Italy. His comedies *Se sa minga* and *Nella Luna* (1867–68) were successful but international recognition came with *Il Guarany* (La Scala, 1870), whose exotic score includes colourful Latin American and Indian dances. After *Fosca* (1873), *Salvator Rosa* (1874) and *Maria Tudor* (1879), Gomes repeated his success with *Lo Schiavo* ('The Slave', 1889), again on a Brazilian subject. His last opera *Condor* evinced the new *verismo* style; his oratorio *Colombo* (1892) was performed on the Columbus Anniversary in Rio.

Gottschalk, Louis Moreau

(Got'shôk, Lōō-ē' Mō-rō') 1829–69

AMERICAN COMPOSER

Gottschalk was a charismatic piano virtuoso distinguished by his New Orleans upbringing and French-Creole ancestry. He dazzled the salons and saloons of New Orleans as a child prodigy, and at 13 went to study in Paris, where his skill was admired by Chopin and Berlioz. He toured as pianist and conductor until his untimely death. His piano works, over 300, such as *Bamboula* (1845), a scintillating rondo on 'Sweet Potatoes', are influenced by Creole-Caribbean folk music. In ballads and variations such as *The Last Hope* and *The Dying Poet*, folk themes combine with sophisticated Romantic idioms, as also in larger symphonic poems including *La nuit des tropiques* ('Night in the Tropics', 1859). His works were significant in the development of American music.

FAURÉ'S SONGS

Fauré is central to late-Romantic vocal repertory. His oeuvre of over 100 songs, in three collections (1879, 1897, 1908) and four major cycles, offers challenges to even the greatest singers. Many of the earliest were written for the charismatic Spanish soprano Pauline Viardot, to whose sister Fauré was briefly engaged. Most popular of his first stylistic period (1870–85) are *Lydia*, with its punning use of the Lydian mode, the beguiling *Aprés un reve* ('After a Dream') and the plangent *Les Berceaux* ('The Cradles'). Here, the gently swaying accompaniment symbolizes the rocking of both the babies' cradles and of the ships that transport their fathers through threatening seas. Fauré's second style peroid (1885–1906) is significant for its masterly settings of *Verlaine*, the famous *Clair de Lune* and two cycles, in which individual songs are related thematically. In his late period (1906–24), Fauré set poetry by the Belgian symbolist Van Lerberghe in the cycles *La Chanson d'Eve* ('Song of Eve') and *Le Jardin Clos* ('The Secret Garden'), which attain a refined and visionary style of great expressive heights.

Gounod, Charles-François

(Goō-nō, Shârl Frān-swà') 1818–93

FRENCH COMPOSER

Gounod is best known as the composer of one of the most popular French lyric operas, *Faust*. His teachers at the Paris Conservatoire were the opera composers **Fromental Halévy** (1799–1862) and Jean François Le Sueur (1760–1837) and in 1839 he won the coveted Prix de Rome. Alongside much sacred music, such as the florid *Messe solonnelle de Sainte Cecile* (1855), Gounod's outstanding gift for word-setting was shown in his lyric operas, a genre midway between grand and comic opera. Early successes include *Sapho* (1851) and *Le médecin malgré lui* ('Doctor in Spite of Himself', 1858), but it was *Faust* (1859) that established his enduring fame. Based on Goethe's play, the plot centres on the character of Marguerite, for whom Gounod composed his finest melodies, such as the 'Ballad of the King of Thule'. *Faust* enjoyed great popularity in England, where Gounod stayed in 1870–74, composing the oratorio *The Redemption* (1868–81) for the English public. After *Faust*, his most important operas were *Roméo et Juliette* (1867), with its famous Love music, and *Mireille* with its Provençal setting; his songs influenced the younger French composers including Fauré. Among his other popular works is the charming *Petite Symphonie* for wind (1888).

Granados, Enrique

(Grā-nā'-thōs, En-rē'-kā) 1867–1916

SPANISH COMPOSER

Born in Lérida, Granados studied with Pedrell in Barcelona and then in Paris. He later founded and directed a music academy in Barcelona. Like his compatriots Albéniz and Falla, he forged a new Spanish style, with strumming effects, ornamentation, modes and exuberant dance rhythms. His best-known works are the *Goyescas* (1911), two sets of imaginative piano pieces inspired by the great Spanish painter Goya, of which 'The Maiden and the Nightingale' is one of the most famous. The pieces were reworked into *Goyescas*, one of his seven completed operas. It was while returning from its première in 1916 at the Metropolitan Opera, New York, that Granados and his wife drowned tragically, when their ship was torpedoed in the English Channel.

Grieg, Edvard

(Grēg, Ed'-värd) 1843–1907

NORWEGIAN COMPOSER

Of Scottish ancestry, Grieg studied music with his mother and later in Leipzig (1858–62) with Ignaz Moscheles and Carl Reinecke, and with Gade in Copenhagen. There he became organizer of the Euterpe Society for Scandinavian Music and subsequently, in Norway, founded the Norwegian Academy of Music (1867). The same year he married his cousin Nina Hagerup, a soprano who gave the premières of many of his songs. Grieg's style combines the early German Romanticism of Schumann and Mendelssohn with nationalistic Norwegian elements, yet filtered through his distinctive lyrical imagination. His best-known works are his Piano Concerto (1868), still a concert favourite (which Liszt sight-read perfectly when they met in Weimar), and the incidental music for *Peer Gynt*, from which he made two suites that won him international fame. Grieg was above all a master of the miniature, exemplified in the 10 sets of *Lyric Pieces* for piano (1867–1901) based on Norwegian folk themes, the neo-classical *Holberg Suite* (1884) and much beautiful chamber music. Honoured all over Europe in his final years, Grieg retired to a house near Bergen, yet continued to be an influential mentor to younger colleagues including **Frederick Delius** (1862–1934) and **Percy Grainger** (1882–1961). Grieg's music, some of which is still unfamiliar, continues to exert its popular melodic appeal, as for instance in the film *The Song of Norway*.

Humperdinck, Engelbert

(Hoom'-per-dink, Eng'-el-bârt) 1854–1921

GERMAN COMPOSER

Humperdinck studied in Cologne with Ferdinand Hiller and joined Wagner's circle in Bayreuth. He assisted in the publication of *Parsifal* and was music tutor to Wagner's son Siegfried, who later praised *Hänsel und Gretel* (1893) as 'the most important opera since *Parsifal*'. Based on a tale by the brothers Grimm, the opera was composed while Humperdinck was professor and critic in Frankfurt. Its success was due to its refreshing melodic charm (the 'Sleeping Song' is a children's favourite) set within an exciting Wagnerian style. Of five later operas, the best is *Königskinder* ('The King's Children', 1910) also based on a fairy story; other works include a symphony, choral pieces and songs.

Joachim, Joseph

(Yō'-ā-khēm, Yō'-zef) 1831–1907

GERMAN VIOLINIST

Joachim studied with Ferdinand David, leader of the Gewandhaus Orchestra in Leipzig, where he made his début in 1843. After a spell as leader of the Court Orchestra in Weimar under Liszt (1850–51), he distanced himself from Liszt's 'New German School' in favour of Brahms's classicism. Appointed violinist to the king in Hanover (1852), he became great friends with Brahms, championing his music across Europe. He played Brahms's Violin Concerto to great acclaim in 1852, gave the premières of many of the chamber works with his Hanover Quartet, and conducted the première of Brahms's First Symphony in England, where he received the honorary doctorate at Cambridge University. His playing was renowned for its singing quality and depth.

(L) Reinhold Moritsovich Glière

Although Glière crosses the line between the modern and Romantic eras, his style was firmly in the tradition of Russian romanticism.

(TR) Engelbert Humperdinck

Humperdinck was part of Wagner's circle in Bayreuth; he based many of his works on fairy tales.

Delius ▶ p. 288 Enescu ▶ p. 289 Grainger ▶ p. 290 Halévy ▶ p. 193 Ravel ▶ p. 294

Lalo, Edouard

(Lä-lō', Ā-dwär) 1823–92

FRENCH COMPOSER

After studies at the Paris Conservatoire, Lalo joined a string quartet, composing salon music and songs. In 1874, after a fallow period, he first achieved success with the *Symphonie espagnole* ('Spanish Symphony', 1874), a scintillating violin concerto whose five movements exude Spanish rhythmic zest and lyricism (he was of Spanish descent). This was followed by the impressive Cello Concerto (1877), the colourful *Rapsodie norvégienne* ('Norwegian Rhapsody') for violin and orchestra (1878), the opera *Le roi d'Ys* ('The King of Ys', 1888), and numerous songs. His finest work is the ballet *Namouna* (1882), much admired by younger French composers such as D'Indy and Debussy. Among the favourite movements are the atmospheric 'Serenade', the 'Valse de Cigarette' and 'La Sieste'.

Leoncavallo, Ruggero

(Lā-ōn-kă-văl'-lō, Rood-jâ'-rō) 1858–1919

ITALIAN OPERA COMPOSER

Leoncavallo's masterpiece was the one-act opera *Pagliacci* ('Clowns', 1892), for which he wrote the libretto, based on an incident in the Italian town where his father was a judge. In its realistic subject and passionately expressive style, it embodies the *verismo* movement pioneered by Mascagni, with whose *Cavalleria rusticana* ('Rustic Cavalry', 1890) it is often twinned in performance. *Pagliacci* was performed with great success across the world months after its première in Milan in 1892, and was popularized by the great Italian tenors and divas of the day. Though *La bohème* (1897), appearing a year after the famous opera by Puccini, is no longer performed, *Zazà* (1900), the story of love and betrayal of a cabaret singer in *fin-de-siècle* France, remains a favourite of the *verismo* repertory.

MacDowell, Edward

1861–1908

AMERICAN COMPOSER

Although his training and early career were European, with studies in Paris and Frankfurt and posts in Darmstadt, MacDowell was a pioneer of American music, which he felt reflected 'the youthful optimistic vitality and the undaunted tenacity of spirit that characterize the American man'. His strong European influences, with echoes of Grieg and Liszt, who admired his First Piano Concerto (1882), combine with an individual lyricism in many of the character pieces for piano for which he is best known: *Woodland Sketches* (1896), *Fireside Tales* (1902) and *New England Idylls* (1902). MacDowell lived in Boston (1886–96) and was later a professor at Columbia University (1896–1903) and founder-member of the American Academy of Arts and Letters. His other works include two piano concertos, four piano sonatas whose titles, *Tragica*, *Eroica*, *Norse* and *Keltic*, display the influence of his Celtic ancestry, orchestral suites and songs.

Mahler, Gustav

(Mä'-ler, Goos'-täf) 1860–1911

AUSTRIAN COMPOSER AND CONDUCTOR

Gustav Mahler bestrode the world of music at the end of the nineteenth century. 'My time will come', he remarked about his often misunderstood compositions. For Mahler the conductor, due recognition did come during his lifetime, but another half-century had to pass before a fully sympathetic appreciation of his creative achievement was possible – nine completed symphonies, conceived on a vast scale, orchestrated with unprecedented richness and refinement, and the series of songs and cycles that inspired many of these great symphonic canvases and impregnated them with sweeping lyricism as well as elements of folk, military and even street music. His large and permanent niche in today's concert repertory is surely owed, at least in part, to the congruity of his own expressive attitudes with the *Zeitgeist* of our modern world. 'As long as my experience can be summed up in words,' he said, 'I write no music about it; my need to express myself musically – symphonically – begins at the point where the dark feelings hold sway, at the door which leads into the "other world" – the world in which things are no longer separated by space and time.'

MAHLER'S YOUTH

Gustav Mahler was born on 7 July 1860 in Kalischt (Kaliště), Bohemia, a village about 60 miles south-east of Prague. That year the family moved to nearby Iglau (now Jihlava), a larger, German-speaking Moravian town, where Gustav went to school, took piano lessons and played his first public recital at the age of 10. Death was a regular visitor to his home – eight of his 13 younger siblings perished in childhood. Mahler also had to endure the unhappy marriage of his ill-tempered, womanizing father and his gentle, long-suffering, lame mother. The emotional residue of these experiences permeates the music he would later compose. His father, to his credit, acknowledged his son's talents when a local businessman encouraged him to take the 15-year-old Gustav to Vienna to audition for the Conservatory. There the youth won prizes for piano and composition and performed his first surviving work, a piano quintet, in July 1876. After leaving the Conservatory in 1878, Mahler supported himself by giving piano lessons while working at his first large-scale composition, *Das klagende Lied* ('The Plaintive Song'), a cantata on his own text. To its failure to win the prestigious Vienna Beethoven Prize in 1881 he later attributed his years of wandering in 'that hell', the theatre.

YEARS OF WANDERING

From a summer job in 1880 conducting operettas at the Upper Austrian spa of Bad Hall, Mahler began his steady climb up the musical ladder: in 1881 to Laibach (now Ljubljana); in 1883 to Olmütz (now Olomouc), where a company member observed that he 'was not liked, but they learned to fear him'; in 1883–85 he was in Kassel, where his precision and fire were praised but his unconventional interpretations criticized (an unhappy affair with a Kassel singer inspired his first masterpiece, the *Songs of a Wayfarer*); in 1885–86, at the German Theatre in Prague, he scored his first great successes conducting operas by Mozart and Wagner; in 1886–88 he was a junior conductor under Nikisch in Leipzig. There he was entrusted with the completion of **Weber**'s opera sketch *Die drei Pintos* ('The Three Pintos') by the composer's grandson, and through the Weber family he got to know poems of *Des Knaben Wunderhorn* ('The Youth's Magic Horn'), a powerful inspiration for his music. He was then recommended to the Budapest opera, where in January 1889 he was acclaimed for Wagner performances in Hungarian. The première of his First Symphony in November (a month after his beloved mother's death) was not well received, though some Budapest critics recognized his genius and originality.

(L) Gustav Mahler
Mahler photographed in New York in 1909, two years before his death.

(TR) Mahler the Conductor
Front page of a Vienna newspaper showing a caricature of Mahler conducting.

(BR) The Eighth Symphony
Poster for Mahler's Eighth Symphony, performed in Munich in 1910.

MAHLER THE CONDUCTOR

Notwithstanding his dismissal of conducting as a mere means to an end, Mahler put his heart and soul into his opera and concert activities. He loved the superb Court Opera house, and loved its great orchestra – the Vienna Philharmonic – for its responsiveness to his demands. The reviews of his Viennese début with *Lohengrin* in 1897 were in agreement about his unprecedented grasp and power: 'He noticed everything. He was in close and constant touch with the chorus, the orchestra and each individual; not one performer missed his smallest gesture.' Mahler concerned himself not only with the music, but also with every aspect of staging. His famous 1903 *Tristan* production, restoring traditional cuts, with partly symbolic sets by the artist Alfred Roller, has been called the birth of modernism in opera production. His exacting standards probably contributed to the tide of negative feelings that swelled up in Vienna, as elsewhere, against his tyrannical rule. 'What a storm I bring down on my head,' he once said, 'whenever I depart from normal routine and try out some idea of my own.'

MAHLER AND THE 'SECOND VIENNESE SCHOOL'

Mahler was already a musical father-figure to the next generation of Viennese composers in his lifetime – he supported **Schoenberg** and **Alexander Zemlinsky** (1871–1942), for example, even at the risk of jeopardizing his own position. Soon after his death, writes the musical scholar Constantin Floros, he became 'the spiritual leader, the artistic ideal for those few inspired musicians who recognized his stature….'. Schoenberg called him a martyr and a saint. For **Anton Webern** (1883–1945) and **Alban Berg** (1885–1935), he was the most influential figure apart from Schoenberg.

Instrumental Colour

One aspect of Mahler that made a particularly deep impression on these younger composers was his organic sense of instrumental colour. 'He writes down only what is absolutely necessary,' Schoenberg observed. 'His sound never comes from ornamental additions.... Among the most beautiful … are the delicate, fragrant ones [in which] … he brings unheard-of novelty.' Schoenberg included guitar and mandolin in his own *Serenade*, a direct expression of his esteem for the Seventh Symphony's scoring. Mahler's subtle changes of tone colour between different instruments or groups sharing musical material foreshadow Schoenberg's concept of *Klangfarbenmelodie* (tone-colour melody), so characteristic of his works and those of his disciples, especially Webern, who was not only a great admirer of Mahler, but also a great interpreter of the symphonies. Once, while rehearsing the Sixth, Webern made the orchestra hold a certain chord for what seemed an eternity, apologizing to the musicians: 'I simply must revel in this sonority for a little while.'

GUSTAV MAHLER: WORKS

- **Symphonies:** No. 1 in D (1888); No. 2 in c–E flat ('Resurrection') with solo soprano and contralto and mixed chorus (1894); No. 3 in d–D with solo contralto, boys' and women's choruses (1896); No. 4 in G–E with solo soprano (1900); No. 5 in c sharp–D (1902); No. 6 in a (1905), No. 7 in e–C (1905); No. 8 in E flat with 3 soprano, 2 contralto, tenor, baritone and bass soloists, boys' and mixed choruses (1906); No. 9 in D-D flat (1909); No. 10 in f sharp/F sharp (unfinished, 1910)
- **Cantatas and orchestral songs:** *Das klagende Lied* (1880); *Lieder eines fahrenden Gesellen* (1885); *Des Knaben Wunderhorn* (1892–98); Late Rückert and *Wunderhorn* settings (1899–1902); *Kindertotenlieder* (1904);, *Das Lied von der Erde* (1909)
- **Songs with piano:** 3 early Lieder (1880); 19 *Lieder und Gesänge* (1880–90)
- **Other works:** Piano Quartet (unfinished, ?1876–78); *Rübezahl* (opera, lost, ?1879–83); *Der Trompeter von Säkkingen* (incidental music, lost, 1884)

REACHING THE SUMMIT

By the time he resigned from Budapest in 1891, Mahler was already in negotiations with Hamburg, where critics had praised his performance of Tchaikovsky's *Eugene Onegin*, attended by the composer. The great conductor Bülow took him under his wing, grooming him as his successor. His reputation abroad was now growing rapidly too – in London in 1892 he conducted his first *Ring* – but his ambition was fixed on one goal, directorship of the Vienna Court Opera. Realizing it would be closed to him as a Jew, he converted to Catholicism and, following secret negotiations, was appointed in 1897.

Although he experienced phenomenal artistic success at the Court Opera, Mahler still regarded conducting as no more than a means to an end: 'Only when I experience do I "compose" – only when I compose do I experience.' Each summer from 1892 he devoted himself entirely to a routine of physical activity and composition, escaping from the gruelling pace of the opera-house to a series of idyllic Austrian mountain retreats. In 1901 he met Alma Schindler, the beautiful 22-year-old daughter of a well-known painter, and they married in March 1902. Alma was a talented musician, but Mahler forbade her to play the piano because it disturbed his composing, or to write music herself, because he abhorred the thought of a husband and wife in competition. It was to be a turbulent marriage.

Berg ▶ p. 286 Schoenberg ▶ p. 295 Weber ▶ p. 205 Webern ▶ p. 299 Zemlinsky ▶ p. 299

YEARS OF CRISIS

Their beloved elder daughter died at the age of five, leaving Mahler and Alma heartbroken and estranged. He was then diagnosed with a heart defect that forced him to give up the strenuous summer routine on which his sense of physical and psychological well-being had depended. As his international career burgeoned, Mahler was frequently absent from Vienna conducting his own works. Meanwhile, anti-semitic attacks against him in the Viennese press were increasing. By mutual agreement with the opera administration, he resigned the position and accepted an offer from the Metropolitan Opera. He made his New York début conducting *Tristan* on New Year's Day 1907. His popularity with his American public and critics was a match for Vienna, and he now had the world's greatest singers at his disposal. During his second season he also conducted concerts, including his own Second Symphony, at Carnegie Hall, but his relations with the Met's new Italian régime soured, especially after **Arturo Toscanini** (1867–1957) insisted on being allowed to make his own début with *Tristan*. Mahler protested and eventually prevailed, but he later left the Met to take over the New York Philharmonic.

Summering in the South Tyrol, Mahler completed his symphonic song-cycle *Das Lied von der Erde* ('The Song of the Earth'), sometimes called his farewell to life, in 1908, and his fateful Ninth Symphony, the last work he was to finish, the following year. In 1910 he prepared for the première in Munich of the monumental Eighth, which he dedicated to Alma even as their marriage, already under strain for over a year, was in shreds (driving him to visit Freud to rediscover his love for her). The performance, before an audience studded with Europe's intellectual elite, was perhaps the single greatest triumph of Mahler's life. He returned to New York for the last time in the autumn, still in good health, but in February 1911 he contracted a bacterial infection. Seriously ill when the couple returned to Europe in April, he was seen but not helped by specialists in Paris, then taken by train to Vienna where he died on 18 May.

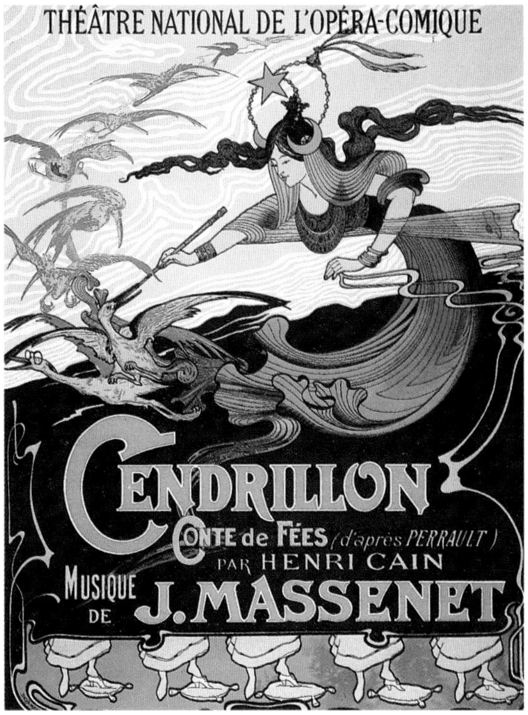

MAHLER'S VIENNA

'With its acutely felt tremors of social and political disintegration', *fin-de-siècle* Vienna was described (by historian Carl Schorske) as one of the most fertile breeding grounds of the century's culture. Although their sponsorship of music and the other arts may have originated in emulation of the aristocracy, by the end of the nineteenth century, Vienna's new *haute bourgeoisie* 'manifested more genuine enthusiasm for these arts than its counterparts in any other city in Europe'. When Mahler moved to Vienna to direct the Court Opera, artists, writers and musicians had supplanted politicians as the heroes of the upper-middle class. On the other hand, few cities treated the artists they later proclaimed cultural heroes so shabbily during their lifetime as did Vienna. Mahler suffered more than most from this duplicity. He was simultaneously lionized as the greatest of conductors, who had raised the Court Opera to new heights, and denounced by the anti-semites for being a derivative composer and for monopolizing the city's musical life. Yet the same Mahler who called himself 'thrice homeless: as a native of Bohemia in Austria, as an Austrian among Germans, and as a Jew throughout the whole world' also admitted, homesick in New York: 'I shall never be anything but a dyed-in-the-wool Viennese.'

Mascagni, Pietro

(Más-kán'-yē, Pe-ā'-trō) 1863–1945

ITALIAN OPERA COMPOSER

The son of a baker, Mascagni studied law before becoming a conductor and piano teacher. In 1890, while a conductor in Cerignola, he shot into the limelight with his prize-winning one-act opera *Cavalleria rusticana* which, at its legendary première at the Teatro Costanzi in Rome, received an unprecedented 60 curtain calls. Based on Giovanni Verga's story of love and jealousy in a Sicilian village, *Cavalleria* symbolized the new

verismo movement in Italian opera, characteristically lyrical yet also highly passionate, capable of portraying powerful complex emotions. The style continued in Mascagni's dozen or so less well-known operas including *Iris* (1898), *L'amico Fritz* (1905) and *Nerone* (1935), as well as *Pagliacci* by Leoncavallo, often given as a companion piece to *Cavalleria*, and the operas of Puccini.

Massenet, Jules

(Mas-nā', Jōōl) 1842–1912

FRENCH COMPOSER

Shortly after his first operatic success with *Le roi de Lahore* ('The King of Lahore', 1877) Massenet became Professor at the Paris Conservatoire; he was subsequently elected to the French Academy instead of his rival Saint-Saëns. Massenet's 28 operas include several enduring masterpieces: *Manon* (1884) remains one of the most popular French Romantic operas, while *Werther* (1892), after Goethe, arguably his finest work, is intensely dramatic. *Thaïs* (1894) displays a post-Wagnerian exoticism, described by D'Indy as 'semi-religious eroticism', illustrated in the seductive lyricism of its famous 'Méditation', often played as a violin encore. The gutsy *verismo* style of Bizet's *Carmen* infuses *La Navarraise* (1894, aptly set in Spain) and *Sapho* (1897) with expressive power, while the medievalism of his later operas (*Esclarmonde*, 1888 and *Grisélidis*, 1894) – for which he requested pre-Raphaelite sets) foreshadows Debussy's *Pelléas et Mélisande* (1902). *Don Quichotte* (1910), based on Cervantes, is an elegiac romance of appealing simplicity.

(NL) Esclarmonde
Massenet wrote Esclarmonde *for Sybil Sanderson, with whom he was infatuated.*
(FL) Cendrillon
Poster advertising Jules Massenet's opera based on the story of Cinderella.
(TFR) The Tales of Hoffman
Stage design for Act II of Offenbach's operatic masterpiece, Tales of Hoffman.

Musorgsky, Modest Petrovich

(Mōō-zôrk'-skē, Mōd-yest' Pyä-trō'-vich) 1839–81
RUSSIAN COMPOSER

Musorgsky was the most radical of the Russian composers known as 'The Five'. Born to a land-owning family, he joined the army in 1856, where he encountered Borodin, then a military doctor, and Cui, who introduced him to Balakirev, with whom he studied. In 1858 he resigned to pursue a musical career, but the Tsar's emancipation of the serfs in 1861 obliged him to contribute to the family's welfare and he joined the civil service, composing in his spare time. Often mixing with wild intellectuals, Musorgsky developed alcoholic tendencies and finally collapsed, shortly after a performance of his choral work *The Destruction of Sennacherib* (1867) conducted by his friend Rimsky-Korsakov.

RUSSIAN REALISM

Musorgsky injected a new realism into Russian music, fired by the strong belief that art should be true to life. Rejecting the techniques of Western Romanticism, he forged a daringly original style, raw and often dissonant, evocatively orchestrated as in the tone poem *St John's Night on the Bare Mountain* (1867). His outstanding vocal and operatic works employ a radical declamatory style based on everyday speech patterns, as in his masterpiece, the opera *Boris Godunov* (1868–73). Boris's noble soliloquies and the splendid choruses show a concern for the plight of the Russian masses. Another opera, *Khovanshchina* ('The Khovansky Affair', 1873), followed three masterly song cycles: *The Nursery* (1872), a brilliant depiction of childhood, *Sunless* (1874) and *Songs and Dances of Death* (1877), in which the vivid depictive piano parts recall those of his most famous piano work, *Pictures at an Exhibition* (1874, later orchestrated by Ravel among others).

Offenbach, Jacques

(Of'-fen-bäkh, Zhäk) 1819–80
FRENCH COMPOSER

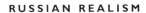

Offenbach's tuneful, witty and often outrageous satires on Greek mythology and the Second Empire enthralled the French public, including the Emperor Louis-Napoleon, and continue to cast their spell on audiences worldwide. After only one year at the Paris Conservatoire, he joined the Opéra-Comique orchestra, studying with Halévy, and toured as a virtuoso cellist. After conducting at the Théâtre Français, he launched his famous Bouffes-Parisien in 1855, scoring huge successes with some hundred operettas produced in collaboration with his chief librettist, Ludovic Halévy (nephew of the composer and librettist for Bizet's *Carmen*), and the singer/actress Hortense Schneider. In hits such as *Orphée aux enfers* ('Orpheus in the Underworld', 1858), with its daring 'Can-Can' in the final scene, *La belle Hélène* (1864), and *La vie parisienne* (1866), memorable tunes are interspersed with piquant musical parodies of great composers such as **Christoph Willibald von Gluck** (1714–87), **Meyerbeer** or **Rossini**. Offenbach's enduring operatic masterpiece is *Les Contes d'Hoffmann* ('The Tales of Hoffman', completed after his death by Guiraud, 1881), with its famous 'Barcarolle'.

Paderewski, Ignacy

(Pä-de-ref'-skē, Ig-nät'-si) 1860–1941
POLISH PIANIST AND COMPOSER

Paderewski achieved fame as a virtuoso pianist following studies in Vienna with Theodor Leschetizky (1830–1915), and a triumphal Paris début (1888). During his 50-year career he toured worldwide to immense acclaim. In 1909 he was appointed Director of the Warsaw Academy. A fervent patriot and among the highest-paid artists, he gave much financial support to Poland and in 1919 became its prime minister. In 1939, with the invasion by Germany and Russia, he was appointed President of the Polish government-in-exile in France. His most popular works, in a Romantic style influenced by Chopin and Liszt, include the Minuet in G, Piano Concerto in A minor, *Polish Fantasy* for piano and orchestra, Symphony in B minor and the opera *Manru* (1892–1901).

WOMEN AS POPULAR SONGWRITERS

The Victorian drawing-room ballad is a much-derided musical genre – perhaps partly due to the way in which it was so successfully and stylishly cultivated by women composers. In fact, in the mid nineteenth century, some male composers even used female pseudonyms, as, for example, 'Florence Fare', pen name of Alfred William Rawlings. Two of the most successful songwriters of this period were Virginia Gabriel (1825–77), whose songs have an appealing Italianate quality, and the immensely popular 'Claribel', pseudonym of Charlotte Alington Barnard (1830–69). A later generation of successful songwriters included the American composer Carrie Jacobs-Bond (1861–1946), who reluctantly resorted to singing and publishing her songs when she found herself financially destitute, the French composer 'Guy d'Hardelot', pseudonym of Helen Rhodes (1858–1936), and the British composer Amy Woodforde-Finden (1860–1919), whose best-selling *Four Indian Love Lyrics* (1902) appealed to the Edwardian obsession with the Orient.

British songwriters who produced more subtle and inventive songs included Maude Valerie White (1855–1937) and Liza Lehmann (1862–1918), both of whom left fascinating memoirs. At the peak of their careers, at the turn of the century, these two women were regarded as leading composers of British song, irrespective of gender. White's songs are characterized by an effective and expansive lyricism while Lehmann was responsible for popularizing the song cycle in Britain. Although her finest work, such as the powerful *In Memoriam* (Tennyson, 1899) for tenor and piano, is in this genre, she became best known for her lighter songs, such as 'There are Fairies at the Bottom of our Garden' (Rose Fylemen, 1917).

Gluck ▶ p. 158 Meyerbeer ▶ p. 198 Rossini ▶ p. 200 Toscanini ▶ p. 300

Parker, Horatio

1863–1919

AMERICAN COMPOSER

Parker studied in Boston with the European-trained George Chadwick and in Munich with Josef Rheinberger, and later taught in New York and Yale, where his students included **Charles Ives** (1874–1954) and **Roger Sessions** (1896–1985). As a virtuoso organist he held a prestigious post at Trinity Church, Boston, and founded and conducted the New Hampshire Symphony Orchestra and Choir. The first of his two operas, *Mona* (1910), won an award and was given its première at the Metropolitan Opera, New York in 1912. Alongside his organ concerti and chamber music he is best known for his choral music, including the *Hora Novissima* (1893), much admired by Elgar and frequently performed in England.

Parry, (Sir) Charles Hubert

1848–1918

ENGLISH COMPOSER

Parry's precocious musical talents earned him an Oxford music degree while still a schoolboy at Eton. From 1867 he studied with Sterndale Bennett and Macfarren at Oxford, where he became Professor of Music (1900–08); he then succeeded Sir George Grove as director of the Royal College of Music. Although he produced four symphonies and chamber music, Parry excelled in vocal genres: the opera *Guinevere* (1885–86), several oratorios including *Job* (1892), and numerous anthems and songs. His expansive, noble melodies and a certain English flavour are exemplified in his Milton setting *Blest Pair of Sirens* (1887) and the uniquely popular 'Jerusalem', a setting of Blake, still sung regularly at The Last Night of the Proms, the BBC Promenade Concerts held every summer at the Royal Albert Hall.

Puccini, Giacomo

(Pōot-chē'-nē, Jä'-kō'mō) 1858–1924

ITALIAN COMPOSER

Puccini wrote 12 operas, three of which rank among the most popular in the world: *La bohème*, *Tosca* and *Madama Butterfly*. The composer came from a long line of musicians. His great-great-grandfather, the first Giacomo Puccini (1712–81), was organist and choirmaster at the cathedral of S Martino in the Tuscan town of Lucca. His son Antonio (1747–1832) was also a composer of church music, while Antonio's son Domenico (1771–1815) wrote both serious and comic operas, as well as church music. Domenico's son Michele (1813–64) composed two operas and much religious music.

Michele had eight children, of whom Giacomo was the fifth. Although he wrote some church music in his youth, it was soon evident that he would become an opera composer. After the triumph of his third attempt, *Manon Lescaut* (1893), he was hailed as the long-awaited successor to Verdi. Although more than half his operas were written in the twentieth century, his style remained firmly anchored in the late Romantic tradition.

GIACOMO PUCCINI: WORKS

- **Operas:** *Le villi* (1884); *Edgar* (1889); *Manon Lescaut* (1894); *La bohème* (1895); *Tosca* (1900); *Madama Butterfly* (1904); *La fanciulla del West* (1910); *La rondine* (1916); *Il tabarro*, *Suor Angelica*, *Gianni Schicchi*, together as *Il trittico* (1918); *Turandot* (1926)
- **Church, choral and vocal music:** *Mass* (1880); cantatas; songs
- **Orchestral music:** 'Capriccio sinfonico' (1883)

STUDENT DAYS AND EARLY OPERAS

Puccini was born in Lucca on 22 December 1858. From the age of 10 he sang in the cathedral choir, and at 14 played the organ. He became interested in opera at an early age and when he was 18 he walked the 20 miles to Pisa, where Verdi's *Aida* was being performed. He studied first in Lucca then, with the aid of a scholarship, at the Milan Conservatory. Throughout his student days he was acutely short of money. In 1883 he entered the Sonzogno competition for a one-act opera, and though his entry, *Le villi* ('The Willis', 1884), did not win, money was raised to have it performed at the Teatro dal Verme in Milan.

The opera was a fair success, but the most important result of its production was a contract with Giulio Ricordi, the most influential music publisher in Italy. Ricordi paid Puccini a small monthly stipend and *Le villi*, expanded into two acts, was staged in Turin and at La Scala, Milan.

Meanwhile, in Lucca, Puccini gave music lessons to improve his income. One of his pupils was Elvira Gemignani, a married woman with whom he began to live openly, causing such a scandal that the couple moved to Milan. Puccini's second opera, *Edgar* (1889), had its première at La Scala, but was not a great success.

THE YEARS OF FAME

Puccini always had trouble finding suitable subjects. For his third opera he chose *The Story of the Chevalier des Grieux and of Manon Lescaut* by the Abbé Prévost. This eighteenth-century French novel had already been set by Massenet, whose highly successful *Manon* was produced in Paris in 1884. Puccini used different scenes for his opera and *Manon Lescaut*, first performed in Turin in February 1893, scored a triumph: Puccini took 30 curtain calls, becoming a celebrity overnight.

Puccini's next opera, *La bohème*, was adapted from *Scenes from Bohemian Life* by Henry

LIBRETTISTS

Like many other opera composers, Puccini had recurrent trouble with his librettists. Ferdinando Fontana, who wrote the texts for his first two operas, *Le villi* and *Edgar*, did not greatly inspire the composer, but he was well-connected and instrumental in getting them performed. For *Manon Lescaut*, his third opera, no less than five writers had a hand in the libretto. Two among them, Giuseppe Giacosa and Luigi Illica, were to collaborate again with him on his three most popular operas, *La bohème*, *Tosca* and *Madama Butterfly*.

Giacosa died in 1906, and Puccini was never to find such sympathetic librettists again. Carlo Zangarini was asked to write the libretto for *La fanciulla del West* ('The Girl of the Golden West'), partly because his mother was American. He worked too slowly for Puccini and Guelfo Civinini provided the third act. Giuseppe Adami, who made an Italian translation of the German text of *La rondine*, ended by providing a complete libretto. Adami also wrote the libretto for *Il tabarro*, the first opera of *Il trittico*. Giovacchino Forzano wrote the other two, *Suor Angelica* and *Gianni Schicchi*. For his final opera, *Turandot*, Puccini returned to Adami, who collaborated with Renato Simonov on the excellent libretto.

PUCCINI'S PERFORMERS

Puccini provided superb roles for his singers. Chevalier des Grieux, hero of *Manon Lescaut*, was sung by the young **Enrico Caruso** (18731921) in 1895, two years after the première. The great tenor became a famous Rodolfo in *La bohème* and Cavaradossi in *Tosca*, before creating Dick Johnson in *La fanciulla del West*. The title role of this opera, Minnie, was sung at the première by the Czech soprano Emmy Destinn, who had been London's first Butterfly at Covent Garden. Another famous Butterfly was the American soprano Geraldine Farrar, first to sing the role at the Metropolitan Opera, where she created the title-role of *Suor Angelica*.

Many baritones have found Scarpia, the sadistic Chief of Police in *Tosca*, a rewarding part, among them Giuseppe De Luca, who created Sharpless, the American Consul in *Madama Butterfly*, at La Scala and the title-role of *Gianni Schicchi* at the Metropolitan Opera. Tito Gobbi sang Scarpia to the Tosca of **Maria Callas** (1923–77), and was also an excellent Michele in *Il tabarro* and a superb Gianni Schicchi. The English soprano **Dame Eva Turner** (1892–1990), magnificent in the title-role of *Turandot*, and the Italian tenor Giovanni Martinelli, a very fine Calaf, sang these roles at Covent Garden in the Coronation Season of 1937. Liu, the slave girl, was sung by Licia Albanese, who had seven Puccini heroines in her repertory.

Murger. By now he and Elvira, still unable to live in Lucca, had moved to Torre del Lago, about 15 miles away, where he rented a house by the lake.

Inspired by his own impecunious days as a student, Puccini paints a vivid and convincing picture of everyday Parisian life in *La bohème*, first performed in Turin in 1896. The conductor was Toscanini. The opera, though not at first well received, soon began a triumphant progress round the world.

A SUCCESS AND A FIASCO

For some time Puccini had considered an opera based on *La Tosca*, a play by the French dramatist Victorien Sardou. It received its first performance in January 1900 at the Teatro Costanzi in Rome, chosen because the action takes place in that city. The opera was performed at La Scala in March and reached London in July the same year, earning a rapturous reception at Covent Garden.

While in London for the British première, Puccini saw an American play, *Madam Butterfly* by David Belasco. He understood little English, but the character of Butterfly appealed to him and he decided on Belasco's play for his next opera. *Madama Butterfly* had its première at La Scala in February 1904; it was a fiasco, and was withdrawn after one performance. Puccini made cuts and alterations, reshaping the opera from two acts to three. The revised version was performed at the Teatro Grande, Brescia, in May 1904. This time it was a tremendous success.

PREMIÈRES IN NEW YORK AND MONTE CARLO

In 1907, Puccini travelled to New York, where four of his operas were being performed at the Metropolitan Opera House. In search of a new subject, he saw three more plays by Belasco. One of these was *The Girl of the Golden West*, which he settled upon as his next opera. The first performance of *La fanciulla del West* took place at the Metropolitan in 1910.

In 1913, Puccini was asked to write an operetta for the Carl Theatre in Vienna. He accepted, but World War I broke out in 1914, with Italy and Austria on opposite sides. *La rondine* ('The Swallow'), now a full opera, was first performed in neutral Monte Carlo in 1917, and was not given in Vienna until 1920. During the war Puccini wrote a triple bill of one-act operas: *Il tabarro* ('The Cloak', 1916), *Suor Angelica* ('Sister Angelica', 1917) and *Gianni Schicchi* (1918). *Il trittico* ('The Triptych') was produced in December 1918 at the Metropolitan; the war had finished only a month before, and for the first time, the composer was unable to attend the première.

FINAL, UNFINISHED OPERA

Puccini considered several subjects for his next opera before he finally settled on *Turandot*, by the Venetian playwright Carlo Gozzi. He began composition in 1921. By March 1924 the opera was ready, leaving only the final duet between Turandot and Calaf to complete. By this time Puccini was seriously ill with throat cancer. He had an operation in Brussels, but died on 29 November 1924. His body was taken to Milan and in 1926 transferred to Torre del Lago.

The final duet of *Turandot* was orchestrated from the composer's sketches by Franco Alfano. The première took place at La Scala on 23 April 1926. The conductor, Toscanini, laid down his baton after the death of Liu, saying 'at this point in the opera, the composer died'.

Puccini had an unrivalled sense of the theatre, and in particular of how to draw an audience's sympathy for suffering – above all, a suffering young woman (Mimì in *La Bohème*, Butterfly, Liù in *Turandot*) – with his remarkable gift for conveying sentiment through lyrical melody and expressive harmony. He was at his most powerful in music that combined erotic, sensual feeling with tenderness and pathos: most of his chosen librettos give him opportunities for this. But cruelty and high spirits also have a place in his palette. The three operas he wrote around the turn of the century – *La Bohème* (1896), *Tosca* (1900) and *Madama Butterfly* (1904) – remain at the centre of the repertory of every opera house today.

(BL) A Composer of World Renown
After the success of Manon Lescaut, *Puccini was hailed as the long-awaited successor of Verdi.*
***(TL)* Madama Butterfly**
Madama Butterfly *ranks among the world's most popular and frequently performed operas.*
(NR) Maria Callas
Callas singing Tosca, *the role in which she made her debut in 1942.*
***(FR)* Turandot**
Turandot *remained unfinished at Puccini's death in 1924; it was premièred in 1926.*

Callas ▶ p. 303 Caruso ▶ p. 303 Ives ▶ p. 291 Sessions ▶ p. 297 Turner ▶ p. 303

Rachmaninov, Sergey Vasilyevich

(Rákh-ma'-nē-nof, Sâr'-gā Vá-sil-yā'-vēch) 1873–1943

RUSSIAN COMPOSER

Rachmaninov studied with Arensky and Taneyev in Moscow, graduating with the Great Gold Medal in 1892. The same year, he composed his famous Prelude in C sharp minor. In 1897, the première of his First Symphony had a hostile reception and he ceased composing for three years. However, he was able to complete his masterly Second Piano Concerto in 1901. By 1917 Rachmaninov had composed three piano concertos, two symphonies and several major piano works and songs. After the Revolution, he decided to move, first to Switzerland, then in 1935 to the US. There, alongside a legendary virtuoso concert career, he composed his Fourth Piano Concerto (1926), the dramatic *Rhapsody on a Theme by Paganini* (1934), the Third Symphony (1938) and *Symphonic Dances* (1940).

Though sometimes labelled 'conservative' for its Romanticism in a modern age, Rachmaninov's music has won enduring recognition on account of its expressive breadth and melodic appeal, coloured with a Russian nostalgia. His piano works, the 24 Preludes, *Etudes-Tableaux*, *Moments Musicaux* and concertos are influenced by the European Romantics Schumann, Chopin and Liszt, yet there is a noble individuality to the sweeping melodies, yearning 'Russian' harmony and exciting rhythms of his distinctive style.

Reger, Max

(Rā'-ger, Máks) 1873–1916

GERMAN COMPOSER

A student of Hugo Riemann (1849–1919), Reger bridged the divide between nineteenth-century Brahmsian academicism and Liszt's 'New German School', with music that combined Bachian counterpoint and Wagnerian chromaticism. Reger was among the most frequently performed composers at Schoenberg's 'Society for the Performance of New Music'. After army service, he worked in Munich (1901) then as a Professor at the Leipzig Conservatory (1907), where his pupils included Othmar Schoeck (1886–1957), the Swiss composer, and conductor George Szell (1897–1970). His notable works include the lyrical *Psalm 100* (1908–09), ingenious and elaborate orchestral variations on themes by Mozart and Hiller, and much chamber and organ music.

Rimsky-Korsakov, Nicolai

(Rim'-skē Kôr'-sà-kôf, Nï'-ku-lī) 1844–1908

RUSSIAN COMPOSER

Born to a land-owning family, Rimsky-Korsakov served in the Russian navy and composed the first 'Russian' symphony while on duty off Gravesend. He joined Balakirev's circle, 'The Five', in 1861 and following the success of *Sadko* (1867), a tone-poem about the sea, was appointed professor at the new St Petersburg Conservatory. In addition to his use of nationalist elements including folk themes, speech-inflected vocal writing, exotic harmonies and modes, he was a master of orchestration. His orchestral brilliance conjures up magical and fantastic tableaux, particularly in descriptive works including three symphonies, the *Capriccio Espagnol* op. 34 (1887), *Russian Easter Overture* (1888) and the suite *Sheherazade* (1888). His 15 operas on Russian subjects, including *The Snow Maiden* (1881), *Ivan the Terrible* (also called *The Maid of Pskov*, 1872–92), *Sadko* (1896), *The Legend of the Invisible City of Kitezh* (1906) and *The Golden Cockerel* (1909) contain much attractive music and are frequently performed. Rimsky-Korsakov revised and orchestrated many of his contemporaries' operas, including Dargomïzhsky's *The Stone Guest*, Borodin's *Prince Igor* and Musorgsky's *Boris Godunov* and *Khovanshchina*. The revisions were often questionable 'corrections' to the more radical originals, yet they served to ensure their wider reception.

Rubinstein, Anton

(Rōō'-bēn-stīn, An'-tōn) 1829–94

RUSSIAN PIANIST AND COMPOSER

Rubinstein's younger brother Nikolai (1835–81) founded the Moscow Conservatory. As a child prodigy Anton played to Liszt. His legendary virtuosity was acclaimed across Europe and the US, where he toured with Wieniawski in 1872. He espoused German Romanticism and thus, as founder-director of the St Petersburg Conservatory (1862), represented the 'conservative' opposition to the radical nationalism of 'The Five'. Rubinstein founded the Russian Music Society and also composed several 'Russian' works, such as the overture *Ivan the Terrible*, first given by Balakirev, among a large output of 20 operas, six symphonies and piano works, including the *Melody in F* (1852). His five piano concertos were very popular and strongly influenced Tchaikovsky's First Piano Concerto.

FINLANDIA

Finlandia still stirs audiences as it did when Sibelius unleashed this rousingly patriotic music at a Finnish historical pageant in 1899. Hollywood has used it to dramatic effect in two grandiose action films, *The Hunt for Red October* and *Die Hard 2*.

POPULAR MELODY *Sibelius*

Saint-Saëns, Camille

(San-San, Ka-mel') 1835–1921

FRENCH COMPOSER

Saint-Saëns was the founder of the National Society for French Music (1871) and influenced the development of the French style through his immense output and through his pupil Fauré. His music epitomizes French qualities of formal elegance, clarity of texture and craftsmanship, all allied to techniques of Romanticism. He was a prodigy, beginning his studies aged 13 at the Paris Conservatoire. Saint-Saëns introduced Liszt's symphonic poems to the French public and also composed the first French symphonic poems, of which *Danse macabre* (1884) is the most famous. Similarly, his five virtuoso piano concertos, the second of which is still frequently played, are the first French examples of their genre. Among his most significant works are the popular 'Organ' Symphony No. 3 (1886), which employs 'thematic metamorphosis', and *Samson and Delilah* (1877), the finest of his 13 operas. He also composed much chamber music including the entertaining *Carnival of the Animals* (1886), originally intended as a private joke, which has become one of the most universally enjoyed pieces of all time.

Sibelius, Jean

(Sē-bāl-yoos, Zhán) 1865–1957

FINNISH COMPOSER

When Jean (Johan) Sibelius, Finland's greatest composer, was born on 8 December 1865 at Hämeenlinna, his homeland had been ruled by

Russia since Napoleon snatched it from Sweden (which still dominated it culturally). As a child he composed and played the violin, but he was 14 before taking up the instrument seriously. He enrolled in 1886 at the Music Institute of Martin Wegelius, the pioneer of Finnish music education. His strongest impressions there came from a young teacher, the German-Italian composer-pianist **Ferruccio Busoni** (1866–1924), and in 1889 he went abroad to study in Germany and then Vienna. His sights were still set on a violin career, but a failed audition for the Vienna Philharmonic ended that dream.

THE FINNISH HERO

On his return in 1891 to a Finland seething under mounting Russian repression, Sibelius made his living from teaching. Then, the success of *Kullervo* in 1892 made him a hero at home virtually overnight and put his name on the musical map abroad. This ambitious and accomplished choral symphony, based on the *Kalevala*, Finland's national epic, revealed a new and original musical voice. It also proclaimed Sibelius's commitment to the Finnish-language movement (he mastered the tongue only in adulthood), consolidated by his marriage that year to a leading nationalist's daughter. During this decade he would focus on tone-poems ('Here I can move freely without feeling the weight of tradition') – including the Lemminkinen legends, also inspired by the *Kalevala* – and incidental music, including *Karelia* (1893; named for the Finns' old cultural heartland, now largely in Russia) and composed what would become his most popular work, the stirring *Finlandia*.

(BL) *Nicolai Rimsky-Korsakov*
The Russian composer at his home in St Petersburg.
(TL) Sheherazade
Costume design by León Bakst for Rimsky-Korsakov's suite Sheherazade.
(NR) *Sibelius at Ainola*
The Finnish composer with his wife and daughter, 1915.

JEAN SIBELIUS: WORKS

Symphonies: *Kullervo* (1892); Symphony No. 1 in e (1899); Symphony No. 2 in D (1902); Symphony No. 3 in C (1907); Symphony No. 4 in a (1911); Symphony No. 5 in E flat (1915, rev. 1916, 1919); Symphony No. 6 in d (Dorian mode, 1923); Symphony No. 7 in C (1924); Symphony No. 8 (1929, destroyed)
Tone poems: *The Wood Nymph* (1895, unpubd); *Spring Song* (1894); *Lemminkäinen Suite* (4 tone poems: 'Lemminkäinen and the Maidens of the Island', 1895, 'Lemminkäinen in Tuonela', 1895, 'The Swan of Tuonela', 1893, 'Lemminkäinen's Return', 1895); *Tiera* (1898); *Finlandia* (1900); *The Dryad* (1910); *Pohjola's Daughter* (1906); *Nightride and Sunrise* (1907); *Luonnotar* (with soprano, *c.* 1910); *The Bard* (1913); *The Oceanides* (1914); *Tapiola* (1926)
Incidental music: *Karelia* (1893, unpubd; Suite also 1893); *King Christian* (1898); *Kuolema* ('Death', 1903, unpubd; incl. 'Valse triste'); *Pelléas et Mélisande* (1905); *Belshazzar's Feast* (1906, unpubd; Suite, 1907); *Swanwhite Feast* (1908, unpubd; Suite, 1909); *Scaramouche* (1913); *Everyman Feast* (1916, unpubd); *The Tempest* (1925); and others
Violin Concerto (1903, rev. 1905); shorter orchestral works incl. *En saga* (1892); cantatas, male, female, mixed and children's choruses, orchestral songs, many songs with piano, chamber music incl. String Quartet *Voces intimae* (1909), piano pieces

THE PUBLIC FIGURE

This phase of his development culminated in 1899 with his first numbered symphony. Performances on the Helsinki Philharmonic's European tour the next year spread the composer's name (and drew attention to his nation's intensifying plight). But setbacks – including failure to be named professor of music in Helsinki in 1897 – had drained his resources. He would be plagued by debt well into the new century. The first of several gifts from a Finnish music-lover allowed him to travel to Italy, where he began the Second Symphony in 1901, completing it back in Helsinki and conducting its triumphant première by the Helsinki Symphony Orchestra on 8 March 1902. Further performances on the Continent and in England, and extensive travel by Sibelius in the years before the outbreak of World War I, widened and deepened his fame.

THE PRIVATE FIGURE

Meanwhile, the increasingly private nature of his music was already manifested in the neo-classical Third Symphony, completed in 1907. He had begun it in 1904, the year of his retreat to a country home at nearby Järvenpää, where he would live for the rest of his life. Nature now stimulated his composition as Finnish culture and politics had done earlier. He reached an extreme of austerity and 'modernism' in the Fourth Symphony, whose brooding darkness may have reflected a diagnosis and operation for throat cancer (Sibelius was a heavy cigar-smoker). Its powerful formal concentration remained a feature of all his subsequent music: tone-poems like *Luonnotar* (with soprano) and *The Bard*, the heroic Fifth Symphony, the poetic Sixth, and two consummately integrated late works, the single-movement Seventh Symphony and the tone-poem *Tapiola* (1926), again based on the Kalevala, which stunningly evokes the primeval northern forests.

THE RECLUSE

After that, Sibelius grew silent. He worked on an Eighth Symphony in the late 1920s, possibly even completing it, but the work disappeared, or he destroyed it. Though venerated worldwide, he did not leave Finland during the 1930s, and his physical isolation was paralleled by an artistic isolation – from the 'progressive' tendencies of contemporaries such as Schoenberg, Stravinsky and **Bartók**. He was showered with tributes on his 90th birthday, but by his death a critical 'reaction against his dominant position in the Anglo-Saxon world' (Robert Layton) had set in. Since the 1970s, however, the scope of his achievement has once again been duly recognized: his search, in the words of the Sibelius expert James Heposki, 'to uncover a deeply intuitive and nature-mystical relationship to sound itself through a process of meditative inwardness and ruthless self-criticism.

A SIGNIFICANT ASPECT OF THEORY

Sibelius brought his own version of 'Classicism' to the modern symphony. The eighteenth-century form of Haydn and Mozart had been crystallized by Beethoven into a model for the nineteenth, and the Romantics essentially poured their ever bigger and bolder wine into the classical bottle. To the composer of monumental, all-encompassing symphonic worlds, Mahler, his opposite pole in the genre's evolutionary bifurcation, Sibelius remarked that for him the essence of a symphony was 'severity of style and the profound logic that created an inner connection among all the motifs'. Beginning with his Third, he moved away from lyrical expansiveness towards an increasing economy of gesture, a formal condensation that actually intensified the expressive content of his music. Each succeeding symphony marks a new structural experiment until, in the single-movement Seventh, an epic distilled into 20 minutes, the integration and compactness reach an apogee.

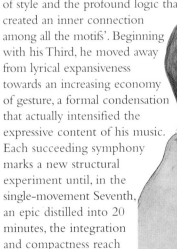

Bartók ▶ p. 285 Busoni ▶ p. 288

Smetana, Bedřich

(Smā'-tā-nā, Be'-der-zhikh) 1824–84

Smetana was the founding father of the Czech national musical revival. Born to middle-class parents on 2 March 1824, he showed considerable talent as a pianist by the time he was six. He went to study in Prague in 1839, subsequently making a living as a teacher and player. In 1848 he opened a music school, but it did not prosper. With nationalistic fervour, he helped man the barricades in the revolution of 1848 but, depressed by the lack of political emancipation and a stagnant musical scene in Prague during the next five years, he left for Göteborg in Sweden in 1856, where he had considerable success as a conductor and performer.

THE PRAGUE PROVISIONAL THEATRE

Inspired by the prospect of a theatre for the performance of opera in Czech (Prague Provisional Theatre, opened 1862), Smetana returned to Prague in 1861. Although he failed to become the theatre's first conductor, and experienced considerable antagonism from Prague's artistic establishment, he spent the next few years at work on two operas for its stage. In 1866 his first opera, *The Brandenburgers in Bohemia*, was a great success, winning first prize in a competition for new operas for the theatre; following this, he became the Provisional Theatre's chief conductor. This work was followed by *The Bartered Bride* and six more operas.

DEAFNESS

In 1874, as a result of syphilis, Smetana became rapidly and completely deaf. Forced to retire from his post as conductor he experienced hardship but continued to compose, including the cycle of symphonic poems *Má vlast* ('My Country'). Towards the end of his life composition became difficult, though Smetana had the consolation of seeing his festival opera, *Libuše*, performed at the opening of the National Theatre in 1881. He died in an asylum in Prague on 23 April 1884.

Smyth, (Dame) Ethel

1858–1944

BRITISH COMPOSER

A determined and talented composer, Smyth studied in Germany and returned to England in the 1890s to well-received performances of her orchestral works and her dynamic Mass in D (1891). Although she wrote compelling songs and chamber music, her main musical attention was devoted to six operas, the most successful of which was *The Wreckers* (1902–04), a powerful tragedy in which two lovers defy their close-knit Cornish community. In this work Smyth's musical language moved away from a rich Germanic Romanticism towards the sparer clarity of her later works, such as her inventive Double Concerto for violin and horn (1926).

BEDŘICH SMETANA: WORKS

Operas: *The Brandenburgers in Bohemia* (1863); *The Bartered Bride* (1866, rev. 1870); *Dalibor* (1868); *Libuše* (1872); *The Two Widows* (1874); *The Kiss* (1876); *The Secret* (1878); *The Devil's Wall* (1882)
Symphony, symphonic poems: *Triumph Symphony* (1854); *Richard III* (1858); *Wallenstein's Camp* (1859); *Haakon Jarl* (1861); *Má vlast* comprising 'Vyšehrad', 'Vltava', 'Šárka', 'From Bohemia's Woods and Fields', 'Tábor', 'Blaník' (1872–79); *Prague Carnival* (1883)
Choruses: *Czech Song* (1860), *Song of the Sea* (1877); *Our Song* (1883)
Chamber works: Piano Trio in G (1855); String Quartet No. 1 in E, *From My Life* (1876); String Quartet No. 2 in D (1883)
Piano: *Dreams* (1875); *Czech Dances* I and II (1877, 1879)
Choruses, chamber music, piano music

Stanford, (Sir) Charles Villiers

1852–1924

BRITISH COMPOSER

Born in Dublin where he studied organ, Stanford moved to London at the age of 10 to study piano with Ernst Pauer. At Cambridge he was organist of Trinity College (1873–92) and founder-conductor of the Cambridge University Musical Society, where he gave the premières of many of Brahms's works. He also studied in Leipzig and Berlin. From the 1880s onwards he taught at the RCM, where his students included **Vaughan Williams**, and from 1888 was a professor at Cambridge. In addition to his still-popular Anglican liturgical music and part-songs, several of his 10 operas, including *The Canterbury Pilgrims* (1884), achieved success. Stanford frequently drew on Irish folk music, an interest reflected in many orchestral works including the 'Irish' Symphony (1887) and in his folksong editions.

BLUE DANUBE

This most well-known of waltz tunes was composed in the 1870s by Johann Strauss the Younger. It is regularly performed at the New Year's Day Concert held each year in the elegant hall of the Musikverein in Vienna. Its lilting rhythm epitomizes the Viennese style.

POPULAR MELODY *J. Strauss*

Strauss, Richard

(Shtrous, Rē-khart) 1864–1949

GERMAN COMPOSER

During an amazingly productive career, Strauss wrote 15 operas, five ballets, several orchestral masterpieces, well over 200 songs and many other works. As a conductor he contributed in countless practical ways to the musical life of Europe and the US in the flourishing period from the last two decades of the nineteenth century to the start of the 1930s. His roots were in the great German Romantic tradition and to the end – despite increasing criticism – he refused to abandon them. His apparent indifference to technical advances in music, however, has to be measured

SMETANA'S OPERAS

Smetana's operas provided the backbone for the development of a native Czech repertory. The success of the 'historical' opera, *The Brandenburgers in Bohemia*, was crucial for his career and the health of Czech opera at an early stage, but *The Bartered Bride*, with its national dances and use of popular elements, set the agenda for Czech comic opera for the next 40 years and influenced numerous composers, including Dvořák. The rural setting and pungent characterization of Sabina's libretto created a vogue for the depiction of comic events in the Bohemian countryside, which was only supplanted by the realism favoured by **Janáček** in his opera *Jenůfa* (1904). It is interesting that in an opera which seems to epitomize nationalism, the word setting is often very awkward. Like many of his contemporaries, Smetana was primarily a German-speaker and learned Czech only as the national revival gained impetus; with the accent on the first syllable, Czech proved a problematic language for many native composers brought up with fundamentally German musical precepts.

THE SOPRANO VOICE

Strauss's career as a composer of vocal music lasted well over 70 years. He began writing songs when he was only eight and a sketch for a song was said to be on his desk when he died. Many of his songs were written after his marriage in 1894 to Pauline de Ahna, a general's daughter and an accomplished singer. She was the inspiration for some of the best of them, including the marvellous group of four in op. 27 which Strauss gave to her as a wedding present.

Strauss continued his love affair with the female voice in his operas. Aware that women's voices have an especially powerful impact on audiences, he often devoted the most memorable moments in his operas to them. The concluding trio of *Der Rosenkavalier* (1909–10), in which three sopranos (or two sopranos and a mezzo) voices soar above the orchestra with ecstatically entwined melodies, is perhaps the most inspired. Fittingly, Strauss concluded his operatic output with the monologue of the Countess at the end of *Capriccio* (1940–41), a gorgeous outpouring of meditative song about the relative value of words and music, that sums up a lifetime's experience of writing for voices.

The *Four Last Songs* (1946–48) are probably Strauss's most enduring monument to the soprano voice. Written in his last years, and beautifully orchestrated, they are vivid proof of his genius, undimmed to the end, for marrying instrumental sound and song. Strauss orchestrated many of the songs, well over 200, that he composed – a testimony to his lifelong ambition to bring the spirit of his orchestral writing into line with the power of the human voice.

against his astounding feats of orchestration and harmonic invention. His political opportunism, too, came to an abrupt end in 1935 when he was asked to resign his official posts after refusing to break off contact with his Jewish librettist Stefan Zweig. At the end of his life in the immediate aftermath of World War II, when musical Modernism began to pass through its most hermetic phase, he continued to write lavish and exquisitely refined music that expressed a heroic ideal to which he thought the modern age should aspire.

EARLY YEARS

Strauss was born in Munich on 11 June 1864. His father, Franz Strauss, was one of Germany's leading horn players and his mother, Franz's second wife Josephine Pschorr, belonged to a family of brewers. Josephine's wealth ensured a sunny childhood for Richard and also gave her husband the independence to do and to say what he liked, including expressing a negative opinion of Wagner.

Strauss began composing when he was six. One of his first compositions was a polka, written for his sister, notated and orchestrated by his father. Like Mozart's father, Franz Strauss was an all-round musician who taught his son everything he could. Richard's early works include songs, orchestral marches, a String Quartet in A (1880), a Sonata in B minor for piano (1881) and two symphonies, all influenced by classical models and frequently by later composers such as Mendelssohn and Brahms.

(NL) **The Bartered Bride**
The Bartered Bride *was a celebration of Czech national dances and popular themes.*
(TR) Poster Advertisement
Salome *was less well received by Strauss's critics than his previous works.*
(BR) **Salome *in Performance***
New York production of Strauss's opera.

RICHARD STRAUSS: WORKS

- **Operas:** *Guntram* (1887–93); *Feuersnot* (1900–01); *Salome* (1904–05); *Elektra* (1906–08); *Der Rosenkavalier* (1909–10); *Ariadne auf Naxos* (1911–12); *Die Frau ohne Schatten* (1914–17); *Intermezzo* (1917–23); *Die ägyptische Helena* (1923–27); *Arabella* (1930–32); *Die schweigsame Frau* (1933–34); *Friedenstag* ('Peace Day', 1935–36); *Daphne* (1936–37); *Die Liebe der Danae* (1938–40); *Capriccio* (1940–41)
- **Orchestral works:** *Macbeth* (1887–88); *Don Juan* (1888); *Tod und Verklärung* (1888–89); *Till Eulenspiegels lustige Streiche* (1894); *Also sprach Zarathustra* (1895–96); *Don Quixote* (1896–97); *Ein Heldenleben* (1897–98); *Symphonia domestica* (1902–03); *Eine Alpensinfonie* (1911–15); *Metamorphosen* (1944–45)
- **Songs:** over 200, including 4 Lieder, op. 27: 'Ruhe, meine Seele!', 'Cäcilie', 'Heimliche Aufforderung', 'Morgen!' (1894), and Four Last Songs (1946–48)
- Ballets, concertos, chamber music, piano music, melodramas, choral works

TOWARDS MATURITY

Strauss's early Piano Quartet in C minor (1884) is influenced by Brahms. But it is also his first work to demonstrate the paradoxical mixture of skilful economy and provocative lavishness that became the hallmark of his later style. It was first performed in Meiningen where, at the age of only 21, he had been appointed assistant to Bülow, the greatest conductor of the time. Also in Meiningen, Strauss met Alexander Ritter, a violinist in Bülow's orchestra, to whom he later gave the complete credit for putting him on the right road as a composer. Discussing ideas and music with his new friend was 'like a whirlwind', which converted him for life to the philosophy of Schopenhauer and the composers his father hated most: Berlioz, Liszt and Wagner.

THE HEIGHT OF FAME

After his conversion to the latest ideas in philosophy and music, Strauss wrote a series of tone poems for large orchestra based on well-known literary models and strongly influenced by Berlioz and Liszt. The first, *Macbeth*, was dedicated to his friend Ritter, who continued to support his advocacy of the New German School. Indeed, the Weimar première in 1889 of the second, *Don Juan*, was such a sensation that it established Strauss practically overnight as the most exciting figure in German music since Wagner. A group of brilliant tone-poems followed, including *Till Eulenspiegel* (1894–95), *Also sprach Zarathustra* ('Thus Spake Zarathustra') after Nietzsche and *Don Quixote* after Cervantes, which made Strauss world-famous by the time he was only 34. Moreover, his appointment to the prestigious post of Royal Prussian Court Conductor in Berlin in 1898 further underscored his status as a member of an illustrious line of musicians going back to Haydn and Mozart.

MOON-STRUCK DECADENCE

Initially, operatic success eluded Strauss. His first opera, *Guntram*, was a failure. To distance himself from Wagner, his new-found spiritual father, became as inevitable as it had been to do so from his real father. There are still traces of Wagner in *Salome*, his third opera, based on Oscar Wilde's French Orientalist drama. But compared with Wagner's noble dramatic ideals, its moon-struck decadence could hardly be more different. The dead lips on the severed head of Jokanaan (John the Baptist), the breathless trills imitated by Stravinsky in *The Rite of Spring* (1913), and the deranged counterpoint of Strauss's score caused a sensation. After its première in Dresden in 1905, the opera was condemned by many as allegedly obscene and blasphemous. For others it was already the high point of Strauss's career.

Janácek ▶ p. 291 Vaughan Williams ▶ p. 298

DECLINING REPUTATION

Strauss's next work, *Elektra*, delved still further into the psychopathology of human nature and consolidated his reputation as the foremost avant-garde composer of his day. But it also marked a turn of creative events in his life that will always divide opinion. With the librettist of *Elektra*, Hugo von Hofmannsthal (1874–1929), Strauss embarked on a series of operas on more beguiling themes. Their second, and possibly greatest, success was *Der Rosenkavalier* ('The Knight of the Rose'), with its extravagant Rococo world of the silver rose, the mature married princess and her young lover. Other notable works followed, including *Ariadne auf Naxos* ('Ariadne on Naxos'), *Die Frau ohne Schatten* ('The Woman without a Shadow') and *Arabella*.

But for his critics, Strauss had gone 'soft'. The jagged dissonances of *Salome* and *Elektra* were no longer in evidence, and in their place was an almost Mozartian elegance, both melancholic and luxurious. Particularly in the brittle cultural climate of Germany's Weimar Republic after World War I, this elegiac opulence found few admirers. Once a radical modernist, Strauss was now perceived in many quarters to be deeply reactionary. He had become in the last 25 years of his life, as he said himself, a modern composer who was 'out of season'.

LAST YEARS

Strauss once humorously described *Salome* as a scherzo with a fatal conclusion. Similarly, his life can be seen as rapidly successful, lively and vastly inventive, yet at the very end also suddenly clouded by catastrophe. His disillusionment with the future of German music was confirmed in the early months of 1945, when the opera houses of Dresden, Munich and Vienna, where many memorable performances of his works had taken place, were destroyed during World War II. This probably accounts for the sense of tragedy in the *Metamorphosen* for 23 solo strings which appears with comparable intensity in none of his previous music. It is undoubtedly one of his greatest works, matched only in the final years of his life by the equally remarkable *Vier letzte Lieder* ('Four Last Songs'). The sense of rich fulfilment in these late masterpieces, coloured at the same time by a deep melancholy, is unforgettable.

Suk, Josef

(Sook, Yō'-sef) 1874–1935

CZECH VIOLINIST AND COMPOSER

Suk was second violinist with the Czech String Quartet from 1892 to 1922, then became a professor at the Prague Academy where, in 1892, he had been a favourite student of Dvořák. He later married Dvořák's daughter, Otilie, and his love for her inspired many works, such as the *Fantasy* for violin and orchestra. Suk's grief at the loss of both Dvořák and Otilie in 1904–05 was expressed in his best-known work, the *Asrael Symphony* (1906). Otilie is also the subject of the evocative piano suite *About Mother*, part of a substantial piano output. Though his early influence was Dvořák, his later atonality anticipates the Czech modernism of his pupil Martinů.

Sullivan, (Sir) Arthur

1842–1900

ENGLISH COMPOSER

Sullivan was a Chapel Royal chorister, the first-ever Mendelssohn scholar and a student of Sterndale Bennett. He was already a composer of distinction when, in 1867, he collaborated with the playwright W. S. Gilbert (1836–1911) in *Cox and Box* (1866). Their *Trial by Jury* (1875) set the seal on a historic partnership that spawned a string of gems culminating with *The Gondoliers* (1889). Produced by the impresario Richard D'Oyly Carte at the Savoy theatre, Gilbert and Sullivan's 'Savoy operas' swept through audiences like a whirlwind, rivalling Offenbach in Paris and Johann Strauss in Vienna. *The Pirates of Penzance* (1879), *Patience* (1881), *Iolanthe* (1882), *The Mikado* (1885) and many others ran for extended seasons on both sides of the Atlantic, and still retain their immense appeal. Gilbert's witty satires on contemporary English culture were matched in Sullivan's piquant parodies of Italian opera and ***bel canto***, Handelian choruses and attractive melodies that were instant hits (his famous ballad 'The Lost Chord' sold some 10,000 copies within a few days). Sullivan's finely crafted serious output includes the oratorios *The Prodigal Son* (1869) and *The Light of the World* (1873), the opera *Ivanhoe* (1890), symphonies, stage music and songs.

Suppé, Franz von

(Zōō-pā', Frànts fun) 1819–95

AUSTRIAN COMPOSER

Suppé's full name was Francesco Ezechiele Ermenegildo Cavaliere Suppé-Demelli. He came from Dalmatia, but received his musical education with Ignaz Xaver Seyfried (a pupil of Haydn) in

TRIAL BY JURY

Trial by Jury, which ran for 131 performances at the Royalty Theatre, Soho, in 1875 exemplifies many of the essential ingredients that made Gilbert and Sullivan's Savoy Operas so successful. Its witty libretto about a breach-of-promise trial was set to a sparkling score which abounds with familiar choruses.

POPULAR MELODY *Sullivan*

Vienna, in whose famous theatres (an der Wien, Carl and Leopoldstadt) he conducted operetta. He composed over 150 operettas, including *Boccaccio* (1879), highly popular in their day and rivals to those of Offenbach. Despite their charm, Suppé's achievement was eclipsed by that of Johann Strauss the Younger and only a small portion of his music survives, notably the overtures *Poet and Peasant* (1846) and *Light Cavalry* (1866).

Svendsen, Johann Sverin

(Svent'sen, Yō'-hán Se'-ve-rin) 1840–1911

NORWEGIAN COMPOSER

Svendsen followed his father's career as a bandmaster, but in his early twenties went to study in Leipzig under Ferdinand David and Reinecke. He moved to Paris as a theatre violinist, but returned in 1870 to Leipzig and thence to the US, where he married. He returned to Norway to conduct at the Christiania (Oslo) Music Association in the 1870s and 80s, and later went to Denmark as conductor of the Copenhagen Royal Orchestra and Theatre. Apart from his popular *Romance* (1881) for violin and orchestra, his best-known works include four *Norwegian Rhapsodies* and the folk-inspired *Carnival of Norwegian Artists*, as well as symphonies, chamber music and songs.

bel canto ▶ p. 356

Taneyev, Sergey Ivanovich

(Tā-nā'-yof, Sâr'-gā Ē-vā-nō'-vich) 1856–1915

RUSSIAN COMPOSER

Taneyev studied in Moscow with Nicolai Rubinstein and Tchaikovsky, a lifelong friend. He gave the Moscow premières of all Tchaikovsky's piano concertos and in 1878 succeeded him at the Conservatory, becoming Director, 1885–89. His music was, like Tchaikovsky's, cosmopolitan, especially skilful in his use of Bachian counterpoint (about which he wrote a book) applied to Russian folk-like themes. He excelled in large-scale works, the opera *Oresteia* (1894), the masterly Symphony No. 4 in C minor (1898), dedicated to Glazunov, and much chamber music. An influential teacher, he included among his pupils **Alexander Scriabin** (1872–1915), Rachmaninov, Sergey Lyapunov (1859–1924) and Glière.

Thomas, Ambroise

(Tō-màs', Âm-brwàz') 1811–96

FRENCH COMPOSER

Thomas studied with Le Sueur at the Paris Conservatoire, where he became Director in 1871. After winning the 1832 Prix de Rome, he composed the first of his 20 operas, *La double*

échelle ('The Double Ladder', 1837). His first successes, *Le Caïd* ('The Cadi', 1849) and *Songe d'une nuit d'été* ('A Midsummer Night's Dream', 1850), show the influence of Gounod and Rossini. Yet *Mignon* (1866), based on Goethe's novel, introduced into French opera a radical new dramatic intensity, with expansive melodies and colourful orchestration to convey the heroine's passions and jealousies. *Mignon* was an immediate hit; at its thousandth performance (1894) Thomas was awarded the Légion d'Honneur. While *Hamlet* (1868), with a contrived happy ending, was a success, his final opera, *Françoise de Rimini* (1882), was not.

Wieniawski, Henri

(Vēn-yov'-skē, Hen'-ri) 1835–80

POLISH COMPOSER

Wieniawski was a child prodigy; after studies with Massart at the Paris Conservatoire, he was the youngest at 11 years old to graduate with the Gold Medal. He was also influenced by the Belgian School of Charles-Auguste de Bériot and Henri Vieuxtemps, whom he succeeded as professor at the Brussels Conservatory, following a post at the St Petersburg Conservatory (1860–72). During his short life, Wieniawski gave hundreds of concerts across Europe and America with his brother Josef and with Anton Rubinstein. Renowned for his Bohemian lifestyle, he was also a notable composer. His best-known works include the Second Violin Concerto, a stirring *Légende* for violin and orchestra (1860), dedicated to his bride Isabella, 'Russian' pieces such as the *Souvenir de Moscou* and the sparkling, virtuoso *Polonaise* (1853), still a favourite encore.

Wolf, Hugo

(Vulf, Hoō'-gō) 1860–1903

GERMAN COMPOSER

A fervent Wagnerian, Wolf worked in Vienna as a music critic. As a composer he was master of the miniature: his songs are mini-dramas which encapsulate Wagnerian expression within a lyrical, intimate form, the subtle vocal melodies matched by an equally important, symphonic piano part. The first collections, settings of poems by Mörike (1889) and Goethe (1890), display an almost erotic chromatic idiom, contrasting with the more lucid lyricism and irony of the *Spanish* (1891) and *Italian Songbooks* (1892, 1896), based on translations by Paul Heyse of sacred and folk poetry; a more intimate passion colours the later, austere *Michelangelo Sonnets* (1897). His immensely wide expressive range reflects his nervous intensity. This may be related to the syphilis that led him to insanity: Wolf spent his final years in a mental asylum. Apart from a striking String Quartet (1878–84, his first work) and a few symphonic poems, his larger works, such as the failed comic opera *Der Corregidor* ('The Magistrate', 1896), were less successful than his masterly Lieder.

***(BL)* The Pirates of Penzance *and* The Mikado**
A modern performance of The Pirates of Penzance, *one of Gilbert and Sullivan's most popular operettas (NL) and a cover of an early twentieth-century score of* The Mikado *(FL).*

(FR) Hugo Wolf
Best known for his Lieder compositions, Wolf was a dedicated follower of the Wagnerian tradition.

***(NR)* Promenade Quadrille**
Poster for Johann Strauss's promenade concert in London's Covent Garden.

THE STRAUSS FAMILY

The four most prominent members of Austria's leading musical family were Johann Strauss the Elder (1804–49) and his three sons, Johann Strauss the Younger (1825–99), Josef Strauss (1827–70) and Eduard Strauss (1835–1916). Johann the Elder came from humble origins. By his twenties he had already established himself and his orchestra as – in the words of the young Wagner – 'the magic fiddler' and 'the genius of Vienna's musical spirit'. He was a pioneer in the evolution of the Viennese waltz – some of his waltz collections are still played – and his *Radetzky March* (1848) quickly became a symbol of Habsburg military strength.

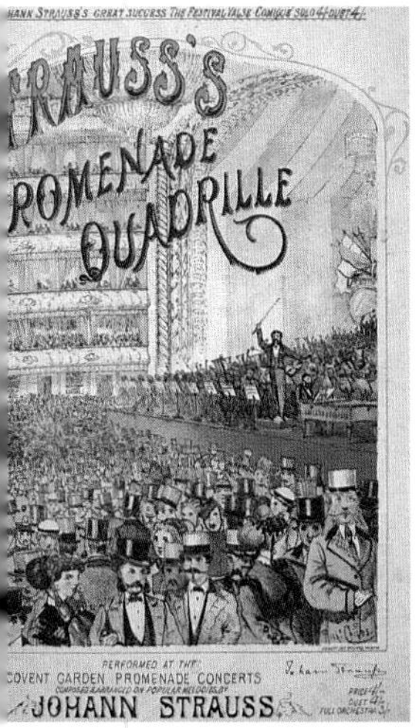

Johann the Younger

He was outshone, however, by his son, Johann the Younger, also a composer, conductor and violinist like his father, whose waltzes, polkas and quadrilles swept nineteenth-century imperial Vienna almost literally off its feet with their vivacity and elegance. Johann the Younger wrote some of Vienna's most famous waltzes, including the *Blue Danube* and *Wine, Women and Song*, both greatly admired by Brahms. He also had considerable success as a composer of operettas. The light sentimental irony of *Die Fledermaus* imitates Offenbach's Parisian operettas, though its charm is wholly Viennese. *The Gypsy Baron* (1885), however, is not at all like Offenbach, and its more ambitious scope greatly influenced later composers like **Franz Lehár** (1870–1948). Johann the Younger's two brothers, Josef and Eduard, were less eminent, but made their own highly individual contributions to the creation and interpretation of Viennese dance music.

Lehár ▶ p. 292 Scriabin ▶ p. 296

The Late Romantic
STYLES AND FORMS

That music has a double history – a social and a stylistic one – is amply proven by its development in the second half of the nineteenth century. Its progress was marked, though not entirely determined, by the revolutions that swept Europe in 1848. There were perceptible changes of emphasis, not only in concert and operatic life from the salon to the public recital, and from loosely planned operas on commission to rigorously worked-out masterpieces in which the composer did exactly what he or she wanted, but also in styles and forms that make them far less straightforward to define than in previous epochs. At mid-century, new creative directions in music multiplied and the idea of the 'new', already a watchword among artists such as Robert Schumann who saw themselves at the forefront of progress, was aggressively promoted. In February 1848, when Louis-Philippe was overthrown in France, Liszt left behind his career as a world-famous piano virtuoso and eventually settled in Weimar where, among other things, he invented a new kind of orchestral work he called the symphonic poem. Soon after the Paris uprising and the revolutions in Vienna and Berlin, Wagner began to plan an epoch-making work that eventually became the *Ring* and changed the nature of opera for ever. Even Schumann, a shy and outwardly conservative man, struck out on new paths which, often to the puzzlement of his admirers, lent a quite different tone to his late works.

Sound Worlds

Broadly speaking, the new musical aesthetic that emerged after 1848 placed a much stronger emphasis on the individuality of each work, its unique 'sound world'. The idea of music belonging to a genre in which forms and styles traditionally differed from one work to another, was fading fast. Not the least significant feature of **Verdi**'s three great operas *Rigoletto*, *Il trovatore* and *La traviata*, which marked his emergence in the early 1850s from his 'years in the galleys' (as Verdi himself put it) with a new operatic realism and intensity of expression, was the fact that they were so different from one another. Each opera had its own highly individual vocal, instrumental and dramatic style. It is far from a coincidence, too, that in exactly the same period, Wagner publicly announced that he was going 'to write no more operas', by which he meant that the new works for the stage he was planning to compose were finally to be cut loose from opera's traditional moorings. Liszt's invention of the new 'genre' of the symphonic poem had the same ambition: each work turned out to have not just its own extramusical programme, but also its own form, thematic character, instrumentation and time-scale.

Serious and Popular Music

The reaction against this pronounced rejection of traditional style and form was twofold. First, the new generation of composers that began to emerge after mid-century, including **Brahms**, took the more conservative view that chamber music and the symphony were not as moribund as the New German School claimed they were. Secondly, the 'light' music written in vastly increasing quantities for the ballroom and the popular theatre relied for its effectiveness in part on a deliberately anti-progressive feature: an exaggerated sense of 'belonging' to a specific style and form. The elegant and highly successful waltzes

THE NEW GERMAN SCHOOL

In 1859, at a conference of musicians in Leipzig, the representatives of a musical 'party of progress' under the leadership of Liszt gave itself the name New German School in conscious opposition to Brahms and his followers, who were still committed to composing in the spirit of the classical style. During his sojourn in Weimar (1848–61), Liszt had gathered around him several musicians who thought of themselves as progressives, including **Bülow** and **Cornelius**, and had conducted performances of new works by **Berlioz** and Wagner which, along with his own symphonic poems, promoted and successfully established a new musical sensibility which can be briefly described as programme music and musical drama. Liszt's opponents disdainfully referred to this new sensibility as *Zukunftsmusik* or 'Music of the Future'. An abortive manifesto published in 1860, signed by Brahms and the violinist **Joachim** among others, even went so far as to describe it as 'contrary to the innermost essence of music'.

THE CHANGING ORCHESTRA

By the early nineteenth century, the orchestra was fairly standardized: strings, divided into first and second violins (typically about 16 each in a full-size group), violas (12), cellos (12) and double basses (8); woodwind, consisting of two each of flutes, oboes, clarinets and bassoons; and brass, usually two or four horns, two trumpets, occasionally three trombones, with percussion, generally just timpani. It expanded and extended its range of colour during the century. The strings were unaltered, though increased in number. The flutes could be augmented with a piccolo, the oboes with an English horn, the clarinets with a bass clarinet or a smaller high-pitched clarinet (or both) and the bassoons with a double bassoon; each of these four sections might have as many as four players, some playing two or more instruments of the same type as the music might demand (the fingering on a flute, a piccolo or an alto flute, for example, was virtually the same, enabling the player to switch over easily). The horns generally numbered four, possibly even eight in a large-scale work; there would be two or three trumpets, three trombones (two tenor, one bass) and a tuba. The percussion offered a wide range of possibilities beyond the standard timpani; sometimes there were two harps. An orchestra of this size needed conducting, with a baton, from a raised podium.

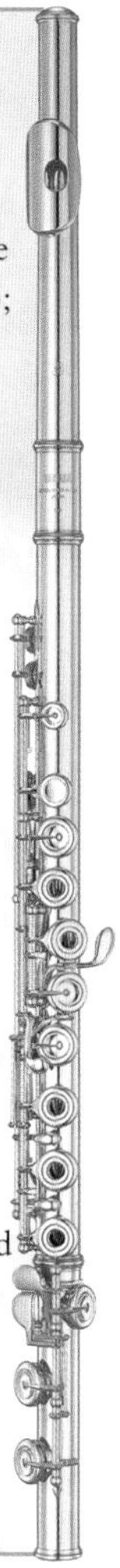

of the Strauss family were an example, as were the neo-classical operettas of **Offenbach**, which were often open parodies of contemporary art music and its self-conscious efforts to be 'new'. Both the classical revival, which moved effortlessly from concert hall to drawing room, with familiar styles and forms specially prepared for 'easy' playing and listening, and the mass appeal of light music by composers such as Offenbach and Johann Strauss, helped to consolidate the widening gulf between the serious and the popular that characterized the music of the second half of the nineteenth century. The gulf exists to this day.

Programme Music

Instrumental music is referred to as programme music when it is associated with an extramusical image or literary text, which the composer usually indicates with a descriptive title or accompanying text. The term 'symphonie à programme' was coined as early as 1800 in Paris, but only with the composition of Berlioz's *Symphonie fantastique* (1830), of which Liszt made a well-known piano transcription, did it gain real currency. Berlioz's overtures and symphonies on literary subjects such as *King Lear* (1831) and *Harold in Italy* (1834) were the main influences on the best-known form of programme music, the symphonic poem, which was eventually established by Liszt as one of the flagships of the new music after 1850. Liszt defined the symphonic poem as an extended instrumental work in one movement (or more), provided with a definite programme, the purpose of which was to render the 'indistinct impressions of the soul more distinct [...] with the suggestion or detailed description of specific concepts or images'. Liszt did not intend a literal musical interpretation of something that was extramusical. Rather, he wanted to offer the listener a starting point from which he or she could begin to grasp the poetic 'idea' of a subject in musical terms and to follow its poetic or philosophical thread.

(L) Rigoletto
Verdi's operas all differed from one another in terms of vocal, instrumental and dramatic styles.
(TR) Ballroom Dancing
Light music saw a rise in popularity in the second half of the nineteenth century.
(BR) At the Opera
Wagner struggled to establish a distinction between opera and musical drama, wanting to differentiate his dramatic works from the more traditional operas of the time.

PROGRAMME COMPOSERS

The idea was enormously influential on a variety of composers, whose sources of inspiration were equally as varied. Like Berlioz's *Symphonie fantastique*, the programme could be invented by the composer, as in **Smetana**'s First String Quartet *From My Life* (1876) or **Richard Strauss**'s *Symphonia domestica* (1902–03). It could be based on great literature by Shakespeare or Goethe, a mythological figure like Orpheus or Prometheus, or even a series of paintings, as in **Musorgsky**'s *Pictures at an Exhibition* (1874). Straightforward musical landscape painting as in Smetana's *Má vlast* (1872–79) and **Ottorino Respighi**'s (1879–1936) *Pines of Rome* (1924), or symphonic pieces associated with philosophical poems and texts such as Liszt's *Die Ideale* (1857, after Schiller) and Strauss's *Also sprach Zarathustra* (1896, after Nietzsche) were by no means exceptional.

Opera and Musical Drama

Some of the most significant innovations in style and form in the latter half of the nineteenth century were in opera and musical drama. The distinction between opera and drama was made by Wagner in 1851, in order to distinguish his own works for the stage from those of others. On closer examination the distinction is hard to uphold, if only because Wagner's techniques of attaining greater realism and flexibility in musical drama were, broadly speaking, not dissimilar to the methods of very different composers who also sensed that the tastes of audiences after the political upheavals in Europe at mid-century had significantly changed. Whether what emerged was 'drama' – a new form of music-theatre akin to the complexities of the greatest examples of spoken theatre – or merely 'opera' in a fresh and more sophisticated guise, is an issue that will always preoccupy historians of music. But the techniques that link, say, the glorification of heroic myth in Wagner's *Ring* (the music of which was begun in 1853) and the discovery of heroism in the low-born and the disreputable in Verdi's *Rigoletto* and *La traviata* are plain to hear.

NEW THEATRE ORCHESTRATION

The blending of recitative and aria to accommodate a more flexible movement from one dramatic moment to the next was a goal both composers shared. And so was the telescoping of narrative and psychological time which they achieved with unexpected twists in operatic convention and an identification of melody and harmony with orchestration. Although they sound entirely different, Wagner's and Verdi's orchestras 'sing' with a previously unheard-of passion and virtuosity. Indeed, both composers brought about a transformation in theatre orchestration that perhaps did more than anything else to influence the extraordinary increase in expressiveness of purely instrumental music towards the end of the nineteenth century.

Operetta

In the mood of realism that spread through Europe after the failure of the revolutions of 1848, it was inevitable that the high-minded seriousness of 'progressive' musicians and dramatists should be countered by light music and frothy entertainment that went out of its way to avoid anything smacking of idealism and the momentousness of 'history'. The operettas and waltzes of Offenbach and Johann Strauss the Younger probably contributed more than anything else to the serious business of deliberately not being serious about the second half of the nineteenth century. Their punishment was eventual respectability and, for a time at least, undeserved historical neglect. But their reward was phenomenal social success. Rooted in the song and dance music of the day, the musical 'numbers' of Offenbach's operettas were comfortingly predictable. And everyone knew that the plot, no matter how convoluted or sharply satirical, would finally dissolve in an intoxicating dance.

Berlioz ▶ p. 186 Brahms ▶ p. 240 Bülow ▶ p. 243 Cornelius ▶ p. 244 Joachim ▶ p. 249 Liszt ▶ p. 194 Musorgsky ▶ p. 253 Offenbach ▶ p. 253
Respighi ▶ p. 295 R. Schumann ▶ p. 201 Smetana ▶ p. 258 R. Strauss ▶ p. 258 Verdi ▶ p. 230 Wagner ▶ p. 226

The Theatre of the Absurd?

Offenbach's first full-length work in the genre was *Orphée aux enfers*, a merciless parody of the mythological plays and operas beloved of the French aristocracy since the days of Louis XIV, in which the gods take a holiday in hell at the end to the accompaniment of a stately minuet that turns into a *galop infernal* (can-can). Similarly, *La belle Hélène* (1864) is a lightly disguised satire of corrupt Parisian society: the plot climaxes in a waltz which not only mocks the operatic convention of the ensemble finale, but also at the last minute dips the sharply satirical tangles of the plot in waves of pleasure. Johann Strauss repeated the formula in his two best Viennese operettas, *Die Fledermaus* ('The Bat', 1874) and *Der Zigeunerbaron* ('The Gypsy Baron', 1885), though without Offenbach's sharp wit and tantalizing ambivalence. The element of the theatre of the absurd that Offenbach invented in his operettas, however, did find its way into the Savoy operas of Gilbert and **Sullivan**. Two of their most successful collaborations, *The Pirates of Penzance* (1879) and *The Mikado* (1885), are thinly veiled satires on the British Establishment and its hypocritical moral codes, with the added bonus of Sullivan's genius for placing 'straight' imitations of the great masters from **Schubert** to Verdi in incongruous and hilarious contexts.

Chamber Music

The history of chamber music in the second half of the nineteenth century was influenced at first by **Beethoven** and very different views of his legacy. Liszt and von Bülow were renowned for their performances of the piano sonatas, and Wagner went out of his way to encourage musicians to play the composer's late string quartets in concert – a public status these works had hardly enjoyed in Beethoven's lifetime because of their confinement to private circles of connoisseurs. Liszt and Wagner both wrote piano sonatas in the early 1850s. But Brahms, a protégé of Robert Schumann, discreetly adopted Beethoven's mantle as a composer of finely wrought chamber music in conscious opposition to their progressivist views. Brahms began his composing career with a series of piano sonatas, songs and chamber music for strings with and without piano, advancing gradually to more public works, yet never relinquishing his passion for small ensembles and the rigours of musical logic. Even his earliest published song, *Liebestreu* ('Faithful in Love', 1853), the first of many great Brahms songs, showed a density of form and motivic detail that was conspicuously unlike the boldly extrovert methods of Berlioz, Liszt and Wagner. Although he was branded a conservative by them, Brahms's faith in the ideal of chamber music eventually came into its own.

THE SOCIÉTÉ NATIONALE DE MUSIQUE

The renewed interest in chamber music in France that went hand in hand with the founding of the Société Nationale de Musique in 1871 by **Saint-Saëns** and **Fauré**, amongst others owed not a little to Brahms's example, even though Saint-Saëns' more relaxed view of form and the almost pastoral simplicity of Fauré's melodies seemed light years away from Brahms' 'pedantic' methods. The French honoured Brahms' achievement by emulating it quantitatively and by trying to oppose it aesthetically – not always with complete success. The same was true of **Wolf**, whose song collections on poetry by Mörike, Eichendorff and Goethe, published between 1888 and 1890, established him as one of the great song-writers of the nineteenth century.

THE LEITMOTIF

The term leitmotif ('leading motif') usually designates a distinct musical shape associated with a specific poetic or dramatic moment (an idea, a thing or a person), recurring during the musical work when this moment is recalled or elaborated upon. Since the nineteenth century, Wagner's famous system of leitmotifs has found great resonance because of an inclination among many listeners to hear music 'leitmotivically'. This applies not just to the music of Wagner, but also to that of Liszt and Berlioz, whose adventures in musical syntax – incomprehensible to many – were compensated by commentaries that encouraged audiences to hear salient motifs, and the links between them, according to a narrative chain of associations or 'thread'. Too often derided as an anti-intellectual substitute for 'correct' hearing, the use of leitmotif by the New German School is, on the contrary, an important facet of any history of musical listening. The technique is an extension of Berlioz's ***idée fixe*** – a resilient theme symbolizing a central figure that returns in different shapes and sizes during the course of the narrative.

Wagner's Leitmotifs

The metamorphosis of themes in Liszt's symphonic poems that links together different sections and movements, is a similar technique. But the sheer quantity of motifs Wagner needed to fill out about 15 hours of music in the *Ring* already suggests an important difference. His decision in the *Ring* finally to abolish the contrast between unstructured recitative and musically highly organized set-pieces typical of conventional opera meant that the invention of a new kind of leitmotif was inevitable. He basically set out to create a continuous musical-dramatic dialogue that relies for its coherence not on predictable changes of style or a simple recurrence of musical shapes, but on a steady interchange of symphonically related motifs that can be joined, combined and varied in countless ways without loss of identity. Wagner's leitmotifs not only represent significant aspects of the unfolding drama, but also relate to each other to provide its narrative with a semblance of logic and a scaffold for its monumental structure on a musical level. The technique was emulated, often in starkly modified form, by many later composers of opera, including Richard Strauss.

idée fixe ▶ p. 359

MUSICAL PROSE

Wolf at first took his cue from the fragile open-endedness of Schumann's Lieder rather than Brahms's motivic cohesiveness. Yet in his later songs, such as the *Michelangelo* settings (1897), he was propelled into the conundrum, which had pre-occupied Brahms from the start, of how to balance form and motivic logic with advanced harmony and the increasing tendencies of the singing voice to appropriate the rhythms and melodies of speech. **Schoenberg** used the terms 'musical prose' and 'developing variation' to describe this process. In a spectacular turnabout, Brahms's chamber music was, by the end of the nineteenth century, no longer outside 'history', as it had been in the eyes of the New German School. According to Schoenberg, whose string sextet *Verklärte Nacht* ('Transfigured Night'), his first major chamber work, was completed in 1899; its revitalization of traditional form, its harnessing of advanced harmony and innovation in musical syntax were beacons of light on the way to the music of the future.

Drame Lyrique

The first performance of **Gounod**'s *Faust* (after Goethe) in Paris in 1859, was the inception of a type of opera in the latter part of the nineteenth century that came to be known as *drame lyrique*. It differed from *grand opéra* and *opéra comique*, the two main genres already well established in Paris, by its lyric character and the seriousness of its librettos. Formal elegance, subtle instrumentation, themes of reminiscence and rhythmically lively and gracious melodies, which avoided becoming saccharine by a hair's breadth, were its main characteristics. Critics were not slow to point out the frequent disparity between the sentimental tone of Gounod's opera and the complexity of its literary model. Yet the opera seemed to thrive on its audience's understanding of great literary subjects in terms of heightened lyricism. It was followed by *Mignon* (1866) and *Hamlet* (1868) by **Thomas**, and later by **Massenet**'s *Werther* (1892), based on another Goethe novel. Although it was not an immediate success, the combination of a great literary subject and intense vocal lyricism eventually made *Werther* one of the most popular operas in Paris.

OPERATIC REALISM AND *DRAME LYRIQUE*

The *drame lyrique* was a foil for **Bizet**'s *Carmen*, the most famous French opera of the period. Don José's lyrical pleading is rudely rejected by Carmen, while Micaëla, the decent girl he is supposed to marry, seems to isolate herself from her surroundings with extended melodic lines worthy of Gounod or Thomas. *Carmen* is also based on a distinguished literary source – the novel by Prosper Mérimée – with the difference from the *drame lyrique* that Bizet and his librettists placed the realism of its Spanish setting and the all-or-nothing passion of its heroine to the fore instead of the vulnerable sentiments of its characters. A similar tension between operatic realism and *drame lyrique* is noticeable, too, in the epic style of Musorgsky's *Boris Godunov* (1873) and **Tchaikovsky**'s *Eugene Onegin* (1879), both based on texts by the great Russian author Pushkin. The characters in *Boris* who express their emotions in lyrical song, pale before the realistic recreation of sixteenth-century Russia and the intense interior monologues of the opera's protagonist. And despite *Onegin*'s subtitle – 'lyric scenes' – Tchaikovsky created realistic effects of conversation and colourful dance while, also expressing the pathos of his characters in exquisitely crafted arias and duets.

The Symphony

The genre of the symphony experienced what appeared to be a remarkable revival in the last 30 years of the nineteenth century. Whether it is true to speak of a 'revival' in terms of style and form, however, is an issue that has still not been resolved by historians. Brahms famously emulated classical procedures in his symphonies (1876–85) and for the most part kept within the dimensions of the classical orchestra. Yet despite his objections to the aesthetics of the New German School, the advanced harmony and instrumental colour he invented within these limitations still reflected in part the development in musical resources that had taken place in Europe since the time of Schumann. Tchaikovsky's six symphonies (1868–93) and both of **Borodin**'s (1869, 1877) borrowed a number of techniques from Liszt's symphonic poems, including the metamorphosis of themes and a redistribution of the individual components of classical forms which served to heighten dramatic contrast and an almost theatrical intensity of expression.

INFLUENCES AND INFLUENCED

The terracing of dynamics and musical texture in **Bruckner**'s nine symphonies (1865–96) paid homage to the Baroque, and the inevitable forward movement of each work towards a triumphant apotheosis in its final movement was undoubtedly a confrontation with Beethoven's symphonies, which Bruckner was determined to surpass. The monumental scale of Bruckner's symphonies, however, would have been unthinkable without Wagner's symphonic music drama. Similarly, Franck's single symphony (1888), **Dvořák**'s nine (1865–93) and **Mahler**'s 10 symphonies (1888–1911), despite their vast differences, owed a profound debt to Wagner's harmony and orchestration. The breathtaking range of style, form, time-scale and not least orchestration in Mahler's works, however, summed up the enormous scope of the late nineteenth-century symphony. Its sources were extraordinarily diverse and the breadth of its influence can scarcely be underestimated.

(NL) Das Rheingold
The Ring *cycle, of which* Das Rheingold *was part, uses leitmotif, a technique enabling significant moments or themes to be emphasized using a distinct musical shape.*
(FL) The Pirates of Penzance
Sullivan's musical explored the hypocrisy of moral codes through absurd theatre.
(TR) Eugene Onegin
An example of drame lyrique*, the new type of opera that arose in the latter part of the nineteenth century.*
(BR) A Debt to Wagner
Mahler was of many composers whose symphonies were indebted to Wagner's harmony and orchestration.

Beethoven ▶ p. 150 Bizet ▶ p. 239 Borodin ▶ p. 240 Bruckner ▶ p. 242 Dvořák ▶ p. 245 Fauré ▶ p. 248 Gounod ▶ p. 249 Mahler ▶ p. 250 Massenet ▶ p. 252
Saint-Saëns ▶ p. 256 Schoenberg ▶ p. 295 Schubert ▶ p. 182 Sullivan ▶ p. 260 Tchaikovsky ▶ p. 234 Thomas ▶ p. 261 Wolf ▶ p. 261

The Late Romantic INSTRUMENTS

INSIDE THE LATE ROMANTIC ORCHESTRA

Piccolo

Half the size of the flute, the piccolo is played the same way: held sideways to the mouth. The player blows not into but across a small hole. It sounds an octave above the flute and came into orchestral use in the late classical age, making an appearance in **Beethoven**'s Fifth and Sixth Symphonies and the 'Egmont' Overture. It was written for by **Verdi** in his *Requiem* and **Mahler** in his First Symphony, both of whom seem to have overestimated how low it could play. Perhaps its most famous appearance is in **Tchaikovsky**'s *Nutcracker*.

Clarinet

The German player and maker Iwan Müller had developed a 13-keyed instrument in about 1812 and the music being written for the clarinet at the beginning of the nineteenth century by **Weber**, among others, made an instrument with 13 keys essential. While its chamber music life in the classical period had produced such masterpieces as the Beethoven Septet (op. 20) and **Mozart**'s Clarinet Quintet in A (K581), in the Romantic period, before **Brahms**'s quintet of 1891, it was limited. However, it became an ever more important member of the orchestra. Different instruments, variously pitched, were all included in the instrumentation of orchestral music from the time of **Berlioz**.

The modern clarinet is commonly pitched in B flat, and family members include the higher E flat clarinet, the lower (and rarer) basset horn and, still lower, the bass and contrabass clarinets.

Bass Clarinet

Commonly pitched in B flat like the standard orchestral clarinet, but sounding an octave below it, the bass clarinet began life as an eighteenth-century instrument that looked faintly like a dulcian, though with an upward-pointing bell. Adolphe Sax (1814–94) and L. A. Buffet (fl. 1839–43) both worked on the instrument in the nineteenth century. Sax developed one with two speaker keys, one high up and one halfway down the column of the instrument, which break the continuity of the blown air and allow the instrument to reach its higher notes. The greater size of the bass clarinet and its larger finger-holes meant that it made an early move into comprehensive keywork.

Because many instruments were manufactured with lower notes, **Wagner** scored for bass clarinet in A and used the low E, which requires the modern instrument to have extra length and an extra key. Similar depths are required by **Shostakovich**, who wrote for instruments with this extra range.

Oboe

Although two-keyed oboes continued to be made as late as 1820, it was around 1825 that a Viennese oboist of the court orchestra developed a 13-keyed instrument. Joseph Sellner's development continued to be used in Germany throughout the nineteenth century, and is the basis of the modern Viennese instrument.

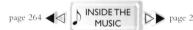

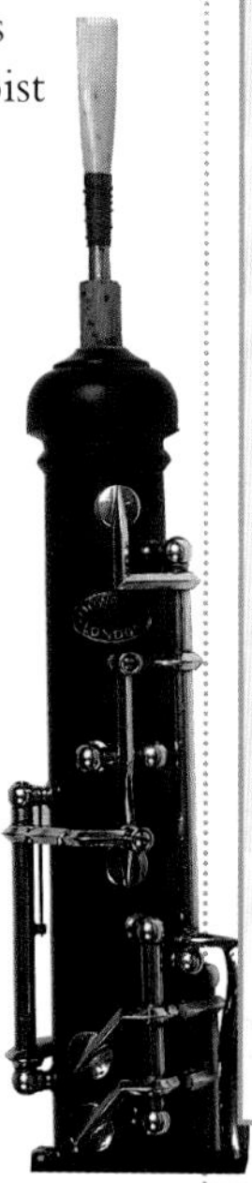

In France, instrument-makers pursued a different path. Henri Brod began manufacturing oboes in 1839. His contemporary, Guillaume Tribert, was a member of a family of makers who developed the modern French oboe. In addition to differences in the workings of keys, the sound quality sought by French makers was different: they valued the warmth of sound less than German makers and thus pursued a more refined sound. Outside Vienna, it is now usually the French model that is used. Although there were experiments with a bass or baritone oboe in the eighteenth century, it was in the 1820s that a firm called Tribert began manufacturing the modern instrument. The tube was folded up like that of a bassoon, and the first straight baritone oboe was produced by F. Lore in 1889. Like the English horn, its reed is carried on a curved metal crook.

XYLOPHONE

The xylophone (the name means 'sounding wood') is a percussion instrument consisting of a series of wooden bars of ascending size, capable of producing a range of notes when struck. It originated possibly in Asia or Africa; an instrument thought to be of Chinese origin fell into the hands of **Jean-Philippe Rameau** (1683–1764). Early instruments consisted of blocks strung together with cords, or resting on a bed of straw. In the modern instrument, the blocks are arranged in the pattern of a piano keyboard and beneath each is a hollow tube which resonates when the bar is struck.

A folk instrument, it attracted the attention of composers in the nineteenth century. Its most famous appearance in the Romantic period is in **Saint-Saëns**' *Carnival of the Animals*. Here it gives the impression of dancing bones in the section entitled 'Fossils'. It is also bones that are in the programme in the same composer's *Danse macabre* . The xylophone went on to be the most commonly used tuned percussion instrument in the twentieth century, the standard instrument to learn on, with a wide orchestral repertory.

crook ▶ p. 357

Heckelphone

The heckelphone was developed by William Heckel after he heard from Wagner in 1879 that the orchestra lacked a powerful baritone double-reed instrument. Accordingly, he experimented with the oboe family and produced the first heckelphone in 1904. Built in three sections, it has a wider bore than the oboe, and is played using a bassoon-type reed mounted on a curved crook. The instrument in C has a compass running A to G sharp; the E flat instrument runs C sharp to F sharp and the piccolo heckelphone plays E to A sharp. Instead of ending in a flaring bell it ends in a bulb, similar in shape to an English horn. The heckelphone can be heard in **Richard Strauss**'s opera *Salome*.

English Horn (Cor Anglais)

The English horn or cor anglais is a member of the oboe family. It is neither English nor a horn, and the name is usually written off as a mystery. Pitched a fifth below the oboe, it had been developed in 1760 by Ferlandis of Bergamo, but was rarely heard in the orchestra before the Romantic period. Brod produced a modern instrument in 1839, for the first time using a curved brass **crook** to carry the reed. There are notable parts for it in the third act of Wagner's *Tristan und Isolde* and, perhaps most famously of all, it depicts the swan in **Sibelius**'s 'Swan of Tuonela', one of the *Lemminkäinen* legends.

Bassoon

Attempts were made in the nineteenth century to turn the bassoon into a metal instrument: Charles and Adolphe Sax experimented with brass bassoons and the latter patented such an instrument, with 24 keys, in 1851. There were rival arrangements of keys (which implied different ways of fingering) available in the nineteenth century. There continue to be French and German models available.

The Heckel family worked on developing the instrument, and their Heckel double bassoon (developed in 1876 and revised in 1879) won the approval of Wagner, who wrote for it in *Parsifal*. The loop-shaped double bassoon, or contrabassoon, has a larger reed than the bassoon. The contrabassoon will play up to C and down to C sharp; by adding a downward-facing metal bell, the range was extended to B flat and later A sharp.

(TL) Musicians Outside an Inn
A shared love of music facilitates the coming together of different sectors of society.
(NR) The Ring
Whilst writing his famous Ring, *Wagner found he needed an instrument that bridged the gap between French horns and trombones; from this the Wagner tuba was developed.*

French Horn

The nineteenth century saw several attempts at remaking the French horn when a valved horn along the lines of the trumpet competed with an omnitonic horn. The latter looks like a bowl of spaghetti and includes enough tubing for the instrument to be played in any key. The problem was controlling the tubing: models with various kinds of valving were tried. Rotary valves, which are to be found in the modern instrument, were only one of several available systems until some way into the twentieth century. While the piston valve works as a plunger, the rotary valve is operated by a lever and the internal mechanism swivels, not unlike a stopcock.

Wagner Tuba

A brass instrument with the tubing curled in an elliptical loop ending in a small bell and fingered using four valves, this is a type of tuba probably based on the saxhorn.

When writing the *Ring*, Wagner wanted a brass instrument to bridge the gap between the French horns and the trombones. The 1853 sketch for *Das Rheingold* specifies trombones at one stage. This is later marked for Wagner tubas. Wagner recorded that he had visited Adolphe Sax's workshop in 1853, but that on returning to Germany he found that band instruments there did not offer anything to match the saxhorns he had seen. A quartet of instruments was specially made (two tenor tubas in B flat, two bass ones in F). Although they were doubled by French horns, the sound was intended to be less bright and more dignified than the horns.

The bass trumpet was also developed specifically to play in Wagner's *Ring*. The composer approached the Berlin maker C. W. Moritz with an idea for a four-valve trumpet capable of playing in C, B flat and A. With a wider bore than the orchestral trumpet, it is pitched an octave deeper and played by a trombonist. The range runs from G flat to G flat. The instrument commanded the interest of both Richard Strauss and **Stravinsky**.

Harp

By the early eighteenth century, a harp furnished with pedals had been developed in Bavaria. In this instrument, each of the foot-operated pedals directed a mechanism that could sharpen every string playing notes of the same name. Initially there were five such pedals, controlling C, D, F, G and A.

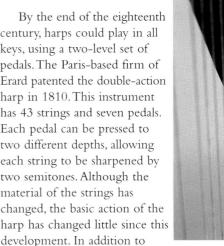

By the end of the eighteenth century, harps could play in all keys, using a two-level set of pedals. The Paris-based firm of Erard patented the double-action harp in 1810. This instrument has 43 strings and seven pedals. Each pedal can be pressed to two different depths, allowing each string to be sharpened by two semitones. Although the material of the strings has changed, the basic action of the harp has changed little since this development. In addition to Erard, the outstanding name in the early history of the double-action harp is Elias Parish Alvars, who was both a composer and a virtuoso.

Paris had been a centre of harp manufacture and performance at least since Marie Antoinette popularized the single-action pedal harp. Notable French harp music includes a concerto by **Boieldieu**. **Debussy**'s *Prélude à 'l'après midi d'un faune* (1892–94) features a famous role for two harps, while **Ravel**'s *Introduction et allegro* (1905) for string quartet, clarinet, flute and harp is among the most famous works in the harp repertory.

Organ

While the medieval, Renaissance and even Baroque organs produced effects with the keyboard (or 'manual') and the stops, the Baroque period in England saw the first development of the 'swell box'. The front of the swell box comprises a set of movable shutters connected to pedals which, lying under the organist's feet, allow the sound to grow louder or softer. Even in England, swell boxes were insignificant in both number and effect for most of the eighteenth century, and virtually unknown elsewhere until the nineteenth. The became a standard feature only in the Romantic period.

Despite all such developments, the medieval organist would have continued broadly to recognize his instrument not only through the nineteenth but indeed well into the twentieth century, when electronic technology first helped the organist to manage the stops of a pipe organ and then produce the sound without benefit of pipes. Although pipe organs continue to be built, the advent of transistors in the 1960s, silicon chips in the 1980s and MIDI interface in the 1990s has made a very different construction possible.

Beethoven ▶ p. 150 Berlioz ▶ p. 186 Boeildieu ▶ p. 189 Brahms ▶ p. 240 Debussy ▶ p. 282 Mahler ▶ p. 250 Mozart ▶ p. 144 Rameau ▶ p. 120 Ravel ▶ p. 294
Saint-Saëns ▶ p. 256 Sibelius ▶ p. 256 Shostakovich ▶ p. 297 R. Strauss ▶ p. 258 Stravinsky ▶ p. 280 Tchaikovsky ▶ p. 234 Verdi ▶ p. 230 Wagner ▶ p. 226 Weber ▶ p. 205

OUTSIDE THE ORCHESTRA

Bugle

The history of the bugle is usually traced to the Seven Years' War (1756–63), when the semicircular metal hunting horn came into use on the battlefield. It settled down as a single loop, pitched in C or B flat around 1800, while a two-loop version developed later in the nineteenth century following the Crimean War (1853–56). This instrument was used for military calls and signals, some of which can be traced back to the instrument's pre-military life on the hunting field.

Keyed bugles were developed by Joseph Halliday in Dublin (1810) and these were taken up in early nineteenth-century military and wind bands. Keys were used, not to close holes in the usual manner, but to open them: the springing was such as to keep all fingerholes closed except when the keys were used. They became popular in the developing brass bands of the time and were used by the Besses o' th' Barn, founded in Manchester around 1815.

Cornet

The cornet is a looped brass instrument with a wide bore and three valves. Beginning life as a development of the circular looped posthorn, it became a valved instrument in France in the late 1820s. It apparently reached Britain in the 1830s, where its bright sound soon displaced the keyed bugle from amateur wind bands.

Most often to be heard as a brass band instrument, it did make occasional appearances in the orchestra (it was more popular with French composers), where it was doubled by horn players. The cornet is usually said to have made an early appearance in **Rossini**'s *William Tell* (1829) and Berlioz's *Symphonie fantastique* (1830), though the naming of instruments at this time can be confusing, as designs were changing and composers occasionally referred to instruments by the wrong name. Even in the very eclectic twentieth century, it remained a rare visitor to the concert hall, but it can be heard in **Vaughan Williams**'s *London Symphony* and Constant Lambert's (1905–51) *Rio Grande* (1927).

Bass Tuba

The invention of valves meant that brass instruments could now explore the bass register, and soon after 1835 bass tubas started being manufactured in Germany. Essentially a keyed bugle by descent, the bass tuba (confusingly, the name tuba comes from the Latin word for trumpet) has a very wide conical bore and as a result requires a good deal of puff. Although the modern instrument is oval with a vertical-facing bell, some mid nineteenth-century instruments were longer and thinner in overall design, with less of the tubing wound up. In the symphony orchestra, the tuba gradually replaced the ophicleide, on which it was in part based, and was written for by Wagner, Richard Strauss and Mahler. Vaughan Williams's tuba concerto of 1954 remains an unusual – though not unique – work for it as a solo instrument.

Euphonium

The euphonium (the name is coined from Greek and means 'sweet-voiced') is a brass instrument with a compass of three octaves. Developed from the bass saxhorn, it has a wide conical profile and an upward-facing bell. Although prototypes were known in Germany in the 1820s and an instrument was patented in 1838 by Carl Moritz of Berlin, the first euphonium was made by Sommer of Bavaria in 1843. Adopted by brass bands in several countries, the euphonium is a rare visitor to the symphony orchestra, though it is often heard playing the Wagner-horn part in Strauss's *Ein Heldenleben* and the ophicleide parts in Berlioz.

BRASS BANDS IN INDUSTRIAL SOCIETY

While in the US and several European countries there a tradition is of mixed wind bands, Britain developed bands made up of brass instruments with saxophone and percussion. The repertory of such ensembles tended to be arrangements of dance music, opera overtures and marches. (Twentieth-century British composers have pioneered original music for brass band.) The brass band developed from civic wind bands, called 'waits', and military bands. It was the development of valved instruments that made the brass band possible, while the work by Sax on the concept of a unified family of brass instruments laid the foundations for the modern ensemble.

In the north of England and in Wales, brass bands were an essential element in industrial culture, with large firms sponsoring bands that would bear their name. M. Blaina Ironworks saw the creation of a band in 1832; the Cyfarthfa Brass Band was formed in 1838, funded by coal and iron money and staffed with musicians from London's theatres and orchestras. Amateur bands regularly met for banding competitions – and still do – the first on record taking place in 1818.

Sousaphone

The sousaphone was made to the specifications of the American bandmaster John Philip Sousa (1954–1932). A type of tuba, it has a dramatically wide bell, although it has been argued that the size of the bell has nothing to do with sound production or tone quality and everything to do with being eye-catching. The instrument encircles the player, passing across the right hip and over the left shoulder in the manner of the shoulder-band of a Sam Brown military belt, with the bell rising over the player's left shoulder to point forwards. An alternative model, with the bell pointing directly upwards – therefore nicknamed the 'rain-catcher' – proved less saleable. Also known as the 'helicon' from its helical shape, the instrument has proved popular with American wind and military bands, but it has not taken off in Europe.

Flugelhorn

The flugelhorn (or flügelhorn: *Flügel* means 'wing' in German) is a cornet-like valved brass instrument, a member of the bugle family. It has a conical bore and three valves; in Britain these are invariably piston valves, but German and Austrian ones have rotary valves. The flugelhorn's ancestor was a type of semicircular hunting horn carried by the hunt-master who directed the wings of a ducal hunt, and in German the name Flügelhorn predates the instrument with which we are familiar by a couple of centuries.

The flugelhorn can be heard in British brass bands and European (though not British or American) military bands. It has made only very occasional appearances in the orchestra, examples including **Respighi**'s *Pines of Rome* and, most famously, Vaughan Williams's Ninth Symphony (1956–58).

Saxhorn

Adolphe Sax patented the saxhorn in 1845. Seizing on the idea of valved brass instruments which was already current, Sax conceived the idea of a family of such instruments, with a shared playing technique and a shared quality of sound. After early experiments with a shape modelled on the trumpet, he built the entire family on the tuba model. Although the expression 'saxhorn' has largely dropped out of currency, the effects of Sax's conception have endured. The E flat soprano saxhorn can be heard today in the form of the soprano cornett, the E flat instrument is now the tenor horn, the B flat instrument is the baritone, the B flat bass is the euphonium and the E flat contrabass was replaced by the E-flat bass tuba.

Saxophone

Sax's most famous invention, the saxophone, was patented in 1846. This new family of instruments is a cross between the single-reed woodwind family and the keyed brass instruments of the early nineteenth century such as the ophicleides, which are said to have influenced him. Each member of the family combines the single reed and mouthpiece, familiar from the clarinet, with a wide, conical brass body. It is fingered entirely with keys and is another instrument to have felt the effects of Theobald Boehm's arrangement for flute keywork and fingering.

The saxophone, which is generally thought to come in four sizes (soprano, alto, tenor and bass are the most frequently encountered), was originally conceived of as a family of fourteen, comprising orchestral and military band subsets of seven each. The early instruments could manage about three octaves between them, though the highest notes were of poor quality. The range has been extended since Sax's lifetime and additional instruments, such as the sub-contrabass, have been built. The sopranino in E flat, the highest of the family, can be heard in Ravel's *Boléro*. In the orchestra, the saxophone was initially written for by French composers such as Saint-Saëns, **Delibes** and **Bizet**. Because the saxophone's early successes were in France and in band music, when Strauss took his *Symphonia domestica* to New York in 1904 finding the necessary four saxophonists proved a major headache.

Ophicleide

Patented in 1821, the ophicleide was a French invention. Although the name is intended to mean 'keyed serpent', the instrument is not a serpent, but rather a development of the keyed bugle, undertaken by Halary in Paris. The instrument comes in various sizes with various ranges, but all built to the same pattern. Built in a tight U-shape, the ophicleide is held upright, with the bell opening a little above the player's crown and the mouthpiece at the end of a crook at 45 degrees to the instrument's body. Generally made of brass (wooden instruments were known: the maker Thomas McBean Glen of Edinburgh called his 'serpentkleides'), it had anything from nine to 12 keys.

The ophicleide was taken up by military bands, but can also be found in the scores of Berlioz, Verdi and Wagner.

WOMEN AND THE VIOLIN

Towards the end of the nineteenth century, women throughout Europe and the US were entering the music profession as instrumentalists, singers, teachers, journalists, musicologists, administrators and composers of all genres of music, from song to symphony. One of the most significant advances was the appearance of the female violinist. There had been isolated instances of successful female violin virtuosos for centuries but in general the violin was deemed to be an unfeminine instrument. The pioneer violinist who made the instrument respectable in Europe was the Czech-born Wilhelmine Norman-Neruda (1839–1911), Lady Hallé after her second marriage. The French-born violinist Camilla Urso (1842–1902) had the same effect in the US. By the 1880s, both amateur and professional women were taking up the instrument in large numbers and wanting to play with others in orchestras.

The first professional all-woman orchestra since the *cori* of the Venetian *ospedali* was the internationally famous Viennese Ladies' Orchestra, founded in the 1860s. Soon numerous women's orchestras and bands were to be found throughout Europe and the US. Amateur groups played to raise money for charity; the inaugural concert of Lady Radnor's String Band, for example, raised £1,000 towards the foundation of London's Royal College of Music.

(BL) Brass Band
A marching band at the Durham Miners' Gala bears testimony to the origins of such ensembles.
(TNL)* The Muscians *by Albertina Palau
A late nineteenth-century painting inspired by a group of musicians in a tavern.
(TR) Ophicleide
The ophicleide originated in France as a development of the keyed bugle.

Bizet ▶ p. 239 Delibes ▶ p. 245 Respighi ▶ p. 295 Rossini ▶ p. 200 Vaughan Williams ▶ p. 298

The Late Romantic

LISTENING GUIDE

Pyotr Ilyich Tchaikovsky
Symphony No.6, 'Pathétique'

WORK: Pyotr Ilyich Tchaikovsky, Symphony No. 6 in B minor, op. 74 ('Pathétique'), composed in 1893
SCORING: piccolo, two flutes, two oboes, two clarinets, two bassoons, four horns, two trumpets, three trombones, tuba, timpani, bass drum, cymbals, strings
EXCERPT: First movement: *Adagio – Allegro non troppo* Track 3 of CD II.
TIMINGS BASED ON: Symphony No. 6, Leningrad Philharmonic Orchestra conducted by Yevgeny Mravinsky (see Recommended CDs)

RECOMMENDED CDs

1. Leningrad Philharmonic Orchestra. Yevgeny Mravinsky, conductor. Deutsche Grammophon 419 745-2 (2 CDs)

   The classic balance of passion with precision, containing the hellfire of Tchaikovsky's outer movements with some of the most keenly articulated playing on disc. Here it follows the Fourth and Fifth Symphonies in recordings made at the time of Mravinsky's 1960 visit to London with the orchestra.

2. St Petersburg Philharmonic Orchestra. Yuri Temirkanov, conductor. RCA Red Seal 09026 613772 (2 CDs)

   A more extreme reading than Mravinsky's from the current music director, who has his own distinctive views on interpretation. Temirkanov follows his predecessor's example in presenting the last three symphonies as a sequence.

3. Russian National Orchestra. Mikhail Pletnev, conductor. Virgin VC7 59661 2

   The celebrated début recording of Russia's latest super-orchestra. The players still have some way to go to form a truly distinctive whole, but Pletnev is well within the Mravinsky tradition in balancing white heat with structural control.

4. Berlin Philharmonic Orchestra. Ferenc Fricsay, conductor. Deutsche Grammophon 445 409-2

   Another master at combining intensity and sheer hard work, the brilliant Hungarian Ferenc Fricsay left us the ultimate testament to his conducting greatness – recorded in 1949 in vivid mono sound, and coupled with a vintage Menuhin performance of the Violin Concerto.

At the beginning of 1893, the 52-year-old Tchaikovsky seemed to have reached the peak of personal and international success. Revered as Russia's leading composer since the lavish staging of his operas at the Imperial Theatres in the mid-1880s and the more recent success of his two later ballets, *The Sleeping Beauty* and *Nutcracker*, he was also an expert ambassador for his own music as a conductor throughout Western Europe and the US. He had found a personal stability in his homeland following years of self-imposed exile after the failure of his marriage and a suicide attempt in 1877. In the spring and summer of 1893, he worked with exhilaration on a 'symphony with a secret programme'. Although he had 'wept copiously' planning it out the previous year, as he came to complete it he told his publisher he had never in his life 'felt so pleased' with himself, 'so proud, so happy in the knowledge that I really have written something good'.

Within months he was dead. The cause remains uncertain; there is some evidence to support both the likelihood of cholera and the rather more implausible theory of suicide by decree to hush up a homosexual scandal in court circles. Only one thing is certain: the end was shockingly sudden, never so much as hinted at in any of Tchaikovsky's correspondence earlier that year. And yet the second performance of the Sixth Symphony nine days after the composer's death fuelled the romantic legend that he had composed his own requiem.

1. 0'00" (*Adagio*)
A slow introduction added after the rest of the symphony was completed; Tchaikovsky foreshadows the wailing main subject of the movement on solo bassoon against low strings playing *pp*.

2. 1'49" (*Allegro non troppo*)
The main theme appears at a faster tempo, but still in dark colouring: the violas are divided into two parts, but violins do not make their entry until later (2'14").

3. 2'41"
As violins dance along in a linking passage, the simple descending scales that are to be a hallmark of the symphony appear – first in the double basses, then in the woodwind.

4. 3'34"
The music builds to a fateful climax, with the trumpets, trombones and tuba making their first appearance in a combative fanfare.

5. 4'31" (*Andante*)
The second main theme of the symphony makes its appearance in what seems like a self-contained slow movement. It is introduced with the utmost tenderness and flexibility by muted first violins and cellos.

6. 5'29"
A wistful sequence led by the first flute leads to a fuller statement of the melody (6'56"). This subsides to a quiet reminiscence on clarinet (8'40"), and ends with descending bassoon *pppppp* (9'22"; Mravinsky employs a bass clarinet here).

coda ▶ p. 357

THE HAND OF FATE

The composer's attitude to fate had changed a great deal since the Fourth Symphony of 1877. There fate, 'that inexorable force which prevents our aspirations to happiness from reaching their goal', is represented by the same fierce brass fanfare throughout. In the Fifth Symphony it has become 'providence', in the shape of a motto theme which moves from gloom to glory. In the Sixth, the composer's attitude to fate is charted by the favourite device of his final years – the descending scale, or portions of it. Scales flit across the canvas of the first movement, dictate its climax and provide its **coda**; they appear rather more briefly at the ends of the second-movement waltz in the lilting metre of 5/4 and the brazen march. The *Adagio lamentoso's* two main themes are both portions of the scale: a five-note figure in B minor at the start, which touches base (the note of B) but refuses to settle there, and a contrasting group of four notes descending from D to A. It begins as a consolation but finally finds itself sucked into the all-enveloping gloom and comes to rest on cellos and basses in an ultimate gesture of tragedy.

The symphony's French subtitle, *Pathétique* or (in Russian) *Pateticheskaya* to convey the primary emotion of suffering, was Modest's idea, and his brother approved it (with 'No. 6' in brackets) for the title-page of the publication he never lived to see.

A SOUL IN TORMENT

It seems unlikely that Tchaikovsky had his own death in mind when composing the Sixth Symphony; although the piece begins and ends in the depths of the orchestra, in the gloomiest key of B minor, the composer's brother Modest thought it was more in the nature of a confessional, purging any negative feelings Tchaikovsky may have had about his unhappy past, than the cry of a soul in torment. There is a suggestion of autobiography in the breathtakingly original idea of developing a brash, euphoric march out of a scintillating scherzo in the third movement and following it with a finale that, for the first time in the history of the symphony, happens to be an *adagio* and not a noisy *allegro*. Yet Tchaikovsky took pride in this as a departure from the symphonic norm, and referred to it specifically when he wrote that 'from the point of view of form there will be much that is new in this symphony'.

(TR) The House at Klin
Tchaikovsky's house at Klin, just north of Moscow.

7. 9'27" (*Allegro vivo*)
Six *pianos* are followed by two *fortes* for full orchestra; followed by a hellfire development sequence with strings in ferocious *counterpoint* (9'41"). At the first climax the trumpets blare out a version of the descending scale (10'09").

8. 10'27"
As the music momentarily subsides, the first trumpet, three trombones and tuba quote a passage from the Russian Orthodox Mass for the dead.

9. 11'13"
Against the unsteady heartbeat of the horns, the violins and violas sigh the main theme. This is the nearest Tchaikovsky comes to the standard recapitulation of sonata form; the music continues to develop towards greater terrors.

10. 12'18"
The most devastating double climax of the movement: a brass-laden statement of the 'supernatural' octatonic scale, followed by regular scales voiced by the strings in protest at the brass (12'50").

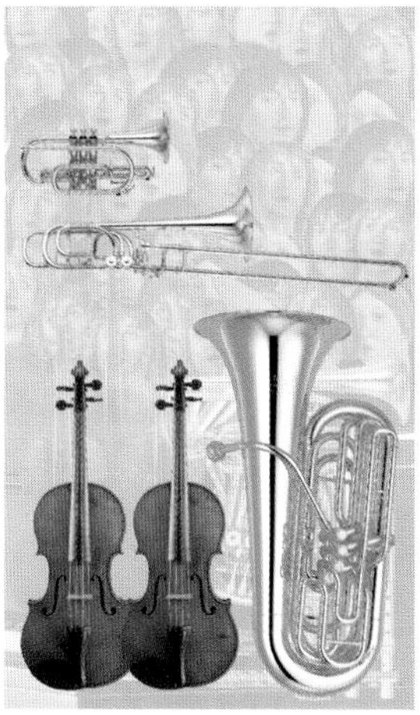

11. 13'47" (*Andante come prima*)
Only the lyrical theme returns as it was before, to bring sweet relief and guide the movement towards an unexpected final haven. The clarinet returns to echo the melody supported by flutes, bassoons, horns and timpani (15'30").

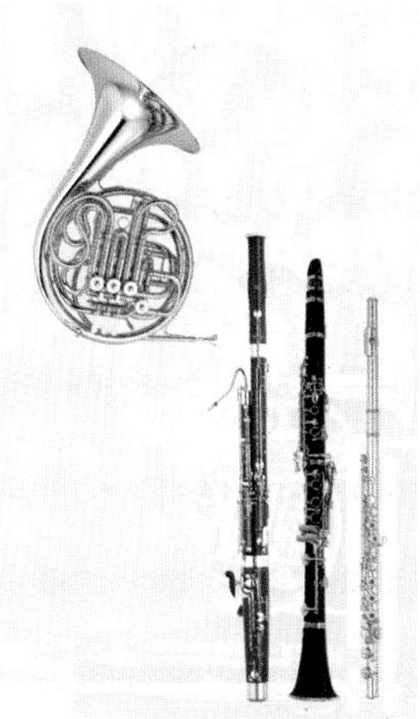

12. 16'26" (*Andante mosso*)
The coda maintains the sense of calm with the descending scales constantly repeated on *pizzicato* strings and a new, religious chorale-like theme on brass and woodwind.

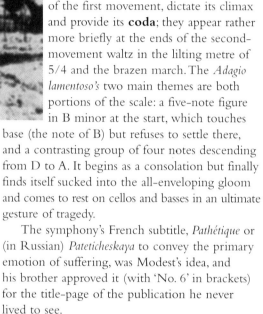

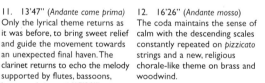

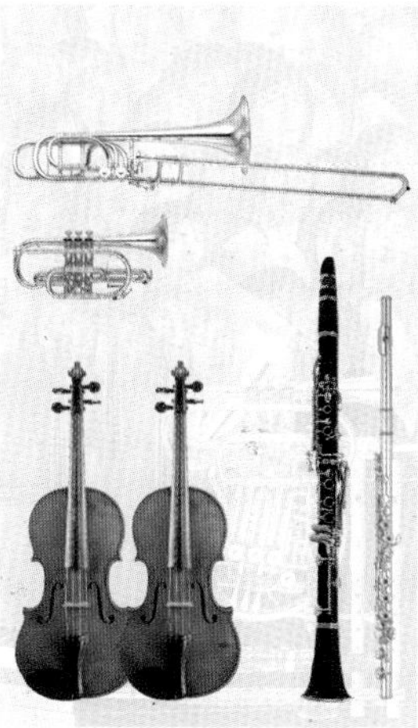

Tchaikovsky ▶ p. 234

GIUSEPPE VERDI: *OTELLO*

As an experienced man of the theatre, **Verdi** was capable of writing to order, producing an astonishingly high number of masterpieces among the 24 operas he composed between *Oberto* in 1838 and *Aida* in 1871. Thirteen years were to elapse, however, between the Cairo première of *Aida* and the old master's willingness to turn to a new subject in 1885. The seed had been sown by his publisher Ricordi in connection with the fiery young composer and librettist **Boito**.

By the time of *Otello*, Verdi's art had become astonishingly concise. He now wanted fast-moving acts, preferably each of no more than half an hour's length, and Boito's quicksilver paraphrasing of Shakespeare fitted the bill perfectly. His adaptation of the tragedy, in which a proud Moorish warrior in the service of the Venetian Republic believes a suave troublemaker's false accusations of his blameless young wife and is driven to a state of murderous jealousy, moves swiftly to the core of the action.

A Farewell to Opera

Before that happens, Verdi has a chance to expand upon the short-lived happiness of Otello and Desdemona in his most tender love duet, initiated by four solo cellos and shared equally between the soprano and the tenor in a sequence of narratives; their voices only join briefly at the end of the duet. Free-flowing passages using the ***arioso*** style replace conventional arias and there is only one grand operatic scene in the standard *pezzo concertato* (concerted-piece) form, motivated by Otello's savage treatment of Desdemona in front of the assembled company. The searing drama of *Otello* is enriched by a comparison with its comic sequel *Falstaff*, the second joint homage of Verdi and Boito to Shakespeare and the octogenarian composer's remarkable farewell to the operatic stage.

RECOMMENDED CD

Giuseppe Verdi: *Otello*. Ramón Vinay (Otello), Giuseppe Valdengo (Iago), Herva Nelli (Desdemona), Virginio Assandri (Cassio), Nan Merriman (Emilia), NBC Symphony Orchestra and Choruses. Arturo Toscanini, conductor. RCA GD60302 (2 CDs)

Italy's greatest conductor returned to this magnificent masterpiece at an even more advanced age than Verdi was when he composed it, and with equal fire and energy. The pace is electrifying, the playing always in control and the 1947 mono radio recording crisp; Ramón Vinay is the perfect heroic-tenor Otello and Valdengo insinuates superbly as the evil Iago.

RICHARD WAGNER: *DIE WALKÜRE*

In 1850, with the successes of *The Flying Dutchman*, *Tannhäuser* and *Lohengrin* already behind him, **Wagner** embarked on the most ambitious project in the history of opera, *Der Ring des Nibelungen* – a massive saga adapting the events of Norse and German mythology to underline a contemporary message, in three long operas preceded by a 'preliminary evening'. The richly human world of *Die Walküre* followed the wrangling of gods and giants in *Das Rheingold*, which introduces the main ideas to be developed. The music was begun in 1854 and completed two years later.

'ADAGIETTO', FIFTH SYMPHONY

Many movie-goers will have enjoyed Mahler's music watching Dirk Bogarde in the 1971 film *Death in Venice*. Director Luchino Visconti underlays images of turn-of-the-century Venice with the yearning strains of the Adagietto and even turns the story's protagonist, originally a writer, into Mahler himself.

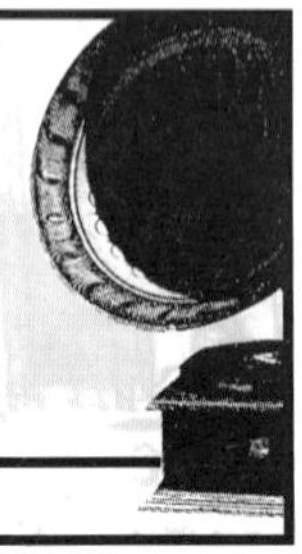

POPULAR MELODY *Mahler*

In it, Wagner develops the elaborate system of the 'leading theme' or **leitmotif** he had begun to lay down in *The Rhinegold*. Some leitmotifs retain their identity throughout, such as the shining trumpet theme of the sword which the god Wotan plants in the trunk of a tree to be retrieved by his part-mortal son Siegmund, or the vigorous horn melody associated with the wild war-maiden daughters of Wotan, immortalized out of the context of the opera in the 'Ride of the Valkyries', the prelude to the third act. Other themes develop in true symphonic style.

NATURE IN WAGNER'S *DIE WALKÜRE*

The art of representing natural elements in music, which **Beethoven** had maintained was 'more a question of feeling than painting' in his Pastoral Symphony (No. 6), reached its Romantic apogee in Wagner's *Ring* cycle. Having launched the entire saga at the beginning of *Das Rheingold* with a series of liquid arpeggios rising upward from the elemental note of E flat in the basses to depict the pure, untainted waters of the river Rhine, Wagner went on in *Die Walküre* to depict a storm and the power of fire in unforgettable terms, while the 'Forest Murmurs' section of *Siegfried* is filled with entrancing birdsong.

The tempest which launches the first act of *Die Walküre* is suggested by a rapidly ascending and falling **ostinato** figure in the cellos and basses against fierce tremolos on a single note from second violins and violas. It is only when the music builds towards a climax that Wagner's specially devised low horns – the so-called 'Wagner tubas' – give out the theme of the thunder-god Donner from *Das Rheingold*, revealing a divine hand in the storm. Even more effective is the development of the fire-god Loge's music in Act 3 as Wotan conjures up a ring of fire to surround his sleeping daughter Brünnhilde and provide a barrier against all but the most fearless of would-be rescuers. The increasingly elaborate orchestration includes flickering tongues of fire from two piccolos, a specified six harps and glockenspiel.

THE EXOTIC IN EARLY TWENTIETH-CENTURY MUSIC

The element of oriental quaintness which Mahler brings to the more extrovert Chinese poems in *Das Lied von der Erde* appeared towards the end of a decade in which composers found themselves increasingly fascinated by the musical allure of

seemingly exotic cultures. Mahler may have been influenced by **Puccini**'s *Madam Butterfly*, which reached the Vienna Opera (where he was music director) late in 1907 and which spiced lush Italianate song with liberal helpings of the oriental pentatonic scale (playable on the five black notes of the piano). Puccini's creation of atmosphere, like Mahler's, was necessary to his subject, and *Madam Butterfly* had an honourable 'exotic' ancestry in the lighter operas and operettas by French and English composers of the previous century (chiefly **Saint-Saëns**' *La princesse jaune* and **Sullivan**'s *The Mikado*).

Instrumental music was slower to incorporate oriental features, though a trend was established by **Debussy** in several piano pieces, chiefly *Pagodes* and *Poissons d'or*, which reflect his fascination with the pentatonic aspect of the Javanese gamelan orchestras visiting the Paris international exhibitions of 1889 and 1900.

arioso ▶ p. 356 chaconne ▶ p. 357 leitmotif ▶ p. 359 ostinato ▶ p. 361

They help to chart the psychological progress of the four main characters in *The Valkyrie* – Wotan, trapped by the moral law into allowing his son to be killed, the brother and sister Siegmund and Sieglinde who fall in love as they discover their true relationship, and the Valkyrie of the title, Brünnhilde, who defies her father when she learns what human love is through her meeting with Siegmund and his devotion to Sieglinde. The final scene of the opera, in which Wotan strips the disobedient Brünnhilde of her supernatural powers and puts her to sleep on a mountain- top ringed by fire, inspires Wagner's supreme lyrical and illustrative gifts.

RECOMMENDED CD

Richard Wagner: *Die Walküre*. Birgit Nilsson (Brünnhilde), Theo Adam (Wotan), James King (Siegmund), Leonie Rysanek (Sieglinde), Annelies Burmeister (Fricka), Bayreuth Festival Orchestra. Karl Böhm, conductor. Philips 412 478-2PH4 (4 CDs)

All the best *Ring* cycles on CD have been captured live at Wagner's festival theatre of Bayreuth, and this production, from 1967, brought together an outstanding team of Wagnerian singers under the volatile baton of Karl Böhm.

GUSTAV MAHLER: *DAS LIED VON DER ERDE*

In 1906, **Mahler** found that the mortality which had always been a central issue in his symphonic world suddenly had to be faced head-on. His doctor's diagnosis of a potentially fatal heart lesion meant a drastic reduction in the exercise he had always taken so vigorously during his summers in the Austrian countryside, and the start of 'the greatest calamity that has ever befallen me'. Under the shadow of death, his last three major works – *Das Lied von der Erde*, the Ninth Symphony and a Tenth he never lived to complete – took on a new urgency in the tension they revealed between a love of the world and a terror of the unknown.

Das Lied von der Erde is a symphony conducted through the medium of six song-settings for two soloists – contralto (or baritone) and tenor. Beginning with desperation and loneliness, the sequence moves to a more relaxed incorporation of Chinese pentatonic (or five-note) music in its third and fourth movements. Mahler's ultimate achievement, though, rests with the 'Farewell' (*Der Abschied*), almost as long as the other five movements put together. The sense of isolation

in the face of death is represented by exposed, graphic solos for oboe and flute, often very free in expression, while the love of the 'green earth' is represented by a blossoming of string sound, kept to a minimum elsewhere in the movement. After a long interlude in the form of a funeral march with dark orchestral colours and threatening trombones, the pattern of loneliness followed by spiritual release is repeated, with the extra colours of celesta and harp suggesting infinity while the soloist's exclamations of 'ewig, ewig' ('eternally, eternally') fade beyond the threshold of audibility.

RECOMMENDED CD

Gustav Mahler: *Das Lied von der Erde*. Christa Ludwig (mezzo-soprano), Fritz Wunderlich (tenor), New Philharmonia and Philharmonia Orchestras. Otto Klemperer, conductor. EMI CDM 5 66892 2

A rare team for this work in that the tenor soloist is as sensitive to nuance as his female counterpart. Klemperer twists the knife with orchestral playing of knife-edge intensity.

JOHANNES BRAHMS: SYMPHONY NO. 4 IN E MINOR, OP. 98

Brahms worked painstakingly on the first of his four symphonies over the course of 20 years. Shortly after its first performance it was dubbed 'Beethoven's Tenth', and he immediately achieved recognition as the late-nineteenth-century heir to the Austro-German symphonic tradition. The rigour with which he undertook the symphonic design of the First's successors more than repaid the compliment, though after the high drama of that initial essay in the form, he seemed to relax into the song-related worlds of the Second and Third Symphonies.

The Fourth Symphony of 1884–85 marked a return to an architectural grandeur and a sense of high tragedy which in this case persists to the end; only an exuberant, big-boned *Allegro giocoso* taking the role of the scherzo allows the mood of tension to relax for long. The first three movements are all highly original specimens of what **Schoenberg** referred to as Brahms's 'epic-lyric genius'; but it is in the finale that Brahms effects the shock of the new by building on old foundations. Taking a varied form of the **chaconne** bass employed by **J. S. Bach** in his Cantata No. 150, Brahms builds above its regular eight-bar repetitions 30 variations.

The austere, powerful framework is reinforced right at the beginning of the movement by the trombones, making their first appearance in the symphony. With the twelfth variation, we reach the introspective heart – a flute solo playing over the bass in broken phrases. The following variations move into the major key – and there is a magical moment when the trombones enter playing chords pianissimo. But the sorrowful vein of E minor returns and the inexorable tragedy is hammered home in a coda of unrelenting power.

RECOMMENDED CD

Johannes Brahms: Symphony No. 4 in E minor, op. 98. Vienna Philharmonic Orchestra. Carlos Kleiber, conductor. Deutsche Grammophon 457 706-2

Viennese warmth joins with Carlos Kleiber's celebrated brand of spring-heeled intensity to provide an overwhelming reading of this mighty symphony.

(BL) Madama Butterfly
Opera drew inspiration from the Orient at the end of the Romantic era.
(TL) Rose Caron
Caron in the role of Desdemona at the first Paris performance of Verdi's Otello.
(TR) The Eighth Symphony
Poster for Mahler's Eighth Symphony, performed in Munich, 1910.
(BR) Brahms in Vienna
Brahms's Fourth Symphony was dubbed 'Beethoven's Tenth' in honour of the classical tradition it represented.

THE MODERN ERA

There is no escaping the crucial importance of World War I (1914–18) in the formation of the Modern Age (as the first half of the twentieth century has come to be known). The war changed irrevocably the development and directions of almost all pre-war innovations in politics, society, the arts and ideas in general. Declining economic conditions also altered the political face of Europe. The Austro-Hungarian Empire collapsed, and its Habsburg emperor, like the German kaiser, resigned. The Russian Tsar lost both the throne and his life following the revolutions of 1917. New self-governing countries emerged in Central Europe as part of the fragmentation of the Habsburg Empire. Republican governments became the norm in the new countries and the breadth of the public franchise became greatly enlarged.

CRACKS AND COLLAPSE

The war deeply affected the economies of Europe and the US. By the end of the 1920s a collapse came, epitomized in the Wall Street Crash of 1929. Left and Centre governments became torn by internal disputes. Disillusion followed, leading to dictatorships in Russia, Italy, Spain and Germany. Fascism became the ideology of the new Right. Eventually Europe became embroiled in another war between 1939 and 1945. In its aftermath, as after World War I, economic conditions and collapses changed political structures and governments. Europe became divided into two major power blocs: one governed by the Soviet Union, the other a looser organization of Western European nations allied to the US.

THE MARCH OF CHANGE

The first half of the twentieth century was a period of almost unrelenting experimentation. No major area escaped the march of change. Realism in painting was challenged by Cubism, abstraction and action painting. New narrative techniques in literature transformed the novel. In music, atonality and the 12-tone system challenged the dominance of tonality in musical structure and harmony. New instruments, the use of unusual folk scales and an increased awareness of and experimentation with rhythm similarly altered its character. Music was also affected by profound changes in aesthetics and ideologies. New technology had its effect, not only aesthetically in Futurism, but also in the rise of electronically generated sounds.

The Modern Era

INTRODUCTION

The Modern Age was characterized by rapid and radical change and political turmoil. By 1918 the Russian tsar, the Habsburg emperor and the German kaiser had lost their thrones. The two Russian revolutions of 1917 resulted in a Communist government led by Vladimir Ilyich Lenin. The Austro-Hungarian Empire was fragmented to allow self-determination to the newly formed countries of Czechoslovakia, Yugoslavia, Romania and a now-independent Hungary.

In Germany, a succession of weak governments, compounded by severe economic difficulties, widespread poverty, rampant post-war corruption and national resentment of crippling war reparations provided ideal conditions for the emergence of right-wing factions. Some were eager to restore Germany's aristocratic leadership, others, above all the National Socialists, were more intent on appealing to a revived sense of national identity and racial superiority. Eventually the former came to support the latter (the Nazi party), culminating in 1933 with the election of the Austro-German Nazi leader Adolf Hitler as German chancellor. Between 1933 and 1939, Hitler set about recovering lands lost in World War I, ignoring unfavourable treaties, until eventually Europe was at war again.

MOVES TO THE RIGHT

Germany was not the only country to move to the political right. Italy also became ruled by a Fascist party after Benito Mussolini – installed as prime minister in 1922 – became sole ruler in 1925 and dictator in 1926, having suppressed all opposition parties. Mussolini and Hitler also assisted the emergence of another dictator, General Francisco Franco who, in 1936, led a successful military revolt against the Republican Popular Front in Spain.

KEY EVENTS

1905	Bloody Sunday in Russia, storming of the Winter Palace
1907	Birth of Cubist style in art
1914	Assassination of Habsburg heir in July leads to world war by August
1915	Germans use poison gas in warfare for the first time at Langemark
1916	Battle of the Somme; Allies suffer 60,000 casualties, Germany 450,000
1917	February Revolution in Russia establishes parliament, which is overturned by October Bolshevik Revolution
1918	Armistice between defeated Germany and Allies comes into force on 11 November
1920	League of Nations brought into effect by Versailles Treaty
1921	First Salzburg festival; D. H. Lawrence publishes *Women in Love*; Chanel No. 5 scent launched
1926	Great Britain experiences first and only General Strike, 3–12 May
1929	Shares crash in New York; market is closed 24–29 October
1933	Adolf Hitler appointed German chancellor; German civil liberties suspended after Reichstag fire; Franklin Roosevelt elected president of the US
1936	Following Republican victory in Spanish elections, General Franco begins Civil War (–1939)
1939	Britain and France declare war on Germany after its refusal to quit Poland
1940	Winston Churchill elected prime minister of the UK
1941	Germany invades Russia, aiming to capture Leningrad and Moscow in Operation Barbarossa; Japan's attack on Pearl Harbor leads to US entry into the war
1944	D-Day: Anglo-US forces land on beaches in Normandy
1945	May: war ends in Europe; 6 August: Americans drop atomic bomb on Japan, compelling surrender
1953	Death in the Soviet Union of dictator Joseph Stalin and composer Prokofiev

The most unexpected, but strategically important, alliance Hitler made was with the Soviet Union, which after Lenin's death in 1924 had been ruled as a dictatorship by Joseph Stalin, one-time general secretary of the Communist party. Stalin imposed extreme restrictions on political opposition and ideological freedom. Keen to avoid involvement in a costly European war, he signed a non-aggression treaty with Hitler, but this was broken when Hitler invaded Russia in 1941. Stalin then allied with Britain and the US, but in the final stages of the war he acquired political dominance over much of central-eastern Europe, parts of Germany and a sector of Berlin. The resulting military stand-off between East and West, known as the 'Cold War', lasted from 1945 until 1989.

THE ARTISTIC ROOTS OF MODERNISM

Reaction and innovation distinguish much of early twentieth-century arts and ideas. The sense of decline in humanism and civilization gave rise to a number of works that continued the pessimism of Arthur Schopenhauer and Friedrich Nietzsche. They included such varied works as the *Decline of the West* by the German historical philosopher Oswald Spengler, and a parable of decay in the novel *Buddenbrooks* by the German writer Thomas Mann.

The traumatic effects of World War I transformed such pessimism into more bitter and objective satire, particularly in Germany. Typical were Bertolt Brecht's Expressionist drama *Baal* and anti-Wagnerian 'epic' plays with music, such as his collaboration with **Kurt Weill** (1900–50), *Aufstieg und Fall der Stadt Mahagonny* ('Rise and Fall of the City of Mahagonny', 1930), in which he exploited a number of 'distancing effects' (*Verfremdungseffekte*), or 'alienation', to avoid the audience 'falling under the spell' of illusion as in Wagner. Brecht's satire found parallels in the bitter exposés of the German bourgeoisie of the Weimar Republic in the paintings of George Grosz, Otto Dix and Max Beckmann.

ESCAPING REALISM

Such critical pessimism was but one end of a spectrum of a much wider critique of previous arts and ideas. One innovation was an anti-synaesthetic focus on the uniqueness of each art, concerned only about itself. Radical painters sought to escape the limits of realism, as in the Cubism (begun 1907) of Pablo Picasso and Georges Braque and, later, abstract art. The new emphasis on the non-referentialism of the medium led to even more radical experiments such as action painting, a term first coined in 1952.

Literature followed suit. Nineteenth-century realistic narrative with its naturalist dialogue, quasi-chronological time sequence and authorial story-telling was challenged by innovatory transformations in the Irish novelist James Joyce's *Ulysses* and *Finnegans Wake*, the French novelist Marcel Proust's *À la recherche du temps perdu* and the 'stream of consciousness' novels of Virginia Woolf: *Mrs Dalloway*, *To the Lighthouse* and *The Waves*.

(L) Hitler and Mussolini
The first half of the twentieth century was an era of Fascism and dictatorship, led by Hitler in Germany and Mussolini in Italy.
(TR) Salome
Front page from the score for Richard Strauss's opera Salome.
(BR) Over the Top
Allied soldiers make their way from the trenches into the dangers of No Man's Land.

chromaticism ▶ p. 357 dissonance ▶ p. 358

IMAGISM

Radical developments also took place in poetry. The American Ezra Pound pared down and de-emotionalized his early pre-Raphaelite aestheticism to the more elusive and allusive imagism, of which movement he was the leader. He also became a great translator, particularly of Chinese, early Italian, Provençal and northern European poetry, and his often unfavourable comparisons of European poetry of the eighteenth and nineteenth centuries to this material stimulated yet further innovations in both content and poetic style. Pound often used early poetry as an imaginative springboard, copying and updating it. His self-conscious use of the past had many artistic parallels, from the neo-classicism of **Igor Stravinsky** (1882–1971) to Brecht and Weill's satirical *Dreigroschenoper* ('Threepenny Opera'). Pound's dissociation from the recent past and evocation of works of far-distant ages found many other artistic parallels.

REFERENTIALISM

Pound encouraged many other poets. His most influential praise was for his fellow American T. S. Eliot, whose *The Waste Land* he helped refine. Eliot's use of past references was typical of the Modern Age. In part, it was a way of achieving a required emotional distance by both author and reader. In part, it was inspired by his indebtedness to Symbolism, with its veiled layers of inner meaning. This intellectual referentialism allied Eliot to a wide range of dissimilar works, from Thomas Mann's use of symbolic music sessions in *The Magic Mountain* and *Doktor Faustus* to the American playwright Eugene O'Neill's use of Greek tragedy in *Mourning Becomes Electra*, Pound's massive sequence of *Cantos* and the works of the British poet W. H. Auden.

THE MUSICAL SEARCH FOR NOVELTIES FOR THE MODERN AGE

Reactions to the techniques and aesthetics of **Richard Wagner** (1813–83) propelled much music of the early twentieth-century. Before 1914, Wagnerian adherents explored increasing **chromaticism**, often allied to the expression or exploration of ever-more powerful emotions. The corresponding artistic movement was Expressionism. Representative were the operas *Salome* (1905) and *Elektra* (1909) by **Richard Strauss** (1864–1949), the opera *Wozzeck* (1914–20) by **Alban Berg** (1885–1935) and **Arnold Schoenberg**'s (1874–1951) monodrama *Erwartung* ('Expectation', 1909) and song cycle *Pierrot Lunaire* (1912). In all these, **dissonance**, rhythmic unpredictability, use of extreme registers and melodic angularity reached new extremes.

WORLD WAR I

The origins of World War I are complex and much disputed. The emergence of Germany as a united country seeking an ever-more powerful position in Europe, and the consequent alliances among the US, France, Britain and Russia, played their part. Austro-Hungarian governments dealt badly with the increasingly bitter aspirations of and disputes between Slavs, Slovaks, Germans and Magyars in their empire. The war was triggered by the assassination by a Serb nationalist in June 1914 of the Habsburg heir, Archduke Franz Ferdinand, in Sarajevo. By the first week of August, Russia had mobilized, Germany and Austria had formed a pact and war was declared on Russia and France. On 4 August, Britain declared war on Germany.

The Changing Face of Warfare

Many thought the war would end by Christmas, but a complex web of contributory factors, many unforeseen, played a part in prolonging it. One was recent technological development: trains could transport more men and supplies over a much wider distance than in earlier European wars. Old-fashioned strategies were used at the outset, but they were overtaken by new weaponry and different conditions, and by December 1914, the characteristic mode of warfare emerged: opposing armies dug into trenches; living in squalor; engaging in battles which cost many lives with little or no advance. The end – a bitter peace – finally came in 1918, and was followed by savage financial reparations imposed on defeated Germany.

The Artistic Response

The pointless waste of life, the miscalculated strategies and the horrors of trench warfare, profoundly changed European psychology. This change found many outlets in the arts, from the savage attacks on bourgeois life in the Brecht/Weill collaborations or the paintings of George Grosz in Germany to the 'ephemeral' and emotional detachment of much Parisian art, to the sense of profound loss and despair to be found in the works of the soldier poets and music such as Symphony No. 3 (1921) by **Ralph Vaughan Williams** (1872–1958). Perhaps the most abiding images were those of No-Man's Land, as painted by Paul Nash, which, echoing photographs of the American Civil War, symbolized waste, desolation and the high price paid not by governments or generals but by ordinary young, men.

Berg ▶ p. 286 Schoenberg ▶ p. 295 R. Strauss ▶ p. 258 Stravinsky ▶ p. 280 Vaughan Williams ▶ p. 298 Wagner ▶ p. 226 Weill ▶ p. 299

MUSICAL CONSEQUENCES OF WORLD WAR I

The war had a profound effect on music. New aesthetics and consequent experiments emerged. One distinct trend leaned toward anti-emotional objectification and a greater emphasis on observable compositional craft. This aim has lain behind such widely differing works as *Kleine Kammermusik* op. 24 No. 2 ('Little Chamber Music', 1922) by **Paul Hindemith** (1895–1963) and Stravinsky's *Octet* (1922–23). Schoenberg also moved from overt Expressionism after his adoption of the **12-note** system to a greater use of abstract forms. His pupil **Anton Webern** (1883–1945), though still claiming allegiance to musical expressiveness, in fact moved further away from it than Schoenberg in his pursuit of brevity and the pre-determination of the sequences of pitches, as in his Symphony op. 21 (1928).

TECHNICAL EXPERIMENTS

Modern technology has had a marked effect in the Modern Age, both in its introduction of new sounds and methods of producing sounds, and its modernist symbolism and non-human objectivity. The Futurist manifestos of the Italian painter Luigi Russolo advocated using modern sounds for the new age. Parallel to his aesthetics and technical experiments were the development of the theremin by the Russian Lev Theremin in 1920 and the ondes martenot by the Frenchman Maurice Martenot in 1928.

Modern composers have sought new sounds and often favoured the instruments least associated with the emotional world of nineteenth-century music. One marked development has been the increased use of percussion in such works as *Ionisation* (1931), by the French composer **Edgard Varèse** (1883–1965), or the opera *The Nose* (1927–28) by the Russian composer **Dmitri Shostakovich** (1906–75). Elsewhere, composers have de-humanized the voice and used it merely as a sonority, either as an ethereal effect, as in *The Planets* (1914–16) by **Gustav Holst** (1874–1934), or as semi-spoken chant, as in *Les choephores* (1915) by **Darius Milhaud** (1892–1974).

DEMOCRACIES IN MUSIC

One effect of World War I and its accompanying political upheavals was a change both in the desired effect of music and in its relation to the audience. Jean Cocteau, in *Coq et l'Harlequin*, attacked the Wagnerian aesthetic: 'Music to be listened to with the head in the hands is immediately suspect. Wagner's music is the prototype of such music.' Cocteau found a highly sympathetic spirit in **Erik Satie** (1866–1925) whose anti-emotional, often witty or ironic style was much to his liking. From the 1920s onwards, Cocteau became occasionally involved with a loosely knit group of composers known as 'Les Six'. Though generalizing about these six very different composers (Francis Poulenc, Darius Milhaud, Arthur Honegger, Germaine Tailleferre, Louis Durey and Georges Auric) is difficult, most of them experimented in the 1920s with popular musical styles either borrowed from the newly imported American jazz or echoing the music-hall songs of the Parisian Montmartre.

MUSIC FOR THE PEOPLE

Hindemith evolved another kind of musical democratization in his desire to compose music that could be more easily understood than that of his more avant-garde contemporaries (Schoenberg, Berg and Webern) and did not need a virtuoso technique to perform. His evolution of ***Gebrauchsmusik*** ('utility music') was very much in the spirit of the *Neue Sachlichkeit* ('new objectivity') of the Weimar Republic. The same desire for comprehensibility led **Aaron Copland** (1900–90) in the US to abandon his earlier avant-garde style in favour of a more melodic, more deliberately American style with his ballets such as *Billy the Kid* (1938) and *Appalachian Spring* (1944).

Several attempts were made early in the Modern Age to write music ostensibly 'for the people'. These ranged from works for amateurs or for children by Holst (*St Paul's Suite*, 1905) and Vaughan Williams, to those for multiple pianists by the Australian **Percy Grainger** (1882–1961) or choral works by **Carl Orff** (1895–1982; *Carmina Burana*, 1938).

In the Soviet Union, the populism of the Communist government encouraged works about the 'people's struggle' or the new Soviet industrial development. After the mid-1930s Stalin's government grew strongly hostile to avant-garde music, and composers such as Shostakovich, **Sergei Prokofiev** (1891–1953) and **Aram Khachaturian** (1903–78) were forced to find innovative ways of using tonal harmonies and lyrical melodies in, for the most part, nineteenth-century structures.

NATIONALISM VERSUS INTERNATIONALISM

In the nineteenth century, composers had already used folk music as a means of national identification. This continued in the twentieth century, particularly after the emergence of newly self-governing countries, or countries wishing to establish a place in the Western canon. Spain and Latin America in particular made a bid, with **Isaac Albéniz** (1860–1909), **Enrique Granados** (1867–1916) and **Manuel de Falla** (1876–1946) quickly establishing a Spanish style

12-note music ▶ p. 363 *Gebrauchsmusik* ▶ p. 358 Albéniz ▶ p. 238 Bartók ▶ p. 285 Copland ▶ p. 288 Debussy ▶ p. 282 Falla ▶ p. 289 Glinka ▶ p. 192 Grainger ▶ p. 290 Granados ▶ p. 249 Hindemith ▶ p. 290 Holst ▶ p. 290 Ives ▶ p. 291

and the presence of Spanish composers with a distinct voice. In Latin America, Silvestre Revueltas (1891–1940), **Heitor Villa-Lobos** (1887–1959) and Alberto Ginastera (1916–83) each did the same for Mexico, Brazil and Argentina respectively. Each explored in particular his country's dance rhythms, and in this way found common ground, not only with European composers such as Milhaud, who had used Brazilian rhythms after a period spent there during World War I, but also with the general trend towards elevating rhythm to much greater prominence.

FOLK MUSIC

Folk materials in the Modern Age seeped more deeply into musical syntax than they did in the nineteenth century. **Béla Bartók** (1881–1945) and **Zoltán Kodály** (1882–1967) collected and codified enormous amounts of Central European folk music, in part to determine a distinct Hungarian style. Bartók in particular transformed his harmonic and melodic vocabulary and his musical structures in the light of his explorations, and in the process created one of the century's most innovative genres.

Similarly, in Czechoslovakia **Leoš Janáček** (1854–1928), by combining the short-phrased style of his early choral music, the speech-patterns of his native Moravia and an enriched harmonic language derived from new acoustical theories, evolved another of the early modern period's most distinctive voices, especially in the decade following World War I.

(NL) Manuel de Falla
Falla helped bring Spanish composers to the forefront of new music.
(FL) Ondes Martenot
Developments in instruments led to the invention of the ondes martenot in 1928.
(FR) Olivier Messiaen
Messiaen, with his second wife, the French pianist Yvonne Loriod.
(NR) Vie Parisienne
Paris became the centre of musical innovation during the first half of the twentieth century.

PARIS: THE CENTRE OF MODERNISM

In the twentieth century, Paris regained its place as the centre of musical innovation, especially in the years either side of World War I.

In the late nineteenth century, **Claude Debussy**'s (1862–1918) influential musical innovations and explicitly anti-Wagnerian stance made Paris the centre of post-Wagnerian modernity. This was confirmed in the early modern period by the arrival of Serge Diaghilev in 1907, with Russian art exhibitions, concerts and, later, ballets. The last, with the works of Stravinsky as much as anything, made Paris the centre of non-Wagnerian musical innovation, particularly with the scandalous success of *Le sacre du printemps* ('The Rite of Spring', 1913). Music in Paris was only one part of what was almost a frenzy of creation. Exhibitions by Picasso and Braque, the appearance of the Ballets Russes' rival Ballet Suédois and the immigration of such writers as Gertrude Stein, James Joyce and later Ernest Hemingway guaranteed Paris hegemony.

Characteristic of the 1920s were the extravagant ephemerality of such fashion-setters as Gabrielle 'Coco' Chanel, the cult of such music-hall *chansonnières* as Mistinguett and the emergence of Surrealism. During the grimmer 1930s, much of this disappeared, coming to an end in the war-time occupation by the Nazis. More typical of the seriousness with which such events had to be met were the poems of Paul Eluard, the works of Poulenc and the work written in a prisoner-of-war camp by the young **Olivier Messiaen** (1908–92), *Quatuor pour la fin du temps* ('Quartet for the End of Time', 1941), a voice that ensured Paris's musical centrality throughout the twentieth century.

NATIONALISM IN THE MODERN ERA

Nationalism in the twentieth century could be said to have broadened from the mere use of folk materials to a much larger-scale, but less clearly defined, national evocation. Typical of this were such contrasted composers as **Jean Sibelius** (1865–1957), **Carl Nielsen** (1865–1931) and **Charles Ives** (1874–1954), each of whom could be said to have established his country's identity through music and in the process produced abstract music that has had as profound an effect on the Modern Age as any other style.

The absorption of folk materials into a distinctly individual language was the hallmark of Stravinsky. He apparently abandoned the obvious Russian-ness of his early ballets in his neo-classical period from 1920 and his later 12-note period. But recent musicological explorations have demonstrated how indebted all his music was to the scales, melodic patterns and rhythms of his native country. His transformation of these elements into one of the most influential and characteristic voices of the century is itself a mark of the importance and use of nationalism in the modern period.

SERGE DIAGHILEV

Few non-performing or non-composing figures have had as much effect on the development of twentieth-century music as Serge Diaghilev (1872–1929). Born in Russia, he became enamoured early of Russian national music, memorizing *Ruslan and Lyudmila* by **Mikhail Glinka** (1804–57) as a child.

Though he studied composition with **Nicolai Rimsky-Korsakov** (1844–1908), Diaghilev abandoned it to concentrate on promoting, rather than creating, Russian works. In 1898, he organized an exhibition of Russian national art and became the founder-editor of the enormously influential magazine *Mir Iskusstva* ('The World of Art'). A lover of ballet, he was annoyed by the conservatism of the Russian Imperial Ballet and found a company with some younger dancers, including Anna Pavlova, Vaslav Nijinsky and Michel Fokine. Their collective impact on the rest of the world took place when Diaghilev, failing to make headway with his ideas, decided to leave Russia after the Russo-Japanese War (1904) and the 1905 Winter Palace Massacre. His move to Paris both ensured him publicity and in turn transformed ballet, stage-design and music, through his celebrated collaborations with famous choreographers, painters, dancers and composers, including **Maurice Ravel** (1875–1937), Stravinsky and Debussy.

Undaunted though not unaffected by the financial crises following World War I, Diaghilev pointed Stravinsky and Poulenc in the direction of neo-classicism, the former with his ballet *Pulcinella* (1919–20), the latter with his witty social satire *Les Biches* ('The Darlings', 1923).

Janáček ▶ p. 291 Khachaturian ▶ p. 292 Kodály ▶ p. 292 Messiaen ▶ p. 293 Milhaud ▶ p. 293 Nielsen ▶ p. 293 Orff ▶ p. 293 Prokofiev ▶ p. 294 Ravel ▶ p. 294
Rimsky-Korsakov ▶ p. 256 Satie ▶ p. 295 Shostakovich ▶ p. 297 Sibelius ▶ p. 256 Varèse ▶ p. 298 Villa-Lobos ▶ p. 299 Webern ▶ p. 299

The Modern Era
IGOR STRAVINSKY

FANTASIA

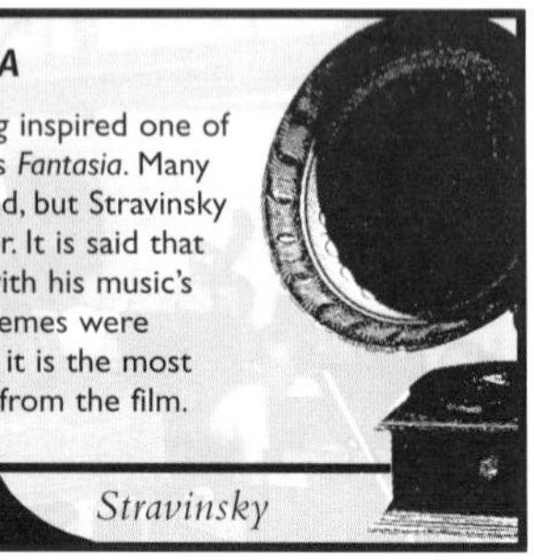

Stravinsky's *The Rite of Spring* inspired one of the sections in Walt Disney's *Fantasia*. Many well-known pieces were used, but Stravinsky was the only living composer. It is said that he was not entirely happy with his music's treatment, as many of his themes were moved around. Despite this, it is the most instantly recognizable piece from the film.

POPULAR MELODY *Stravinsky*

Igor Stravinsky (1882–1971) was a Russian composer, naturalized to French citizenship, then ultimately became American. He was one of the most formative influences on twentieth-century music. He came from a musical background (his father was principal bass singer at the Imperial Opera in St Petersburg) and studied with Rimsky-Korsakov, from whom he acquired a mastery of orchestration and an interest in Russian folk music. Influenced by his teacher and by Debussy, he wrote two short orchestral works, *Feu d'artifice* ('Fireworks', 1908) and *Scherzo fantasque* ('Fantastic Scherzo', 1909), which attracted the attention of Sergei Diaghilev, who was busy preparing his second season of Russian ballet in Paris. Stravinsky was asked first to orchestrate two pieces by Frédéric Chopin (1810–49) for a new production of *Les Sylphides*, then, to a tight deadline, to supply a new ballet score. The result – the brilliantly colourful and Rimsky-Korsakovian *The Firebird* (1910) – immediately made him famous, a success intensified by his second ballet for Diaghilev, *Petrushka* (1911), a sinister tale set in a Russian fairground, which greatly outdoes Rimsky-Korsakov in its orchestral wizardry. But his third ballet, *The Rite of Spring* (1913), the most ground-breaking and revolutionary score of the century, was greeted at its first performance by a tumultuous riot.

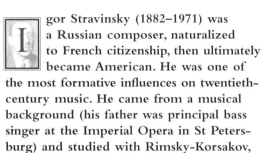

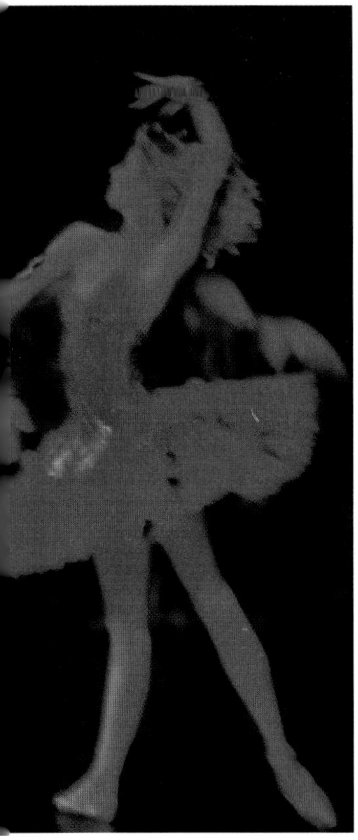

IGOR STRAVINSKY: WORKS

- **Operas:** *The Nightingale* (1909); *Mavra* (1922); *Oedipus Rex* (1927); *The Rake's Progress* (1951)
- **Ballets:** *The Firebird* (1910); *Petrushka* (1911); *The Rite of Spring* (1913); *Pulcinella* (1920); *Les Noces* (1923); *Apollo* (1929); *Le baiser de la fée* (1928); *Orpheus* (1947); *Agon* (1954)
- **Other stage pieces:** *Renard* (1916); *The Soldier's Tale* (1918); *Perséphone* (1934); *The Flood* (1962)
- **Orchestral works:** Piano Concerto (1924);Violin Concerto (1931); *Symphony in C* (1940); Symphony in Three Movements (1945); Movements (1959);Variations Aldous Huxley 'In Memoriam' (1964)
- **Choral works:** Symphony of Psalms (1930); Mass (1948); Cantata (1952); *Canticum Sacrum* (1955); *Threni* (1958); *Requiem Canticles* (1966)
- Piano music, songs, chamber music

FORWARD FROM *THE RITE*

World War I caused the temporary disbandment of Diaghilev's company, and Stravinsky spent the war years in Switzerland, where his wife was receiving treatment in a tuberculosis sanatorium. His works of this period continued to explore Russian folk music (an important, though unacknowledged, constituent of *The Rite of Spring*), but now much more economically, using a handful of instruments for songs in folk style such as *Pribaoutki* ('Tellings', 1914) and *Berceuses du chat* ('Cat's Cradle Songs', 1916), for the miniature drama *Renard* ('The Fox', 1916) and for the culminating work of this period, the choral ballet *Les Noces* ('The Wedding', 1917), an 'orchestra' of four pianos and percussion.

This period is also marked by an intensifying melodic economy (short, pithy ideas are varied by the addition or alteration of single notes) and by a growing interest in non-Russian music. *Histoire du Soldat* ('The Soldier's Tale', 1918), for two actors, dancer and seven instruments, incorporates a French waltz, a Spanish *paso doble*, an Argentinian tango and a ragtime (Stravinsky's rhythm, with its insitence on pulse and syncopation had points of contact with jazz). With his first ballet for the post-war Diaghilev company – *Les Noces* was delayed because Stravinsky was having difficulty deciding on its final scoring – he disconcerted his admirers by going a great deal further in this 'internationalizing' of his style, departing in an apparently retrogressive direction: the music of *Pulcinella* (1920) consisted of arrangements of music by **Giovanni Battista Pergolesi** (1710–36) or his contemporaries.

NEO-CLASSICISM

Pulcinella, its music by other composers 'merely' but radically arranged by Stravinsky, is an extreme instance – another is the ballet *Le baiser de la fée* ('The Fairy's Kiss', 1928), based almost entirely on music by Tchaikovsky – of his long period of absorption with the past. This is usually called his 'neo-classical' phase, although he did not like the expression. During it he did not refer only to the classical period of Haydn and Mozart; his miniature opera *Mavra* (1922) holds up an affectionate distorting mirror to his great nineteenth-century Russian predecessor Glinka and to Glinka's Italian operatic models, **Vincenzo Bellini** (1801–35) and **Gaetano Donizetti** (1797–1848). *The Symphony of Psalms* (1929) echoes **J. S. Bach** and Russian Orthodox chant, and the 'opera-oratorio' *Oedipus Rex* (1927), with its Latin libretto, refers both to the choruses of **George Frideric Handel** (1685–1759) and the arias of **Giuseppe Verdi** (1813–1901).

Reworking of Former Styles

In all Stravinsky's neo-classical works, and there are many spread over more than 30 years, he uses the stylistic conventions of earlier music entirely for his own ends: a repeating accompaniment figure may recall Bach, but it would not serve any function that Bach would have recognized. In many ways, Stravinsky's neo-classicism recalls his friend Pablo Picasso's revisitings and transformations of earlier styles. The idea of *Pulcinella*, on an old Italian ***commedia dell'arte*** subject, had first occurred to Stravinsky when he and Picasso were visiting Naples with Diaghilev's company. Seeing a burlesque group of traditional comedians reinforced Picasso's interest in clowns and the circus, and for the first production of *Pulcinella* he designed sets and costumes in a style recalling popular music-hall, a close parallel to the pungent twentieth-century orchestral colours that Stravinsky applied to his eighteenth-century originals.

commedia dell'arte ▶ p. 357 dissonance ▶ p. 358 serial music ▶ p. 362

AFTER DIAGHILEV

In the later years of Diaghilev's company, and especially after the impresario's death in 1929, Stravinsky wrote fewer stage works and far more concert pieces, many of them for him to play as piano soloist. The Piano Concerto of 1924 (his first appearance in the West as a pianist) was followed by a sonata, a serenade and a concerto for two solo pianos (for himself and his younger son). This was also the period of his brief but absorbed fascination with the pianola: he wrote a study specifically for it (unplayable by a human pianist) and laboriously recorded many of his works on piano rolls.

AMERICA BECKONS

By now, Stravinsky had four children and a bed-ridden wife, supported numerous relatives who had fled Soviet Russia and maintained a separate household with his mistress, later his second wife, the artist Vera Sudeikina. Finding his earnings from composing still uncomfortably inadequate, he began conducting. In his later years he depended on conducting and recording for the greater part of his income. Already traumatized by exile from Russia ('exile from his native language', he called it, but the Russian Revolution had also deprived him of a small estate and the income from it), he viewed the move towards a second world war with anxiety. After the deaths of his widowed mother and his wife, he left France for the US in 1939, and settled in Hollywood for the rest of his life.

(BL) The Firebird
Kirov Ballet Company production of Stravinsky's The Firebird.
(TR) Igor Stravinsky *by Milein Cosman*
Contemporary painting of the composer conducting.
(MR) Stravinsky Rehearsing
Stravinsky rehearsing his opera The Rake's Progress *at La Scala in Milan.*
(BR) Lad's Costume
Design for one of the costumes used in the first performance of The Rite of Spring.

AN EXPATRIATE IN HOLLYWOOD

On Stravinsky's arrival in the US, where he and Vera were soon naturalized and married, he had not only to adapt to a new language (his English was imperfect, Vera's almost non-existent), but also to a new economic way of life. The US was not a signatory to the Berne Copyright Convention, which meant that Stravinsky's earlier and more profitable works, originally published in Russia, could be performed without him receiving a fee. He remedied this, but only in part, by producing revised editions of those scores, and also made repeated attempts – all unsuccessful – to obtain work writing music for Hollywood films. Greater financial stability arrived only after the war, partly because of a fruitful working relationship with the choreographer George Balanchine (1904–83). By 1948 Stravinsky was able to contemplate his first full-length opera and his first major setting of English, *The Rake's Progress*, to a libretto based on Hogarth by W. H. Auden.

The neo-Mozartian opera was preceded by a setting of the Mass and followed by a cantata, which both refer to medieval prototypes. These and the opera were his last 'neo-classical' works, but during the writing of the cantata, Stravinsky experienced a creative crisis, from which he found an escape, prompted in part by his musical assistant Robert Craft, through a gradual and wholly individual adaptation of **Schoenberg**'s **serial** technique.

STRAVINSKY AND SCHOENBERG

Stravinsky and Schoenberg had been regarded as opposite poles, their followers ranged in incompatible camps, for 40 years. Stravinsky's 'conversion' to serialism disconcerted one group and delighted the other, of the possibilities of small groups of notes, he had in fact been a sort of 'serialist' since as far back as *The Rite of Spring*. He began with a quite un-Schoenbergian use of rows of less than 12 notes (thus by no means denying a sense of key), and even in more strict pieces continued his fascination with the techniques of the past, going further than Schoenberg in devising ways of using the system's severity while keeping his creative options open.

His discovery and adaptation of serialism gave Stravinsky a new lease of life, enabling him to continue working into his eighties, with such eloquent masterpieces as *Threni* (1958), a choral setting of texts from the Lamentations of Jeremiah, the *Canticum Sacrum* (1956), in praise of St Mark and the city of Venice, and the *Requiem Canticles* (1966). His last original work, at 84, was a gentle (but serial) setting of Edward Lear's 'The Owl and the Pussy-Cat', inscribed 'To Vera'. He continued to conduct and to make recordings up to an even greater age, and from 1959 until his death published a series of autobiographical recollections and trenchant comments on his own music and that of others, in the form of transcribed conversations with Robert Craft.

THE PREMIÈRE OF *THE RITE OF SPRING*

It was predictable that Stravinsky's score, with its harsh **dissonances** and jagged rhythms, would arouse some disapproval at its première in Paris on 29 May 1913, and during the unearthly sounds of the Prelude there were already protests. But when the curtain rose, as the music increased in rhythmic energy and violence and the audience got its first sight of Vaslav Nijinsky's (1890–1950) anti-classical, deliberately ungraceful choreography, the storm broke, and from that point on the music was drowned by shouting, booing and counter-demonstrations from Stravinsky's and Nijinsky's admirers. One of them, the composer Florent Schmitt (1870–1958), shouted coarse abuse at the fashionable ladies yelling from their boxes. The noise was so great that the dancers could not hear the music, and Nijinsky had to shout directions to them from the wings, while Diaghilev repeatedly had the house-lights raised and lowered in a vain attempt to quell the uproar. During the culminating 'Sacrificial Dance' the spasmodic movements of the Chosen Victim drew satirical cries of 'A doctor! Two doctors!', but when she raised her hands to her face this was replaced by 'No: a dentist!'. There are differing reports of Diaghilev's reaction to the scandal: according to Stravinsky it was 'Just what I wanted'. Later performances, however, were received respectfully, and when Stravinsky's score had its concert première later the same year, he was given a standing ovation and carried back to his hotel on the shoulders of a group of cheering students.

The Modern Era

CLAUDE DEBUSSY

Claude Debussy (1862–1918) was one of the father figures of twentieth-century music, often associated with the Impressionist movement. He was not only influential on subsequent French composers such as Ravel and Messaien, but also on other major European figures, including Stravinsky and Bartók. His early songs experimented with an intimate kind of word-setting, while his piano music developed a style more dependent on static washes of sound than on clearly defined melodies. In such pieces as *La mer* ('The Sea', 1903–05), he drew novel sounds from the orchestra and organized them in unpredictable ways. It was partly his use of evocative titles that caused him to be dubbed an 'Impressionist', while his songs and the opera *Pelléas et Mélisande* (1893–1902) allied him to the poetic and artistic movement known as Symbolism. Some of his pieces, such as 'Clair de lune' ('Moonlight', *c.* 1890), have become popular classics, while others are elusive and highly subtle, liberating sound itself from the shackles of conventional form, harmony and melody. Towards the end of his life, aware of the developments of Stravinsky and Schoenberg, he abandoned his fanciful titles and returned to the very form he had despised in his youth, namely the sonata.

CLAUDE DEBUSSY: WORKS

- **Piano music:** *Arabesques* (1888–91); *Suite bergamasque* (1890–1905); *Pour le piano* (1894–1905); *Estampes* (1903); *L'Isle joyeuse* (1904); *Images I* and *II* (1904–07); *Children's Corner* (1906–08); *Préludes* Books I and II (1909–12); *Etudes* (1915)
- **Orchestral works:** *Fantaisie* (piano and orchestra, 1889–90); *Prélude à l'après-midi d'un faune* (1892–93); *Nocturnes* (1897–99); *La mer* (1903–05); *Images* (1905–12)
- **Stage works:** *Rodrigue et Chimène* (1890–92); *Pelléas et Mélisande* (1893–1902); *La chute de la maison Usher* (1908–17); *Le martyre de Saint Sébastien* (1911); *Jeux* (ballet, 1912–13)
- **Chamber music:** String Quartet (1893); Rhapsody for clarinet (1909–10); *Syrinx* (Solo flute, 1913); Sonatas (cello and piano; violin and piano; flute, viola and harp, 1915–17)
- **Songs:** Early songs (for Mme Vasnier, 1881–83); *Ariettes oubliées* (Verlaine, 1885–87); five poems of Baudelaire (1887–89); *La Damoiselle Elue* (cantata after D. G. Rossetti, 1887–88), *Fêtes Galantes I* and *II* (Verlaine, 1891 and 1904), *Proses lyriques* (Debussy, 1892–93); *Chansons de Bilitis* (Louÿs, 1897–98); *Trois ballades de François Villon* (1910); *Trois poèmes de Stéphane Mallarmé* (1913)
- Other singly published songs and cycles; many abandoned works and projects; arrangements, editions, transcriptions; reviews and articles

REBELLIOUS YOUTH

While his mother taught him to read and write, his father 'intended him for the sea'. Someone (Debussy never remembered who) convinced him of his son's musical talents and one Madame Mauté brought his piano-playing up to the entry standard for the Paris Conservatoire, where he was accepted at the age of 10 – his first formal education. Sometimes he 'almost charged at the piano', recalled a fellow student, while at other times he produced soft effects of considerable beauty. He reacted against formal training in composition, constantly challenging established principles. Delighting in playing 'forbidden' harmonies, he proclaimed that the only rule was 'mon plaisir' – 'my own pleasure'.

THE PRIX DE ROME

Debussy's first surviving works date from when he was 16. Two years later, accompanying pupils for a singing teacher, he met a cultured soprano

'CLAIR DE LUNE'

Debussy's most popular piece, arranged for many combinations of instruments, must be 'Clair de lune' from the *Suite bergamasque*. The moonlight of its title refers to nocturnal antics at a masked ball; associations which are long forgotten. Also popular is 'The Girl with the Flaxen Hair', based on a poem about a Scottish girl.

POPULAR MELODY *Debussy*

14 years his senior, Marie-Blanche Vasnier. They became lovers and he wrote over 20 songs for her, setting the leading avant-garde poets of the day, Paul Verlaine and Stéphane Mallarmé in particular. His break came with the cantata *L'enfant prodigue* ('The Prodigal Son'), which won the Prix de Rome in 1884, giving him a year to compose at his leisure and fraternize with fellow musicians as well as with artists and literary people. These latter – more avant-garde in their attitudes than his musical colleagues – nurtured his preference for the half-stated and left an imprint on his compositions of the 1890s, which were mostly indebted to literature or the visual arts.

TOWARDS THE NEW CENTURY

Debussy had spent his year in Rome searching for the ideal text which, he claimed, would leave him space 'to graft his dream onto his poet's'.

LANDSCAPE INTO MUSIC

Debussy was fascinated by the musical evocation of nature. In *Pelléas*, nature music was several times demanded: the stillness of the dark forest; the changing effects of light on the water; a newly watered rose-garden. It was only after numerous settings of texts that Debussy began to compose orchestral and piano pieces representational in their own right. In 'Nuages' ('Clouds') from the *Nocturnes* (1900), the passage of grey clouds over a river is portrayed with strings representing the clouds and the oboes a boat's foghorn. In 'Sirènes', the imagined singing of mermaids is heard. The *Préludes* (1909–12) for piano have a wide variety of evocative titles, added to the pieces in parentheses as if their associations might provide a key, or could be ignored. Among the best-known are 'La fille aux cheveux de lin' ('The Girl with the Flaxen Hair') and 'La cathédrale engloutie' ('The Submerged Cathedral'), evoking the Cathedral of Ys, said to emerge from the sea on occasion. Sometimes exotic landscapes are evoked with pastiche music from outside the classical tradition. Several pieces (for example the orchestral Image 'Les parfums de la nuit' from *Ibéria*) use Cuban scales and dance rhythms such as the **habanera**.

habanera ▶ p. 358 leitmotif ▶ p. 359

A NEW KIND OF OPERA

Debussy's search for an ideal libretto ended when he discovered Maeterlinck's play *Pelléas et Mélisande*, which tells of a young girl, Mélisande, rescued from the forest by the older Golaud. Golaud marries her but his half-brother, Pelléas, falls in love with her. Golaud becomes jealous and kills Pelléas. Mélisande inexplicably dies, having given birth to a child. Debussy sets the play verbatim, in a conversational style which only occasionally broadens out towards the lyrical singing generally heard in the opera-house. The love story is accompanied by beautiful and gentle music, the most celebrated scene being the one in which Mélisande leans out of her tower, with her long hair enveloping Pelléas below. In direct contrast, the darker side of the play, where the increasingly distraught Golaud takes Pelléas into the vaults to 'smell the scent of death', draws terrifying music from Debussy. The symbolism of certain sections allowed him to 'complete Maeterlinck's dream', set in a fairytale landscape, but with strong portrayals of raw emotion. Debussy uses orchestral effects and careful pacing to underline the symbolism and prolongs each act into resonant interludes while the scene changes occur. There is nothing of grand opera here, more an orchestral backcloth over which the play gently unfolds.

MUSICAL EFFECTS

Many of Debussy's colleagues were smitten with the music of **Wagner** and believed that imitation of his music was the way forward. Debussy begged to differ. He greatly admired *Tristan und Isolde* (1857–59) for its adventurous harmony and *Parsifal* (1882) for its luminous orchestral effects, but he ultimately thought that Wagner was 'a sunset mistaken for a sunrise', although *Pelléas et Mélisande* uses Wagner's celebrated **leitmotif** technique to represent characters and symbolic themes. Debussy ended one era and began another. While the Art Nouveau and pre-Raphaelite elements of his earlier music are a culmination of the Romantic traditions of nineteenth-century music, other aspects of his work are fundamental to the modern school.

Debussy's momentary effects, which are neither prepared nor resolved, have been admired by many twentieth-century composers, as have his harmonic discoveries, often based on scales he evolved himself. Many of his pianistic and orchestral effects have been carefully studied by modern composers. His forms, which turned their back on the repetition of material inherent in the sonata, were dependent on a principle of perpetual variation: 'Why hear the same music again if you have already heard it once?' he asked. This principle, notably exemplified in the constantly varying lines of the faun's flute, became an important element in his work and the *Prélude à l'après-midi d'un faune* has been called 'the first piece of twentieth-century music'.

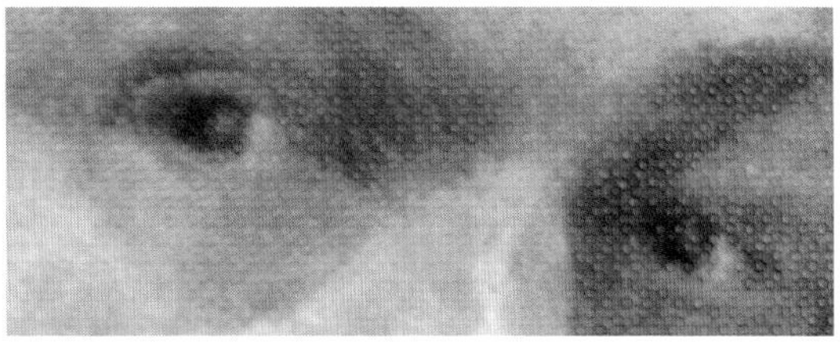

'I don't think I shall ever be able to cast my music in a rigid mould', he wrote prophetically, and back in Paris continued setting poetry either as cantatas, for example *La Damoiselle Elue* ('The Blessed Damozel', 1889), after Dante Gabriel Rossetti, or as songs with piano. His discerning literary tastes resulted in his first masterpiece, the *Prélude à l'après-midi d'un faune* ('Prelude to the Afternoon of a Faun', 1892–93), originally intended to accompany a reading of Mallarmé's lengthy and obscure poem.

In 1893, he attended the single Paris performance of the play *Pelléas et Mélisande*, by the young Belgian playwright Maurice Maeterlinck. He decided this was his ideal opera libretto, and began work almost immediately. At first little more than salon music, his style developed and deepened and he used more static and rippling effects. He also continued to produce songs, particularly inspired by the symbolist poetry of Verlaine, whose dictum 'De la musique avant toute chose' ('Music before everything') lay behind much Symbolist poetry, and led to a coming together of the arts.

RETURN TO CLASSICISM

Pelléas, first given at the Opéra-Comique in Paris in 1902, was a major success and became the most frequently performed French opera of the twentieth century, on the one hand chiming in with the popularity of the Pre-Raphaelites (a major influence on its playwright) and on the other offering composers a model for a new kind of opera. Before 1910, sets of pieces entitled *Images* appeared, for both piano and orchestra. Their titles give a hint as to their associations, but none was a narrative tone-poem with a storyline. 'Reflets dans l'eau' ('Reflections in the Water') and 'Cloches à travers les feuilles' ('Bells Through the Leaves') bear comparison with the paintings of Claude Monet and Georges Seurat, capturing the effects of light on water or bells through rustling leaves with washes or rapid 'dots' of sound.

LA MER

Begun in 1903, the celebrated sea-piece *La mer* was subtitled *Esquisses symphoniques* ('Symphonic Sketches'), heralding a return to a use of terms which Debussy had before avoided: he had never been interested in prolonging the symphonic tradition and considered the 'two-theme sonata' outmoded. By using the titles *Préludes* and *Études*, he allied himself to an ongoing tradition which went back through **Chopin** to **J. S. Bach**. His series of six sonatas, of which only three were completed, seemed to confirm that Impressionism had had its day, and presaged a new period of neo-classicism which was to be explored by Stravinsky among others.

(BL) Water Lilies ***by Claude Monet***
Debussy earned himself a reputation as an 'Impressionist' in music, after the contemporary artistic movement, begun by Monet.
(FR) Waterfall ***by Hokusai***
With La mer, *Debussy used his music to conjure up impressions of eastern landscapes.*
(NR) Pelleas et Melisande
Modern production of Debussy's opera, first performed in 1902.

J. S. Bach ▶ p. 106 Bartók ▶ p. 285 Chopin ▶ p. 190 Messaien ▶ p. 293 Ravel ▶ p. 294 Schoenberg ▶ p. 295 Stravinsky ▶ p. 280 Wagner ▶ p. 226

The Modern Era

PERSONALITIES

Arnold, Malcolm

b. 1921

ENGLISH COMPOSER

Arnold began his career as an orchestral trumpet player, but soon attracted attention with music that combined tunefulness, orchestral brilliance and engaging humour (the comedy overture *Beckus the Dandipratt* and two sets of *English Dances*). His symphonies and concertos combine these qualities with deeper, sometimes troubled emotions; they have attracted a smaller, but a deeply admiring, audience. Among his most characteristic – and most popular – works is his guitar concerto, memorably melodious and with a bittersweet elegy for the jazz guitarist Django Reinhardt (1910–53) at its centre. He has also written much film music.

BARTÓK AND FOLK MUSIC

At the end of the nineteenth century, 'Hungarian music' – to Hungarians as well as foreigners – meant **Franz Liszt** (1811–86), whose Hungarian Rhapsodies and other nationalist works were world-famous. Bartók, travelling through the Hungarian countryside and eventually throughout Eastern Europe and beyond, in search of ancient folk songs, soon discovered that what Liszt had taken to be Hungarian national melodies were often the music of commercial gypsy bands heard in the cafés of Budapest. Bartók was excited to discover that genuine Hungarian melodies were not only often of very high quality, but also that many of them used scales other than the major and minor of Western classical music. Bartók collected thousands of these melodies, recording them on a cylinder phonograph so that he could replay them in order to capture their complex rhythms and melodic subtleties. In the process, he discovered that He also discovered that folk tunes are oblivious to national boundaries, and that some songs previously thought to be Hungarian actually originated in Romania, Bulgaria or even further afield, in the Middle and Near East. The richness of a folk culture, he came to believe, depended on receiving and sharing influences. These discoveries profoundly affected his own music and his political beliefs.

Babbitt, Milton

b. 1916

AMERICAN COMPOSER

An enthusiastic exponent of Modernism, Babbitt is an influential teacher. In a famous essay, 'Who cares if you listen?', he argued that modern composers should not address the mass concert audience but, like scientists communicating research to their fellows, a specialist, almost private one. Strongly influenced by Schoenberg and Webern, he has extended their principles of organization to areas other than pitch. His works are abstract and complex, but not without drama, wit (*All Set*, for jazz octet) or lyricism (*Philomel*, for soprano and electronic tape).

Bacewicz, Grażyna

(Bát-sä'-vĕch, Grä-zhē'-nä) 1909–69

POLISH COMPOSER

Bacewicz was a pupil of Nadia Boulanger. She became one of Poland's leading composers as well as being an accomplished violinist. Her music is characterized by an individual neo-classicism and a clear sense of structure. She wrote a great deal for her own instrument (including seven violin concertos and five violin sonatas) as well as a series of seven string quartets, four symphonies and many other chamber and orchestral works.

'ADAGIO' FOR STRINGS

Originally the slow movement of a string quartet, Barber's 'Adagio' was taken up by such conductors as Toscanini and Koussevitzky and was played on occasions of national mourning or solemnity. Its haunting melody has been used for many soundtracks, most notably the war films *Platoon* and *The Killing Fields*.

POPULAR MELODY *Barber*

Barber, Samuel

1910–81

AMERICAN COMPOSER

Barber came from a musical family, and was trained in singing as well as composition. At 21 he gave the première of his own *Dover Beach*, for baritone and string quartet. Many of his works are vocal, including two full-length operas, *Vanessa* (1957) and *Antony and Cleopatra* (1966), numerous fine songs and, perhaps his masterpiece, the hauntingly beautiful *Knoxville: Summer of 1915* (1947), for soprano and orchestra. His two symphonies and his concertos for piano, for violin and for cello received high praise, but his conservative, lyrical style was later disdained by some critics; his later years were embittered by neglect, but produced his finest set of songs, *Despite and Still* (1969).

atonality ▶ p. 356

Bartók, Béla

(Bàr'-tok, Bā'-là) 1881–1945

HUNGARIAN COMPOSER AND PIANIST

Bartók's earliest works were influenced by **Johannes Brahms** (1833–97), by Hungary's famous Liszt and by **Richard Strauss**, then regarded as the last word in Modernism. Bartók's personal style, though, was formed by his discovery of **Debussy** and of Hungarian folk music. The strongly rhythmic, percussive, sharply dissonant music that resulted, earned him a leading position among the European avant-garde. His folk-music studies, partly undertaken from patriotic motives, soon led him towards a passionate internationalism, and he reacted strongly and courageously to Nazi ideas of racial superiority. In 1940 he left Europe for America, where he was little known and for a while close to poverty.

A STYLE ENRICHED BY DIVERSE INFLUENCES

The influences of folk music and of Debussy are audible in Bartók's first mature works: the First String Quartet, numerous volumes of short piano pieces (including *For Children*, 85 easy pieces for beginners) and his solitary opera, the one-act *Bluebeard's Castle* (1911). He was impressed by the revolutionary rhythmic language and vivid dissonance of **Stravinsky**'s *The Rite of Spring* (1913), and sympathetic to Schoenberg's exploration of music without a sense of key. These influences enriched and expanded his musical language until, in the dance drama *The Miraculous Mandarin* (1923), violent imagery is reflected in savage rhythms and lurid colour (the plot concerns a prostitute who lures men to be robbed by her associates; the Mandarin, though beaten and stabbed, will not die until she yields to him). In the Second and Third String Quartets he approached Schoenbergian **atonality**, but his awareness of Stravinsky's neo-classicism and his own study of folk music led him towards inclusiveness rather than exclusiveness. Another factor in his final maturing was a growing preoccupation with order and symmetry.

STRUCTURE AND SYMMETRY

In his folk music studies, Bartók had discovered that Hungarian and other folk melodies often build a satisfying sense of structure by not repeating, but constantly varying melodic ideas. This became an important feature of his own music, together with a strong feeling for structure. In several of his works, for example, five movements are arranged symmetrically in an ABCBA pattern, the 'A' and 'B' sections being transformed reflections of each other, not literal repeats. He also used the ancient proportioning system known as the Golden Section, whereby two parts of a work or movement are divided in such a way that the ratio of the length of the shorter to the longer is the same as that of the longer to the whole. In many of his works, partly as a consequence of this, partly as guidance to performers, the duration of movements and sections of movements is precisely timed.

(BL) Béla Bartók
Bartók collecting Slovak folk songs in the village of Zobordaraxes (now in the Czech Republic), in 1907.

BÉLA BARTÓK: WORKS

- **Stage works:** *Bluebeard's Castle*, opera (1911); *The Wooden Prince*, ballet (1917); *The Miraculous Mandarin*, dance pantomime (1923)
- **Concertos:** Piano Concerto No. 1 (1926); Piano Concerto No. 2 (1931); Piano Concerto No. 3 (1945); Violin Concerto No. 2 (1938); Viola Concerto (1945)
- **Orchestral works:** Suite No. 1 (1905); Suite No. 2 (1907); Dance Suite (1923); Music for Strings, Percussion and Celesta (1936); Divertimento for Strings (1939); Concerto for Orchestra (1943)
- **Chamber music:** String Quartet No. 1 (1908); String Quartet No. 2 (1917); String Quartet No. 3 (1927); String Quartet No. 4 (1928); String Quartet No. 5 (1934); String Quartet No. 6 (1939); Sonata for Two Pianos and Percussion (1937); Contrasts (violin, clarinet and piano, 1938); Solo Violin Sonata (1944)
- **Piano music:** 14 Bagatelles (1908); *For Children* (1909); *Allegro barbaro* (1911); *Sonatina* (1915); *Sonata* (1920); *Out of Doors* (1926); *Mikrokosmos* (six volumes of graded piano studies, 1926–39)
- **Choral music:** Village Scenes (1926); *Cantata profana* (1930) Songs, folk music transcriptions and arrangements

BARTÓK IN EXILE

When the Nazis promulgated their racial laws, Bartók announced that, despite the fact that most of his income from composition came from Germany, for the purposes of these laws he wished to be considered Jewish. In exile, he lived just long enough to see Hungary liberated from pro-Nazi rule. Some of his later works (the Second Violin Concerto and the Concerto for Orchestra) are in a less astringent, warmly lyrical style, but he died (of leukaemia) just as these were beginning to achieve widespread popularity.

Bax, (Sir) Arnold

1883–1953

ENGLISH COMPOSER

Bax was strongly affected by Richard Strauss, Debussy and Ravel, but the formative influence on him was a Romantic image of Ireland, first encountered through the poetry of W. B. Yeats and reflected in such tone-poems as *The Garden of Fand* (Fand was the goddess of the Western Sea). His music is passionate (the tone-poem *Tintagel* was partly inspired by a love affair), subtle and richly coloured, marked by rapid changes of emotion. He later turned to the symphony, writing seven, in which his Romanticism is tinged with deep melancholy and nostalgia.

WOMEN COMPOSERS IN THE MODERN ERA

During the twentieth century, increasing numbers of women worked as composers, and there is little that links them together other than the varying degrees of resistance that they encountered as they forged their careers, often complicated by the demands of marriage and motherhood. But while there are the disheartening stories of women such as Alma Mahler (1879–1964), agreeing to the demand of her husband **Gustav Mahler** (1860–1911) that she give up her own composition when they married (although when he later heard songs she had written as a young woman he made amends by having them published), there continued to be plenty of women who ignored the strictures of family or society and developed successful and lasting musical careers.

Graceful, Pretty and Undemanding

In the earlier twentieth century, there was still a general belief that women were not capable of creating the complex structures of large-scale music and that they should concentrate on genres which mirrored society's understanding of the feminine – something graceful, pretty and undemanding. Needless to say, the women composers of this period created a wide variety of music, from the simple to the intricate, the delicate to the grandiose, the unashamedly melodic to the courageously avant-garde. The music of the generation of women composers whose careers began in 1930s Britain, for example, includes the finely judged serialism of Elisabeth Lutyens (1906–83), the impassioned contrapuntal arguments of Elizabeth Maconchy (1907–94), the broad orchestral canvases of Grace Williams (1906–77) and the innovative sounds of Priaulx Rainier (1903–86). Of the preceding generation, the violist Rebecca Clarke (1886–1979) produced some striking songs and chamber works, including her well-known viola sonata (1919), before abandoning composition in her fifties.

Other talented musicians and composers of the era included Lili Boulanger, who became the first woman to win the Prix de Rome, and her sister Nadia, who became a teacher, numbering the female Polish composer and violinist Bacewicz among her pupils. Another teacher and composer was the Soviet Galina Ustvolskaya (b. 1919), herself one of Shostakovich's pupils at the Leningrad Conservatory.

Brahms ▶ p. 240 Debussy ▶ p. 282 Liszt ▶ p. 194 Mahler ▶ p. 250 R. Strauss ▶ p. 258 Stravinsky ▶ p. 280

Berg, Alban

(Bârg, Al'-bàn) 1885–1935

AUSTRIAN COMPOSER

Berg came from a cultured background, but had little serious musical training until, at 19, he began studying with Schoenberg. His progress was rapid, but although he was Schoenberg's most naturally talented and most devoted pupil, Mahler's influence on him remained strong. His first published work, the Piano Sonata op. 1 (1907–08), confidently uses a multiplicity of themes in a manner that strongly recalls Mahler, but in his next work, the Four Songs op. 2 (1909–10), he is already following Schoenberg in his explorations of atonality. In the remarkable String Quartet op. 3 (1910) he went further than his teacher had yet done in combining atonality with large-scale formal structures.

With the *Altenberg-Lieder* op. 4 (1912), he found his own distinctive voice, a post-Mahlerian world-weariness and profoundly original orchestral palette, mingling with a need to impose order on the disorder of atonality (Schoenberg had not yet invented dodecaphony for this very purpose). With the Three Orchestral Pieces op. 6 (1914–15), completed when he was 30, he was fully equipped for the sequence of masterpieces that occupied the remaining 20 years of his life.

LATER WORKS

The opera *Wozzeck* (1917–22) is a pitying and angry study of the exploitation of an underdog, so powerfully moving, despite its advanced language, that its popular success made Berg financially independent. The *Chamber Concerto* (1923–25), written in honour of Schoenberg's 50th birthday, is an exuberant play on the musical letters of his name, Berg's own and Webern's. *The Lyric Suite* for string quartet (1925–26), a work of extreme emotion and technical demands on its players, has an elaborate secret programme about Berg's love for Hanna Fuchs-Robettin, a passion that also strongly affected his second opera, *Lulu* (1929–35). He broke off working on this story to write first a large-scale concert aria, *Der Wein* ('Wine', 1930) and then, in response to the tragically early death of Manon Gropius – the daughter of Mahler's widow, Alma, by her second marriage – a Violin Concerto (1935). In its bitter protest and poignant tenderness and its incorporation of two folk melodies and a **chorale** by **J. S. Bach**, it has become the most widely popular of all works using Schoenberg's serial technique. Berg died (of blood poisoning following an insect bite) before finishing *Lulu*. Although the opera was very nearly complete, his widow's objections made it impossible for the opera to be heard in full until she died, 42 years later.

Berlin, Irving

1888–1989

AMERICAN COMPOSER

Born in Siberia of Russian-Jewish parents (his real name was Israel Balin) who emigrated to New York when he was a child, Berlin was self-taught and sold his first successful song ('Sadie Salome, Go Home') before his 20th birthday. 'Alexander's Ragtime Band' in 1911 was an international hit. In all, he wrote over 1,000 songs and numerous successful musicals, including *Annie Get Your Gun* (1946) and *Call Me Madam* (1950).

Bernstein, Leonard

1918–90

AMERICAN COMPOSER AND CONDUCTOR

Bernstein studied at Harvard and the Curtis Institute and became a protegé of Koussevitsky during summers spent at Tanglewood. His conducting break came in 1943, when the New York Philharmonic asked him to step in after its guest conductor was taken ill. The following year, still in his twenties, Bernstein wrote a successful Broadway musical, *On the Town* (1944) and a large-scale, critically admired concert work, the *Jeremiah Symphony* (1944). He was also a fine enough pianist to direct concertos from the keyboard. His composing output – at first extensive – was reduced by the success of his career as a conductor (he was appointed Music Director of the New York Philharmonic in 1958), but other musicals followed, notably the quasi-operatic, frequently revised *Candide* (1956) and the hugely successful *West Side Story* (1957). *Jeremiah* was followed by two other symphonies, *Age of Anxiety* (1949), with solo piano, and *Kaddish* (1951), with vocal soloists and chorus. His concert works – including the *Chichester Psalms*, the *Mass* and *Songfest* – often incorporate elements of jazz and popular styles; his musicals and light music are finely and seriously crafted.

WEST SIDE STORY

Based on Shakespeare's *Romeo and Juliet*, with clashing Montagues and Capulets replaced by rival gangs in 1950s New York, Bernstein's *West Side Story* mingles brilliantly the popular dances of the period (including Latin rhythms: one of the gangs is Puerto Rican) with love music not unworthy of Shakespeare's star-crossed lovers.

POPULAR MELODY *Bernstein*

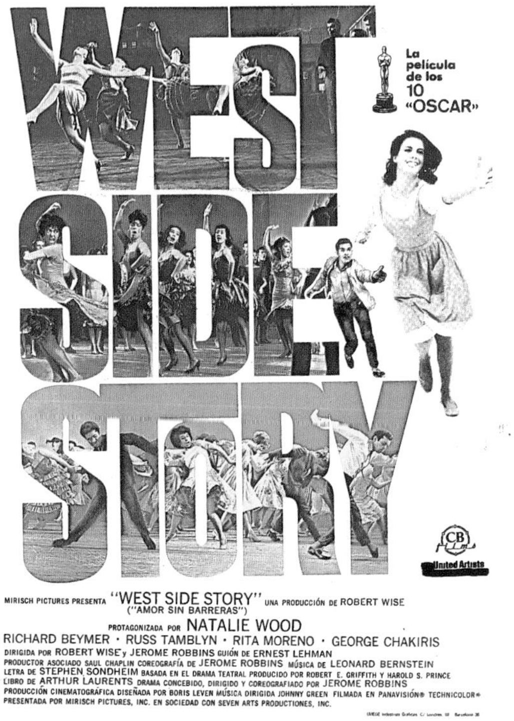

Bloch, Ernest

1880–1959

SWISS/AMERICAN COMPOSER

Bloch studied in Belgium and Germany, and his early works are in a rich late-Romantic style that owes much to Richard Strauss; this stage culminated in his powerful opera *Macbeth* (1909). In the following years, he sought a language which would reflect his Jewish faith in music of fervent solemnity with Eastern colouring: the symphony with voices *Israel* (1916), *Schelomo* ('Solomon', 1916), for cello and orchestra, *Avodath Hakodesh* ('Sacred Service', 1933) and others. Some instrumental works are in a neo-classical style as close to Vaughan Williams as to Stravinsky.

chorale ▶ p. 357

BRITTEN: A GIFT FOR OPERA

The formative influences on Britten's vocal style were **Henry Purcell** (1659–95) and the experience of working with **Peter Pears** (1910–86). From Purcell, much of whose music he transcribed for modern performance, he learned word-setting that was intimately responsive to the meaning and sound of the text. Pears acknowledged that Britten understood the potential of his voice better and sooner than he did himself. Apart from Pears, Britten wrote with deep insight for such singers as the contralto Kathleen Ferrier (1912–53), the soprano Galina Vishnevskaya (b. 1926) and the baritone Dietrich Fischer-Dieskau (b. 1925). This talent was one of the reasons for his quality as an opera composer, enabling him to make vivid character studies of even the minor roles.

Boulanger, Lili

(Bōō-lān-zhā', Lē-lē') 1893–1918

FRENCH COMPOSER

Despite being an invalid for most of her very short life, Lili Boulanger composed some outstanding works, in particular her gripping setting of Psalm 130, *Du fond de l'abîme* ('Out of the Depths', 1910–17) for soloists, choir and orchestra. Her talent was widely acknowledged, especially when, in 1913, she became the first woman to win the coveted Prix de Rome for her cantata *Faust et Hélène*. Lili's music and memory were kept alive by her elder sister Nadia (1887–1979), an equally talented musician who stopped composing after Lili's death and turned to conducting and teaching, something she once described as 'a sacred form of life'. One of the most respected teachers of the century, Lili included among her students Copland, **Philip Glass** (b. 1937) and Thea Musgrave (b. 1928).

Britten, (Lord) Benjamin

1913–76

ENGLISH COMPOSER

The finest English composer of his generation, Britten reacted against the folksong-derived pastoralism of his elder compatriots, finding inspiration in Purcell and influences as various as Mahler and Stravinsky. The international success of his opera *Peter Grimes* (1945) brought financial security, but he continued to appear as a pianist, accompanying his partner and outstanding interpreter, the tenor Peter Pears, and as conductor. He both founded and actively directed the English Opera Group and the Aldeburgh Festival.

Britten was born in Lowestoft, Suffolk (spending most of his adult life nearby in Aldeburgh), and at a very early age began composing with such promise that at 13 he was accepted by Frank Bridge (1879–1941) as his only pupil. After leaving the Royal College of Music at 21, he made his living by writing music for documentary films, soon attracting attention as a composer of outstanding gifts but also, in the view of some British critics of the time, of shallow cleverness and dangerous responsiveness to European Modernism. In 1939, he left England for the US, where his lifelong relationship with Pears began.

BENJAMIN BRITTEN: WORKS

- **Operas:** *Paul Bunyan* (1941); *Peter Grimes* (1945); *The Rape of Lucretia* (1946); *Albert Herring* (1947); *The Beggar's Opera* (arr. after Gay), 1948; *Billy Budd* (1951); *Gloriana* (1953); *The Turn of the Screw* (1954); *A Midsummer Night's Dream* (1960); *Owen Wingrave* (1970); *Death in Venice* (1973)
- **Other stage works:** *The Prince of the Pagodas* (ballet, 1956); *Noyes Fludde* (1957); *Curlew River, The Burning Fiery Furnace, The Prodigal Son* (church parables, 1964, 1966, 1968)
- **Solo voice(s) and orchestra:** *Our Hunting Fathers* (1936); *Les Illuminations* (1939), *Serenade* (1943)
- **Choral:** *A Ceremony of Carols* (1942); *Hymn to St Cecilia* (1942); *St Nicolas* (1949); *Spring Symphony* (1949); *War Requiem* (1961)
- **Solo voice and piano:** *Seven Sonnets of Michelangelo* (1940); *The Holy Sonnets of John Donne* (1945); *Winter Words* (1953)
- **Orchestral works:** *Sinfonietta* (1932); *Variations on a Theme of Frank Bridge* (1937); Piano Concerto (1938); Violin Concerto (1939); *Sinfonia da Requiem* (1940); *The Young Person's Guide to the Orchestra* (1946); *Cello Symphony* (1963)
- **Chamber and instrumental:** String Quartet No. 1 (1941); String Quartet No. 2 (1945); String Quartet No. 3 (1975); Cello Sonata (1961); Cello Suites Nos. 1, 2, 3 (1964, 1967, 1972)
- Five canticles for solo voices and instruments, many folksong arrangements and transcriptions of Purcell

MATURITY AND HOMESICKNESS

In the US, Britten wrote his first work for full orchestra without voices, the *Sinfonia da Requiem* (1940), conceived as a memorial to his parents and as a vision of the war that had already begun. He also wrote his first work for Pears, the virtuoso, Italianate *Seven Sonnets of Michelangelo* (1940), and his first stage work, *Paul Bunyan* (1941). A chance encounter with the poetry of George Crabbe, born in Aldeburgh in 1754, both filled him with nostalgia for his native Suffolk and provided him with the subject for his first true opera, *Peter Grimes* (1945).

CHAMBER OPERA

Britten and Pears returned to England, settling in Aldeburgh, and *Peter Grimes* was performed as soon as World War II ended, to public, critical and soon international acclaim. Several of his subsequent operas, however, were written for chamber forces, and to perform them he founded the English Opera Group, a small company capable of touring to places where opera could not otherwise be performed.

Britten's chamber operas use an orchestra of a dozen or so in which every player is a soloist. Apart from the advantage in terms of touring, chamber opera has great intimacy, giving directness to the genial comedy of *Albert Herring* (1947), poignancy to the heroine of *The Rape of Lucretia* (1946) and a nightmare intensity to *The Turn of the Screw* (1954). Individual instruments play an important role in sketching landscape, mood and character. As a further development of chamber opera, Britten devised the 'church parable', influenced by medieval mystery plays and by Japanese drama, in which all the musicians (including the instrumentalists) appear as monks, entering and leaving in procession.

THE MIDDLE AND LATER YEARS

The middle years of Britten's career were devoted very largely to opera and other vocal music, the former including large-scale works for Covent Garden (*Billy Budd* and *Gloriana*). The works that are arguably his finest were for chamber forces: one of his greatest operas, *The Turn of the Screw*, and his most personal, *Death in Venice* (1973). His concert works for voices reached their climax in the *War Requiem* (1961), a large-scale setting of the Requiem Mass, interspersed with settings of the war poems of Wilfred Owen for soloists and a separate chamber orchestra. In his later years he found new inspiration and challenges in the artistry and personality of the great Russian cellist **Mstislav Rostropovich** (b. 1927), writing for him his first major solo compositions (a sonata and three suites) and his first orchestral work without voices for many years, the Cello Symphony (1963). A severe heart complaint enfeebled him in his last years, but he managed to complete, as his final major work, the Third String Quartet (1975), of remarkable adventurousness and poignant expression.

(FL) Wozzeck
Berg's opera Wozzeck *was his most instant and enduring success.*
(NL) West Side Story
Poster for the film version of Bernstein's adaptation of Romeo and Juliet.

J. S. Bach ▶ p. 106 Glass ▶ p. 325 Pears ▶ p. 335 Purcell ▶ p. 78 Rostropovich ▶ p. 333

Busoni, Ferruccio

(Bōō-zō'-nē, Fer-rōōch'-yō) 1866–1924

ITALIAN/GERMAN COMPOSER

Busoni was a child prodigy, giving concerts from the age of seven and starting to compose soon after. His music was formed from the fruitful tensions between his Latin and Teutonic ancestries and between his reverence for the past – J. S. Bach and **Ludwig van Beethoven** (1770–1827) above all – and his openness to the new. What he called 'Young Classicism' was rather close to Stravinskian neo-classicism, and he welcomed Schoenberg's radicalism. Several of his works, including the monumental *Fantasia Contrappuntistica* (1910), reinterpret Bach for the twentieth century. Many of his later compositions are sketches for, or tributaries from, his masterpiece, the opera *Doktor Faust* (1924), a humanist and optimistic retelling of the ancient legend.

Cilèa, Francesco

(Chē-lā'-ä, Frän-chās'-kō) 1866–1950

ITALIAN COMPOSER

Although he is usually classified as one of the ***verismo*** ('realist') school, of his two well-known operas only *L'Arlesiana* ('The Woman of Arles', 1897), based on Alphonse Daudet's story of obsessive love set in a peasant community in southern France, answers to that description. The more famous *Adriana Lecouvreur* (1902) does not; its heroine is a famous eighteenth-century actress, jealously murdered with a poisoned bunch of violets. Both echo **Giacomo Puccini** (1858–1924) in style, with an almost cinematic sense of timing and with striking stage pictures.

Copland, Aaron

1900–90

AMERICAN COMPOSER

Born in Brooklyn of Russian Jewish parents (his surname is an immigration officer's mishearing of the family name, Kaplan), Copland became the archetypal composer of the American West, his style much imitated by the writers of Hollywood film scores. Trained in Paris by Nadia Boulanger, he was strongly influenced by Stravinsky and began using jazz elements in early works such as the Piano Concerto (1926). He then developed a tougher style, with affinities to Schoenberg in the austere and masterly Piano Variations (1931, later scored as 'Orchestral Variations'). His next and most familiar phase was a more popular style, using folk music (including cowboy songs) in the ballets *Billy the Kid* (1938) and *Rodeo* (1942) and Latin rhythms in *El salón México* (1936), his transparent scoring and plain, open harmonies conjuring up wide-open spaces. The masterpiece of this style is the moving 'pioneer' ballet *Appalachian Spring* (1944), but this was followed by a return to the leaner manner of the Variations and an adoption of Schoenbergian serialism. However, even these works, which included the orchestral *Inscape* (1967) and *Connotations* (1962), retain a characteristic Copland sound, and the late works are not exclusively serial.

Cowell, Henry

1897–1965

AMERICAN COMPOSER

From his childhood, Cowell was interested in 'New Musical Resources' – also the title of an influential book he published in 1930 – experimenting in his teens with **tone-clusters** (groups of adjacent notes played on the piano with the fist, palm or forearm) and, not long after, with plucking or strumming the piano's strings. A pioneer of complex rhythm and of **aleatory music**, in which performers make some of the composing decisions, his output was prolific. He was also an influential teacher, of **John Cage** (1912–92) and Gershwin, among others, and his New Music Edition published the work of Ives and Ruggles.

Crawford Seeger, Ruth

1901–53

AMERICAN COMPOSER

In the early part of her career, Ruth Crawford was associated with experimental 'ultra-modern' American composers such as Cowell. Her music from the 1920s and early 30s is bold and original; and includes a widely played string quartet (1931). After marrying her teacher Charles Seeger in 1932, she then turned, as she put it, to 'composing babies' and to her important work in transcribing and arranging traditional American music and folksong.

RHAPSODY IN BLUE

Written very rapidly (Gershwin did not have time to orchestrate it himself) in 1924 for a concert of 'symphonic syncopation' at New York's Aeolian Hall attended by Rachmaninov, the *Rhapsody* takes jazz and other popular styles and develops them symphonically. No other work of its kind has achieved such lasting popularity.

POPULAR MELODY *Gershwin*

Dallapiccola, Luigi

(Däl'-lä-pēk'-kō-lä, Lōō-ē'-jē) 1904–75

ITALIAN COMPOSER

Of the Italian composers of his generation, Dallapiccola was the first to adopt Schoenbergian serialism and the only one who actively opposed the dictator Benito Mussolini. His use of serialism is lyrical and Italianate. Many of his works are vocal, often subtle and delicate. His overtly anti-Fascist works (the *Canti di prigionia* – 'Prison Songs', 1941, and the opera *Il prigioniero* – 'The Prisoner', 1948) are also indebted to Stravinsky, but most of his later works are marked by restraint, economy and precision. These qualities made him an influential and honourable example to, and teacher of, the post-war generation of Italian composers.

Delius, Frederick

1862–1934

ENGLISH COMPOSER

Bradford-born but of German descent, Delius escaped the family wool business to devote himself entirely to music. He studied in Leipzig, where he met **Edvard Grieg** (1843–1907), and moved to Paris, where his friends included Ravel, but also such painters as Paul Gauguin and Edvard Munch. Affected by all these figures, and by **Wagner** and Debussy, his music is sensuous, richly coloured and filled with a rhapsodic love of nature. In later years syphilis caused blindness and paralysis in the composer, and his last works were dictated to an amanuensis, Eric Fenby (1906–97).

(L) Aaron Copland
Copland became the archetypal composer of the American West.
(TR) George Gershwin
Gershwin (left) with Guy Bolton and Ira Gershwin, 1930.
***(BR)* Porgy and Bess**
Sidney Poitier and Dorothy Dandridge in the film version of Gershwin's classic opera.

aleatory music ▶ p. 356 tone-cluster ▶ p. 363 *verismo* ▶ p. 363

Dohnányi, Ernö

(Dōkh-nän'-yē, Âr-nö) 1877–1960

HUNGARIAN COMPOSER

Less influenced by folk music than his contemporaries Bartók and Kodály, Dohnányi cultivated a late-Romantic style rooted in Brahms, though not without the sense of humour obvious in his *Variations on a Nursery Theme* (1914), nor occasional resort to national melodies, as in *Ruralia Hungarica* ('Rural Hungary', 1924). His success as a conductor diminished his output as a composer until, in his seventies, he emigrated to the US and resumed writing.

Dukas, Paul

(Dü-kä', Pōl) 1865–1935

FRENCH COMPOSER

Acutely self-critical, Dukas allowed only a handful of his compositions to be performed and published and wrote nothing of importance after the age of 47. He admired and was admired by Debussy, but his Symphony in C and his Piano Sonata are in a line traceable to Beethoven, and Debussy's influence is joined by Wagner's in the fine opera *Ariane et Barbe-bleue* ('Ariadne and Bluebeard', 1908). In later years he was a respected teacher, notably of Messiaen.

Eisler, Hanns

(Īz'-le, Häns) 1898–1962

GERMAN COMPOSER

A pupil of Schoenberg, but also a committed Communist, Eisler appalled his teacher by writing political music in a popular style derived from cabaret and marches. A refugee in the US during World War II, he was investigated by Senator McCarthy's House Un-American Activities Committee, and spent the rest of his life in East Germany, writing music for theatre and cinema. In some of his finest works – for example the *Deutsche Sinfonie* ('German Symphony', 1937) – his popularism, Schoenbergian rigour and a nostalgia for the pre-Nazi German past coexist memorably.

Ellington, Duke

1899–1974

AMERICAN COMPOSER

Although his heartland was the chiaroscuro world of jazz, Ellington transcended its boundaries, frequently lauded as 'America's greatest living composer'. A fine pianist, his keyboard skills were overshadowed by his writing abilities – evident in a multitude of jazz standards – and by his arranging. With the Ellington Orchestra he created dynamic unison passages using a palette of subtle textures (epitomized in *Mood Indigo*). Resurgent in the 1960s, Ellington explored his fondness for extended suites, reworking Grieg's *Peer Gynt* and Tchaikovsy's *Nutcracker* and rounded off his prolific career with a triptych of religious pieces, notably *The Majesty of God* (1973), performed at Westminster Abbey.

Enescu, George

(En-es'-kō, Zhôrzh) 1881–1955

ROMANIAN COMPOSER

A pupil of **Jules Massenet** (1842–1912) and **Gabriel Fauré** (1845–1924), Enescu became famous as a composer with his two *Romanian Rhapsodies*, written when he was 20, in a style close to Liszt's *Hungarian Rhapsodies*. His performing career as violinist and conductor was cut short by illness and he was largely forgotten after his death, but his striking opera *Oedipe* (1936) and other works, notably five symphonies, have been rediscovered in recent years. They combine French refinement with a strength drawn from Eastern European folk music.

Falla, Manuel de

(Fä'-yä, Män'-wel dā) 1876–1946

SPANISH COMPOSER

Falla first trained as a pianist and had written five *zarzuelas* (Spanish light operas) before studying composition with Felipe Pedrell (1841–1922), who influenced him profoundly, with his insistence that Spanish composers should write 'Spanish music with a view of Europe'. Falla then moved to Paris, where Ravel and Debussy influenced the exquisite orchestral colour of his *Nights in the Gardens of Spain* (1915). His two vivid ballet scores, *Love the Magician* (1915) and *The Three-Cornered Hat* (1917), made him internationally famous, but his later works are deeplymarked by his admiration for Stravinsky and by his own increasingly austere religious views. Most of them are pungent and epigrammatic, save the dramatic oratorio *Atlántida* (finished after his death by a pupil), an epic combining the legend of Atlantis, the voyage of Columbus and a vision of the world united by Roman Catholicism.

Gerhard, Roberto

(Gâr'-härd, Rō-bâr'-tō) 1896–1970

CATALAN COMPOSER

Like Falla, Gerhard was a pupil of the great apostle of Spanish national music, Pedrell, but Gerhard also studied with Schoenberg. Much of his music reflects this duality, which was sharpened by his exile from Spain after the Civil War (1936–39), when he lived in England. His opera *The Duenna* (1947), his symphonies and chamber music, are now gaining acceptance as modern classics.

Gershwin, George

1898–1937

AMERICAN COMPOSER

As a teenager, Gershwin played the latest hit songs to potential customers in a sheet-music store, and by the age of 21 (with his 'Swanee', made popular by Al Jolson) he had become a successful songwriter himself. After a visit to Europe, when he heard the latest musical shows and operettas that London, Berlin and elsewhere had to offer, he began writing musicals (*Lady be Good*, *Oh, Kay!*, *Funny Face* and others), but also sought a formal musical education, studying briefly with numerous teachers. Alongside his musicals and popular songs, he began to write concert works, beginning with *Rhapsody in Blue* (1924). *An American in Paris* (1927) is a still more successful example of this, but Gershwin's ambition now was to combine his command of large-scale forms and his mastery of musical theatre in a genuinely American opera. This he achieved, two years before his early death, with *Porgy and Bess* (1935), but his popular songs have proved no less enduring.

Giordano, Umberto

(Jôr-dä'-nō, Ōom-bâr'-tō) 1867–1948

ITALIAN COMPOSER

A leading member of the *verismo* school, Giordano has been much criticized for dramatic crudity and melodic short-windedness. He remains popular with singers, however, who value his effectively flattering vocal writing, and with audiences, who respond to his sense of the stage and his emotional power. Such works as *Andrea Chénier* (1895) and *Fedora* (1897) have something of the appeal of a Hollywood movie, with their strong situations, their suspense and the 'star quality' of their leading roles.

Beethoven ▶ p. 150 Cage ▶ p. 324 Fauré ▶ p. 248 Grieg ▶ p. 249 Massenet ▶ p. 252 Puccini ▶ p. 254 Wagner ▶ p. 226

Grainger, Percy

1882–1961

AUSTRALIAN COMPOSER

Influenced by Grieg and by Delius, Grainger spent his early years as a concert pianist and after that, in the US as a teacher. He was also particularly interested in folksong and much of his repertory consists of arrangements of such pieces. He is best known for such brief and catchy pieces as 'Country Gardens' (1918) and 'Handel in the Strand' (1930/1947), but other works investigate 'elastic scoring' and defy conventional rules, most notably the 'Hill Song No. 1' (1921) and *The Warriors* (1916), an imaginary ballet whose complex rhythms ideally require three conductors. Most of his works are characterized by this experimental nature and originality. In later life he invented machines for producing 'free music'.

Hanson, Howard

1896–1981

AMERICAN COMPOSER

Hanson's symphonies suggest an American **Sibelius**; his choral music is grandly optimistic (*Song of Democracy*, 1957; *Songs of Human Rights*, 1963) and his opera, *Merry Mount*, was well received at its première in 1933. He was Director of the Eastman School of Music for many years, where he made a notable reputation as promoter of American music.

Harris, Roy

1898–1979

AMERICAN COMPOSER

Born in a log cabin, ~~Harris paid~~ for his musical studies by driving a truck. He studied in Paris with Nadia Boulanger, but his rugged style owes as much to American folksong and hymn tunes and to his love of J. S. Bach. Of his 16 symphonies only the Third (1937), a work of epic striving and nobility, has achieved wide recognition, but some of the others are no less striking, and he wrote fine string quartets, choral and piano music.

Hindemith, Paul

(Hin'-de-mit, Poul) 1895–1963

GERMAN COMPOSER AND VIOLIST

Hindemith began his career as an *enfant terrible*, shocking conservative audiences with a ragtime based on a theme by J. S. Bach and a trilogy of one-act operas – *Mörder, Hoffnung der Frauen* ('Murder, Hope of Women'), *The Nusch-Nuschi*, *Sancta Susanna* ('Saint Susannah') – that mingled themes of sexual obsession with quotations from Wagner and strangely beautiful lyrics. His full-length opera *Cardillac* (1926) was no less disturbing in its portrayal of a goldsmith so obsessed with his own work that he murders to regain it. This phase ended in the early 1930s, and his next opera *Mathis der Maler* ('Matthis the Painter', 1933) is a serious essay, to music of sometimes grave beauty, on the artist's role in a society at war; a symphony drawn from it achieved lasting popularity. He had given the first performance of Walton's viola concerto in London in 1929, and in 1935, composed his own, *Der Schwanendreher* ('The Swan-Turner').

Denounced by the Nazis, Hindemith emigrated to America and began to formulate a harmonic system based on a hierarchy of intervals. He also radically revised some of his earlier works in the light of this system, even equipping *Cardillac* with a modified plot. Once highly influential, not least as a modern but palatable alternative to Schoenberg, he was regarded as a conservative in his later years; new interest in him has been sparked by the rediscovery of his youthful works.

Holst, Gustav

(Hōlst, Goos'-tav) 1874–1934

ENGLISH COMPOSER

As young men, Holst and Vaughan Williams were musically and personally close, collecting folk songs together and playing through each other's works. Unlike Vaughan Williams, Holst had no private income; he made his living first by playing the trombone, then as an inspiring teacher, at St Paul's Girls' School, London, and at Morley College (in a then largely working-class area of London). His suite *The Planets* (1919) achieved great popularity, but the influence of Stravinsky and Holst's interest in oriental philosophy led him into other areas, sometimes mystical ones, epitomized in *The Hymn of Jesus* (1917) and *Ode to Death* (1919).

'MARS' FROM *THE PLANETS*

'Mars, the Bringer of War' is the first movement of a suite in seven sections. It was begun before World War I, but was seen by many as a prediction of it, its remorseless savagery depicted in Holst's barbarically vivid scoring and insistent use of a crushing five-beat rhythm.

POPULAR MELODY *Holst*

Honegger, Arthur

(Ô-ne-gâr', Är-tür') 1892–1955

SWISS COMPOSER

Honegger studied in Paris, and was soon bracketed with five French contemporaries as 'Les Six', but his idiom was tougher and less Gallic than theirs. He made his name with a powerful, neo-Handelian scenic cantata *Le roi David* ('King David'; first performed at an outdoor festival in Switzerland, 1921). He wrote orchestral works on such subjects as *Rugby* (football) and *Pacific 231* (a locomotive) and a distinguished series of five symphonies. His dramatic works include operas such as *Judith* (1926), *Antigone* (1927) and the staged oratorio *Jeanne d'Arc au bûcher* ('Joan of Arc at the Stake', 1938).

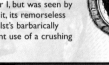

THREE PLACES IN NEW ENGLAND

Ives' 'Orchestral Set No. 1' (he preferred the English 'set' to the French 'suite'), evokes its three places with different types of music heard simultaneously. 'The St Gaudens on Boston Common' describes a monument to a regiment of black soldiers largely wiped out during the American Civil War (1861–65): a solemn march, dark with foreboding but also with an epic quality. Ives' father had brought a young, orphaned black bandsman back with him from the War, and his parents had given him an education. 'Putnam's Camp' is about a place near Ives' home which commemorates the American War of Independence (1775–81). A young boy (Ives himself, surely) wanders off from the noisy Fourth of July celebrations to the historic site itself, where he has a vision of Putnam's troops preparing for battle. They are led by a winged woman of great beauty (later the boy recognizes her in one of his father's books: she is Liberty). The vision fades, and the boy returns to the hubbub of the bands and the fair. In 'The Housatonic at Stockbridge', Ives recalls a Sunday stroll with his wife shortly after their marriage: sunlight through leaves, rippling water, the sound of hymns from a distant church; perhaps the Ives' love for each other and what they talked of.

Ibert, Jacques

(Ē-bâr', Zhàk) 1890–1962

FRENCH COMPOSER

Ibert won the coveted Prix de Rome, and shocked those who awarded it with the non-academic levity of the pieces he wrote in Rome. His best-known work is the uproarious *Divertissement* (1930), but it has distracted attention from an accomplished opera (*L'Aiglon*, 'The Young Eagle', 1937, written in collaboration with Honegger), some fine chamber music including a string quartet and such effective 'serious' orchestral works as the suite *Escales* ('Ports of Call', 1922).

Ireland, John

1879–1962

ENGLISH COMPOSER

Ireland's style is fundamentally English, drawing on his teacher, **Charles Villiers Stanford** (1852–1924), and on **Edward Elgar** (1857–1934), but he was fruitfully aware of Ravel and Debussy and, more guardedly, of the young Stravinsky. His attractive Piano Concerto (1930), *London* overture (1936) and his *Satyricon* (1946) have an agreeable wit; in other works he was influenced by the legends attached to prehistoric monuments. In mid-career he taught composition.

Ives, Charles

1874–1954

AMERICAN COMPOSER

Ives was drawn to music largely by the example of his father George, who had been a bandsman in the American Civil War and who encouraged his son in such experiments as playing a tune in one key and its accompaniment in another. Ives studied with the conservative composer **Horatio Parker** (1863–1919), but soon turned to his own unique style of writing, most notably with his *Unanswered Question* (1906). He realized, however, that he would not be able to support a family with the sort of music that he wanted to write and therefore moved (very successfully) into insurance, composing prolifically in his spare time. A heart condition eventually caused his retirement, and he wrote almost nothing after the age of 50.

Ives made little attempt to get his music performed, convinced that if it had quality people would discover it eventually. At his own expense he published the 'Concord' Sonata for piano (1918) and a collection of his songs, but his music remained largely unknown until the 1930s, and many major works were not heard until after his death.

THE THINGS OUR FATHERS LOVED

Ives wrote music using complex simultaneous rhythms, music in more than one key at once (polytonality) and in no key at all (atonality); in some works the orchestra is divided into two or more independent groups (sometimes requiring more than one conductor) and he often juxtaposed hymn-tunes, marches and rags in the manner of a collage. These pioneering discoveries (most of his major works were written before 1915) anticipate many of the century's later musical developments, but they are often intended to evoke the past, especially the idealistic America of his father's youth and the homelike but noble principles of the New England Transcendentalists, evoked in his 'Concord' Sonata. He believed that a key to this world was to be found in its tunes, which speak 'of the things our fathers loved'.

LEOŠ JANÁČEK WORKS

- **Operas:** *Šárka* (1888); *The Beginning of a Romance* (1891); *Jenufa* (1903); *Fate* (1905); *The Excursions of Mr Broucek* (1917); *Katya Kabanová* (1921); *The Cunning Little Vixen* (1923); *The Makropulos Case* (1925); *From the House of the Dead* (1928)
- **Cantatas:** *Amarus* (c. 1897); *Glagolitic Mass* (1926)
- **Songs:** 'The Diary of One Who Disappeared' (1919)
- **Orchestral works:** *Taras Bulba* (1925); *Sinfonietta* (1926)
- **String quartets:** No. 1 *The Kreutzer Sonata* (1923); No. 2 *Intimate Letters* (1928)
- **Piano music:** *On the Overgrown Path* (1901–8); Sonata '1 x 1905' (1905); *In the Mist* (1912)

Janáček, Leoš

(Yă'-nà-chek, Lā'-ōsh) 1854–1928

CZECH COMPOSER

Janáček came from a teaching family and initially followed that calling, though he later studied music in Prague, Leipzig and Vienna. He made his mark by fostering musical life in the Moravian capital Brno as teacher and conductor, and by collecting and publishing folksong. His musical voice crystallized in the realist opera *Jenufa*, given its successful première in 1904. A late starter, he consolidated his style in music for piano and choir, and two more operas, over the next 12 years. Acclaim in Prague eluded him until the triumphant success of *Jenufa* there in 1916. At the same time, Janácek met and fell in love with a married woman, Kamila Stösslová, nearly 40 years younger, who became the muse of his last 12 years. Images of Kamila dominate the depiction of women in his next three operas, *Katya Kabanová* (1921), *The Cunning Little Vixen* (1924) and *The Makropulos Case* (1926), and his unrequited love for her was celebrated in his second string quartet, *Intimate Letters* (1928). New-found love and the encouraging prospect of a free Czechoslovak state – realized in 1918 – released huge creative energy in Janáček. Nearly all of his best-known works come from the 1920s and are marked by a buoyant enthusiasm which communicates itself markedly in the well-known *Sinfonietta* (1926).

JANÁČEK'S MUSIC

Janáček is the greatest Czech composer of the twentieth century. Folksong and the sound of the Czech language had a major impact on his style. His early works have affinities with his friend and mentor **Antonín Dvořák** (1841–1904), but his explosive originality owes very little to conventional influence. Short melodic ideas, succinctly communicating enormous sentiment, set against strongly conceived tonal paragraphs, which often build to overwhelming climaxes – notably at the end of *Jenufa* and in the outer movements of the *Sinfonietta* – result in a craggy but extremely compelling musical language. These qualities and an uncanny ability for characterization, especially of female figures, have made him one of the most popular and successful of twentieth-century opera composers.

(FL) Percy Grainger
Grainger, best-known for his popular songs 'Handel in the Strand' and 'Country Garden', with his mother.
(NL) Arthur Honegger
Honegger surrounded by his students at the École Normale Superieure de Musique.

Dvorák ▶ p. 245 Elgar ▶ p. 247 Parker ▶ p. 254 Sibelius ▶ p. 256 Stanford ▶ p. 258

Joplin, Scott

1868–1917

AMERICAN COMPOSER

More than any other composer, Joplin brought ragtime to its pinnacle: his *Maple Leaf Rag* (1899) is characteristic of his joyous and infectious but disciplined art, while 15 years later *Magnetic Rag*, with its dramatic and unexpected shifts of key, suggests a composer ready to expand into other areas. Joplin evidently thought so, since he wrote two operas, one destroyed, the other (*Treemonisha*, 1911) unperformed until 1974.

Kabalevsky, Dmitri

(Kā-bā-lef-skē, D'mē'-trē) 1904–87

RUSSIAN COMPOSER

A rather late developer, Kabalevsky made a career as a pianist before beginning composition studies in his twenties. His style is conservative but, especially in his opera *Colas Breugnon* (1938) and in music for his own instrument (three concertos, three sonatas, numerous preludes and **fugues**), freshly and often catchily melodious.

Kern, Jerome

1885–1945

AMERICAN COMPOSER

Like Gershwin, Kern began his career as a song-plugger (playing new songs to potential customers in a publisher's showroom) and then gained invaluable experience writing additional or replacement numbers for musicals imported to the US from Europe. In 1915, he formed a partnership with the writer Guy Bolton (soon joined by P. G. Wodehouse as lyricist). Their earliest shows included *Very Good Eddie* (1915) and *Oh, Boy* (1917), culminating in the hugely successful *Sally* (1920). Kern's greatest triumph was *Show Boat* (1927), to a libretto by Oscar Hammerstein II, with whom he also wrote *Music in the Air* (1932), and with Otto Harbach *The Cat and the Fiddle* (1931) and *Roberta* (1933). He wrote over 40 musicals, some specifically for Hollywood. His best-known songs include 'The Way You Look Tonight', 'Smoke Gets in Your Eyes', 'Ol' Man River' and 'All the Things You Are'.

Khachaturian, Aram

(Khā-chā-tōōr'-yān, Ā'-rām) 1903–78

ARMENIAN COMPOSER

Khachaturian's music is conservative, winning popularity with its ample tunefulness, sometimes with local colour derived from Armenian folk music. His ballets *Gayane* (1942) and *Spartacus* (1954) were very successful in the Soviet Union, and extracts from them (the 'Sabre Dance' from *Gayane*, the ***pas-de-deux*** from *Spartacus*) became world-famous. His concertos, concerto-rhapsodies and symphonies are in a similar, opulently Romantic style.

Kodály, Zoltán

(Kō-dā'-ē, Zōl'-tān) 1882–1967

HUNGARIAN COMPOSER

Kodály was closely associated with Bartók in folksong collecting and research, but his own music takes less radical paths. Apart from his compositions – notably the colourful *Peacock Variations* (1939) on a Hungarian folk tune, the *Dances of Marosszek* (1930) and *Dances of Galánta* (1933), the impressive choral *Psalmus Hungaricus* (1923), a fine sonata for unaccompanied cello and the comic opera *Háry János* (1926) – he had a major influence on music education, believing that all children can be taught music by means of choral singing. He wrote much music for this purpose, and his method was widely admired and emulated.

Lehár, Franz

(Lā'-här, Frāntz) 1870–1948

AUSTRIAN COMPOSER

Of Hungarian ancestry and Czech training (Dvořák helped him as a young man), Lehár began his career as an army bandmaster, while also writing waltzes. These were so successful that he was able to leave the army in his early thirties to begin a long career composing operettas. Welcomed by the Viennese as the successor to Johann Strauss the Younger (1825–99), his background enabled him to add Eastern European local colour to such works as *The Merry Widow* (1905, his first international success) and *Zigeunerliebe* ('Gipsy Love', 1910).

Malipiero, Gian Francesco

(Mā-lē-pē-ā'-rō, Jān Fran-chā-skō) 1882–1973

ITALIAN COMPOSER

Although unevenly prolific, he was described by his younger contemporary Dallapiccola as the most important figure in Italian music since Puccini. He was influenced by Stravinsky, no less radically by his discovery of early Italian music – **Claudio Monteverdi** (1567–1643) and **Antonio Vivaldi** (1678–1741), both of whose music he edited for publication – and, late in life, by Schoenberg. In opera (he wrote dozens of unconventional stage pieces) he rejected realism and Romantic grandiloquence; in instrumental music, he preferred dramatic juxtaposition of themes to traditional symphonic development. In his finest operas, among them the extraordinary *Torneo Notturno* ('Nocturnal Tournament', 1931) and *L'Orfeide* (1925), especially its central 'act', *Sette Canzoni* ('Seven Songs'), and the best of his symphonies and string quartets, he is a powerfully original composer, and is still much underrated.

THE STING

On the whole a light-hearted and debonair crime-story, the film *The Sting* found not only ideally exuberant period music in Joplin's rags, but brought them to a new audience. Joplin might well have approved: he made his living not only by publishing his music, but also by distributing it through the new medium of the piano roll.

POPULAR MELODY *Joplin*

Martin, Frank

(Mär-tan', Frånk) 1890–1974

SWISS COMPOSER

Martin was an eclectic, but with his own voice. His best-known composition, the *Petite Symphonie Concertante* (1945) for harp, harpsichord, piano and strings, adopts systematic discipline from Schoenberg and rhythmic vigour from Stravinsky and jazz, but its combination of brooding solemnity and Gallic wit is Martin's own. His concertos and chamber music are no less accomplished, but another, important, group of works reflects his devout religious belief: four oratorios (one of them staged) and a Requiem. He wrote operas in French and German and a secular oratorio, *Le vin herbé* ('The Drugged Wine', 1942), on the legend of Tristan and Isolde.

Menotti, Gian Carlo

(Me-nôt'-tē, Jān Kär'-lō) b. 1911

ITALIAN/AMERICAN COMPOSER

The best of Menotti's stage works combine something of the melodic appeal of Puccini and his successors with a dramatic punch that is Menotti's own, but owes something to the American musical. His macabre *The Medium* (1946) and the chilling *The Consul* (1950), about refugees attempting to escape an unnamed country, have both enjoyed many performances worldwide, while his one-act comedies *Amelia Goes to the Ball* (1937) and *The Telephone* (1947) demonstrate an elegant gift for humour. His Christmas parable *Amahl and the Night Visitors* (1951) was

pas-de-deux ▶ p. 361

shown on American television annually for many years. His later operas have been criticized as melodramatic and musically thin, but his best tunes are obstinately memorable. For many years he lived with his fellow composer Barber, for whose opera *Vanessa* (1957) he wrote the libretto.

Messiaen, Olivier

(Mes-sē-än', Ō-lēv-yā') 1908–92

FRENCH COMPOSER

Messiaen's music is unmistakably personal, drawn from a wide range of interests rather than influences. A church organist from his twenties, he was aware of the 'church modes' (scales used in Western music before the development of the key system) and investigated other modes, including rhythmic ones. He studied Asian and ancient Greek music and was an insatiable collector of birdsong.

Central to his work was his Roman Catholic faith, but secular and personal concerns also surfaced, in the ecstatic love songs – *Poèmes pour Mi* (1936) and others – addressed to his first wife and then, after she was struck down by a disease which robbed her of her faculties, a series of works inspired by his love for an outstandingly gifted pupil, the pianist Yvonne Loriod (b. 1924). Central to these, and Messiaen's most widely performed work, is the huge *Turangalîla-Symphonie*, a rapturous love-song and hymn to joy in 10 movements. Inspired by Loriod's virtuosity, he wrote for her the evening-long cycles of piano pieces *Vingt regards sur l'enfant-Jesus* ('Twenty Gazes at the Child Jesus', 1944) and *Catalogue d'oiseaux* ('Catalogue of Birds', 1946–48), as well as *Visions de l'Amen* ('Visions of the Amen', for two pianos, 1943) and an important series of multi-movement works for his own instrument, the organ. These include *La nativité du Seigneur* ('The Nativity of the Lord', 1935), *Messe de la Pentecôte* ('Pentecost Mass', 1945–50), *Livre d'orgue* ('Organ Book', 1951) and *Méditations sur le mystère de la Sainte-Trinité* ('Meditations on the Mystery of the Holy Trinity', 1969). In the 1960s, the imagery of his music became grander, and a series of late works act as a final confession of faith as well as a conspectus of the areas his work had explored: an oratorio, *La transfiguration de notre Seigneur Jésus-Christ* ('The Transfiguration of Our Lord Jesus Christ', 1969), an orchestral cycle, *Des canyons aux étoiles...* ('From the Canyons to the Stars', 1974), and an opera, *Saint-François d'Assise* ('St Francis of Assisi', 1983). His learning and non-doctrinaire openness to new musical ideas made him an inspiring teacher and his pupils included **Pierre Boulez** (b. 1925), **Karlheinz Stockhausen** (b. 1928), **Iannis Xenakis** (b. 1922), **Alexander Goehr** (b. 1932) and **George Benjamin** (b. 1960).

Milhaud, Darius

(Mē-yō', Där-yüs') 1892–1974

FRENCH COMPOSER

One of the group known as 'Les Six', Milhaud was perhaps the most prolific composer of the twentieth century. Jazz was an important influence on him, as was the carnival music of South America, and he was famous for writing music in two or more keys at once (polytonality). He composed in most musical forms (12 symphonies, 18 string quartets), but is especially remembered for some of the most famous ballet scores of the 1920s, including *La création du monde* ('The Creation of the World', 1923), *Le boeuf sur le toit* ('The Ox on the Roof', 1920).

Nielsen, Carl

(Nēl'-sen, Kärl) 1865–1931

DANISH COMPOSER

Nielsen was born of working-class parents on the island of Funen; his father was well known locally as a folk fiddle-player. After a period in a military band, he studied the violin and for some years made his living as an orchestral violinist, then as a conductor. At the centre of his output are six symphonies, among the greatest of the century, which dramatize huge aspirations and conflicts with powerful tensions between keys, strongly contrasting melodic ideas and a remarkable sense of 'concert drama'. In the Fourth Symphony (1916) two kettledrummers on opposite sides of the platform engage in battle, in the Fifth (1916), a side-drum improvises 'as though at all costs to stop the progress of the orchestra'. He also wrote, for the newly established Danish state schools, simple, direct and instantly memorable unison songs, many of which became universally familiar. These two worlds approach each other in the sometimes gruff good humour of his Wind Quintet (1922) and the humane comedy of his opera *Maskarade* ('Masquerade', 1905), and meet in the exquisite lyricism and nostalgia of his cantata *Springtime on Funen* (1922).

Orff, Carl

(Ôrf, Kärl) 1895–1982

GERMAN COMPOSER

Orff's enduringly popular *Carmina Burana* ('Songs of Beuren', 1937), with its simple melodies and pounding rhythms, is characteristic of his work. He wrote comic and satirical operas in this manner, including *Der Mond* ('The Moon', 1939) and *Die Kluge* ('The Clever Girl', 1943). Some later compositions use orchestras consisting almost entirely of percussion instruments; they also include settings of classical Greek dramas (*Antigone*, 1949) and a trilogy of Christian mystery plays. He devised an influential system of musical education using singing and percussion instruments.

Pfitzner, Hans

(Fits'-ner, Hänz) 1869–1949

GERMAN COMPOSER

An opponent of all forms of modernism, Pfitzner composed his own music in a late-Romantic but highly individual style. His opera *Palestrina* (1917) – his confession of faith and his masterpiece – is about the cumulative wisdom of tradition, but also its renewal. His German nationalism was more idealistic than political, but his reputation was harmed by his cantankerous nature and by the title of one of his cantatas: *Vom deutscher Seele* ('Of the German Soul', 1921), which was assumed to be Nazi propaganda. It was not – he wrote it long before the rise of the Nazis – and its radiant depictions of nature went unheard for many years. He wrote three other operas, distinguished orchestral and chamber music and many fine songs.

Piston, Walter

1894–1976

AMERICAN COMPOSER

Piston studied in Paris with Nadia Boulanger and Dukas, then taught at Harvard University (Bernstein and **Elliott Carter**, b. 1908, were among his pupils), publishing several composition textbooks. His music, including eight symphonies, is neo-classical, athletically energetic and graceful.

(L) Franz Lehár
Caricature showing Lehár 'At the Peak of Success', after the opening of his Endlich Allein.
***(FR)* Carmina Burana**
Production of Carl Orff's famous Carmina Burana*, the music of which is known and loved the world over.*

Benjamin ▶ p. 324 Boulez ▶ p. 324 Carter ▶ p. 325 Goehr ▶ p. 325 Monteverdi ▶ p. 76 Stockhausen ▶ p. 329 Vivaldi ▶ p. 122 Xenakis ▶ p. 330

Pizzetti, Ildebrando

(Pid-zet'-tē, Ēl-dā-brán'-dō) 1880–1968

ITALIAN COMPOSER

Like many Italian composers of his generation, Pizzetti was more influenced by older music than by the recent Italian past; he was little affected by trends post-Debussy. He wrote in most musical . forms, but is best known for his operas. With dignified solo writing rooted in Monteverdi and sonorously effective choral scenes, they are on classical (*Fedra* – 'Phaedra', 1909), biblical (*Debora e Jaele*, 1922) and historical subjects (*Assassinio nella cattedrale* – 'Murder in the Cathedral', 1958).

Poulenc, Francis

(Pōō-lank', Frán-sēs) 1899–1963

FRENCH COMPOSER

Poulenc was the youngest member of the group of composers known as 'Les Six'; his urbanity and humour and his many masterly songs have given him a reputation as a light-hearted miniaturist. His range, however, is better indicated by his three operas: *Les mamelles de Tirésias* ('Tiresias' Breasts', 1947), a joyously Gallic and absurd wartime rejection of Teutonic seriousness (many of his works are in this vein), *Dialogues des Carmélites* ('Carmelite Dialogues', 1957), the story of a community of nuns executed during the French Revolution (Poulenc returned to the Catholic faith in his thirties, and wrote numerous sacred works), and *La voix humaine* ('The Human Voice', 1958), the monologue of a woman abandoned by her lover.

Prokofiev, Sergei

(Pru-kôf'-yef, Syir'-gā) 1891–1953

RUSSIAN COMPOSER

Prokofiev's music oscillates between motor rhythm and lyricism, and between irony and expressive sincerity. This gives his compositions extreme variety: works composed closely in time, even adjacent movements in the same work, are of quite different characters.

He began composing as a child, and had his first success (with his First Piano Concerto, which he played himself) while still a student. He soon attracted the attention of Diaghilev, who commissioned a score (*Ala and Lolly*) for his Ballets Russes, but rejected it: Prokofiev had imitated Stravinsky's *The Rite of Spring* too closely. In rapid succession he then wrote *Chout* ('The Clown', 1915), a ballet in his ironic, strongly rhythmic manner, an opera, *The Gambler* (1917), in which a recurring theme – compulsive obsession – is first sketched, the Haydnesque 'Classical' Symphony (1917) and his elegantly melodious First Violin Concerto (1917).

LATER YEARS

He spent the years after World War I in the US and Paris, writing *The Love for Three Oranges* (1920), a fairytale operatic fantasy, and *The Fiery Angel* (1923), a wildly frenetic story of demonic possession. Two new ballets were as strongly contrasted: *Le pas d'acier* ('The Steel Step', 1925), a machine-age fantasy, and *The Prodigal Son* (1927), filled with nobility and balletic grace.

In 1933 he visited Russia for the first time in 16 years, and returned there for good in 1936, but his *Romeo and Juliet* (1935), commissioned by the Kirov Ballet in Leningrad, was at first rejected. For a while Prokofiev devoted himself to propaganda music and film scores, including Sergei Eisenstein's (1898–1948) *Ivan the Terrible* and *Alexander Nevsky*. His Fifth Symphony (1944) was welcomed by Soviet authorities and audiences, but his later operas, including *The Duenna* (1940) and the epic *War and Peace* (1941), had a mixed reception, and his final years were troubled by official denunciation and worsening health.

Ravel, Maurice

(Rá-vel', Mō-rēs') 1875–1937

FRENCH COMPOSER

Ravel is often described (like Debussy, but still more misleadingly) as an 'Impressionist', but Ravel's music is in fact precisely and delicately crafted, subtly perfect in its artifice (in the best sense of the word). Influenced by **Alexis-Emmanuel Chabrier** (1841–94), Satie and his close friend Stravinsky, attracted to Spain temperamentally (he never visited the country, but his mother came from the Basque region), he absorbed all these factors – and jazz – to produce a style that was entirely his own. Each of his works, even those in the same form, is unique: the sprightly comic opera *L'heure espagnole* ('The Spanish Hour', 1907) is as different from the touching child-like fantasy of *L'enfant et les sortilèges* ('The Child and the Spells', 1925) as his brilliant, Gershwinesque but **Mozart**-centred Piano Concerto in G is from the sombre and sinewy Concerto for Left Hand (1931).

Ravel wrote very little that was second-rate (though he described his *Boléro* of 1928 as 'a piece for orchestra without music'). His ballet *Daphnis et*

BOLÉRO

Ravel's rousing *Boléro* has become his best-known piece, thanks to two ice-skaters. Jayne Torvill and Christopher Dean used *Boléro* to accompany their perfect-six ice dance in the 1986 Olympics. It won them the gold medal.

POPULAR MELODY *Ravel*

TONALITY AND ATONALITY

Music is said to be 'in C' (or any other key) when it uses predominantly the seven notes of the scale (major or minor) starting on the stated note, the other five available notes being used as expressive colouring, often suggesting the imminence of another key and thus building tension. Throughout the nineteenth century, composers, seeking increasingly expressive subtlety, tended to use notes extraneous to the home key more and more often until, in the super-expressive 'Prelude' to Wagner's opera *Tristan und Isolde*, it became very hard to tell what key the music was in, and thus to perceive any sense of the music's destination.

After writing a number of works, including *Verklärte Nacht* ('Transfigured Night', 1899) for string sextet or string orchestra, and the enormous *Gurrelieder* ('Songs of Gurre', 1903) for soloists, chorus and orchestra, which are deeply indebted to Wagner, Schoenberg began to believe that the days of tonality were numbered, and that what had happened must be accepted and taken as a new starting-point, not as an *impasse*. He began to write 'atonal' music, in which any sense of key was as rigorously excluded as possible, producing works of astonishing imagination and power, but, because it is difficult to impose a sense of form without repetition or a sense of key, they either tended towards brevity or relied on a story or text to give them form and articulacy.

12-note music ▶ p. 363 minimalism ▶ p. 360

Chloé (1912), his orchestral *Rapsodie espagnole* (1907) and *Le tombeau de Couperin* ('The Grave of Couperin', 1917), his String Quartet (1903) and the late sonatas are among his major works, but none of his songs and very few of his orchestral miniatures or short piano pieces can be called 'minor'.

Respighi, Ottorino

(Res-pē'-gē, Ot-tō-rē'-nō) 1879–1936

ITALIAN COMPOSER

As a young man, making his living as a violinist, Respighi studied briefly with **Rimsky-Korsakov**. This, and a remarkable ear, made him a master orchestrator, and his three sets of Roman Pictures (*Pines*, *Fountains* and *Festivals of Rome*) are vividly colourful and dramatic. His popular suites of *Ancient Airs and Dances* (1917) reflect his interest in early music, which is evident in many of his works (*Botticelli Triptych*), including his operas.

Ruggles, Carl

1876–1971

AMERICAN COMPOSER

Ruggles wrote only a handful of works, of which the most important are the orchestral *Men and Mountains* (1924) and *Sun-Treader* (1926), *Portals* (1926) for strings and *Angels* (1924) for brass ensemble. They exhibit a boldly powerful, big-boned atonal style that at times approaches his friends Ives and Varèse, but remains independent. He worked slowly and painstakingly, and ceased composing in his early seventies.

Satie, Erik

(Sà-tē', Á-rĕk') 1866–1925

FRENCH COMPOSER

For a long time regarded as a mere joker because of his apparently absurd and flippant titles – 'Genuine Limp Preludes (For a Dog)', 'Bureaucratic Sonatina' – Satie is now regarded as a major figure in his own right, as well as an influence both on his contemporaries Debussy and Ravel and on many more recent composers. He is anti-Romantic in his rejection of portentousness, while his lucid simplicity was admired both by 'Les Six' and, half a century later, by the **minimalists**. Inspired by the ancient modes and by cabaret (he made his living playing a piano in a night club), his music is both simple and profound, humorous and nostalgic.

(FL) Sergei Prokofiev *by Pyotr Konchalovsky*
Portrait of the Russian composer, 1934.
(NL) ***Maurice Ravel***
The French composer who, like Debussy, was often associated with 'Impressionism' in music.
(FR) Arnold Schoenberg
Self-portrait by the Austrian composer and inventor of the 12-note technique.
(NR) Gymnopedie
First page of the manuscript score of Satie's Gymnopedie.

ARNOLD SCHOENBERG: WORKS

- **Operas:** *Erwartung* (1909); *Von Heute auf Morgen* (1929); *Moses und Aron* (1932)
- **Orchestral works:** *Pelleas und Melisande* (1903); Chamber Symphony No. 1 (1922); Orchestral Variations (1928); Violin Concerto (1936); Chamber Symphony No. 2 (1939); Piano Concerto (1942)
- **Choral works:** *Gurrelieder* (1911); *Die Jakobsleiter* (unfinished; 1922); *Kol Nidre* (1938); *A Survivor from Warsaw* (1947)
- **Chamber works:** *Verklärte Nacht* (1899); String Quartet No. 1 (1905); String Quartet No. 2 (1908); String Quartet No. 3 (1927); String Quartet No. 4 (1936); Serenade (1923); Wind Quintet (1924); Suite (1926); String Trio (1946)
- **Melodramas (speaker and instruments):** *Pierrot lunaire* (1912); *Ode to Napoleon Bonaparte* (1942)
- Many songs, piano pieces and arrangements

Schmidt, Franz

(Shmit, Frånts) 1874–1939

AUSTRIAN COMPOSER

A remarkably versatile musician, Schmidt played the piano, the organ and the cello and was a skilful conductor; he was also a vastly learned one (he knew much of the standard orchestral and chamber repertory by heart). He was both a friend of Schoenberg and his opposite: his comprehensive knowledge of the Austro-German tradition led him to develop it, in a style that is close to **Anton Bruckner** (1824–96). His most important compositions include two operas, four symphonies, five major chamber works and, above all, his visionary oratorio *Das Buch mit sieben Siegeln* ('The Book with Seven Seals').

Schoenberg, Arnold

(Shön'-bârg, Är'-nōlt) 1874–1951

AUSTRIAN COMPOSER

Together with Stravinsky, Schoenberg has become the most influential figure in twentieth-century music. In his youth he wrote music in a ripe and sumptuously orchestrated late-Romantic style, but came to believe that the later music of Wagner, and that of Mahler and Richard Strauss, as well as his own, was undermining the great tradition from which it sprang: the Austro-German tonal tradition in which a sense of key and of tensions between keys is structurally crucial. He at first resolved to accept this development as inevitable and necessary, writing music in which there is no sense of key. He found, however, that this atonal music could not generate the powerfully logical forms that had made tonal music so durable, and over a period devised the **12-note**, or serial, system to replace them. His music was slow to achieve acceptance, and he was regarded as dangerously destructive.

NEW MEANS OF EXPRESSION

Schoenberg's one-act monodrama *Erwartung* ('Expectation', 1909) is a key work of this phase: a hypnotic monologue for solo soprano and large orchestra, in which a woman seeks her lover in a forest at night. It is sheer expressive intensity, not any sense of a 'home' key or of melodic recurrence, that gives the work its power and unity. His 'melodrama' *Pierrot lunaire* (1912) is more elaborately structured: a setting of 21 poems (arranged in a dramatic sequence of three groups of seven) of nocturnal, dream-like, bizarre and violent imagery for voice and five instrumentalists. The voice employs Sprechstimme or Sprechsgesang (half-way between speech and song), the actor/ singer enunciating a precise pitch but not holding it; the instrumental ensemble is enriched by doublings – violinist also plays viola, etc.). *Pierrot lunaire* is a hallucinatory Expressionist masterpiece, its scoring, vocal style and dramatic implications enormously influential on composers as various as Stravinsky and Boulez.

Bruckner ▶ p. 242 Chabrier ▶ p. 244 Mozart ▶ p. 144 Rimsky-Korsakov ▶ p. 256

A 14-YEAR SEARCH

At this stage, despite some early successes, Schoenberg was receiving very few performances, and made his living primarily by teaching. In Vienna, he founded a Society for Private Musical Performance, at which works were very thoroughly rehearsed, performed to subscribers and their guests only, the concert programmes unannounced in advance, and at which critics and applause were equally unwelcome. He also began painting at this period, in a dream-like, Expressionist manner, and his work drew praise fom Wassily Kandinsky of the Munich Blaue Reiter, but between *Pierrot lunaire* and the first signs of a new way forward, the Five Piano Pieces op. 23 (1920), there is a gap of only one opus number (*Pierrot* is op. 21). In the years 1912–23, Schoenberg gradually invented and clarified the principles of dodecaphony.

COMPOSING WITH 12 NOTES

Accepting the end of tonality brought an extraordinary richness, and a music untrammelled by rules, but it also brought a disorder that was difficult to discipline and threatened chaos. His solution to this was an alternative to the key system. In the strictest use of his method, a work would be based on a particular arrangement (a '**note-row**') of all 12 notes of the **chromatic** scale. No note should be repeated until all 11 others have been heard (thus ensuring that no note acquires primacy, which might suggest a sense of key). Four versions of the row are permitted, a complete statement of any one of them could be a 12-note melody, three chords of four notes, two three-note chords and six melody notes, or any such permutation.

DESCENT FROM THE MOUNTAIN

Schoenberg's relief at finding a way forward that was intellectually coherent, richly varied in its potential yet firmly disciplined, is immediately obvious in the number and variety of works that followed the development of serialism. Within the next 10 years he wrote several major chamber works, piano and choral music, his Orchestral Variations, a comic opera and the first two acts (the third was never written) of his statement of religious and moral faith, the opera *Moses und Aron* (1932), a parable of the search for truth, which was not heard until after the composer's death.

It was at this time that the Nazis came to power, and Schoenberg (nominally a Christian since his twenties) publicly returned to the Jewish faith. He emigrated to the US, where he continued to teach and to write works (tonal as well as serial) that avowed his religion and explored the richness that serialism offered. They include the *Ode to Napoleon Bonaparte* (1942), using Lord Byron's poem for an implacable denunciation of Hitler, and *A Survivor from Warsaw* (1947), an eye-witness account of Jews being deported to death-camps breaking into an ancient Hebrew prayer. Schoenberg was a man of iron principle, sensitive and deeply loved by all his pupils.

Schreker, Franz

(Shrek'-er, Fränts) 1878–1934

AUSTRIAN COMPOSER

A contemporary and friend of Schoenberg (he conducted the first performance of his *Gurrelieder*), Schreker never followed him into atonality. He was strongly influenced by Mahler (in his fine Chamber Symphony, by the chamber textures often found in late Mahler) and in his operas by Richard Strauss. The operas, among them *Der ferne Klang* ('The Distant Sound', 1910), *Die Gezeichneten* ('The Stigmatized', 1918) and *Der Schatzgräber* ('The Treasure-Seeker', 1920), were successful and an influence on Berg.

Schuman, William

1910–92

AMERICAN COMPOSER

Schuman was a pupil of Harris, whose work much influenced him, especially in his 10 strongly dramatic, brilliantly scored symphonies. He also wrote two short operas – including perhaps the only opera ever written about baseball, *Casey at the Bat* (1976) – and was an influential teacher and musical administrator.

Scriabin, Alexander

(Skrē-ä'-bin Äl-yek-sän'-der) 1872–1915

RUSSIAN COMPOSER AND PIANIST

Scriabin's early music, nearly all for piano, is close to **Chopin**, but his philosophical and religious views (he was influenced by Nietzsche and, more strongly, by theosophy) brought a rhapsodic and visionary quality that continued to intensify throughout his short life. Convinced that music has a religious power and function, he planned a sort of ceremonial 'Mysterium' combining all the arts, and at the time of his death had begun drafting it. His Third Symphony (*The Divine Poem*, 1902) and the orchestral *The Poem of Ecstasy* and *Prometheus* (*The Poem of Fire*) (1908) may be considered preparatory sketches for the 'Mysterium'; so may such piano sonatas as the Seventh ('White Mass', 1911) and the Ninth ('Black Mass', 1913) and the late piano piece 'Towards the Flame'. His ecstatic, hovering melodies and static harmony tend, in his last works, to approach atonality.

Sessions, Roger

1896–1985

AMERICAN COMPOSER

Influenced early in his career by Stravinsky and Bloch, whose teaching assistant he was in the early 1920s, resident for some years in Europe (where he encountered Schoenberg's music and witnessed the rise of Fascism), Sessions was regarded in the US as a more European than American composer. Though friendly with Copland (they organized a concert series together) he wrote disparagingly of 'Americana'. He eventually adopted serialism, but his music (including two operas and eight symphonies) is in fact characteristically American in its tough, uningratiating honesty.

CYPHERS AND HIDDEN MESSAGES

In the apparently jubilant finale of his Fifth Symphony, regarded in the Soviet Union as a positive response to his critics, Shostakovich quotes from **Modest Musorgsky**'s (1839–81) opera *Boris Godunov*, a passage in which peasants are being violently forced to hail the usurping Tsar. From this point onwards he used quotations and his musical cypher extensively, and these have been widely interpreted as ironic or protesting coded messages, but they are also sometimes private (quotations from his works that had not yet been performed) or perplexing. His Fifteenth Symphony (1971), for example, repeatedly quotes from **Gioacchino Rossini**'s (1792–1868) *William Tell* overture and from Wagner's *Ring* cycle and *Tristan und Isolde*, where they may be a wry comment on the artist as hero. The DSCH cypher is often used as an indication of personal feeling. Another aspect of this 'secret' language is the use from the mid 1940s of themes of a pronouncedly 'Jewish' cast: Shostakovich had many Jewish friends, some ill-treated in the Soviet Union, and is said to have admired the capacity of Jewish folksongs to be both happy and sad.

chromaticism ▶ p. 357 note-row ▶ p. 360

DMITRI SHOSTAKOVICH: WORKS

- **Operas:** *The Nose* (1928); *Lady Macbeth of the Mtsensk District* (1932)
- **Ballets:** *The Age of Gold* (1930); *The Bolt* (1931); *The Limpid Stream* (1935)
- **Symphonies:** 15, including No. 1 (1925); No. 4 (1936); No. 5 (1937); No. 7 ('Leningrad', 1941); No. 8 (1943); No. 10 (1953); No. 13 (Babiy Yar, 1962); No. 14 (1969); No. 15 (1971)
- **Concertos:** for piano and trumpet (1933); for piano (1957); for violin No. 1 (1948); No. 2 (1967); for cello No. 1 (1959); No. 2 (1966)
- **Chamber music:** 15 String Quartets, including No. 8 (1960); No. 10 (1964); No. 15 (1974); Piano Trio No. 2 (1944); Piano Quintet (1940)
- **Piano music:** 24 Preludes and Fugues (1933)
- Songs, other piano music, choral music, film scores

Shostakovich, Dmitri

(Shus-tă-kō'vich, D'mē'-trē) 1906–75

RUSSIAN COMPOSER

Shostakovich was the first of his country's composers to come to attention after the Russian Revolution of 1917, and since Stravinsky, Rachmaninov and (until the 1930s) Prokofiev were all living abroad, his early successes made him the great hope of Soviet music. He became associated with the Western-influenced Modernist movement in the Soviet Union, but with the rise of Stalin his music came under attack. A successful opera, *Lady Macbeth of the Mtsensk District* (1934), and a ballet, *The Age of Gold* (1930), were driven from the stage and Shostakovich prudently withdrew his harsh Fourth Symphony (1936). He soon wrote a Fifth (1937), and did not object to it being described as 'a Soviet artist's creative reply to justified criticism'. During World War II, he regained a degree of official approval, notably with the Seventh ('Leningrad') Symphony (1939), ostensibly a portrayal of the city's resistance to privation and German bombardment, but he was one of a number to be publicly disgraced again in 1948, and from then until the death of Stalin in 1953 he wrote little but film music and propaganda cantatas.

(NL) Alexander Scriabin
Portrait of the Russian composer and pianist by A.Y. Golovin.
(TR) Taking a Bow
Shostakovich (centre) with Svyatoslav Richter and David Oistrakh, after a performance of his Sonata for Violin and Pianoforte, 1970.
(BR) Young Shostakovich
Shostakovich playing with the Glazunov Quartet in 1940.

MUSIC IN A COMMUNIST STATE

The new post-revolutionary régime at first accepted modernism as the natural language of a revolutionary society, but another faction held that art should serve the Revolution, and in order to do so, should appeal to the working classes. This group became dominant, and music not following its precepts was condemned as 'formalist': more concerned with form than content, influenced by decadent Western trends. Shostakovich was probably too internationally prominent a figure to be in physical danger on the occasions when he was denounced for formalism, but the Union of Composers was all-powerful. No non-member could have work performed or published, income and many other benefits depended on membership, and the Union, an arm of the state, interpreted and enforced its policies.

Even after the death of Stalin, Shostakovich was not in an easy position, but in the 1960s his Fourth Symphony was at last performed, and *Lady Macbeth*, albeit in a slightly softened revision, was staged again. His Tenth Symphony (1953) – internationally hailed as a masterpiece in the very year of Stalin's death – is marked by deep ambiguity, by now a cardinal element of Shostakovich's style, and, no less characteristically, incorporates his musical cypher, DSCH (in German musical notation D, E flat, C, B).

LATE SHOSTAKOVICH

His Thirteenth Symphony (*Babiy Yar*, 1962) set poems by Yevgeny Yevtushenko (b. 1933), including one that by implication condemned Russian anti-semitism. In his later years he was warily honoured by the Soviet state, and enjoyed a late friendship of mutual admiration with Britten but, since he was by now in poor health, his last works are often austere and several are concerned with death: his penultimate symphony is a song-cycle about death, the last of his great cycle of string quartets is in six, mostly sombre, slow movements.

Stenhammar, Wilhelm

(Sten'-hàm-här, Vil'-elm) 1871–1927

SWEDISH COMPOSER

Like his friends Sibelius and Nielsen, Stenhammar sought a national language independent of nineteenth-century Romanticism. He wrote two symphonies, two concertos for his own instrument, two operas, choral music, six fine string quartets and numerous songs, in a style that is distinctively Nordic but owes something to Mahler.

Chopin ▶ p. 190 Musorsky ▶ p. 253 Rossini ▶ p. 200

Szymanowski, Karol

(Shi-mán-ov'-skē, Kär'-ōl) 1882–1937

POLISH COMPOSER

Szymanowski came from a wealthy family whose estate in the Ukraine was lost after the Russian Revolution. He suffered from tuberculosis, and as a child was able to study only at home. He later lived in Germany and in Vienna, also travelling to Russia, North Africa, Italy and Sicily, returning to Poland in 1919. From 1927 he directed the Warsaw Conservatoire, but recurrences of his illness forced him to spend more and more time in sanatoriums.

He was the greatest intermediate Polish composer after Chopin, who influenced his earliest works. Affected by Debussy, Scriabin and his travels, his music then took on a florid and harmonically sumptuous character (the Second and Third Symphonies and his remarkable opera *King Roger*). In his latter years, inspired by Polish folk music but also by Stravinsky, he turned to more primary colours and sparer textures, in the Fourth Symphony, the folk ballet *Harnasie* and the *Stabat Mater*.

Thomson, Virgil

1896–1989

AMERICAN COMPOSER

Thomson was trained in Paris (where he lived for many years) by Nadia Boulanger, and was friendly with several of 'Les Six', but his own music is more influenced by Satie and is deeply rooted in American folk music and hymns. It is melodically fresh, harmonically plain and of great simplicity; he was an influence on the later minimalists. His most important works are two operas – *Four Saints in Three Acts* (1928) and *The Mother of Us All* (1946) – to texts by Gertrude Stein, several film and ballet scores and a large number of musical portraits, composed 'from life'. For 14 years he was the trenchantly brilliant music critic of the *New York Herald Tribune*.

Turina, Joaquin

(Tōō-rē'-nā, Hwa-kēēn') 1882–1949

SPANISH COMPOSER

A friend of Falla, Turina was, like him, a composer of nationalist music, but his style was also affected by his eight years of study in Paris. His orchestral music is full of Spanish local colour, and is often richly, sometimes heavily scored. His best-known orchestral works are *La procesion del roc'o* ('The Procession of the Dew', 1913) and the *Danzas fantasticas* (1920). He wrote more chamber music than most Spanish composers of his period, and some fine songs.

Ullman, Viktor

(Ūhl'-mán, Vikh'-tōr) 1898–c. 1944

CZECH COMPOSER

Ullman studied in Vienna with Schoenberg and also in his native Prague with the pioneer of microtonal music, Alois Hába. In his own music their influence is joined by those of Mahler, Zemlinsky (with whom he studied conducting), Debussy and Weill, among others. His powerful opera *Der Sturz des Antichrists* ('The Rise of Antichrist', 1935) was not performed due to the German occupation of Czechoslovakia, and in 1942 Ullman was arrested and interned in the Terezin ghetto. In his two years there he wrote prolifically, notably the courageously satirical and movingly humane opera *Der Kaiser von Atlantis* ('The Emperor of Atlantis', 1943). In 1944 he was transferred to the concentration camp at Auschwitz, where he presumably died or was executed (no records survive) soon thereafter. Since most of his music was unpublished his name was forgotten until the posthumous premiere of *Der Kaiser von Atlantis* in 1975. Numerous other productions, and performances and recordings of his surviving music, show him to have been one of the most gifted of the group of composers who worked at Terezin before their deaths at Auschwitz.

Varèse, Edgard

(Vâ-rez', Ed-gâr') 1883–1965

FRENCH/AMERICAN COMPOSER

As a young man, Varèse became convinced that the twentieth century needed its own music, untrammelled by the legacy of the nineteenth. He emigrated to the US and began to write music (*Amériques*, *Offrandes*, 1921) that took the **dissonance** and rhythmic energy of Stravinsky's *Rite of Spring* as a starting-point. He gave more and more importance to percussion, writing *Ionisation* (1931) for percussion alone, used the pioneering instrument ondes martenot in *Ecuatorial* (1934) and then fell silent for 16 years until, with the development of tape recording, he could manipulate urban sounds and other noise (*Déserts*, 1954) and invent the new sounds (*Poème electronique*, 1958) he had imagined.

Vaughan Williams, Ralph

1872–1958

ENGLISH COMPOSER

He studied with **Charles Hubert Parry** (1848–1918), Stanford and, in Berlin, with **Max Bruch** (1838–1920), but was slow to find his unique personal voice. This was released by his study of English folksong (which he began collecting in 1903) and of Tudor church music, and by a further period of study with Ravel in 1908. He realized that there were links between folksong and early English church music (both using the modal scales, not the prevalent minor and major) and his work as editor of the *English Hymnal* confirmed this perception. The first masterpiece to be drawn from it is his *Fantasia on a Theme of Thomas Tallis* (1910), in which rhapsodic pastoral and radiant mysticism can hardly be separated. His pastoral aspect has been ridiculed by some (one critic said that Vaughan Williams's music reminded him of a cow looking over a gate), but the most notable example of this style, the *Pastoral Symphony*, is in large part a poignant elegy prompted by memories of World War I, in which the composer served as a medical orderly. Although an agnostic, he was deeply affected by English religious mysticism, and some of his finest works were inspired by William Blake (the ballet *Job*) and by John Bunyan (his long-meditated opera *The Pilgrim's Progress* and the closely related Fifth Symphony).

HENRY V

Walton's music is ideally suited to the Romantic style and the topically patriotic message (in 1944) of Laurence Olivier's film, providing rousing music for battle sequences, a delicately scored French folk song for a love scene and a magnificent rendering of the 'Agincourt Song', which Henry must have heard sung in his praise.

POPULAR MELODY *Walton*

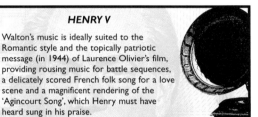

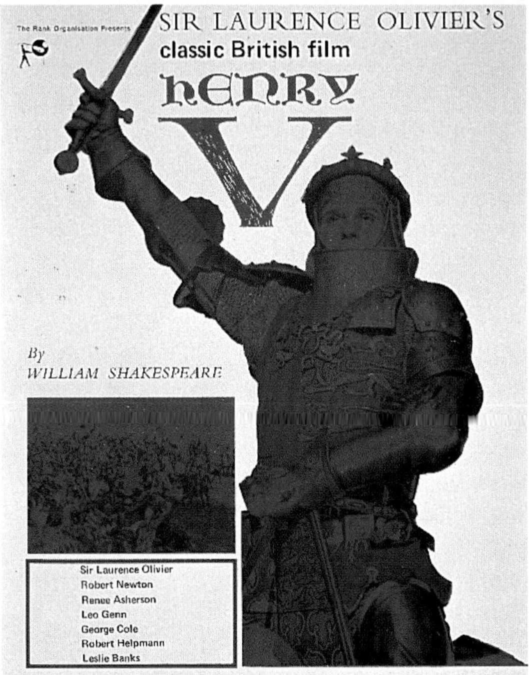

(L) Henry V
Title page of the score for the 1944 film Henry V, for which Walton provided the music.
(R) Heitor Villa-Lobos
Portrait of the Brazilian composer on a bank note from his native country.

dissonance ▶ p. 358

Villa-Lobos, Heitor

(Vēl'-lä Lō'-bōs, Ā'-tôr) 1887–1959

BRAZILIAN COMPOSER

As a boy, Villa-Lobos played in dance bands and travelled throughout Brazil, soaking himself in its folk music, before studying composition. Concerts in Rio de Janeiro made him sufficient money to travel to Paris, where the colourful exoticism of his music became very popular. He then returned to Brazil, where he taught as well as composed. He wrote many symphonies, concertos and chamber works, but his most characteristic pieces are the 14 *Chôros* (1920–29) and the nine *Bachianas Brasileiras* (1930–44), both for various instrumental groups and based on Brazilian folk models, in the latter combined with forms derived from J. S. Bach.

Walton, (Sir) William

1902–83

ENGLISH COMPOSER

After singing in the choir at Christ Church, Oxford, Walton became an undergraduate there, his talent attracting the attention of the Sitwell family (the poets Edith and Osbert and their writer brother Sacheverell). They supported him for 10 years, enabling him to write music at leisure until he earned enough to become independent. At first he was something of an *enfant terrible*, epitomized in a Schoenberg-influenced string quartet, later withdrawn, and the 'entertainment' *Façade* (1926), instrumental music accompanying rhythmically declaimed poems by Edith Sitwell, but his astringently melancholy Viola Concerto (1929, first performed with Hindemith as violist) demonstrated affinities with both Elgar and Prokofiev. The short and powerful oratorio *Belshazzar's Feast* (1931) blew an enlivening blast of fresh air through the venerable English choral tradition, and his tense First Symphony (1935) deepened his emotional range while profitably learning from Sibelius. After his rhapsodic Violin Concerto he was criticized for repeating himself, but his atmospheric scores for Laurence Olivier's three Shakespeare films (*Henry V*, *Hamlet* and *Richard III*) in fact prepared the way for his unfashionably Romantic opera *Troilus and Cressida* (1954).

Webern, Anton

(Vā'-bern, Än'-tōn) 1883–1945

AUSTRIAN COMPOSER

Webern was the most orthodox of Schoenberg's pupils – more rigorous in his exclusive use of serialism than Schoenberg himself – and, after his sudden death (he was accidentally shot by an American soldier), the most influential upon the post-war avant-garde. Even before Schoenberg developed the 12-note system, whose pieces tended towards crystalline formal perfection and extreme brevity (some are only a few seconds long, one consists of a mere 20 notes), his entire output (31 opus numbers) could be played in a single evening. Many of his serial works only achieve longer dimensions by using words or elaborate formal working, related to those of Renaissance composers that he had studied. Often described as austere or coldly cerebral, his music was in fact inspired by nature, an attempt to use the discipline of serialism to parallel the perfection of the ice crystals and alpine flowers that he saw on his expeditions into the mountains. In many of his works, his preoccupation with economy, rigour and symmetry extends to the basic note-row itself (the latter six notes may be a 'mirror' of the first six, or the row may be made up of four audibly related three-note cells) which make the serial processes of his music very clearly perceptible and their precision both exhilarating and beautiful.

Weill, Kurt

(Vīl, Ko͞ort) 1900–50

GERMAN/AMERICAN COMPOSER

Weill was influenced by his teacher Busoni, by Stravinsky and by the ideal of *Zeitoper* (opera on contemporary subjects and themes). In his early, successful stage pieces, including *Der Protagonist* ('The Protagonist', 1926) and *Royal Palace* (1927), he soon moved towards a style, related to jazz and cabaret, that made him an ideal collaborator with Brecht on *Die Dreigroschenoper* ('The Threepenny Opera', 1928) – an updating of the eighteenth-century *Beggar's Opera* – and *Aufstieg und Fall der Stadt Mahagonny* ('Rise and Fall of the City of Mahagonny', 1929). These were so successful (*The Threepenny Opera* had 3,000 performances in many theatres in its first year) that Weill could give up his teaching and conducting commitments, but he fled the rise of Hitler, first to Paris, then to the US. Until recently, the works he wrote in the US (*Johnny Johnson*, *Lady in the Dark*, *Knickerbocker Holiday*, *Lost in the Stars* and others) have been unfavourably compared (in Europe) to his collaborations with Brecht, but serious study of them has suggested that Weill continued to develop, and was no reluctant immigrant to Broadway and Hollywood.

BRECHT AND WEILL

Most of Bertolt Brecht's poems and plays have a political message – he was a lifelong Communist – and many of them call for music. Weill was not his only collaborator (his partnership with Eisler was longer and voluminously productive), but Weill's music parallels the bitterness and the irony of Brecht's words with precision. Their songs have become known primarily through performances by Weill's wife Lotte Lenya (1898–1981), whose unmistakable world-weary growl made her a third collaborator in such numbers as 'Pirate Jenny' and 'Surabaya-Jonny'.

Zemlinsky, Alexander

(Zem-lin'skē, Ä-lek-sän'-der) 1871–1942

AUSTRIAN COMPOSER

Zemlinsky was a friend, teacher and (for a while) brother-in-law of Schoenberg; unlike him he never severed his stylistic roots in the music of Strauss and Mahler. His work was long neglected or ignored, but recent interest in his four string quartets, his operas – notably *Eine florentinische Tragödie* ('A Florentine Tragedy', 1917) and *Der Zwerg* ('The Dwarf', 1922) – and his Lyric Symphony (1923) have revealed an individual of very high stature in the modern world.

Bruch ▶ p. 242 Parry ▶ p. 254

CONDUCTORS

Barbirolli, (Sir) John *1899–1970*
ENGLISH CONDUCTOR

Born in London to an Italian musical family, Barbirolli made his debut as a cellist at the age of 17 before pursuing a career conducting. In the 1920s and 30s he conducted the British National Opera Company, the Covent Garden Opera Company and the Scottish Orchestra. He succeeded Toscanini as permanent conductor of the New York Philharmonic in 1937. In 1943 he became permanent conductor of the Hallé Orchestra in Manchester, with which he remained for the rest of his life, appearing as a guest with the Berlin Philharmonic and other orchestras.

Beecham, (Sir) Thomas *1879–1961*
ENGLISH CONDUCTOR

Beecham conducted the operas of Richard Strauss at Covent Garden before World War I, and advocated the works of Delius. He founded the London Philharmonic Orchestra in 1932 and the Royal Philharmonic in 1946. He was admired for his springy rhythms and elegant phrasing.

Böhm, Karl *1894–1981*
AUSTRIAN CONDUCTOR

Music director of several German opera houses before the World War II, Böhm was director of the Vienna State Opera 1943–45 and 1954–56. He championed Berg's *Wozzeck*, and gave many performances of operas by Richard Strauss, who dedicated *Daphne* to him. He was also renowned for his interpretations of Mozart and Wagner.

Boult, (Sir) Adrian *1889–1983*
ENGLISH CONDUCTOR

Boult studied under Nikisch at the Leipzig Conservatory before joining the music staff at Covent Garden in 1914. In 1918 he conducted the first performance of Holst's *The Planets*, soon becoming known as a champion of contemporary English music. He was musical director of the newly formed BBC Symphony Orchestra 1930–50 and of the London Philharmonic Orchestra 1951–58. He enjoyed an Indian summer of recordings in the 1970s.

Furtwängler, Wilhelm *1886–1954*
GERMAN CONDUCTOR

After various positions in German opera houses, Furtwängler became conductor of the Berlin Philharmonic Orchestra 1922–45 and 1947–54. He was guest conductor of the New York Philharmonic Orchestra in the 1930s, and he conducted at Bayreuth and Covent Garden. His treatment of the German classics as works to be interpreted anew at each performance won him a huge following.

Kleiber, Erich *1890–1956*
AUSTRIAN CONDUCTOR

In 1923, Kleiber was appointed music director of the Berlin State Opera, where he performed several new works, including Berg's *Wozzeck*. He spent World War II in South America and conducted regularly at Covent Garden 1950–53. He made fine recordings of *Le nozze di Figaro* and *Der Rosenkavalier*.

Koussevitzky, Serge *1874–1951*
AMERICAN CONDUCTOR

Born in Russia, Koussevitzky started out as a double bass recitalist, turning conductor in 1908. He left Russia in 1917, and was conductor of the Boston Symphony Orchestra, 1924–49. His commissioning of many new works for Boston eventually led to the establishment of the Koussevitzky Music Foundation.

Kubelik, Rafael *1914–96*
CZECH CONDUCTOR

Kubelik left his native country, where he had been conductor of the Czech Philharmonic Orchestra, in 1948. He was music director of the Chicago Symphony Orchestra, 1950–53, and Covent Garden Opera 1955–58, and principal conductor of the Bavarian Radio Symphony Orchestra 1961–79, making many recordings, including the complete Mahler symphonies and much Czech music.

Nikisch, Arthur *1855–1922*
HUNGARIAN CONDUCTOR

Principal conductor at the Leipzig Opera in 1879, Nikisch became conductor of the Boston Symphony Orchestra 10 years later, and conductor of both the

Leipzig Gewandhaus Orchestra and the Berlin Philharmonic Orchestra from 1895 until his death. He performed the works of many contemporary composers, including Bruckner, Tchaikovsky, Mahler and Strauss.

Ormandy, Eugene *1899–1985*
AMERICAN CONDUCTOR

Born in Hungary, where he later had a career as a violinist, Ormandy started conducting in the US. After five years with the Minneapolis Symphony Orchestra, he moved to the Philadelphia Orchestra, where he was music director 1938–73. He specialized in large-scale Romantic orchestral works, but he also conducted new music.

Reiner, Fritz *1888–1963*
AMERICAN CONDUCTOR

Born in Hungary, Reiner held operatic positions in Budapest, Ljubljana and Dresden. In the US he conducted in Cincinnati and Pittsburgh, at the Metropolitan Opera and, most famously, was music director of the Chicago Symphony Orchestra from 1953. Renowned as a martinet, he brought great power to his performances.

Richter, Hans *1843–1916*
HUNGARIAN CONDUCTOR

Richter worked closely with Wagner, leading the first performances of the complete *Ring* cycle at Bayreuth in 1876. He was also conductor of the Court Opera and the Philharmonic Orchestra in Vienna. He performed Wagner at Covent Garden and was conductor of the Hallé Orchestra 1897–1911.

Sabata, Victor de *1892–1967*
ITALIAN CONDUCTOR

After an early career as a composer, de Sabata became conductor of the Monte Carlo Opera. In 1930 he began his association with La Scala, Milan, which lasted beyond his retirement in 1957. He conducted fiery performances of Wagner and Verdi, and made an outstanding recording of *Tosca*.

Serafin, Tullio *1878–1968*
ITALIAN CONDUCTOR

Serafin was principal conductor at La Scala, Milan, 1909–14 and 1917–18, and conductor at the Metropolitan Opera, New York, 1924–34. After World War II he returned to La Scala, where he conducted the Italian première of Britten's *Peter Grimes*. At Covent Garden in 1959 he conducted Joan Sutherland in her triumphant performance of *Lucia di Lammermoor*.

Stokowski, Leopold *1882–1977*
AMERICAN CONDUCTOR

Born in London, Stokowski was organist of St James's, Piccadilly, and of St Bartholomew's, New York. A conducting post in Cincinnati led to his appointment as music director of the Philadelphia Orchestra, 1912–36, where he created the world-famous 'Philadelphia sound'.

Toscanini, Arturo *1867–1957*
ITALIAN CONDUCTOR

Trained as a cellist, Toscanini was artistic director of La Scala, Milan 1898–1903, 1906–08 and 1920–29, and of the Metropolitan Opera, New York 1908–15. A strict disciplinarian, he inspired devotion for his artistic integrity, his respect for the composer's intentions and the electricity of his performances. He conducted the New York Philharmonic Orchestra in the 1920s and 30s; the NBC Symphony Orchestra was formed for him and he led it 1937–54.

Walter, Bruno *1876–1962*
GERMAN CONDUCTOR

After conducting at the Vienna Court Opera, Walter was music director at the Munich Opera 1913–22, and at the Städtische Oper, Berlin 1925–29. He worked at the Vienna Opera in the 1930s, but left Austria after the Anschlüss in 1938 and settled in the US. He conducted regularly at Covent Garden 1924–31, and at the Metropolitan Opera 1941–57. An early advocate of Mahler's music, he was noted for the intense expressiveness of his performances.

Weingartner, Felix *1863–1942*
AUSTRIAN CONDUCTOR

Weingartner conducted opera and concerts in Berlin and, in 1908, succeeded Mahler as head of the Vienna Court Opera. During World War I, he was conductor at

Darmstadt, and director of the Vienna Volksoper 1919–24. In 1927 he moved to Switzerland, returning briefly to the Vienna State Opera as director in 1935. He was particularly renowned for his performances of Beethoven.

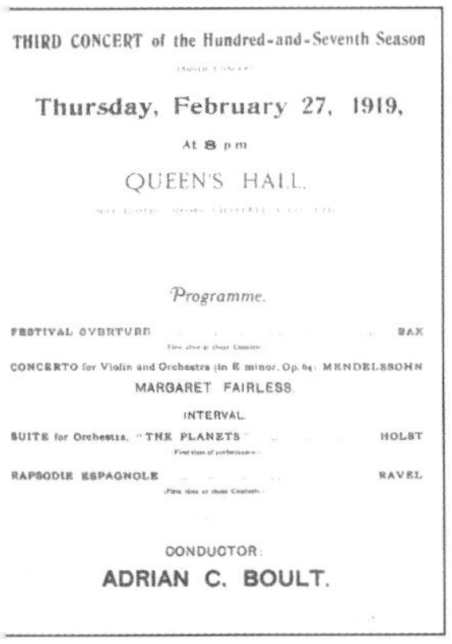
THIRD CONCERT of the Hundred-and-Seventh Season

Thursday, February 27, 1919,

At 8 p.m

QUEEN'S HALL.

Programme.

FESTIVAL OVERTURE ... BAX

CONCERTO for Violin and Orchestra (in E minor, Op. 64) MENDELSSOHN

MARGARET FAIRLESS.

INTERVAL.

SUITE for Orchestra, "THE PLANETS" ... HOLST

RAPSODIE ESPAGNOLE ... RAVEL

CONDUCTOR:

ADRIAN C. BOULT.

Wood, (Sir) Henry *1869–1944*

ENGLISH CONDUCTOR

After studying at the Royal Academy of Music and working with opera companies, Wood established the Queen's Hall Promenade Concerts in 1895. These concerts, now held at the Royal Albert Hall, have become an enduring British tradition. He was noted for his adventurous choice of repertory and his professionalism.

INSTRUMENTALISTS

Brain, Dennis *1921–57*

BRITISH HORN-PLAYER

The son and grandson of horn-players, Brain was principal in Beecham's Royal Philharmonic Orchestra and in the Philharmonia Orchestra. He played with brilliance and delicacy, recording the Mozart concertos under **Herbert von Karajan** (1908–89). He be heard anonymously in many Philharmonia recordings of the 1950s.

Casals, Pablo *1876–1973*

SPANISH CELLIST

Casals, a musician of intense and visionary power, is responsible for the present-day appreciation of the cello as a solo instrument. His career as an international soloist was complemented by his membership of the Cortot-Thibaud-Casals piano trio and by his conducting. His recording of the unaccompanied suites by J. S. Bach brought these works to a new audience.

Cortot, Alfred *1877–1962*

FRENCH PIANIST

In his early years, Cortot combined the piano with conducting, directing the first performance in Paris of *Götterdämmerung* at the age of 24. As a pianist he specialized in Romantic music, especially Schumann and Chopin, and in music by contemporary French composers. He co-founded the Cortot-Thibaud-Casals piano trio in 1906.

Dupré, Marcel *1886–1971*

FRENCH ORGANIST

Dupré was organist of St Sulpice in Paris 1934–71. He was the first to play the complete works of J. S. Bach (Paris Conservatoire, 1920). Famous for his improvisations, he was also an influential teacher at the Conservatoire.

(TR) Queen's Hall Programme
Playlist for the Queen's Hall concert, showing works by Bax, Mendelssohn, Holst and Ravel, conducted by Boult.
(BR) Royal Opera House, Covent Garden
View of the auditorium of the Royal Opera House; Sian Edwards became the first woman to conduct there in 1988.

Feuermann, Emanuel *1902–42*

AMERICAN CELLIST

Born in Austria, Feuermann made his début in Vienna under Weingartner in 1912. He taught at the Berlin Hochschule 1928–33, and settled in the US in 1938. He played piano trios with Schnabel and Bronislaw Huberman, and with Rubinstein and Heifetz. He was noted for his warm tone and rare technique.

Fischer, Edwin *1886–1960*

SWISS PIANIST

Fischer taught in Berlin 1905–14 and succeeded Schnabel at the Hochschule in 1931. He was one of the first modern pianists to direct concerto performances from the keyboard, for which purpose he founded a chamber orchestra in Berlin. After World War II, he appeared in recitals and gave master classes in Lucerne.

Fournier, Pierre *1906–86*

FRENCH CELLIST

Fournier studied the piano, but turned to the cello after an attack of polio. He was a student and a teacher at the Paris Conservatoire, and in 1943 replaced Casals in the Cortot-Thibaud-Casals piano trio. His elegant and refined playing can be heard in recordings of the Bach suites and the Dvořák Cello Concerto.

Gieseking, Walter *1895–1956*

GERMAN PIANIST

Born in France to German parents, Gieseking was particularly associated with the music of Debussy and Ravel. He studied in Hanover, where he performed a near-complete cycle of the Beethoven sonatas. His recitals in the 1920s included much contemporary music, and he was admired as an interpreter of Mozart and Beethoven.

Goossens, Leon *1897–1988*

ENGLISH OBOIST

Goossens became principal oboe of the Queen's Hall Orchestra at the age of 17 and of the London Philharmonic Orchestra when it was founded in 1932. His refined playing and exquisite tone led many English composers to write for him, including Arthur Bliss (1891–1975) and Vaughan Williams.

Grumiaux, Arthur *1921–86*

BELGIAN VIOLINIST

Grumiaux made his début in Brussels with the Mendelssohn Violin Concerto, but his career was immediately interrupted by the war. He made his British début in 1945. Noted for his fastidious playing, he made many recordings, including the unaccompanied Bach sonatas and the sonatas of Mozart and Beethoven.

Heifetz, Jascha *1901–87*

AMERICAN VIOLINIST

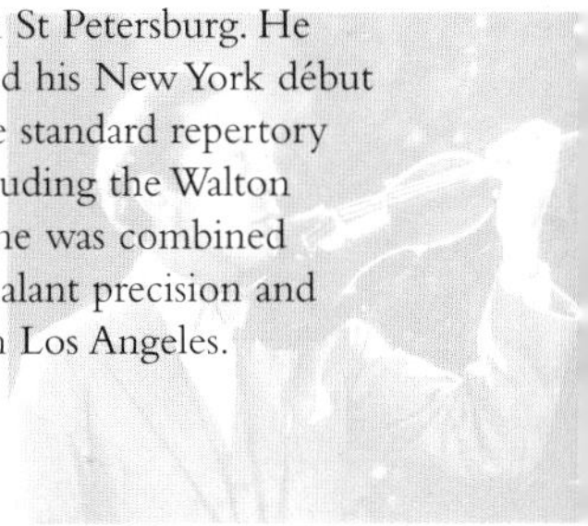

Born in Russia, Heifetz studied in St Petersburg. He made his Berlin début in 1912, and his New York début in 1917. As well as performing the standard repertory he commissioned new works, including the Walton Violin Concerto. His powerful tone was combined with a technique of almost nonchalant precision and brilliance. From 1962 he taught in Los Angeles.

Hess, Myra *1890–1965*

ENGLISH PIANIST

Hess studied at the Royal Academy under Tobias Matthay, and made her debut under Beecham in 1907. The warmth and spirituality of her playing endeared her to audiences across Europe and the US. During World War II she organized recitals at the National Gallery to boost morale. She was best known for her warm, mellow interpretations of J. S. Bach, Mozart and Schubert.

WOMEN AS CONDUCTORS

As the conductor is placed in a very visible position of power over other musicians, conducting has been a particularly difficult career for women to pursue. While women have, in fact, conducted throughout history, it is still rare to find them working with professional symphony orchestras. In the late nineteenth and early twentieth centuries, women such as Frédérique Petrides (1903–83), director of the American Orchestrette Classique, often conducted all-women ensembles, while female composers such as **Ethel Smyth** (1858–1944) frequently took the baton for performances of their own works.

The pioneering Ethel Leginska (1886–1970) began her conducting career in the 1920s, appearing with orchestras in Germany, France, Britain and the US. The Dutch-born Antonia Brico (1902–89) established her conducting career with professional orchestras in the US in the 1920s and 30s. From the 1940s she was the conductor of the semi-professional Brico Symphony Orchestra. The British composer and conductor Ruth Gipps (1921–99) also worked for most of her career with a semi-professional orchestra, the London Repertoire, as well as founding the professional Chanticleer Orchestra which specialized in contemporary British music. Several women conductors have concentrated on conducting opera, including the American Sarah Caldwell (b. 1924), the first woman to conduct at the New York Metropolitan Opera House (in 1976), and the British Sian Edwards (b. 1959), musical director of English National Opera in the early 1990s and the first woman to conduct at the Royal Opera House, Covent Garden (in 1988). The British Jane Glover (b. 1949) is also a prominent conductor.

Karajan ▶ p. 331 Smyth ▶ p. 258

Kempff, Wilhelm *1895–1991*
GERMAN PIANIST

Kempff studied at the Berlin Hochschule and appeared with the Berlin Philharmonic in 1918. He toured throughout the world, but made his US début only in 1964. He was noted for his lyrical playing. His recordings include the complete sonatas of Beethoven and Schubert.

Kincaid, William *1895–1967*
AMERICAN FLAUTIST

After studying in New York, Kincaid joined the New York Symphony Orchestra and, later, the New York Chamber Music Society. He was principal flute of the Philadelphia Orchestra 1921–26 and taught at the Curtis Institute.

Kreisler, Fritz *1875–1962*
AMERICAN VIOLINIST

Kreisler's international career began with the Berlin Philharmonic under Nikisch in 1899. His London début was in 1902. Elgar wrote his Violin Concerto for him, and he gave the first performance in 1910. He was known for the perfection of his playing and the pieces that he composed and passed off as the work of eighteenth-century composers.

Landowska, Wanda *1879–1959*
POLISH HARPSICHORDIST

Landowska studied the piano, but soon took up the then-unfashionable cause of playing the music of J. S. Bach and his contemporaries on the harpsichord. She founded a school of early music near Paris. She was influential through her writings and recordings, which show her vigour and rhythmic strength. Falla and Poulenc wrote for her.

Lipatti, Dinu *1917–50*
ROMANIAN PIANIST

Lipatti studied with Cortot in Paris. His concert career after 1945 was cut short by cancer. The delicacy and clarity of his playing made him an ideal interpreter of J. S. Bach, Mozart and Chopin. He made a number of recordings, including his last recital a few weeks before his death.

Moyse, Marcel *1889–1994*
FRENCH FLAUTIST

Moyse was principal flute at the Opéra Comique in Paris 1913–38, and professor of flute at the Paris Conservatoire 1932–49. He appeared as a soloist in concerts and on recordings. He formed the Moyse Trio (flute, piano and violin) with his son and daughter-in-law in 1933.

Neveu, Ginette *1919–49*
FRENCH VIOLINIST

Neveu studied at the Paris Conservatoire, and with Enescu. She won the International Wieniawski Competition in 1935. She toured Europe, the US and Canada, making her London début in 1945. Her recordings of the Brahms and Sibelius concertos show the force and passion of her playing. She died in a plane crash.

Piatigorsky, Gregor *1903–76*
AMERICAN CELLIST

Piatigorsky left his native Russia in 1921, having been principal cellist in the Bolshoi Theatre orchestra. In 1929, after four years with the Berlin Philharmonic Orchestra, he embarked on a solo career. He gave the first performances of concertos by Hindemith and Walton. A player of great taste and virtuosity, he devoted much time to chamber music, especially with the piano trio that he founded in 1949 with Heifetz and Rubinstein.

Primrose, William *1903–82*
SCOTTISH VIOLA PLAYER

Primrose played as a soloist and as a member of the London String Quartet before moving to the US to become principal viola of the NBC Symphony Orchestra under Toscanini, 1937–42. He continued with his solo career, and commissioned a concerto from Bartók in 1944. He taught in Los Angeles and at Bloomington, Indiana.

Rampal, Jean-Pierre *1922–2000*
FRENCH FLAUTIST

Rampal was principal flute in the Vichy Opera orchestra, 1946–50, and the Paris Opera, 1956–62. He toured widely as a soloist, specializing in the music of the eighteenth century but using a modern flute. He founded the Quintette à Vent Française in 1945 and the Ensemble Baroque de Paris in 1953.

Rubinstein, Arthur *1887–1982*
AMERICAN PIANIST

Born in Poland, Rubinstein gave his first concert at the age of seven. His début in Berlin came in 1900. By World War I, he had appeared in Paris, Austria, Italy, Russia, the US and London. With a break in the 1930s for private study, he continued touring for the rest of his life. He played classical and modern music, and was particularly highly regarded for his poised Chopin playing.

Schnabel, Artur *1882–1951*
AMERICAN PIANIST

Born in Austria, Schnabel studied in Vienna, moving to Berlin in 1900. He gave concerts with his wife, the contralto Therese Behr, and appeared with many other performers including Casals, Feuermann and Fournier. He was an outstanding, deeply intellectual interpreter of the sonatas of Beethoven and Schubert, and an inspiring teacher. He emigrated to the US in 1939.

Schweitzer, Albert *1875–1965*
GERMAN/FRENCH ORGANIST

Born in Alsace, at that time part of the German Empire, Schweitzer studied in Paris with Charles Widor (1844–1937), who encouraged him to write his book on J. S. Bach. Schweitzer also studied organ building, and was convinced of the unsuitability of the modern organ for Bach's music.

Segovia, Andrés *1893–1987*
SPANISH GUITARIST

Self-taught, Segovia made his début at the age of 15. Considering it his mission to have the guitar taken seriously, he transcribed music written for the lute and the vihuela. Contemporaries who wrote for him included Falla, Joaquín Rodrigo (1901–99) and Villa-Lobos; he played with much passion and intensity.

Serkin, Rudolf *1903–91*
AMERICAN PIANIST

Born in Austria, Serkin studied in Vienna, making his début there in 1915. After World War I, he formed a duo with the violinist Adolf Busch, and played with the Busch Chamber Players. From 1926 he worked in Switzerland, moving to the US in 1939. He was artistic director of the Marlboro festival in Vermont, and head of the piano department at the Curtis Institute, Philadelphia. A thoughtful and powerful musician, he specialized in the classical and Romantic repertory.

Szigeti, Joseph *1892–1973*
AMERICAN VIOLINIST

Born in Hungary, Szigeti made his Berlin début in 1905. He lived in England 1907–13, where he gave many concerts. In the 1920s he toured the Soviet Union, and made his US début with the Philadelphia Orchestra in 1925. He was a keen advocate of contemporary music: Bartók, Bloch and Prokofiev wrote works for him, and he played the concertos of Berg and Stravinsky as well as the standard repertory.

Tertis, Lionel *1876–1975*
ENGLISH VIOLA PLAYER

The title of his autobiography, *Cinderella No More*, indicates the lowly status of the viola when Tertis was young. He transcribed works written for other instruments to build up a repertory for the viola, of which he designed a larger model with an especially rich tone.

Thibaud, Jacques *1880–1953*
FRENCH VIOLINIST

Thibaud studied at the Paris Conservatoire and began his European career with the Concerts Colonne. He is best known for his membership of the Cortot-Thibaud-Casals trio, but was also a distinguished interpreter of the sonata and concerto repertory.

SINGERS

Björling, Jussi *1911–60*
SWEDISH TENOR

Björling spent much of his career at the Metropolitan Opera, New York. His evenly produced voice, with its effortless top notes, was well suited to the French repertory, but he specialized in Verdi and Puccini. One of his finest memorials is the recording of *La bohème* under Beecham.

Callas, Maria *1923–77*
AMERICAN SOPRANO

Callas left the US for Greece in 1937, and made her début as Tosca in Athens in 1942. Her early post-war repertory included Wagner's Brünnhilde and Isolde, but under the guidance of Serafin she concentrated on the Italian repertory. She was a singing actress of great power who made an indelible impression as Bellini's Norma, the part in which she made her London, Chicago and New York débuts.

Caruso, Enrico *1873–1921*
ITALIAN TENOR

Caruso's first great success was in *L'elisir d'amore* at La Scala in 1901, followed by his Covent Garden (1902) and Metropolitan (1903) débuts in *Rigoletto.* He sang regularly at the Metropolitan thereafter, mainly in Verdi and Puccini, and also sang the French repertory including *Faust*, *Manon* and *Samson et Dalila.* He is considered by many to have been the greatest tenor of the twentieth century.

Deller, Alfred *1912–79*
ENGLISH COUNTERTENOR

Deller was responsible for the revival of the male alto voice in the concert hall and opera house. With his ensemble, the Deller Consort, he made many recordings of early music, and he recorded English lute-songs with Desmond Dupré.

Ferrier, Kathleen *1912–53*
ENGLISH CONTRALTO

Ferrier sang in concerts during World War II and made her opera début in Britten's *The Rape of Lucretia* at Glyndebourne in 1946. The two performances she sang at Covent Garden in 1953 were her last appearances in public before her death from cancer. She was a famous Angel in Elgar's *The Dream of Gerontius*, and recorded Mahler's *Das Lied von der Erde* under Walter.

(FL) Wanda Landowska
The Polish harpsichordist with the French composer Poulenc.
(NL) Jean-Pierre Rampal
Rampal playing his flute, 1965.
(R) Maria Callas
Callas singing Tosca, the role in which she made her debut in 1942.

Flagstad, Kirsten *1895–1962*
NORWEGIAN SOPRANO

After many years performing in Scandinavia, Flagstad made her Metropolitan Opera début in 1935 as Wagner's Sieglinde. Before and after World War II she sang at Covent Garden, and gave the first performance of Strauss's *Four Last Songs* at the Royal Albert Hall under Furtwängler in 1950. She was the leading Wagnerian soprano of her day.

Gigli, Beniamino *1890–1957*
ITALIAN TENOR

Gigli made his début in Italy in 1914, and sang Faust in Boito's *Mefistofele* at Bologna and Naples the following year. He made his Metropolitan Opera début in *Mefistofele* in 1920. The operas in which he appeared at the 'Met', where he sang for 12 seasons, included *La bohème*, Ponchielli's *La Gioconda* and Meyerbeer's *L'Africaine.* His first role at Covent Garden was Andrea Chénier in 1930, and his last was Rodolfo (*La bohème*) in 1946.

Hotter, Hans *b. 1909*
AUSTRIAN BASS-BARITONE

Hotter's international career began in Mozart with the Vienna State Opera's visit to Covent Garden in 1947. He made his Metropolitan Opera début in 1950 and first sang at Bayreuth in 1952. He was renowned for his Wotan, but he also sang other Wagnerian roles. He created roles in three Strauss operas, including Olivier in *Capriccio.*

Ludwig, Christa *b. 1928*
GERMAN MEZZO-SOPRANO

Ludwig made her début at Frankfurt in 1946, and from 1955 was based at the Vienna State Opera. She appeared all over the world in Wagner and Strauss mezzo roles, and occasionally sang soprano parts. Her many recordings include Oktavian (*Der Rosenkavalier*) under Karajan and the Marschallin (the same opera) under Bernstein.

McCormack, John *1884–1945*
IRISH TENOR

McCormack sang the French and Italian opera repertory at Covent Garden, the Metropolitan Opera, and in Boston and Chicago. After World War I he abandoned the stage for the concert platform. His repertory included Handel and German Lieder, but it was his performance of ballads and other light pieces that brought him great popularity.

Melchior, Lauritz *1890–1973*
AMERICAN TENOR

Having started as a baritone in his native Denmark, Melchior made his début as Wagner's Siegmund at Covent Garden in 1924. Between the wars he sang at Covent Garden, Bayreuth and the Metropolitan. He was best known for his Wagnerian roles, especially Tristan, which he sang over 200 times.

Ponselle, Rosa *1897–1981*
AMERICAN SOPRANO

Ponselle's first appearance on stage was opposite Caruso in Verdi's *La forza del destino* at the Metropolitan Opera in 1918. She sang there regularly till 1937, mostly in nineteenth-century Italian opera; she did not sing Puccini. Her most celebrated role was Norma, with which she made her début at Covent Garden in 1929.

Ruffo, Titta *1877–1953*
ITALIAN BARITONE

Ruffo sang for one season only at Covent Garden, before appearing at La Scala, Milan 1903–04, as Verdi's Rigoletto. His US début was in 1912; he first sang at the Metropolitan Opera in 1922. His repertory included Don Carlo (*Ernani*), Tonio (*Pagliacci*), Rossini's Figaro and **Ambroise Thomas**'s (1811–96) Hamlet.

Schorr, Friedrich *1888–1952*
AMERICAN BASS-BARITONE

Born in Hungary, Schorr spent his early career in central Europe. He made his name as the leading Wagner bass-baritone of the inter-war years, appearing at Bayreuth 1925–31, Covent Garden 1925–33 and the Metropolitan 1924–43. He was in particular demand as Wotan and Hans Sachs.

Tauber, Richard *1891–1948*
AUSTRIAN TENOR

After his début in Chemnitz in 1913, Tauber was engaged by the Dresden Opera as a lyric tenor. He achieved his greatest fame in operettas, especially those by Lehár; London heard him in *Das Land des Lächelns* ('The Land of Smiles') in 1931. He sang Don Ottavio (Mozart's *Don Giovanni*) at Covent Garden shortly before his death.

Tebaldi, Renata *b. 1922*
ITALIAN SOPRANO

Tebaldi sang regularly at La Scala, Milan 1949–54. She made her début with the Covent Garden company as Tosca in 1955; in the same year she joined the Metropolitan Opera. She also appeared in San Francisco, Chicago and South America. A powerful soprano, her roles included Aida, Cilèa's Adriana Lecouvreur and Catalani's La Wally.

Teyte, (Dame) Maggie *1888–1976*
ENGLISH SOPRANO

Teyte started in Paris, where she appeared at the Opéra-Comique. In 1908 she was chosen by Debussy to succeed Mary Garden as Mélisande, a part she sang in England and, though not until 1948, in New York. She sang with the Beecham Opera Company as well as in Chicago and Boston.

Turner, (Dame) Eva *1892–1990*
ENGLISH SOPRANO

Turner's early career was spent with the Carl Rosa company, with which she appeared at Covent Garden in 1920. As Madam Butterfly she was spotted by Toscanini's assistant at La Scala; her subsequent Italian career included her first Turandot, at Brescia in 1926. At Covent Garden, 1928–39 and 1947–48, she sang not only Turandot and Aida among Italian roles, but also Wagner's Sieglinde and Isolde.

Thomas ► p. 261

The Modern Era

STYLES AND FORMS

Nineteenth-century music had developed with an unprecedented awareness of its own history, and by 1900 the European musical legacy seemed as permanent and unshakeable as the institutions – the opera houses, concert halls and conservatories – that nurtured it. Above all, classical tonality and its associated forms and genres, now the everyday stuff of textbooks, had acquired for the majority the status of an entirely natural musical language. Though challenges to this apparently stable order had been evident late in the nineteenth century, it was in the first decade of the twentieth that their full impact was felt. The result amounted to the most far-reaching changes music had experienced for 300 years.

Radical Change

These changes took a variety of forms. Some composers completely abandoned the pitch materials of tonal music – major and minor scales, **triads** and other standard harmonic combinations – along with the formal and rhythmic structures associated with them. Some deployed those familiar materials in unfamiliar ways, assigning them new structural and functional roles. Others looked elsewhere – to the distant past, folk traditions and the new popular styles – for the means to enrich their language. Still others looked beyond the realm of sounds hitherto regarded as 'musical', turning to the noise available from percussion instruments, or from mechanical or environmental sources.

Many composers, too, continued to write in an essentially tonal, late-Romantic style. But increasingly they did so from conscious aesthetic choice, rather than mere instinct or habit. Style was no longer something unthinkingly inherited, but rather something consciously adopted or even invented. Nothing is more striking about twentieth-century composition than this heightened self-consciousness on the part of its creators.

Departing from Tonality

During the nineteenth century, it was the very stability of tonality, the familiarity to composers and listeners of its network of stable functional relationships, that had allowed the progressively wider exploration of its possibilities. Early in the century composers started to make regular use of **modulations** to distantly related keys, while in the music of **Wagner** especially, the perfect **cadence**, the conventional key defining motion from the **dominant** to the **tonic** chord, was increasingly avoided in favour of less conclusive ways of marking the ends of phrases or even of longer musical paragraphs. The tonic, in other words, was often merely implied rather than actually stated. At other times, it was the sheer number of **chromatic** alterations, notes not belonging to the harmony or key being asserted, that set the identity of that harmony into question.

Extended Tonality

The consequences of this 'extended tonality' are evident, too, in **Schoenberg**'s early works. In the tone poem *Pelleas und Melisande* (1902–03), on the other hand, the pervasive contrapuntal interweaving of the work's chromatic **leitmotifs** makes for an uncertain tonal foundation. Five years later a decisive break

IMPRESSIONISM IN MUSIC

The term 'Impressionism' is associated in music primarily with the work of **Debussy**, but is also used in connection with **Ravel**, **Stravinsky** (the early works especially), **Szymanowski** and others. While Debussy did not enjoy a personal association with any of the leading Impressionists, certain analogies between his aesthetic and techniques and those of painters such as Monet, Renoir and Pissarro are striking. In their attempts to capture transient effects of light and atmosphere, Impressionist painters used small dashes and dabs of contrasted colours which, when viewed from a distance, give the canvas a slightly blurred quality, lacking in sharp outlines and clear directional movements, but with an effect of rapid surface vibration. Debussy's music displays comparable qualities. In the orchestral works, subtle and highly individual blends of sound are created, whose individual instrumental components are hard to isolate. The harmony meanwhile, often lacking clear functional implications, seems static, whatever rapid surface figurations or other 'shimmering' effects (such as the use of a rapidly repeated note or a string ***tremolando***) might animate the surface.

cadence ▶ p. 356 chromaticism ▶ p. 357 dominant ▶ p. 358 leitmotif ▶ p. 359 mode ▶ p. 360 modulation ▶ p. 360 tonic ▶ p. 363 *tremolando* ▶ p. 363 triad ▶ p. 363 12-note music ▶ p. 363

SPRECHGESANG

Sprechgesang (also called *Sprechstimme*) is a type of vocal production lying somewhere between speech and song. The idea of combining speech, sometimes rhythmical, with music (familiar from the well-established genre of melodrama) was taken a step further by Schoenberg at the conclusion of his oratorio *Gurrelieder* (1911) where the intended rise and fall of the speaker's voice is notated precisely using diamond-shaped noteheads on the stave. *Sprechgesang* proper emerged for the first time in *Pierrot lunaire* (1912). Here the notes in the vocal part have crosses in the middle of their stems: the singer is instructed to touch briefly on the notated pitch, gliding from there to the next note, thereby creating a disembodied effect entirely suited to the work's eerie, moonlit atmosphere. Schoenberg demonstrated the technique's adaptability to a variety of dramatic contexts: it underlines the biting satire of *Ode to Napoleon Bonaparte* (1942), where a less precisely pitched notation is used, and characterizes the voice of the prophetic in the unfinished opera *Moses und Aron* (1930–32), soloistically in the character of Moses and chorally in the voice from the burning bush. As well as Berg, who used it in both his operas, **Britten** and **Boulez** have used varieties of the technique.

was made: in the last movement of the Second String Quartet (1907–08), Schoenberg noted how 'the overall multitude of dissonances cannot be counterbalanced any longer by occasional returns to such tonal triads as represent a key'. The consequences of what he later called 'the emancipation of the dissonance' would be with him for the remainder of his creative life.

Schoenberg was under no illusions as to the radical consequences of his step. Whereas previously all dissonance had been understood as an inflection of the basic harmonic building block of tonality, the major or minor triad, into which they would ultimately resolve, dissonances were now equally free not to resolve. This meant that the triad might no longer be present at all as a functional reference point: without it there was no way of articulating cadences or of otherwise defining a single pitch as the tonic or key note.

Atonality

Schoenberg's critics dubbed this new musical universe 'atonal' and, despite Schoenberg's objections to it, the term has stuck. Schoenberg and his students **Berg** and **Webern** – the three composers often collectively referred to as the 'Second Viennese School' (the first being **Haydn**, **Mozart** and **Beethoven**) – now had to find ways of navigating this new musical universe in which, theoretically at least, no note predominates any other. General characteristics of the atonal music of this period are hard to define. Major or minor triads tend to be avoided, as do octaves: also, the 12 notes of the chromatic scale will often be found in very close proximity. Webern later recalled how, during the composition of his Bagatelles for String Quartet, op. 9 (1911–13), all tiny miniatures each of around a minute's duration, he 'had the feeling, "When all twelve notes have gone by the piece is over"'. This was the principle which, after 1920, came to provide the basis of a more rigorous means of controlling the atonal universe, namely the **12-note** technique.

THE RITE OF SPRING

Stravinsky's third ballet for Diaghilev was no piece of naive primitivism: he worked painstakingly with an expert on ancient Slavonic customs, Nikolay Roerich, to ensure the scenario's ethnographic accuracy, and worked a number of published folk melodies into the score. Of those many already embodied the irregularities of metre and accentuation that *The Rite* exploits to such violent and ultimately explosive effect. Harmonically, too, the score was Stravinsky's most complex to date, its pounding, dissonant chordal complexes created from the superimposition of distantly related triads and seventh chords. The score itself, as well as the production, elicited strong reactions. Pierre Lalo wrote of Stravinsky that 'nobody has practised the system and cult of the false note with so much ambition, zeal and sourness of temper'. Debussy, on the other hand, confessed to being 'dumbfounded, overwhelmed by the hurricane that had come from the depths of the ages and taken life by the roots'.

The 'School of Paris'

In 1923 **Milhaud** spoke of 'two opposed currents in music … the school of Paris and the school of Vienna'. 'Each,' he wrote, is only 'of slight acquaintance with that for which the other stands'. Milhaud was writing after World War I, which had created an inevitable breach between the two cultures. But even before the war, musical developments in Paris were taking a very different course from those in Vienna, where Schoenberg and his school were active. Composers based in Paris in the first two decades of the century – including Debussy, Ravel and Stravinsky – sought less the abandonment than the enrichment of tonality, and to provide that enrichment they looked to a variety of heterogeneous sources.

Paris was a flourishing cosmopolitan centre, with a growing émigré population drawn from all parts of Europe, Spain in particular. Russian artistic culture was also very much in evidence, especially with the productions brought to the city by the Ballets Russes and their impresario Diaghilev after 1909. The Great Exhibitions of 1878, 1889 and 1900 also exposed Parisians to Far Eastern cultures, and Debussy was impressed by the Javanese gamelan he heard there in 1889.

Exotic Harmonies

It is hard to tell the degree to which Debussy's use of **modes** was motivated by these exotic cross-cultural encounters. Still, his work came increasingly to incorporate the 'church modes', such as Dorian, Lydian and Phrygian, as well as artificial symmetrical scales such as the whole-tone. Some pieces play on the possibility of subtle switches from one mode to another: the piano piece *L'isle joyeuse* ('The Happy Island', 1904) uses the Phrygian mode, with its characteristic sharpened fourth as a bridge between the major and whole-tone scales.

Even before the arrival of the Ballets Russes in Paris, interest in Russian music was strong, Debussy being drawn especially to the work of **Musorgsky**. Musorgsky's novel harmonies exerted a particular fascination: for instance, the resonant chord dominating the Coronation Scene of his opera *Boris Godunov* (1868–73). A harmony such as this octatonic 'Boris' chord, attractive though it may be as a sonority, implies no continuation, certainly no resolution, and the same can be said for the major-seventh and major-ninth enriched triads which so often, in the music of Debussy, form the basis of large static planes of sound. This emphasis on harmony's 'being' rather than its 'becoming', on rich sonorities exploited for their own sake, was reinforced by the renewed attention to timbre, to instrumental and orchestral colour, often associated with musical Impressionism.

(BL) Impression – Sunrise ***by Claude Monet***
Debussy's music has often been associated with the visual aesthetic of the Impressionist painters; he tried to capture light and atmosphere in his music.
(TL) The Paris Exhibition
Fountains outside the Palace of Electricity at the 1900 Exhibition.
(BR) The Second Viennese School
Anton Webern (left) and Alban Berg; these two composers, along with Arnold Schoenberg, have become known as the 'Second Viennese School'.

Beethoven ▶ p. 150 Berg ▶ p. 286 Boulez ▶ p. 324 Britten ▶ p. 287 Debussy ▶ p. 282 Haydn ▶ p. 140 Milhaud ▶ p. 293 Mozart ▶ p. 144 Musorgsky ▶ p. 253 Ravel ▶ p. 294 Schoenberg ▶ p. 295 Stravinsky ▶ p. 280 Szymanowski ▶ p. 298 Wagner ▶ p. 226 Webern ▶ p. 299

The 'Call to Order' in France

After the chaos and devastation of World War I, the tone and character of modernism in all the arts, not just music, seemed to undergo a radical change. The emphasis on subjective, personal expression was supplanted by detachment and objectivity. Reliance on intuition was widely replaced by a reliance on method. The drive towards the transcendental and the spiritual, considered proper to 'high' art throughout the nineteenth century, gave way to a desire to serve the needs of the present, and at times to a consciously frivolous preoccupation with 'low' art, the commonplace and the ephemeral.

This 'call to order' was made nowhere more explicitly than in the 1918 essay *Le coq et l'harlequin* by the French writer Jean Cocteau. In it, Cocteau railed against not just the predictable adversary, Wagner, but also Debussyan Impressionism and the Russian 'primitivism' of *The Rite of Spring*. Cocteau singled one composer out for particular praise, the maverick Satie, with whom he had collaborated the previous year on the ballet *Parade*. The frivolous style of Satie's score (which included orchestral parts for a revolver, a typewriter and a lottery wheel) naturally seemed the model for what Cocteau called in his essay 'everyday music', a style which looked for inspiration not to the overblown pretensions of the concert hall and opera-house, but to the direct appeal of the music-hall, the circus and jazz. Satie had considerable influence on the younger generation, notably a group of French composers dubbed 'Les Six' by the critic Paul Collaer in analogy to the Russian Five. The six composers, Poulenc, Milhaud, Honegger, Auric, Tailleferre and Durey, enjoyed but a brief collective identity, giving just a handful of concerts together and collaborating as an entire group on only two projects. But, especially in the work of two of its most prominent members, Poulenc and Milhaud, especially, the spirit of Cocteau and Satie enjoyed an extended lease of life.

Neo-Classicism

'Le nouveau classicisme' had been a pervasive aspect of French music in the final decades of the nineteenth century: in Debussy's *Suite bergamasque* (1890–1905), all the movements, apart from the famous 'Clair de lune', are based on eighteenth-century dances. The neo-classicism prevalent after World War I, however, abandoned this nostalgic tone of reverential homage, replacing it with a spirit of irony and detachment. The work to which the critic Boris de Schloezer first applied the term was Stravinsky's *Octet* (1922–23), a work whose first movement, though given the title 'Sinfonia', is effectively a sonata movement with a slow introduction. In his own programme note on the piece, Stravinsky declared it to be 'not an "emotive" work but a musical composition based on objective elements which are sufficient in themselves'.

The term neo-classical should not imply that Stravinsky restricted himself to eighteenth-century models. In fact, he plundered many aspects of the musical past: the Baroque in the *Dumbarton Oaks* concerto (1937–38) and the Concerto for Piano and Wind Instruments (1923–24), **Tchaikovsky** in *Le baiser de la fée* ('The Fairy's Kiss', 1928) and **Verdi** in *Oedipus Rex* (1926–27). Nevertheless, anti-Romanticism and objectivity, together with a taste for strict form and pared-down instrumentation, was characteristic of Stravinsky's neo-classicism in all its varied guises. Gone are the dense, chromatically charged chords of *The Rite of Spring*, and its constant changes of time signature (now replaced by more subtle shifts of metrical emphasis). The basic materials of tonal music – major and minor scales, major and minor triads – are constantly in evidence, though radically defamiliarized by their context. Dominant and tonic functions often find themselves locked in superimposed stalemate, while at other times, balanced sonorities built from the shared notes of third-related triads create genuine and seemingly unresolvable tonal ambiguities.

THE 12-NOTE TECHNIQUE

Towards the beginning of the 1920s, Schoenberg sought a way of codifying the atonal methods of pitch organization that he had been exploring since 1908. The result was the method of ' composing with 12-tones related only to one another'. While the use of all 12 notes of the chromatic scale in a single melody was hardly unprecedented in Western art music the idea of basing an entire composition on a single, fixed 12-note ordering signalled a radical break with existing compositional methods. Schoenberg's technique involves placing the 12 notes of the chromatic scale in a chosen order to form a 'row' or 'series'. The row can then be retrograded (stated in reverse order) or inverted (the direction of its intervals reversed), the inversion itself retrograded and any resulting form of the row transposed. Pitches can be placed in any octave register.

The row is not in itself a melody: though its pitches, when each assigned rhythmic values, can be used to form all or part of a melodic line, they can equally be distributed between simultaneous instrumental or vocal lines. Alternatively, the composer can use a number of forms of the row (say the original form, known as the 'prime', the inversion and the retrograde inversion) at the same time, giving each to a different voice or instrument. Despite its basic constraints, therefore, 12-note technique still leaves the composer considerable compositional freedom, with the result that 12-note works can differ strikingly in style and sound.

Few composers still use 12-note technique as the sole basis of their music. Nonetheless, it was probably the single most influential of twentieth-century compositional methods, and its use in such emotionally powerful works as Berg's Violin Concerto, Schoenberg's *A Survivor from Warsaw* and **Dallapiccola**'s opera *Il prigioniero*, belies its reputation for creating sterile, emotionless products.

diatonic ▶ p. 358 *Gebrauchsmusik* ▶ p. 358

'New Objectivity' in Germany

In Germany, a comparable spirit of objectivism manifested itself in the slogan of *Neue Sachlichkeit* ('new objectivity'), which symbolized a rejection of Expressionist complexity in favour of greater accessibility. This prompted many to incorporate jazz and dance band idioms into their work, as well as more familiar historical styles, such as that of the Baroque concerto. An archetypal medium of the *Neue Sachlichkeit* was the *Zeitoper* ('everyday opera'), which treated modern social and cultural issues in a mixture of operatic and popular idioms. *Royal Palace* (1927) by **Weill** was one of the genre's early successes and Weill went on to explore with Brecht a more politically engaged type of music theatre, notably in *Rise and Fall of the City of Mahagonny*, a sardonic allegory of Weimar decadence, and the well-known *Threepenny Opera*.

Some sought instead to counter the dangers of 'an esoteric isolationism' through music which had a clearly defined social or educational function. One of those was **Hindemith**, whose name became inextricably associated with the concept of ***Gebrauchsmusik***, literally 'music for use', designed for pedagogical or social purposes and often oriented towards children or amateurs.

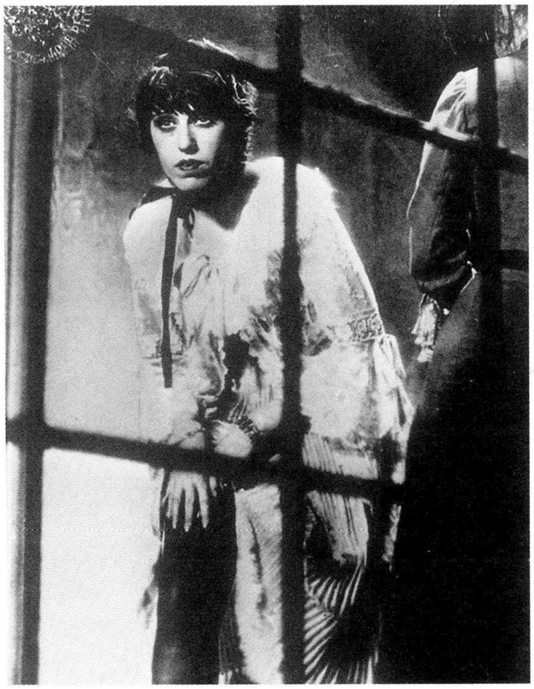

JAZZ

The influence of jazz on concert music stretches back almost to the emergence of jazz itself from roots in gospel, ragtime and blues. One of the most popular black American dances of the 1890s was taken up by Debussy in his 'Golliwog's Cakewalk' (from the piano suite *Children's Corner*, 1906–08). Ragtime found its way into Satie's ballet *Parade* and works by Stravinsky (notably *Piano Rag Music*, 1919). Ravel, for his part, adopted blues melodic inflections in his Violin Sonata (1923–27) and Piano Concerto in G (1929–31). Milhaud's ballet *La Création du Monde* (1923) offers perhaps the most thoroughgoing assimilation of early jazz: both its instrumentation and the quasi-improvised woodwind solos over blues harmonic progressions successfully mimic the authentic Harlem sound. Jazz also featured regularly in German instrumental and stage works (those of Hindemith, Ernst Krenek, 1900–91, and Weill especially) until outlawed as 'degenerate' by the Nazis. Among practitioners of the new idioms, **Gershwin** made forays into concert music with his *Rhapsody in Blue* (1924) and Piano Concerto in F (1925), while others contented themselves with commissioning works: in addition to Bartók's chamber work *Contrasts* (1938), the clarinettist Benny Goodman elicited concertos from Hindemith (1947) and Copland (1947–48).

National Traditions and the New Music

As more and more nations freed themselves from imperial rule in the decades flanking the turn of the century, the political imperative which had been the driving force behind nineteenth-century musical nationalism lost much of its urgency. Still, national traditions remained of central interest to many twentieth-century composers. To be distinctive was not only their serious scholarly engagement with folk music in its cultural context – many of them collecting and transcribing folksongs themselves – but also the radical extent to which they allowed it to transform their personal musical language.

One composer anxious to explore the potential of truly authentic folk sources was the Hungarian **Bartók**. For some of the melodies he collected he composed settings, which keep the tunes themselves intact while providing them with often adventurous harmonizations. But Bartók aimed at more than mere quotation, seeking rather to absorb 'as a child learns his mother tongue' the complex modal structure of peasant melodies, which he saw as a means of freedom 'from the tyrannical rule of the major and minor keys'. This led him – in such mature masterpieces as the Fourth and Fifth String Quartets (1928 and 1934) and the Sonata for Two Pianos and Percussion (1937) – to a highly distinctive post-tonal style, in which densely chromatic textures often result from the superimposition of separate modal fragments.

THE MUSICAL VERNACULAR

Folk music also led many composers to reassess their rhythmic practices. Bartók made considerable use of the irregular rhythmic patterns of Hungarian and Bulgarian dances (the fourth movement of the *Concerto for Orchestra* (1943) uses a Bulgarian rhythm of nine quavers subdivided 4+3+2 distributed between bars of 2/4 and 5/8). Meanwhile, the rhythmic properties of Russian folksong, evident above all in the complex accentual structure of many of the themes in *The Rite of Spring*, left a permanent imprint on Stravinsky's musical style. **Janáček** undertook extensive research into Moravian folksong: never is this material quoted, but it leaves its mark on the short-breathed quality of his melodies, often built up through the varied repetition of small melodic cells.

In England, **Vaughan Williams** had a lifetime preoccupation with English folksong, as well as English polyphony of the Tudor period. For him, as for **Holst** in his formative years, the modal language common to both seemed an ideal basis on which to reconstruct a characteristically English idiom. Others made use of vernacular styles closer to their immediate cultural environment. For the Brazilian **Villa-Lobos**, it was the dance rhythms of the Rio de Janeiro street bands with which he played as a teenager that penetrated both the complex, multi-layered textures of the 14 *Chôros* (1920–29) and the more restrained **diatonic** language of the *Bachianas Brasilieras* (1930–44). In the US, **Ives** and **Thomson** made extensive use of the hymn-tunes of the Sunday School and revival meetings, while **Copland** quoted published cowboy melodies in his popular ballets *Billy the Kid* (1938) and *Rodeo* (1942).

(BL) Les Six with Jean Cocteau
Left to right: Milhaud, Cocteau, Auric, Honegger, Tailleferre, Poulenc, Durey.
(TL) Gymnopedie
Score for Satie's popular Gymnopedie.
(FR) Béla Bartók
Bartók travelled around collecting authentic folk music from his native Hungary, to use in his music.
(NR) The Threepenny Opera
Lotte Lenya in the 1931 film version of Kurt Weill's music theatre work.

Bartók ▶ p. 285 Copland ▶ p. 288 Dallapiccola ▶ p. 288 Gershwin ▶ p. 289 Hindemith ▶ p. 290 Holst ▶ p. 290 Ives ▶ p. 291 Janáček ▶ p. 291
Tchaikovsky ▶ p. 234 Thompson ▶ p. 298 Vaughan Williams ▶ p. 298 Verdi ▶ p. 230 Villa-Lobos ▶ p. 299 Weill ▶ p. 299

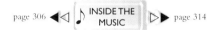

Opera After Wagner

If, in the twentieth century, opera could no longer spearhead the most radical musical developments, it continued to reflect almost every significant trend and to attract many composers primarily active in other genres. A few, nevertheless, chose to specialize in opera composition. For instance, **Richard Strauss**, composer of a remarkable series of orchestral tone-poems in the decade before 1900, turned his attention after that date principally to the stage. While Wagnerian music drama cast its shadow over his first two operas, *Guntram* (1892–93) and *Feuersnot* (1900–01), it stood at some remove from the two works that followed, *Salome* (1903–05) and *Elektra* (1906–08). Both are nerve-jangling psychological dramas which underline the depraved obsessions of their protagonists with violent dissonance and writhing chromaticism. Strauss never sought to recapture this degree of feverish intensity: his next opera, *Der Rosenkavalier* (1909–10), attempts to recapture the spirit of eighteenth-century Vienna with music enriched, rather than destabilized, by chromaticism. Rather, it was Schoenberg in his monodrama *Erwartung* (1909) who produced an opera most worthy of the Expressionist epithet, charting its lone female character's traumatized complex of emotions with music of terrifying immediacy and rapidly fluctuating pace.

THE CHANGING FACE OF OPERA

In Italy, the most important opera composer to emerge after the death of Verdi was **Puccini**. Puccini resisted the banal, regionalist subject matter characteristic of the late nineteenth-century ***verismo*** tradition, drawing instead on a variety of literary sources ranging from the novels of Abbé Prévost to the contemporary American plays of David Belasco. Still, his operas remain 'realist' in the looser sense, featuring strong, 'true-to-life' characterization and brisk dramatic pacing. While no composer could match Puccini in sheer popularity, his operas have, since World War II, been joined in the international repertory by those of Janáček. Janáček broke early from the restrictive mould of Czech nationalist opera, *Jenůfa* was the first of eight mature essays in the genre, strikingly diverse, at times idiosyncratic, in their subject matter, but sustained by music of often glowing intensity and unflagging urgency.

Two Symphonic Radicals

While the symphony could not claim in the twentieth century quite the centrality it had enjoyed in the nineteenth, it retained its importance for many composers, a number of whose works have taken up secure places in the concert repertory. The extremes of approach to the twentieth-century symphony are nowhere illustrated better than in a reported exchange between two of its most celebrated exponents, **Sibelius** and **Mahler** in 1907. Sibelius spoke of the genre's 'severity of form and the profound logic that creates an inner connection between all the motifs'. Mahler contradicted him, suggesting that the symphony instead 'must be a world. It must embrace everything'. Mahler's symphonies were certainly conceived on an enormous scale. None of them lasts much less than an hour, all employ large orchestras, four use vocal soloists (Nos. 2, 3, 4 and 8) and of those three (Nos. 2, 3 and 8) involve massed choirs. On the other hand, of Sibelius's seven purely orchestral symphonies, only the first two are significantly over half an hour long, the one-movement Seventh (1924) lasting barely 20 minutes. Mahler's symphonies juxtapose ideas of contrasted, often seemingly unrelated character, at times incorporating parodies of popular styles, such as the sound of the folk band which bursts in on the bleak funeral march of the third movement of the First. Sibelius's themes, by contrast, are terse and lapidary, tending towards a constant development and merging of their separate identities.

STRUGGLE AND SURVIVAL

The Danish composer **Nielsen** shared Sibelius's view of the symphony as an essentially abstract drama. Many of his symphonies display 'progressive tonality', ending in a key other than that in which they began. Indeed his Fourth, *The Inextinguishable* (1916), can be understood in terms of a quest to recapture the triumphant thematic statement which had closed the first movement exposition along with the key of E which, though it made only a brief and seemingly disruptive appearance in the first movement, ultimately closes the whole work.

The 15 symphonies of **Shostakovich** frequently aspire to Mahlerian dimensions, but the banal patriotism of the texts set in the finales of the Second (1927) and Third (1929) could hardly be further removed from the visionary spirituality of Mahler's choral perorations. More genuinely Mahlerian is the recurrent tone of

MODES AND 'ARTIFICIAL' SCALES

The term 'mode' tends to be used in twentieth-century music to refer to a scale other than major or minor (though these can be called modes as well). The so-called 'church modes', given their prominence in the folk music of both Eastern and Western Europe, are frequently encountered in music that draws on those traditions (e.g. Bartók, Janáček, Vaughan Williams). It is easy to get an idea of their basic scale patterns from a piano keyboard by playing all the white notes in succession within an octave: moving from any D to the D above it gives the interval pattern of the Dorian mode, the scale taken from E gives the Phrygian mode, that from F the Lydian mode and that from G the Mixolydian mode (these are the names originally chosen in the Renaissance). Any of these modes can appear in transposition: for instance, a Dorian mode starting on E would run E-F sharp-G-A-B-C sharp-D-E.

Of the church modes the Dorian and Phrygian are close to the natural minor scale, the Lydian and Mixolydian to the major. They can therefore adapt quite easily to an otherwise tonal context, while providing it with a distinctive colouring. More disruptive of tonality are the 'symmetrical' scales based on the division of the octave into equal intervals (and their further subdivisions). The whole-tone scale (e.g. C-D-E-F sharp-G sharp-A sharp-C) contains no major or minor triads and therefore of itself defines no tonic or key-note. Other symmetrical scales include the octatonic (e.g. C-C sharp-D sharp-E-F sharp-G-A-A sharp-C), consisting of alternate semitones and whole tones (associated especially with Stravinsky) and what is sometimes called the hexatonic (e.g. C sharp-E-F-G sharp-A-C-C sharp), consisting of alternate semitones and minor thirds, whose resemblance to the harmonic minor scale is exploited by Bartók in the third movement of his *Concerto for Orchestra* (1943). What is probably the most universal scale of all, the pentatonic (playable on the black notes of the piano) was often used in early twentieth-century music for its 'oriental' or 'exotic' connotations.

verismo ▶ p. 363

irony and alienation, which proved an essential expressive tool for a composer chafing under the constraints of Soviet cultural policy. It is especially pervasive in the Tenth Symphony (1953), widely regarded as his masterpiece, where, after a bleak first movement, austere in its thematic economy, a terrifying scherzo (a portrait of Stalin according to the composer's unauthenticated memoirs), and an ambivalent *allegretto*, the apparently jubilant helter-skelter of the final movement rings distinctly hollow.

Russia also produced two of the other most widely performed twentieth-century symphonists. The three works by **Rachmaninov**, of which the Second (1906–08) has enjoyed the most popularity, compensate in melodic opulence for what they occasionally lack in formal cohesion. **Prokofiev**'s Symphony No. 1, 'Classical' (1917), is a superbly crafted piece, modelled after Haydn but far removed in tone and character from the neo-classical trends emergent in Europe. Otherwise, of his seven, the Fifth (1944) and Sixth (1945–47) are arguably the finest, consistently innovative in their flexible approach to form and tonality.

TURANDOT

Turandot's significance within the history of twentieth-century opera is twofold. Not only was it Puccini's last opera and, for many, his finest, even though he did not live to finish Act 3 (which was completed from sketches by Franco Alfano). It is also the last work in the Italian grand opera tradition to enter the permanent international repertory. For Puccini it represented a new departure in terms of its choice of subject – a fairytale by the eighteenth-century Venetian playwright Carlo Gozzi about a prince who seeks (where countless others have failed and paid with their lives) to win the hand of the haughty and enigmatic Chinese princess Turandot. Puccini brings his characteristic human warmth to this austere drama, though this serves if anything to accentuate its elements of brutality, notably in the Act 3 torture scene. The music is richly colourful, incorporating transcriptions of Chinese folksong and elements of modal (including whole-tone and pentatonic) harmony. It also contains some of Puccini's most justly celebrated arias, including 'In questa reggia' ('In this Palace') for Turandot herself and Calaf's 'Nessun Dorma' ('None Shall Sleep').

New Worlds of Sound

While the majority of twentieth-century composers found sufficient scope for innovation in the chromatic scale and the sonorities of traditional instruments, others felt the need to move beyond both. The first manifesto in 1910 of the Italian Futurists, whose movement encompassed artists and writers as well as musicians, called for music to be invaded by the sounds of modern industrial society, of factories, trains, motor cars and planes. Their leading 'composer', Luigi Russolo (1885–1947), attempted to recreate these noises using specially constructed mechanical instruments. The composer **Varèse** was among those who saw these so-called *intonarumori* ('noise-intoners') demonstrated in Paris, but he chose instead to concentrate on developing the orchestra's 'noise' component, the percussion section. He introduced to it many new instruments, notably the sirens employed in (among other works) *Ionisation*, one of the very first pieces for percussion alone. Other composers sought to extend the percussive possibilities of pitched instruments: **Cowell** was the first to systematize the use on the piano keyboard of 'tone-clusters', greater or lesser numbers of chromatically adjacent notes played simultaneously. He also explored the inside of the instrument: pieces such as *Aeolian Harp* (1923) require the strumming of the piano strings, while his informal experiments with inserting cutlery, coins and rubber bands between them appear to have prompted **Cage**'s postwar development of the prepared piano.

Microtonal Music

Other composers sought finer differentiation of pitch. As early as 1907, in his *Sketch of a New Aesthetic of Music*, **Busoni** had outlined a system of sixth-tones. But it was the Czech composer Alois Hába (1893–1973) who, from the 1920s, produced the first substantial body of so-called 'microtonal' (mainly quarter-tone) music, including a full-length opera, *Matka* ('The Mother', 1929). The Mexican Julián Carrillo (1875–1965) and the Paris-based Russian émigré Ivan Vïshnegradsky (1893–1979) quickly followed him in exploring divisions of the standard semitone. The American composer Harry Partch (1901–74), on the other hand, rejected that interval along with the entire Western system of equal temperament. Seeking to recreate the spirit of ancient Greek and Chinese musical cultures, he developed a 43-note scale of 'pure', untempered intervals, along with instruments that could play them – by the late 1940s these included such colourfully named objects as Cloud Chamber Bowls and the Mazda marimba, the latter made entirely of light-bulbs.

The early twentieth century also saw the development of the first electronic instruments. Before the famous Hammond organ in 1929 came Thaddeus Cahill's telharmonium in 1906, Lev Theremin's eponymous theremin in 1920 and the ondes martenot, named after its French inventor Maurice Martenot, in 1928. The latter, with its uninterrupted pitch continuum and its eerie, hollow sonority, was much used by French composers, including **Messiaen** and Maurice Jarre (in the score for David Lean's film *Lawrence of Arabia*, 1962). But it was not until after World War II, above all with the availability of magnetic tape as a storage medium, that the potential of these new resources could be thoroughly explored.

(BL) Wozzeck
Modern production of Berg's successful opera Wozzeck.
(TL) Janáček
The Czech composer Janáček moved away from the traditions of his native nationalist opera with Jenůfa.
(R) Turandot
Puccini's opera Turandot, *from which the well-known 'Nessun Dorma' is taken.*

Busoni ▶ p. 288 Cage ▶ p. 324 Cowell ▶ p. 288 Mahler ▶ p. 250 Messiaen ▶ p. 293 Nielsen ▶ p. 293 Prokofiev ▶ p. 294 Puccini ▶ p. 254
Rachmaninov ▶ p. 256 Sibelius ▶ p. 256 Shostakovich ▶ p. 297 R. Strauss ▶ p. 258 Varèse ▶ p. 298

The Modern Era

INSTRUMENTS

Guitar

In the Renaissance, both four- and five-course (eight- or 10-stringed) guitars were played, both of them notably smaller than the modern instrument and with only a shallow waist. In the Baroque period, players seem to have switched over to an instrument with six courses (six or 12 strings), which remains the standard guitar configuration. The instrument at this time became less like the lute and makers invariably built guitars with flat, rather than curved, backs. Tuning varied, but seems to have been in a pattern of thirds between the middle courses, with a fourth between them and the two outer strings at the top and bottom of the range, reflecting the tuning of viols (after all, viols are a kind of bowed vihuela; early guitar). Modern tuning is E, A, D, g, b, e'.

GUITAR MAKERS

The great name in the latter part of the nineteenth century was that of the maker, Antonio de Torres Jurado (1817–92). He is often said to have standardized the instrument's size and shape, increasing the dimensions and fixing string length at 65 cm (30 in), but in fact the guitar family continues to contain the distinct classical and flamenco types and acoustic instruments custom-built for blues, jazz, folk and rock music, as well as characteristic instruments only heard locally in Mexican or Portuguese music. Credit is also given to Torres for the change from gut frets on the fingerboard to metal ones, and a redesign of the internal structure of the sound box to use a fan-shaped pattern of struts.

COMPOSITIONS FOR THE GUITAR

The guitar continues to be associated with the Hispanic world and the repertory tends to reflect this. The best-known guitar composition is without doubt the guitar concerto by Joaquín Rodrigo (1901–99), blind from the age of three. The *Concierto de Aranjuez* was first performed in 1940 and rapidly became an international success story, a rare thing for a piece of contemporary classical music. Although he wrote other music, including the *Fantasia para un gentilhombre* for guitar and orchestra, for Segovia (1955), and a number of guitar solos, no other piece ever had the same impact, much to the composer's annoyance. Other important guitar music has been written by **Britten, Walton** and **Arnold**. In addition, composers such as **Mahler** and **Schoenberg** have included it in chamber ensemble or orchestral works.

The guitar was a central part of the personal iconography of Pablo Picasso. The most famous example of this, from his so-called 'blue period', is a painting of an old man bent over a guitar. This is part of the inspiration for a wonderful, though difficult, long poem by the American Wallace Stevens, *The Blue Guitar*. The title was adopted for a piece by **Michael Tippett** (1905–98), of which the first performance was given in 1983 by **Julian Bream** (b. 1938), who did more than anyone else to establish the guitar as a classical instrument in Britain.

THE MODERN GUITAR

The modern age has seen the introduction of nylon strings and the development of the electric guitar. Acoustic guitars fitted with pickups are still used, but the electric guitar as such is a solid-bodied instrument, with treble and bass pickups and a set of controls determining volume. Through link-up to synthesizing equipment, a guitar can be made to sound like any instrument, just as an electronic keyboard can. The bass guitar works on the same principles, but playing at a lower register, it has adopted a role similar to that of the ***pizzicato*** double bass in jazz.

Although electric guitars of all kinds are most commonly seen in jazz and rock music, there is a part for electric guitar in Michael Berkeley's (b. 1948) secular oratorio of the nuclear age *Or Shall We Die* and Tippett's final opera *New Year*. **Stockhausen** and **Berio** have also written for the electric guitar.

Player Piano

The player piano (usually known by one of its manufacturers' trade names as the 'pianola') was a mechanical device for causing the piano to play a fixed composition in a fixed way. The music has been cut into a roll of paper and when this is fed through a mechanism built into the specially designed piano, a bellows system causes the keyboard to be automatically played. The score of *Ballet Mecanique* (1924–26) by George Antheil (1900–59) was intended to be for an astonishing 16 synchronized player pianos and performed accompanying a film. As things turned out, the link with the film was abandoned and the resulting score was merely

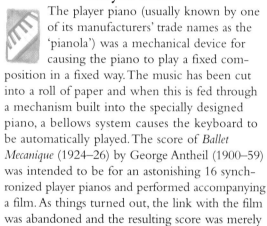

THE FUTURISTS

Futurism was an artistic movement of the early twentieth century with influence on literature and the visual arts as well as music. The force behind the movement was the Italian writer Filippo Marinetti, who published the definitive manifesto in 1909. With declared enthusiasm for modernity and the new inventions, such as the motor car, it is not surprising that the members would experiment with electronic music. One of the greatest living Italian composers of the time, **Busoni**, who had already declared an interest in **microtonal** music and had prophesied that the future would be electric, had been living in Berlin since 1894 (and was not, besides, a 'joiner' by nature). Deprived of his contribution, the group contained Francesco Pratella (1880–1955), a composer who wrote three futurist music manifestos, as well as Luigi Russolo and Uto Piatti.

glissando ▶ p. 358 microtone ▶ p. 360 *pizzicanto* ▶ p. 361 polyrhythm ▶ p. 361

for eight pianos, one player piano, four xylophones, two electric bells, two propellers, tam-tam, four bass drums and a siren. However, it is the American composer Conlon Nancarrow (1912–97) who devoted his career to the player piano, composing directly on to piano rolls, by means of a specially developed punching machine. This approach enabled him to explore complex rhythmic and temporal textures which lie beyond the capacities of a pianist.

Dynaphone

While in Paris, **Varèse** became interested in the dynaphone. Invented by René Bertrand and Nadal in 1927, this monophonic instrument was placed on a table. The right hand turned a knob controlling the pitch of an oscillator, while the left hand controlled volume and timbre. **Honegger** wrote for four dynaphones and a piano in his ballet score *Roses de Metal*; despite his interest, Varèse himself never collaborated with Bertrand in developing new electronic instruments.

In 1931, **Cowell** collaborated with Lev Theremin on developing an electronic machine capable of playing **polyrhythmic** music, the 'rhythmicon'. Cowell also wrote a concerto specially for it, which was not performed until 1971, and then with a computer, not with the original device.

(NL) Julian Bream
Bream helped to establish the guitar as a classical instrument in Britain.
(TR) Player Piano
The player piano, or pianola, allowed the music to be played automatically.
(BR) Ondes Martenot
The ondes martenot – its name means 'martenot waves' – was invented in 1928.

Synthesizer

In the 1950s, the American composer **Babbitt** was the first composer to work on a synthesizer which the US company RCA had developed. The resulting *Composition for Synthesizer* (1961) was Babbitt's first fully synthesized work. It was followed in the same year by *Vision and Prayer* for soprano and synthesizer, and then *Ensembles for Synthesizer* (1962–64). Babbitt appreciated the accuracy which the instrument offered: changes of dynamics on both single and consecutive pitches could be not merely requested of the performers in a score, they could be programmed into the instrument.

Telharmonium

We think of electronic music as a late twentieth-century phenomenon, but one of the earliest electronic instruments, the telharmonium, dates from as early as 1895. Invented in the US by Thaddeus Cahill (who also interested himself in electric typewriters and pianos), the instrument was an electro-mechanical keyboard instrument. It used charge-bearing metal brushes and a rotating wheel with alternating conducting and insulating regions. Current was supplied by a dynamo and the performer sat at a keyboard. In a second design, a large cylinder (the size of a small child) carried eight alternators. Played from three 144-key manuals, the telharmonium possessed a five-octave range, but did not have the volume control of the earlier model. In all, three instruments were built, each different from the other. They were huge, heavy and enormously expensive to build. None survives.

Noise-Intoners

A notable entry into the field of electronic music was made by Luigi Russolo and Ugo Piatti. Members of the Futurist movement, they developed a family of machines called 'noise-intoners'. One of these contained a wheel with a rosined or toothed circumference, which could be brought into contact with a string, whose tension could be varied and which was attached to a diaphragm. In another, the diaphragm was struck by a beater. The result was a pounding and groaning electronic hurdy-gurdy. One gramophone recording of their performance survives; the instruments themselves were destroyed in World War II.

Theremin

The theremin was invented by the Franco-Russian physicist Lev Theremin (or Termen) in 1920. It is unique in the manner by which it is played, as the performer never actually touches the instrument. When the player's hand approaches or retreats from a vertical antenna, the sound generated by two radio-frequency oscillators swings up or down. The pitch can vary across as much as five octaves and the sound, which is not unlike that of the glass armonica, is characterized by continual **glissando**.

The theremin has retained a degree of interest and a new version of it is now in use in music education, particularly with physically handicapped musicians. The two rods around which the hands play give it a disembodied appearance to match its unearthly sound. **Ives**, **Grainger** and **Martin** have all written for the theremin.

Ondes Martenot

Invented by Maurice Martenot in 1928, the ondes martenot or 'martenot waves' possesses a keyboard for separate notes, a sliding mechanism for glissando, and a range of seven octaves. It is probably best known for its appearance in **Messiaen**'s *Turangalîla-Symphonie* and *Trois petites liturgies de la presence divine*. Honegger, who wrote for it in *Jeanne d'Arc au bûcher*, recommended that it should replace the double bassoon! Another electronic keyboard was developed by Brune Helberger: a first version was built in 1936 and a second in 1947. With a seven-octave range, this had two manuals, two knee levers to control vibrato and six pedals directing volume. Players today can be seen controlling vibrato by lateral movements of the keys, not unlike clavichord technique.

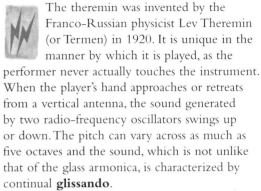

Arnold ▶ p. 284 Babbitt ▶ p. 284 Berio ▶ p. 324 Bream ▶ p. 332 Britten ▶ p. 287 Busoni ▶ p. 288 Cowell ▶ p. 288 Grainger ▶ p. 290 Honegger ▶ p. 290
Ives ▶ p. 291 Mahler ▶ p. 250 Martin ▶ p. 292 Messiaen ▶ p. 293 Schoenberg ▶ p. 295 Stockhausen ▶ p. 329 Tippett ▶ p. 330 Varèse ▶ p. 298 Walton ▶ p. 299

Orchestral Percussion

The percussionists of the twentieth century often found themselves faced by an array of different instruments whose only common theme is that they are all idiophones: they are played by being struck. Some of these are known as 'tuned percussion', because the beaten sound is actually tuned to a specific note. Some are known as 'untuned percussion', since the pitch is indefinite and could not usefully be written anywhere specific on the stave.

Timpani

The most widely used tuned percussion in early twentieth-century classical music are the timpani. These instruments, often called 'kettle drums', are metal hemispheres with a tense membrane (formerly leather, now plastic) across the top and are tuned to play a single note. An instrument with military origins (as the timpani/trumpets combination in **Monteverdi**'s *Orfeo*, 1607, reminds us), timpani had intervened only occasionally in classical music to provide strictly limited local effects: the surprise chord in **Haydn**'s 'Surprise' Symphony No. 94 involves timpani and his 'Drum Roll' Symphony No. 103 (1795) opens with a roll on the timpani.

THE MODERN ORCHESTRA

By the end of the nineteenth century, or early in the twentieth, every self-respecting city in Europe or North America expected to have an orchestra of its own, playing regularly in a purpose-built concert hall or civic hall. Some, like the Vienna Philharmonic, the Dresden State Symphony or the Leipzig Gewandhaus, continued long traditions (Dresden can claim continuity from the time of **Heinrich Schütz**'s, 1585–1672); others were the proud creations of new industrial cities, such as the Cleveland Orchestra or the Hallé Orchestra (Manchester), and some were organized by concert societies (as in Paris). As radio developed, many radio stations in larger cities set up their own orchestras, and opera houses employed their own. In the middle of the century, many chamber orchestras, of between 15 and 30 players, came into existence – partly in reaction to the overblown Romantic orchestra, partly on economic grounds, partly because they seemed more suitable for pre-Romantic music anyway; and in the late twentieth century, orchestras of period instruments were established to play earlier music in a style and producing a sound closer to that envisaged by the composer.

Classical orchestration used timpani to emphasize the **tonic** and **dominant** in unison with the natural trumpets, and the timpanist as a result usually had two instruments to play; the modern orchestral timpanist will usually have three, sometimes more.

REVOLUTIONIZING RHYTHM

In the early twentieth century, as composers began to experiment with rhythm in an unparalleled way, so the role of percussion was revolutionized. In Stravinsky's *The Rite of Spring*, the time signature changes not from movement to movement but from bar to bar. Here, the percussion has a vital role in establishing the pounding, driving force of the music. There is no sense in this piece that the percussion is providing local effects or is in a supporting role.

The tension in the membrane of the eighteenth-century timpani had been maintained either by rods or ropes. In the nineteenth century, mechanically tuned drums had made rapidly changing pitch possible and Adolphe Sax patented a pedal-operated system. Nevertheless, timpani continued to be used to provide such operatic and programmatic effects as thunder, drum rolls and gunshots (as in **Prokofiev**'s *Peter and the Wolf*). However, in his Sonata for Two Pianos and Percussion (1937), **Bartók** made use of the pedal timpani for a novel effect. Here, the pedal alters the tension in the membrane while it is actually being played, making the instrument capable of glissando.

Snare Drum

The snare drum is cylindrical. It has a wooden or metal frame with parchment stretched across either end. Stretched across the lower of these is a metal 'snare' which rattles when the drum is beaten. Another name for snare drums is 'side drums' because they were carried at the hip by army drummers.

Snare drums are often used in **Handel**'s *Music for the Royal Fireworks* (1749) and contribute to a bright, martial sound. They act in agreement with the rest of the ensemble. Although the snare drum does act as part of a team in **Ravel**'s *Boléro*, it is far from providing a brief roll for local effect. Here, the drumming builds gradually to a climax through 300 bars of the same rhythm. In similar relentless mode, **Shostakovich**'s Seventh Symphony, the 'Leningrad', takes a two-bar pattern on the snare drum and repeats it, gradually reaching a climax over the course of 176 bars, before fading into silence. His Twelfth Symphony, 'The Year 1917', scores timpani, snare drum and bass drum playing in unison over 95 bars. Bridging the first and second movement, this combination advances from very quiet to violently loud, before receding once more into silence.

Orchestral Piano

The twentieth century saw the piano return to the orchestra: notable works including the orchestral piano are **Kodály**'s *Háry János* (1926), Prokofiev's Fifth Symphony and **Orff**'s *Carmina Burana* (1937). Modern composers realized that, as it creates sound with hammers that strike strings, the piano is technically a member of the percussion family. Indeed, in Grainger's *The Warriors* (1916) the pianist has to lean inside and strike the strings directly with marimba mallets (the piece boasts three grand pianos and one upright, part of an enormous percussion department). Similarly, in solo piano repertory, Cowell's *Aeolian Harp* (1923) requires the piano strings to be strummed or plucked. The percussive possibilities of the piano are also seen to advantage in George Antheil's music of the 1920s and later in Boulez's conventionally played but nevertheless 'Hammer-klavier' piece, the Second Piano Sonata (1948).

dominant ▶ p. 358 tonic ▶ p. 363

Additional Percussion

Composers of the early twentieth century sought out further percussion instruments to add to their sound palette. **Berg**'s *Three Pieces for Orchestra* (1913) requires a xylorimba: a composite instrument, with a top end sounding like a xylophone, the bass end like a marimba. Walton's *Façade* (1926) requires wood blocks: stemming from Africa, these are a series of resonant wooden blocks stuck by drumsticks. Wood blocks are also to be found in **Gershwin**'s two Piano Concertos, while Ravel's Piano Concerto demands the slapstick, an instrument also known as a 'whip', in which two hinged, flat-sided pieces of wood are brought together sharply to make a 'crack' sound when the slapstick is flicked abruptly. **Debussy** often requires a large orchestra and the percussion section in his music may contain timpani, drums both large and small, cymbals, tam-tams, glockenspiel and xylophone. Cowell introduced bullroarers (also known as thundersticks) into the score of his *Ensemble* (1924). His *Ostinato* (1951) was written entirely for percussion ensemble and his Percussion Concerto (1958–59), though not the first in the genre, is a notable landmark.

Cimbalom

The dulcimer is a type of box zither whose name derives from *dulce melos* or 'sweet sound'. Usually with four sides, none of them running parallel to each other (though as this is an instrument to be found under various names in practically every country on earth, it is difficult to be definite), it has several strings but no keyboard. The strings run between two sets of pins and through bridges, and are played by being struck by a pair of hammers. A lap-top or table-top instrument, the dulcimer was well known in the Middle Ages and continued to be played through the Baroque period. By the nineteenth century, it had come to be regarded largely as a folk or dance-music instrument.

The cimbalom, one of the many varieties of dulcimer, was rediscovered by composers from southeastern Europe as a result of the late nineteenth-century interest in folk culture. Consequently, it plays a notable role in the music of Kodály and Bartók in particular.

(BL) Percussion Instruments
A multi-percussion set-up, including drums, chimes and xylophone.
(TL) Timpani and Snare Drum
Pedal timpani, also known as a 'kettle drum' and the familiar snare or 'side' drum.
(TR) The Gamelan
Part of a gamelan orchestra in a village in central Java.
(BR) Carmina Burana
Performance of Orff's Carmina Burana*; Orff deployed many percussion instruments in his works.*

THE GAMELAN ORCHESTRA

Gamelan is an orchestral tradition in Java and Bali, where every instrument – various gongs and drums – is a member of the percussion family. The tradition emphasizes respect for the instruments and co-operation between the players. In 1887, the Paris Conservatoire acquired a gamelan. In 1889, Debussy went to the Paris Exhibition, where he heard the sound of the Javanese gamelan; the experience influenced his music. Debussy sought to reflect its use of the pentatonic scale by using whole-tone scales on the piano in pieces like Pagodes (part of *Estampes*, 1903). Similarly, 'The Girl with the Flaxen Hair' (part of the Préludes Book 1, 1909–10) is played entirely on black notes. Of his *Et la Lune descende sur le temple qui fût* ('And the Moon Sets Over the Ruined Temple', 1908), Boulez has commented that it was a transformation of oriental influence at the deepest levels, not merely a piece of pastiche.

Britten visited Bali to listen to the gamelan and worked to take the sound into his ballet *Prince of the Pagodas* (1955–57). As well as transferring the gamelan's gong strokes to a conventional orchestral gong (with double-bass doubling), Britten used staccato notes played with hard sticks on a piccolo timpani. Xylophone, vibraphone, celesta, cymbals, tam-tams and a rack of gong chimes all help Britten recreate something of the effect of gamelan.

Recreating the Gamelan in Western Music

Prominent among composers to be influenced by the gamelan sound was Messiaen, for example in his *Turangalîla-symphonie*, probably his most widely performed orchestral work. His *Et Exspecto resurrectionem mortuorum* ('I look for the resurrection of the dead') boasts six gongs and three tam-tams. Stockhausen, who also visited Bali, and **Cage** both studied gamelan instrumentation and procedures. The American composer and ethnomusicologist Colin McPhee (1901–64) visited Bali in 1934, the influence of which can be seen in his *Tabuh-tabuhan* (1936) and *Balinese Ceremonial Music* (1940). Following a study of world music, Lou Harrison (b. 1917) wrote for a combination of percussion and prepared piano, and his *Pacifika Rondo* (1963) is scored for a chamber orchestra bringing together western instruments such as the violin, celesta, two tack pianos (where the keys have added drawing pins to create a deliberately honky-tonk quality) and two percussionists with Javanese instruments.

The gamelan has become prominent in British music education in recent years, with some universities, local authorities and concert venues owning their own gamelan orchestras. This reflects partly the rise in importance of world musics in both schools and universities, and partly the world-wide impact of Orff's use of percussion in education, making access to a sophisticated percussion tradition such as gamelan an attractive option. Orff's experience of teaching led him to develop instruments to allow students to improvise their own music without first learning instrumental skills. There was tuned and untuned percussion: alloyed steel triangles, silver-bronze (not brass as it is conventional) cymbals, rosewood castanets, woodblocks, claves, xylophone bars and spruce resonance boxes of bar instruments. Each type of instrument was built in three sizes.

Bartók ▶ p. 285 Berg ▶ p. 286 Cage ▶ p. 324 Debussy ▶ p. 282 Gershwin ▶ p. 289 Handel ▶ p. 112 Haydn ▶ p. 140 Kodály ▶ p. 292 Monteverdi ▶ p. 76 Orff ▶ p. 293 Prokofiev ▶ p. 294 Ravel ▶ p. 294 Schütz ▶ p. 86 Shostakovich ▶ p. 297

The Modern Era
LISTENING GUIDE

Igor Stravinsky
The Rite of Spring

WORK: Igor Stravinsky, *The Rite of Spring (Le sacre du printemps; Vesna Svyashchennaya),* composed in 1911–13
SCORING: (brackets indicate doublings): piccolo, 3 flutes (piccolo 2), alto flute, 4 oboes (cor anglais 2), cor anglais, 3 clarinets (E flat clarinet, bass clarinet 2), bass clarinet, 4 bassoons (contra-bassoon 2), contra-bassoon, 8 horns (2 tenor tubas), 5 trumpets (bass trumpet), 3 trombones, 2 bass tubas, timpani (two players), percussion, strings
EXCERPT: First three sections of work (Introduction; The Augurs of Spring – Dances of the Young Girls; Ritual of Abduction).
TIMINGS BASED ON: City of Birmingham Symphony Orchestra/Sir Simon Rattle (see Recommended CDs)

RECOMMENDED CDs

1. *The Rite of Spring/Apollo.* City of Birmingham Symphony Orchestra. Sir Simon Rattle, conductor. Recorded in 1989. EMI CDC7 49636-2.

The Rite of Spring, once thought almost unplayably difficult but now in danger of becoming a vehicle for showman conductors, receives a performance whose accuracy and attack restores its ferocious impact. Apollo, one of Stravinsky's most gracious neo-classical scores, is both elegant and eloquent.

2. *Les Noces*/Mass. English Bach Festival Chorus. Leonard Bernstein, conductor. Recorded in 1977. Deutsche Grammophon 423 251-2GC.

Les Noces, Stravinsky's evocation of a Russian peasant wedding, has both humour and solemnity to it; Bernstein finds both, and a sense of ancient ritual in the bell-like sonorities of its 'orchestra' of four pianos and percussion. The austerely beautiful Mass is an ideal coupling.

3. *Oedipus Rex*/Symphony of Psalms. Czech Philharmonic Chorus and Orchestra. Karel Ancerl, conductor. Recorded in 1964 and 1966. Supraphon 11 1947-2.

The secular and sacred masterpieces of Stravinsky's neo-classicism, with Verdi and Handel among the points of reference in *Oedipus Rex,* Bach and Russian Orthodox chant in the Symphony. Karel Ancerl's sensitive performances have never been surpassed.

4. *The Rake's Progress.* Soloists, Sadler's Wells Chorus, Royal Philharmonic Orchestra. Igor Stravinsky, conductor. Recorded in 1964. Sony Classical SM2K 46299 (2 CDs).

Stravinsky's only full-length opera, to a libretto by W. H. Auden, is a homage to Mozart: an eighteenth-century tragi-comedy (complete with harpsichord-accompanied recitatives) but pure Stravinsky in every bar. His own performance sparkles with wit and energy.

Stravinsky's *The Rite of Spring* has become one of the best-known pieces in the twentieth-century repertory, helped along by the notoriety it gained from its very first performance. It was the culmination of his association with Diaghilev and a turning point in the composer's career, not to mention Western music as a whole. The score was based on folksong, but Stravinsky moved away from the symphonic treatment, describing it as a primitive ballet. Stravinsky's rejection of traditional forms, together with Nijinksy's unprecedented choreography led to almost universal dismissal when the work was first performed, but it has long since been recognized as a masterpiece.

THE ROOTS OF GENIUS

Stravinsky had been given piano lessons as a child and soon showed signs of musical talent, but his father insisted that at university he should study not music but law. A fellow student, however, was the son of Rimsky-Korsakov, one of the most famous Russian composers of the period and Russia's most distinguished teacher of composition. Stravinsky showed him some of his youthful pieces and was soon accepted as a private pupil, benefiting from Rimsky-Korsakev's encyclopedic knowledge and his renowned mastery of orchestration.

(NL) Costume Design
Design for the 'Lad's Costume' that was used in the now-notorious première of Stravinsky's The Rite of Spring.
***(TNR)* The Firebird**
Modern performance for the fairy-tale based Russian opera, in which the influence of Rimsky-Korsakov was evident.

1. 0'00"
Very high solo bassoon; other woodwind instruments join in; eight changes of bar-length in 13 bars.

2. 0'58"
Cor anglais and three bassoons; rhythm becomes a little more regular.

3. 1'12"
High clarinet melody with bird-like replies from flutes. Melody passes to oboe, cor anglais; first point of rest...

4. 1'51"
... but a flute flourish injects more energy.

5. 2'17"
New tune in the oboe; rejoinder from high clarinet, more and more instruments join in....

6. 2'52"
... and abruptly fall silent; opening bassoon solo returns, seems to fade, but *pizzicato* strings herald rise of curtain.

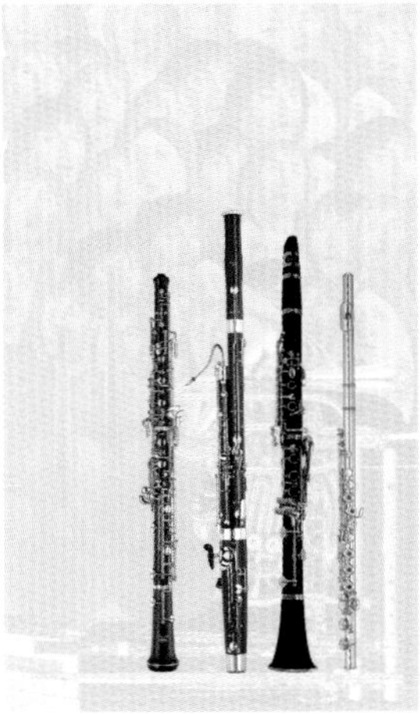
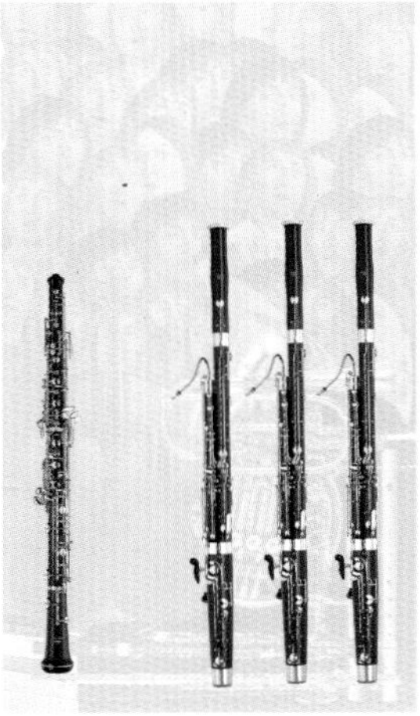

dissonance ▶ p. 358

DIAGHILEV

For five years, until his teacher died in 1908, all Stravinsky's works were written under his detailed supervision. Rimsky-Korsakov also arranged for some of them to be published and performed, and in this way Stravinsky came to the attention of Sergei Diaghilev, who needed a new ballet for his second Ballets Russes season in 1910. Diaghilev invited him to write the music for a ballet based on a Russian fairytale, *The Firebird*. This vivid score was a huge success at its première at the Paris Opéra in June 1910, and Stravinsky became famous overnight.

THE SHOCK OF THE NEW

If *The Firebird* was audibly by a pupil of Rimsky-Korsakov, its successor *Petrushka*, given its première by the Ballets Russes a year later, was a huge step forward, with its tingling rhythmic drive and acidly bright orchestral colours. It, too, was an overwhelming public success and Stravinsky's third work for Diaghilev, *The Rite of Spring*, was eagerly anticipated. To reflect its subject-matter (a pagan ritual in prehistoric Russia at the height of which a chosen virgin dances herself to death to propitiate the gods) its language was far more revolutionary than that of *Petrushka*. Its rhythms were unprecedentedly violent and irregular, its harmonies no less innovatively harsh and its melodies often brusquely brief. It profoundly shocked the first-night audience, and a full-scale riot ensued.

The violent scenes of the first night were not repeated at subsequent performances, and the work was soon recognized as one of those rare masterpieces that have changed the whole of musical history. Its influence on the rest of twentieth-century music has been profound.

BREAKING THE RULES

Most Western music before *The Rite of Spring* was written in regularly repeating patterns of two or three (or their multiples: four or six) beats to the bar. In *The Rite* Stravinsky often uses bars of five, seven, even 11 beats, and no less often changes the number of beats every bar; the listener is aware of powerful rhythm, but cannot tap his foot to it. Most music before *The Rite* used **dissonance** (notes that clash when played together) only as expressive 'seasoning'; in *The Rite*, dissonance becomes the norm. Before *The Rite*, most music used recurring themes and ordered contrast of key to give a sense of gradual development and evolving form. There is little development in *The Rite of Spring* and no formal growth: blocks of music are juxtaposed, even superimposed, and many of its melodies are in no recognizable key at all.

Not all of these departures are entirely original. Russian composers before Stravinsky had been uncomfortable with Western European ideas of musical form; some (including Stravinsky's teacher **Rimsky-Korsakov**) had experimented with scales, derived from folk music, that were neither major nor minor. Under the impact of his savage subject-matter, Stravinsky took all these tendencies, greatly expanded them and fuelled them with the huge power of his wholly original rhythmic language. The result denied all the rules of the composition text-books, but liberated melody, harmony, counterpoint and rhythm from those rules with its sheer expressive force and urgency. No piece of twentieth-century music has been more influential.

7. 3'26"
Stamping string chords, eight horns on off-beat accents; two-note cor anglais 'tune', brief muted-trumpet figure; climax and stamping dance returns...

8. 4'15"
... now with primitive tune on three bassoons; music collapses, but rhythm soon picks up.

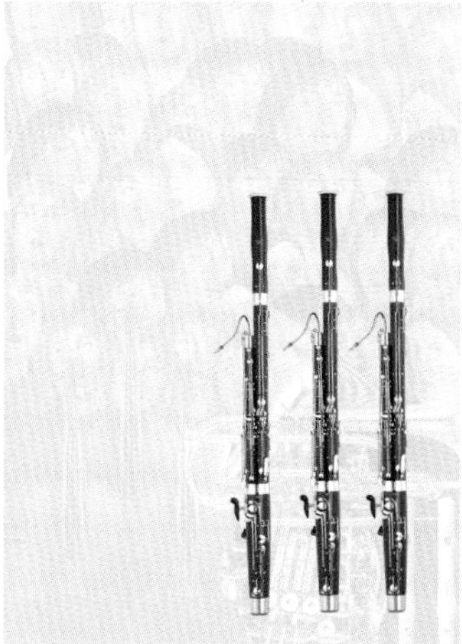

9. 5'10"
Solo horn, echoed by flute, introduces new melody; earlier two-note tune and trumpet figure return.

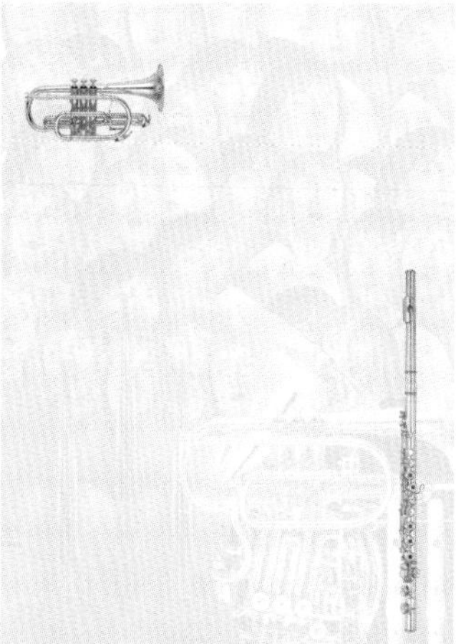

10. 5'42"
Using all this material, the texture grows ever more dense as other instruments join, building tension...

11. 6'47"
... to very fast music whose speed remains constant, increasing rhythmic excitement due to growing irregularity of bar lengths.

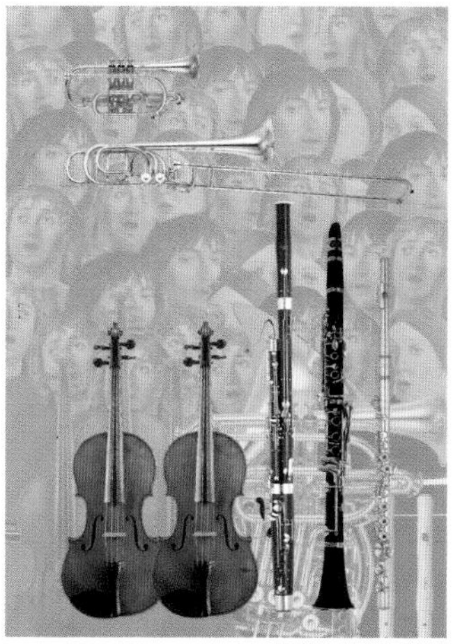

Rimsky-Korsakov ▶ p. 256 Stravinsky ▶ p. 280

page 312 ◀◁ ARTS AND CULTURE ▷▶ page 322
page 314 ◀◁ INSIDE THE MUSIC ▷▶ page 330
◀◁ THE VOICE ▷▶

CLAUDE DEBUSSY: *LA MER*

La mer (1903–05) is often described as Impressionist, by analogy with the paintings of Claude Monet *et al*, and it is easy to hear foam-crested waves and the sparkle of sunlight on water in **Debussy**'s music. He, however, was less interested in the Impressionists than in J. M. W. Turner, whom he called 'the greatest creator of mystery in the whole world of art', and he was fascinated by the formal perfection and sense of order of Japanese art. The melodies of *La mer* are often rooted not in any major or minor key but in the five-note or pentatonic scale, used in Eastern and Western folk music. None of its movements is in an established musical form, and its orchestral colour is highly original. Listen to the opening of the third movement ('Dialogue of the Wind and Waves'): a low rumble of drums, abrupt figures in cellos and double-basses, quiet gong strokes; then, high above, hovering phrases on oboes and clarinets, their attack almost imperceptibly intensified by two trumpets. Eventually, two melodies are heard (one on muted trumpet, the other on woodwind and horns), both from the first movement, but now seen in a new light. 'Painters and sculptors,' Debussy said, 'can only give us a very free and always fragmentary interpretation of the beauties of the universe. They can only seize and fix one of her aspects, only one of her moments. Only musicians have the privilege of capturing all the poetry of the night and the day, of the earth and the sky, to reconstitute their atmosphere and give rhythm to their immense vibration."

RECOMMENDED CD

La mer etc. Royal Concertgebouw Orchestra. Bernard Haitink, Eduard van Beinum, conductors. Recorded in 1959-80. Philips 438 742-2 (2 CDs)

All of Debussy's major orchestral works, in performances of great strength, subtlety and refinement of colour.

ARNOLD SCHOENBERG: ORCHESTRAL VARIATIONS OP. 31

A misty, impressionistic Introduction hints at the theme and quietly (solo trombone) sketches the notes B flat, A, C, B natural: in German musical notation BACH. The theme (in the cellos, its last phrases on solo viola) consists of all four versions of a **12-note** row.

Variation 1: theme mainly in bass (beginning on bass clarinet, bassoons and double-basses), but with its rhythm changed. Other instruments present short melodic fragments that reflect each other, like images in a kaleidoscope.

Variation 2: theme upside-down, played by violin with oboe imitating. Similar games played by other pairs of instruments.

Variation 3: another rhythmic transformation of the theme, in the horns; related phrases flung from one section of the orchestra to another.

Variation 4: a waltz, beginning in solo strings and woodwind; the theme is in the accompaniment, for harp, celesta and mandolin.

Variation 5: theme first heard in bass (trombone, contra-bassoon and double-basses), transformations of it soon invade the whole orchestra.

Variation 6: chamber music texture; theme half-hidden in solo cello line, phrases from other instruments imitating and reflecting each other.

Variation 7: slow and glittering music, fragments of theme heard around winding melody that passes from bassoon to clarinet, oboe, flute, solo violin and bass clarinet.

Variation 8: brief and very fast, phrases from transformed theme hurled back and forth by oboes and bassoons, then high and low strings.

Variation 9: longer phrases pass from instrument to instrument, like questions and answers.

Finale begins with recollection of introduction, revisits moods of several earlier variations, with frequent returns to the BACH motif.

UNANSWERED QUESTION

Subtitled, 'A Contemplation of a Serious Matter', this was the piece with which Ives really broke with tradition in 1906. Different groups within the orchestra contribute layers that are not precisely synchronized. The result is a fascinating and poetic work, pioneering the use of aleatory or chance elements in music.

POPULAR MELODY *Ives*

RECOMMENDED CD

Orchestral Variations/*Pelleas und Melisande*. Chicago Symphony Orchestra. Pierre Boulez, conductor. Recorded in 1991. Erato 2292-45827-2

Schoenberg's serial masterpiece and his early, massively Straussian tone-poem in performances that ideally distil the essence of both.

LISTENING TO SERIALISM

In pre-Schoenberg tonal music, the ear finds its way around a composition by recognizing even quite disguised repetitions and variants and by sensing tensions between keys. Neither of these is possible in a piece of strict **serial music**. With a bit of practice, the ear can recognize the inversion of a phrase but not very readily a pattern of notes played backwards; still less upside-down and backwards. Serial composers sometimes compensate for this by using easily recognizable classical forms (as in Schoenberg's Variations, where if the precise relationship of the various forms of the row is unclear the work is audibly a series of contrasted variations). Schoenberg's pupil **Webern**, in his Concerto op. 24, devised a 12-note row in which a three-note cell is inverted, played backwards (retrograde) and in retrograde inversion. This intensification of Schoenberg's method in fact makes the serial process easier to hear, the entire work being audible as a dazzling interplay of closely related three-note fragments. Webern said that this extreme concentration, far from being a restriction, in fact liberated his imaginative fantasy. His influence on the post-war avant-garde was profound.

EXPANDING THE LANGUAGE OF MUSIC

Western classical music since the seventeenth century, because it placed great emphasis on harmonic subtlety and tensions between keys, had been less interested in melodic flexibility (a maximum of 12 notes to the octave, while Indian music uses 22) and in rhythm (regular division into bars, normally of two, three, four or six beats; Indian music, again, uses rhythmic structures much longer than Western bars). Twentieth-century composers have investigated these neglected areas. **Ives**, in his Fourth Symphony, calls for an (optional) piano tuned in quarter-tones (24 notes to the octave) and in several passages divides his orchestra into groups playing simultaneously in different rhythms. Other composers (notably **Stockhausen**, **Berio**, **Boulez** and **Babbitt**) have invented entirely new sounds, using electronic means, or have incorporated into their music sounds that an earlier age would have dismissed as noise. *Déserts* by **Varèse** alternates orchestral music with a pre-recorded tape of sounds collected in factories, saw-mills and iron-works. At the outset of his career he had declared that 'I refuse to submit solely to sounds that have been heard before'.

adagio ▶ p. 356 cadenza ▶ p. 356 dissonance ▶ p. 358 serial music ▶ p. 362 12-note music ▶ p. 363

BÉLA BARTÓK: SECOND PIANO CONCERTO

Like his First Piano Concerto, **Bartók**'s Second (1933) was written for himself to play; its huge difficulty is evidence of the steely virtuosity of his technique. As with several of his works of this period (for example the Fourth and Fifth String Quartets) it is roughly symmetrical in structure, the outer movements being closely related, the central ***adagio*** having a powerful scherzo at its centre.

The first movement has several themes, most of them close relatives of the trumpet figure heard at the beginning. In this movement, the warm sound of string instruments is absent, intensifying the music's percussive brilliance. The piano part is exuberant as well as demanding; near the end there is a very taxing solo **cadenza**. The slow movement begins with hushed and beautiful string chords; the piano's ornate phrases, accompanied only by quiet drum rolls, have a marked Hungarian flavour. The centre of the movement is an example of Bartók's 'night music', the whirrings and chirrupings of nocturnal creatures growing to a powerful climax before the peaceful opening gradually returns. The brilliant finale begins with a driving new theme, but it soon turns to transformed variants of ideas first heard in the first movement, including the trumpet figure.

RECOMMENDED CD

Piano Concertos 1–3. András Schiff, piano. Budapest Festival Orchestra. Iván Fischer, conductor. Recorded in 1996. Teldec 0630-13158-2

Schiff has all the virtuosity and power this music needs, but finds humour and fantasy as well; he is closely matched by the fiery brilliance of an outstanding Hungarian orchestra.

CHARLES IVES: 'COUNTRY BAND' MARCH

Encouraged by his remarkable father, Ives very soon began to question the established 'rules' of harmony, counterpoint and form which, he felt, merely imprisoned the imagination within outworn conventions. The most withering term of contempt in his vocabulary, for music that obeyed all the rules but had not a spark of life, was 'nice'. He loved the anything-but-nice music of the country bands that he heard as a child, whose players would throw in fragments of favourite tunes jovially without worrying whether they were in the right key or not, who would sometimes mis-read their parts or get out of step with each other. In the 'Country Band' March of 1903, the main tune is a sort of amalgam of well-known marches of the period; Ives used it in many of his works. He lovingly portrays all the foibles of the town-band musicians that he knew, including their way of getting ahead of the conductor's beat, the total confusion near the end where no one is quite sure where they are, and the unfortunate saxophonist who goes on playing when everyone else has stopped.

The 'Country Band' March is what Ives called a 'stunt', but in its enjoyment of **dissonance** and its very precise noting-down of unsynchronized musical strands it is characteristic of many of his major works. He re-used parts of it in the 'Putnam's Camp' section of *Three Places in New England*, in the 'Hawthorne' movement of his 'Concord' Sonata for piano and in the extraordinary scherzo ('not a scherzo but a comedy,' Ives insisted) of his Fourth Symphony.

RECOMMENDED CD

'Country Band' March/Set for Theatre Orchestra/Three Places in New England etc. Orchestra New England. James Sinclair, conductor. Recorded in 1990. Koch 3-7025-2 H1

Noted Ives scholar conducts orchestra of Ives enthusiasts in a cross-section of his works given ideally exuberant performances.

(BL) Luciano Berio
Berio, a pioneering composer, used electronic means to generate entirely new sounds in his music.
(TL) Eastern Influences
La mer *demonstrated Debussy's fascination with the Japanese sense of order.*
(TR) Béla Bartók
Bartók's wrote his Second Piano Concerto for himself to play.
(BR) Charles Ives
Ives moved away from all that was formal and organised in music; he called his 'Country Band' March a 'stunt'.

Babbitt ▶ p. 284 Bartók ▶ p. 285 Berio ▶ p. 324 Boulez ▶ p. 324 Debussy ▶ p. 282 Ives ▶ p. 291 Schoenberg ▶ p. 295 Stockhausen ▶ p. 329 Varèse ▶ p. 298 Webern ▶ p. 299

THE LATE 20TH CENTURY

Music of the late twentieth century whose ancestry lies in the Western classical tradition finds itself in a curious position. Nothing illustrates this better than the fact that we are not entirely sure what to call it. The label 'classical', even 'contemporary classical', seems anachronistic, especially when applied to composers who have challenged some of the fundamental assumptions of the classical tradition. 'Concert music' is similarly problematic, as many of the more radical expressions of the last few decades have overspilled the boundaries of conventional performance spaces. 'Contemporary art music' remains perhaps the safest term. But to use it is not to suggest that jazz or other popular music never aspires to or attains the condition of art, nor that there is no art music that does not actively resist that label, even as it continues to operate within traditional musical institutions.

A WORLD OF POSSIBILITY?

There was an immense expansion in the variety, scope and influence of communications media in the second half of the twentieth century. The arrival of satellite links in the 1970s and the Internet in the 1990s further dissolved the barriers of space and time first breached by telecommunications. These developments, coupled with unprecedented population mobility through travel, emigration and displacement, mean that today a given musical style is rarely restricted to a single geographical location. Indeed, Western art music is no longer the exclusive preserve of the Western countries in which it originated. It is now practised, often in fruitful dialogue with indigenous traditions, in countries as diverse as Taiwan, Egypt, Indonesia and Turkey. East Asian composers especially, such as the Japanese Toru Takemitsu (1930–96), have made a significant impact on the international scene.

GIANT STEPS

But the effect of communications technology, broadcasting and recording above all, has been double-edged. While the greater accessibility of recording facilities after World War II created new possibilities for composition, potentially freeing it from both notation and live performers, it also fuelled a classical recording industry which concentrated not on new music as such, but on new interpretations of old music. The conservatism which had already taken root in the concert hall thus became still more entrenched, making the gap between contemporary composers and the concert-going, let alone the mass, public seem wider than ever.

The Late 20th Century

INTRODUCTION

After the devastation wrought in Europe by World War II, the urgent task of rebuilding the continent's war-torn urban fabric demanded radical solutions. These were found in the centralized urban planning advocated before the war by architects such as Le Corbusier and Ludwig Mies van der Rohe. Writing in 1953, the composer Karlheinz Stockhausen (b. 1928) created an explicit analogy between the projects of urban and musical reconstruction: 'the "cities have been razed to the ground",' he wrote, 'and we can start completely from scratch, paying no attention to the ruins and "tasteless" remains'. Ignoring the 'remains' was indeed a widely perceived necessity. Few forms of European cultural expression had escaped Fascist appropriation – even aspects of Bauhaus design had been pressed into service in the construction of concentration camps. Composers and literary writers alike now sought a completely renewed language, free of nostalgia and inherited rhetoric.

LA DOMENICA DEL CORRIERE
Si pubblica a Milano ogni settimana
Supplemento illustrato del "Corriere della Sera"
Anno 43 — N. 2
12 Gennaio 1941 XIX
Centesimi 50 la copia
Tra le rovine della "City". Dopo i bombardamenti tedeschi, soldati inglesi e vigili del fuoco completano la distruzione del centro di Londra, facendo saltare con la dinamite le mura rimaste ancora in piedi e pericolanti. Sullo sfondo la cattedrale di San Paolo, rimasta intatta in mezzo a tanto sfacelo.

BUILDING-BLOCKS

Electronic music allowed composers to start from scratch in a literal way, by artificially constructing complex sounds using the 'pure' sine-tone as an elementary building-block. While the pioneering experiments in ***musique concrète*** undertaken by Pierre Schaeffer (1910–95) in Paris used sounds derived from real-life environments (such as the railway in the *Etude aux chemins de fer*, 'Study for Railways, 1948), he too wanted to make them 'new', to transform them out of all recognition into pure 'sound objects'. The highly ramified post-war developments in serial technique, led in Europe by **Stockhausen**, **Pierre Boulez** (b. 1925), **Henri Pousseur** (b. 1929) and **Luigi Nono** (1924–90), likewise aimed at an objective structural logic that, in large measure, would bypass considerations of personal taste and aesthetic preference.

KEY EVENTS

1952	Completion of Unité d'Habitation in Marseilles, a celebrated post-war housing project designed by Le Corbusier
1953	Death in the Soviet Union of dictator Joseph Stalin
1956	Hungarian revolt crushed by USSR
1957	Democracy in Ghana marks the beginning of colonial independence in Africa
1958	Nikita Krushchev becomes Soviet prime minister
1961	US send military aid to Vietnam, beginning their involvement in the war between North and South; Yuri Gagarin of the USSR becomes first man in space
1963	Martin Luther King leads Freedom March on Washington, a turning point in the black civil rights movement; Betty Friedan writes *The Feminine Mystique*
1968	Student riots in several European cities
1971	The Intel company begins marketing the microchip, the catalyst for the subsequent microcomputer revolution
1978	The Piazza d'Italia, a landmark in postmodernist architecture, completed in New Orleans to a design by Charles W. Moore
1980	Phillips release the first compact discs
1985	Mikhail Gorbachev becomes president of the USSR, initiating the economic and political reforms of *perestroika* ('restructuring')
1987	Crash of London and New York stock markets leads to the second major post-war recession in Western economies
1989	End of Communist rule in Czechoslovakia, Hungary, Poland and Romania; demolition of Berlin Wall begins
1991	Soviet states granted independence from the union; dissolution of Warsaw Pact
1992	World Wide Web enters the public domain
1999	The Euro, a single currency for Europe, goes into circulation

MUSIC AND THE POLITICS OF THE COLD WAR

After World War II, it took the Soviet Union just a few years to consolidate its hold over Eastern Europe. With the formation of the Commission for Mutual Economic Assistance in 1949, the Soviet bloc became an economic and political reality. The West responded with the formation of the NATO military alliance and, by the following year, when the USSR announced its possession of the atomic bomb, the Cold War had begun in earnest.

Cold War politics had a direct impact on the cultural policies of the new Eastern bloc, which defined its doctrine of 'socialist realism' in explicit opposition to the 'over-bourgeois' trends in Europe and America, with their rejection of heritage 'under the guise of apparent novelty'. Much Western music, that of not only Schoenberg and **Igor Stravinsky** (1882–1971) but also **Benjamin Britten** (1913–76) and **Darius Milhaud** (1892–1974), was banned. The state also turned on the supposed enemy within. In 1948, resolutions were passed by the Communist party condemning, among others, **Dmitri Shostakovich** (1906–75), **Sergei Prokofiev** (1891–1953) and **Aram Khachaturian** (1903–78) for maintaining a 'formalism … alien to the people and leading to the destruction of music'. These pronouncements had repercussions throughout the Eastern bloc. A few composers, such as the Hungarian **György Ligeti** (b. 1923), managed to flee to the West. Others, notably Shostakovich, were banned from teaching and all but a handful of their works suppressed. After the death of the dictator Joseph Stalin in 1953, the situation gradually improved. The effects of the subsequent cultural 'thaw' were particularly visible in Poland, where the Warsaw Autumn Festival became (from 1956) a virtually unrestricted platform for international contemporary music, and composers such as **Witold Lutosławski** (1913–93) and **Krzysztof Penderecki** (b. 1933) appropriated avant-garde techniques to their own highly individual expressive ends. But elsewhere, especially in the USSR and East Germany, composers continued to endure sudden blocks on performances and arbitrary censure in the official press.

COMPOSING IN POST-WAR AMERICA

By contrast, the activity of composers in the US seemed increasingly divorced from the political and social sphere. **John Cage**'s (1912–92) desire, through techniques of indeterminacy, to 'let sounds be themselves rather than vehicles for man-made theories or expressions of human sentiments', apparently absolved music from the responsibility of carrying any message at all, let alone an overtly political one. The post-war expansion of higher education created a natural home for composers

(L) Blitz
Italian magazine cover showing the effects of the Blitz in London.
(FR) Concerto for Piano and Orchestra
The complicated score for John Cage's work.
(NR) Anti-War Demonstration
Rebellion against institutions characterized the 1960s, it was a decade of the individual against the institutions, the minorities against the majorities.

minimalism ▶ p. 360 *musique concrète* ▶ p. 360

as teachers within universities, and this served only to heighten their isolation from the social mainstream. Some, like **Milton Babbitt** (b. 1916), styled themselves as 'specialists', their audiences inevitably consisting of other 'specialists'. But that composers themselves felt contemporary social conditions limited their audiences did not, at least to some, make their activities politically insignificant. The fact that modernist art flourished in the US, while it was suppressed in Stalinist Eastern Europe, was upheld as proof of America's championing of liberal intellectual values in the face of the Communist totalitarian threat. Experimental art was thus co-opted in the Cold War struggle: through organizations such as the Congress for Cultural Freedom, even the CIA channelled funds which ended up supporting performances of new music in Europe and the US.

DARMSTADT

The summer courses held in the German city of Darmstadt from 1946 enabled otherwise isolated young composers, in the words of Berio, 'to stand side by side in defence of a new idea of music'. In their first decade, the courses introduced to many for the first time the music which had been suppressed in Nazi-occupied countries during the war, including that of **Paul Hindemith** (1895–1963), **Arnold Schoenberg** (1874–1951) and **Anton Webern** (1883–1945). But they soon became one of the most important platforms for the rising avant-garde generation, not only its composers – Boulez, Stockhausen, Nono, Pousseur, Ligeti and Kagel – but also its virtuoso performers, including the oboist **Heinz Holliger** (b. 1939), also a composer, the cellist Siegfried Palm (b. 1927) and the piano duo of Alfons (b. 1932) and Aloys (b. 1931) Kontarsky. Guests from the US included **Edgard Varèse** (1883–1965), **Morton Feldman** (1926–87) and, most notably, Cage, whose 1958 visit proved a vital catalyst for growing European interest in indeterminacy.

Though the 1950s tend to be viewed as Darmstadt's heyday, the courses have continued to thrive (biennially from 1970) under such influential teachers as **Brian Ferneyhough** (b. 1943), Rihm and Helmut Lachenmann (b. 1935).

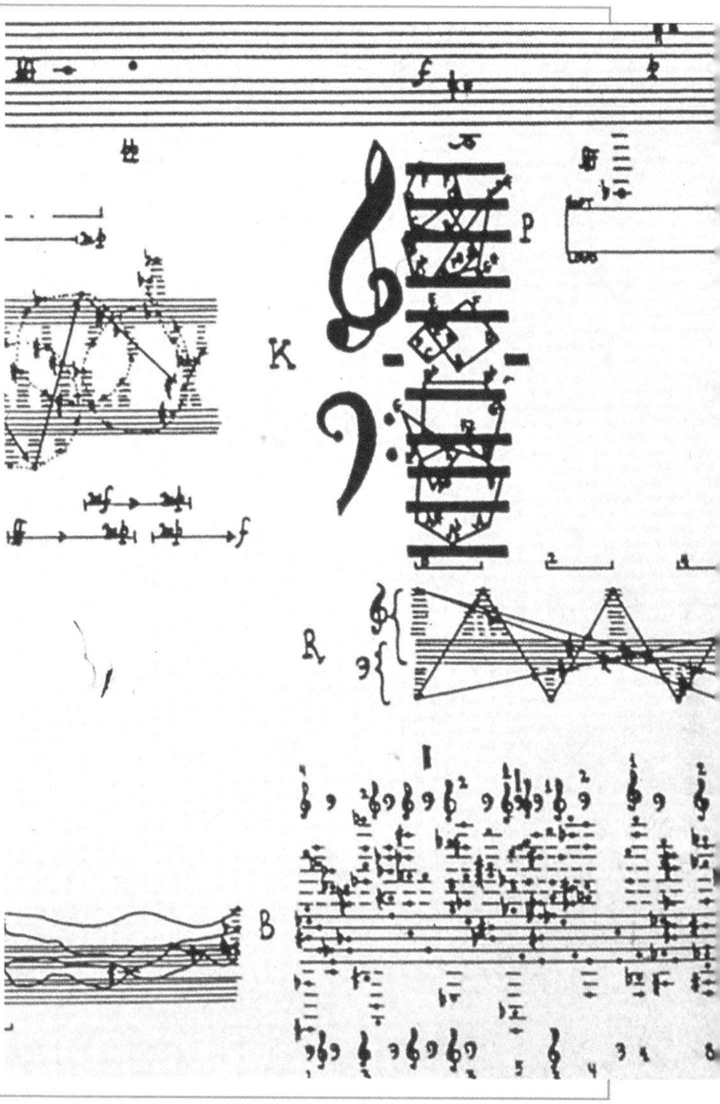

THE COUNTER-CULTURAL REACTION

By the dawn of the 1960s, many had a sense that the avant-garde's relationship to the Establishment had become a little too comfortable. The very idea of an avant-garde, a single, authoritative élite which set a unified agenda and pace for artistic developments, started to lose credibility. This was, after all, to be the decade of the civil rights protests, the anti-nuclear and anti-Vietnam demonstrations and the student riots, each seeking greater empowerment for the individual against institutions, for minorities against the majority. Belief in any kind of centralized authority seemed to be crumbling.

In music the 'counter-culture' manifested itself in a variety of ways. Where the serial and even the indeterminate works of the 1950s had required specialist performers, many composers turned to more open, 'democratic' kinds of music-making, based on improvisation, collaboration or both. While the Fluxus movement took up the threads of the Dadaist heritage, the Scratch Orchestra, founded in London by Cornelius Cardew (1936–81), brought together amateurs and professionals under the banner of revolutionary politics. Co-operation was also a feature of such early **minimalist** compositions as *In C* (1964) by **Terry Riley** (b. 1935), in which performers proceed at a mutually negotiated pace through a group of simple melodic fragments. Listeners too found minimalism accessible: the use of synthesizers and amplified instruments by groups such as Steve Reich and Musicians and the Philip Glass Ensemble won them an enthusiastic following among rock-music audiences.

Babbitt ▶ p. 284 Britten ▶ p. 287 Boulez ▶ p. 324 Cage ▶ p. 324 Khachaturian ▶ p. 292 Ligeti ▶ p. 326 Lutosławski ▶ p. 327 Milhaud ▶ p. 293 Nono ▶ p. 327
Penderecki ▶ p. 328 Pousseur ▶ p. 328 Prokofiev ▶ p. 294 Riley ▶ p. 328 Shostakovich ▶ p. 297 Stockhausen ▶ p. 329 Stravinsky ▶ p. 280

NEW METHODS OF COMPOSITION

Many of the former avant-garde composers also became disillusioned with the orthodoxies of the 1950s. Stockhausen turned increasingly towards 'intuitive composition', involving graphics and text rather than conventional notation, and also demonstrated an increasing interest in the music of non-Western cultures: *Telemusik* (1966) absorbs into its electronic fabric music from Bali, Japan, the Amazon and the southern Sahara. Nono, meanwhile, turned to electronics to voice his strong socialist commitment: not only did *La fabbrica illuminata* ('The Enlightened Factory', 1964) use the sounds of a factory as raw material, it was also designed to be played to factory employees in their working environment. During the 1950s, few avant-garde composers had ventured into the theatre: now people such as Nono and Pousseur, made up for lost time with works which, while written for the opera-house, challenged the very legitimacy of that institution. And as European composers invaded the theatre, so 'the theatre' began to invade their works for the concert hall, which increasingly incorporated speech, movement and gesture.

'Music theatre', as this hybrid genre came to be described, attracted not only Ligeti, Kagel and **Luciano Berio** (b. 1925), but also the American **George Crumb** (b. 1929) and the British composers **Harrison Birtwistle** (b. 1934) and **Peter Maxwell Davies** (b. 1934).

ART MUSIC IN THE 'GLOBAL VILLAGE'

The pluralism in evidence in the late 1960s and early 70s was a harbinger of the extreme fragmentation which characterized the musical scene in the 1980s and 90s. Fragmentation and instability were just as endemic in the socio-economic sphere during these two decades. As manufacturers scoured the East and the southern hemisphere in search of cheaper labour markets, Western economies turned their attention from the production of goods to the production of demand for goods, through advertising, information technology and image production. Unstable conditions of employment became for many a permanent reality, while the increasingly volatile global currency markets demonstrated on more than one occasion how a single crisis of confidence could plunge whole continents into recession.

Within a culture dominated by the fashion industry's values of instantaneity and the ephemeral, a modernist's aspiration towards artworks of permanent value or significance might seem futile. Still, at the end of the century, modernism remained one of the most resilient compositional trends, composers such as **Elliott Carter** (b. 1908) and **György Kurtág** (b. 1926) working more confidently and productively than ever. The

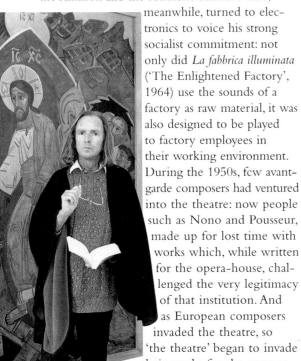

response of others to the confusion of postmodern cross-currents has been to root their music in particular places and environments – Davies in the landscape and literature of the Orkney Islands, where he settled at the beginning of the 1970s, and **Peter Sculthorpe** (b. 1929) in the aboriginal traditions of his native Australia. Expressions of personal faith and spirituality

(FL) John Tavener
Tavener's works embraced his spiritual beliefs.
(NL) Compact Disc
The arrival of the CD in 1980 heralded a new era of mass production and dissemination.
(FR) La Monte Young
Young was a member of the 1960s informal arts group Fluxus.
(NR) Destruction of the Berlin Wall
The end of Communism brought new freedoms to the arts.

CROSS-CURRENTS AND CONNECTIONS

Though art music in the second half of the twentieth century tended more often to define itself in opposition to rock and commercial pop music, signs of mutual regard were already emerging in the 1960s. While it is Stockhausen's face that stands out from the crowd on the front cover of the Beatles' 1967 album *Sergeant Pepper's Lonely Hearts Club Band*, it was Berio who returned the compliment that same year on behalf of the avant-garde, with his arrangements of the Lennon-McCartney songs 'Michelle', 'Yesterday' and 'Ticket to Ride'. In American music especially, quotations from rock and pop have crept often surreptitiously into quite alien styles and genres – from James Tenney's (b. 1934) *musique concrète* manipulation of Elvis Presley's 'Blue Suede Shoes' in the undemonstratively titled *Collage No. 1* (1961) to the music of Michael Torke (b. 1961), whose chamber work *The Yellow Pages* (1987) develops its ironically disjointed minimalist process from the bass line of a Chaka Khan song.

Mixing Genres

If some art music composers' attempts at stylistic imitation have been less than convincing – as with the rap of the character Donny in *New Year* (1986–88), the last opera of **Michael Tippett** (1905–98) – concert works by composers such as **Andrew Lloyd Webber** (b. 1948, *Requiem*, 1985) and **Paul McCartney** (b. 1942, *Liverpool Oratorio*, 1991) have, despite initial commercial success, tended to be routine in their handling of traditional choral and orchestral forces. Contemporary art music has periodically captured the imagination of rock music audiences, from the cult success of the 1968 recording of Tavener's *The Whale* to the punchy, aggressive post-minimalism of Steve Martland (b. 1959) in England and the composers – David Lang (b. 1957), Julia Wolfe (b. 1958) and Michael Gordon (b. 1956) – associated with the downtown New York Bang-on-a-Can Festival. But what generally remains a clearly demarcated institutional separation between the two kinds of music makes most of these cross-currents 'strange meetings' rather than lasting rapprochements. Some have built bridges in other ways: one of the more surprising developments of the 1990s was the emergence of the Rex Foundation, set up to sponsor performances and recordings of complex contemporary scores (of Birtwistle, Carter, Ferneyhough and others) by Phil Lesh, formerly of the rock band The Grateful Dead.

Berio ▶ p. 324 Birtwistle ▶ p. 324 Carter ▶ p. 325 Crumb ▶ p. 325 Davies ▶ p. 325 Feldman ▶ p. 325 Ferneyhough ▶ p. 325 Górecki ▶ p. 326

also characterize the work of a number of composers: **John Tavener** (b. 1944) and **Arvo Pärt** (b. 1935) draw on the Eastern Orthodox tradition, **Henryk Górecki** (b. 1933) and James Macmillan (b. 1959) on Roman Catholicism and **Sofiya Gubaydulina** (b. 1931) on elements of both.

THE AGE OF MASS PRODUCTION

A musical culture already dominated by recording received further impetus with the arrival of the compact disc in the early 1980s. Whereas LPs had had to be pressed in their thousands in order to make a commercially viable release, CDs required an edition of only hundreds. This meant that an even greater variety of recorded music could remain in circulation. In an environment saturated by so much music, some composers seemed to doubt the possibility of creating anything genuinely new. All that was left was the endless recombination of existing fragments, in a spirit ranging from the near-pastiche of **Michael Nyman** (b. 1944), which revels unashamedly in its own artificiality, to the anxiety and disorientation of **Wolfgang Rihm** (b. 1952) and **Alfred Schnittke** (1934–98), whose allusions to past styles often seem to lament the loss of that same authenticity, that ability to speak clearly in one's 'own' voice.

BEGINNING THE TWENTY-FIRST CENTURY

The sheer amount of contemporary art music composition in progress would seem enough to guarantee its survival in the new millennium. Throughout the world more musicians than ever consider composition their primary activity, though most rely on other occupations, such as performing or teaching, to generate the backbone of their income. With the major publishing and recording companies signing up fewer individuals, many composers now promote and distribute their own scores and recordings, a process facilitated of late by the greater accessibility of digital recording techniques and the development of highly sophisticated music notation software, which allows the desktop publishing of scores to a previously unattainable standard.

That classical music-making in general will likewise survive in some form or other is in little doubt. The future of its institutions, however, seems less certain, as state subsidies in Europe show no sign of increasing. The audience for classical music in the twenty-first century seems set to become even more fragmented, and still further orientated towards recording (in any case a more lucrative source of income for performers) than towards live concerts.

THE COLLAPSE OF THE SOVIET BLOC

The events which brought about the end of Communist rule in Eastern Europe and the Soviet Union unfolded with remarkable rapidity in the space of little more than a year. Mikhail Gorbachev had made his liberalizing intentions evident soon after gaining power in March 1985, and in July 1988 his proposals had received the official endorsement of the Communist party conference. But the following year, events elsewhere in Eastern Europe started to overtake him. In August 1989, Poland elected its first non-Communist prime minister; a month later Hungary announced its transition to democracy, opening its borders and allowing in refugees from East Germany. Within three weeks, East Germany's dictator Erich Honecker had resigned, and in November the destruction of the Berlin Wall began. As the best-known physical embodiment of the 'Iron Curtain' began to crumble, so did the régimes in Romania, Bulgaria and Czechoslovakia and the Communist monopolies in Lithuania, Latvia, Yugoslavia and Mongolia. After a wave of independence declarations throughout the following year, the Warsaw Pact was finally disbanded on 1 July 1991.

Democracy

The first decade of democracy was not without upheaval. Most catastrophic were the consequences in the former Yugoslavia, where the end of Communist rule reopened former conflicts between ethnic populations, resulting in a decade of military conflict and mass civilian slaughter on a scale compared by some commentators to genocide.

Elsewhere, the problems were financial as the new states struggled to adapt to market economics. Many cultural institutions, including orchestras and opera companies, suffered grievously from the loss of their comparatively luxurious state subsidies. And while individual artists welcomed their now unrestricted freedom, a number, including the Russians Viktor Suslin (b. 1942), Dmitry Smirnov (b. 1948) and Elena Firsova (b. 1950), chose to exercise it by moving to Western Europe.

FLUXUS

Inspired by Cage's pioneering mixed-media events of the 1950s, Fluxus was an informal group of composers, artists and perfomers founded by the Lithuanian-born artist and architect George Maciunas (1931–78). After its first concert in Wiesbaden (1962), it remained active in Europe and the US intermittently until Maciunas's death. The group also included the composers La Monte Young (b. 1935), Tenney and Nam June Paik (b. 1932), and the artist and performer Yoko Ono (b. 1933), who later married John Lennon. While it had no formal manifesto, the group shared Cage's resistance to the conventional distinctions between art and everyday life. Fluxus performances centred around 'events', actions usually described in short verbal instructions to the performer. Many of these involved critiques of familiar concert-hall rituals, subverting conventional relationships both between performers and musical instruments (which Paik would often destroy on stage) and between performers and audiences (in Young's *Composition 1960 No. 6*, the performers are instructed simply to sit and watch the audience). By the 1980s and 1990s, Fluxus-type 'performance art' was more commonly encountered in art galleries than in concert halls, but its activities did much to demonstrate to composers that within a concert environment, anything and everything was possible.

TURNING BACK THE CLOCK

In other respects, however, the clock seems to be turning back. Whereas nineteenth-century aesthetics had stressed its separateness from everyday life, music now seems to be reassuming the kinds of social functions it played up until the eighteenth century. Classical music is becoming an inescapable part of our environment. In advertising it is used to manipulate moods and desires, often carrying connotations of refinement, sophistication and elevated social status. On telephone queuing systems and in bus stations it is used to induce relaxation and to lower stress levels. It is now even played in kindergartens, following academic studies that suggest it stimulates children's reasoning faculties. Whether these developments are regarded as positive or negative symptoms, one thing seems certain that as the millennium progresses, music will play a greater, rather than a smaller, role in our everyday lives.

Gubaydulina ▶ p. 326 Hindemith ▶ p. 290 Holliger ▶ p. 326 Kurtág ▶ p. 326 Lloyd Webber ▶ p. 327 McCartney ▶ p. 327 Nyman ▶ p. 327 Pärt ▶ p. 327
Rihm ▶ p. 328 Schnittke ▶ p. 328 Schoenberg ▶ p. 295 Sculthorpe ▶ p. 328 Tavener ▶ p. 329 Tippett ▶ p. 330 Varèse ▶ p. 298 Webern ▶ p. 299

The Late 20th Century
PERSONALITIES

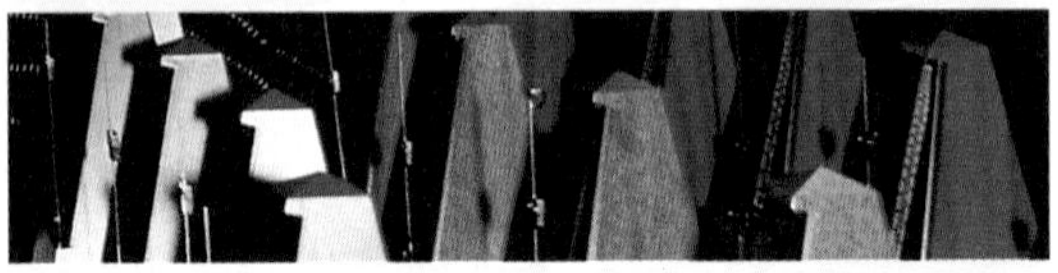

Adams, John
b. 1947
AMERICAN COMPOSER
Adams has played a significant role in introducing contemporary music to American audiences, working as adviser to a number of organizations, including the San Francisco Symphony Orchestra. Although Adams' basic compositional style is made up of **minimalist** processes, he is set apart from the style by his strong lyrical voice. Adams has been particularly taken by vocal works and both *Harmonium* (1980) and the opera *Nixon in China* (1985–87) have shown a refreshing approach to the voice.

Barraqué, Jean
(Bār-rà'-kē, Zhân) 1928–73
FRENCH COMPOSER
A pupil of **Olivier Messiaen** (1908–92), Barraqué was profoundly affected by his relationship with Michel Foucault. He also shared many of Boulez's concerns and believed in the necessity of **serial** technique, but did not follow the general trend of the 1950s into total serialism. Barraqué's vision of music was far grander and he shared **Ludwig van Beethoven**'s (1770–1827) colossal view of music. His high philosophical standpoint can be clearly heard in *Séquence* (1950–54). Barraqué completed only seven works, but his writing has a fullness and breadth almost unparalleled in the serial output.

Benjamin, George
b. 1960
ENGLISH COMPOSER
Benjamin studied at the Paris Conservatoire under Messiaen and later at Cambridge with Goehr, both of whom proved to have a lasting influence on his work. His orchestral piece *Ringed by the Flat Horizon* (1980) first brought the young composer into the limelight. He swiftly followed up the success of his debut with *A Mind of Winter* the following year and a chamber ensemble piece *At First Light* in 1982.

Berio, Luciano
(Bâr'-yō, Lōōch-yà'-nō) b. 1925
ITALIAN COMPOSER
Study with Giorgio Ghedini and **Luigi Dallapiccola** (1904–75) led Berio to an early interest in the possibilities offered by serialism. *Nones* (1954) demonstrates not only this, but also a typical joy in the human voice. In 1955, Berio and Bruno Maderna (1920–73) jointly opened the *Studio di fonologia* for electronic composition. Berio was also fascinated by virtuosity and discovering new means of expression with all instruments, to which end he composed the series of *Sequenze* for solo instruments. The *Sinfonia* (1968–69) is one of Berio's best-known works and one in which his fertile imagination and incredible control are in abundant display. Since the 1970s, Berio has concentrated on creating strong, dramatic structures by using functional harmony to make the passing of time musically consequential.

Birtwistle, (Sir) Harrison
b. 1934
ENGLISH COMPOSER
Birtwistle, member of the Manchester New Music Group, says his juvenilia are pastiche **Ralph Vaughan Williams** (1872–1958). Study with Richard Hall opened his ears to **Stravinsky**, **Webern** and **Varèse**, altering his musical style radically. In many ways his music is utterly individual; Birtwistle has said that he was driven to compose in order to try to create the music which existed only in his head. He owes much to stylized ritual and theatre as well as to the **heterophonic** style of early composers such as the fourteenth-century **Guillaume de Machaut** (*c.* 1300–77). He creates music that feels three-dimensional, shifting textures around to create audible sculptures. His naturally dramatic temperament has led to him making a huge contribution to twentieth-century opera, beginning with *Punch and Judy* (1966–67).

Boulez, Pierre
(Bōō-lez', Pē-âr') b. 1925
FRENCH COMPOSER AND CONDUCTOR
A student of Messiaen and René Leibowitz (1913–72), Boulez is perhaps the arch-modernist of the twentieth century. His early piano works clearly show the influence of **Schoenberg** (*Notations*, 1945). A visit from Cage in 1949 sparked a friendship and correspondence that was to be central to the progress of twentieth-century music. He was ruthless in his development of a new musical language; for him, Schoenberg's innovations were not courageous enough and were too rooted in classical

2001: A SPACE ODYSSEY

Stanley Kubrick's cult science fiction film *2001: A Space Odyssey* famously used music by composers such as Ligeti to evoke the dawn of civilization and the awesome expanse of time and space. Many pieces will be familiar, including Richard Strauss's *Also sprach Zarathustra*.

POPULAR MELODY *Ligeti*

forms. Boulez believed that 'in order to create effectively one has to consider delirium and, yes, organize it'. Serialism was a means for him to take control of all elements of music – pitch, timbre, duration, instrumentation, dynamic – and bind them together. *Le marteau sans maître* ('The Masterless Hammer', 1953–55), as well as being a wonderful example of such techniques, is now regarded as one of the cornerstones of twentieth-century music. Boulez's approach to composition gradually opened out and *Pli selon pli* ('Fold Upon Fold', 1959–62) shows an expressive simplicity. He began the 'progressing' work *Éclats/Multiples* in 1965, but began to devote more time to conducting and to re-working older compositions from the 1970s. Between 1975 and 1991 Boulez held the post of director at IRCAM in Paris, during which time he produced *Répons* (1983).

Cage, John
1912–92
AMERICAN COMPOSER
Cage's initial studies led to a devotion to Schoenberg, but this early fascination did not stay long in his music. In 1939 he composed *First Construction (In Metal)*, which bases its structure on durations and not harmony. It was also around this time that Cage first began to use the prepared piano, an instrument which was to become central to his compositional aesthetic. This is a normal piano with everyday items such as rubber bands and screws inserted between the strings to alter the sound. It was

(NL) Pierre Boulez
The French composer and conductor Boulez (right) with Olivier Messiaen and John Cage.
(FL) John Adams
Adams has played an important role in introducing contemporary music to his audiences in the US.
(R) Silent Studies
John Cage's complicated scores base their structure on durations, not harmonies.

aleatory music ▶ p. 356 diatonic ▶ p. 358 heterophony ▶ p. 359 minimalism ▶ p. 360 *pizzicato* ▶ p. 361 polyrhythm ▶ p. 361 register ▶ p. 362 serial music ▶ p. 362

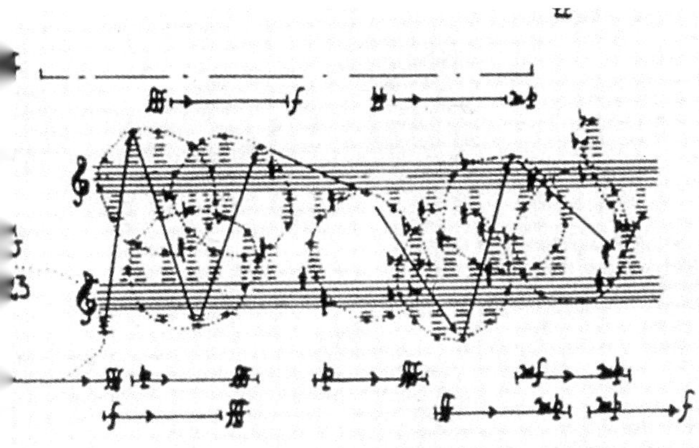

one such work – *Sonatas and Interludes* (1946–48) – which impressed Boulez when Cage visited Paris in 1949. In the late 1940s, he began to develop a strong interest in silence, rooted in the philosophies of Asian religions. Initially Cage used such means as the prepared piano to write music with 'silent' harmony, but on hearing Feldman's *Extensions 1* (a graphic composition where only the number and **register** of pitches are indicated) he found a whole new level of compositional silence. This reached its zenith in *4'33"* (1952), which consists only of the noises made by audience members and the outside world. The late 1950s and 60s were largely spent in discussion of his own musical philosophy. From the 1970s onwards, Cage began to write prolifically again, with the same chance elements, often in response to commissions from performers.

Carter, Elliott

b. 1908

AMERICAN COMPOSER

An early relationship with **Charles Ives** (1874–1954) and a period of study with Nadia Boulanger (1887–1979) led to a synthesis of European modernism and American ultra-modernism, which can be heard in the String Quartet No. 1 (1950–51). By the second quartet (1959), Carter was following an entirely different style: the four string players are instructed to sit as far apart as possible so they appear to be playing different works. This middle period is characterized by Carter's increased development of **polyrhythm** (several rhythms performed at the same time) and tempo modulation (an evolutionary change of speed). Carter's late works show greater focus on continuity and expression. His orchestral writing of this time is dazzling in its lightness (*Allegro scorrevole*, 1997).

Crumb, George

b. 1929

AMERICAN COMPOSER

Crumb studied with Boris Blacher (1903–75) and Ross Lee Finney (b. 1906). A strong identification with the writer García Lorca is reflected in the surreal, other-worldly soundscapes he has composed (*Ancient Voices of Children*, 1970). As a means of creating these he used unusual performance instructions, such as playing woodwind instruments with thimbles. Crumb also has an inclination towards parody, for instance quoting a Bach fugue in *Music for a Summer Evening* (1974).

Davies, (Sir) Peter Maxwell

b. 1934

ENGLISH COMPOSER

Early use of serialism (Trumpet Sonata, 1955) led Davies to a less systematic method of composing with smaller sets of pitches (*Prolation*, 1958). Alongside this grew a fascination for the pre-Baroque. Davies makes particular use of plainsong themes, which he then subjects to transformations such as octave displacement and rhythmic shifts. A peculiar leaning towards parody was central to Davies's early work. In *Eight Songs for a Mad King* (1968) the wild ravings of George III are further enraged by crazed adaptations of music from the period, an effect enhanced by having the musicians perform from songbird cages onstage. In 1971 Davies moved to Orkney, which led to a calmer outlook and the establishment of the St Magnus Festival. His appointment in 1985 as Associate Composer/Conductor of the Scottish Chamber Orchestra resulted in a series of Strathclyde Concertos, which were completed in 1993.

Dutilleux, Henri

(Dü-te-yö', On-re') b. 1916

FRENCH COMPOSER

Despite success as a young composer, Dutilleux disowned almost his entire oeuvre before the Piano Sonata (1946–48). He followed a very different path from his compatriot Boulez and his two symphonies (1950–51 and 1955–59) exhibit strong links with the traditional Germanic form. Variation is a key feature of Dutilleux's music, but he tends not to show an idea in its bare form initially, instead allowing it to be discerned gradually during the course of the work. He is also particularly interested in symmetrical forms, such as palindromes. Dutilleux's writing is beautifully colourful and always crafted with poise.

Feldman, Morton

1926–87

AMERICAN COMPOSER

Associated with the musical group surrounding Cage, Feldman was also strongly affected by the aesthetic of the abstract Expressionist painters in New York. Feldman's music displays a distrust of intellectual, rigorous systems of writing, exploring instead abstract forms and an instinctive approach to composition. He is well known for his graphic scores, such as his five *Projections* (1950–51). In these scores he gives only the approximate register (high, middle or low), who plays together, the type of sound (***pizzicato***, harmonic, and so on), the tempo and duration of notes.

Ferneyhough, Brian

b. 1943

ENGLISH COMPOSER

Ferneyhough spent time with Lennox Berkeley (1903–89) and then Klaus Huber (b. 1924), though he is essentially self-taught. Along with Webern, Boulez and Stockhausen, Ferneyhough felt himself at the forefront of modern music. His works are often extremely difficult, and in the early 1970s some **aleatory** elements were included (*Sieben Sterne*, 'Seven Stars', 1970). From the 1980s, he became more aware of his relationship with the lineage of the great German composers. His String Quartet No. 4 looks towards Schoenberg with its use of a soprano in the final movement.

Glass, Philip

b. 1937

AMERICAN COMPOSER

Glass studied with Nadia Boulanger and Alla Rakha, Ravi Shankar's tabla player, but the influence of Indian music is not overt; rather it is evident in the additive, repetitive rhythmic processes (*Music in Similar Motion*, 1969). Parallel lines, simple **diatonic** harmony and unspecified instrumentation are characteristic of Glass's early music. From the early 1970s, the harmony became fuller and Glass began to use pedal points. With the opera *Einstein on the Beach* (1975–76), Glass found public acclaim. Here, the normal linear narrative of opera is replaced by an exploration of various symbols related to Einstein, such as the Theory of Relativity. Glass's objective approach to minimalism was gradually infused with expressiveness (*The Canyon*, 1988). A strong aspect of Glass's music has been his collaborations with artists as varied as Paul Simon ('Song from Liquid Days', 1986) and Doris Lessing (the operas *The Making of the Representative for Planet 8*, 1986; *The Marriages between Zones Three, Four and Five*, 1996).

Goehr, Alexander

b. 1932

ENGLISH COMPOSER

A member of the Manchester New Music Group, Goehr studied also with Messiaen. He initially explored the ideas of the prevailing avant-garde, particularly Boulez, but soon grew tired of what he felt were constrictive systems. Instead, he turned to slight elements of pastiche and in-depth study of the formal proportions of **Johann Sebastian Bach** (1685–1750). Further interest in methods of combinatorial sets and modality led to a more distinct and expressive style (Little Symphony, 1963). Goehr has a strong interest in harmonic control (String Quartet No. 2, 1967). Later, he returned to the examples afforded by older music including a reinvention of **Claudio Monteverdi**'s (1567–1643) opera *Arianna*.

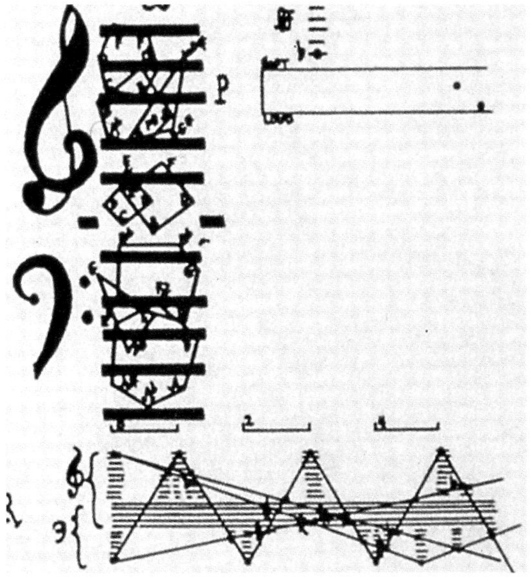

J. S. Bach ▶ p. 106 Beethoven ▶ p. 150 Dallapiccola ▶ p. 288 Ives ▶ p. 291 Machaut ▶ p. 29 Messiaen ▶ p. 293 Monteverdi ▶ p. 76 Schoenberg ▶ p. 295 Stravinsky ▶ p. 280 Varèse ▶ p. 298 Vaughan Williams ▶ p. 298 Webern ▶ p. 299

Górecki, Henryk

(Gôr'-rěk-kē, On-rĭkh) b. 1933

POLISH COMPOSER

As a young composer, Górecki made a name for himself as a leading member of the Polish avant-garde. In the 1950s he quickly adopted techniques from Webern and Boulez which gave him a new expressive dimension. Górecki's music follows an underlying Polish belief in the importance of emotion over rhetoric. To this end, he gradually pared down his technique to its essentials, eventually abandoning serialism. The Symphony No. 3, *Symfonia piesni zalosnych* ('Symphony of Sorrowful Songs', 1976), demonstrates a searing spiritual directness. His shift towards a wholly **modal** musical language has its essence in folk and religious music as well as his interest in incorporating older composers' music into his own. During the 1980s and 90s, Górecki's music became more vivacious, while stemming from the same emotional base.

Gruber, Heinz Karl (H. K.)

(Groō-bâr, Hīnts Kärl) b. 1943

AUSTRIAN COMPOSER

Gruber studied with Alfred Uhl (1909–92) and Hanns Jelinek (1901–69). In spite of early work in the serial idiom, Gruber is extremely open to all types of music, particularly pop and light music. At the end of his violin concerto *... aus Schatten Duft gewebt* ('Scent Weaving from the Shadows', 1977–78) he quotes a pop song, alluding to a violin concerto by **Alban Berg** (1885–1935). He easily combines a wide variety of styles while retaining a strongly personal voice.

Gubaydulina, Sofiya

(Gōō'-bä-du'-lēna, Zô-fyä) b. 1931

RUSSIAN COMPOSER

Gubaydulina's innovative works grew from her belief in the spiritual power of music. She creates a mesmerizing sound-world which explores many different structures and sounds, often using traditional instruments. One of her best-known works is the violin concerto *Offertorium* (1980), built on a transfiguration of the theme from J. S. Bach's *Musical Offering*. *Garten von Freuden und Traurigkeiten* ('Garden of Joys and Sorrows', 1980) for flute, viola and harp is a chamber work of haunting beauty, while the choral and orchestral *Jetzt immer Schnee* ('Now Always Snow', 1993) creates an atmosphere of intense mysticism.

Henze, Hans Werner

(Hent'-se, Häns Vâr'-ner) b. 1926

GERMAN COMPOSER

A prolific composer, Henze was born into a musical family and gew up at a time when the Nazi party in Germany was exerting a strong hold over family life. Stravinsky remains the strongest influence on his style, in which underlying diatonic harmony is covered by heavy **chromaticism** and **bitonality**. Henze also composed in more traditional genres, producing the ballets *Jack Puddling* (1951) and *Labyrinth* (1951) as well as operas (*Boulevard Solitude*, 1952). Henze's early dalliance with serialism was soon rejected as he found the technique too dogmatic; following his move to Italy in 1953 his natural tendency to highly expressive, dramatic music was further fostered and he wrote many operas, including König Hirsch ('King Stag', 1956) and *Elegy for Young Lovers* (1961). In the 1960s he was drawn to be more active in expressing his political views, resulting in compositions such as the collective work *Jüdische Chronik* ('Jewish Chronicle', 1960). The height of his success during this period, however, is epitomized in his opera *The Bassarids* (1966). His socialism was not long restrained, though, and over the next few years it found its way into works such as his Sixth Symphony (1970), which used the tunes from revolutionary songs, and the opera *We Come to the River* (1976). He continued to compose, in his own inimitable style, into the 1980s.

Holliger, Heinz

(Hō'-lig'-âr, Hīnts) b. 1939

SWISS COMPOSER AND OBOIST

Holliger's work is characterized by a constant striving to push the boundaries of the expressive possibilities offered by all instruments. His scores often contain detailed instructions with regard to **embouchure** and breathing, finger pressure, placing of the bow etc. Holliger has been powerfully inspired by themes of the state between life and death and by the feelings of outsiders, setting texts by Georg Trakl and Samuel Beckett. As an oboist he has had many works composed for him, by Berio, Henze, Lutoslawski and Stockhausen.

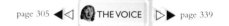

JOSEPH

Lloyd Webber's songs have become an institution, none more so than those from the musical *Joseph and the Amazing Technocolour Dreamcoat*. Tunes such as 'Any Dream Will Do' have been chart hits and the stage musical has been a success from London's West End to Broadway.

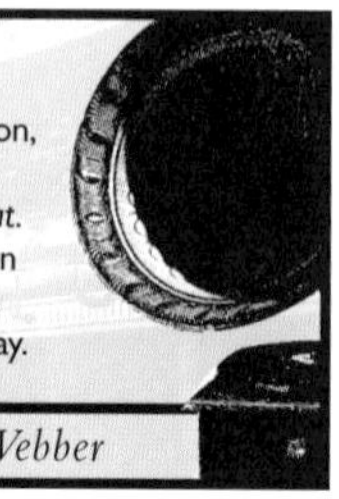

POPULAR MELODY *Lloyd Webber*

Kagel, Maurizio

(Kä'-gel, Mou'-rēs'-yō) b. 1931

ARGENTINIAN COMPOSER

Kagel studied at the University of Buenos Aires and later with Juan Carlos Paz (1901–72), but was largely self-taught as a composer. He worked as a pianist and conductor at the Teatro Colón from 1949. His works embrace many of the styles of the twentieth century, including the 12-tone technique, aleatory music, tonality and atonality. Kagel's interest in the theatrical led to pieces such as *Die Erschöpfung der Welt* ('The Exhaustion of the World', 1985) and several radio dramas.

Kurtág, György

(Kōōr-tāg, Jörd'-ji) b. 1926

HUNGARIAN COMPOSER

Kurtág's music is unusual in the period for the depth and intensity with which it addresses human concerns. He has never been interested in forging new musical paths and often revisits familiar territory. The one abiding concern of his work is to strip away everything that is inessential structurally or emotionally (*Messages of the Late R. V. Troussova*, 1976–80). Kurtág's concern with the tiniest of links has inevitably imposed brevity on his works, but he experienced a flowering in the late 1980s with the expressive directness of pieces such as *Grabstein für Stephan* ('Stephen's Gravestone', 1989).

Ligeti, György

(Lē-get'-ē, Jörd'ji) b. 1923

HUNGARIAN COMPOSER

Although Ligeti composed a great deal of music before the end of Stalinist tyranny in Hungary in 1953, most was kept privately. His limited knowledge of twentieth-century music was then opened up to Stockhausen, Webern, Boulez and others. In 1956 he travelled to Vienna; there he produced *Apparitions* (1958–59), which led to *Atmosphères* (1961). These works express Ligeti's distrust of systems of composition, particularly serialism, and show his delight in pure sound. They eschew control of harmony, pitch or rhythm and instead contrast clouds of static sound. Central to their creation is micropolyphony, where canons of tiny motifs occur repeatedly inside the texture. Ligeti gradually added elements to his writing, such as functional harmony in *Lontano* (1967) and melody in *Melodien* (1971). His more recent works have shown an

(TL) Hans Werner Henze
The German composer in his role as conductor, demonstrating his passion.

***(FR)* Joseph and his Amazing Technicolour Dreamcoat**
Jason Donovan in the stage musical of Lloyd Webber's popular musical.

(NR) György Ligeti
Ligeti with his metronomes, at a rare performance of his Poème symphonique pour 100 metronomes.

bitonality ▶ p. 356 chromaticism ▶ p. 357 embouchure ▶ p. 358 mode ▶ p. 360 12-note music ▶ p. 363

FALSETTIST, ALTO, COUNTERTENOR?

English church music readily accommodates the high male alto voice, but only in the last half of the twentieth century was the countertenor (or 'male alto') welcomed into the opera house. After hearing the alto Alfred Deller singing in Canterbury Cathedral in 1944, Tippett remarked that the 'centuries rolled back'. Tippett encouraged Deller to extend his repertory, which coincided with the beginning of the Baroque opera revival. Many roles in that repertory, written for castratos but for many years assigned to mezzo-sopranos, were reclaimed by countertenors.

Deller, and others encouraged by his success, made a new voice-type available to contemporary composers. Among those to benefit was **Britten**, who wrote the role of Oberon (*A Midsummer Night's Dream*, 1960) for Deller, and had James Bowman (b. 1941) create the part of Apollo in *Death in Venice* (1973).

Composers usually follow Britten and consign counter-tenors to roles indicating other-worldliness, as in *Lear* (1978) by Aribert Reimann (b. 1936), in which Edgar switches into countertenor register when feigning madness. In *Akhnaten* (1984), Glass gave the title-role to a countertenor, acknowledging the hermaphroditism of the historic figure, an Egyptian king of the fourteenth century BC.

increased interest in African music and polymetre, a close identification with his Hungarian musical roots (*3 Phantasien*, 1983) and the Caribbean and Latin influence of his former student Roberto Sierra.

Lloyd Webber, (Sir) Andrew

b. 1948

ENGLISH COMPOSER AND PRODUCER

Lloyd Webber met the lyricist Tim Rice in 1965 and within three years they had written *Joseph and the Amazing Technicolour Dreamcoat* (1968), which displays a strong lyricism and a close affinity to pop. His most successful musical was *Cats*, based on the poems by T. S. Eliot, which was oneof the longest-running shows in London and on Broadway. Lloyd Webber's musicals are essentially episodic, although he has shown an inclination to through-composition, for example his motivic writing in *Sunset Boulevard* (1993). Besides musicals, he has also written film scores and *Variations* (1977) for cello and rock band. Lloyd Webber's scores are always emotionally direct with a silky sheen, which makes them highly appealing.

Lutosławski, Witold

(Lōō-tō-slwăf'-skē, Vē'-tōld) 1913–94

POLISH COMPOSER

A talented violinist and pianist, Lutosławski studied composition with Witold Maliszewski (1873–1939). Early works show the influence of Debussy, Stravinsky and Bartók. In the late 1950s, Lutosławski began to work with **12-note** rows, though not actual serialism. This led to his use of aleatory techniques from the 1960s, which involved freedom of the timing of entries, as in *Jeux vénitiens* ('Venetian Games', 1960–61). Lutosławski had a strong interest in folk melodies, frequently incorporating them into his own style (*Little Suite*, 1950). His later works display a wonderfully beautiful sound-world, often associated with surrealism, such as *Les espaces du sommeil* ('The Intervals of Sleep', 1975). Among his best-known works is his Third Symphony, commissioned by the Chicago Symphony Orchestra in 1972 and completed in the 1980s.

McCartney, (Sir) Paul

b. 1942

ENGLISH COMPOSER AND SINGER

Most famous for his contribution to The Beatles, McCartney broke away from the group in 1970 with the album *McCartney*. He then formed his own group, Wings, with whom he created a number of successful albums, notably *Band on the Run* (1973). McCartney pays much attention to detail in his songwriting. He is acutely aware of the nuances of his lyrics and forms clear structures to articulate them. His two ventures into classical genres (*Liverpool Oratorio*, 1991, written with Carl Davis; *Standing Stone*, 1997, written with Richard Rodney Bennett and others) have gained much public attention.

Nono, Luigi

(Nō'-nō, Lōō-ē'-jē) 1924–90

ITALIAN COMPOSER

Nono studied with Hermann Scherchen (1891–1966) and through him attended Darmstadt. He was influenced by many art forms, especially painting and theatre. He worked extensively with electronics, often in combination with acoustic instruments, allowing him a high degree of control over his expressive needs, as can be seen in *La fabbrica illuminata*. His work starts from a serial standpoint, extending the technique to an astonishing degree.

Nyman, Michael

b. 1944

ENGLISH COMPOSER

The influence of Cage and Feldman can be heard in Nyman's creation of elastic, intuitive sound-worlds. *1–100* (1976) is simply a series of 100 chords descending through a circle of fourths. Nyman's early music is full of allusions to and quotations from music of the past, in addition to the use of amplification and rhythms and sounds from rock music. During the 1990s, his work began to grow in expressivity and replaced quotations from classical music with folksongs from a number of sources. He has composed several scores for the films of Peter Greenaway.

Pärt, Arvo

(Pairt, Ar'-vō) b. 1935

ESTONIAN COMPOSER

Pärt initially wrote in a neo-classical style, gradually shifting to serial techniques as previously banned scores filtered into the country. Works such as *Perpetuum mobile* ('Continuous Motion', 1963) attracted the wrath of the state. A love of Baroque music and particularly J. S. Bach is revealed in works such as *Collage teemal B-A-C-H* (1964). He often contrasted the ordered Baroque with more chaotic modernism, a technique that reached its zenith with *Credo* (1968) in which Bach's famous C major prelude is contorted through 12-note transformations. From 1968, Pärt focused on simpler, tonal music and in 1976 wrote *Für Alina*, in which he first used the 'tintinnabuli' technique, so called because of its bell-like sonority. This is essentially a two-part texture, with one melodic line focusing on a central pitch and another tintinnabuli voice playing notes from the tonic triad. Characteristic of all his work from 1968 onwards is a passionate commitment to Christianity.

Berg ▶ p. 286 Britten ▶ p. 287

Penderecki, Krzysztof
(Pen-de-ret'-skē, K'zhēsh'-tôf) b. 1933

POLISH COMPOSER

Following the early influence of Stravinsky and Webern, Penderecki took a place at the forefront of the avant-garde with *Tern ofiarom Hiroszimy* ('Threnody for the Victims of Hiroshima', 1960), which uses **tone-clusters, quarter-tones** and graphic notation. His music of this time is searingly intense and passionate. His music softened during the late 1970s, becoming much more open and tonal (Violin Concerto No. 1). Penderecki has also made a significant contribution to opera with four works, including *Die schwarze Maske* ('The Black Mask', 1984–86). Since 1988 Penderecki has worked on a number of symphonies and concertos, including the Violin Concerto No. 2 (1992–95).

Pousseur, Henri
(Pōō-ser', On-rē') b. 1929

BELGIAN COMPOSER

During the 1950s and early 60s, Pousseur was at the forefront of the avant-garde, collaborating on electronic music with Berio and Maderna. Although he was strongly influenced by Webern, Pousseur concentrated particularly on finding a means to create coherent harmonic organization (*Quintette à la mémoire d'Anton Webern*, 'Quintet in Memory of Anton Webern', 1955). Pousseur became increasingly interested in using non-musical sounds to add to the dramatic effect of his works (*Votre Faust*, 'Your Faust', 1960–67). Added to this were quotations from, or passages in the style of, older composers.

Reich, Steve
b. 1936

AMERICAN COMPOSER

Reich studied with Hall Overton (1920–72), Vincent Persichetti (b. 1915), William Bergsma (b. 1921), Milhaud and Berio. A particular focus of his development was Asian music, especially its rhythmic structures. Much of Reich's music is characterized by phasing, in which a number of instruments play identical music starting one after the other, giving an echo effect (*Clapping Music*, 1972). Up to the 1970s, Reich's music was fairly static harmonically. From the mid-1970s he became more adventurous and *Music for 18 Musicians* (1976) shifts in its harmonies and uses a degree of polyphony. Later works show international influences: *Tehillin* (1981) based on Hebrew psalms, and *Electric Counterpoint* (1987) which combines African and jazz influences. His best-known work of later years is *The Cave* (1989–93), in which he uses video footage and speech. As a minimalist composer, Reich has found much public success.

Rihm, Wolfgang
(Rēēm, Volf-găng) b. 1952

GERMAN COMPOSER

Rihm studied with Stockhausen. He was influenced by a diverse range of composers, including Webern, Bartók, Mahler and Beethoven. His early music is strongly expressive, even Romantic (Symphony No. 3, 1976–77). From the 1980s a more distinctive and personal voice emerged as his music became more economical of means and extreme in expression (*Chiffre*, 1982–88). Rihm also contributed significantly to opera and music theatre with such works as *Jakob Lenz* (1977–78) and *Oedipus* (1986–87).

Riley, Terry
b. 1935

AMERICAN COMPOSER

Initially influenced by Stockhausen, Riley was profoundly affected by the sustained, minimalist style of La Monte Young, whom he met at the University of California at Berkeley. His use of tape loops allowed him to experiment with echo effects, which eventually led to the seminal *In C* (1964). Viewed as the first fully minimalist work, *In C* is written for an unspecified number of players and consists of 53 short motifs, each one of which is repeated freely until the individual player decides to move on. Following a period in the early 1970s of adding improvised sections to his work, Riley devoted himself almost entirely to the study, teaching and performing of Indian music.

Sallinen, Aulis
(Săl'-li-năn, Ŏr'-liss) b. 1935

FINNISH COMPOSER

An early dabble with serialism was swiftly replaced with a strong feeling for simple, expressive themes, diatonicism and clarity of structure (*Elegy for Sebastian Knight*, 1964). Like his compatriot **Jean Sibelius** (1865–1957), Sallinen developed a strong interest in the folk tradition of his country, which can be heard both in his use of folk melodies and in the use of texts from the Finnish national epic, *Kalevala* (*Kullervo*, 1992). It was in opera that Sallinen made his biggest contribution. His operas often deal with contemporary issues such as the first Finnish general election, in the piece *Punainen viiva* ('The Red Line', 1978).

Schnittke, Alfred (also Shnitke)
(Shnit'-kė, Ăl-fred) 1934–98

RUSSIAN COMPOSER

The most striking aspect of Schnittke's music is its combination of a multitude of styles. His Symphony No. 1 (1972) contains quotations from many composers – from **Joseph Haydn** (1732–1809) to **Pyotr Ilyich Tchaikovsky** (1840–93). The Concerti Grossi parody Baroque styles with some wit. Unlike other exponents of collage style, Schnittke makes it a personal voice, gradually refining and paring down the technique to the taut expression of the Symphony No. 5 (1988). Schnittke's wit is presented in wonderful form in the opera *Life with an Idiot* (1991), a form to which he made striking contributions, following up later with *Gesualdo* (1995) and *Historia von D. Johann Fausten* (1995).

Sculthorpe, Peter
b. 1929

AUSTRALIAN COMPOSER

Following a period of study in Oxford (1958–1960), Sculthorpe returned to Australia, where he has remained ever since. A slightly self-conscious style of writing, whereby he adds together many tiny parts, gives his work a clear personal stamp. Sculthorpe has had a strong relationship with the Aboriginal culture, writing works which are evocative of certain areas (*Mangrove*, 1979), the spirituality of the people (*The Loneliness of Bunjil*, 1954, rev. 1965) and events (*Port Essington*, 1977). Although often uneasy, Sculthorpe's music regularly displays his gift for beautiful melody.

Sondheim, Stephen
b. 1930

AMERICAN COMPOSER AND LYRICIST

Sondheim studied with Oscar Hammerstein II (1895–1960) and **Babbitt**. Early work as a lyricist for Jules Styne's (1905–89) *Gypsy* (1959) and Bernstein's *West Side Story* (1957) brought his name to public attention, but it was not until *Follies* (1971) that he achieved recognition as a composer. His work is marked by a biting wit and strong feeling for irony alongside a symphonic conception of the musical. *Sweeney Todd, the Demon Barber of Fleet Street* (1979) uses a number of character motifs, glued together by the 'Ballad of Sweeney Todd' theme. Sondheim's capacity to take a wide variety of genres and adapt them to his own needs can be clearly heard in *Assassins* (1991), in which pop, gospel and folk music rub shoulders.

melisma ▶ p. 360 quarter-tone ▶ p. 361 tone-cluster ▶ p. 361

Takemitsu, Toru

(Tă-ke-mit-sōō, Tō-rōō) 1930–96

JAPANESE COMPOSER

Although he studied with Yasuji Kiyose, Takemitsu was largely self-taught. He was interested in the effect and internal make-up of sound and his early work confounded many critics. Although he wanted to write in the Western classical tradition, Takemitsu's background in traditional Japanese music led to his concern for releasing sound from the confines of a beat structure (*Masque*, 1959–60; *Landscape*, 1960). This led in turn to an interest in tape composition, where he was freer to work with sound. *Water Music* (1960) creates rhythms from recorded patterns of dripping water. From the late 1960s, Takemitsu began to use tone-clusters (*November Steps*, 1967) as a colouristic inflection. Throughout the late 1970s and into the 80s, he became more concerned with the beauty of sound and particularly with writing in a tonal idiom (*To the Edge of Dream*, 1983). A central part of all Takemitsu's work was in film, for which he wrote over 80 scores, including *Ran* (1985), a Japanese interpretation of *King Lear*.

Tavener, John

b. 1944

ENGLISH COMPOSER

Perhaps the biggest influence on Tavener's early writing was Stravinsky (*In memoriam Igor Stravinsky*, 1971). Tavener's reception into the Orthodox Church in 1977 affected his writing and his life deeply, leading initially to the *Liturgy of St John Chrysostom* (1980). Tavener's Orthodoxy complemented an earlier interest in Russia and Byzantine chant, which can be heard strongly in *Orthodox Vigil Service* (1984). The pervasion of Orthodoxy in Tavener is reflected in his use of **melisma**, monody and repetition. In addition, he has been drawn to the creation of musical 'Ikons', such as the *Ikon of St Cuthbert of Lindisfarne* (1986). More recent commissions include *The Hidden Face* (1996), *The Last Discourse* (1997) and the epic *Fall and Resurrection* (2000).

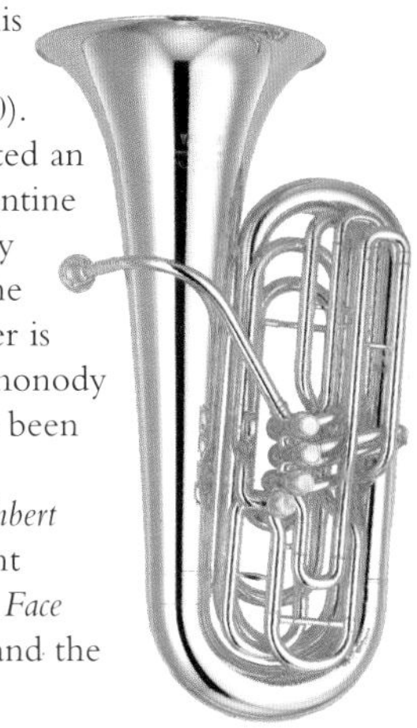

Stockhausen, Karlheinz

(Shtŏk'-hou-zen, Kärl'-hīnts) b. 1928

GERMAN COMPOSER

Stockhausen studied with **Frank Martin** (1890–1974) and then with Messiaen in Paris, where he met Boulez. Stockhausen's use of serialism differs from Boulez's: where the latter wanted to find a means of creating relations between diverse elements, the former was concerned to provide a smooth path between extremes. This can be clearly seen in *Gesang der Jünglinge* ('Song of the Youths', 1956), which tries, through electronic means, to achieve a union of music and language. With *Gruppen* ('Groups', 1955–57), Stockhausen created a way of serializing duration by treating tempo in the same way as pitch. His particular method necessitated a number of different tempos co-existing; consequently, *Gruppen* is scored for three orchestras, each with its own conductor. Stockhausen's most protracted composition has been his *Licht* ('Light') cycle of operas, which he began with *Donnerstag* ('Thursday') in 1977 and which is still in progress. During the course of the *Licht* cycle, Stockhausen became increasingly interested in extending performance techniques, to the extent that in his *Helikopter-Streichquartett* ('Helicopter String Quartet', 1992–93) each player performs the work in a helicopter, the playing transmitted into the auditorium via screens and loudspeakers.

(BNL) Stephen Sondheim
Sondheim's Assassins *combines pop, gospel and folk music, with fascinating results.*
(TL) Peter Sculthorpe
Sculthorpe draws much of his inspiration tfrom the aboriginal heritage of his native Australia.
(TR) Toru Takemitsu
Takemitsu's scores express his interest with the beauty of sound.
(BR) Judith Weir
Weir's King Harald's Saga *demands that the solo soprano sings all the roles.*

WOMEN COMPOSERS OF OPERA AND FILM MUSIC

Several women composers of the late twentieth century have a particular affinity for opera, while also writing works in a wide variety of other genres. For the Scottish composer Thea Musgrave (b. 1928), writing her first full-length opera, *The Decision* (1965), led to the development of what she describes as her 'dramatic-abstract' instrumental style. Her later operas, which make effective use of traditional music, include *Harriet, the Woman Called Moses* (1985), based on the life of the African-American slave Harriet Tubman; and *Simón Bolivar* (1995), which tells the story of the South American liberator. The operas of the British composer Nicola LeFanu (b. 1947) involve rewarding and powerful roles for women. LeFanu's dramatic works include the opera *Blood Wedding* (1992), in which her intensely **chromatic** musical language, with its strong sense of melodic line, illustrates Lorca's story of passionate but illicit love.

Weir and Larsen

In 1979 Judith Weir (b. 1954), one of Britain's best-known living composers, produced *King Harald's Saga*, a remarkable 10-minute 'Grand Opera' for solo soprano, who sings all roles (including the entire Norwegian army). Weir's other operas display her fascination with historically or geographically distant cultures, such as medieval China in *A Night at the Chinese Opera* (1987) or traditional Scotland in The *Vanishing Bridegroom* (1990). The American composer Libby Larsen (b. 1950) wrote her first operas during the coffee breaks of a secretarial job. Her later dramatic works often use texts written by women, such as *Frankenstein, or the Modern Prometheus* (1990), after Mary Shelley and *Mrs Dalloway* (1993), after Virginia Woolf.

Writing for the Modern Media

Several British female composers have had notable successes writing music for film and television. Rachel Portman (b. 1960) was the first female composer to win an Academy Award, for the music to *Emma* (1996). Anne Dudley (b. 1956) also won an Academy Award for *The Full Monty* (1997) and her score for *American History X* (1998) was widely acclaimed. Debbie Wiseman has written much music for television and for films such as *Tom and Viv* (1994) and *Wilde* (1997), while the versatile musician Jocelyn Pook composed the score for Stanley Kubrick's last film *Eyes Wide Shut* (1999).

Babbitt ▶ p. 284 Haydn ▶ p. 140 Martin ▶ p. 292 Sibelius ▶ p. 256 Tchaikovsky ▶ p. 234

Tippett, (Sir) Michael
1905–98

ENGLISH COMPOSER

Tippett's open receptivity to a myriad of cultures and musical styles made him one of the most profoundly communicative composers of the twentieth century. His left-wing politics were to surface many times in his music and were of central importance in his life. His first acknowledged works were Piano Sonata No. 1 (1936–37) and Concerto for Double String Orchestra (1938–39). One of the most fascinating aspects of his music is the belief in the principle of Austro-German music, particularly Beethoven. Alongside this lies a deep interest in early English music. *The Fantasia Concertante on a Theme of Corelli* (1953) is one work of many to explore the rhythmic inflections of the Baroque. Perhaps his most personal thoughts are carried in his vocal works. The choral works *A Child of Our Time* (1939–41) and *The Mask of Time* (1980–82) and the operas all explore Tippett's social and human preoccupations.

Williams, John
b. 1932

AMERICAN COMPOSER

Early work as a studio pianist in Hollywood led to pockets of work in the 1960s. During the 1970s, he produced music for a number of films including *The Towering Inferno* (1974). Following collaborations with Steven Spielberg in the mid-1970s, Williams wrote music to *Star Wars* (1977). He adopts music from a wide variety of genres: initially the romantic breadth of composers such as **Gustav Holst** (1874–1934) and **Edward Elgar** (1857–1934), later more avant-garde techniques (the velociraptor music in *Jurassic Park*, 1993).

Wolpe, Stefan
(Vŏl'-pe, Stef'-ăn) 1902–72

AMERICAN COMPOSER

Wolpe studied with **Ferruccio Busoni** (1866–1924) and later with Webern. He was compelled by the deteriorating political situation in Germany to express his opinions in music, and his left-wing views are often present (*Zeus und Elida*, 1928). Forced to flee by the Nazis, he ended up in Palestine in 1933, where he was strongly attracted to Jewish and Arabic music as well as the **octatonic** scale. Settling in the US in 1938, Wolpe began to assimilate elements of conventional tonality (*The Man from Midian*, 1942) and jazz (*Saxophone Quartet*, 1950) into his 12-note base.

Xenakis, Iannis
(Ze-nă'-kis, Yăn'-nis) b. 1922

FRENCH/GREEK COMPOSER

Xenakis took up the formal study of music late, having lessons with **Arthur Honegger** (1892–1955), Milhaud and Messiaen in Paris in the early 1950s. He developed a technique in which masses of sound were manipulated according to laws of mathematical probability. This can be clearly heard in the masses of overlapping string glissandos in *Metastasis* (1954), his first acknowledged composition and the foundation of his musical ideology. Throughout the late 1970s and early 80s Xenakis concentrated on a series of pieces combining sound and light, including *Polytope de Mycènes* (1978) and *Diatope* (1978).

Zimmermann, Bernd Alois
(Tsim'-mer-màn, Bârnt Ă-lō'-ēs) 1918–70

GERMAN COMPOSER

Milhaud and Stravinsky were formative influences on Zimmermann's music, but it was Webern who exerted the strongest hold on him (*Perspektiven*, 1955). The almost geometrically balanced forms of much of his music clearly reflect this. Zimmermann's best-known work is the opera *Die Soldaten* ('The Soldiers', 1958–64). This is an example of the most pervasive aspect of his music, **pluralism**, where materials from a number of different composers are woven together along with Zimmermann's own music.

CONDUCTORS

Abbado, Claudio *b. 1933*

ITALIAN CONDUCTOR

Abbado studied in Milan and Vienna. He first conducted at La Scala, Milan in 1960 and held a number of posts there 1969–86. He was principal conductor of the London Symphony Orchestra 1979–96, music director of the Vienna State Opera 1986–91, and has been principal conductor of the Berlin Philharmonic Orchestra since 1990. He made his Covent Garden début in 1968 with *Don Carlo*.

Barenboim, Daniel *b. 1942*

ISRAELI CONDUCTOR AND PIANIST

Barenboim studied at Salzburg and Rome, and under Nadia Boulanger in Paris. He made his UK debut as a pianist in 1956, but turned to conducting in the 1960s with the English Chamber Orchestra. In 1975 he was appointed music director of the Orchestre de Paris, where he showed a commitment to contemporary music. He succeeded Solti at the Chicago Symphony Orchestra in 1991 and became General Music Director of the Deutsche Staatsoper, Berlin, in 1992. He continues to conduct other orchestras, touring with the Vienna Philharmonic in 1997 and making regular appearances with the Berlin Philharmonic.

Christie, William *b. 1944*

AMERICAN CONDUCTOR

Christie moved to France in 1971, where he founded Les Arts Florissants, a flexible vocal and instrumental group, in 1979. With them he has staged and recorded many French works, including operas by **Jean Baptiste Lully** (1632–87) and **Jean-Philippe Rameau** (1683–1764). Their production of *King Arthur* by **Henry Purcell** (1659–95) was seen at Covent Garden in 1995.

STAR WARS

By associating characters with clear themes Williams was able to give his music an active role across the *Star Wars* films. Parts of Anakin's theme, for instance, is clearly drawn from Darth Vader's. Such recognizability allows Williams to change the mood of a theme without losing its identity.

POPULAR MELODY *Williams*

Davis, (Sir) Colin *b. 1927*

ENGLISH CONDUCTOR

Davis came to public notice as the conductor of early performances by the Chelsea Opera Group. He made his début at Sadler's Wells Opera in 1958, and was music director 1961–65. He was principal conductor of the BBC Symphony Orchestra 1967–71, music director of the Royal Opera 1971–86 and of the Bavarian State Radio Orchestra 1983–92, and principal conductor of the London Symphony Orchestra from 1995. He is particularly associated with the music of Mozart, Berlioz and Tippett.

Gardiner, (Sir) John Eliot *b. 1943*

ENGLISH CONDUCTOR

Gardiner founded the Monteverdi Choir in 1964 and the Monteverdi Orchestra in 1968, when he conducted the Monteverdi *Vespers* at the Promenade Concerts in London. He was artistic director of the Göttingen

LA MONTE YOUNG AND THE BIRTH OF MINIMALISM

La Monte Young was saxophonist and jazz musician as a youth, but his postgraduate work at the University of California at Berkeley (where he met Riley) led to a performance of his Trio for Strings (1958) arranged by his composition teacher, Seymour Shifrin (b. 1926), in an attempt to show Young how much he had miscalculated. The work, consisting entirely of long notes and rests, is now regarded as the source of minimalist composition. Young's music uses a limited number of pitches and a high degree of repetition, but his biggest contribution to minimalism was his use of **drones**. This can be heard highly effectively in *Drift Studies* (1964), where two or more **sine waves** shift gradually in phase relationship so that volumes and harmonics are subtly altered. In Berkeley, Young performed numerous works by Cage, which attracted the derision of most but found sympathy with his fellow student Riley. Although Young had experimented with shifting repetitions as early as 1960, it was Riley's *In C* from which the most popular style of minimalism grew.

drone ▶ p. 358 octatonic ▶ p. 360 pluralism ▶ p. 361 sine wave ▶ p. 362

Handel Festival 1981–90 and music director of the Lyons Opera 1983–88. He has given many performances of French Baroque opera, including the first staging of Rameau's *Les Boréades* ('The Sons of Boreas', Aix-en-Provence, 1982). He founded two period instrument orchestras, the English Baroque Soloists and the Orchestre Révolutionnaire et Romantique.

Giulini, Carlo Maria *b. 1914*
ITALIAN CONDUCTOR

Giulini first conducted at La Scala, Milan in 1952, and was principal conductor 1953–56. He conducted Verdi's *Falstaff* at the Edinburgh Festival in 1955 and *Don Carlo* at Covent Garden in 1958. He returned to Covent Garden for *Il barbiere di Siviglia* (1960), *Il trovatore* (1964) and *La traviata* (1967), but shortly after abandoned opera until 1982. In the 1960s he conducted the Philharmonia Orchestra. He was principal conductor of the Chicago Symphony Orchestra 1969–78, and music director of the Los Angeles Philharmonic Orchestra 1978–84.

Haitink, Bernard *b. 1929*
DUTCH CONDUCTOR

Haitink studied with Felix Hupka and Ferdinand Leitner, who gave him a post as second conductor at the Netherlands Radio Union. He became principal conductor of the Concertgebouw Orchestra in 1961 (shared intitially with Eugen Jochum), and of the London Philharmonic Orchestra 1967–79. He was music director at Glyndebourne 1977–88, and at Covent Garden Opera 1987–2002.

Harnoncourt, Nikolaus *b. 1929*
AUSTRIAN CONDUCTOR

Harnoncourt was a cellist in the Vienna Symphony Orchestra 1952–62. He founded the Vienna Concentus Musicus, a period instrument orchestra, in 1953. He conducted and recorded Monteverdi operas in Zürich in the 1970s and Mozart operas in the 1980s; since then he has broadened his repertory and often conducts the Vienna Philharmonic Orchestra.

(L) Sir Michael Tippett
Tippett greeting applause at a performance of his The Mask of Time.
(TR) Sir John Eliot Gardiner
Gardiner with the London-based Monteverdi Orchestra, which he founded in 1968.
(BR) Sir Simon Rattle
Rattle will succeed Abbado as director of the Berlin Philharmonic Orchestra in 2002.

Hogwood, Christopher *b. 1941*
ENGLISH CONDUCTOR

Hogwood began his career as a harpsichord player, and was a founding member of the Early Music Consort in 1967. In 1973 he founded a period instrument orchestra, the Academy of Ancient Music, with which he recorded the complete Mozart symphonies and two Mozart operas. He was director of music of the St Paul Chamber Orchestra in the US 1987–92, and has been artistic director of the Handel and Haydn Society, Boston, since 1986.

Karajan, Herbert von *1908–89*
AUSTRIAN CONDUCTOR

Appointed music director at Aachen in 1934, he conducted *Tristan und Isolde* three years later in Berlin. From 1948 to 1960 he had a close association with the Philharmonia Orchestra. He succeeded his rival **Wilhelm Furtwängler** (1886–1954) as chief conductor of the Berlin Philharmonic Orchestra in 1955, was artistic director of the Salzburg Festival 1956–60, and director of the Vienna State Opera 1957–64. He also conducted at La Scala and Bayreuth, and founded the Salzburg Easter Festival in 1967.

Kempe, Rudolf *1910–76*
GERMAN CONDUCTOR

After seven years as oboist in the Leipzig Gewandhaus Orchestra, Kempe joined the music staff of the Leipzig Opera in 1935. He conducted at the Chemnitz Opera during and after the war, before becoming music director at Dresden 1949–52 and Munich 1952–54. He succeeded **Thomas Beecham** (1879–1961) as principal conductor of the Royal Philharmonic Orchestra in 1961 and was appointed principal conductor of the BBC Symphony Orchestra in 1975. He was a noted interpreter of Wagner.

Klemperer, Otto *1885–1973*
GERMAN CONDUCTOR

On Mahler's recommendation, Klemperer was appointed chorus-master at the German opera house in Prague in 1907. Subsequent conducting posts included Hamburg, Strasbourg and Cologne. He was music director of the Kroll Opera, Berlin 1927–31. He emigrated to the US where he became conductor of the Los Angeles Philharmonic Orchestra 1933–39. He was at the Budapest Opera 1947–50, but it was only when he became principal conductor of the Philharmonia Orchestra in 1955 that his qualities as an interpreter of the classical repertory came to be recognized.

Mravinsky, Evgeny *1906–87*
RUSSIAN CONDUCTOR

After studying at the Leningrad Conservatory, Mravinsky was conductor of the Leningrad Academic Opera and Ballet Theatre – now the Mariinsky Theatre, housing the Kirov companies – between 1932 and 1938. From 1938 he was chief conductor of the Leningrad Philharmonic Orchestra, which he built up into a world-class ensemble. He excelled in the music of Tchaikovsky and Shostakovich; the latter dedicated his Eighth Symphony to him.

Muti, Riccardo *b. 1941*
ITALIAN CONDUCTOR

Muti studied in Naples and Milan, and won the Guido Cantelli International Conductors' Competition in 1967. He was appointed principal conductor of the Florence Maggio Musicale in 1969. Principal conductor and music director of the New Philharmonia (now Philharmonia) Orchestra 1973–82, and of the Philadelphia Orchestra 1980–92, he succeeded Abbado as music director of La Scala, Milan, in 1986.

Ozawa, Seiji *b. 1935*
JAPANESE CONDUCTOR

Ozawa intended to become a pianist, but took up conducting and composing when he broke both his index fingers. He toured Japan with Bernstein in 1961 and was made assistant conductor of the New York Philharmonic later that year. He was appointed music director of the Boston Symphony Orchestra in 1973.

Rattle, (Sir) Simon *b. 1955*
ENGLISH CONDUCTOR

Rattle won the John Player International Conductors' Competition in 1974, which gave him two years as assistant conductor with the Bournemouth Orchestras. After posts with the Royal Liverpool Philharmonic Orchestra and the BBC Scottish Symphony Orchestra, he was principal conductor and music director of the City of Birmingham Symphony Orchestra, 1980–97. In 1999 he was appointed Abbado's successor, from 2002, at the Berlin Philharmonic Orchestra. He has conducted the London Sinfonietta, the Orchestra of the Age of Enlightenment and the Vienna Philharmonic Orchestra.

Solti, (Sir) Georg *1912–97*
BRITISH CONDUCTOR

Born in Hungary, Solti joined the Budapest Opera as a répétiteur (coach), and assisted **Arturo Toscanini** (1867–1957) at the 1936 and 1937 Salzburg Festivals. After spending the war years in Switzerland, he was music director at the Bavarian State Opera 1946–52, in Frankfurt 1952–61, and at the Royal Opera, Covent Garden 1961–71. He was also music director of the Chicago Symphony Orchestra 1969–90, and the London Philharmonic Orchestra 1977–83. He made many recordings, including the first studio version of Wagner's *Ring*.

Beecham ▶ p. 300 Busoni ▶ p. 288 Elgar ▶ p. 247 Furtwängler ▶ p. 300 Holst ▶ p. 290 Honegger ▶ p. 290 Lully ▶ p. 84 Purcell ▶ p. 78 Rameau ▶ p. 120 ▶ Toscanini p. 300

INSTRUMENTALISTS

Arrau, Claudio *1903–91*
CHILEAN PIANIST

Arrau studied at Stern's Conservatory in Berlin – where he taught 1924–40 – giving his first recital in 1914. He toured Europe in 1918, and gave concerts in Argentina and Chile in 1921. He made his London début in 1922 and US in 1923. After founding a piano school in Santiago, he moved to New York. Arrau was especially admired for his performances of Beethoven.

Ashkenazy, Vladimir *b. 1937*
RUSSIAN PIANIST AND CONDUCTOR

Ashkenazy studied at the Central School of Music and the Moscow Conservatory. He won second prize at the Chopin Competition in Warsaw in 1955, first prize at the Queen Elizabeth Competition in Brussels in 1956, and joint first prize at the Tchaikovsky Competition in Moscow in 1962. His London début came in 1963 and since then he has given recitals and concerto performances all over the world and has made many recordings including the complete Mozart, Beethoven and Rachmaninov concertos.

Since the 1970s he has had a parallel career as a conductor and has held the positions of principal guest conductor with the Philharmonia Orchestra and the Cleveland Orchestra, music director with the Royal Philharmonic Orchestra and chief conductor and music director with the Deutches Symphonie-Orchester in Berlin. He has also made guest appearances with a number of orchestras. In 1998 he became chief conductor of the Czech Philharmonic Orchestra. Alongside this position, he was also appointed Conductor Laureate of the Philharmonia Orchestra and music director of the European Union Youth Orchestra in 2000.

Bashmet, Yuri *b. 1953*
RUSSIAN VIOLIST

Bashmet studied at the Moscow Conservatory, and won the International Viola Competition, Munich, in 1976. He has given the first performance of viola concertos by Schnittke (Amsterdam, 1986) and Gubaydulina (Chicago, 1997) and of Britten's Double Concerto for violin and viola with Gidon Kremer (Manchester, 1998).

Biggs, E. Power *1906–77*
AMERICAN ORGANIST

Born in England, Biggs made his US début in 1930. He did much to popularize organ music through concerts and recordings, and through broadcasting a weekly programme from Harvard on national radio 1942–58. He played organ music of all periods including his own, with new works by **Walter Piston** (1894–1976) and others.

Blades, James *1901–99*
ENGLISH PERCUSSIONIST

Blades played as a drummer in the band of a travelling circus, and in orchestras for silent films. He joined the London Symphony Orchestra in 1940, and later worked with the Melos Ensemble and the English Opera Group. It was Blades who was actually heard (though not seen) when the Roman gladiator struck the gong at the beginning of the films produced by J. Arthur Rank.

Bream, Julian *b. 1933*
ENGLISH GUITARIST AND LUTENIST

Bream made his London début on the guitar in 1950, and his US début in 1958. Having begun to study the lute in 1950, he formed a partnership with Pears, with whom he performed and recorded Elizabethan lute songs. He formed the Julian Bream Consort in 1959. Among composers who wrote guitar works for him were Britten and **William Walton** (1902–83).

Brendel, Alfred *b. 1931*
AUSTRIAN PIANIST

Brendel studied in Zagreb and Graz and later attended classes with Edwin Fischer. He made his debut in Graz in 1948 and became well known in the 1950s through his many recordings. He is widely admired for his performances of the sonatas of Beethoven and Schubert.

Coin, Christophe *b. 1958*
FRENCH CELLIST

Coin studied the cello in Caen, at the Paris Conservatoire, and in Vienna with Harnoncourt. He studied the viola da gamba at the Basle Schola Cantorum, 1977–79. He played with the Vienna Concentus Musicus, Hesperion XX and the Academy of Ancient Music, 1977–83. Since 1984 he has followed a career as a soloist on the Baroque cello. He is also a member of the Mosaïques string quartet.

Curzon, (Sir) Clifford *1907–82*
ENGLISH PIANIST

Curzon studied in Berlin and Paris. He toured Europe from 1932 and America from 1939. He gave the first performance of works by Lennox Berkeley and Alan Rawsthorne, but was associated mainly with the Classical repertory, especially Mozart. His recordings include the First Piano Concerto by **Johannes Brahms** (1833–97), conducted by George Szell (1897–1970).

Du Pré, Jacqueline *1945–87*
ENGLISH CELLIST

Du Pré studied with William Pleeth and made her début in London in 1961. At the age of 20 she recorded the Elgar Cello Concerto under Sir John Barbirolli. She was married to Barenboim, who often accompanied her as pianist and conductor. Her career was cut short by multiple sclerosis.

Fox, Virgil *1912–80*
AMERICAN ORGANIST

Fox studied in America, and with Marcel Dupré in Paris. He made his début at the age of 14 and appeared in London when he was 19. From 1946 to 1965 he was well known as organist of the Riverside Church, New York. As well as making recordings, he went on tours with a large portable electronic organ and accompanying light show.

Galway, James *b. 1939*
BRITISH FLAUTIST

Galway studied in London and Paris before becoming an orchestral player, first in England, then with the Berlin Philharmonic Orchestra 1969–75. Since leaving Berlin he has been active as a soloist. He has enlarged the flute repertory by adapting works written for other instruments, and several composers have written pieces for him.

Gilels, Emil *(1916–85)*
RUSSIAN PIANIST

Gilels studied at the Odessa Conservatory, winning prizes in Moscow, Vienna and Brussels before his career was interrupted by the war. From 1947 he was able to travel abroad, making his New York début in 1955 and his London début in 1959. He played large-scale Romantic works, but was also a delicate Mozartian.

Gould, Glenn *1932–82*
CANADIAN PIANIST

Although renowned as a concert pianist from the age of 14, Gould constantly sought new ways of communicating music through the popular media of the time. To this end, he gave up concerts in 1964 and concentrated on making recordings. His interpretations, notably of J. S. Bach, were controversial but had many admirers. He also composed, wrote articles and made television and radio documentaries.

Horowitz, Vladimir *1904–89*
AMERICAN PIANIST

Horowitz studied in his native Russia and gave concerts in Kiev, Moscow and Leningrad before his début in Berlin in 1925. His New York and London débuts followed in 1928. He settled in the US in 1940. In later life he restricted his concert appearances, but he continued to make recordings. He performed again in the USSR three years before his death.

Leonhardt, Gustav *b. 1928*
DUTCH HARPSICHORDIST

After studying at the Schola Cantorum in Basle, Leonhardt made his début as a harpsichord player in Vienna in 1950. He was professor of harpsichord at the Vienna Academy of Music 1952–55. Since 1954 he has taught at the Conservatory in Amsterdam, where he is organist of the Nieuwe Kerk.

Marsalis, Wynton *b. 1961*
AMERICAN TRUMPET-PLAYER

Marsalis studied at the Juilliard School in New York. In 1980 he joined Art Blakey and the Jazz Messengers, and toured with Herbie Hancock the following year. He formed his own group in 1982. He has performed and recorded much of the classical trumpet repertory, appearing with the New York Philharmonic, Los Angeles Philharmonic and Cleveland Orchestras, and the London Symphony Orchestra.

Menuhin, Yehudi *1916–99*
AMERICAN/BRITISH VIOLINIST

Menuhin studied with **Georges Enescu** (1881–1955). As a child prodigy he appeared in San Francisco in 1924 and in New York in 1926. He made his début in Paris in 1927, in Berlin in 1928 and in London in 1929. His famous 1932 recording of the Elgar concerto under the composer's baton is still in the catalogue. He gave many concerts for Allied troops during the war. He settled in London in 1959, and devoted the latter part of his musical career to conducting. He took British citizenship, and was raised to the peerage and appointed to the Order of Merit.

Mutter, Anne-Sophie *b. 1963*
GERMAN VIOLINIST

After studying in Germany and Switzerland, Mutter performed at the Lucerne Festival in 1976. She appeared at the Salzburg Festival in 1977, the same year as her English début with the English Chamber Orchestra under Barenboim at the Brighton Festival. She has recorded all the Beethoven sonatas.

(FL) Julian Bream
Bream has become renowned for his virtuoso guitar and lute playing.
(NL) Jacqueline du Pré
English cellist Du Pré, who made a seminal recording of Elgar's Cello Concerto.
(TR) Yehudi Menuhin
Menuhin, a prodigious violinist, maintained a parallel career as a conductor in later years.
(BR) James Galway
Galway, one the most eminent flautists of his era, has had works written for him by several composers.

Oistrakh, David *1908–74*
RUSSIAN VIOLINIST

Oistrakh studied at the Odessa Conservatory and made his Leningrad début in 1928. He won several competitions in the 1930s, and came second to **Ginette Neveu** (1919–49) in the 1935 Wieniawski competition. His international career developed after the war. Many composers wrote works for him, notably Shostakovich, whose First Concerto he played at his New York début in 1955.

Perahia, Murray *b. 1947*
AMERICAN PIANIST

After studying in New York, Perahia won the Leeds International Piano Competition in 1972. In 1973 he appeared at the Aldeburgh Festival, where he worked with Britten and Pears. He has recorded all the Mozart concertos (directing the English Chamber Orchestra from the keyboard), and the Beethoven concertos with the Concertgebouw Orchestra under Haitink.

Perlman, Itzhak *b. 1945*
ISRAELI VIOLINIST

Perlman studied at the Juilliard School in New York and made his début at the Carnegie Hall in 1963. His London début followed in 1968. He has made many recordings, including the Beethoven Triple Concerto with Barenboim and Yo Yo Ma, and the violin solos on the soundtrack of the film *Schindler's List*. He performed as director/soloist with the English Chamber Orchestra in 1997.

Pollini, Maurizio *b. 1942*
ITALIAN PIANIST

After studying at the Milan Conservatory, Pollini won the 1960 Warsaw Chopin Competition. His repertory includes works by J. S. Bach and the Viennese Classical composers. He is also an advocate of twentieth-century music, including works by Schoenberg and Boulez.

Richter, Sviatoslav *1915–97*
SOVIET PIANIST

Self-taught as a pianist, Richter gave his first recital in 1934. After studying at the Moscow Conservatory, he toured the USSR in 1940. He gave the first performances of Prokofiev's Sixth, Seventh and Ninth Sonatas. His fame had already spread to the West by the time he

made his first appearance there in 1960. His virtuosity encompassed composers as diverse as J. S. Bach and Debussy.

Rostropovich, Mstislav *b. 1927*
RUSSIAN CELLIST

Rostropovich studied at the Moscow Conservatory, where he was appointed professor in 1956, the year of his London and New York débuts. Composers who wrote works for him include Shostakovich and Britten. He left the USSR in 1974. As well as accompanying his wife, the soprano Galina Vishnevskaya, on the piano, he has frequently appeared as a conductor.

Stern, Isaac *b. 1920*
AMERICAN VIOLINIST

Born in Russia, Stern was taken by his parents to America as a baby. He studied in San Francisco, where he played the Brahms concerto under Pierre Monteux in 1936. He played for Allied troops during the war, and made his European début at the Lucerne Festival in 1948. He formed a piano trio with Eugene Istomin and Leonard Rose in 1936; as a soloist he has performed works by Bernstein, Penderecki, Dutilleux and Davies as well as the standard repertory.

Vengerov, Maxim *b. 1974*
RUSSIAN VIOLINIST

Vengerov gave his first recital when he was five, and played his first concerto at the age of six. Since winning the Carl Flesch competition in 1990 he has given recitals and played concertos in Europe, America and the Far East. He gave the first performance of Rodin Shchedrin's *Concerto cantabile* in 1998. His many recordings include both concertos of Prokofiev and Shostakovich.

PROMOTING WOMEN'S MUSIC

The promotion of women's work in music is not a late twentieth-century phenomenon. Organizations such as the British Society of Women Musicians (1911) or the American Society of Women Composers (1920s) worked hard to improve the opportunities available for their members. But a new wave of feminism in the late 1960s brought an increased awareness of the position of women in the musical world and musicologists began to study historical women musicians and investigate the way that issues of gender function within the musical world.

Several membership organizations grew up which aimed to encourage and promote women's music: the International Alliance of Women in Music, created in 1995 through the merging of the International League of Women Composers (1974), American Women Composers (1976) and the International Congress on Women in Music (1980) – as well as Germany's Frau und Musik, Finland's NaMu, the Netherlands's Stichting Vrouw en Muziek and Britain's Women in Music. Two all-women orchestras were formed specifically to play music by women composers: the American Women's Philharmonic (1981) and the European Women's Orchestra (1990s).

Brahms ▶ p. 240 Enescu ▶ p. 289 Neveu ▶ p. 302 Piston ▶ p. 293 Walton ▶ p. 299

SINGERS

Allen, (Sir) Thomas *b. 1944*
ENGLISH BARITONE

Allen's early career was spent with the Welsh National Opera, in works ranging from Mozart to Britten. He made his Covent Garden début as Donald in Britten's *Billy Budd* in 1971, and his Metropolitan Opera début as Papageno (*The Magic Flute*) in 1981. He appeared at English National Opera as Busoni's Faust in 1986 and as Billy Budd in 1988.

Baker, (Dame) Janet *b. 1933*
ENGLISH MEZZO-SOPRANO

Baker studied in London, and made her début in Smetana's *The Secret* in Oxford in 1956. She sang Handel roles early in her career, and made a particular impression as Purcell's Dido, which she recorded several times. At Covent Garden, where she first appeared as Hermia in Britten's *A Midsummer Night's Dream*, her roles included Berlioz's Dido, Kate in *Owen Wingrave* (which Britten wrote for her), Mozart's Vitellia and Gluck's Alceste. At Glyndebourne she sang in Cavalli's *La Calisto*, Monteverdi's *Il ritorno d'Ulisse in patria* and Gluck's *Orfeo*.

Bartoli, Cecilia *b. 1966*
ITALIAN MEZZO-SOPRANO

Bartoli made her début at Verona in 1987. Her most celebrated role is Rosina in Rossini's *Il barbiere di Siviglia*, which she has sung in Cologne, Catania, Schwetzingen, Zürich and Barcelona. Other parts include Cenerentola (Rossini), Cherubino and Dorabella (Mozart) and Haydn's Eurydice. She made her Metropolitan Opera debut in 1996 as Despina in *Cosí fan tutte*.

Berganza, Teresa *b. 1935*
SPANISH MEZZO-SOPRANO

Berganza made her début as Mozart's Dorabella at Aix-en-Provence, and sang Cherubino (*The Marriage of Figaro*) at Glyndebourne the next year. Her roles included Sesto (*La clemenza di Tito,* 'The Clemency of Titus'), Zerlina (*Don Giovanni*) and, later, Carmen, but she was most sought after for Rossini heroines.

Bergonzi, Carlo *b. 1924*
ITALIAN TENOR

Bergonzi studied as a baritone, singing Rossini's Figaro in Lecce in 1948 before retraining as a tenor. His second début was as Giordano's Andrea Chénier in 1951. He sang regularly at the Metropolitan Opera 1956–88. At Covent Garden, where he made his début in 1962, he sang many roles including Verdi's Alvaro, Manrico (conducted by Giulini) and Gustavus.

Caballé, Montserrat *b. 1933*
SPANISH SOPRANO

Caballé studied at the Barcelona Liceo, and joined the Basle Opera in 1956, where she sang the Italian and German repertory. She appeared at La Scala and in Vienna, before consolidating her reputation in several operas by Donizetti. She made her Glyndebourne and Metropolitan Opera débuts in 1965, and her Covent Garden début in 1972. Though she was associated mainly with Italian opera, her many recordings include Richard Strauss's *Salome*.

Carreras, José *b. 1946*
SPANISH TENOR

Carreras was born and studied in Barcelona. He also made his professional debut there in 1970 as Ismaele in *Nabucco*. He made his London debut in 1971. In 1974 he appeared at Covent Garden as Alfredo in *La traviata* and at the New York Met as Cavaradossi in *Tosca*. Leukaemia halted his career for some time, but he returned in 1988. Most recently he has experienced much popularity as one of the Three Tenors.

Christof, Boris *1914–93*
BULGARIAN BASS

Christof made his début in Italy in *La bohème* (1946). He was most famous as Boris Godunov in the Rimsky-Korsakov version of the Musorgsky opera. He made his US début in San Francisco in 1956 in the same role. His Verdi roles included Philip II in the Giulini-Visconti *Don Carlo* at Covent Garden in 1958, and as Fiesco in *Simon Boccanegra*. He recorded *Boris Godunov* twice, singing all three of the main bass roles.

Domingo, Plácido *b. 1941*
SPANISH TENOR

Domingo was brought up in Mexico, where he made his début as a baritone in 1957. He appeared as a tenor in Dallas in 1961, and was a member of the Israeli National Opera 1962–65. He sang Pinkerton (*Madama Butterfly*) at the New York City Opera in 1965, Maurizio in Cilea's *Adriana Lecouvreur* at the Metropolitan Opera in 1968, Verdi's Ernani at La Scala, Milan, in 1969, and Puccini's Cavaradossi at Covent Garden in 1971. He has sung Verdi's Otello on stage, on film and three times on record. In recent years he has moved into the Wagnerian repertory.

Evans, (Sir) Geraint *1922–92*
WELSH BARITONE

Evans joined the Covent Garden company in 1948, singing Mozart's Figaro in his second season. He sang at Glyndebourne 1950–61, and made his début at La Scala in 1960 and in Vienna in 1961. Appearances in America included Beckmesser in *Die Meistersinger* (Chicago, 1959) and Verdi's Falstaff (Metropolitan Opera, 1964). Renowned for many years in Mozart roles, in later life he added the *buffo* parts of Donizetti's Dulcamara and Don Pasquale and Rossini's Bartolo to his repertory.

Fischer-Dieskau, Dietrich *b. 1925*
GERMAN BARITONE

Fischer-Dieskau made his opera début in Berlin as Posa (*Don Carlos*) in 1948. The following year he appeared in Vienna and Munich, and in 1952 at Salzburg. He sang at Bayreuth 1954–56, and appeared at Covent Garden in 1965 as Richard Strauss's Mandryka (*Arabella*) and in 1967 as Verdi's Falstaff. He is widely known as a Lieder singer, having extensively recorded Beethoven, Schubert, Schumann, Brahms and Wolf songs.

Ghiaurov, Nicolai *b. 1929*
BULGARIAN BASS

After studying in Leningrad and Moscow, Ghiaurov made his début as Rossini's Don Basilio in 1955. From 1958 he often performed in Italy; débuts followed at Covent Garden (Padre Guardiano in *La forza del destino*, 'The Force of Destiny', 1962) and the Metropolitan Opera (Gounod's Méphistophélès, 1965). His most famous roles are Boris Godunov, which he recorded with Karajan, and Philip II (*Don Carlo*), which he recorded with Solti.

Gobbi, Tito *1913–94*
ITALIAN BARITONE

Gobbi studied in Rome, and sang regularly at the Opera from 1938. He made his La Scala début in 1942, when he also sang Berg's Wozzeck in Rome. He made his US début in San Francisco in 1948, and his Metropolitan Opera début in 1956. He often appeared at Covent Garden, in roles by Mozart, Verdi and Puccini. He both sang in and directed the Covent Garden première of Verdi's *Simon Boccanegra* in 1965.

Horne, Marilyn *b. 1934*
AMERICAN MEZZO-SOPRANO

After three years in Europe, Horne sang Marie (*Wozzeck*) in San Francisco in 1960, repeating the role in her Covent Garden début in 1964. She often sang with Sutherland, notably as Arsace in *Semiramide* (Rossini) and Adalgisa in *Norma* (Bellini). She made her Metropolitan opera début in 1970 as Adalgisa. She sang many Rossini roles, including Malcolm (*La donna del lago*, 'The Lady of the Lake') and Isabella (*L'italiana in Algeri*). She was also the voice of Carmen in the film *Carmen Jones* (1954), based on the Bizet opera.

(L) Cecilia Bartoli
Bartoli at a concert performance at Avery Fisher Hall.

(TR) Bryn Terfel
Young baritone Terfel as Verdi's Falstaff. He sang this role at the 1999 reopening of Covent Garden.

(BR) Joan Sutherland
Sutherland in the title role of Lehár's opera The Merry Widow.

bel canto ▶ p. 356

Kirkby, Emma *b. 1949*
ENGLISH SOPRANO

Kirkby was known early in her career primarily as a member of the early music group the Consort of Musicke and as a recitalist with the lutenist Anthony Rooley. She has subsequently performed music from all eras up to the time of Mozart. Her many recordings include Purcell's *Dido and Aeneas*, Handel's *Orlando*, *Athalia* and *Messiah*, and Hasse's *Cleofide*.

Nilsson, Birgit *b. 1918*
SWEDISH SOPRANO

Nilsson made her début as Agathe (*Der Freischütz*) in Stockholm in 1946. She sang many German and Italian roles there before her Glyndebourne début as Mozart's Elettra (*Idomeneo*) in 1951. In the 1950s she became known as a Wagner specialist, singing regularly at Bayreuth 1957–70. She frequently appeared at Covent Garden from 1957, singing Turandot, Leonore (*Fidelio*) and Elektra, as well as Brünnhilde and Isolde. Her Metropolitan Opera début was in 1959 as Isolde. Notable recordings are her Brünnhilde and Isolde under both Solti and Böhm.

Norman, Jessye *b. 1945*
AMERICAN SOPRANO

Norman made her operatic début in 1969 in Berlin as Elisabeth in *Tannhäuser*, followed by Mozart's Countess (*The Marriage of Figaro*), which she recorded under Colin Davis. Débuts followed in 1972 at La Scala (*Aida*) and Covent Garden (Berlioz's Cassandra in *The Trojans*), and in 1983 she appeared at the Metropolitan Opera (Cassandra, then Dido). She sang Elisabeth at Covent Garden in 1973, and Strauss's Ariadne in 1985.

Pavarotti, Luciano *b. 1935*
ITALIAN TENOR

After winning the international competition at the Teatro Reggio Emilia in 1961, Pavarotti made his début there as Rodolfo (*La bohème*), the role of his Covent Garden début in 1963. In 1964 he sang Idamante (*Idomemeo*) at Glyndebourne. His many roles at Covent Garden included Tonio in *La fille du régiment* ('the Daughter of the Regiment'), Verdi's Alfredo, Gustavus and Radames, Cavaradossi (*Tosca*), and Donizetti's Nemorino. He made his Metropolitan Opera début in 1968 as Rodolfo. In recent years he has reached a wide audience through his concert appearances as one of the 'Three Tenors'.

Pears, (Sir) Peter *1910–86*
ENGLISH TENOR

Pears was the life-long companion of Britten, who wrote all his tenor roles and many of his concert works for him. He was a choral singer in the 1930s; in 1943, after returning with Britten from the US, he joined Sadler's Wells Opera, singing mainly lyrical parts. At Covent Garden in the 1950s his roles included David in *Die Meistersinger von Nürnberg*. His Britten performances ranged from *Peter Grimes* (1945) to *Death in Venice* (1973). His recordings included the *War Requiem* and nearly all the Britten operas.

Scholl, Andreas *b. 1967*
GERMAN COUNTERTENOR

Scholl studied at the Schola Cantorum in Basle. He has worked with many leading Baroque specialists, including William Christie, Philip Herreweghe, Christopher Hogwood and Ton Koopman, singing oratorios and cantatas by J. S. Bach and Handel. His recordings include Handel's *Messiah* and *Solomon*, and Bach's Christmas Oratorio and B minor Mass. He made his stage début as Bertarido in Handel's *Rodelinda* at Glyndebourne in 1998.

Schreier, Peter *b. 1935*
GERMAN TENOR

Schreier made his début as the First Prisoner in *Fidelio* (Dresden, 1961), before joining the Berlin State Opera. On the death of Fritz Wunderlich in 1966, he became the best-known exponent of Mozart's Belmonte, Don Ottavio, Ferrando and Tamino (*The Magic Flute*), the part with which he made his Metropolitan Opera début in 1968. He was a noted singer of Lieder and of the Evangelist in Bach's Passions.

Schwarzkopf, (Dame) Elisabeth *b. 1915*
GERMAN SOPRANO

Schwarzkopf made her début at the Städtische Oper in 1938 as a flower maiden in *Parsifal*. She joined the Vienna State Opera, with which she appeared on the company's visit to Covent Garden in 1947. She then joined the resident company at Covent Garden, singing many German and Italian roles. She made her Salzburg and La Scala débuts in 1949 as Mozart's Countess, and her Metropolitan Opera début in 1949 as Strauss's Marschallin. She created the role of Anne Trulove in Stravinsky's *The Rake's Progress* (Venice, 1951).

Sutherland, (Dame) Joan *b. 1926*
AUSTRALIAN SOPRANO

Sutherland studied in Sydney and sang in public there before travelling to London for further study at the Royal College of Music. She joined the Covent Garden company in 1952 and sang many roles, including Jenifer in the première of Tippett's *The Midsummer Marriage*. Her performance as Donizetti's Lucia di Lammermoor under Serafin in 1959 launched her career as an international star in the ***bel canto*** repertory, with débuts in the role at Paris (1960), La Scala (1961)

and the Metropolitan Opera (1961). In the 1960s and 70s she performed and recorded many Donizetti and Bellini roles, usually conducted by her husband, Richard Bonynge.

Terfel, Bryn *b. 1965*
WELSH BARITONE

Terfel studied at the Guildhall School of Music and Drama in London and in 1989 won the Lieder prize in the Cardiff Singer of the World competition. He made his début in 1990 as Guglielmo (*Così fan tutte*) for the Welsh National Opera. He has performed Figaro worldwide. He sang Verdi's Falstaff at the reopening of Covent Garden in 1999. His recordings include Figaro, Strauss's Jokanaan, both Don Giovanni and Leporello, and discs of arias, Lieder and English songs.

Vickers, Jon *b. 1926*
CANADIAN TENOR

Vickers joined the Covent Garden company in 1957, singing Verdi's Gustavus and Berlioz's Aeneas. In 1958 he sang the title-role in the Giulini-Visconti production of *Don Carlo*, and Siegmund at Bayreuth, followed by Jason in Cherubini's *Medea* in Dallas. He sang Siegmund and three other roles in Vienna in 1959. He made his Metropolitan Opera début in 1960 with Canio (*Pagliacci*). The many roles he sang at Covent Garden included Florestan (*Fidelio*), Samson (both Handel's and Saint-Saëns'), Wagner's Tristan, Verdi's Otello and Britten's Peter Grimes.

The Late 20th Century

STYLES AND FORMS

After the cataclysmic upheaval of World War II subsided, it was clear that a very different musical world would result. The conflict had led to the dislocation, destruction and occupation of major cities in Germany and central Europe, coupled with the dispersal of their leading creative figures around the globe. It was inevitable that fresh centres, directions and personalities would emerge, and they were quick to appear.

In Paris, Messiaen's composition class at the Conservatoire provided a forum for a radical intelligentsia to develop, determined upon a thoroughgoing re-evaluation of modernism as it had existed pre-war. Boulez emerged early on as a charismatic leader, able to back his compositional skills with a savage polemical gift. Stravinsky's neo-classicism was scornfully dismissed as retrogressive, whilst Messiaen's structural techniques were criticized for substituting, as Boulez saw it, juxtaposition for composition. Nor did the senior generation of serialists, Schoenberg, Webern and Berg, escape wholly, being variously pulled up for temporizing with pre-serial formal models or for failing to develop a correspondingly radical approach to rhythmic organization, as they had established for pitch.

A New World Order

Nevertheless, it was upon their example that Boulez and his contemporaries set about building a new world order for music. Taking as a starting point the aesthetic of Schoenberg's early **atonal** works and the organizational methods of late Webern, Boulez aimed at what he called an 'organized delirium', an intensification of the **12-note** method that involved a melodic style spread over extremes of **register** and a use of rhythm, derived from a detailed manipulation of small melodic and rhythmic cells, that disrupted any conventional notion of pulse. This early style found its fullest expression in the Second Piano Sonata (1948), a work consciously conceived as a successor to the great Romantic sonatas of the past, in particular **Beethoven**'s *Hammerklavier* (1818).

Serialism

But soon Boulez, along with his colleagues, was exploring a still more fundamental interpretation of the 12-note ideal: 'total serialism'. Aspects of Webern's work had hinted at the extension of serialism to cover not just the organization of pitched notes, but of other parameters too, including rhythm, mode of attack, dynamics and timbre. These composers found inspiration in a pioneering piano piece by Messiaen, the *Mode de valeurs et d'intensitées* ('Forms of Value and Intensity', 1949), which attempted to unify four of these elements by forging numerical links between them and the pitch row. Boulez and **Stockhausen** elaborated this idea in a series of experimental works composed between 1950 and 1952. In Stockhausen's case, the music took the form of 'points', individualized notes each with their own highly specific duration, dynamic and mode of attack.

Eventually, however, this extraordinary experiment in aesthetic unity could not be sustained. The difficulties experienced in live performance and an instinctive feeling that too rigid a system might stifle a composer's individual creativity led its chief proponents to seek other paths. For Boulez, this involved the development of a highly embellished and exotic style that re-integrated some elements of total serialism with his earlier rhythmic flexibility. For Stockhausen, total serialism eventually led to the exploration of a new medium, offering the potential for control over the elements of sound itself: electronic music.

(BL) James Joyce
Portrait of the writer James Joyce, whose soliloquies were adopted by Berio.
(TL) Pierre Boulez
Boulez worked in a style known as 'total serialism', an experimental method of composition.
(TR) Conch-shell Composition
The composer John Cage experimented with new forms of music-making.
(BR) Karlheinz Stockhausen
Stockhausen was leader of the international avant-garde, a pioneer of electronic music.

MUSIC AND LITERATURE

The ground-breaking literature of the twentieth century had a major impact on composers, particularly in the 1950s and 60s. The work of **Berio** has consistently drawn upon the works of James Joyce for parallels between verbal and musical technique, particularly 'stream of consciousness' chapters such as Molly Bloom's soliloquy from *Ulysses*, while **Barraqué** based his entire later output on Hermann Broch's poetic novel, *The Death of Virgil*. The poets e.e. cummings and Stéphane Mallarmé were also important, particularly for Boulez, whose Third Piano Sonata, in its presentation of the score as a map or maze through which the performer must plan a route, has parallels with the appearance on the page of Mallarmé's *Un coup de dès* ('A Throw of the Dice'). Mallarmé was even more influential on Boulez's major orchestral work *Pli selon pli*, which seeks not to 'set' the poems in any conventional sense, but rather to absorb their structure into the music itself.

STRAVINSKY AND SERIALISM

By the 1950s, Modernism in its new manifestations was well established, with strongholds in the Darmstadt courses and at the Donaueschingen Festival, as well as in Paris and Cologne. Its strength was increasingly felt in the US as well as Europe, with **Babbitt**, **Wolpe** and **Carter** all evolving individual lines of development. The most striking instance of its impact, however, was on Stravinsky, widely regarded as the greatest composer living. Although in his seventies and resident in America, he remained acutely alert both to Viennese serialism and the music of Europe's younger generation. If the ballet score *Agon* (1954–57) represented the point of Stravinsky's transition from neo-classical to serialist composer, *Movements for Piano and Orchestra* (1958–59) shows the traces of Webern and Schoenberg even more clearly. Stravinsky rarely adopted serialism in its purest form, however, often using repeated notes and making independent use of smaller units from within the note-row to suit his own ends, while distinctive fingerprints in orchestration, chord spacing, **sprung rhythms** and verse/refrain forms remained to the end.

aleatory music ▶ p. 356 atonality ▶ p. 356 *musique concrète* ▶ p. 360 register ▶ p. 362 sine waves ▶ p. 362 sprung rhythm ▶ p. 362 12-note music ▶ p. 363

The Mechanical World

Although experiments had been carried out in the 1920s and 30s in the manipulation of sound by electronic means, it was not until the creation in 1948 by Paul Schaeffer (b. 1910) of a studio in Paris that the world heard the first truly electronic compositions. Schaeffer called them ***musique concrète***, by which he meant the creation of new sounds from existing or 'concrete' sources. These could be drawn from the mechanical world – for instance railway trains – as much as instrumental, human or environmental sounds. The interest for composers, however, was less in creating a sort of collage, more in transforming these 'sound objects' into new sounds, by such means as playing recordings backwards, faster, slower, or by removing the initial attack to create pure tone. Schaeffer's means for manipulating material were gramophone records, but from 1950 the arrival of tape recorders multiplied the possibilities for a more comprehensive deconstruction of the very components of sound.

INFLUENCES FROM THE EAST

From the late 1940s onwards, **John Cage** was a figure of major significance as a thinker, inventor and exemplar whose approach drew crucial sustenance from outside the Western tradition. A different conception of time and sound informed Cage's music from the start, including his influential makeover of the conventional piano, which he 'prepared' by inserting bolts, pieces of rubber and other objects between its strings. The result, as heard in *Sonatas and Interludes* (1946–48), is a kind of crazy Balinese gamelan, in which clunks and rattles coexist alongside ordinary sounding notes and unexpectedly beautiful, muted tones. But while the prepared piano music was as organized, in its way, as total serialism, Cage's increasing involvement with Zen philosophy led to his gradual withdrawal as a willed agent in his pieces and the introduction of the use of chance events, such as tossing a coin, to determine their fabric. Resistant to anything that smacked of goal-directedness, in 1952 Cage produced *4'33"*, a piece that comprised four minutes 33 seconds of silence, during which the audience is invited to listen to environmental sounds or contribute some noises of its own. Cage's work, to some a provocation, offered others an alternative and a release from what they saw as the didacticism of much modernist thought.

Electronic Music

In 1952, the opening of the Studio für Elektronische Musik in Cologne by West German Radio led Stockhausen to the first of a visionary series of compositions using electronic resources. Initially he attempted to create new timbres by the combination of **sine waves**, a synthetic process which led to the coining of the term 'electronic music'. Subsequent courses in phonetics and communication studies led Stockhausen to analyse speech by its formants (its emphasized bands of frequencies) and from there to attempt a synthesized language through tape transformations that would break down the artificial barriers between speech and sound. The resulting tape piece, *Gesang der Jünglinge*, transforms a recording of a choirboy singing the Benedicite by means of editing and studio techniques. Its extraordinary mixture uses superimposition to create the illusion of virtual choirs, reverberation effects, intentional jumblings and scramblings of words or parts of words, juxtaposed with suddenly clear delivery, and rapid changes of register and velocity; it was all relayed through five spatially separated loudspeakers. It went on to exercise enormous influence on other composers.

Stockhausen's ongoing preoccupation with getting behind notes to the sounds themselves, led to a further substantial electronic piece, *Kontakte* ('Contacts', 1959–60), which deals not only with the way complex sonic events can be broken down or built up from their constituent parts, but also introduces live participants (piano and percussion) to perform simultaneously with the tape.

Aleatory Music, Mobile Forms, Graphic Scores

Inspired by Cage, many composers in the late 1950s began to introduce an **aleatory** or free element into their music, and to experiment with notation. In the case of **Lutosławski** this took the form of areas set aside for musicians to play a given cycle of notes, unsynchronized. Stockhausen, in *Klavierstück XI*, provided groups of material, with the pianist determining their order of execution by means of random glances across the page. The introduction of pieces with movements or parts of movements, whose order could be transposed also fed the development of graphic scores, in which conventional notation and layout were abandoned. Composers such as **Penderecki** increasingly wrote with their own notational symbols and systems, first heard to fiercely expressive effect in *Threnody for the Victims of Hiroshima*.

Babbitt ▶ p. 284 Barraqué ▶ p. 324 Beethoven ▶ p. 150 Berio ▶ p. 324 Berg ▶ p. 286 Boulez ▶ p. 324 Cage ▶ p. 324 Carter ▶ p. 325 Lutosławski ▶ p. 327
Messiaen ▶ p. 293 Penderecki ▶ p. 328 Schoenberg ▶ p. 295 Stockhausen ▶ p. 329 Stravinsky ▶ p. 280 Webern ▶ p. 299 Wolpe ▶ p. 330

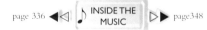

IRCAM

From the early 1950s onwards, studios for electro-acoustic music had provided an alternative crucible to the concert hall and opera house for music's development. In the mid 1970s, the French government took this to a further level with the creation of IRCAM, the Institut de Recherche et de Co-ordination Acoustique/Musique. Headed by Boulez, lavishly funded and based at the Pompidou Centre in central Paris, it quickly became a magnet from all over the world for both musicians and scientists engaged in electro-acoustic and, increasingly, computer music. The first work Boulez composed at IRCAM, *Répons* ('Response', 1980), represented a characteristically ambitious attempt to mould the language of music, combining live performance with sounds transformed both by electro-acoustic means and through a computer, the 4X. Boulez developed IRCAM as a centre for the new in other ways, including a concert hall and a performance group, the Ensemble InterContemporain. This last initiative was a response to the resistance of many orchestras and established chamber groups to the demands made on them by new music, and the consequent need to establish specialist ensembles of committed performers skilled in the necessary techniques. Groups such as the London Sinfonietta and Ensemble Modern, in Britain and Germany respectively, provide similar examples and have also done much to generate new repertory.

The Rise of Minimalism

If many of the immediate post-war developments were led by Europe, minimalism gave American music another movement which, like jazz, had widespread international influence. Its three most essential characteristics were use of tonality, an almost hypnotic approach to rhythmic repetition and the capacity to absorb a variety of world music. The first two of these features implied a fundamental criticism of the new modernist tenets.

Minimalism's early protagonists, mostly based in New York, included La Monte Young, whose group, Theatre of Eternal Music, performed work strongly influenced by Cage and by Indian music in its use of mixed media, drones, repetition, slow tempos and extremes of length, with pieces lasting hours rather than minutes. An early collaborator with Young was **Riley**, whose *In C* was the first seminal work of minimalism, presenting its musicians with 53 optional phrases, all in C major, to be performed around a pounding **ostinato** pulse which persists throughout the piece.

GLASS AND REICH

Shortly after this, two composers emerged with whom minimalism has subsequently become synonymous: **Glass** and **Reich**. Glass's early music, influenced by his studies with Ravi Shankar, was almost entirely composed for his own small ensemble. Characterized by driving repetitions played at very high volume and speed, it was organized by small sections, which would be repeated over and over, until a prearranged signal enabled the musicians to move on to the next. While Glass's works did not usually specify which instruments should perform them, Reich's music, almost from the start, showed more interest in specific timbres; taped sounds were also of key importance. It was while experimenting with a tape loop that Reich stumbled across the technique upon which his early music is based – phasing. By bringing identical strands of music gradually out of synchrony and then bringing them inexorably back together, Reich created a repetitive process in which systemic change was clearly audible, with new patterns constantly emerging for the listener.

THE 'CLASSIC' PERIOD

In the early 1970s, Reich, inspired by an extended visit to Ghana, produced lengthy works such as *Drumming* (1971), which has no melody or changes of key, but relies on variations of pitch, timbre and time to maintain its structure.

The 'classic' period of minimalism lasted perhaps 10 years. By the 1970s, both Glass and Reich began to abandon the almost ascetic severity of their earlier music for more diverse paths, in Glass's case film and opera, including *Einstein on the Beach*. Reich developed colourful scores for ensemble such as *Music for 18 Musicians*, integrating harmony with the familiar repetitive patterns and insistent rhythms. These works sealed minimalism's transition from the lofts of SoHo to commercial success in little over a decade, with far-reaching repercussions for music of the 1980s and 90s.

The End of the Millennium

The last two decades of the twentieth century would seem, at least on the surface, to present a bewildering plurality of styles. Yet although no dominant strand became apparent, some of the main threads can be picked out. Many of the leading figures of modernism from the 1950s and 1960s remained alive, active and influential. **Ligeti**, for example, reinvented himself as a post-Romantic composer in works such as *Horn Trio* (1982), which revisits the music of **Brahms** but from an entirely distorted, late-twentieth-century viewpoint. His recent music, expressed in a series

MUSIC AND POLITICS

Ideological divisions and oppressive régimes had a significant impact on the first four decades of post-war music, particularly in Eastern Europe. The 15 symphonies of **Shostakovich** are now widely seen as political statements, sometimes overt, sometimes covert, as with the Tenth Symphony (1953) and its haunting depiction of Russia under Stalinism. Dissent also found expression in the music of **Schnittke**, whose use of serial techniques was sufficient to ensure his marginalization within the Soviet Union, and in works such as *Miserere* (1981) by **Górecki**, explicitly written in response to the crushing of Solidarity in Poland.

In the West, the turbulence of the late 1960s led some composers to challenge the political implications of contemporary modernism, which they saw as elitist and divorced from the needs of ordinary people. Composers such as **Nono**, however, saw political progress and the advance of musical modernism as interlinked, integrating modernist techniques with tapes of revolutionary speeches and everyday sounds and performing the results in workers' canteens and factories.

ostinato ▶ p. 361

MUSIC THEATRE

Opera presented a problem for many post-war composers, who considered it hidebound by backward-looking institutions and conservative repertory. Boulez famously declared that all opera houses should be blown up. This did not mean, however, that composers were uninterested in the theatre or the idea of musicians making music before a public, or that they would give up on exploring new paths. **Britten** wrote works such as *Curlew River* (1964), which developed a style of chamber church opera, based in part on Japanese Noh drama. The 1960s also saw the development of music theatre, works for a few instrumentalists and singers that did not need a stage environment. Drawing on the examples of Schoenberg's *Pierrot lunaire* (1912) or the Stravinsky of *A Soldier's Tale* (1918) and *Renard* (1916), music theatre works often depicted extremes of expression to shocking effect. Ligeti, in *Aventures* and *Nouvelles Aventures* (1962–65), largely dispensed with conventional communication through language in favour of extended vocal techniques for the soloists – extremes of range, shouts, grunts, screams, ululations, hissing, all precisely detailed in the score.

OLIVIER MESSIAEN: COLOURS AND BIRDS

Messiaen's creative personality and influence as a teacher were fundamental to the development of new music in Europe after 1945. He was Debussy's natural successor, taking the French master's innovative approach to harmony and rhythm to a new plane, while sharing his openness to the music of other cultures. Although by the late 1940s the main elements of Messiaen's harmonic language were already in place, he continued to develop as a 'rythmicien', creating an influential synthesis derived from Hindu and classical Greek poetic metre and Western models, particularly Stravinsky. Birdsong, collected from all corners of the planet, came to occupy a central role, starting with the almost literal transcriptions of *Réveil des oiseaux* ('Awakening of the Birds', 1953) but quickly developing a more orchestral range in *Oiseaux exotiques* ('Exotic Birds', 1955–56). The brightly coloured plumages evoked in the bird pieces co-existed with his belief that chord sequences could directly describe the sensation of colour, expressed in works such as *Couleurs de la cité céleste* ('Colours of the Heavenly City', 1963), where the colours represented are listed in the score. While many of his pupils might regard these ideas as eccentric, the influence of Messiaen's teaching remained vast, with eminent students including Boulez, Stockhausen and Barraqué.

of concertos and an ongoing collection of Piano Studies (1985–), has explored rhythmic complexity, inspired by new mathematical concepts such as chaos theory, and also the cross-rhythms of Brazil and the Caribbean. 'Classic' Modernism, however, has continued to develop and even intensify through the so-called 'complexity music' of composers such as **Ferneyhough**, whose work features an extreme density of detailed event and makes exceptional demands on a performer's virtuosity.

Ligeti's late work is perhaps closest to postmodernism, a term borrowed from contemporary architecture to describe composers who draw from the past with a mixture of open admiration and ironic detachment. Postmodernism's most successful and imitated exponent is the American **Adams**, whose orchestral work *Harmonielehre* ('Theory of Harmony', 1985) creates a powerful fusion between the New York minimalism of Reich and late Romantic models, Schoenberg, **Wagner** and **Debussy**.

Post-minimalism

Minimalism's influence has proved crucial in shifting the centre of gravity back from atonality towards tonality. Much minimalism from the mid-1970s onwards, including that of Reich, might be better described as post-minimal in its willingness to add elements from other quarters. The Dutch composer Louis Andriessen (b. 1939) has been an increasingly significant figure in this regard, taking the repetitive thrust of minimalism but bringing to the mix European dissonance, political radicalism, intellectual literariness and rock music. A further development saw the emergence of **Górecki**, **Pärt** and **Tavener**, all of whom achieved large-scale success and CD sales in the early 1990s. Works such as Górecki's Third Symphony (1976), Pärt's *Passio* (1981) and Tavener's *The Protecting Veil* (1987) led to the term 'sacred minimalism' to describe their music. In common is a radical simplicity and use of tonality, combined in Pärt's case with an interest in medieval techniques, in Tavener's with Greek Orthodox liturgy and music, and in Górecki's with the folk culture of Poland's Tatra mountains.

Global Music

At the beginning of the new millennium, new music is more than ever before a global phenomenon. The emergence, after the Cultural Revolution, of a generation of Chinese composers willing to fuse Chinese traditions with Western modernism, with Tan Dun (b. 1957) the best known, is perhaps globalization's most striking manifestation to date. Although the pace of change may become less hectic, the plethora of ideas from Modernism's cornucopia still to be worked through, the growing consciousness of other world traditions and the challenge of popular music all seem set to play a big part in shaping the new music of the future.

(FL) Steve Reich
Reich was one of the best-known exponents of minimalism.
(NL) The London Sinfonietta
One of the groups who have embraced the new challenges of the twentieth-century repertory.
(R) John Adams
Adams was a leading exponent of post-modernism in music.

Adams ▶ p. 324 Brahms ▶ p. 240 Britten ▶ p. 287 Debussy ▶ p. 282 Ferneyhough ▶ p. 325 Glass ▶ p. 325 Górecki p. 326 Ligeti ▶ p. 326 Nono ▶ p. 327
Pärt ▶ p. 327 Reich ▶ p. 328 Riley ▶ p. 328 Schnittke ▶ p. 328 Shostakovich ▶ p. 297 Tavener ▶ p. 329 Wagner ▶ p. 226

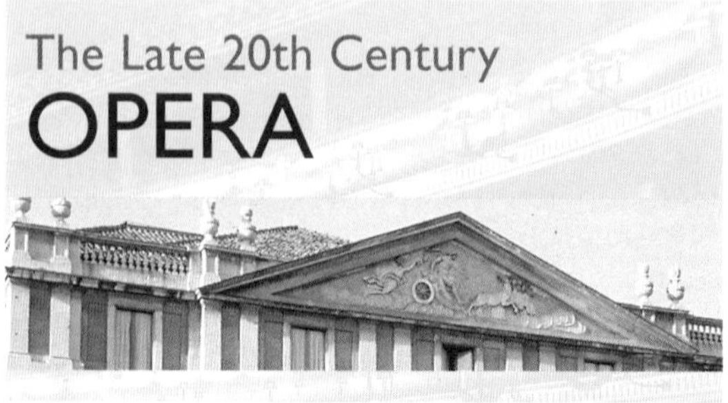

European culture lay in ruins after the end of World War II. There were many who, in company with the philosopher Theodor Adorno, felt that Nazi atrocities such as Auschwitz rendered art impossible, at least temporarily. Others, though, felt that humanity could only establish itself anew by rediscovering the potency of art, including opera. On the one hand, that meant rebuilding opera houses destroyed during the war; on the other, opera had to rediscover its moral authority, and that could best be done by the creation of new works.

In some senses, the old had died and the new been born during the war. *Capriccio*, the last opera by Richard Strauss, had its première in Munich in 1942, with Allied air-raids a nightly threat. Meanwhile Britten, who spent the duration of the war in America, had written his first opera, *Paul Bunyan*, staged in a student production at Columbia University, New York, in 1941. Where *Capriccio* seemed lost, both musically and dramatically, in an agony of nostalgia for a world eradicated by the war, *Paul Bunyan*, a work rooted as much in American as in European idioms, was filled with energy and optimism.

The Shock of the New

Britten was to emerge as the first great opera composer of the post-war era. Yet while composers attempted to renew opera, most opera houses relied increasingly on a repertory that had been fixed, not even in the 1930s, but in the 1920s. This was especially true in the US, where new work emerged only with the greatest difficulty. Faced with a culture resistant to the shock of the new, many composers abandoned opera altogether. Others sought to change the form, while still others continued to explore the possibilities that opera traditionally offered. The rich, and in many ways unprecedented, diversity of opera since 1945 derives from the interaction of these responses.

European Opera After the War

Several composers whose reputations were established before the war contributed significantly to the post-war repertory. When Schoenberg died, he left incomplete his last stage work, *Moses und Aron*, on which he had begun work in the 1930s. Acts One and Two were first given in concert in Hamburg in 1954, and staged in Zürich in 1957. Two months after Schoenberg's death came the Venice première of *The Rake's Progress* by **Stravinsky**, written in the United States by a Russian composer, to a libretto in English by a British poet (W. H. Auden) and an American (Chester Kallman). The last of Stravinsky's neo-classical works, it is among the most successful operas written since the death of **Giacomo Puccini** (1858–1924), thanks in part to its quasi-Mozartean music and dramaturgy, well served by a sardonic libretto.

KEY EVENTS

1945	Sadler's Wells Opera presents first performance of Britten's *Peter Grimes*
1947	Columbia University student cast gives première of Virgil Thomson's *The Mother of Us All*
1951	La Fenice in Venice stages première of Stravinsky's *The Rake's Progress*; first of many TV broadcasts of Menotti's *Amahl and the Night Visitors*
1952	Bernstein's one-act opera *Trouble in Tahiti* first performed
1954	First two acts of Schoenberg's *Moses und Aron* given in Hamburg
1956	Bernstein's *Candide* first performed in Boston
1959	Joan Sutherland's Covent Garden performances as Lucia announce a major talent
1965	Callas gives last operatic performances, as Tosca at Covent Garden
1966	Première of Barber's *Antony and Cleopatra* reopens New York Metropolitan Opera
1969	The Covent Garden Opera Company, established 1946, becomes the Royal Opera
1974	Sadler's Wells Opera, established 1935, changes name to English National Opera
1979	Boulez conducts première of Berg's three-act *Lulu* at Paris Opera; Sondheim's *Sweeney Todd* premiered
1981	Stockhausen gives première of first instalment ('Thursday') of operatic cycle *Licht*
1983	Canadian Opera Company introduces surtitles for a performance of Strauss's *Elektra*
1987	Adams' *Nixon in China* receives first performance from Houston Grand Opera
1990	Pavarotti, Domingo and Carreras give first 'Three Tenors' concert in Rome
1991	Corigliano's *The Ghosts of Versailles*, first new work at Metropolitan Opera since 1967
1992	Finnish National Opera gives première of Sallinen's *Kullervo* in Los Angeles
1999	After controversial closure, London's rebuilt Royal Opera House opens again

'NESSUN DORMA'

When Italy hosted football's World Cup in 1990, they chose 'Nessun Dorma' from Puccini's *Turandot* as its theme. Pavarotti, long a football fan, suggested to his fellow tenors, Domingo and Carreras, that they perform together; the resulting Three Tenors concert earned them superstar status.

POPULAR MELODY *Puccini*

THE PRE-WAR TRADITION

Francis Poulenc (1899–1963) wrote his first opera, *Les Mamelles de Tirésias* ('Tiresias's Breasts') in 1944, but it was not staged until 1947. The riotous musical business, fondly evoking broad swathes of French musical history, contrasts starkly with *Dialogues des Carmélites* ('Carmelite Dialogues', 1957), a sombre dramatization of the fate of Carmelite nuns during the French Revolution. Poulenc's last opera, *La Voix humaine* ('The Human Voice', 1959), is a 40-minute monodrama, in which we hear one end only of a telephone conversation between a woman and her soon-to-be ex-lover.

Post-war operas by **Hindemith**, **Carl Orff** (1895–1982), **Milhaud** and **Ildebrando Pizzetti** (1880–1968), although varying in significance, can be seen as continuations of a pre-war tradition. Although in some senses *Il Prigioniero* ('The Prisoner', 1950) by

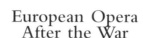

opera seria ▶ p. 361 serial music ▶ p. 362 Berg ▶ p. 286 Berio ▶ p. 324 Birtwistle ▶ p. 324 Britten ▶ p. 287 Cage ▶ p. 324

Dallapiccola** returned to pre-war concerns, its fusion of Schoenbergian **serialism** and Italianate lyricism provided inspiration for younger composers. Its depiction of a prisoner tortured by hope that is eventually betrayed, also demonstrated that modern opera could accommodate left-wing politics.

(NL) Royal Opera House
The Royal Opera House in London was reopened in 1999.
***(FL)* Gloriana**
Performance of Britten's opera Gloriana.
(R) The Three Tenors
Domingo, Carreras and Pavarotti produced the world's best-selling classical album.

HANS WERNER HENZE

The lessons were not lost on **Henze** who, after serving in the German army during the war, worked on the music staff at several opera houses. That experience engendered a practicality that has helped make Henze one of the most prolific and most lyrical post-war composers of opera. Early works included the 'opera for actors' *Das Wundertheater* ('The Magic Theatre', 1949) and two radio operas. His first full-length stage work was *Boulevard Solitude* (1952), a successful marriage of disparate stylistic elements (serialism, cabaret, jazz) that separated Henze from more doctrinaire contemporaries.

After his move to Italy in 1953, subsequent operas embraced a diversity of genres: comic opera (*Der junge Lord*, 'The Young Lord', 1963); chamber opera (Elegy for Young Lovers, 1961); even ***opera seria*** (*The Bassarids*, 1966). For a time Henze abandoned the opera house for politicized music theatre (*El Cimarrón*, 1970; *La cubana*, 1974); when he wrote *We Come to the River* (1976, to a libretto by Edward Bond, socialist playwright) for Covent Garden, the results were no less political. Henze's commitment to opera, and to left-wing politics, has remained undiminished. In 1988, he founded the Munich Biennale, a source of commissions for many younger composers.

Post-war Opera in Britain

For nearly 200 years after the death of **George Frideric Handel** (1685–1759), Britain contributed little to the history of new opera. Benjamin Britten changed that. Ironically, Britten styled his first stage work a 'Broadway opera'; first seen in New York, *Paul Bunyan* was moderately successful with audiences, but ridiculed by critics. Weeks after its première, Britten, now in California, discovered the work of the nineteenth-century poet George Crabbe, a Suffolk man like himself. Crabbe's *The Borough* included the story of a fisherman, Peter Grimes, ostracized for mistreating his apprentices: this, Britten determined, would become his next opera. Returning to Britain in 1942, he secured a contract from the Sadler's Wells Opera Company, which gave the première of *Peter Grimes* on 7 June 1945.

Presciently, the opera caught the mood of paranoia and persecution that would settle over post-war Europe. Its moving 'Sea Interludes' (often performed in concert), its arias, ensembles and choruses, show the influence of nineteenth-century opera. Yet its complex structure and its subject matter, profoundly influenced by **Berg**'s *Wozzeck* (1925), remain contemporary. Like Britten's next grand opera *Billy Budd* (1951), it dramatizes the tension between innocence and evil, between individual and community.

BRITTEN AND THE ENGLISH OPERA GROUP

Although never an avant-garde composer, Britten often worked outside opera's conventional boundaries. He wrote for children and amateurs (*Noye's Fludde*, 1958), for church performance (the 'parables', *Curlew River*, 1964; *The Burning Fiery Furnace*, 1966; *The Prodigal Son*, 1968), for television (*Owen Wingrave*, 1971); and in 1947 founded the English Opera Group (it folded in 1980). In Venice in 1954 the company gave the première of Britten's *The Turn of the Screw*, scored for an orchestra of 13 players, whom Britten deployed with such skill that the listener senses no lack of weight, texture or colour.

Other than Britten's work, few operas commissioned by the English Opera Group remained in the repertory. Yet the company gave important commissions to many composers, including **Walton**, Lennox Berkeley (1903–89), Thea Musgrave (b. 1928) and Birtwistle. Perhaps more important still has been the company's practical example: its fostering of collaborations between composers, poets and playwrights; and its development of notions of small-scale, even portable opera. In that sense, the company's influence has been as profound as that of Britten himself.

MUSIC THEATRE

The ideas behind Britten's English Opera Group implied less a rejection of the opera house than an acknowledgement of other possibilities. During the 1960s and 70s many composers, not necessarily influenced by Britten, sought to rescue music drama from the perceived bourgeois stranglehold of the opera-house. Besides Britten, significant predecessors included Stravinsky's *The Soldier's Tale* (1918), a work conceived in terms of portability; and the 'epic theatre' of Bertolt Brecht and **Kurt Weill** (1900–50).

Diverse in form and content, such works are often labelled 'music theatre'. Among the characteristics implied by the term are smallness of scale, though not of imagination; a theatricality closer to contemporary drama than to opera; sometimes the use of non-operatic voices and venues; and an insistence on the importance of text, even if that text is nonsensical.

In Britain, **Birtwistle** and **Davies** formed the Pierrot Players, named for Schoenberg's *Pierrot lunaire* (they later became The Fires of London, after Birtwistle had left) in 1967 as a conduit for their and others' works. In continental Europe, **Berio**, **Nono** and Henze sought forms to serve a radical political agenda, while the Argentinian **Kagel** and the Americans **Cage** and Meredith Monk (b. 1943) were among those creating non-narrative theatre through music.

Eventually many composers found the label 'music theatre' itself constricting. Nevertheless music theatre in all its variety altered perceptions of what the combination of music and theatre might achieve; operas as different as Birtwistle's *Gawain* (1991) or *Marco Polo* (1996) by Tan Dun show its influence.

Dallapiccola ▶ p. 288 Davies ▶ p. 325 Handel ▶ p. 112 Henze ▶ p. 326 Hindemith ▶ p. 290 Kagel ▶ p. 326 Milhaud ▶ p. 293 Nono ▶ p. 327 Orff ▶ p. 293
Pizzetti ▶ p. 294 Poulenc ▶ p. 294 Puccini ▶ p. 254 Schoenberg ▶ p. 295 R. Strauss ▶ p. 258 Stravinsky ▶ p. 280 Walton ▶ p. 299 Weill ▶ p. 299

CARMEN JONES

Of many attempts to popularize opera, perhaps the most successful was Oscar Hammerstein's musical *Carmen Jones*. Hammerstein substituted post-war black America for the Spain of Bizet's original, and provided Broadway style arrangements of the opera's tunes.

POPULAR MELODY *Hammerstein*

POST-WAR PREMIÈRES

Although both Arthur Bliss (1891–1975) and **Vaughan Williams** had operas given in the immediate post-war period (respectively, *The Olympians*, 1949, and *The Pilgrim's Progress*, 1951), it was **Tippett** who came closest to matching Britten's success. Tippett always provided his own librettos, and their oddities of language and plot, their exploration of abstract myths and archetypes, have dismayed many. Nevertheless, his highly personal lyricism and capacious humanity won him admirers world-wide. *The Midsummer Marriage* (1955) and *The Knot Garden* (1970), idiosyncratic studies of personal relationships, are frequently revived, while the Homeric *King Priam* (1962), an altogether darker work, may be his operatic masterpiece.

THE 1960s AND BEYOND

When the English Opera Group gave the première of Birtwistle's *Punch and Judy* at the 1968 Aldeburgh Festival, Britten was famously unimpressed. His opinion symbolizes a break between 'old' and 'new' opera. Subtitled 'tragicomedy or comitragedy', *Punch and Judy* is loudly expressionistic, but there are counterbalancing moments of rapture in its ritualistic account of Punch's serial murders. *The Mask of Orpheus* (1986) is yet more ritualistic, returning to opera's founding myth via a libretto of bewildering complexity, to which Birtwistle's music (including electronic tape) responds with rugged beauty.

European opera over the following decades readily embraced the primitive and the complex. In *Die Teufel von Loudun* ('The Devils of Loudun', 1972), the Polish composer **Penderecki**, a devout Christian, graphically depicted demonic possession (or sexual obsession) in a seventeenth-century convent. The special vocal and instrumental devices Penderecki demanded represented a search for new forms of expression. More recently Penderecki has retreated somewhat from such avant-gardisms, but both *Die schwarze Maske* ('The Black Mask', 1986) and *Ubu Rex* ('King Ubu', 1991) are acerbic satires.

LIBRETTISTS

The most successful librettist of the modern era was W. H. Auden, who provided texts for Britten's first opera, *Paul Bunyan* and, in collaboration with Chester Kallman, for operas by Stravinsky (*The Rake's Progress*), Henze (*Elegy for Young Lovers*, 1961; *The Bassarids*, 1966), and for less acclaimed works by John Gardner (b. 1917) and Nicolas Nabokov (1903–78).

Few opera librettists in recent history have been as prolific. Many composers have preferred to supply their own librettos, notably Tippett, Rautavaara and (not invariably) **Davies**. Several directors have involved themselves in writing texts, usually for operas which they would be staging: David Freeman (b. 1952) wrote the libretto for *Hell's Angels* (1986) by Nigel Osborne (b. 1948), which Freeman directed; while Harry Kupfer (b. 1935) collaborated with the composer on the libretto of *Die schwarze Maske* by Penderecki.

For the most part, though, the job of librettist has gone to poets or playwrights. Among the former, notable contributors have been Tony Harrison (librettos for Birtwistle and Jacob Druckman), Paavo Haavikko (two for **Sallinen**), and Alice Goodman (two for **Adams**); while the playwright Edward Bond has written two librettos for Henze.

Opera from Communist Nations

Penderecki is one of the few composers from former Communist nations whose works have reached the West. The Russian **Schnittke** had left the Soviet Union by the time his bleakly parodistic *Life with an Idiot* (1992) was premièred, while *Historia von D. Johann Fausten* (1995) is a wild collage of musics in what Schnittke referred to as his polystylistic mode. Operas by Giya Kancheli (Georgian, b. 1935), Sándor Szokolay (Hungarian, b. 1931) and Rodion Shchedrin (Russian, b. 1932) remain rarities in the West.

The German **Zimmermann** wrote only one opera before his suicide. *Die Soldaten* ('The Soldiers', 1965) benefits from the composer's experience of writing for radio and theatre; like Berg's *Lulu*, it incorporates film footage, and calls for a huge cast and orchestra. It has been called the most important German opera since the war, but while Zimmermann's musical skill is not in doubt, the opera's anti-militaristic stance is facilely dramatized.

STOCKHAUSEN AND BERIO

Stockhausen initially found the medium of opera unattractive, but in 1977 he embarked on a vast operatic sequence of Wagnerian ambition. Much influenced by Asian dramatic forms, *Licht: Die sieben Tage der Woche* ('Light: The Seven Days of the Week') functions as a kind of didactic and religious ceremony. So far, Stockhausen has unveiled *Donnerstag* ('Thursday', 1981), *Samstag* ('Saturday', 1984), *Montag* ('Monday', 1988), *Dienstag* ('Tuesday', 1992), *Freitag* ('Friday', 1996) and *Mittwoch* ('Wednesday', 2000), all ending with 'aus Licht' ('from Light').

***(FL)* The King Goes Forth to France**
Aulis Sallinen uses voice and orchestra to dramatic effect in his operas.

***(NL)* Carmen Jones**
Dorothy Dandridge in the 1954 film version of this popular opera.

(NR) Tito Gobbi
The Italian baritone in his most widely remembered role as Falstaff.

(FR) Judith Weir
Weir has a gift for storytelling, complemented by her musical talent.

bel canto ▶ p. 356 coloratura ▶ p. 357

BARITONES

Baritones, it is said, sing and act, while tenors merely sing. That may tell us more about the roles they take than about the singers themselves, but certainly the finest baritones excel in both skills, none more than **Tito Gobbi**, whose most noted roles were Falstaff in Verdi's eponymous opera, and Scarpia in Puccini's *Tosca*. By contrast, **Fischer-Dieskau** was at home in Wagner and Richard Strauss, while in Verdi he was thought stern and unsmiling.

If Gobbi and Fischer-Dieskau are the most celebrated baritones of the last half-century, they have not occupied an empty stage. While the United States produced such fine baritones as Robert Merrill (b. 1917), Sherrill Milnes (b. 1935) and, more recently, Thomas Hampson (b. 1950), the former Soviet Union nurtured two of the most exciting singers to be heard today, Sergei Leiferkus (b. 1946) and Dmitri Hvorostovsky (b. 1962). In Britain the young **Bryn Terfel** launched a successful career after making a great impression at the 1989 Cardiff Singer of the World competition.

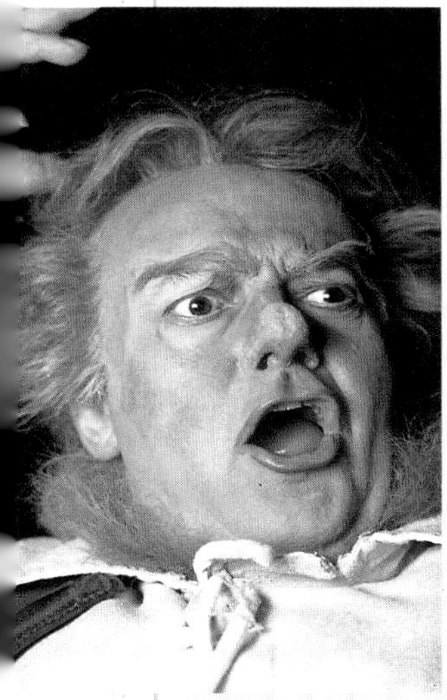

Singers as diverse as **Hans Hotter** (b. 1909) and José van Dam (b. 1940) have been labelled 'bass-baritones', but it is debatable whether this denotes a separate voice-type, or simply indicates perceived extra weight, depth or colour. What is not in doubt is that, baritones or bass-baritones, these men have been uncommonly talented as singers and as actors.

Unlike Stockhausen, Berio was drawn to opera while still young, working as an opera conductor, and in 1950 marrying the soprano Cathy Berberian, an important collaborator. Early music theatre pieces displayed an adventurous – sometimes irreverent – theatricality that would sustain more operatic works such as *La vera storia* ('The True Story', 1982), a complex political debate that is also a deconstruction of traditional operatic fare. *Un Re in Ascolto* ('A King Listens', 1984) is similarly as much about opera as itself.

Europe Today

The Finnish composer Sallinen has suffered charges of conservatism, but his operas show a refined understanding of how to use voice and orchestra in an inherently dramatic way. His most recent opera, *King Lear* (2000), derives from Shakespeare's play, but of his previous five operas, the most powerful is *Kullervo* (1992). This cool depiction of communal barbarism draws elements of its plot from the *Kalevala*, the bardic epic that is one of the cornerstones of Finnish literature.

The *Kalevala* also provided inspiration for two operas by Sallinen's compatriot Einojuhani Rautavaara (b. 1938), *Marjatta, The Lowly Maiden* (1975) and *Rune 42: The Abduction of Sampo* (1983). Rautavaara's international reputation rests on his orchestral works, and his eight operas display an idiosyncratic sense of drama that might suggest opera is not his natural medium. Yet he writes sympathetically for the voice (his wife Sini is a singer for whom he has written several roles), and the eccentricities of his plotting conspire to create a dreamlike atmosphere, as in *Thomas* (1985), about a thirteenth-century bishop who was one of the first to propose the idea of Finnish nationhood.

TURNAGE AND WEIR

A generation younger than Sallinen and Rautavaara, the British composer Mark-Anthony Turnage (b. 1960) sought an altogether more abrasive style in *Greek* (1988), which relocated the Oedipus myth to contemporary London. A caustic parable of Thatcherite Britain, *Greek* acquired universality thanks to Turnage's skills as an orchestrator. Since *Greek*, Turnage's commitment to opera has been fitful. *Twice Through the Heart* (1997) is more a song-cycle than an opera; while *The Country of the Blind* (1997), based on H. G. Wells's story, lacks the individuality of *Greek*. Turnage's largest opera to date, *The Silver Tassie* (2000), derives from Sean O'Casey's anti-war play (1929).

The music-dramas of Judith Weir include a dance-opera, *HEAVEN ABLAZE in his Breast* (1989); a televisual adaptation of Mozart, *Scipio's Dream* (1991); and a 10-minute 'Grand Opera in Three Acts', *King Harald's Saga* (1979), for soprano singing nine roles, including impersonating an army. Her unorthodox wit is no less apparent in her full-length operas, *A Night at the Chinese Opera* (1987), *The Vanishing Bridegroom* (1990) and *Blond Eckbert* (1994). Weir's storytelling gift is complemented by a musical talent that is as much at home with folk idioms from her native Scotland as with the many languages of contemporary music.

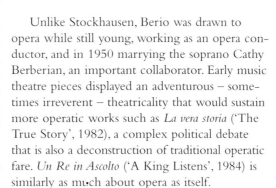

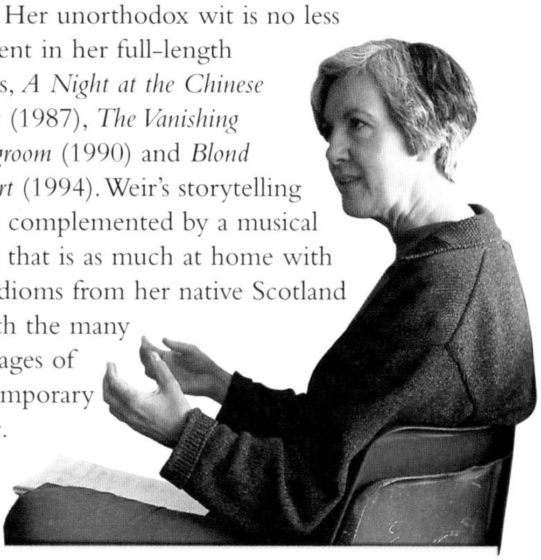

BEL CANTO REVIVED

Since Puccini's death in 1924, opera houses have made little room for living composers. While the core repertory has remained more or less fixed, the need for novelty has necessitated the rediscovery of works long forgotten. This in turn has required singers able to cope with different technical and aesthetic problems; indeed, it is usually the prominence of such a singer that has fostered the kind of archeology that uncovers neglected works.

So it was with the soprano **Maria Callas** (1923–77), whose extraordinary vocal and dramatic intensity encouraged the revival of many operas previously deemed unworkable. They included eighteenth-century works, notably Haydn's *L'anima del filosofo* ('The Spirit of the Philosopher'), unperformed in the composer's lifetime but given in Florence in 1951 in a staging conceived for Callas. More significant was the restoration of nineteenth-century ***bel canto*** works such as Bellini's *Il Pirata* ('The Pirates'), Donizetti's *Anna Bolena* ('Anne Boleyn') and Rossini's *Il Turco in Italia* ('The Turks in Italy'). These, Callas proved, could work with a singer with solid technique, dramatic charisma, dazzling **coloratura**, and above all, perhaps, a belief in the music.

Fitting the Opera to the Voice

Shortly after Callas's rise to stardom, the Australian soprano **Joan Sutherland** began to make an impact. Although less dramatically gifted than Callas, Sutherland had a voice that was purer, less vulnerable at the top of its range. Her husband, the conductor Richard Bonynge, was assiduous in his quest for rare works suited to her voice: not only many of the nineteenth-century Italian operas which Callas had revived, but also operas by Handel, early works by Verdi, and French operas by Meyerbeer, Delibes and Massenet.

Many, though not all, of the operas exhumed for Callas and Sutherland were recorded by them. Although some have subsequently found themselves reinterred, both singers proved that scholarship, interpretation and exceptional technique can rescue operas from obscurity, to the enrichment of the repertory. Similar work has been done by contemporary singers such as the mezzo-sopranos **Cecilia Bartoli** and Vesselina Kasarova (b. 1965), who have, in different ways, continued what Callas and Sutherland began.

Adams ▶ p. 324 Bartoli ▶ p. 334 Callas ▶ p. 303 Davies ▶ p. 325 Fischer-Dieskau ▶ p. 334 Gobbi ▶ p. 334 Hotter ▶ p. 303 Penderecki ▶ p. 328
Sallinen ▶ p. 328 Schnittke ▶ p. 328 Stockhausen ▶ p. 329 Sutherland ▶ p. 335 Terfel ▶ p. 335 Tippett ▶ p. 330 Vaughan Williams ▶ p. 298 Zimmerman ▶ p. 330

WOLFGANG RIHM

The career of the German composer **Rihm** has followed a trajectory from narrative-based opera towards stage-works that emulate the ritual-based theatre proposed by the French playwright Antonin Artaud (1896–1948). Artaud's writings have been the direct source of several of Rihm's compositions, notably the opera *Die Eroberung von Mexico* ('The Conquest of Mexico', 1992), a densely layered, imaginatively orchestrated allegory.

Rihm resists the label 'opera', but his consistent search for original ways of telling stories through music shows that opera's originating impulse still functions powerfully, whatever the problems of form, finance and audience that opera faces today.

American Opera After the War

While European opera dominates the repertory in the United States, the quest for an American form, separate from the musical, has not been neglected. **Virgil Thomson** (1896–1989) described *The Mother of Us All* (1947, libretto by Gertrude Stein) as a 'musical memory book', for the way it incorporated fragments of pre-existing American styles. It was an exuberant experiment, more adventurous than Thomson's later *Lord Byron* (1972).

Born in Italy, **Gian Carlo Menotti** (b. 1911) arrived in America in 1928. While a student in Philadelphia he met **Samuel Barber** (1910–81); the two were life-long companions, and between them did much to establish American opera, albeit of a distinctly European complexion. In all his works, pre- and post-war, Menotti displays an innate gift for expansive, heartfelt melody.

MENOTTI'S OPERAS

Among his more than two dozen operas (all to his own librettos) are a monodrama, *The Telephone* (1947), children's operas (including *Help, Help, the Globolinks!*, 1968), church operas and television operas: *Amahl and the Night Visitors* (1951), the first opera to be written for American television, has been broadcast annually at Christmas, reaching an audience undreamt of by any composer living or dead. Other Menotti operas, including *The Consul* (1950), a sinister political drama, have pleased audiences, who appreciate his directness, while exasperating critics, especially in Europe, where his music has often been thought facile.

Menotti provided librettos for Barber's first two operas. *A Hand of Bridge* (1959) is a caustic nine-minute miniature, but *Vanessa* (1958) is a

THE GREAT OPERA HOUSES

The history of opera is dominated by Italian and Austro-German composers. Correspondingly it is in Italy and Germany that we find the greatest number of opera houses. La Scala in Milan lays claim to be the most famous opera house in the world, and its opening night every season is a major event in the country's social calendar. The theatre, opened in 1778, has been the venue for the premières of major operas by Rossini, Bellini and Donizetti, as well as of Verdi's last two operas, *Otello* and *Falstaff*. Other famous opera houses in Italy include La Fenice ('The Phoenix') in Venice, currently undergoing massive restoration after being destroyed by fire in 1996; the Teatro Comunale in Bologna; and the Teatro dell'Opera in Naples.

Since reunification, Germany possesses an even richer variety of opera houses. There is considerable doubt whether Berlin can continue to support three large houses (the Deutsche Oper in former West Berlin, the Komische Oper and the Staatsoper unter den Linden in former East Berlin); for now, the city has access to an unparalleled diversity of opera. Elsewhere in Germany, the most celebrated opera houses are in Munich and at Bayreuth, where Wagner opened his custom-built Festspielhaus in 1876. Only Wagner's operas are performed in the Festspielhaus, though there is pressure for that to change.

Modern Opera Houses

While most opera houses are nineteenth-century edifices, Drottningholm in Sweden is a Baroque building in full working order. As for the twentieth century, Australia's Sydney Opera House, designed by Jørn Utzon and opened in 1973, has perhaps the most easily recognized architectural profile in the world. Other significant modern opera houses include New York's Lincoln Center Met, opened in 1966, and the Opéra de la Bastille in Paris, a controversial structure opened in 1990. Although plans for completely new opera houses in London have been mooted several times, none has materialized. After many difficulties, a redesigned Covent Garden opened in late 1999; a few hundred yards away, the city's biggest theatre, the London Coliseum, is home to English National Opera. The country's only new opera house in recent years has been the rebuilt Glyndebourne, which opened in 1994.

TENORS

Although he made his début in the pre-war era, the Swedish tenor **Jussi Björling** (1911–60) was thought among the finest if not the most imaginative tenors of the post-war years. A fellow Swede, Nicolai Gedda (b. 1925), proved able to encompass virtually the entire tenor repertory from the Baroque to the twentieth century, though he was most impressive in Italian opera.

Through the 1950s, a succession of Italian singers dominated in their national repertory. **Carlo Bergonzi** made his début as a baritone but, switching to tenor in 1951, he proved one of the most elegant singers of his day. Mario del Monaco (1915–82), Franco Corelli (b. 1921) and Giuseppe di Stefano (b. 1921) sang more brashly, but for many listeners, that was what the music required. Di Stefano made many notable recordings and appearances with Callas. The Spaniard Alfredo Kraus (1927–99) was perhaps Bergonzi's equal in refinement.

Beyond the Italian Repertory

Peter Pears had a distinctive voice that is inseparably linked to the music of Britten, who wrote several operatic roles especially for him, including *Peter Grimes*. When the Canadian **Jon Vickers** took that role at Covent Garden and on disc, Britten was reportedly unhappy with his interpretation. Vickers was nevertheless a tenor of genuinely heroic timbre, able to sing Monteverdi and Handel with the same intensity he brought to works by Verdi.

Leading Wagnerian singers have included Wolfgang Windgassen (1914–74) and Siegfried Jerusalem (b. 1940). Had he not died so young, the German Fritz Wunderlich (1930–66) might have become a fine Wagnerian; as it is he is particularly remembered for his elegance in Mozart. For two decades and more after his death, the famous Three Tenors ruled the world's stages: **Luciano Pavarotti**, **Placido Domingo** and **José Carreras** each brought imagination and vocal athleticism to everything they sang. In the wake of their success, any promising new tenor is labelled the 'Fourth Tenor', a sobriquet that does no justice to singers as individual as Roberto Alagna (b. 1963), José Cura (b. 1963) or Ramon Vargas (b. 1960).

full-scale four-act opera. The lush orchestral scoring supports powerful singing in the European grand opera tradition, but the story has overtones of sentimental 1940s Hollywood. Franco Zeffirelli's (b. 1923) libretto for Barber's last opera, *Antony and Cleopatra* (1966), consists entirely of Shakespeare's words, which generated some of Barber's most impassioned music, but he wrote no more for the opera house.

MOORE AND FLOYD

Douglas Moore (1893–1969) inflected European idioms with something more American, as in *The Ballad of Baby Doe* (1956), which at times seems lost in reminiscence of American popular styles, though the attractive tunes are mostly Moore's own. Like Menotti, Carlisle Floyd (b. 1926) writes his own librettos; his most successful work has been *Susannah* (1955), a Southern Gothic drama derived from the Apocrypha. The score incorporates American folk idioms to frame more fulsome melodies that, with cinematic ease, assume darker hues when plot demands. It has been one of America's most popular operas, although its popularity has yet to spread elsewhere.

(L) Great Opera Houses
La Scala in Milan (BL) and the famous façade of the Sydney Opera House (TL).

(R) Britten and Pears
One of the most successful partnerships of modern times: the singer Peter Pears with composer Benjamin Britten, seen here playing the piano.

IN THE AMERICAN MAINSTREAM

The stage works of **Bernstein** largely belong to the category of musical, but *On the Town* (1944), *Candide* (1956: Bernstein called it a 'comic operetta') and, particularly, *Trouble in Tahiti* (1952) and *West Side Story* (1957), refused to accept that musicals are inferior to opera. *A Quiet Place* (1983), unequivocally labelled 'opera', imperceptibly fuses classical idioms with popular and jazz styles. The works of New York-born **Sondheim**, who worked with Bernstein on *West Side Story,* also lean towards opera, from *Sweeney Todd* (1979) to *Passion* (1994).

Hugo Weisgall (1912–97) and Dominick Argento (b. 1927), both of European parentage, retained musical affinities with Europe. Weisgall's operas, including *The Tenor* (1952) and *Six Characters in Search of an Author* (1959), fashioned a modern, though never avant-garde, American idiom from Germanic expressionism and Italianate neo-classicism. In his 13 operas, including *Postcard from Morocco* (1972) and *The Aspern Papers* (1988), Argento combined a highly literate dramatic sense with intensely melodic vocal writing.

John Corigliano (b. 1938) wrote *Naked Carmen* (1970), an 'electric rock opera', specifically to be recorded. More conventional, *The Ghosts of Versailles* (1991) derives in part from Beaumarchais' third 'Figaro' play, *La mère coupable* ('The Guilty Mother'), and includes quotations from Mozart and Rossini in a thick pastiche of styles ancient and modern. With this piece the composer wanted to show an ironic detachment from Europe.

Barber ▶ p. 284 Bergonzi ▶ p. 334 Bernstein ▶ p. 286 Björling ▶ p. 303 Carreras ▶ p. 334 Domingo ▶ p. 334 Menotti ▶ p. 292 Pavarotti ▶ p. 335 Pears ▶ p. 335
Rihm ▶ p. 328 Sondheim ▶ p. 328 Thomson ▶ p. 298 Vickers ▶ p. 335

PIONEERS AND EXPERIMENTERS

Cage wrote of his *Europeras 3 & 4* (1990), 'Europe has been sending us its operas for 150 years. Now I'm sending them all back'. His five *Europeras* have singers performing, in random order, arias from European operas: an amusing reminder that not all American composers are in thrall to the European tradition.

Glass frequently collaborates with the director Robert Wilson to produce multimedia spectacles that stretch the definition of opera. *La Belle et la Bête* ('Beauty and the Beast', 1994) created its own genre, 'film opera': the score is performed in synchronization with a silent screening of Jean Cocteau's 1945 film. Glass's chamber opera *The Fall of the House of Usher* (1988) is closer to Old World models.

Adams writes political operas on subjects from recent history: President Nixon's 1972 visit to Mao-Tse Tung in *Nixon in China* (1987); the 1985 hijacking of the cruise liner *Achille Lauro* in the oratorio-like *The Death of Klinghoffer* (1991). Adams calls *I Was Looking at the Ceiling and Then I Saw the Sky* (1995) a 'Songspiel'. Its rock-oriented songs, interspersed with spoken dialogue, tell of the effect of the 1994 earthquake on Los Angelenos.

The Growth of the Director

The notion that there was something sacrosanct in a composer's vision of how a work should be staged began to lose ground before World War II. The need for change became urgent after the war, particularly at Wagner's theatre in Bayreuth, a Nazi shrine during the Third Reich.

When Bayreuth reopened in 1951, Wagner's grandson Wieland (1917–66) attempted to purge his grandfather's work of the taint of Nazism. Wieland dispensed with pictorial sets that sought to fulfil Wagner's instructions to the letter, preferring abstract designs that, combined with stylized acting and movement, produced a network of symbolic meanings. No element of Wieland's *mise-en-scène* was merely decorative.

While Wieland Wagner was revolutionizing Bayreuth, productions developed differently at the Komische Oper in East Berlin, where Walter Felsenstein (1910–75) was director from 1947 until 1975. Alert to the symbiosis between text and music, Felsenstein sought to build ensemble performances based on detailed realism and psychological identification with the characters.

There was political intent in both directors' works, and in that of several German directors who continue to follow their lead. Götz Friedrich (b. 1930), Joachim Herz (b. 1924) and Harry Kupfer have been called Felsenstein's 'disciples'; Herz and Kupfer have staged controversial productions at Bayreuth. Their work, like that of Ruth Berghaus (1927–96), unites didactic intent with a powerful theatricality, both derived from Bertolt Brecht. At first known mostly in Germany, all eventually worked throughout Europe.

New Methods of Staging

In the United States, Peter Sellars (b. 1957) and David Alden (b. 1949) are at the forefront of attempts to rid opera of superfluous pageantry. Sellars' productions stress contemporary relevance: his Glimmerglass staging of Mozart's *Don Giovanni* cast the black twins Eugene and Herbert Perry as Giovanni and Leporello, leather-clad drug dealers ruling Harlem's ghetto. Alden, notably in Verdi stagings at English National Opera during the 1980s, presents opera in a hallucinatory, unspecific time and place.

David Pountney (b. 1947), ENO's Director of Productions from 1982 to 1993, mixes carnivalesque vulgarity with grotesquerie and a distinctive morbidity: his Janácek stagings for ENO, Scottish Opera and Welsh National Opera consolidated that composer's reputation in Britain. While traditional stagings survive everywhere, directors such as Peter Stein (b. 1937) and Jonathan Miller (b. 1934) occupy a middle ground between traditionalism and iconoclasm.

These directors work through extended rehearsals, and this usually precludes working with opera's biggest stars, who prefer undemanding rehearsal schedules. For all of them, design is integral to their productions, so that the terms 'produceritis' and 'designer's opera' are used to deride their work and that of like-minded directors.

(BL) Modern Interpretations
Modern productions, such as this version of Mozart's Don Giovanni *attempt to look at familiar opera's in a different light.*
(TL) **Nixon in China**
Adams writes political operas commemerating significant events in recent history.
(NR) Leontyne Price
The American soprano was one of the leading singers of the 1950s and 60s.
(FR) American Sopranos
Kathleen Battle and Jessye Norman have found success throughout Europe and America.

FILM, RADIO, TELEVISION

Opera at the cinema can be traced back as far as 1903, when a silent version of Gounod's *Faust* was made (live musicians provided accompaniment for cinema showings). Post-war opera films have included adaptations by Ingmar Bergman of Mozart's *Die Zauberflöte* ('The Magic Flute', 1975), by Joseph Losey of Mozart's *Don Giovanni* (1979) and by Francesco Rosi of Bizet's *Carmen* (1984: there have been over three dozen films of *Carmen* in one form or another).

If nobody has written opera specifically for the cinema, the younger media of radio and television have occasionally commissioned new works. Although radio lacks the visual dimension, composers as various as Martin (*The Voice of the Forest*, Czech Radio, 1935), Menotti (*The Old Maid and the Thief*, NBC, 1939) and Henze (*Ein Landarzt*, 'A Country Doctor', Norddeutscher Rundfunk, 1951) have risen to the challenge of writing purely acoustic operas, some of which later received staging.

Television has been less willing to risk commissioning operas. Nevertheless, there is a solid corpus of works written for television (again, many later made their way into the theatre). Among the most successful are Menotti's *Amahl and the Night Visitors* (NBC, 1951), and Britten's *Owen Wingrave* (BBC, 1971). For the most part, though, opera on television means transmission of pre-existing stage productions.

Film, radio and television use opera as a means to underwrite their cultural status, but they have also provided fresh opportunities and challenges. No doubt the new technologies of the future will offer further possibilities; whether opera composers are allowed to exploit them remains to be seen.

SOPRANOS

If **Birgitte Nilsson** dominated Wagnerian singing in the post-war era, their success in the *bel canto* repertory made Callas and Sutherland the first soprano superstars on a global scale. As commanding in Austro-German repertory as they were in Italian, **Elisabeth Schwarzkopf** excelled in Mozart and Richard Strauss.

Renata Tebaldi (b. 1922), meanwhile, was hailed by some as Callas's vocal superior, damned by others as lacking true expressivity; **Montserrat Caballé** divided opinion along similar lines. Kiri Te Kanawa (b. 1944) has carefully restricted her career to a short list of roles ideally suited to her superbly lyrical voice.

Leontyne Price (b. 1927) was one of the leading sopranos of the 1950s and 60s. Black singers remain comparatively rare in opera, but more recently both **Jesse Norman** and Kathleen Battle (b. 1948) have been outstandingly successful; Norman, like Price, has a voice of sumptuous richness, Battle's is lighter. These singers' prowess confirmed the United States as Europe's equal in vocal expertise.

Through the last decade a new generation of American sopranos has risen to prominence: Renée Fleming (b. 1959) and Dawn Upshaw (b. 1960) have impressed across a broad repertory. Unusually for singers of such stature, both have proved willing interpreters of contemporary music. By contrast, the Romanian Angela Gheorghiu (b. 1963), alone and with her husband Roberto Alagna, has brought new lustre to established Italian and French repertory.

Rediscovering the Baroque

The success of the period instrument movement introduced previously neglected Baroque operas to the repertory. Landmarks on the way to that achievement included Britten's English Opera Group edition of Purcell's *Dido and Aeneas* (1951), Hindemith's edition of Monteverdi's *Orfeo* for Vienna (1954) and the founding of the Handel Opera Society in Britain (1955), while in the 1960s, Raymond Leppard (b. 1927) brought Monteverdi and Cavalli to Glyndebourne.

If none of these events met the criteria of what would come to be called 'authenticity', they suggested the viability of Baroque opera. That viability was finally established in the 1970s and 80s, thanks to conductors such as **Gardiner** and **Hogwood** in Britain, and, in mainland Europe, **Harnoncourt** (notably in productions of Monteverdi staged in Zürich by Jean-Pierre Ponnelle, 1932–88) and Arnold Östman (b. 1939) (at the eighteenth-century opera house at Drottningholm in Sweden).

With contemporary works marginalized, it has often fallen to Baroque operas to refresh the repertory through such inventive staging as Nicholas Hytner's (b. 1956) of Handel's *Xerxes* (1985). There have also been attempts to revive these works in a genuinely Baroque style: experimenters in this area have included Roger Norrington's Early Opera Project and Lina Lalandi's English Bach Festival. So far have these productions been from everyday convention that they influenced contemporary ideas about design and movement, including the incorporation of dance.

PAYING HOMAGE

Contemporary composers have also taken note, several returning to Monteverdi's work to prepare performing editions that amount to personal homages. Besides Hindemith and **Vincent d'Indy** (1851–1931, who edited Monteverdi's *L'Incoronazione di Poppea*, 'The Coronation of Poppea', as early as 1908), others include Dallapiccola's realization of *Il ritorno di Ulisse* ('The Return of Ulysses', 1942), Berio's ultra-modernized rendition of *Orfeo* (1984), and Henze's *Il ritorno d'Ulisse* (1985). An engaging variation was **Goehr**'s 'lost opera by Monteverdi', *Arianna* (1995): apart from the famous 'Lamento d'Arianna', all that survives of this Monteverdi opera is Ottavio Rinuccini's libretto. It was this that Goehr set, for an orchestra including saxophones, bass clarinet and sampler.

The success of Baroque opera has enriched the repertory and also expanded vocal and instrumental resources: composers such as **Reich**, for whom the traditional operatic voice is an anachronism, have welcomed the purer, less vibrato-ridden voices, including the countertenor required for early opera. Other composers have composed works (though not so far operas) for period instruments.

Caballé ▶ p. 334 D'Indy ▶ p. 244 Gardiner ▶ p. 330 Glass ▶ p. 325 Goehr ▶ p. 325 Harnoncourt ▶ p. 331 Hogwood ▶ p. 331 Nilsson ▶ p. 335
Norman ▶ p. 335 Reich ▶ p. 328 Schwarzkopf ▶ p. 335

The Late 20th Century INSTRUMENTS

Recording Classical Music

The high quality of performance and sound on modern CDs, as well as the sheer range of recordings available, has had a dramatic effect on the reception of classical music. On the one hand, recording has brought the music to much larger audiences than concert halls could ever accommodate. On the other hand, it has altered the way music is performed and the way we hear it. The increasing prevalence of recorded classical music has meant that some listeners can have unrealistic expectations of music in a concert hall. When a live performance differs from their favourite CD in terms of balance, tempo or interpretation, they can sometimes be disappointed.

The purpose of recording is to extend the life of an individual performance, making it available to a wide audience by distribution via CDs, tapes, broadcasting or the Internet. How this is achieved is often more complex than many listeners may realize. To begin with, the musicians rarely – if ever – play a piece of music from beginning to end, as they would in concert. Instead, a recording is made in a series of 'takes'. For each 'take', the musicians play a section of music, which can be as long as a movement or as short as a few bars. The producer then advises on passages that did not go well and these are re-recorded.

MICROPHONES AND MULTI-TRACKING

Developments in the use of microphones in recording music have radically altered the way classical music is heard. The principle of using two microphones to reproduce stereophonic sound was first demonstrated by the British company EMI in 1933, but stereo recordings did not become widely available until the late 1950s. This development gave listeners a dramatically improved sense of the spatial environment in which music was played. Later, increasing flexibility was offered by the development of multi-track tape recorders, famously used by The Beatles and their producer George Martin to make the aurally complex *Sergeant Pepper's Lonely Hearts Club Band* (1967) vinyl album. By the mid-1970s recording studios could record 24 separate sounds simultaneously on the same magnetic tape. This profoundly affected the attitudes of musicians and producers to the act of recording music, giving them the flexibility to place microphones around an orchestra and record each section and soloist separately. By the 1990s there had grown a reaction in classical music recording against such complex microphone set-ups in favour of the simplicity of a 'stereo pair' of microphones carefully positioned in front of the orchestra.

ACOUSTICS AND REVERBERATION

We can all form a mental 'picture' of the space in which a recording takes place, even while listening to a **mono** recording. This is called the 'acoustic' of a space – it can sound as small as a cupboard or as large as Westminster Abbey. The aural clues

COMPOSERS OF FILM SCORES

Camille Saint-Saëns (1835–1921) is said to have written the first film score with *L'assassinat du duc de Guise* ('The Assassination of the Duke of Guise', *c.* 1908). Many composers in the US and Europe followed suit, although few wished to make a career in films. A famous exception was Erich Wolfgang Korngold (1897–1957), whose scores include the Academy Award-winning *The Adventures of Robin Hood* (1938). Other American composers to write for film include **Copland**, whose score for *The Heiress* (1949) won an Academy Award, and **Thomson**, winner of the first Pulitzer Prize for film music, for *Louisiana Story* (1948). Film scores by British composers that contributed memorably to the success of films include *Henry V* (1945) by **Walton**, *Bridge on the River Kwai* (1957) by **Malcolm Arnold** (b. 1921) and Arthur Bliss's (1891–1975) *Things to Come* (1936).

Films with Pre-Composed Music

Pre-composed music has also been used in films, sometimes becoming more famous through its filmic associations. The director Stanley Kubrick memorably used passages from **Richard Strauss**'s *Also sprach Zarathustra* and **Ligeti**'s *Atmosphères, Lux aeterna* and *Requiem*. The slow movement from the Piano Concerto No. 21 by **Mozart** is now often called the 'Elvira Madigan' after its popularity in the Swedish director Bo Widerberg's eponymous film of that name. The Adagietto movement of **Mahler**'s Symphony No. 5 became indelibly linked in popular imagination with sequences in *Death in Venice* (1971), directed by Luchino Visconti. One of the most popular – and controversial – uses of pre-existing music was Walt Disney's Fantasia (1940) – and the recent *Fantasia 2000* – whose cartoon treatment of **Stravinsky**'s *The Rite of Spring* induced contempt from the composer.

POST-PRODUCTION

After a conventional CD recording session comes the post-production session, in which the recorded sounds are analysed, mixed and edited. The mixing involves making precise adjustments to the relative loudness and tone quality of individual instruments and different parts of the music. This is achieved using a mixing desk – a large sloping console, often with dozens of sets of controls.

Editing is an aspect of post-production in classical music recording that receives little attention. This is the process in which the various 'takes' from the recording session are selected and assembled. Even a solo can be constructed in this way to form a seamless musical line from different versions of the same melody. In the days of analogue recording, it was the task of the recording engineer physically to cut and splice pieces of magnetic tape to string all the best bits together. Now the engineer carries out this task using digital editing software on a computer. The result is a second recording, the 'master', which is then used to press the CDs.

collage ▶ p. 357 mono ▶ p. 360

(BL) Disney's **Fantasia**
Stravinsky was famously unimpressed with the use of his music in Fantasia.
(TL) Recording Studio
Recording pieces of music extends the life of a performance and widens its audience.
(TR) Early Recordings
Edward Elgar, conducting the first recording of his Carrisma *in 1914.*
(BR) Ute Lemper
The singer recording at the famous Abbey Road Studios in London.

MICROPHONES AND SINGING PRACTICE

No factor has had a more profound influence on singing practice in the twentieth century than the use of microphones. Just as recording equipment and the acoustics of a space can alter the sound of instrumental music, so the apparent nature of the singing voice can be changed. The distance between the singer and the microphone makes a huge difference and singers have had to master a new skill called 'mike technique' – the moving towards and away from the microphone for loud and soft passages. This technique means that singers do not need to produce as much volume to be heard, and allows them to retain the best qualities of quieter singing when singing louder passages.

Recorded Versus Live Vocal Performances

It has always been the case that different voices and venues suit different kinds of music, but with the increasing use of microphones in live performance, hard and fast assumptions about voices and venues are being challenged. Singers were traditionally expected to have been trained to project their voices and would specialize in the repertory which suited their voice type. Singers with reputations based on smaller venues and studio work, however, are sometimes encouraged to appear, using discrete microphones, in large opera-houses and perform works for which their voices are not suited. Such techniques are controversial; some singers are believed to be incapable of effectively reproducing recorded performances on stage.

that allow us to detect this are the sound waves, or reverberations, reflected from the inside surfaces of the room in which the music is played. Music is often suited to a particular location (much was written with a specific venue in mind) and it is possible to simulate 'reverb' in a recording studio so that the music sounds, for example, as though it is being played in a large church rather than a small studio. However, this technique is disliked by a number of classical musicians and listeners who want recordings to sound more authentic and less artificial.

The alternative, preferred by many musicians, is to set up the equipment and make recordings 'on location'. Halls and churches with good acoustics are regularly used for this purpose. Recording engineers are aware that the acoustics of recording spaces vary according to the size, shape and materials used in the buildings. Victorian plaster and a rectangular hall give a rounded acoustic which can suit a chamber ensemble well. High ceilings can enhance a large orchestra and chorus performing a work from the late Romantic repertory.

MUSIC IN FILMS

In cinema's infancy, films were silent, whereas audiences and early projecting machinery were, by contrast, noisy. Film was also a new art form and there was a need to explain what was happening. Live musical accompaniment helped to alleviate these problems and was initially improvised by a solo pianist or organist. Producers soon recognized that music could play a vital role in conveying emotional and narrative force in films. The pioneer director D.W. Griffith collaborated on the score for his own milestone epic, *The Birth of a Nation* (1915). Major silent films were often released with a score of either commissioned or library music which, in large city cinemas, would be played live by a full orchestra.

The commercial success of pre-recorded synchronized film sound was heralded by *The Jazz Singer* in 1927. Early synchronized film music was little more than aural wallpaper, usually comprising arrangements of pre-existing compositions. By the mid 1930s, original music was being composed for most American and European feature films and the technique of synchronizing music with moving images became a new discipline for composers and musicians alike.

COMPOSING AND RECORDING A FILM SCORE

Although a composer is likely to be commissioned before the completion of the film, the real work starts when the composer views the initial edit of the film with the editor and director, noting where music is required and what its function will be. The beginning of each musical passage is called a 'cue' and is marked on a videotape so that it appears onscreen. The composer then works alone, moulding the music to fit the cues on the videotape. The composition process often continues to be collaborative as both the edited film and the score undergo further refinement.

To record a full orchestral score requires a large studio or 'sound stage'. The film is projected so that the conductor and musicians can see the cues marked on the film. These appear as diagonal lines that move across the screen, allowing the performers to anticipate when a cue is coming. Although much film music still traditionally uses musical language associated with the late Romantic period and employs a full orchestra to record it, scores can call for all kinds of instrumentation and ensemble. Electronic and synthesized sound is increasingly used, often modified so that music and other sound effects are combined to form a sound **collage**.

Arnold ▶ p. 284 Copland ▶ p. 288 Ligeti ▶ p. 326 Mahler ▶ p. 250 Mozart ▶ p. 144 Saint-Saëns ▶ p. 256 R. Strauss ▶ p. 258 Stravinsky ▶ p. 280 Thomson ▶ p. 298 Walton ▶ p. 299

Twentieth-century Instruments and Inventions

Varèse was particularly interested in the sounds of the modern urban world. His music takes a sound world derived from factories and industrialization and turns them into music. But it took the off-beat genius of Ligeti to compose a work entirely for special effects: his *Poème symphonique* (1962) has passed into musical folklore as the piece of music written for 100 wind-up metronomes that tick away at different speeds, gradually winding down until there is only one, and finally silence.

Crockery is thrown into a dustbin in Ligeti's opera *Le Grand Macabre* (1977), which also scores 12 car horns (the recapitulation is for 12 doorbells). Car keys have been jingled, paper bags burst, telephones rung, transistor radios tuned to different frequencies and an enormous range of objects have been variously rubbed, rattled and banged together. The American Harry Partch (1901–74) developed an entire collection of novel percussion instruments, using bamboo, glass and other materials. The conservative reader, disregarding the long history of such experiments, might question their sense and thus the value of the music containing them, but the saxophone in the age of Richard Strauss and the oboe in the age of **J. S. Bach** were novelties with an uncertain future. The fact is that a creative age is an age of experiment.

Musique Concrète

The tape recorder, invented in 1935, had been used early on to record concerts by the Berlin Philharmonic, but it was not until 1948 that Pierre Schaeffer, a technician at the Radiodiffusion Française studio in Paris, conceived his *Etude aux chemins de fer*. This was the first piece of *musique concrète*, an experimental technique that used a tape recorder to combine pre-recorded sounds – natural as well as musical – to make musical compositions. The tape recorder itself became a musical instrument on which sounds were edited, played backwards and speeded up and down. Pierre Henry (b. 1927) was a prolific composer of *musique concrète* and collaborated with Schaeffer on many compositions.

Varèse had stopped writing before World War II, waiting for technology to catch up with his ambitions. In 1953, he was presented with a tape recorder and returned to composition, collecting sounds for the tape sections of his *Déserts* (1954), for ensemble and tape. Two years after its première, *Poème électronique* (1956) was performed over 350 loudspeakers in a Le Corbusier-designed pavilion at the 1958 Brussels world exhibition.

Radio Stations and Studios

From the 1950s, several composers began to discover the compositional possibilities in the technology of radio stations and specialized studios. Important centres were: Columbia-Princeton Electronic Music Center, New York, founded in 1951 by Vladimir Ussachevsky and Otto Luening; Studio für Elektronische Musik, Cologne, established by Herbert Eimert in 1951; Studio di Fonologia, Milan, established in 1953 and used by many avant-garde composers including **Berio**, **Pousseur**, **Nono** and **Cage**; Institut de Recherche et de Coordination Acoustique/Musique (IRCAM), Paris, established in 1976 under the direction of **Boulez**.

Roberto Gerhard's (1896–1970) Third Symphony ('Collages', 1960) incorporated sounds recorded in the composer's garden, assisted by the BBC's Radiophonic Workshop in London. Other fruits of collaborations with radio stations include Berio's *Visage* (1961), which combined synthesized sounds with the electronically treated voice of his wife, the soprano Cathy Berberian.

Computers

From the 1980s, the new sound-worlds discovered by **Stockhausen** and others, using tape recorders and recording studio equipment, began to be further extended by the use of computers. The computer enables composers to examine and modify their work in unprecedented detail. Whereas the synthesizer can control pitch and timbre with ease, the computer can go a stage further and control musical time. IRCAM in Paris is an important centre for advanced music computing and many composers, including Berio, have used its facilities. For his opera *The Mask of Orpheus*, **Birtwistle** used the IRCAM computer to construct six taped inserts for use in performance, transforming notes originally played on a harp into enormous percussion sounds like bongos, bass drums, marimbas and vibraphones.

Marimba

A type of xylophone, the marimba is a percussion instrument. The percussionist strikes a row (or two rows) of wooden blocks – laid out like a keyboard – beneath which are attached a series of echo chambers that resonate the sound. The compass of the instrument varies, but generally covers three or four chromatic octaves from the C below middle C. Music written for this range will move between bass and treble clefs, or may use both, like piano music, for which the player can use four mallets to play chords. The player uses mallets bound in yarn, sometimes rubber beaters, as hard sticks will damage the bars.

The instrument originated in Africa, where it used calabashes as resonators. Possibly because of the trans-atlantic slave trade, the marimba reached Latin America, where it acquired enormous popularity. Marimbas began to be manufactured in the US in 1910. These instruments used stopped metal tubes of graduated lengths as resonators.

(BL) Karlheinz Stockhausen
Stockhausen was among the first composers to use tapes and recording equipment in composition.
(TL) Gyorgy Ligeti
Ligeti's Poème symphonique *was written for 100 wind-up metronomes.*
(R) Harmonica
Concertos have been written for the harmonica by Vaughan Williams and Milhaud.

microtone ▶ p. 360 music theatre ▶ p. 360 quarter-tone ▶ p. 361 Adams ▶ p. 324 Babbitt ▶ p. 284 J. S. Bach ▶ p. 106 Berg ▶ p. 286 Berio ▶ p. 324
Birtwistle ▶ p. 324 Boulez ▶ p. 324 Cage ▶ p. 324 Gerhard ▶ p. 289 Glass ▶ p. 325 Grainger ▶ p. 290 Hindemith ▶ p. 290 Ibert ▶ p. 291 Messiaen ▶ p. 293

Initially joining the stock-in-trade of light entertainment, the marimba was picked up by **Percy Grainger** (1882–1961), who wrote for it a 10-minute fantasia on 'Campdown Races' called *Tribute to Foster* (1915). Koechlin opened the second movement of his Symphony No. 2 (1943–44) with a marimba solo. Milhaud wrote a concerto for marimba and orchestra in 1947, which required playing with two hammers in each hand. It is also to be heard in Richard Rodney Bennett's (b. 1936) first symphony, and in music by Japanese composers such as **Takemitsu** and Mayazumi.

Vibraphone

The vibraphone is a kind of electronic steel marimba, initially produced in the US in 1916. The player uses rubber-topped beaters to strike two rows of metal bars. The sound is not amplified electronically: it is amplified by the action of the resonators (like the marimba) which enhance the sound. Each resonator has a fan, and all are joined together along a long rod which is turned by a fan-belt. The belt is driven by an electric motor and the speed of the fans can be altered. This arrangement produces the vibraphone characteristic sound. The instrument has a pedal which controls duration. The compass is three octaves, running f to f'''. Having begun life in the dance orchestra, the vibraphone forms part of the instrumentation of **Berg**'s opera *Lulu* (1934) and later Walton's Cello Concerto (1956). In his *Le marteau sans maître* ('The Masterless Hammer'), Boulez wrote for vibraphone and the the xylorimba, a composite of the xylophone and marimba, with an extended range.

ELECTRONIC INSTRUMENTS OF THE TWENTIETH CENTURY

The synthesizer has become hugely influential since the 1960s, but it had many antecedents in twentieth-century electronic instruments.

The theremin, invented in 1920 by the Russian Lev Theremin, consists of a box containing thermionic valves producing ethereal oscillations which were modified by moving a hand around an attached antenna.

The ondes martenot was first demonstrated in 1928 by the French inventor Maurice Martenot. It produced oscillating frequencies in a similar way to the theremin. **Messiaen** used its disembodied sounds in his *Trois Petites Liturgies de la Présence Divine* ('Three Small Liturgies of the Divine Presence', 1944).

The trautonium was introduced by the German Friedrich Trautwein in 1930, assisted by Oskar Sala who became the instrument's virtuoso. Tones were produced by touching a fingerboard, altering the pitch of the oscillation, which was then amplified through a loudspeaker. **Hindemith** was inspired to write a *Concertino for Trautonium and Strings* (1931).

The electric organ emerged in the early twentieth century, originally designed as a compact substitute for the larger pipe organ. The best-known of its type is the Hammond organ, patented by its American inventor Laurens Hammond in 1934. It can be heard in Stockhausen's *Momente* (1965) and **Tavener**'s *The Whale* (1966).

Harmonica

A small free-reed instrument, the harmonica, or mouth organ, is placed between the lips and moved to and fro to reach the rows of channels which house vibrating reeds, played by blowing into it. The arrival of the Chinese sheng in Europe in the eighteenth century encouraged a great deal of experimentation with free-reed instruments. In 1821, Christian Friedrich Ludwig Buschmann (1805–64) built such an instrument, the *Mundäoline*, with 15 reeds. Intended merely as a pitch pipe, used to tune instruments, it turned out to be capable of being played itself. A German clockmaker began manufacturing small numbers of Buschmann's invention: a hand-carved wooden body holding 'reeds' made out of beaten brass wire and fitted into brass or bronze reed plates. A fully chromatic (12-note) harmonica was developed in the 1920s and

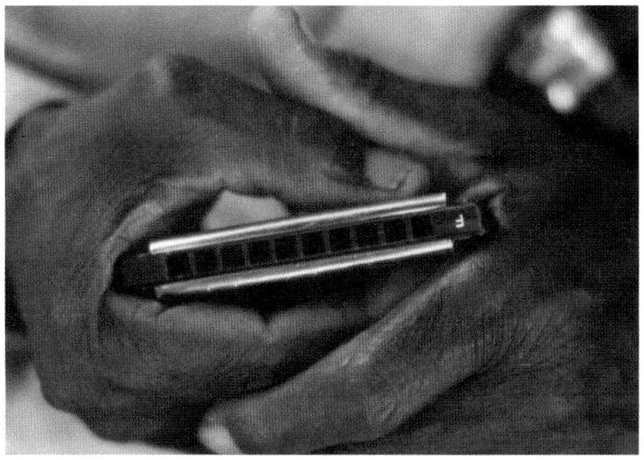

achieved fame in the hands of Larry Adler (b. 1914). Concertos have been written for the instrument by Vaughan Williams, Milhaud, Arnold and many others.

Synthesizer

The world's first synthesizer was the American RCA Mk I, made in 1951, whose bulk occupied a laboratory. To play it, composers such as **Babbitt** had to tap in punched-tape instructions – there was no keyboard. In 1964, Robert Moog (b. 1934) developed the first commercially successful synthesizer. It was capable of generating a wide range of sounds but was monophonic – able to sound only one key at a time. Walter (later Wendy) Carlos popularized the instrument with her record *Switched on Bach* (1968). From the 1970s ever more sophisticated and miniaturized polyphonic instruments were developed. Tristan Murail's (b. 1947) *Les Sept Paroles* ('The Seven Last Words', 1986–89), written in **quarter-tones**, uses the synthesizer's ability to play **microtones** – intervals smaller than the modern Western semi-tone. **Adams**'s *The Wound Dresser* (1988), **Reich**'s *The Cave* (1989–93) and a host of works by **Glass** also make significant use of the synthesizer.

SPECIAL EFFECTS

The twentieth century has seen a wealth of special effects employed in music, beginning with the *intonarumori* ('noise intoners') invented by Luigi Russolo. A football rattle (called a 'bird scare' by the composer) was required by Havergal Brian (1876–1972) for his Gothic Symphony No. 1 (1927). The sound of dragging chains is called for in **Schoenberg**'s mammoth choral work *Gurrelieder* ('Songs of Gurre', 1912). The typewriter has made several musical appearances, for instance in **Satie**'s *Parade* (1917). **Ibert**'s *Divertissement* includes a role for police and sports whistles. **Milhaud** required a saw to be struck with a beater in his *Cinq Etudes* op. 63 (1920) for piano and orchestra. His *Les Choëphores* ('The Libation Bearers', 1915) demands rushing wind created by a barrel cranked round at speed inside a canvas loop; other wind machines are to be found in Richard Strauss's *Don Quixote* (1896–97), Schoenberg's visionary *Jakobsleiter* (1917–22) and **Vaughan Williams**'s bleak *Sinfonia Antarctica* (1953).

The last work began life as a film score (*Scott of the Antarctic*, 1952) and certainly the rise in importance of the special effect is linked to the central importance of **music theatre** in the twentieth-century repertory. The percussionist in any production of **Poulenc**'s *Dialogues des Carmelites* (1953–56) is likely to find him- or herself visiting the local builders' yard in search of the means to produce the sound of the guillotine. After emigrating to New York, the radical Franco-American composer Varèse wrote for a battery of unusual percussion effects in his seminal *Ionisation* (1933), including chains, anvils and wailing sirens.

Milhaud ▶ p. 293 Nono p. 327 Poulenc p. 294 Pousseur ▶ p. 328 Reich ▶ p. 328 Satie ▶ p. 295 Schoenberg ▶ p. 295 Stockhausen ▶ p. 329 Takemitsu ▶ p. 329 Tavener ▶ p. 329 Varèse ▶ p. 298 Vaughan Williams ▶ p. 298

The Late 20th Century

LISTENING GUIDE

At the beginning of the twentieth century no one would have been able to predict the shock of Stravinsky's *The Rite of Spring*, which arrived only 13 years later. At the mid-point of the century some theorists and composers insisted that the only logical way forward for the art of music was to take the invention of serialism as a starting-point. Many composers ignored this or, while respecting Schoenberg, found his methods irrelevant to them; others reacted angrily against the idea of serialism and its developments becoming a rigid orthodoxy. The result by the end of the century was a plethora of styles with no perceptible mainstream. It is not even possible to isolate a number of identifiable 'schools', into which a majority of late twentieth-century composers can be conveniently categorized. The four works described here can at best be regarded as indications of the extraordinary variety of music our time has produced. Each is a planet from which a whole constellation of different music can not only be glimpsed but explored. There has never been a time in human history when the variety of new music waiting to be explored has been richer.

Pierre Boulez

Le marteau sans maître (1953–55)

SCORING: alto voice, alto flute, xylorimba, vibraphone, guitar, viola, percussion.
EXCERPT: fourth movement, 'Bourreaux de solitude' (see Recommended CD)

Le marteau sans maître ('The Masterless Hammer' – the title is from a collection of surrealist poems by René Char) was first performed in 1955 and soon recognized as the crucial score of its period. Stravinsky, not much given to praising the work of other living composers, admired it unreservedly. On the printed page it occasionally looks superficially like the music of **Webern**; its sound-world distantly evokes **Ravel**; in all other respects it is unprecedented.

It calls, very unusually, for alto voice and a group of instruments that play mostly in the alto register. Each movement is differently scored, all seven musicians appearing continuously in only one of them. The nine movements unfold in three interlocked 'cycles', each associated with a short poem by Char. *Bourreaux de solitude* ('Executioners of Solitude'), for example, has a vocal setting and three instrumental 'commentaries' upon it; *L'artisanat furieux* ('The Furious Handicraft') has a separate prelude and postlude; *Bel édifice et les pressentiments* ('Fine Building and Premonitions') appears as a 'first version' and a 'double'.

RECOMMENDED CD

Le marteau sans maître: Jeanne Deroubaix, instrumental ensemble/Pierre Boulez. Recorded in 1964. Adès 14.073-2, tracks 6–7 (duration 4'28").

One reason for Boulez's ingenious and very influential instrumentation was his desire to evoke non-European musics, not literally, but 'to enrich European vocabulary with non-European hearing'. Thus the xylorimba 'represents' the African balaphon, the vibraphone the Balinese gender, the guitar the Japanese koto, and so on (n.b.: the recommended CD is wrongly labelled and tracked. 'Bourreaux de solitude' occupies tracks 6 and 7).

The compositional technique of *Le marteau sans maître* is of huge complexity. Exhaustive development of the **serial** technique had led Boulez and others to a point at which it was possible to derive not only every pitch but every other element of a composition – note-values, rhythm, the loudness of each individual note, and so on – from a basic **note-row**. In such a work, however, despite maximum logical order, the composer might be seen to have minimum creative input. *Le marteau* escapes from this dilemma by confronting it head-on. The row itself is subject to serial processes in order to generate further rows; almost limitless harmonic possibilities are produced by subjecting these rows to numerical proportioning systems, and so on. The result is rigidly organized, yet requires the composer to make constant judgments and choices. Hence the impression it gives of almost manic intensity combined with strict scientific logic.

1. 0'00"
Angular but linear counterpoint for alto flute and viola; xylorimba, vibraphone and guitar more percussive.

2. 0'29"
First vocal entry, unaccompanied; counterpoint more bare; a long pause.

3. 1'13"
Instruments alone, their melodies now more amply curving.

4. 1'59"
Voice returns, leading to climax and pause.

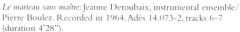

5. 3'14"
Epilogue and coda

note-row ▶ p. 360 serial music ▶ p. 362

György Ligeti

Horn Trio (1982)

SCORING: violin, horn, piano
EXCERPT: second movement, *Vivacissimo molto ritmico* (see Recommended CD)

Because of the disruption of World War II and the subsequent Communist régime in Hungary, Ligeti did not become aware of Western European musical Modernism until he was over 30. Until then he wrote in the folk-song-based, Bartók-influenced style that was officially approved in his country. He left Hungary during the 1956 uprising, arriving in Cologne in a period of vigorous and optimistic avant-garde activity in music, which he enthusiastically joined. He became especially well known for works in which dense webs of lines weave in micropolyphony (an example of this, *Apparitions*, became world-famous after Stanley Kubrick used part of it in his film *2001: A Space Odyssey*).

Ligeti retained a critical detachment from the avant-garde, however, and from the 1960s began to rediscover and redefine in a uniquely personal way first harmony, then melody. The Horn Trio dates from late in this process, after a long silence (partly due to illness) following his opera *Le grand macabre*. It is subtitled 'Hommage à Brahms', no doubt because **Brahms** wrote the first masterpiece for this combination of instruments, partly perhaps as a good-humoured side-swipe at the avant-garde (Ligeti's sharp sense of humour, including self-mockery, is audible in many of his works). He had become fascinated with the music of the American minimalists, **Reich** and **Riley**, and with the music for player-piano (able to perform music which was unplayable by human hands) of Conlon Nancarrow, as well as with the complex rhythms of African music. These interests pervade the Trio, but they are not incompatible with a rediscovery of roots in the past (a half-quotation from **Beethoven**) or of emotion: the last movement is a lament.

(TL) Arnold Schoenberg
Boulez developed Schoenberg's 12-note serial technique so that it was possible to produce every element of a composition.
***(R)* 2001: A Space Odyssey**
Ligetti's Apparitions *was widely recognized after being used in Kubrick's film.*

An epic drama of adventure and exploration
Space Station One: your first step in an Odyssey that will take you to the Moon, the planets and the distant stars.
STANLEY KUBRICK'S
2001: a space odyssey
KEIR DULLEA · GARY LOCKWOOD · STANLEY KUBRICK AND ARTHUR C. CLARKE
STANLEY KUBRICK · IN SUPER PANAVISION® · METROCOLOR
G GENERAL AUDIENCES
MGM
United Artists

RECOMMENDED CD

Horn Trio: Saschko Gawriloff (violin), Marie-Louise Neunecker (horn), Pierre-Laurent Aimard (piano). Recorded in 1996. Sony SK 62309. (Track 2, duration 5'28")

Ligeti describes this movement as 'folk music from non-existent peoples, as if Hungary, Romania and all the Balkan countries lay somewhere between Africa and the Caribbean'. The exoticism is increased by the horn being played in natural harmonics, sounding at times out of tune with its colleagues.

1. 0'00"
Pizzicato violin, then piano; is rhythm 4+4 or 3+3+2? Horn enters out of tune.

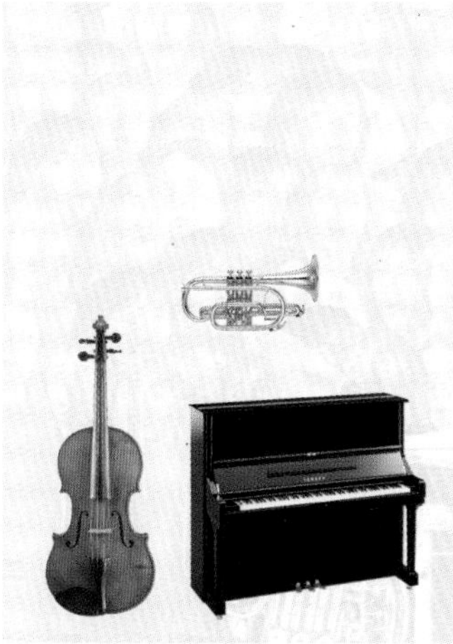

2. 1'21"
Violin introduces new melody: very nearly (but not quite) 'BACH' motto.

3. 1'51"
More lyrical, but still the ceaseless rhythm.

4. 3'12"
Horn gymnastics lead to even wilder activity.

5. 4'50"
Abrupt silence; violin's misquotation of Beethoven leads to eerie coda.

Beethoven ▶ p. 150 Boulez ▶ p. 324 Brahms ▶ p. 240 Ligeti ▶ p. 326 Ravel ▶ p. 294 Reich ▶ p. 328 Riley ▶ p. 328 Schoenberg ▶ p. 295 Stravinsky ▶ p. 280 Webern ▶ p. 299

RECOMMENDED CD

In C: Piano Circus. Recorded in 1990. Argo 430 380-2, track 2.

The score of *In C* is a single sheet of paper with 53 short melodic figures. All the performers work from this but may start when they wish and repeat each figure as often as they wish. Every player is of equal importance, no part is to be construed as 'accompaniment' or background. Any combination of melody instruments may be used; on the recommended CD they are three pianos (grand, amplified and upright), two harpsichords and vibraphone.

Terry Riley
In C (1964)

SCORING: any number of instruments capable of playing the specified pitches
EXCERPT: first five minutes approximately (see Recommended CD)

Riley studied music at the San Francisco State College and San Francisco Conservatoire, and his earliest compositions were influenced by Stockhausen. He had paid for his studies, however, by playing ragtime in a saloon. He soon became interested in improvised music and 'happenings' and made a serious study of Indian music. For his early solo keyboard and saxophone performances he used both tape loops (where a pre-recorded tape repeats a short figure endlessly, the live player adding further layers of music) and tape delay, where every phrase from the live player is repeated after a brief pause by a tape recorder. He subsequently developed this technique using the 'time-lag accumulator' where, by means of a bank of tape recorders, a solo performer can build up numerous layers of sound. Improvisation is central to his work, and very few of his pieces have any pre-determined form (though *A Rainbow in Curved Air* uses a rhythmic structure akin to the Indian *tal*). In this he differs from the other minimalists, Reich and **Glass**, both of whom have shown interest in articulating their longer works in formal structures. Riley has said that the fault with Western music is that it adds too much material; his own music investigates very simple material very exhaustively.

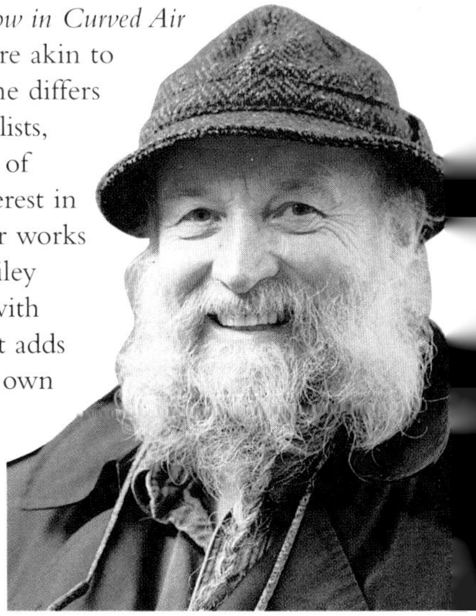

In his more recent work he has renewed his interest in Indian music, writing for the sitar and tabla, and has written extensively for string quartet. His influence on popular music has been widespread: the American groups Talking Heads and Soft Machine are two examples.

***(TL)* Talking Heads**
Talking Heads are one of the American rock groups to have been inspired by Riley's work.
***(TR)* BBC Philarmonic Orchestra**
The BBC Philarmonic have enabled some of the best recordings of a wide variety of music.
***(BR)* King Priam**
A production of Tippett's King Priam *at the Royal Opera House, London.*

1. 0'00"
Repeated octave Cs and regular pulse; will continue until end of performance.

2. 1'21"
First occurrence of a note shorter than a quaver.

3. 2'45"
Grace-notes and shorter note-values; overlaps contradict basic pulse.

4. 4'06"
Dissonance!

5. 4'41"
Descending phrase in longer note-values: suggestion of gamelan music.

Michael Tippett

Triple Concerto (1978–79)

SCORING (brackets indicate doublings): solo violin, viola and cello. Flute (piccolo, alto flute), oboe, cor anglais (bass oboe), 2 clarinets, 2 bass clarinets, bassoon, contra-bassoon, 4 horns, 2 trumpets, 2 trombones, harp, celesta, timpani, percussion (including 5 gongs, vibraphone, glockenspiel, marimba, tubular bells), strings
EXCERPT: central section (score no. 79)

In a famous definition of what composers are for, Tippett said that their function was 'to create images from the depths of the imagination and to give them form ... for it is only through images that the inner world communicates at all. Images of vigour for a decadent period, images of calm for one too violent. Images of reconciliation for worlds torn by division. And in an age of mediocrity and shattered dreams, images of abounding, generous, exuberant beauty'. Making such images was a constant in his long life's work, together with an undimmed inquisitiveness which led him to enrich his music with elements from a bewildering variety of sources. At the deepest level they were Beethoven, jazz, Stravinsky and the English madrigal, but at the end of his life he was excitedly discovering rap and the amplified guitar, using the sound of brake-drums struck with a hammer and the recently invented rototoms (drums whose pitch can instantly be changed by rotating them).

His music often confronted contemporary issues, from the early *A Child of Our Time*, an oratorio prompted by the Nazi persecution of the Jews, to his late opera *New Year*, which deals with relationships broken by inner-city violence and racial conflict. But images of 'generous, exuberant beauty' occur in all of them, and in the Triple Concerto, a late work that uses many of the discoveries he had made in 50 years of composing, he also recaptures the radiant lyricism of his first opera, *The Midsummer Marriage*, completed 20 years earlier.

RECOMMENDED CD

Triple Concerto: Ernst Kovacic (violin), Gerard Caussé (viola), Alexander Baillie (cello). BBC Philharmonic Orchestra/Sir Michael Tippett. Recorded in 1990. Nimbus NI 5301 (Track 3, duration 9'40")

While preparing to write the Triple Concerto, and considering the problem of treating its soloists as individuals, not as a string trio, Tippett visited Java for the first time, and the gamelan music he heard there gave the concerto's central movement the character of an exotic 'paradise garden'. The form of the concerto – three movements separated by interludes – is reflected in the five-part structure of this movement.

1. 0'00"
Rapturous lyricism from soloists; dark background with xylophone and gongs.

2. 1'32"
First interlude: cello and bass oboe duet. Impassioned cello leads into ...

3. 3'32"
... main theme in woodwind, rhapsodic commentary from soloists. Fanfares herald ...

4. 5'14"
... second interlude: violin and alto flute duet. Gamelan-like passage and violin/viola duet introduce ...

5. 7'56"
... main theme, now surrounded by gong and bell sounds.

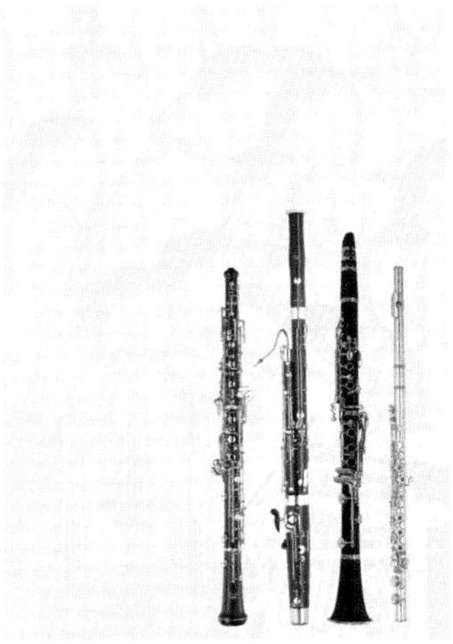

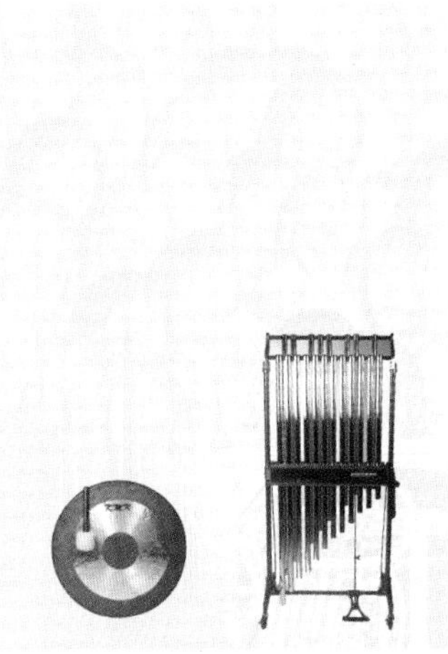

Glass ▶ p. 325 Riley ▶ p. 328 Tippett ▶ p. 330

GLOSSARY

***An asterisk indicates a cross-reference to another entry in the Glossary.**

accent

A stress on a single note caused by increased loudness, by a melodic leap, by a rhythmic feature such as syncopation, or by a combination of any or all of these elements.

acoustics

The science of acoustics is about the way sound is generated, the way it travels through the air, and the way it is perceived by listeners. A distinction is usually made between sounds of definite pitch (like the low C that can be played on the deepest-sounding string of a cello) and noise (like the apparently pitchless sound of clashed cymbals). Both types of sound are made by causing the instrument to vibrate (or by making a column of air vibrate in a wind instrument). These vibrations are then converted into compressions and decompressions of the surrounding air that spread out in all directions like waves made by a stone thrown in a pond. The sound is then modified by the enclosed space in which the instrumentalist is performing (a small, heavily furnished room will deaden the sound, a large empty hall will amplify it). When sound waves, direct and reflected, reach the eardrums of a listener they are made to vibrate in sympathy with this modified sound. Finally, nerves convert the vibrations of the eardrums into electrochemical impulses which the brain decodes as a particular type of sound.

PITCH

Pitch (the highness or lowness of a sound) is determined by frequency (the number of vibrations per second, scientifically expressed as cycles per second or cps). Vibrating at 64 cps the deepest string of a cello generates a sound that is heard as the C two *octaves below middle C (**Example 2d**). Other things being equal, a string half the length of this cello string will vibrate twice as fast (128 cps), generating a sound exactly an octave above the longer string. A cellist can play this higher note by pressing the C string firmly halfway along its length so that only half of it is free to vibrate. A whole range of pitches can be played on the same string by shortening it to a greater or lesser extent in this way, and the frequency will always be proportional to the vibrating length of the string.

These principles apply to many other instruments. For instance a half-size flute (the piccolo) has a range of notes pitched an octave above that of an ordinary flute because the column of air inside it vibrates twice as fast as that in a full size flute. And just as a cellist can effectively shorten the length of a string by stopping it, so a flautist can shorten the vibrating column of air by progressively opening holes in the instrument so as to produce a complete *chromatic scale.

The weight and tension of a string also help determine its pitch. The greater the weight the lower the basic pitch will be, and the greater the tension the higher it will be. This explains why four strings of equal length on a cello sound at different pitches. The lowest string has the greatest weight (it actually looks fatter than the others), and the cellist tunes the strings to C, G, d and a by adjusting their tensions with tuning pegs. The same principles apply to other instruments. For instance a heavy gong makes a deeper sound than a light cymbal of the same size, and a timpanist can adjust the tension of a drum's membrane, so altering the pitch of the instrument. (*See melody.*)

TIMBRE AND HARMONICS

Everyone can distinguish between the tone colour of a cello and a piano, even when they are playing notes of the same pitch. The most important factor that contributes to this difference in timbre is the harmonic content of each note. When a string is bowed or struck by a felted hammer, it not only vibrates along its whole length to generate the pitch of a particular note (**Example 2e**), it simultaneously vibrates in halves (**Example 2f**), in thirds (**Example 2g**) and in several other *modes. These vibrations generate subsidiary pitches (known as harmonics) that cannot normally be heard separately, but which are vital to the tone colour of the instrument. They are always pitched an octave, an octave and a fifth, two octaves and so on above the fundamental (the pitch generated by the string vibrating along its whole length). The harmonics thrown off by the C string of a cello or piano are shown in **Example 2d**. The presence of the fourth, fifth and sixth harmonics in the sound of a piano string can be verified by silently depressing and holding down the three notes labelled 'C major triad'. When the C two octaves below middle C is struck forcefully and released it will cease to sound almost immediately, but the notes of the triad, excited by harmonics 4, 5 and 6, will continue to sound. It is the relative strength of these harmonics which most determines the timbre of an instrument. If the fundamental is strong and the higher harmonics are weak or absent (as is the case in flute tone) the sound will be relatively pure. If the upper harmonics (especially the 'flat' seventh harmonic) are strong the sound will be more biting (as is the case in oboe tone).

The air inside wind instruments vibrates in much the same way as the vibrations that produce the harmonics on string instruments (**Example 2e–g**). Wind players depend on these harmonics in order to achieve a wide range of notes. Thus a trombonist can play seven notes of an ascending chromatic scale by progressively pulling the slide in (thus shortening the effective length of tubing). However, to extend the scale beyond these seven notes, both *embouchure and wind pressure have to be adjusted so that a set of harmonics can be produced above each of the seven notes played by altering the position of the slide. In this way a trombonist can play a chromatic scale extending over some three octaves. (*See texture.*)

acte de ballet

An eighteenth-century French opera-cum-ballet in one act.

adagio

1. At a slow *tempo.
2. A slow movement.

air

A song, or a song-like instrumental composition such as Bach's 'Air on the G String'. The term covers a multitude of vocal genres ranging from simple songs like Purcell's 'Fairest Isle' to elaborate *arias such as 'The Trumpet Shall Sound' from Handel's *Messiah*.

aleatory music

Music wholly or partially governed by chance such as the indeterminacy evident in Cage's *Music of Changes* (1952). (*See Styles and Forms: Late Twentieth Century.*)

alto

1. A low female voice (*contralto) or a high male voice (*countertenor).
2. The second highest part in a four-part instrumental composition.

anthem

1. A setting of an English text sung by the choir (full anthem) or by choir and soloists (verse anthem) at the end of the Anglican offices of Matins and Evensong.
2. A patriotic hymn.

antiphon

A *plainsong setting of a Latin text derived from a psalm or canticle and sung before and after it. Britten frames his *Ceremony of Carols* in this way with the Christmas antiphon *Hodie Christus natus est.*

antiphonal music

1. Singing in which two groups of voices alternate (as they do in the chanting of psalms in monastic churches and Anglican cathedrals).
2. Similar alternations of groups of instruments (as in Vaughan Williams's *Fantasia on a Theme of Thomas Tallis*).

(*See Styles and Forms: Renaissance.*)

aria

1. *Air.
2. A self-contained solo song with instrumental accompaniment in a *cantata, *opera, *oratorio or *Passion.
3. An independent solo song known as a concert aria.

(*See Styles and Forms: Early Baroque.*)

ariette

1. In early eighteenth-century France, a virtuoso operatic solo like its Italian counterpart, the *aria.
2. In the late eighteenth century, a song from a comic *opera.

arioso

1. A passage of measured, song-like music in a *recitative.
2. An independent solo vocal movement that is shorter and less complex than an *aria (for example 'Betrachte meine Seel' from Bach's *St John Passion*).

arpeggio

The notes of a *chord performed successively rather than simultaneously. The notes in bar 3 of **Example 6a** form an arpeggio of the chord of C major.

atonality

Music in which no one *pitch assumes greater importance than another, so that it is impossible to feel a sense of *tonality. **Example 10** is atonal.
(*See Styles and Forms: Modern.*)

augmentation, diminution

The recurrence of a theme in uniformly longer (augmentation) or shorter (diminution) note-values. The devices are commonly used in music based on imitation, including *fugue and *ricercare.

ballade

One of the three **formes fixes* in fourteenth- and fifteenth-century French music; the ballade normally has three stanzas each of seven or eight lines with the same rhyme and metre, and the same refrain.

ballet de cour

An entertainment of the sixteenth- and seventeenth-century French court. It consisted of an *overture followed by sets of dances, each introduced by a spoken prologue or *recitative.

bar

A unit of musical time defined by bar lines (vertical lines extending over one or more staves). The space between two bar lines (see **Example 3**).

bass

1. The lowest male voice.
2. The lowest-sounding part of a composition for voices, instruments or both.

basso continuo

A continuous bass part in baroque ensemble music. It forms the basis for *chords improvised by harmony instruments such as lutes, harpsichords or organs. The bass melody can itself be reinforced by instruments such as cellos or bassoons.
(*See Styles and Forms: Early Baroque.*)

bel canto

'Beautiful singing': an Italian term originating in the nineteenth century and referring back to a supposed golden age of vocal production coinciding with the flowering of the eighteenth-century operatic *aria.

binary form

Two-part form in which a decisive *cadence marks the end of each of the two sections (both of them repeated). The structure is often clarified by a *modulation to a related key at the end of the first section, with a return to the original key in the second section. The theme of the variations in Schubert's 'Trout' Quintet is a binary-form structure of this type.

bitonality

The use of two *keys simultaneously. The term is often used more loosely to mean the simultaneous use of chords from two different keys. For instance, at the start of Part 2 of Stravinsky's ballet *Petrouchka*, a clarinet plays an *arpeggio of C major (C, E, G, C) at the same time as another clarinet plays an arpeggio of F sharp major (A#, C#, F# A#).

broken consort

See consort.

buffa, buffo

'Comical'. **Opera buffa* is the comic antithesis of eighteenth-century **opera seria*, while a *basso buffo* might well sing a comic patter song such as Figaro's famous 'Largo al factotum' from Rossini's *Barber of Seville*.

cabaret

A satirical singing and dancing entertainment staged in venues such as night clubs. 'Mack the Knife' from Weill's *Threepenny Opera* is a stylized version of a cabaret song which achieved universal popularity in the context of the stage and screen versions of Isherwood's *Goodbye to Berlin* (appropriately re-named *Cabaret*).

caccia

Fourteenth-century Italian musical style, often taking the form of dialogue, characterized by its realistic thematic content.

cadence, cadenza

A point of repose in a *melody or *harmonic progression. A *phrase ending on the *tonic suggests closure, while a phrase ending on any other note suggests partial closure. This is illustrated in the two phrases of **Example 9a** in which accompanying chords reinforce these melodic effects. In **Example 9b**, however, the effect of the tonic note at the end of phrase 1 is negated by the accompanying *chord. (*See harmony.*)

canon

A musical device in which a *melody heard in one part is repeated note for note in a second part, while the melody of the first part continues to unfold. This *imitative process continues until the melody of the first part ends. In a canon for more than two voices, all of them repeat the melody of the first part. 'Three Blind Mice' is a special type of canon (a round), in which each voice can return to the beginning and repeat the melody ad infinitum.

cantabile

In a singing style. Smoothly flowing and expressive.

cantata

An instrumental and vocal genre, usually containing *recitatives and *arias. Lutheran cantatas were closely related to the prescribed biblical readings and sermon that preceded and followed them. In most of Bach's cantatas a sequence of recitatives and arias is framed by a *polyphonic chorus (often based on a *chorale melody associated with a particular day of the church's year) and a simple four-part harmonization of the same melody.
(*See Styles and Forms: Late Baroque.*)

cantus firmus

A previously composed melody that is heard in long notes in one voice part of a *polyphonic composition. Many settings of the Mass are based on sacred or secular melodies treated in this way, while Lutheran *cantata movements often make similar use of *chorale melodies.

canzona

The sixteenth-century canzona (lit. 'a song') began life as an instrumental transcription of the French chanson. Later, as a freely composed instrumental piece, it still retained the sectional structure of the chanson and some of its rhythmic fingerprints.

capriccio

A caprice. Any composition which defeats normal expectations. Thus the last movement of Bach's Keyboard Partita (*suite) in C minor ends with a capriccio in 2/4 time instead of the expected gigue in compound time.

castrato
An emasculated male capable of singing operatic *soprano or *alto parts such as that of the eponymous hero of Handel's *Julius Caesar*.

chaconne
Originally a dance in triple time with a repeating bass melody (*ground bass), the chaconne later lost its function as a dance, but retained the original metre and variation form.

chamber music
Music for two or more solo instruments designed for domestic performance.
(*See Styles and Forms: Late Romantic.*)

chanson
'Song'. Normally applied to the secular tradition of fifteenth and sixteenth centuries.

chant
Any unaccompanied song of a simple and often repetitive nature, usually (like *plainchant) associated with religious celebrations.

chorale
A protestant hymn with German words and a melody designed for congregational singing. See **Example 9**. (*See Styles and Forms: Early Baroque.*)

chord
Three or more notes sounded simultaneously. Some say two notes form a chord, but most call this an *interval or a dyad. (*See harmony.*)

chromaticism
The use of notes foreign to the scale of the prevailing *key. Because they do not belong to the scale of F major (the prevailing key) the two notes marked with an asterisk in **Example 6a** are chromatic. (*See harmony.*)

coda
The final section of a movement or complete work. The original key is usually strongly emphasised to suggest finality.

collage
The simultaneous or successive combination of pre-existent music. The third movement of Berio's *Sinfonia* combines music from two of Mahler's symphonies with quotations from the music of Schoenberg, Debussy and Hindemith (among others).

coloratura
1. An elaborately ornamented *soprano song like that sung by the Queen of the Night in Mozart's *The Magic Flute*.
2. A virtuoso soprano capable of singing such music.

combinatorial tone row
A *tone row so constructed that, when the first six notes are transposed (moved to another *pitch level) and inverted (turned upside down), they produce the same set of pitches as the last six notes of the original row. **Example 10a** shows that the pitches of the cello melody below it form a 12-tone row that can be divided into two six-note sections (x and y). **Example 10c** shows x transposed down an octave and a third and inverted (the same intervals between successive notes are maintained, but they move in the opposite direction). This transposed inversion of x begins and ends with the same notes as those in the box on the bass staff of **Example 10b**. Between the G natural and A flat Schoenberg has verticalized notes 2–5 to form a *chord. This set of six pitches is the same as the set of six pitches (y) in the second half of Schoenberg's cello melody (though they are arranged in a different order and at different *octaves). Thus the transposed inversion of the first six-note segment of Schoenberg's row contains the same set of pitches as the last six notes of the same row (y).

comédie-ballet
A French opera-cum-ballet of the late seventeenth and early eighteenth centuries such as Lully's *Le bourgeois gentilhomme* (1670).

comédie-lyrique
One of the many types of *opera cultivated in eighteenth-century France, notably by Rameau, whose three-act *comédie-lyrique*, *Platée*, was first performed at Versailles in 1745.

commedia dell'arte
A comic entertainment including improvised songs. It originated in sixteenth-century Italy then spread throughout Europe. Some of the stock characters of the *commedia dell'arte* continued to appear in musical works through to the twentieth century (such as Punch in Stravinsky's *Pulcinella*, and Pedrolino the Clown in Schoenberg's *Pierrot Lunaire*).

concertato style
A style of the early Baroque era in which contrasting groups of instruments and/or voices alternated and combined. The variety of *textures produced by these forces was unified by a *continuo group.

Example 1

(a)

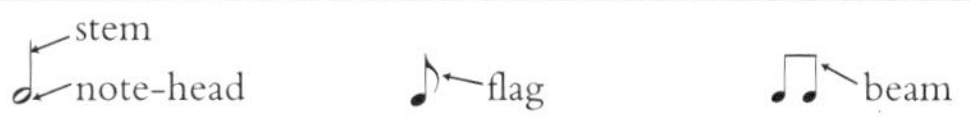

(b)

English names	Notes	American names	Rests
semibreve	(= +)	whole note	
dotted minium	(= +)	dotted half note	or
minium		half note	
crotchet		quarter note	
quaver	(=)	eighth note	
semiquaver	(=)	sixteenth note	
demisemiquaver	(=)	thirtysecond note	

Example 2

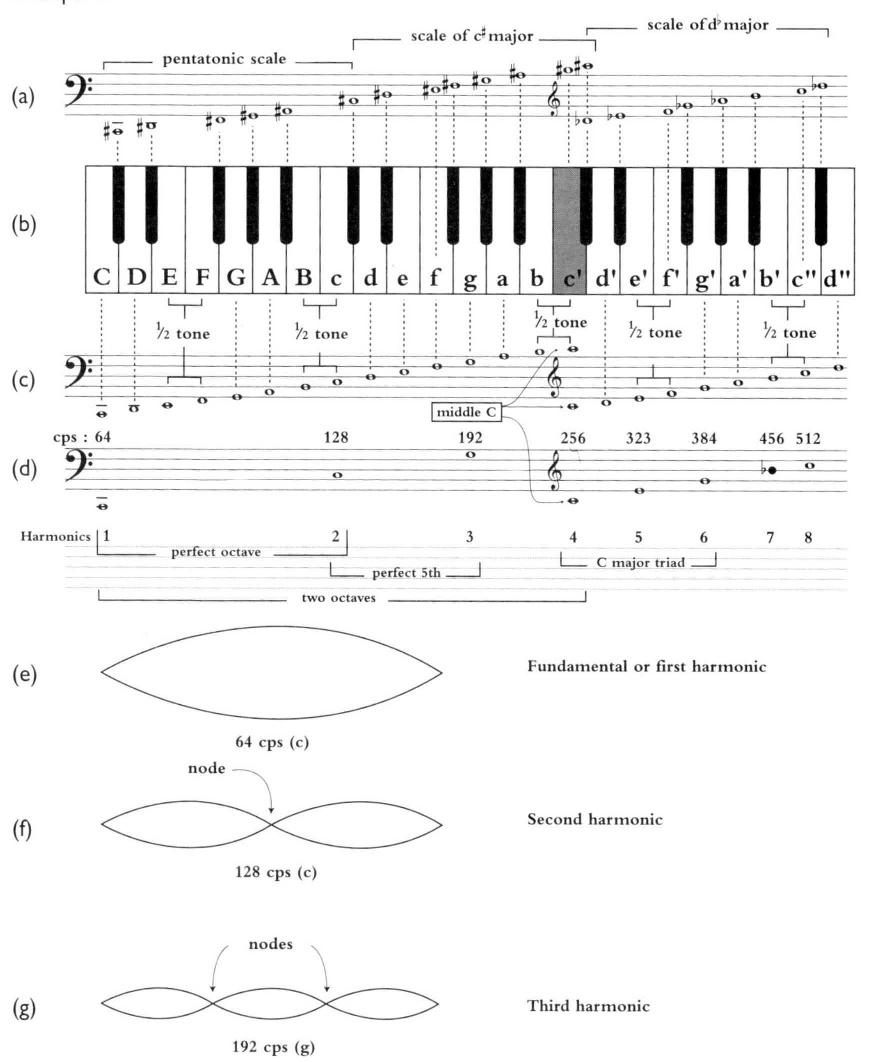

concertino
1. In a Baroque **concerto grosso*, a small group of soloists with *continuo.
2. In the nineteenth and twentieth centuries, a short concerto for one or more soloists and orchestra.

concerto
1. A Baroque composition in **concertato* style (some of Bach's cantatas are thus entitled).
2. A multi-movement instrumental composition for one or more soloists and orchestra (see **Example 6**).

(*See Styles and Forms: Early Baroque, Classical, Early Romantic.*)

concerto da camera, concerto da chiesa
A Baroque instrumental *concerto intended for performance in a secular venue (*da chiesa*) or a church (*da camera*).

concerto grosso
A Baroque instrumental *concerto contrasting a small group of soloists (**concertino*) with a larger string ensemble (**ripieno*), both supported by a *continuo group.
(*See Styles and Forms: Late Baroque.*)

concord, consonance
Two or more notes which together create a sense of repose (for example the last *chord of **Example 3**). The interval of an *octave has always been regarded as a concord, but some intervals now regarded as consonant were in earlier periods regarded as *discords.

consort, broken consort
A late Renaissance English term for an *ensemble of instruments. A whole consort was an ensemble of instruments of one family (such as viols), a broken consort an ensemble of instruments from different families (such as recorders and viols).

continuo
One or more accompanimental instruments playing from a **basso continuo*.

contralto
The lowest female voice.

counterpoint
The simultaneous combination of two or more *melodies. See **Example 3f** and the entry on texture. (*See Styles and Forms: Early Baroque.*)

countertenor
The highest male voice, equivalent in range to that of a *contralto. The tone is produced by tightening the vocal chords in such a way that they vibrate in shorter lengths than usual.

crescendo
A graduated increase in volume.

crook
On a brass instrument, a length of tubing which can be adjusted or replaced to alter the fundamental pitch of the instrument. On a bassoon, the bent metal tube that joins the body of the instrument to the reeds through which the player blows.

da capo
A direction requiring the performer to return to the beginning of the movement and repeat the first section. The *da capo* *aria is a *ternary structure (A–B–A) in which the repeat is rarely written out: instead the words *da capo* or the letters DC at the end of the second section are sufficient indication of the composer's intentions.

diatonic
Notes belonging to the *scale of the prevailing *key. All of the notes in **Example 9a** are diatonic since they all belong to the scale of C major.

diminuendo
A graduated reduction of volume.

diminution
See augmentation, diminution.

discord, dissonance
Two or more notes which together create a sense of tension that seeks resolution by movement to a *concord. In the chord on the eleventh beat of **Example 9a** the bass G natural is dissonant with the tenor A natural above it. The tension is resolved when the bass moves down to an F natural (a note that is concordant with the other three chord notes above it). Dissonance is relative. In any other context than *serial music the six-part *chord in the first bar of **Example 10** would sound extremely dissonant, but in these variations it sounds no more dissonant than most of the other chords in this piece.

displacement
In *serial music, the notion that any note of the series can be moved up or down one or more *octaves and still retain its original function in the *tone row. Thus the C sharp in the first chord of **Example 10b** and the C sharp in **Example 10c** are displaced by an octave but retain the same function in the row.

dissonance
See discord, dissonance.

divertissement
1. In seventeenth-century French *opera, a group of pieces performed within or between the acts.
2. In the late eighteenth century, an entertaining instrumental composition such as a divertimento, cassation or serenade.

division
A type of variation of the English Baroque era, in which the notes of a *melody were 'divided' by the substitution of two or more shorter notes for one long note. Thus a crotchet G in the original melody might become a quaver G and a quaver B in the division. See **Examples 3a–d**.

dominant
The fifth degree of a *diatonic scale (see **Example 4e**). As an adjective, the term can refer to the *key a fifth above the *tonic, or to a chord on the fifth degree (for example the last chord of **Example 9a**).

double stopping
On a string instrument, the performance of an *interval by pressing two strings with two left-hand fingers and bowing both strings simultaneously. The term is loosely applied to the performance of a two-note chord whether or not both strings are stopped.

drame lyrique
Expression used from the mid-1800s to describe French operas that do not fit neatly into the categories of **opera comique* or *grand opera*.

drone
A sustained note (most often in the bass), or two sustained notes (most often the *tonic and *dominant). On bagpipes the *melody is played on the chanter (a pipe with finger holes), while the drone pipes provide unavoidable sustained notes throughout the performance.

dynamics
Relative levels of volume ranging from *ff* (**fortissimo* or very loud) to *pp* (**pianissimo* or very soft). Some composers add extra letters to encourage extreme dynamic levels.

echos
A set of *melodic formulae associated with the eight tones of Byzantine ecclesiastical *chant.

embouchure
The shape and tension of the mouth, facial muscles and jaw when playing wind instruments.

ensemble
1. A group of two or more performers.
2. The degree of unanimity in group performance.
3. An operatic movement involving several characters and sometimes a chorus.

entr'acte
Music performed between the acts of an *opera or play.

entrée
1. A group of dances in a **ballet de cour*.
2. The entrance of an *operatic character, or the music for such an entrance.
3. The first movement of a *suite.

exposition
1. The first part of a fugue in which the *subject is stated in every part.
2. The first section of a movement in sonata form (a structure common in many *symphonies and *chamber works as well as *sonatas), containing all or most of the thematic material of the movement disposed in two chief keys.

eye music
Technique used in the fifteenth and sixteenth centuries to emphasize a non-musical meaning or emotion, such as sorrow by e.g. colouring the notes.

fantasia
An imaginative instrumental piece, consciously avoiding conventional forms and structures.

figured bass
A **basso continuo* part with figures beneath it indicating the *chords that should be played by one or more members of the *continuo group. Thus the figures 64 under a C indicate that, as well as the written C, an A (a sixth above C) and an F (a fourth above C) should also be played.

formes fixes
A group of forms popular in fourteenth-century French music and poetry, the three main *formes fixes* are *ballade, *rondeau and *virelai.

forte, fortissimo
Italian: loud, very loud (*f*, *ff*).

free reed
A tongue of metal in a wind instrument that is secured at one end only and so is free to vibrate according to its size and natural properties. A free reed is capable of sounding only one pitch, so free-reed instruments (such as a mouth organ) contain as many reeds as the number of pitches that can be played.

frottola
Piece from a secular repertory common in late fifteenth and early sixteenth century northern Italy. The frottole repertory favoured different poetic forms set in a variety of musical styles.

fugue
1. In the Middle Ages, a *canon.
2. In the Renaissance, *imitation.
3. A *contrapuntal movement in which a *melody (called the *subject) is heard alone in one part and is then imitated in turn by each of the other parts (usually a fourth or fifth up or down in relation to the previous entry). Having stated the subject, each part continues with a melody which is contrapuntally combined with the subject. The completion of the subject in the last part to enter marks the end of the fugal *exposition. What happens thereafter differs from one fugue to another, but the subject is likely to be heard again in different keys before returning to a final statement in the *tonic key. **Example 8** shows the opening bars of a fugue.

(See Styles and Forms: Early Baroque.)

Gebrauchsmusik
Music intended to fulfil a particular need. Thus there was no sonata for tuba until Hindemith wrote one to provide *chamber music for this neglected instrument.

glissando
A slide from one *pitch to another, encompassing many distinct pitches on a piano or harp, but producing continuous change in which individual pitches can not be distinguished on other string instruments and trombone.

grand motet
A *motet for large *ensembles of voices and instruments performed in the liturgies of the court chapel of Louis XIV and as a concert piece elsewhere in eighteenth-century France.

(See Styles and Forms: Early Baroque.)

ground bass
A variation form in which a repeating *phrase in the bass supports an evolving melody in an upper part.

(See chaconne.)

habanera
A dance of Cuban origin in moderate 2/4 time with a characteristic rhythm of a dotted quaver and semiquaver followed by two quavers (usually heard in the bass).

harmonics
1. Naturally occurring *pitches, the relative volumes of which largely determine the *timbres of various voices and instruments.
2. Notes produced on a string instrument by lightly touching one of the strings at one of a number of critical points (nodes) along its length so that, when the string is bowed or plucked, a very high-pitched silvery sound is produced (see **Examples 2e–f**).
3. Notes produced on wind instruments by altering the *embouchure and wind pressure. *(See acoustics.)*

harmony
TRIADS

Harmony is the sounding together of notes to produce a series of *chords. In Western music of the last three centuries most of these chords have consisted of *pitches derived from the superimposition of thirds above a bass note. **Example 9b** shows a *scale of C major with *triads (three-note chords) built in this way on the first, fourth, fifth and sixth degrees of the scale (chords I, IV, V and VI respectively). Arrows show that these triads can be expanded into four-note chords by repeating one of the pitches an *octave or two octaves away.

SPACING

Example 9a shows how the *intervals between the constituent notes of the same chord can be altered. Chord I is heard at the beginning and end of phrase 1. Both contain the pitches C, E and G, but in the first chord there is an octave between the two C naturals, whereas there are two octaves between them in the last chord. The first chord is said to be closely spaced because the chord notes are as close to each other as possible. The last is said to be widely spaced because the intervals between parts are a fifth or more.

INVERSIONS

Any note of a triad can be sounded in the bass. The chords in a box at the end of **Example 9b** show how chord I can be 'inverted' so E instead of C becomes the bass note. The arrow shows how Bach spreads out this inverted triad (chord Ib) in the penultimate chord of **Example 9a**. The same chord in a different spacing is used on the third beat of phrase 1.

PRIMARY TRIADS

Because chords I, IV and V and their inversions clearly establish tonality, they are known as primary triads. All but one of the chords in phrase 1 are derived from primary triads, so leaving no doubt about the key of C major that is already so clearly implied by the rising scale of the chorale melody. These chords also reinforce the melodic *cadences. The sense of closure engendered by the last two *melody notes of phrase 1 is reinforced by a perfect cadence (chords V and I). Similarly the sense of partial closure of the last two melody notes of phrase 2 is mirrored in the imperfect cadence formed by chords Ib and V.

DISCORDS

Chords can be built by the superimposition of thirds on all other degrees of the scale. A triad on the sixth degree (chord VI) is heard on the first beat of the penultimate bar. On the last beat of this bar a G natural (again a superimposed third) is added to the triad to form a four-note *discord (the interval between the bass note and the G natural being a dissonant seventh). Similar discords occur immediately before and after this chord.

FUNCTIONAL HARMONY

The harmonic progressions in **Example 9a** are said to be functional: every chord is related to its neighbours in a chain that extends from the tonic chord (heard twice at the start of **Example 9a**) to a conclusive return to the same chord. That goal is achieved in the first phrase, but the second phrase sounds incomplete precisely because it does not end on the tonic (the complete chorale does, of course, end on a tonic chord). Functional harmony is clearest when only primary triads are used, but a *tonal chord progression can include many other chords that function in similar ways to chords I, IV and V, as the following summary shows:

(a) The tonic chord - the eventual goal of all tonal harmonic progressions.

(b) Chords of *dominant function. These create a sense of tension that is released by resolution to the tonic. As well as the dominant chord itself, this category can include any chord containing the *leading note, for example chord VIIb (the third chord of phrase 1) contains the leading note and so functions as a dominant chord in relation to its immediate neighbours.

(c) Chords of *subdominant function. These can be considered as satellites of the dominant or the tonic. As well as the subdominant chord itself (the sixth chord of **Example 9a**), this category can include any chord (other than the tonic) that does not contain the leading note (for example all of the chords in the penultimate bar of **Example 9a**).

CHROMATIC HARMONY

Bach's harmony in **Example 9a** is entirely *diatonic. In another harmonisation of the same chorale melody (**Example 9c**) Bach introduces *chromatic chords. All of them (beats 3 and 4 of bars 2 and 4) can be regarded as chromatic secondary dominants of chords V, VI and II respectively. Since V of VI actually cadences on chord VI at the end of phrase 1, it is possible to view this progression as a brief *modulation to A minor, but the chromatic progression in phrase 2 leads to a clear cadence in the *home key, so these chromatic chords simply colour the C major tonality of the whole extract. Secondary dominants such as these are among the most common of a whole range of chromatic chords that composers used more and more frequently in the tonal harmony of the eighteenth and nineteenth centuries.

ATONAL HARMONY

In some twentieth-century music, chromatic harmony became so pervasive that it is impossible to detect any tonal centre. This is particularly true of *serial music in which chords are generated, not by the superimposition of thirds above the various degrees of a tonal scale, but by manipulations of *tone rows including all 12 chromatic pitches. For instance the six-note chord on the second beat of **Example 10b** is a verticalization of five pitches of one tone row (notes 1–5 in **Example 10c**) together with the second note of another (the E natural in **Example 10a**). The other chords in **Example 10b** are formed in a similar manner, so the cohesive element in this music is not tonality, it is the tone row heard in the cello part. *(See tonality.)*

Example 3: Extracts from Handel's Suite in G (1733)

heterophony
The simultaneous sounding of two *melodies, the second being a more elaborate version of the first. If played together **Examples 3b** and **3c** would produce heterophony.

historia
Title given to some biblical *oratorios, such as *The Christmas History* by Schütz.

home key
The *tonic key of a movement; the key in which the movement begins and ends.

homophony
A musical texture in which a prominent *melody is supported by a subservient accompaniment. The English national anthem is an example of four-part homophony (a *treble melody with three subservient lower parts).

idée fixe
A cyclic technique used by Berlioz in his *Symphonie fantastique*, in which a similar musical theme recurs throughout the movements.

idiophone
Any instrument that produces sound solely by the vibrations of its whole body, such as a pair of cymbals.

imitation
The exact or varied repetition of a musical phrase in another contrapuntal part. See **Example 8**.

incidental music
Music that adorns a dramatic production but which is not an essential part of it, for example Mendelssohn's music for *A Midsummer Night's Dream*.

intermedio, intermedium
Vocal and instrumental music performed between the acts of a play. In sixteenth-century Florence, these could be elaborately staged dramas on allegorical or mythical subjects involving more than 80 performers. In the next century *intermedi* were performed between the acts of full-scale *operas.
(See Styles and Forms: Renaissance.)

intermezzo
1. A comic version of the **intermedio* that was performed between acts of eighteenth-century serious *operas.
2. A diverting movement between more demanding movements of a large-scale work, for example the third movement of Brahms's Second Symphony.
3. A characteristic piano piece in no set form, such as 'Paganini' from Schumann's *Carnival*.

interval
The distance between two *pitches. This is best calculated by counting letter-names including the first and last. Thus the interval from C up to E is a third (C, D, E) and the interval from D up to G sharp is a fourth (D, E, F, G sharp). The difference between major and minor intervals is explained in the entry on tonality.

jazz
At the turn of the nineteenth century, the music of black Americans, characterized by improvisation, syncopation and the use of emotive effects such as the blue note (a pitch 'in the crack' between two adjacent notes on a keyboard). Later jazz spread to white Americans, eventually becoming a worldwide phenomenon diverging into a bewildering variety of styles.
(See Styles and Forms: Modern.)

Example 4: English National Anthem

key
1. A system of pitch relationships in which one of seven *pitches (the *tonic) assumes a privileged position over the others. *(See tonality.)*
2. One of the levers on a piano, organ etc., which, when touched, activates a sound-making device. A set of such keys is called a keyboard.
3. A lever on a woodwind instrument, which, when pressed, closes one of the holes in the body of the instrument.

lauda
A religious song – usually in Italian, sometimes Latin – not based on liturgical texts; important in the thirteenth, fifteenth and sixteenth centuries.

leading note
The seventh degree of a *major or *minor scale (shown in **Examples 4e** and **4g**).

leitmotif (Fr), leitmotiv (Ger), leading motive
A striking melodic fragment or *chord representing a dramatic character, a significant object, an emotion or an idea. In Wagnerian *opera leitmotifs are often used in a subtle manner to recall an earlier stage of the drama or to prefigure new developments. As parts of complex *polyphonic *textures they can also generate a purely musical drama and function as unifying elements that give shape to large musical structures.
(See Styles and Forms: Late Romantic.)

libretto
The text of an extended vocal work such as an *opera or *oratorio.

Lied
A German poem set to music by a composer; most popular during the late eighteenth and nineteenth centuries, usually for solo voice accompanied by piano.

madrigal
A medieval or late Renaissance song for several voices, often with a vernacular text of an amatory nature. The madrigal is most familiar as a late sixteenth-century Italian genre that was exported to England where it flowered briefly and brilliantly around the turn of the century.
(See Styles and Forms: Renaissance.)

major, minor
1. Adjectives that describe larger and smaller *intervals, such as the falling major third in bars 1–2 of **Example 7**, a semitone wider than the falling minor third in bars 3–4.
2. Scales whose first and third degrees form intervals of a major or a minor third respectively (compare **Examples 4e** and **4g**).
3. Chords that prominently feature these intervals.

maqam
Middle Eastern modality based on *scales that include *microtones.

Example 5: Extracts from a plainsong sequence

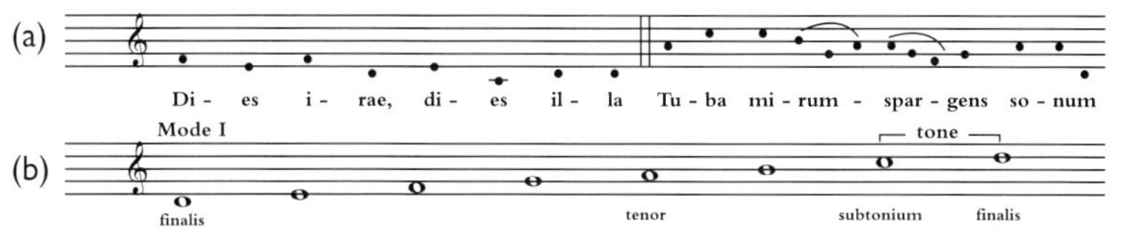

masque
A dramatic entertainment with vocal and instrumental music deriving from the Italian **intermedio* and reaching its apogee in seventeenth-century England.
(*See Styles and Forms: Early Baroque.*)

Mass
1. The Roman Catholic celebration of the Eucharist or Holy Communion.
2. A musical setting of texts that are common to most celebrations of the Mass (Kyrie, Gloria, Creed, Sanctus and Agnus Dei).

(*See Styles and Forms: Medieval, Renaissance, Classical.*)

melisma
A portion of *melody sung to one syllable, for example the second syllable of 'mirum' and the first syllable of 'spargens' in **Example 5a**.
(*See Styles and Forms: Renaissance.*)

melody
Melody is a generic term that covers any single line of organized *pitches and *rhythms. It is not quite synonymous with the colloquial term 'tune', since this usually refers to a self-contained and independent melody such as the English national anthem (**Example 4**), whereas other melodies might be a part of a larger musical design. What nearly all melodies have in common is *tonality (the national anthem is in the *key of G major), a limited range of rhythmic patterns (**Example 4a** contains just two) and exact or varied repetition. Even in such an apparently simple tune, this last melodic feature can be quite complex. In **Example 4a** bars 3–4 initially sound as though they are a repetition of the first two bars at a higher pitch (a *sequence), but in fact bar 4 is an upside-down version of bar 2. It is such features that engender both unity and variety in the simplest as well as the most complex melodies.

PHRASE
Melodies more than a few bars long usually fall into sections which, though not complete in themselves, make the same sort of sense as does a phrase in a verbal sentence. Melodies of the classical period often divide into two equal phrases that balance each other like a question and answer. **Example 6a** shows a melody which divides into two three-bar phrases, the first rising through the notes of the *tonic chord of F major, the second rising through the notes of the *dominant chord. Both end with a *chromatic note rising to a *diatonic note, thus further uniting the two phrases in a wonderfully poised melodic statement.

THEME
The melody shown in **Example 6a** is a theme – a melody that is part of a larger design (in this case the slow *movement of a piano *concerto). Within this design Mozart returns to his first theme in new contexts and new *keys. **Example 6b** shows one such repeat. It is considerably varied and in the new key of A flat major, so throwing a new light on the original theme.

MOTIF
Some themes are constructed from tiny melodic cells known as motifs. **Example 7** shows how Beethoven manipulates the famous four-note motif (x) heard at the start of his Fifth Symphony. Out of this tiny acorn grows the theme shown in **Example 7**, and out of this theme grows a complete movement. The letters and brackets under the staves show the following motivic manipulations:
1. Transpositions of motive x (i.e. the same motive at a different pitch level).
2. Contractions of the falling interval in motive x (from a third to a second).
3. Expansions of the falling interval in motive x (from a third to a fourth).
4. In-filling of the falling interval in motive x (the third note changed from G to F).
5. Melodic inversion (i.e. motive d is played upside down).

SUBJECT
The potential of a short, pithy melody known as a subject is exploited in *contrapuntal music such as a *fugue. **Example 7** shows how Beethoven uses a subject only four notes long at the start of a gigantic fugue, throughout which this melody keeps reappearing in combination with two other subjects. Note that when the subject is played at a different pitch in the first section of a fugue it is called an answer. (*See texture.*)

mensural music
A system of notation developed in medieval times to indicate the duration of a note, in which they have a fixed value in relation to one another. The fundamental principles of the Franconian system (after Franco of Cologne) were developed in the fourteenth century.

metre
The organization of the underlying pulse of music into strong and weak beats in a manner similar to the pattern of strong and weak syllables in a poetic foot. 'Time' is often used as a synonym for 'metre'. Thus **Example 3a** can be described as being in duple time because of the alternation of strong and weak beats, while **Example 4a** is in triple time because of the repeating pattern strong-weak-weak.

mezzo soprano
A female voice, the range of which falls between the ranges of *sopranos and *altos.

microtone
An *interval smaller than that between a white note and an adjacent black note on a keyboard.
(*See Styles and Forms: Modern.*)

minimalism
Late twentieth-century music that exploits the potential of very short and simple ideas, often employing a minimum of performers. In Reich's *Clapping Music* an extended movement develops from an oft-repeated and unvarying eight-note *rhythm clapped by two performers.
(*See Styles and Forms: Late 20th Century.*)

minor
See major, minor.

minuet
A dance of French origin in moderate 3/4 time found in some Baroque *suites. It features as the last movement of early classical multi-movement works and the third movement of later *symphonies and *chamber works.

mode
1. *Rhythmic notation and organization in medieval music.
2. Seven-note *scales that antedate modern *major and *minor scales. (*See tonality*).
3. The behaviour of vibrating strings and columns of air. (*See acoustics*).

(*See Styles and Forms: Modern.*)

modulation
A *harmonic process that leads to the establishment of a new *key. (*See tonality.*)

mono
In recording, an abbreviation of 'monaural': the reproduction of an original performance through one electronic channel so that the original spatial separation of sounds heard in that performance can no longer be heard.

monophony
Music comprising only a single line or melody, without accompaniment, as distinct from *homophony or *polyphony.

motet
1. In the Middle Ages, a multi-voice vocal composition based on a pre-existent *melody in long notes heard in one of the *contrapuntal parts.
2. In the Renaissance, an independent *polyphonic vocal setting of a sacred Latin text. Most such motets were specific to a particular day in the church's year.
3. After 1700, a title for almost any sacred work other than a *Mass movement (for example Bach referred to at least one of his cantatas as a motteto).

(*See Styles and Forms: Medieval, Renaissance, Early Baroque.*)

movement
A self-contained section of a larger work.

multiple stopping
The performance of three or four-part *chords on a string instrument. (*See double stopping.*)

music theatre
A twentieth-century genre in which drama and music are combined in semi-staged performances that deliberately reject the traditions of conventional *opera.

musique concrète
Music composed of electronically manipulated natural sounds.

notation
The two most important elements of music that can be represented in written or printed notation are rhythm (patterns in time made by a succession of sounds and silences) and pitch (the highness or lowness of sounds). Rhythms are usually shown by symbols called notes and rests, while pitches are determined by the position of notes on, between, above or below a set of five horizontal lines called a staff.

NOTES AND RESTS
The length of a note is usually represented by a note-head (an empty or filled circle) that can be attached to a vertical stem (**Example 1a**). For shorter time-values one or more flags (or tails) can be attached to the stem. Alternatively a group of short notes can be joined together by one or more horizontal beams, each additional beam (or flag) halving the length of the note.

For every note there is a rest that signifies a silence of the same duration as the note with which it is associated. **Example 1b** shows some of the most common types of notes and rests together with their British and American names (the latter defining shorter notes as fractions of a semibreve). The precise relationships between shorter notes and crotchet are evident in the extracts from Handel's Suite in G (**Example 3**). The vertical dotted lines show that in the time taken to play one crotchet (**Example 3a**) two quavers or four semiquavers can be performed (**Examples 3b** and **3d**).

A dot added to a note makes it 50 per cent longer. Thus the dotted minim in **Example 1b** is equivalent in length to the minim (half note) plus crotchet (quarter note) shown in brackets. Similarly the dotted crotchet towards the end of **Example 3e** lasts as long as the bracketed crotchet and quaver shown beneath it (the curved line or tie showing that the two notes are to be played as one longer note).

In **Example 3c** quavers are beamed together in threes, and the figure 3 is printed above each group. This is the conventional way of notating triplets – groups of three notes played in the time normally occupied by two notes of the same type. More complex ratios of long to short notes can be shown in similar ways. For instance, the figure 11 under the second group of demisemiquavers at the end of **Example 3d** means that all 11 notes must be fitted into the time normally occupied by eight demisemiquavers. (*See melody.*)

PITCH
The pitch of a note is designated by one of the first seven letters of the alphabet. **Example 2b** shows these letters on the white notes of a keyboard, and it will be seen that once all seven letters have been used to identify adjacent keys the same pattern is repeated an *octave higher. These repeating series are distinguished from one another by the use of capital letters (for the lowest octave shown in **Example 2b**), lower case letters (for the next higher octave) and apostrophes after the letters (for the highest notes). It is best to get one's bearings from the C that is near the centre of a real keyboard (shaded in **Example 2b**) and that is commonly known as middle C.

The precise pitches of the lines and spaces of a staff are fixed by a clef (the symbol printed at the start of each line of music). To accommodate a wider range of pitches the staff can be extended in both directions by the use of ledger lines, like those that effectively make a seven-line staff immediately after the clef at the start of **Example 2c**. With this bass clef middle C is written on a ledger line above the staff. This allows a wide range of low pitches to be written (as shown by the first 15 notes of **Example 2c**). With the treble clef middle C is written on a ledger line below the stave, thus allowing a wide range of high pitches to be written (as shown by the last 10 notes of **Example 2c**).

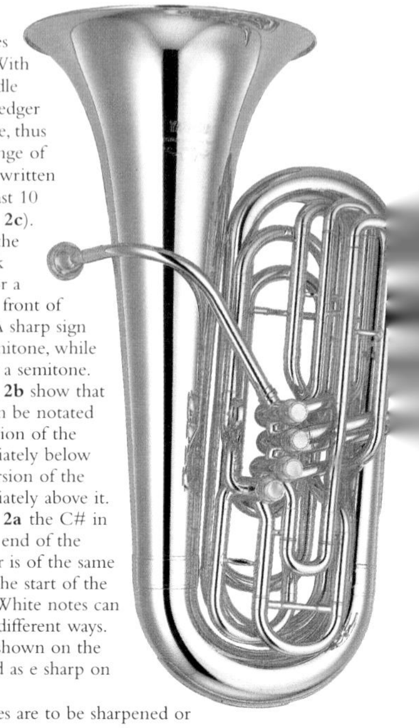

To represent the pitches of the black notes a sharp (#) or a flat (♭) is placed in front of the relevant note. A sharp sign raises a note a *semitone, while a flat sign lowers it a semitone. **Examples 2a** and **2b** show that each black note can be notated as a sharpened version of the white note immediately below it or a flattened version of the white note immediately above it. Thus in **Example 2a** the C# in the bass clef at the end of the *scale of C# major is of the same pitch as the D♭ at the start of the scale of D♭ major. White notes can also be notated in different ways. For instance the f shown on the keyboard is notated as e sharp on the staff above it.

If certain notes are to be sharpened or flattened throughout a substantial passage of music, a key signature is placed just after the clef to show which notes are to be changed throughout the stave on which it appears. Thus the sharp after the clef on every staff of **Example 3** shows that every F should be raised a semitone throughout. (*See acoustics.*)
(*See Styles and Forms: Medieval.*)

note-row
English for the much more widely accepted American term *tone row.

obbligato
A part that must be played, or the instrument that must play it. The trumpet is an obbligato instrument in the *aria 'The Trumpet Shall Sound' from Handel's *Messiah*.

octatonic
Music using the eight pitch-classes of an artificial *scale of alternating tones and semitones, for example C sharp, D, E, F, G, A flat, A sharp, B, C sharp. This scale can be heard very clearly towards the end of the last movement of Stravinsky's *Symphony of Psalms* when the sopranos sing 'Laudate Dominum, laudate eum in cordis et organo'.

octave
An *interval formed between any note and the next note above or below it that has the same letter-name (for example the bracketed notes in the penultimate bar of **Example 3f**).

ode
An extended vocal composition written to celebrate the prowess of a person, the personification of an emotion or idea, or a particular day, such as Handel's 'Ode for St Cecilia's Day'.

opera
An extended drama in which, in its most serious versions, the text is sung throughout. The first extant operas were produced in Italy at the start of the seventeenth century (for example Monteverdi's *Orfeo* of 1607), and it is still one of the most popular and lavish of musical genres.
(*See Styles and Forms: Early Baroque, Late Baroque, Classical, Early Romantic, Late Romantic, Modern.*)

opéra-ballet
An opera-cum-ballet that flourished in France in the late seventeenth and early eighteenth centuries.

opera buffa
Comic opera sung in Italian.

Example 6: Extracts from the Andante of Mozart's concerto K467

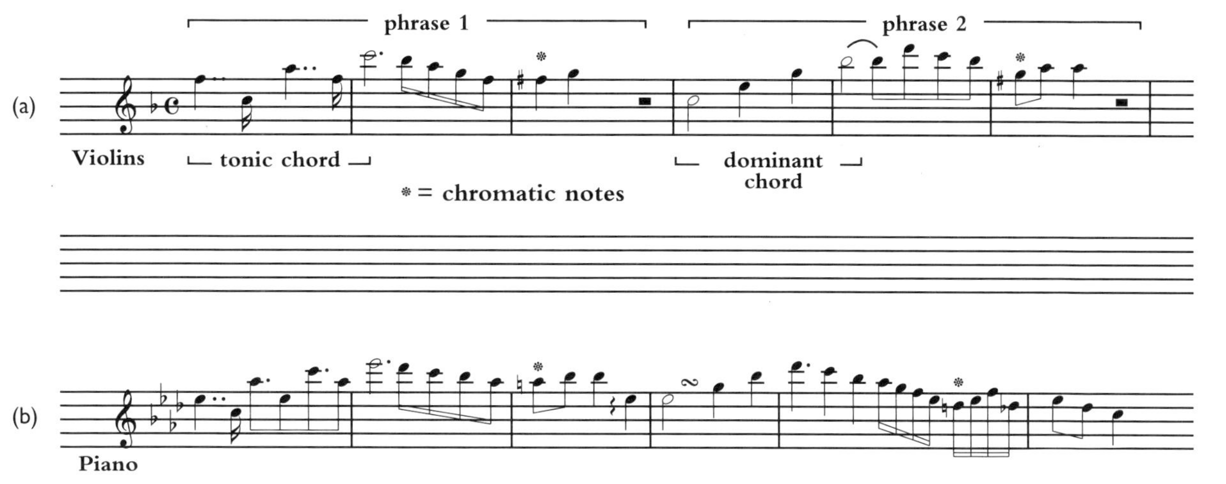

opéra comique
An *opera based on a French text including music and dialogue; it developed from being lighthearted, to incorporating more serious elements throughout the eighteenth century.

opera seria
Serious *opera of the eighteenth century. It was a highly stylized art form, largely consisting of a series of *recitatives and **da capo* arias presented in three acts. Later in the century vocal *ensembles, choruses and ballets figured more prominently.

oratorio
A religious drama first cultivated by the Congregation of the Oratory in sixteenth-century Italy. Like *opera it contains *recitatives and *arias. Unlike opera most oratorios were not staged, relied to a greater extent on the dramatic use of choruses and excluded ballet.
(*See Styles and Forms: Early Baroque, Classical.*)

ordre
A large collection of instrumental pieces in the same *key composed in the French classical period. Most *ordres* contain some of the dance movements that figured in the contemporary *suite as well as the programmatic pieces and *rondeaux that were more specifically French in style.

organum
Medieval polyphonic music, frequently based on **cantus firmus*.

ornamentation
The addition of notes that beautify a piece of music, but which are not essential to the underlying *harmonic and formal structure of it. These range from conventional *cadential trills to the elaborate embellishments of classical French harpsichord music. Ornaments may be fully *notated, represented by conventional symbols, or added by the performer.

ostinato
The repetition of a musical pattern (*melodic, *harmonic or *rhythmic) throughout a movement or a substantial portion of it, for example the rhythm in 5/4 time heard at the start of the first movement of Holst's *Planets Suite*.

overture
An instrumental prelude to a dramatic work such as an *opera or *oratorio.
(*See Styles and Forms: Early Baroque.*)

part
A single *melodic line. In **Example 3** the melody on the top *staff can be described as the *treble part, the other melody being the *bass part.

partita
Italian term for a Baroque *suite.

pas-de-deux
Music for two dancers.

paso doble
Twentieth-century quick Spanish dance in 6/8 or 2/4 time, for example the 'Tango-Pasodoblé' from Walton's *Façade*.

Passion
A setting of texts associated with the Passion and death of Christ. In its original form *plainsong was the vehicle for the whole biblical text. The German Baroque Passion (for example Bach's *St John Passion*) was a type of *oratorio in which *recitative replaced plainsong, and the words of the crowds were set *polyphonically. The narrative was divided into short scenes by reflective *arias and four-part harmonizations of Lutheran *chorale melodies.

pastorale héroïque
A French operatic genre in one or more acts which evoked a golden age when heroes conducted their affairs in Elysian rural seclusion. It was cultivated by Lully and Rameau in the period 1686–1753.

Example 7: Bars 1–21 of the first movement of Beethoven's Fifth Symphony

pentatonic music
Music based on five *pitches that can be arranged into a scale such as that represented by the black notes on a piano (see **Examples 2a** and **2b**). There are many other such scales, some including *semitones and *microtones.

petit motet
A French *motet for a small vocal *ensemble with *continuo. (*See grand motet.*)

phrase
A section of music of indefinite length analogous to a phrase in a sentence. Two phrases are shown in **Example 9a**.

piano, pianissimo
Italian: soft, very soft (*p*, *pp*).

pitch
The height or depth of a note. **Example 3a** moves steadily from low-pitched notes to high-pitched notes. (*See acoustics and notation*).

pizzicato
Plucked notes played on string instruments that are normally bowed.

plainchant, plainsong
A corpus of unaccompanied *melodies of great antiquity associated with the liturgical texts of the Roman Catholic church. See **Example 5a**.
(*See Styles and Forms: Medieval.*)

pluralism
In relation to the arts, an acceptance and integration of differing cultures within society at large or an art work in particular.

polychoral
Musical *textures in which two or more groups of instruments and/or voices are contrasted and combined.

polymetre
Music that combines two or more conflicting *metres. In his opera *Don Giovanni* Mozart combines a minuet in 3/4 time with a contradance in 2/4 and a German dance in 3/8.

polyphony
Originally meaning music in more than one part, polyphony is now most often used as a synonym of *counterpoint.
(*See Styles and Forms: Medieval, Renaissance.*)

polyrhythm
The combination of two or more conflicting *rhythms. If **Examples 3b**, **3c** and **3d** were played together they would form polyrhythms.

polytonality
Music in which music in two or more *keys are combined. See also *bitonality.

prima pratica
A term invented in the early seventeenth century to distinguish between the equal-voice *polyphony of the Renaissance (*prima pratica* or 'first practice') and the new harmonically conceived music of the Baroque Era (*seconda pratica* or 'second practice').
(*See Styles and Forms: Renaissance.*)

quarter-tone
Half a *semitone.

raga
The framework for improvised compositions in Indian music. A given raga prescribes the type of *scale, the characteristic melodic figures used in ascending and descending the scale, the mood of the piece and the types of *ornament that are appropriate to the mood.

recitative
A single vocal line designed to replicate the *rhythms of spoken words and express their meaning through the use of appropriate melodic *intervals. In Baroque *opera and *oratorio the resulting fragmented *melody was usually supported by a *continuo group, but in later periods orchestral accompaniments took over this role.

register
A characteristic part of the pitch-range of a voice or instrument. The chalumeau register of a clarinet is lower, darker and more oily sounding than its other registers.

reprise
A repetition, whether exact or varied. **Example 6b** is a varied reprise of **Example 6a**.

rhythm
A pattern of durations of sounds and silences. The first three notes of Beethoven's Fifth Symphony have a rhythmic pattern that can be approximately represented as 'short-short-short-long'. (*See notation.*)
(*See Styles and Forms: Modern.*)

rhythmic shift
A change from one *rhythmic pattern to another.

ricercar, ricercare
Initially a transcription of a vocal work for keyboard or instrumental *ensemble, the ricercar became an independent work that was widely cultivated in the sixteenth and seventeenth centuries. There were two types, homophonic and contrapuntal, the latter better exemplifying the literal meaning of the term 'to seek out' (the potential of one or more *contrapuntal *subjects).

ripieno
The full orchestra in a **concerto grosso* or similar concertante composition.

ritornello
1. A passage of instrumental music heard in a Baroque vocal movement. In a **da capo* aria the instrumental *ritornello* heard at the start is often repeated at the end.
2. A passage of music for the **ripieno* recurring in whole or in part in a Baroque *concerto movement.

rondeau
In Baroque music, a movement in which a refrain beginning and ending in the *tonic (A) is repeated after contrasting passages (B) in the pattern ABACA etc.

scale
A set of *pitches derived from a composition and arranged in ascending or descending order. *Major, *minor and *modal scales are shown in **Examples 4e**, **4g** and **5b** respectively.
(*See Styles and Forms: Modern.*)

scordatura
An unusual tuning of the strings of a guitar or violin etc. In Saint-Saëns' *Danse Macabre* the highest string is tuned down a *semitone so that the *diabolus in musica* (the devil's interval – in this case A and E flat) can be played on vibrant open strings.

secco
Dry or detached. In a *secco* *recitative the *continuo group plays short, detached chords whether or not the composer has written sustained notes in the **basso continuo* part.

seconda pratica
'Second practice'. (*See Prima pratica.*)
(*See Styles and Forms: Renaissance.*)

semi-opera
English dramas of the late seventeenth and early eighteenth centuries in which the leading roles were spoken, but music was composed for lesser characters together with *incidental instrumental music, for example Purcell's *Dioclesian*.

semitone
The smallest *interval heard in most Western music. The distance between a white note and an adjacent black note on the piano, or the distance between two white notes that do not have a black note between them (see **Example 2b**).

sequence
An immediate repetition of a melodic *phrase in the same part but at a different *pitch, or similar treatment of a *harmonic progression. In **Example 4f** the tune for the words 'Send her victorious, happy and glorious' is sequential, 'happy and glorious' being the same musical phrase as 'Send her victorious', but pitched a step lower.

serenata
A type of serenade performed outdoors in the evening.

serial music
Music constructed from a pre-conceived series of musical events such as a *tone row. (See **Example 10**.)
(*See Styles and Forms: Late 20th Century.*)

Siciliana, Siciliano, Sicilienne
A Baroque vocal or instrumental movement in slow compound time (for example 6/8 or 12/8). 'La Paix' from Handel's *Fireworks Music* is a *Largo alla Siciliana* (a slow movement in the style of a Siciliana).

sine wave
In music, the graphic representation of a pure sound (a single pitch unmixed with *harmonics) such as that produced by a tuning fork.

sinfonia
See symphony, sinfonia.

solmization
The use of a set of symbols to represent the relative *pitches of notes, for example *do, re, mi, fa, sol, la, si* (representing the seven pitches of a major scale).

sonata
In a majority of cases, a multi-movement instrumental composition for one or more solo performers.
(*See Styles and Forms: Late Baroque, Classical, Early Romantic.*)

sonata da camera, sonata da chiesa
A Baroque *sonata intended to be performed in secular surroundings (*da camera*) or in a church (*da chiesa*).

sopranino
Diminutive of *soprano, thus a very small treble instrument such as the highest-pitched recorder.

soprano
The highest female voice, or the uppermost part of an *ensemble of voices or instruments.

sprung rhythm
A theory of poetic rhythm developed by Gerard Manley Hopkins to account for poetry that did not fall into regular metrical feet. In the following line from his *The Wreck of the Deutschland* sprung rhythms range from the six-syllable foot 'and the recovery' to the monosyllabic foot 'sides': *The recurb and the recovery of the gulf's sides* (stressed syllables underlined). The fact that Hopkins himself compared such poetry to music perhaps justifies the use of this term for similarly irregular rhythms in music.

staff
A set of five horizontal lines upon and between which note-heads can be placed. (*See notation.*)

stile concitato
An agitated style of the Baroque period characterised by fast repeated notes, for example the accompaniment to the aria 'Why do the Nations so Furiously Rage Together' from Handel's *Messiah*.

strophic
A setting of a poem in which the same music is used for every stanza.

style brisé
The 'broken style' of French or French-influenced lute and harpsichord music in which a quasi-contrapuntal *texture emerges from broken *chords and melodic fragments in a varying number of parts, for example the 'Sarabande simple' from Bach's Suite in A minor, BWV 818.

subdominant
1. The fourth degree of a *diatonic scale (see **Example 4e**).
2. A *chord built on this degree (see **Example 9a** and **b**).
3. The *key a fourth above the *tonic key.

subject
1. In a *fugue or similar *contrapuntal work, the *melody (most often unaccompanied) heard in one contrapuntal part at the start, then heard in each of the other parts in turn. See **Example 8**.
2. In many classical instrumental pieces, a theme, or a group of themes in the same key. **Example 7** shows the start of the first subject of a symphonic movement.

suite
In the Baroque era, a collection of instrumental movements, all or most of them in the same *key, often beginning with an *overture, and usually including dance movements, for example Handel's *Fireworks Music*. Later suites might consist of a number of movements taken from a larger work (for example Tchaikovsky's *Nutcracker Suite*), or a set of movements linked by a common idea (for example Holst's *Planets Suite*).
(*See Styles and Forms: Early Baroque, Late Baroque.*)

suspension
A sustained or repeated note that causes a *discord with one or more of the other notes heard at the point of suspension. Immediately after this, the part containing the suspension usually moves by step to a *concord. The tied notes in bars 5 and 7 of **Example 8** are suspensions.

symphony, sinfonia
1. In the Baroque era, an instrumental movement in an extended vocal work. Thus Handel calls the *overture to *Messiah* a *Sinfony* and, conversely, the *Pifa* in the same work is generally known as the *Pastoral Symphony*.
2. In the classical era, an independent orchestral work, most often in four movements.
3. In the nineteenth century, an extended version of the classical symphony or a vehicle for programme music (for example Berlioz's *Symphonie fantastique*).
4. In the twentieth century the title Symphony or Sinfonia could take on any of these different meanings.

(*See Styles and Forms: Classical, Early Romantic, Late Romantic, Modern.*)

tablature
A form of notation, distinct from traditional Western staff notation, in which pitch is specified by letters, numerals or diagrams.

tala
A repeating rhythmic pattern in Indian music.

temperament
Adjustments of *acoustically pure *intervals to make them compatible with other intervals in a tuning system. (*See acoustics.*)

tempo
The speed of the underlying pulse in metrical music.

tenor
A high male voice, or the third melodic line down in conventional four-part *harmony.

ternary form
A three-part structure, A-B-A, in which A is usually a closed section beginning and ending in the *tonic, and B is a section in a contrasting *key. The third *movement of many classical *symphonies and *chamber compositions consists of a *minuet and *trio which, together with the repeat of the minuet, make a ternary structure (minuet-trio-minuet).
(*See Styles and Forms: Early Baroque.*)

tetrachord
A set of four *pitches, for example the first four notes of the *diatonic *scale of G major shown in **Example 3a**.

texture
The texture of music is the pattern made by a single part, or, more often, the blending of specific numbers of parts. Thus the texture of unaccompanied *plainsong (**Example 5a**) is monophonic, while **Example 3**, the last two bars of **Example 8**, and **Example 9a** can be described as two, three and four-part textures respectively.

The way in which a given number of parts relate to one another is more complex. A *heterophonic texture is formed by the simultaneous combination of a simple *melody with more elaborate versions of it (for example the combination of any or all of **Examples 3a–d**). A *contrapuntal (or *polyphonic) texture is formed when two or more rhythmically independent melodies are combined (as they are in **Example 3f**). An imitative texture is a special type of counterpoint in which the same melody appears successively in a number of parts (as in the three-part fugal texture of **Example 8**). The texture of the music of most hymns is chordal – all four parts have the same *rhythm. This is a special type of *homophony – another sort is shown in **Example 11**, where the all-important melody is supported by a subservient broken-chord accompaniment.

Other aspects of texture are relative and less easy to define, for example the texture of **Example 11** could be described as high and thin compared with the low and muddy texture of **Example 10b**. In fact most textures are not so clear cut as these examples would suggest. At first hearing, **Example 9a** might sound chordal with some independent quaver movement, but a performance of the bass and treble parts alone reveals that the former is just as melodic as the latter. This is even more evident in the second phrase of **Example 9c**, where homophony and counterpoint are finely balanced in a texture that refuses to be neatly categorized.

timbre
The tone colour that distinguishes one instrument or voice from another even when they sound the same notes of the same *pitch. (*See acoustics.*)

toccata
A brilliant display piece, most often for a keyboard instrument.

tombeau
A musical memorial.

Example 8: Opening of J. S. Bach's fugue BWV 849

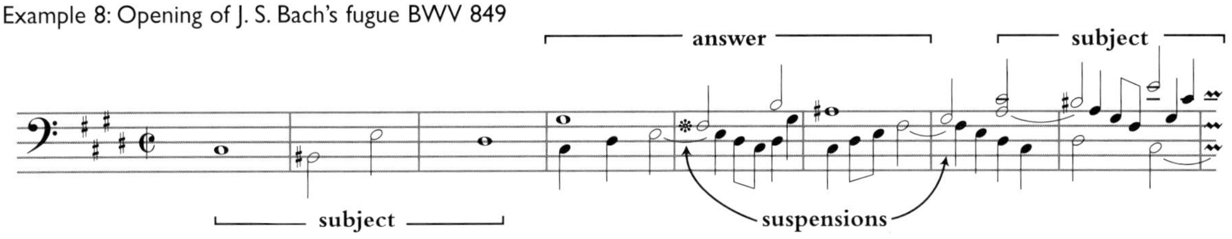

Example 9: Extracts from Bach's harmonizations of the chorale melody 'O Ewigkeit, du Donnerwort' (transposed to C major).

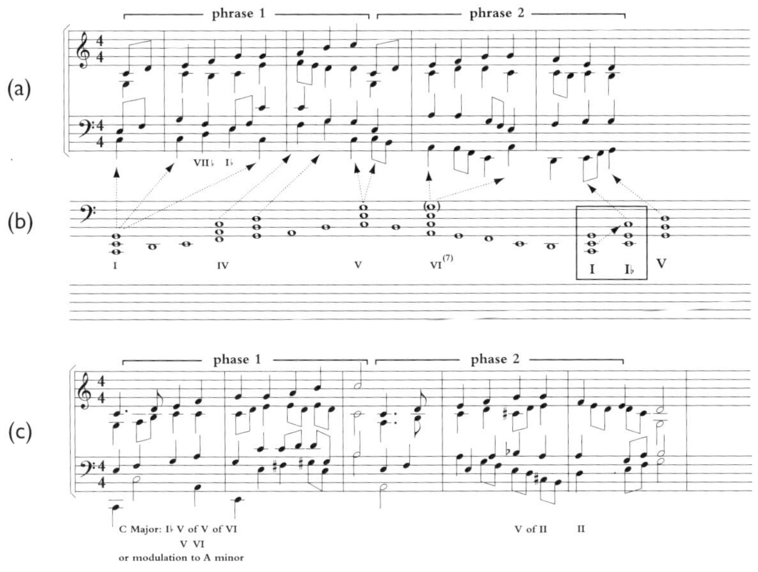

Example 10: An extract from Schoenberg's Variations Op.31

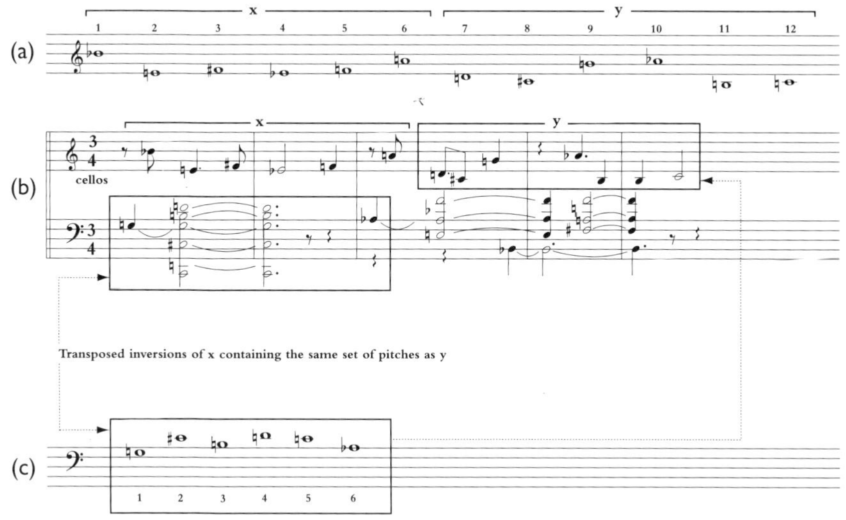

tonality

The organizing principle that creates a web of relationships between a set of *pitches (such as the notes of a *diatonic scale) so that one of them (the *tonic) becomes pre-eminent.

Tonality, like gravity, is an elemental binding force which, like gravity, cannot be directly perceived. Just as the force of gravity only became apparent to Newton when he saw the effect the earth had on his apple, so the effect of tonality only becomes apparent when musical sounds begin to react with one another. If we sing the English national anthem and pause on the fifteenth note (**Example 4a**) we will feel the force of tonality. There is an almost irresistible urge to move from this note (F#) to the sixteenth note (G). If we replace the F# with a D or an A (**Example 4b**) the urge to move on to a G will still be felt. If, however, we replace the F# with a low E the tonal force of G will be less strong. Instead we may feel that an as yet unseen and unheard low D is exerting as much attractive force as the G, so the *phrase could end with equal tonal logic on either note (**Example 4c**). Finally, if we replace the original F# with a high E (**Example 4d**), the tonal force of the D a step below it will be so strong that it will almost completely negate the attractive force of the G on which the original phrase ended.

Our experiments have demonstrated some of the complex relationships between the set of seven pitches deployed in the *melody of the national anthem. These pitches can be arranged in ascending order as a *scale (with the first note repeated an *octave higher as shown in **Example 4e**). The experiments have also shown that the first degree of the scale (known as the tonic) is pre-eminent because it exerts a greater attractive force than any other note (the nouns 'tonic' and 'tonality' are inextricably linked). Furthermore, they have shown that the fifth degree of the scale (known as the dominant) can, in certain localized circumstances, exert as much attractive force on its neighbours as the tonic does on the seventh degree (the leading note), the second degree (the supertonic) or the dominant itself.

MAJOR KEYS

Examples 4a–d are said to be in the key of G major because they are based on a set of seven pitches disposed in such a way that G becomes the pre-eminent note – the tonic that is the centre and goal of the whole melody. (G functions as a tonic in exactly the same way throughout the whole of **Example 3**.) But, as the first four bars of **Example 4f** show, the national anthem can be sung at a lower pitch. The tonic is now F, so these bars are said to be in F major. Despite starting on a different note it remains recognizable as the national anthem because the *intervals between successive notes have been maintained (compare the first four bars of **Examples 4a** and **4f**). In fact it is possible to begin on any one of the 12 pitches used in Western music, and, provided exactly the same intervals are maintained, the melody will still be that of the national anthem. Thus the key of a piece of music is tonality expressed through a particular set of seven pitches.

MODULATION

In **Example 4f** the sixteenth note of the melody has been altered. Instead of the expected tonic (F) the first phrase of the melody ends on D (the last note on the first staff). This leads to a whole new set of expectations which are fulfilled in the melody on the second staff. Now the music revolves around a new tonic, D, and it is on this note that the rather sad second phrase of the melody ends. This process, by which a new tonal centre is established, is known as modulation.

MINOR KEYS

Once having established D as the new tonal centre, it will be apparent that a sadder mood is expressed through the melody on the second staff of **Example 4f**. This is because, among other things, the interval between the first and third degrees of the new scale is smaller than that between the first and third degrees of the scale of G major. A comparison of **Examples 4e** and **4g** will reveal that the major third in the former encompasses four *semitones, whereas the minor third in the latter encompasses just three semitones. It is chiefly for this reason that the music shown in **Examples 4a–e** is said to be in G major, while the music shown on the second staff of **Example 4f** is said to be in D minor. In fact, like major scales, minor scales can be constructed on any of the 12 pitches commonly used in Western music. Thus there is a total of 24 possible keys, 12 major and 12 minor. (*See harmony.*)

MODALITY

The church modes are sets of seven pitches derived from *plainsong melodies by medieval theorists. Two phrases from one of the most famous of these chants are shown in **Example 5**, together with the modal scale that can be constructed from their constituent pitches. This scale differs from modern major and minor scales in several ways, the most obvious being the flattened seventh degree (there is a tone between the subtonium and finalis in **Example 5b**, but a semitone between the leading note and tonic of **Examples 4e** and **4g**). Theoretically, all plainsong melodies can be classified as versions of church modes I (C–C on the white notes of a keyboard), III (E–E on the keyboard), V (G–G) and VII (F–F). (*See melody.*)
(*See Styles and Forms: Modern.*)

tone-cluster

A *chord of notes a step apart.

tone row

A pre-determined ordering of a set of *pitch used as a matrix for composition. In most *serial music all 12 *chromatic tones are used. See **Example 10a**.

tonic

1. The first degree of a *diatonic scale. **Example 4a** begins and ends on the tonic of G major.
2. A *chord built on this degree (for the first chord of **Example 9a**).

tragédie lyrique

French seventeenth- and eighteenth-century tragic or epic *opera.

treble

A high child's voice, or the uppermost part of a *polyphonic composition.

tremolando

The rapid repetition of one note, or the rapid alternation of two notes.

triad

A three-note *chord. (*See harmony.*)

trill

An *ornament consisting of a rapid alternation of the written note and the note a step above it. A trill is indicated in the last bar of **Example 6b**.

trio

1. Music for three to play, or the *ensemble that plays it.
2. The second of a pair of dances, the first being repeated after the trio (for example minuet-trio-minuet).

trio sonata

A Baroque multi-movement composition written on three *staffs – one each for two melody instruments, and a third for the *continuo group. Since the bass part implied the participation of a *melody bass instrument (such as a cello) and a *harmony instrument (such as a harpsichord), the trio sonata paradoxically required the participation of at least four performers.
(*See Styles and Forms: Early Baroque.*)

triplet

A group of three equal notes played in the time normally taken up by two notes of the same type. See **Example 3c** and the entry on notation.

trope

The addition or insertion of newly composed words and/or music into a pre-existent composition.

12-note, 12-tone music

See serial music and tone row.
(*See Styles and Forms: Modern.*)

verismo

A late Romantic style of *opera in which violent and sordid events were realistically portrayed in contemporary settings.

virelai

One of the three main **formes fixes* of fourteenth-century French music and poetry.

voluntary

An organ piece played before or after an Anglican church service.

Example 11: Melody dominated homophony at the start of Mozart's Piano Sonata K.

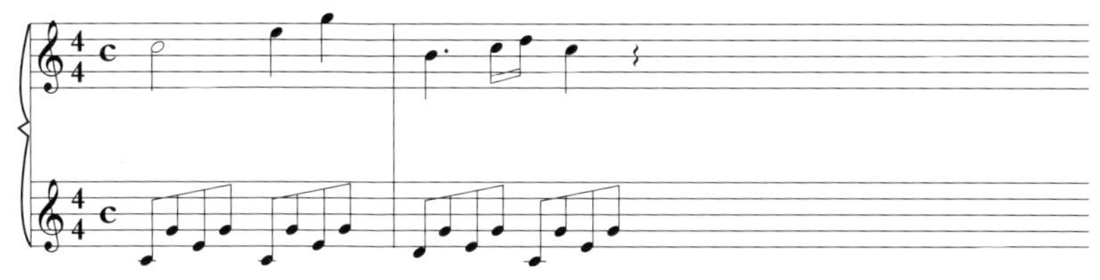

BIBLIOGRAPHY

THE WORLD OF MUSIC

Anderson, Warren D., *Ethos and Education in Greek Music. The Evidence of Poetry and Philosophy*, Harvard University Press, Cambridge, Mass., 1966

Baké, Arnold, 'The Music of India' in *The New Oxford History of Music*, vol. 1, Egon Wellesz (ed.), Oxford University Press, London, 1957, pp. 195–227

Farmer, Henry George, 'The Music of Ancient Egypt' in *The New Oxford History of Music*, vol. 1, Egon Wellesz (ed.), Oxford University Press, London, 1957, pp. 255–81

Farmer, Henry George, 'The Music of Islam' in *The New Oxford History of Music*, vol. 1, Egon Wellesz (ed.), Oxford University Press, London, 1957, pp. 421–503

Fenlon, Iain, *Early Music History*, Cambridge University Press, Cambridge

Festschrift fair Johannes Wolf, Breslauer, Berlin, 1929, facsimile edition, Olm, Hildesheim, 1978, pp. 97–106

Fleischhauer, Gunter, 'Etruria' in *The New Grove Dictionary of Music and Musicians*, Stanley Sadie (ed.), vol. 6, 1980, pp. 287–91

Galpin, Francis W., *The Music of the Sumerians and their Immediate Successors – the Babylonians and Assyrians*, Cambridge University Press, Cambridge, 1937; 2nd ed, 1955

Henderson, Isobel, 'Ancient Greek Music' in *The New Oxford History of Music*, vol. 1, Egon Wellesz (ed.), Oxford University Press, London, 1957, pp. 336–403

Idelsohn, Abraham Zvi, *Jewish Music in its Historical Development*, Schocken Books, New York, 1967

Jairazbhoy, Nazir Ali, *The Ragas of North Indian Music*, Faber and Faber, London, 1971

Kolinski, Myczeslaw, 'Modes, musical' in *Encyclopedia Britannica*, 15th ed., vol. 12, 1974, pp. 295–98

Kraelin, Carl H. and Mowry, Lucetta, 'Music in the Bible' in *The New Oxford History of Music*, vol. 1, Egon Wellesz (ed.), Oxford University Press, London, 1957, pp. 283–312

Landels, John Gray, *Music in Ancient Greece and Rome*, Routledge, London, 1999

Malm, William P., *Music Cultures of the Pacific, the Near East, and Asia*, Prentice-Hall, Englewood Cliffs, New Jersey, 1967

Music and Musicians in Ancient Greece, Ithaca; London, Cornell University Press, 1994

Myers, Helen (ed.), 'South Asia' in *Ethnomusicology: Historical and Regional Studies*, W.W. Norton, London, 1993

Neubauer, Eckhard, 'Islamic Religious Music' in *The New Grove Dictionary of Music and Musicians*, vol. 9, Stanley Sadie (ed.), Macmillan, London, 1980, pp. 342–49

Picken, Laurence, 'China' in *The New Oxford History of Music*, vol. 1, Egon Wellesz (ed.), Oxford University Press, London, 1957, pp. 135–94

Powers, Harold S., 'India, I and II,' in *The New Grove Dictionary of Music and Musicians*, vol. 9, Stanley Sadie (ed.), Macmillan, London, 1980, pp. 69–141

Rowell, Lewis, *Music and Musical Thought in Early India*, University of Chicago Press, Chicago, 1992

Scott, J. E., 'Roman Music' in *The New Oxford History of Music*, vol. 1, Egon Wellesz (ed.), *Oxford University Press*, London, 1957, pp. 404–20

Shiloah, Amnon, *Music in the World of Islam: A Socio-cultural Study*, Scolar Press, Aldershot, 1995

Stauder, Wilhelm, 'Mesopotamia' in *The New Grove Dictionary of Music and Musicians*, vol. 12, Macmillan, London, 1980, pp. 196–200

Strunk, Oliver, and James McKinnon (eds.), *Source Readings in Music History*, W. W. Norton, 1998

'The Music of Ancient Mesopotamia' in *The New Oxford History of Music*, vol. 1, Egon Wellesz (ed.), Oxford University Press, London, 1957, pp. 228–54

'The Pentatonic Tuning of the Greek Lyre: A Theory Examined', *Classical Quarterly* (new series), vi, 1956

Thrasher, Alan R., 'China' in *The Norton/Grove Handbooks in Music*, Helen Myers (ed.), W. W. Norton, London, 1993

van Gulik, R. H., *The Lore of the Chinese Lute. An Essay in the Ideology of the Ch'in*, Sophia University, Tokyo, 1968

Wellesz, Egon (ed.), *The New Oxford History of Music*, vol. 1, Oxford University Press, London, 1957

Werner, Eric, *The Sacred Bridge. The Interdependence of Liturgy and Music in Synagogue and Church during the First Millennium*, Dennis Dobson, London; Columbia University Press, New York; 1959, rev. 1970

West, Martin Litchfield, *Ancient Greek Music*, Clarendon Press, Oxford, 1992

Widdess, Richard, *The Ragas of Early Indian Music: Modes, Melodies, and Musical Notations from the Gulta Period to c. 1250*, Clarendon Press, Oxford, 1995

Winnington-Ingram, R. P., *Mode in Ancient Greek Music*, Cambridge University Press, Cambridge, 1936, rev. ed. 1968

Wiora, Walter, *The Four Ages of Music*, W.W. Norton, New York, 1965

Yung, Bell, Evelyn S. Rawski and Rubie S. Watson (eds.), *Harmony and Counterpoint: Ritual Music in Chinese Context*, Stanford University Press, Stanford, California; Cambridge University Press, Cambridge, 1996

THE MEDIEVAL ERA

Apel, Willi, *The Notation of Polyphonic Music, 900–1600*, Medieval Academy of America, Cambridge, Mass., 1961

Arnold, Joan, *Medieval Music*, Oxford University Press, London, 1982

Bauml, Franz H., *From Symbol to Mimesis, the Generation of Walter von der Vogelweide*, Alfred Kümmerle, Göppingen, 1984

Boone, Graeme M. (ed.), *Essays on Medieval Music*, Harvard University Press, Cambridge, Mass., 1995

Brothers, Thomas, *Chromatic Beauty in the Late Medieval Chanson*, Cambridge University Press, Cambridge, 1997

Caldwell, John, *The Oxford History of English Music*, Clarendon Press, Oxford, 1991

Crocker, Richard and David Hiley (eds), *The Early Middle Ages to 1300*, Oxford University Press, Oxford, 1990

Dronke, Peter, *The Medieval Lyric*, D. S. Brewer, 1996

Everist, Mark (ed.), *French Motets in the Thirteenth Century*, Cambridge University Press, Cambridge, 1994

Fallows, David, *A Catalogue of Polyphonic Songs 1415–1480*, Clarendon Press, Oxford, 1999

Fallows, David, *Dufay*, Dent, London, 1987

Flanagan, Sabina, *Hildegard of Bingen, A Visionary Life*, Routledge, London, 1989

Harris, Simon (ed.), *The Communion Chants of the Thirteenth-century Byzantine Asmatikon*, Harwood Academic, 1998

Higgins, Paula (ed.), *Antoine Busnoys*, Clarendon Press, Oxford, 1998

Hollister, C. Warren, *Medieval Europe: a Short History*, McGraw-Hill, Boston, Mass., 8th edition, 1998

Hoppin, Richard H., *An Anthology of Medieval Music*, Norton, New York, 1978

Hoppin, Richard H., *Medieval Music*, Norton, New York, 1978

Hughes, Andrew, *Style and Symbol – Medieval Music 800–1453*, Ottawa, 1989

Kenyon, Nicholas (ed.), *Authenticity and Early Music*, Oxford University Press, 1988

Knighton, Tess, and David Fallows (eds.), *Companion to Medieval and Renaissance Music*, Dent, London, 1992

Mabey, Richard, *Medieval Music – Gregorian Chants*, Penguin Books, 1999

Marrocco, Thomas and Nicholas Sandon (eds.), *Medieval Music*, Oxford University Press, London, 1977

Martindale, Andrew, *Gothic Art*, Thames & Hudson, London, 1967

McKinnon, James (ed.), *Man & Music: Antiquity and the Middle Ages*, Macmillan, London, 1990

Moll, Kevin N. (ed.), *Counterpoint and Compositional Process in the Time of Dufay*, Garland Publishing Inc., 1998

Montagu, Jeremy and Gwen, *Minstrels and Angels, Carvings of Musicians in Medieval English Churches*, Fallen Leaf Press, Berkeley, California, 1998

Musik des Mittelalters und der Renaissance, Musikgeschichte in Bildern, III, especially vols. 3–5, Deutscher Verlag für Musik, Leipzig, 1969–75

Page, Christopher, *Music and Instruments of the Middle Ages*, London, 1998

Page, Christopher, *Voices and Instruments of the Middle Ages*, University of California Press, Berkeley, 1986

Palisca, C.V., *Anthology of Western Music vol. 1: Ancient/Baroque*, W. W. Norton, 1996

Rastall, Richard, *Notation of Western Music*, Dent, London, 1983; 2nd edition, 1998

Remnant, Mary, *English Bowed Instruments from Anglo-Saxon to Tudor Times*, Oxford, 1986

Robertshaw, Alan, *Oswald von Wolkenstein, The Myth and the Man*, Alfred Kümmerle, Göppingen, 1977

Silverstein, *English Lyrics Before 1500*, Northwesterm University Press, 1989

Wilkins, Nigel, *Music in the Age of Chaucer*, D. S. Brewer, 1999

Williams, Peter, *The Organ in Western Culture, 750–1250*, Cambridge University Press, 1993

Wilson, David Fenwick, *Music of the Middle Ages*, Schirmer, New York, 1990

Woolf, Rosemary, *The English Religious Lyric in the Middle Ages*, Oxford University Press, London, 1968

THE RENAISSANCE

Abraham, Gerald, and Anselm Hughes (eds.), *Ars Nova and the Renaissance 1300–1540*, Oxford University Press, 1960

Arnold, Dennis, *Giovanni Gabrieli and the Music of the Ventian High Renaissance*, Oxford University Press, Oxford, 1979

Atlas, Allan W., *Renaissance Music*, W. W. Norton, 1998

Binkley, Thomas, and Margit Frenk, *Spanish Romances of the Sixteenth Century*, Indiana University Press, 1995

Blackburn, Bonnie J., et al (ed.), *A Correspondence of Renaissance Musicians*, Clarendon Press, Oxford, 1991
Blume, Friedrich, *Renaissance and Baroque Music: A Comprehensive Survey*, W. W. Norton
Bond, Ann, *A Guide to The Harpsichord*, Amadeus Press
Bowers, Jane and Judith Tick (eds.), *Women Making Music: The Western Art Tradition 1150–1950*, University of Illinois Press, Urbana, 1986
Brookes, Virginia, *British Keyboard Music to c. 1660*, Clarendon Press, Oxford, 1996
Chater, James, *Luca Marenzio and the Italian Madrigal*, UMI, Ann Arbor, 1981
Comberiati, Carmelo Peter, *Late Renaissance Music at the Hapsburg Court*, Gordon & Breach Science Publishing, 1987
Cunningham, Walker, *The Keyboard Music of John Bull*, Bowker, Epping, 1984
D'Accone, Frank, *The Civic Muse: Music and Musicians in Siena During the Middle Ages and the Renaissance*, University of Chicago Press, 1997
Eisenbichler, Konrad (ed.), *Crossing the Boundaries: Christian Piety and the Arts in Italian Medieval Renaissance Confraternities*, Western Michigan University, 1991
Fenlon, Iain (ed.), *The Renaissance: From the 1470s to the End of the Sixteenth Century*, Prentice Hall, Englewood Cliffs, New Jersey, 1989
Haar, James, *Essays on Italian Poetry and Music in the Renaissance, 1350–1600*, University of California Press, Berkeley, 1986
Haar, James, et al, *The Science and Art of Renaissance Music*, Princeton University Press
Harley, John, *Orlando Gibbons and the Gibbons Family of Musicians*, Ashgate, Aldershot, 1999
Harley, John, *William Byrd: Gentleman of the Royal Chapel*, Scholar Press, Aldershot, 1997
Jacobson, Bernard, *A Polish Renaissance*, Phaidon Press, 1996
Kerman, Joseph, *The Masses and Motets of William Byrd*, Faber and Faber, London, 1981
Kmetz, John (ed.), *Music in the German Renaissance: Sources, Styles, and Contexts*, Cambridge University Press, 1994
Knighton, Tess and David Fallows (eds.), *Companion to Medieval and Renaissance Music*, Schirmer, New York, 1992
Kovacs, Sandor, *Kozepkor Es Reneszansz (The Music of the Middle Age and Renaissance)*, Magus Kiado, 1998
Lacy, Norris J. (ed.), *26 Chansons d'Amour de la Renaissance*, University Press of Kansas, 1986
Lasso, Orlando Di, *The Complete Motets 17: Motets from Printed Anthologies and Manuscipts*, A–R Editions, 1999
Lewis, M. S., *Antonio Gardano Venetian Music Printer 1538–1569*, Garland Publishing Inc., 1996
Lindley, David, *Thomas Campion*, E. J. Brill, Leiden, 1986
Lockwood, Lewis, et al (ed.), *Music in Renaissance Cities and Courts: Studies in Honor of Lewis Lockwood*, Harmonie Park Press, 1996
Lowinsky, Edward E. and Bonnie Blackburn (eds.), *Josquin des Prez: Proceedings of the International Josquin Festival*, Oxford University Press, London, 1976
Mayer Brown, Howard and Louise K. Stein, *Music in the Renaissance*, Prentice Hall, 1998
Mould, Charles and Donald H. Boalch, *Makers of Harpsichords and Clavichords 1440–1840*, Clarendon Press, Oxford
Perkins, Leeman L., *Music in the Age of the Renaissance*, W. W. Norton, 1999
Pesce, Dolores (ed.), *Hearing the Motet: Essays on the Motet of the Middle Ages and Renaissance*, Oxford University Press, Oxford, 1998
Reese, Gustav, et al, *The New Grove High Renaissance Masters*, Macmillan, London, 1984
Reese, Gustave, *Music in the Renaissance*, W. W. Norton, 1959
Roche, Jerome, *Lassus*, Oxford University Press, London, 1982
Schubert, Peter, *Modal Counterpoint, Renaissance Style*, Oxford University Press, Oxford, 1999
Selfridge-Field, Eleanor, *Venetian Instrumental Music from Gabrieli to Vivaldi*, Dover Publications, 1994
Stove, R. J., *Prince of Music, Palestrina and his World*, Quakers Hill Press, New South Wales, 1990
The Complete Motets 15: Cantica Sacra Sex Et Octo Vocibus (Recent Researches in the Music of the Renaissance), A–R Editions, 1999
Thomson, John (ed.), *Cambridge Companion to the Recorder*, Cambridge University Press, Cambridge
Treitler, Leo (ed.), *Source Readings in Music History*, New York, Norton, 1998
Turbet, R. B., *William Byrd: Lincoln's Greatest Musician*, Hollywood Press, Lincoln, 1993
Watkins, Glenn, *Gesualdo, The Man and his Music*, Clarendon Press, Oxford, 1991
Watson, Thomas, and Chatterley, Albert (eds,), *Italian Madrigals Englished (1590) vol. 74*, Stainer & Bell Ltd, 1999
Wegman, Rob C., *Born for the Music, The Life and Masses of Jacob Obrecht*, Clarendon Press, Oxford, 1994
Woetmann Christoffersen, Peter, *French Music in the Early Sixteenth Century*, Museum Tusculanum Press, 1994
Woodfield, I., *The Early History of the Viol*, Cambridge, 1984

THE EARLY BAROQUE

Agay, Denes, *The Baroque Period (Anthology of Piano Music, vol 1)*, Music Sales Corporation, 1981
Alfassy, Leo, *Baroque and Folk Tunes for the Recorder*, Music Sales Corporation, 1975
Allsop, Peter, *Arcangelo Corelli; New Orpheus of Our Times*, Oxford University Press, Oxford, 1999
Anderson, Nicholas, *Baroque Music from Monteverdi to Handel*, Thames & Hudson, London, 1994
Anthony, James, *French Baroque Music*, London, 1974 (rev. 1978)
Anthony, James, et al, *French Baroque Masters*, Macmillan, London, 1986
Arnold, Denis and Nigel Fortune (eds.), *The New Monteverdi Companion*, London, 1985
Arnold, Denis, *Monteverdi (The Master Musicians)*, Oxford University Press, Oxford
Bathe, William, *A Briefe Introduction of the Skill of Song c. 1587*, D. S. Brewer, 1982
Bianconi, Lorenzo, *Music in the Seventeenth Century*, Cambridge University Press, Cambridge, 1987
Bianconi, Lorenzo, *Music in the Seventeenth Century*, Cambridge, 1987
Bokina, John, *Opera and Politics, from Monteverdi to Henze*, Yale University Press, New Haven and London, 1997
Bowers, Jane and Judith Tick (eds.), *Women Making Music: The Western Art Tradition 1150–1950*, University of Illinois Press, Urbana, 1986
Bukofzer, M. F., *Music in the Baroque Era*, W. W. Norton, 1947
Burden, Michael, *Purcell Remembered*, Faber and Faber, 1995
Bute, P., *The Flute*, London, 1967 and 1979
Campbell, M., *Henry Purcell: Glory of His Age*, Hutchinson, London, 1993; Oxford University Press, 1995
Carroll, Paul, *Baroque Woodwind Instruments*, Ashgate Publishing Limited, 1999
Carter, Tim, *Jacopo Peri, His Life and Works*, Garland Publishing, New York and London, 1989
Crowther, Victor, *The Oratorio in Bologna 1650–1730*, Clarendon Press, Oxford, 1999
Dennison, Peter, *Pelham Humfrey*, Oxford University Press, Oxford, 1986
Dixon, Graham, *Carissimi*, Oxford University Press, Oxford, 1986
Donington, Robert, *Interpretation of Early Music*, Faber and Faber, London, 1989
Gianturco, *Alessandro Stradella, His Life and Works*, Clarendon Press, Oxford, 1994
Hammond, Frederick, *Girolamo Frescobaldi*, Harvard University Press, Cambridge, Mass., 1983
Holman, Peter, *Henry Purcell (Oxford Studies of Composers)*, 1994
Keates, Jonathan, *Purcell, A Biography*, Chatto and Windus, London, 1995
King, R., *Henry Purcell: A Greater Musical Genius England Never Had*, Thames & Hudson, London, 1994
Kölneder, Walter, *Amadeus Book of the Violin: Construction, History and Music*, Amadeus Press
Koneman Music, *The Baroque Pianiste*, Konemann
Kurtzman, Jeffrey, *The Monteverdi Vespers of 1610*, Clarendon Press, Oxford, 1999
Mundy, Simon, *Purcell*, Omnibus, London, 1995
Price, Curtis (ed.), *The Early Baroque Era*, London, 1993
Price, Curtis (ed.), *The Early Baroque Era: from the Late Sixteenth Century to the 1660s*, Prentice Hall, Englewood Cliffs, New Jersey, 1994
Rifkin, Joshua, et al, *French Baroque Masters*, Macmillan, London, 1985
Sadie, Julie Anne (ed.), *Companion to Baroque Music*, London, 1990
Schrade, Leo, *Monteverdi, Creator of Modern Music*, Gollancz, London, 1972
Stevens, Denis, *The Letters of Claudio Monteverdi*, Clarendon Press, Oxford, 1995
Stowell, Robin (ed.), *Cambridge Companion to the Violin*, Cambridge University Press
Tellart, Roger, *Claudio Monteverdi*, Fayard, Paris, 1997
Thistlethwaite, Nicholas and Geoffrey Webber (eds.), *Cambridge Companion to the Organ*, Cambridge University Press
Tomlinson, Gary, *Monteverdi and the End of the Renaissance*, University of California Press, Berkeley, 1985
Treitler, Leo (ed.) *Source Readings in Music History*, Norton, New York, 1998
Webber, Geoffrey, *North German Church Music in the Age of Buxtehude*, Clarendon Press, Oxford, 1996
Westrup, J. A., *Purcell*, Oxford University Press, Oxford, 1995
Whenham, John, *Monteverdi, Vespers (1610)*, Cambridge University Press, Cambridge, 1997

THE LATE BAROQUE

Bartel, Dietrich, *Musica Poetica: Musical-Rhetorical Figures in German Baroque Music*, University of Nebraska Press, 1997
Booth, John, *Vivaldi*, Omnibus Press, 1989
Boyd (ed.), *Oxford Composer Companions: J. S. Bach*, OUP, 1999
Boyd, Malcolm, *Bach (The Master Musicians)*, Oxford University Press, London, 1983
Boyd, Malcolm, *Domenico Scarlatti*, London, 1986
Brown, Pam, *Antonio Vivaldi*, Exley, Watford, 1992
Buelow, George J. (ed.), *The Late Baroque Era*, London, 1993
Burrows, Donald, *Handel*, Oxford University Press, Oxford, 1996
Butt, John (ed.), *The Cambridge Companion to Bach*, Cambridge University Press, Cambridge, 1997
Catucci, Stefano, et al, *Bach and Baroque Music*, Barron's, 1998
Cessac, Catherine, *Marc-Antoine Charpentier*, Paris, 1988 (English translation, Amadeus Press, 1995)
David and Mendel (eds.), revised by Christoph Wolff *The New Bach Reader*, Norton, 1998
Dean, Winton, *Handel*, London, 1982
Dean, Winton and John Merrill Knapp, *Handel's Operas, 1704–1726*, Clarendon Press, Oxford, 1995
Deane, Seamus, *Vivaldi: The Four Seasons*, Penguin Books
Dreyfuss, Laurence, *Bach and the Patterns of Invention*, Harvard University Press, Cambridge, Mass. and London, 1996
Dürr and Kobayashi (eds.), *Bach-Werke Verzeichnis – Kleine Ausgabe*, Breitkopf, 1998
Girdlestone, Cuthbert, *Jean-Philippe Rameau*, London, 1957 (rev. New York, 1969)
Grey, Charlotte, *Johann Sebastian Bach*, Exley, Watford, 1994
Headington, Christopher, *Johann Sebastian Bach*, Pavilion, London, 1997
Heller, Karl, *Antonio Vivaldi, The Red Priest of Venice*, Leipzig, 1991 (English translation, Amadeus Press, 1997)
Hutchings, Arthur, *The Baroque Concerto*, London, 1961
Johnson, Theodore, *Analytical Survey of the Fifteen Two-part Inventions by J. S. Bach*, University Press of America, 1983
Keates, Jonathan, *Handel, The Man and His Music*, Hamish Hamilton, 1986
Landon, H. C. Robbins, *Vivaldi: Voice of the Baroque*, Thames & Hudson, London, 1993
Ledbetter, David, *Continuo Playing According to Handel*, Clarendon Press, 1990
Lewis, Anthony and Nigel Fortune (eds.), 'Opera and Church Music, 1630–1750', in *The New Oxford History of Music*, vol. 5,
Little, Meredith, and Jenne, Natalie, *Dance and the Music of J. S. Bach*, Indiana University Press, 1998
Mellers, Wilfred, *François Couperin and the French Classical Tradition*, London, 1949 (rev. 1986)
Neumann, Frederick, *Ornamentation in Baroque and Post-Baroque Music: with Special Emphsis on J. S. Bach*, Princeton University Press, 1983
Newman, Anthony, *Bach and the Baroque: European Source Materials from the Baroque and Early Classical Periods with Special Emphasis on the Music of J. S. Bach*, Pendragon Press, 1995
Owen, Barbara, *The Registration of Baroque Organ Music*, Indiana University Press, 1999
Palisca, Claude V., *Baroque Music*, Yale, 1968 (rev. 1981)
Radice, Mark A. (ed.), *Opera in Context: Essays on Historical Staging from the Late Renaissance to the Time of Puccini*, Amadeus Press, 1998
Seth, Vikram, *Wind Concertos of Vivaldi*, Penguin Books, 1999
Smith, Ruth, *Handel's Oratorios and Eighteenth-Century Thought*, Cambridge University Press, Cambridge, 1995
Smither, Howard E., *A History of the Oratorio*, University of North Carolina Press, 1977
Stowell, Robin (ed.), *Cambridge Companion to the Cello*, Cambridge University Press
Swan, Claudia (ed.), *Perceptible Processes: Minimalism and the Baroque*, EOS Music Inc., 1997
Talbot, Michael, *Tomaso Albinoni: the Venetian Composer and his World*, Oxford University Press, Oxford, 1990
Talbot, Michael, *Vivaldi (The Master Musicians)*, Oxford University Press, Oxford, 1993
Thompson, Wendy, *Handel*, Omnibus Press, 1994
White, Harry, *Johann Joseph Fux and the Music of the Austro-Italian Baroque*, Scholar Press, Aldershot, 1992
Wilson, Ruth M., *Anglican Chant and Chanting in England, Scotland, and America, 1660 to 1820*, Clarendon Press, Oxford, 1996
Wolff, Christoph, *The Bach Family*, Macmillan, London, 1983

THE CLASSICAL ERA

Altman, Gail S., *Beethoven: A Man of His World*, Anubian Press
Bailie, John, *The Hamlyn History of Classical Music*, Hamlyn, 1999
Baines, A. C., *Woodwind Instruments and their History*, London, 1967
Brown, Clive, and Norrington, Roger, *Classical and Romantic Performing Practice 1750–1900*, Clarendon Press, Oxford, 1999
Braunbehrens, V., trans. T. Bell, *Mozart in Vienna*, Oxford, 1991
Butterworth, Neil, *Haydn*, Omnibus Press, 1983
Charlton, David, *Grétry and the Growth of Opéra-Comique*, Cambridge University Press, Cambridge, 1986
Cook, Nicholas, *Beethoven*, Cambridge University Press, Cambridge, 1993
Cooper, Barry (ed.), *The Beethoven Compendium*, London, 1996
Cooper, Barry, *Beethoven and the Creative Process*, Clarendon Press, Oxford, 1992
Cooper, Barry, *Beethoven (The Master Musicians)*, Oxford, in press
Downs, Philip G., *Classical Music*, Norton, New York, 1992
Fortune, John, *Beethoven's Violin Concerto/ Romances for Violinerto*, Penguin Books, 1999
Forbes, Elliot, (ed.), *Thayer's Life of Beethoven*, 2nd edn, Princeton, 1967
Fowles, John, *Beethoven: Piano Sonatas Nos. 14, 21 and 23*, Penguin Books, 1999
Heartz, Daniel, *Haydn, Mozart and the Viennese School, 1740–80*, Norton, 1995
Hildesheimer, Wolfgang, *Mozart*, J. M. Dent, 1983
Hopkins, A., *The Nine Symphonies of Beethoven*, London and Seattle, 1981
Hughes, Rosemary, *Haydn Master Musicians Series*, Oxford University Press, Oxford, 1950, rev. 1989 and 1994
Hutchings, Arthur, and Eisen, Cliff, *A Companion to Mozart's Piano Concertos*, Clarendon Press, Oxford, 1998
Jenkins, John, *Mozart and the English Connection*, Cygnus Arts, London, 1998
Jones, David Wyn, *The Life of Beethoven*, Cambridge University Press, Cambridge, 1998
Jones, Tim, *Beethoven: "The Moonlight" and Other Sonatas Opp. 27 and 31*, Cambridge University Press, Cambridge, 1999
Kerman, Joseph, and Alan Tyson, *The New Grove Beethoven*, London, 1983
Landon, H. C. Robbins, *Beethoven: His Life, Work and World*, London, 1992
Landon, H.C. Robbins, *Haydn Symphonies*, Ariel Music, 1986
Landon, H. C. Robbins, *Haydn at Eszterhaza 1766–1790*, Thames & Hudson, 1978
Landon, H. C. Robbins, *1791: Mozart's Last Year*, Thames and Hudson, 1999
Lawson, Colin (ed.), *Cambridge Companion to the Clarinet*, Cambridge University Press, Cambridge
Matthews, Denis, *Beethoven*, Oxford University Press, Oxford, 1997
Pestellf, Giorgio, *The Age of Mozart and Beethoven*, cambrdige University Press, Cambridge, 1994
Plantinga, Leon, *Beethoven's Concertos*, Norton, New York and London, 1999
Rice, John A., *Antonio Salieri and the Viennese Opera*, University of Chicago Press, Chicago and London, 1998
Rosen, Charles, *The Classical Style*, Faber and Faber, London, 1971
Rosselli, John, *The Life of Mozart*, Cambridge University Press, Cambridge, 1998
Rushton, Julian, *Classical Music*, Thames & Hudson, 1986
Sipe, Thomas, *Beethoven: the "Eroica" Symphony*, Cambridge University Press, Cambridge, 1998
Sonneck, O. G., *Beethoven: Impressions by his Contemporaries*, New York, 1967
Stanley, John, *Classical Music*, Mitchell Beazley, 1994
Sutcliffe, W. Dean, *String Quartets, Op. 50*, Cambridge Music Handbooks, Cambridge University Press, Cambridge, 1992
Temperley, Nicholas, *The Creation*, Cambridge Music Handbooks, Cambridge University Press, Cambridge, 1991
Thompson, Wendy, *Composer's World: Beethoven*, Faber Paperbacks, 1990
Wellesz, Egon and Stemfeld, Frederick, *The New Oxford History of Music, vii: The Age of Enlightenment 1745–1790*, Oxford University Press, Oxford, 1973
Wyn-Jones, David and H. C. Robbins Landon, *Haydn: His Life and Music*, Thames & Hudson, 1988
Zaslaw, Neal (ed.), *The Classical Era*, Macmillan, London, 1989

THE EARLY ROMANTIC

Cairns, David (trans. and ed.), *The Memoirs of Hector Berlioz*, Cardinal, London, 1990
Cairns, David, *Berlioz*, Vol. One, 'The Making of an Artist', Allen Lane, Penguin, 2nd Edition, 1999; Vol. Two, 'Servitude and Greatness', Allen Lane et al
Caldwell, John, *The Oxford History of English Music, ii: c . 1715 to the Present Day*
Chissell, *Schumann*, Oxford University Press, Oxford, 1977
Gibbs, Christopher (ed.), *The Cambridge Companion to Schubert*, Oxford University Press, Oxford, 1997
Hedley, A., *Chopin (The Master Musicians)*, Dent, 1974
Holoman, D. Kern, *Berlioz*, London, 1989

Johnson, James H., *Listening in Paris: A Cultural History*, University of California Press, Berkeley, 1995
Kimbell, David, *Italian Opera*, Cambridge University Press, Cambridge, 1991
le Huray, Peter and James Day, *Music and Aesthetics in the Fifteenth and Early-Nineteenth Centuries*, Cambridge University Press, Cambridge, 1981
Loesser, Arthur, *Men, Women and Pianos*, Simon & Shuster, New York, 1954
McKay, Elizabeth Norman, *Franz Schubert: a Biography*, Oxford University Press, 1996
New Grove Composer Biographies – The Early Romantics: Chopin, Schumann and Liszt, Macmillan, 1980
Newbould, Brian, *Schubert: The Music and the Man*, Victor Gollancz, 1997
Osborne, Richard, *Rossini*, Dent, London, 1993
Parker, Roger (ed.), *The Oxford Illustrated History of Opera*, Oxford University Press, Oxford, 1994
Pollens, Stewart, *The Early Pianoforte*, Cambridge University Press, Cambridge
Reed, John, *Schubert (The Master Musicians)*, Oxford University Press, Oxford 1987
Reed, John, *The Schubert Song Companion*, Manchester University Press, 1985
Ringer, Alexander (ed.), *The Early Romantic Era*, Macmillan, London, 1990
Rink, John, *Chopin: The Piano Concertos*, Cambridge University Press, Cambridge, 1997
Romanticism, 1830–1890, Oxford University Press, Oxford, 1990
Rosen, Charles, *The Romantic Generation*, HarperCollins, London, 1995
Rosselli, John, *Music and Musicians in Nineteenth-Century Italy*, Batsford, London, 1991
Rowland, David (ed.), *Cambridge Companion to the Piano*, Cambridge University Press
Samson, Jim, *Chopin*, Oxford University Press, Oxford, 1998
Sillitoe, Alan, *Berlioz's Symphonie Fantastique*, Penguin, 1999
Strauss, Richard (ed), *Berlioz: Treatise on Instrumentation*, New York, 1948
Todd, Larry, *Nineteenth-Century Piano Music*, Schirmer, New York, 1990
Walker, Alan (ed.), *Robert Schumann: the Man and his Music,* London, 1972
Whittall, Arnold, *Romantic Music*, Thames & Hudson, London

THE LATE ROMANTIC

Adorno, Theordor W., *In Search of Wagner*, trans. R. Livingstone, New Left Books, London, 1981
Anderson, Robert, *Elgar*, Dent, London, 1993
Avins, Styra, *Johannes Brahms, Life and Letters*, Oxford University Press, 1997
Bailey, Paul (trans.), *Dvorák: Symphony No. 9*, Penguin, London, 1999
Beckerman, Michael, *Dvorák and his world*, Princeton, 1993
Between Tchaikovsky and Nadezhda von Meck, 1876–78, Oxford, 1993
Brown, David, *Tchaikovsky: A Biographical and Critical Study*, Victor Gollancz, 1978–91
Budden, Julian, *Verdi*, Dent, 1985
Butterworth, Neil, *Dvorák*, Omnibus Press
Camer, Mosco, *Puccini, A Critical Biography*, 3rd edition, Gerald Duckworth, London, 1992
Clapham, John, *Dvorák,* London, 1979
Clapham, John, *Smetana*, London, 1971
Cooke, Deryck, *Gustav Mahler: An Introduction to his Music*, Faber, 1980
Cooke, Deryck, *I Saw The World End: A Study of Wagner's Ring*, Oxford University Press, Oxford, 1979, rev. 1991
Dahlhaus, Carl, *Nineteenth-Century Music*, trans. J. B. Robinson, University of California Press, Berkeley and Los Angeles, 1989
Dahlhaus, Carl, *Between Romanticism and Modernism: Four Studies in the Music of the Later Nineteenth Century*, trans. M. Whittall, University of California Press, Berkeley and Los Angeles, 1980
Dean, Winton, *Bizet*, J. M. Dent & Sons Ltd, London, 1975
Deathridge, John and Carl Dalhaus, *The New Grove Wagner*, Macmillan, London, 1984
del Mar, Norman, *The Anatomy of the Orchestra*, London, Faber and Faber
Garden, Edward and Nigel Gotteri (eds.), *To My Best Friend: Correspondence*
Gilliam, Bryan (ed.), *Richard Strauss and His World*, Princeton University Press, Princeton, New Jersey, 1992
Herbert, Trevor and John Wallace (eds.), *Cambridge Companion to Brass Instruments*, Cambridge University Press, Cambridge
Holmes, Paul, *Brahms*, Omnibus Press Paperback, 1987
Hussey, Dyneley, *Verdi*, Dent, London, 1963
Ingham, Richard, *The Cambridge Companion to the Saxophone*, Cambridge University Press, Cambridge
Kennedy, Michael, *Richard Strauss*, Cambridge University Press, Cambridge, 1999
Large, Brian, *Smetana*, London, 1970
MacDonald, Malcolm, *Brahms*, Oxford University Press, 2000
Mann, Thomas, *Pro and Contra Wagner*, trans. A. Blunden with introduction by E. Heller, Faber and Faber, London, 1985
Martin, George, *Verdi, His Music, Life and Times*, Macmillan, London, 1965
Millington, Barry (ed.), *The Wagner Companion*, Thames & Hudson, London, 1992
Nice, David, *Tchaikovsky*, Pavilion, 1997
Orlova, Alexandra (ed.), *Tchaikovsky: A Self-Portrait*, Oxford, 1990
Osborne, Charles, *The Complete Operas of Giacomo Puccini*, Victor Gollancz, London, 1981
Osborne, Charles, *The Complete Operas of Verdi*, Victor.Gollancz, London, 1969
Plantigna, Leon, *Romantic Music: A History of Musical Style in Nineteenth-Century Europe*, W. W. Norton, New York and London, 1984
Poznansky, Alexander, *Tchaikovsky*, Methuen, 1993
Samson, Jim (ed.), *The Late Romantic Era*, Macmillan, London, 1991
Tovey, D. F., *Essays in Musical Analysis*, Vol. II Symphonies, Oxford University Press, London
Walker, Frank, *The Man Verdi*, J. M. Dent, London, 1962
Warrack, John, *Tchaikovsky*, Hamish Hamilton, 1973
Watson, Derek, *Master Musicians*, Oxford University Press, 1996
Whittall, Arnold, *Romantic Music: a Concise History from Schubert to Sibelius*, Thames & Hudson, London, 1987
Wilson, Conrad, *Giacomo Puccini*, Phaidon Press, London, 1997

THE MODERN ERA

Blades, James, *Percussion Instruments and Their History*, London, 1970
Cooper, David, *Bartok: "Concerto for Orchestra"*, Cambridge University Press, Cambridge, 1996
Dahlhaus, C., *Schoenberg and the New Music*, Cambridge, 1989
Hall, Michael, *Leaving Home: a Conducted Tour of Twentieth Century Music with Simon Rattle*, Faber and Faber, London
Nichols, David, *American Experimental Music 1890–1940*, Cambridge, 1996
Nichols, Roger and Langham Smith, Richard, *Pelléas et Mélisande*, Cambridge Opera Book, cambridge University Press, 1989
Nichols, Roger, *The Life of Debussy*, Cambridge, 1998
Schrader, R., *Introduction to Electro-Acoustic Music*, Englewood Cliffs, New Jersey, 1982
Tisdall, O. and A. Bozzola, *Futurism*, London, 1977
Thompson, Wendy, *Claude Debussy*, Faber Paperbacks, 1993
Tyrrell, *Janácek's Operas – A Documentary Account*, London, 1992
Video: *Pelléas et Mélisande*, Hagley, Archer, Maxwell etc. Welsh National Opera, conducted by Pierre Boulez. Directed by Peter Stein. Deutsche Gramophon 072 431-3
Vogal, Jaroslav, *Leos Janácek*, London, 1981

THE LATE 20TH CENTURY

Cook, Nicholas, *Analysing Musical Multimedia*, Oxford University Press, Oxford, 1998
Gough-Yates, K., M. and Tarratt, *The Film Music Book: a Guide to Film Composers*, New Rochelle, 1978
Griffiths, P., *Modern Music: The Avant-garde Since 1945*, Dent, London, 1981
Lindenberger, Herbert, *Opera: The Extravagant Art*, Cornell University Press, Ithaca and London, 1984
Maccalum, F., *The Book of the Marimba*, New York, 1968
Maconie, Robin, *The Works of Karlheinz Stockhausen*, London, 1990
Mellers, Wilfrid, *The Masks of Orpheus*, Manchester University Press, Manchester, 1987
Nyman, M., *Experimental Music: Cage and Beyond*, London, 1999
Sayre, H., *The Object of Performance the American Avant-garde since 1970*, Chicago, 1989
Sohm, H. (ed.), *Happenings and Fluxus*, Cologne, Germany, 1970
Steane, J. B., *The Grand Tradition: Seventy Years of Singing on Record*, Duckworth, London, 1993
Sutcliffe, Tom, *Believing in Opera*, Faber and Faber, London, 1996
Tambling, Jeremy, *Opera, Ideology and Film*, Manchester University Press, 1987

WOMEN IN MUSIC

Block, Adrienne Fried, *Amy Beach, Passionate Victorian: The Life and Work of an American Composer (1867–1944)*, Oxford University Press, Oxford, 1998
Cook, Susan C., and Judy S. Tsou (eds.), *Cecilia Reclaimed: Feminist Perspectives on Gender and Music*, University of Illinois Press, Urbana and Chicago, 1994
Fuller, Sophie, *The Pandora Guide to Women Composers: Britain and the United States, 1629–Present*, Pandora, London, 1994
Glickman, Sylvia and Furman Schleifer, Martha (eds.), *Women Composers: Music Through The Ages*, 12 vols., G. K. Hall, New York, 1996
Neuls-Bates, Carol (ed.), *Women in Music: An Anthology of Source Readings from the Middle Ages to the Present*, Northeastern University Press, Boston, 1996
Pendle, Karin (ed.), *Women and Music: A History*, Indiana University Press, 1991
Reich, Nancy B., *Clara Schumann: The Artist and the Woman*, Victor Gollancz, London, 1985
Sadie, Julie Anne and Samuel Rhian (eds.), *The New Grove Dictionary of Women Composers*, Macmillan, London, 1994
Tick, Judith, *Ruth Crawford Seeger: A Composer's Search for American Music*, Oxford University Press, Oxford, 1997

DISCOGRAPHY

H *after an entry denotes a historic recording which is listed because the performance is particularly outstanding.*

P *after an entry in the Baroque, Classical or Romantic sections indicates a performance employing period instruments.*

THE WORLD OF MUSIC

West Meets East, Yehudi Menuhin, Ravi Shankar, Alla Rakha (EMI)

Inspiration – India: Duets for Sitar, Surbahar, Shehnai, Vilayat Khan, Imrat Khan, Bismillah Khan (EMI)

The Genius of Ustad Vilayat Khan, Vilayat Khan, Kashinath Mishra (EMI)

Shakuhachi – The Japanese Flute, Kohachiro Miyata (Nonesuch Explorer)

China: Classical Music, various artists of the 1950s (Ocora)

China: The Art of the Qin, Li Xiangting (Ocora)

THE MEDIEVAL ERA

Adam de la Halle: *Vocal, Choral & Instrumental Music*, Sequentia (Deutsche Harmonia Mundi)

A Dance in the Garden of Mirth: Medieval Instrumental Music, Dufay Collective (Chandos)

Carmina Burana, New London Consort, Philip Pickett (L'Oiseau-Lyre)

Dufay: *Missa L'homme armé; Motets*, Hilliard Ensemble (dir) Paul Hillier (EMI)

Dufay: *Complete Secular Music*, Medieval Ensemble of London (dirs) Peter and Timothy Davies (Decca)

Dunstable: *Motets*, Hilliard Ensemble (dir) Paul Hillier (EMI)

Dunstable: *Missa Rex seculorum; Motets*, Orlando Consort (Metronome)

Essential Gregorian Chant, Pro Cantione Antiqua (dir) James O'Donnell (United)

Hildegard of Bingen: *A Feather on the Breath of God – Sequences & Hymns*, Emma Kirkby, Gothic Voices (dir) Christopher Page (Hyperion)

Leonin: *Vocal & Choral Works*, John Potter, Richard Wistreich, Capella Amsterdam (Hyperion)

Machaut: *Messe de Nostre Dame, etc.*, Hilliard Ensemble (dir) Paul Hillier (Hyperion)

Ockeghem: *Missa Mi-Mi; Salve Regina; Alma redemptoris mater*, Clerks' Group (dir) Edward Wickham (ASV Gaudeamus)

Ockeghem: *Mass De plus en plus and songs*; Orlando Consort (Archiv)

Ockeghem: *Requiem; Fors seulement; Missa Fors seulement*; De la Rue: *Fors seulement;* Brumel: *Du tout plongiet/Fors seulement*, Clerks' Group (dir) Edward Wickham (ASV Gaudeamus)

Passion Music by Tinctoris, Dufay, des Prez, Isaac, Compère & Obrecht, Orlando Consort (Metronome)

Perotin: *Viderunt omnes; Sederunt principes*, etc., Hilliard Ensemble (dir) Paul Hillier (ECM)

Power: *Sacred Choral Works*, Hilliard Ensemble (dir) Paul Hillier (Virgin Veritas)

Tinctoris: Missa L'Homme armé; Missa Sine nomine, Clerks' Group (dir) Edward Wickham (Cyprès)

THE RENAISSANCE

Agricola: *Mass, motets and songs*, Huelgas Ensemble (dir) Paul van Nevel (Sony Classcial SK)

Art of the Netherlands, Early Music Consort of London (dir) David Munrow (Virgin Classics)

Byrd: *The Complete Keyboard Music*, Davitt Moroney (Hyperion)

Byrd: *The Three Masses*, Tallis Scholars (dir) Peter Phillips (Gimell)

Byrd: *Music for Viols, Voices & Keyboard*, Tessa Bonner, Timothy Roberts, Red Byrd, Rose Consort (Naxos)

Consort Music of the English Renaissance, Extempore String Ensemble, (Meridian)

Dowland: *Lachrimae*, Hespèrion XX (Auvidis Astrée)

Dowland: *Lute Songs & Lute Solos*, Alfred Deller, Robert Spencer, Consort of Six (Harmonia Mundi)

Gabrieli, G.: *Music for San Rocco*, Gabrieli Consort & Players (dir) Paul McCreesh (Archiv)

Gibbons: *Anthems, Madrigals & Fantasies*; Morley: *Madrigals*, Deller Consort (dir) Alfred Deller, Ambrosian Singers (dir) Denis Stevens (Archiv) **H**

Gibbons: *Choral & Organ Music*, Oxford Camerata (dir) Jeremy Summerly, Laurence Cummings, organ (Naxos)

Gombert: *Regina caeli* etc., Huelgas Ensemble (dir) Paul van Nevel (Sony Classical SK)

Guerrero: *Sacred Choral Works, incl. 'Missa Sancta at immaculata'*, Westminster Cathedral Choir (dir) James O'Donnell (Hyperion)

Janequin: *Chansons*, Ensemble Clément Janequin (Harmonia Mundi)

Josquin: *Motets & Chansons*, Hilliard Ensemble (Virgin Veritas)

Josquin: *Mass Pange lingua*, Ensembles Organum (dirs) Marcel Pérès and Dominique Visse (Harmonia Mundi)

Josquin: *Sacred Choral Works, incl. 'Missa L'homme armé'*, Tallis Scholars (dir) Peter Phillips (Gimell)

Lassus: *Lagrima di san Pietro*, Ensemble Vocal Européen (dir) Philippe Herreweghe (Harmonia Mundi)

Lassus: *Chansons et Moresche*, Ensemble Clement Janéquin (dir) Dominique Visse (Harmonia Mundi)

Lassus: *Villanelle, moresche a altre canzoni*, Concerto Italiano (dir) Rinaldo Alessandrini (Opus 111)

Le Jeune: *Le Printans*, Huelgas Ensemble (dir) Paul Van Nevel (Sony)

Le Jeune: *Chansons et fantaisies de violes*, Ensemble Clément Janequin, Ensemble Les Élements (Harmonia Mundi)

Le Jeune: *Missa ad placitum; Magnificat; Motets*, Ensemble Clément Janequin (dir) Dominique Visse (Harmonia Mundi)

Les Cris de Paris: Chansons de Janequin & Sermisy, Ensemble Clément Janequin (Harmonia Mundi)

Morales: *Sacred Choral Works, incl. 'Missa Queramus cum pastoribus'*, Westminster Cathedral Choir (dir) James O'Donnell (Hyperion)

Palestrina: *Canticum Canticorum Salomonis*, Pro Cantione Antiqua (dir) Bruno Turner (Hyperion)

Palestrina: *Music for Good Friday incl. 'Improperia'*, Musica Contexta (dir) Simon Ravens (Chandos)

Palestrina: *Missa Papae Marcelli; Missa brevis*, Westminster Cathedral Choir (dir) David Hill (Hyperion)

Praetorius: *Dances from Terpsichore; Motets*, Early Music Consort of London (dir) David Munrow (Virgin Veritas)

Rore: *Mass Praeter rerum serium and motets*, Tallis Scholars (dir) Peter Phillips (Gimmell)

Sheppard: *Sacred Choral Music*; Tye: *Mass Euge bone*, Clerkes of Oxenford (dir) David Wulstan (Proudsound)

Sixteenth-Century English Keyboard Music, Trevor Pinnock (CRD)

Songs & Dances from Shakespeare, Broadside Band (dir) Jeremy Barlow (Saydisc)

Spanish & Mexican Renaissance Vocal Music, Hilliard Ensemble (EMI)

Tallis: *Lamentations*, Deller Consort (dir) Alfred Deller (Vanguard) **H**

Tallis: *Sacred Choral Works, incl. 'Spem in alium'*, Tallis Scholars (dir) Peter Phillips (Gimell)

Taverner: *Sacred Choral Works, incl. 'Missa Gloria tibi Trinitas'*, Sixteen (dir) Harry Christophers, (Hyperion)

Taverner, Tye & Sheppard: *Western Wind Masses*, Tallis Scholars (dir) Peter Phillips (Gimell)

Victoria: *Officium defunctorum*, Westminster Cathedral Choir (dir) David Hill (Hyperion)

Victoria: *Tenebrae Responsories*, Pro Cantione Antiqua (dir) Bruno Turner (EMI)

Victoria: *Sacred Choral Works, incl. 'Missa O magnum mysterium'*, Westminster Cathedral Choir (dir) David Hill (Hyperion)

THE EARLY BAROQUE

An Excess of Pleasure, Palladian Ensemble (Linn) **P**

Biber: *Mystery Sonatas*, Eduard Melkus, Huguette Dreyfus, Lionel Rogg, Karl Scheit (Archiv) **P**

Blow: *Venus and Adonis*, Soloists, New London Consort (dir) Philip Pickett (L'Oiseau-Lyre) **P**

Buxtehude: *Works for Organ*, Marie-Claire Alain (Erato) **P**

Charpentier: *La descente d'Orphée aux enfers*, Les Arts Florissants (dir) William Christie (Erato)

Corelli: *Violin Sonatas, Op. 5*, The Locatelli Trio (Hyperion)

Corelli: *Concerti grossi, Op. 6*, Europa Galante (dir) Fabio Biondi (Opus 111) **P**

German 17th-Century Church Music, Robin Blaze, Parley of Instruments (Hyperion) **P**

Grand Tour: Music from 16th- & 17th-century Italy, Spain & Germany, His Majesties Sagbutts & Cornetts (Hyperion) **P**

Lamento d'Arianna, Consort of Musicke (dir) Anthony Rooley (Deutsche Harmonia Mundi) **P**

Monteverdi: *L'Orfeo*, Soloists, New London Consort (dir) Philip Pickett (L'Oiseau-Lyre) **P**

Monteverdi: *Madrigali Concertati*, Tragicomedia (Teldec Das Alte Werk)

Monteverdi: *Ottavo Libro dei Madrigali*, Concerto Italiano (dir) Rinaldo Alessandrini (Opus 111)

Monteverdi: *Selva Morale e Spirituale*, Taverner Consort, Choir & Players (dir) Andrew Parrott (Virgin Veritas) **P**

Monteverdi: *Vespro della Beata Vergine 1610*, Taverner Consort, Choir & Players (dir) Andrew Parrott (Virgin Veritas) **P**

Monteverdi: *Vespers of 1610*, Moteverdi Choir and Orchestra (dir) John Eliot Gardiner (Decca)

Monteverdi: *Vespers*, Les Arts Florissants (dir) William Christie (Erato)

Monteverdi: *Vespers*, Monteverdi Choir (dir) John Eliot Gardiner (DG Archiv)

Monteverdi: *Musica Sacra*, Concerto Italiano (dir) Rinaldo Alessandrini (Opus 111)

Musica Dolce, Julianne Baird, Colin Tilney (Dorian) **P**

Opera Baroque: les moments forts, Les arts florissants & others, (Harmonia Mundi) **P**

Pachelbel: *Canon & Gigue; Two Suites; Aria con variazioni*; Buxtehude: *Three Sonatas*, Musica Antiqua Cologne (dir) Reinhard Goebel (Archiv) **P**

Purcell: *A Purcell Miscellany*, Catherine Bott, Purcell Quartet (Chandos) **P**

Purcell: *Dido and Aeneas*, St Anthony Singers, English Chamber Orchestra (dir) Anthony Lewis (Decca)

Purcell: *Fantasias,* Phantasm (Simax) **P**

Purcell: *Choral Works*, Soloists, Choir of Christ Church Cathedral, Oxford, English Concert (dir) Simon Preston (Archiv) **P**

Purcell: *Music for Queen Mary*, Soloists, Westminster Abbey Choir, New London Consort (dir) Martin Neary (Sony) **P**

Purcell: *Odes*, Soloists, Choir & Orchestra of the Age of Enlightenment (dir) Gustav Leonhardt (Virgin Veritas) **P**

Schütz: *Psalms of David*, Cantus Cölln, Concerto Paladino (dir) Konrad Junghänel (Harmonia Mundi) **P**

Schütz: *Weihnachtshistorie*, Tavener Consort, Choir and Players (dir) Andrew Parrott (Virgin Veritas)

Schütz: *Psalms, Motets, Concertos*, Cantus Cölln, Musica Fiata, Hanover Boys' Choir (Deutsche Harmonia Mundi) **P**

Strozzi: *Virtusissima Cantatrice (Various vocal works)* (Hyperion)

Strozzi: *Sacri musicali affetti, Bk 1 (extracts)*, Maria Cristina Kiehr, Concerto Soave (Harmonia Mundi) **P**

Sweelinck: *Cantiones sacrae*, Trinity College Choir, Cambridge (dir) Richard Marlow (Hyperion)

Venetian Vespers, Gabrieli Consort & Players (dir) Paul McCreesh (Archiv) **P**

THE LATE BAROQUE

Bach: *Italian Concerto; Chromatic Fantasia & Fugue, etc.*, Scott Ross (Erato) **P**

Bach: *Goldberg Variations*, Scott Ross (EMI) **P**

Bach: *The Well-Tempered Clavier, Bks 1 & 2*, Gustav Leonhardt (Deutsche Harmonia Mundi) **P**

Bach: *Art of Fugue*, Gustav Leonhardt (Deutsche Harmonia Mundi) **P**

Bach: *Toccata & Fugue in D minor, etc.*, Ton Koopman (Teldec or Archiv) **P**

Bach: *Six Solo Cello Suites*, Jaap ter Linden (Harmonia Mundi) **P**

Bach: *Solo Violin Sonatas & Partitas*, Sigiswald Kuijken (Deutsche Harmonia Mundi) **P**

Bach: *Viola da Gamba Sonatas*, Laurence Dreyfus & Ketil Haugsand (Simax) **P**

Bach: *Concertos*, Les Solistes Romandes, New Philharmonia Orchestra (dirs) Arpad Gerecz, Edo de Waart (Philips) **P**

Bach: *Brandenburg Concertos; Orchestral Suites*, Busch Chamber Players (dir) Adolf Busch (Pearl) **H**

Bach: *Brandenburg Concertos*, Camerata of the 18th Century (dir) Konrad Hünteler (MDG Gold) **P**

Bach: *Cantatas 140 and 147*, Monteverdi Choir, English Baroque Soloists (dir) John Eliot Gardiner (DG Archiv) **P**

Bach: *Mass in B Minor*, Soloists, Collegium Musicum of the Netherlands Bachvereniging, La Petite Bande (dir) Gustav Leonhardt (Deutsche Harmonia Mundi) **P**

Bach: *St Matthew Passion*, Soloists, Tölz Boys' Choir, La Petite Bande (dir) Gustav Leonhardt (Deutsche Harmonia Mundi) **P**

Couperin: *Quatrième livre de clavecin*, (harpsichord) Kenneth Gilbert (Harmonia Mundi) **P**

Couperin: *Concerts royaux*, Kuijken Ensemble (Sony) **P**

Couperin: *Les Apothéoses*, Hespèrion XX (Auvidis Astrée) **P**

Couperin: *Les Nations*, Kuijken Ensemble (Accent) **P**

Eighteenth Century Music by Women Composers, keyboard music by Cecilia Barthelemon, Marianne Martinez, Marianna d'Auenbrugg, Elisabetta de Gambarini & Maria Hester Park (Gasparo) **P**

Geminiani: *Concerti grossi, Op. 3*, Europa Galante (dir) Fabio Biondi (Opus 111) **P**

Handel: *Harpsichord Suites*, Paul Nicholson (Hyperion) **P**

Handel: *Trio Sonatas, Op. 2*, London Baroque (Harmonia Mundi) **P**

Handel: *Organ Concertos*, Amsterdam Baroque Orchestra (sol & dir) Ton Koopman (Erato) **P**

Handel: Concerti grossi, Op. 6, Busch Chamber Players (dir) Adolf Busch (Pearl) **H**

Handel: Concerti grossi, Op. 6, English Concert (dir) Trevor Pinnock (Archiv) **P**

Handel: *Water Music*; Telemann: *Water Music*, Il Fondamento (dir) Paul Dombrecht (Vanguard) **P**

Handel: *Music for the Royal Fireworks; Coronation Anthems*, King's Consort (dir) Robert King (Hyperion) **P**

Handel: *Cantata 'Lucrezia' & Arias*, Janet Baker, English CO (cond) Raymond Leppard (Philips)

Handel: *Messiah*, Soloists, Les Arts Florissants (dir) William Christie (Harmonia Mundi) **P**

Handel: *Messiah*, English Concert and Choir (dir) Trevor Pinnock (DG Archiv)

Handel: *Messiah*, Gabrieli Consort and Players (dir) Paul McCreesh (DG Archiv)

Handel: *Messiah*, Royal Philharmonic Orchestra and Chorus (dir) Thomas Beecham (RCA)

Handel: *Solomon*, Soloists, Gabrieli Consort & Players (dir) Paul McCreesh (Archiv) **P**

Handel: *Partenope*, Soloists, La Petite Bande (dir) Sigiswald Kuijken (Deutsche Harmonia Mundi) **P**

Handel: *Alessandro*, Soloists, La Petite Bande (dir) Sigiswald Kuijken (Deutsche Harmonia Mundi) **P**

Jacquet de la Guerre: *Sonatas; Trio Sonatas*, Camerata Moderna (MDG Gold) **P**

Jacquet de la Guerre: Pieces for Harpsichord, Blandine Verlet (Auvidis) **P**
Leclair: *Ouvertures & Trio Sonatas*, Purcell Quartet (Chandos) **P**
Locatelli: *Concerti grossi; Sinfonia in F minor*, Europa Galante (sol & dir) Fabio Biondi (opus 111) **P**
Lully: *Dies Irae; Miserere*; Dumont: *Memorare*, Soloists, Choir & Orchestra of the Chapelle Royale (cond) Philippe Herreweghe (Harmonia Mundi) **P**
Marais: *Pièces de Viol, Bk 5*, Wieland Kuijken, Robert Kohnen, Kaori Uemura (Accent) **P**
Pergolesi: *Stabat Mater*; A. Scarlatti: *Stabat Mater*, Concerto Italiano (dir) Rinaldo Alessandrini (Opus 111) **P**
Pergolesi: *La serva padrona; Livietta e Tracollo*, Soloists, Le Petite Bande (dir) Sigiswald Kuijken (Accent) **P**
Rameau: *Pièces de Clavecin en concerts*, Barthold, Sigiswald & Wieland Kuijken, Robert Kohnen (Accent) **P**
Rameau: *Suite 'Les Paladins'*, Orchestra of the Age of Enlightenment (dir) Gustav Leonhardt (Philips) **P**
Rameau: *Hippolyte et Aricie*, Soloists, Les Arts Florissants (dir) William Christie (Erato) **P**
Scarlatti, D.: *Harpsichord Sonatas*, Scott Ross (Erato) **P**
Scarlatti, D.: *Harpsichord Sonatas*, Andreas Staier (Teldec or Deutsche Harmonia Mundi) **P**
Tartini: *Five Violin Sonatas*, Fabio Biondi, Rinaldo Alessandrini et al (Opus 111) **P**
Tartini: *Violin Concertos*, Uto Ughi, I Solisti Veneti (dir) Claudio Scimone (Erato)
Telemann: *12 Paris Quartets*, Barthold, Sigiswald & Wieland Kuijken, Gustav Leonhardt (Sony Vivarte) **P**
Telemann: *Ouverture 'La Bourse', Suites*, Il Fondamento (dir) Paul Dombrecht (Vanguard) **P**
Telemann: Christmas Oratorio, Cantatas, Soloists, Michaelstein Telemann Chamber Choir & Orchestra (dir) Ludger Rémy (CPO) **P**
Vivaldi: *L'estro armonico, Op. 3*, Europa Galante (sol & dir) Fabio Biondi (Virgin Veritas) **P**
Vivaldi: *The Four Seasons*, The Amserdam Baroque Orchestra (dir) Tom Koopman (Erato)
Zelenka: *Concerto; Hipocondrie; Ouverture; Simphonia*, Il Fondamento (dir) Paul Dombrecht

THE CLASSICAL ERA

Bach, J. C.: *Quintets, Op. 11*, Camerata of the 18th Century (MDG Gold) **P**
Bach, C. P. E.: *Cello Concertos*, Anner Bylsma, Orchestra of the Age of Enlightenment (dir) Gustav Leonhardt (Virgin Veritas) **P**
Bach, C. P. E.: *Symphonies*, Orchestra of the Age of Enlightenment (dir) Gustav Leonhardt (Virgin Veritas) **P**
Bach, C. P. E.: Magnificat, Gächinger Cantorei Stuttgart, Bach Collegium Stuttgart (dir) Helmuth Rilling (Hänssler)
Beethoven: *32 Piano Sonatas, Diabelli Variations*, Artur Schnabel (Pearl) **H**
Beethoven: *32 Piano Sonatas*, Richard Goode (Nonesuch)
Beethoven: *Diabelli Variations*, Alfred Brendel (Philips)
Beethoven: *String Quartets*, Gabrieli Quartet, Aeolian Quartet (Decca)
Beethoven: *Late String Quartets*, Busch Quartet (Pearl) **H**
Beethoven: *Late String Quartets*, Lindsay Quartet (ASV)
Beethoven: *Piano Concertos; Violin Concerto; Triple Concerto*, Emil Gilels, David Oistrakh, Lev Oborin, Sviatoslav Knushevitzky, Nathan Milstein, French National & Philharmonia Orchestras (cond) André Vandernoot, André Cluytens, Sir Malcolm Sargent, Leopold Ludwig (EMI) **H**
Beethoven: *Piano Concertos*, Steven Lubin, Academy of Ancient Music (cond) Christopher Hogwood (L'Oiseau-Lyre) **P**
Beethoven: *Violin Concerto; Two Romances*, Thomas Zehetmair, Orchestra of the 18th Century (cond) Frans Bruggen (Philips) **P**
Beethoven: *Symphonies Nos 1-9*, NBC SO (cond) Arturo Toscanini (RCA) **H**
Beethoven: *Symphonies Nos 1-9*, North German Radio SO (cond) Günter Wand (RCA)
Beethoven: *Symphonies Nos 5 & 7*, Vienna PO (cond) Carlos Kleiber (Deutsche Grammophon)
Beethoven: *Fidelio*, Soloists, Deutsche Oper Chorus, Berlin PO (cond) Herbert von Karajan (EMI)
Beethoven: *Missa Solemnis*, Soloists, Netherlands Radio Chorus, Royal Concertgebouw Orchestra (cond) Eugen Jochum (Philips)
Boccherini: *Three String Quintets*, Europa Galante (Opus 111) **P**
Boccherini: *Two Cello Concertos; Three Cello Sonatas*, Steven Isserlis, Maggie Cole, Ostrobothnian CO (cond) Juha Kangas
Boyce: *Symphonies*, English Concert (dir) Trevor Pinnock (Archiv) **P**
Cimarosa: *Il matrimonio segreto*, Soloists, Orchestra of La Scala, Milan (cond) Nino Sanzogno (EMI) **H**
Clementi: *Piano sonatas op. 13/6, op. 24/2, op. 25/5, op. 37/1*, Jos van Immerseel (Accent) **P**
Dittersdorf: *Sinfonia concertante; Viola Concerto; Divertimento in D*, Petr Pribyl, David Rejchrt, Jakub Waldmann, South Bohemian PO (sol & dir) Ondrej Kukal
Gluck: *Orfeo ed Euridice*, Stuttgart Chamber Choir, Tafelmusik (cond) Frieder Bemius (Sony) **P**
Haydn: *Piano Sonatas*, Alfred Brendel (Philips)
Haydn: *Baryton Trios*, John Hsu, David Miller, Fortunato Arico (ASV) **P**
Haydn: *'Joke' and 'Fifths' Quartets;* Hofstetter: *'Serenade' Quartet*, Janácek Quartet (Decca)
Haydn: *Op. 1/1, 'Lark' & 'Rider' Quartets*, Hagen Quartet (Deutsche Grammophon)
Haydn: *String Quartets, Op. 76*, Alban Berg Quartet (EMI)
Haydn: *String Quartets, Op. 77*, Quatuor Mosaïques (Auvidis Astrée) **P**
Haydn: *Trumpet Concerto;* Hummel: *Trumpet Concerto*, Reinhold Friedrich, Wiener Akademie (cond) Martin Haselböck (Capriccio) **P**
Haydn: *The Seven Last Words*, I Solisti di Zagreb (cond) Antonio Janigro (Vanguard)
Haydn: *'Le Matin', 'Le Midi' & 'Le Soir' Symphonies*, English Concert (dir) Trevor Pinnock (Archiv) **P**
Haydn: *'Sturm und Drang' Symphonies (2 Vols)*, Radio Zagreb SO (cond) Antonio Janigro (Vanguard)
Haydn: *Paris Symphonies, Nos 82-87*, Orchestra of the Age of Enlightenment (cond) Sigiswald Kuijken (Philips) **P**
Haydn: *Symphonies Nos 88-92*, La Petite Bande (cond) Sigiswald Kuijken (Philips) **P**
Haydn: *London Symphonies, Nos 94-104*, La Petite Bande (cond) Sigiswald Kuijken (Philips) **P**
Haydn: *Nelson Mass; Te Deum*, Soloists, English Concert Choir, English Concert (cond) Trevor Pinnock (Archiv) **P**
Haydn: *The Creation*, Soloists, Monteverdi Choir, English Baroque Soloists, Sir John Eliot Gardiner (Archiv) **P**
Haydn: *Missa in augustiis*, (incl. Handel, Vivaldi), Choir of King's College, Cambridge, London Symphony Orchestra (dir) David Willcocks (Decca)
Mozart: *Piano Concerto No. 20 in D minor*, English Chamber Orchestra (dir) Murray Peahia (Sony Classical) **P**
Mozart: *Piano Concerto No. 20 in D minor*, English Chamber Orchestra (dir) Jeffrey Tate (Philips)
Mozart: *Piano Concerto No. 20 in D minor*, Orpheus Chamber Orchestra (Nonesuch)
Mozart: *Piano Concerto in D minor*, English Baroque Soloists (dir) John Elior Gardiner (DG Archiv)
Mozart: *The 'Haydn', 'Hoffmeister' & 'Prussian' String Quartets*, Quatuor Mosaïques (Auvidis Astrée) **P**
Mozart: *Piano Quartets*, Mozartean Players (Harmonia Mundi) **P**
Mozart: *Clarinet Quintet; 'Kegelstatt' Trio*, Wolfgang Meyer, Patrick Cohen, Quatuor Mosaïques (Auvidis Astrée) **P**
Mozart: *Four String Quintets*, Hausmusik (Virgin Veritas) **P**
Mozart: *Wind Music (3 Vols)*, Ensemble Zefiro (Auvidis Astrée) **P**
Mozart: *Clarinet, Oboe & Flute Concertos*, Joy Farrell, Nicholas Daniel, Kate Hill, Britten Sinfonia (cond) Nicholas Cleobury (Classic FM)
Mozart: *Horn Concertos*, Anthony Halstead, Academy of Ancient Music (dir) Christopher Hogwood (L'Oiseau-Lyre) **P**
Mozart: *Piano Concertos (Various Vols)*, Robert Levin, Academy of Ancient Music (dir) Christopher Hogwood (L'Oiseau-Lyre) **P**
Mozart: *Piano Concertos Nos 19 & 27; Piano Sonata in F*, Clara Haskil, Berlin Philharmonic & Bavarian State Orchestras (cond) Ferenc Fricsay **H**
Mozart: *String Quartet in C*, Alban Berg Quartet (Teldec)
Mozart: *Violin Concertos; Sinfonia concertante in E flat*, Orchestra of the Age of Enlightenment (sol & dir) Monica Huggett (Virgin Veritas) **P**
Mozart: *Sinfonia concertante in E flat; Concertone; Rondo in C*, Pavlo Beznosiuk, Portland Baroque Orchestra (sol & dir) Monica Huggett (Virgin Veritas) **P**
Mozart: *Mass in C minor*, Soloists, La Chapelle Royale, Collegium Vocale, Orchestre des Champs Élysées (cond) Philippe Herreweghe (Harmonia Mundi) **P**
Mozart: *Requiem*, Solists, La Chapelle Royale, Collegium Vocale, Orchestre des Champs Élysées (cond) Philippe Herreweghe (Harmonia Mundi) **P**
Mozart: *Le nozze di Figaro*, Soloists, Glyndebourne Festival Chorus & Orchestra (cond) Vittorio Gui (Classics for Pleasure)
Mozart: *Don Giovanni*, Soloists, Philharmonia Chorus & Orchestra (cond) Carlo Maria Giulini (EMI)
Mozart: *Così fan tutte*, Soloists, Philharmonia Chorus & Orchestra (cond) Herbert von Karajan (EMI) **H**
Mozart: *Così fan tutte*, Soloists, Cologne Chamber Chorus & Orchestra (cond) René Jacobs (Harmonia Mundi) **P**
Mozart: *Die Zauberflöte*, Soloists, Vienna State Opera Chorus, Vienna PO (cond) Sir Georg Solti (Decca)
Salieri: *Falstaff*, Soloists, Milan Madrigalists, Guido Cantelli Orchestra (cond) Alberto Veronesi

THE EARLY ROMANTIC

Bellini: *Norma*, Soloists incl. Maria Callas, Chorus & Orchestra of La Scala, Milan (cond) Tullio Serafin (EMI) **H**
Berlioz: *Symphonic fantastique*, Orchestre Révolutionnaire et Romantique, Sir John Eliot Gardiner (Philips) **P**
Berlioz: *Symphonie fantastique*, Royal Concertgebouw Orchestra (cond) Sir Colin Davis (Philips or Decca)
Berlioz: *Symphonie fantastique*, Orchestre de l'Opera Bastille (cond) Myung-Whun Chung (Deutsche Grammophon)
Berlioz: *Symphonie fantastique*, The London Classical Players (cond) Roger Norrington (EMI)
Berlioz: *Harold in Italy*, Laurent Verney, Orchestre de l'Opéra Bastille (cond) Myung-Whun Chung (Deutsche Grammophon)
Berlioz: *Nuits d'Ete; Mélodies*, Soloists, Orchestre de l'Opéra de Lyon (cond) Sir John Eliot Gardiner (Erato)
Berwald: *Sinfonie singulière; Symphony in E flat*, LSO (cond) Sixten Ehrling (Bluebell)
Berwald: *Sinfonie sérieuse; Overtures; Tone Poems*, Swedish Radio SO (cond) Sixten Ehrling (Bluebell)
Berlioz: *La Damnation de Faust*, Riegel, Von Stade, Van Dam, King, Chicago Chorus & SO, Sir Georg Solti (Decca)
Cherubini: *Requiem in D minor*; Mozart: *'Coronation' Mass*, Soloists, Czech Philharmonic Chorus & Orchestra, Brasseur Choir Lamoureux Orchestra (cond) Igor Markevitch (Deutsche Grammophon)
Chopin: *14 Waltzes; Barcarolle; Nocturne; Mazurka*, Dinu Lipatti (EMI) **H**
Chopin: *Chopin Favourites (2 Vols)*, Vladimir Ashkenazy (Decca)
Chopin: *Nocturnes; Polonaises; Waltzes*, Yevgeny Kissin (RCA)
Chopin: *Ballades; Scherzos; Tarantelle*, Artur Rubinstein (RCA)
Chopin: *Scherzos; Études; Mazurkas*, Ivan Moravec (Dorian)
Chopin: *Ballades*, Murray Perahia (Sony SK)
Chopin: *Nocturnes*, Ivan Moravec (Erato)
Chopin: *15 Mazurkas*, André Tchaikovsky (Dante)
Chopin: *Piano Concerto No. 1, etc.*, Emanuel Ax, Orchestra of the Age of Enlightenment (cond) Sir Charles Mackerras (Sony) **P**
Donizetti: *L'Elisir d'amore*, Soloists, Tallis Chamber Choir, English CO (cond) Marcello Viotti (Erato)
Donizetti: *Don Pasquale*, Soloists, Ambrosian Opera Chorus, Philharmonia (cond) Riccardo Muti (EMI)
Donizetti: *Lucia di Lammermoor*, Soloists, Royal Opera House Chorus & Orchestra (cond) Richard Bonynge (Decca)
Glinka: *Ruslan and Lyudmila*, Soloists, Kirov Opera Chorus & Orchestra (cond) Valery Gergiev (Philips)
Kuhlau: *Overtures*, Danish State Radio SO (cond) Michael Schønwandt (Chandos)
Liszt: *19 Hungarian Rhapsodies*, Various Pianists (VAI) **H**
Liszt: *Années de pèlerinage (excerpts); Gondoliera; Deux Légendes*, Wilhelm Kempff (Deutsche Grammophon)
Liszt: *Sonata in B minor*; Schubert: *Sonata in D*, Emil Gilels (RCA)
Liszt: *Symphonic poems: 'Mazeppa', 'Les Préludes', 'Prometheus', 'Tasso'*, Polish National RSO (cond) Michael Halász (Naxos)
Loewe: *'Carl Loewe zu Ehren': Lieder & Ballads*, Elisabeth Rethberg, Julia Culp, Sigrid Onegin, Karl Erb, Gerhard Hüsch, Heinrich Schlusnus, Hans Hotter, Paul Bender et al (Preiser) **H**
Mendelssohn: *Octet, Quintet No. 1*, Hausmusik London (Virgin Veritas) **P**
Mendelssohn: *Quartet No. 2, Quintet No. 2*, Hausmusik London (Virgin Veritas) **P**
Mendelssohn: *Violin Concerto in E minor*, Bamberg SO, Kyoto Takazawa, (cond) Claus Peter Flor (RCA Victor)
Mendelsson: *'Scottish' & 'Italian' Symphonies*, San Francisco SO (cond) Herbert Blomstedt (Decca)
Mendelssohn: *'Italian' & 'Reformation' Symphonies*, Vienna PO (cond) Sir John Eliot Gardiner (Deutsche Grammophon)
Mendelssohn: *Elijah*, Soloists, Philharmonia Chorus & Orchestra (cond) Rafael Frühbeck de Burgos (EMI)
Mendelssohn Hensel: *Piano Trio in G minor;* Mendelssohn: *Piano Trios*, Abegg Trio (Tacet)
Mendelssohn Hensel: *Lieder*, Susan Gritton, Eugene Asti (Hyperion)
Meyerbeer: *Les Huguenots*, Soloists, New Philharmonia Orchestra (cond) Richard Bonynge (Decca)
Paganini: *24 Caprices*, Salvatore Accardo (Deutsche Grammophon)
Rolla: *Gran duetti concertanti*, Salvatore Accardo, Luigi Alberto Bianchi (Dynamic)
Rossini: *Overtures*, Philharmonia Orchestra, Carlo Maria Giulini (EMI)
Rossini: *Il barbiere di Siviglia*, Soloists, Glyndebourne Chorus & Orchestra (cond) Vittorio Gui (EMI)
Rossini: *La Cenerentola*, Soloists, Chorus & Orchestra of Teatro Communale, Bologna (cond) Riccardo Chailly (Decca)
Rossini: *L'Italiana in Algeri*, Soloists, Prague Philharmonic Chorus, i Solisti Veneti (cond) Claudio Scimone (Erato)
Rossini: *Semiramide*, Soloists, Ambrosian Opera Chorus, LSO (cond) Richard Bonynge (Decca)
Rossini: *Il Turco in Italia*, Soloists, Chorus & Orchestra of La Scala, Milan (cond) Riccardo Chailly (Decca)
Schubert: *Music for Piano Four Hands*, Duo Tal & Groethuysen (Sony)
Schubert: *Piano Sonata in B flat*, Radu Lupu (Decca)
Schubert: *String Quartet in D minor; Quartet in G major*, Busch Quartet (EMI) **H**
Schubert: *String Quartet in D minor; Quartet in E flat*, Alban Berg Quartet (EMI)
Schubert: *String Quintet in C; Symphony No. 5*, Isaac Stern, Alexander Schneider, Milton Katims, Pablo Casals, Paul Tortelier et al (Sony) **H**

Schubert: *Octet*, Academy of Ancient Music Chamber Ensemble (L'Oiseau-Lyre) **P**
Schubert: *Symphonies Nos. 3 & 8*, Vienna PO, Carlos Kleiber (Deutsche Grammophon)
Schubert: *Symphony No. 9*; Wagner: *Siegfried Idyll*, Vienna PO, Sir Georg Solti (Decca Legends)
Schubert: *Die schöne Müllerin*, Aksel Schiøtz, Gerald Moore (Danacord) **H**
Schubert: *Die schöne Müllerin*, Dietrich Fischer-Dieskau, Gerald Moore (EMI)
Schubert: *Winterreise*, Peter Schreier, András Schiff (Decca)
Schubert: *Winterreise*, Dietrich Fischer-Dieskau, Jörg Demus (Deutsche Grammophon)
Schubert: *Schwanengesang*, Peter Schreier, András Schiff (Decca)
Schubert: *Songs, incl. 'Gretchen am Spinnrade', 'Die junge Nonne', 'Nur wer die Sehnsucht kennt'*, Janet Baker, Gerald Moore (EMI)
Schubert: *Mass in E flat*, Soloists, Leipzig Radio Chorus, Dresden Staatskapelle, Wolfgang Sawallisch (Philips)
Schumann: *Carnaval*, Sergei Rachmaninov (RCA) **H**
Schumann: *Fantasia in C*, Svyatoslav Richter (EMI)
Schumann: *Humoresque*, Svyatoslav Richter (Melodiya) **H**
Schumann: *Kreisleriana*, Vladimir Horowitz (Sony or Philips)
Schumann: *Piano Quintet in E flat,* Kodály Quartet, Jenö Jandó (Naxos)
Schumann: *Piano Concerto, Symphony No. 2*, Andreas Staier, Orchestre des Champs Elysées (cond) Philippe Herreweghe **P**
Schumann: *Symphonies Nos 1-4, Overture, Scherzo & Finale*, Dresden Staatskapelle, Wolfgang Sawallisch (EMI)
Schumann: *Dichterliebe*, Aksel Schiøtz, Gerald Moore (Danacord) **H**
Schumann: *Liederkreis Op. 24; Dichterliebe; Der arme Peter*, Peter Schreier, Norman Shetler (Berlin Classics)
Spohr: *Violin Concerto No. 8, 'Gesangsszene'*; Mendelssohn: *Violin Concerto in E minor*, Albert Spalding, Philadelphia Orchestra (cond) Eugene Ormandy (Biddulph) **H**
Viotti: *Violin Concertos (Various Vols)*, Symphonia Perusina (sol & dir) Franco Mezzena (Dynamic)
Weber: *Der Freischütz*, Soloists, German Opera Chorus, Berlin PO, Joseph Keilberth (EMI)

THE LATE ROMANTIC

Albéniz: *Iberia*; Granados: *Goyescas*, Alicia de Larrocha (Decca)
Bax: *Tintagel; Garden of Fand; November Woods; Northern Ballad No. 1; Mediterranean*, LPO (cond) Sir Adrian Boult (Lyrita)
Beach: *Piano Quintet*; Clarke: *Piano Trio & Viola Sonata* (ASV)
Bizet: *Carmen*, Soloists, French Radio Chorus, French National Orchestra (cond) Lorin Maazel (Erato)
Borodin: *String Quartet No. 2; String Quintet, etc.*, Alexander Gotthelf, Moscow Quartet (Saison Russe)
Borodin: *Prince Igor*, Soloists, Kirov Opera Chorus & Orchestra (cond) Valery Gergiev (Philips)
Brahms: *Piano Concertos*, Emil Gilels, Berlin PO (cond) Eugen Jochum (Deutsche Grammophon)
Brahms: *Violin Concerto*; Beethoven: *Violin Concerto*; Lalo: *Symphonie espagnole*; Tchaikovsky: *Violin Concerto; Sérénade mélancolique*, Leonid Kogan, Various Orchestras (cond) Kyrill Kondrashin, Constantin Silvestri (EMI)
Brahms: *Symphonies Nos 1-4; Tragic Overture; St Antoni Variations*, Dresden Staatskapelle (cond) Kurt Sanderling (RCA)
Brahms: *Symphony No. 4*, Vienna PO (cond) Carlos Kleiber (Deutsche Grammophon)
Bruch: *Violin Concerto No. 1; Scottish Fantasy*; Vieuxtemps: *Concerto No. 5*, Jascha Heifetz, New SO (cond) Sir Malcolm Sargent (RCA)
Bruch: *Violin Concerto No. 2*; Conus: *Concerto in E minor*; Wieniawski: *Concerto No. 2*; Tchaikovsky: *Sérénade mélancolique*, Jascha Heifetz, RCA Victor SO (cond) Izler Solomon (RCA)
Bruckner: *Symphony No. 4*, Vienna PO (cond) Karl Böhm (Decca)
Bruckner: *Symphony No. 7*, Vienna PO (cond) Herbert von Karajan (Deutsche Grammophon)
Bruckner: *Symphony No. 8*, Vienna PO (cond) Herbert von Karajan (Deutsche Grammophon)
Chaminade: *Piano Music*, Peter Jacobs (Hyperion)
Duparc: *Mélodies*, Bernard Kruysen, Noel Lee (Auvidis Valois)
Dvorák: *Piano Trio in F minor; 'Dumky' Piano Trio*, Guarneri Trio (Supraphon)
Dvorák: *String Quartets Nos 11, 12 ('American'), 13 & 14 (2 Vols)*, Panocha Quartet (Supraphon)
Dvorák: *String Quintets*, Panocha Quartet, Josef Kluson (Supraphon)
Dvorák: *Piano Quintets*, Panocha Quartet, Jan Panenka (Supraphon)
Dvorák: *Cello Concerto No. 2*; Saint-Saëns: *Cello Concerto No. 1*, Mstislav Rostropovich, RPO (cond) Sir Adrian Boult, Philharmonia (cond) Sir Malcolm Sargent (Testament)
Dvorák: *Cello Concerto No. 2*, Michaela Fukacová, Prague SO (cond) Jirí Belohlavek (Panton)
Dvorák: *Slavonic Dances*, Czech PO (cond) Sir Charles Mackerras (Supraphon)
Dvorák: *Symphonies Nos 7 & 8*, Czech PO (cond) Václav Neumann (Supraphon)
Dvorák: *Symphony No. 9, 'New World'; Symphonic Variations*, London PO (cond) Zdenek Macal (Classics for Pleasure)
Dvorák: *Rusalka*, Soloists, Czech PO & Chorus (cond) Vaclav Neumann (Supraphon)
Elgar: *The Elgar Edition: Complete Electrical Recordings*, Various Soloists & Orchestras (cond) Sir Edward Elgar (EMI) **H**
Elgar: *Cello Concerto; Sea Pictures*, Jacqueline du Pré, Dame Janet Baker, LSO (cond) Sir John Barbirolli (EMI)
Elgar: *Enigma Variations; Pomp and Circumstance Marches*, RPO (cond) Norman del Mar (Deutsche Grammophon)
Elgar: *Symphony No. 1; Serenade for Strings, etc.*, LPO (cond) Sir Adrian Boult (EMI)
Elgar: *Symphony No. 2; Cockaigne Overture*, LPO (cond) Sir Adrian Boult (EMI)
Elgar: *The Dream of Gerontius; The Music Makers*, Soloists, London Philharmonic Chorus, New Philharmonia, LPO (cond) Sir Adrian Boult (EMI)
Fauré: *Mélodies incl. La bonne chanson & L'horizon chimerique*; Duparc: *Mélodies*, Charles & Magdeleine Panzéra (Dante Lys) **H**
Fauré: *Requiem*; Fauré/Messager: *Messe des Pêcheurs de Villerville*, Soloists, Chapelle Royale, Petits Chanteurs de Saint-Louis, Ensemble Musique Oblique (cond) Philippe Herreweghe (Harmonia Mundi)
Franck: *Violin Sonata*; Szymanowski: *Mythes, etc.*, Kaja Danczowska, Kristian Zimerman (Deutsche Grammophon)
Franck: *Symphony*; Stravinsky: *Petrushka*, Chicago SO, Boston SO (cond) Pierre Monteux (RCA)
Gounod: *Faust*, Soloists, Capitole Chorus & Orchestra, Toulouse (cond) Michel Plasson (EMI)
Grieg: *Lyric Pieces*, Emil Gilels (Deutsche Grammophon)
Grieg: *Piano Concerto; Sonata*; Schumann: *Piano Concerto*, Steven Kovacevich, Zoltán Kocsis, BBC SO (cond) Sir Colin Davis (Philips)
Grieg: *Peer Gynt (excerpts)*, Ilse Hollweg, Beecham Choral Society, RPO (cond) Sir Thomas Beecham (EMI)
Mahler: *Symphony No. 1*; Lieder eines fahrenden Gesellen, Dietrich Fischer-Dieskau, Bavarian Radio SO (cond) Rafael Kubelík (Deitsche Grammophon)
Mahler: *Symphony No. 2*; Schmidt: *Symphony No. 4*, Vienna PO (cond) Zubin Mehta (Decca)
Mahler: *Symphony No. 4*, Kathleen Battle, Vienna PO (cond) Lorin Maazel (Sony)
Mahler: *Symphony No. 5*, Vienna PO (cond) Leonard Bernstein (Deutsche Grammophon)
Mahler: *Symphony No. 6*, Vienna PO (cond) Pierre Boulez (Deutsche Grammophon)
Mahler: *Symphony No. 8*, Soloists, Choirs, Chicago SO, Sir Georg Solti (Decca)
Mahler: *Symphony No. 9*, Vienna PO (cond) Claudio Abbado (Deutsche Grammophon)
Mahler: *Das Lied von der Erde*, Kathleen Ferrier, Julius Patzak, Vienna PO (cond) Bruno Walter (Decca) **H**
Mahler: *Das Lied von der Erde*, Christa Ludwig, Fritz Wunderlig, New Philharmonia and Philharmonia Orchestras (cond) Otto Klemperer (EMI)
Massenet: *Manon*, Soloists, Capitole Chorus & Orchestra, Toulouse (cond) Michel Plasson (EMI)
Musorgsky: *Pictures at an Exhibition*, Svyatoslav Richter (Philips or Melodiya)
Musorgsky: *Pictures at an Exhibition (orch. Ravel)*, Berlin PO (cond) Herbert von Karajan (Deutsche Grammophon)
Musorgsky: *Boris Godunov*, Soloists, Kirov Opera Chorus & Orchestra (cond) Valery Gergiev (Philips)
Offenbach: *La vie parisienne; La belle Hélène; Orphée aux enfers (excerpts)*, Soloists, Choeurs Raymond Saint-Paul, Lamoureux Orchestra (cond) Jules Gressler (EMI) **H**
Offenbach: *La fille du tambour major; La grande duchesse de Gerolstein* (excerpts), Soloists, Choeurs René Duclos, Paris Conservatoire Orchestra (cond) Félix Nuvolone, Jean-Pierre Marty (EMI)
Parry: *Symphony No. 5; Symphonic Variations; Blest Pair of Sirens etc.*, London Philharmonic Choir, LPO (cond) Sir Adrian Boult (EMI)
Puccini: *La Bohème*, Soloists, Accademia di Santa Cecilia Chorus & Orchestra (cond) Tullio Serafin (Decca)
Puccini: *Madama Butterfly*, Soloists, Rome Opera Chorus & Orchestra (cond) Sir John Barbirolli (EMI)
Puccini: *Tosca*, Soloists incl. Maria Callas, Chorus & Orchestra of La Scala, Milan (cond) Victor De Sabata (EMI) **H**
Puccini: *Turandot*, Soloists, Choirs, LPO (cond) Zubin Mehta (Decca)
Rachmaninov: *Piano Concertos Nos 2 & 3*, Vladimir Ashkenazy, Moscow PO (cond) Kyrill Kondrashin, LSO (cond) Anatole Fistoulari (Decca)
Rachmaninov: *Symphony No. 2*, Leningrad PO (cond) Kurt Sanderling (Deutsche Grammophon) **H**
Rachmaninov: *Symphonic Dances; The Bells*, Soloists, Russian Republican Cappella, Moscow PO (cond) Kyrill Kondrashin (Melodiya)
Rachmaninov: *All-Night Vigil (Vespers)*, St Petersburg Cappella (cond) Vladislav Chernushenko (Saison Russe)
Raff: *Symphony No. 3; Abends-Rhapsodie; Romeo and Juliet Overture*, Philharmonia Orchestra (cond) Francesco d'Avalos (ASV)
Reger: *Mozart Variations*; Hindemith: *Symphonic Metamorphosis*, Bavarian Radio SO (cond) Sir Colin Davis (Philips)
Reger: *Serenade; Suite im alten Stil*, Bamberg SO (cond) Horst Stein (Koch Schwann)
Reger: *A Ballet Suite; Konzert im alten Stil; Beethoven Variations*, Berlin Staatskapelle (cond) Otmar Suitner
Rimsky-Korsakov: *Scheherazade*, Royal Concertbegouw Orchestra (cond) Kyril Kondrashin
Rimsky-Korsakov: *The Snow Maiden*, Soloists, Bulgarian Radio Chorus & Orchestra (cond) Stoyan Angelov (Capriccio)
Saint-Saëns: *Carnival of the Animals; Septet*, Michel Beroff, Jean-Philippe Collard, Maurice André, Michel Debost, French String Trio et al (EMI)
Schmidt: *Das Buch mit Sieben Siegeln*, Soloists, Wiener Singverein, Vienna SO (cond) Horst Stein (Calig)
Sibelius: *Symphonies Nos 1-3 & 5; Belshazzar's Feast; Karelia Suite; Pohjola's daughter; Tapiola*, LSO (cond) Robert Kajanus (Finlandia) **H**
Sibelius: *Symphony No. 5*; Nielsen: *Symphony No. 4; Pan and Syrinx*, Philharmonia, CBSO (cond) Sir Simon Rattle (EMI)
Sibelius: *Symphonies Nos 6 & 7*, Lahti SO (cond) Osmo Vänska (BIS)
Smetana: *String Quartets*, Panocha Quartet (Supraphon)
Smetana: *Má vlast*, Czech PO (cond) Rafael Kubelík (Supraphon)
Smetana: *The Bartered Bride*, Soloists, Czech PO & Chorus (cond) Zdenek Kosler (Supraphon)
Smyth: *Concerto for Violin, Horn & Orchestra; Serenade in D*, Sophie Langdon, Richard Watkins, BBC PO (cond) Odaline de la Martinez (Chandos)
Strauss, J.: *1989 & 1992 New Year Concerts*, Vienna PO (cond) Carlos Kleiber (Sony)
Strauss, J.: *Die Fledermaus*, Soloists, Vienna State Opera Chorus, Vienna PO (cond) Herbert von Karajan (Decca)
Strauss, R,: *Four Last Songs; Ein Heldenleben*, Arleen Augér, Vienna PO (cond) André Previn (Telarc)
Strauss, R,: *Don Juan; Don Quixote*, Soloists, Vienna PO (cond) André Previn (Telarc)
Strauss, R,: *Death and Transfiguration; Metamorphosen*, Berlin PO (cond) Herbert von Karajan (Deutsche Grammophon)
Strauss, R,: *Der Rosenkavalier*, Soloists, Vienna State Opera Chorus, Vienna PO (cond) Erich Kleiber (Decca) **H**
Suk: *Asrael Symphony; Fairy Tale; Serenade for Strings*, Czech PO (cond) Jirí Belohlávek (Chandos)
Szymanowski: *Stabat Mater; Litany to the Virgin Mary; Symphony No. 3*, Soloists, CBSO & Chorus (cond) Sir Simon Rattle (EMI)
Tchaikovsky: *Piano Concerto No. 1*; Rachmaninov: *Concerto No. 3*, Martha Argerich, Bavarian Radio SO (cond) Kyrill Kondrashin, Berlin Radio SO (cond) Riccardo Chailly (Philips)
Tchaikovsky: *Francesca da Rimini; Hamlet*, New York Stadium Orchestra (cond) Leopold Stokowski (Everest)
Tchaikovsky: *Symphony No. 6*, Leningrad PO (cond) Yevgeny Mravinsky (Deutsche Grammophon)
Tchaikovsky: *Symphony No. 6*, St Petersburg PO (cond) Yuri Temirkanov (RCA Red Seal)
Tchaikovsky: *Symphony No. 6*, Russian National Orchestra (cond) Mikhail Pletnev (Virgin)
Tchaikovsky: *Symphony No. 6*, Berlin PO (cond) Ferenc Fricsay (Deutsche Grammophon)
Tchaikovsky: *The Nutcracker*, Kirov Orchestra (cond) Valery Gergiev (Philips)
Tchaikovsky: *The Sleeping Beauty*, Royal Opera House Orchestra (cond) Mark Ermler (Conifer)
Tchaikovsky: *Swan Lake*, Royal Opera House Orchestra (cond) Mark Ermler (Conifer)
Tchaikovsky: *Eugene Onegin*, Soloists incl. Galina Vishnevskaya, Bolshoi Theatre Chorus & Orchestra, Boris Khaikin (Melodiya) **H**
Verdi: *Aida*, Leontyne Price, Jon Vickers, Rome Opera Chorus & Orchestra (cond) Sir Georg Solti (Decca)
Verdi: *Falstaff*, Soloists, RCA Italiana Chorus & Orchestra (cond) Sir Georg Solti (RCA)
Verdi: *Otello*, NBC Symphony Orchetsra and Choruses (cond) Arturo Toscanini (RCA)
Verdi: *La Traviata*, Soloists, Chorus & Orchestra of Bavarian State Opera (cond) Carlos Kleiber (Deutsche Grammophon)
Verdi: *Rigoletto*, Soloists, Accademia di Santa Cecilia Chorus & Orchestra (cond) Giuseppe Sinopoli (Philips)
Verdi: *Requiem*, Soloists, Philharmonia Chorus & Orchestra (cond) Carlo Maria Giulini (EMI)
Wagner: *Overtures*, Vienna PO (cond) Horst Stein (Belart)
Wagner: *Die Meistersinger*, Soloists, Bavarian Radio Chorus & Orchestra (cond) Rafael Kubelík (Calig)
Wagner: *Die Walküre*, Bayreuth Festival Orchestra (cond) Karl Böhm (Philips)

THE MODERN ERA

Bacewicz: *String Quartets Nos 4 & 7; Piano Quintet*, Grazyna Bacewicz Quartet, Warsaw Piano Quintet (Olympia)
Bacewicz: *Divertimento; Pensieri notturni; Concerto for Orchestra; Viola Concerto; Concerto for Two Pianos*, Stefan Kamasa, Jerzy Maksymiuk, Jerzy Witkowski, Warsaw PO (cond) Witold Rowicki, Stanislaw Wislocki (Olympia)

Barber: *Adagio for Strings*; Gershwin: *Rhapsody in Blue*; Copland: *Appalachian Spring Suite*, Los Angeles PO (dir) Leonard Bernstein (Deutsche Grammophon)
Bartók: *Two Rhapsodies; Violin Sonatas; Violin Duos; Sonatine; Solo Violin Sonata; Contrasts; Violin Concertos*, André Gertler, Josef Suk, Diane Andersen, Milan Etlík, Czech PO (cond) Karel Ancerl (Baltic)
Bartók: *String Quartets*, Hungarian Quartet (Deutsche Grammophon)
Bartók: *Piano Concertos 1-3*, András Schiff, Budapest Festival Orchestra (cond) Iván Fischer (Teldec)
Bartók: *Violin Concerto; Viola Concerto*, Pinchas Zukerman, St Louis SO (cond) Leonard Slatkin (RCA)
Bartók: *Concerto for Orchestra; Music for Strings, Percussion & Celesta*, Los Angeles PO, Esa-Pekka Salonen (Sony)
Berg: *Chamber Concerto*; Schoenberg: *Chamber Symphony No. 1*, Thomas Zehetmair, Oleg Maisenberg, CO of Europe (cond) Heinz Holliger (Teldec)
Berg: *Violin Concerto*; Stravinsky: *Violin Concerto*; Ravel: *Tzigane*, Itzhak Perlman, Boston SO (cond) Seiji Ozawa (Deutsche Grammophon)
Berg: *Altenberg-Lieder; Lulu Suite; Three Pieces from the Lyric Suite*, Juliane Banse, Vienna PO (cond) Claudio Abbado (Deutsche Grammophon
Berg: *Wozzeck*; Schoenberg: *Erwartung*, Soloists, Vienna PO (cond) Christoph von Dohnányi (Decca)
Boulanger: *Du fond de l'abime; Psalm 24; Faust et Hélène, etc.*, Soloists, CBSO Chorus, BBC PO (cond) Yan Pascal Tortelier (Chandos)
Britten: *Peter Grimes*, Soloists, Orchestra of the Royal Opera House (cond) Benjamin Britten (Decca)
Britten: *War Requiem*, Soloists, Choirs, Melos Ensemble, LSO (cond) Benjamin Britten (Decca)
Debussy: *Complete Works for Solo Piano*, Walter Gieseking (EMI) **H**
Debussy: *Three Sonatas; Syrinx; String Quartet*, Arthur Grumiaux, Maurice Gendron, Jean Francaix, Quartetto Italiano et al (Philips)
Debussy: *Images; Prélude à l'après-midi d'un faune; Printemps*, Cleveland Orchestra (cond) Pierre Boulez (Deutsche Grammophon)
Debussy: *Nocturnes; Première Rhapsodie; Jeux; La Mer*, Cleveland Orchestra & Chorus (cond) Pierre Boulez (Deutsche Grammophon)
Debussy: *Pelléas et Mélisande*, Soloists, Choeurs Yvonne Gouverné, Symphony Orchestra (cond) Roger Desormière; *Mélodies*, Maggie Teyte, Mary Garden, Alfred Cortot, Claude Debussy (EMI) **H**
Debussy: *la mer*, Royal Concertgebouw Orchestra (conds) Bernard Haitinck, Eduard van Beinum (Philips)
Falla: *The Three-Cornered Hat; Love the Magician*, Soloists, Montreal SO (cond) Charles Dutoit (Decca)
Henze: *The Henze Collection* (14 Vols), Various Artists (Deutsche Grammophon)
Henze: *Undine*, London Sinfonietta (cond) Oliver Knussen (Deutsche Grammophon)
Hindemith: *'Mathis der Maler' Symphony; Nobilissima Visione; Symphony in E flat; Symphonia Serena, etc.*, Dresden PO (cond) Herbert Kegel (Berlin Classics)
Holst: *The Planets; The Perfect Fool (Ballet Music); Egdon Heath*, New Philharmonia (cond) Sir Adrian Boult, LSO (cond) André Previn (EMI)
In Praise of Woman: 150 Years of English Women Composers, songs by Virginia Gabriel, Maude Valérie White, Liza Lehmann, Amy WoodfordeFinden, Ethel Smyth, Rebecca Clarke, Elisabeth Lutyens, Elizabeth Maconchy & others (Hyperion)
Ives: *'Country Band' March, Set for Theatre, Three Places in New England*, Orchestra New England (cond) James Sinclair (Koch
Janácek: *String Quartets*, Panocha Quartet (Supraphon)
Janácek: *Sinfonietta, Taras Bulba*, Vienna PO (cond) Sir Charles Mackerras (Decca)
Janácek: *The Cunning Little Vixen*, Soloists, Czech Philharmonic Chorus & Orchestra (cond) Vaclav Neumann (Supraphon)
Janácek: *Katya Kabanová*, Soloists, Vienna State Opera Chorus, Vienna PO (cond) Sir Charles Mackerras (Decca)
Kodály: *Hary Janos Suite; Dances of Galanta & Marosszék*, Budapest Festival Orchestra (cond) Iván Fischer (Philips)
Lourié: *A Little Chamber Music; Little Gidding; Concerto da camera*, Thomas Klug, Kenneth Riegel, Deutsche Kammerphilharmonie (sol & dir) Gidon Kremer (Deutsche Grammophon)
Maconchy: *String Quartets (3 Vols)*, Hanson, Bingham & Mistry Quartets (Unicorn-Kanchana)
Martinu: *The Parables; The Frescoes; Symphony No. 6*, Czech PO (cond) Karel Ancerl (Supraphon) **H**
Martinu: *Double Concerto; Symphony No. 1*, Czech PO (cond) Jirí Belohlávek (Chandos)
Messiaen: *Works for Organ*, Olivier Messiaen (EMI) **H**
Messiaen: *Turangalîla-symphonie*, Jeanne & Yvonne Loriot, Orchestre de l'Opéra Bastille, Myung-Whun Chung (Deutsche Grammophon)
Messiaen: *Saint François d'Assise*, Soloists, Arnold Schoenberg Choir, Hallé Orchestra (cond) Kent Nagano (Deutsche Grammophon)
Milhaud: *Les Choéphores*; Honegger: *Symphony No. 5*; Roussel: *Bacchus et Ariane Suite No. 2*, Soloists, Chorale de l'Université, Lamoureux Orchestra (cond) Igor Markevitch (Deutsche Grammophon) **H**
Milhaud: *La création du monde; Saudades do Brasil; Le boeuf sur le toit*, French National Orchestra (cond) Leonard Bernstein (EMI)
Nielsen: *Symphonies 1, 2, 4 & 5; Helios Overture (2 Vols)*, Danish State Radio SO (cond) Erik Tuxen, Thomas Jensen, Launy Grøndahl (Dutton) **H**
Orff: *Carmina Burana*, Soloists, Vienna Boys' Choir, Arnold Schoenberg Choir, Vienna PO (cond) André Previn (Deutsche Grammophon)
Poulenc: *Édition du centenaire (4 Vols) – Mélodies & Chansons; Piano & Chamber Music; Concertos, Orchestral & Sacred Music; Vocal Works*, Various Artists incl. Francis Poulenc (EMI)
Prokofiev: *Piano Sonatas Nos 3 & 8; Visions fugitives; March*; Stravinsky: *Three Movements from Petrushka*; Medtner: *Sonata reminiscenza*, etc., Emil Gilels (Philips)
Prokofiev: *Piano Concertos Nos 1 & 3*; Bartók: *Piano Concerto No. 3*, Martha Argerich, Montreal SO (cond) Charles Dutoit (EMI)
Prokofiev: *Violin Concerto No. 1*; Shostakovich: *Violin Concerto No. 1*, Maxim Vengerov, LSO (cond) Mstislav Rostropovich (Teldec)
Prokofiev: *Violin Concerto No. 2*; Sibelius: *Violin Concerto*; Glazunov: *Violin Concerto*, Jascha Heifetz, Chicago SO, Boston SO et al (cond) Walter Hendl, Charles Munch (RCA)
Prokofiev: *Symphonies Nos 1-7*, Royal Scottish National Orchestra (cond) Neeme Järvi (Chandos)
Prokofiev: *Romeo and Juliet (excerpts)*, Berlin PO (cond) Esa-Pekka Salonen (Sony)
Ravel: *Piano Concertos; Valses nobles et sentimentales*, Krystian Zimerman, Cleveland Orchestra, LSO (cond) Pierre Boulez (Deutsche Grammophon)
Ravel: *Alborada del gracioso; Une barque sur l'ocean; Boléro; Ma Mère l'Oye; Menuet antique; Pavane pur une infante défunte; Rapsodie espagnole; Le tombeau de Couperin; La valse; Valses nobles et sentimentales*, Paris Conservatoire Orchestra (cond) André Cluytens (EMI)
Ravel: *Daphnis et Chloé*, New England Conservatory Choir, Boston SO (cond) Charles Munch (RCA)
Ravel: *L'enfant et les sortilèges*, Soloists, French National Radio Chorus & Orchestra (cond) Ernest Bour (Testament)
Rodrigo: *Concierto de Aranjuez*, Craig Ogden, BBC PO, S. Fujioka (Chandos)
Schoenberg: *Pierrot lunaire; Herzgewächse; Ode to Napoleon Bonaparte*, Christine Schäfer, David Pittman-Jennings, Ensemble Intercontemporain (dir) Pierre Boulez (Deutsche Grammophon)
Schoenberg: *Orchestral Variations, Op. 31*, Chicago SO (cond) Pierre Boulez (Erato)
Schoenberg: *Gurrelieder*, Soloists, Choirs, Dresden Staatskapelle (cond) Giuseppe Sinopoli (Teldec)
Seeger: *Orchestral Works; String Quartet; Suite for Wind Quintet*, Schoenberg Ensemble (cond) Oliver Knussen (Deutsche Grammophon)
Shostakovich: *String Quartets*, Borodin Quartet (Melodiya)
Shostakovich: *Piano Concertos*, Dmitri Alexeev, English CO (cond) Jerzy Maksymiuk (Classics for Pleasure)
Shostakovich: *Cello Concertos*, Heinrich Schiff, Bavarian Radio SO (cond) Maxim Shostakovich (Philips)
Shostakovich: *Violin Concertos*, Leonid Kogan, David Oistrakh, Moscow PO (cond) Kyrill Kondrashin (Russian Disc)
Shostakovich: *Symphonies Nos 1-15*, Moscow PO (cond) Kyrill Kondrashin (Melodiya)
Stenhammar: *Symphony No. 2*, Stockholm PO (cond) Stig Westerberg (Caprice)
Stravinsky: *The Fairy's Kiss; Symphony in C; Pulcinella; The Soldier's Tale Suite; Octet*, Soloists, Cleveland Orchestra (cond) Igor Stravinsky (Sony Masterworks Heritage) **H**
Stravinsky: *Les Noces*, English Bach Festival Chorus (cond) Leonard Bernstein (Deutsche Grammophon)
Stravinsky: *The Rite of Spring*, City of Birmingham SO (cond) Simon Rattle (EMI)
Stravinsky: *Oedipus Rex, Symphony of Psalms*, Czech Philharmonic Chorus and Orchestra (cond) Karel Ancerl (Supraphon)
Stravinsky: *The Rake's Progress*, Soloists, RPO (cond) Igor Stravinsky (Sony Classical)
Vainberg: *Violin Concerto; Symphony No. 4*, Leonid Kogan, Moscow PO (cond) Kyrill Kondrashin (Olympia)
Vaughan Williams: *Serenade to Music; In the Fen Country; The Lark Ascending; Norfolk Rhapsody; English Folk Song Suite; Fantasia on 'Greensleeves'*, New Philharmonia Orchestra, LPO, LSO, Sir Adrian Bou;lt (EMI)
Vaughan Williams: *Symphonies Nos 4 & 5; On Wenlock Edge; Tallis Fantasia; Folk Songs & Carols*, Peter Pears, Benjamin Britten, Zorian Quartet, Boyd Neel String Orchestra, BBC SO (cond) Ralph Vaughan Williams, Hallé Orchestra (cond) Sir John Barbirolli (Pearl) **H**
Vaughan Williams: *Symphonies Nos 3 & 5*, New Philharmonia Orchestra, LPO, Sir Adrian Bou;lt (EMI)
Vaughan Williams: *Symphony No. 5; Flos Campi*, Christopher Balmer, Liverpool Philharmonic Choir, RLPO, Vernon Handley (EMI Eminence)
Vaughan Williams: *Symphony No. 6; Tallis Fantasia; The Lark Ascending*, BBC SO, Sir Andrew Davis (Teldec)
Walton: *Viola Concerto; Symphony No. 1 etc.*, Frederick Riddle, LSO (cond) Sir William Walton, Sir Hamilton Harty (Dutton) **H**
Walton: *Symphony No. 1; Belshazzar's Feast*, Thomas Hampson, Cleveland Orchestra Chorus, CBSO & Chorus (cond) Sir Simon Rattle (EMI)
Walton: *Symphony No. 2; Partita; Hindemith Variations*, Cleveland Orchestra (cond) George Szell (Sony)

THE LATE 20TH CENTURY

Adams: *The Chairman Dances; Harmonielehre; Tromba lontana; Short ride in a fast machine*, CBSO (cond) Sir Simon Rattle (EMI)
Adams: *Nixon in China*, Soloists, St Luke's Chorus & Orchestra (cond) Edo de Waart (Nonesuch)
Berio: *Sinfonia; Canticum Novissimi Testamenti II*, Electric Phoenix, Orchestre de Paris (cond) Semyon Bychkov (Philips)
Birtwhistle: *Secret Theatre*, Ensemble Intercontemporain (cond) Pierre Boulez (Deutsche Grammophon)
Birtwistle: *The Mask of Orpheus*, BBC SO (cond) Sir Andrew Davis & Martyn Brabbins (NMC D050)
Boulez: *Le marteau sans maître*, Jeanne Deroubaix, instrumental ensemble/Pierre Boulez (Adés)
Carter: *Concerto for Orchestra*; Ives: *Holidays; The Unanswered Question; Central Park in the Dark*, Camerata Singers, New York PO (cond) Leonard Bernstein (Sony)
Crumb: *Black Angels*, Kronos Quartet (Nonesuch)
Glass: *Einstein on the Beach*, Soloists, Philip Glass Ensemble (dir) Michael Riesman (Sony)
Gorecki: *Symphony of Sorrowful Songs*, Zofia Kilanowicz, Polish National Radio SO (cond) Antoni Wit (Naxos)
Gubaydulina: *Jetzt immer Schnee; Perception*, Soloists, Netherlands Chamber Choir, Schoenberg Ensemble (cond) Reinbert de Leeuw (Philips)
Gubaydulina: *Offertorium; Hommage à T. S. Eliot*, Gidon Kremer, Christine Whittlesey et al, Boston SO (cond) Charles Dutoit (Deutsche Grammophon)
Knussen: *Horn Concerto etc.*, Barry Tuckwell, London Sinfonietta (cond) Oliver Knussen (Deutsche Grammophon)
Knussen: *Where the Wild Things Are; Higglety Pigglety Pop!*, Soloists, London Sinfonietta (cond) Oliver Knussen (Unicorn Kanchana)
Kurtág: *Játékok*, Márta & György Kurtág (ECM)
Ligeti: *Horn Trio*, Saschko Gawriloff, marie-Louise Neunexker, Pierre-Laurent Aimard (Sony)
Ligeti: *Le grand macabre*, Soloists, Choirs, Austrian Radio SO (cond) Elgar Howarth (Wergo)
Lutoslawski: *Cello Concerto*; Dutilleux: *Cello Concerto*, Mstislav Rostropovich, Paris Orchesatra (cond) Witold Lutoslawski, Serge Baudo (EMI)
Lutoslawski: *Chain 2*; Rihm: *Gesungene Zeit*, BBC SO (cond) Witold Lutoslawski, Chicago SO (cond) James Levine (Deutsche Grammophon)
Matthews, C.: *Broken Symmetry*, London Sinfonietta (cond) Oliver Knussen (Deutsche Grammophon)
Maxwell Davies: *Eight Songs for a Mad King*, Julius Eastman, Fires of London (cond) Sir Peter Maxwell Davies (Unicorn-Kanchana)
Panufnik: *Sinfonia sacra; Arbor cosmica*, Royal Concertgebouw Orchestra, New York Chamber Symphony (cond) Sir Andrzej Panufnik (Elektra Nonesuch)
Pärt: Fratres; *Cantus in memory of Benjamin Britten; Tabula rasa*, Gidon Kremer, Tatiana Grindenko, Alfred Schnittke, Keith Jarrett, Berlin PO Cellists, Staatsorchester Stuttgart (cond) Dennis Russell Davies (ECM)
Pärt: *Arbos; An den Wassern zu Babel; Pari intervallo; De profundis; Es sang vor langen Jahren; Summa; Stabat Mater*, Gidon Kremer, Vladimir Mandelssohn, Thomas Demenga, Hilliard Ensemble, Staatsorchester Stuttgart (cond) Dennis Russell Davies (ECM)
Reich: *Clapping Music etc.*, Steve Reich, Russell Hartenberger (Nonesuch)
Reich: *Different Trains etc.*, Kronos Quartet (Nonesuch)
Rihm: *Die Eroberung von Mexico*, Philharmonisches Staatsorchester Hamburg (cond) Ingo Metzmacher (CPO)
Riley: *In C*, Piano Circus (Argo)
Schnittke: *Concerto grosso No. 1; Viola Concerto, Piano Concerto; Monologue; Praeludium in memoriam Dmitri Shostakovich; Suite in the Old Style*, Gidon Kremer, Tatiana Grindenko, Yuri Bashmet, Vladimir Krainev, Various Orchestras (cond) Gennady Rozhdestvensky, Mstislav Rostropovich, Vladimir Spivakov (RCA)
Takemitsu: *Viola Concerto; November Steps; Eclipse*, Nobuko Imai, Katsuya Yokoyama, Kinshi Tsuruta, Saito Kinen Orchestra (cond) Seiji Ozawa (Philips)
Takemitsu: *Day Signal; From Heaven; Quotation of Dream; How Slow the Wind; Twill by Twilight; Archipelago S; Dream/Window; Night Signal*, Paul Crossley, Peter Serkin, London Sinfonietta (cond) Oliver Knussen (Deutsche Grammophon)
Tavener: *The Protecting Veil; Thrinos*, Steven Isserlis, LSO (cond) Gennadi Rozhdestvensky (Virgin Classics)
Tavener: *The Akathist of Thanksgiving*. Soloists, Westminster Abbey Choir, BBC SO & Singers (cond) Martin Neary (Sony)
Tippett: *Triple Concerto*, BBC PO/Michael Tippett (Nimbus)
Tippett: *The Rose Lake; The Vision of St Augustine*, LSO (cond) Sir Colin Davis (Conifer)
Varèse: *Ionisation*, Ensemble Intercontemporain (cond) Pierre Boulez (Auvidis Astrée)

MUSIC ORGANIZATIONS

The selection of music organizations listed here is intended to provide information on some of the best-known orchestras, ensembles, events, venues and record companies. For further information and a more comprehensive list of organizations and addresses, please contact *www.foundry.co.uk/*. Website addresses are given wherever available. Area codes are given in brackets.

ORCHESTRAS

UK

BBC National Orchestra of Wales
BBC Broadcasting House
Llandaff
Cardiff CF5 2YQ
Tel. (029) 2057 2442
Fax. (029) 2057 2575
www.bbc.co.uk/wales/now

BBC Philharmonic
New Broadcasting House
Oxford Road
Manchester M60 1SJ
Tel. (0161) 244 4001
Fax. (0161) 244 4211
www.bbc.co.uk/orchestras/philharmonic/

BBC Scottish Symphony Orchestra
BBC Broadcasting House
Queen Margaret Drive
Glasgow G12 8DG
Tel. (0141) 338 2606
Fax. (0141) 307 4312

BBC Symphony Orchestra
BBC Maida Vale Studios
Delaware Road
London W9 2LG
Tel. (020) 7765 5751
www.bbc.co.uk/orchestras/so/

Bournemouth Symphony Orchestra
2 Seldown Lane
Poole
Dorset BH15 1UF
Tel. (01202) 670611
Fax. (01202) 687235
www.orchestras.co.uk/

City of Birmingham Symphony Orchestra
Paradise Place
Birmingham B3 3RP
Tel. (0121) 236 1555
Fax. (0121) 233 2423
www.cbso.co.uk

English Northern Philharmonia
Opera North, Grand Theatre
Leeds LSI 6NU
Tel. (0113) 243 9999
Fax. (0113) 244 0418

English Sinfonia
1 Wedgewood Court
Stevenage SG1 4QR
Tel: (01438) 350990
Fax: (01438) 350930
www.stevenage.gov.uk/EnglishSinfonia/

Hallé Orchestra
The Bridgewater Hall
Manchester M2 3WS
Tel. (0161) 237 7000
Fax: (0161) 237 7029
www.bridgewater-hall.co.uk/halleorchestra/index.html

London Philharmonic
35 Doughty Street
London WC1N 2AA
Tel. (020) 7546 1600
Fax. (020) 7546 1666
www.lpo.co.uk

London Symphony Orchestra
Barbican Centre
London EC2Y 8DS
Tel. (020) 7588 1116
Fax (020) 7374 0127
www.lso.co.uk/

Philharmonia Orchestra
First Floor
125 High Holborn
London WC1V 6QA
Tel. (020) 7242 5001
Fax. (020) 7242 4840
www.philharmonia.co.uk/

Royal Liverpool Philharmonic Orchestra
Philharmonic Hall
Hope Street
Liverpool L1 9BP
Tel. (0151) 709 2895
Fax. (0151) 709 0918

Royal Philharmonic Orchestra
16 Clerkenwell Green
London EC1R 0DP
Tel. (020) 7608 2381
Fax. (020) 7608 1226
www.orchestranet.co.uk/rpo.html

Royal Scottish National Orchestra
73 Claremont Street
Glasgow G3 7JB
Tel. (0141) 226 3868
Fax. (0141) 221 4317
www.scot-art.org/rsno/

Ulster Orchestra
Elmwood Hall at Queens
89 University Rd
Belfast BT7 1NF
Tel. (028) 9066 4535
Fax: (028) 9066 2761

Welsh Philharmonic Orchestra
40 Tudor Court
Murton
Swansea SA3 3BB
Tel. (01792) 232387

USA

Atlanta Symphony Orchestra
1280 Peachtree Street NE
Atlanta, GA 30309
Tel. (404) 733 4939
www.atlantasymphony.org/

Baltimore Symphony Orchestra
212 Cathedral Street
Baltimore, MD 21201
Tel. (410) 783 8024
Fax. (410) 783 8077
www.baltimoresymphony.org

Boston Symphony Orchestra
Symphony Hall
301 Massachusetts Avenue
Boston, MA 02115
Tel. (617) 266 1492
Fax. (617) 638 9436
www.bso.org

Chicago Symphony Orchestra
220 S. Michigan Avenue
Chicago, IL 60604
Tel. (312) 294 3000
Fax (800) 223 7114 (toll-free)
www.chicagosymphony.org

Cleveland Orchestra
Severance Hall
11001 Euclid Avenue
Cleveland, OH 44106
Tel. (216) 231 7300
Fax. (216) 231 0202
www.clevelandorch.com

Dallas Symphony Orchestra
Morton H. Meyerson Symphony Center
2301 Flora Street
Suite 300
Dallas, TA 75201-2497
Tel: (214) 871 4000
Fax. (214) 953 1218
www.dallassymphony.com/homepage.html

Detroit Symphony Orchestra
400 Buhl Building
535 Griswold Street
Detroit, MI 48226
Tel. (313) 962 1000
Fax. (313) 962 9107
www.detroitsymphony.com/

Houston Symphony
615 Louisiana Street
Suite 102
Houston, TX 77002
Tel. (713) 224 4240
Fax. (713) 224 6129
www.houstonsymphony.org

Los Angeles Philharmonic
135 North Grand Avenue
Los Angeles, CA 90012
Tel. (213) 972 7300
Fax. (213) 617 3065
www.laphil.org

MET Orchestra (Orchestra of the Metropolitan Opera New York)
Carnegie Hall
New York, NY
Tel. (212) 247 7800
www.carnegiehall.org/

New York Philharmonic
Avery Fisher Hall
10 Lincoln Center Plaza
New York
NY 10023-6990
Tel. (212) 875 5000
Fax. (212) 875 5670
www.nyphilharmon.org

Oregon Symphony
921 SW Washington
Suite 200
Portland, OR 97205
Tel. (503) 228 4294
Fax. (503) 228 4150
www.orsymphony.org

Philadelphia Orchestra
260 South Broad Street
16th Floor
Philadelphia
PA 19102
Tel. (215) 803 1900
www.philorch.org

Pittsburgh Symphony Orchestra
Heinz Hall for the Performing Arts
600 Penn Avenue
Pittsburgh, PA 15222-3259
Tel. (412) 392 4900
www.pittsburghsymphony.org

St Louis Symphony Orchestra
Powell Symphony Hall
718 North Grand Boulevard
St. Louis, MO 63103
Tel. (314) 533 2500
Fax. (314) 533 6000
www.slso.org/

San Francisco Symphony
Davies Symphony Hall
201 Van Ness Avenue
San Francisco
CA 94102
Tel. (415) 552 8000
www.sfsymphony.org

Seattle Symphony Orchestra
PO Box 21906
Seattle, WA 98111-3906
Tel. (206) 215 4700
Fax. (206) 215 4701
www.seattlesymphony.org

CANADA

Orchestre Symphonique de Montréal
260 de Maisonneuve Blvd West
Montreal, Quebec H2X 1Y9
Tel. (514) 842 9951
Fax. (514) 842 0728
www.osm.ca

Toronto Symphony Orchestra
212 King Street West, Suite 550
Toronto, ON, M5H 1K5
Tel. (416) 598 3375
Fax. (416) 598 9522
www.tso.on.ca

Vancouver Symphony Orchestra
601 Smithe Street
Vancouver, BC V6B 5G1
Tel. (604) 684 9100,
Fax. (604) 684 9264
www.culturenet.ca/vso/

AUSTRALIA & NEW ZEALAND

Adelaide Symphony Orchestra
GPO Box 2121, Adelaide,
South Australia 5001
Tel. (8) 8343 4834
Fax. (8) 8343 4808
www.aso.com.au

Melbourne Symphony Orchestra
120–130 Southbank Boulevard
Southbank VIC 3006
Tel. (3) 9626 1111
Fax. (3) 9626 1101
www.mso.com.au/

Sydney Symphony Orchestra
GPO Box 4338
Sydney NSW 2001
Tel. (2) 933 44648
Fax. (2) 9334 4646
www.symphony.org.au

West Australian Symphony Orchestra
191 Adelaide Terrace
Perth WA 6000
Tel. (8) 9326 0011
Fax. (8) 9326 0099
www.waso.com.au/

Auckland Symphony Orchestra
PO Box 56 024, Auckland
New Zealand 1030
Tel. (9) 638 7073
Fax. (9) 630 9687
www.akl-phil.co.nz/

EUROPE

Vienna Philharmonic Orchestra
Bösendorferstraße 12
A-1012 Vienna
Austria
Tel. (1) 505 65 25
www.wienerphilharmoniker.at

Czech Philharmonic Orchestra
Alsovo nabrezi 12
110 01 Prague 1
Czech Republic
Tel. (2) 248 93 352
Fax. (2) 231 68 78
www.czechphilharmonic.cz

Prague Symphony Orchestra
Obecni dum
Namesti Republiky 5
110 00 Prague 1
Czech Republic
Tel. (2) 231 5981
Fax. (2) 231 0784

Copenhagen Philharmonic Orchestra/Sjællands Symfoniorkester/Tivoli Symfoniorkester
Ny Kongensgade 13
1472, Copenhagen K
Denmark
Tel. (33) 91 11 99
Fax. (33) 14 90 34
www.symphony.dk/sjaelland.htm

Danish National Radio Symphony Orchestra (Radiosymfonieorkestret)
Julius Thomsensgade 12
1632, Copenhagen V
Denmark
Tel. (35) 20 62 62
www.dr.dk/p2musik/rso/dan/b/index.htm

Radion Sinfoniaorkesteri (Radio Symphony Orchestra)
PL 14 Fin-00240 Yleisradio
Helsinki
Finland
Tel. (9) 1480 4366
Fax. (9) 1480 3551
www.yle.fi/rso/

Orchestre National de Lille (National Orchestra of Lille)
30 place Mendès France
BP 119 59 027
Lille Cedex
France
Tel. (3) 20 12 82 40
www.onlille.com/

Orchestre National de France (National Orchestra of France)
Radio France
Direction de la musique
Pièce 6344
116, av du Président Kennedy
75220 Paris Cedex 16
France
Tel. (1) 42 30 36 15
www.radio-france.fr/chaines/orchestres/national/

Orchestre Philharmonique de Radio France
116, avenue du Président Kennedy
75220 Paris Cedex 16
France
Tel. (1) 42 30 36 15
www.radio-france.fr/

L'Orchestre de Paris
252, rue du Faubourg Saint-Honoré
75008 Paris
France
Tel. (1) 45 61 65 64
Fax. (1) 42 89 24 49
www.orchestredeparis.com/

WDR Sinfonieorchester
Westdeutscher Rundfunk
Köln
50600 Cologne
Germany
Tel. (221) 280108
Fax. (221) 20408 161
www.wdr.de/radio/orchester/sinfonieorchester/

Dresden Philharmonie
PO Box 120 424
01005 Dresden
Germany
Tel. (351) 4866 202
Fax. (351) 4866 283
www.dresdnerphilharmonie.de/

Berlin Philharmonic
Herbert-von-Karajan-Strasse 1
10785 Berlin
Germany
Tel. (30) 25 488 254
www.berlin-philharmonic.com

Orchester der Beethovenhalle
Wachsbleiche 2
53111 Bonn
Germany
Tel. (228) 63 0031
Fax. (228) 63 0031
www.uni-bonn.de/beethoven/index.html

Leipzig Gewandhaus Orchestra
Gewandhauskasse
Augustusplatz 8
04109 Leipzig
Germany
Tel. (341) 1270 280
Fax. (341) 1270 222
www.leipzig-online.de/gewandhaus/

National Symphony Orchestra of Ireland
RTE
Donnybrook
Dublin 4
Ireland
Tel. (1) 208 2977
Fax. (1) 208 2522

Orchestra del Teatro Comunale di Bologna
Largo Respighi 1
40126 Bologna
Italy
Tel. (051) 52 9999
Fax. (051) 52 9995
www.nettuno.it/bo/teatro_comunale/

Orchestra dell'Accademia Nazionale di Santa Cecilia
Via Vittoria
6-00187 Rome
Italy
Tel. (06) 361 1064/68/72/86
www.santacecilia.it/

Royal Concertgebouw Orchestra
Jacob Obrechtstraat 51
1071 KJ Amsterdam
The Netherlands
Tel. (20) 679 2211
Fax. (20) 676 3331
www.concertgebouworkest.nl

Oslo Philharmonic
PO Box 1607 Vika
0119 Oslo, Norway
Tel. (22) 01 49 00
Fax. (22) 01 49 01
www.oslophil.com

Trondheim Symphony Orchestra
PO Box 774
N-7408 Trondheim
Norway
Tel. (73) 53 98 00
Fax. (73) 53 98 01
www.aksess.no/symfoni/

Russian National Orchestra
Ulitsa Garibaldi 19, Building 2
Moscow 11733
Russia
Tel. (095) 120 7409/128 7811
www.w7.dj.net.tw/~rno/

St Petersburg Symphony Orchestra
Big Hall of the Shostakovich Academy
St Petersburg
Russia
Tel. (812) 311 21 26

Suisse Romande Orchestra
Rue Bovy-Lysberg 2
CH 1204 Geneva
Switzerland
Tel. (22) 807 00 17
Fax. (22) 807 00 18
www.osr.ch/

Tonhalle Orchestra
Gotthardstrasse 5,
8002 Zürich
Switzerland
Tel. (1) 206 3440
Fax. (1) 206 3436

ENSEMBLES

UK

The Academy of Ancient Music
10 Brookside
Cambridge CB2 1JE
Tel. (01223) 301509
Fax. (01223) 327377
www.aam.co.uk

Academy of St Martin in the Fields
Raine House, Raine Street
London El 9RG
Tel. (020) 7702 1377
Fax. (020) 7481 0228
www.academysmif.co.uk/

The Brandenburg Consort
97 Mill Lane
Lower Earley
Reading RG6 3UH
Tel. (0118) 935 2595
Fax. (0118) 935 2627

Chamber Orchestra of Europe
8 Southampton Place
London WC1A 2EA
Tel. (020) 7831 2326
Fax. (020) 7831 8248
www.coeurope.org

Chamber Orchestra of Great Britain
2 Clumber Avenue
Mapperley
Nottingham NG3 5JY
Tel. (0115) 926 7281

English Chamber Orchestra
2 Coningsby Road
London W5 4HR
Tel. (020) 8840 6565
Fax. (020) 8567 7198

The Hanover Band
45 Portland Road
Hove
East Sussex BN3 5DQ
Tel. (01273) 206978
Fax. (01273) 329636
www.orchestranet.co.uk/hanover.htm

London Sinfonietta
1 Wedgewood Court
Stevenage SG1 4QR
Tel. (01438) 350990
Fax. (01438) 350930
www.londonsinfonietta.org.uk/

Monteverdi Orchestra
The Bowring Building
PO Box 145
Tower Place
London EC3P 3BE
Tel. (020) 7480 5183
Fax. (020) 7480 5185
www.monteverdi.co.uk/hallway.html

Orchestra of The Age of Enlightenment
Fifth Floor
Westcombe House
56–58 Whitcomb Street
London WC2H 7DN
Tel. (020) 7930 0646
Fax. (020) 7930 0626
www.orchestranet.co.uk/oae/index.html

Scottish Chamber Orchestra
4 Royal Terrace
Edinburgh EH7 5AB
Tel. (0131) 557 6800
Fax. (0131) 557 6933
www.sco.org.uk/

Sinfonia 21
14 Princes Gardens
London SW7 1NA
Tel. (020) 7584 2759
Fax: (020) 7581 0970
www.orchestranet.co.uk/sinf21.html

Welsh Chamber Orchestra
100 Ystrad Fawr
Bridgend
Mid-Glamorgan CF31 4HW
Tel. (01656) 658891
Fax. (01685) 876675

USA

American Composers Orchestra
1775 Broadway, Suite 525
New York, NY 10019
Tel. (212) 977 8495
Fax. (212) 977 8995
www.americancomposers.org/

Handel & Haydn Society
Horticultural Hall
300 Massachusetts Avenue
Boston, MA 02115
Tel. (617) 262 1815
www.handelandhaydn.org

Dallas Wind Symphony
DWS Guild
PO Box 595026
Dallas, TX 75359-5026
Fax. (214) 421 2263
www.dws.org/guild.html

EVENTS

UK

Aldeburgh Festival of Music
July
www.aldeburgh.co.uk/

Edinburgh International Festival
August–September
www.eif.co.uk/

Henry Wood Promenade Concerts, Royal Albert Hall, London
Held annually in July–September
www.bbc.co.uk/proms/

Leeds International Concert Season
October–May
www.leeds.gov.uk/tourinfo/events/lics/lics_fr.html

USA

Colorado Music festival
June–August
www.coloradomusicfest.com/

Philadelphia Bach Festival
October–February
www.libertynet.org/bach/20th.html

EUROPE

Salzburg Festival, Austria
July and August
www.salzburg.com/festspiele/

Tivoli Gardens, Denmark
Summer months
www.tivoligardens.com

Prague Spring Festival, Czechoslovakia
festival@login.cz

Besançon Festival of Music, France
September
www.besancon.com/intro/francais/

Bayreuth Festival, Germany
July and August
www.festspiele.de/tmt/index.html

Internationale Beethovenfeste Bonn, Germany
September-October
www.beethovenfest-bonn.de/

Schleswig-Holstein Music Festival, Germany
July and August
www.shmf.de/

International Music Festival, Lucerne, Switzerland
August and September
www.LucerneMusic.ch/

VENUES

UK

Barbican Centre
Silk Street
London EC2Y 8DS
Tel. (020) 7638 8891
www.barbican.org.uk/

The Bridgewater Hall
Manchester M2 3WS
Tel. (0161) 907 9000
Fax. (0161) 950 0001
www.bridgewater-hall.co.uk/

Royal Albert Hall
Kennington Gore
London SW7
Tel. (020) 7960 4242

Royal Concert Hall
2 Sauchiehall Street
Glasgow G2 3NY
Tel. (0141) 287 5511
Fax. (0141) 353 8006
www.grch.com/

Royal Festival Hall
South Bank
London SE1
Tel. (020) 7960 4242

Royal Opera House
Bow Street
Covent Garden
London WC2
Tel. (020) 7304 4000
www.royalopera.org/

Royal Philharmonic Hall
Hope Street
Liverpool L1 9BP
Tel. (0151) 210 2895
Fax. (0151) 210 2902

Sadler's Wells
Rosebery Avenue
London EC2
Tel. (020) 7863 8000
www.sadlers-wells.com/

St David's Hall
The Hayes
Cardiff CF10 1SH
Wales
Tel. (01222) 878444

Symphony Hall
International Convention Centre
Broad Street
Birmingham B1 2EA
Tel. (0121) 644 6440

USA

Joseph Meyerhoff Symphony Hall
212 Cathedral Street
Baltimore, MD 21201
Tel. (410) 783 8000

Symphony Hall
301 Massachusetts Avenue
Boston, MA 02115
Tel. (617) 266 1492
Fax. (617) 638 9436

Severance Hall
11001 Euclid Avenue
Cleveland, OH 44106
Tel. (216) 231 1111

Symphony Center
220 South Michigan Avenue
Chicago, IL 60604
Tel. (312) 294 3000
Fax. (312) 294 3035

Morton H. Meyerson Symphony Center
2301 Flora Street
Dallas, TA 75201-2497
Tel. (214) 670 3600

Dorothy Chandler Pavilion
135 North Grand Avenue
Los Angeles, CA 90012
Tel. (213) 972 8001

Avery Fisher Hall
10 Lincoln Center Plaza
New York, NY 10023-6990
Tel. (212) 875 5030
www.lincolncenter.org/
hallinfo/fisher.html

Carnegie Hall
154 West 57th Street
New York, NY
Tel. (212) 247 7800
www.carnegiehall.org/

Heinz Hall for the Performing Arts
600 Penn Avenue
Pittsburgh, PA 15222-3259
Tel. (412) 392 4900

Symphony Hall
718 North Grand Boulevard
St. Louis, MO 63103
Tel. (314) 533 2500
Fax. (314) 533 6000

CANADA

Orpheum
649 Cambie Street
Vancouver BC, V6B 2P1
Tel. (604) 665 3050

Roy Thompson Hall, Toronto
60 Simcoe Street
Toronto
Ontario M5J 2H5
Tel. (416) 872 4255
Fax. (416) 593 9918
www.masseyhall.com/
roythompson/home.html

AUSTRALIA

Sydney Opera House
PO Box R239, Royal Exchange
NSW 1225
Australia
Tel. (2) 9250 7777
Fax. (2) 9251 3943
www.soh.nsw.gov.au/

EUROPE

Grosse Saal der Musikverein
Bösendorferstraße 12
A-1012 Vienna
Austria
Tel. (1) 505 65 25

Vienna Konzerthaus
Lothringerstraße 20
A-1030 Vienna
Austria
Tel. (1) 712 12 11
Fax. (1) 712 28 72
www.konzerthaus.at/

Rudolfinum, Prague
Alsovo nabrezi 12
110 01 Prague 1
Czech Republic
Tel. (2) 248 93 352
Fax. (2) 231 68 78

Smetana Hall
Obecni Dum
Namesti Republiky 5
110 00 Prague 1
Czech Republic
Tel. (2) 248 93 352
Fax. (2) 231 07 84

Tivoli Gardens
Tivoli Billetcenter
Vesterbrogade 3
1630 København V
Copenhagen
Denmark
Tel. (33) 15 10 12
www.tivoligardens.com/

Cité de la Musique
221, avenue Jean-Jaurés
75019 Paris
France
Tel. (1) 44 84 45 45
Fax. (1) 44 84 45 01
www.cite-musique.fr/

Halle aux Grains
Place Dupuy
31000 Toulouse
France
Tel. (5) 61 63 13 13
Fax. (5) 61 62 70 77

Opéra de la Bastille
120 rue de Lyon
Place de la Bastille
12th Arrondissement
Paris
Tel. (1) 44 72 13 99
www.opera-de-paris.fr/

Palais de la Musique et des Congrès
Place de Bordeaux
Wacken
F67082 Strasbourg Cedex
France
Tel. (3) 88 67 67
Fax. (3) 88 35 38 17

Salle Pleyel
252 Faubourg Saint Honoré
75008 Paris
France
Tel. (1) 45 61 53 01

Salle Messiaen of Radio France
116, avenue du Président
Kennedy
75220 Paris Cedex 16
France
Tel. (1) 42 30 36 15

Théâtre des Champs-Elysées
15, avenue montaigne
75008 Paris
France
Tel. (1) 49 52 50 50
Fax. (1) 49 52 07 41

Théâtre du Châtelet
2, rue Edouard Colonne
F75001 Paris
France
Tel. (1) 40 28 28 40
www.chatelet-theatre.com/

Deutsche Oper
Bismarckstrasse 35
10627 Berlin
Germany
Tel. (30) 343 8401
Fax. (30) 343 8455
www.deutsche-oper.berlin.de/

Konzerthaus Berlin
1016 Berlin
Germany
Tel. (30) 20309 2101
Fax. (30) 2043470
www.konzerthaus.de/

Kulturpalast am Altmarkt
PSF 120424
01005 Dresden
Germany
Tel. (351) 486 6306
Fax. (351) 486 6353

Philharmonie
Matthäikirschstraße 1
10785 Berlin
Germany
Fax. (30) 254 88323

Staatsoper Unter den Linden
Besucherservice
Postfach 354
D10109 Berlin
Germany
Tel. (30) 20 35 44 38
Fax. (30) 20 35 44 80
www.staatsoper-berlin.org

The National Concert Hall
Earlsfort Terrace
Dublin 2
Ireland
Tel. (1) 475 1666
Fax. (1) 478 3797
www.nch.ie/

La Scala
Via Filodrammatici
2-20121 Milan
Italy
Tel. (02) 720037 4420
www.lascala.milano.it/

Teatro Comunale
Biglietteria del Teatro
Comunale
Largo Respighi 1
40126 Bologna
Italy
Tel. (051) 529999
Fax. (051) 529995
www.communalebologna.it/

Concertgebouw
Antwoordnummer 17902
100 WR Amsterdam
The Netherlands
Tel. (20) 671 8345
Fax. (20) 573 0460
www.concertgebouw.nl/

Shostakovich Academy
St Petersburg
Russia
Tel. (812) 311 21 26

RECORD COMPANIES

UK

Albany Records
Unit 9B Upper Wingbury
Courtyard, Wingrave
Bucks HP22 4LW
Tel. (01296) 682255
Fax. (01296) 682275
www.albanyrecords.
demon.co.uk

BMG/Telarc/Conifer
Bedford House
69-75 Fulham High Street
London SW6 3JW
Tel. (020) 7384 7500
Fax. (020) 7384 7922
www.bmg.com/

Chandos Records/Chaconne
Chandos House
Commerce Way
Colchester
Essex CO2 8HQ
Tel. (01206) 225200
Fax. (01206) 225201
www.chandos-records.com/

Collins Classics
Windsong International
Electron House
Cray Avenue
St Mary Cray
Orpington
Kent BR5 3RJ
Tel. (01689) 899062
Fax. (01689) 899030

Decca/Double Decca
22 St Peter's Square
London W6 9NW
Tel. (020) 8910 5000
Fax. (020) 8910 5411
www.decca.com/

Deutsche Grammophon & Archiv/Philips Classics/ Polygram Classics
PO Box 1420, 1 Sussex
Place
London W6 9XS
Tel. (020) 8910 5000
Fax. (020) 8910 5411
www.dgclassics.com/

EMI Classics
64 Baker Street
London W1M 1DJ
Tel. (020) 7467 2000
www.emiclassics.com/

Harmonia Mundi
19-21 Nile Street
London N1 7LL
Tel. (020) 7253 0836
Fax. (020) 7253 3237
www.harmoniamundi.com/

Hyperion Records
PO Box 25
London SE9 1AX
Tel. (020) 8294 1166
Fax. (020) 8294 1161
www.hyperion-records.co.uk/

Naxos
Unit 4, Wyllots Manor
Potters Bar
Hertfordshire EN6 2HN
Tel. (01707) 661961
Fax. (01707) 661971
www.hnh.com/

Nimbus Records
Wyatstone Leys
Monmouth
Gwent NP5 3SR
Tel. (01600) 890682
Fax. (01600) 890007

RCA
Bedford House
69-79 Fulham High Street
London SW6 3JW
Tel. (020) 7384 7500
Fax. (020) 7371 9298

Sony Classical/CBS
Columbia/Vivante
10 Great Marlborough
Street
London W1V 2LP
Tel. (020) 7911 8200
Fax. (020) 7911 8600
www.sonymusic.com/

Virgin Classics
Kensal House
553-579 Harrow Road
London W10 4RH
Tel. (020) 8964 6000
Fax. (020) 8968 6533

Warner Classics/Erato/
Nonesuch
The Warner Building
28 Kensington Church Street
London W8 4EP
Tel. (020) 7938 0167
Fax. (020) 7938 3986
www.warner-classics.com/

USA

Allegro
14134 NE Airport Way
Portland, OR 97230-3443

Angel Records (CBS)
304 Park Avenue South
4th Floor
New York, NY 10010
Tel. (212) 253 3000

Atlantic Records (Warner US)
1290 Avenue of the Americas
New York, NY
Fax. (212) 405 5470
www.warner-classics.com/

Boston Skyline Records
73 Hemingway Street
Suite 508
Boston, MA 02115
Tel. (617) 536 5464
Fax. (617) 266 1575
www.bostonskylinerecords.
com/

CBS
550 Madison Avenue
New York
NY 10022
Tel. (212) 833 8000
Fax. (212) 833 4270

Centaur Records Inc.
8867 Highland Road
Suite 206
Baton Rouge, LA 70808
Tel. (225) 336 4877
Fax. (225) 336 9678
www.centaurrecords.com/

Cristofori Records
2936 Lincoln Avenue # 151
San Diego, CA 92104
www.cristofori.com

Deutsche Grammophon
World Wide Plaza
12th Floor
825 Eighth Avenue
New York, NY 10019
Tel. (212) 333 8000

Harmonia Mundi
2037 Granville Avenue
Los Angeles, CA 90025-6103
Tel. (310) 478 1311
www.harmoniamundi.com/
hmUS/

Lyric Records
PO Box 1112
New York
NY 10023
Tel. (212) 613 1655
Fax. (212) 613 1612
www.lyricrecords.com/

Phoenix
200 Winston Drive
Cliffside Park
New Jersey 07010
Tel. (201) 224 8318
Fax. (201) 224 7968
www.phoenixcd.com/

CONTRIBUTOR BIOGRAPHIES

Stanley Sadie
General Editor; Classical: Era Introduction, Mozart, Personalities
Stanley Sadie was music critic for *The Times* for 17 years, Editor of *The Musical Times* for 20 years and music consultant to the television series *Man and Music*, and since 1970 has worked as Editor of the standard reference work, *The New Grove Dictionary of Music and Musicians* (1980, new edition 2000) as well as its associated dictionaries, on instruments, opera and American music. He has written extensively on Mozart and Handel and has been president of the Royal Musical Association (1989–94) and the International Musicological Society (1992–97). He was appointed CBE in 1982. With his wife, Julie Anne Sadie, he is currently completing a survey of European composer museums and memorials.

AUTHORS

(The sections written by each author are indicated under their name; some of the entries incorporated into the Personalities sections were written by specialist authors who are credited separately).

Nicholas Anderson
Early Baroque: Personalities; Late Baroque: Personalities
Nicholas Anderson studied at New College, Oxford and Durham University. For 20 years he worked for the BBC as a music producer, since when he has continued broadcasting, teaching and writing. He is the author of *Baroque Music from Monteverdi to Handel* (1994) and has contributed chapters to *A Guide to the Concerto* (1988) and *The Cambridge Cultural History* (1992) as well as to *The New Grove Dictionary of Music and Musicians* and various symposiums and journals.

Robert Anderson
Late Romantic: Elgar
Robert Anderson has been director of music at Gordonstoun School, an associate conductor at the Spoleto Festival, and has conducted many concerts at the Royal Albert Hall. He has written criticisms for *The Times*, *The Musical Times* and other journals, been co-ordinating editor of the *Elgar Complete Edition* and written on ancient Egyptian music, Wagner and Elgar.

David Bowman
Glossary
David Bowman was for nearly 20 years Director of Music at Ampleforth College where he still teaches. He was Chief Examiner for the University of London Schools Examination Board from 1982–98. His numerous publications include the *London Anthology of Music* (1986), *Aural Matters in Practice* (co-auth. Paul Terry, 1994), *Analysis Matters* (Vol. 1, 1997; Vol. 2, 1998) and analytical articles for *Music Teacher*.

Alison Bullock
Medieval: Era Introduction, Personalities, Styles and Forms
Alison Bullock is an editor on the revised edition of the *New Grove Dictionary of Music and Musicians*. She took her first degree at Cambridge University before studying for her PhD, written at Southampton University, on 'The Musical Readings of the Machaut Manuscripts'.

Margaret Campbell
Early Baroque: Purcell
Margaret Campbell, writer and lecturer, has had features published regularly in leading musical journals and the national press since 1961. She has published four biographies, including *Henry Purcell: Glory of his Age* (1993). She received a Winston Churchill Travelling Fellowship for researching her first book, *Dolmetsch; the Man and his Work* (1975).

Barry Cooper
Classical: Beethoven
Barry Cooper lectured in music at the University of Aberdeen from 1974 to 1990, before moving to the University of Manchester, and is known mainly as a musicologist. He is general editor and co-author of *The Beethoven Compendium* (1991); his other books include *Beethoven and the Creative Process* and *Beethoven's Folksong Settings*, as well as studies of English Baroque keyboard music and of music theory in Britain in the seventeenth and eighteenth centuries.

John Deathridge
Late Romantic: Wagner, R. Strauss, Styles and Forms
John Deathridge is King Edward Professor of Music at King's College, University of London. Previously he was Reader in Music at the University of Cambridge and a Fellow of King's College from 1983 to 1996. He is a pianist, conductor and regular broadcaster. His many publications include his English-language edition of the *Wagner Handbook* (Harvard University Press, 1992).

Richard Evidon
Late Romantic: Mahler, Sibelius
Richard Evidon is a writer on music, critic and editor based in the USA. He was for many years English Editor and Editorial Manager of Deutsche Grammophon, Hamburg, and earlier served on the editorial staff of *The New Grove Dictionary of Music and Musicians* in London.

Fabrice Fitch
Medieval: Listening Guide; Renaissance: Listening Guide
Fabrice Fitch is a composer and musicologist, and currently lectures at the University of Durham (UK). His book *Johannes Ockeghem: Masses and Models* appeared in 1997, and a CD of his music (in collaboration with the composer Paul Archbold) has recently been issued on the Metier label. He is an editorial consultant and contributor to *Gramophone*, and is Recordings Reviews Editor with the journal *Early Music*.

Elizabeth Forbes
Late Romantic: Bizet, Puccini, Verdi
Elizabeth Forbes is a writer on music, critic and translator. Her books include *Mario and Grisi* (1985). She has been a contributor to *Grove 6*, *Opera Grove*, *New Grove Dictionary*, *New DNB*, *Viking Opera Guide*, *The Financial Times*, *The Independent* and many English, American, French and German periodicals. She has also translated opera librettos from French, Italian, German and Swedish.

Edmund Forey
Early Romantic: Chopin, Schumann
Edmund Forey studied as a pianist and singer, and was for some years an editor on the seventh edition of *The New Grove Dictionary of Music and Musicians*; he currently works at the editorial department of Decca Records.

Sophie Fuller
Women in Music and female Personalities
Sophie Fuller is a lecturer in music at the University of Reading and author of *The Pandora Guide to Women Composers: Britain and the United States*. Although her research interests range from representations of music-making in English literature to issues of gender in contemporary songwriting, her specialist field is the place of late Victorian and Edwardian women composers and musicians in British musical life.

Matthew Greenall
Late 20th Century: Styles and Forms
Matthew Greenall was born in London in 1960. After studies at Oxford University and the Royal Academy of Music, he pursued a performing career until becoming Director of the British Music Information Centre, a position he still holds. He is a frequent contributor to many leading music publications, in particular writing on new music.

Sarah Hibberd
Classical: Styles and Forms; Early Romantic: Era Introduction, Berlioz, Mendelssohn, Rossini, Styles and Forms
Sarah Hibberd worked as commissioning editor for the nineteenth century at Grove for four years. She has recently completed a doctorate on opera and theatre in early nineteenth-century Paris, and has published articles on Donizetti and on French adaptations of Goethe's *Faust*. She is currently a research fellow at Royal Holloway, University of London.

Lucien Jenkins
Instruments
Lucien Jenkins is a graduate of Trinity Hall, University of Cambridge and Birkbeck College, University of London. He founded *Early Music Today* in 1993 and was appointed editor of *Music Teacher* in 1996. In 1998–99, he was a consultant with the Qualifications and Curriculum Authority as part of preparing the ground for revising music content of the National Curriculum for England.

Jonathan Keates
Late Baroque: Era Introduction, Handel
Jonathan Keates is the author of *Handel: The Man and His Music* (Gollancz, 1985) and *Henry Purcell: A Biography* (Chatto & Windus, 1995). He has written on music for *The Independent*, *The Times Literary Supplement*, *Early Music News* and *International Record Review* and was the presenter of the Channel 4 documentary *My Night with Handel*.

Nick Kimberley
Late 20th Century: Opera
Nick Kimberley has reviewed television for the *Listener*, crime fiction for the *Guardian*; the *New Statesman* and the *Independent*; film for *Sight and Sound*; and now writes regularly on music, especially opera, for *The Independent*, *Opera*, *Gramophone*, and *BBC Music Magazine*. He was Classical Music Editor of *City Limits* and now edits *The Full Score*.

Richard Langham Smith
Modern: Debussy
Richard Langham Smith graduated from the University of York and studied with Wilfrid Mellers and Edward Lockspeiser. His critical translation of Debussy's complete articles appeared in 1977 and he has subsequently co-authored the Cambridge Opera Guide to Debussy's *Pelléas et Mellisande* as well as writing and broadcasting on French music in general. His completion of Debussy's unfinished opera *Rodrigue et Chimène* opened the new opera house in Lyons in 1993. He is Reader in Music at the University of Exeter.

Richard Lawrence
Early Baroque: Listening Guide; Late Baroque: Listening Guide; Classical: Listening Guide; Early Romantic: Listening Guide; Modern: Conductors, Singers, Instrumentalists; Late 20th Century: Conductors, Singers, Instrumentalists
Richard Lawrence is a writer, lecturer and broadcaster. He was educated at Westminster Abbey Choir School, Haileybury College and Worcester College, Oxford, where he read music under Edmund Rubbra and F. W. Sternfeld. He was the editor of two early music magazines and is a former Music Director of the Arts Council of Great Britain.

Malcolm MacDonald
Late Romantic: Brahms
Malcolm MacDonald edits *Tempo*, the quarterly magazine of modern music, and is a freelance writer on music and broadcaster. His books include *Brahms* and *Schoenberg* in OUP's 'Master Musicians' series, a study of the music of Edgard Varèse and volumes on the British composers Havergal Brian, John Foulds and Ronald Stevenson.

Laura Macy
Renaissance: Era Introduction, Personalities; Early Baroque: Era Introduction, Monteverdi
Laura Macy is a musicologist specialising in the music of the sixteenth and early seventeenth centuries. Her publications include articles on Italian madrigal and on the study of women's role in the musical life of the Renaissance. She is currently writing a book on audiences and their influence on musical style.

Malcolm Miller
Late Romantic: Personalities
Malcolm Miller received his doctorate from King's College, London with a study of Wagner and is currently Associate Lecturer at the Open University, a critic, editor and pianist. He is a regular contributor to leading musical publications including the *New Grove Dictionary of Music*, *MGG*, *Musical Opinion* and *Tempo*.

Helen Myers
The World of Music
Helen Myers is Assistant Professor of Music at Central Connecticut State University. She has taught ethnomusicology at the University of London and the National Centre for the Performing Arts. She is the author or editor of several prize-winning books in ethnomusicology and has served as resident ethnomusicologist for *The New Grove Dictionary of Music* and *The New Oxford Companion to Music*.

Robin Newton
Late 20th Century: Composers
Robin Newton is active as a conductor, specializing in contemporary music. In 1997 he formed his own ensemble e2k, with which he gives regular concerts in London. He has worked on several high-profile academic publications as writer and editor, chiefly for *The New Grove Dictionary of Music and Musicians* and the new Northern Arts magazine *Artscene*.

David Nice
Late Romantic: Tchaikovsky, Listening Guide
David Nice is a writer, lecturer and broadcaster who has written studies of Elgar, Richard Strauss, Tchaikovsky and the history of opera. He has made many contributions to Radio 3's popular *Building a Library* series and writes on a monthly basis for the *BBC Music Magazine*. He is currently working on a major biography of Prokofiev for Yale University Press.

Michael Oliver

Modern: Stravinsky, Composers, Listening Guide; Late 20th Century: Listening Guide

Michael Oliver has written and presented hundreds of programmes for BBC radio; he reviews regularly for *Gramophone*, *Classic CD* and other periodicals and is the editor of *International Opera Collector*. He has published biographies of Stravinsky and Benjamin Britten, and has edited *Settling the Score*, a documentary history of twentieth-century music.

Tim Parry

Early Romantic: Personalities

Tim Parry studied music at Nottingham University, where he specialized in the transcriptions of Liszt and Busoni. He worked as an editor on the second edition of *The New Grove Dictionary of Music and Musicians*, concentrating on the nineteenth century. He is also interested in the piano and reviews regularly for *Gramophone*.

Jan Smaczny

Late Romantic: Dvorák, Smetana; Modern: Janáček

Jan Smaczny studied at Oxford University and the Charles University, Prague. Well-known as a critic and broadcaster, he has written on many aspects of Czech music in general and the life and works of Dvorák in particular. He has been Hamilton Harty Professor of Music at the Queen's University of Belfast since 1996.

Roderick Swanston

Late Romantic: Era Introduction; Modern: Era Introduction

Roderick Swanston is a Reader in Historical and Interdisciplinary Studies at the Royal College of Music, a lecturer at Imperial College of Science, Technology and Medicine, a tutor for the Faculty for Continuing Education of Birkbeck College and a Visiting Professor in music at Dartmouth College, USA. He is a writer, a frequent broadcaster and has lectured extensively in Europe, Asia and the United States.

Ruth Tatlow

Late Baroque: J. S. Bach

Ruth Tatlow studied at the Royal Academy of Music and the Universities of London and Tübingen. A former Leverhulme Fellow, she is consultant to Sir John Eliot Gardiner for the Bach Pilgrimage Project and Honorary Research Fellow at Reading University. Her first book, *Bach and the Riddle of the Number Alphabet* was published in 1991.

Emma Wakelin

Renaissance: Styles and Forms; Early Baroque: Styles and Forms; Late Baroque: Styles and Forms

Emma Wakelin is an editor with *The New Grove Dictionary of Music and Musicians*. Her research interests lie in the late sixteenth-century Italian madrigal; she has made a particular study of madrigal anthologies, in which madrigals by the most renowned composers were published alongside pieces by relatively unknown figures.

Richard Wigmore

Classical: Haydn; Early Romantic: Schubert

Richard Wigmore read modern languages at Cambridge and took a second degree in music theory and performance at the Guildhall School of Music. After a career as a professional singer he now works as a writer and broadcaster, specialising in the Viennese Classical period and in Lieder. He contributes regular reviews and features to *Gramophone*, *BBC Music Magazine* and *The Daily Telegraph*. His first book, *Schubert's Complete Song Texts* was published in 1988, and he is currently working on a new biography of Haydn for the Master Musicians series.

Charles Wilson

Modern: Styles and Forms; Late 20th Century: Era Introduction

Charles Wilson has lectured on twentieth-century music and music theory and analysis at King's College London and other universities and colleges. He is the Area Editor for twentieth-century composers for the second *New Grove Dictionary of Music and Musicians*.

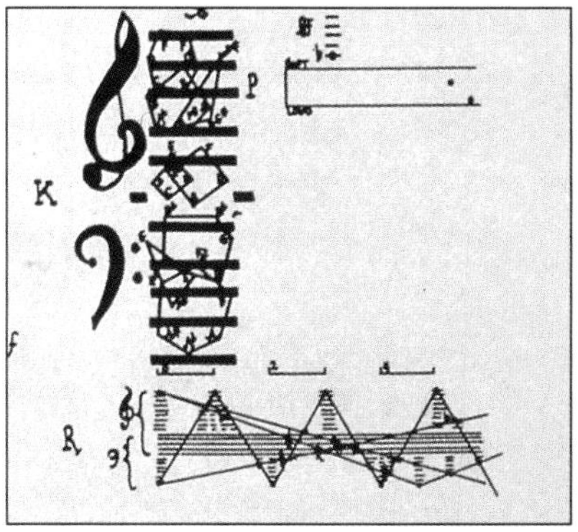

ADVISORY BOARD

Leon Botstein

Leon Botstein has been president of Bard College since 1975. He is music director of the American Symphony Orchestra, founder and co-artistic director of the Bard Music Festival, and music director of the American Russian Young Artists Orchestra. He has been a frequent guest conductor with numerous orchestras around the world and has been the featured conductor on many classical recordings. He is also editor of *The Musical Quarterly* and a member of the board of numerous organizations and professional associations.

Paul Griffiths

Paul Griffiths joined the editorial team of *The New Grove Dictionary of Music and Musicians* in 1973. His first book, *A Concise History of Modern Music* has been translated into several languages. His other books include studies of Boulez, Cage, Messiaen, Ligeti, Davies, Bartók, Stravinsky and the string quartet. Among his fictional writings are several librettos, including *The Jewel Box*, with music by Mozart, which was performed by the Opera North and at Glyndebourne. *Marco Polo*, with music by Tan Dun, was released on record by Sony in 1997 and was given its American premiere by New York City Opera the same year.

Christina Jaremko Porter

Christina Jaremko Porter received a BM (with honours) from Chicago Musical College, Roosevelt University. She went on to receive an MA in Ethnomusicology at the University of California, Los Angeles, where she studied with the famous *p'i-p'a* and *ch'in* player and scholar of Chinese music, Tsun-Yuen Lui. She has published articles on the music of the Baltic region in Eastern Europe.

Lucien Jenkins (See Authors)

Ian Ritchie

Ian Ritchie trained as a singer at the Royal College of Music, Cambridge University (where he was a choral scholar) and The Guildhall School of Music and Drama before embarking on a career as music publisher, festival director and orchestral manager. He was Managing Director of the Scottish Chamber Orchestra for nine years and is currently a consultant specializing in change management, leadership development and recruitment in the arts. He is also Chairman of spnm (society for the promotion of new music).

Julie Anne Sadie

Julie Anne Sadie was born in Oregon and studied the cello there, going on to Cornell to pursue her academic studies and completing the PhD there with a study of French Baroque chamber music (published in book form in 1980); she settled in London after her marriage to Stanley Sadie in 1978. She has published a *Companion to Baroque Music* (1990) and was co-editor of the *New Grove Dictionary of Women Composers* (1994). She is also an authority on musical museums and is completing (with her husband) a survey of European composer museums and memorials.

Laurie Shulman

Laurie Shulman is the program annotator for orchestras, chamber music ensembles, and summer festivals throughout the United States. She holds a BA from Syracuse University in European History and MA and PhD degrees from Cornell University in historical musicology. Her articles have appeared in *The New Grove*, *The New Grove Dictionary of Opera*, *Tempo*, *Stagebill*, and *Chamber Music Magazine*. She has also furnished compact disc liner notes for eight record companies, and is the author of *The Meyerson Symphony Center: Building a Dream* (University of North Texas Press, 2000).

David Stevens

David Stevens has worked in classical music since 1972, after gaining his B. Mus. from the University of Manchester. Between 1981 and 1985 he administered a choir, , worked at the British Music Information Centre and as a freelance TV music researcher. Since 1986 he has worked in the Classical Music Department at BBCTV. He has produced editions of BBC Radio 3's *Hear and Now*, *The Year*, and *Composer of the Week* as well as a 90-minute documentary for Stockhausen's 70th birthday. He also directed a performance of Tippett's *The Mask of Time* for the 1999 First Night of the Proms.

Roderick Swanston (See Authors)

PICTURE CREDITS

AKG London: 19 (bl), 75(r), 99, 107(l), 111(l), 148(br), 154(tl), 155(b), 163(r), 246(b), 301(l), Bibliotheque Nationale, Paris 18(r), 25(l), 32(b), 68(l), Erich Lessing 12(t), 19(tl), 19(r), 44(tr), 46(l), 58(r), 62(l), 73(b), 74, 88(t), 144(bl), 225(r), 282(l), Musee du Berry, Bourges 50, 60(t), Deutsches Theatermuseum 140(bl), 175(br) Kunsthalle, Hamburg 180(r), Kunsthistorisches Museum, Vienna 159(br), Museo Firenze comiera, Florence 39(l), 44(l), 61(br) Musee du Louvre 47(b), 61(t), 136(c), 137(br), Musee Marmottan 304(b), 224(l), Austrian Nationalbibliothek 39(r), Stanford University Museum of Art 173(tr), State Hermitage, St Petersburg 217(c)
Arbiter Group PLC: 212(tl), 214(l), 269(bl), Fender Musical Instruments Inc. 310(l)
Arena Images: 77(bl), 97(t), 114(bl), 121(t), 255(l), 258(br), 260(r), 264(l), 303, 340(l), 342(l), 347(r), 355(r), Jim Caldwell 346(t), Bill Cooper 274-275, 283(l), 346(b), John Fenton 280(l), 315(l), Mike Hoban 335(r), Ron Scherl 115(l), 124(l), 254(t), 262(l), 272(bl), 286(l), 308(l), 335(l), Steve J. Sherman 334, Marty Sohl 145(t), Helen Wilson 255(r), 309
Sir Malcolm Arnold: 284(l)
The Art Archive: 12(r), Archaeological Museum, Lima 16(l)
BBC Philharmonic: Mackenzie 355(t)
Christie's Images: 42-43, 51(l), 55(r), 64, 68(r), 70-71, 77(r), 91(l), 92(b), 94(l), 95(l), 105(t), 118(r), 127(t), 134-135, 146(tl), 150(b), 166(l), 167(l),170, 172(c), 176-177, 191(c), 197(r), 205(r), 212(tc), 212(l), 213(l), 216(c), 218(tl), 220-221, 234(r), 235(tr), 263(r), 266(t), 268(tr), 270(br)
Deutsche Grammophon: 122(r)
English National Ballet: 235(r)
Selwyn Green: 316(b), 324(r), 354(r)
Hobgoblin Music: 38(c)
Image Select: 45, Ann Ronan 22(c), 23(b), 44(br)
Intermusica Artists' Management Ltd: 175(tr)
Lebrecht Collection: 18(l), 20-21, 21, 22(l), 23(t), 24(r), 25(tr), 25(br), 27, 28, 29(l), 30, 31, 32(t), 33, 34, 35, 36, 37(l), 37(tr), 38(t), 40, 41(r), 43(l), 47(t), 48, 49(l), 52(r), 53(t), 53(c), 54, 55(l), 56, 58(l), 59, 61(bl), 62(r), 63(tr), 63(br), 66, 67(t), 69(t), 71(c), 72(r), 73(c), 76(t), 78(t), 79, 80, 81(b), 82(b), 83(l), 84, 85, 86, 87(r), 88(c), 88(b), 91(r), 96, 98(t), 98(b), 100-101, 102(r), 103(r) 104, 105(r), 106(l), 109(r), 111(br) 112, 113, 114(r), 115(r), 116, 117(c), 117(r), 118(l) 119, 120, 121(b), 122(l), 122(b), 123, 124(t), 125, 126, 127(b) 128(t), 129(r), 130(tl), 130(c), 132(tl), 135(cr), 138(b), 140(t), 141, 142, 143(t), 144(t), 145(r), 147(t), 149, 150(t), 151(tr), 152(b), 153(t), 156(r), 157, 158, 159(l), 160, 161, 162(c), 164(t), 164(b), 165(t), 167(r),168, 171(t) 172(tl), 174, 178(l), 182, 183, 184, 185(b), 186(c), 190(l), 190(r), 193, 194(l), 195(t), 196, 197(l), 198(br), 199, 200(t), 200(br), 201, 202(r), 203, 204, 205(l), 206, 207(r), 208(l), 209(l), 210, 211, 215(l), 216(tl), 218(c), 218(r), 219, 223(t), 224(r), 225(l), 226(br), 226(t), 227(tr), 228, 229, 230(t), 231(l), 232(tl), 233(t), 234(t), 236, 236(br) (c) ADAGP, Paris DACS, London 2000. 237, 238(r), 239(r), 240(r), 241, 242, 244, 245, 246(c), 247(t), 248, 249(b), 250, 251, 253(l), 256, 257, 258(bl), 259(br), 263(l), 264(r), 265(tr), 265(br), 267(l), 270(tl), 271(tl), 272(tr), 273, 279(r), 281(b), 282(t), 282(r), 283(c), 282(r), 284(b), 284(r), 289(tr), 290, 291, 293(c), 294, 295(l), 296(r), 297, 298(r), 299, 300(c), 300(r), 305, 306(tl), 306(bl), 307(r), 308(r), 314(c), 314(l), 316(l), 317, 321(t), 325, 327(l), 349(l), 350(l), M. Allen 98(c), 109(l), 226(l), Felix Aprahamian 302(l), Archivo Manuel de Falla 278(r), 289(tl), R. Booth 76(l), 93(bl), 151(br), 202(c) Y. Bouskila 189(t), Milean Cosman 281(t), Mike Evans 233(br), 330(l), 343(l), David Farrell 333(r), 345, Betty Freeman 323(r), 324(l), 328(tr), 328(l), 336(l), 337(b), 338(l), 339, 350(r), 352(l), Joanne Harris 185(tr), 195(r), Richard Haughton 341, C.R. Henderson 268(bl), Matti Kolho 227(br), S. Lauterwasser 347(l), Andre Lecoz 275(c), 293(r), 302(r), 313(b), Laurie Lewis 328(br), Nigel Luckhurst 287, G. Macdomnic 300(l) Suzie Maeder 288(l), 326(t), John Minnion 24(l), 82(tl), 163(l) Morris 181(r), 192(l), 198(t), 252, 261(bl), Kate Mount 329(r), 337(t), 343(r), George Newson 322(l), 329(l), Odile Noel 10-11, 15(b), 130(tr), 278(l), 311(r), 313(t), Wladimir Polak 331(r), Private Collection 156(l), 169(l), 171(b), 177(c), 181(l), 186(r), 187, 189(l), 189(r), 189(b), 192(r), 198(bl), 200(bc), 200(bl), 207(l), 221(c), 230(br), 243, Arthur Reynolds Collection 247(b), Mary Robert 349(r), Celine Rosen 155(t), 344(b), Royal Academy of Music 154(r), 232(bl), 272(tl), 301(r) G. Salter 93(t), 146(tr), 147(br), 261(t) Arnold Schoenberg Institut/ (c) DACS 2000 295(r), 352(r), D. Smirnov 326(bl), Jonathan Smith 238(l), 240(l), Chris Stock 214(tr), 216(b), 266(b), 267(tr), 312, TL 49(r), 77(br), 87(l), 117(l), 165(c), 260(bl), 355(b), Tony Tree 190(b), 191(r), Kurt Weill Foundation 307(l)
London Sinfonietta: 338(r)
Mary Evans: 17, 22(r), 24(c), 26, 29(r), 41(l), 51(r), 52(l), 57, 60(b), 73(l), 75(l), 78(b), 93(br), 94(r), 102(c), 129(l), 131(t), 135(cl), 136(t), 137(t), 137(bl), 138(t), 139, 143(b), 148(tl), 151(l), 152(tl), 153(br), 164(c), 178(r), 179(b), 180(l), 194(c), 213(br), 215(r), 222(r), 223(r), 231(br), 249(l), 249(r), 254(br), 261(br), 268(tl), 269(tr), 276, 304(t), 320, 321(l), 336(b)
Monteverdi Choir and Orchestra Ltd: Jim Four 331(l)
Pictorial Press: 81(t), 106(r), 107(r), 108, 110, 132(br), 133, 208(r), 227(l), 259(tr), 277(l), 280(t), 281(r), 286(r), 289(br), 314(tl), 327(r), 343(r), 348(bl), 353(r)
Redferns: David Farrell 332(r), 333(l), Suzi Gibbons 348(l), Leon Morris 351, Odile Noel 311(l), David Redfern 310(r), 332(l), Ebet Roberts 354(tl)
Royal Opera House: 301(b), 318-319, 340(b)
Bridget Tily: 344(t)
Topham Picturepoint: 46(r), 53(br), 69(b), 101(c), 102(l), 103(tl), 103(bl), 277(r), 279(l), 222(l), 322(r), 323(l), 348(br)
V&A Picture Library: 63(l), 65, 90, 95(r)
Werner Forman Archive: 14, 15(t), National Palace Museum, Taipei 13 Smithsonian Institute, Washington: 12(l), 16(r),
Yamaha-Kemble Music (U.K.) Ltd: 128(br), 169(br), 197(c), 213(tr), 262(r), 296(l), 329(tr)

INDEX

Page references in bold indicate a biographical entry in the Personalities sections.

C

D

H

I

J

K

L

M

N

O

S